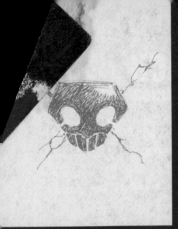

Hello. This is volume 49
of *Bleach*. I worked hard
to create it. Please treat
it kindly.

Sincerely,
-Tite Kubo, 2011

BLEACH is author Tite Kubo's second title. Kubo made his debut
with *ZOMBIEPOWDER.*, a four-volume series for *WEEKLY SHONEN
JUMP*. To date, *BLEACH* has been translated into numerous
languages and has also inspired an animated TV series that
began airing in the U.S. in 2006. Beginning its serialization in
2001, *BLEACH* is still a mainstay in the pages of *WEEKLY SHONEN
JUMP*. In 2005, *BLEACH* was awarded the prestigious Shogakukan
Manga Award in the *shonen* (boys) category.

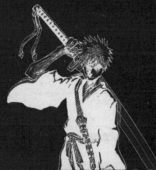

BLEACH
3-in-1 Edition

SHONEN JUMP Manga Omnibus Edition Volume 17
A compilation of the graphic novel volumes 49–51

STORY AND ART BY
TITE KUBO

English Adaptation/Lance Caselman
Translation/Joe Yamazaki
Touch-up Art & Lettering/Mark McMurray
Design - Manga Edition/Kam Li, Yukiko Whitley
Design - Omnibus Edition/Fawn Lau
Editor - Manga Edition/Alexis Kirsch
Editor - Omnibus Edition/Pancha Diaz

BLEACH © 2001 by Tite Kubo. All rights reserved.
First published in Japan in 2001 by SHUEISHA Inc., Tokyo.
English translation rights arranged by SHUEISHA Inc.

Printed in the U.S.A.

Published by VIZ Media, LLC
P.O. Box 77010
San Francisco, CA 94107

10 9 8 7 6 5 4 3 2 1
Omnibus edition first printing, November 2016

www.viz.com

THE WORLD'S MOST POPULAR MANGA
www.shonenjump.com

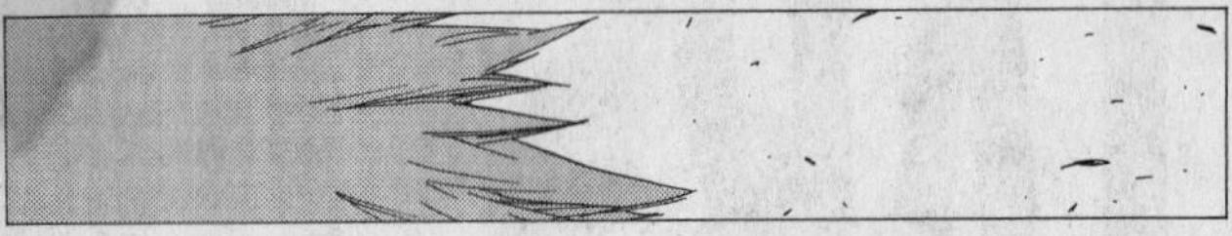

I wonder if I can keep up with...

The speed of a world you're not in.

BLEACH 49 The Lost Agent

STARS AND

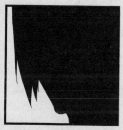

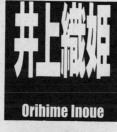

Orihime Inoue

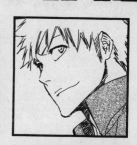

Uryu Ishida

Ichigo Kurosaki

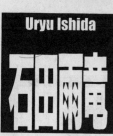

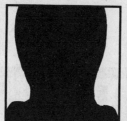

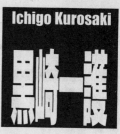

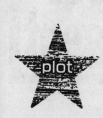

plot

When high school student Ichigo Kurosaki meets Soul Reaper Rukia Kuchiki his life is changed forever. Soon Ichigo is a soul-cleansing Soul Reaper too, and he finds himself having adventures, as well as problems, that he never would have imagined. Later, in the Soul Society, Ichigo stops Rukia's execution but finds out that the entire thing was Aizen's dark plot. Aizen then leads his Arrancar army and declares war on the Soul Society!

As Aizen becomes stronger and stronger, Ichigo continues losing his friends. Ichigo risks his life to master "the final Getsuga Tensho" and trades his Soul Reaper abilities to finally defeat Aizen. Immediately following, the Hogyoku steals Aizen's powers and the battle ends. Ichigo's powers that saved his town and friends start to vanish. Is this the last time he'll ever see Rukia...?

BLEACH ALL

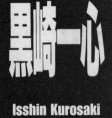

黒崎一心

Isshin Kurosaki

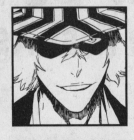

黒崎夏梨

Karin Kurosaki

Kisuke Urahara

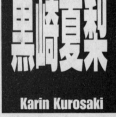

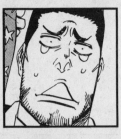

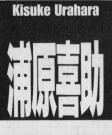

浦原喜助

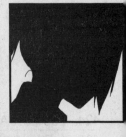

STORIES

BLEACH 49

The Lost Agent

Contents

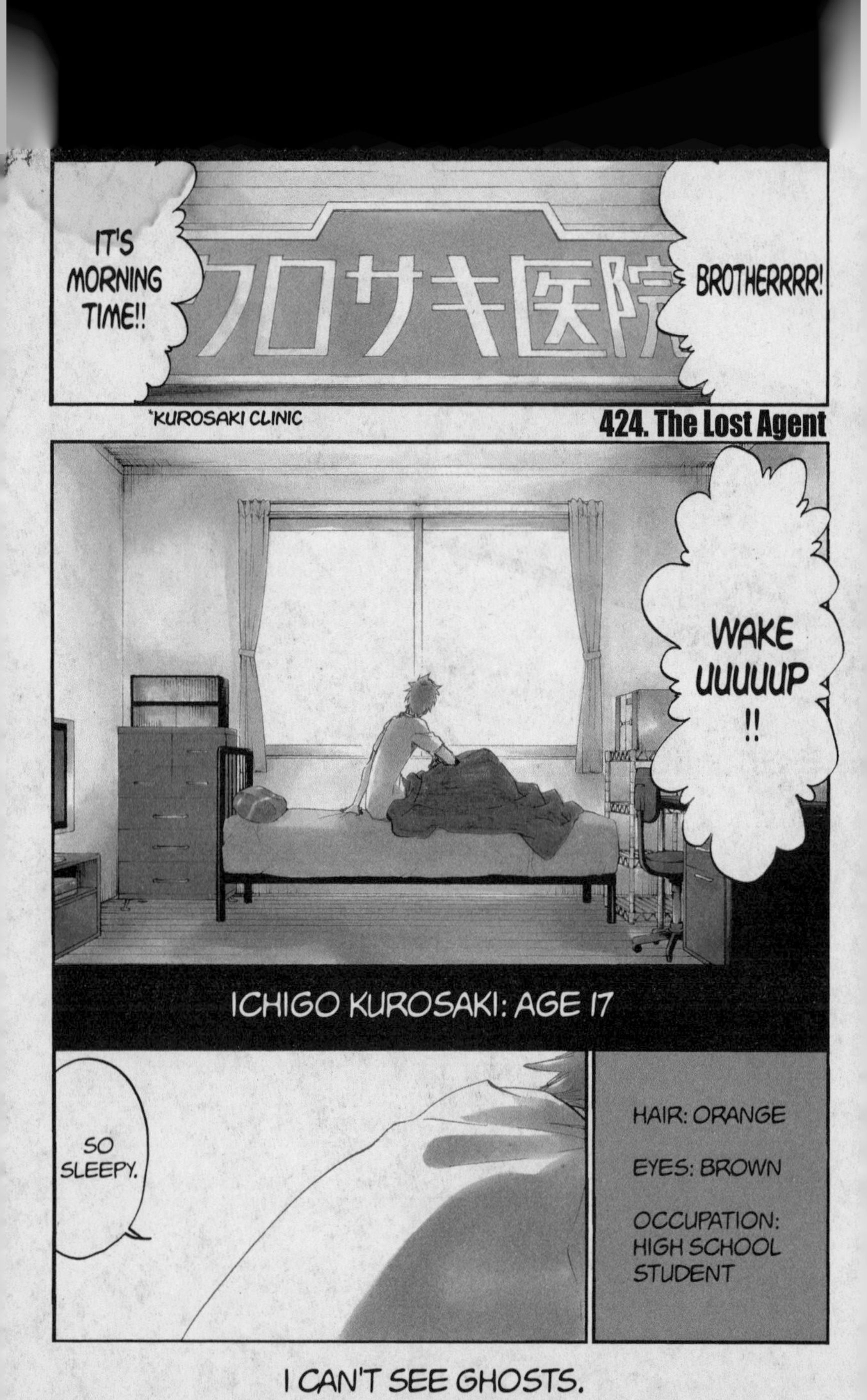

BROTHERRRR!
IT'S MORNING TIME!!
クロサキ医院
*KUROSAKI CLINIC
424. The Lost Agent
WAKE UUUUUP !!
ICHIGO KUROSAKI: AGE 17
HAIR: ORANGE
EYES: BROWN
OCCUPATION: HIGH SCHOOL STUDENT
SO SLEEPY.

I CAN'T SEE GHOSTS.

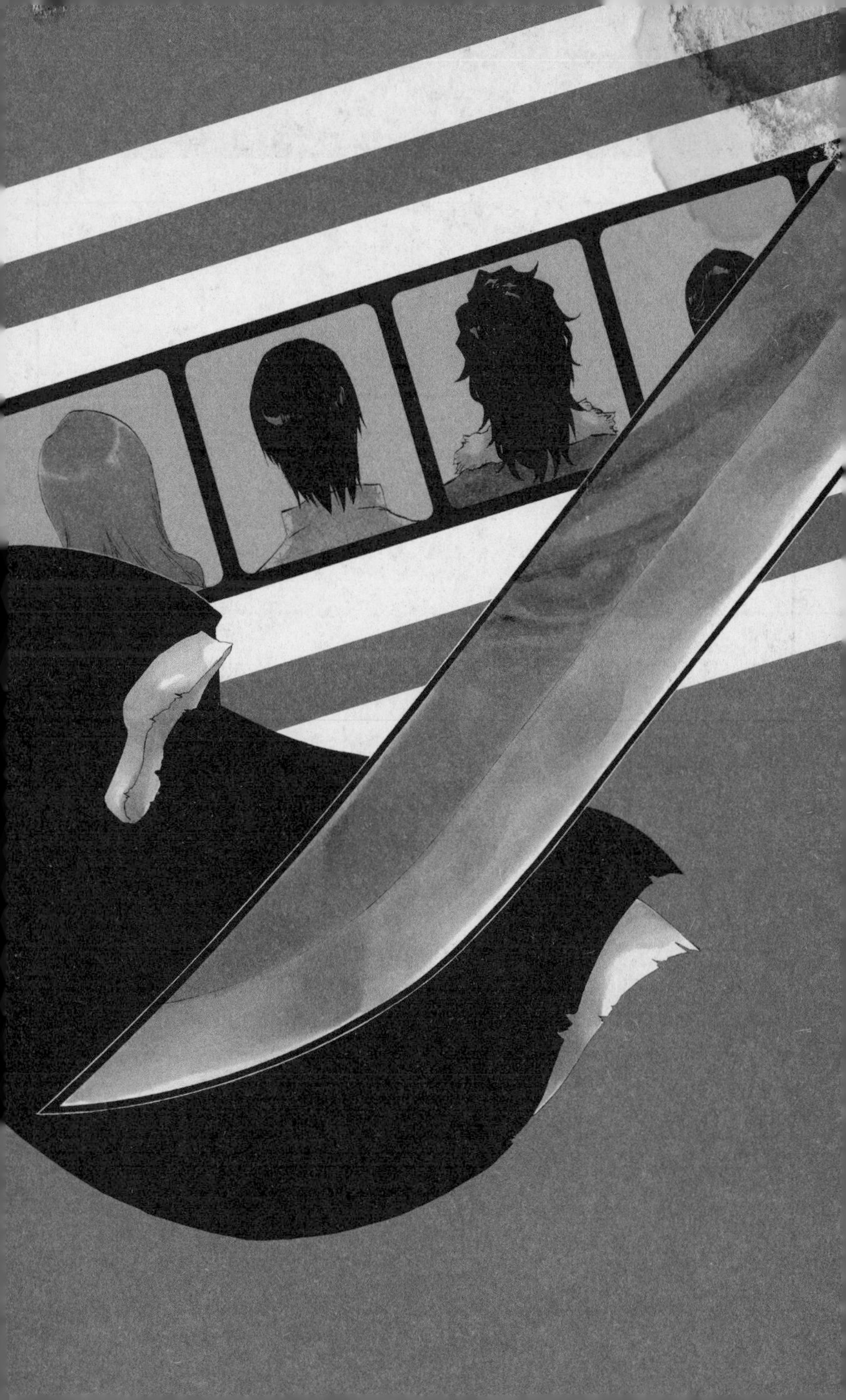

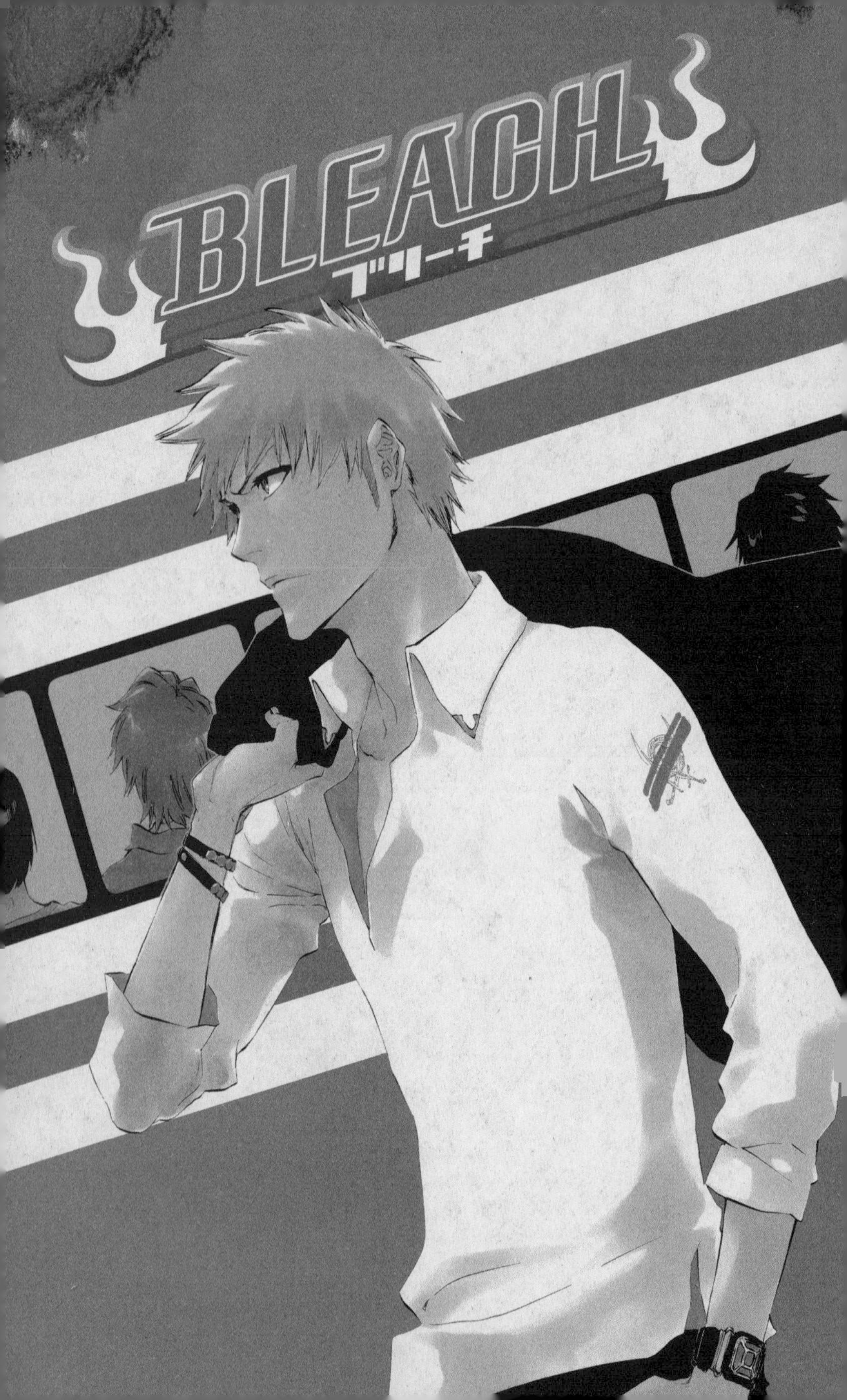
BLEACH
ブリーチ

BLEACH
ブリーチ

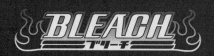

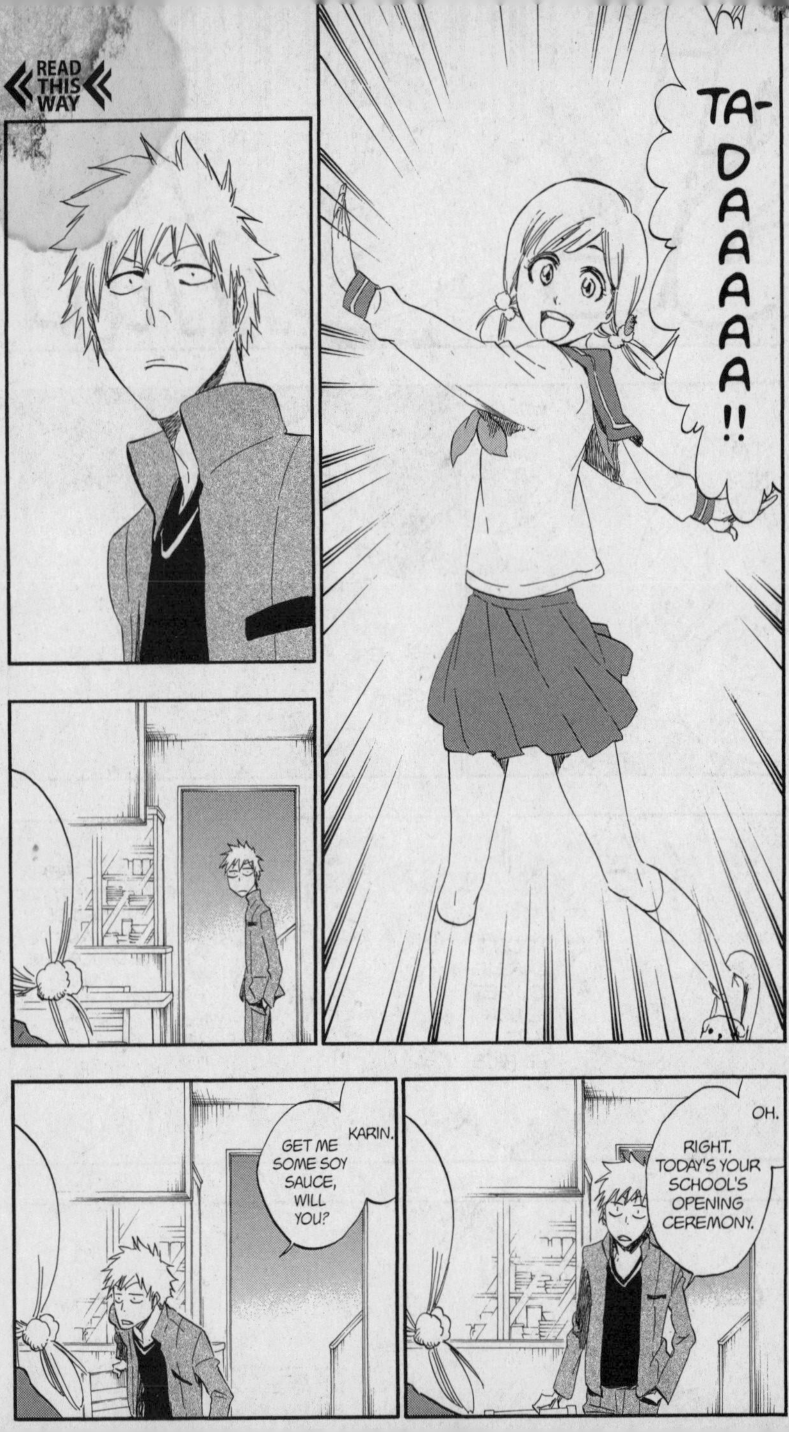
READ THIS WAY
TA-DAAAAAA!!
OH.
RIGHT. TODAY'S YOUR SCHOOL'S OPENING CEREMONY.
KARIN.
GET ME SOME SOY SAUCE, WILL YOU?

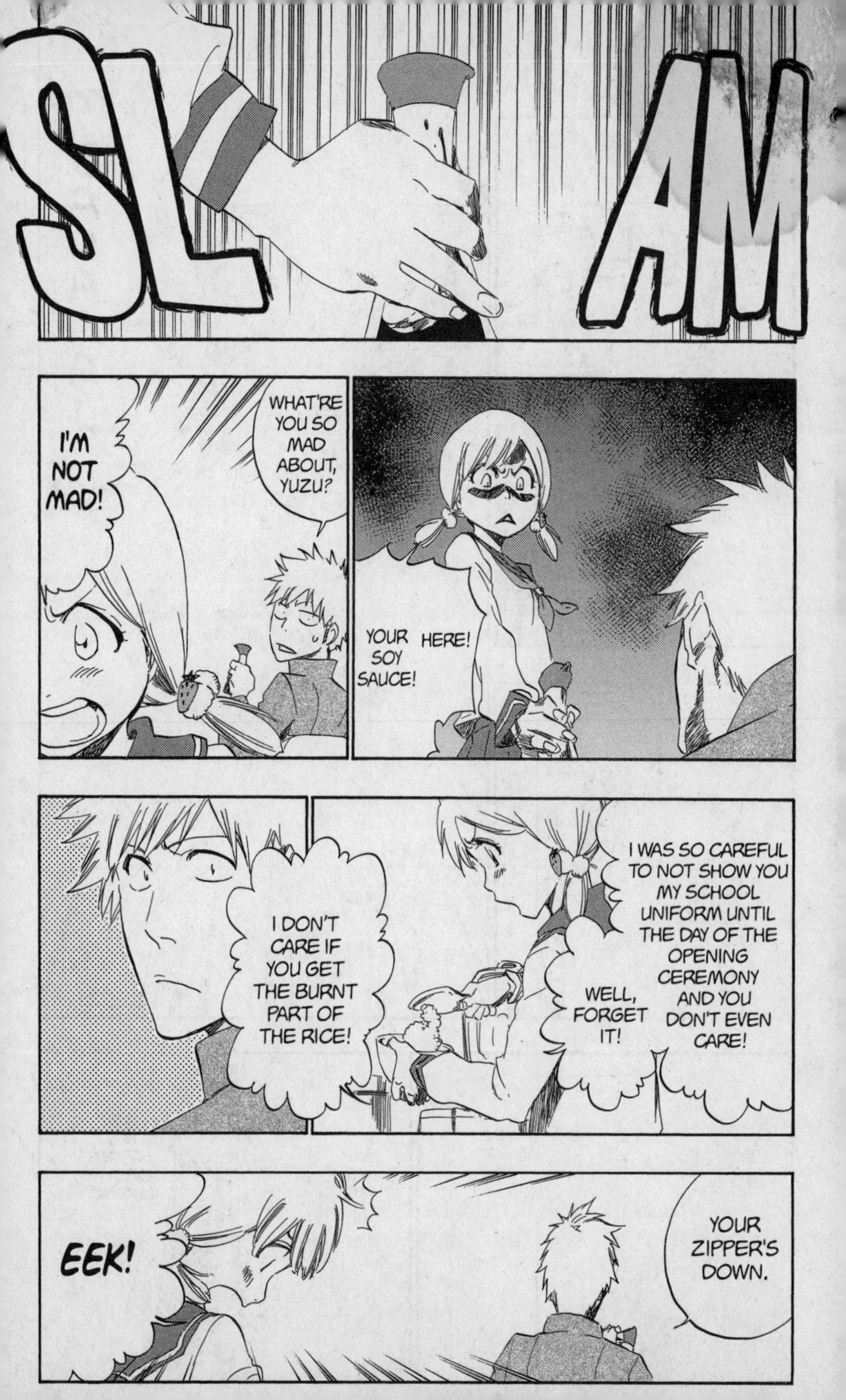
SLAM
HERE!
YOUR SOY SAUCE!
WHAT'RE YOU SO MAD ABOUT, YUZU?
I'M NOT MAD!
I WAS SO CAREFUL TO NOT SHOW YOU MY SCHOOL UNIFORM UNTIL THE DAY OF THE OPENING CEREMONY AND YOU DON'T EVEN CARE!
WELL, FORGET IT!
I DON'T CARE IF YOU GET THE BURNT PART OF THE RICE!
YOUR ZIPPER'S DOWN.
EEK!

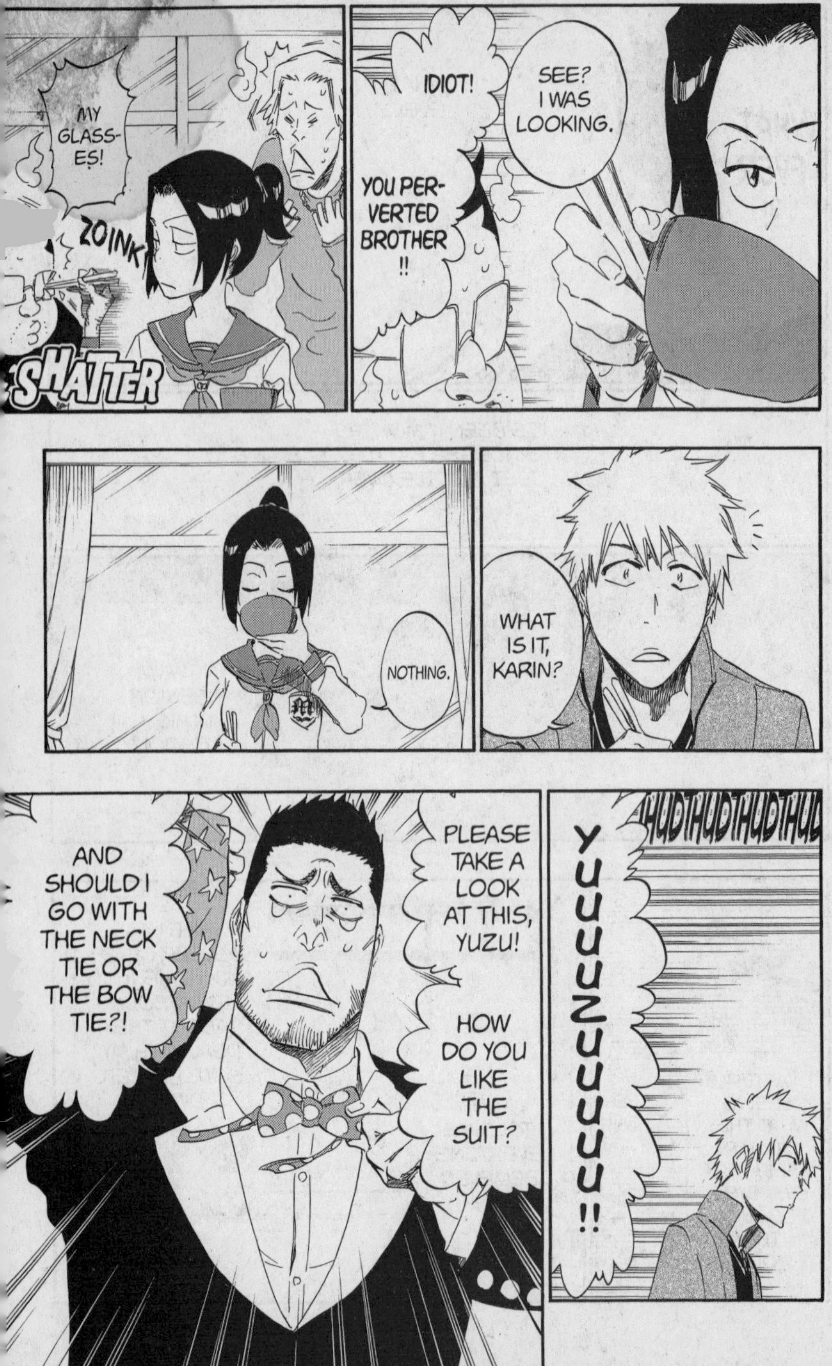
SEE? I WAS LOOKING.
IDIOT!
YOU PERVERTED BROTHER !!
MY GLASSES!
ZOINK
SHATTER
WHAT IS IT, KARIN?
NOTHING.
THUDTHUDTHUDTHUD
YUUUUZUUUUUU!!
PLEASE TAKE A LOOK AT THIS, YUZU!
HOW DO YOU LIKE THE SUIT?
AND SHOULD I GO WITH THE NECK TIE OR THE BOW TIE?!

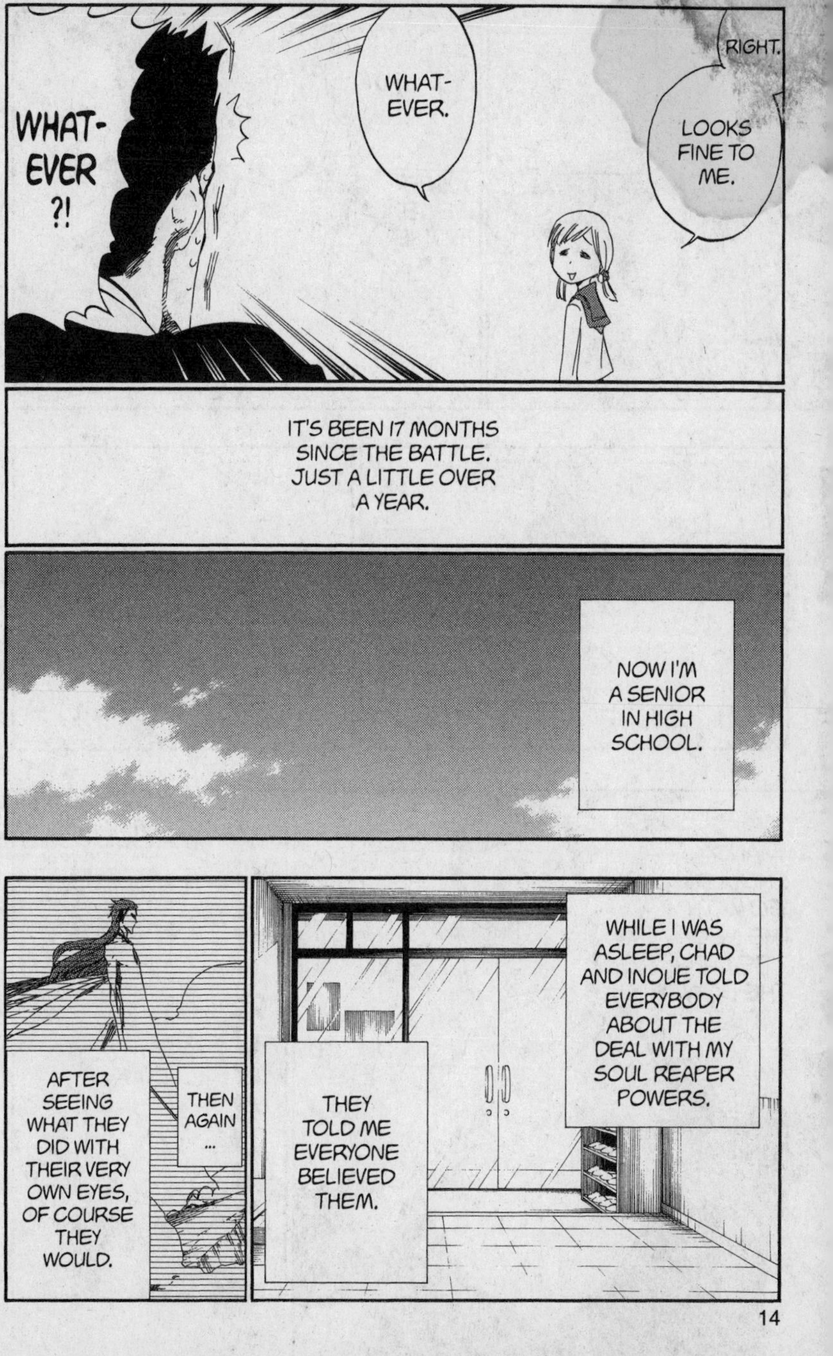
RIGHT.
LOOKS FINE TO ME.
WHAT-EVER.
WHAT-EVER?!
IT'S BEEN 17 MONTHS SINCE THE BATTLE. JUST A LITTLE OVER A YEAR.
NOW I'M A SENIOR IN HIGH SCHOOL.
WHILE I WAS ASLEEP, CHAD AND INOUE TOLD EVERYBODY ABOUT THE DEAL WITH MY SOUL REAPER POWERS.
THEY TOLD ME EVERYONE BELIEVED THEM.
THEN AGAIN...
AFTER SEEING WHAT THEY DID WITH THEIR VERY OWN EYES, OF COURSE THEY WOULD.

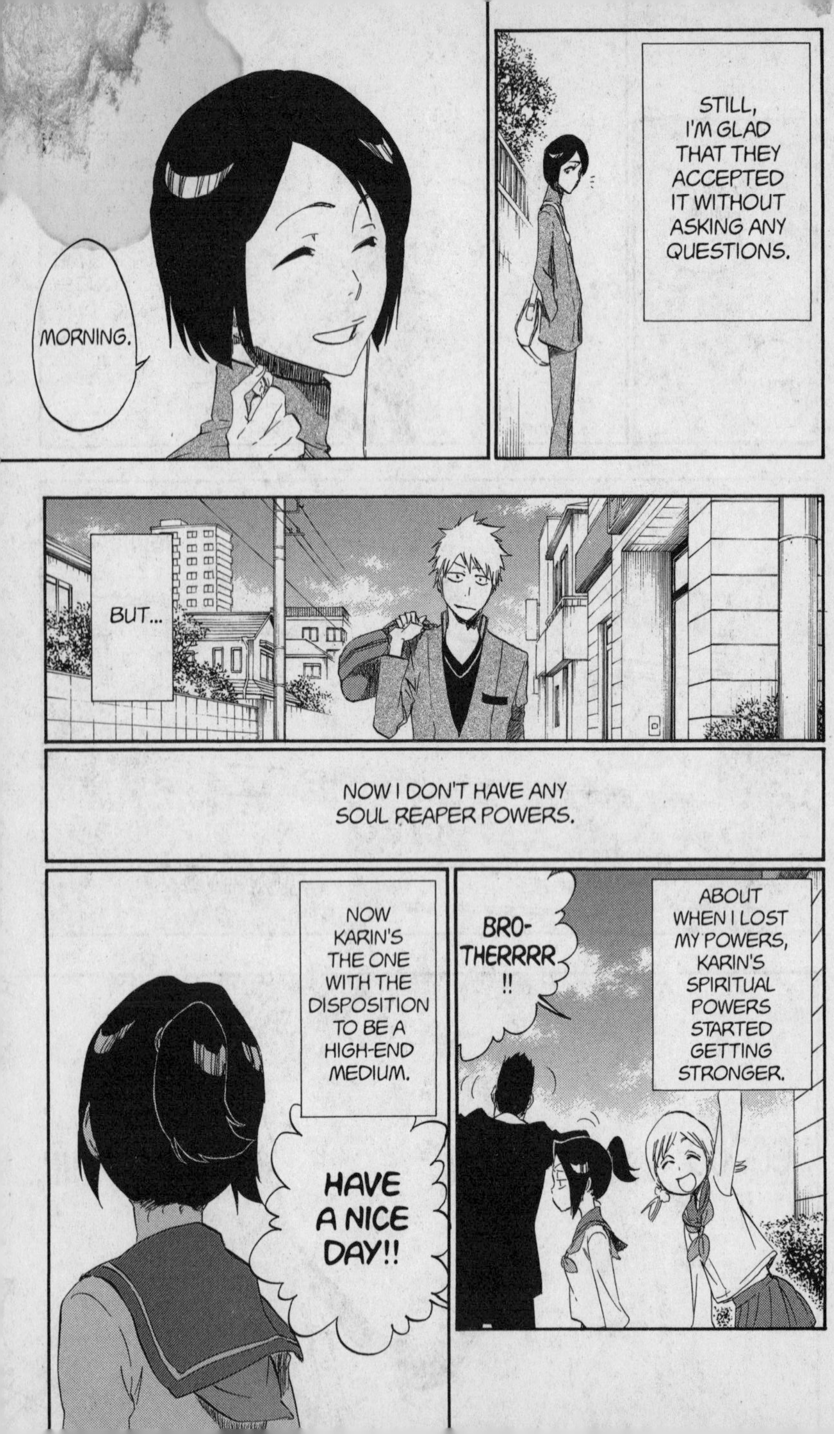
STILL, I'M GLAD THAT THEY ACCEPTED IT WITHOUT ASKING ANY QUESTIONS.
MORNING.
BUT...
NOW I DON'T HAVE ANY SOUL REAPER POWERS.
ABOUT WHEN I LOST MY POWERS, KARIN'S SPIRITUAL POWERS STARTED GETTING STRONGER.
BRO-THERRRR!!
NOW KARIN'S THE ONE WITH THE DISPOSITION TO BE A HIGH-END MEDIUM.
HAVE A NICE DAY!!

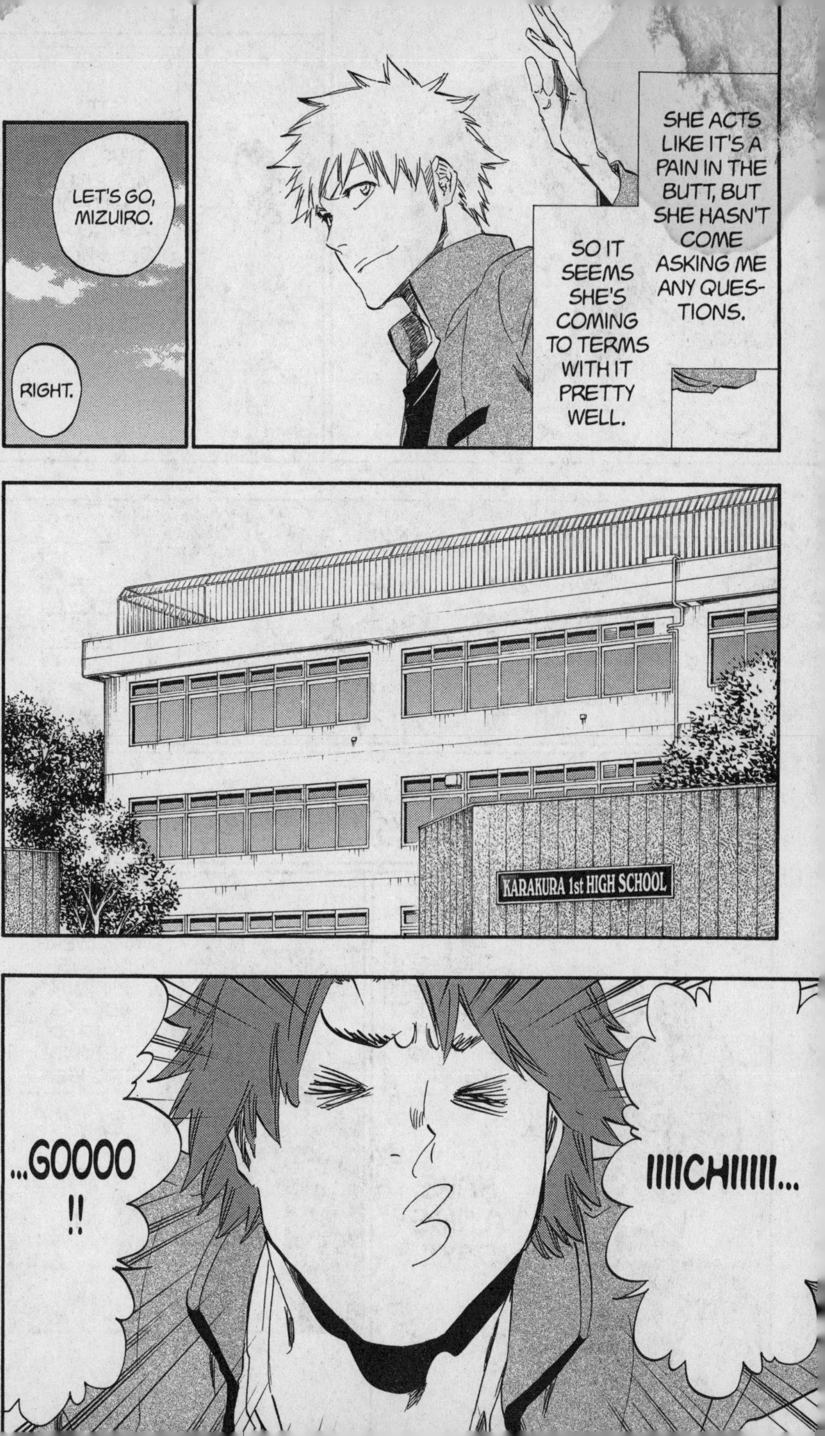
SHE ACTS LIKE IT'S A PAIN IN THE BUTT, BUT SHE HASN'T COME ASKING ME ANY QUESTIONS.
SO IT SEEMS SHE'S COMING TO TERMS WITH IT PRETTY WELL.
LET'S GO, MIZUIRO.
RIGHT.
KARAKURA 1st HIGH SCHOOL
IIIICHIIIII...
...GOOOO !!

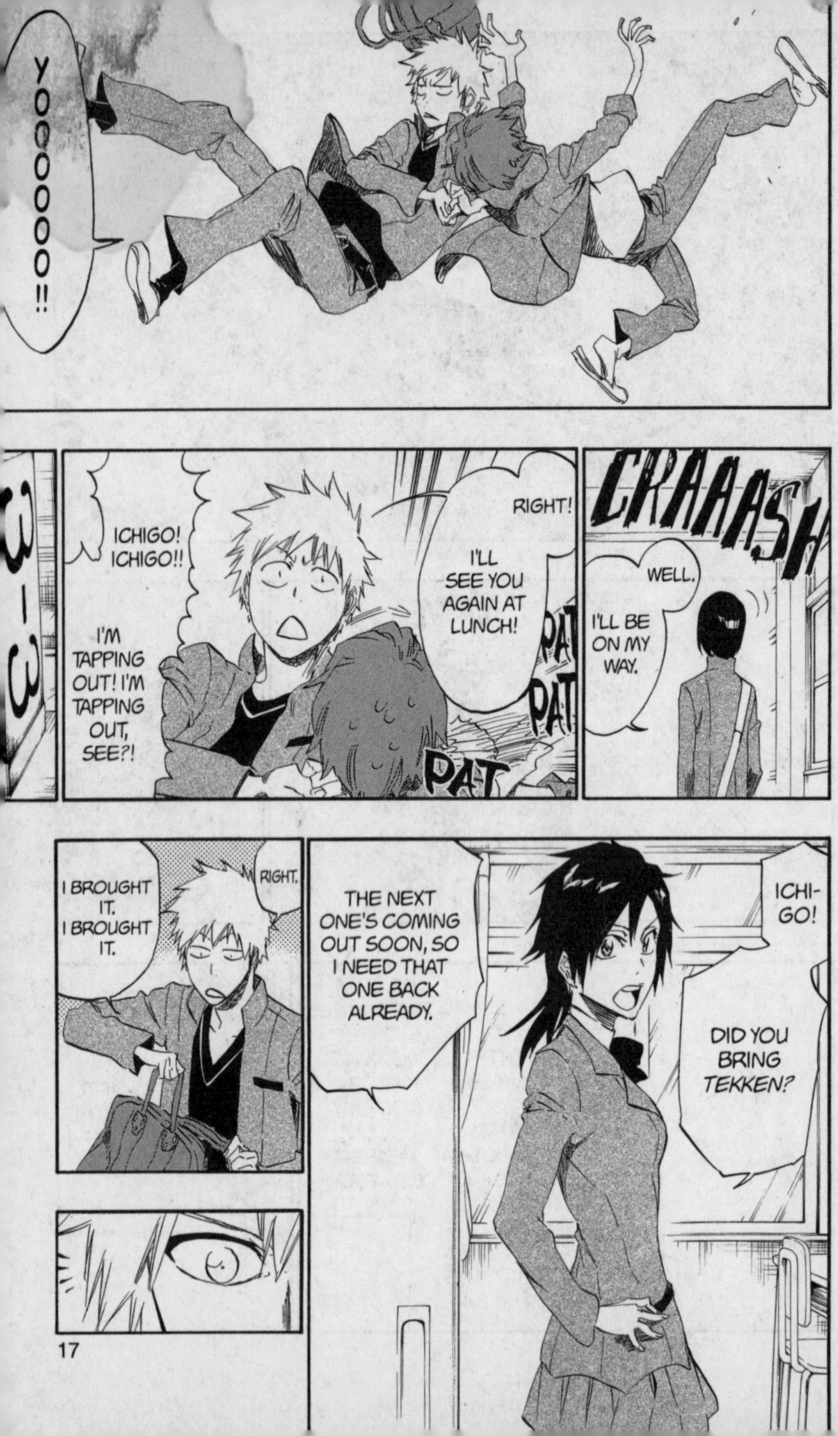
YOOOOOOO!!
CRAAASH
WELL.
I'LL BE ON MY WAY.
RIGHT!
I'LL SEE YOU AGAIN AT LUNCH!
PAT
PAT
PAT
ICHIGO! ICHIGO!!
I'M TAPPING OUT! I'M TAPPING OUT, SEE?!
3-3
ICHI-GO!
DID YOU BRING TEKKEN?
THE NEXT ONE'S COMING OUT SOON, SO I NEED THAT ONE BACK ALREADY.
RIGHT.
I BROUGHT IT. I BROUGHT IT.

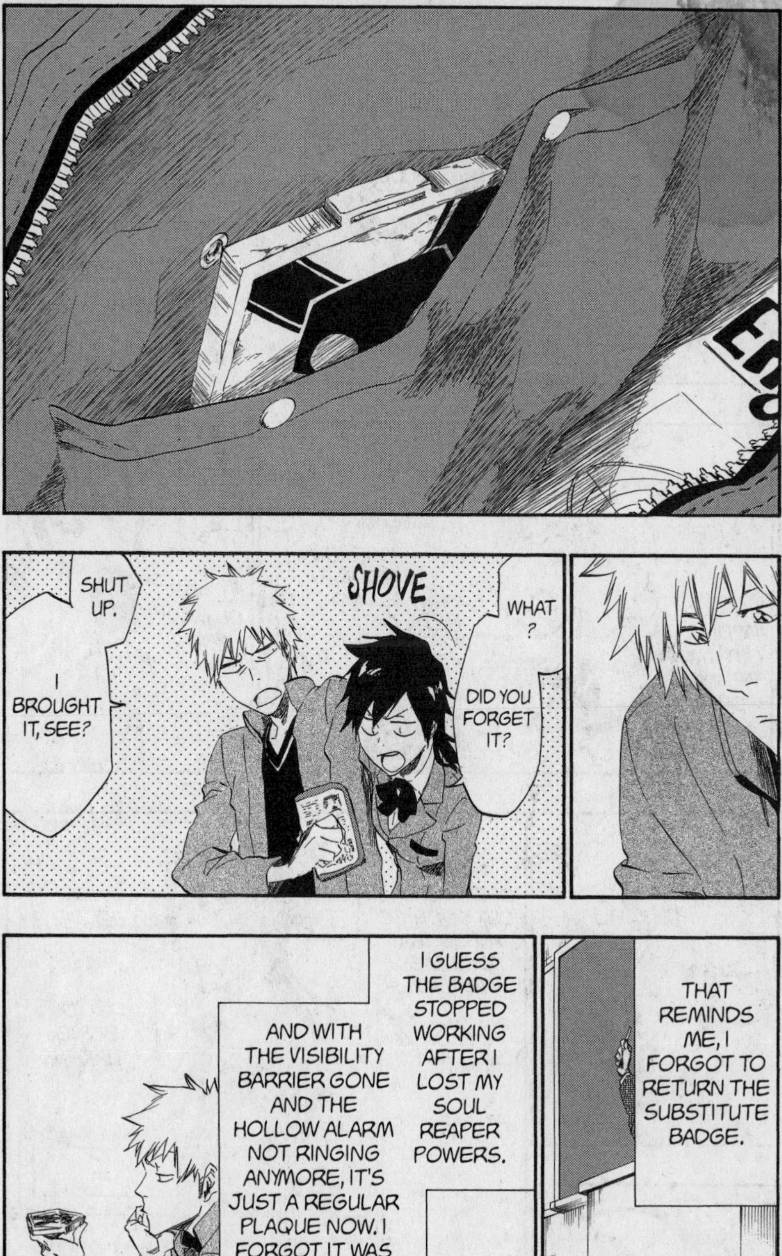
WHAT?
DID YOU FORGET IT?
SHOVE
SHUT UP.
I BROUGHT IT, SEE?
THAT REMINDS ME, I FORGOT TO RETURN THE SUBSTITUTE BADGE.
I GUESS THE BADGE STOPPED WORKING AFTER I LOST MY SOUL REAPER POWERS.
AND WITH THE VISIBILITY BARRIER GONE AND THE HOLLOW ALARM NOT RINGING ANYMORE, IT'S JUST A REGULAR PLAQUE NOW. I FORGOT IT WAS EVEN IN MY BAG.

READ THIS WAY

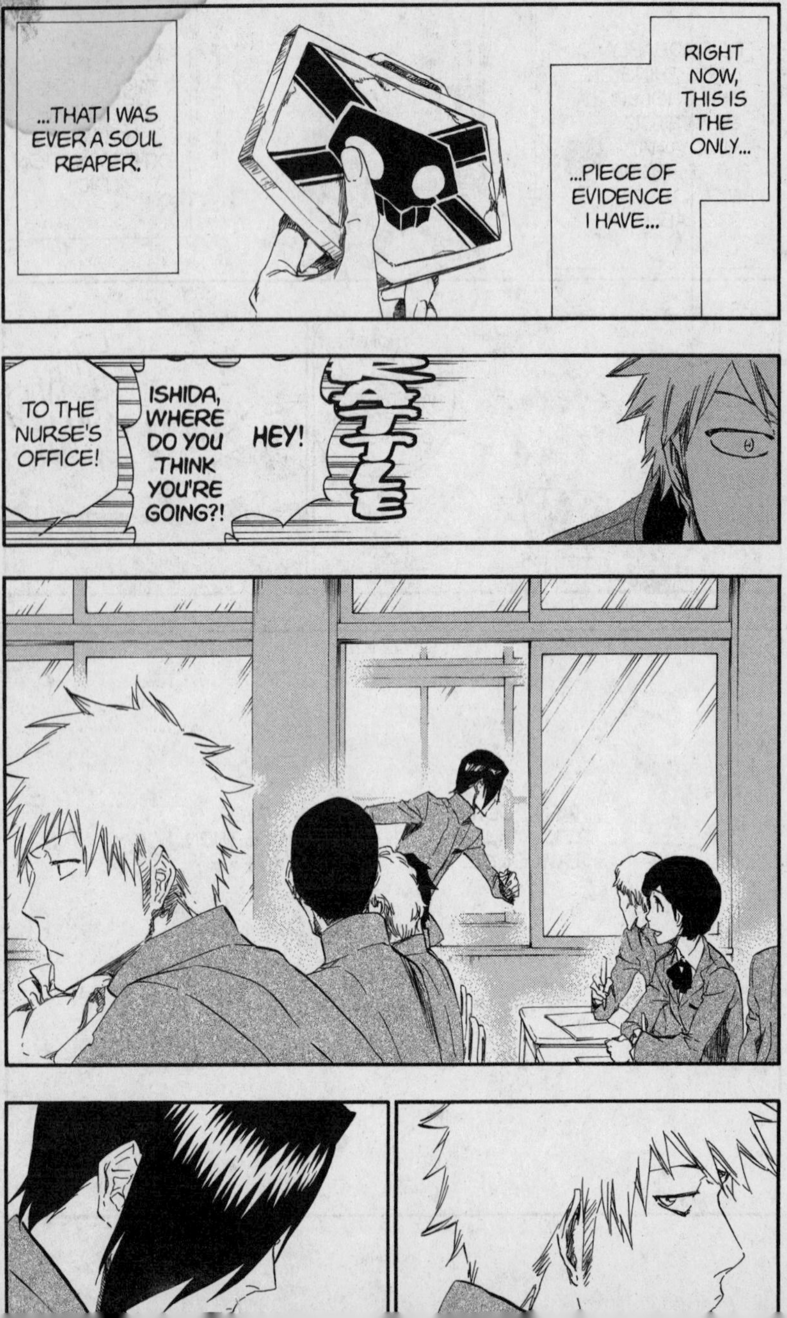
RIGHT NOW, THIS IS THE ONLY...
...PIECE OF EVIDENCE I HAVE...
...THAT I WAS EVER A SOUL REAPER.
HEY!
ISHIDA, WHERE DO YOU THINK YOU'RE GOING?!
TO THE NURSE'S OFFICE!

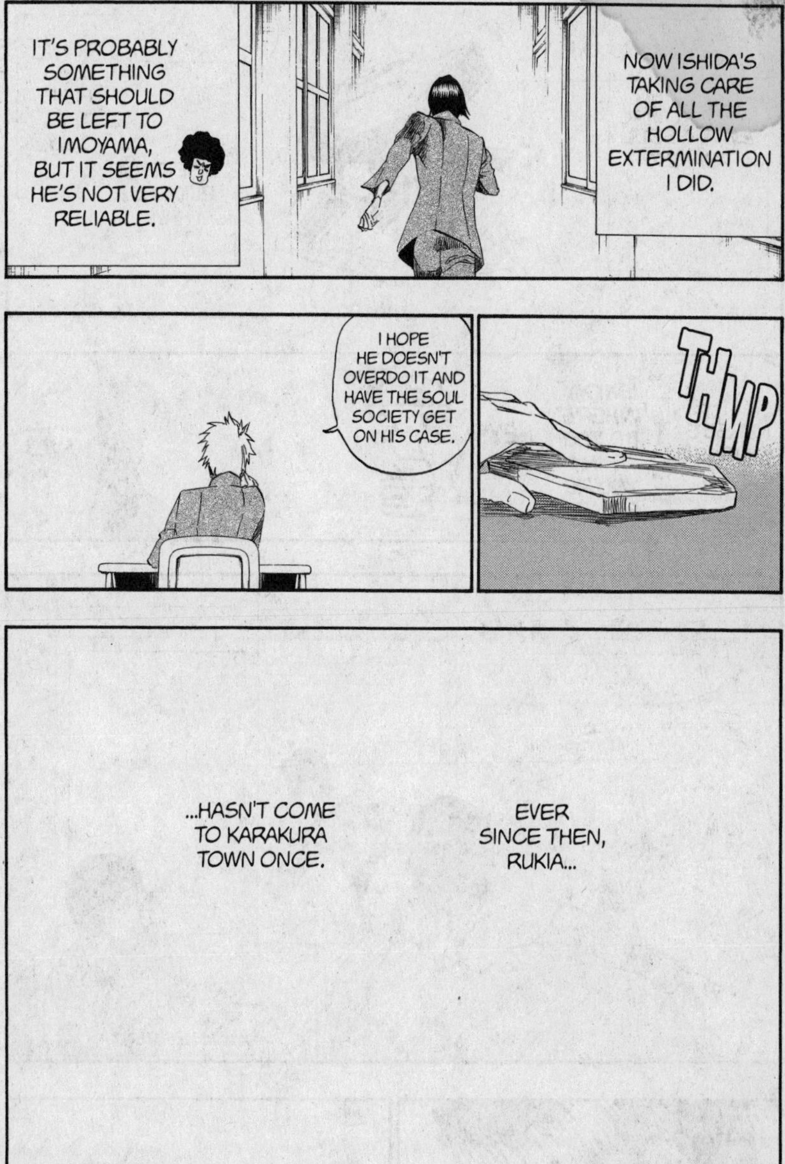
NOW ISHIDA'S TAKING CARE OF ALL THE HOLLOW EXTERMINATION I DID.
IT'S PROBABLY SOMETHING THAT SHOULD BE LEFT TO IMOYAMA, BUT IT SEEMS HE'S NOT VERY RELIABLE.
THMP
I HOPE HE DOESN'T OVERDO IT AND HAVE THE SOUL SOCIETY GET ON HIS CASE.
EVER SINCE THEN, RUKIA...
...HASN'T COME TO KARAKURA TOWN ONCE.

READ THIS WAY

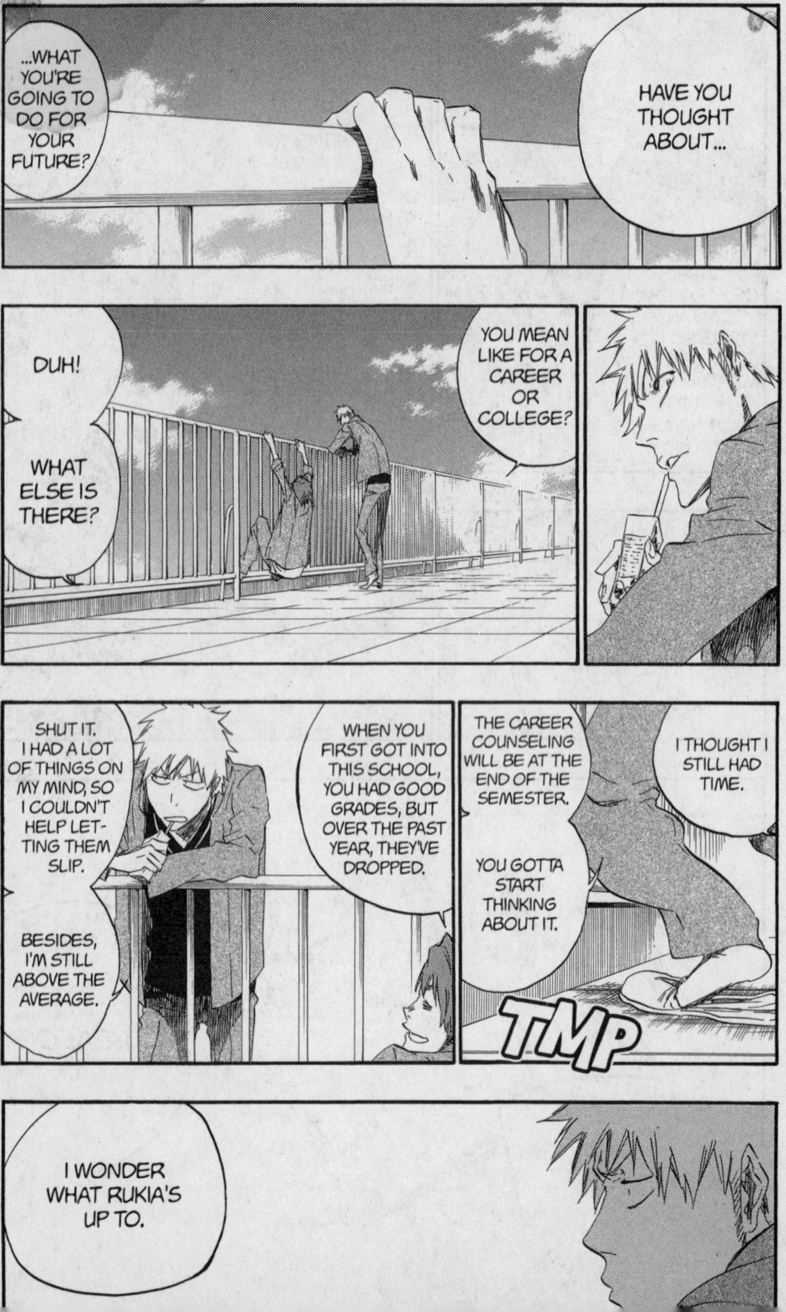
HAVE YOU THOUGHT ABOUT...
...WHAT YOU'RE GOING TO DO FOR YOUR FUTURE?
YOU MEAN LIKE FOR A CAREER OR COLLEGE?
DUH!
WHAT ELSE IS THERE?
I THOUGHT I STILL HAD TIME.
THE CAREER COUNSELING WILL BE AT THE END OF THE SEMESTER.
YOU GOTTA START THINKING ABOUT IT.
TMP
WHEN YOU FIRST GOT INTO THIS SCHOOL, YOU HAD GOOD GRADES, BUT OVER THE PAST YEAR, THEY'VE DROPPED.
SHUT IT. I HAD A LOT OF THINGS ON MY MIND, SO I COULDN'T HELP LETTING THEM SLIP.
BESIDES, I'M STILL ABOVE THE AVERAGE.
I WONDER WHAT RUKIA'S UP TO.

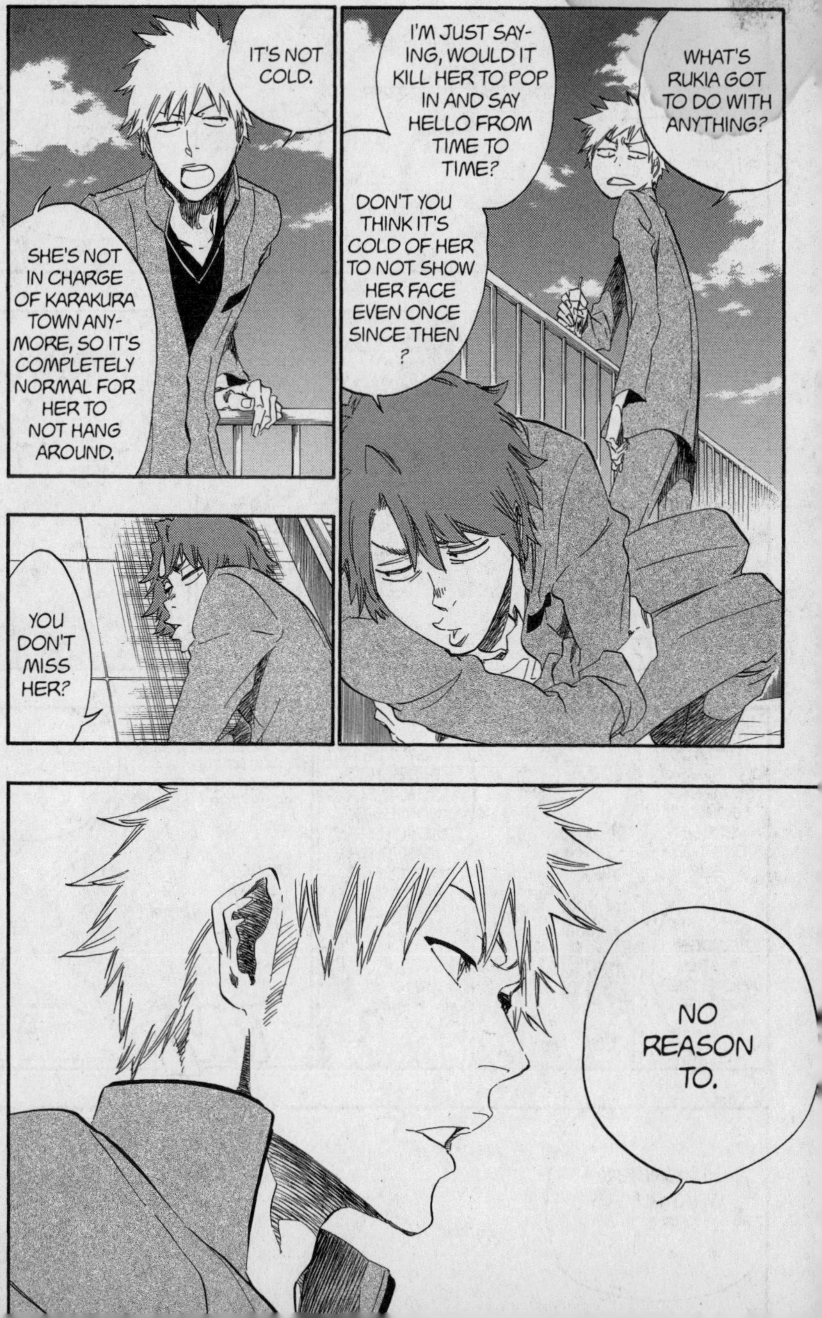
WHAT'S RUKIA GOT TO DO WITH ANYTHING?
I'M JUST SAYING, WOULD IT KILL HER TO POP IN AND SAY HELLO FROM TIME TO TIME?
DON'T YOU THINK IT'S COLD OF HER TO NOT SHOW HER FACE EVEN ONCE SINCE THEN?
IT'S NOT COLD.
SHE'S NOT IN CHARGE OF KARAKURA TOWN ANYMORE, SO IT'S COMPLETELY NORMAL FOR HER TO NOT HANG AROUND.
YOU DON'T MISS HER?
NO REASON TO.

READ THIS WAY

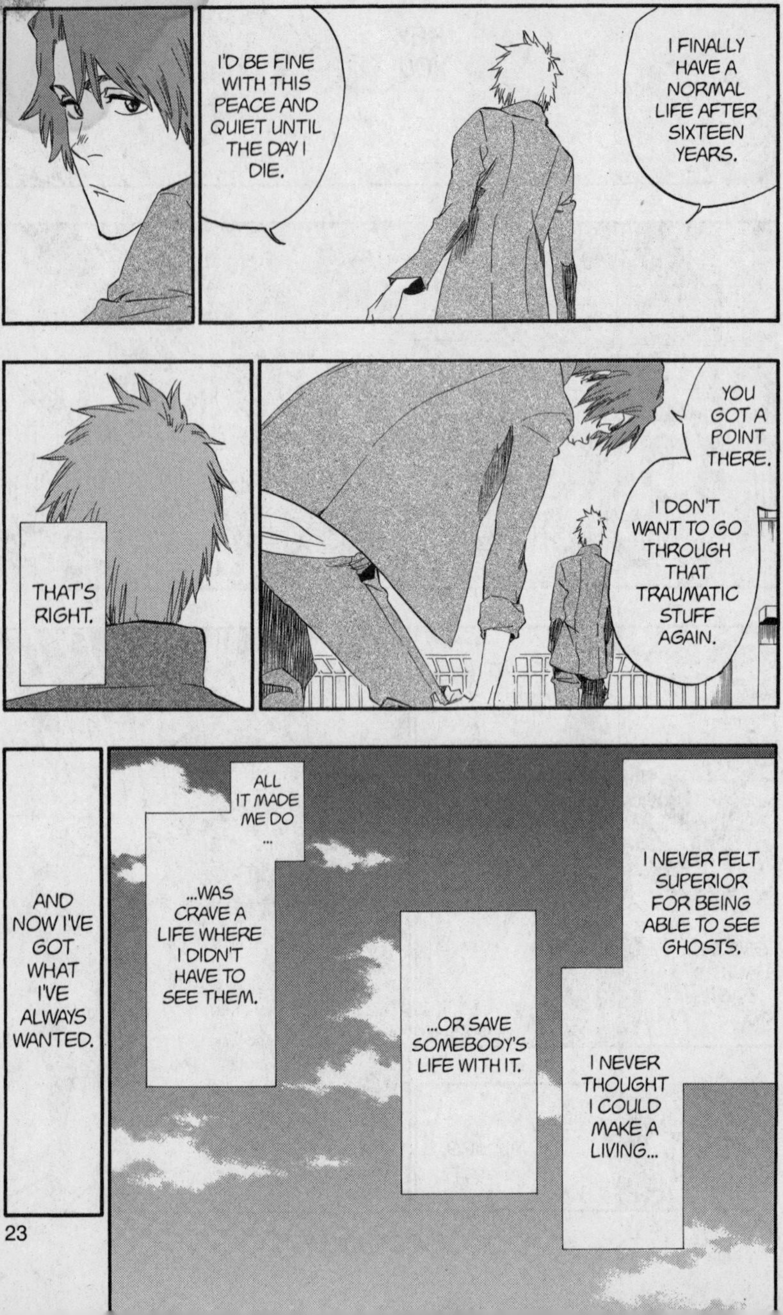

I FINALLY HAVE A NORMAL LIFE AFTER SIXTEEN YEARS.
I'D BE FINE WITH THIS PEACE AND QUIET UNTIL THE DAY I DIE.
YOU GOT A POINT THERE.
I DON'T WANT TO GO THROUGH THAT TRAUMATIC STUFF AGAIN.
THAT'S RIGHT.
I NEVER FELT SUPERIOR FOR BEING ABLE TO SEE GHOSTS.
I NEVER THOUGHT I COULD MAKE A LIVING...
...OR SAVE SOMEBODY'S LIFE WITH IT.
ALL IT MADE ME DO ...
...WAS CRAVE A LIFE WHERE I DIDN'T HAVE TO SEE THEM.
AND NOW I'VE GOT WHAT I'VE ALWAYS WANTED.

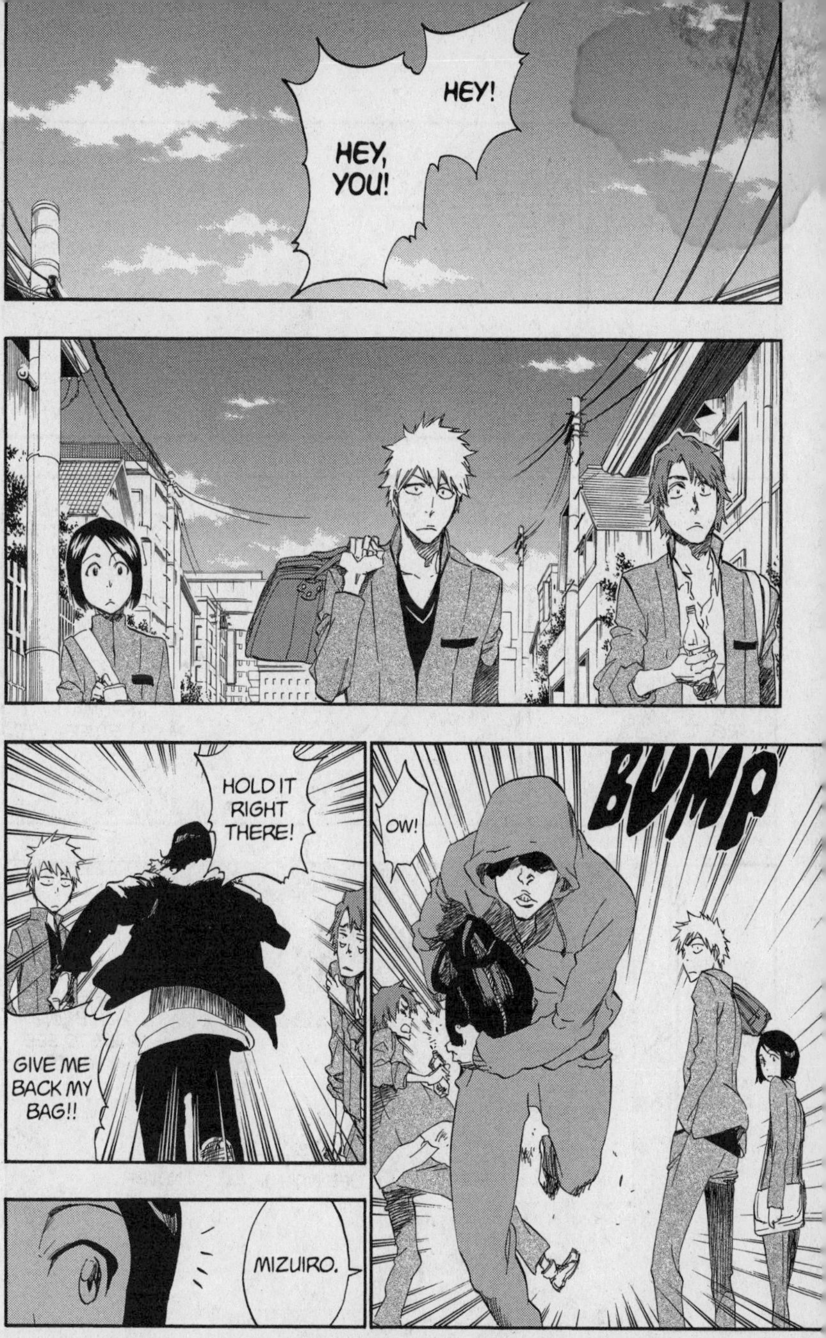
HEY!
HEY, YOU!
BUMP
OW!
HOLD IT RIGHT THERE!
GIVE ME BACK MY BAG!!
MIZUIRO.

ACTUALLY...

READ THIS WAY

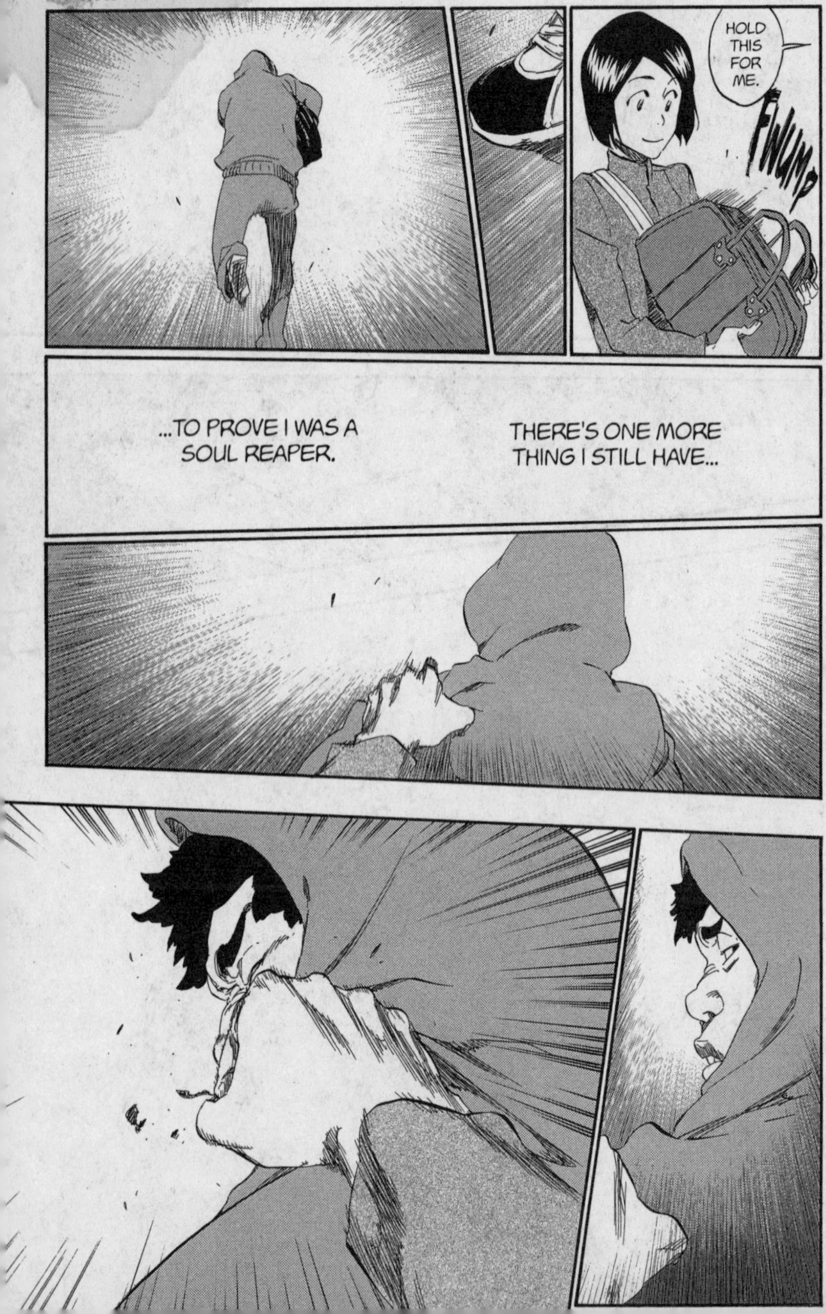

HOLD THIS FOR ME.
FWUMP
THERE'S ONE MORE THING I STILL HAVE...
...TO PROVE I WAS A SOUL REAPER.

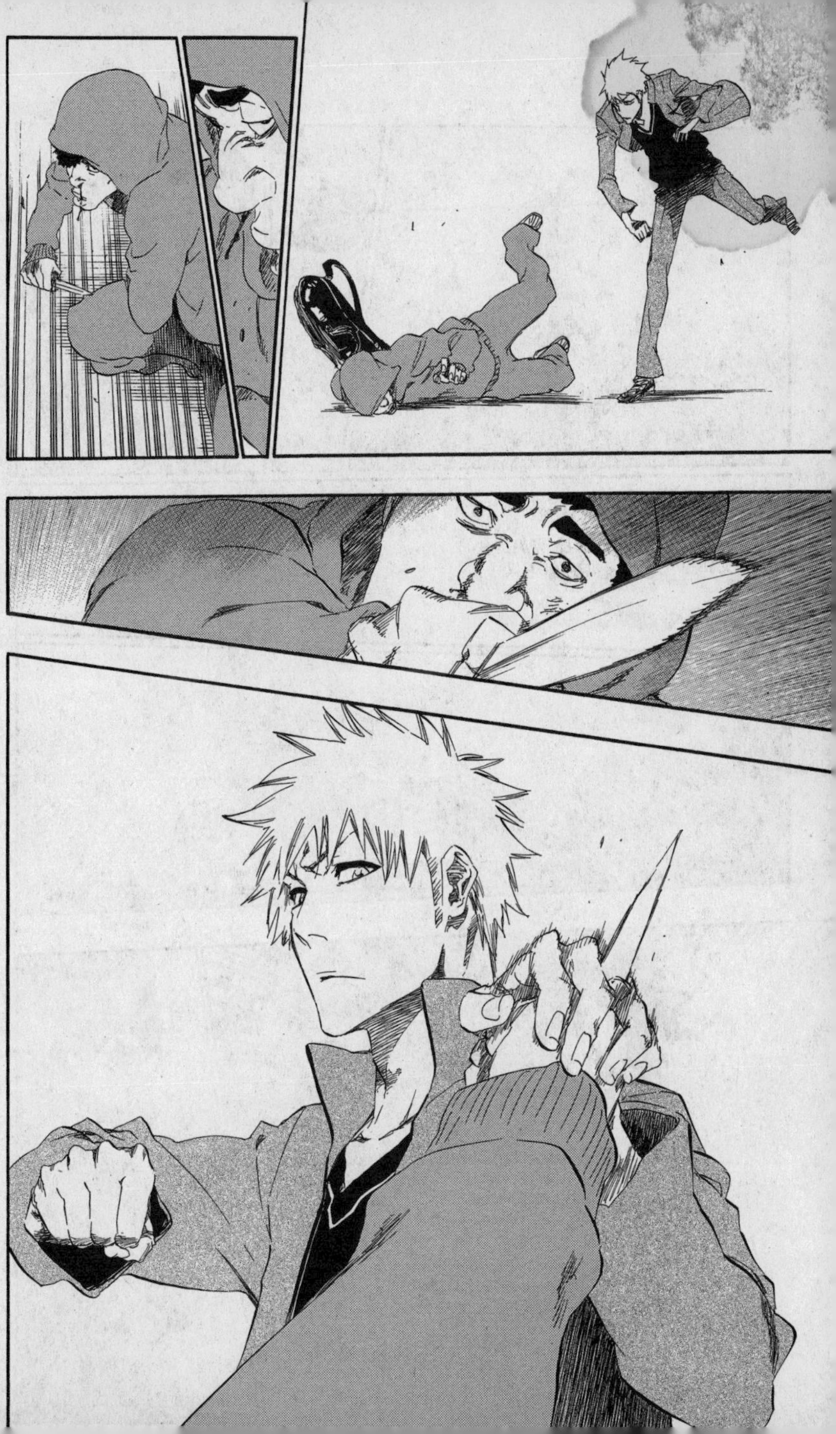

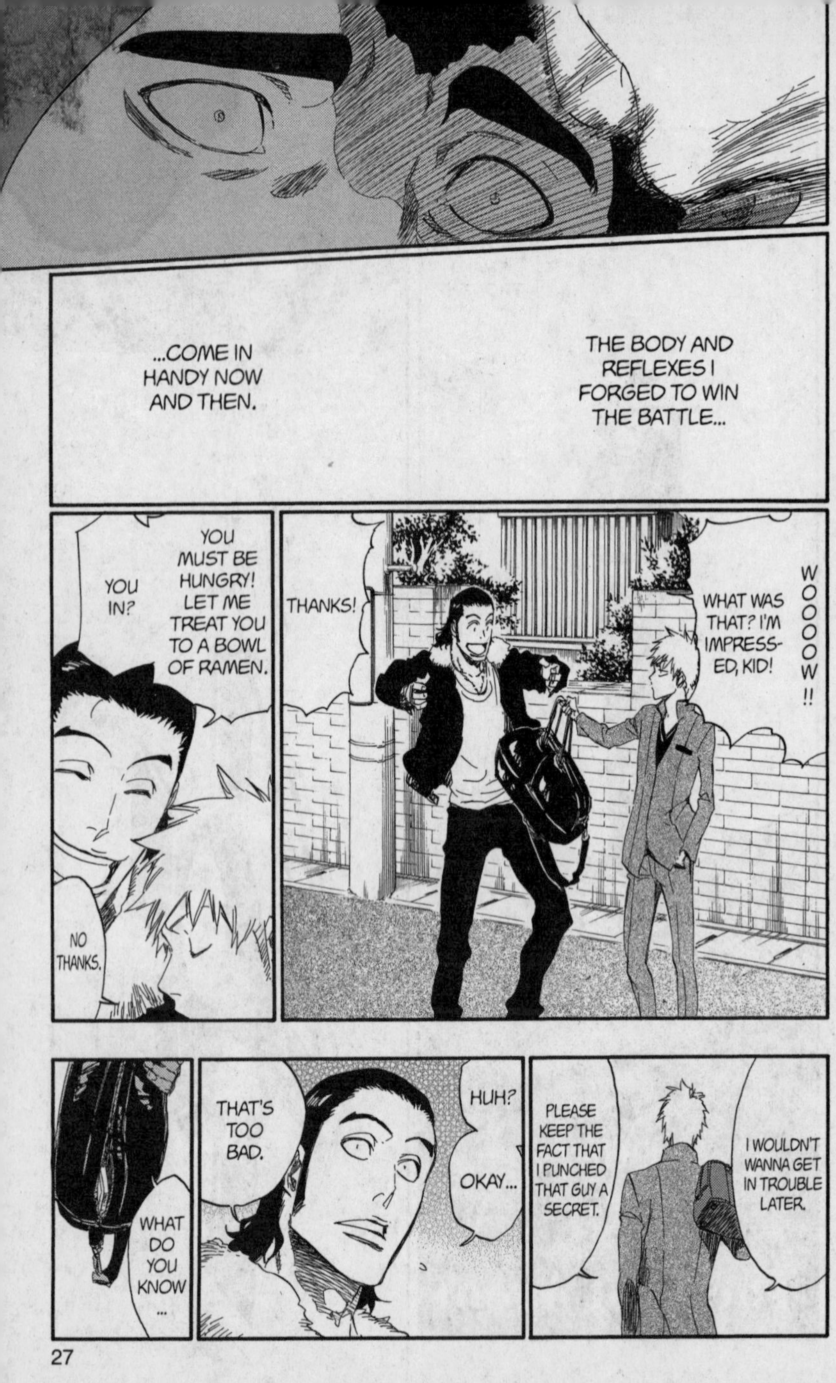
THE BODY AND REFLEXES I FORGED TO WIN THE BATTLE...
...COME IN HANDY NOW AND THEN.
WOOOOOW!!
WHAT WAS THAT? I'M IMPRESSED, KID!
THANKS!
YOU MUST BE HUNGRY! LET ME TREAT YOU TO A BOWL OF RAMEN.
YOU IN?
NO THANKS.
I WOULDN'T WANNA GET IN TROUBLE LATER.
PLEASE KEEP THE FACT THAT I PUNCHED THAT GUY A SECRET.
HUH?
OKAY...
THAT'S TOO BAD.
WHAT DO YOU KNOW...

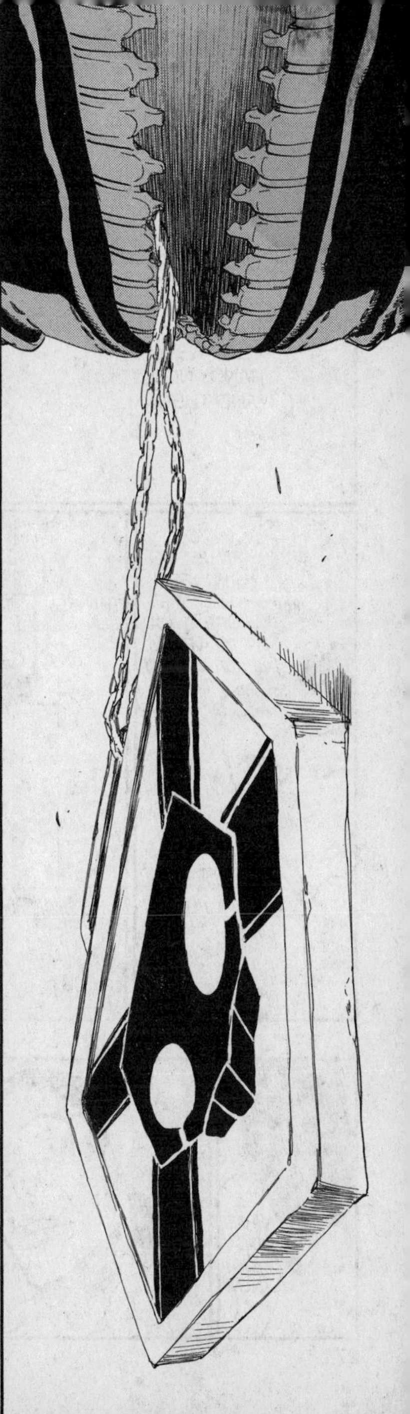

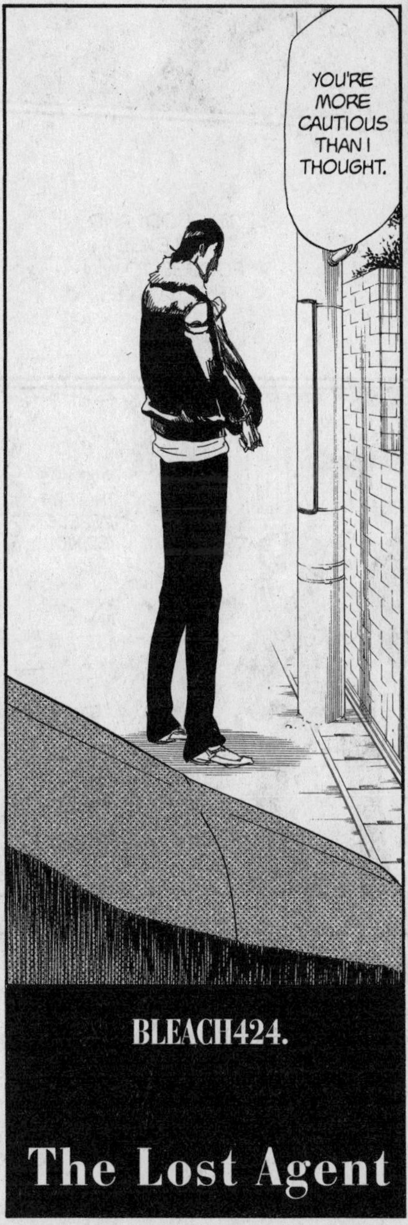
YOU'RE MORE CAUTIOUS THAN I THOUGHT.

BLEACH424.

The Lost Agent

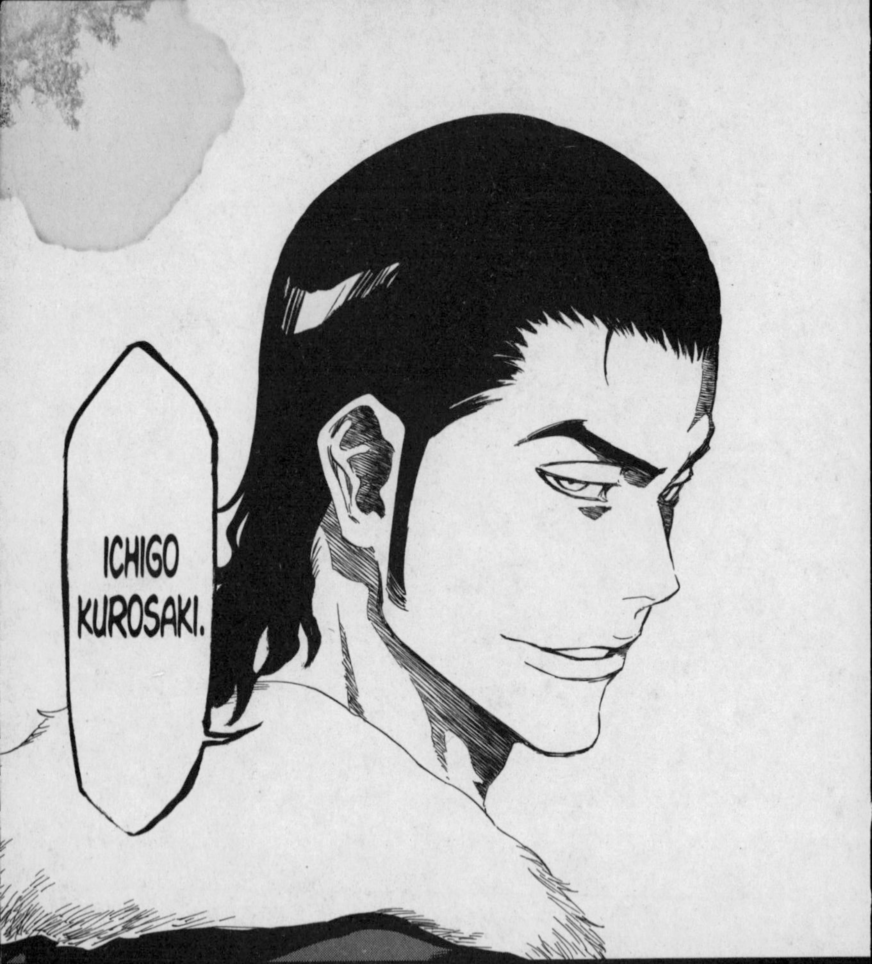
ICHIGO KUROSAKI.

THE LOST AGENT ARC

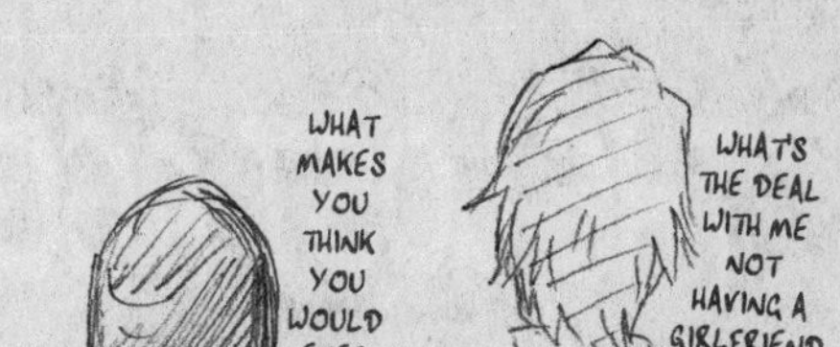
WHAT'S THE DEAL WITH ME NOT HAVING A GIRLFRIEND YET?
WHAT MAKES YOU THINK YOU WOULD EVER HAVE ONE?

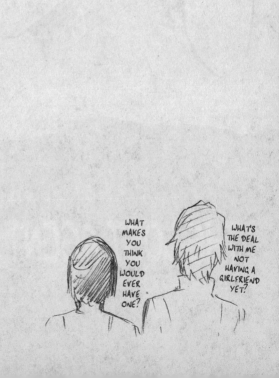

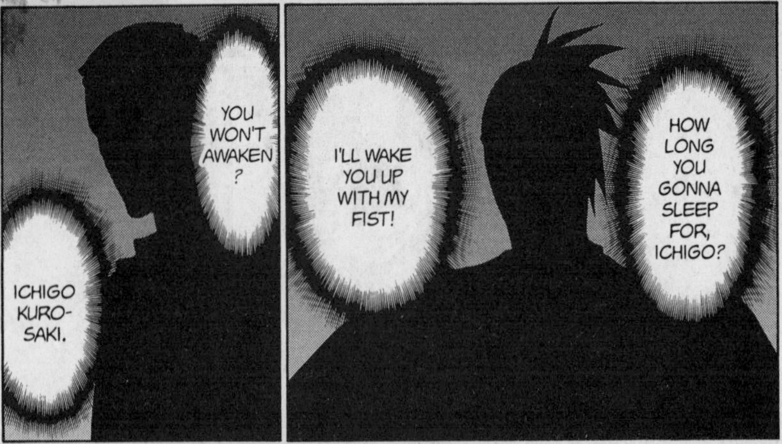
HOW LONG YOU GONNA SLEEP FOR, ICHIGO?
I'LL WAKE YOU UP WITH MY FIST!
YOU WON'T AWAKEN?
ICHIGO KUROSAKI.

425. A Day Without Melodies

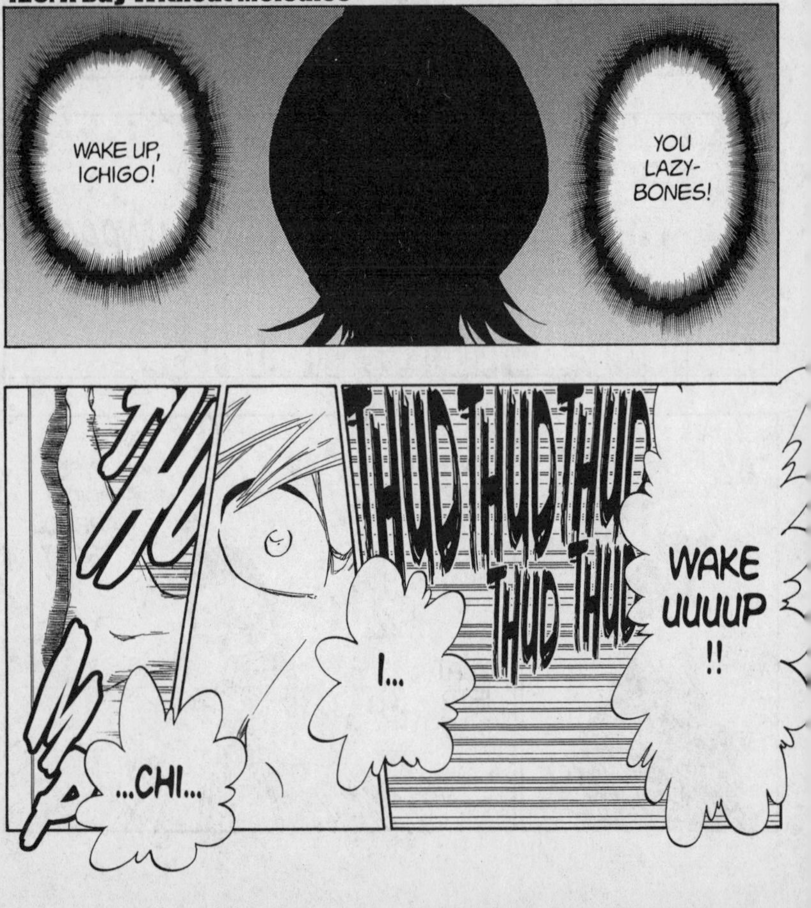
YOU LAZY-BONES!
WAKE UP, ICHIGO!
WAKE UUUUP!!
THUD THUD THUD
THUD THUD
I...
...CHI...
THUMP

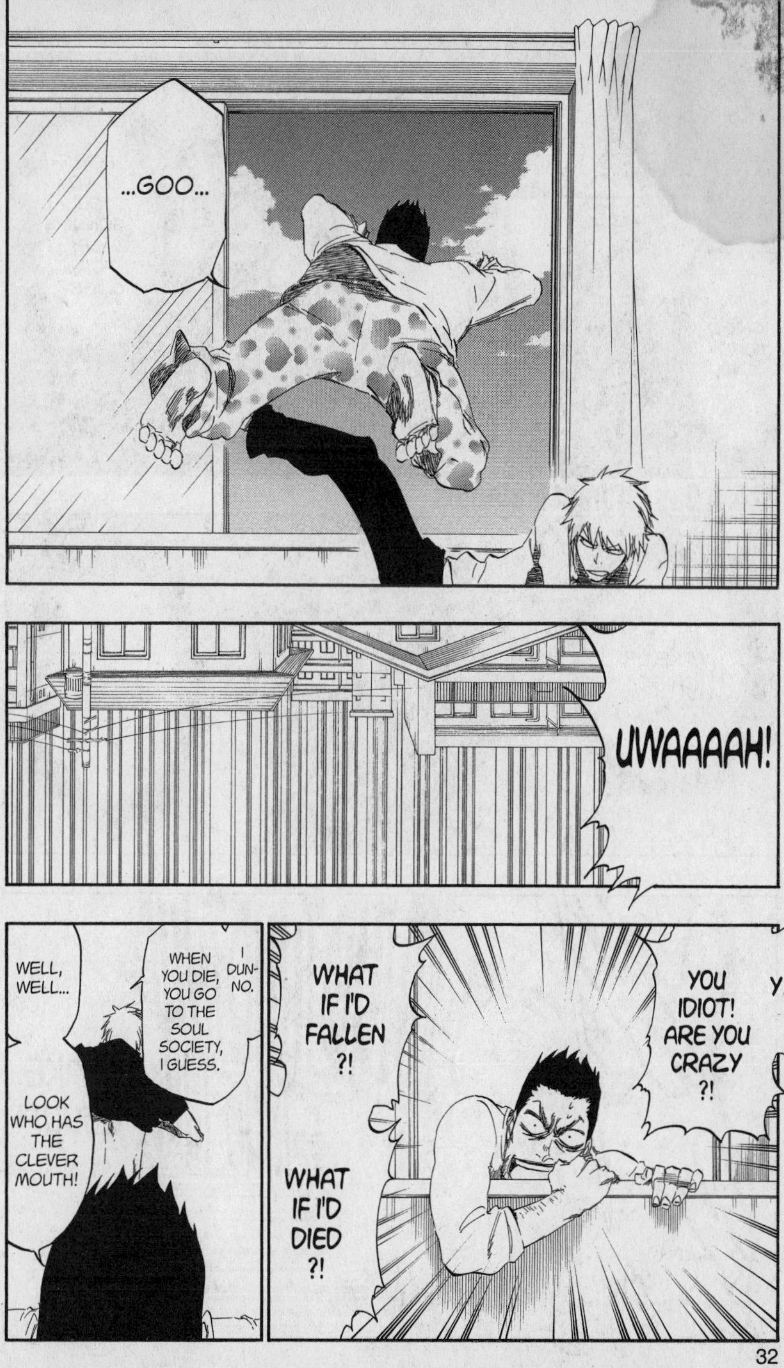
...GOO...
UWAAAAH!
Y...
YOU IDIOT! ARE YOU CRAZY ?!
WHAT IF I'D FALLEN ?!
WHAT IF I'D DIED ?!
I DUN-NO.
WHEN YOU DIE, YOU GO TO THE SOUL SOCIETY, I GUESS.
WELL, WELL...
LOOK WHO HAS THE CLEVER MOUTH!

READ THIS WAY

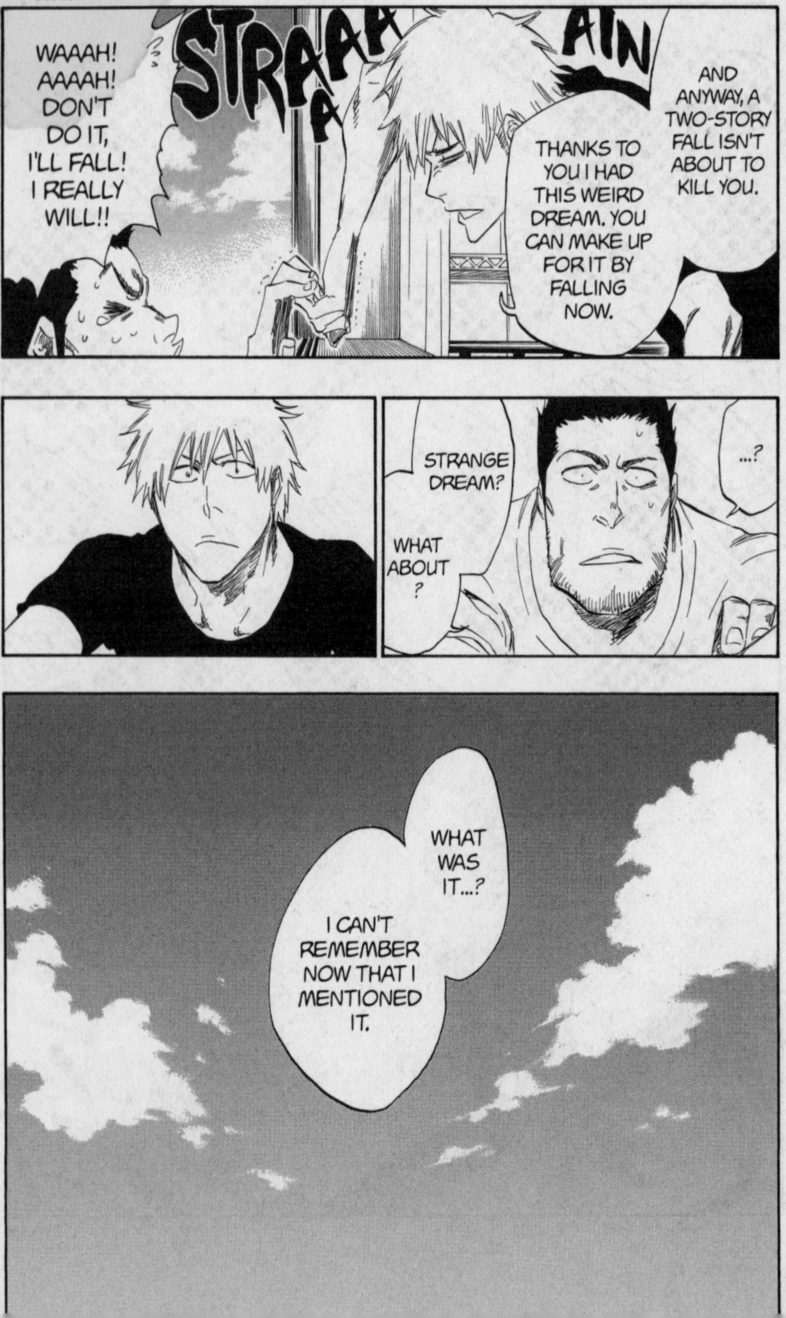

STRAAAAAIN
AND ANYWAY, A TWO-STORY FALL ISN'T ABOUT TO KILL YOU.
THANKS TO YOU I HAD THIS WEIRD DREAM. YOU CAN MAKE UP FOR IT BY FALLING NOW.
WAAAH! AAAAH! DON'T DO IT, I'LL FALL! I REALLY WILL!!
...?
STRANGE DREAM?
WHAT ABOUT?
WHAT WAS IT...?
I CAN'T REMEMBER NOW THAT I MENTIONED IT.

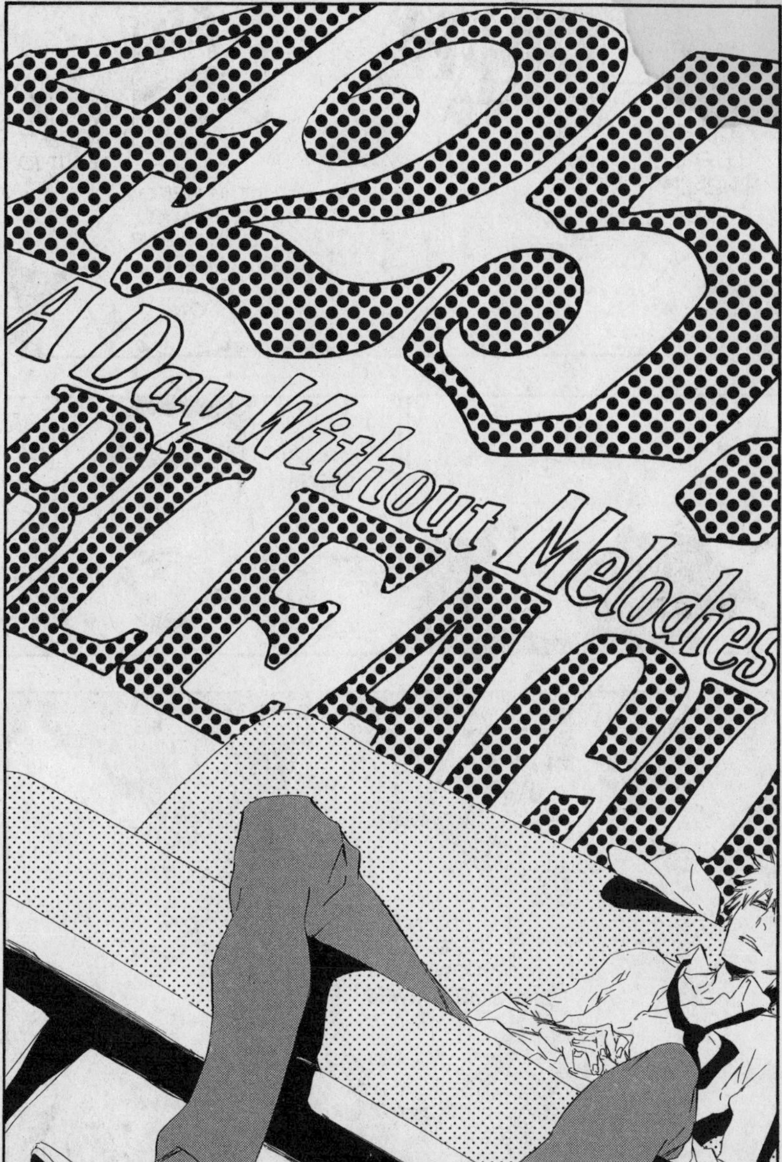
A Day Without Melodies

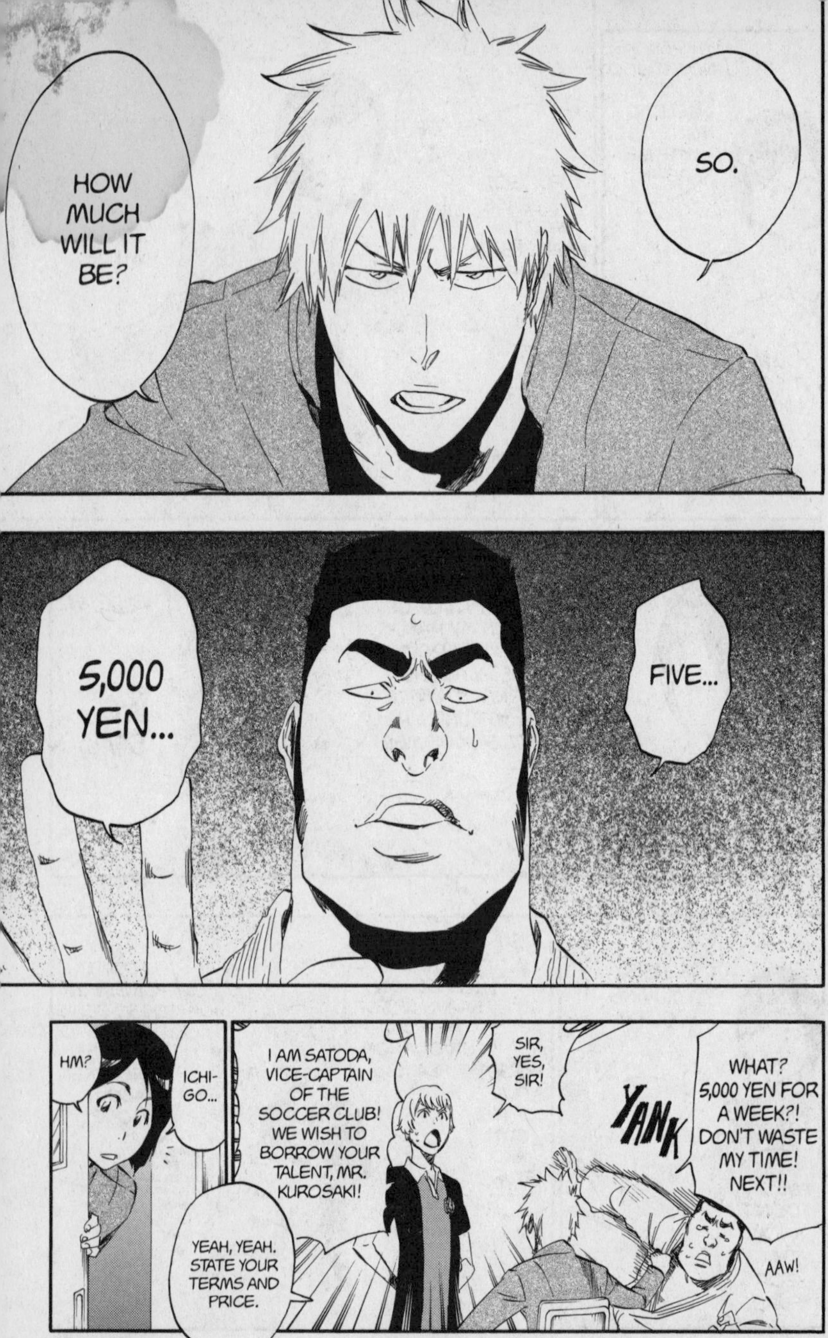
SO.
HOW MUCH WILL IT BE?
FIVE...
5,000 YEN...
WHAT? 5,000 YEN FOR A WEEK?! DON'T WASTE MY TIME! NEXT!!
SIR, YES, SIR!
YANK
I AM SATODA, VICE-CAPTAIN OF THE SOCCER CLUB! WE WISH TO BORROW YOUR TALENT, MR. KUROSAKI!
AAW!
YEAH, YEAH. STATE YOUR TERMS AND PRICE.
ICHI-GO...
HM?

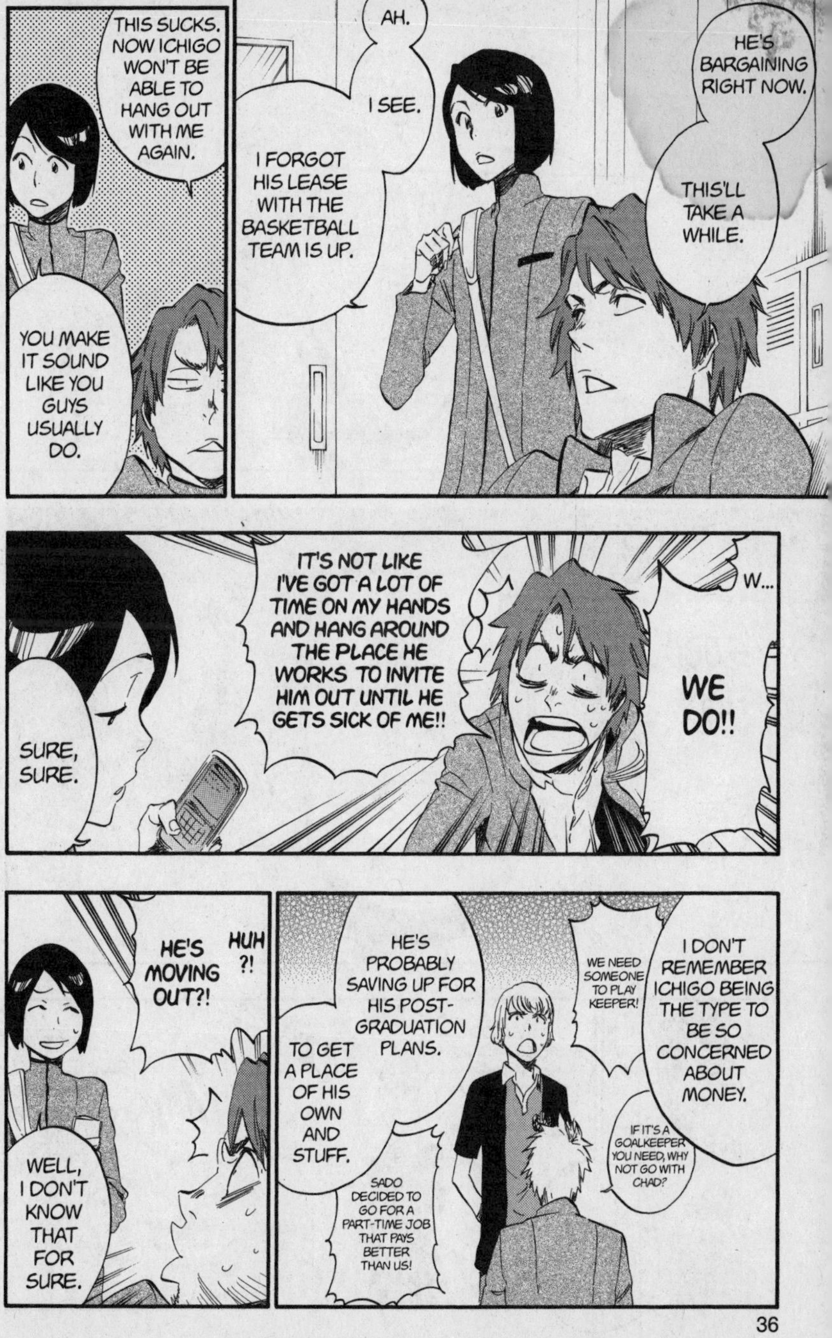
HE'S BARGAINING RIGHT NOW.
THIS'LL TAKE A WHILE.
AH.
I SEE.
I FORGOT HIS LEASE WITH THE BASKETBALL TEAM IS UP.
THIS SUCKS. NOW ICHIGO WON'T BE ABLE TO HANG OUT WITH ME AGAIN.
YOU MAKE IT SOUND LIKE YOU GUYS USUALLY DO.
W...
WE DO!!
IT'S NOT LIKE I'VE GOT A LOT OF TIME ON MY HANDS AND HANG AROUND THE PLACE HE WORKS TO INVITE HIM OUT UNTIL HE GETS SICK OF ME!!
SURE, SURE.
I DON'T REMEMBER ICHIGO BEING THE TYPE TO BE SO CONCERNED ABOUT MONEY.
WE NEED SOMEONE TO PLAY KEEPER!
IF IT'S A GOALKEEPER YOU NEED, WHY NOT GO WITH CHAD?
HE'S PROBABLY SAVING UP FOR HIS POST-GRADUATION PLANS.
TO GET A PLACE OF HIS OWN AND STUFF.
SADO DECIDED TO GO FOR A PART-TIME JOB THAT PAYS BETTER THAN US!
HUH ?!
HE'S MOVING OUT?!
WELL, I DON'T KNOW THAT FOR SURE.

READ THIS WAY

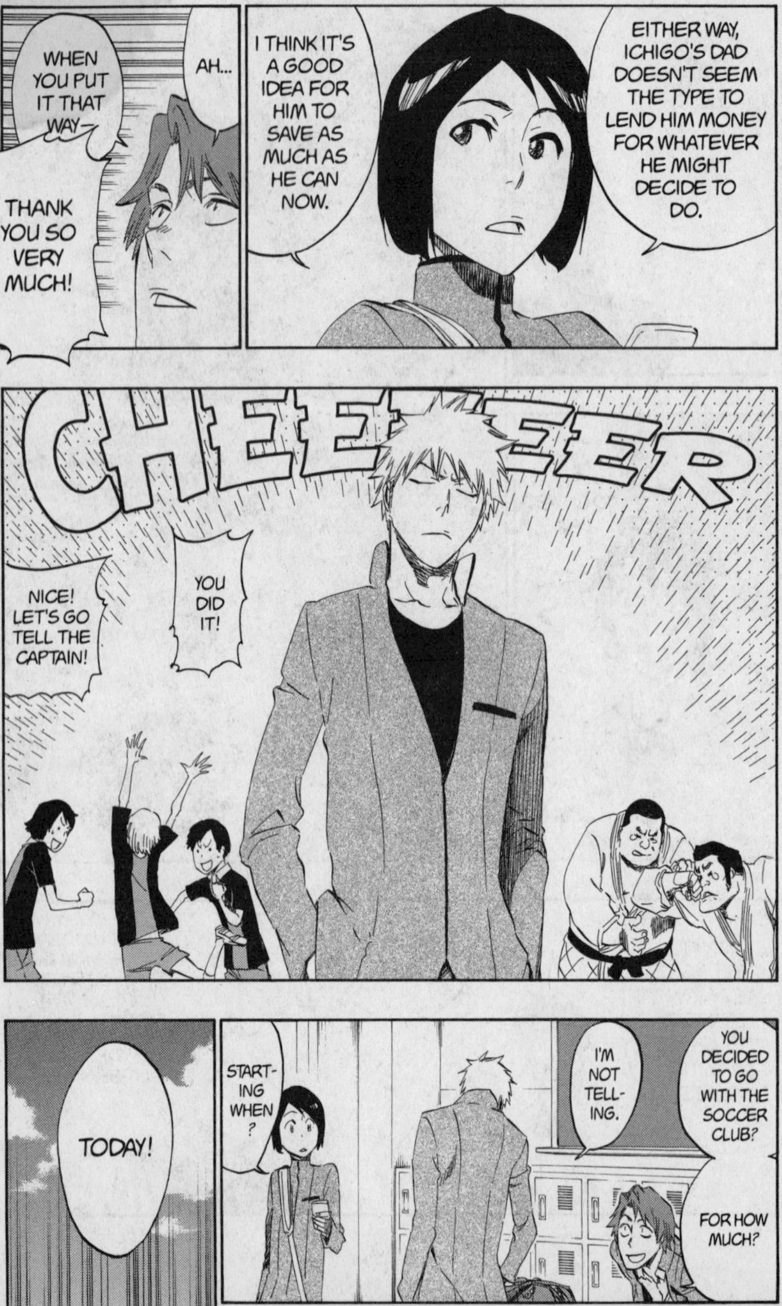
EITHER WAY, ICHIGO'S DAD DOESN'T SEEM THE TYPE TO LEND HIM MONEY FOR WHATEVER HE MIGHT DECIDE TO DO.
I THINK IT'S A GOOD IDEA FOR HIM TO SAVE AS MUCH AS HE CAN NOW.
AH...
WHEN YOU PUT IT THAT WAY—
THANK YOU SO VERY MUCH!
CHEEEER
YOU DID IT!
NICE! LET'S GO TELL THE CAPTAIN!
YOU DECIDED TO GO WITH THE SOCCER CLUB?
I'M NOT TELL-ING.
FOR HOW MUCH?
START-ING WHEN?
TODAY!

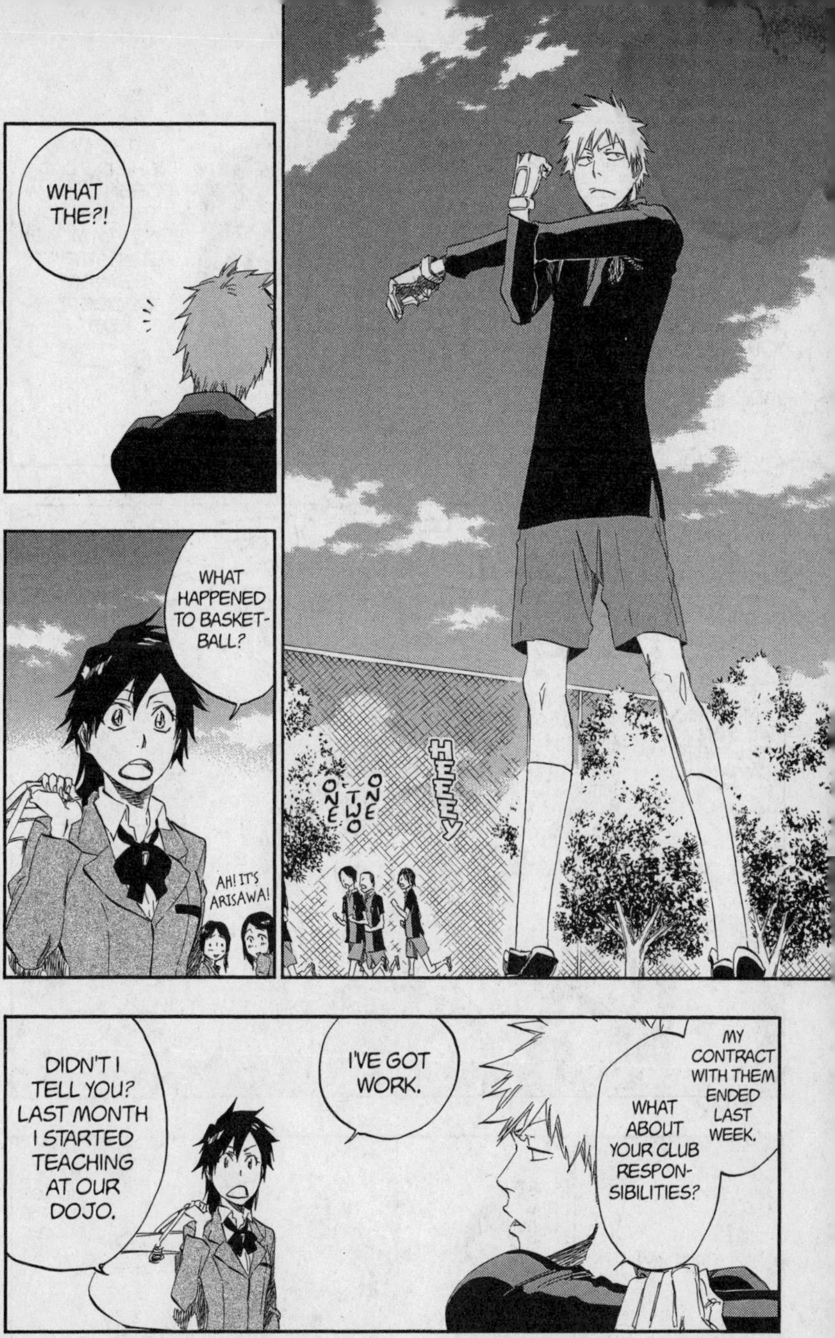
HEEEY
ONE TWO ONE
WHAT THE?!
WHAT HAPPENED TO BASKET-BALL?
AH! IT'S ARISAWA!
MY CONTRACT WITH THEM ENDED LAST WEEK.
WHAT ABOUT YOUR CLUB RESPON-SIBILITIES?
I'VE GOT WORK.
DIDN'T I TELL YOU? LAST MONTH I STARTED TEACHING AT OUR DOJO.

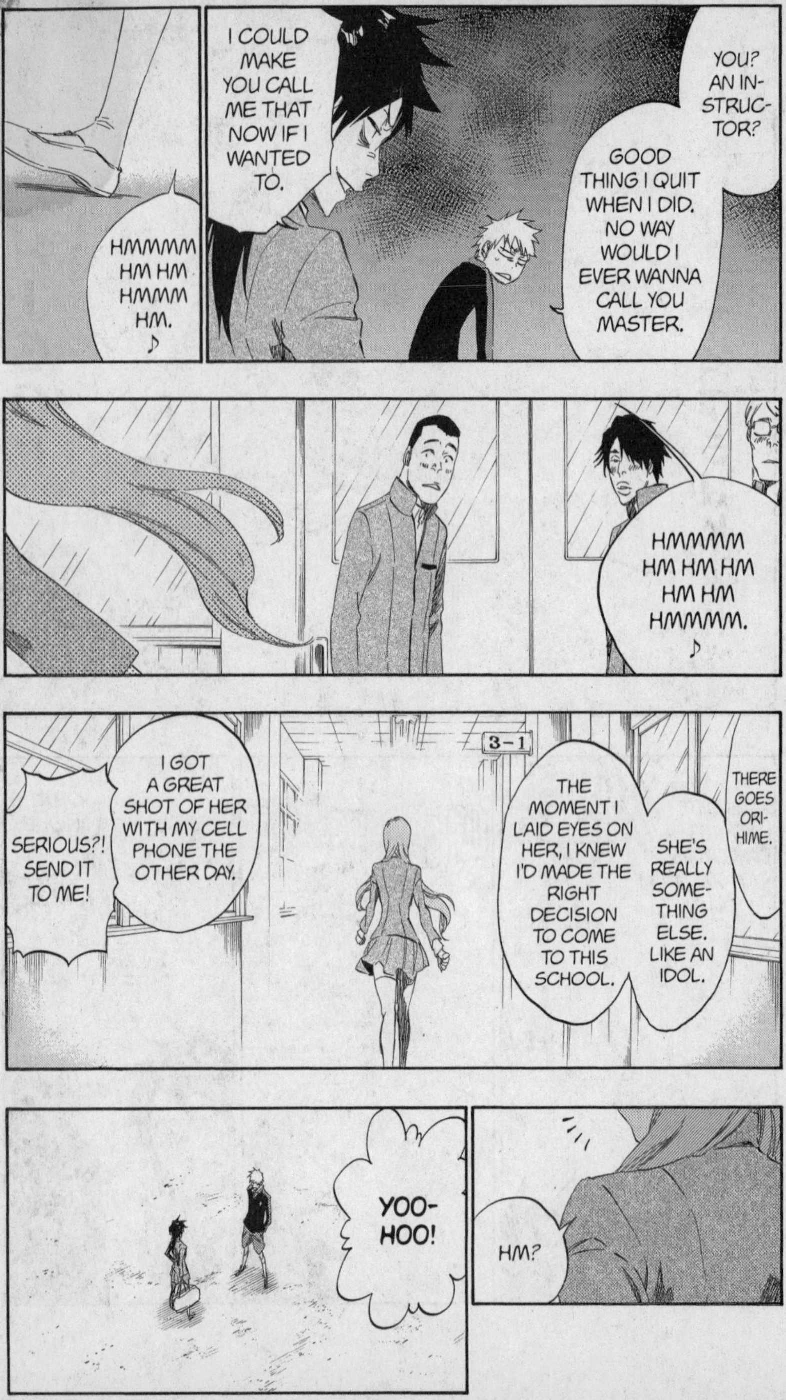
YOU? AN INSTRUCTOR?
GOOD THING I QUIT WHEN I DID. NO WAY WOULD I EVER WANNA CALL YOU MASTER.
I COULD MAKE YOU CALL ME THAT NOW IF I WANTED TO.
HMMMM HM HM HMMM HM. ♪
HMMMM HM HM HM HM HM HMMMM. ♪
3-1
THERE GOES ORIHIME.
SHE'S REALLY SOMETHING ELSE. LIKE AN IDOL.
THE MOMENT I LAID EYES ON HER, I KNEW I'D MADE THE RIGHT DECISION TO COME TO THIS SCHOOL.
I GOT A GREAT SHOT OF HER WITH MY CELL PHONE THE OTHER DAY.
SERIOUS?! SEND IT TO ME!
HM?
YOO-HOO!

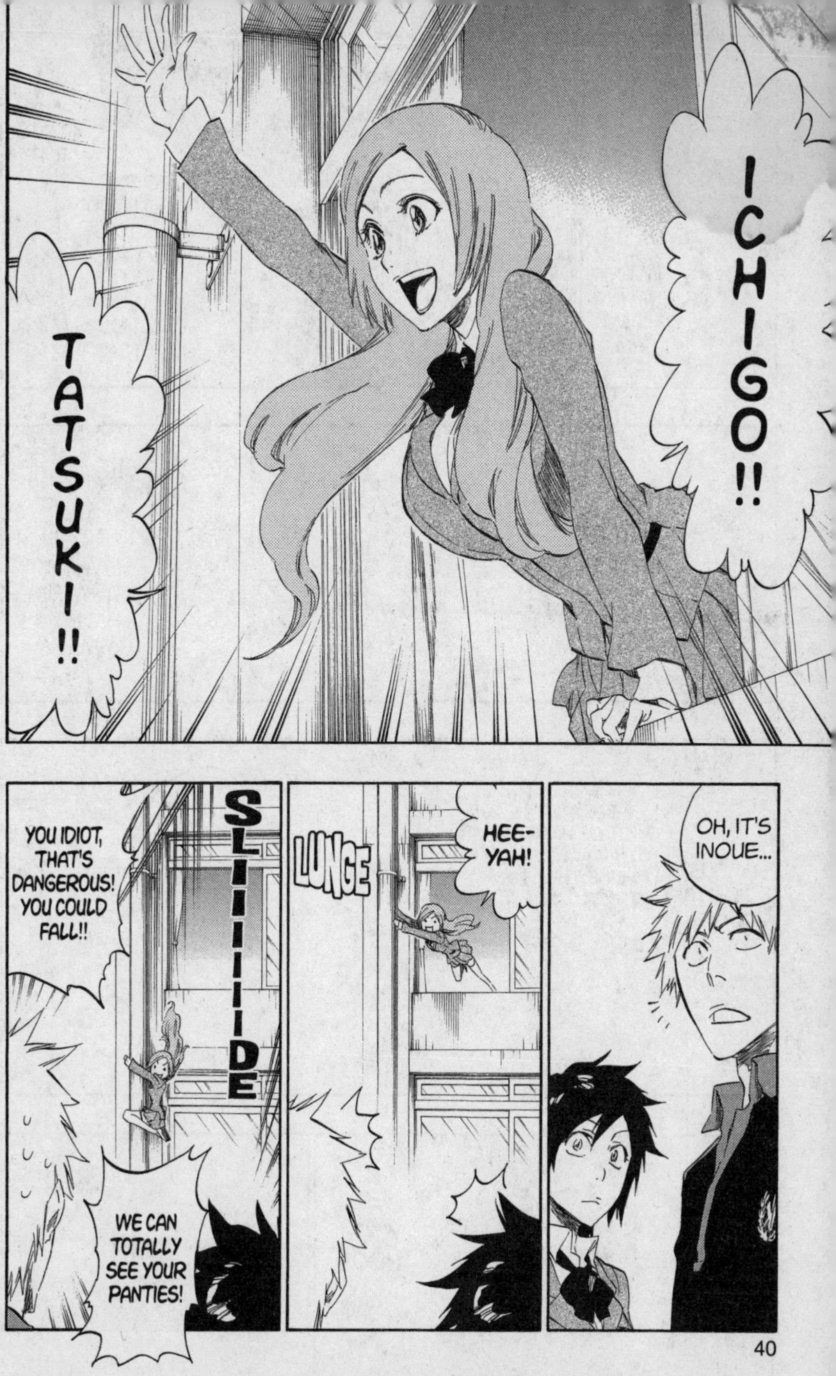
ICHIGO!!
TATSUKI!!
OH, IT'S INOUE...
HEE-YAH!
LUNGE
SLIIIIIIDE
YOU IDIOT, THAT'S DANGEROUS! YOU COULD FALL!!
WE CAN TOTALLY SEE YOUR PANTIES!

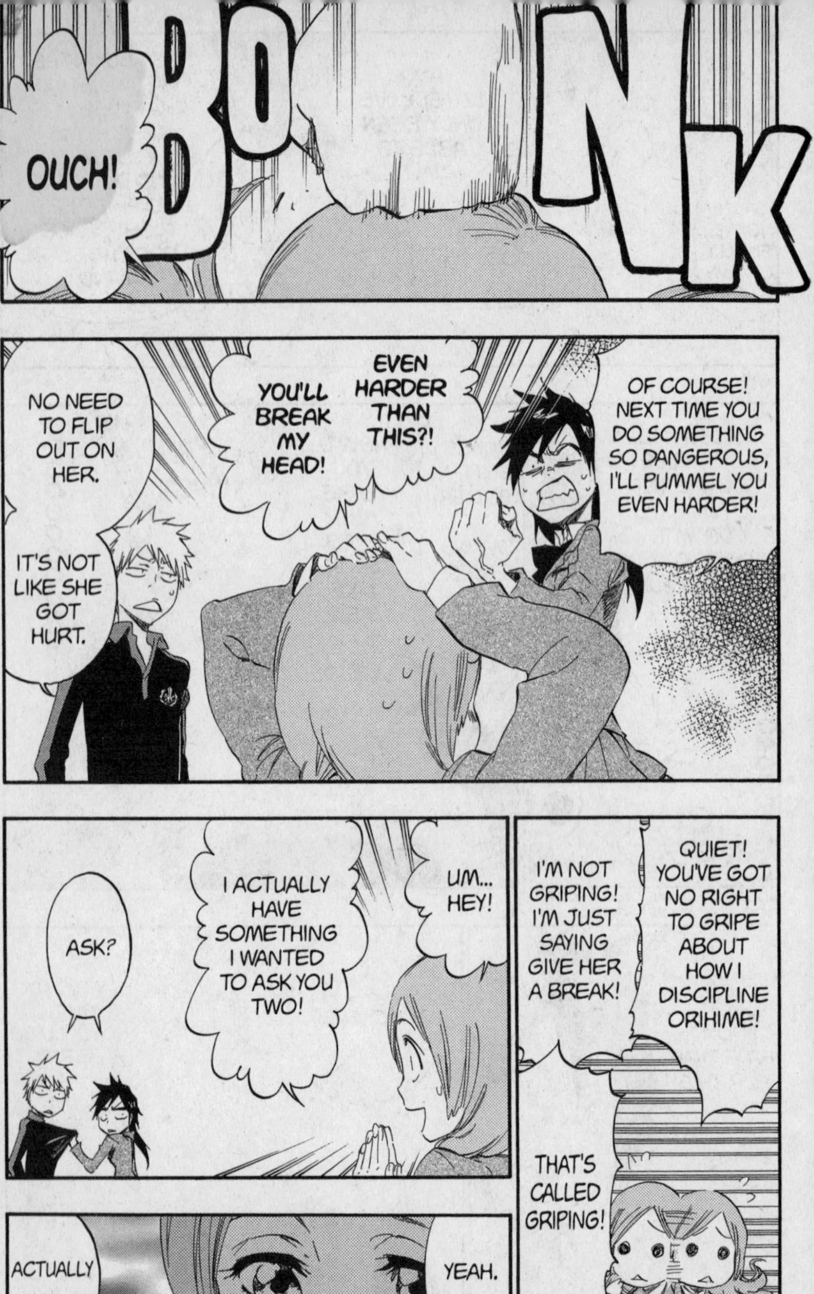
OUCH!
OF COURSE! NEXT TIME YOU DO SOMETHING SO DANGEROUS, I'LL PUMMEL YOU EVEN HARDER!
EVEN HARDER THAN THIS?!
YOU'LL BREAK MY HEAD!
NO NEED TO FLIP OUT ON HER.
IT'S NOT LIKE SHE GOT HURT.
QUIET! YOU'VE GOT NO RIGHT TO GRIPE ABOUT HOW I DISCIPLINE ORIHIME!
I'M NOT GRIPING! I'M JUST SAYING GIVE HER A BREAK!
THAT'S CALLED GRIPING!
UM... HEY!
I ACTUALLY HAVE SOMETHING I WANTED TO ASK YOU TWO!
ASK?
YEAH.
ACTUALLY ...

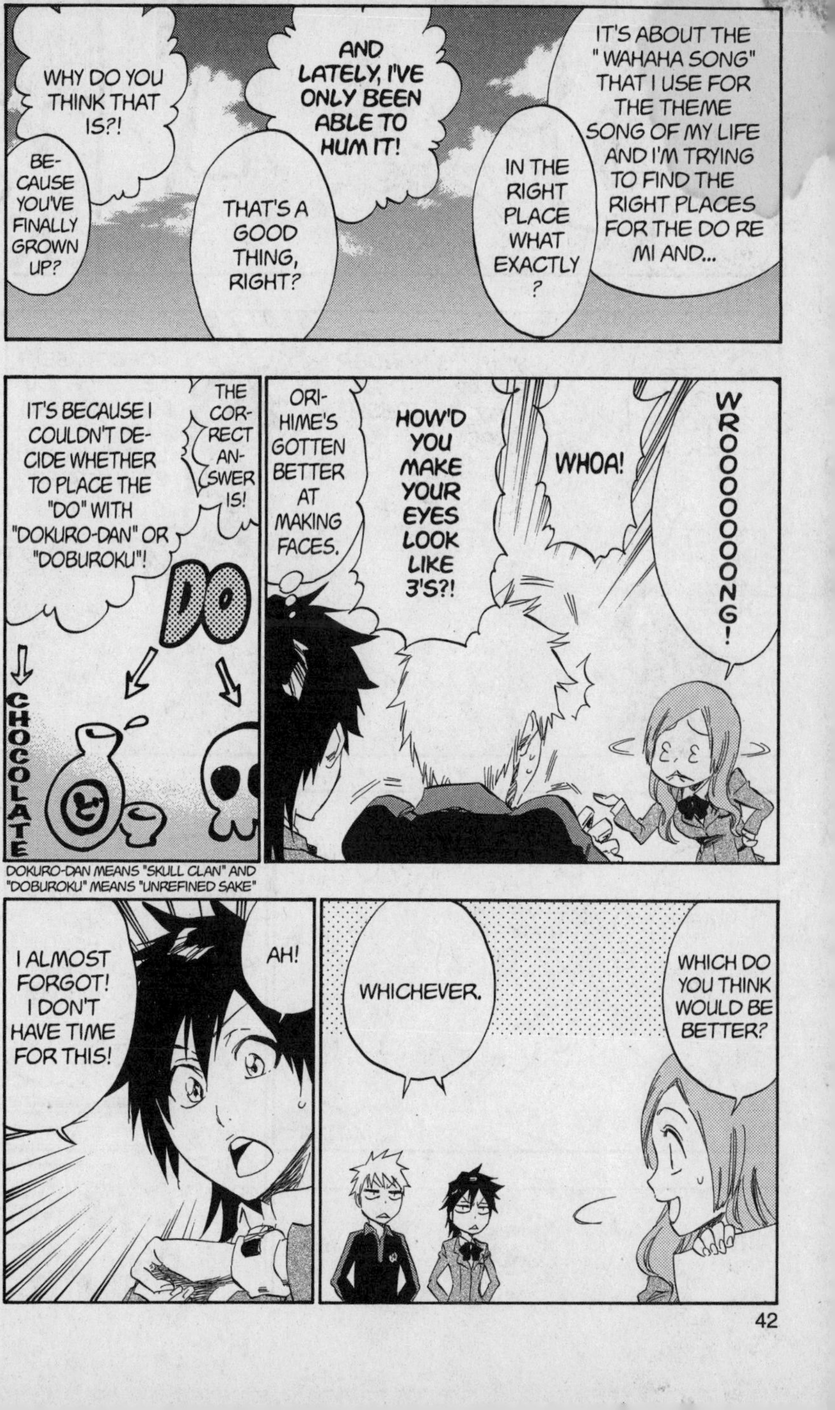
IT'S ABOUT THE "WAHAHA SONG" THAT I USE FOR THE THEME SONG OF MY LIFE AND I'M TRYING TO FIND THE RIGHT PLACES FOR THE DO RE MI AND...
IN THE RIGHT PLACE WHAT EXACTLY?
AND LATELY, I'VE ONLY BEEN ABLE TO HUM IT!
THAT'S A GOOD THING, RIGHT?
WHY DO YOU THINK THAT IS?!
BECAUSE YOU'VE FINALLY GROWN UP?
WROOOOOOOOONG!
WHOA!
HOW'D YOU MAKE YOUR EYES LOOK LIKE 3'S?!
ORIHIME'S GOTTEN BETTER AT MAKING FACES.
THE CORRECT ANSWER IS!
IT'S BECAUSE I COULDN'T DECIDE WHETHER TO PLACE THE "DO" WITH "DOKURO-DAN" OR "DOBUROKU"!
DO
CHOCOLATE
WHICH DO YOU THINK WOULD BE BETTER?
WHICHEVER.
AH!
I ALMOST FORGOT! I DON'T HAVE TIME FOR THIS!

DOKURO-DAN MEANS "SKULL CLAN" AND "DOBUROKU" MEANS "UNREFINED SAKE"

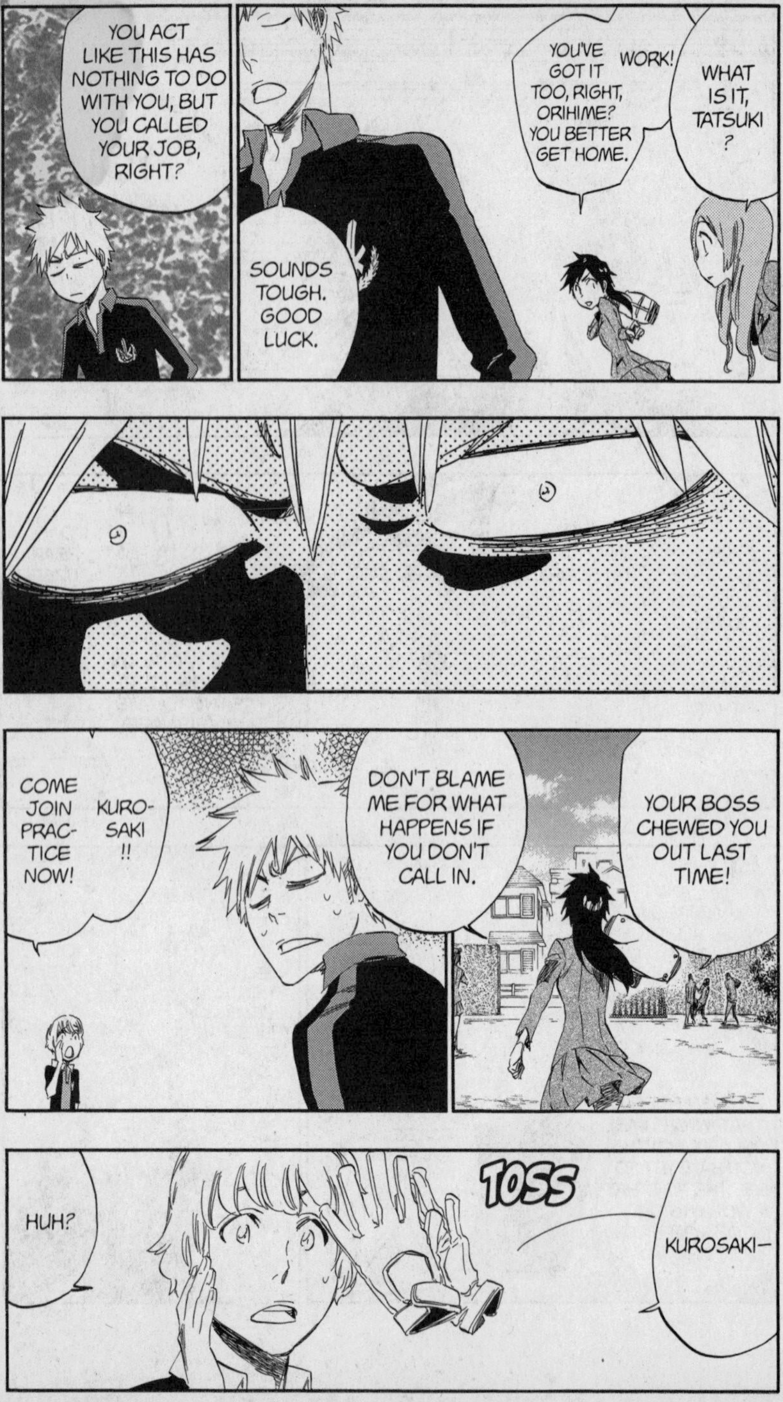
WHAT IS IT, TATSUKI?
WORK!
YOU'VE GOT IT TOO, RIGHT, ORIHIME? YOU BETTER GET HOME.
SOUNDS TOUGH. GOOD LUCK.
YOU ACT LIKE THIS HAS NOTHING TO DO WITH YOU, BUT YOU CALLED YOUR JOB, RIGHT?
YOUR BOSS CHEWED YOU OUT LAST TIME!
DON'T BLAME ME FOR WHAT HAPPENS IF YOU DON'T CALL IN.
KURO-SAKI!!
COME JOIN PRAC-TICE NOW!
KUROSAKI—
TOSS
HUH?

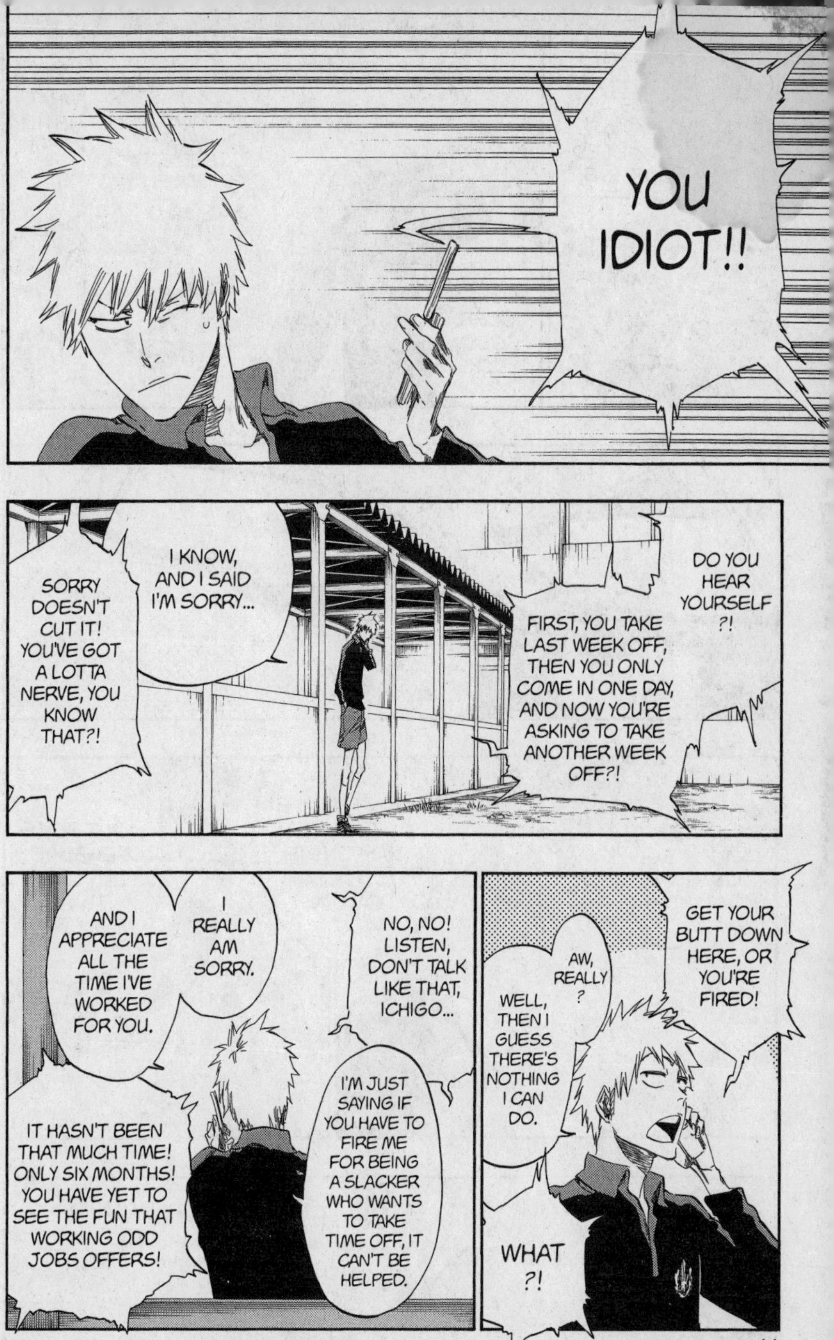
YOU IDIOT!!
DO YOU HEAR YOURSELF?!
FIRST, YOU TAKE LAST WEEK OFF, THEN YOU ONLY COME IN ONE DAY, AND NOW YOU'RE ASKING TO TAKE ANOTHER WEEK OFF?!
I KNOW, AND I SAID I'M SORRY...
SORRY DOESN'T CUT IT! YOU'VE GOT A LOTTA NERVE, YOU KNOW THAT?!
GET YOUR BUTT DOWN HERE, OR YOU'RE FIRED!
AW, REALLY?
WELL, THEN I GUESS THERE'S NOTHING I CAN DO.
WHAT?!
I REALLY AM SORRY.
AND I APPRECIATE ALL THE TIME I'VE WORKED FOR YOU.
NO, NO! LISTEN, DON'T TALK LIKE THAT, ICHIGO...
IT HASN'T BEEN THAT MUCH TIME! ONLY SIX MONTHS! YOU HAVE YET TO SEE THE FUN THAT WORKING ODD JOBS OFFERS!
I'M JUST SAYING IF YOU HAVE TO FIRE ME FOR BEING A SLACKER WHO WANTS TO TAKE TIME OFF, IT CAN'T BE HELPED.

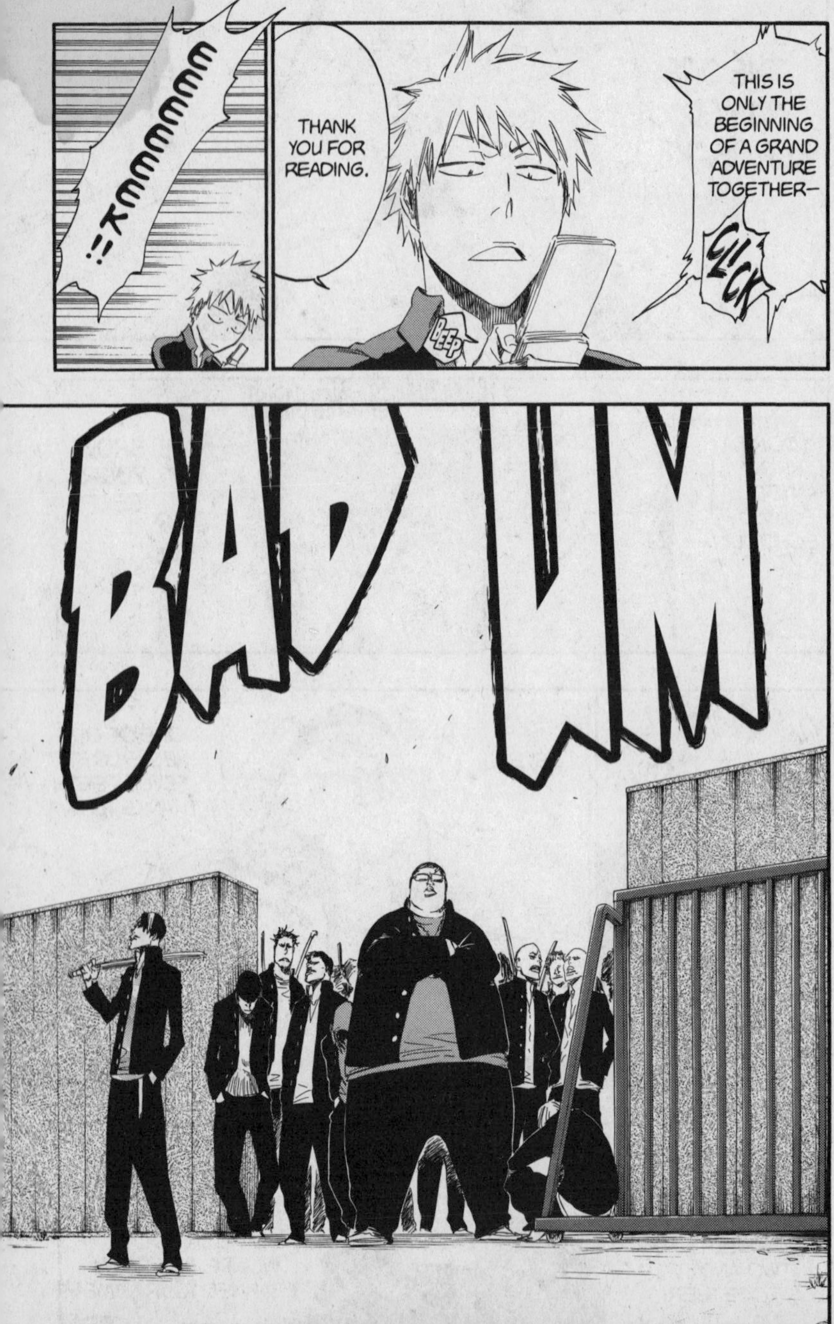
THIS IS ONLY THE BEGINNING OF A GRAND ADVENTURE TOGETHER—
CLICK
THANK YOU FOR READING.
BEEP
EEEEEEEK!!
BADUM

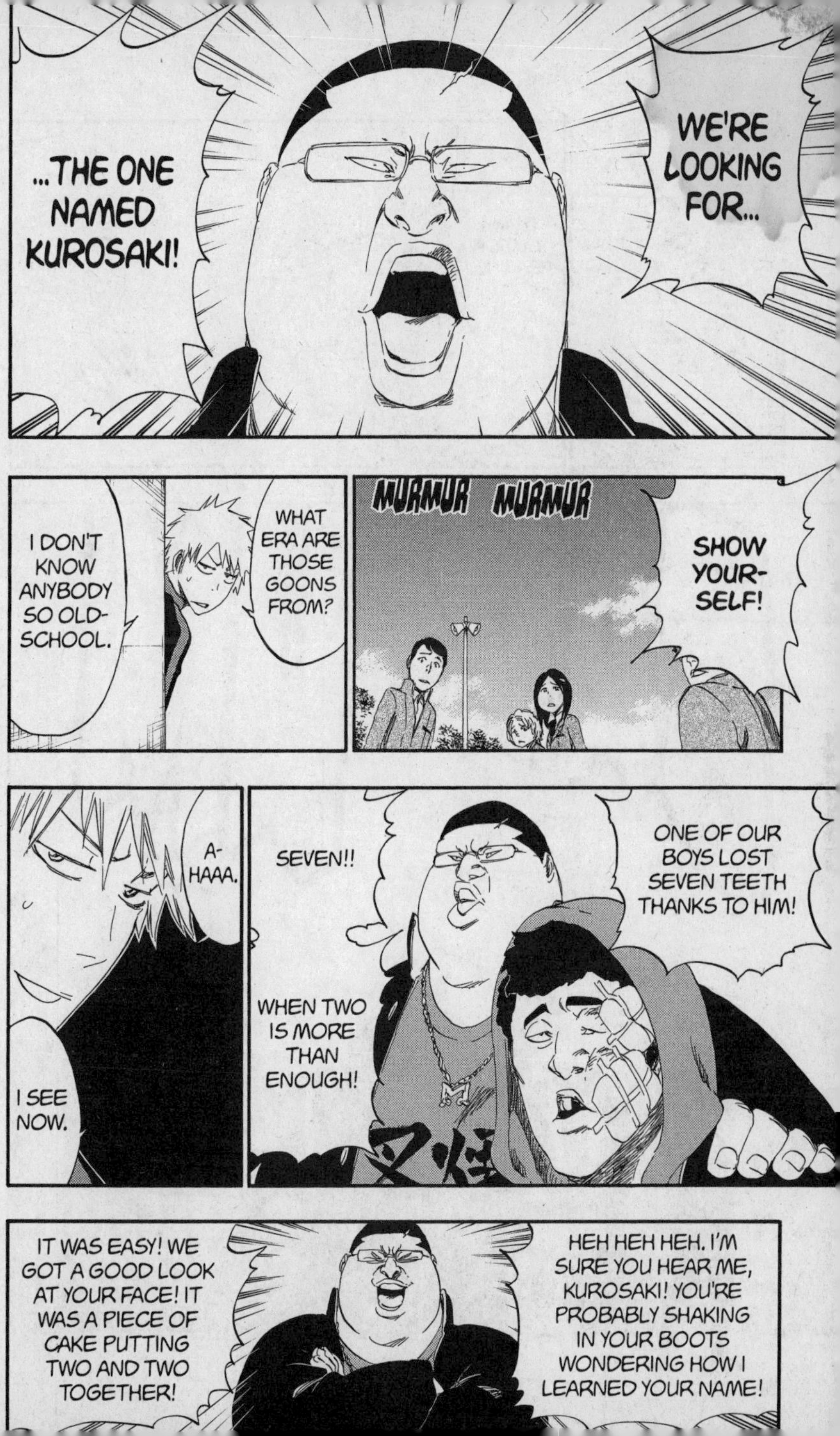
WE'RE LOOKING FOR...
...THE ONE NAMED KUROSAKI!
SHOW YOURSELF!
MURMUR MURMUR
WHAT ERA ARE THOSE GOONS FROM?
I DON'T KNOW ANYBODY SO OLD-SCHOOL.
ONE OF OUR BOYS LOST SEVEN TEETH THANKS TO HIM!
SEVEN!!
WHEN TWO IS MORE THAN ENOUGH!
A-HAAA.
I SEE NOW.
HEH HEH HEH. I'M SURE YOU HEAR ME, KUROSAKI! YOU'RE PROBABLY SHAKING IN YOUR BOOTS WONDERING HOW I LEARNED YOUR NAME!
IT WAS EASY! WE GOT A GOOD LOOK AT YOUR FACE! IT WAS A PIECE OF CAKE PUTTING TWO AND TWO TOGETHER!

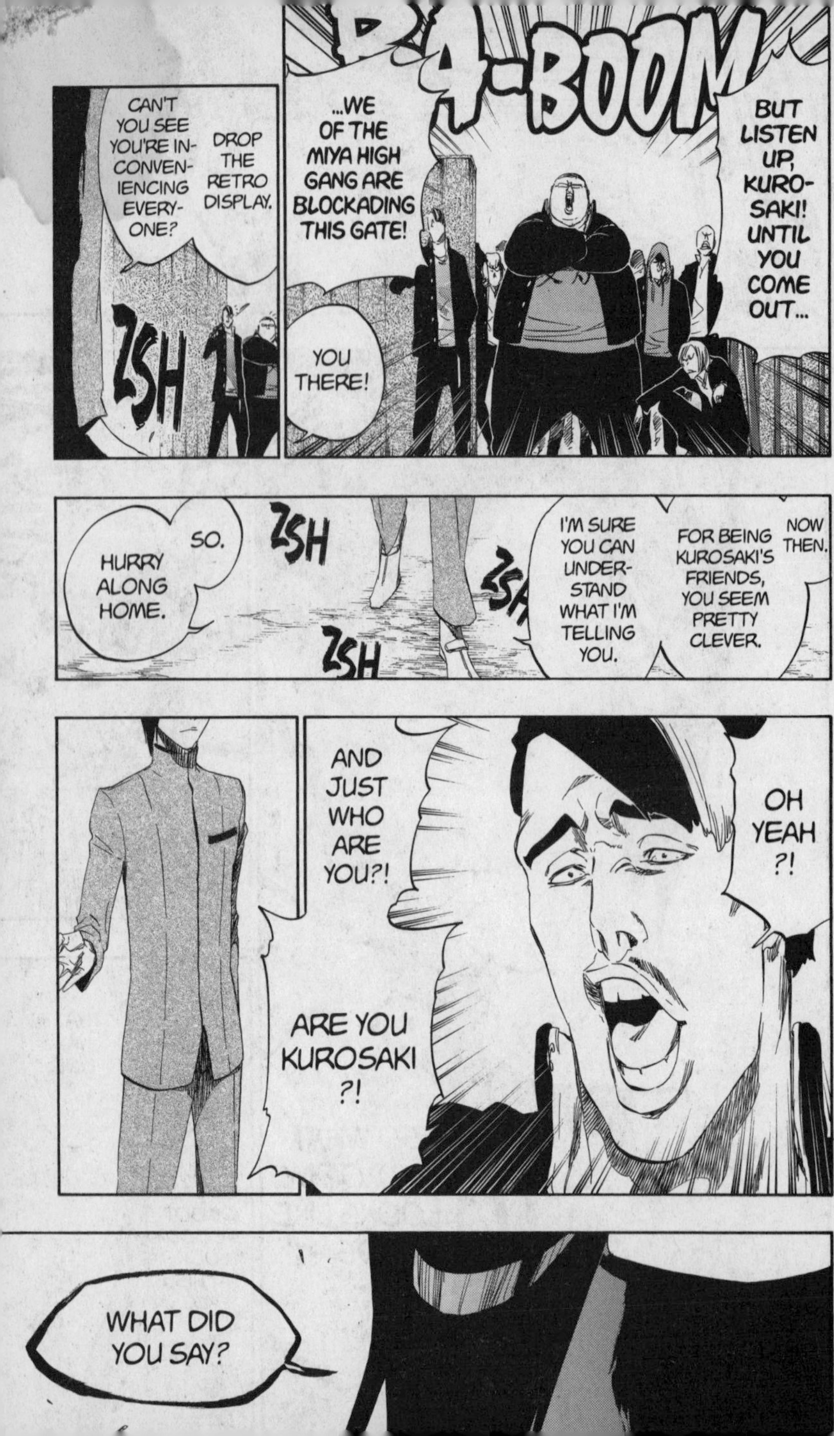
BA-BOOM
BUT LISTEN UP, KUROSAKI! UNTIL YOU COME OUT...
...WE OF THE MIYA HIGH GANG ARE BLOCKADING THIS GATE!
YOU THERE!
DROP THE RETRO DISPLAY.
CAN'T YOU SEE YOU'RE INCONVENIENCING EVERYONE?
ZSH
NOW THEN.
FOR BEING KUROSAKI'S FRIENDS, YOU SEEM PRETTY CLEVER.
I'M SURE YOU CAN UNDERSTAND WHAT I'M TELLING YOU.
ZSH
ZSH
ZSH
SO.
HURRY ALONG HOME.
OH YEAH?!
AND JUST WHO ARE YOU?!
ARE YOU KUROSAKI?!
WHAT DID YOU SAY?

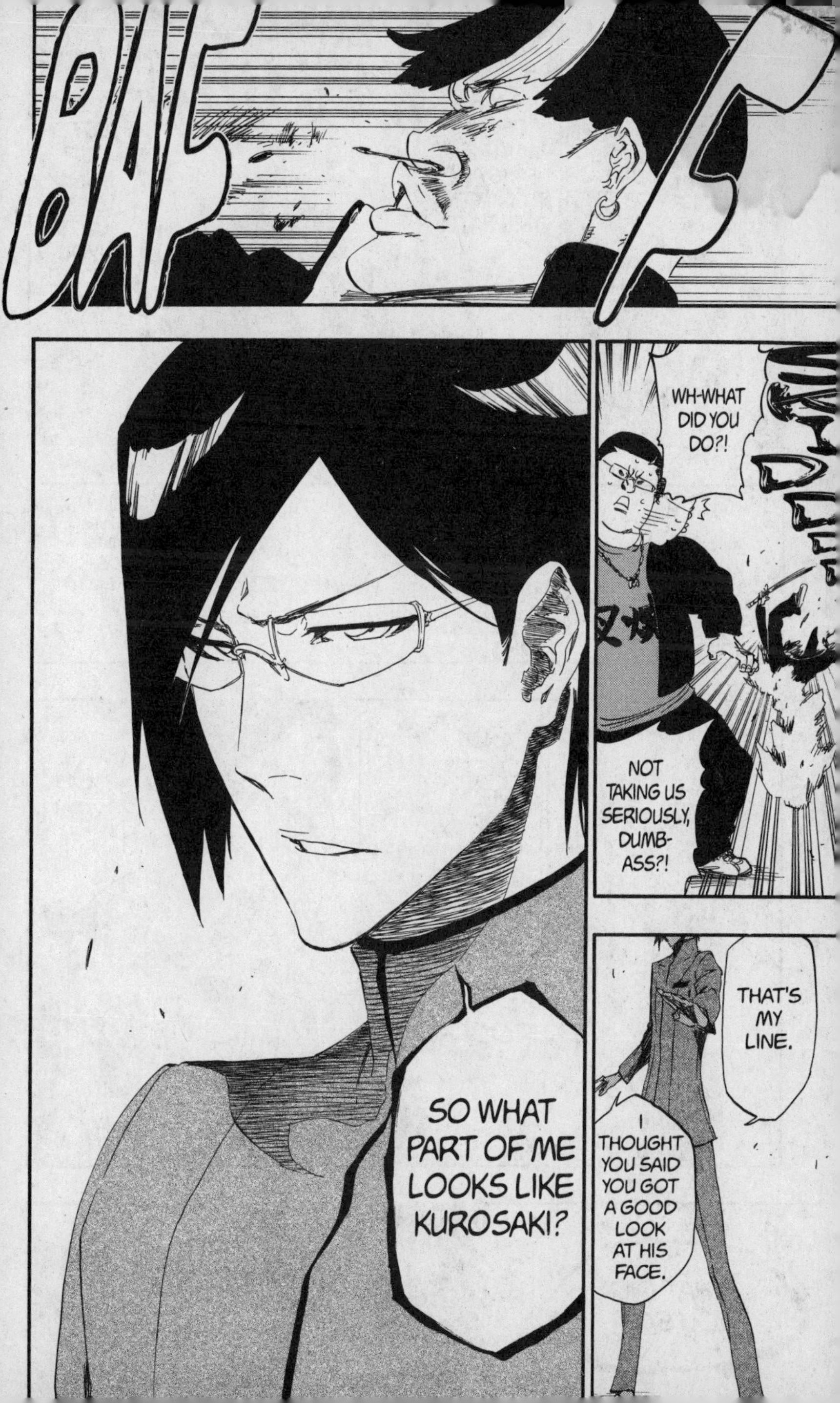
WH-WHAT DID YOU DO?!
NOT TAKING US SERIOUSLY, DUMB-ASS?!
THAT'S MY LINE.
I THOUGHT YOU SAID YOU GOT A GOOD LOOK AT HIS FACE.
SO WHAT PART OF ME LOOKS LIKE KUROSAKI?

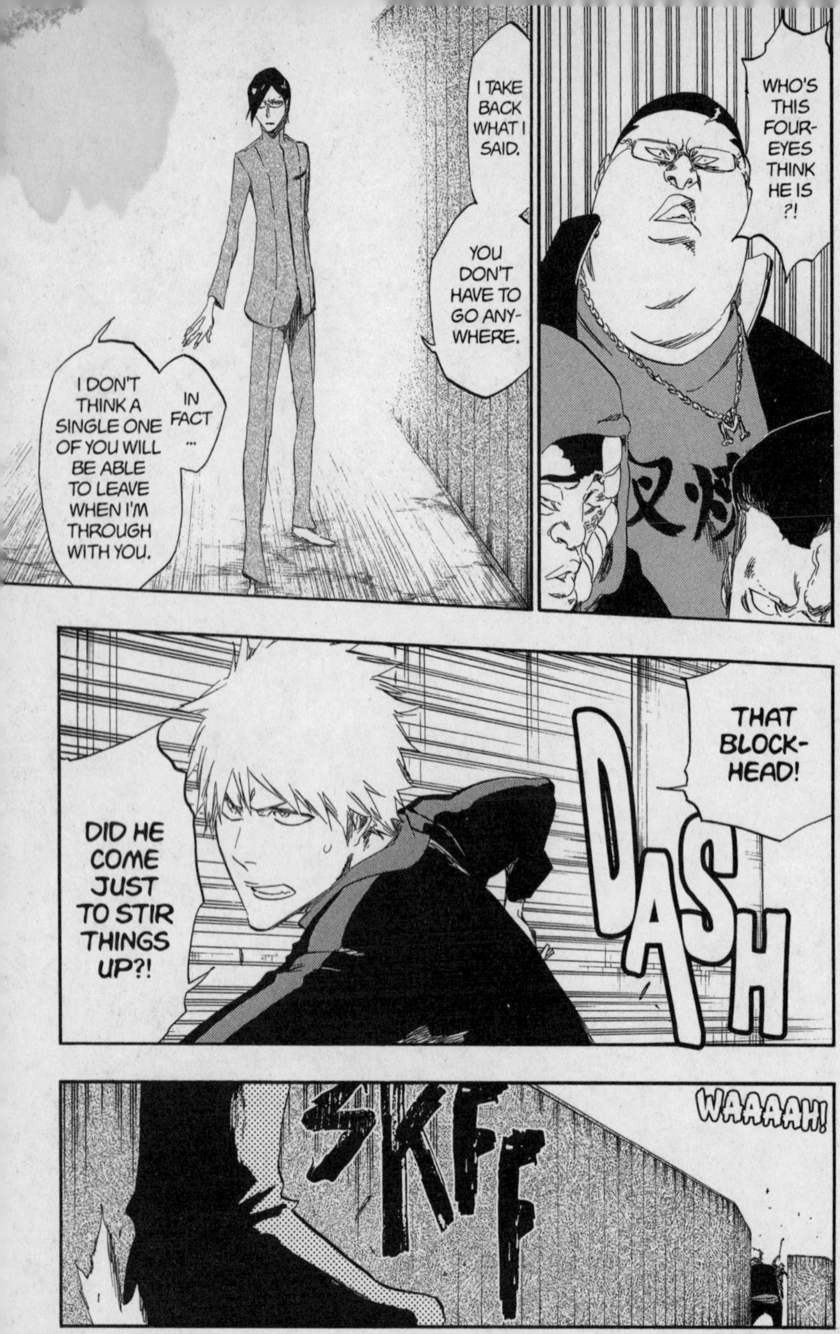
WHO'S THIS FOUR-EYES THINK HE IS?!
I TAKE BACK WHAT I SAID.
YOU DON'T HAVE TO GO ANY-WHERE.
IN FACT...
I DON'T THINK A SINGLE ONE OF YOU WILL BE ABLE TO LEAVE WHEN I'M THROUGH WITH YOU.
THAT BLOCK-HEAD!
DASH
DID HE COME JUST TO STIR THINGS UP?!
WAAAAH!
SKFF

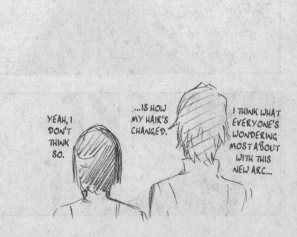

I THINK WHAT EVERYONE'S WONDERING MOST ABOUT WITH THIS NEW ARC...

...IS HOW MY HAIR'S CHANGED.

YEAH, I DON'T THINK SO.

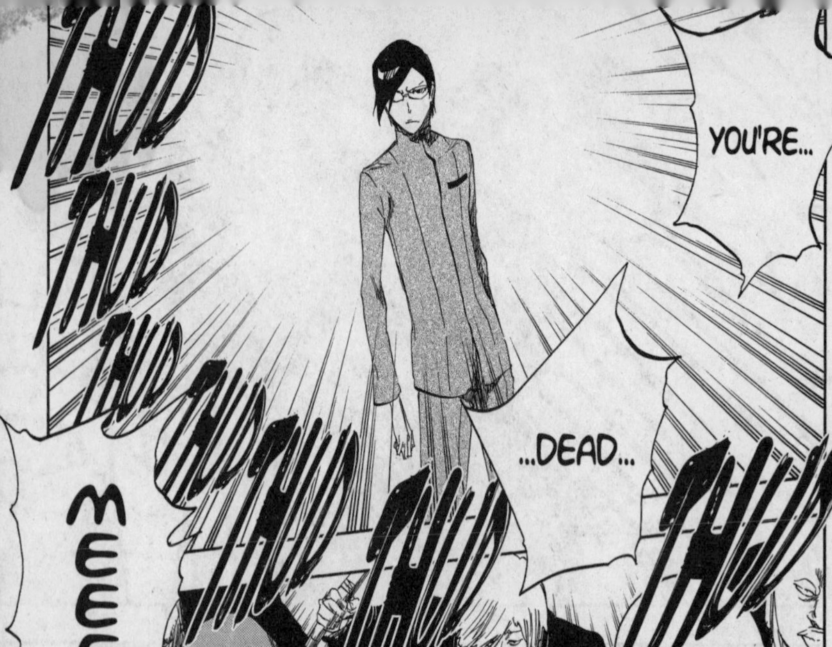
YOU'RE...
...DEAD...
THUD THUD
THUD THUD THUD THUD THUD THUD THUD
MEEEEEEAT!!

426. The Starter 2

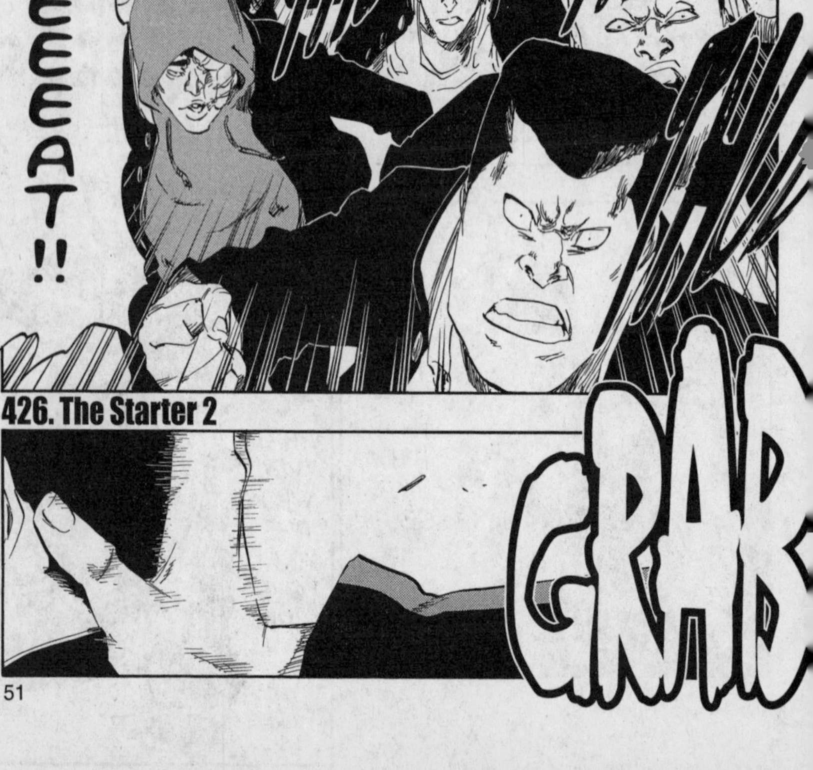
GRAB

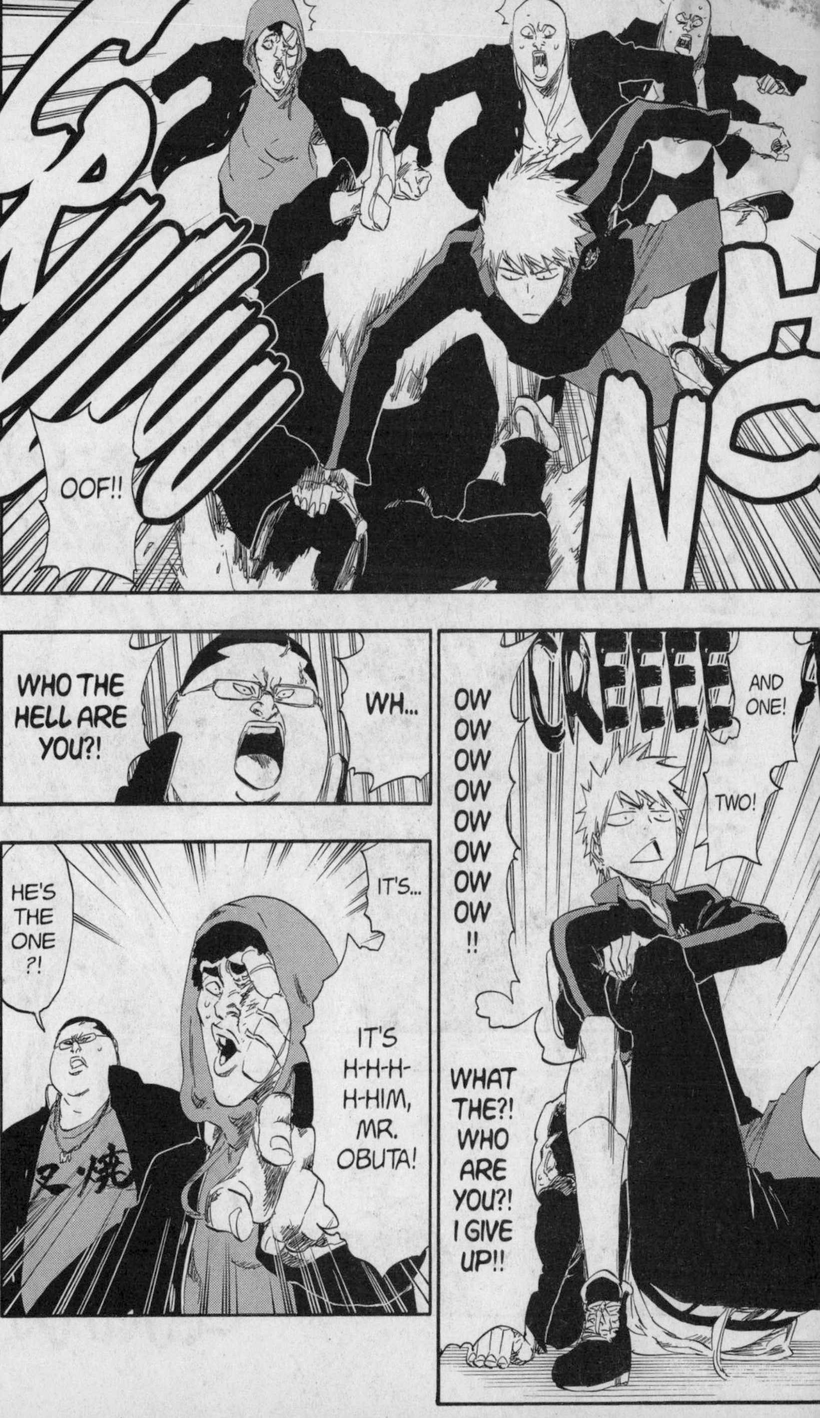
OOF!!
AND ONE!
TWO!
OW OW OW OW OW OW OW OW !!
WHAT THE?! WHO ARE YOU?! I GIVE UP!!
WH...
WHO THE HELL ARE YOU?!
IT'S...
IT'S H-H-H-H-HIM, MR. OBUTA!
HE'S THE ONE ?!

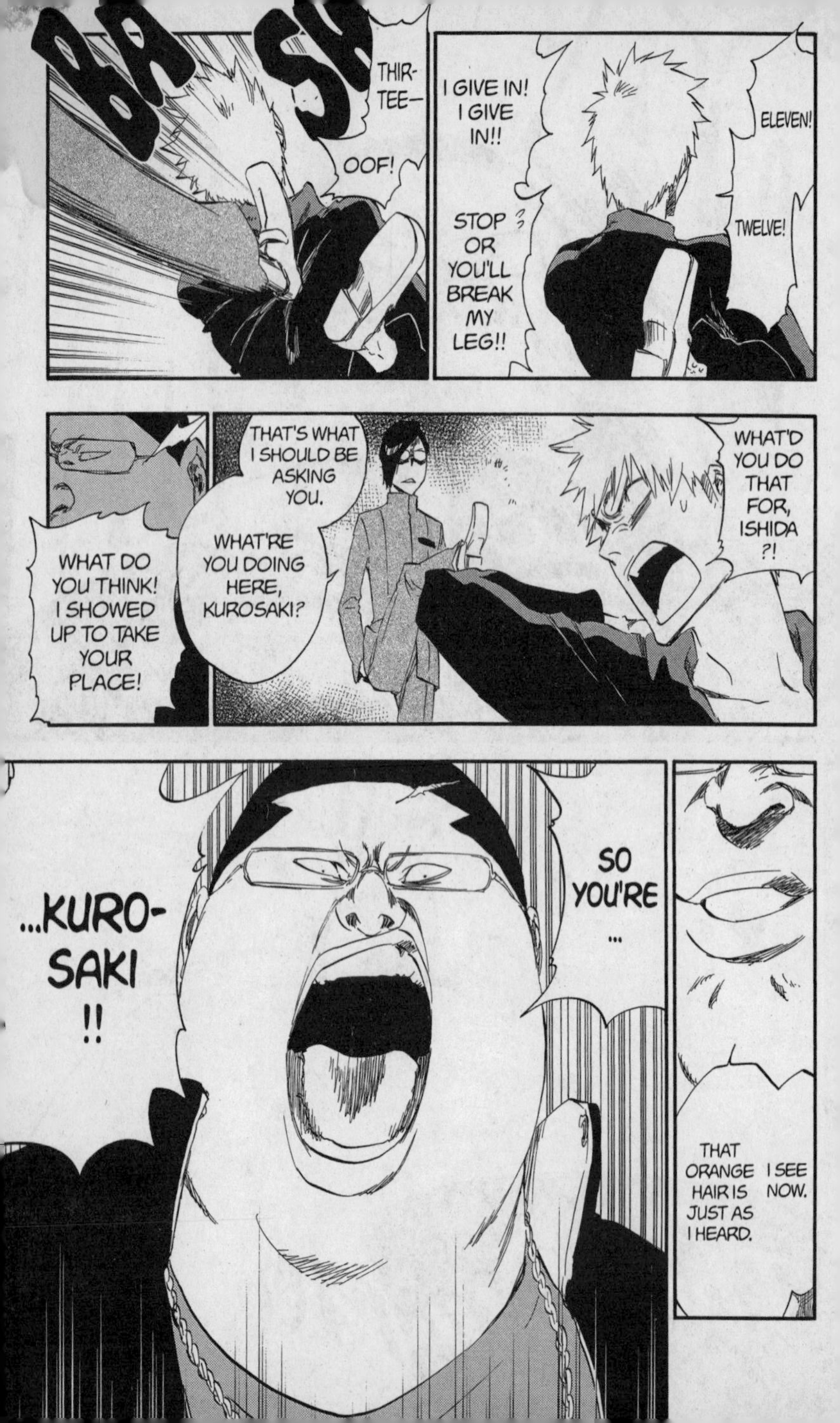
ELEVEN!
TWELVE!
I GIVE IN! I GIVE IN!!
STOP OR YOU'LL BREAK MY LEG!!
THIR-TEE—
BASH
OOF!
WHAT'D YOU DO THAT FOR, ISHIDA?!
THAT'S WHAT I SHOULD BE ASKING YOU.
WHAT'RE YOU DOING HERE, KUROSAKI?
WHAT DO YOU THINK! I SHOWED UP TO TAKE YOUR PLACE!
I SEE NOW.
THAT ORANGE HAIR IS JUST AS I HEARD.
SO YOU'RE...
...KURO-SAKI!!

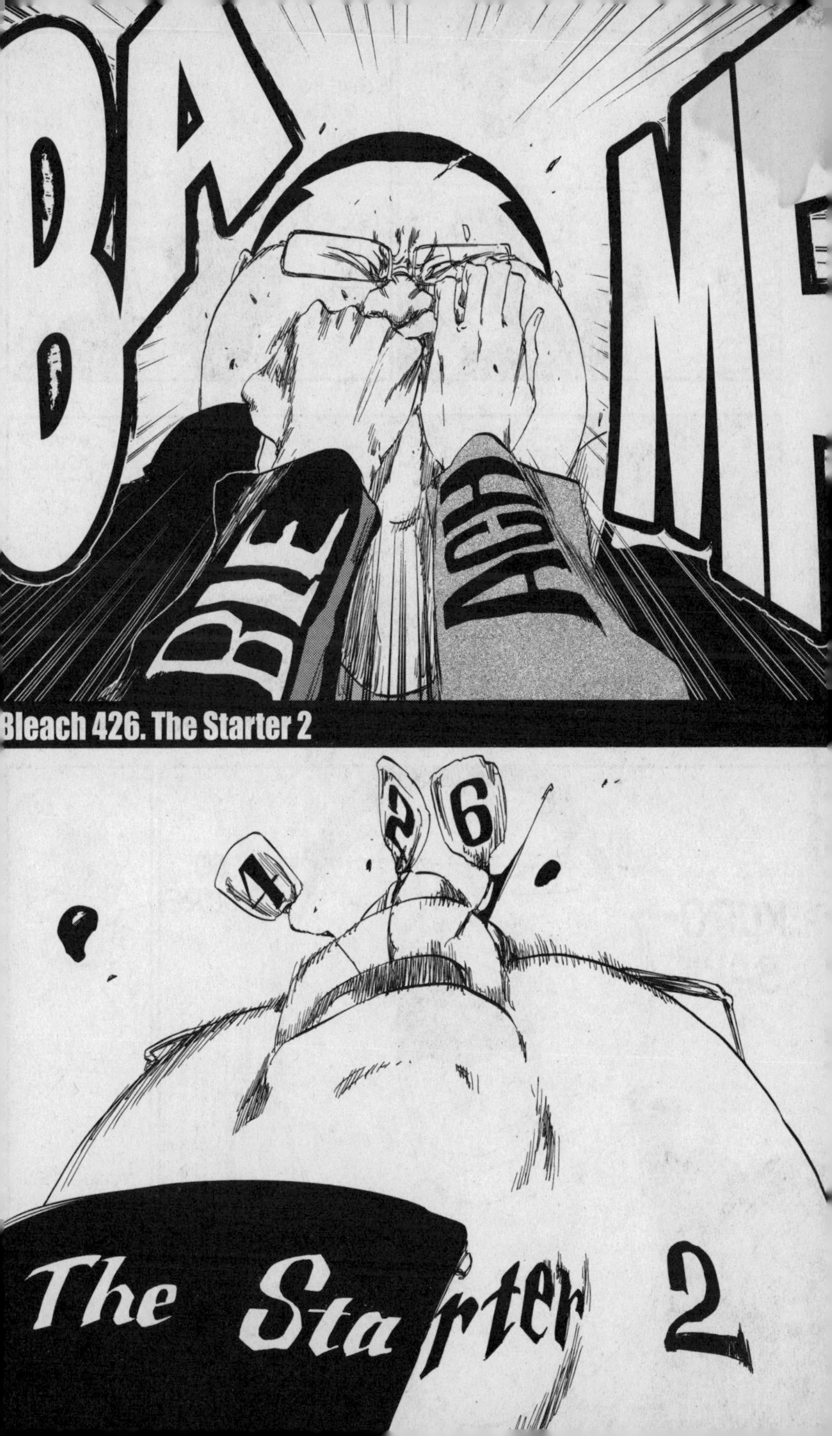
BAM
Bleach 426. The Starter 2
426
The Starter 2

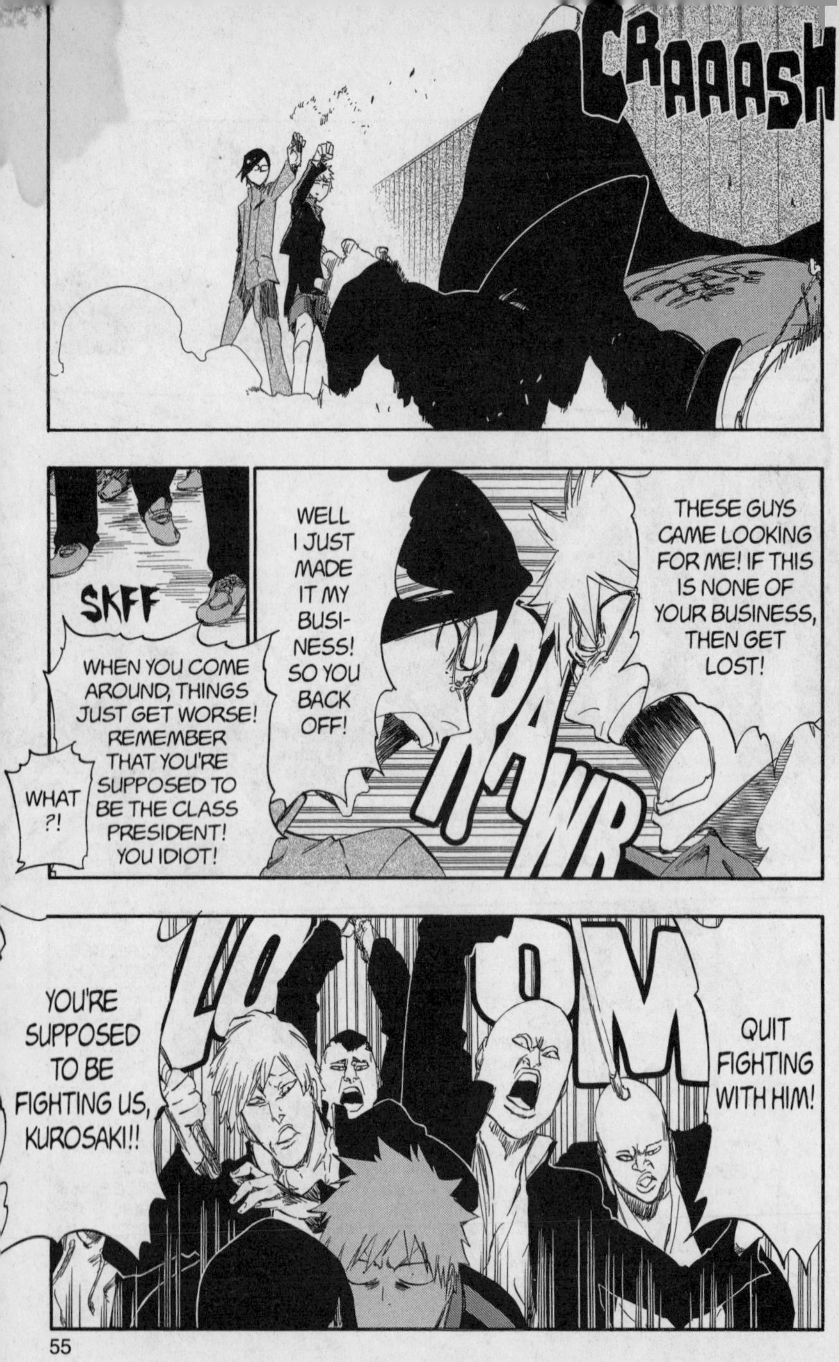
CRAAASH
THESE GUYS CAME LOOKING FOR ME! IF THIS IS NONE OF YOUR BUSINESS, THEN GET LOST!
WELL I JUST MADE IT MY BUSI-NESS! SO YOU BACK OFF!
PAWR
SKFF
WHEN YOU COME AROUND, THINGS JUST GET WORSE! REMEMBER THAT YOU'RE SUPPOSED TO BE THE CLASS PRESIDENT! YOU IDIOT!
WHAT?!
QUIT FIGHTING WITH HIM!
YOU'RE SUPPOSED TO BE FIGHTING US, KUROSAKI!!

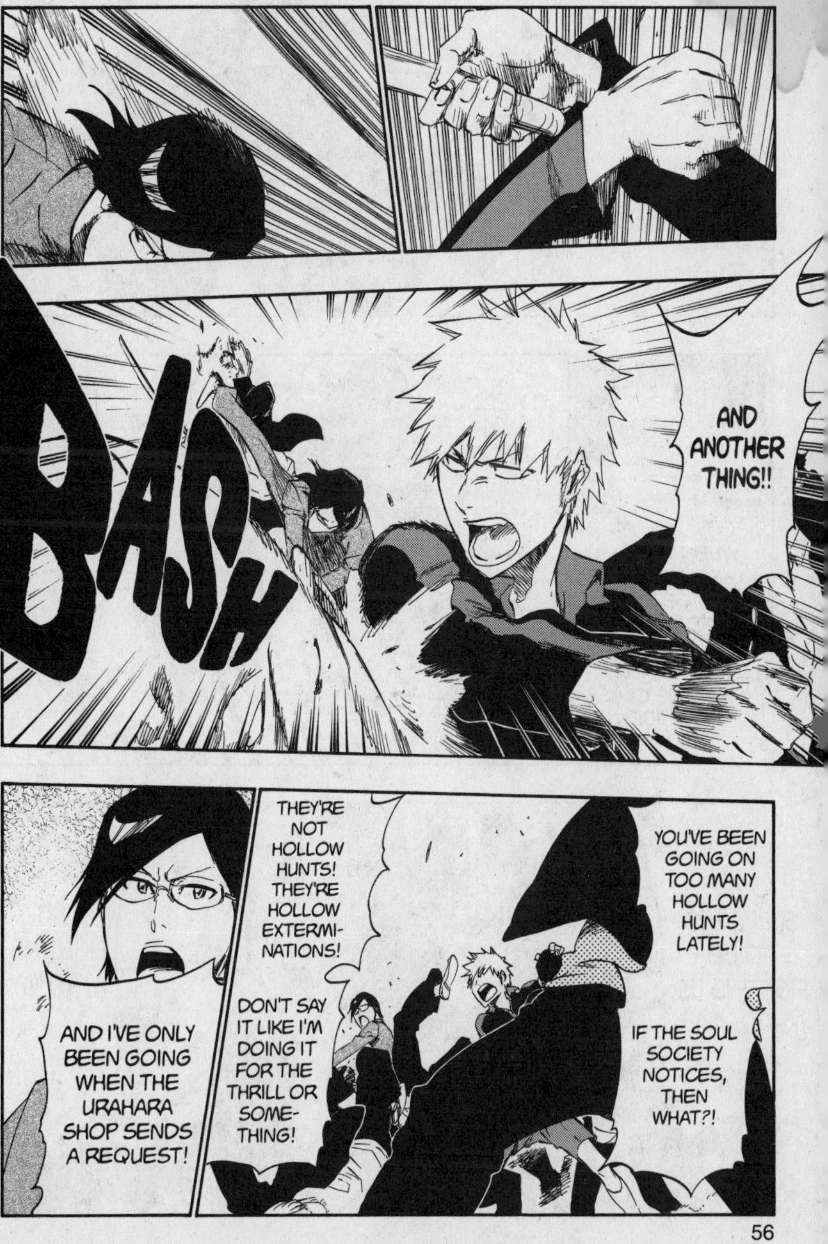
AND ANOTHER THING!!
BASH
YOU'VE BEEN GOING ON TOO MANY HOLLOW HUNTS LATELY!
THEY'RE NOT HOLLOW HUNTS! THEY'RE HOLLOW EXTERMI-NATIONS!
IF THE SOUL SOCIETY NOTICES, THEN WHAT?!
DON'T SAY IT LIKE I'M DOING IT FOR THE THRILL OR SOME-THING!
AND I'VE ONLY BEEN GOING WHEN THE URAHARA SHOP SENDS A REQUEST!

READ THIS WAY

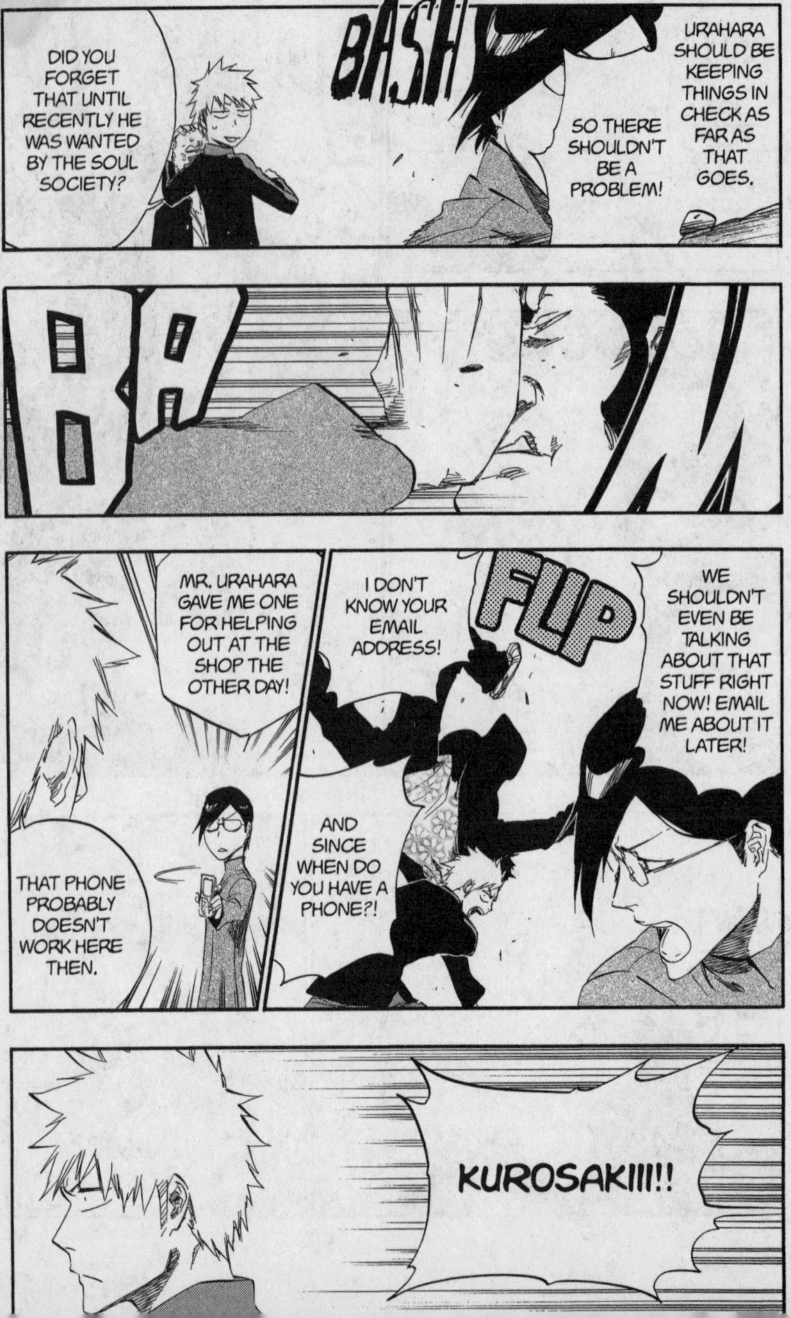
URAHARA SHOULD BE KEEPING THINGS IN CHECK AS FAR AS THAT GOES.
SO THERE SHOULDN'T BE A PROBLEM!
BASH
DID YOU FORGET THAT UNTIL RECENTLY HE WAS WANTED BY THE SOUL SOCIETY?
WE SHOULDN'T EVEN BE TALKING ABOUT THAT STUFF RIGHT NOW! EMAIL ME ABOUT IT LATER!
FLIP
I DON'T KNOW YOUR EMAIL ADDRESS!
AND SINCE WHEN DO YOU HAVE A PHONE?!
MR. URAHARA GAVE ME ONE FOR HELPING OUT AT THE SHOP THE OTHER DAY!
THAT PHONE PROBABLY DOESN'T WORK HERE THEN.
KUROSAKIII!!

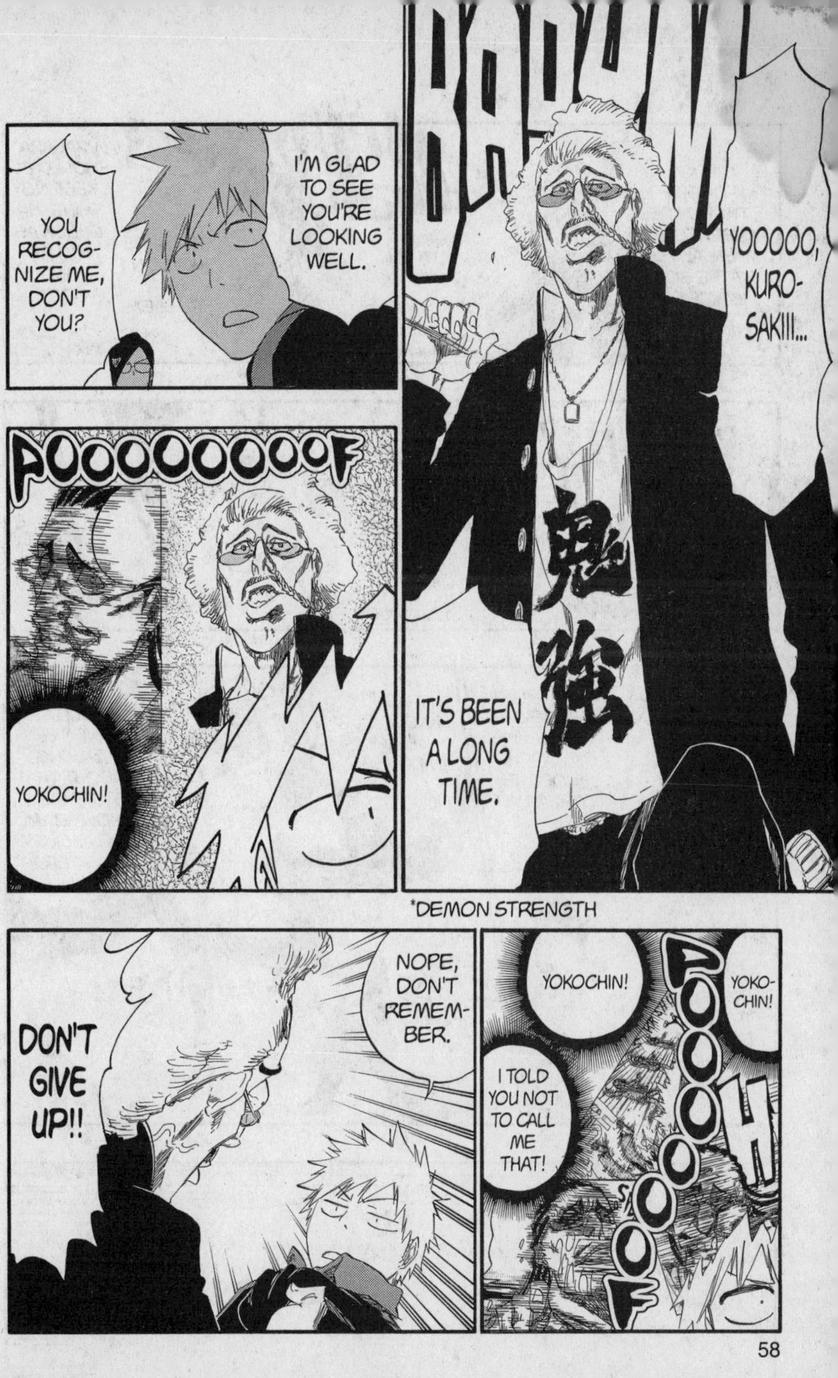
YOOOOO, KURO-SAKIII...
鬼強
IT'S BEEN A LONG TIME.
YOU RECOG-NIZE ME, DON'T YOU?
I'M GLAD TO SEE YOU'RE LOOKING WELL.
POOOOOOOOF
YOKOCHIN!
*DEMON STRENGTH
YOKO-CHIN!
YOKOCHIN!
I TOLD YOU NOT TO CALL ME THAT!
NOPE, DON'T REMEM-BER.
DON'T GIVE UP!!

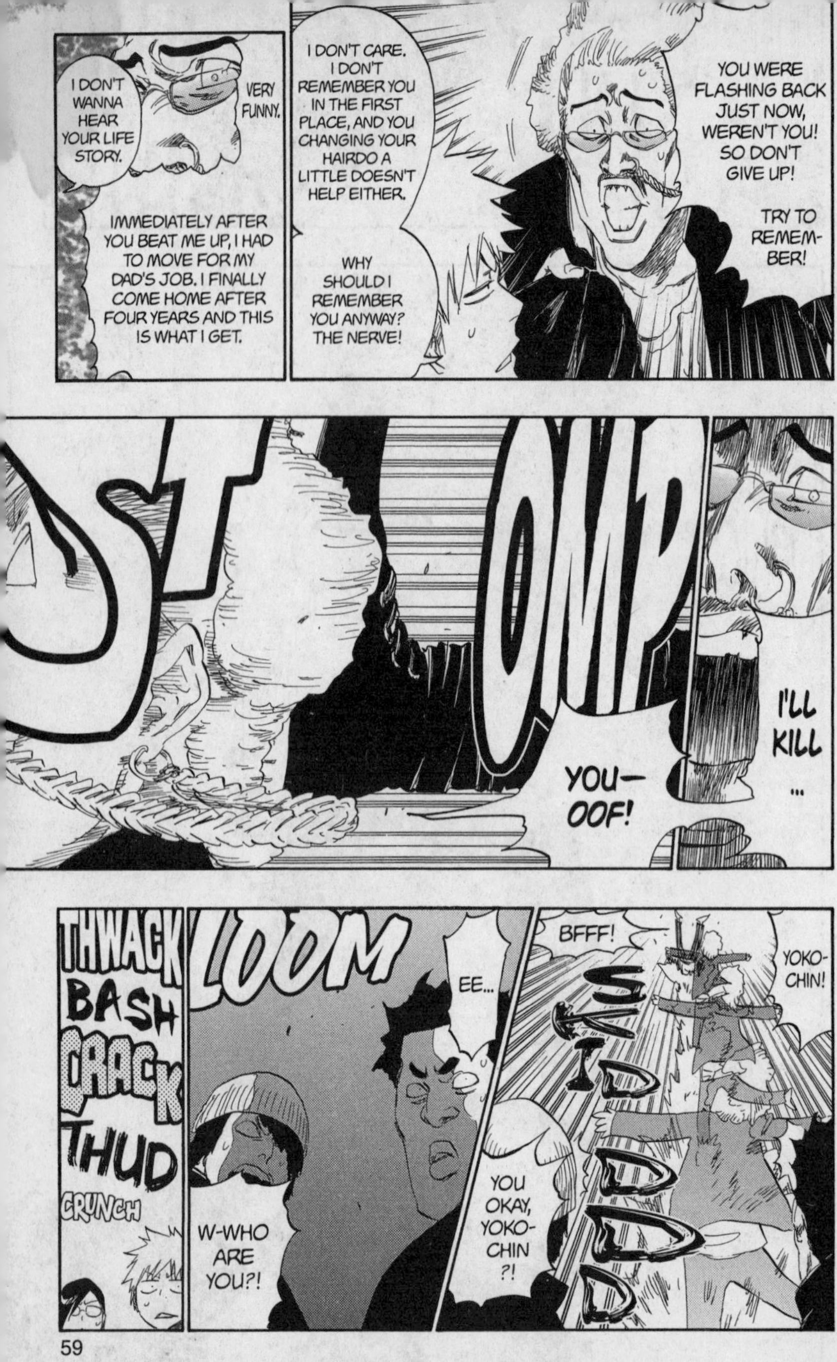
YOU WERE FLASHING BACK JUST NOW, WEREN'T YOU! SO DON'T GIVE UP!
TRY TO REMEMBER!
I DON'T CARE. I DON'T REMEMBER YOU IN THE FIRST PLACE, AND YOU CHANGING YOUR HAIRDO A LITTLE DOESN'T HELP EITHER.
WHY SHOULD I REMEMBER YOU ANYWAY? THE NERVE!
VERY FUNNY.
I DON'T WANNA HEAR YOUR LIFE STORY.
IMMEDIATELY AFTER YOU BEAT ME UP, I HAD TO MOVE FOR MY DAD'S JOB. I FINALLY COME HOME AFTER FOUR YEARS AND THIS IS WHAT I GET.
I'LL KILL ...
YOU— OOF!
ST
OMP!
YOKO-CHIN!
BFFF!
SKIDDDD
YOU OKAY, YOKO-CHIN?!
EE...
LOOM
W-WHO ARE YOU?!
THWACK
BASH
CRACK
THUD
CRUNCH

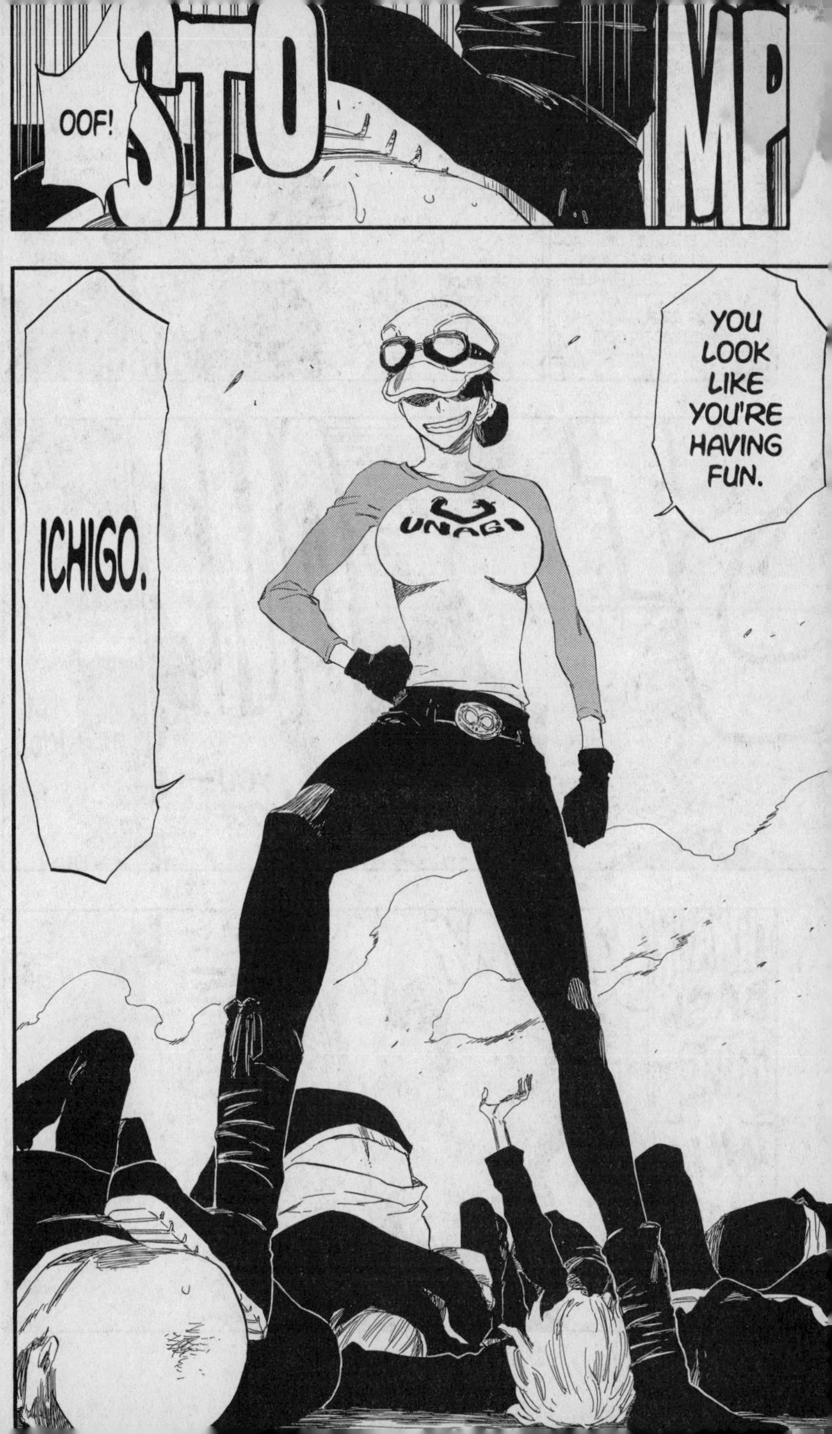
STO
MP
OOF!
YOU LOOK LIKE YOU'RE HAVING FUN.
UNAGI
ICHIGO.

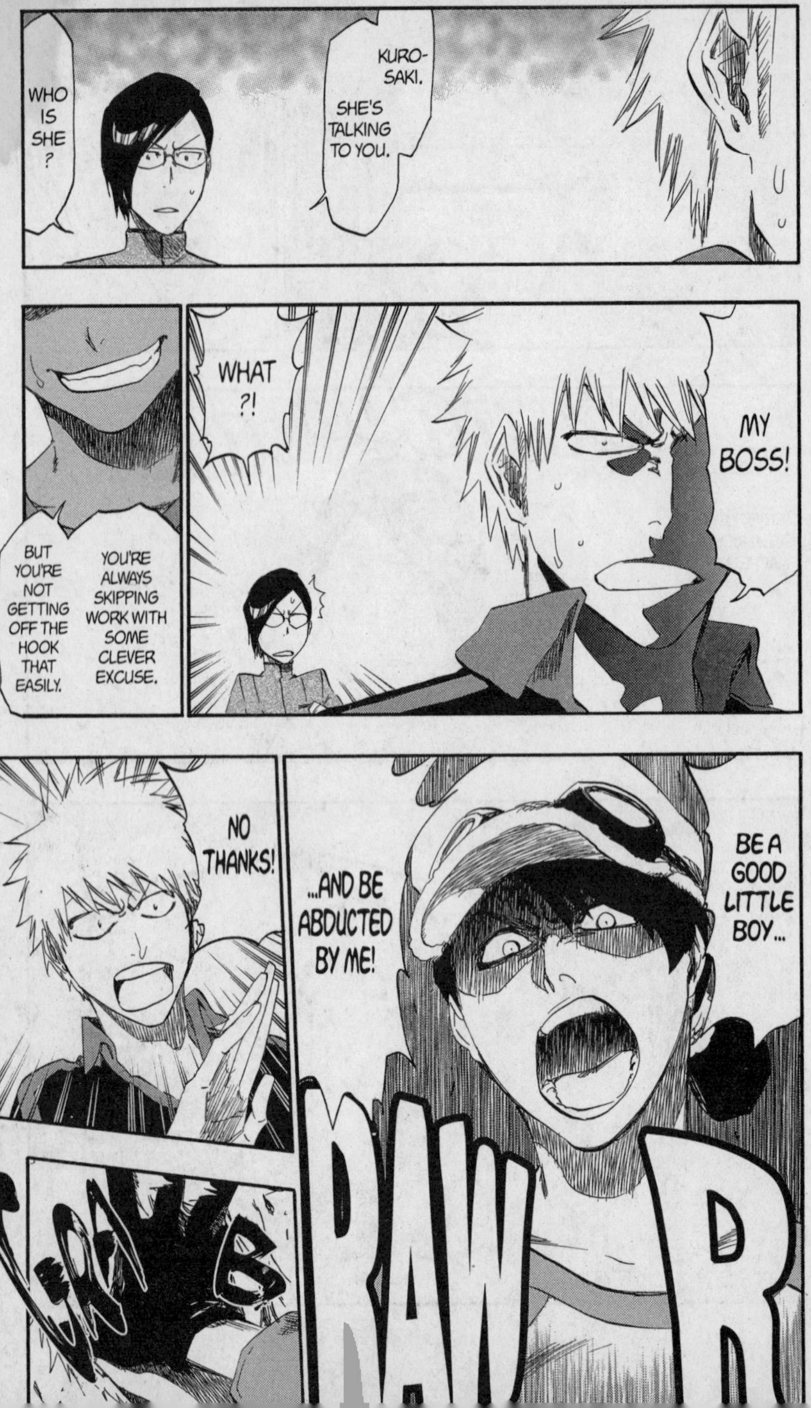
KURO-SAKI.
SHE'S TALKING TO YOU.
WHO IS SHE?
MY BOSS!
WHAT?!
YOU'RE ALWAYS SKIPPING WORK WITH SOME CLEVER EXCUSE.
BUT YOU'RE NOT GETTING OFF THE HOOK THAT EASILY.
BE A GOOD LITTLE BOY...
...AND BE ABDUCTED BY ME!
RAWR
NO THANKS!

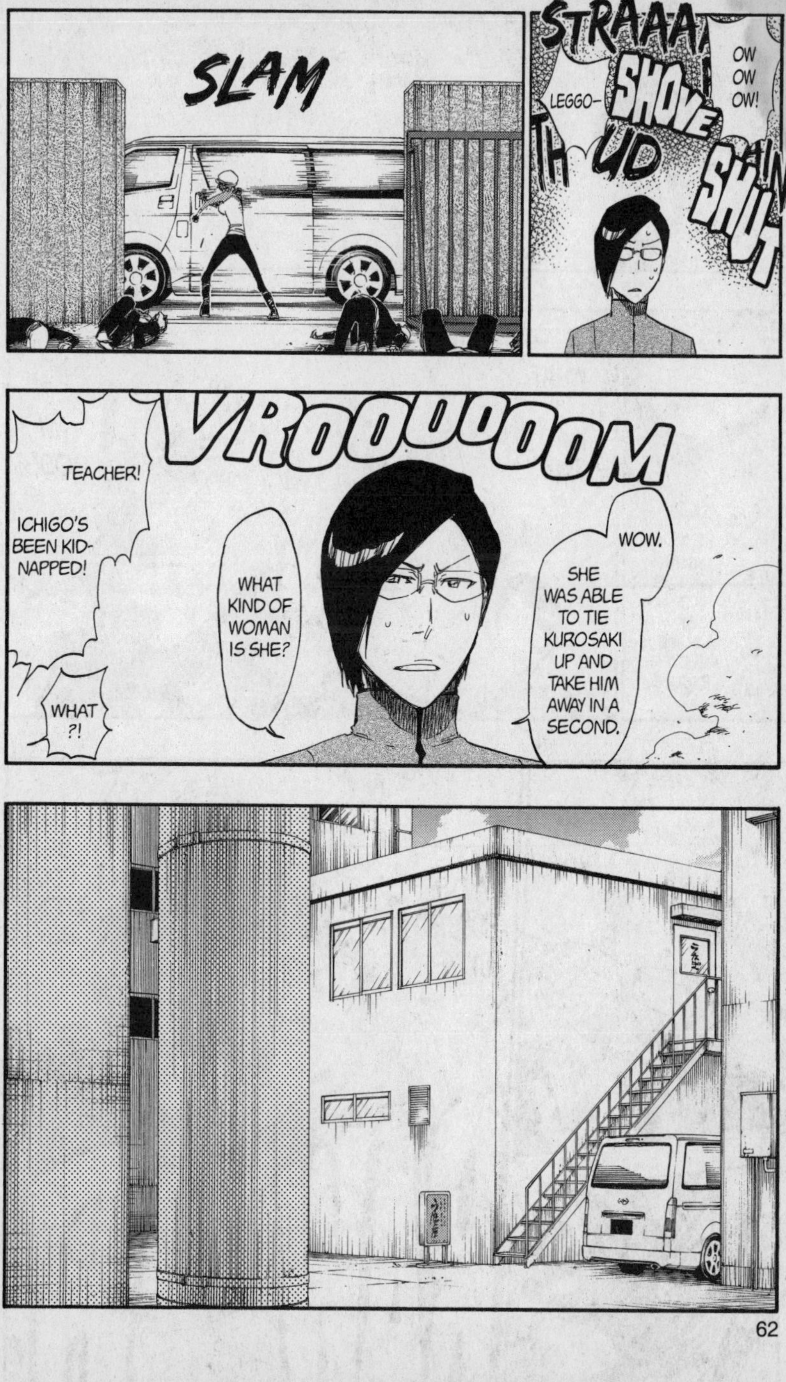
OW OW OW!
LEGGO—
SHOVE
THUD
SHUT
SLAM
VROOOOOOM
WOW.
SHE WAS ABLE TO TIE KUROSAKI UP AND TAKE HIM AWAY IN A SECOND.
WHAT KIND OF WOMAN IS SHE?
TEACHER!
ICHIGO'S BEEN KID-NAPPED!
WHAT?!

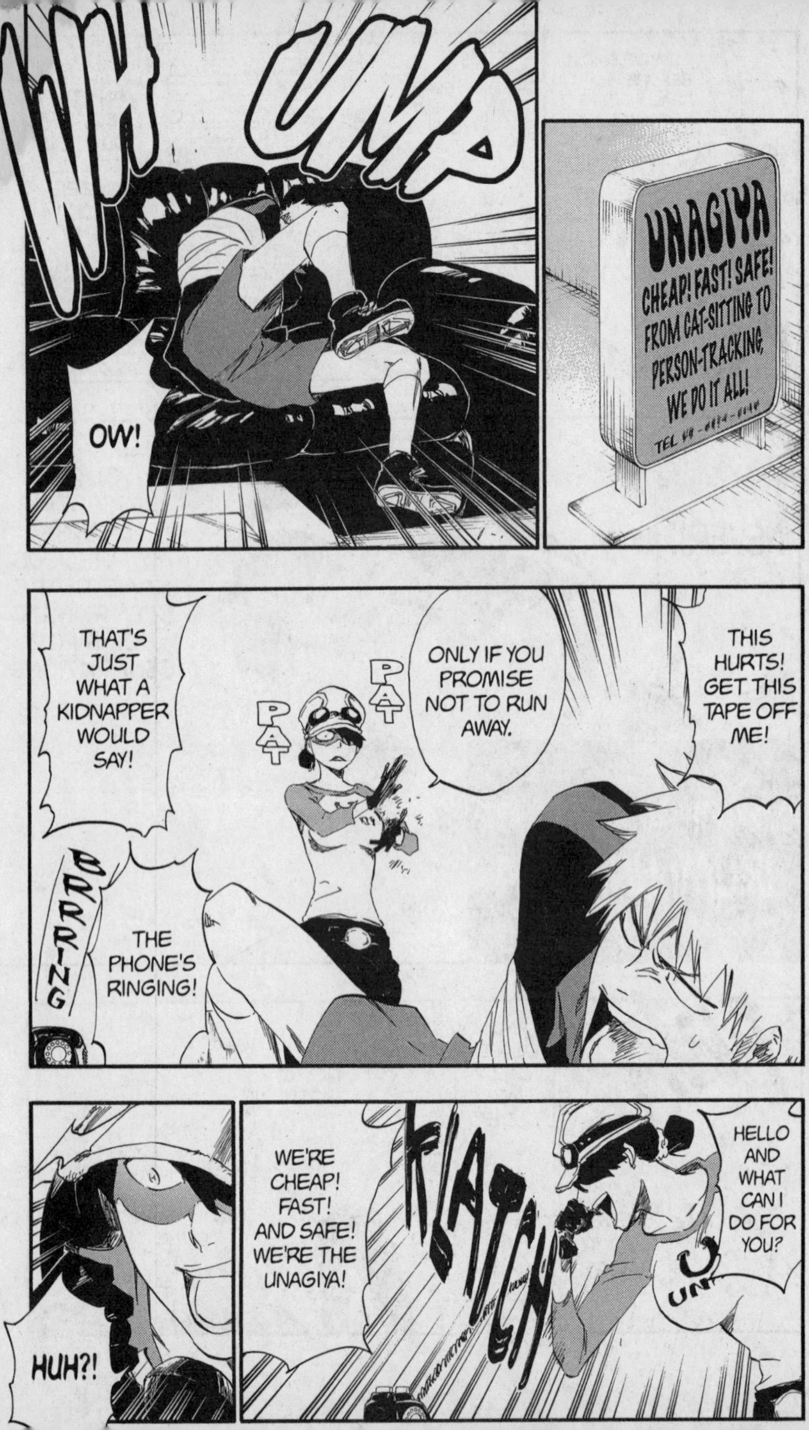
UNAGIYA
CHEAP! FAST! SAFE! FROM CAT-SITTING TO PERSON-TRACKING, WE DO IT ALL!
WHUMP
OW!
THIS HURTS! GET THIS TAPE OFF ME!
ONLY IF YOU PROMISE NOT TO RUN AWAY.
PAT
PAT
THAT'S JUST WHAT A KIDNAPPER WOULD SAY!
BRRRING
THE PHONE'S RINGING!
HELLO AND WHAT CAN I DO FOR YOU?
KLATCH
WE'RE CHEAP! FAST! AND SAFE! WE'RE THE UNAGIYA!
HUH?!

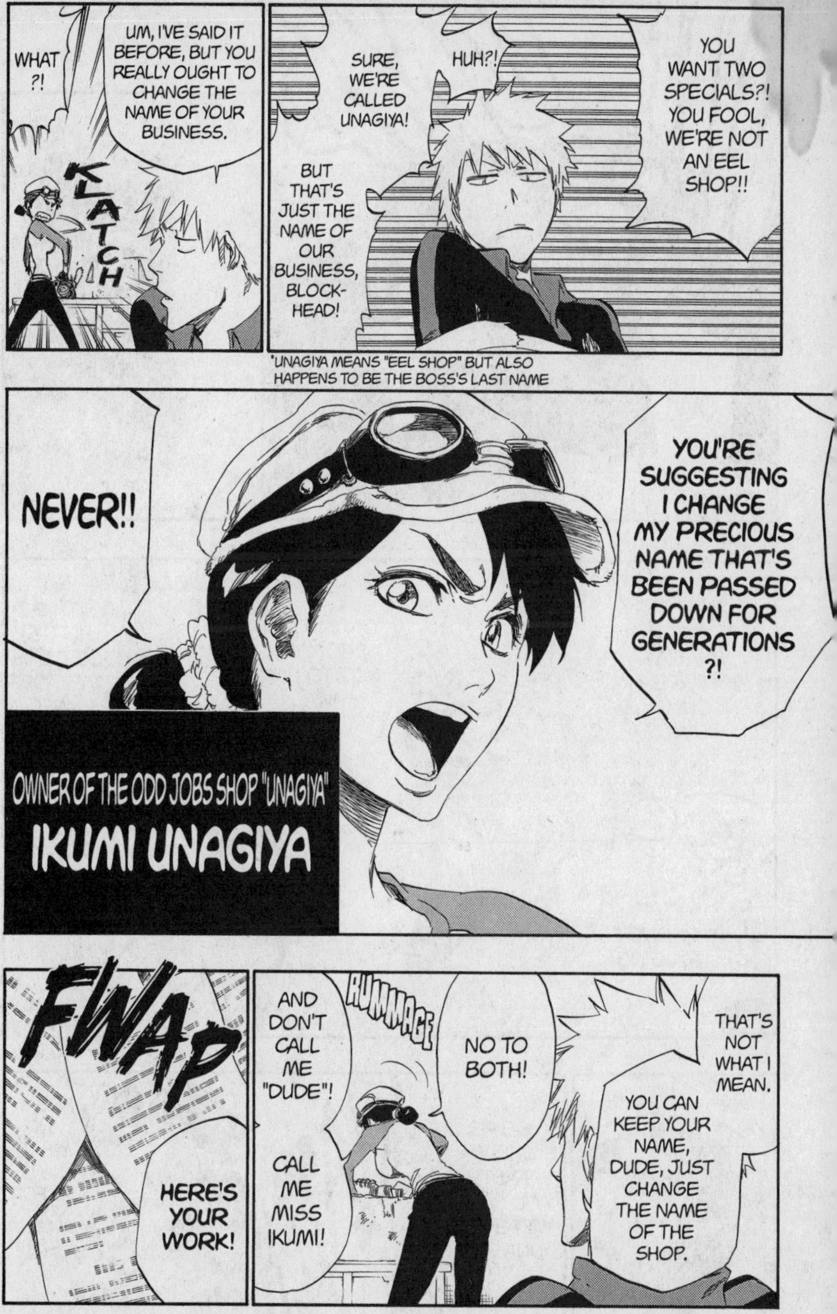
YOU WANT TWO SPECIALS?! YOU FOOL, WE'RE NOT AN EEL SHOP!!
HUH?!
SURE, WE'RE CALLED UNAGIYA!
BUT THAT'S JUST THE NAME OF OUR BUSINESS, BLOCK-HEAD!
UM, I'VE SAID IT BEFORE, BUT YOU REALLY OUGHT TO CHANGE THE NAME OF YOUR BUSINESS.
WHAT?!
KLATCH
YOU'RE SUGGESTING I CHANGE MY PRECIOUS NAME THAT'S BEEN PASSED DOWN FOR GENERATIONS?!
NEVER!!
OWNER OF THE ODD JOBS SHOP "UNAGIYA"
IKUMI UNAGIYA
THAT'S NOT WHAT I MEAN.
YOU CAN KEEP YOUR NAME, DUDE, JUST CHANGE THE NAME OF THE SHOP.
NO TO BOTH!
RUMMAGE
AND DON'T CALL ME "DUDE"!
CALL ME MISS IKUMI!
FWAP
HERE'S YOUR WORK!
*UNAGIYA MEANS "EEL SHOP" BUT ALSO HAPPENS TO BE THE BOSS'S LAST NAME

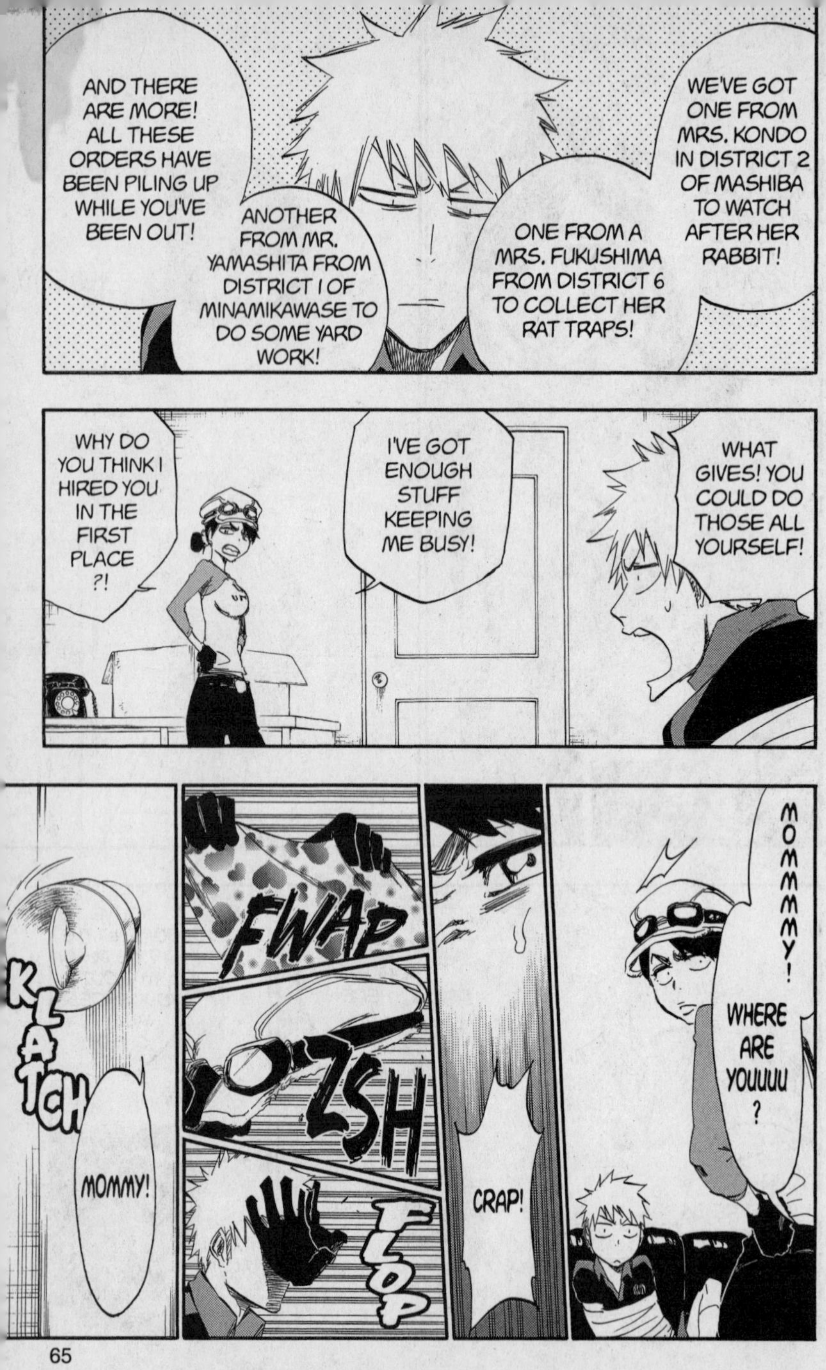

WE'VE GOT ONE FROM MRS. KONDO IN DISTRICT 2 OF MASHIBA TO WATCH AFTER HER RABBIT!
ONE FROM A MRS. FUKUSHIMA FROM DISTRICT 6 TO COLLECT HER RAT TRAPS!
ANOTHER FROM MR. YAMASHITA FROM DISTRICT 1 OF MINAMIKAWASE TO DO SOME YARD WORK!
AND THERE ARE MORE! ALL THESE ORDERS HAVE BEEN PILING UP WHILE YOU'VE BEEN OUT!
WHAT GIVES! YOU COULD DO THOSE ALL YOURSELF!
I'VE GOT ENOUGH STUFF KEEPING ME BUSY!
WHY DO YOU THINK I HIRED YOU IN THE FIRST PLACE?!
MOMMMMY!
WHERE ARE YOUUUU?
CRAP!
FWAP
ZSH
FLOP
KLATCH
MOMMY!

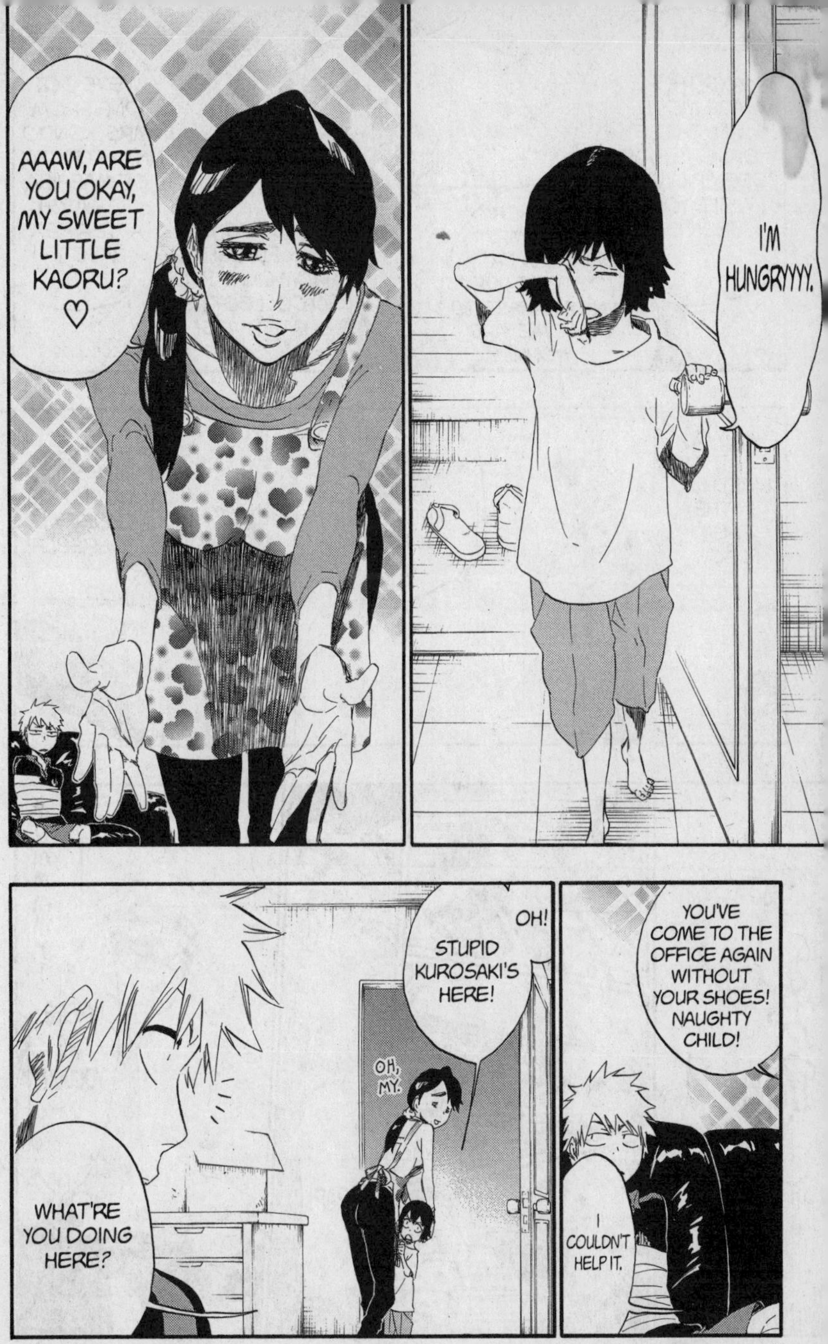
I'M HUNGRYYYY.
AAAW, ARE YOU OKAY, MY SWEET LITTLE KAORU? ♡
YOU'VE COME TO THE OFFICE AGAIN WITHOUT YOUR SHOES! NAUGHTY CHILD!
I COULDN'T HELP IT.
OH!
STUPID KUROSAKI'S HERE!
OH, MY.
WHAT'RE YOU DOING HERE?

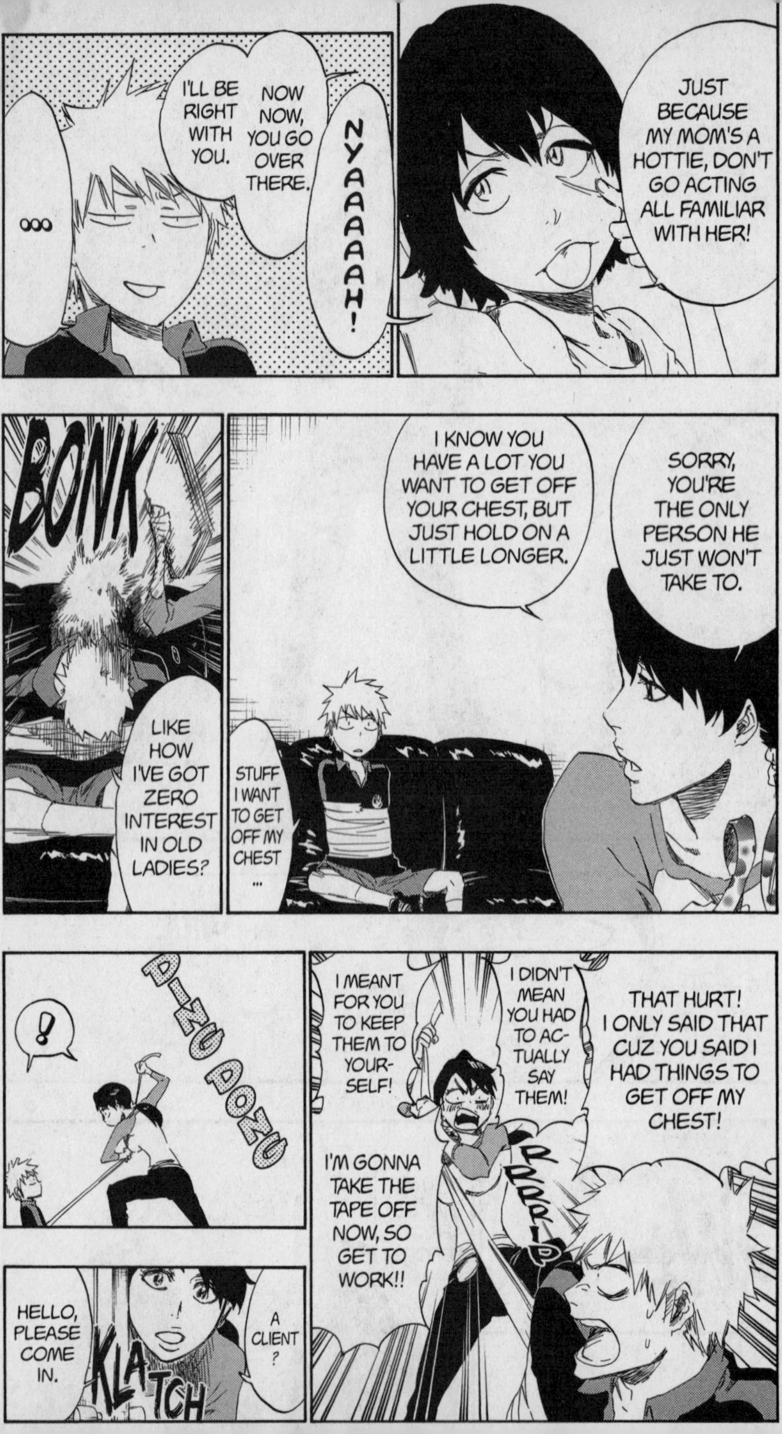
JUST BECAUSE MY MOM'S A HOTTIE, DON'T GO ACTING ALL FAMILIAR WITH HER!
NYAAAAAAH!
NOW NOW, YOU GO OVER THERE.
I'LL BE RIGHT WITH YOU.
...
SORRY, YOU'RE THE ONLY PERSON HE JUST WON'T TAKE TO.
I KNOW YOU HAVE A LOT YOU WANT TO GET OFF YOUR CHEST, BUT JUST HOLD ON A LITTLE LONGER.
STUFF I WANT TO GET OFF MY CHEST...
BONK
LIKE HOW I'VE GOT ZERO INTEREST IN OLD LADIES?
THAT HURT! I ONLY SAID THAT CUZ YOU SAID I HAD THINGS TO GET OFF MY CHEST!
I DIDN'T MEAN YOU HAD TO AC-TUALLY SAY THEM!
I MEANT FOR YOU TO KEEP THEM TO YOUR-SELF!
RRRRIP
I'M GONNA TAKE THE TAPE OFF NOW, SO GET TO WORK!!
DING DONG
!
A CLIENT?
HELLO, PLEASE COME IN.
KLATCH

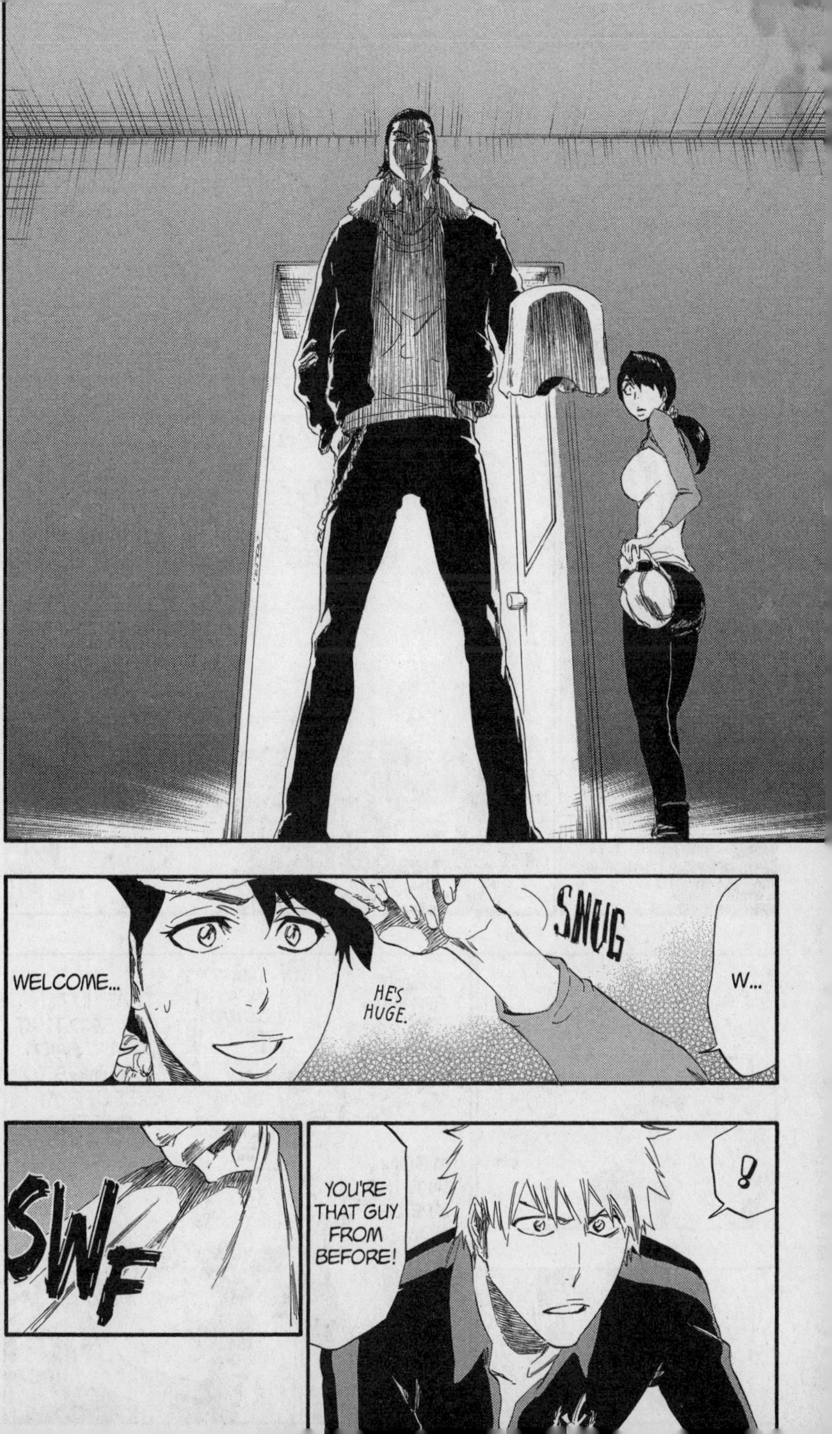
W...
SNUG
HE'S HUGE.
WELCOME...
!
YOU'RE THAT GUY FROM BEFORE!
SWF

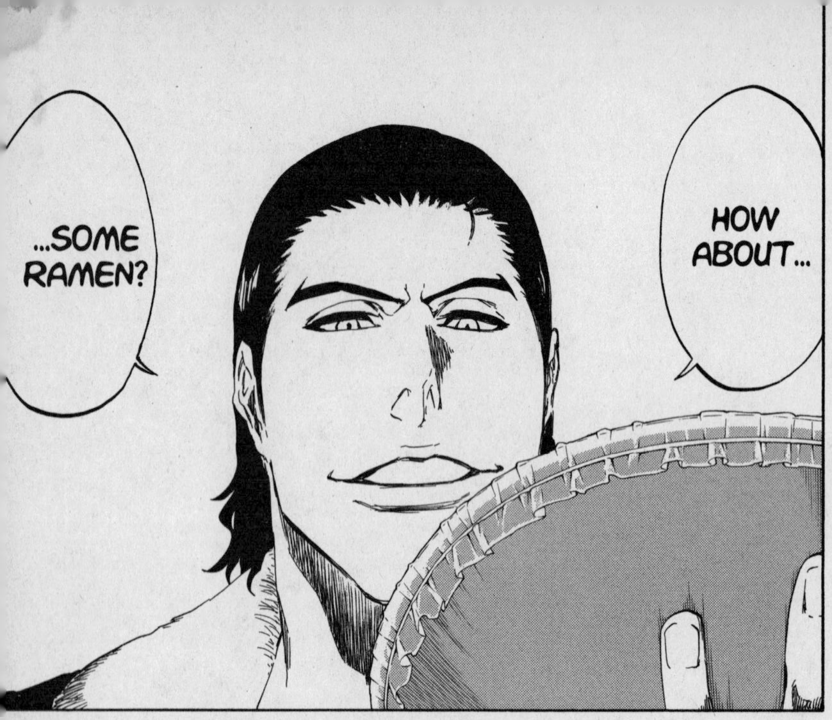
HOW ABOUT...
...SOME RAMEN?

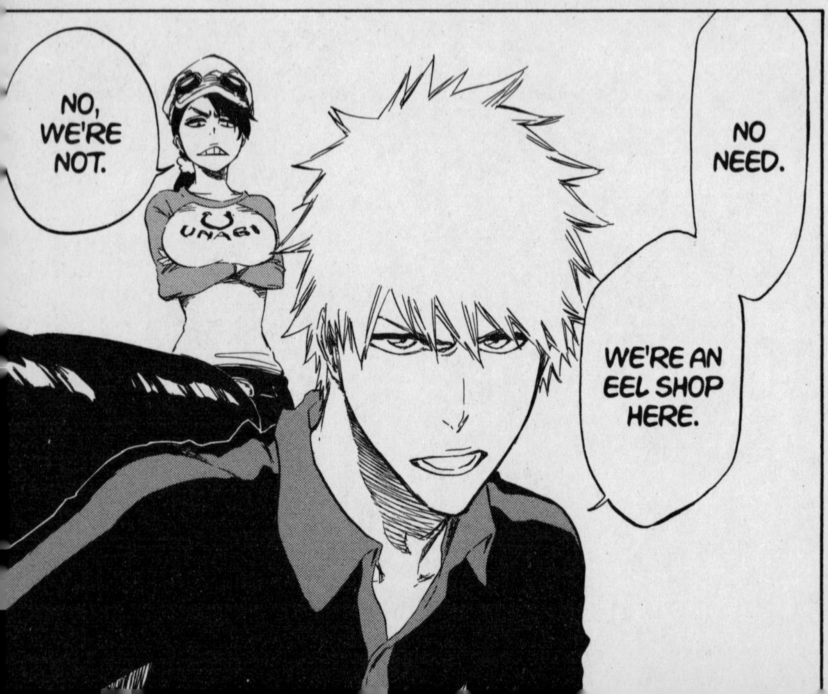
NO NEED.
WE'RE AN EEL SHOP HERE.
NO, WE'RE NOT.
UNAGI

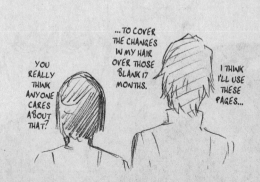

I THINK I'LL USE THESE PAGES...
...TO COVER THE CHANGES IN MY HAIR OVER THOSE BLANK 17 MONTHS.
YOU REALLY THINK ANYONE CARES ABOUT THAT?

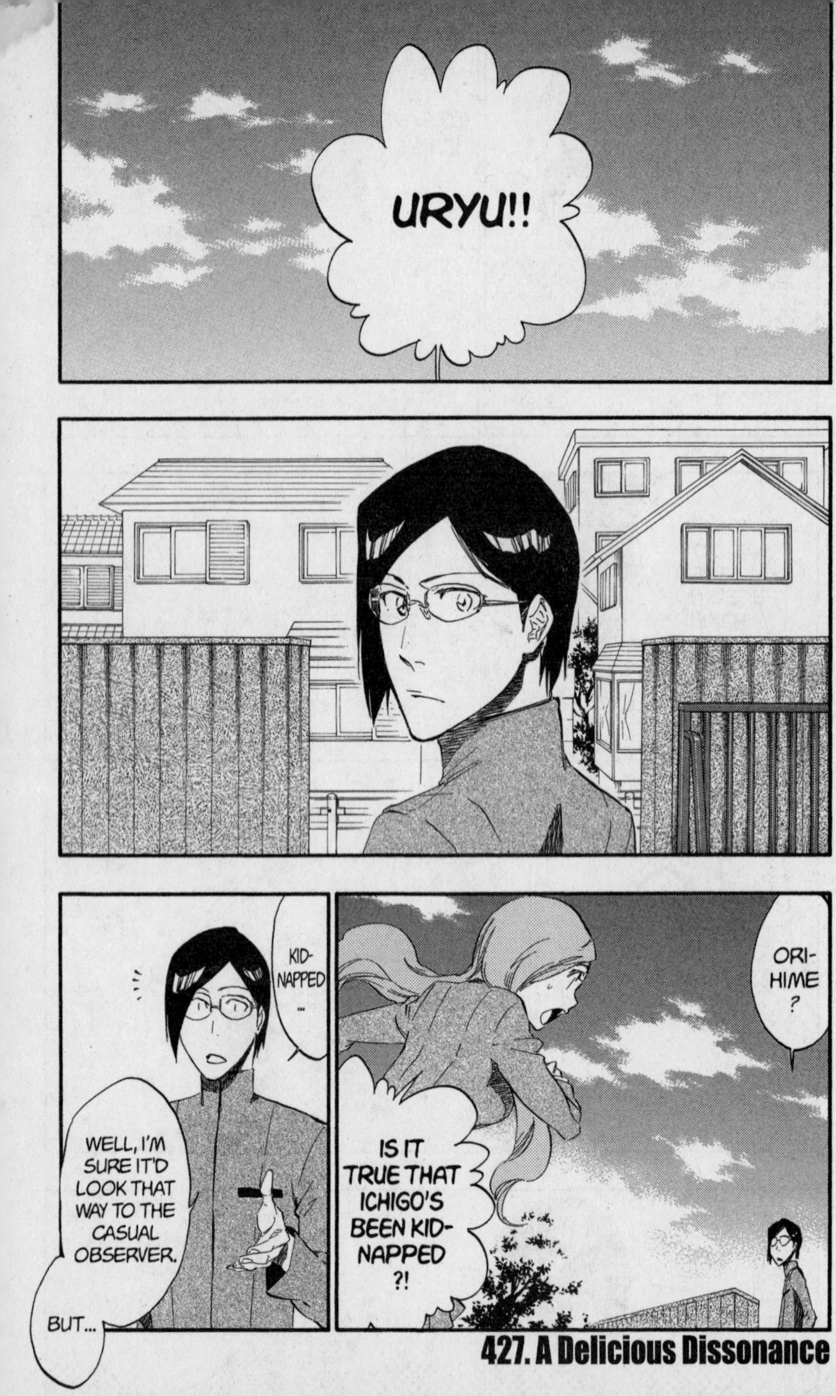
URYU!!
ORI-HIME?
IS IT TRUE THAT ICHIGO'S BEEN KID-NAPPED?!
KID-NAPPED...
WELL, I'M SURE IT'D LOOK THAT WAY TO THE CASUAL OBSERVER.
BUT...

427. A Delicious Dissonance

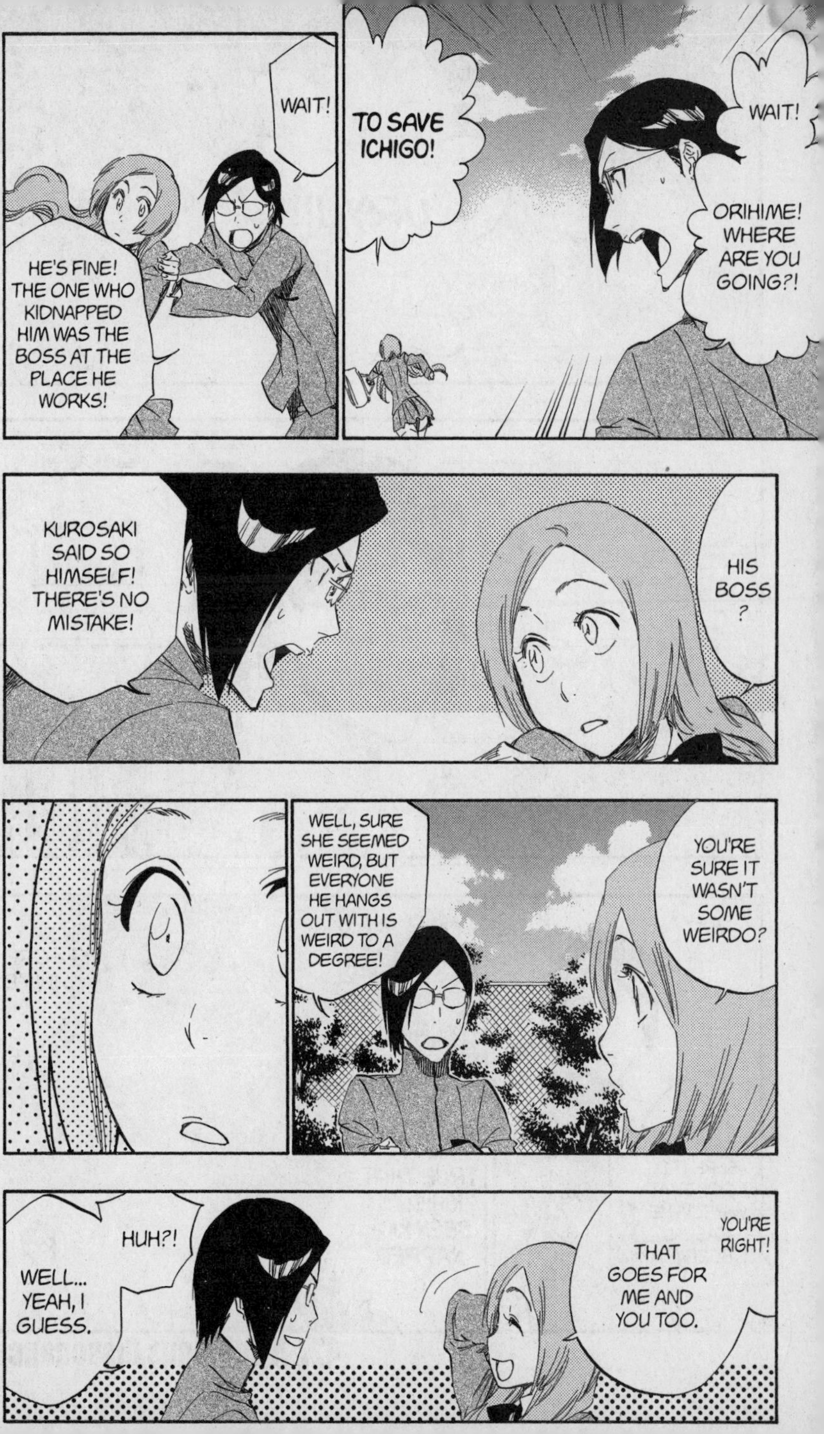
WAIT!
ORIHIME! WHERE ARE YOU GOING?!
TO SAVE ICHIGO!
WAIT!
HE'S FINE! THE ONE WHO KIDNAPPED HIM WAS THE BOSS AT THE PLACE HE WORKS!
HIS BOSS?
KUROSAKI SAID SO HIMSELF! THERE'S NO MISTAKE!
YOU'RE SURE IT WASN'T SOME WEIRDO?
WELL, SURE SHE SEEMED WEIRD, BUT EVERYONE HE HANGS OUT WITH IS WEIRD TO A DEGREE!
YOU'RE RIGHT!
THAT GOES FOR ME AND YOU TOO.
HUH?!
WELL... YEAH, I GUESS.

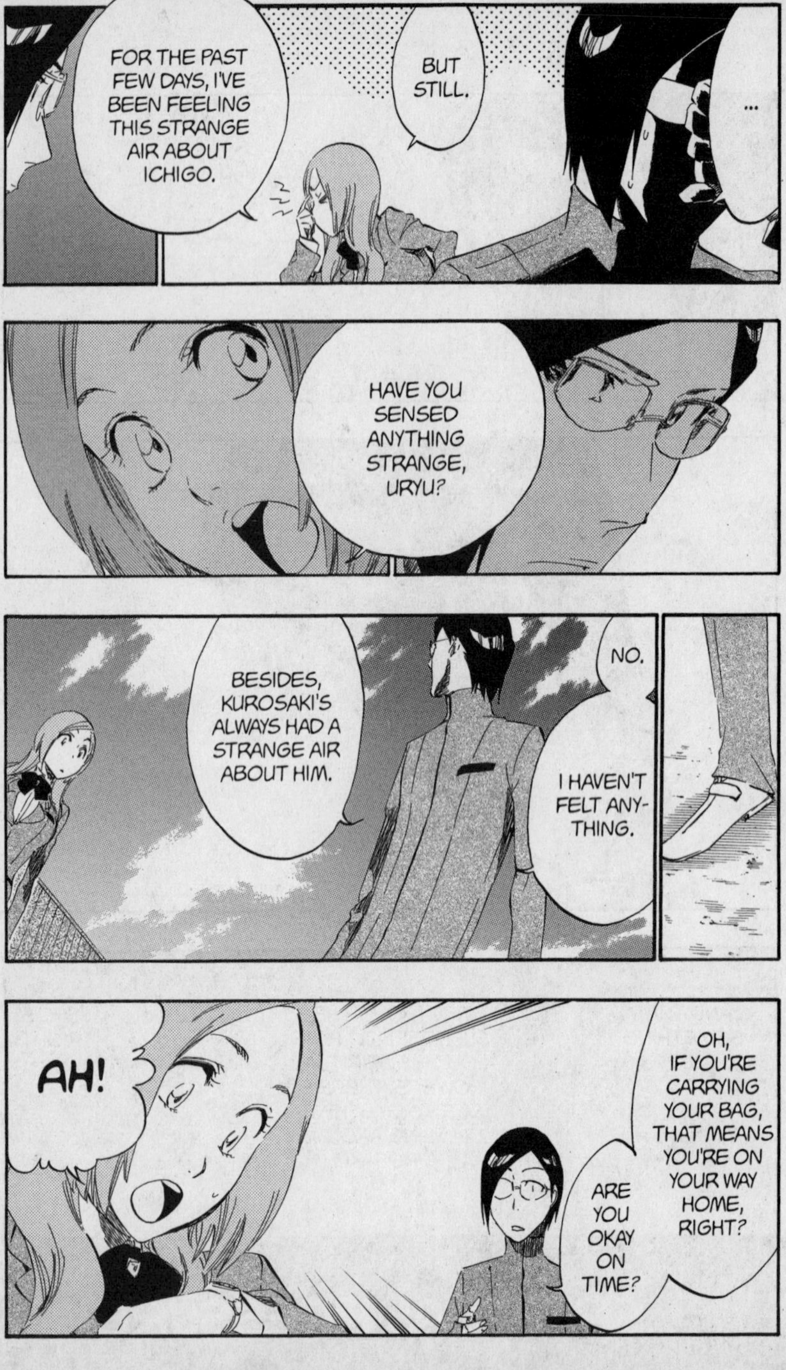
...
BUT STILL.
FOR THE PAST FEW DAYS, I'VE BEEN FEELING THIS STRANGE AIR ABOUT ICHIGO.
HAVE YOU SENSED ANYTHING STRANGE, URYU?
NO.
I HAVEN'T FELT ANY-THING.
BESIDES, KUROSAKI'S ALWAYS HAD A STRANGE AIR ABOUT HIM.
OH, IF YOU'RE CARRYING YOUR BAG, THAT MEANS YOU'RE ON YOUR WAY HOME, RIGHT?
ARE YOU OKAY ON TIME?
AH!

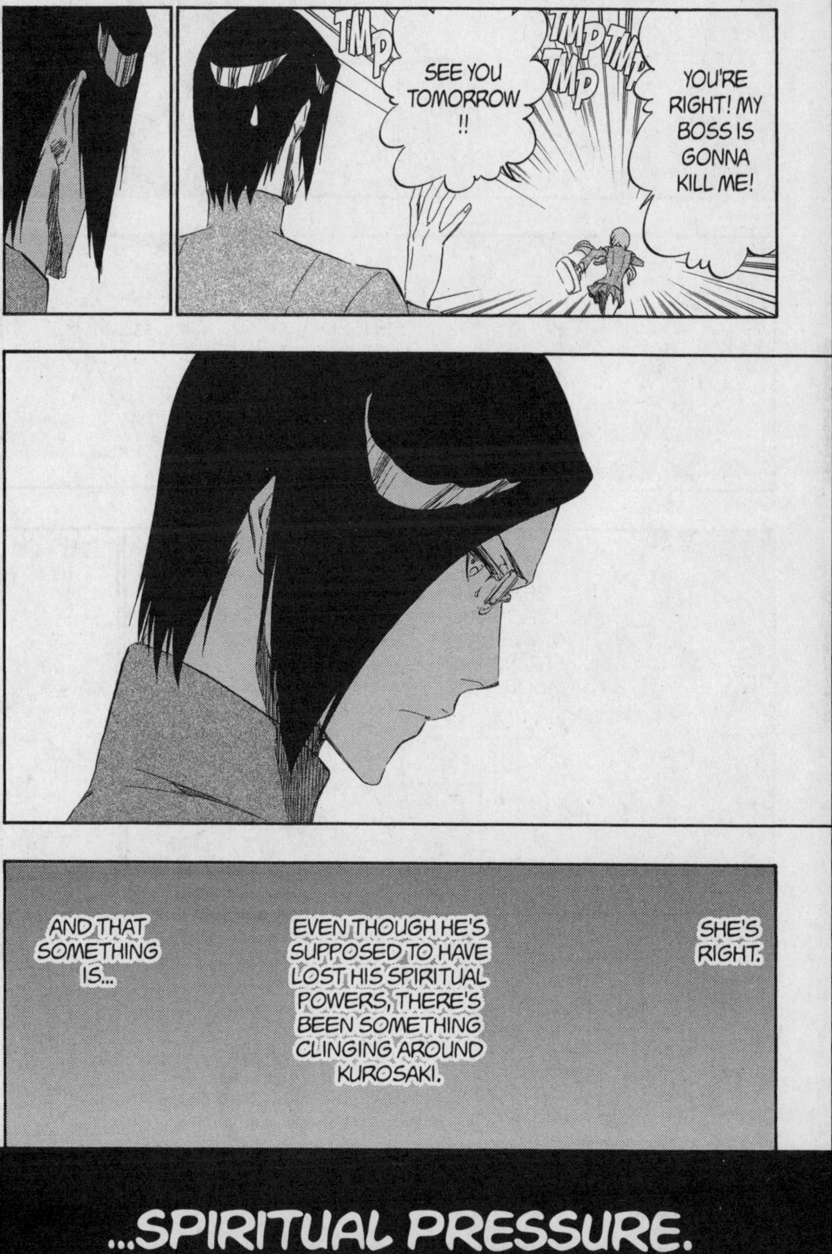
TMP TMP
TMP
YOU'RE RIGHT! MY BOSS IS GONNA KILL ME!
TMP
TMP
SEE YOU TOMORROW !!
SHE'S RIGHT.
EVEN THOUGH HE'S SUPPOSED TO HAVE LOST HIS SPIRITUAL POWERS, THERE'S BEEN SOMETHING CLINGING AROUND KUROSAKI.
AND THAT SOMETHING IS...
...SPIRITUAL PRESSURE.

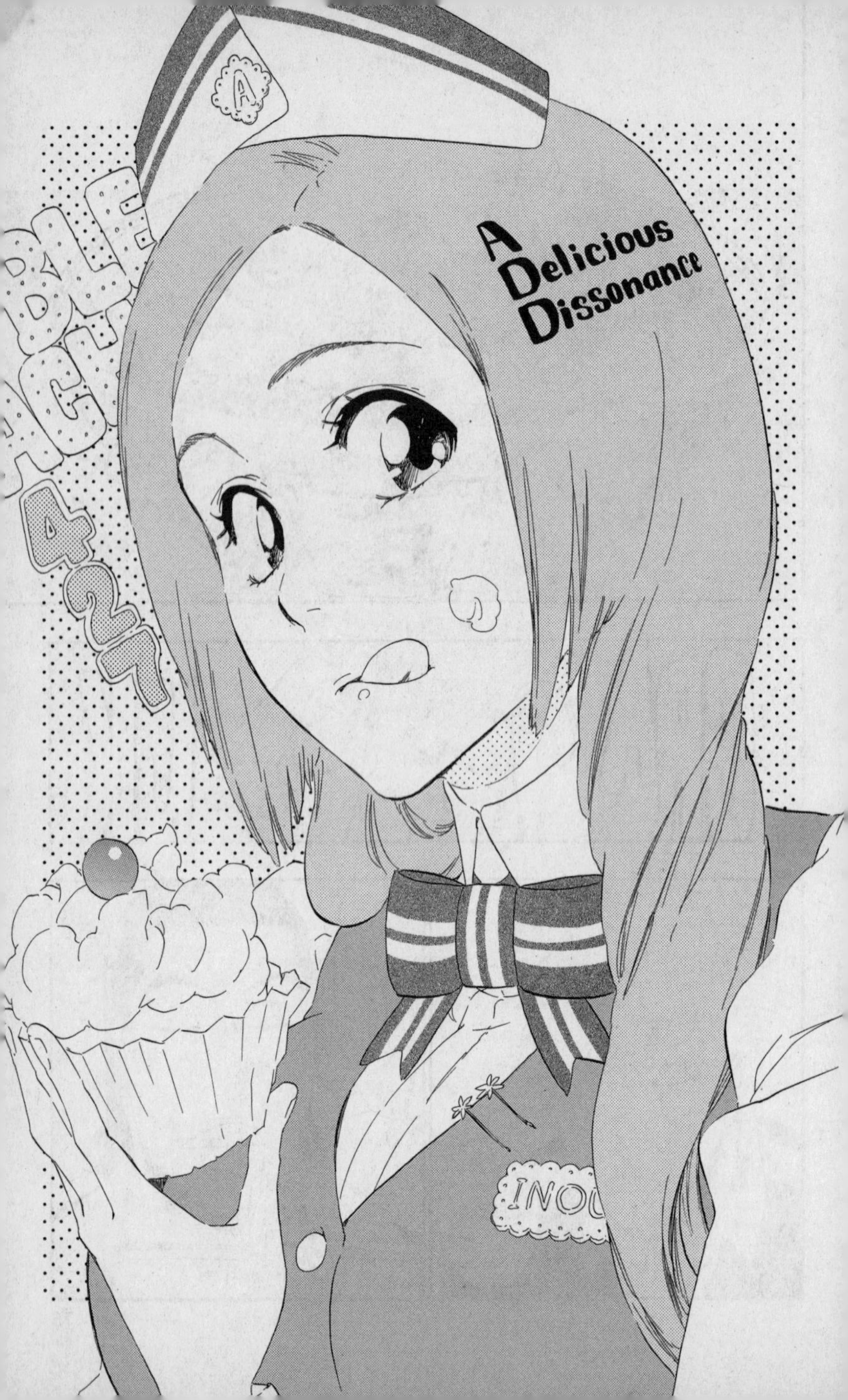
427
A Delicious Dissonance

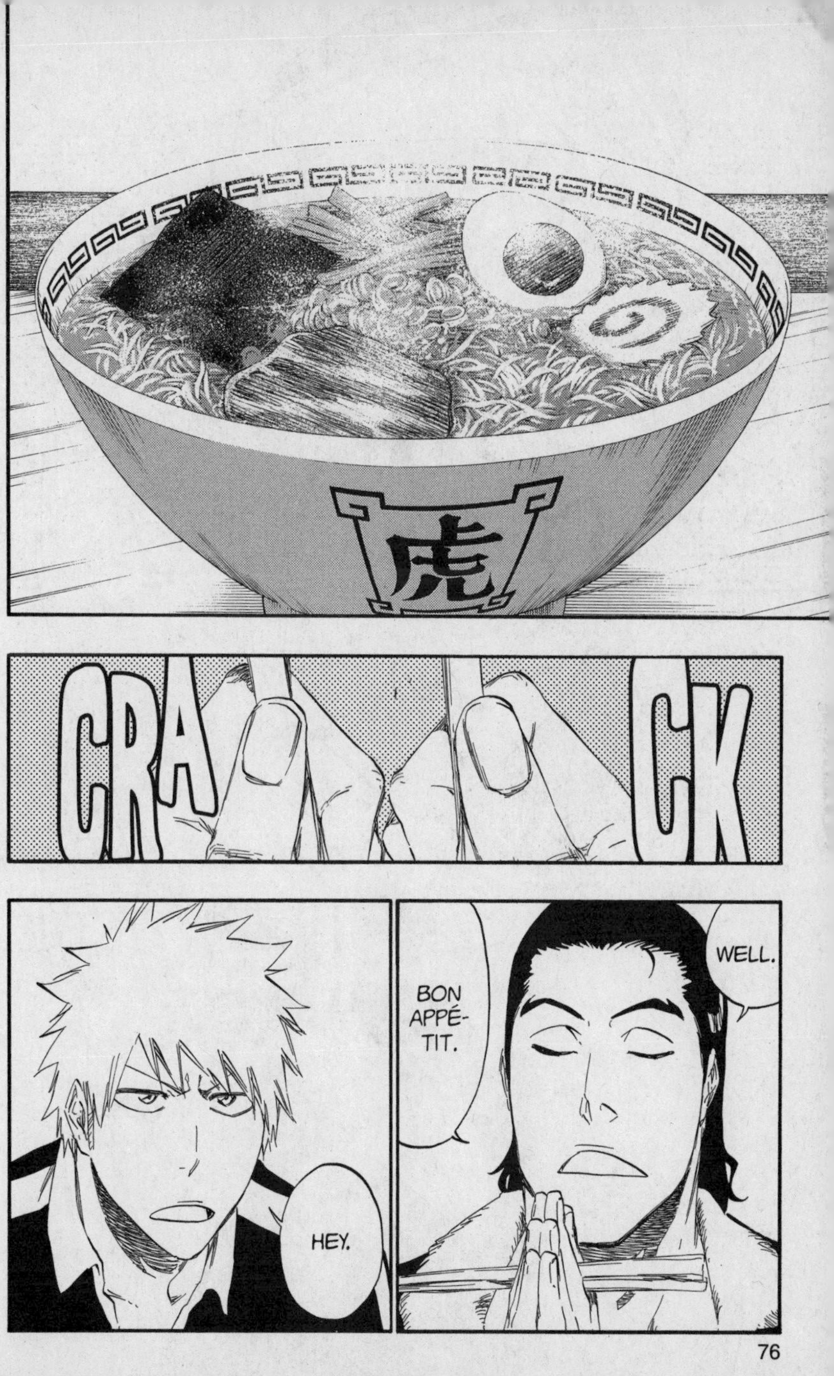
虎
CRACK
WELL.
BON APPÉTIT.
HEY.

READ THIS WAY

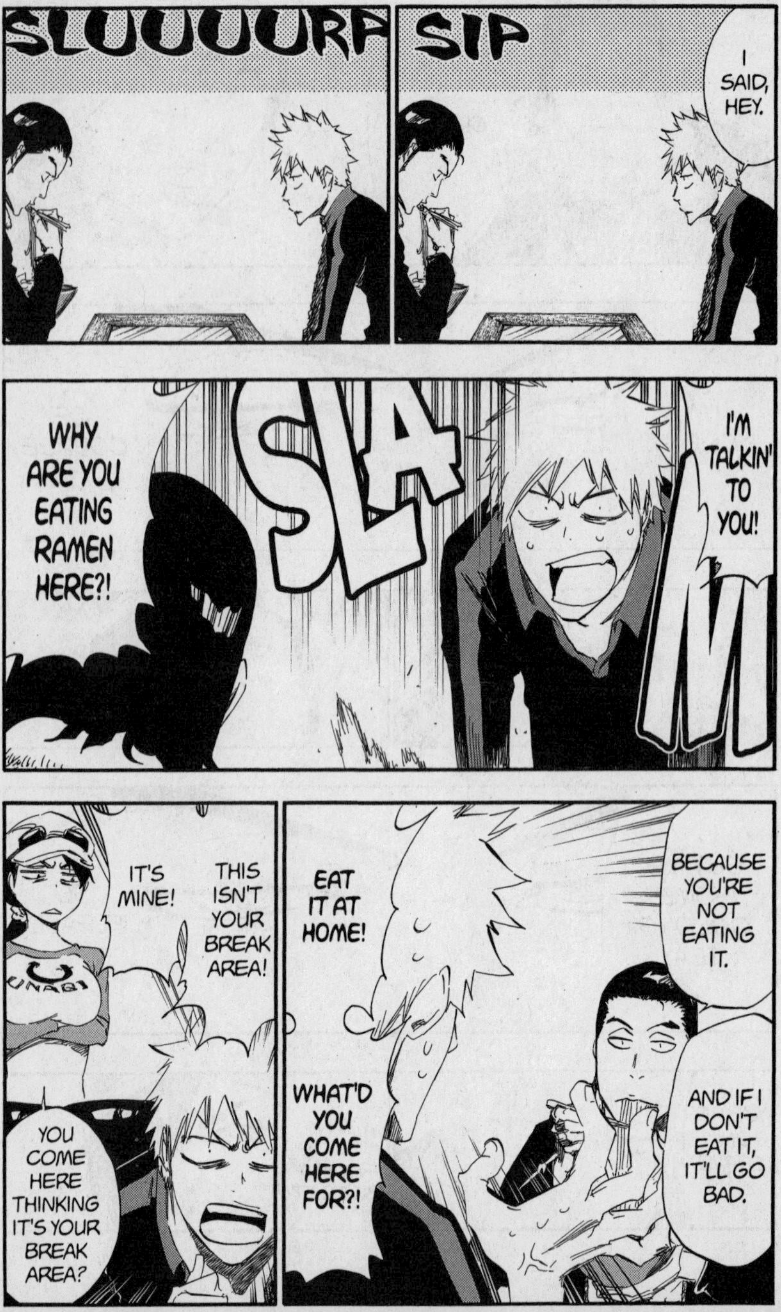
SIP
I SAID, HEY.
SLUUUURP
SLAM
I'M TALKIN' TO YOU!
WHY ARE YOU EATING RAMEN HERE?!
BECAUSE YOU'RE NOT EATING IT.
EAT IT AT HOME!
AND IF I DON'T EAT IT, IT'LL GO BAD.
WHAT'D YOU COME HERE FOR?!
THIS ISN'T YOUR BREAK AREA!
IT'S MINE!
UNAGI
YOU COME HERE THINKING IT'S YOUR BREAK AREA?

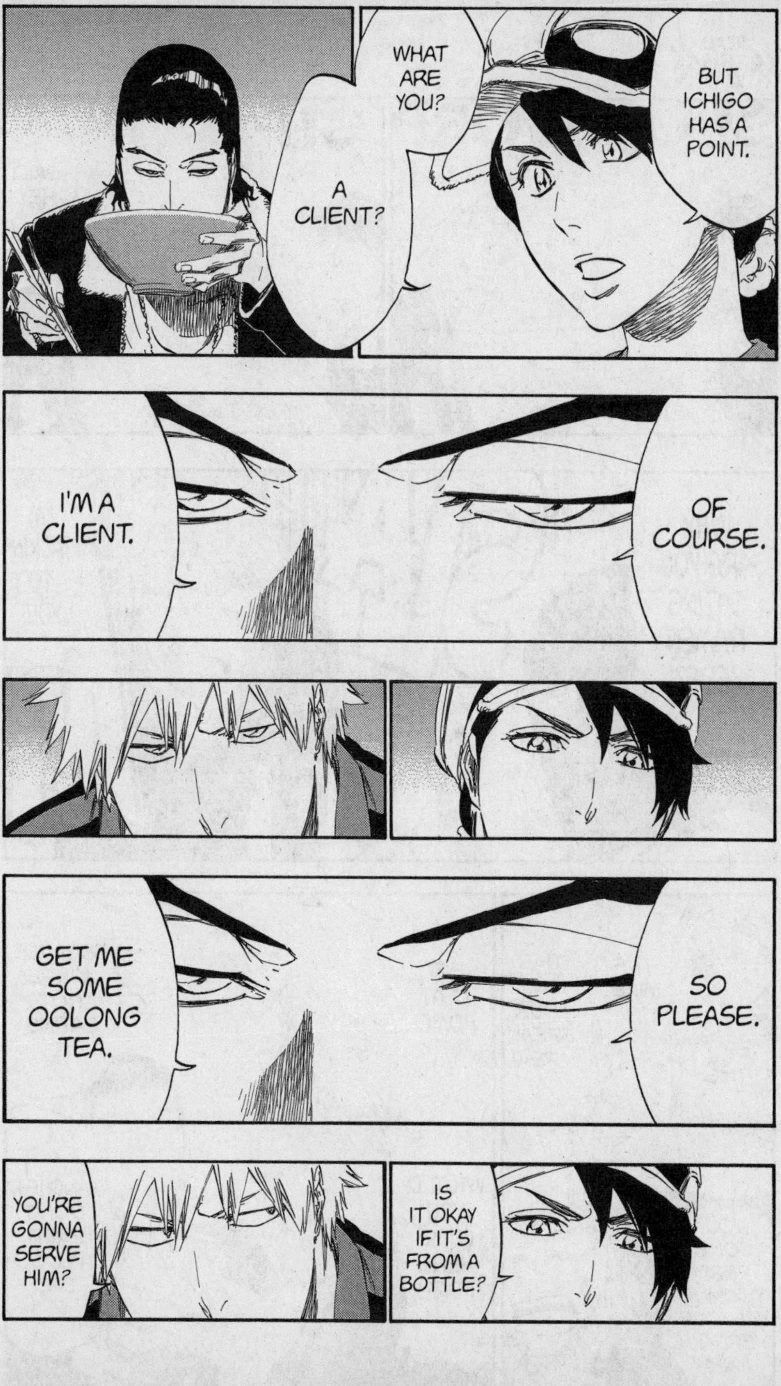
BUT ICHIGO HAS A POINT.
WHAT ARE YOU?
A CLIENT?
OF COURSE.
I'M A CLIENT.
SO PLEASE.
GET ME SOME OOLONG TEA.
IS IT OKAY IF IT'S FROM A BOTTLE?
YOU'RE GONNA SERVE HIM?

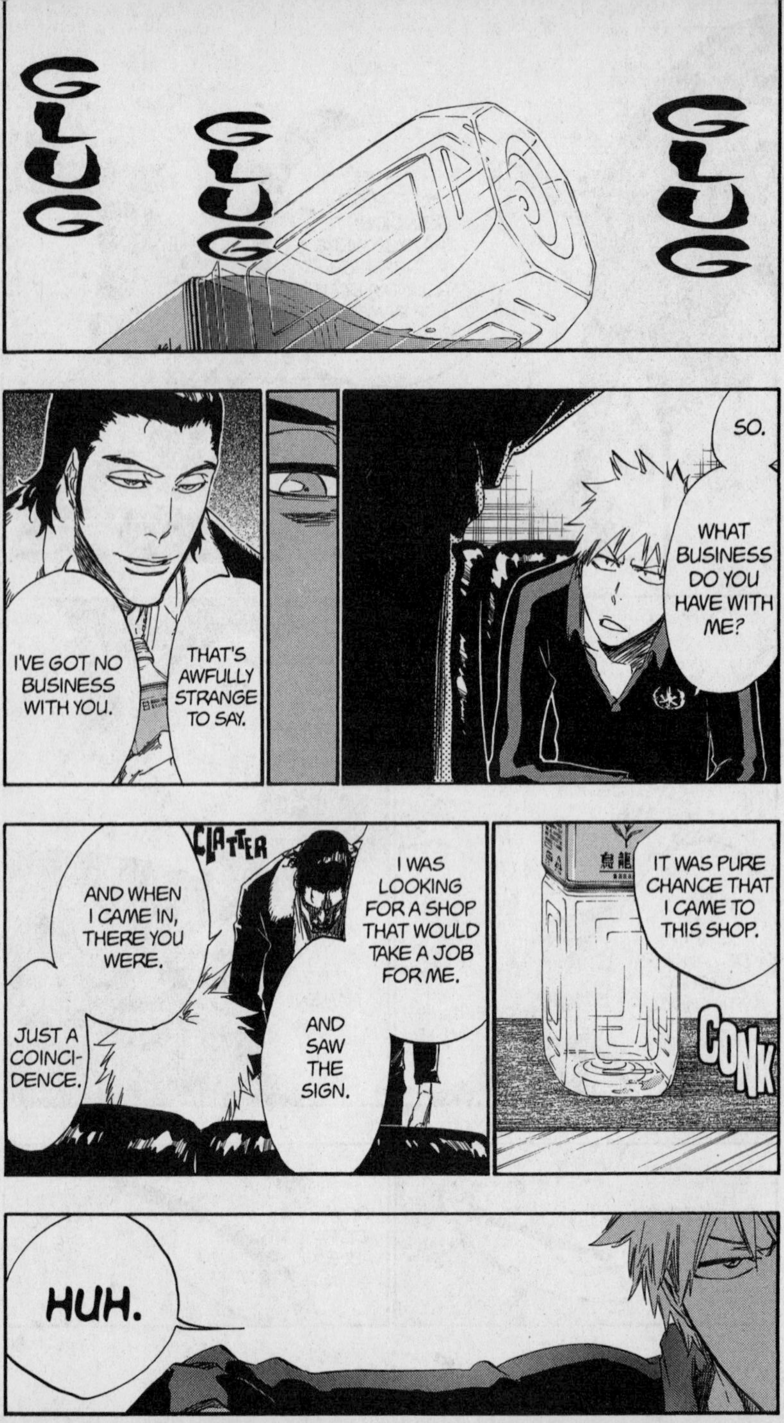
GLUG
GLUG
GLUG
SO.
WHAT BUSINESS DO YOU HAVE WITH ME?
THAT'S AWFULLY STRANGE TO SAY.
I'VE GOT NO BUSINESS WITH YOU.
IT WAS PURE CHANCE THAT I CAME TO THIS SHOP.
CONK
CLATTER
I WAS LOOKING FOR A SHOP THAT WOULD TAKE A JOB FOR ME.
AND SAW THE SIGN.
AND WHEN I CAME IN, THERE YOU WERE.
JUST A COINCIDENCE.
HUH.

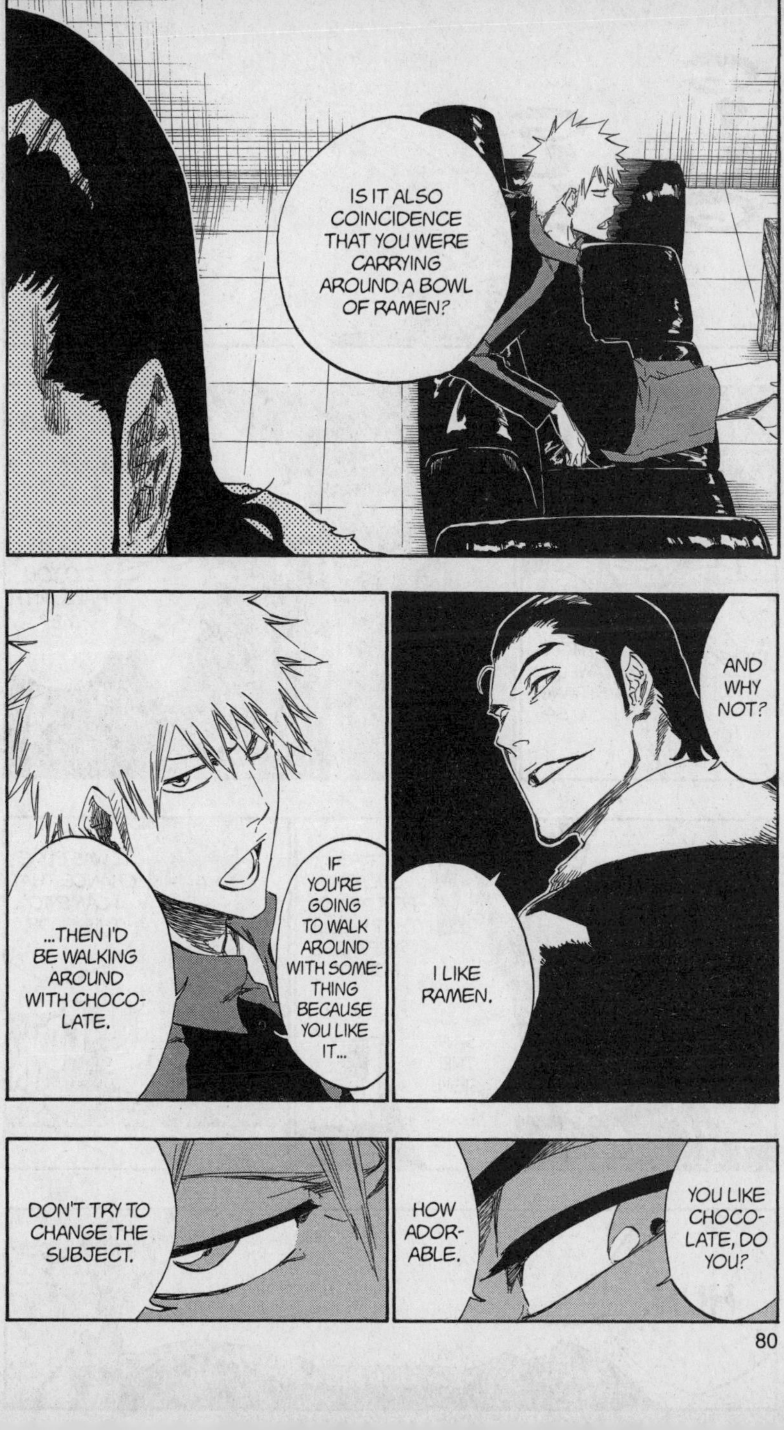
IS IT ALSO COINCIDENCE THAT YOU WERE CARRYING AROUND A BOWL OF RAMEN?
AND WHY NOT?
I LIKE RAMEN.
IF YOU'RE GOING TO WALK AROUND WITH SOME-THING BECAUSE YOU LIKE IT...
...THEN I'D BE WALKING AROUND WITH CHOCO-LATE.
YOU LIKE CHOCO-LATE, DO YOU?
HOW ADOR-ABLE.
DON'T TRY TO CHANGE THE SUBJECT.

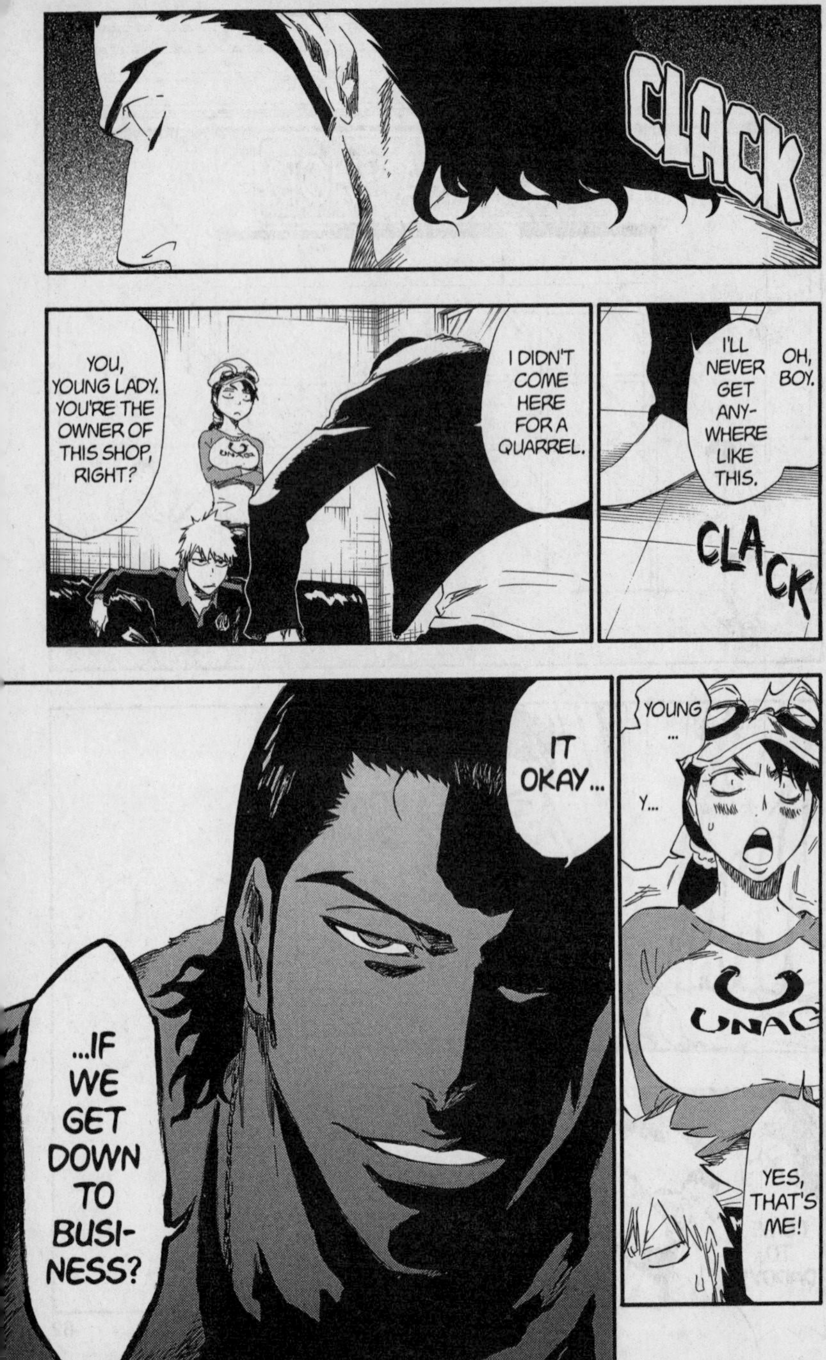
CLACK
OH, BOY.
I'LL NEVER GET ANY-WHERE LIKE THIS.
CLACK
I DIDN'T COME HERE FOR A QUARREL.
YOU, YOUNG LADY. YOU'RE THE OWNER OF THIS SHOP, RIGHT?
YOUNG ...
Y...
YES, THAT'S ME!
IT OKAY...
...IF WE GET DOWN TO BUSI-NESS?

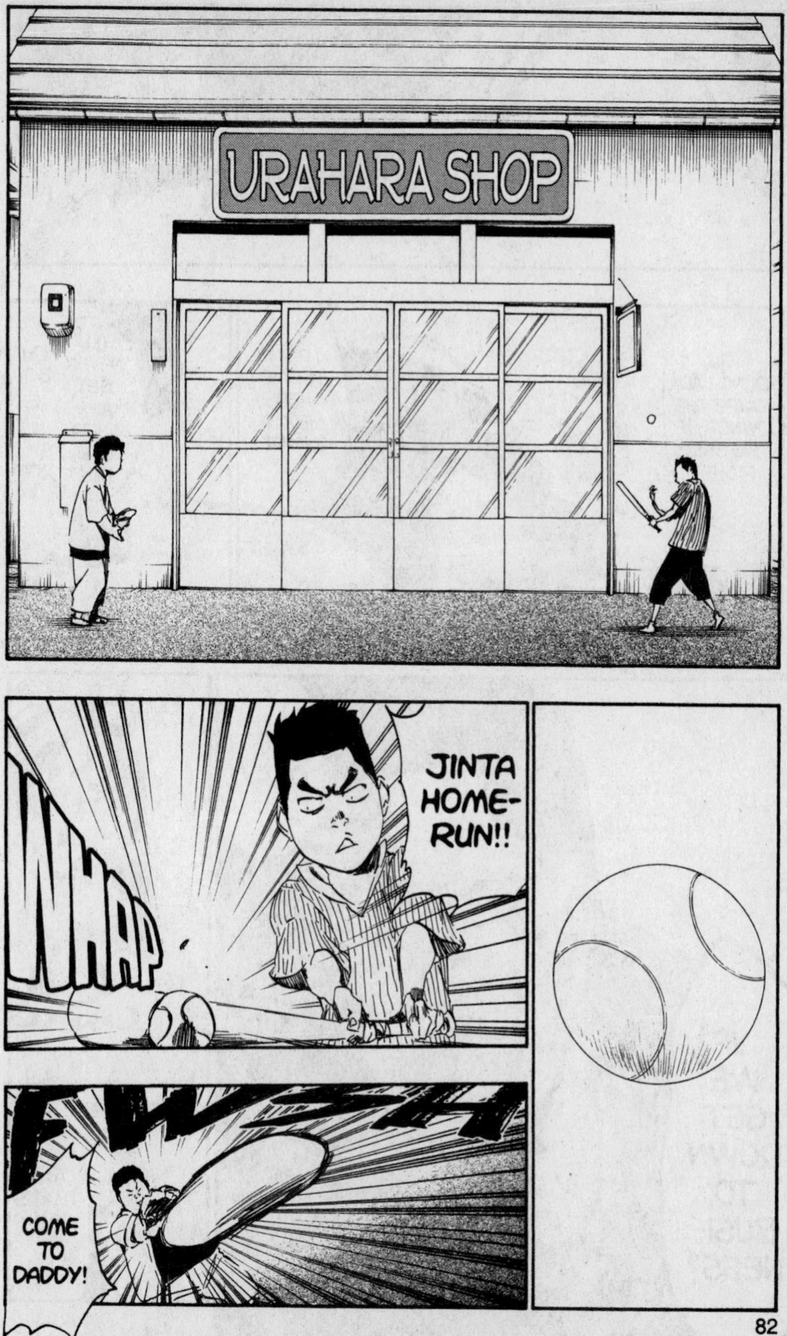
URAHARA SHOP
WHAP
JINTA HOME-RUN!!
COME TO DADDY!

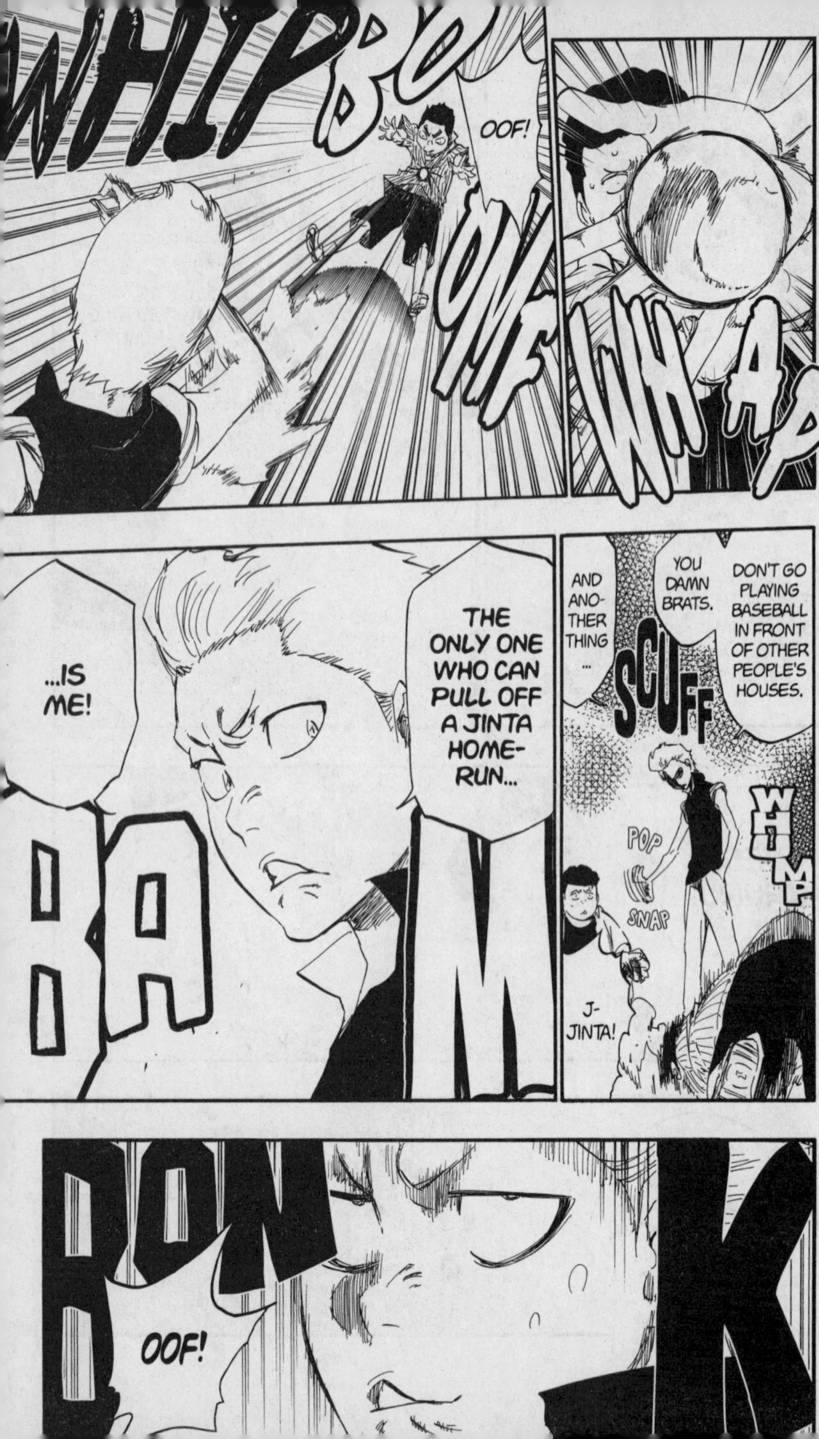
WHAP
WHIP
OOF!
DON'T GO PLAYING BASEBALL IN FRONT OF OTHER PEOPLE'S HOUSES.
YOU DAMN BRATS.
AND ANO-THER THING...
SCUFF
WHUMP
POP
SNAP
J-JINTA!
THE ONLY ONE WHO CAN PULL OFF A JINTA HOME-RUN...
...IS ME!
BAM
BONK
OOF!

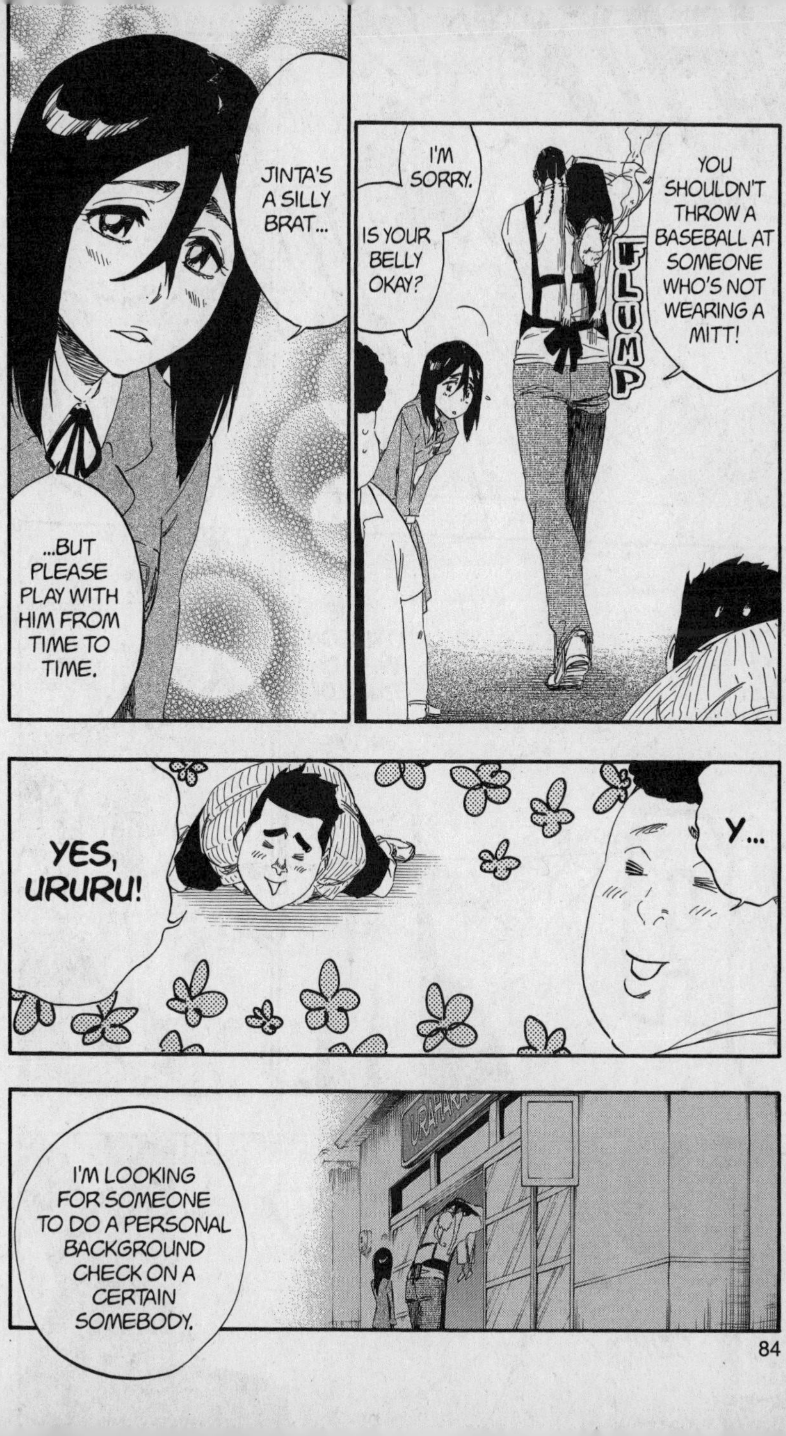
YOU SHOULDN'T THROW A BASEBALL AT SOMEONE WHO'S NOT WEARING A MITT!
FLUMP
I'M SORRY.
IS YOUR BELLY OKAY?
JINTA'S A SILLY BRAT...
...BUT PLEASE PLAY WITH HIM FROM TIME TO TIME.
Y...
YES, URURU!
I'M LOOKING FOR SOMEONE TO DO A PERSONAL BACKGROUND CHECK ON A CERTAIN SOMEBODY.

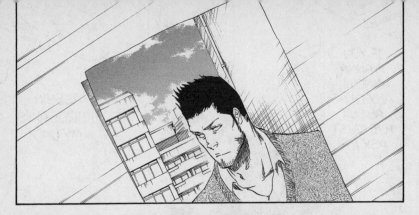

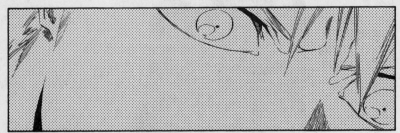

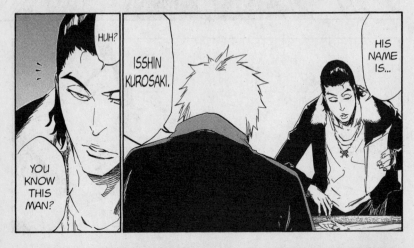

HUH?

ISSHIN KUROSAKI.

HIS NAME IS...

YOU KNOW THIS MAN?

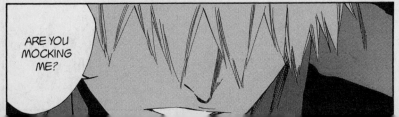

ARE YOU MOCKING ME?

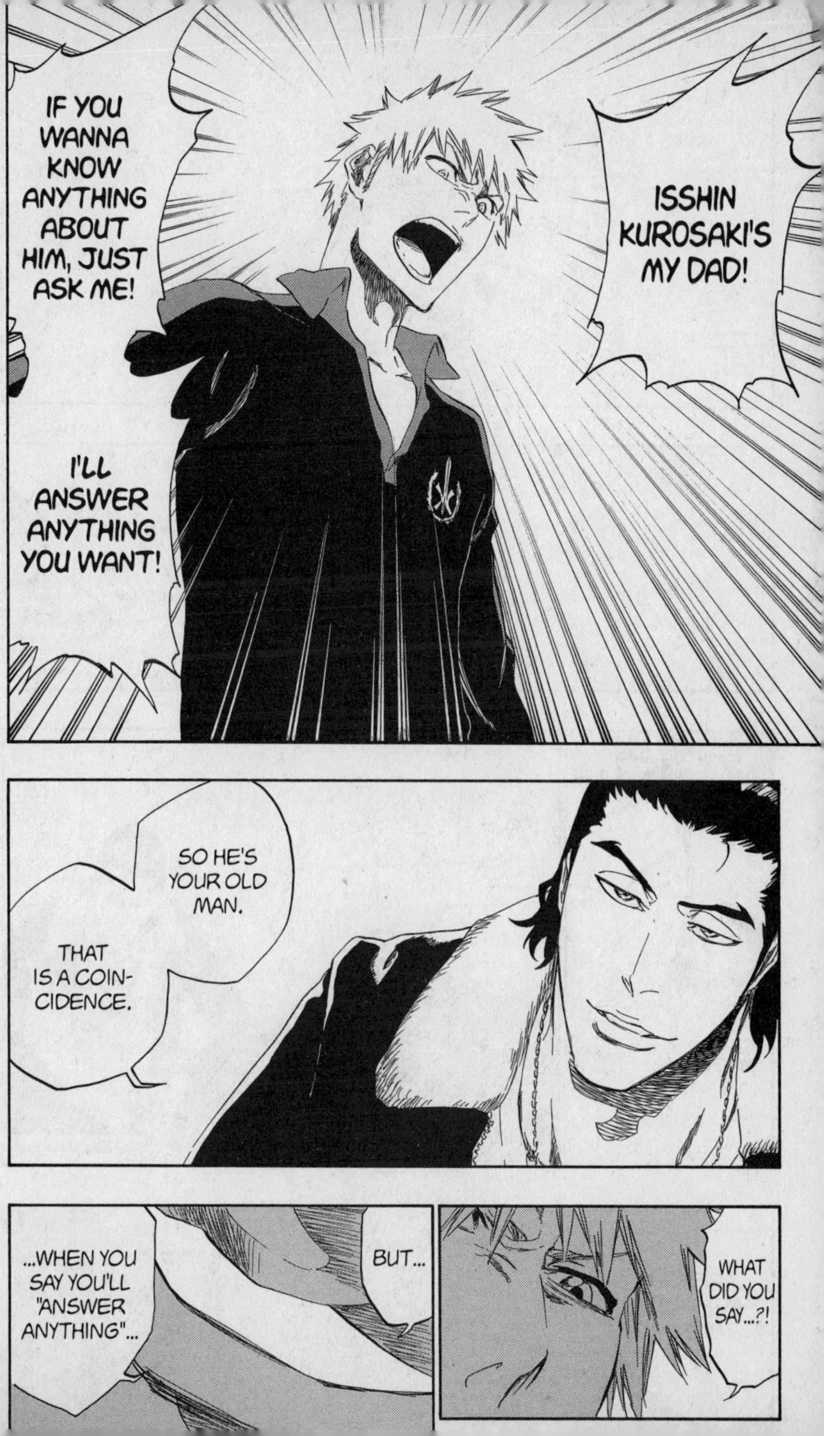
ISSHIN KUROSAKI'S MY DAD!
IF YOU WANNA KNOW ANYTHING ABOUT HIM, JUST ASK ME!
I'LL ANSWER ANYTHING YOU WANT!
SO HE'S YOUR OLD MAN.
THAT IS A COINCIDENCE.
WHAT DID YOU SAY...?!
BUT...
...WHEN YOU SAY YOU'LL "ANSWER ANYTHING"...

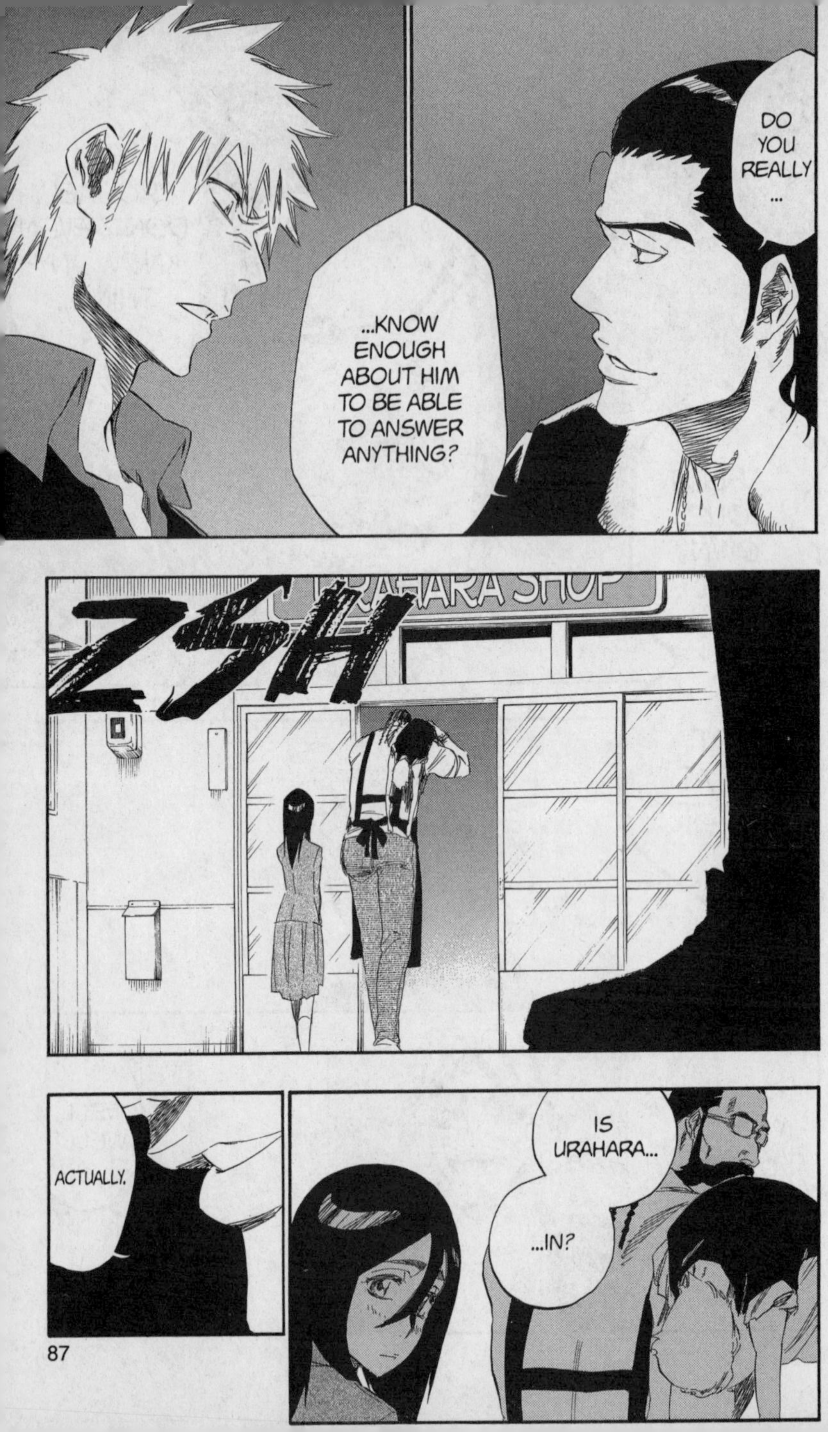
DO YOU REALLY ...
...KNOW ENOUGH ABOUT HIM TO BE ABLE TO ANSWER ANYTHING?
URAHARA SHOP
ZSH
IS URAHARA...
...IN?
ACTUALLY.

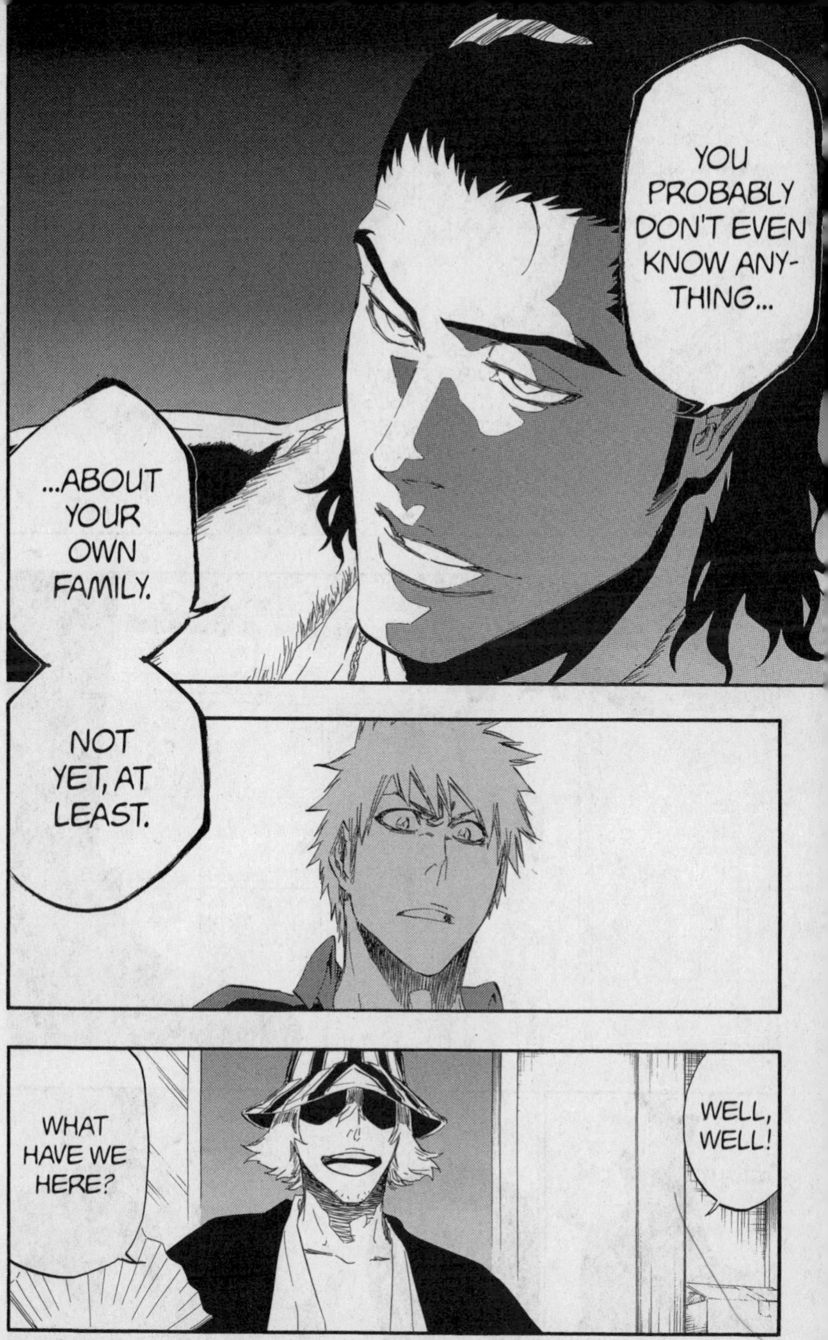
YOU PROBABLY DON'T EVEN KNOW ANY-THING...
...ABOUT YOUR OWN FAMILY.
NOT YET, AT LEAST.
WELL, WELL!
WHAT HAVE WE HERE?

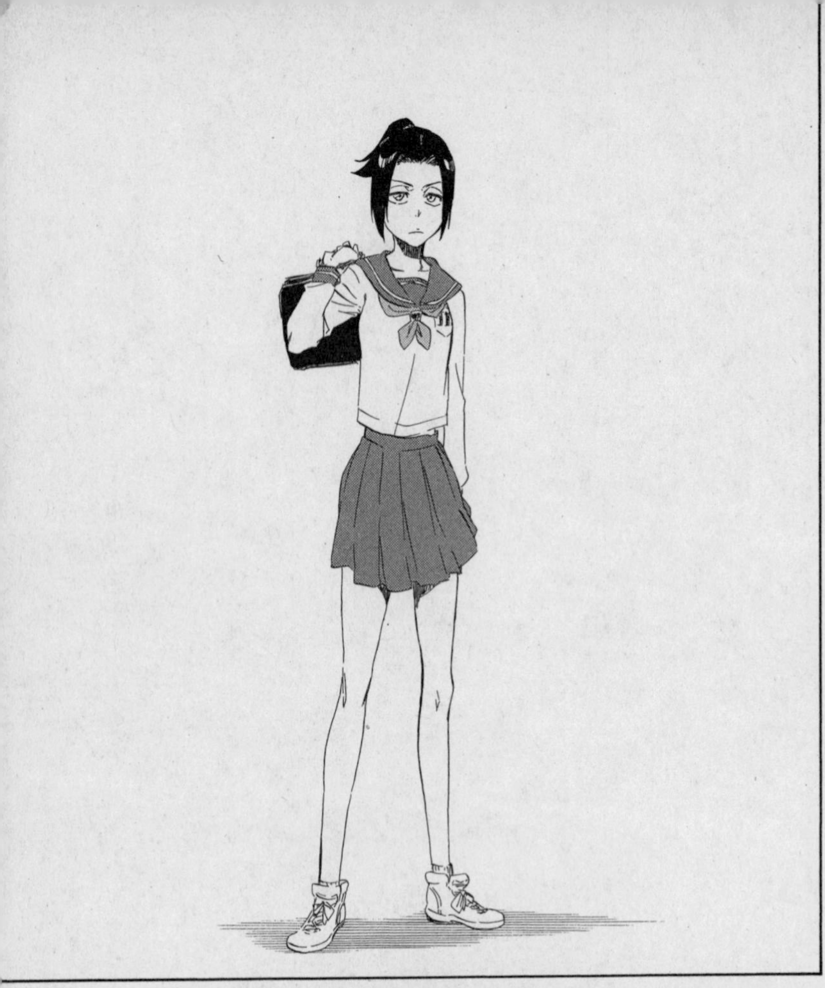

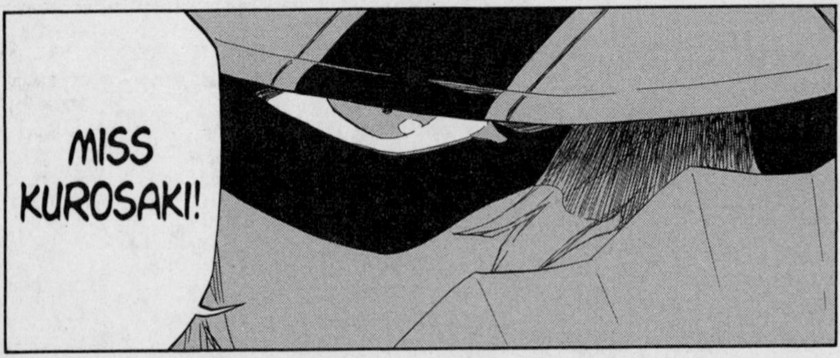
MISS KUROSAKI!

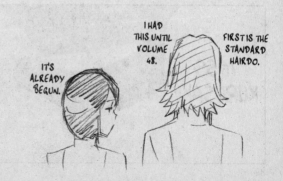

FIRST IS THE STANDARD HAIRDO.

I HAD THIS UNTIL VOLUME 48.

IT'S ALREADY BEGUN.

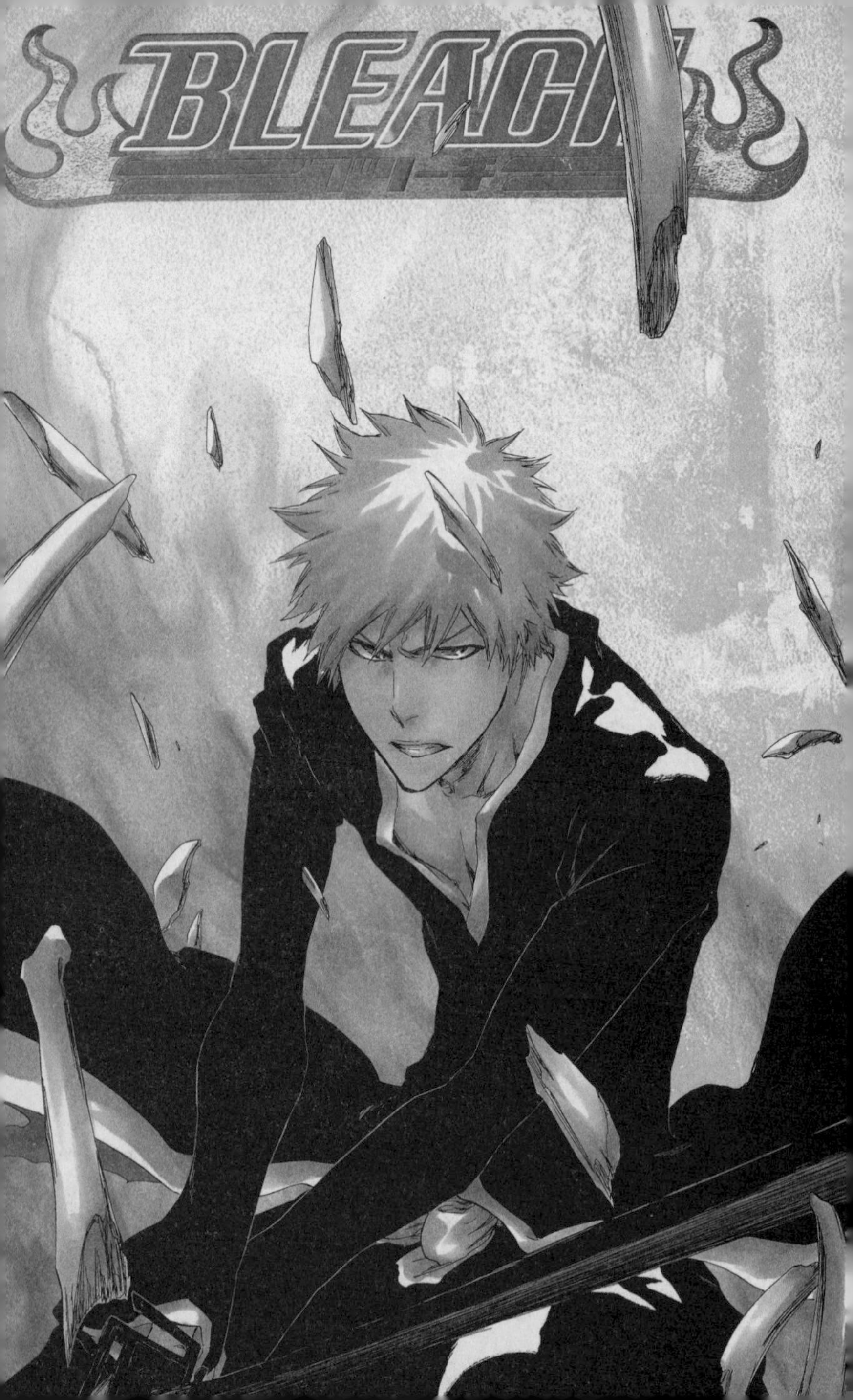

BLEACH
ブリーチ

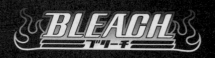

READ THIS WAY

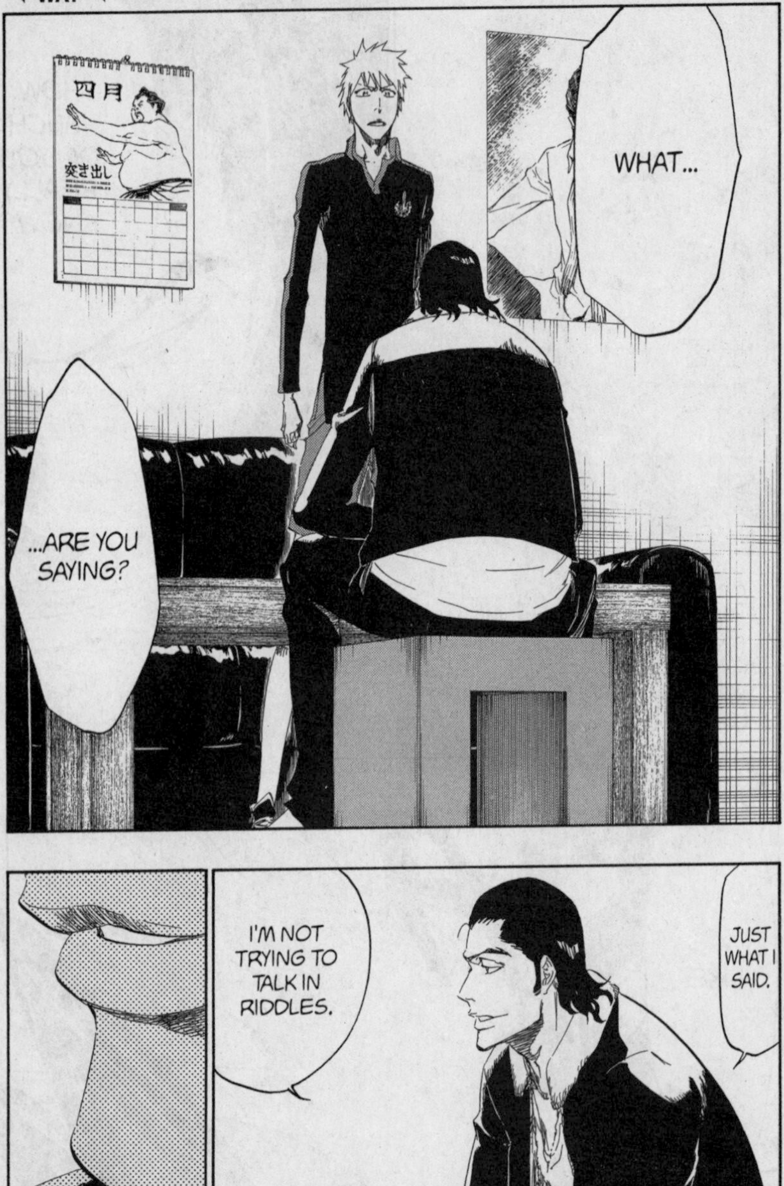
WHAT...
四月
突き出し
...ARE YOU SAYING?
JUST WHAT I SAID.
I'M NOT TRYING TO TALK IN RIDDLES.

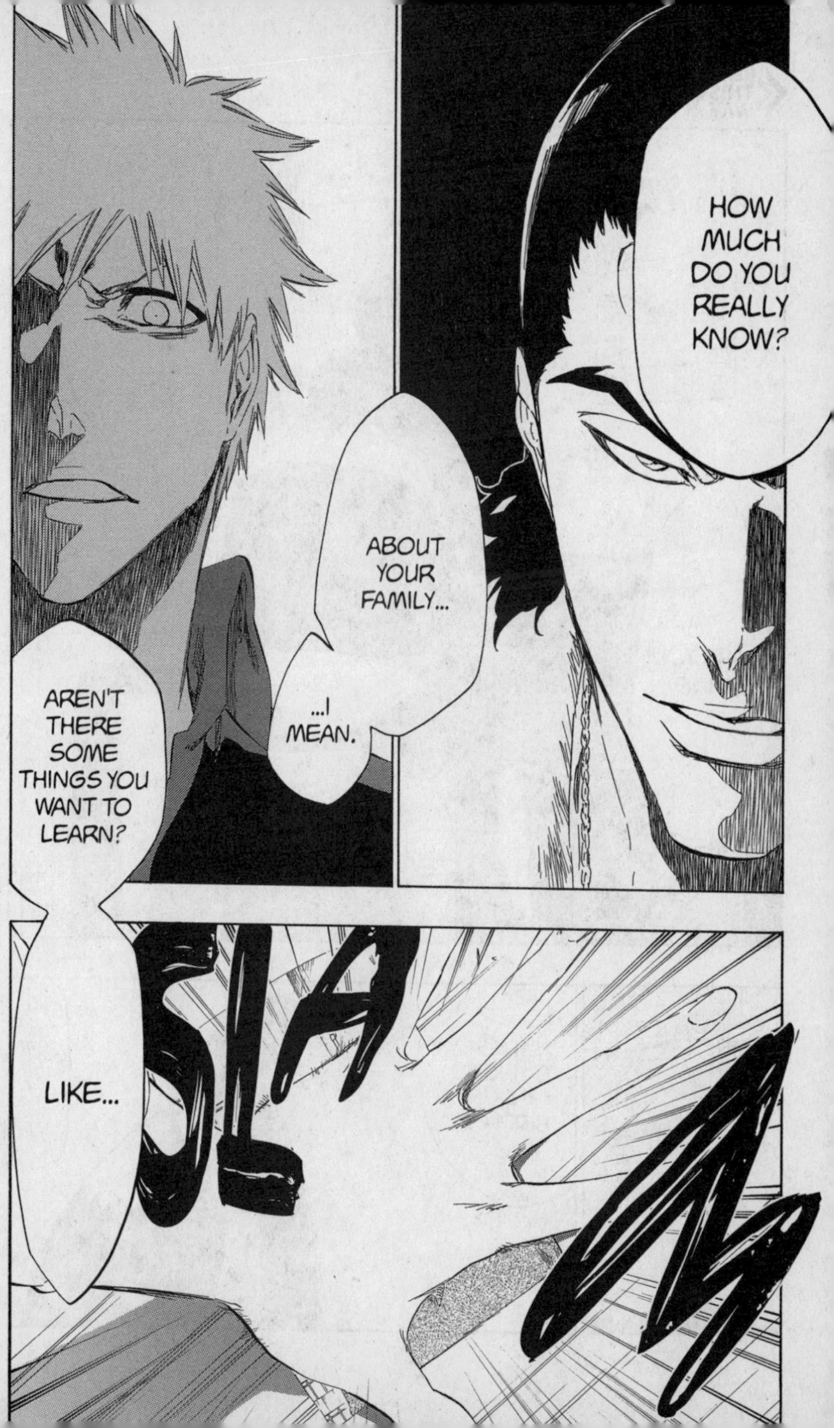
HOW MUCH DO YOU REALLY KNOW?
ABOUT YOUR FAMILY...
...I MEAN.
AREN'T THERE SOME THINGS YOU WANT TO LEARN?
LIKE...
SLAM

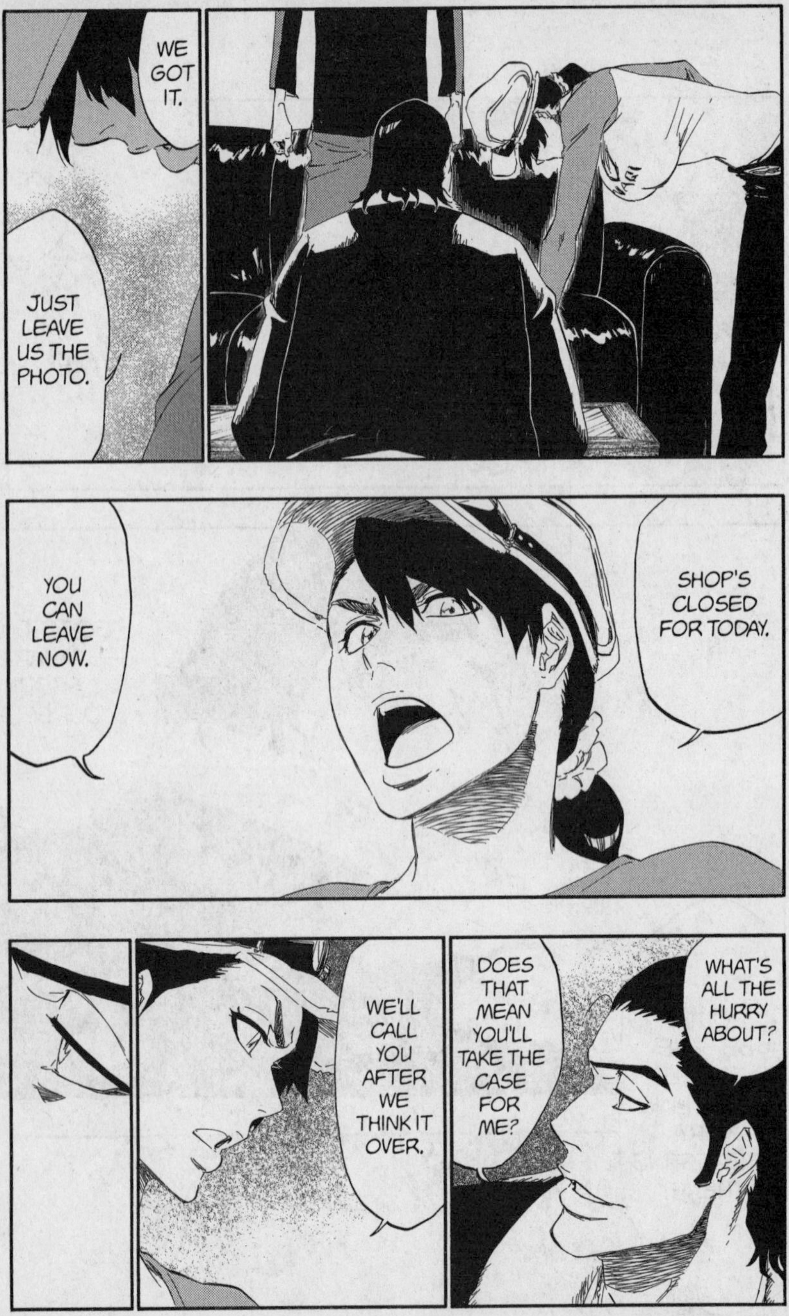

WE GOT IT.
JUST LEAVE US THE PHOTO.
SHOP'S CLOSED FOR TODAY.
YOU CAN LEAVE NOW.
WHAT'S ALL THE HURRY ABOUT?
DOES THAT MEAN YOU'LL TAKE THE CASE FOR ME?
WE'LL CALL YOU AFTER WE THINK IT OVER.

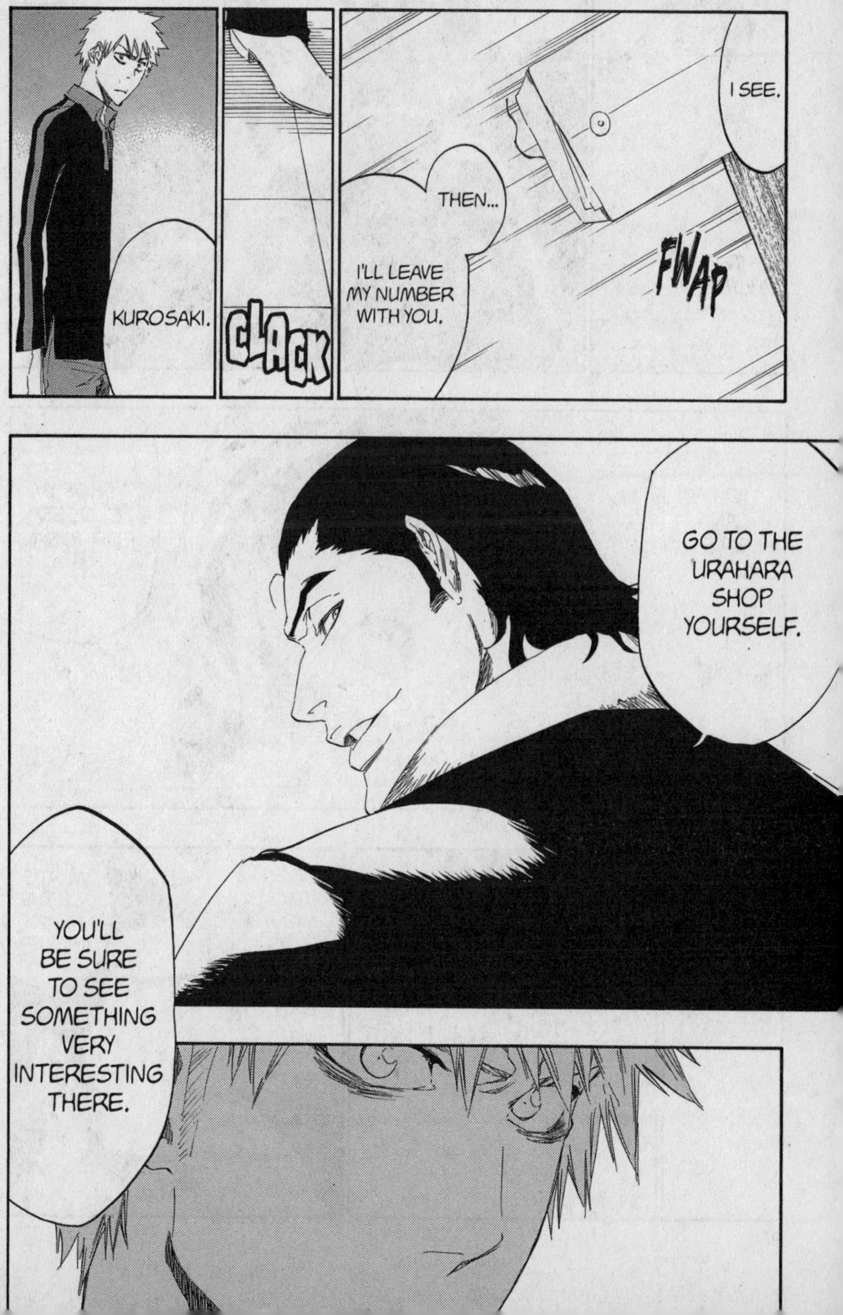
I SEE.
THEN...
FWAP
I'LL LEAVE MY NUMBER WITH YOU.
CLACK
KUROSAKI.
GO TO THE URAHARA SHOP YOURSELF.
YOU'LL BE SURE TO SEE SOMETHING VERY INTERESTING THERE.

READ THIS WAY

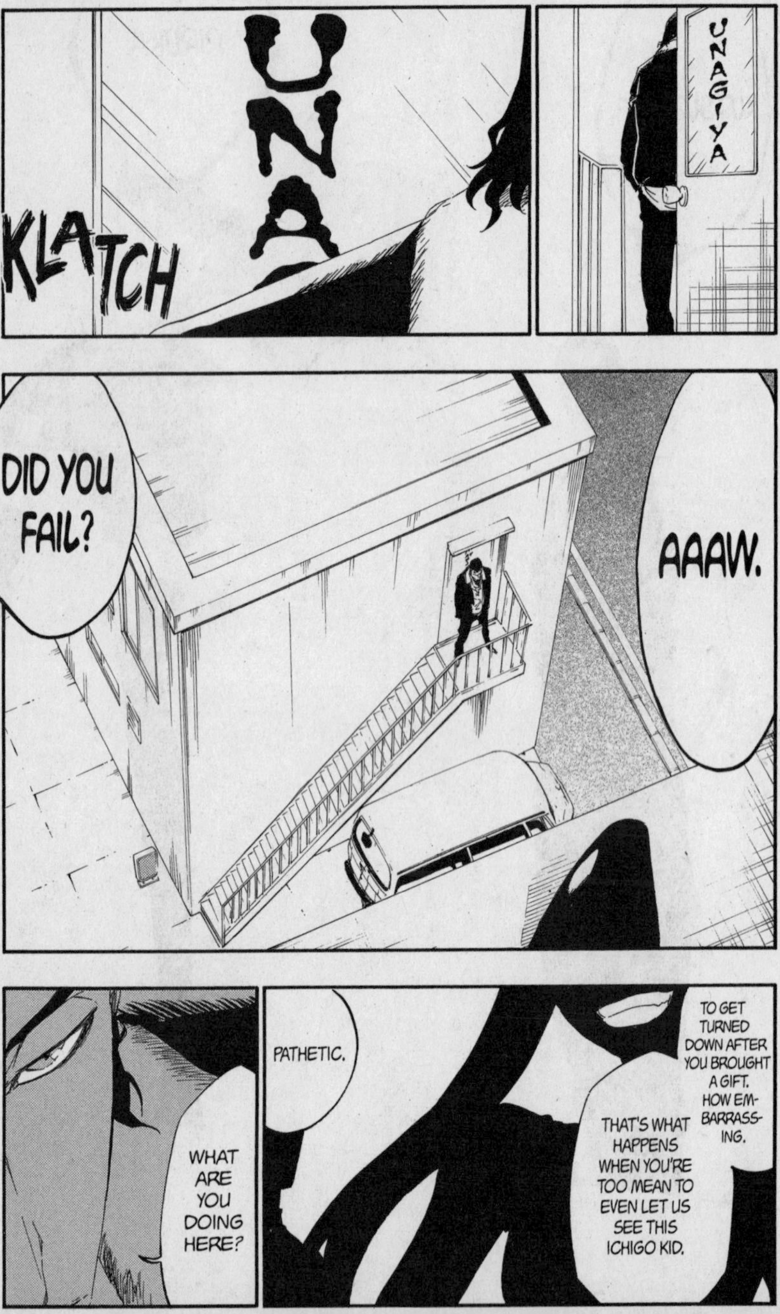
UNAGIYA
KLATCH
UNA
AAAW.
DID YOU FAIL?
TO GET TURNED DOWN AFTER YOU BROUGHT A GIFT. HOW EMBARRASSING.
PATHETIC.
THAT'S WHAT HAPPENS WHEN YOU'RE TOO MEAN TO EVEN LET US SEE THIS ICHIGO KID.
WHAT ARE YOU DOING HERE?

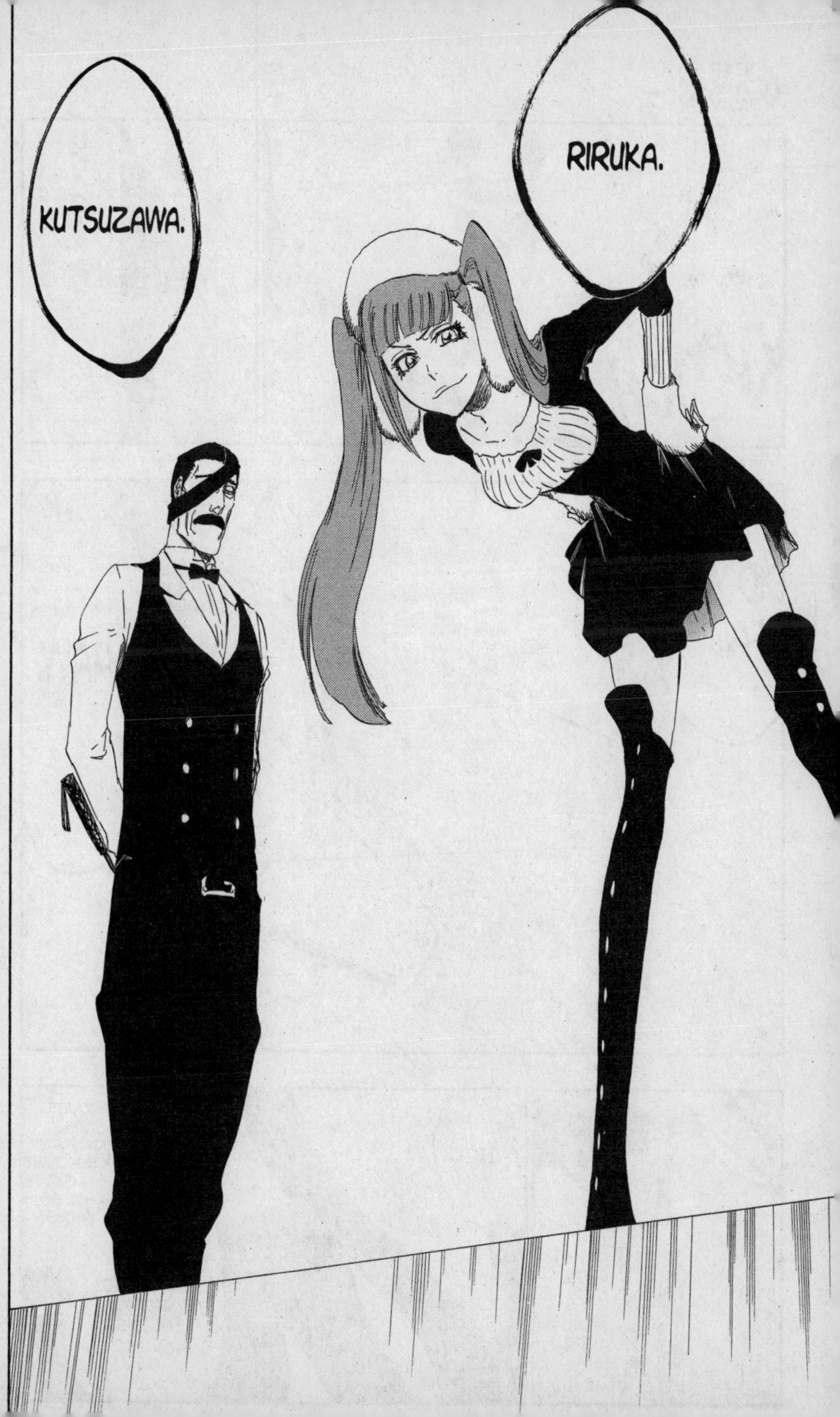
RIRUKA.
KUTSUZAWA.

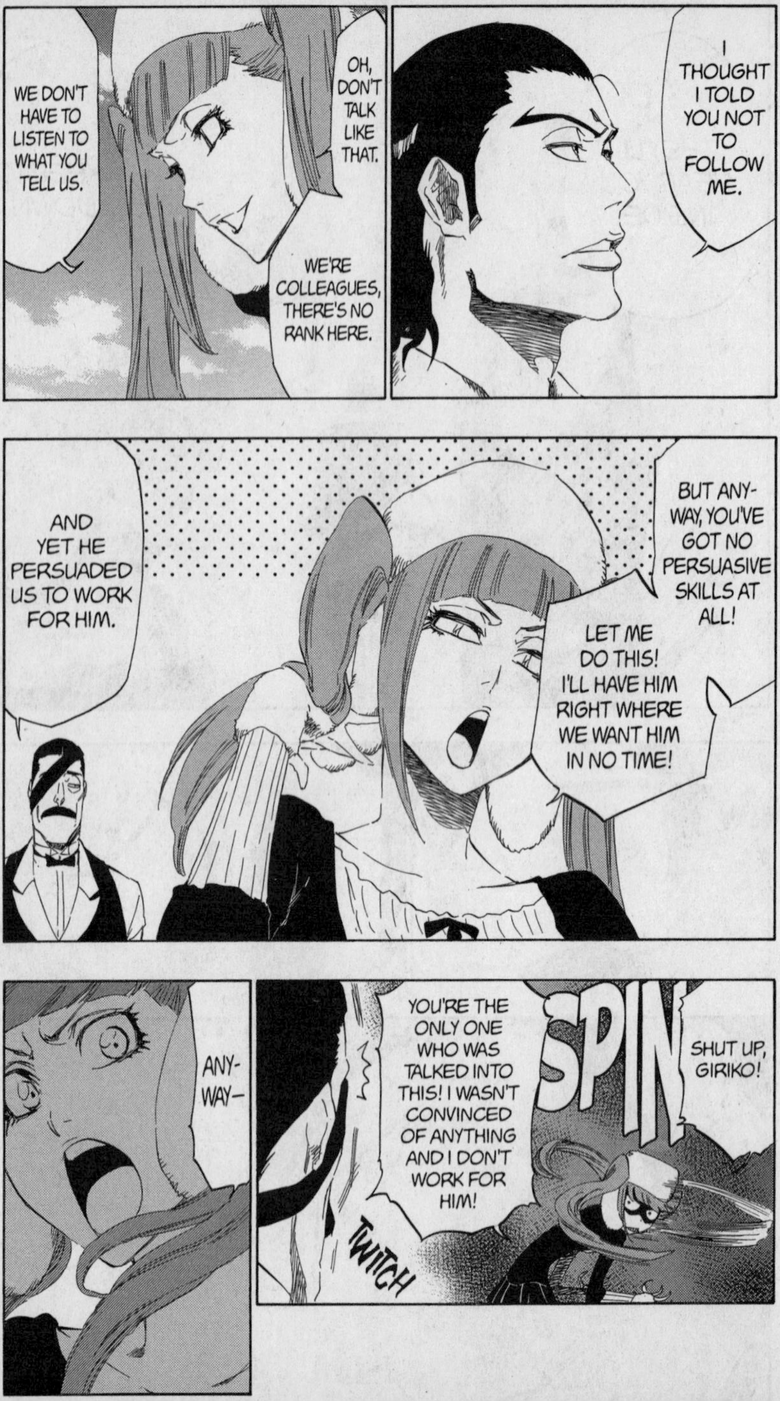
I THOUGHT I TOLD YOU NOT TO FOLLOW ME.
OH, DON'T TALK LIKE THAT.
WE'RE COLLEAGUES, THERE'S NO RANK HERE.
WE DON'T HAVE TO LISTEN TO WHAT YOU TELL US.
BUT ANY-WAY, YOU'VE GOT NO PERSUASIVE SKILLS AT ALL!
LET ME DO THIS! I'LL HAVE HIM RIGHT WHERE WE WANT HIM IN NO TIME!
AND YET HE PERSUADED US TO WORK FOR HIM.
SHUT UP, GIRIKO!
SPIN
YOU'RE THE ONLY ONE WHO WAS TALKED INTO THIS! I WASN'T CONVINCED OF ANYTHING AND I DON'T WORK FOR HIM!
TWITCH
ANY-WAY—

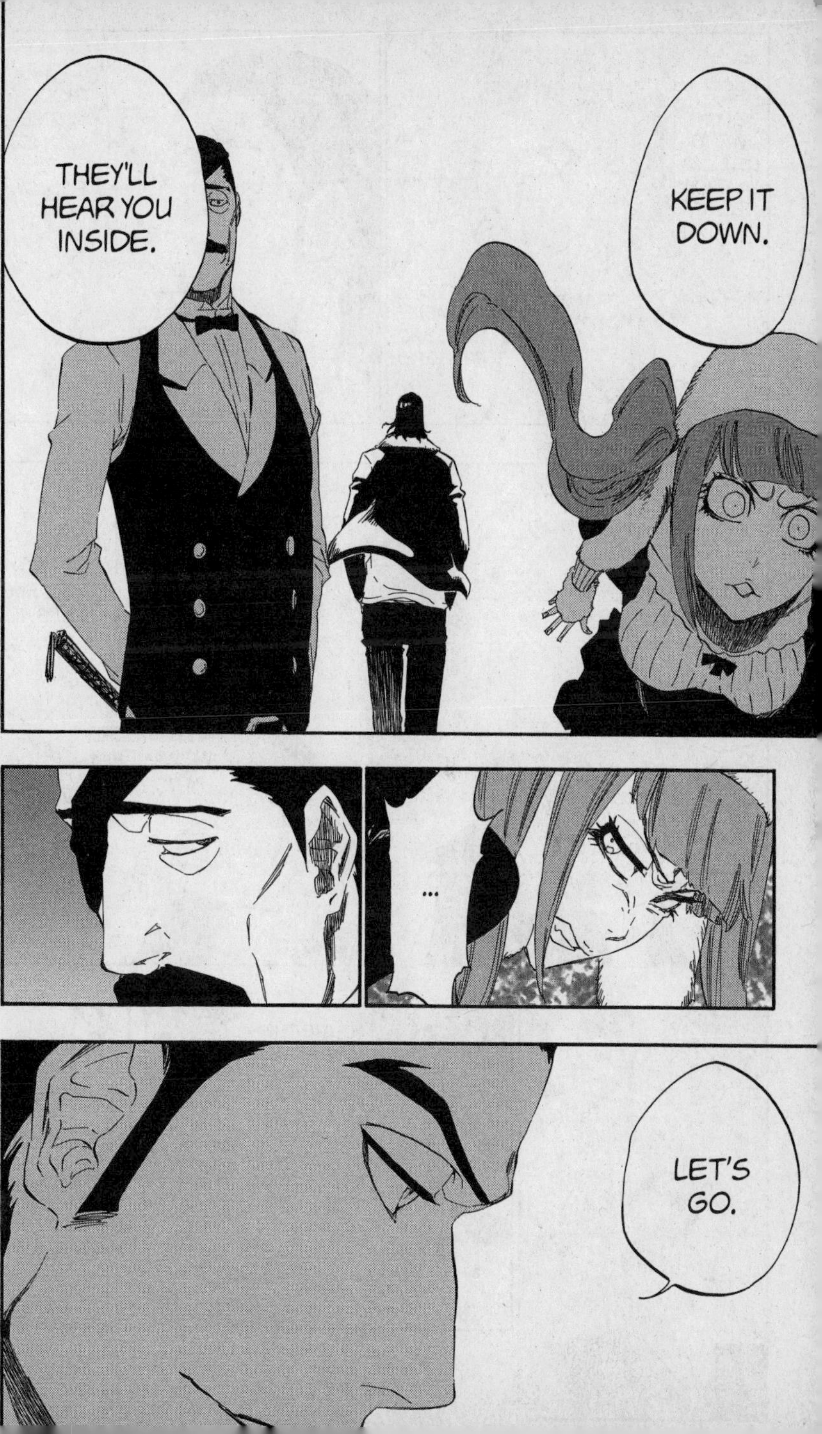
KEEP IT DOWN.
THEY'LL HEAR YOU INSIDE.
...
LET'S GO.

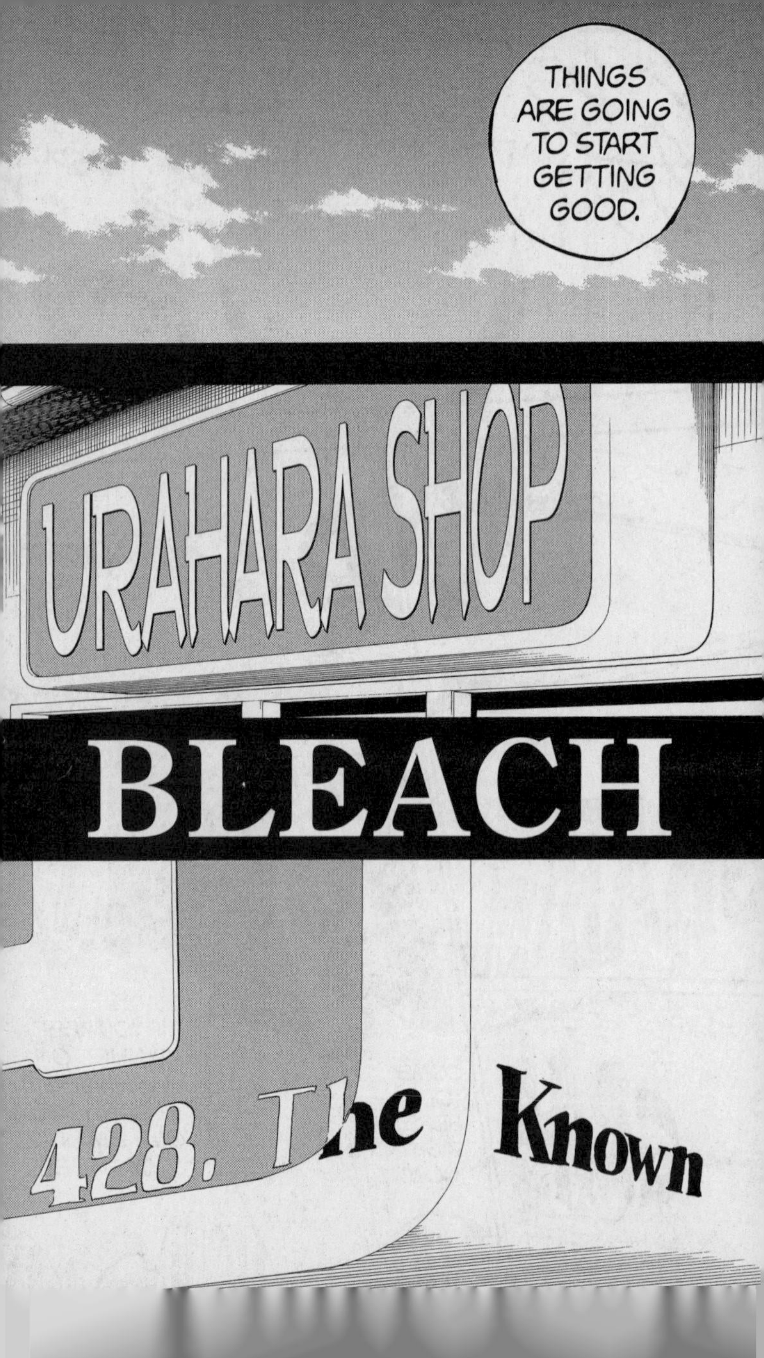
THINGS ARE GOING TO START GETTING GOOD.
URAHARA SHOP
BLEACH
428. The Known

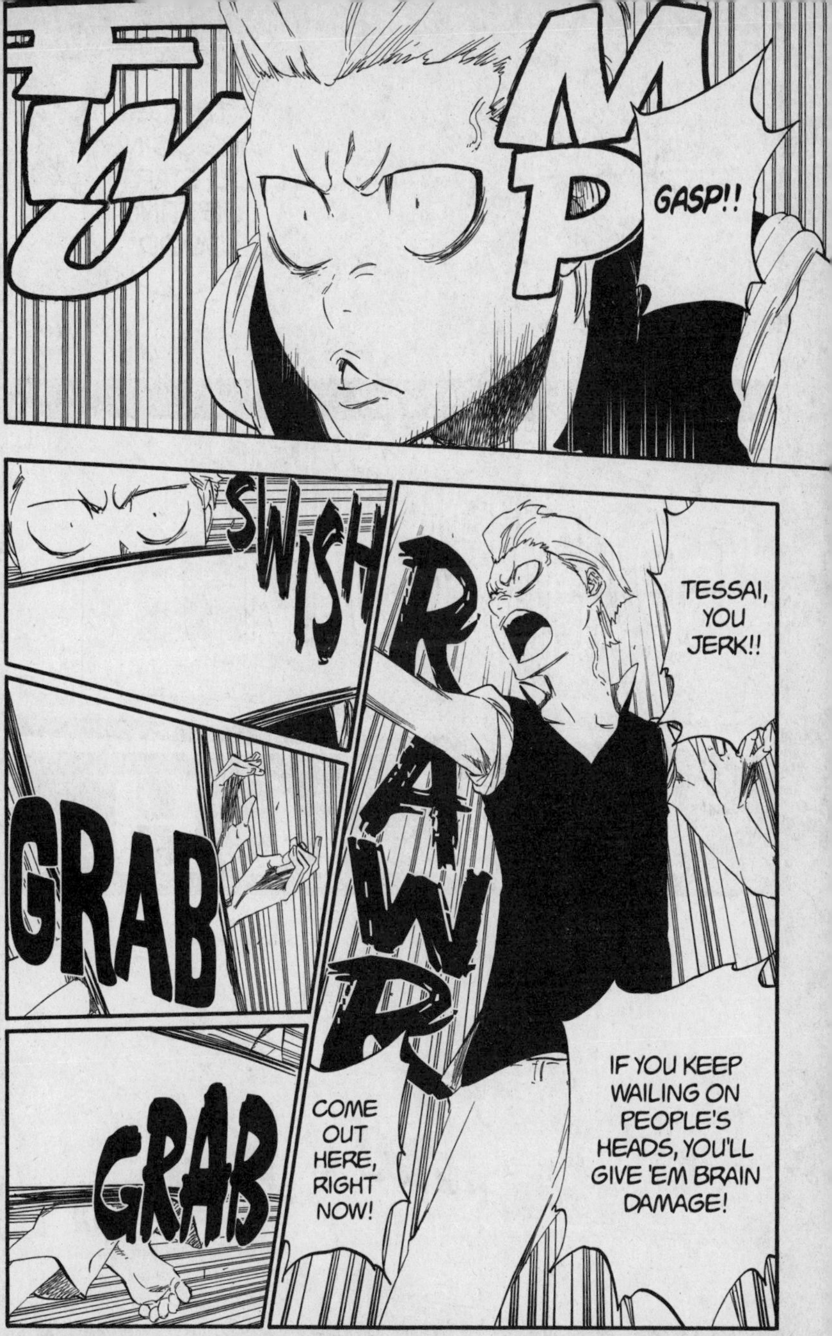
GASP!!
TESSAI, YOU JERK!!
RAWR
IF YOU KEEP WAILING ON PEOPLE'S HEADS, YOU'LL GIVE 'EM BRAIN DAMAGE!
COME OUT HERE, RIGHT NOW!
SWISH
GRAB
GRAB

READ THIS WAY

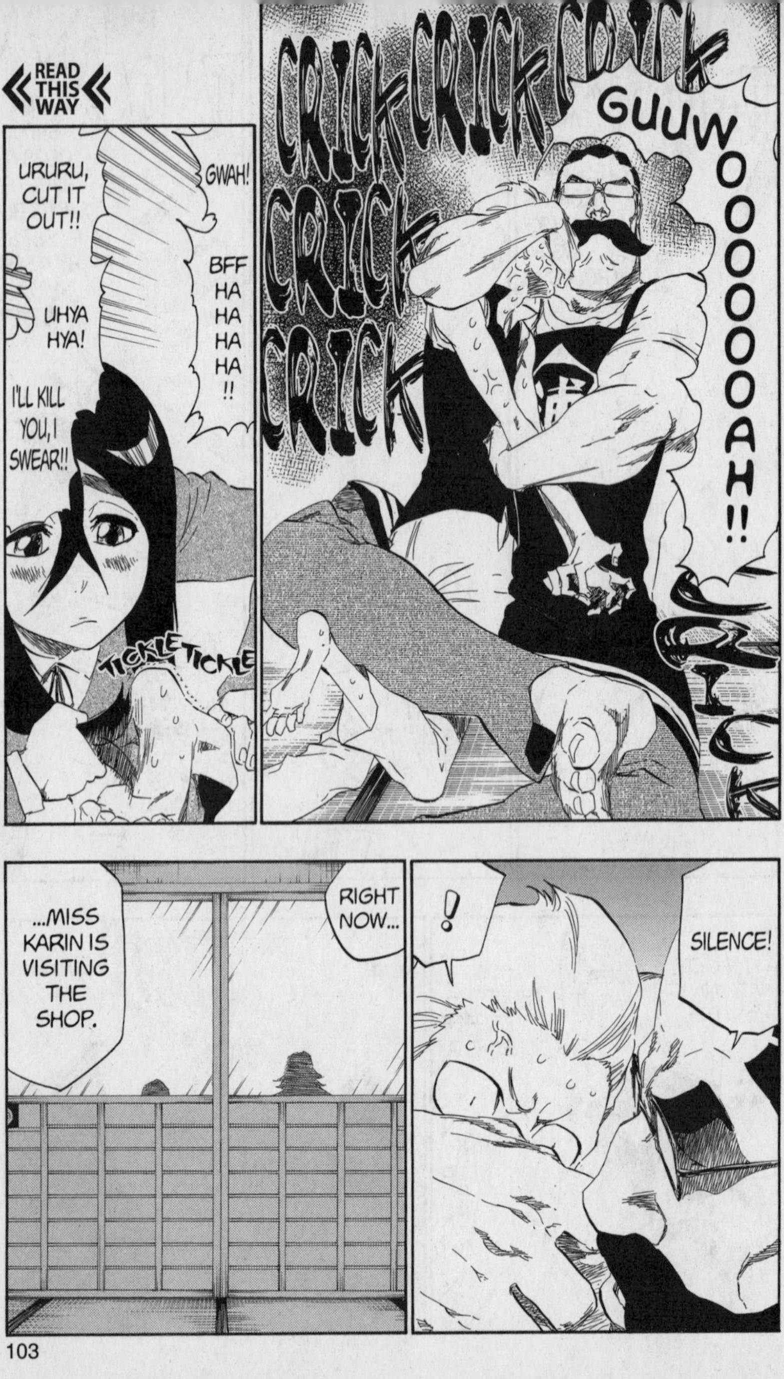

CRICK CRICK CRICK
GUUWOOOOOOOAH!!
CRICK CRICK CRICK
CRICK
GWAH!
BFF HA HA HA HA!!
URURU, CUT IT OUT!!
UHYA HYA!
I'LL KILL YOU, I SWEAR!!
TICKLE TICKLE
SILENCE!
!
RIGHT NOW...
...MISS KARIN IS VISITING THE SHOP.

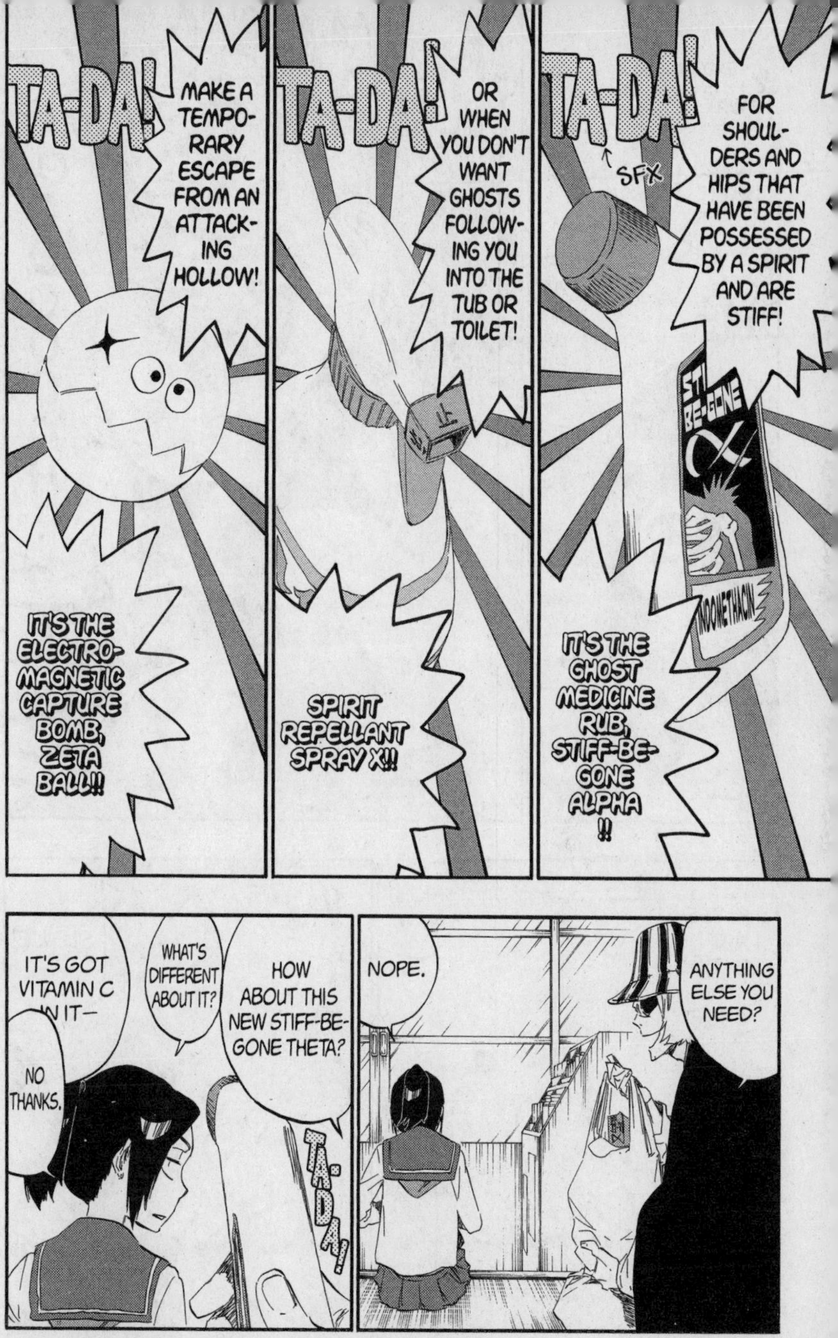
FOR SHOULDERS AND HIPS THAT HAVE BEEN POSSESSED BY A SPIRIT AND ARE STIFF!
TA-DA!
SFX
STI BE-GONE
INDOMETHACIN
IT'S THE GHOST MEDICINE RUB, STIFF-BE-GONE ALPHA!!
OR WHEN YOU DON'T WANT GHOSTS FOLLOWING YOU INTO THE TUB OR TOILET!
TA-DA!
SPIRIT REPELLANT SPRAY X!!
MAKE A TEMPORARY ESCAPE FROM AN ATTACKING HOLLOW!
TA-DA!
IT'S THE ELECTRO-MAGNETIC CAPTURE BOMB, ZETA BALL!!
ANYTHING ELSE YOU NEED?
NOPE.
HOW ABOUT THIS NEW STIFF-BE-GONE THETA?
TA-DA!
WHAT'S DIFFERENT ABOUT IT?
IT'S GOT VITAMIN C IN IT—
NO THANKS.

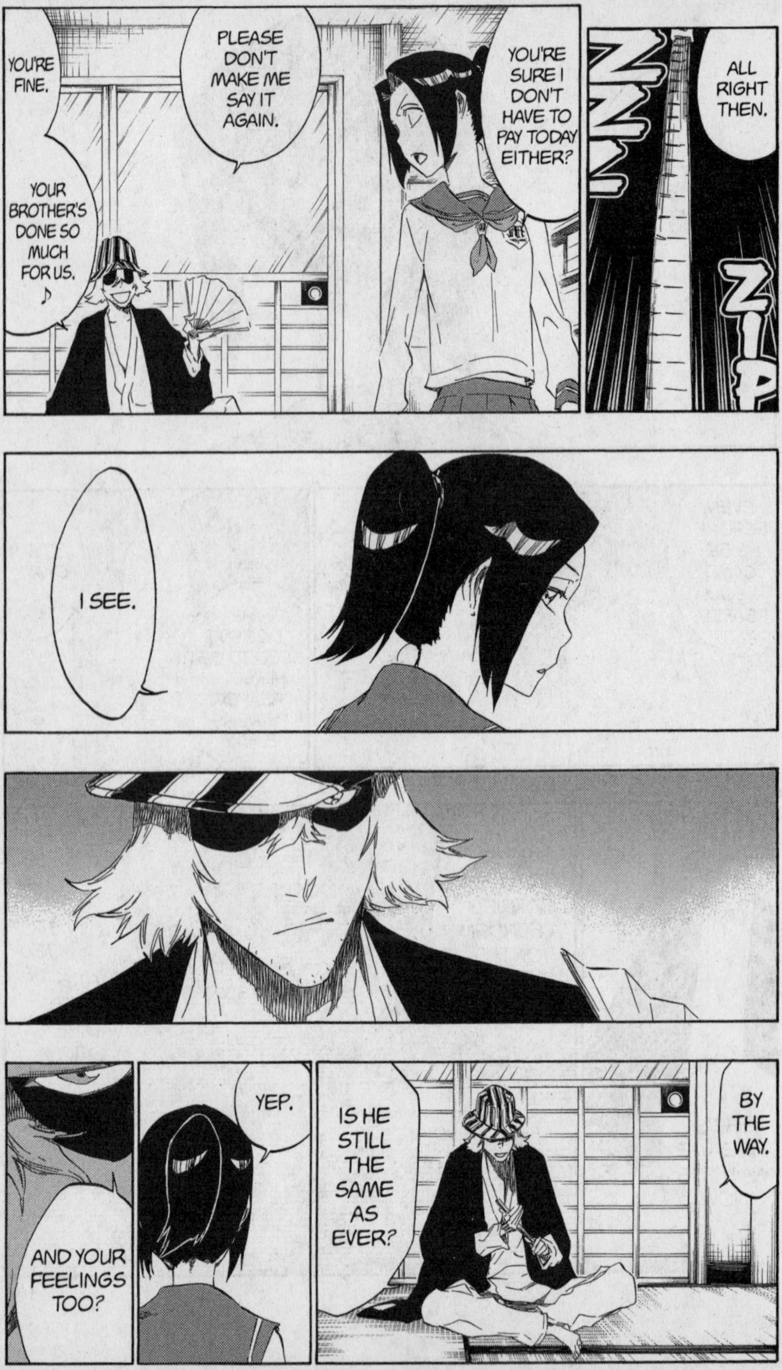
ALL RIGHT THEN.
ZIP
YOU'RE SURE I DON'T HAVE TO PAY TODAY EITHER?
PLEASE DON'T MAKE ME SAY IT AGAIN.
YOU'RE FINE.
YOUR BROTHER'S DONE SO MUCH FOR US. ♪
I SEE.
BY THE WAY.
IS HE STILL THE SAME AS EVER?
YEP.
AND YOUR FEELINGS TOO?

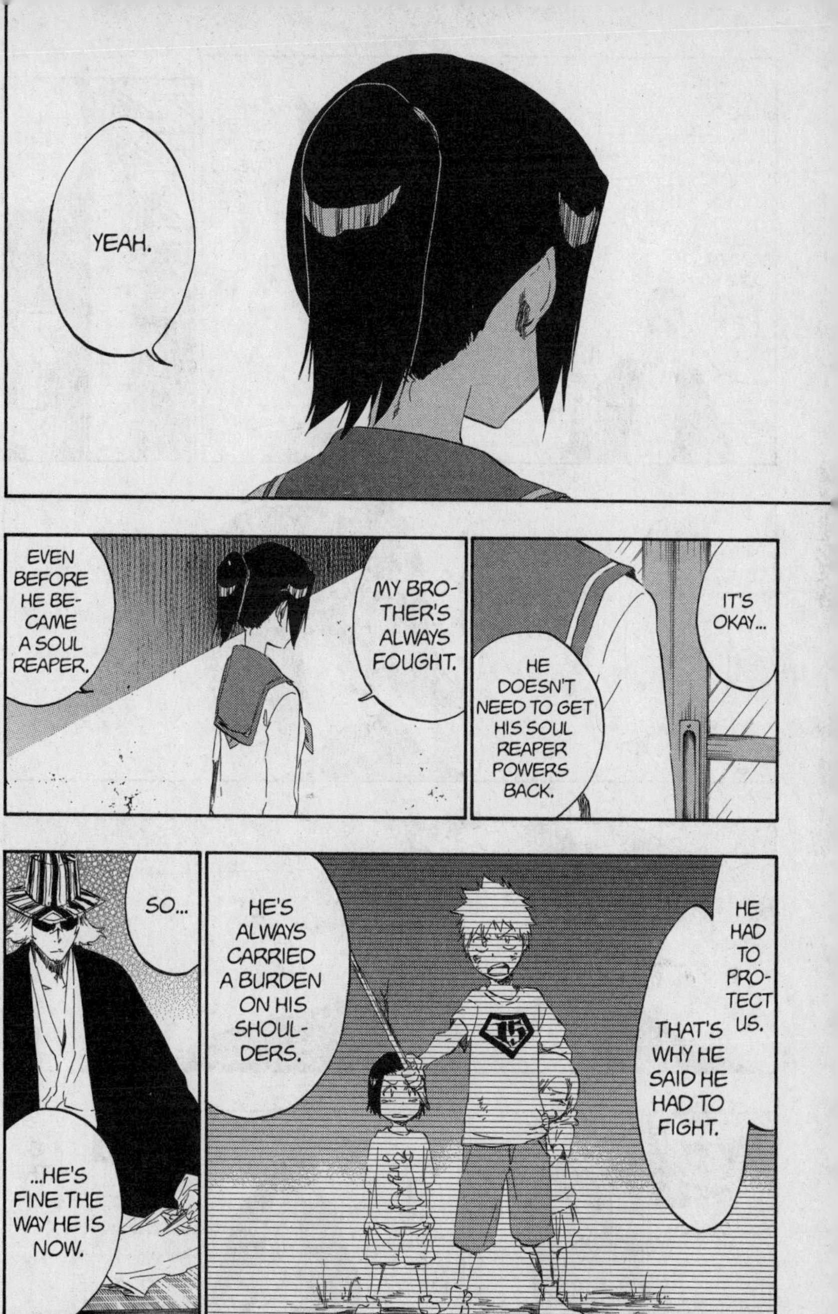

YEAH.
IT'S OKAY...
HE DOESN'T NEED TO GET HIS SOUL REAPER POWERS BACK.
MY BROTHER'S ALWAYS FOUGHT.
EVEN BEFORE HE BECAME A SOUL REAPER.
HE HAD TO PROTECT US.
THAT'S WHY HE SAID HE HAD TO FIGHT.
HE'S ALWAYS CARRIED A BURDEN ON HIS SHOULDERS.
SO...
...HE'S FINE THE WAY HE IS NOW.

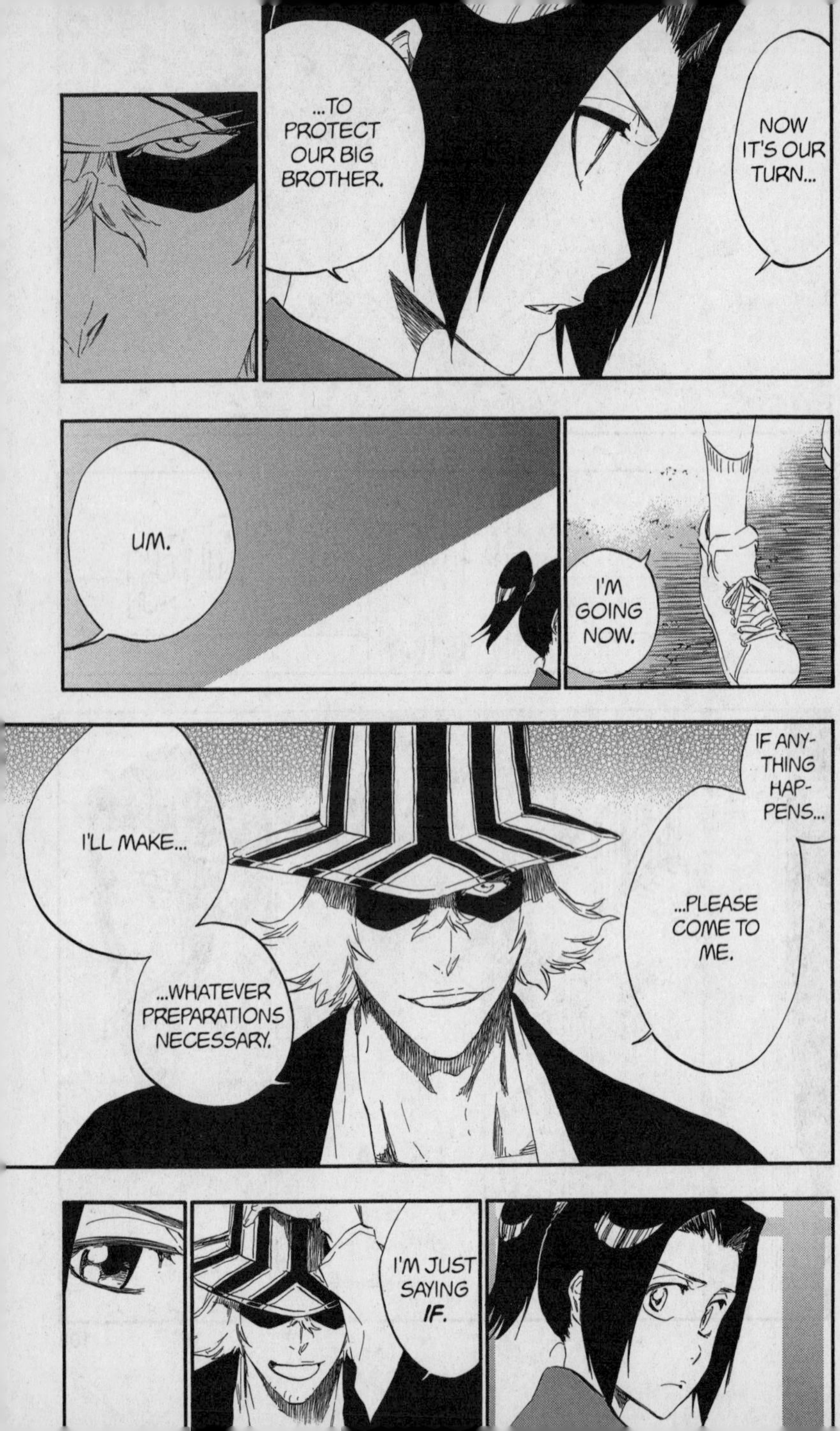
NOW IT'S OUR TURN...
...TO PROTECT OUR BIG BROTHER.
I'M GOING NOW.
UM.
IF ANYTHING HAPPENS...
...PLEASE COME TO ME.
I'LL MAKE...
...WHATEVER PREPARATIONS NECESSARY.
I'M JUST SAYING *IF*.

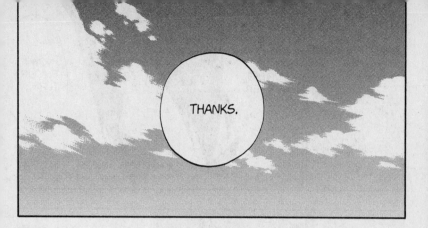

THANKS.

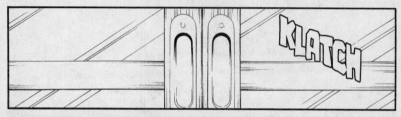

KLATCH

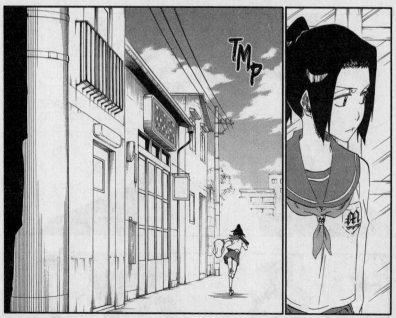

TMP

108

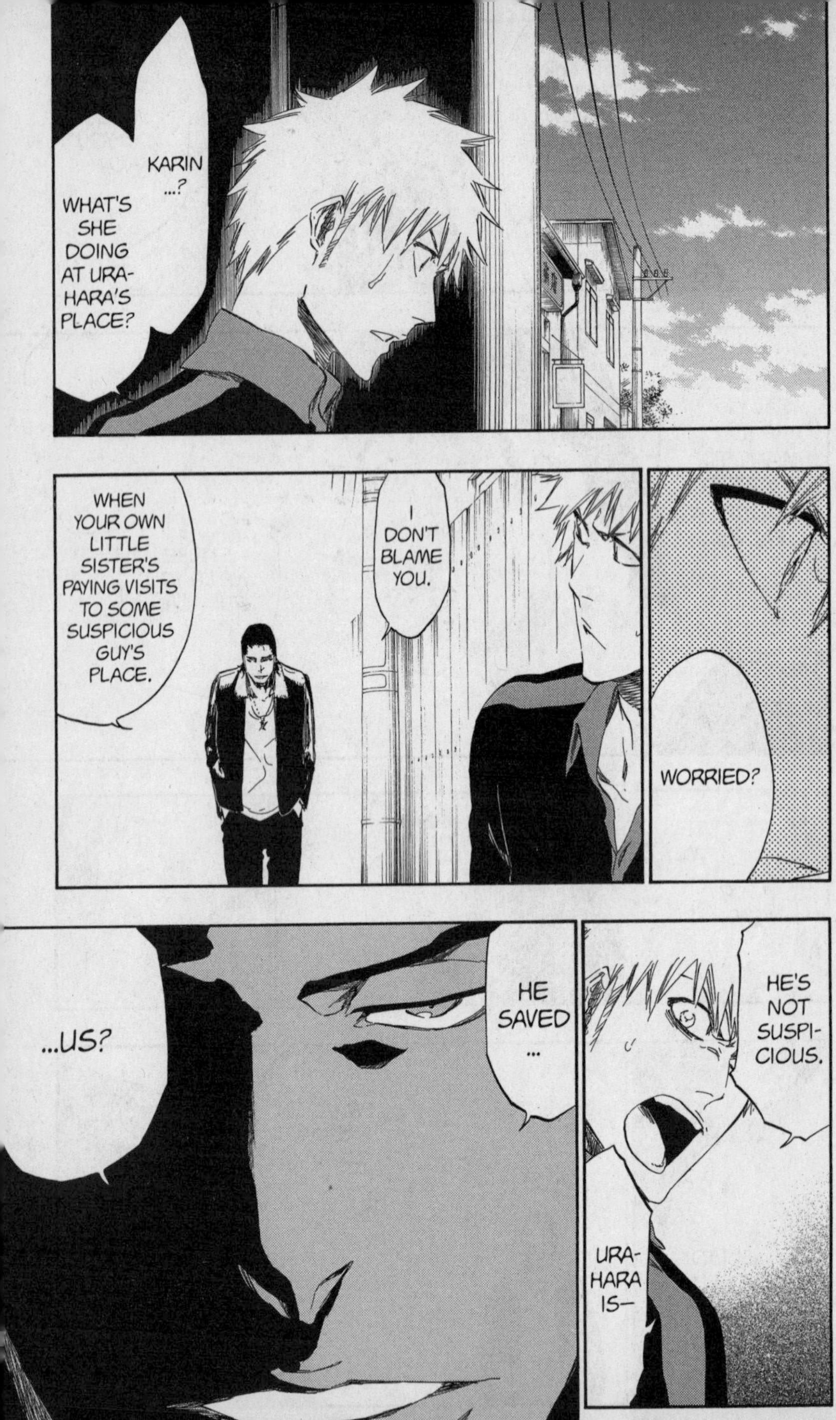
KARIN ...?
WHAT'S SHE DOING AT URA-HARA'S PLACE?
WORRIED?
I DON'T BLAME YOU.
WHEN YOUR OWN LITTLE SISTER'S PAYING VISITS TO SOME SUSPICIOUS GUY'S PLACE.
HE'S NOT SUSPICIOUS.
URA-HARA IS—
HE SAVED ...
...US?

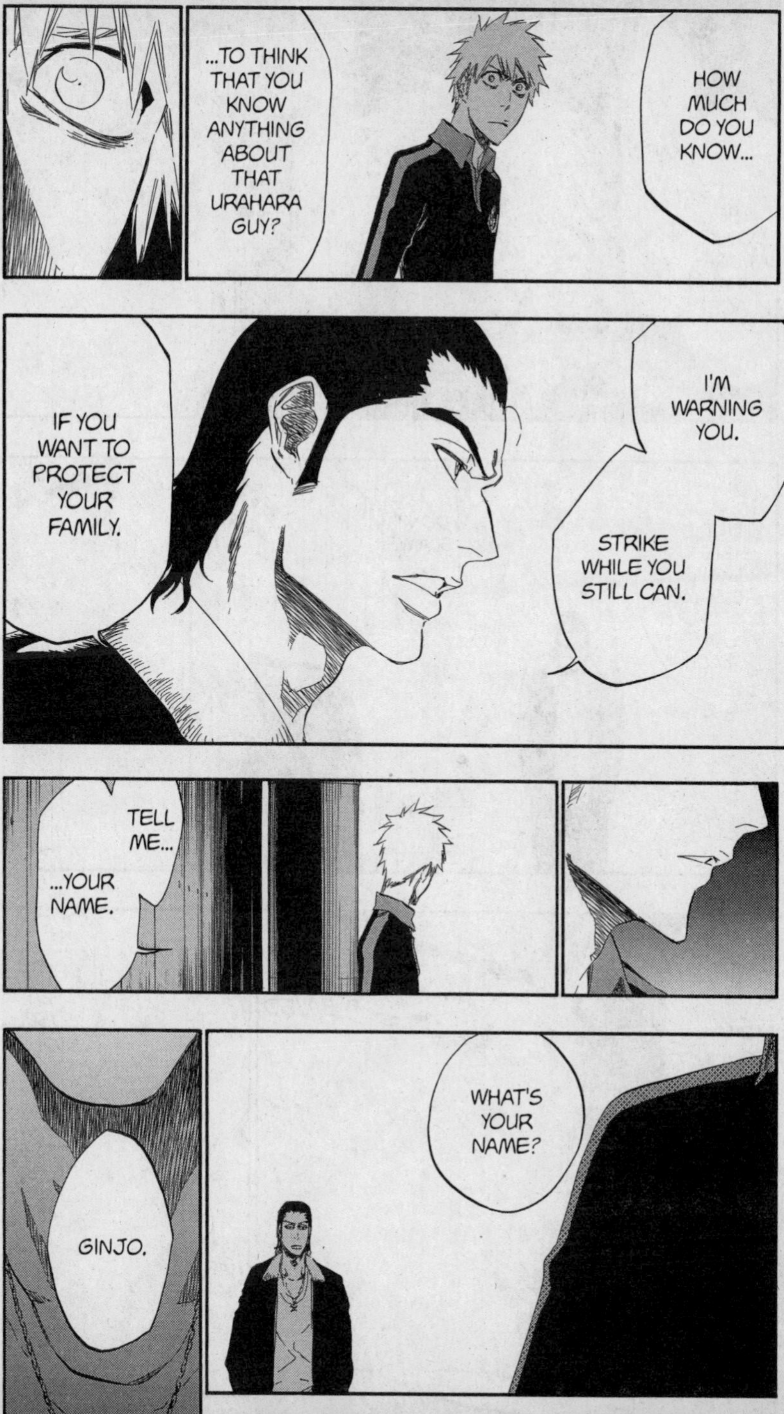
HOW MUCH DO YOU KNOW...
...TO THINK THAT YOU KNOW ANYTHING ABOUT THAT URAHARA GUY?
I'M WARNING YOU.
STRIKE WHILE YOU STILL CAN.
IF YOU WANT TO PROTECT YOUR FAMILY.
TELL ME...
...YOUR NAME.
WHAT'S YOUR NAME?
GINJO.

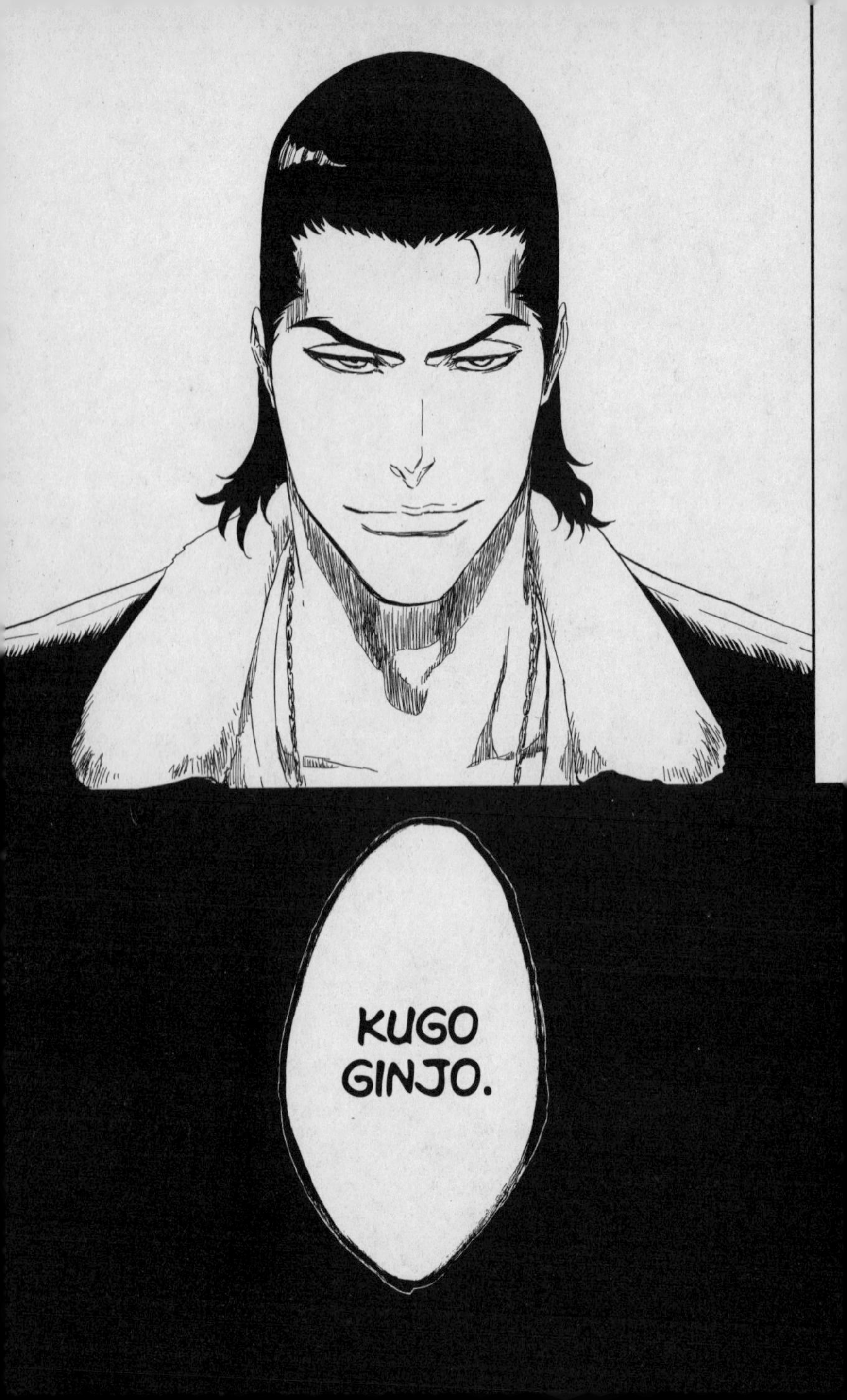
KUGO GINJO.

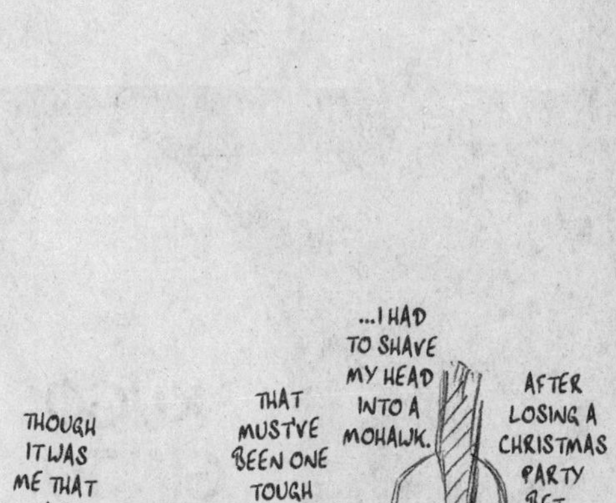
AFTER LOSING A CHRISTMAS PARTY BET...
...I HAD TO SHAVE MY HEAD INTO A MOHAWK.
THAT MUST'VE BEEN ONE TOUGH CHRISTMAS PARTY BET.
THOUGH IT WAS ME THAT MADE YOU DO IT.

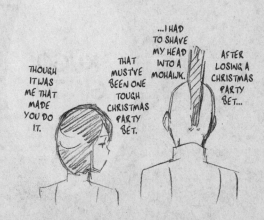

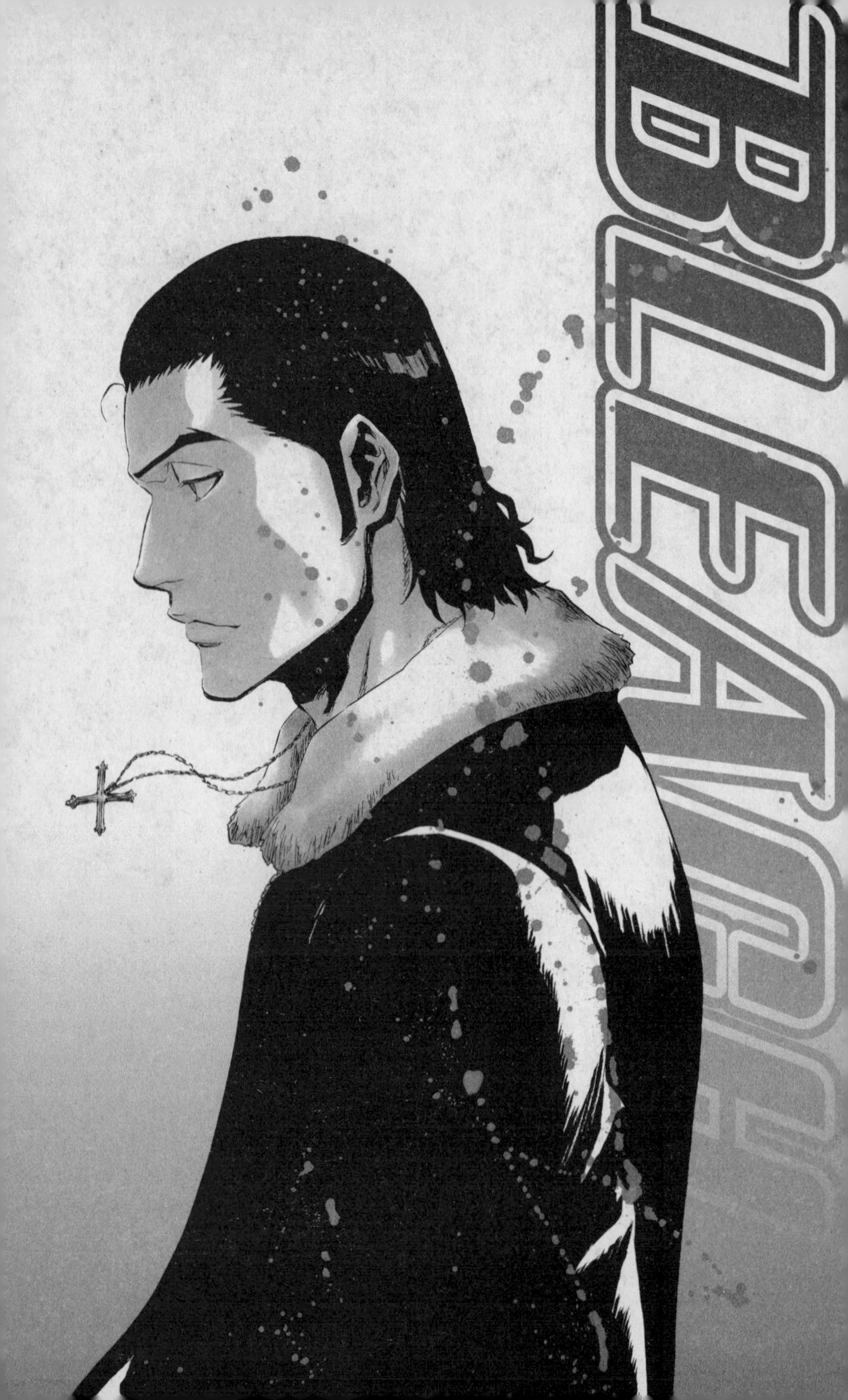
BLEACH

BLEACH
ブリーチ

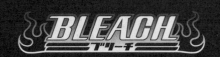

READ THIS WAY

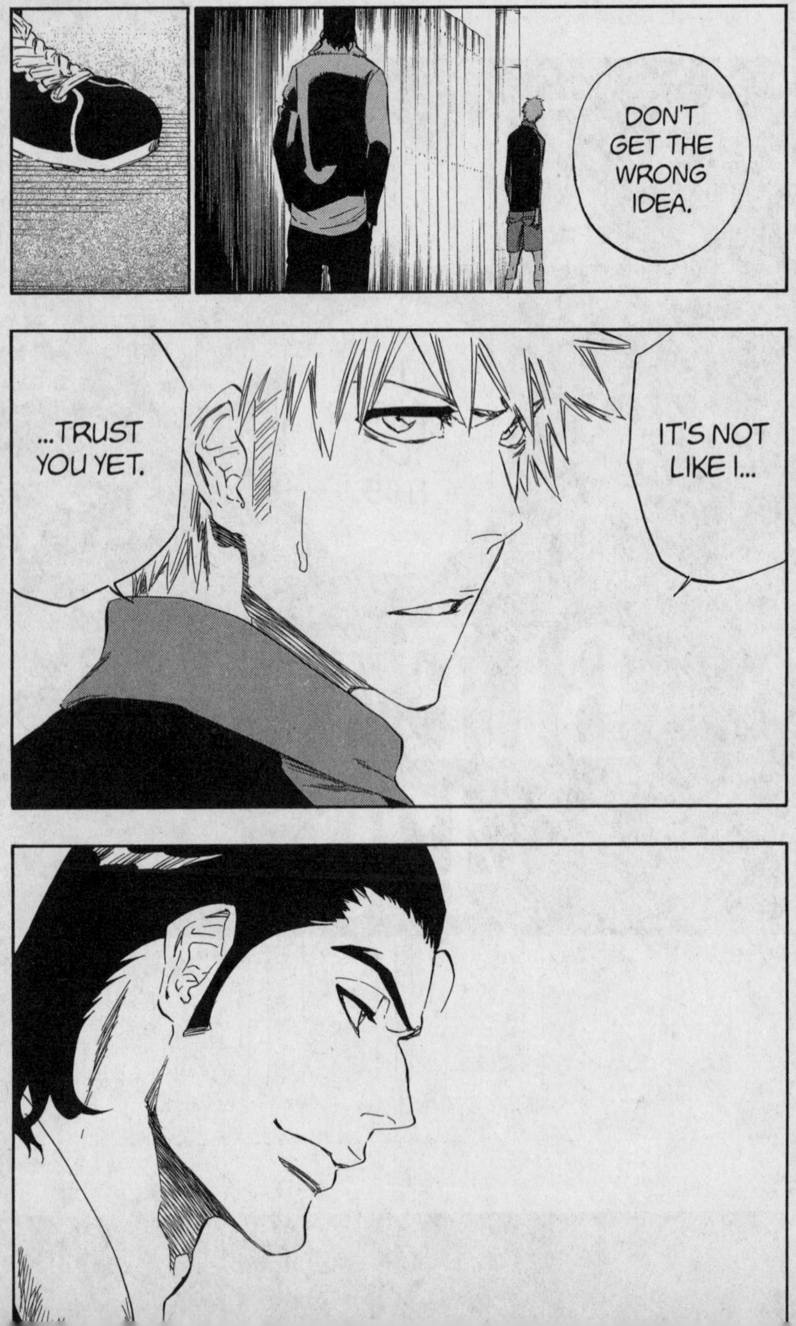
DON'T GET THE WRONG IDEA.
IT'S NOT LIKE I...
...TRUST YOU YET.

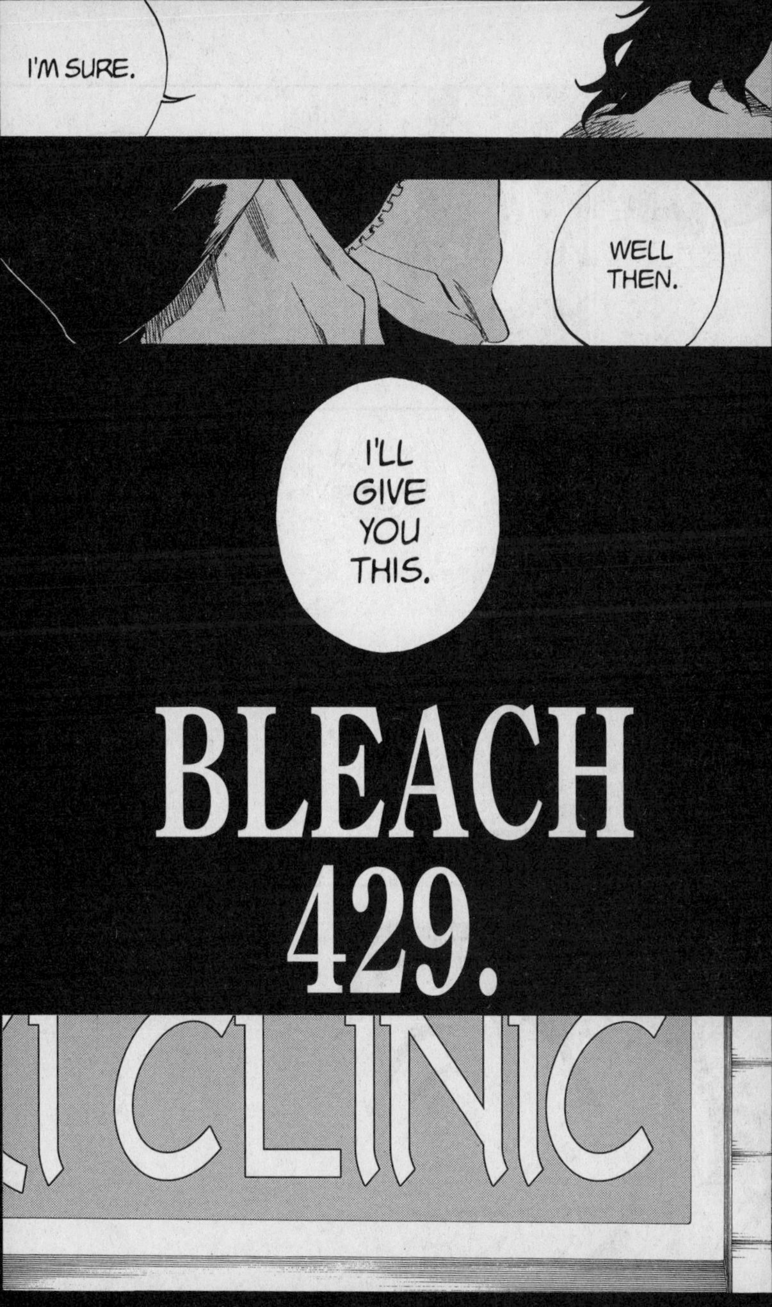
I'M SURE.
WELL THEN.
I'LL GIVE YOU THIS.
BLEACH 429.
CLINIC

READ THIS WAY

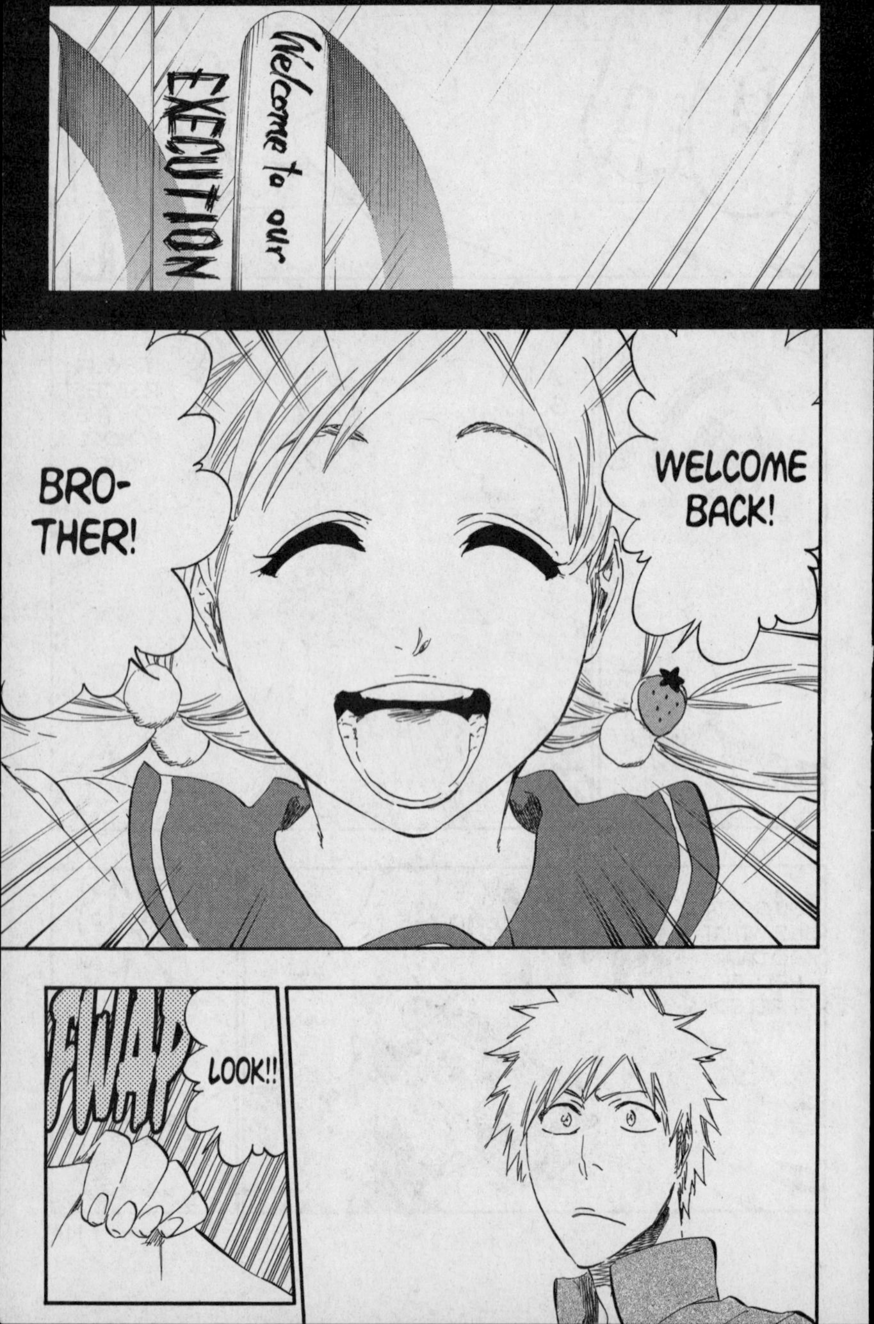
Welcome to our
EXECUTION
WELCOME BACK!
BRO-THER!
FWAP
LOOK!!

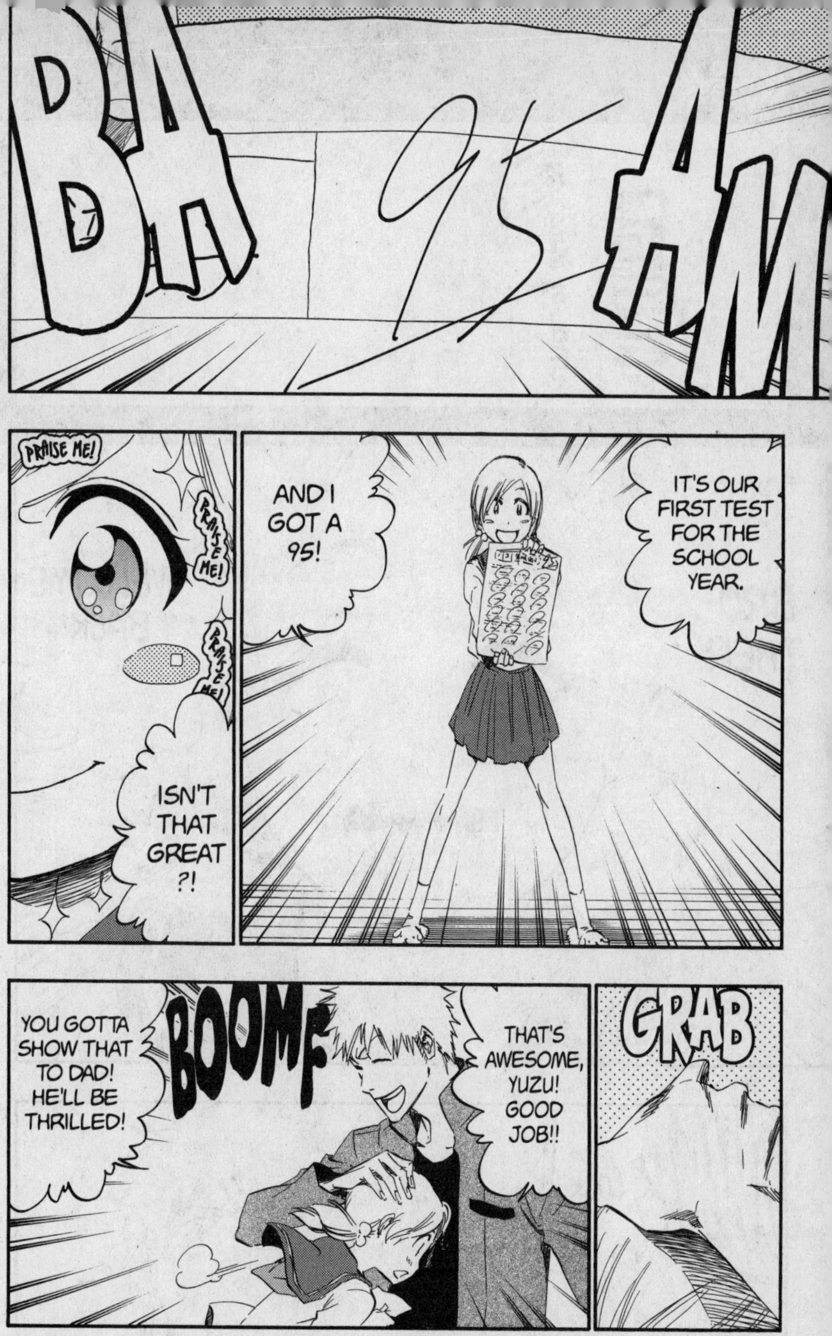

BA
95
AM
IT'S OUR FIRST TEST FOR THE SCHOOL YEAR.
AND I GOT A 95!
PRAISE ME!
PRAISE ME!
PRAISE ME!
ISN'T THAT GREAT?!
GRAB
THAT'S AWESOME, YUZU! GOOD JOB!!
BOOMF
YOU GOTTA SHOW THAT TO DAD! HE'LL BE THRILLED!

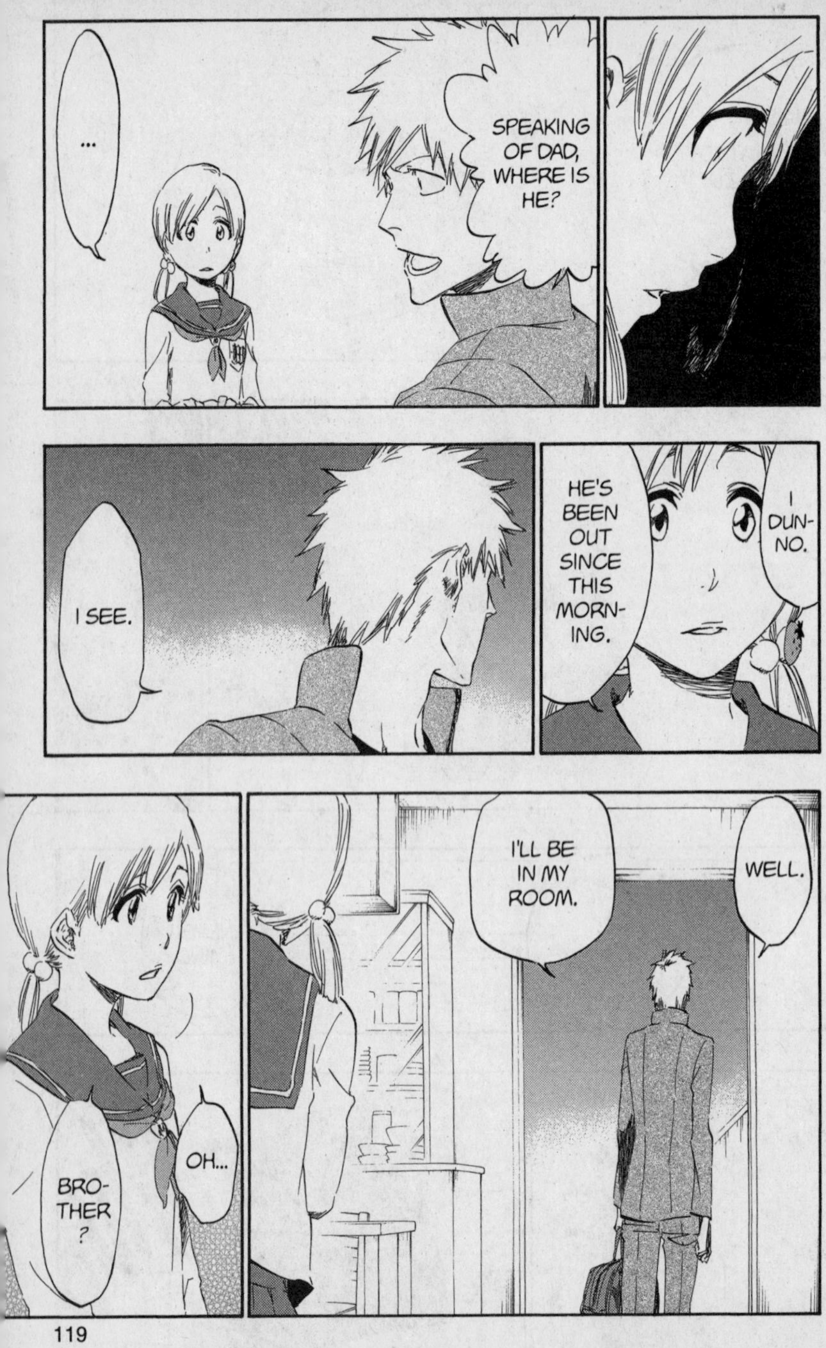
SPEAKING OF DAD, WHERE IS HE?
...
I DUNNO.
HE'S BEEN OUT SINCE THIS MORNING.
I SEE.
WELL.
I'LL BE IN MY ROOM.
OH...
BROTHER?

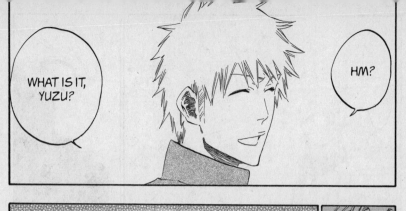

WHAT IS IT, YUZU?

HM?

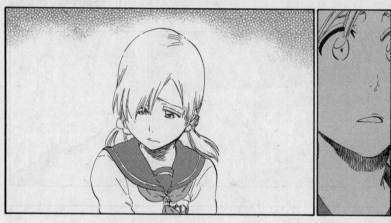

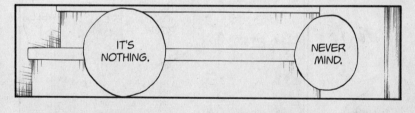

IT'S NOTHING.

NEVER MIND.

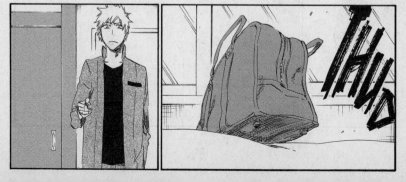

THUD

READ THIS WAY

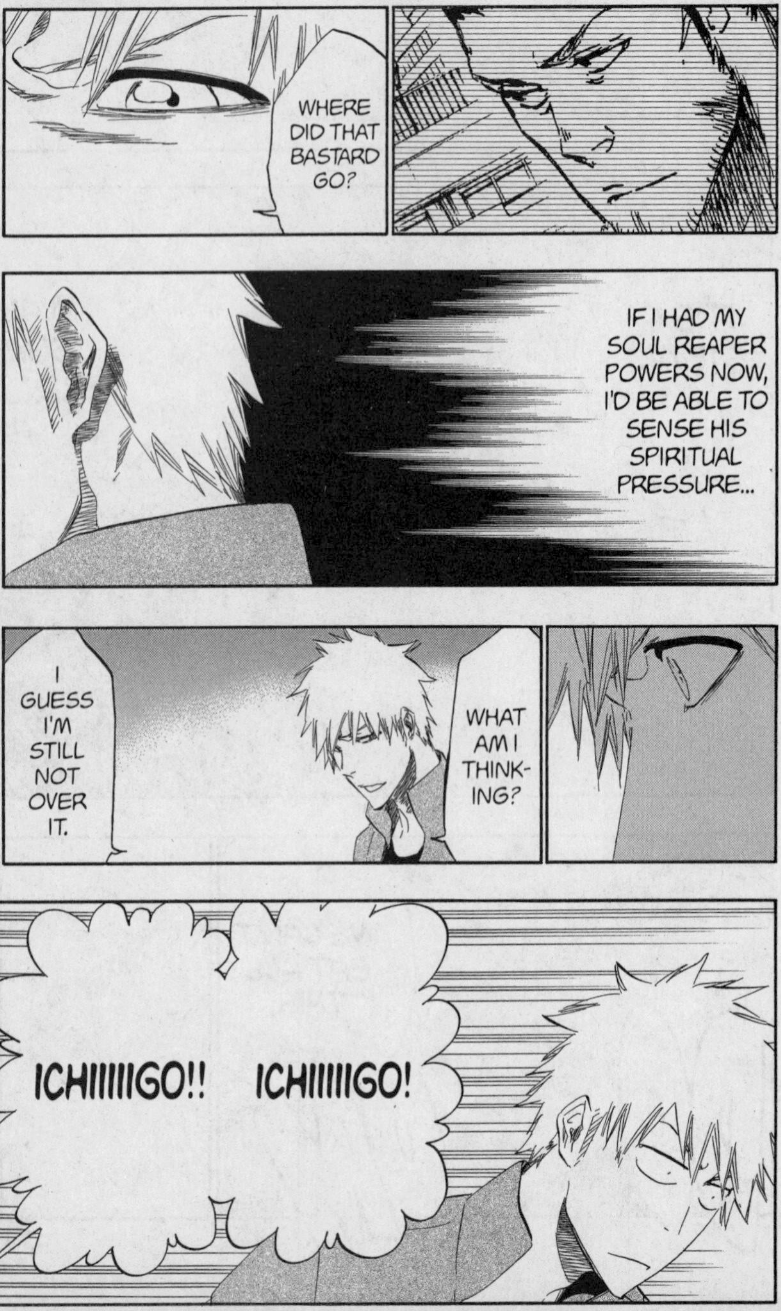

WHERE DID THAT BASTARD GO?
IF I HAD MY SOUL REAPER POWERS NOW, I'D BE ABLE TO SENSE HIS SPIRITUAL PRESSURE...
WHAT AM I THINKING?
I GUESS I'M STILL NOT OVER IT.
ICHIIIIIGO!
ICHIIIIIGO!!

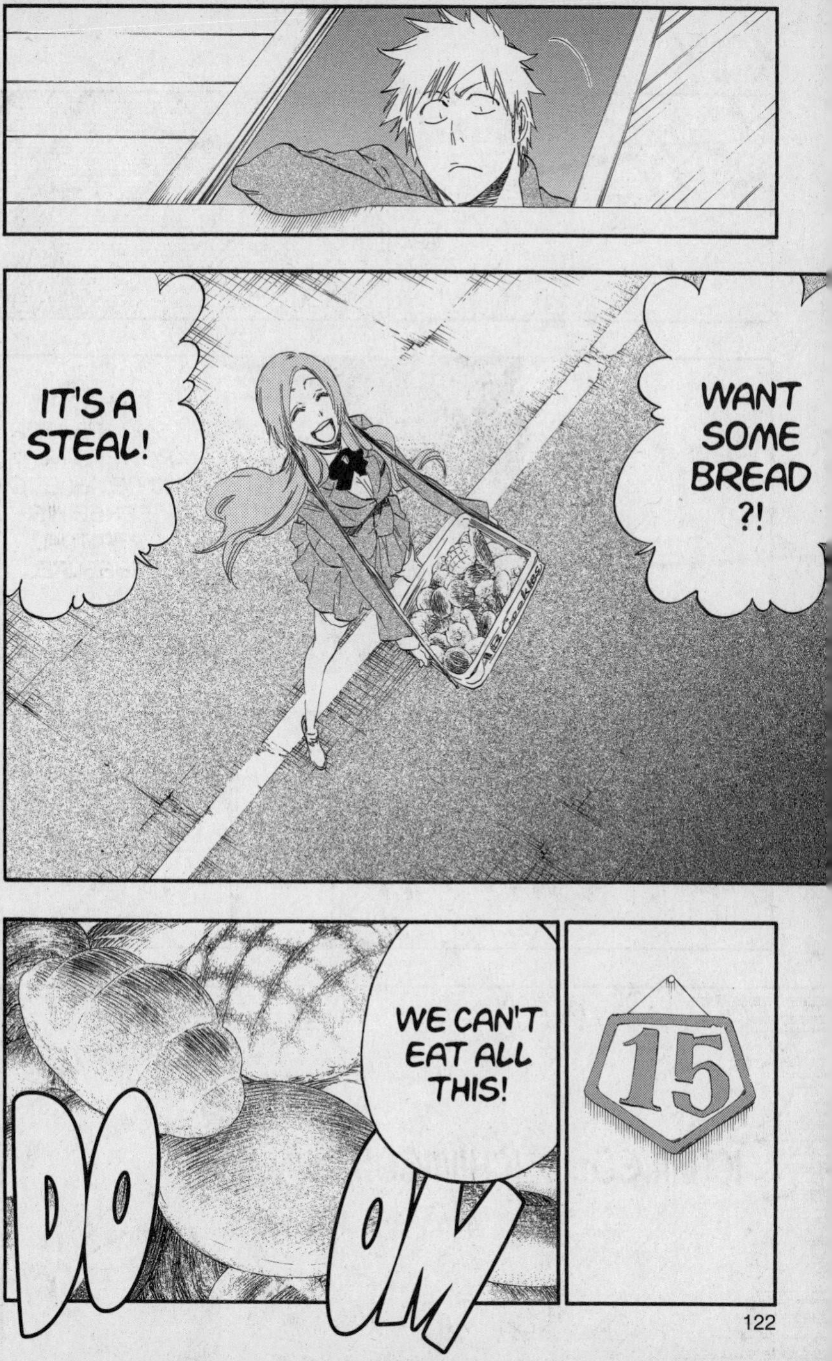
WANT SOME BREAD?!
IT'S A STEAL!
AB Cookies
15
WE CAN'T EAT ALL THIS!
DOOM

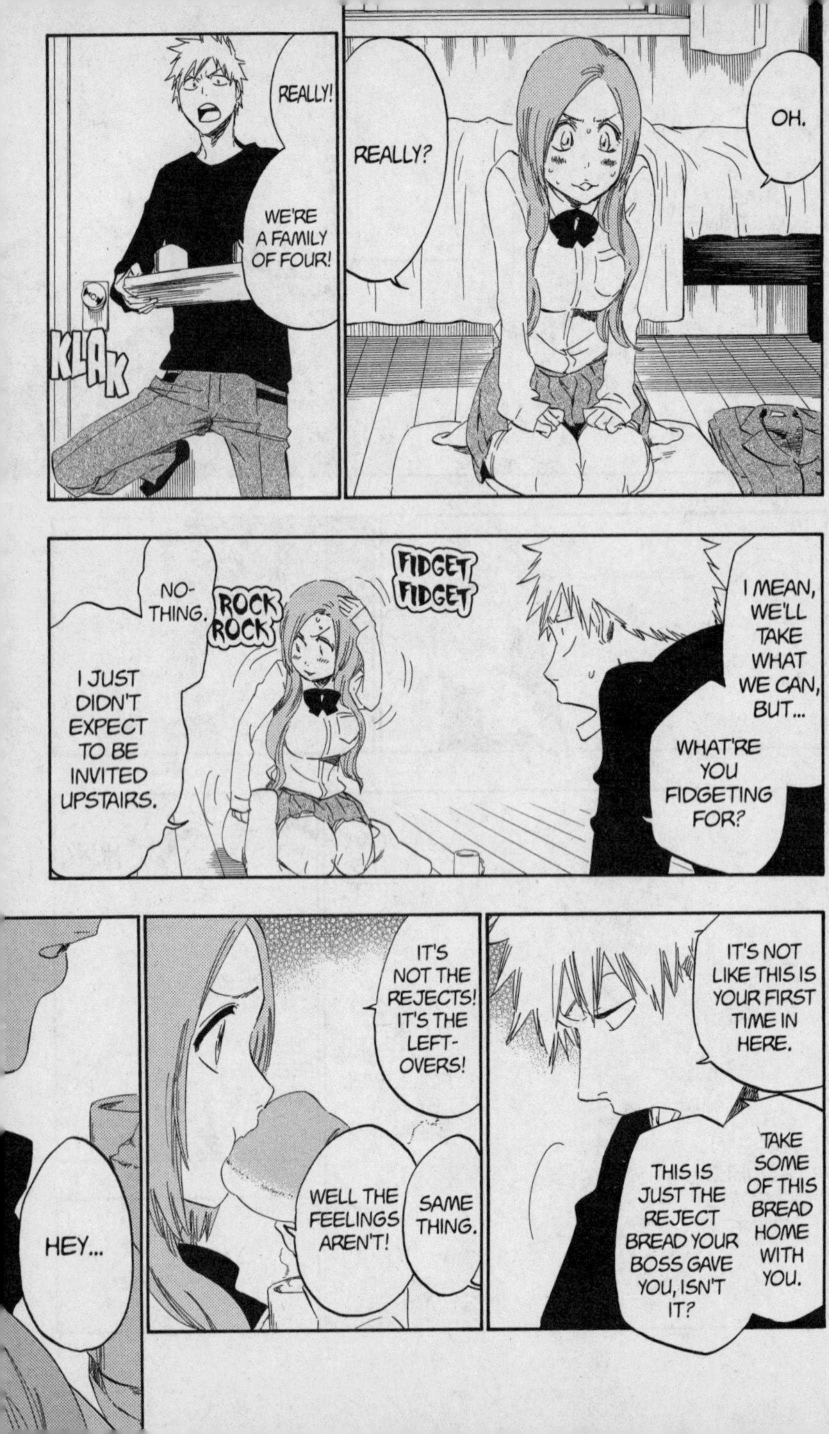
OH.
REALLY?
REALLY!
WE'RE A FAMILY OF FOUR!
KLAK
I MEAN, WE'LL TAKE WHAT WE CAN, BUT...
WHAT'RE YOU FIDGETING FOR?
FIDGET FIDGET
ROCK ROCK
NO-THING.
I JUST DIDN'T EXPECT TO BE INVITED UPSTAIRS.
IT'S NOT LIKE THIS IS YOUR FIRST TIME IN HERE.
TAKE SOME OF THIS BREAD HOME WITH YOU.
THIS IS JUST THE REJECT BREAD YOUR BOSS GAVE YOU, ISN'T IT?
IT'S NOT THE REJECTS! IT'S THE LEFT-OVERS!
SAME THING.
WELL THE FEELINGS AREN'T!
HEY...

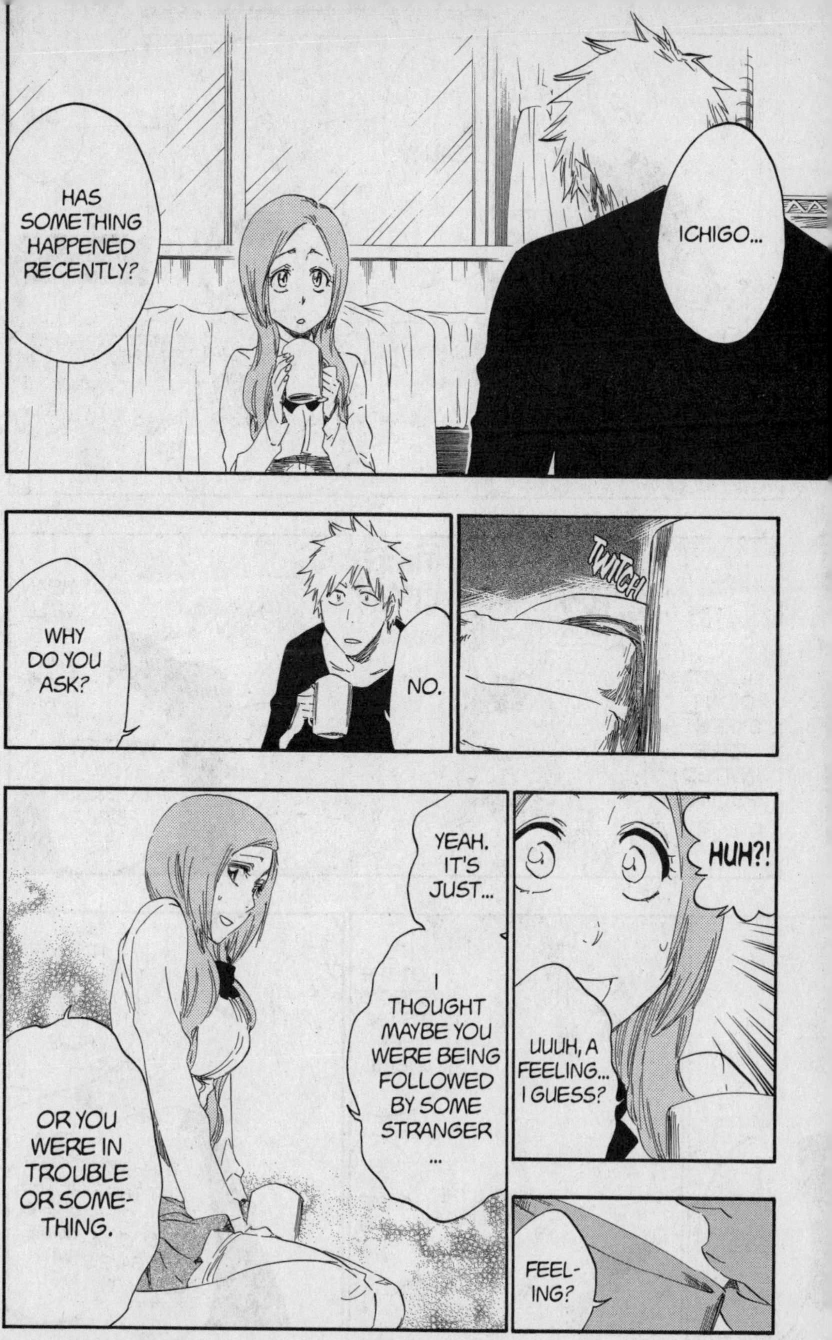
ICHIGO...
HAS SOMETHING HAPPENED RECENTLY?
TWITCH
NO.
WHY DO YOU ASK?
HUH?!
UUUH, A FEELING... I GUESS?
FEEL-ING?
YEAH. IT'S JUST...
I THOUGHT MAYBE YOU WERE BEING FOLLOWED BY SOME STRANGER...
OR YOU WERE IN TROUBLE OR SOME-THING.

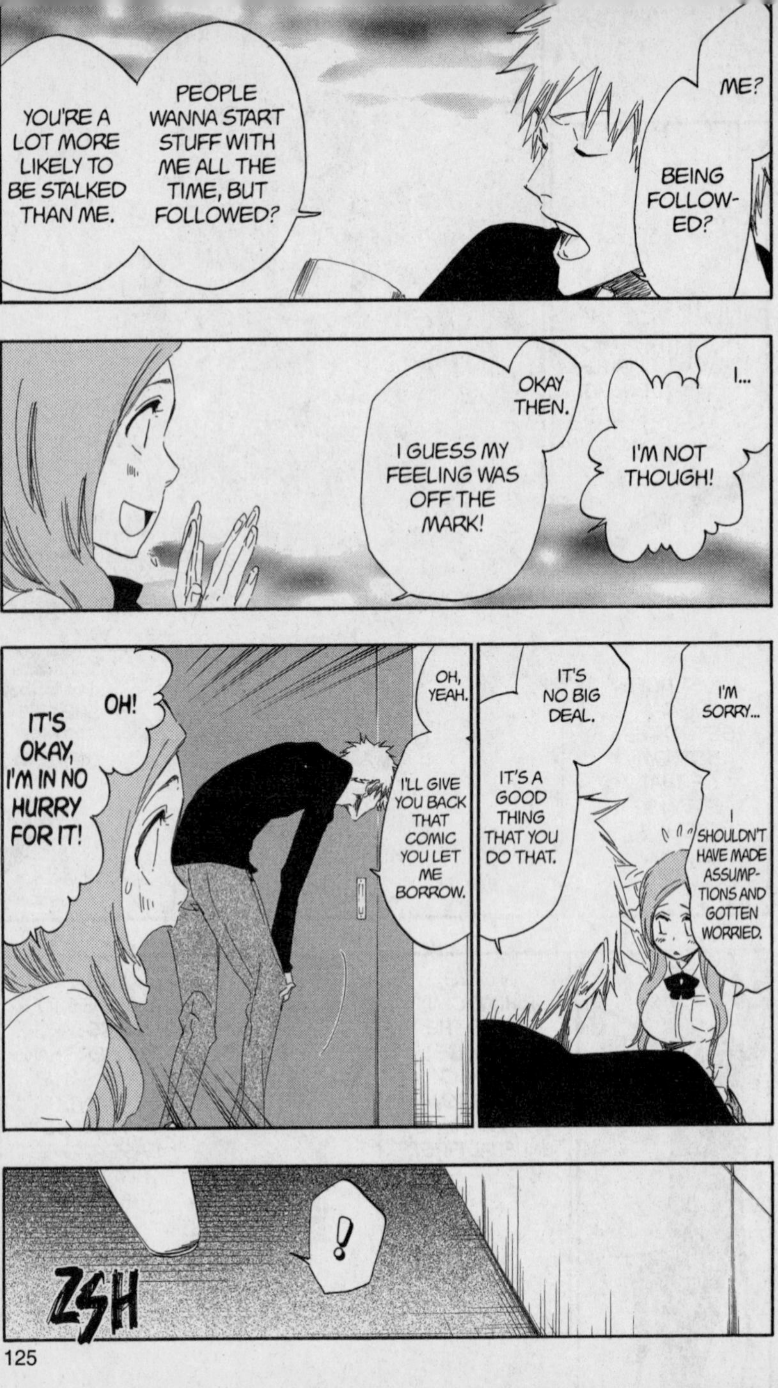
ME?
BEING FOLLOWED?
PEOPLE WANNA START STUFF WITH ME ALL THE TIME, BUT FOLLOWED?
YOU'RE A LOT MORE LIKELY TO BE STALKED THAN ME.
I...
I'M NOT THOUGH!
OKAY THEN.
I GUESS MY FEELING WAS OFF THE MARK!
I'M SORRY...
I SHOULDN'T HAVE MADE ASSUMPTIONS AND GOTTEN WORRIED.
IT'S NO BIG DEAL.
IT'S A GOOD THING THAT YOU DO THAT.
OH, YEAH.
I'LL GIVE YOU BACK THAT COMIC YOU LET ME BORROW.
OH!
IT'S OKAY, I'M IN NO HURRY FOR IT!
!
ZSH

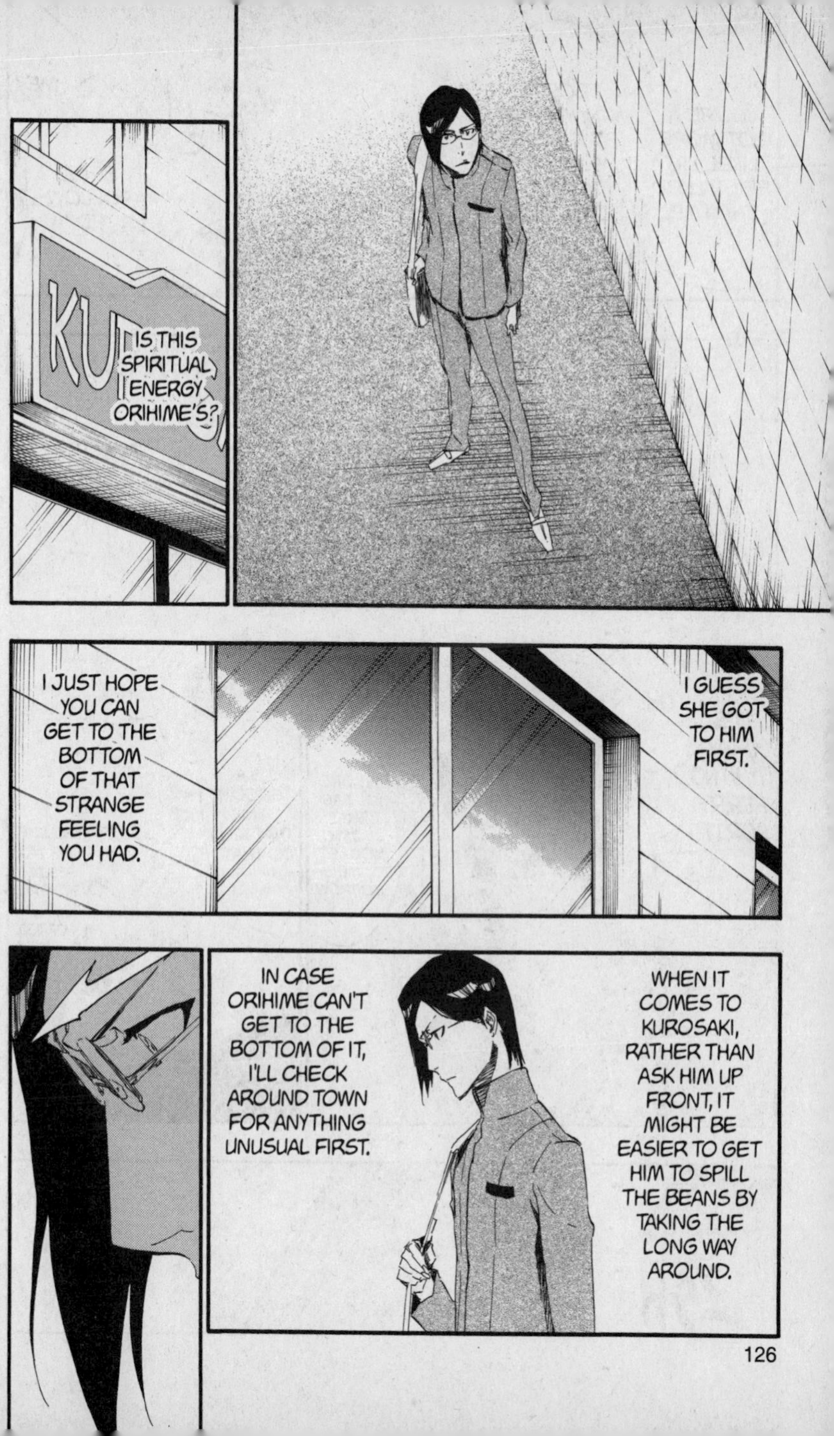
IS THIS SPIRITUAL ENERGY ORIHIME'S?
I GUESS SHE GOT TO HIM FIRST.
I JUST HOPE YOU CAN GET TO THE BOTTOM OF THAT STRANGE FEELING YOU HAD.
WHEN IT COMES TO KUROSAKI, RATHER THAN ASK HIM UP FRONT, IT MIGHT BE EASIER TO GET HIM TO SPILL THE BEANS BY TAKING THE LONG WAY AROUND.
IN CASE ORIHIME CAN'T GET TO THE BOTTOM OF IT, I'LL CHECK AROUND TOWN FOR ANYTHING UNUSUAL FIRST.

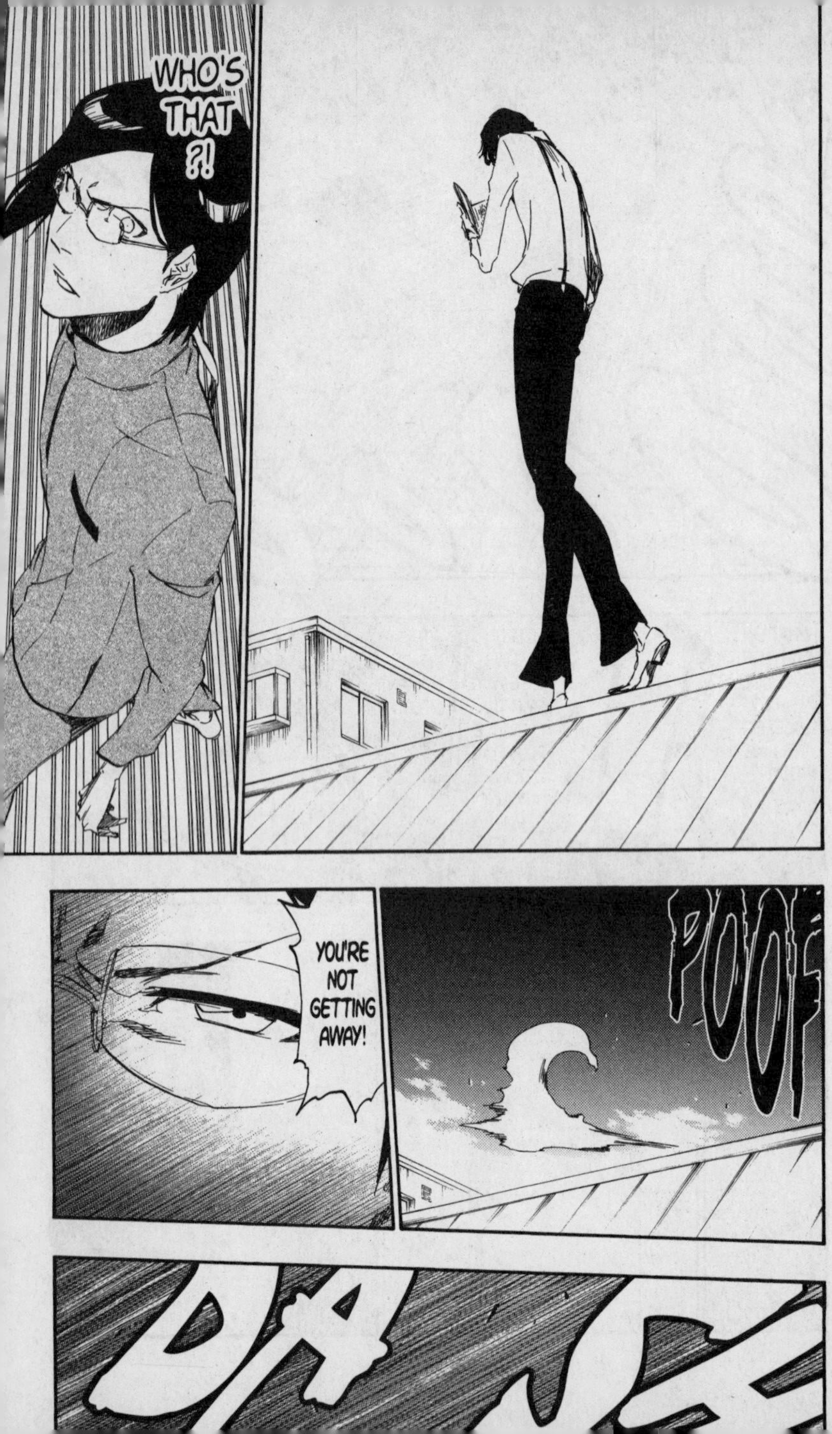
WHO'S THAT ?!
POOF
YOU'RE NOT GETTING AWAY!

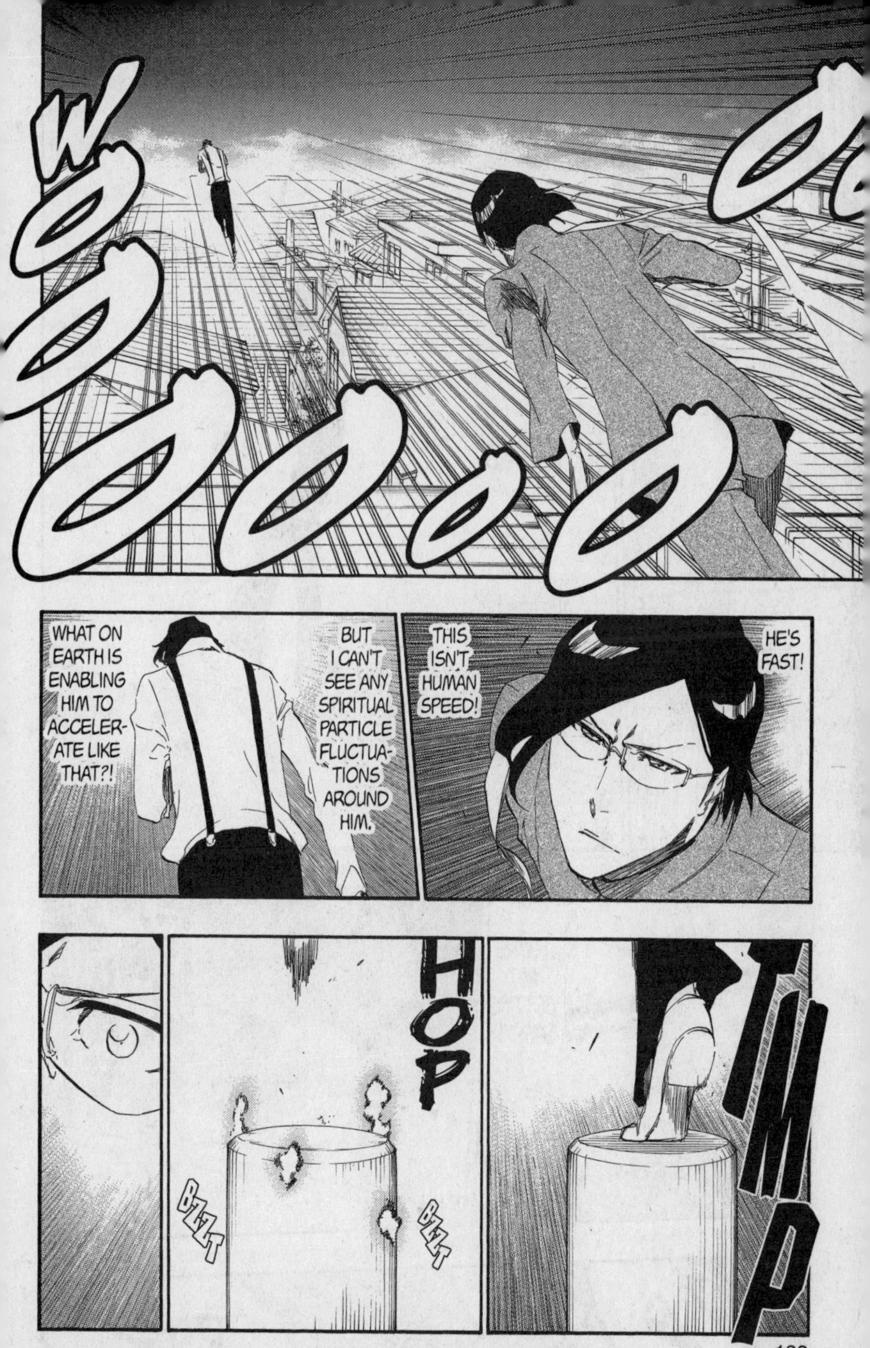
HE'S FAST!
THIS ISN'T HUMAN SPEED!
BUT I CAN'T SEE ANY SPIRITUAL PARTICLE FLUCTUA-TIONS AROUND HIM.
WHAT ON EARTH IS ENABLING HIM TO ACCELER-ATE LIKE THAT?!
TMP
HOP
BZZT
BZZT

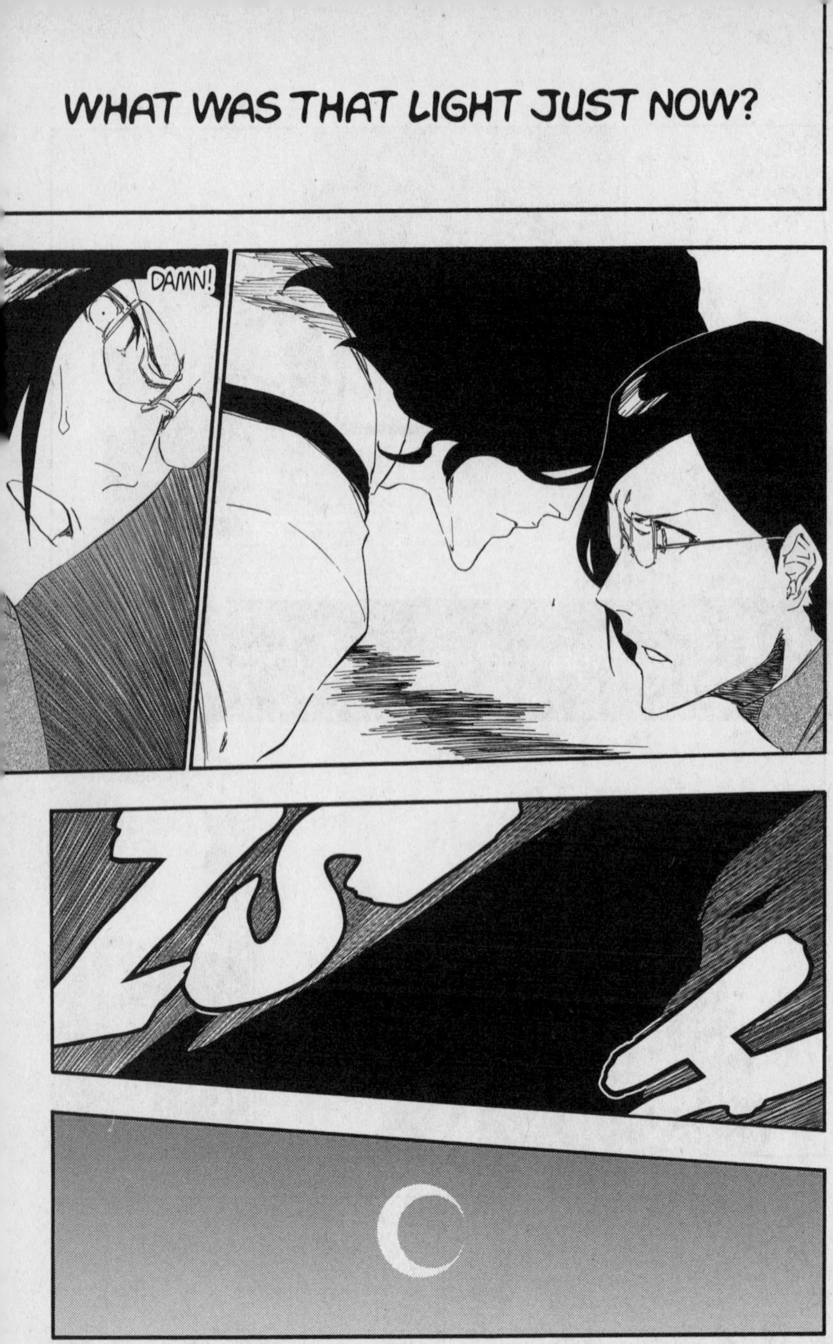
WHAT WAS THAT LIGHT JUST NOW?
DAMN!

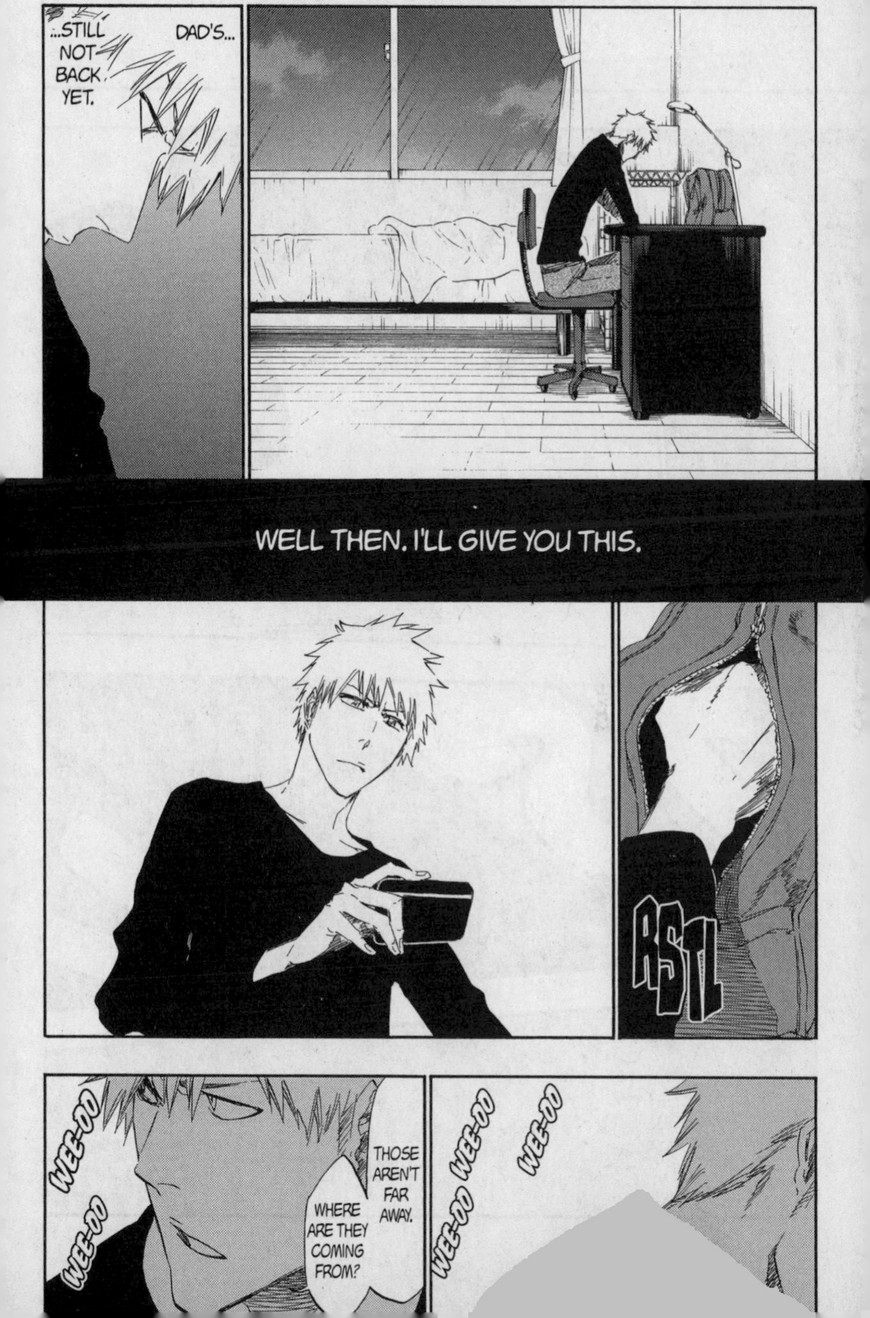
DAD'S...
...STILL NOT BACK YET.
WELL THEN. I'LL GIVE YOU THIS.
RSTL
WEE-OO
WEE-OO
WEE-OO
WEE-OO
WEE-OO
THOSE AREN'T FAR AWAY.
WHERE ARE THEY COMING FROM?

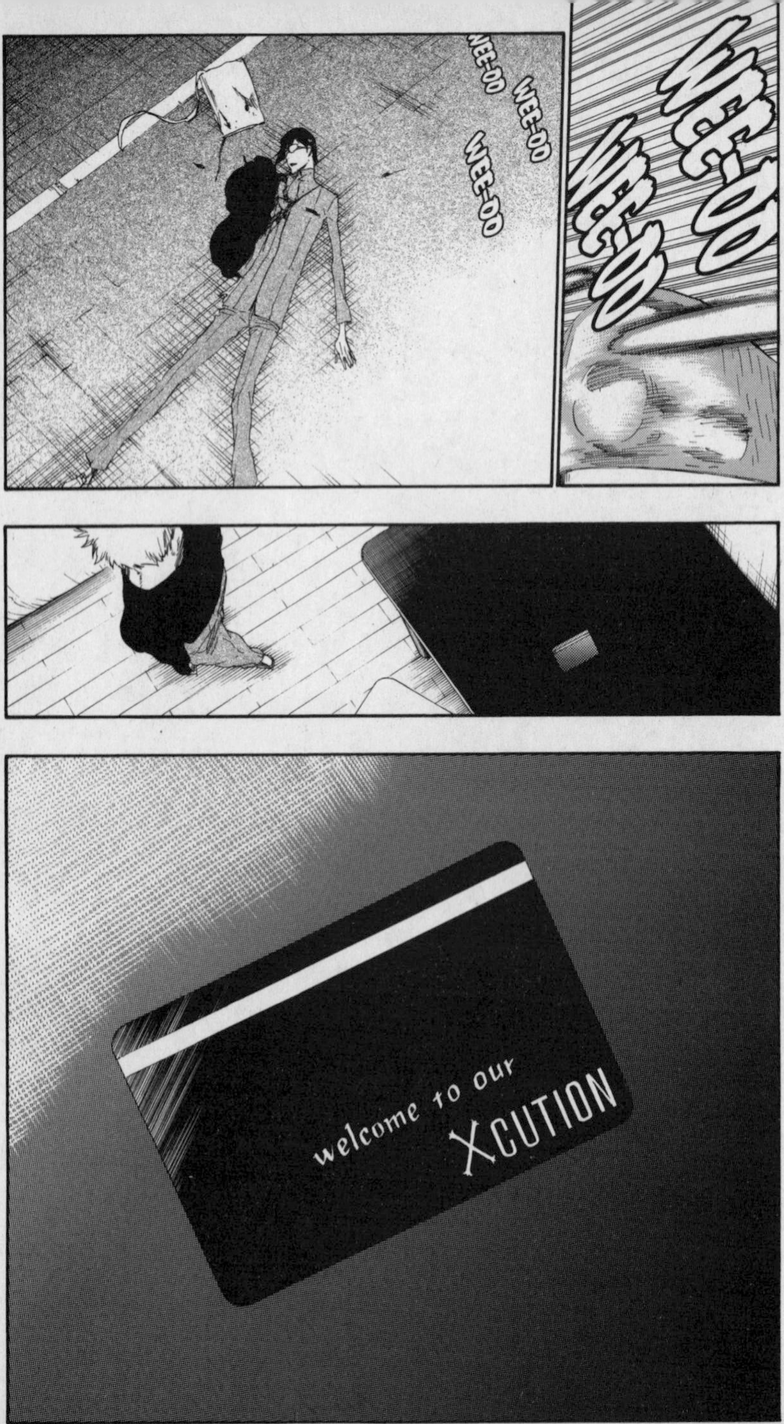
WEE-OO
WEE-OO
WEE-OO
WEE-OO
WEE-OO
welcome to our
XCUTION

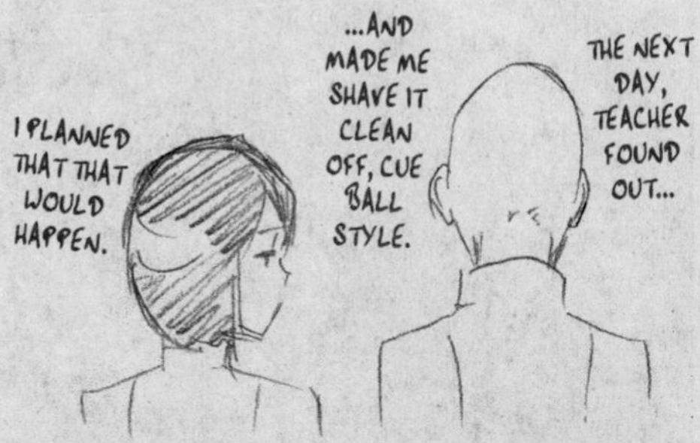
THE NEXT DAY, TEACHER FOUND OUT...
...AND MADE ME SHAVE IT CLEAN OFF, CUE BALL STYLE.
I PLANNED THAT THAT WOULD HAPPEN.

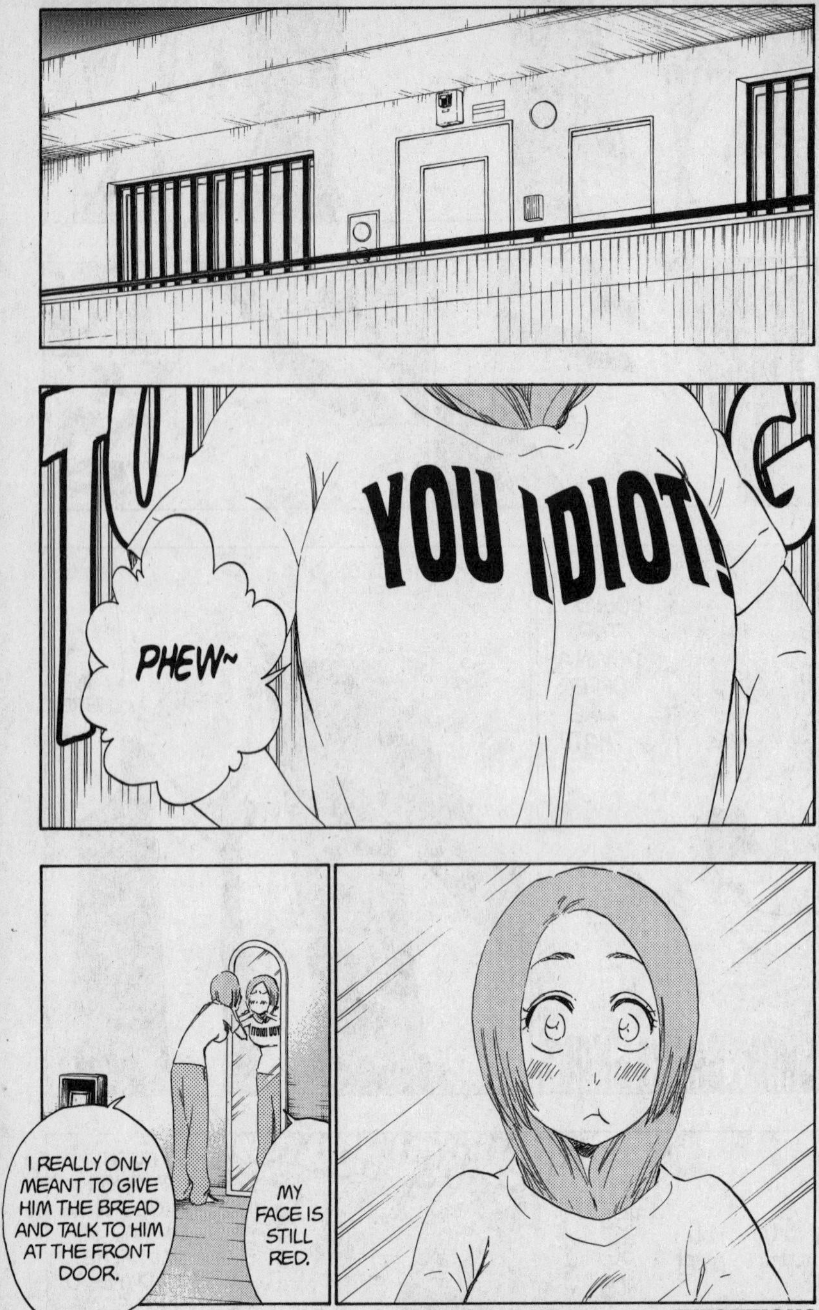
YOU IDIOT!
PHEW~
MY FACE IS STILL RED.
I REALLY ONLY MEANT TO GIVE HIM THE BREAD AND TALK TO HIM AT THE FRONT DOOR.

430. Welcome to our EXECUTION2

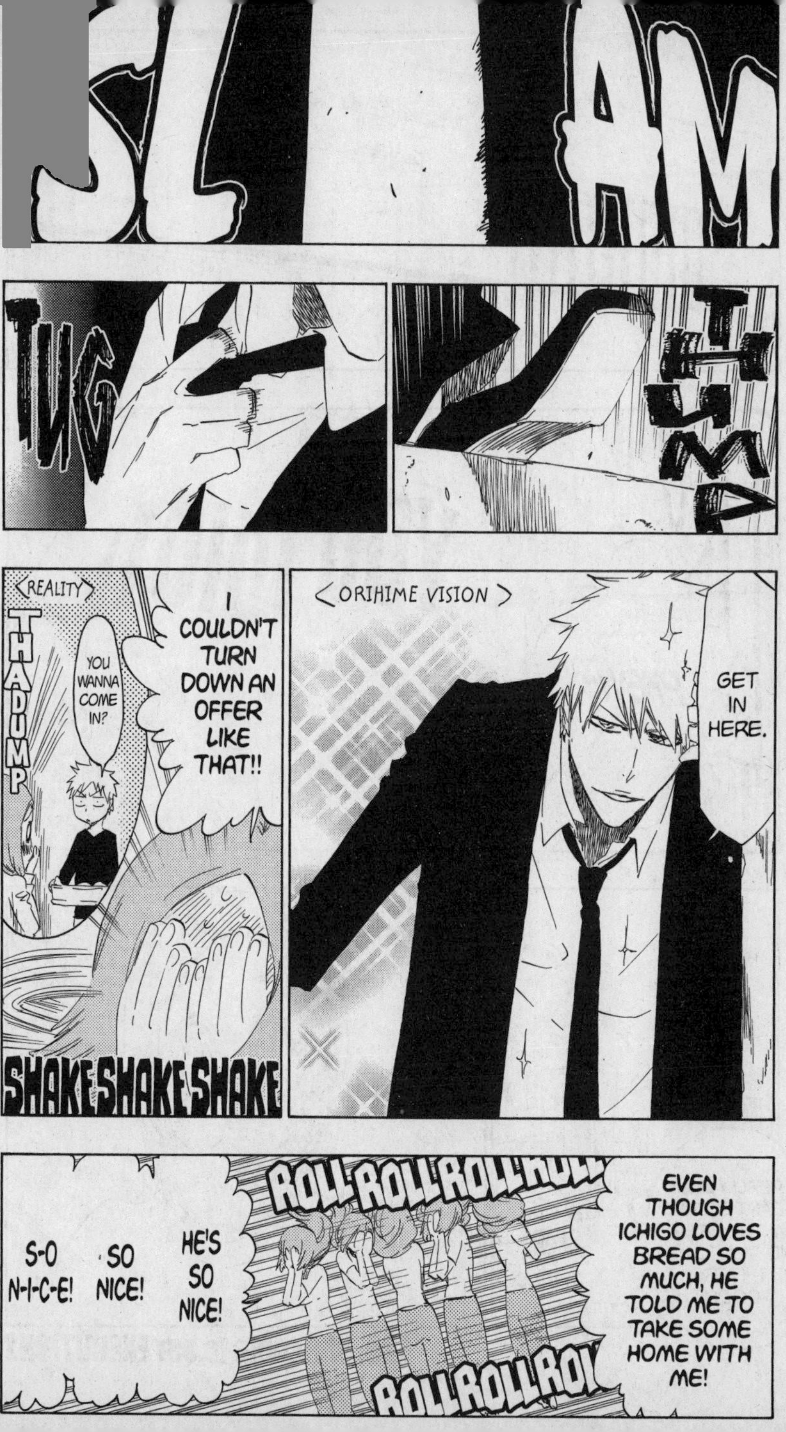
SLAM
THUMP
TUG
<ORIHIME VISION>
GET IN HERE.
<REALITY>
THADUMP
YOU WANNA COME IN?
I COULDN'T TURN DOWN AN OFFER LIKE THAT!!
SHAKE SHAKE SHAKE
EVEN THOUGH ICHIGO LOVES BREAD SO MUCH, HE TOLD ME TO TAKE SOME HOME WITH ME!
ROLL ROLL ROLL
HE'S SO NICE!
SO NICE!
S-O N-I-C-E!
ROLL ROLL

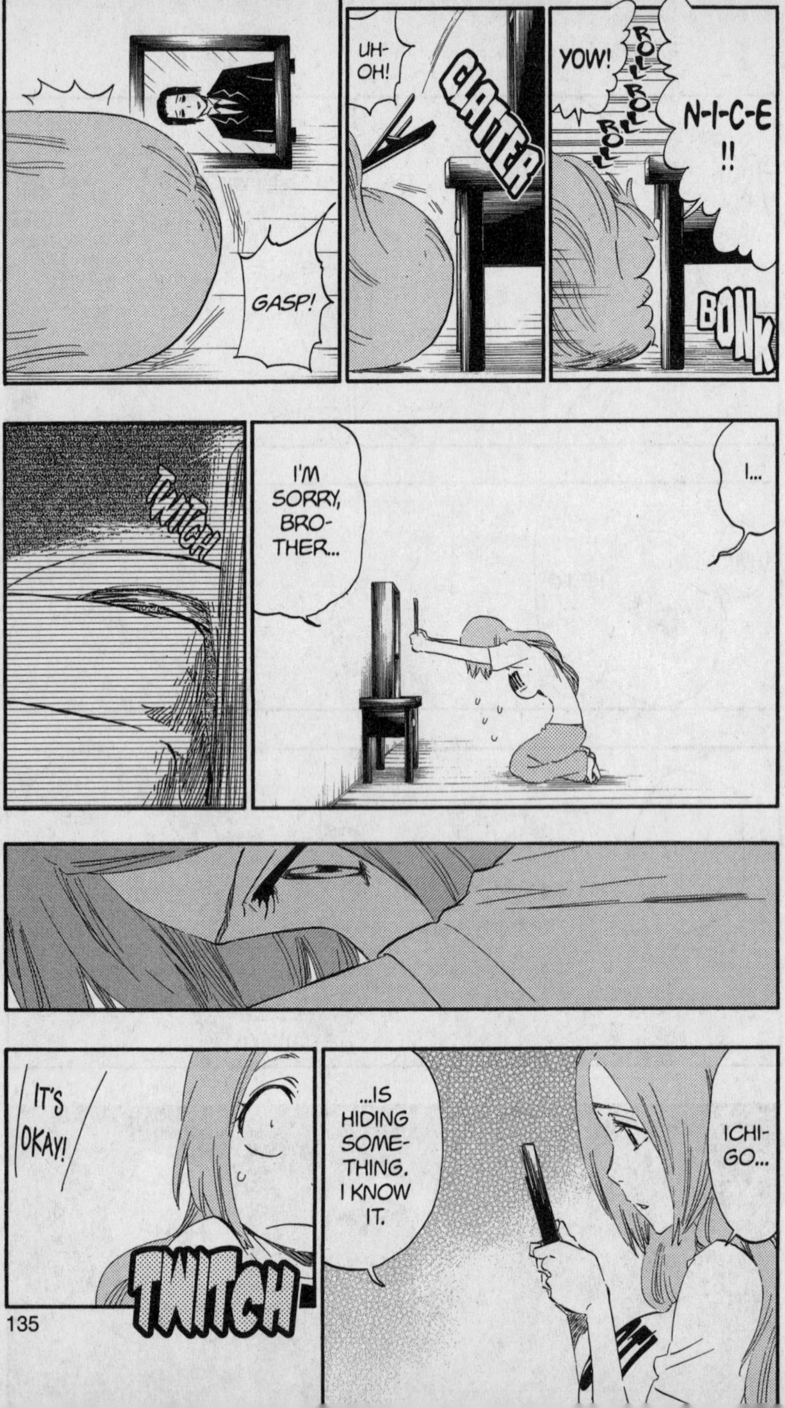
N-I-C-E !!
ROLL ROLL ROLL
YOW!
BONK
UH-OH!
CLATTER
GASP!
I...
I'M SORRY, BROTHER...
TWITCH
ICHI-GO...
...IS HIDING SOMETHING. I KNOW IT.
IT'S OKAY!
TWITCH

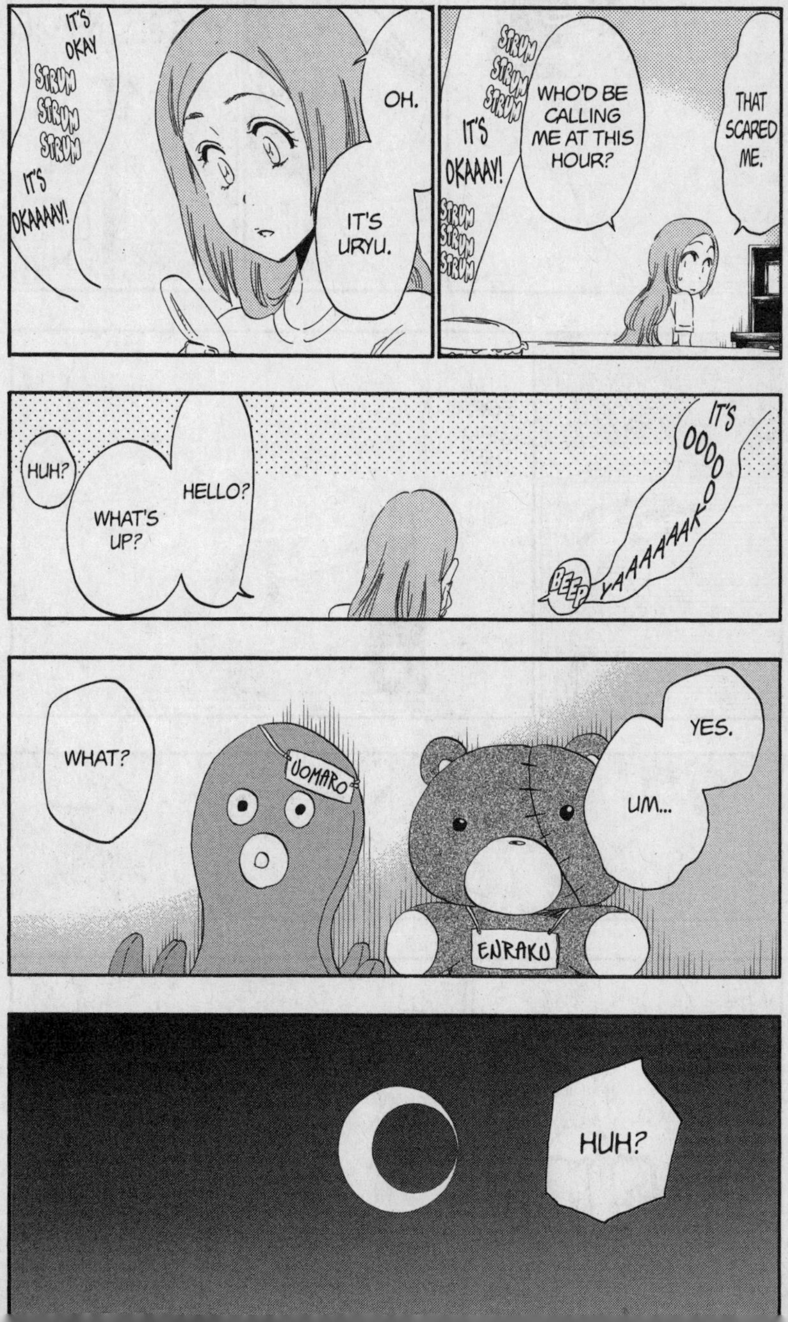
THAT SCARED ME.
WHO'D BE CALLING ME AT THIS HOUR?
STRUM STRUM STRUM
IT'S OKAAAY!
STRUM STRUM STRUM
OH.
IT'S URYU.
IT'S OKAY
STRUM STRUM STRUM
IT'S OKAAAAY!
IT'S OOOOOOKAAAAAAY
BEEP
HELLO?
WHAT'S UP?
HUH?
YES.
UM...
ENRAKU
UOMARO
WHAT?
HUH?

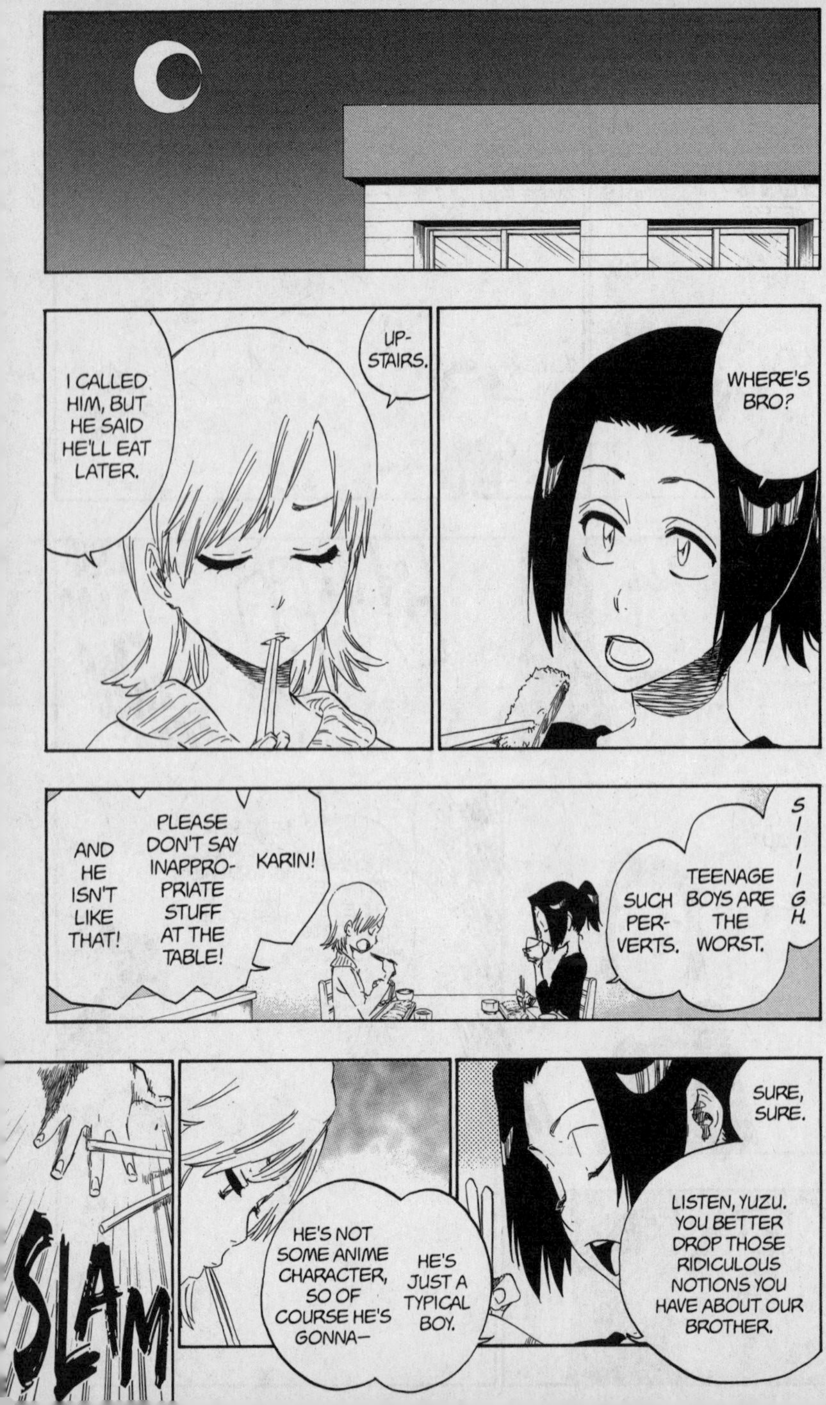
WHERE'S BRO?
UP-STAIRS.
I CALLED HIM, BUT HE SAID HE'LL EAT LATER.
S-I-I-I-I-GH.
TEENAGE BOYS ARE THE WORST.
SUCH PER-VERTS.
KARIN!
PLEASE DON'T SAY INAPPRO-PRIATE STUFF AT THE TABLE!
AND HE ISN'T LIKE THAT!
SURE, SURE.
LISTEN, YUZU. YOU BETTER DROP THOSE RIDICULOUS NOTIONS YOU HAVE ABOUT OUR BROTHER.
HE'S JUST A TYPICAL BOY.
HE'S NOT SOME ANIME CHARACTER, SO OF COURSE HE'S GONNA–
SLAM

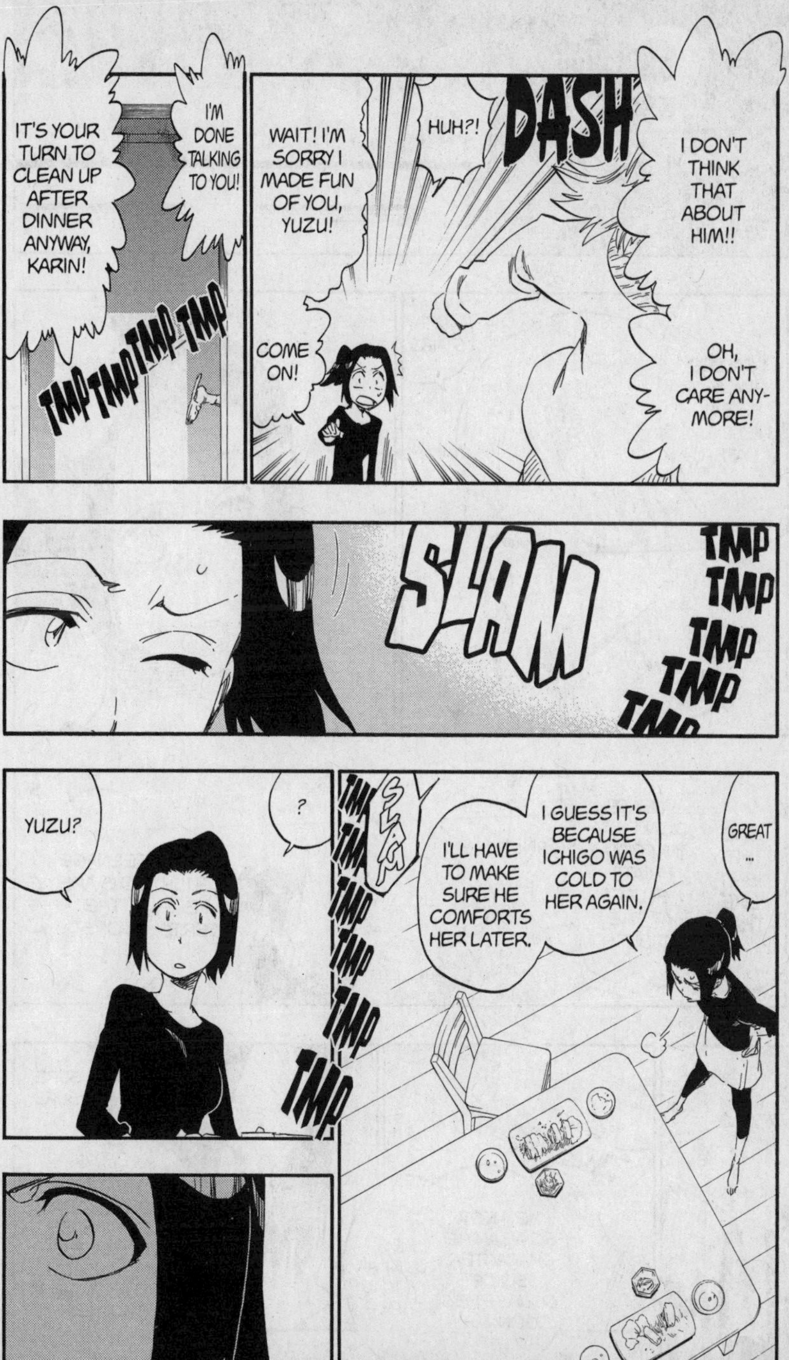
I DON'T THINK THAT ABOUT HIM!!
DASH
HUH?!
WAIT! I'M SORRY I MADE FUN OF YOU, YUZU!
OH, I DON'T CARE ANY-MORE!
COME ON!
I'M DONE TALKING TO YOU!
IT'S YOUR TURN TO CLEAN UP AFTER DINNER ANYWAY, KARIN!
TMP TMP TMP TMP
TMP TMP TMP TMP
SLAM
GREAT ...
I GUESS IT'S BECAUSE ICHIGO WAS COLD TO HER AGAIN.
I'LL HAVE TO MAKE SURE HE COMFORTS HER LATER.
?
SLAM
TMP TMP TMP TMP TMP TMP
YUZU?

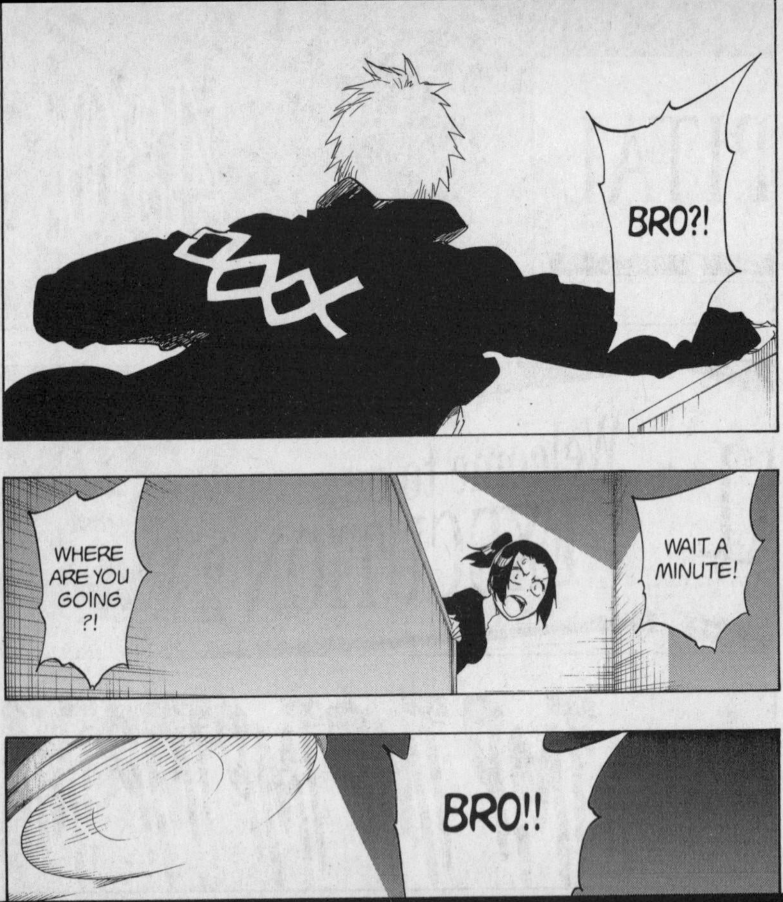
BRO?!
WAIT A MINUTE!
WHERE ARE YOU GOING ?!
BRO!!

BLEACH

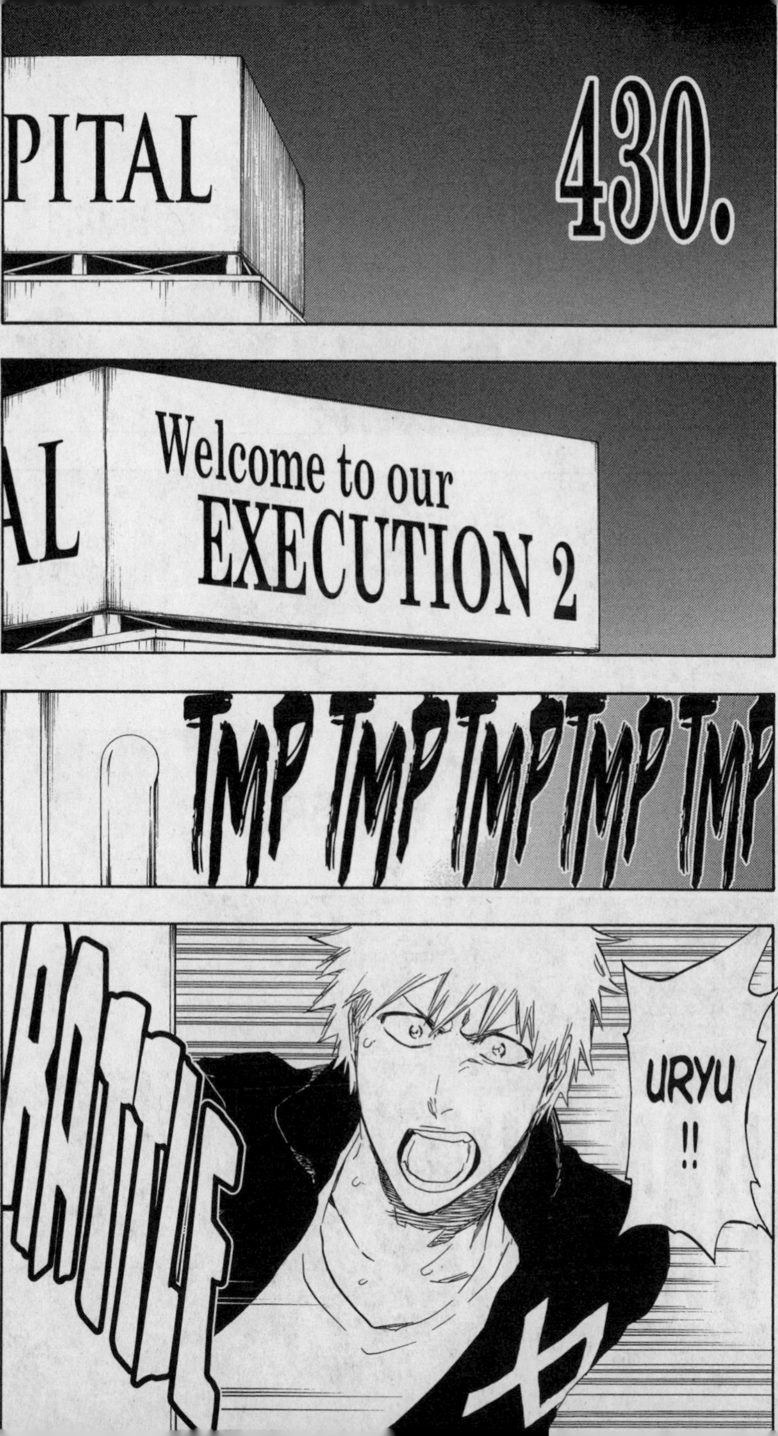
430.
PITAL
AL
Welcome to our
EXECUTION 2
TMP TMP TMP TMP TMP
URYU
!!

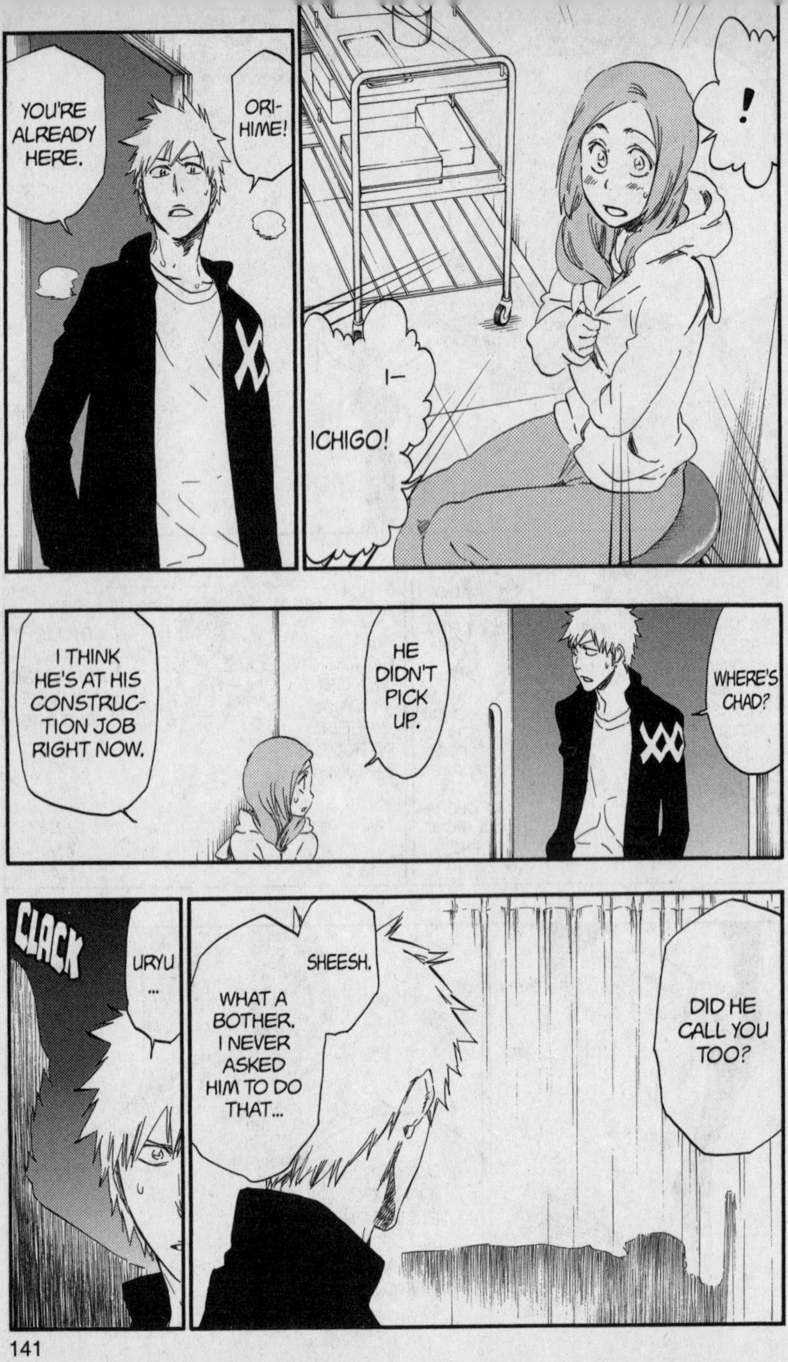
!
I— ICHIGO!
ORI-HIME!
YOU'RE ALREADY HERE.
WHERE'S CHAD?
HE DIDN'T PICK UP.
I THINK HE'S AT HIS CONSTRUCTION JOB RIGHT NOW.
DID HE CALL YOU TOO?
SHEESH.
WHAT A BOTHER. I NEVER ASKED HIM TO DO THAT...
URYU ...
CLACK

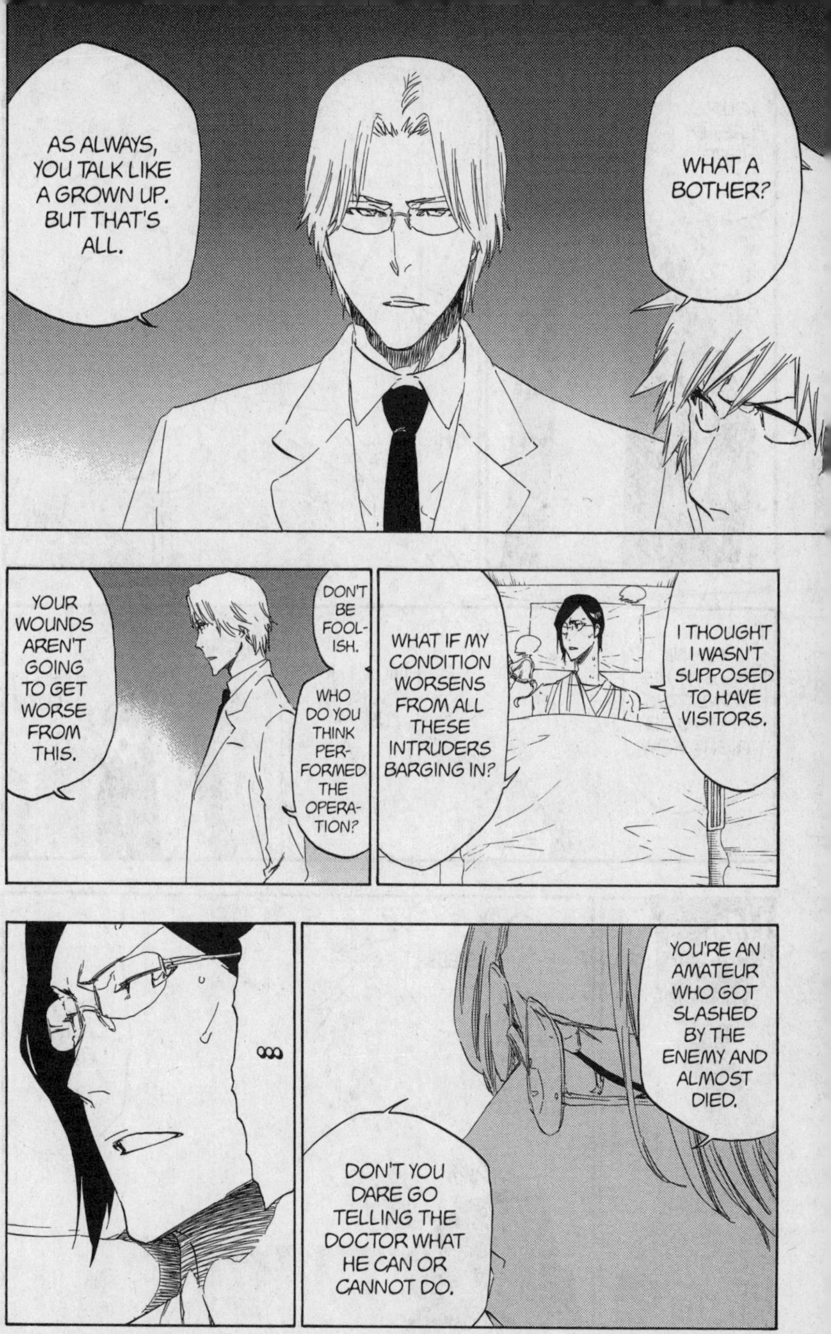

WHAT A BOTHER?
AS ALWAYS, YOU TALK LIKE A GROWN UP. BUT THAT'S ALL.
I THOUGHT I WASN'T SUPPOSED TO HAVE VISITORS.
WHAT IF MY CONDITION WORSENS FROM ALL THESE INTRUDERS BARGING IN?
DON'T BE FOOL-ISH.
WHO DO YOU THINK PER-FORMED THE OPERA-TION?
YOUR WOUNDS AREN'T GOING TO GET WORSE FROM THIS.
YOU'RE AN AMATEUR WHO GOT SLASHED BY THE ENEMY AND ALMOST DIED.
DON'T YOU DARE GO TELLING THE DOCTOR WHAT HE CAN OR CANNOT DO.
...

READ THIS WAY

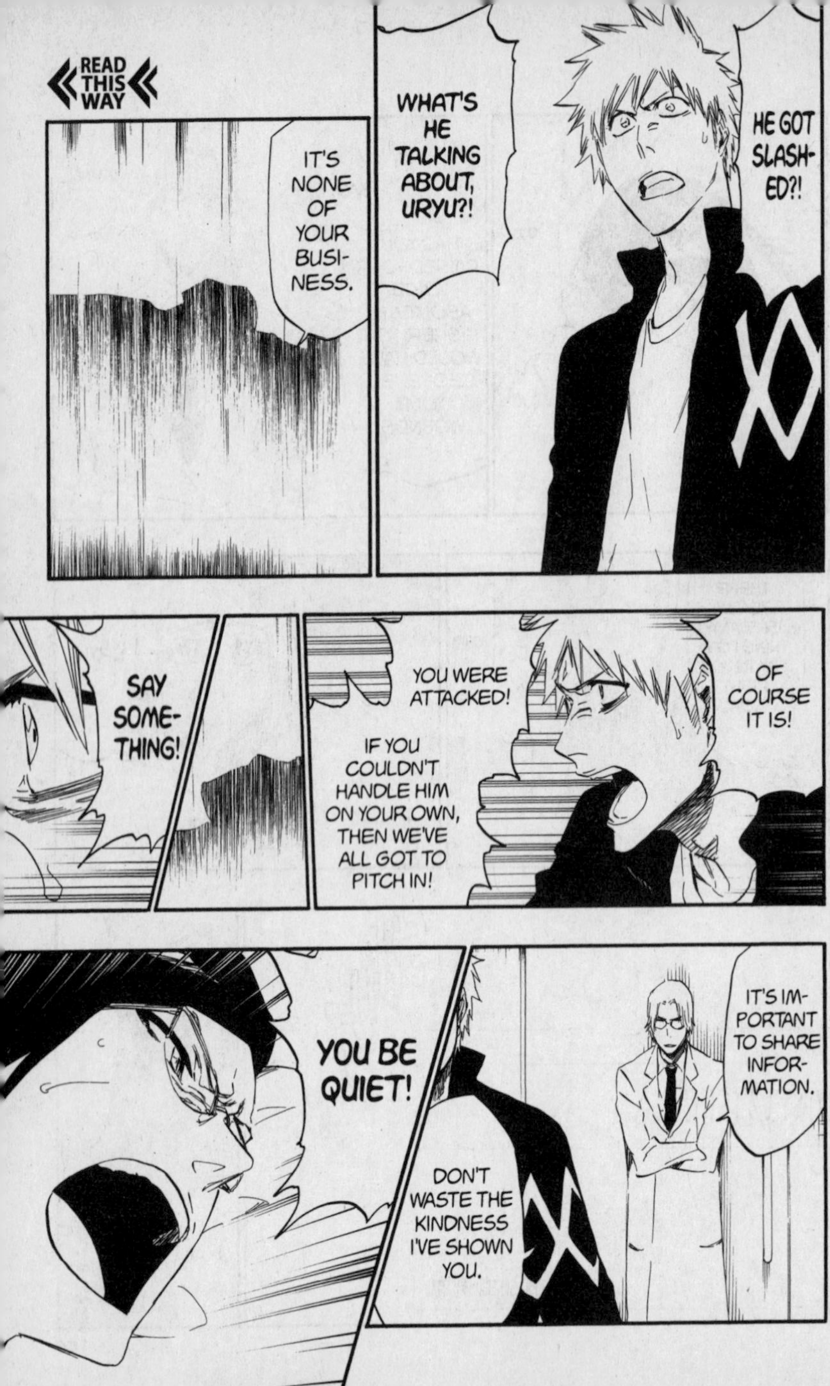
HE GOT SLASHED?!
WHAT'S HE TALKING ABOUT, URYU?!
IT'S NONE OF YOUR BUSINESS.
OF COURSE IT IS!
YOU WERE ATTACKED!
IF YOU COULDN'T HANDLE HIM ON YOUR OWN, THEN WE'VE ALL GOT TO PITCH IN!
SAY SOMETHING!
IT'S IMPORTANT TO SHARE INFORMATION.
DON'T WASTE THE KINDNESS I'VE SHOWN YOU.
YOU BE QUIET!

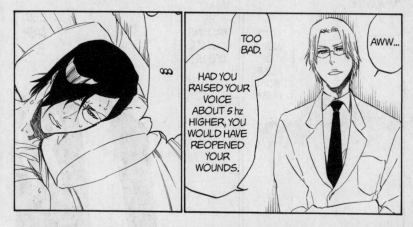

TOO BAD.

HAD YOU RAISED YOUR VOICE ABOUT 5 hz HIGHER, YOU WOULD HAVE REOPENED YOUR WOUNDS.

AWW...

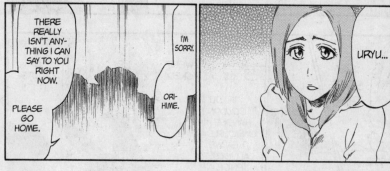

THERE REALLY ISN'T ANY-THING I CAN SAY TO YOU RIGHT NOW.

I'M SORRY.

ORI-HIME.

PLEASE GO HOME.

URYU...

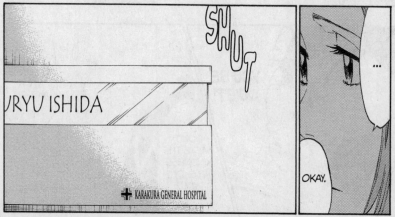

URYU ISHIDA

✚ KARAKURA GENERAL HOSPITAL

SHUT

...

OKAY.

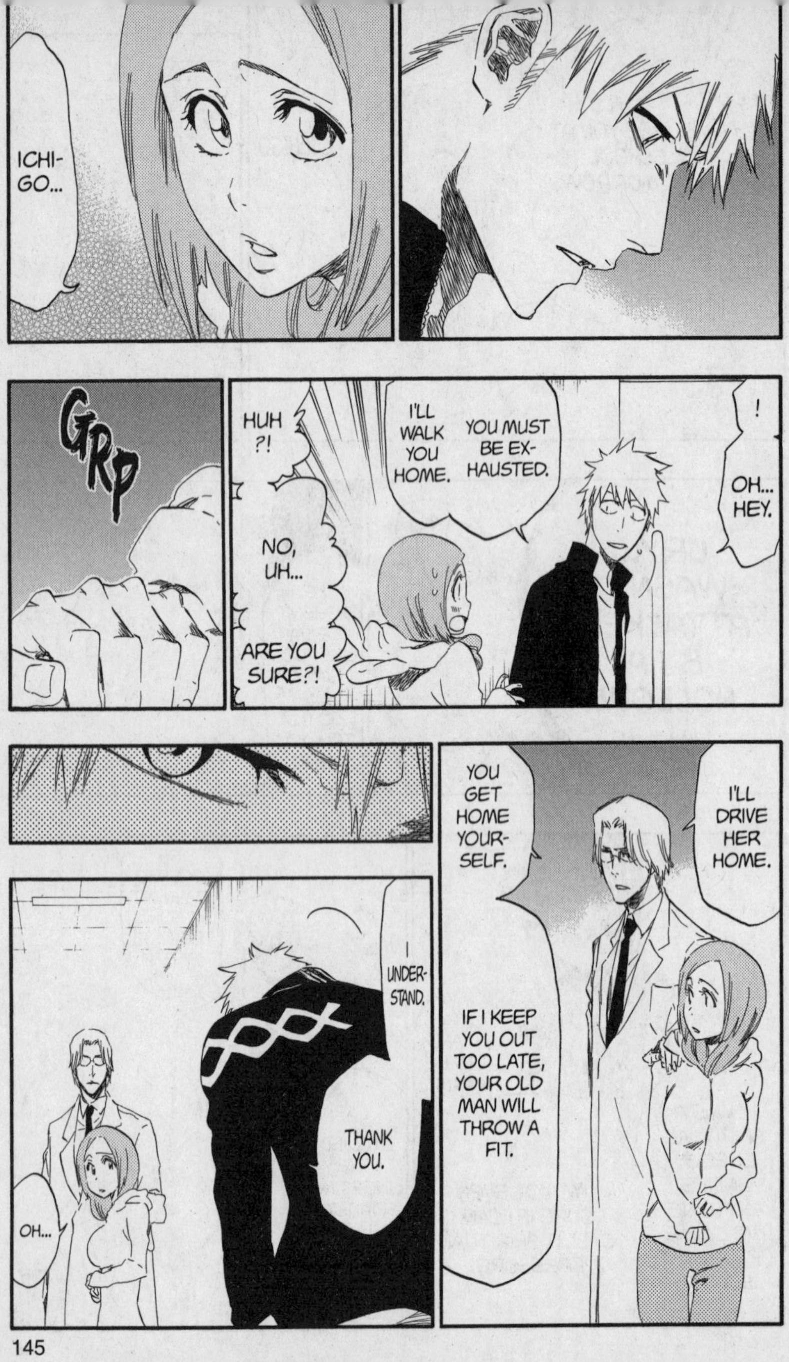
ICHI-GO...
!
OH... HEY.
YOU MUST BE EX-HAUSTED.
I'LL WALK YOU HOME.
HUH?!
NO, UH...
ARE YOU SURE?!
GRP
I'LL DRIVE HER HOME.
YOU GET HOME YOUR-SELF.
IF I KEEP YOU OUT TOO LATE, YOUR OLD MAN WILL THROW A FIT.
I UNDER-STAND.
THANK YOU.
OH...

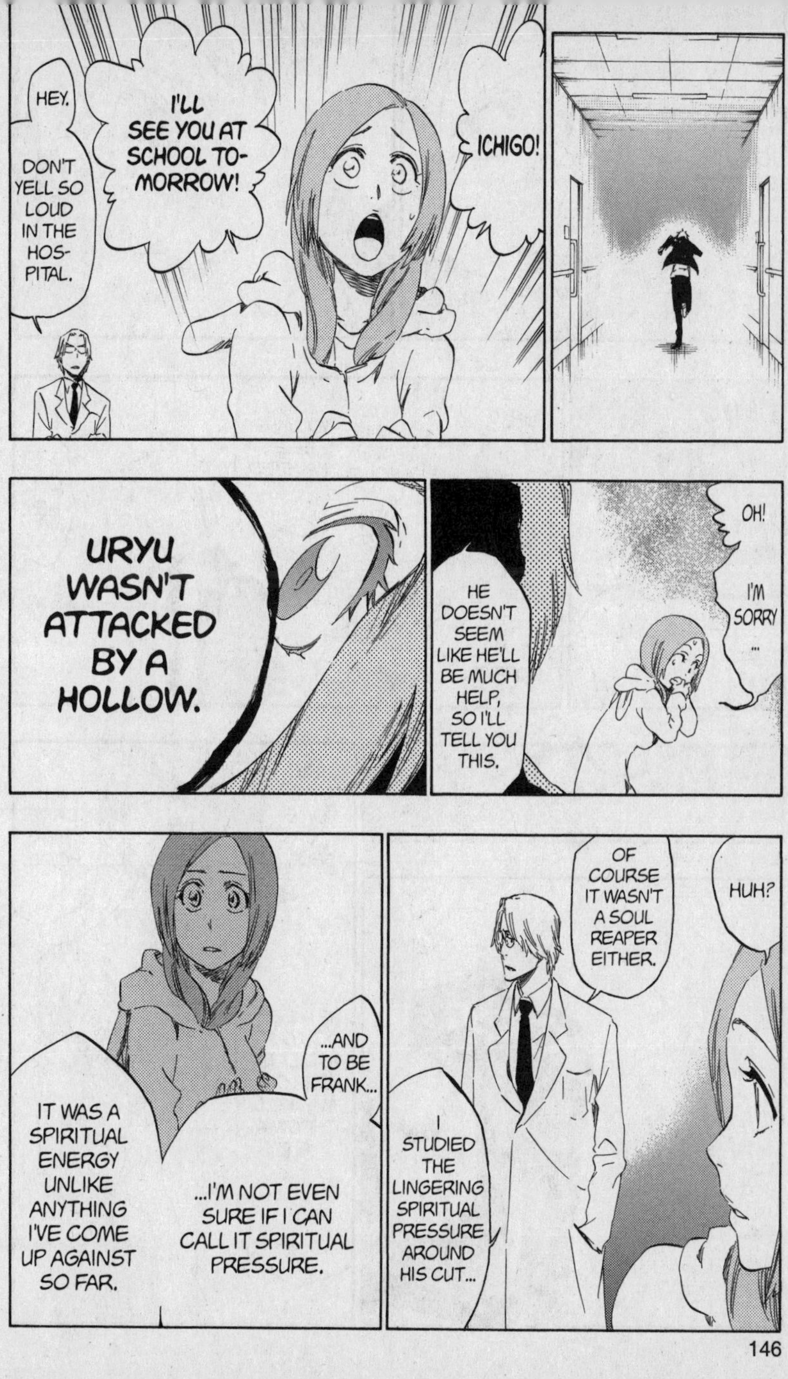
ICHIGO!
I'LL SEE YOU AT SCHOOL TO-MORROW!
HEY.
DON'T YELL SO LOUD IN THE HOS-PITAL.
OH!
I'M SORRY...
HE DOESN'T SEEM LIKE HE'LL BE MUCH HELP, SO I'LL TELL YOU THIS.
URYU WASN'T ATTACKED BY A HOLLOW.
HUH?
OF COURSE IT WASN'T A SOUL REAPER EITHER.
I STUDIED THE LINGERING SPIRITUAL PRESSURE AROUND HIS CUT...
...AND TO BE FRANK...
...I'M NOT EVEN SURE IF I CAN CALL IT SPIRITUAL PRESSURE.
IT WAS A SPIRITUAL ENERGY UNLIKE ANYTHING I'VE COME UP AGAINST SO FAR.

READ THIS WAY

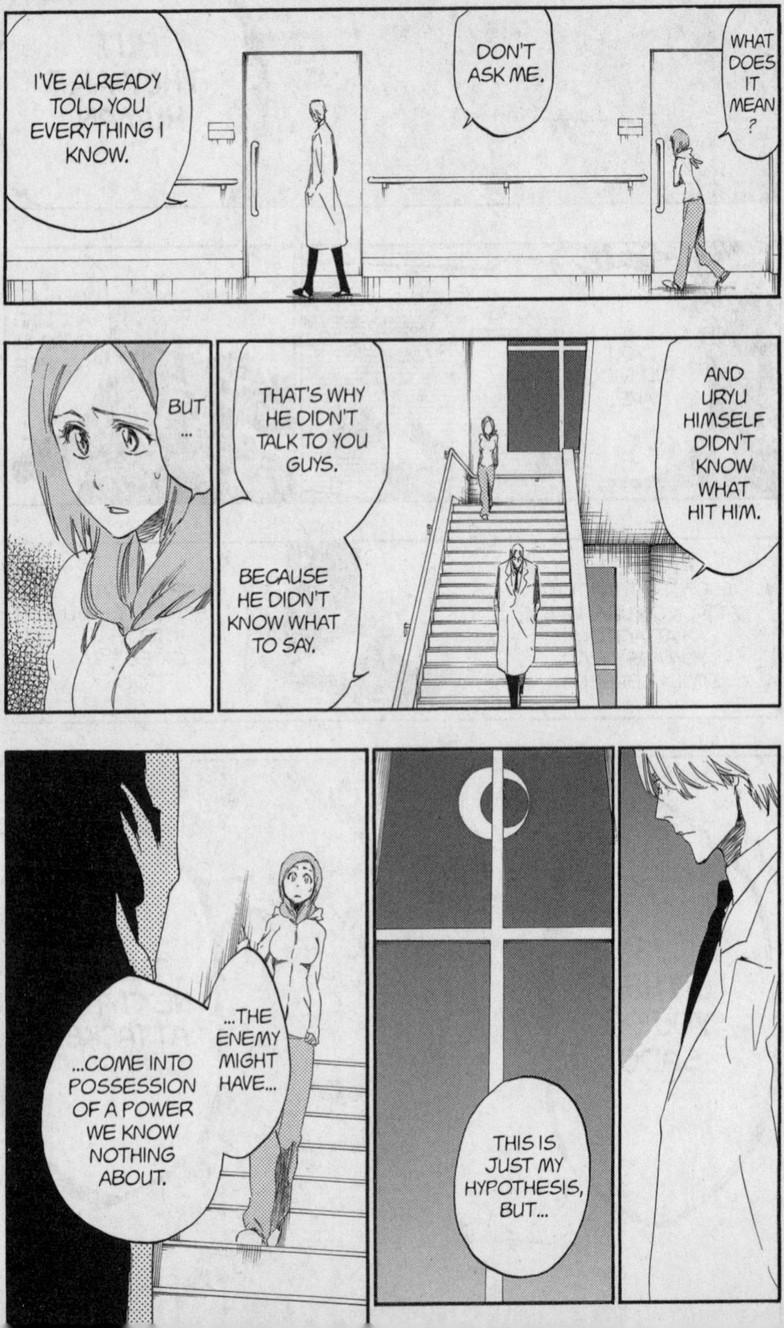
WHAT DOES IT MEAN?
DON'T ASK ME.
I'VE ALREADY TOLD YOU EVERYTHING I KNOW.
AND URYU HIMSELF DIDN'T KNOW WHAT HIT HIM.
THAT'S WHY HE DIDN'T TALK TO YOU GUYS.
BECAUSE HE DIDN'T KNOW WHAT TO SAY.
BUT ...
THIS IS JUST MY HYPOTHESIS, BUT...
...THE ENEMY MIGHT HAVE...
...COME INTO POSSESSION OF A POWER WE KNOW NOTHING ABOUT.

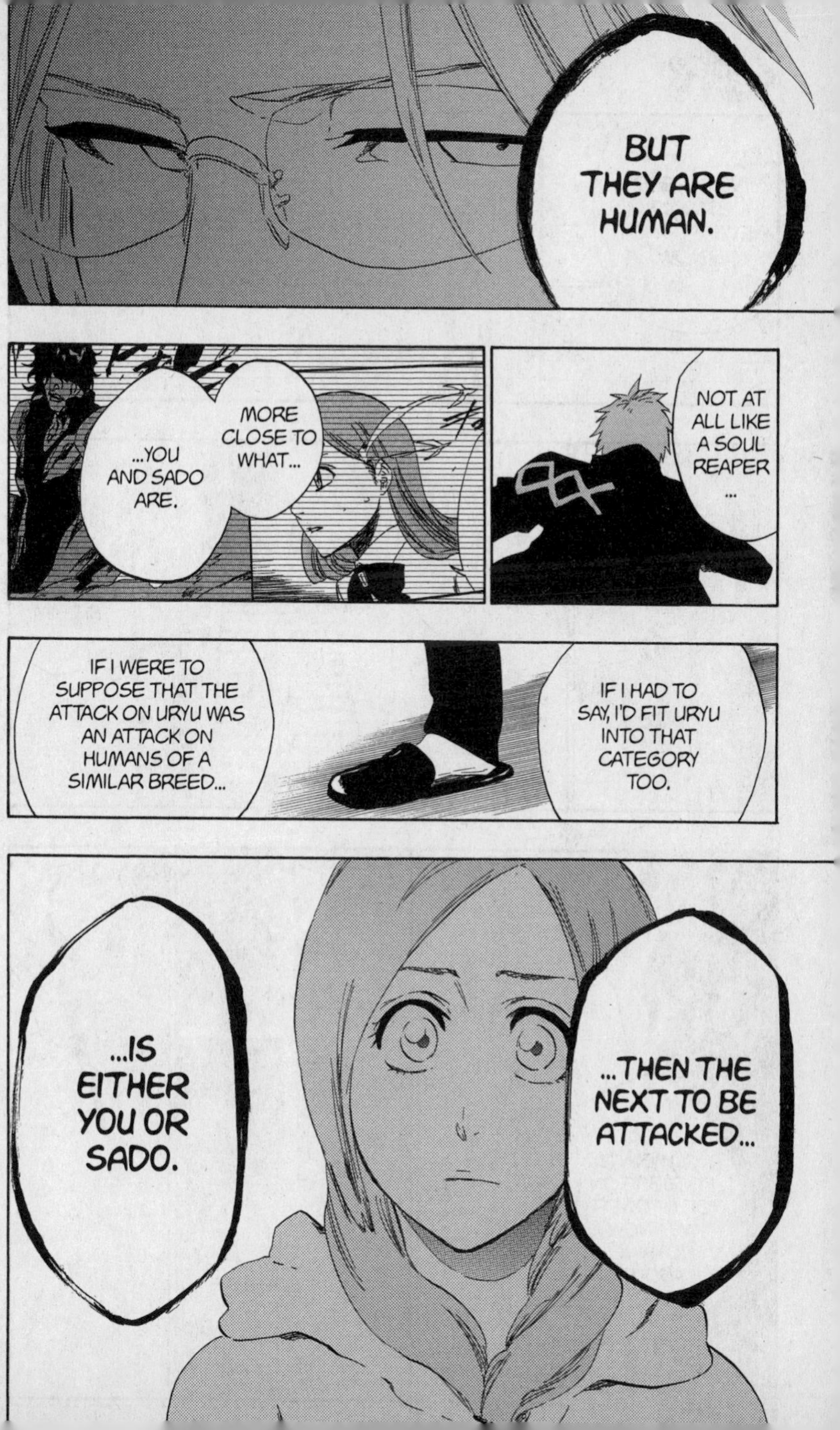
BUT THEY ARE HUMAN.
NOT AT ALL LIKE A SOUL REAPER ...
MORE CLOSE TO WHAT...
...YOU AND SADO ARE.
IF I HAD TO SAY, I'D FIT URYU INTO THAT CATEGORY TOO.
IF I WERE TO SUPPOSE THAT THE ATTACK ON URYU WAS AN ATTACK ON HUMANS OF A SIMILAR BREED...
...THEN THE NEXT TO BE ATTACKED...
...IS EITHER YOU OR SADO.

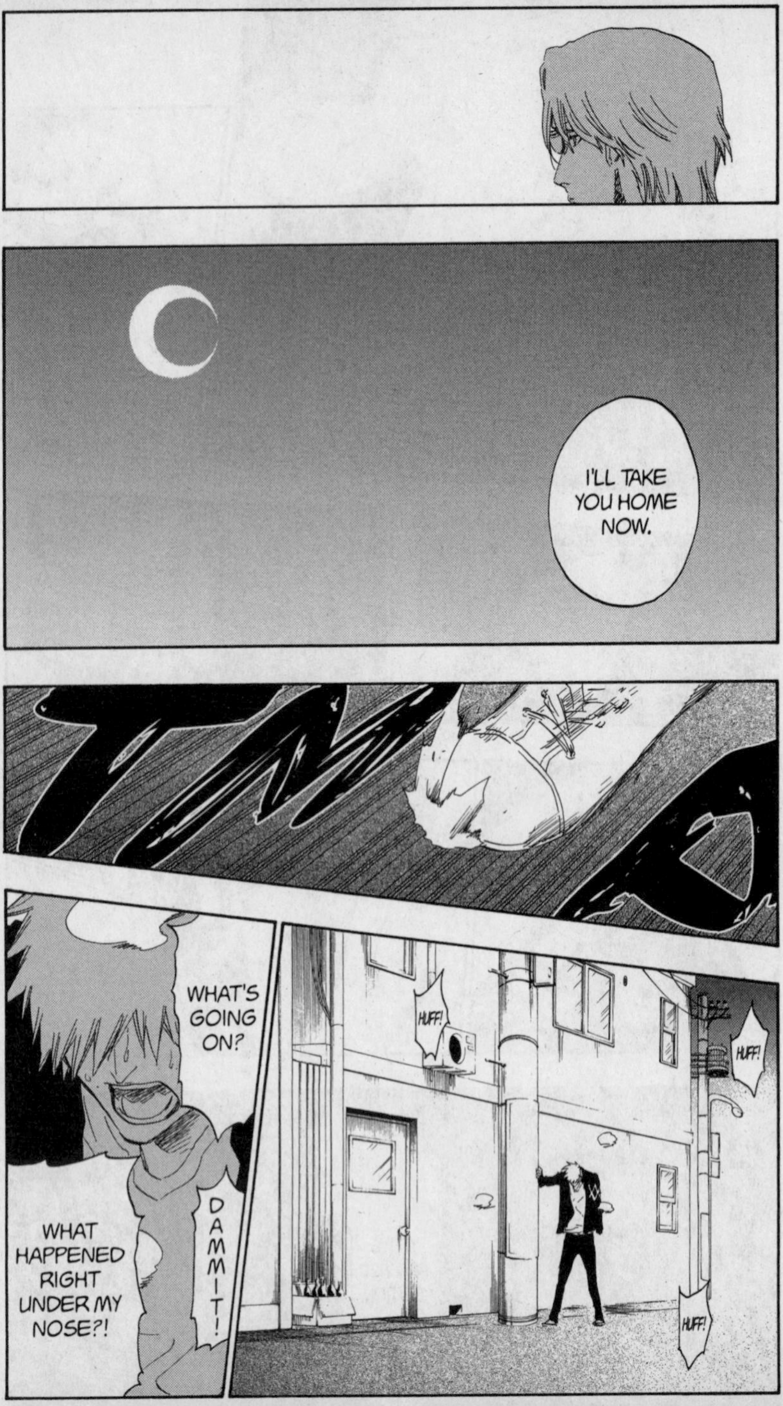
I'LL TAKE YOU HOME NOW.
HUFF!
HUFF!
HUFF!
DAMMIT!
WHAT'S GOING ON?
WHAT HAPPENED RIGHT UNDER MY NOSE?!

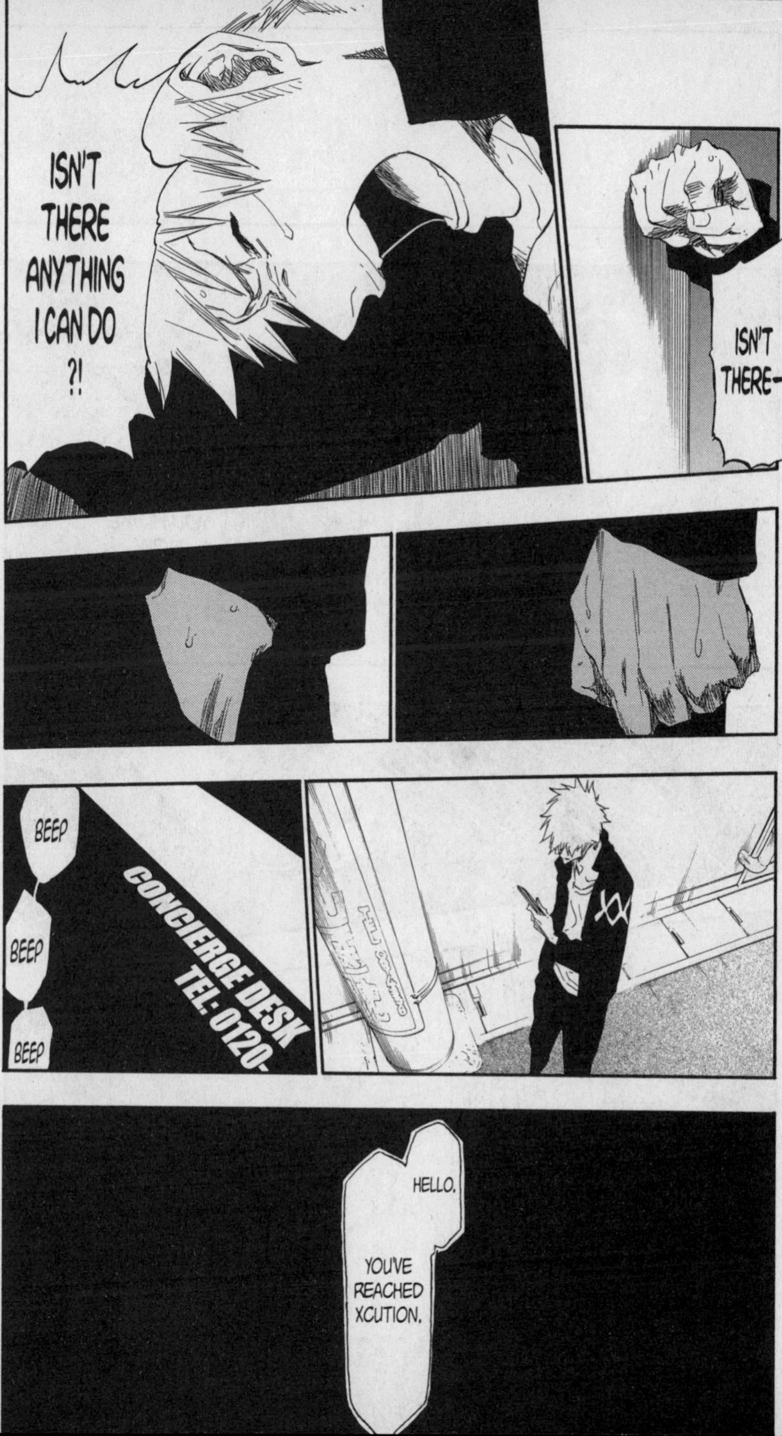
ISN'T THERE-
ISN'T THERE ANYTHING I CAN DO ?!
CONCIERGE DESK TEL: 0120-
BEEP
BEEP
BEEP
HELLO.
YOU'VE REACHED XCUTION.

READ THIS WAY

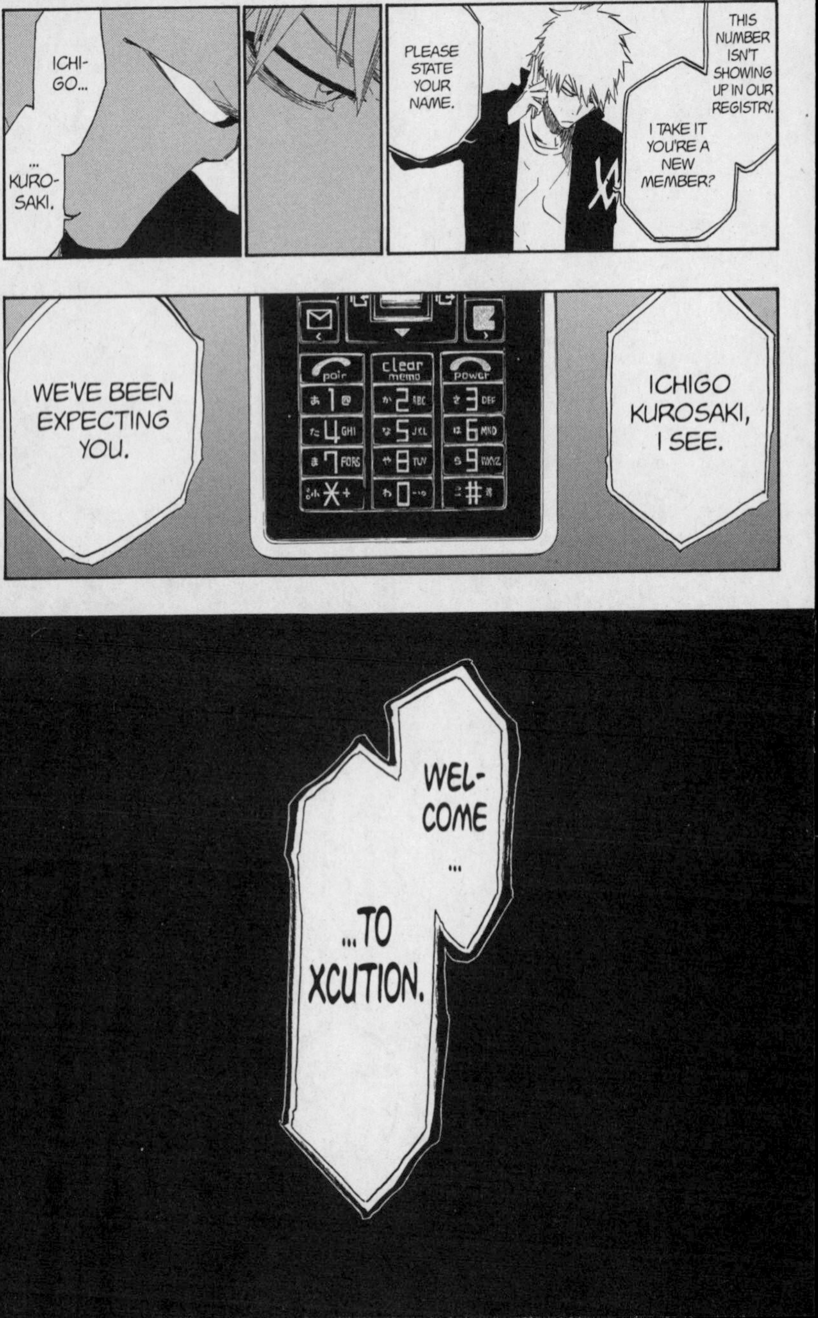
THIS NUMBER ISN'T SHOWING UP IN OUR REGISTRY.
I TAKE IT YOU'RE A NEW MEMBER?
PLEASE STATE YOUR NAME.
ICHI-GO...
...KURO-SAKI.
ICHIGO KUROSAKI, I SEE.
WE'VE BEEN EXPECTING YOU.
WEL-COME...
...TO XCUTION.

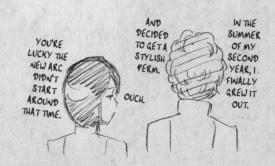

IN THE SUMMER OF MY SECOND YEAR, I FINALLY GREW IT OUT.
AND DECIDED TO GET A STYLISH PERM.
OUCH.
YOU'RE LUCKY THE NEW ARC DIDN'T START AROUND THAT TIME.

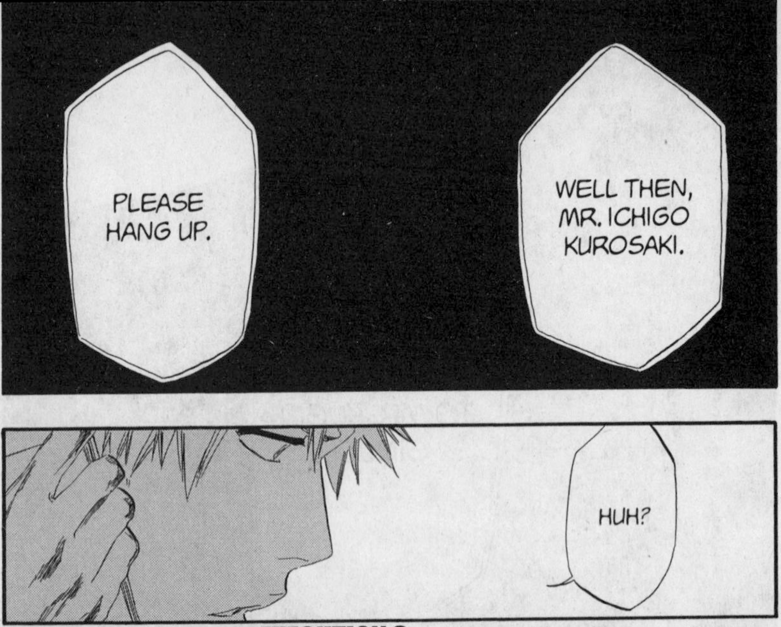
WELL THEN, MR. ICHIGO KUROSAKI.
PLEASE HANG UP.
HUH?

431. Welcome to our EXECUTION 3

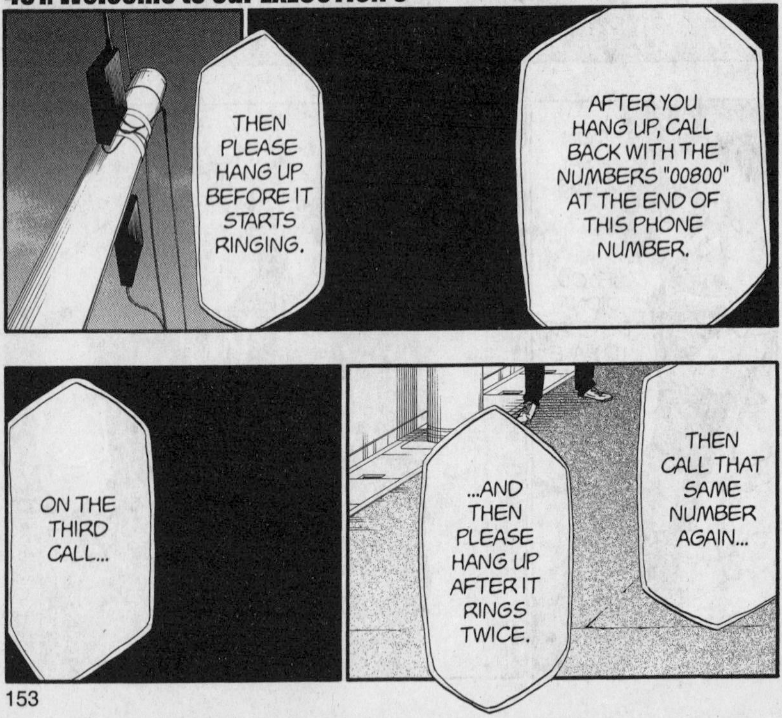
AFTER YOU HANG UP, CALL BACK WITH THE NUMBERS "00800" AT THE END OF THIS PHONE NUMBER.
THEN PLEASE HANG UP BEFORE IT STARTS RINGING.
THEN CALL THAT SAME NUMBER AGAIN...
...AND THEN PLEASE HANG UP AFTER IT RINGS TWICE.
ON THE THIRD CALL...

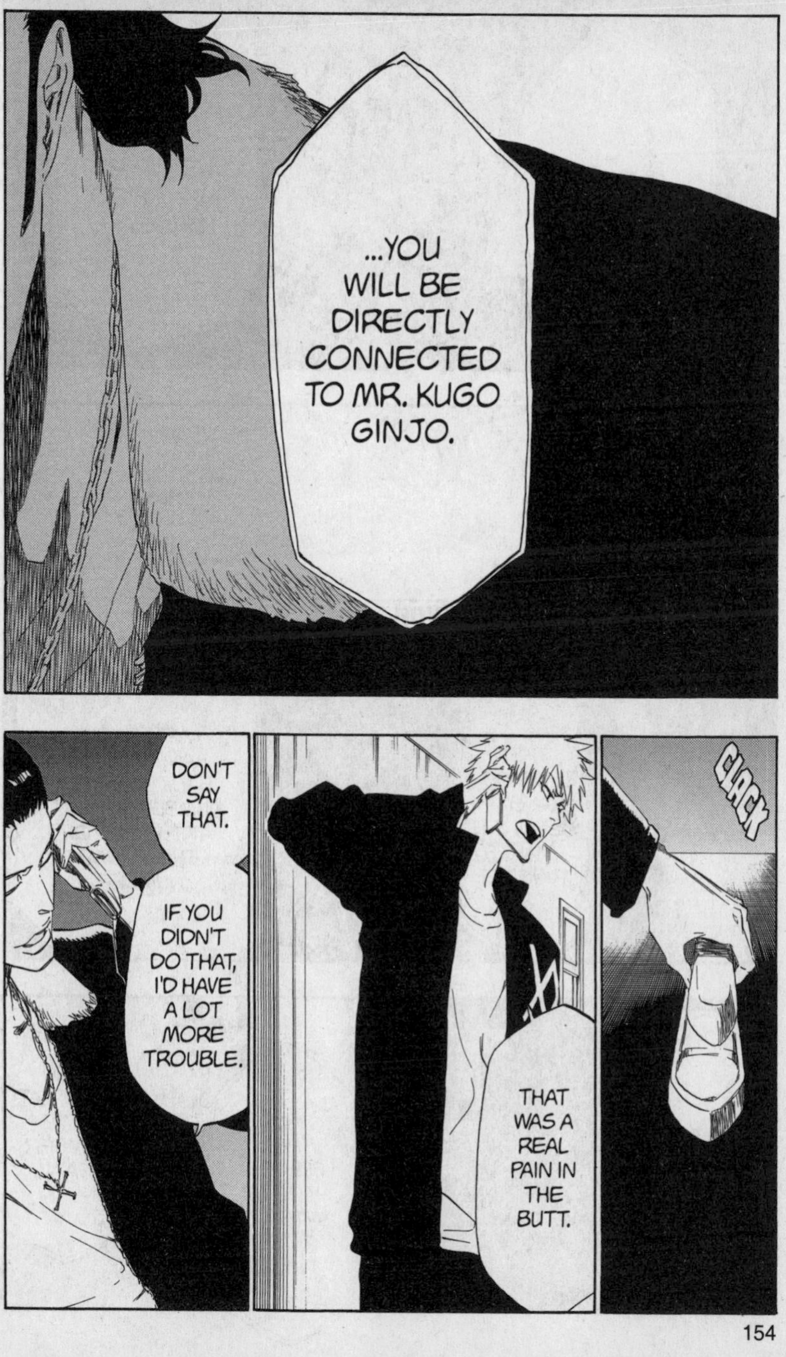
...YOU WILL BE DIRECTLY CONNECTED TO MR. KUGO GINJO.
CLACK
THAT WAS A REAL PAIN IN THE BUTT.
DON'T SAY THAT.
IF YOU DIDN'T DO THAT, I'D HAVE A LOT MORE TROUBLE.

READ THIS WAY

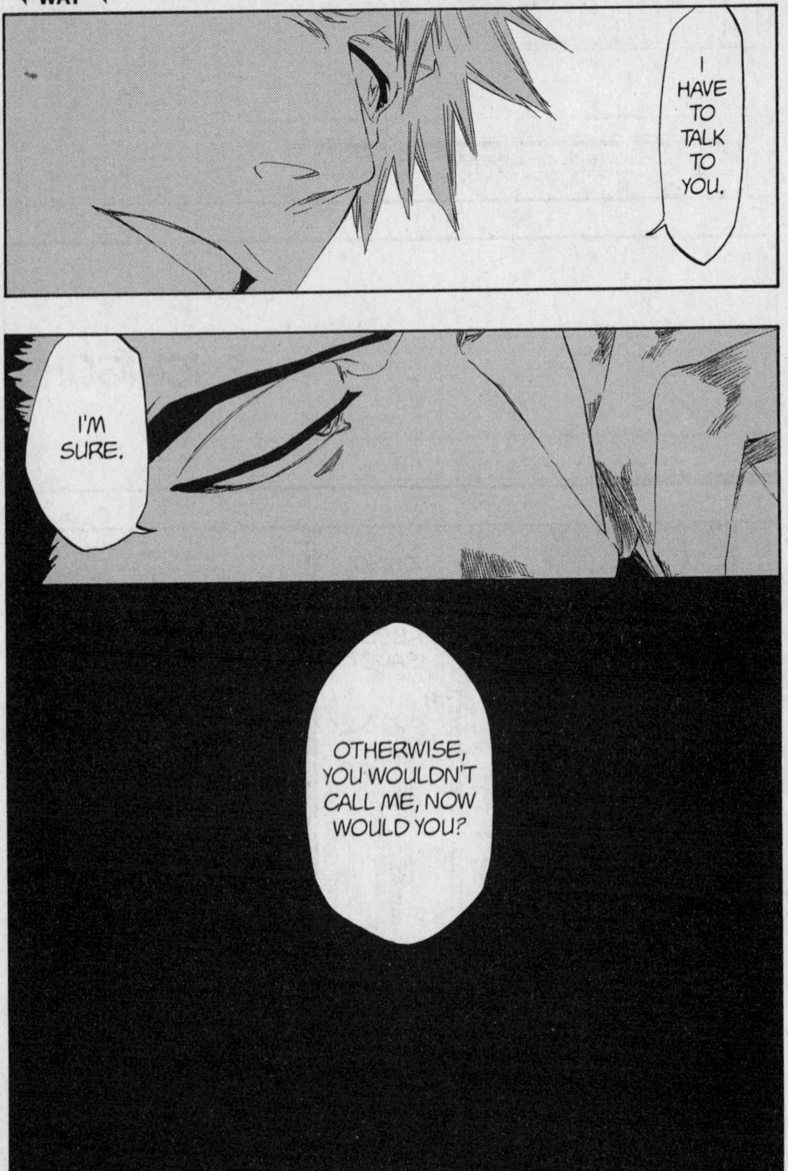
I HAVE TO TALK TO YOU.
I'M SURE.
OTHERWISE, YOU WOULDN'T CALL ME, NOW WOULD YOU?

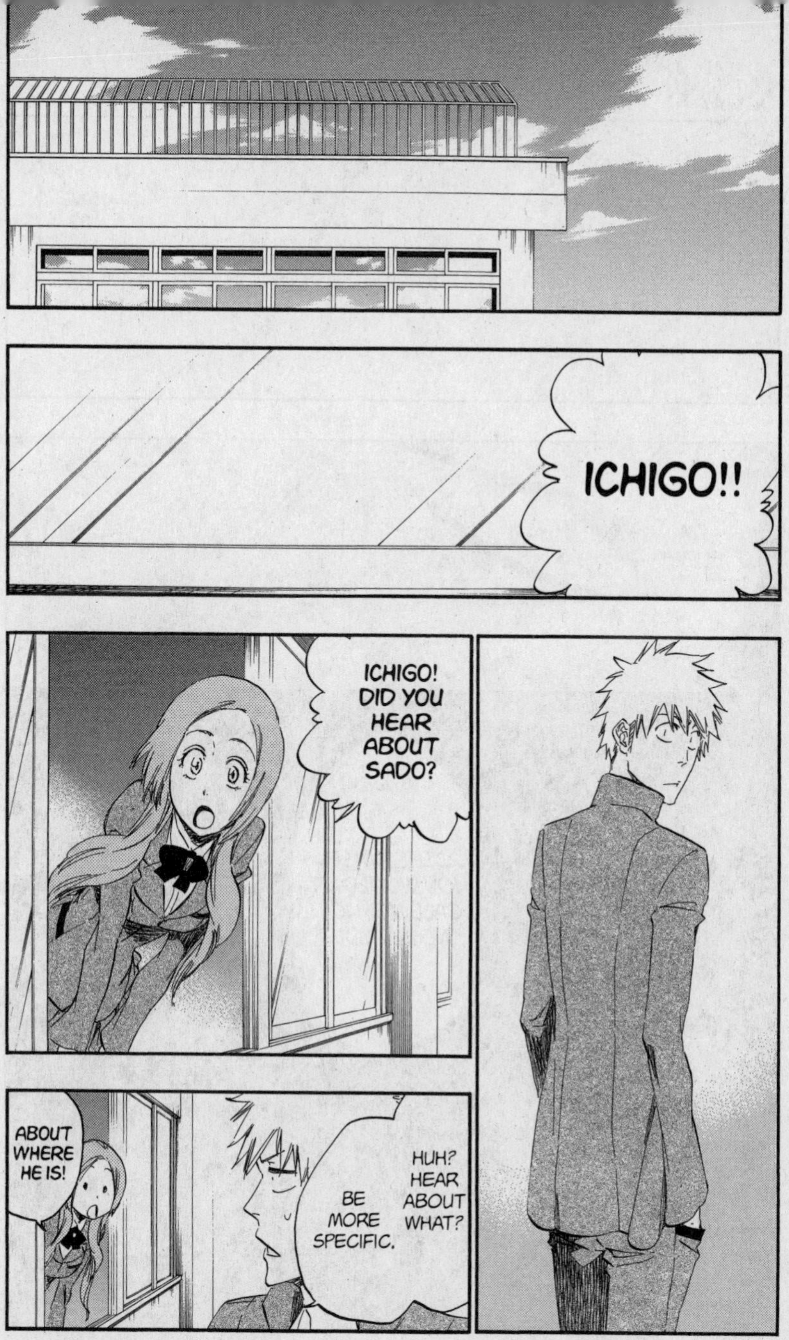
ICHIGO!!
ICHIGO! DID YOU HEAR ABOUT SADO?
HUH? HEAR ABOUT WHAT?
BE MORE SPECIFIC.
ABOUT WHERE HE IS!

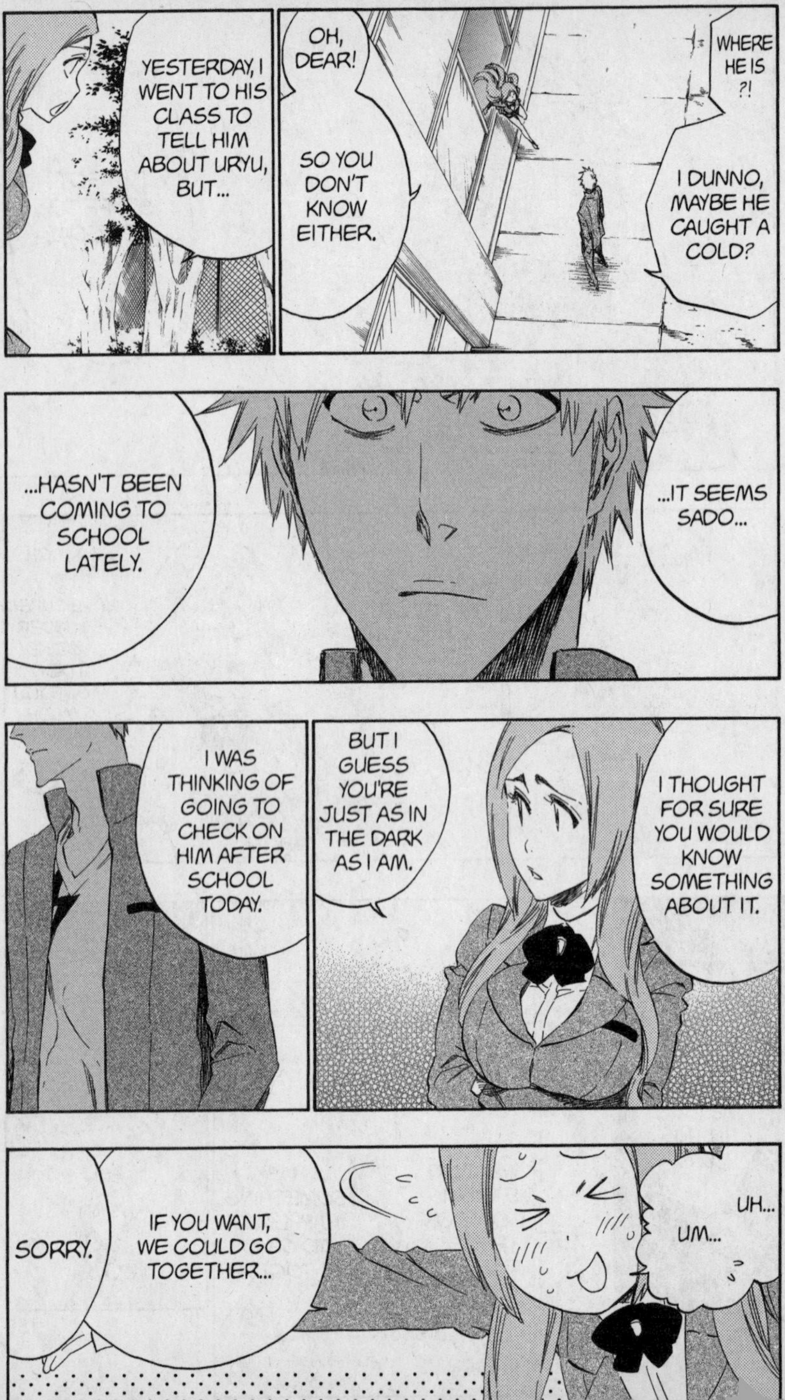
WHERE HE IS ?!
I DUNNO, MAYBE HE CAUGHT A COLD?
OH, DEAR!
SO YOU DON'T KNOW EITHER.
YESTERDAY, I WENT TO HIS CLASS TO TELL HIM ABOUT URYU, BUT...
...IT SEEMS SADO...
...HASN'T BEEN COMING TO SCHOOL LATELY.
I THOUGHT FOR SURE YOU WOULD KNOW SOMETHING ABOUT IT.
BUT I GUESS YOU'RE JUST AS IN THE DARK AS I AM.
I WAS THINKING OF GOING TO CHECK ON HIM AFTER SCHOOL TODAY.
UH...
UM...
IF YOU WANT, WE COULD GO TOGETHER...
SORRY.

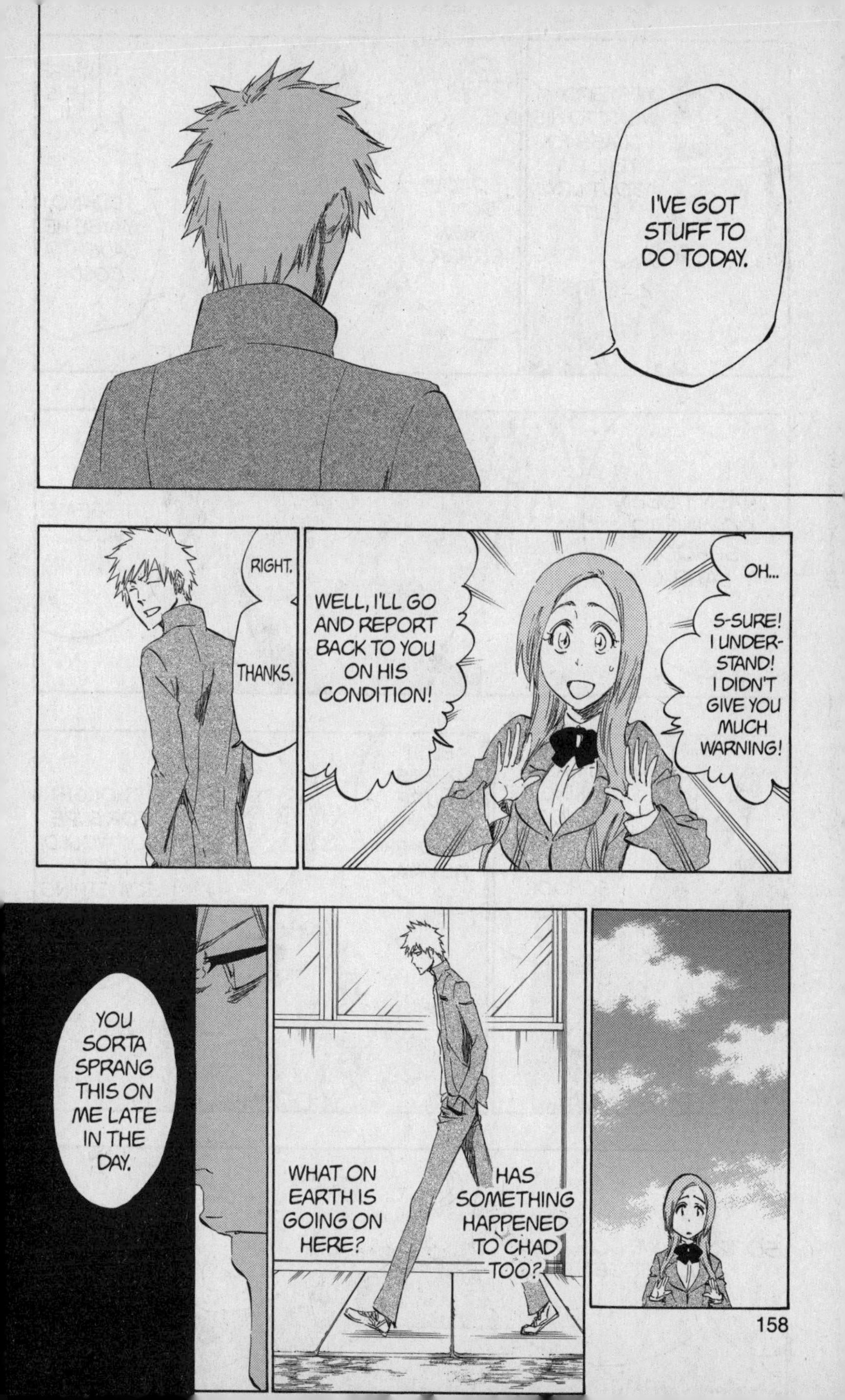
I'VE GOT STUFF TO DO TODAY.
OH...
S-SURE! I UNDERSTAND! I DIDN'T GIVE YOU MUCH WARNING!
WELL, I'LL GO AND REPORT BACK TO YOU ON HIS CONDITION!
RIGHT.
THANKS.
HAS SOMETHING HAPPENED TO CHAD TOO?
WHAT ON EARTH IS GOING ON HERE?
YOU SORTA SPRANG THIS ON ME LATE IN THE DAY.

READ THIS WAY

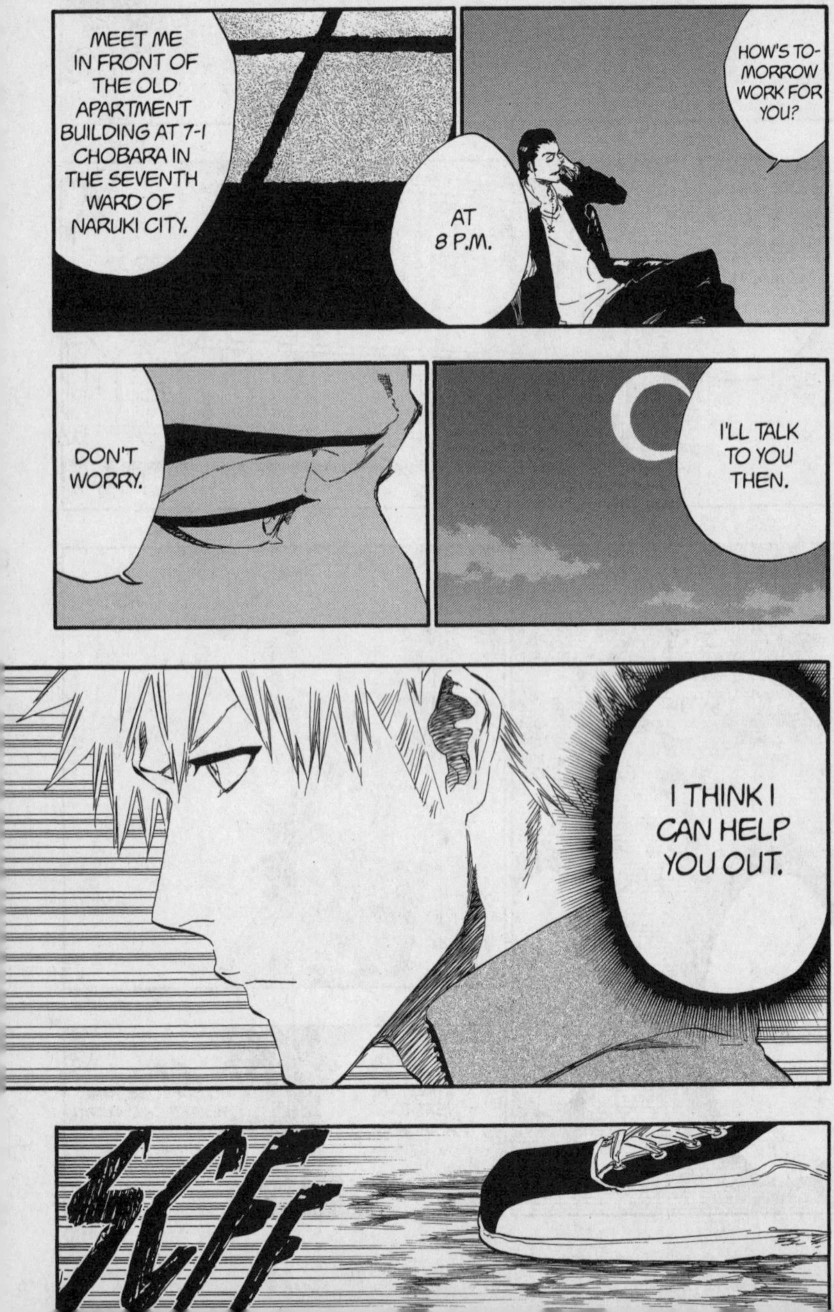
HOW'S TO-MORROW WORK FOR YOU?
AT 8 P.M.
MEET ME IN FRONT OF THE OLD APARTMENT BUILDING AT 7-1 CHOBARA IN THE SEVENTH WARD OF NARUKI CITY.
I'LL TALK TO YOU THEN.
DON'T WORRY.
I THINK I CAN HELP YOU OUT.
SCFF

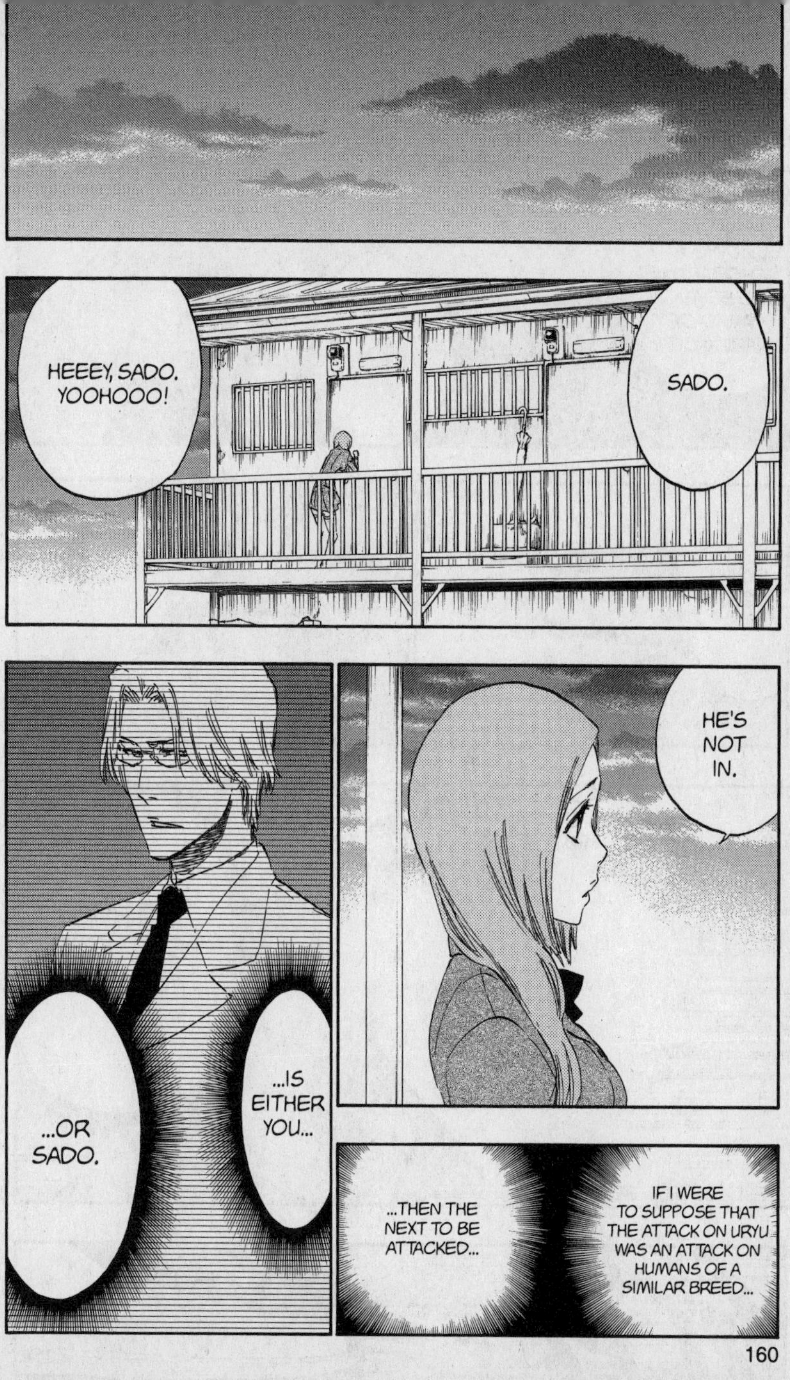
SADO.
HEEEY, SADO. YOOHOOO!
HE'S NOT IN.
IF I WERE TO SUPPOSE THAT THE ATTACK ON URYU WAS AN ATTACK ON HUMANS OF A SIMILAR BREED...
...THEN THE NEXT TO BE ATTACKED...
...IS EITHER YOU...
...OR SADO.

READ THIS WAY

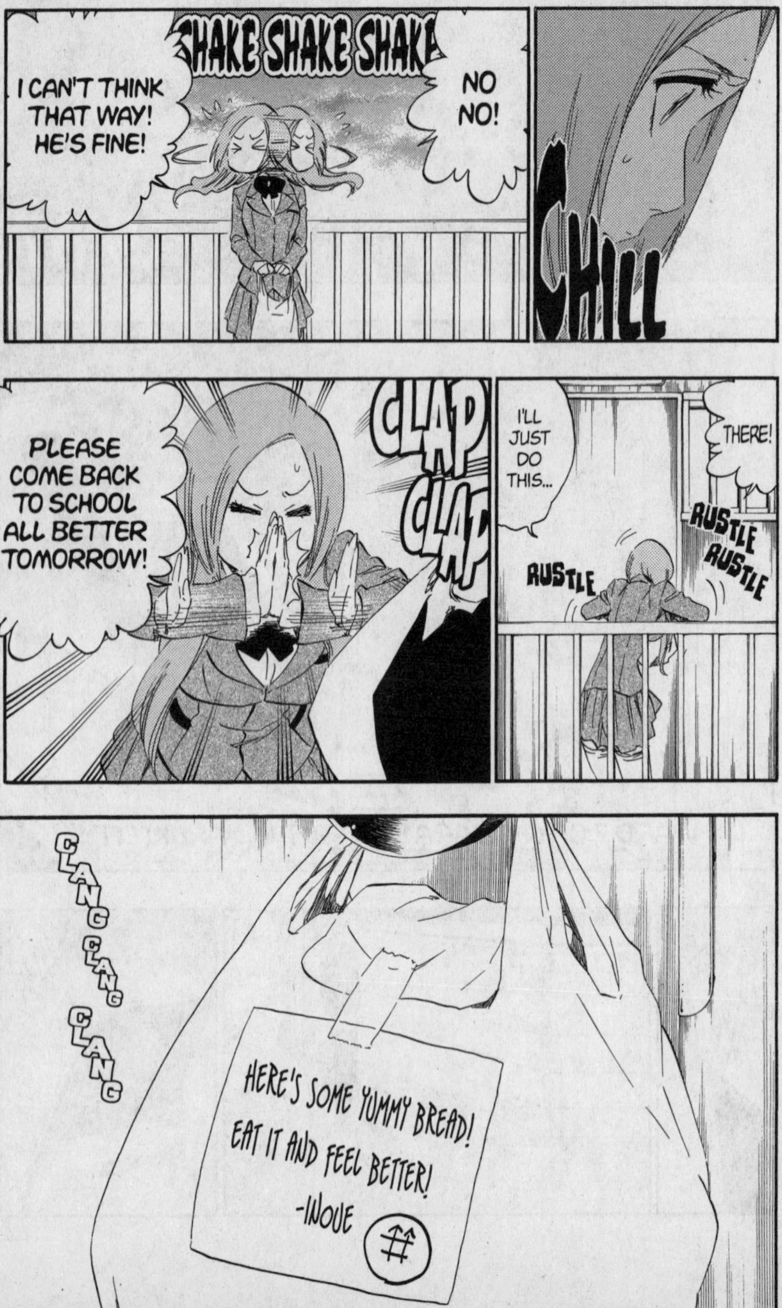
CHILL
SHAKE SHAKE SHAKE
NO NO!
I CAN'T THINK THAT WAY! HE'S FINE!
THERE!
I'LL JUST DO THIS...
RUSTLE RUSTLE
RUSTLE
CLAP CLAP
PLEASE COME BACK TO SCHOOL ALL BETTER TOMORROW!
HERE'S SOME YUMMY BREAD! EAT IT AND FEEL BETTER! -INOUE
CLANG CLANG CLANG

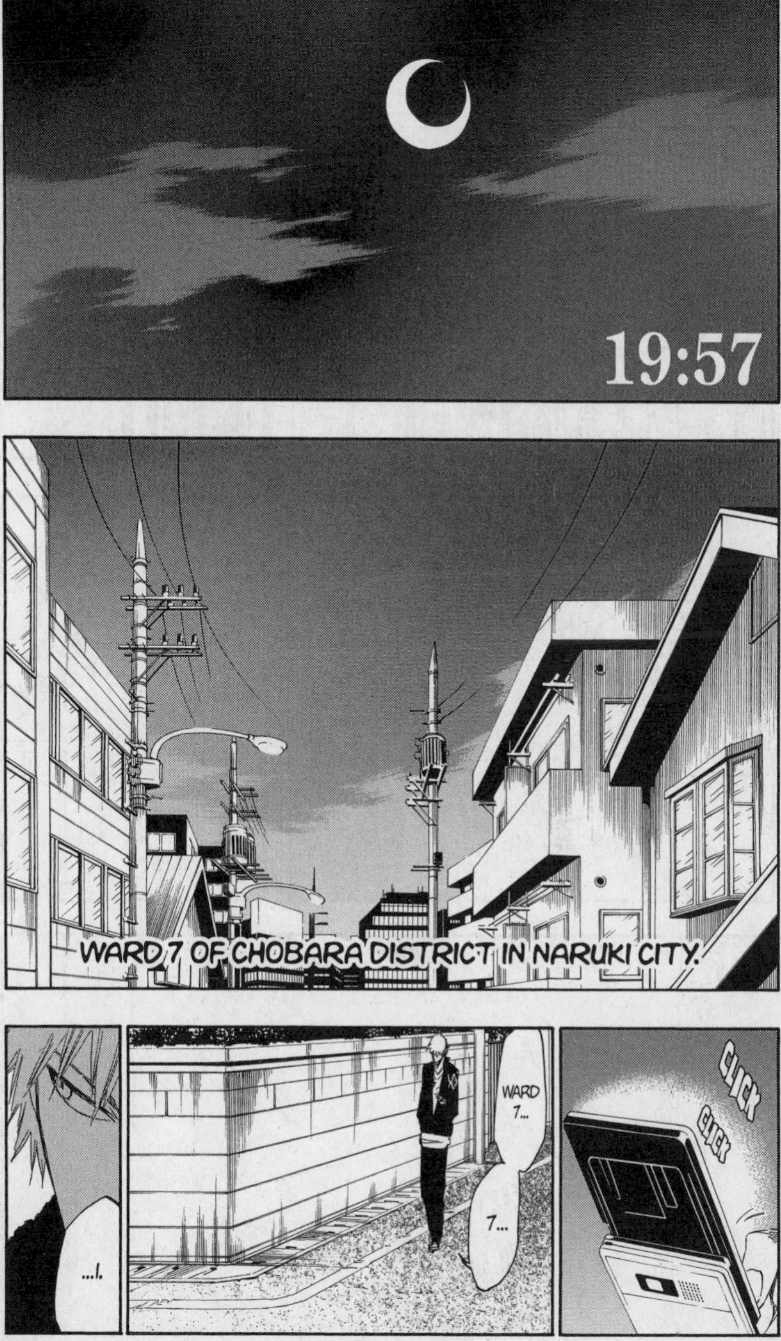
19:57
WARD 7 OF CHOBARA DISTRICT IN NARUKI CITY.
CLICK
CLICK
WARD 7...
7...
...!

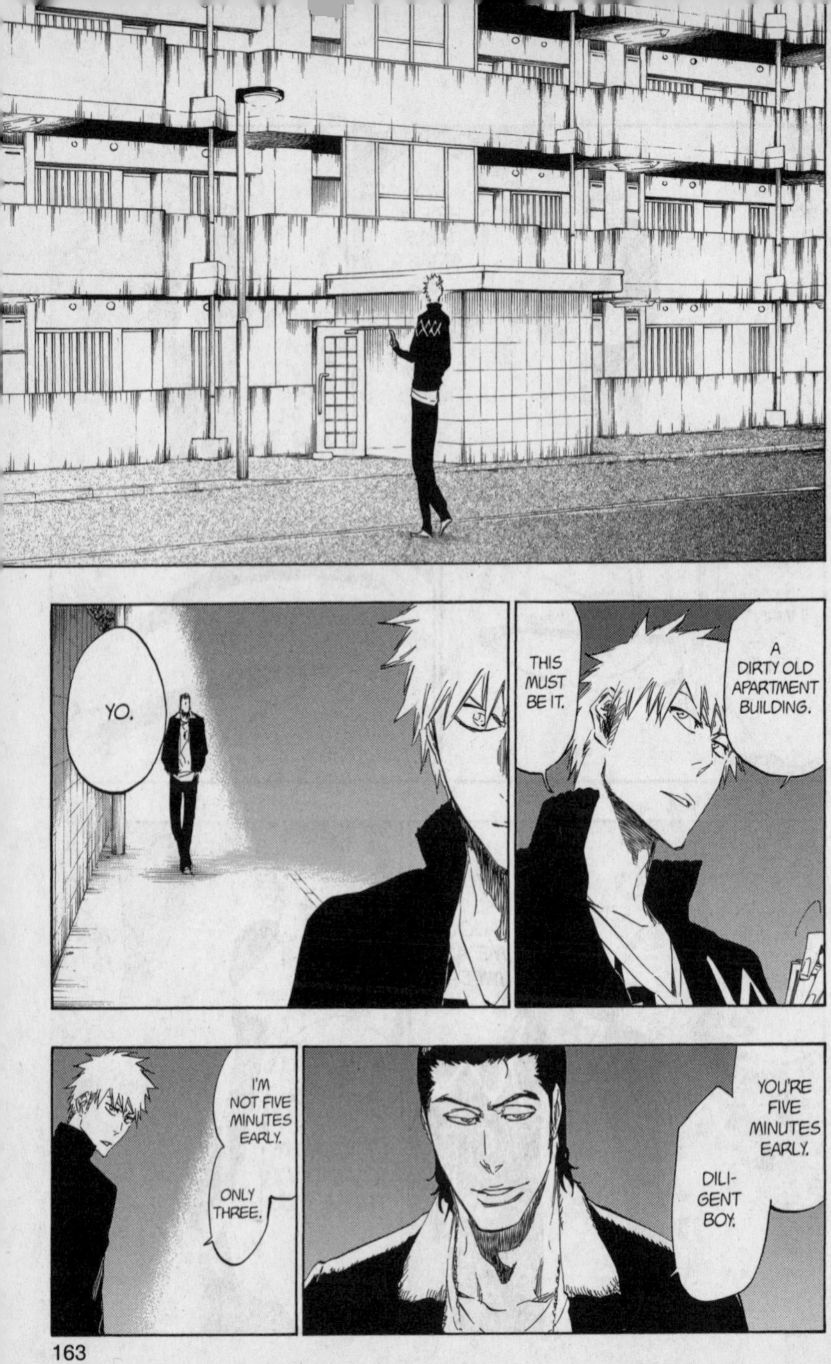
A DIRTY OLD APARTMENT BUILDING.
THIS MUST BE IT.
YO.
YOU'RE FIVE MINUTES EARLY.
DILI-GENT BOY.
I'M NOT FIVE MINUTES EARLY.
ONLY THREE.

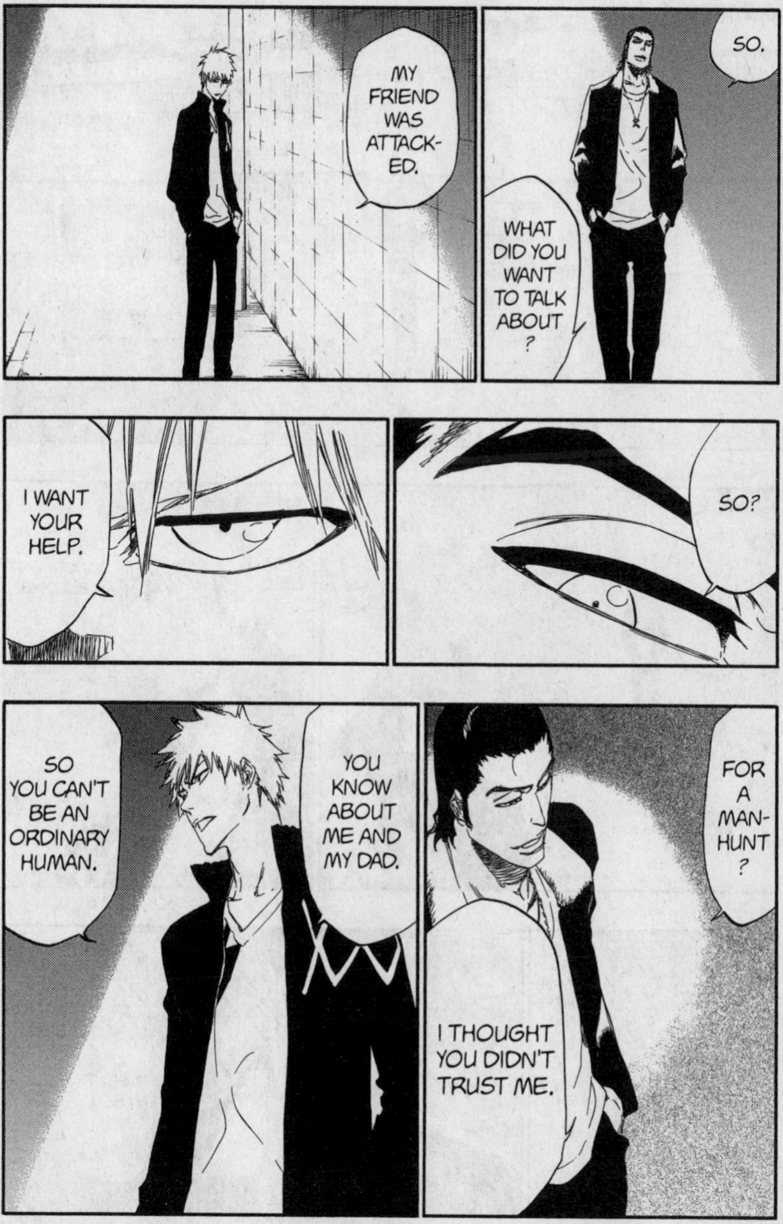
SO.
WHAT DID YOU WANT TO TALK ABOUT?
MY FRIEND WAS ATTACK-ED.
SO?
I WANT YOUR HELP.
FOR A MAN-HUNT?
I THOUGHT YOU DIDN'T TRUST ME.
YOU KNOW ABOUT ME AND MY DAD.
SO YOU CAN'T BE AN ORDINARY HUMAN.

READ THIS WAY

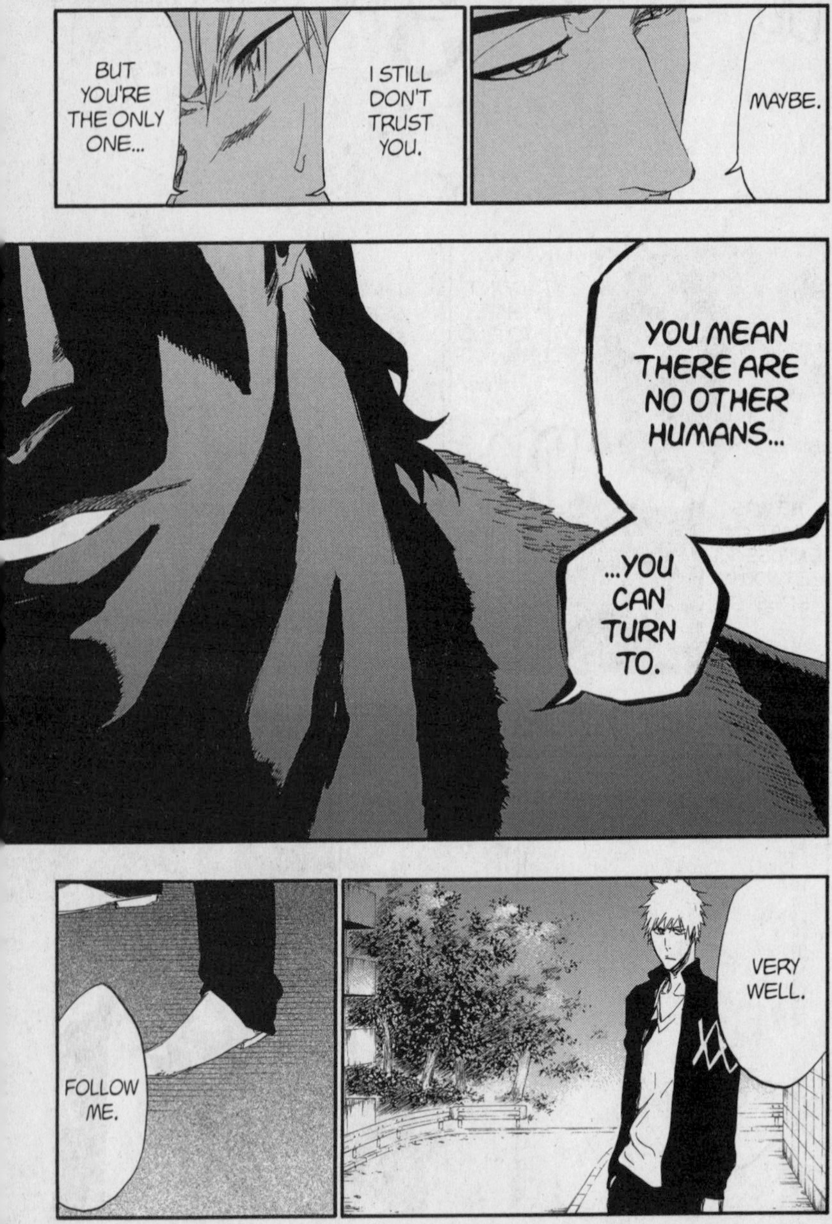
MAYBE.
I STILL DON'T TRUST YOU.
BUT YOU'RE THE ONLY ONE...
YOU MEAN THERE ARE NO OTHER HUMANS...
...YOU CAN TURN TO.
VERY WELL.
FOLLOW ME.

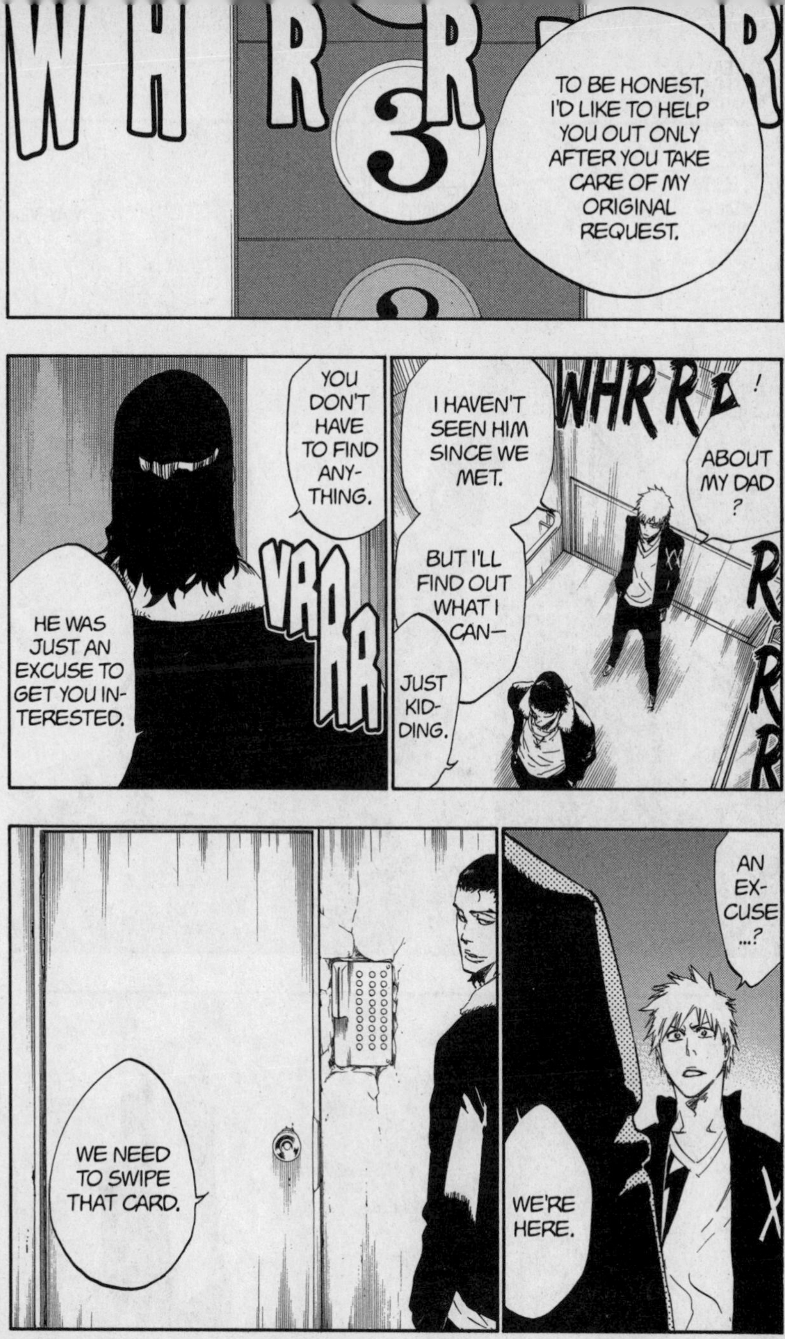
WHRRR
TO BE HONEST, I'D LIKE TO HELP YOU OUT ONLY AFTER YOU TAKE CARE OF MY ORIGINAL REQUEST.
WHRR!
ABOUT MY DAD?
I HAVEN'T SEEN HIM SINCE WE MET.
BUT I'LL FIND OUT WHAT I CAN—
JUST KID-DING.
RRRR
YOU DON'T HAVE TO FIND ANY-THING.
VRRR
HE WAS JUST AN EXCUSE TO GET YOU IN-TERESTED.
AN EX-CUSE...?
WE'RE HERE.
WE NEED TO SWIPE THAT CARD.

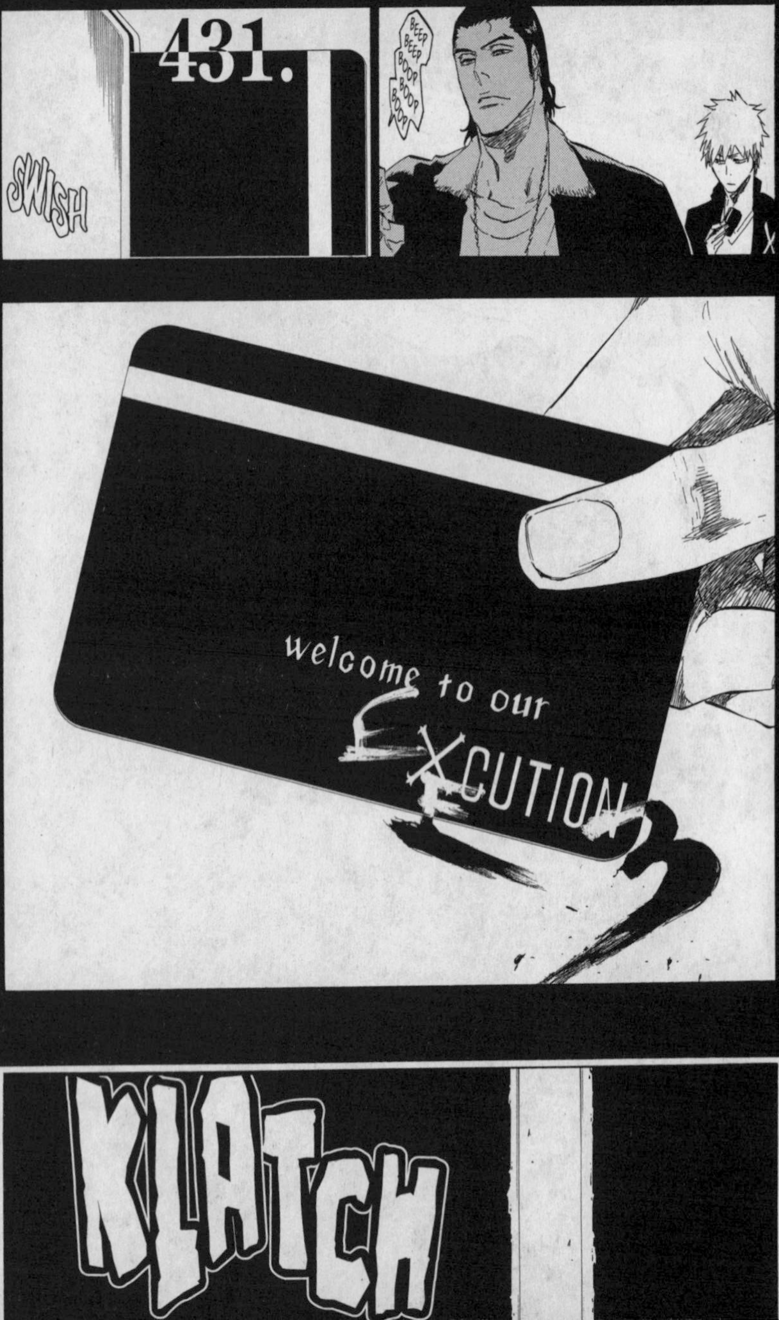
BEEP BEEP BOOP BOOP BOOP
431.
SWISH
welcome to our EXECUTION
KLATCH

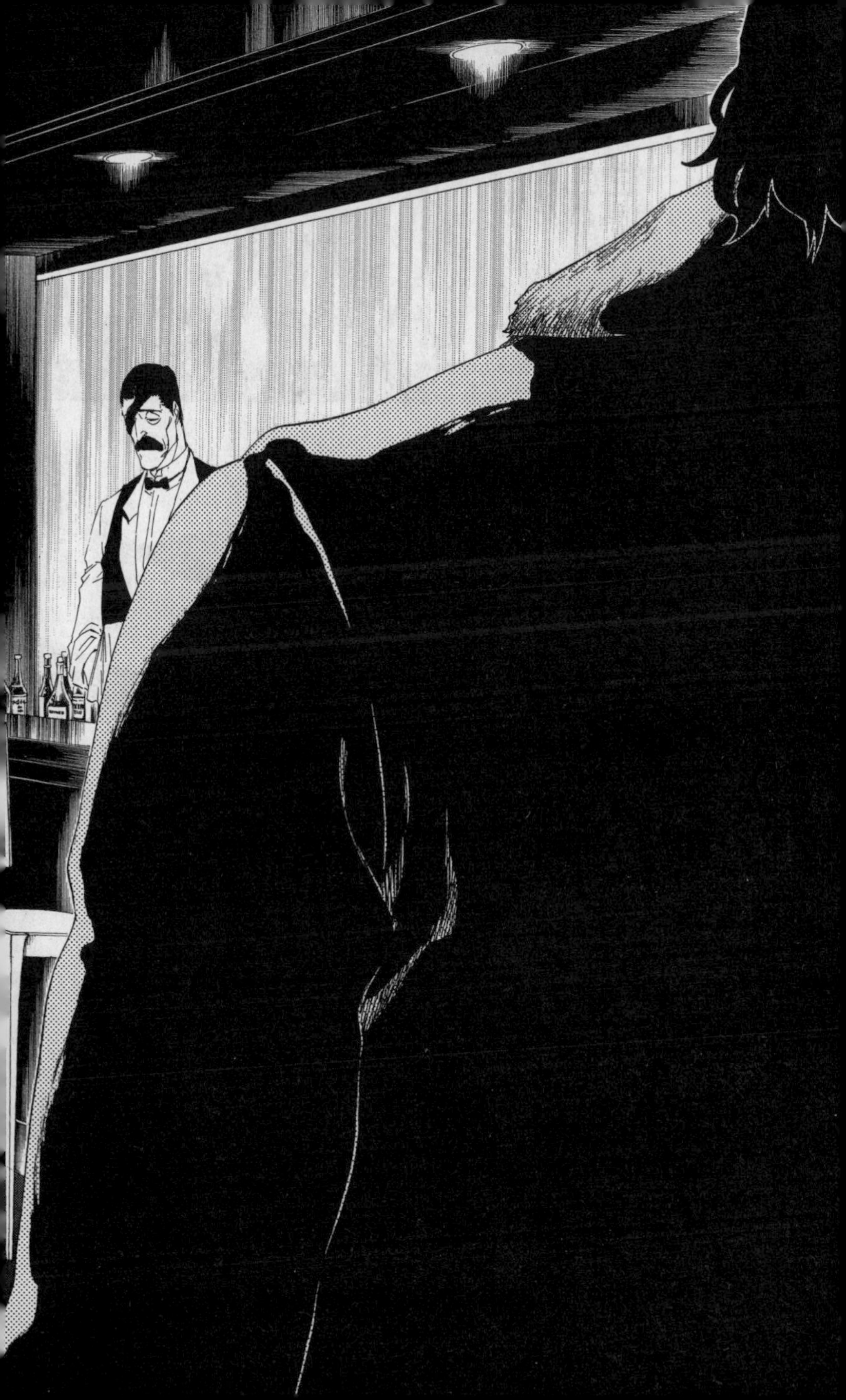

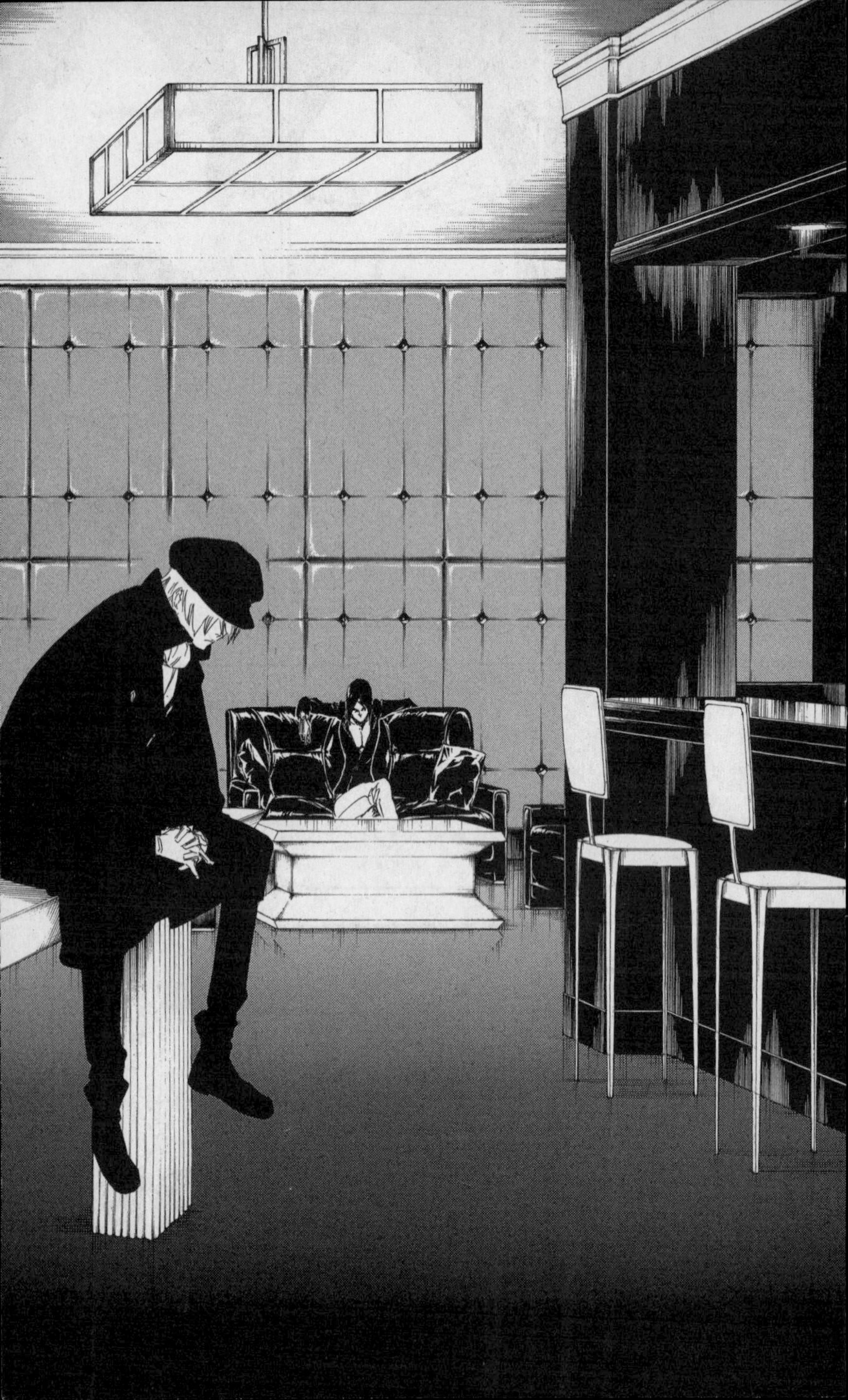

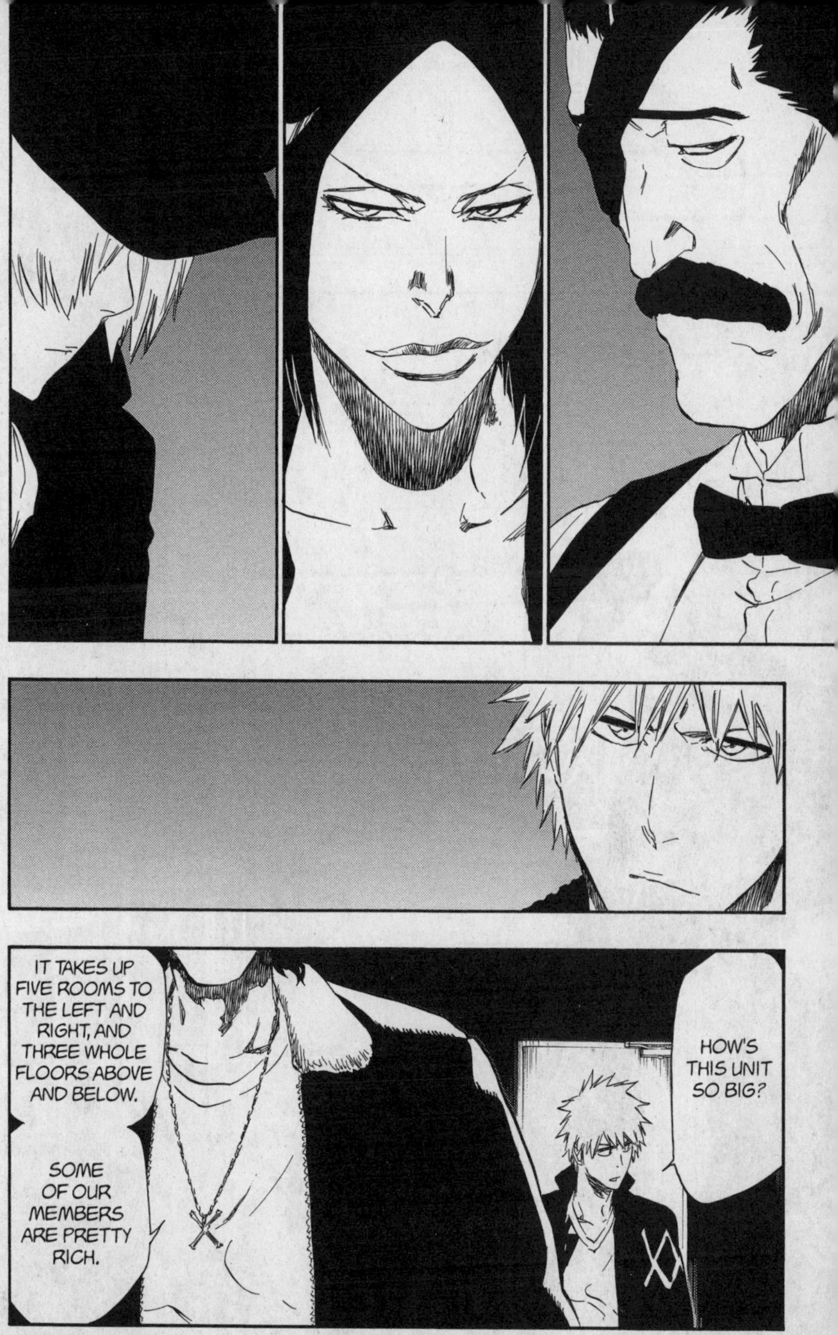
HOW'S THIS UNIT SO BIG?
IT TAKES UP FIVE ROOMS TO THE LEFT AND RIGHT, AND THREE WHOLE FLOORS ABOVE AND BELOW.
SOME OF OUR MEMBERS ARE PRETTY RICH.

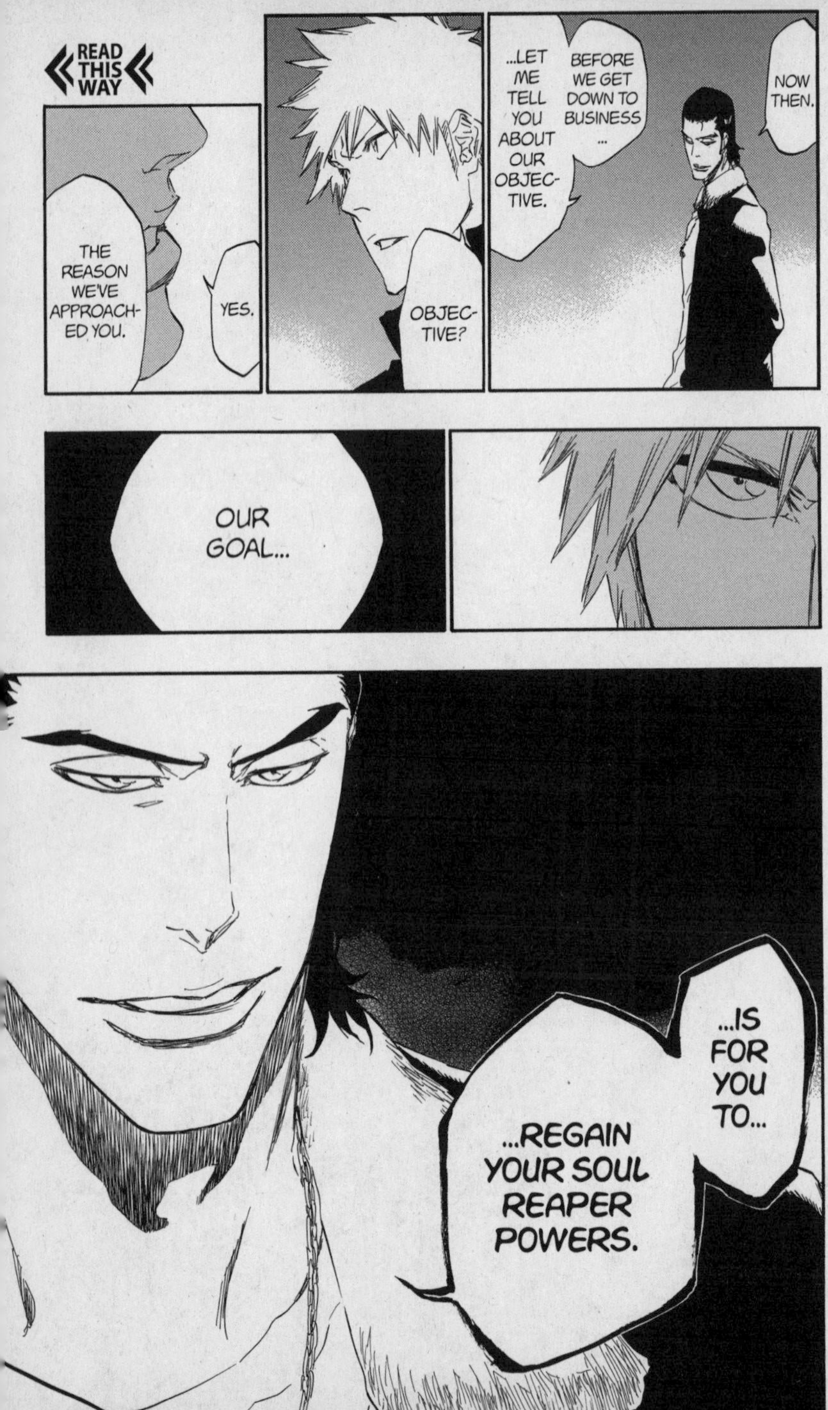
READ THIS WAY
NOW THEN.
BEFORE WE GET DOWN TO BUSINESS...
...LET ME TELL YOU ABOUT OUR OBJECTIVE.
OBJECTIVE?
YES.
THE REASON WE'VE APPROACHED YOU.
OUR GOAL...
...IS FOR YOU TO...
...REGAIN YOUR SOUL REAPER POWERS.

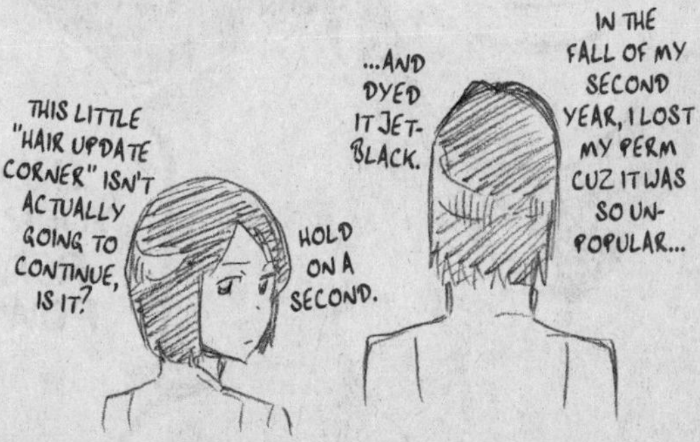
IN THE FALL OF MY SECOND YEAR, I LOST MY PERM CUZ IT WAS SO UN-POPULAR...
...AND DYED IT JET-BLACK.
HOLD ON A SECOND.
THIS LITTLE "HAIR UPDATE CORNER" ISN'T ACTUALLY GOING TO CONTINUE, IS IT?

432. The Soul Pantheism

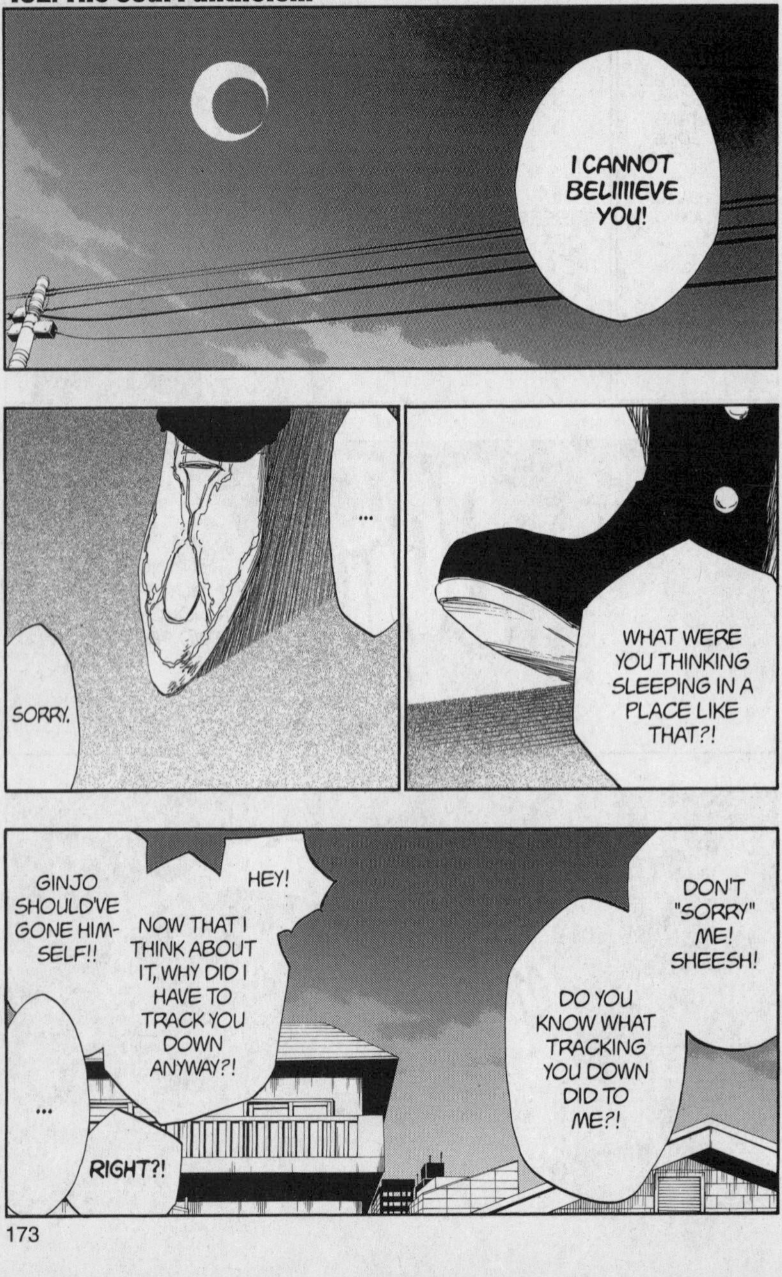
I CANNOT BELIIIIEVE YOU!
WHAT WERE YOU THINKING SLEEPING IN A PLACE LIKE THAT?!
...
SORRY.
DON'T "SORRY" ME! SHEESH!
DO YOU KNOW WHAT TRACKING YOU DOWN DID TO ME?!
HEY!
NOW THAT I THINK ABOUT IT, WHY DID I HAVE TO TRACK YOU DOWN ANYWAY?!
GINJO SHOULD'VE GONE HIM-SELF!!
RIGHT?!
...

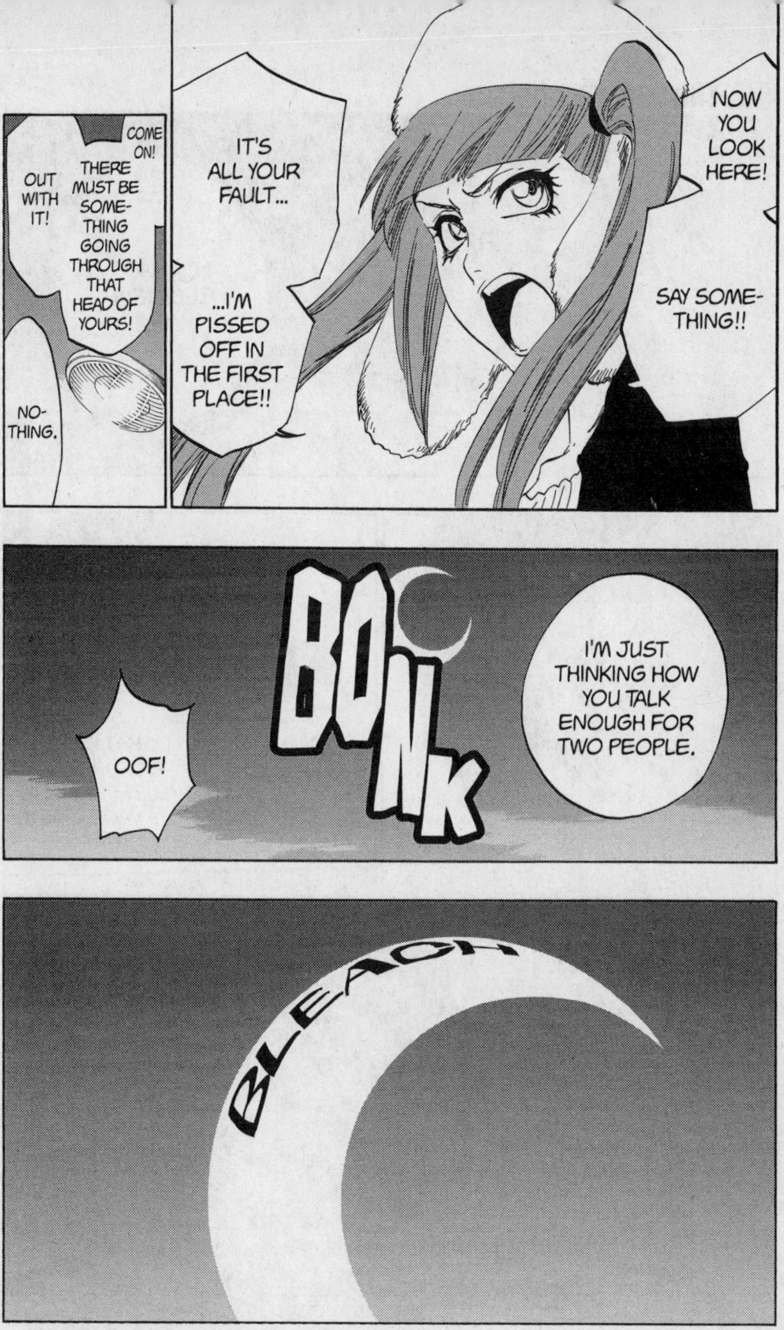
NOW YOU LOOK HERE!
SAY SOMETHING!!
IT'S ALL YOUR FAULT...
...I'M PISSED OFF IN THE FIRST PLACE!!
COME ON! THERE MUST BE SOMETHING GOING THROUGH THAT HEAD OF YOURS!
OUT WITH IT!
NOTHING.
I'M JUST THINKING HOW YOU TALK ENOUGH FOR TWO PEOPLE.
BONK
OOF!
BLEACH

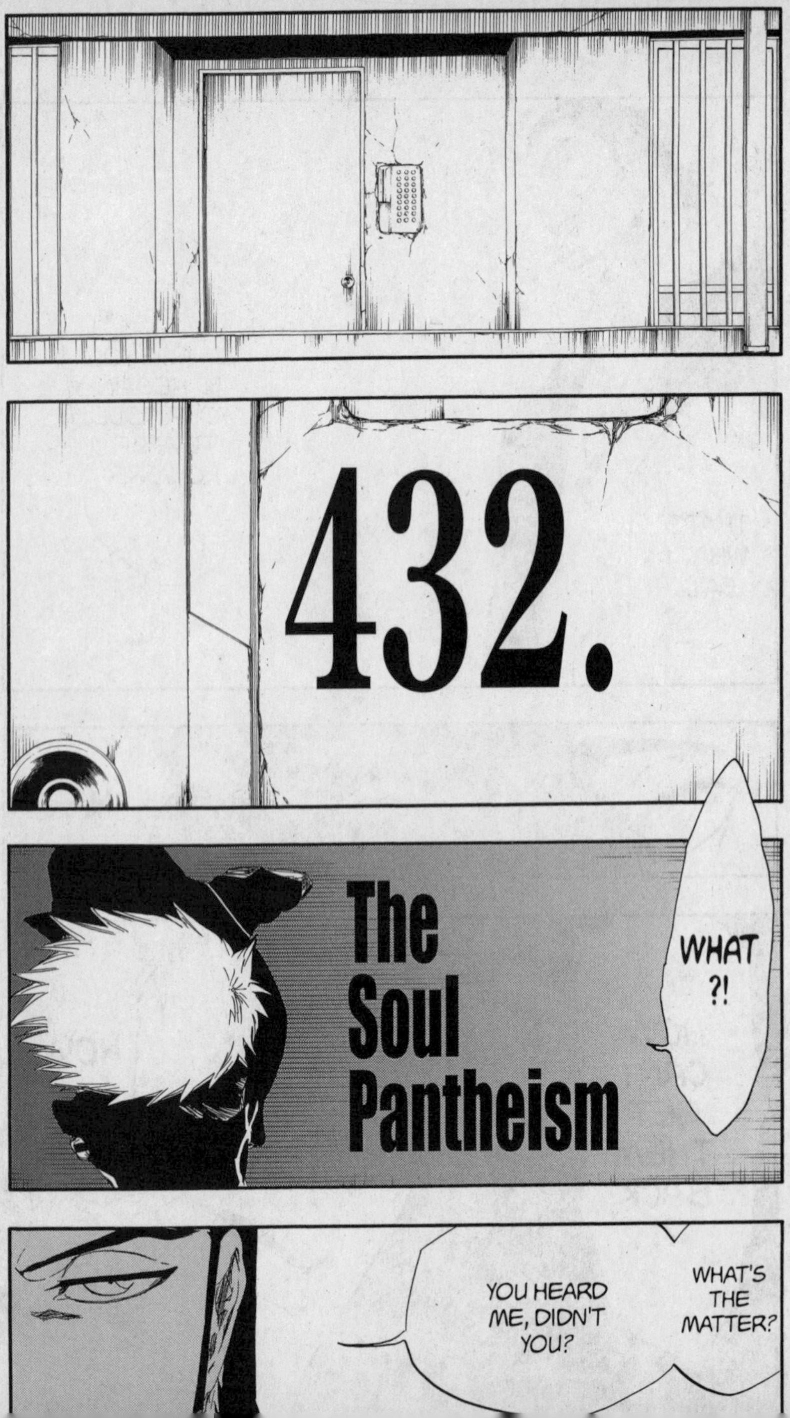
432.
WHAT ?!
The Soul Pantheism
WHAT'S THE MATTER?
YOU HEARD ME, DIDN'T YOU?

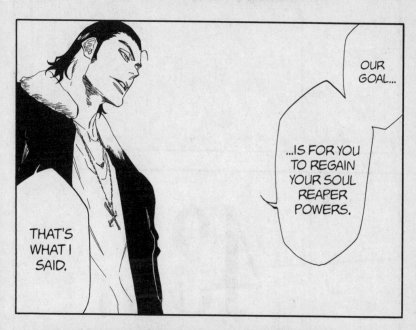

OUR GOAL...

...IS FOR YOU TO REGAIN YOUR SOUL REAPER POWERS.

THAT'S WHAT I SAID.

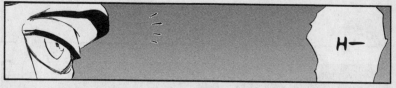

H—

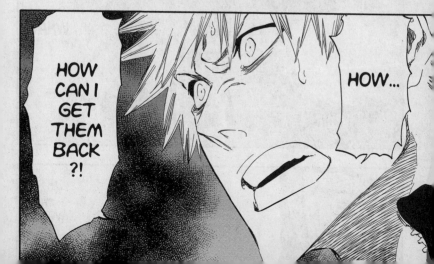

HOW CAN I GET THEM BACK ?!

HOW...

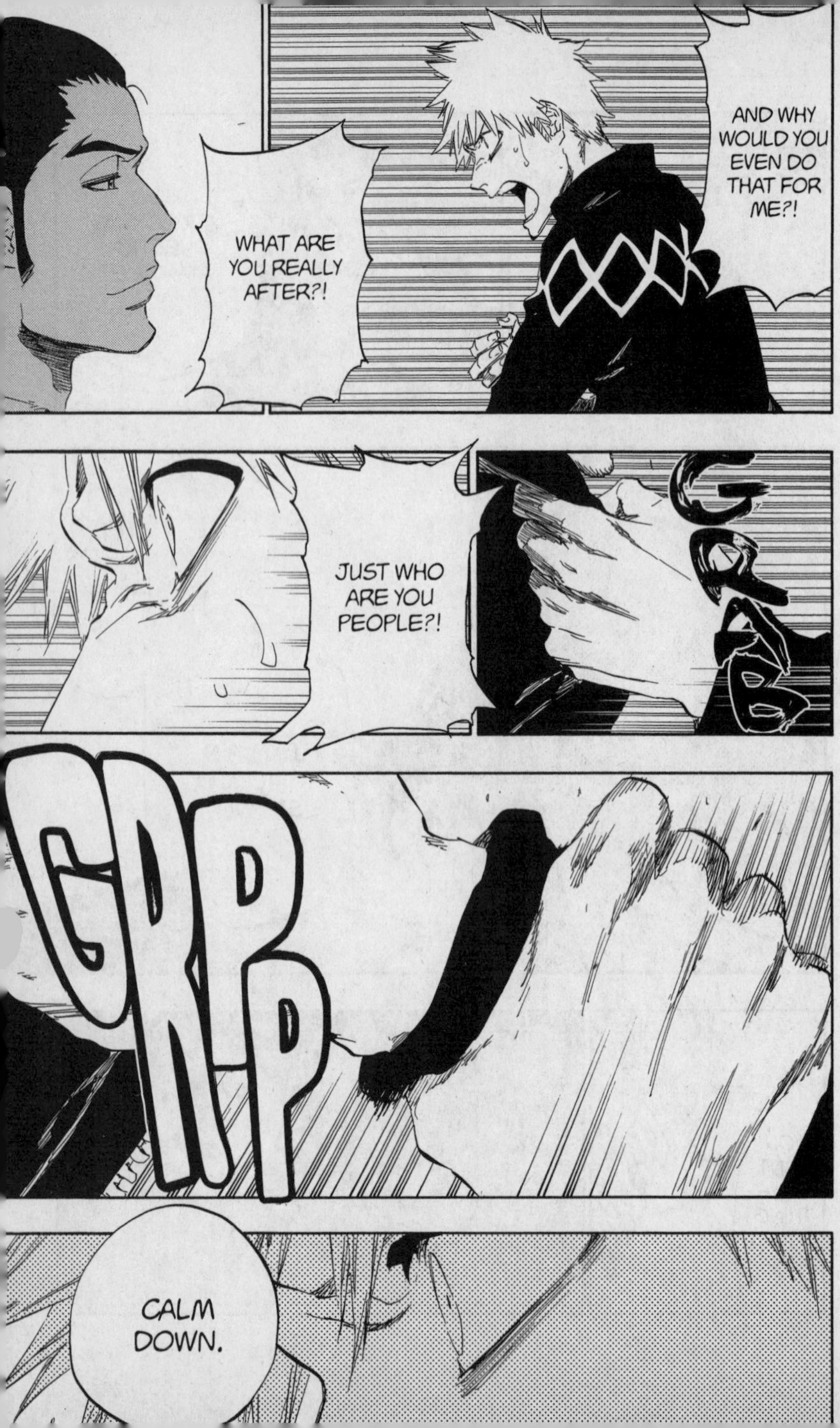

AND WHY WOULD YOU EVEN DO THAT FOR ME?!
WHAT ARE YOU REALLY AFTER?!
GRAB
JUST WHO ARE YOU PEOPLE?!
GRIP
CALM DOWN.

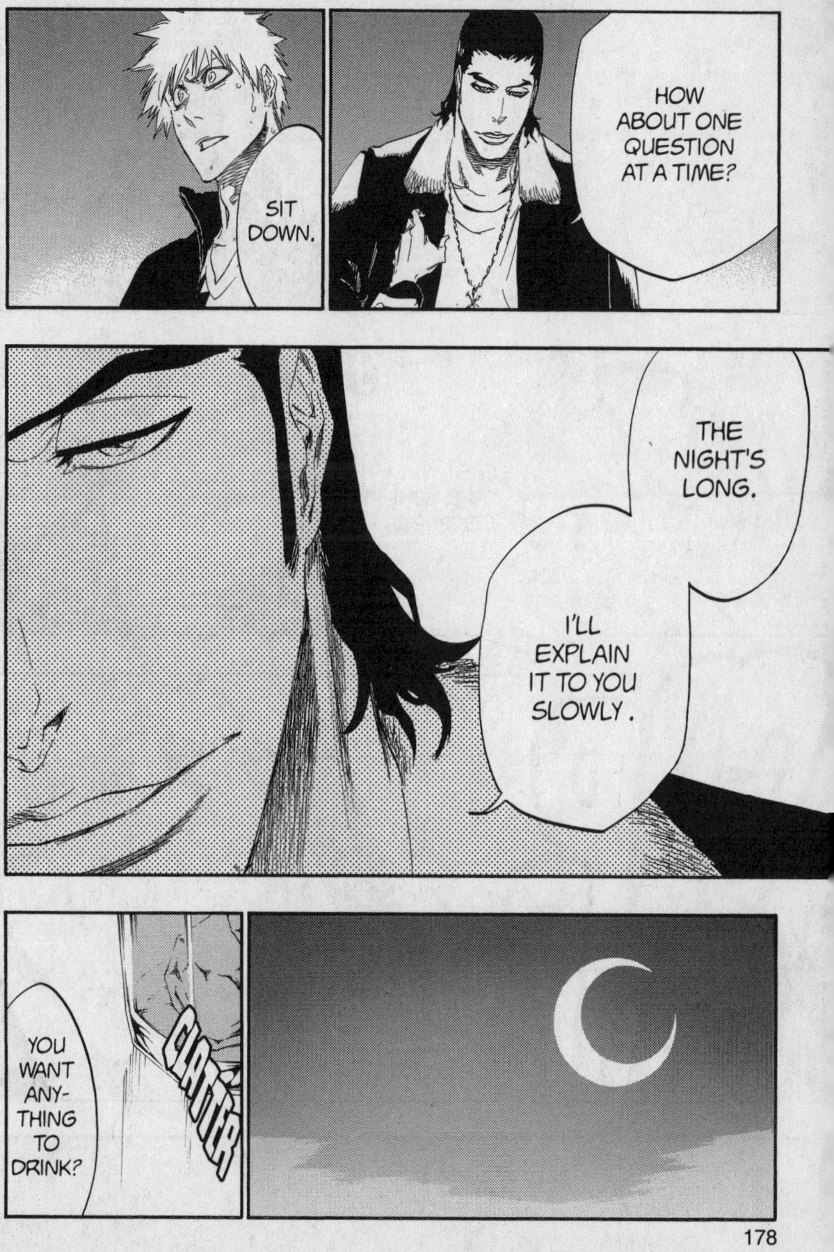
HOW ABOUT ONE QUESTION AT A TIME?
SIT DOWN.
THE NIGHT'S LONG.
I'LL EXPLAIN IT TO YOU SLOWLY.
CLATTER
YOU WANT ANY-THING TO DRINK?

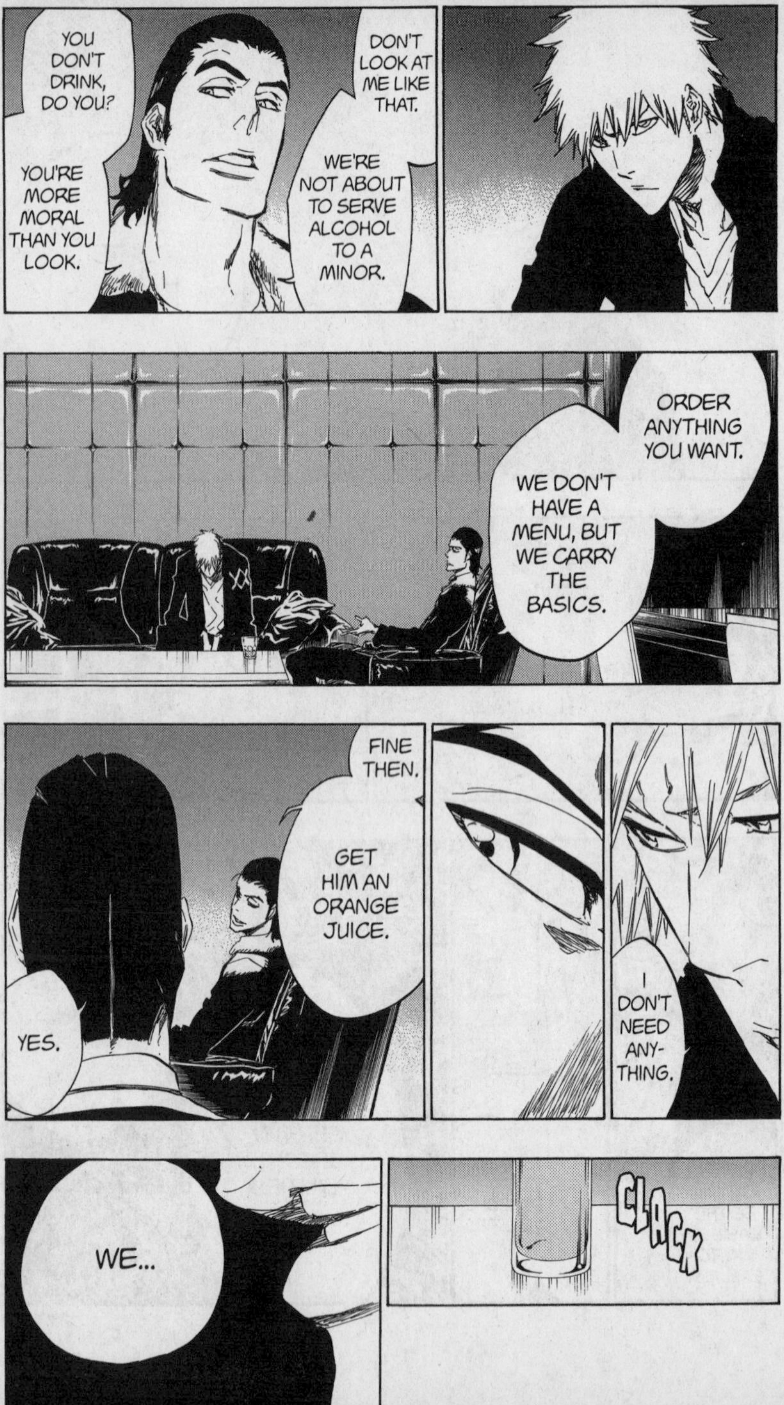
DON'T LOOK AT ME LIKE THAT.
WE'RE NOT ABOUT TO SERVE ALCOHOL TO A MINOR.
YOU DON'T DRINK, DO YOU?
YOU'RE MORE MORAL THAN YOU LOOK.
ORDER ANYTHING YOU WANT.
WE DON'T HAVE A MENU, BUT WE CARRY THE BASICS.
I DON'T NEED ANY-THING.
FINE THEN.
GET HIM AN ORANGE JUICE.
YES.
CLACK
WE...

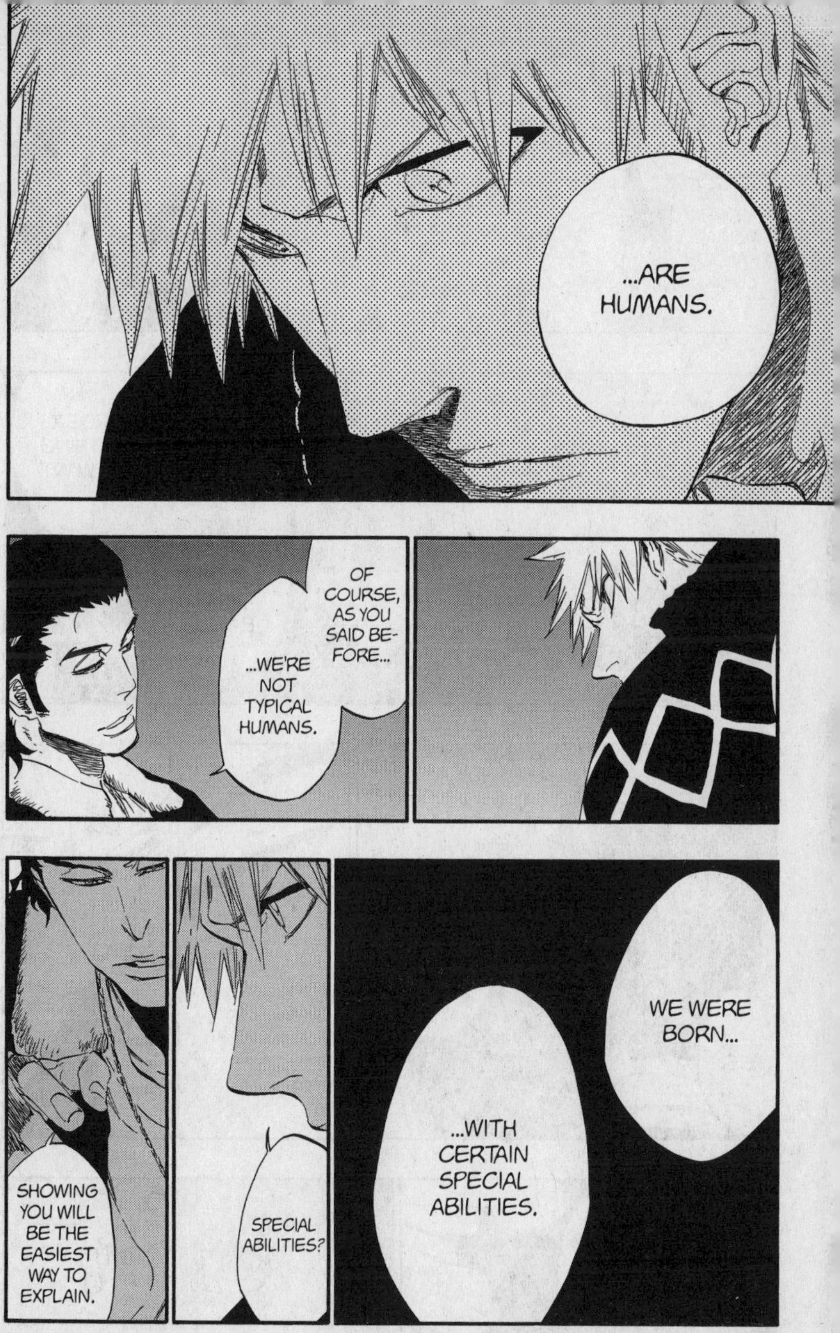
...ARE HUMANS.
OF COURSE, AS YOU SAID BEFORE...
...WE'RE NOT TYPICAL HUMANS.
WE WERE BORN...
...WITH CERTAIN SPECIAL ABILITIES.
SPECIAL ABILITIES?
SHOWING YOU WILL BE THE EASIEST WAY TO EXPLAIN.

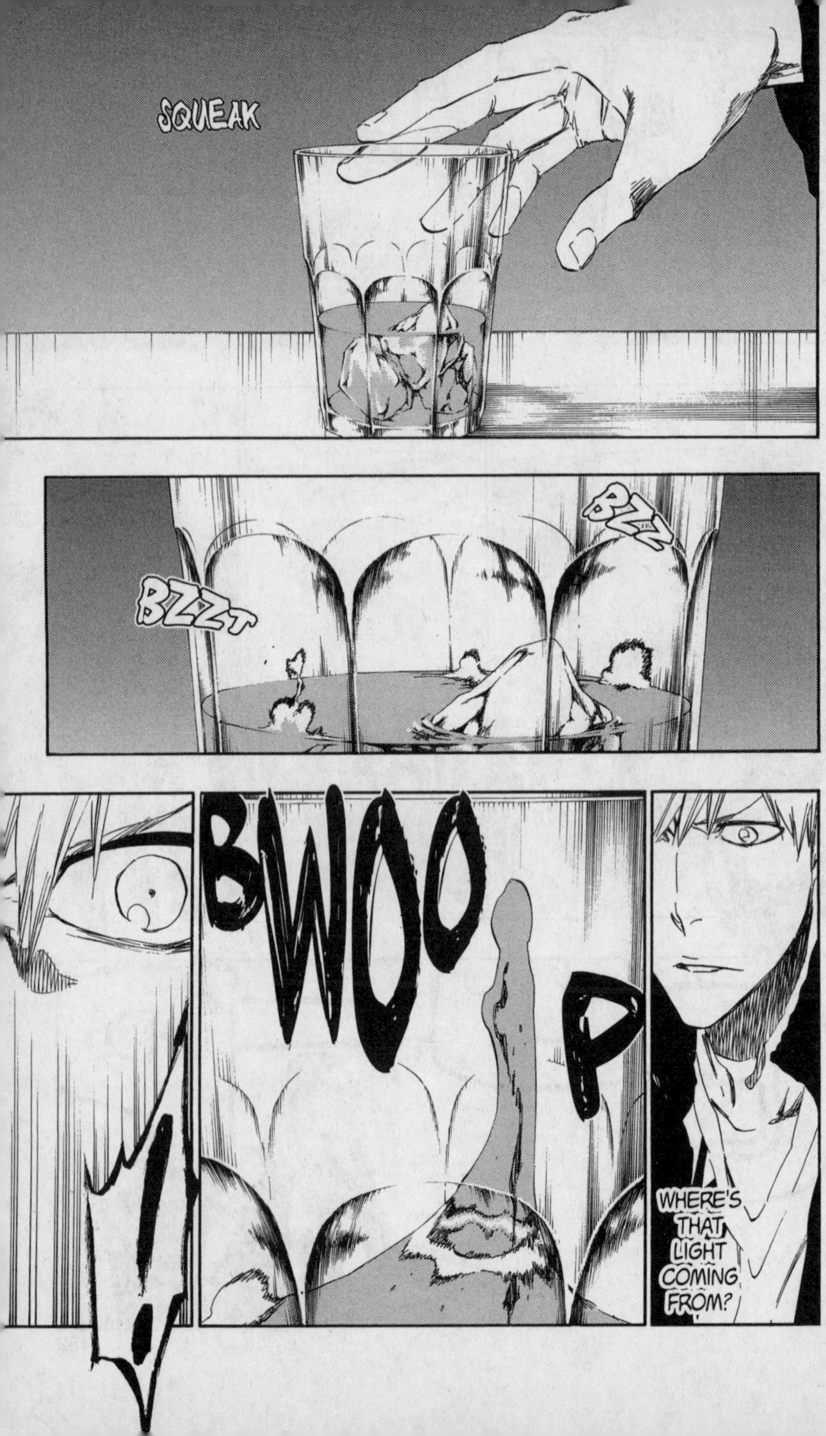
SQUEAK
BZZ
BZZT
WHERE'S THAT LIGHT COMING FROM?
BWOOP
!

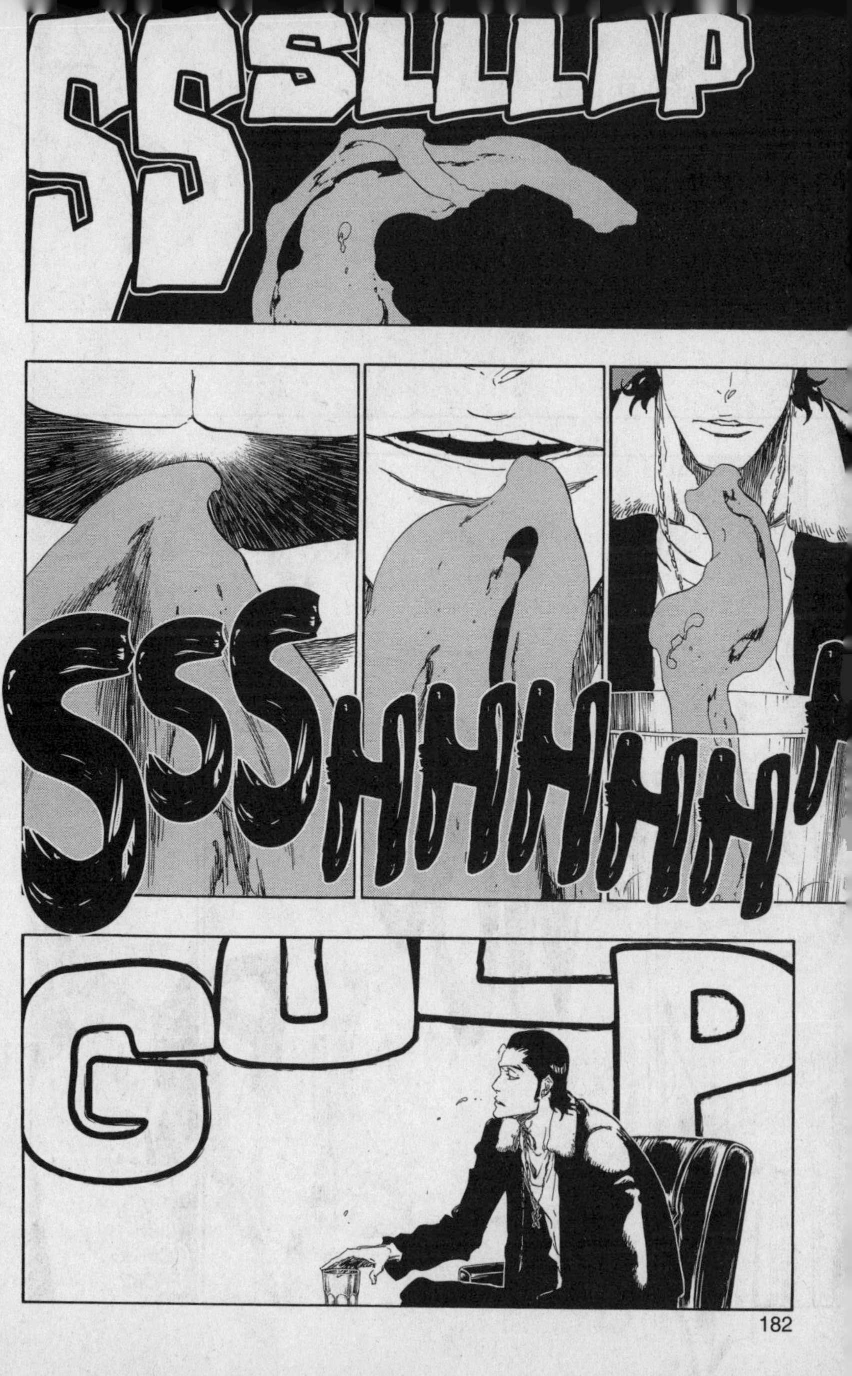
SSSLLLIP
SSSHHHHHHHHH
GULP

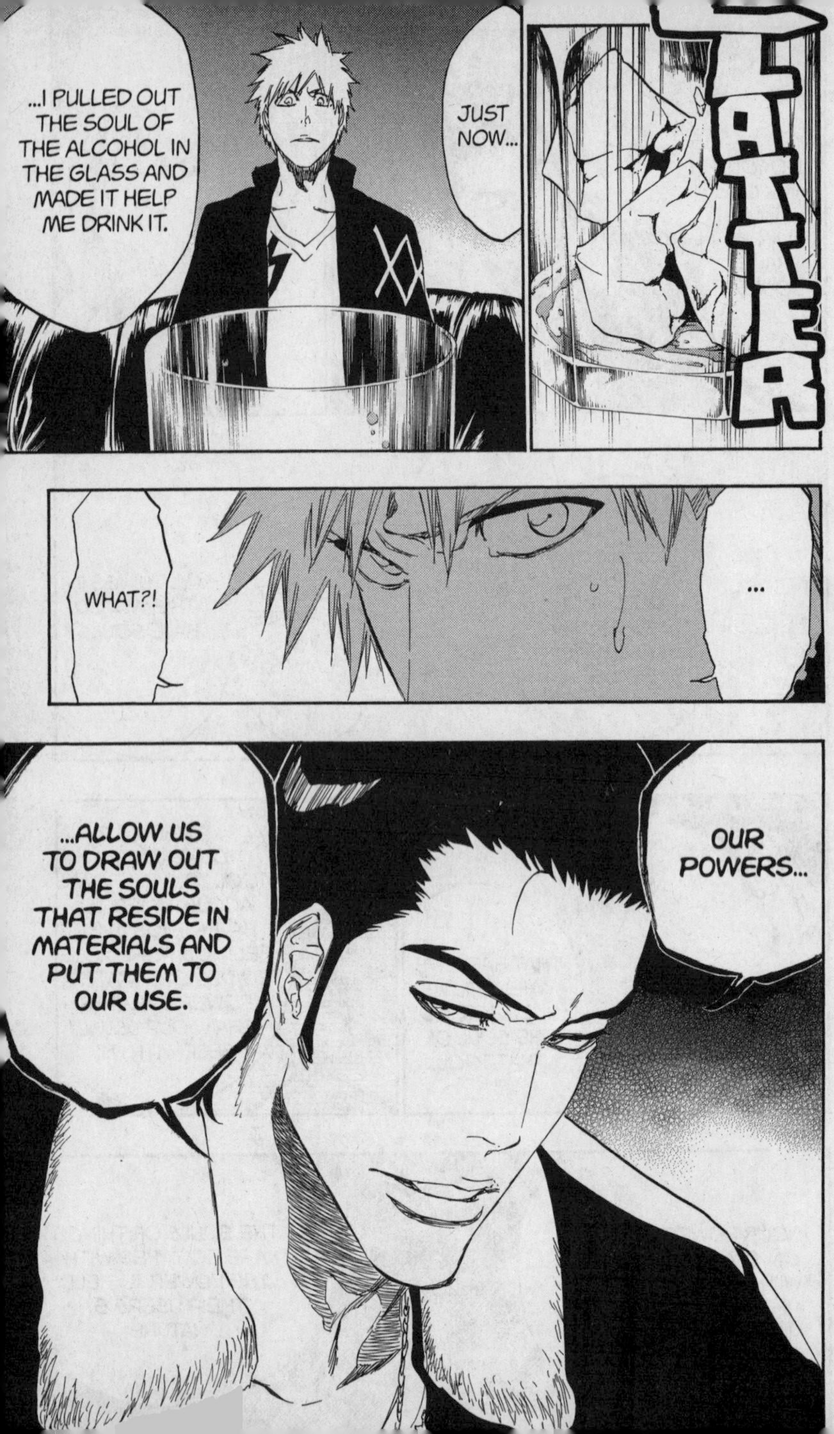
LATTER
JUST NOW...
...I PULLED OUT THE SOUL OF THE ALCOHOL IN THE GLASS AND MADE IT HELP ME DRINK IT.
...
WHAT?!
OUR POWERS...
...ALLOW US TO DRAW OUT THE SOULS THAT RESIDE IN MATERIALS AND PUT THEM TO OUR USE.

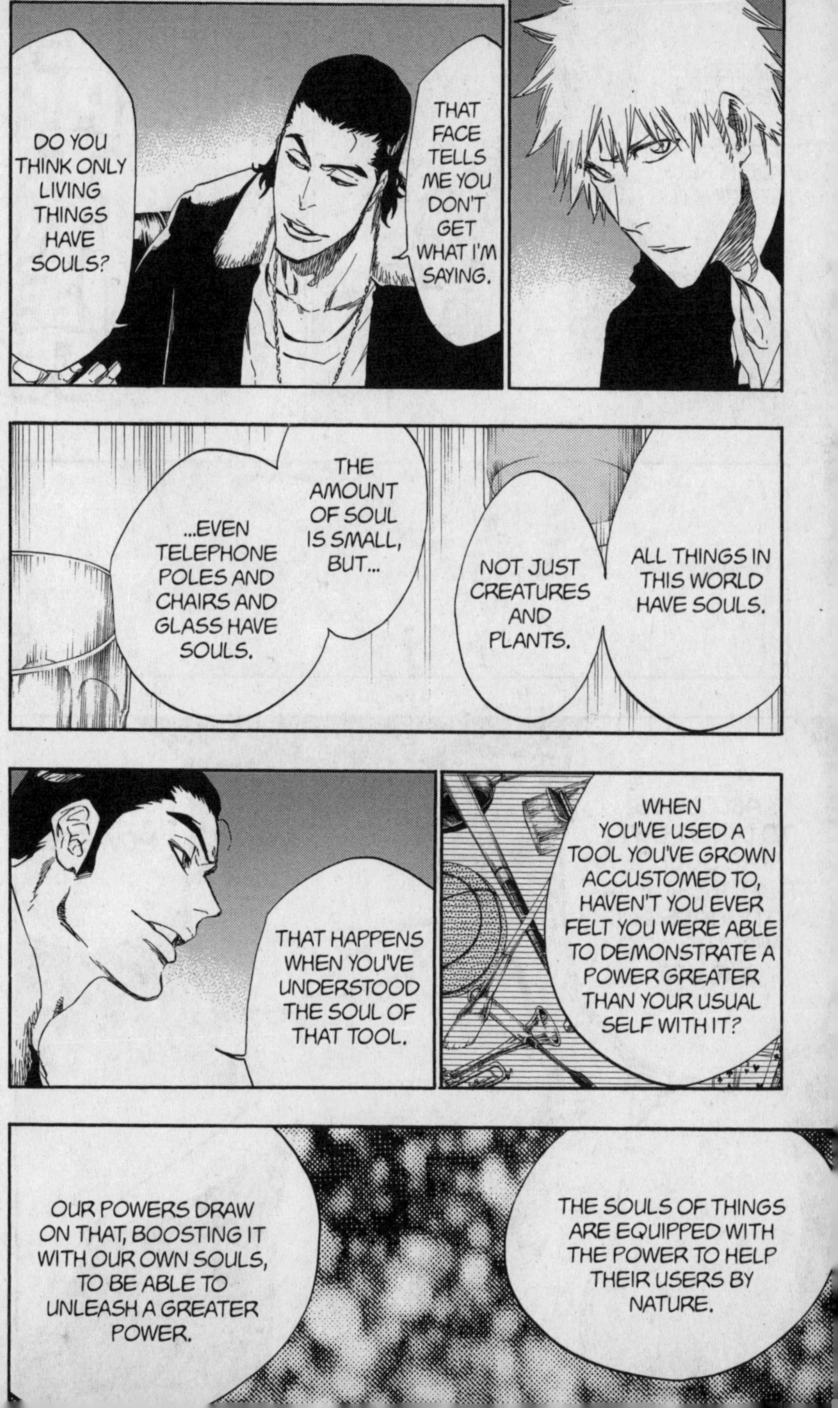
THAT FACE TELLS ME YOU DON'T GET WHAT I'M SAYING.
DO YOU THINK ONLY LIVING THINGS HAVE SOULS?
ALL THINGS IN THIS WORLD HAVE SOULS.
NOT JUST CREATURES AND PLANTS.
THE AMOUNT OF SOUL IS SMALL, BUT...
...EVEN TELEPHONE POLES AND CHAIRS AND GLASS HAVE SOULS.
WHEN YOU'VE USED A TOOL YOU'VE GROWN ACCUSTOMED TO, HAVEN'T YOU EVER FELT YOU WERE ABLE TO DEMONSTRATE A POWER GREATER THAN YOUR USUAL SELF WITH IT?
THAT HAPPENS WHEN YOU'VE UNDERSTOOD THE SOUL OF THAT TOOL.
THE SOULS OF THINGS ARE EQUIPPED WITH THE POWER TO HELP THEIR USERS BY NATURE.
OUR POWERS DRAW ON THAT, BOOSTING IT WITH OUR OWN SOULS, TO BE ABLE TO UNLEASH A GREATER POWER.

READ THIS WAY

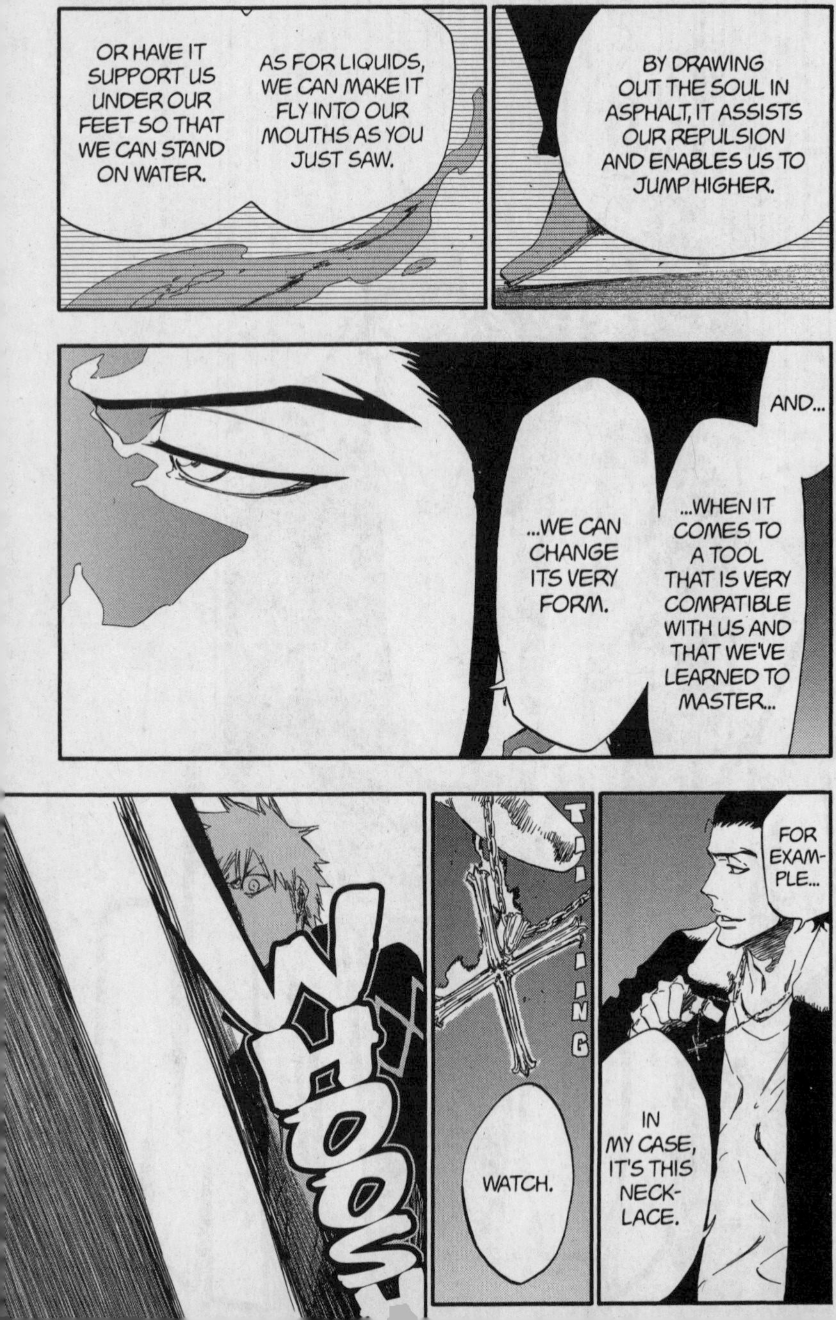
BY DRAWING OUT THE SOUL IN ASPHALT, IT ASSISTS OUR REPULSION AND ENABLES US TO JUMP HIGHER.
AS FOR LIQUIDS, WE CAN MAKE IT FLY INTO OUR MOUTHS AS YOU JUST SAW.
OR HAVE IT SUPPORT US UNDER OUR FEET SO THAT WE CAN STAND ON WATER.
AND...
...WHEN IT COMES TO A TOOL THAT IS VERY COMPATIBLE WITH US AND THAT WE'VE LEARNED TO MASTER...
...WE CAN CHANGE ITS VERY FORM.
FOR EXAM-PLE...
IN MY CASE, IT'S THIS NECK-LACE.
WATCH.

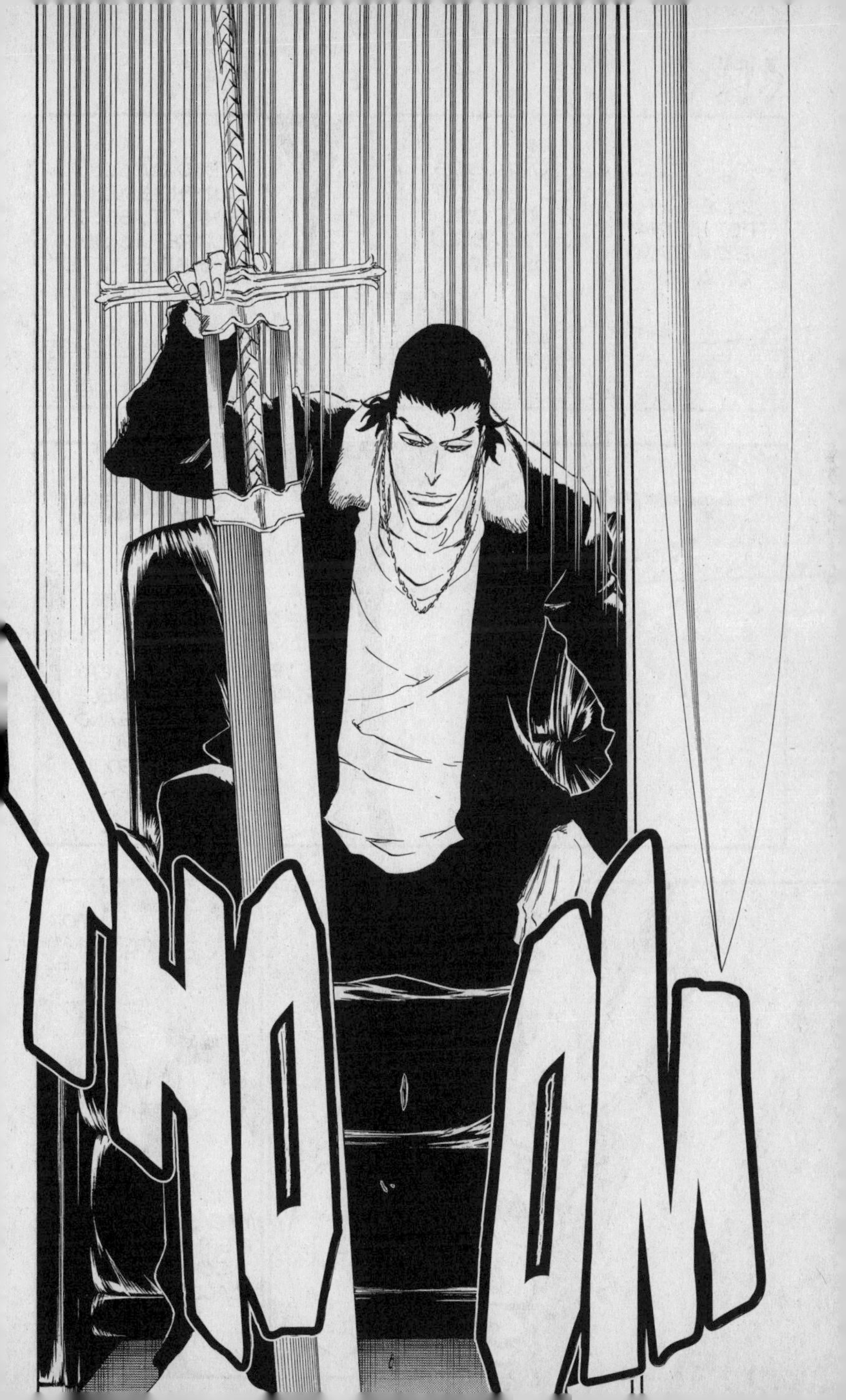

CHOOM

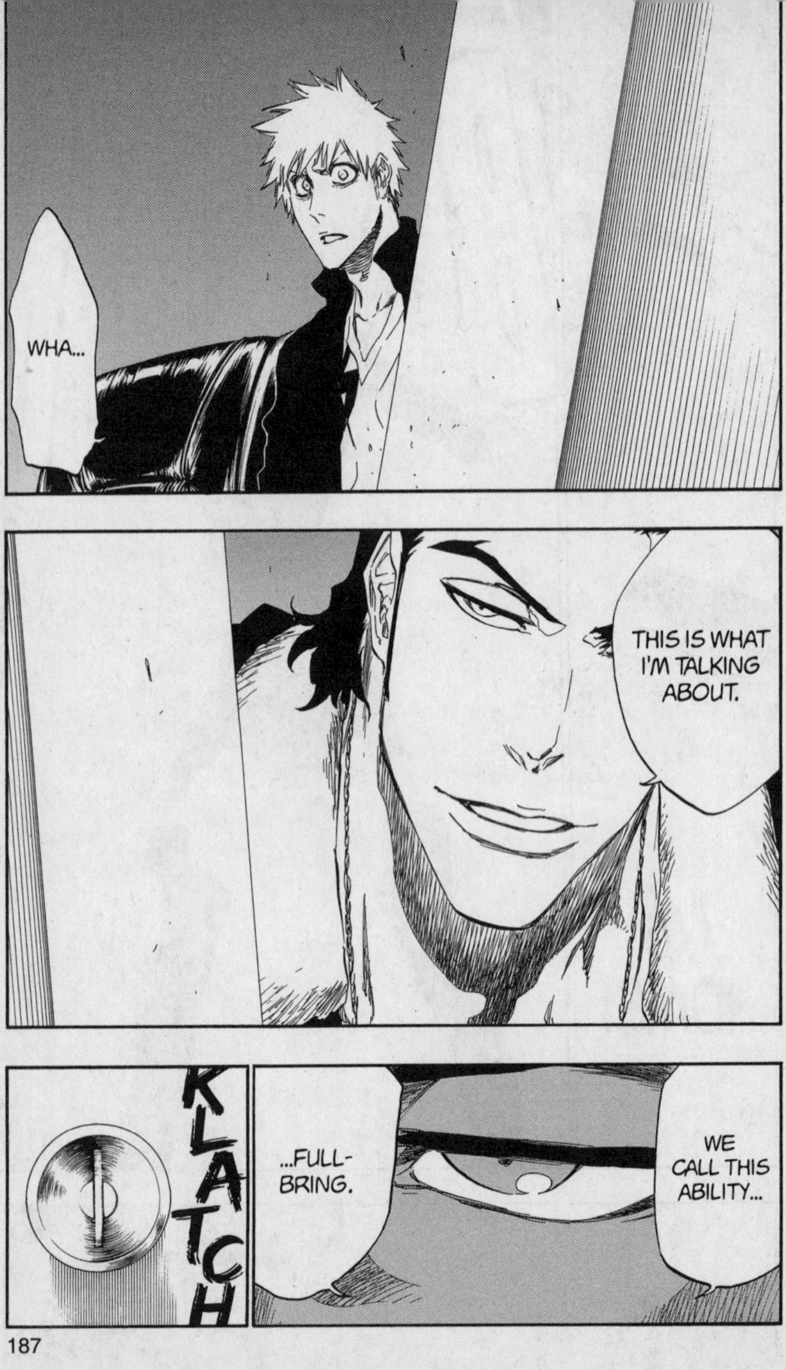
WHA...
THIS IS WHAT I'M TALKING ABOUT.
WE CALL THIS ABILITY...
...FULL-BRING.
KLATCH

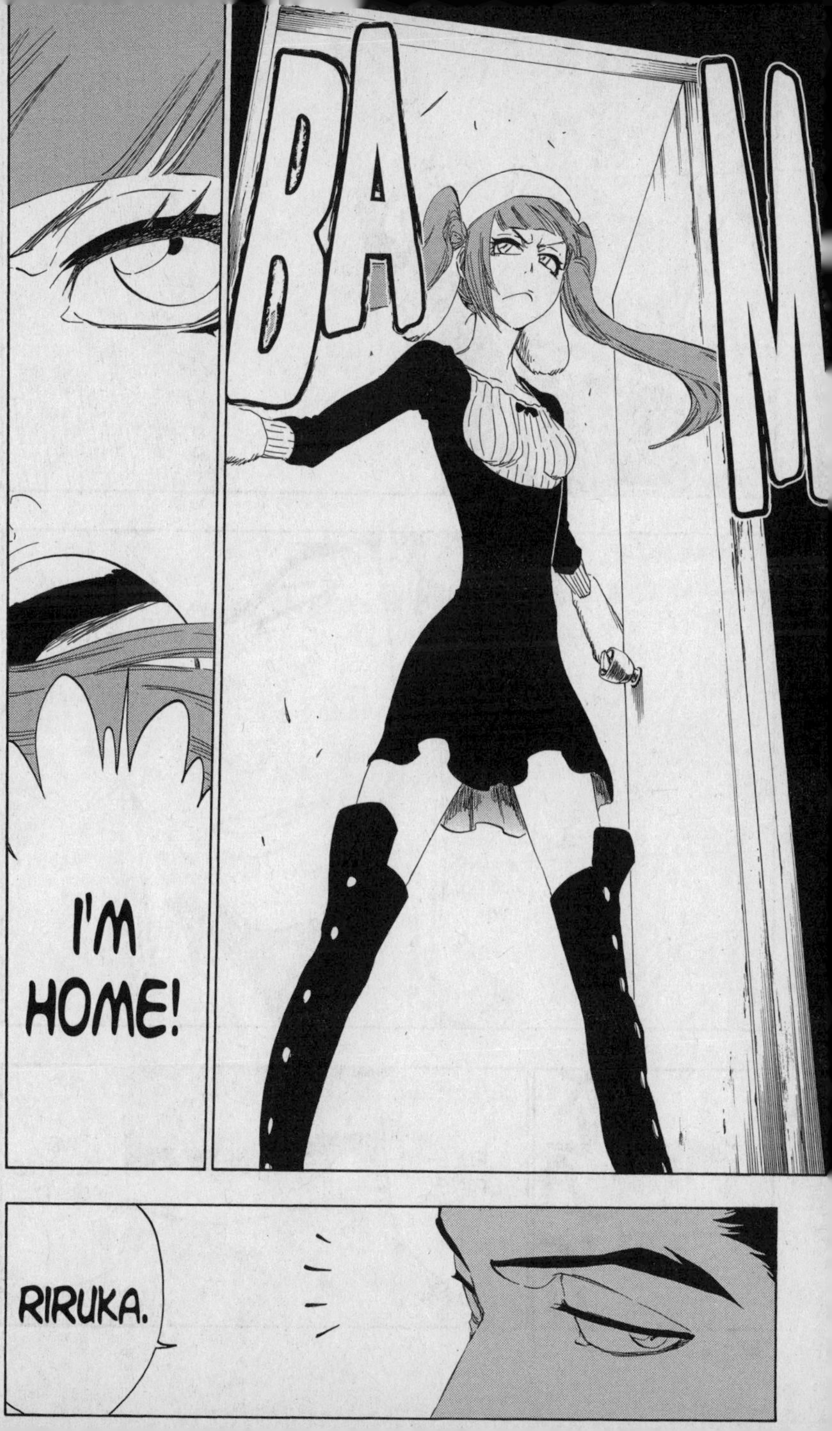
BAM
I'M HOME!
RIRUKA.

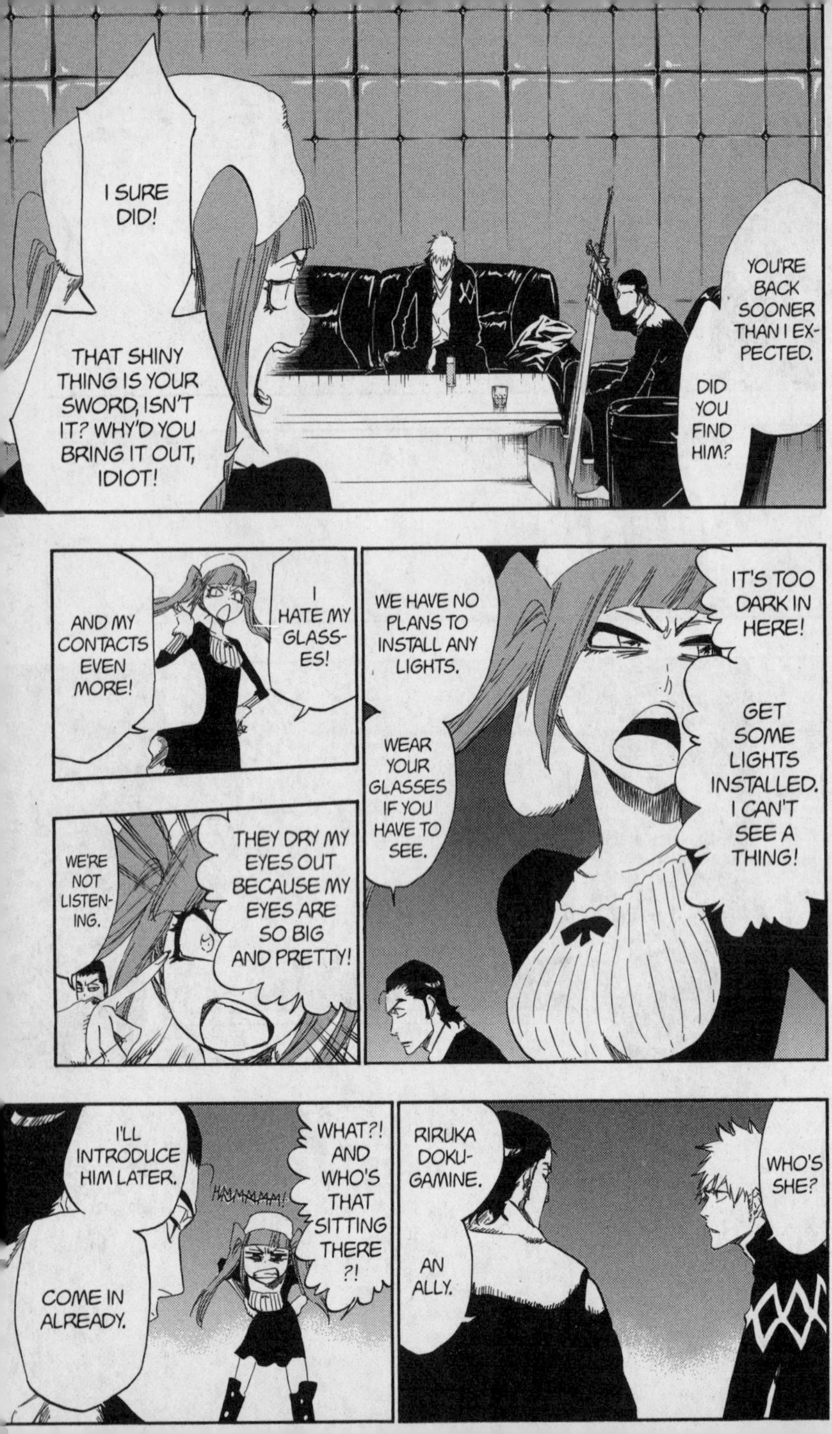
YOU'RE BACK SOONER THAN I EXPECTED.
DID YOU FIND HIM?
I SURE DID!
THAT SHINY THING IS YOUR SWORD, ISN'T IT? WHY'D YOU BRING IT OUT, IDIOT!
IT'S TOO DARK IN HERE!
GET SOME LIGHTS INSTALLED. I CAN'T SEE A THING!
WE HAVE NO PLANS TO INSTALL ANY LIGHTS.
WEAR YOUR GLASSES IF YOU HAVE TO SEE.
I HATE MY GLASSES!
AND MY CONTACTS EVEN MORE!
THEY DRY MY EYES OUT BECAUSE MY EYES ARE SO BIG AND PRETTY!
WE'RE NOT LISTENING.
WHO'S SHE?
RIRUKA DOKUGAMINE.
AN ALLY.
WHAT?! AND WHO'S THAT SITTING THERE?!
I'LL INTRODUCE HIM LATER.
COME IN ALREADY.

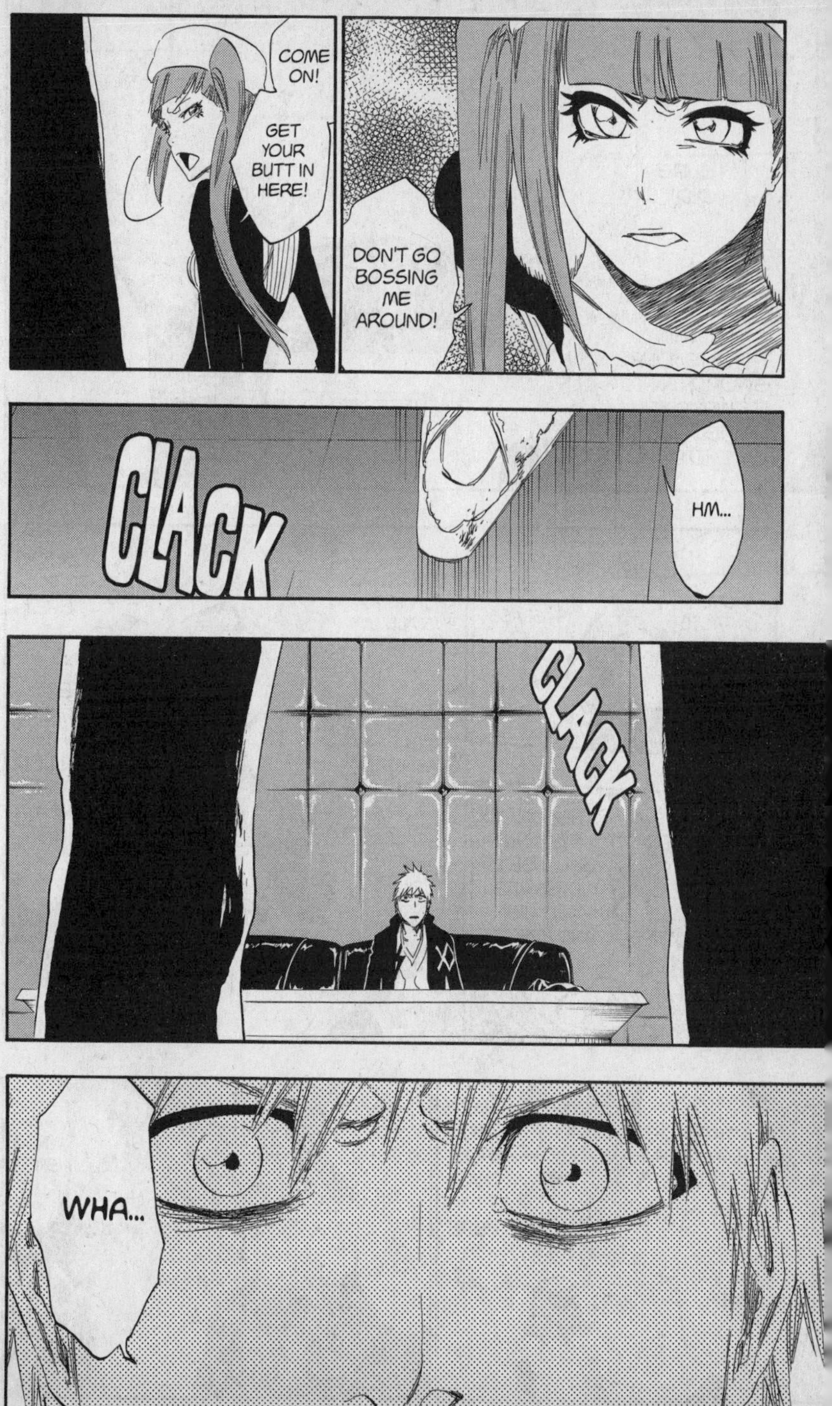
DON'T GO BOSSING ME AROUND!
COME ON!
GET YOUR BUTT IN HERE!
HM...
CLACK
CLACK
WHA...

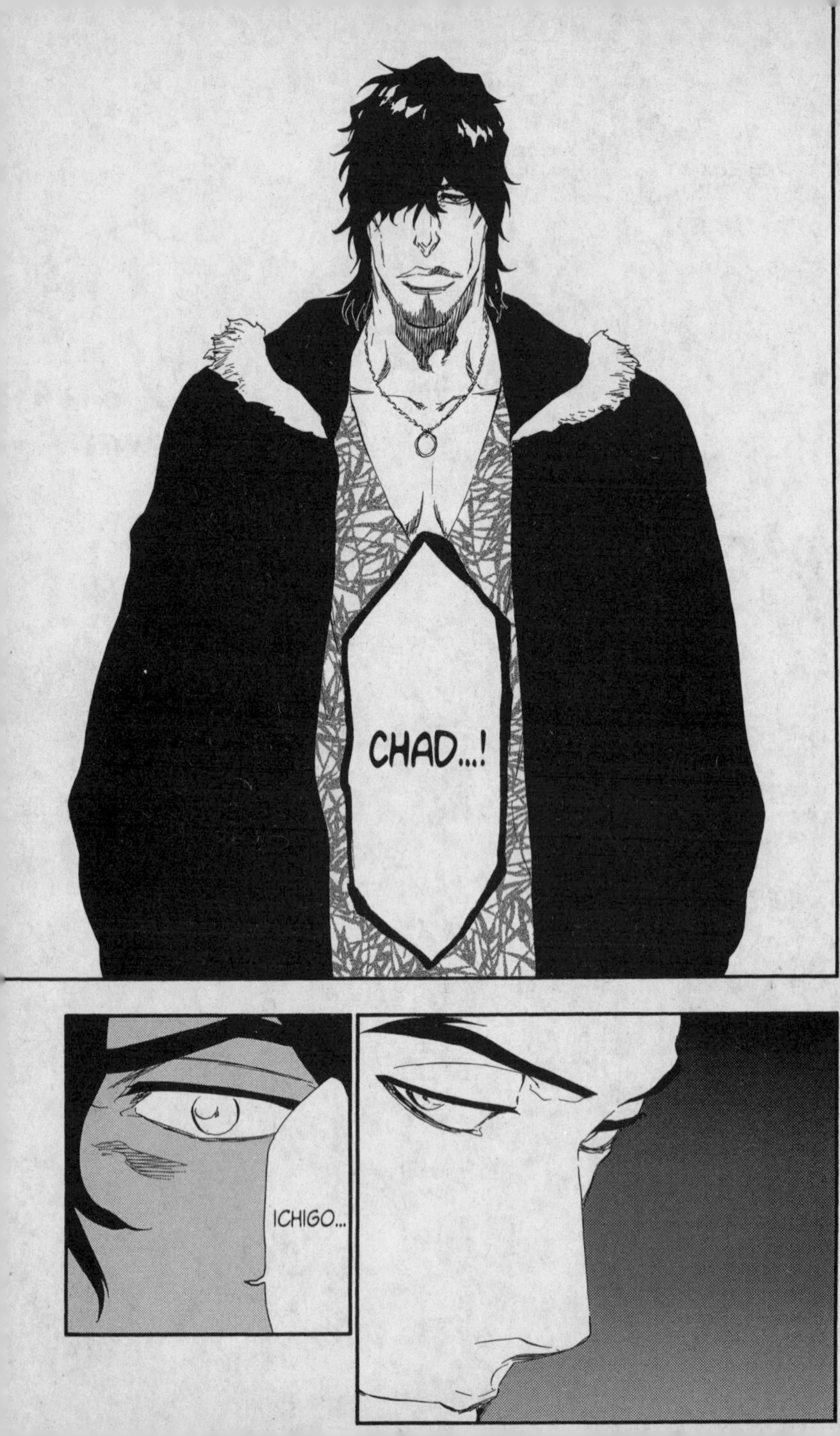
CHAD...!
ICHIGO...

SLEEP

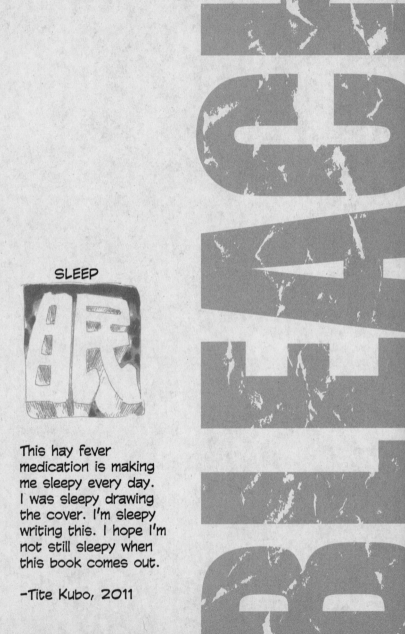

This hay fever
medication is making
me sleepy every day.
I was sleepy drawing
the cover. I'm sleepy
writing this. I hope I'm
not still sleepy when
this book comes out.

-Tite Kubo, 2011

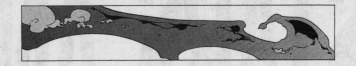

Time always approaches from behind
Growling and flowing past our eyes

Stand your ground
No matter how much time shows its fangs
In order to wash you away to a beautiful past

Do not look forward
Your hopes creep up behind you
Only existing in dark turbid waters

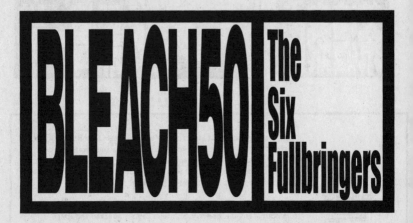

BLEACH 50 The Six Fullbringers

STARS AND

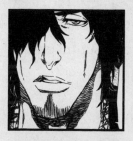

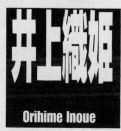

Orihime Inoue

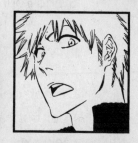

Chad Yasutora

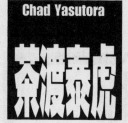

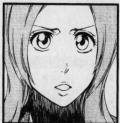

Ichigo Kurosaki

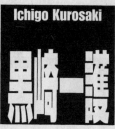

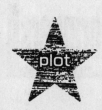
plot

When high school student Ichigo Kurosaki meets Soul Reaper Rukia Kuchiki his life is changed forever. Soon Ichigo is a soul-cleansing Soul Reaper too, and he finds himself facing off against ex-Soul Reaper Aizen and his dark ambitions. In exchange for his Soul Reaper powers, Ichigo is finally able to defeat Aizen and seal him away!

With the long battle over, Ichigo says goodbye to Rukia and returns to a normal life. But one day, his friend Uryu is attacked and Ichigo is confronted by a mysterious man named Kugo Ginjo. Ginjo and his allies say they want to help Ichigo regain his powers. Then suddenly Chad appears…

BLEACH ALL

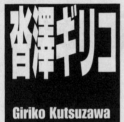

沓澤ギリコ

Giriko Kutsuzawa

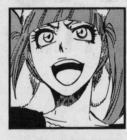

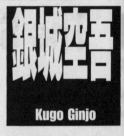

銀城空吾

Kugo Ginjo

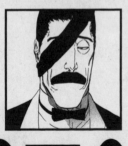

Riruka Dokugamine

毒ヶ峰リルカ

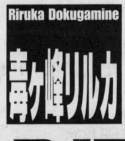

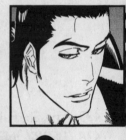

STORIES

BLEACH 50

The Six Fullbringers

Contents

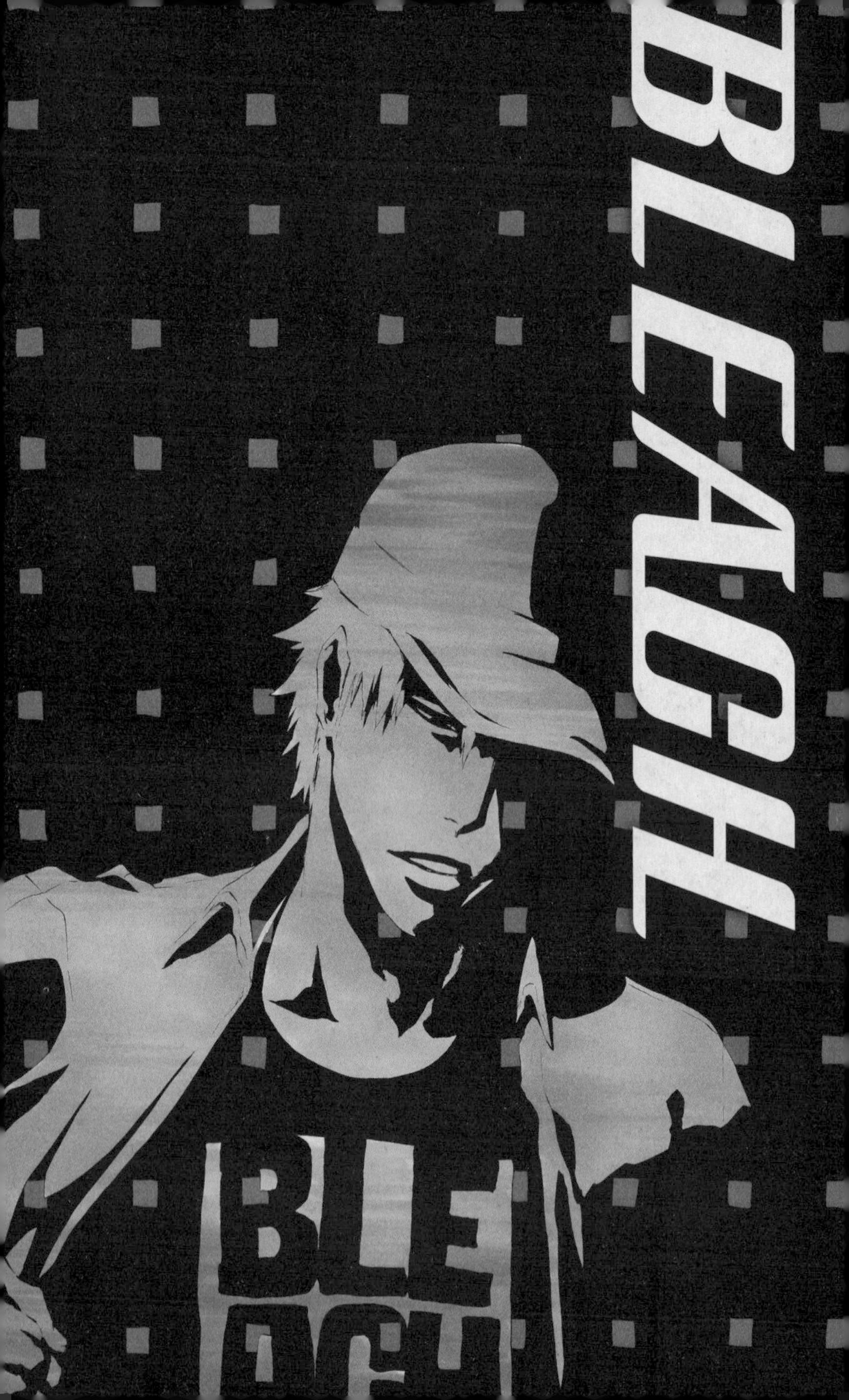
BLEACH

BLEACH
ブリーチ

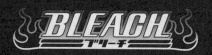

READ THIS WAY

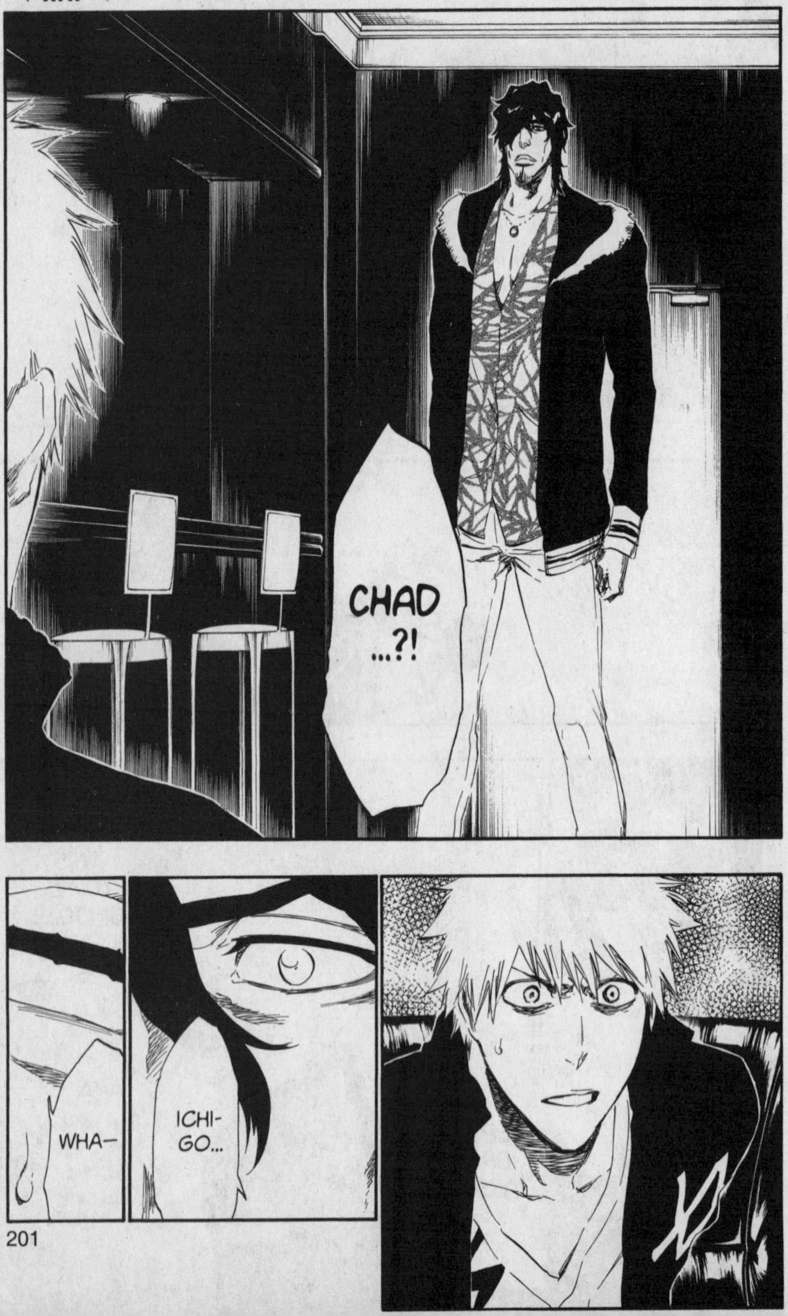
CHAD ...?!
ICHI-GO...
WHA-

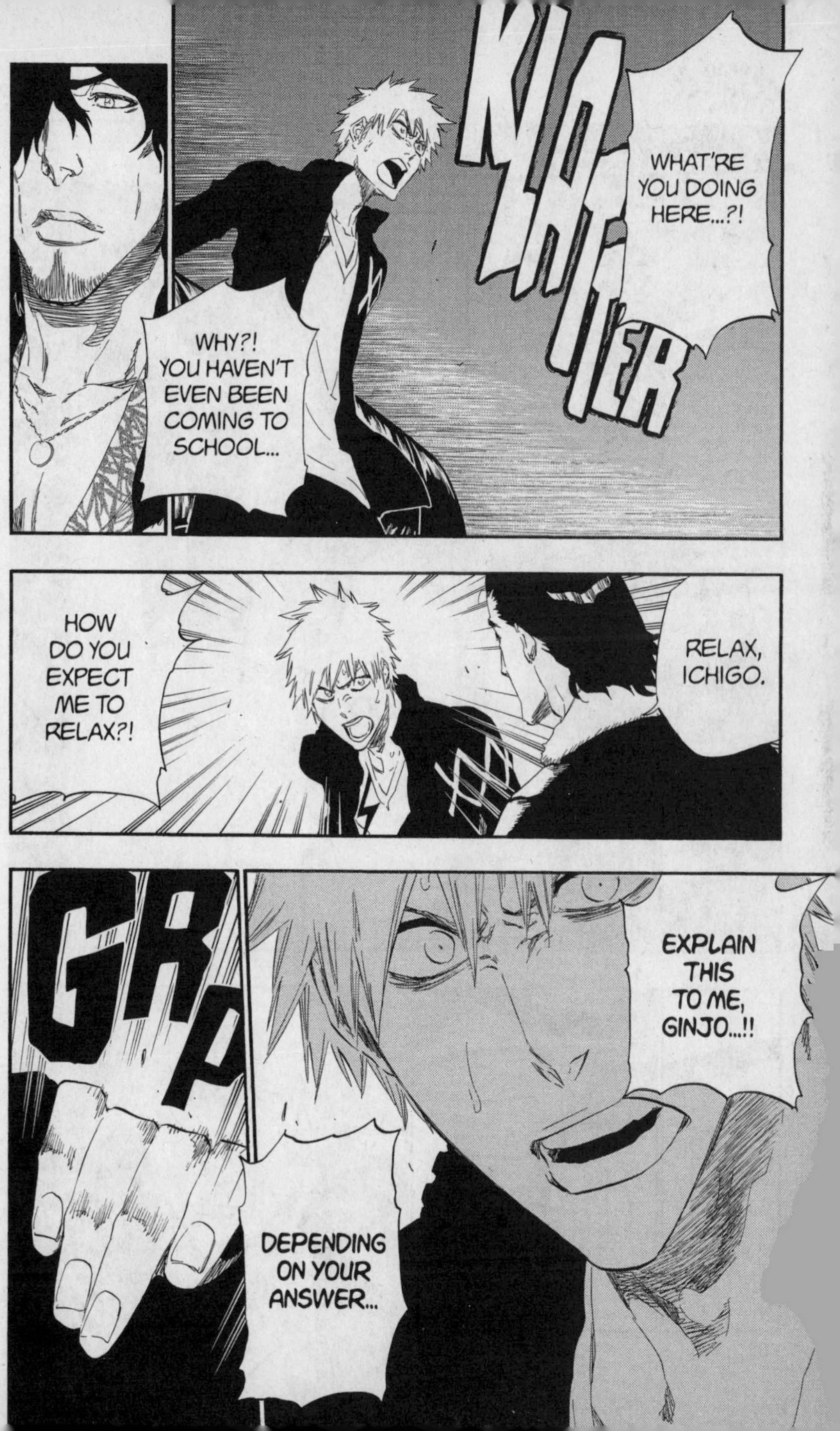
KLATTER
WHAT'RE YOU DOING HERE...?!
WHY?! YOU HAVEN'T EVEN BEEN COMING TO SCHOOL...
RELAX, ICHIGO.
HOW DO YOU EXPECT ME TO RELAX?!
EXPLAIN THIS TO ME, GINJO...!!
DEPENDING ON YOUR ANSWER...

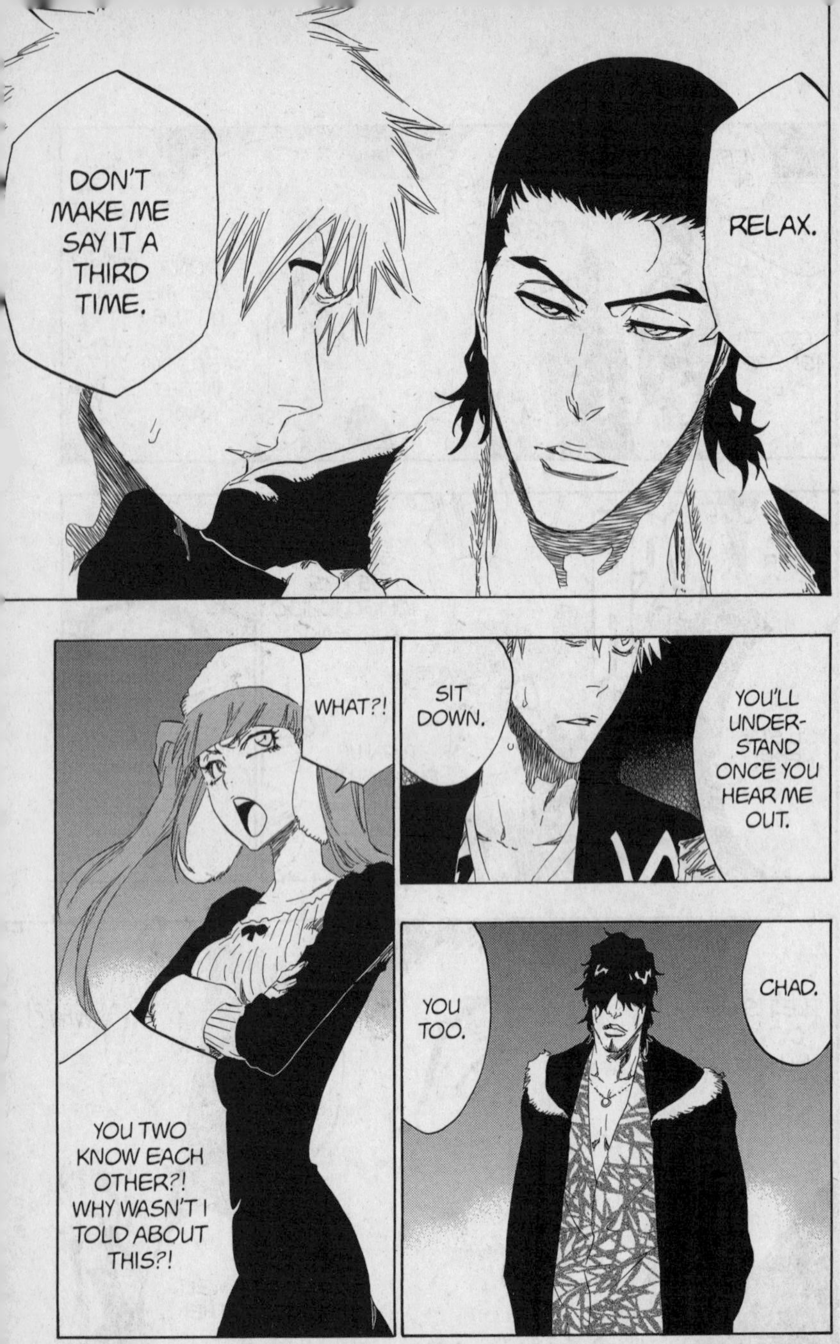
RELAX.
DON'T MAKE ME SAY IT A THIRD TIME.
YOU'LL UNDER-STAND ONCE YOU HEAR ME OUT.
SIT DOWN.
CHAD.
YOU TOO.
WHAT?!
YOU TWO KNOW EACH OTHER?! WHY WASN'T I TOLD ABOUT THIS?!

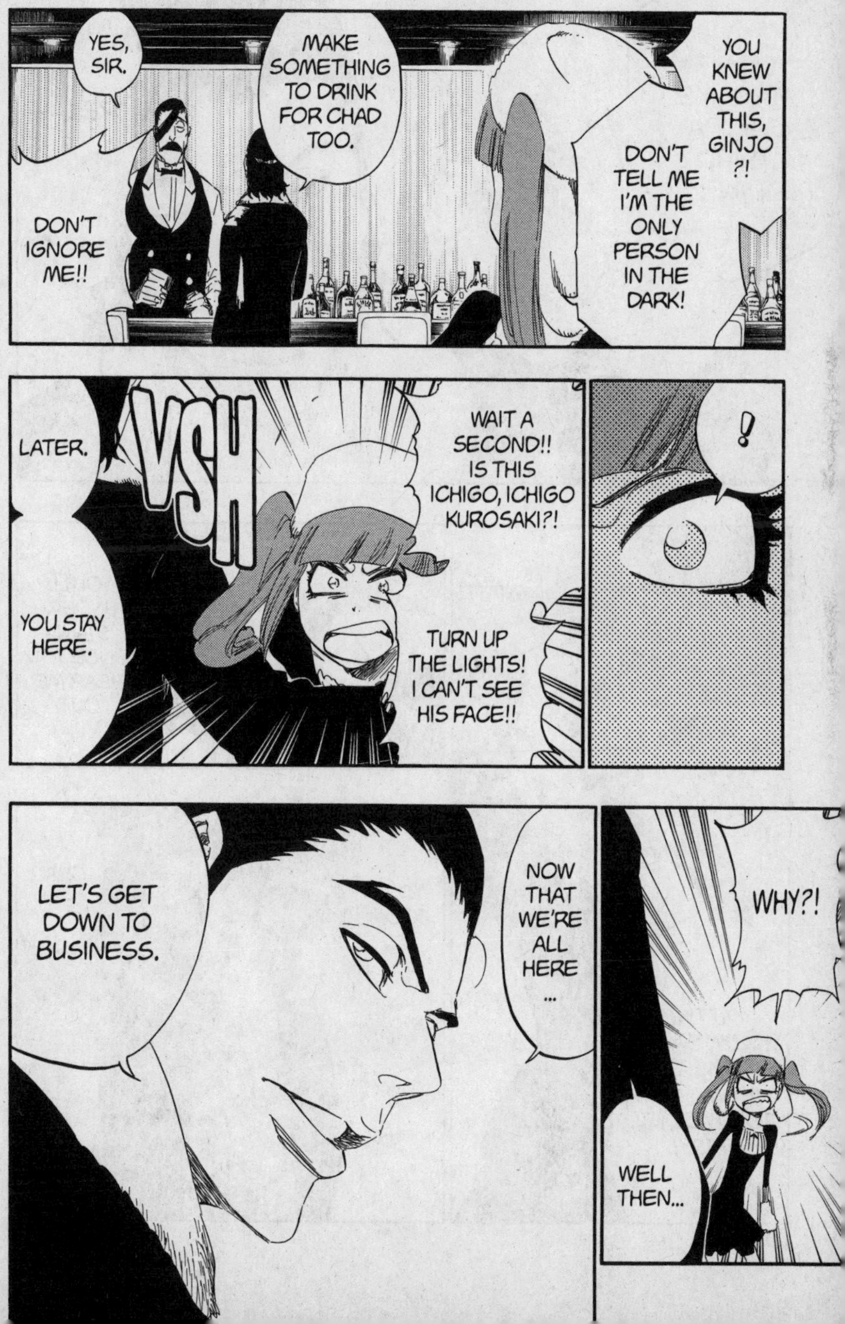
YOU KNEW ABOUT THIS, GINJO?!
DON'T TELL ME I'M THE ONLY PERSON IN THE DARK!
MAKE SOMETHING TO DRINK FOR CHAD TOO.
YES, SIR.
DON'T IGNORE ME!!
!
WAIT A SECOND!! IS THIS ICHIGO, ICHIGO KUROSAKI?!
TURN UP THE LIGHTS! I CAN'T SEE HIS FACE!!
VSH
LATER.
YOU STAY HERE.
WHY?!
WELL THEN...
NOW THAT WE'RE ALL HERE...
LET'S GET DOWN TO BUSINESS.

BLEACH

433.

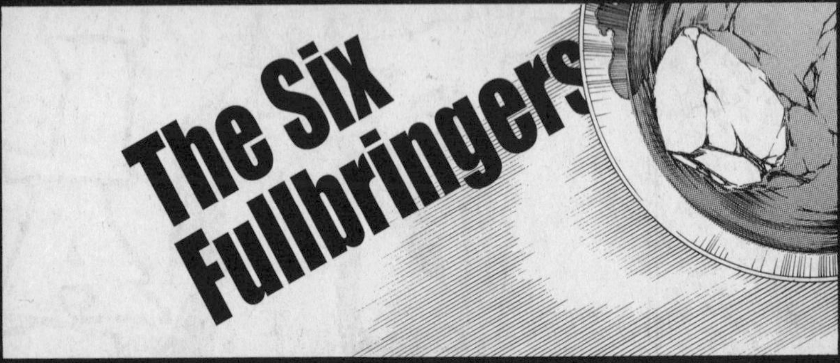
The Six Fullbringers

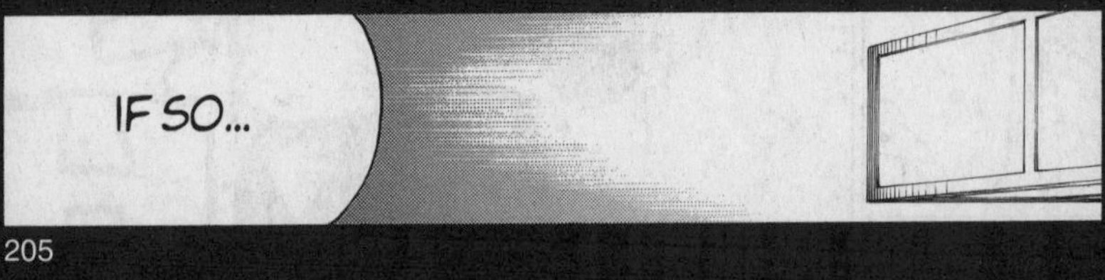
IF SO...

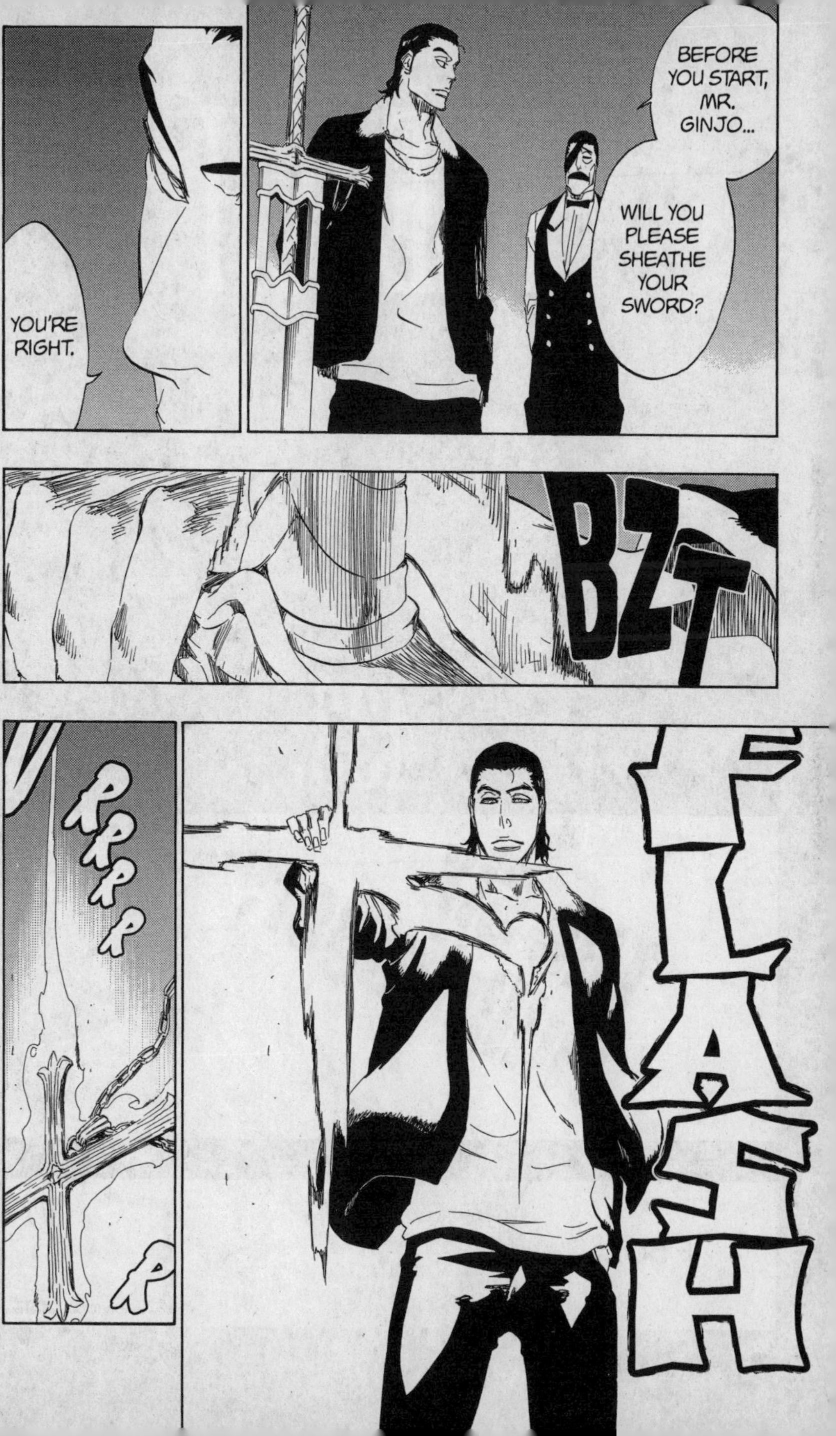
BEFORE YOU START, MR. GINJO...
WILL YOU PLEASE SHEATHE YOUR SWORD?
YOU'RE RIGHT.
BZT
FLASH
RRRRR

READ THIS WAY

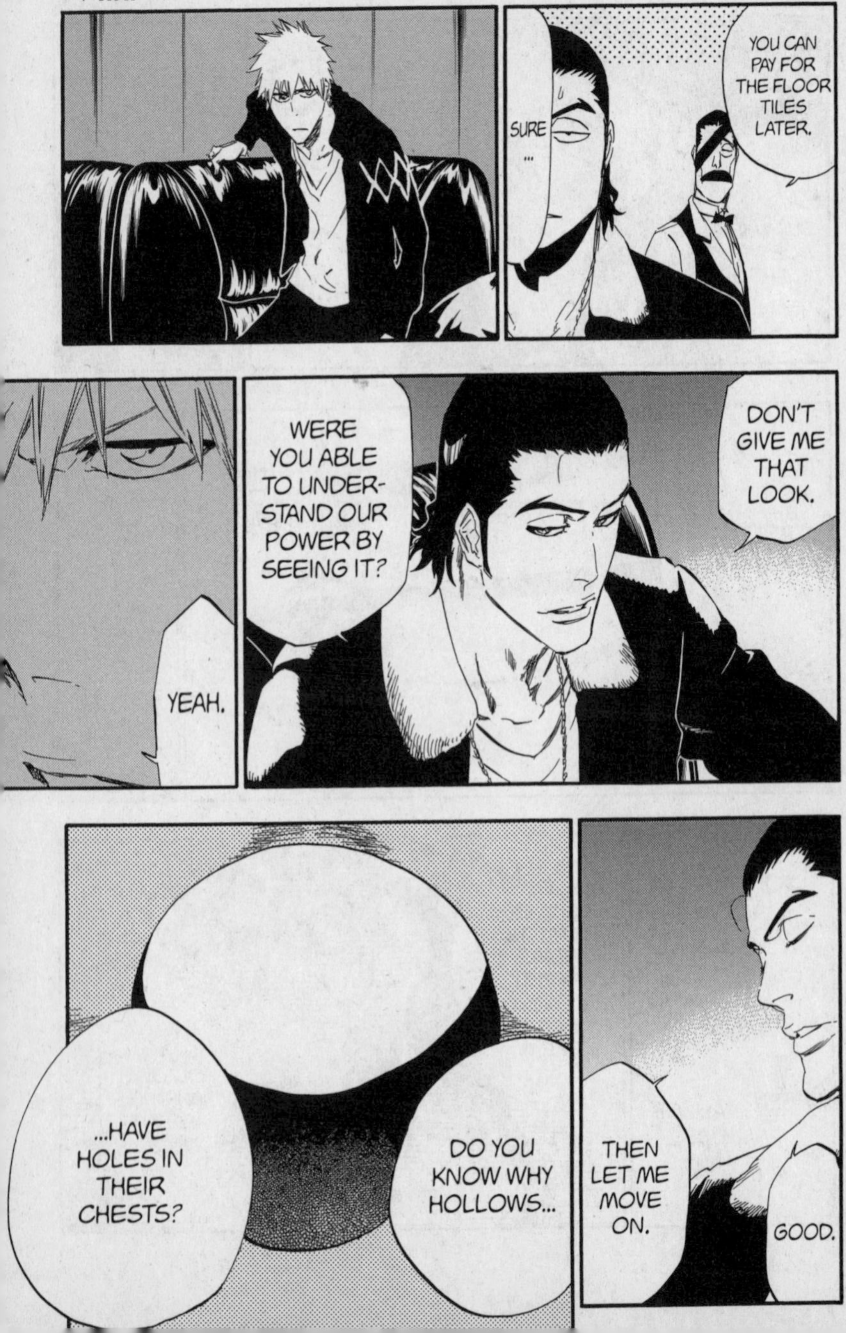
YOU CAN PAY FOR THE FLOOR TILES LATER.
SURE ...
DON'T GIVE ME THAT LOOK.
WERE YOU ABLE TO UNDER-STAND OUR POWER BY SEEING IT?
YEAH.
GOOD.
THEN LET ME MOVE ON.
DO YOU KNOW WHY HOLLOWS...
...HAVE HOLES IN THEIR CHESTS?

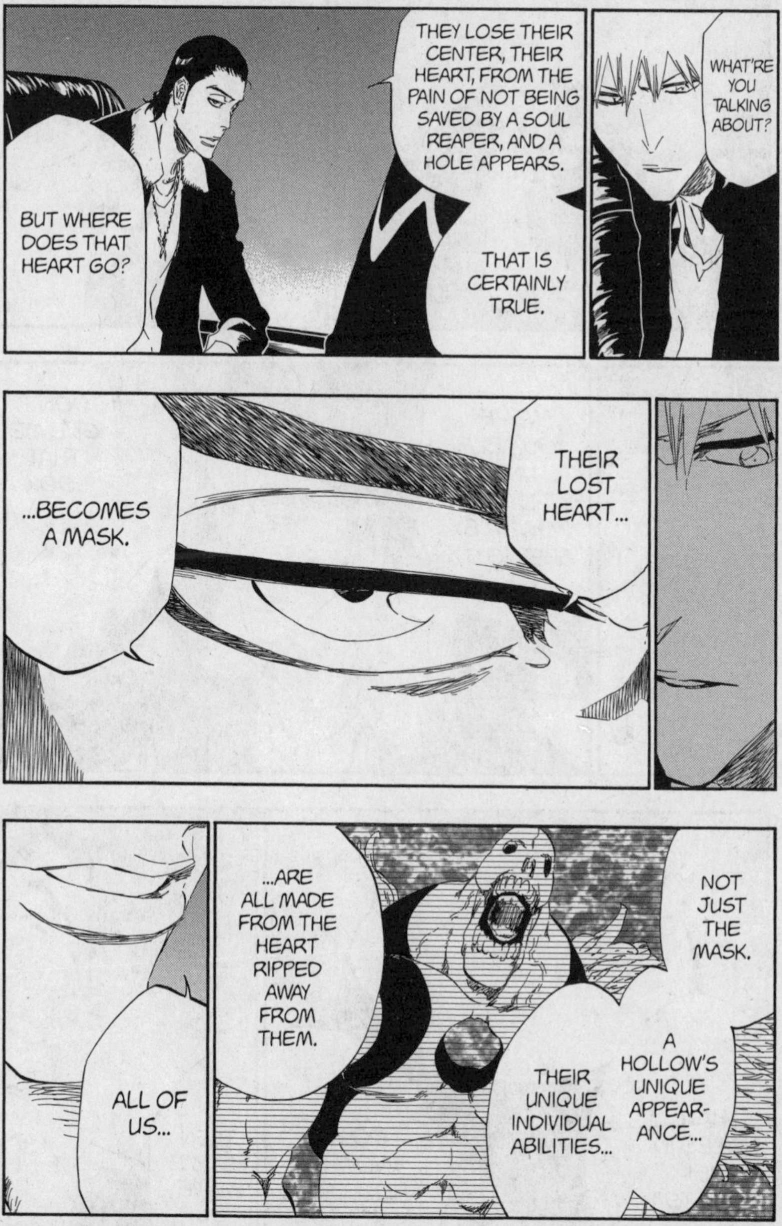
WHAT'RE YOU TALKING ABOUT?
THEY LOSE THEIR CENTER, THEIR HEART, FROM THE PAIN OF NOT BEING SAVED BY A SOUL REAPER, AND A HOLE APPEARS.
THAT IS CERTAINLY TRUE.
BUT WHERE DOES THAT HEART GO?
THEIR LOST HEART...
...BECOMES A MASK.
NOT JUST THE MASK.
A HOLLOW'S UNIQUE APPEAR-ANCE...
THEIR UNIQUE INDIVIDUAL ABILITIES...
...ARE ALL MADE FROM THE HEART RIPPED AWAY FROM THEM.
ALL OF US...

READ THIS WAY

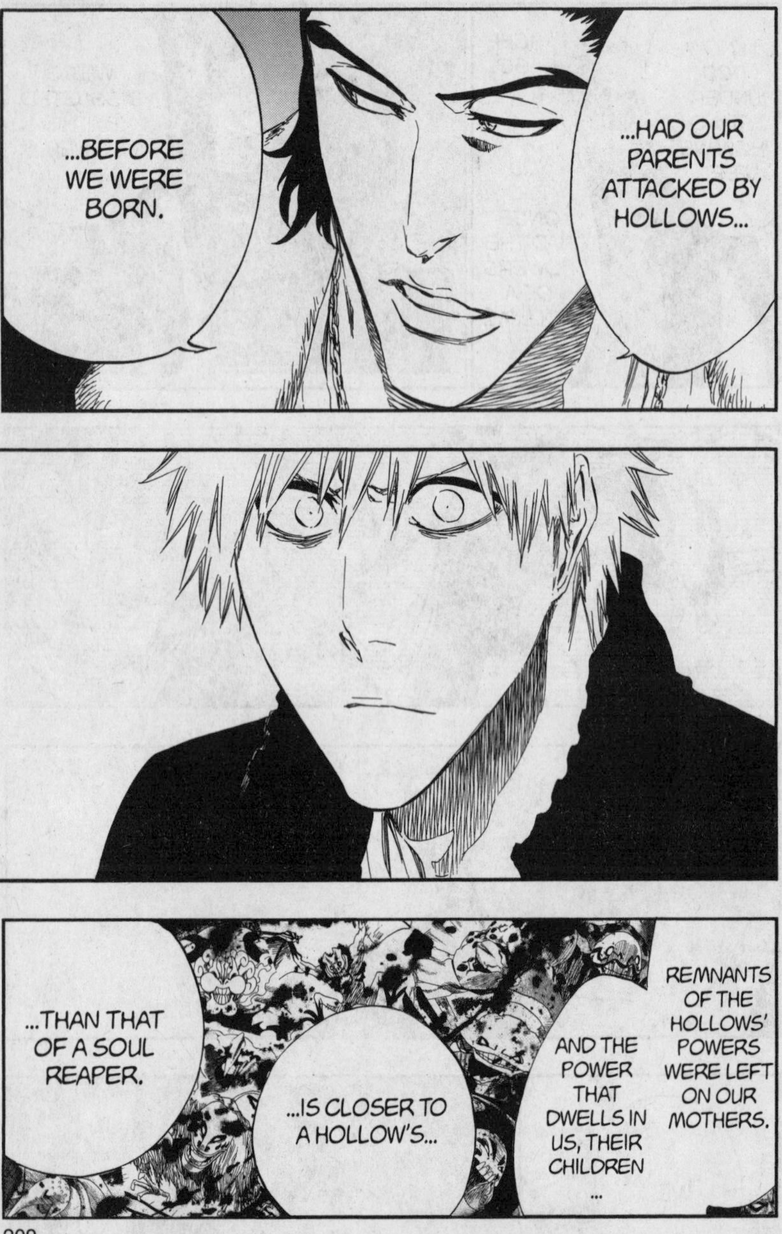
...HAD OUR PARENTS ATTACKED BY HOLLOWS...
...BEFORE WE WERE BORN.
REMNANTS OF THE HOLLOWS' POWERS WERE LEFT ON OUR MOTHERS.
AND THE POWER THAT DWELLS IN US, THEIR CHILDREN ...
...IS CLOSER TO A HOLLOW'S...
...THAN THAT OF A SOUL REAPER.

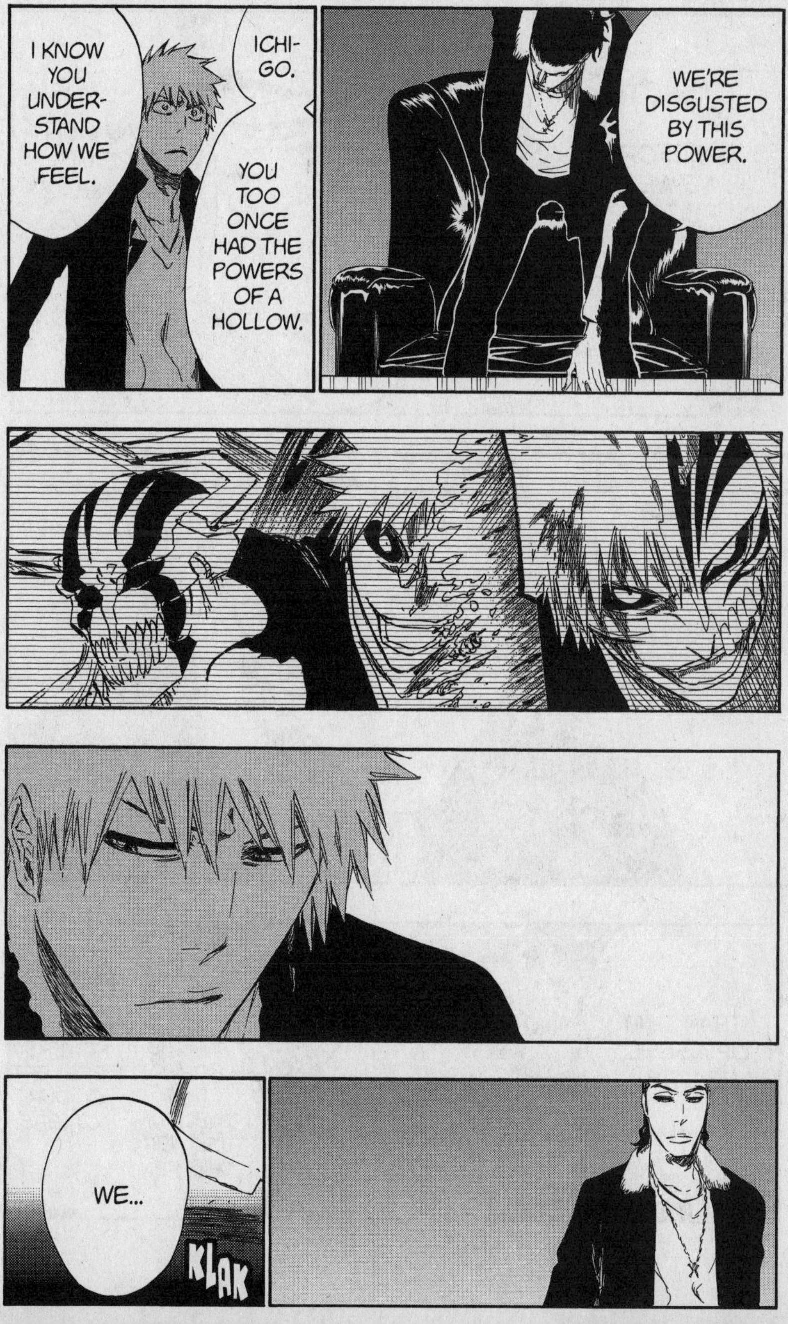
WE'RE DISGUSTED BY THIS POWER.
ICHI-GO.
YOU TOO ONCE HAD THE POWERS OF A HOLLOW.
I KNOW YOU UNDERSTAND HOW WE FEEL.
WE...
KLAK

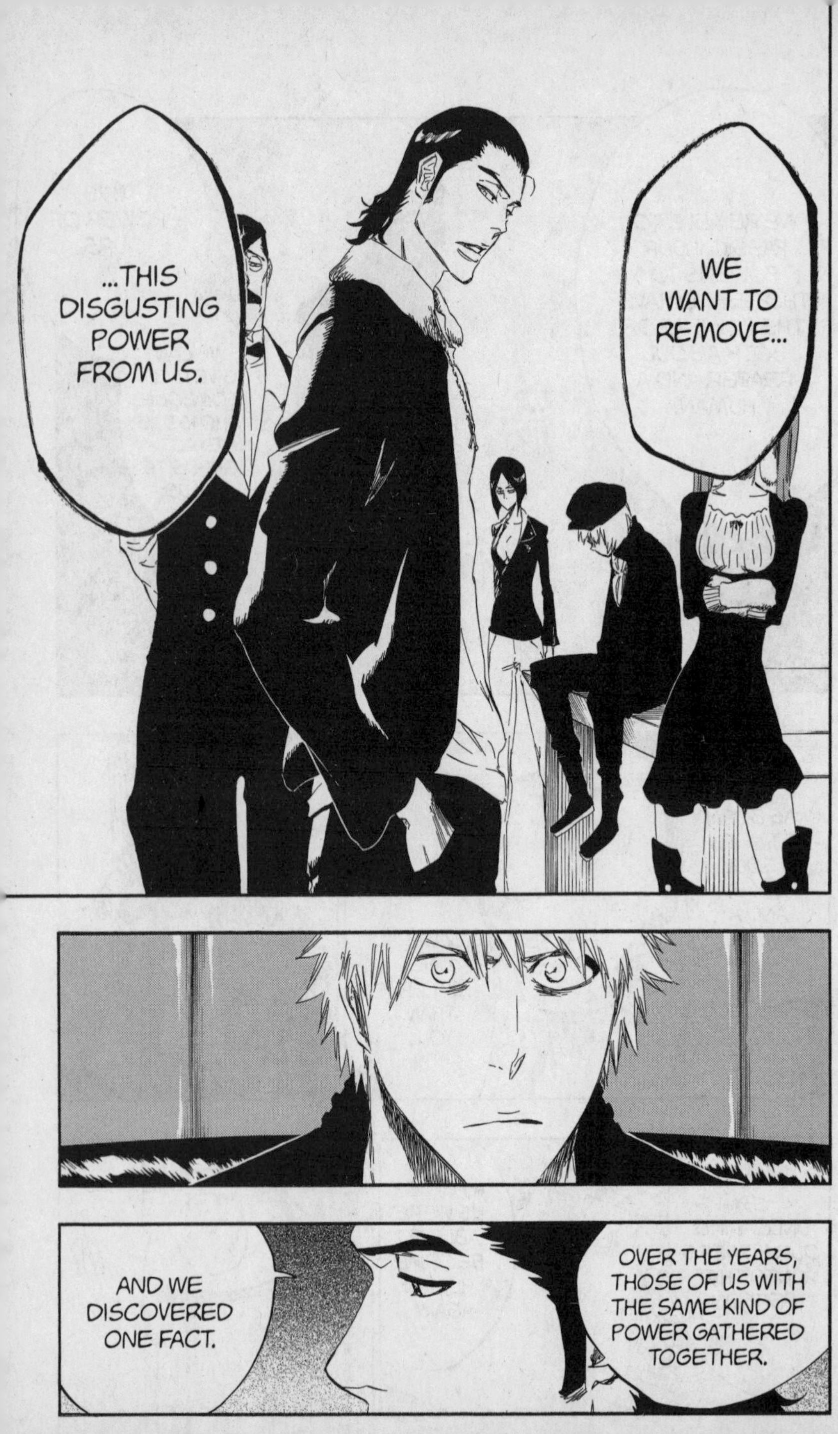
WE WANT TO REMOVE...
...THIS DISGUSTING POWER FROM US.
OVER THE YEARS, THOSE OF US WITH THE SAME KIND OF POWER GATHERED TOGETHER.
AND WE DISCOVERED ONE FACT.

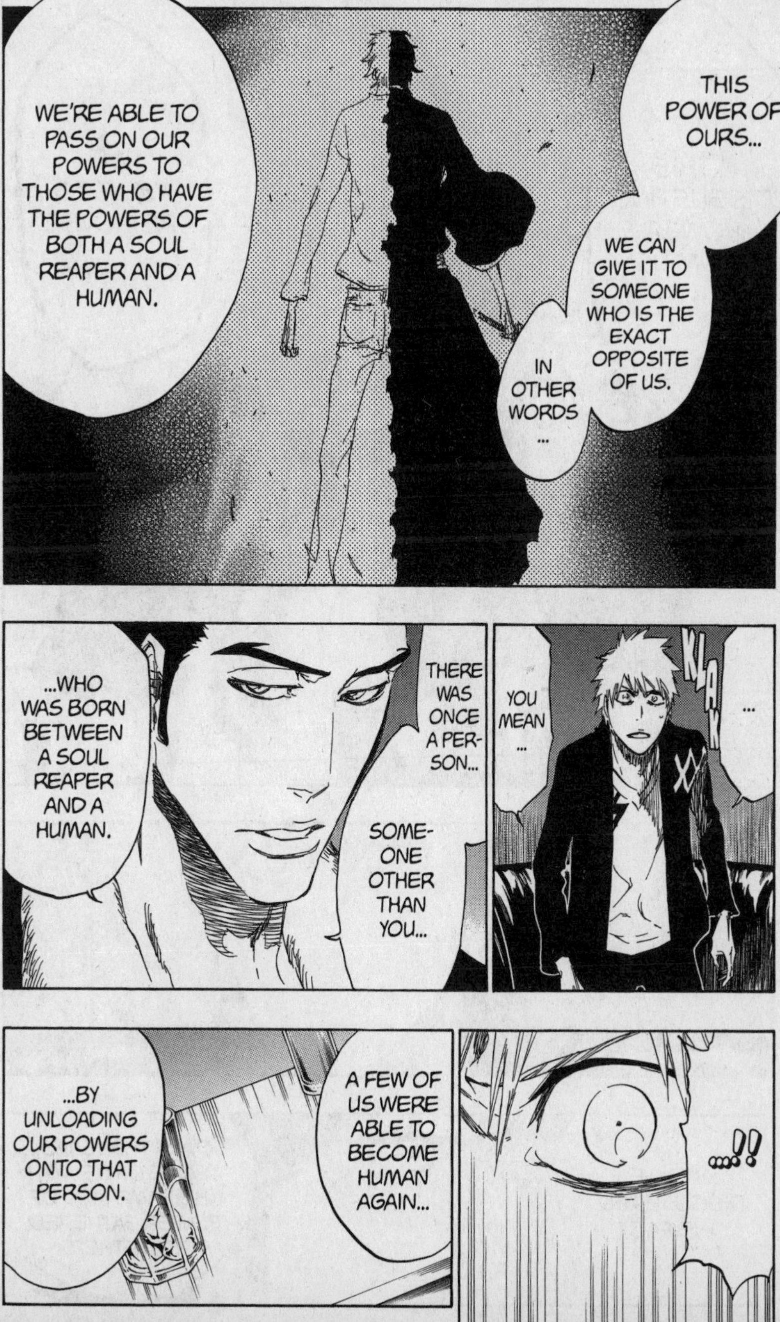
THIS POWER OF OURS...
WE CAN GIVE IT TO SOMEONE WHO IS THE EXACT OPPOSITE OF US.
IN OTHER WORDS...
WE'RE ABLE TO PASS ON OUR POWERS TO THOSE WHO HAVE THE POWERS OF BOTH A SOUL REAPER AND A HUMAN.
...
KLAK
YOU MEAN...
THERE WAS ONCE A PERSON...
SOMEONE OTHER THAN YOU...
...WHO WAS BORN BETWEEN A SOUL REAPER AND A HUMAN.
...!!
A FEW OF US WERE ABLE TO BECOME HUMAN AGAIN...
...BY UNLOADING OUR POWERS ONTO THAT PERSON.

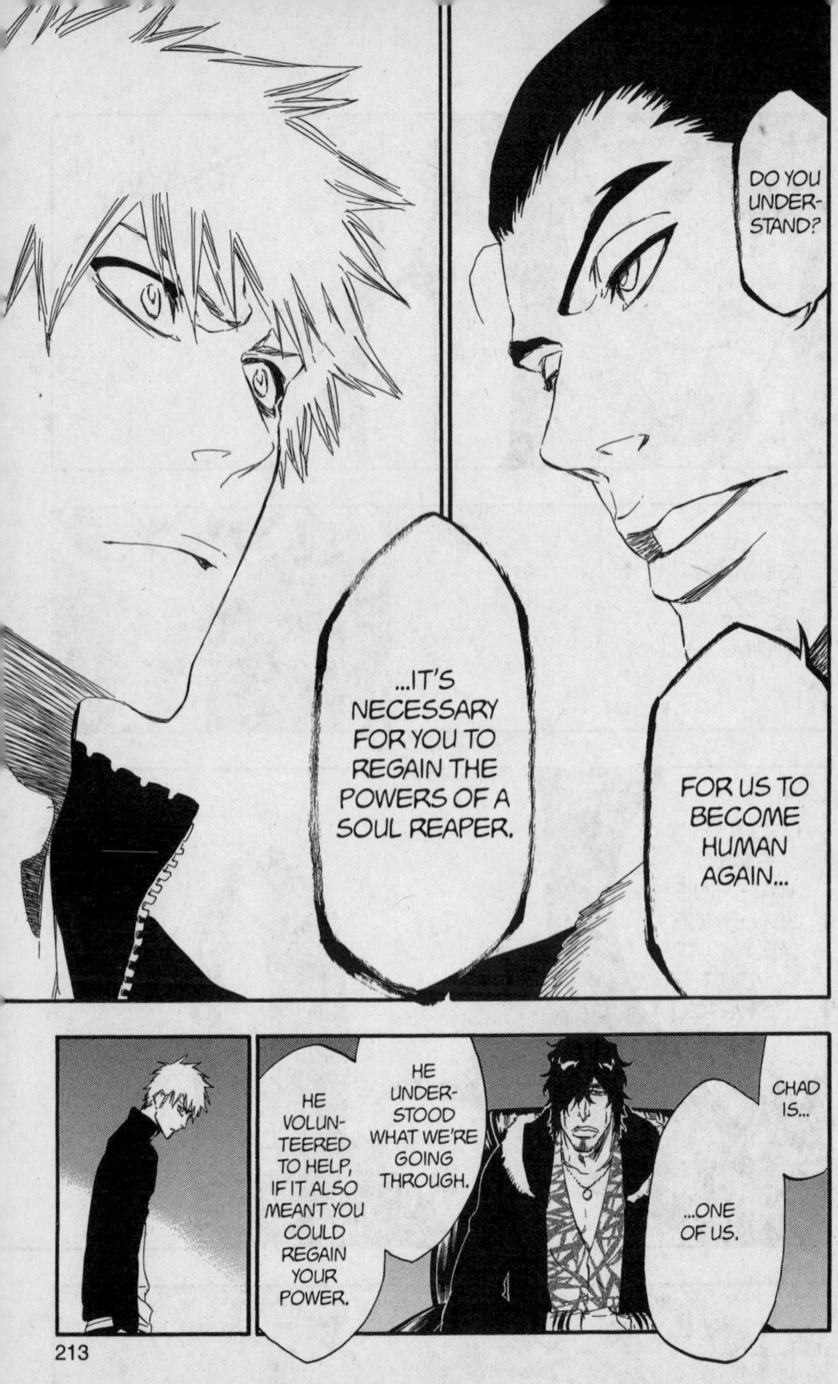
DO YOU UNDER-STAND?
FOR US TO BECOME HUMAN AGAIN...
...IT'S NECESSARY FOR YOU TO REGAIN THE POWERS OF A SOUL REAPER.
CHAD IS...
...ONE OF US.
HE UNDER-STOOD WHAT WE'RE GOING THROUGH.
HE VOLUN-TEERED TO HELP, IF IT ALSO MEANT YOU COULD REGAIN YOUR POWER.

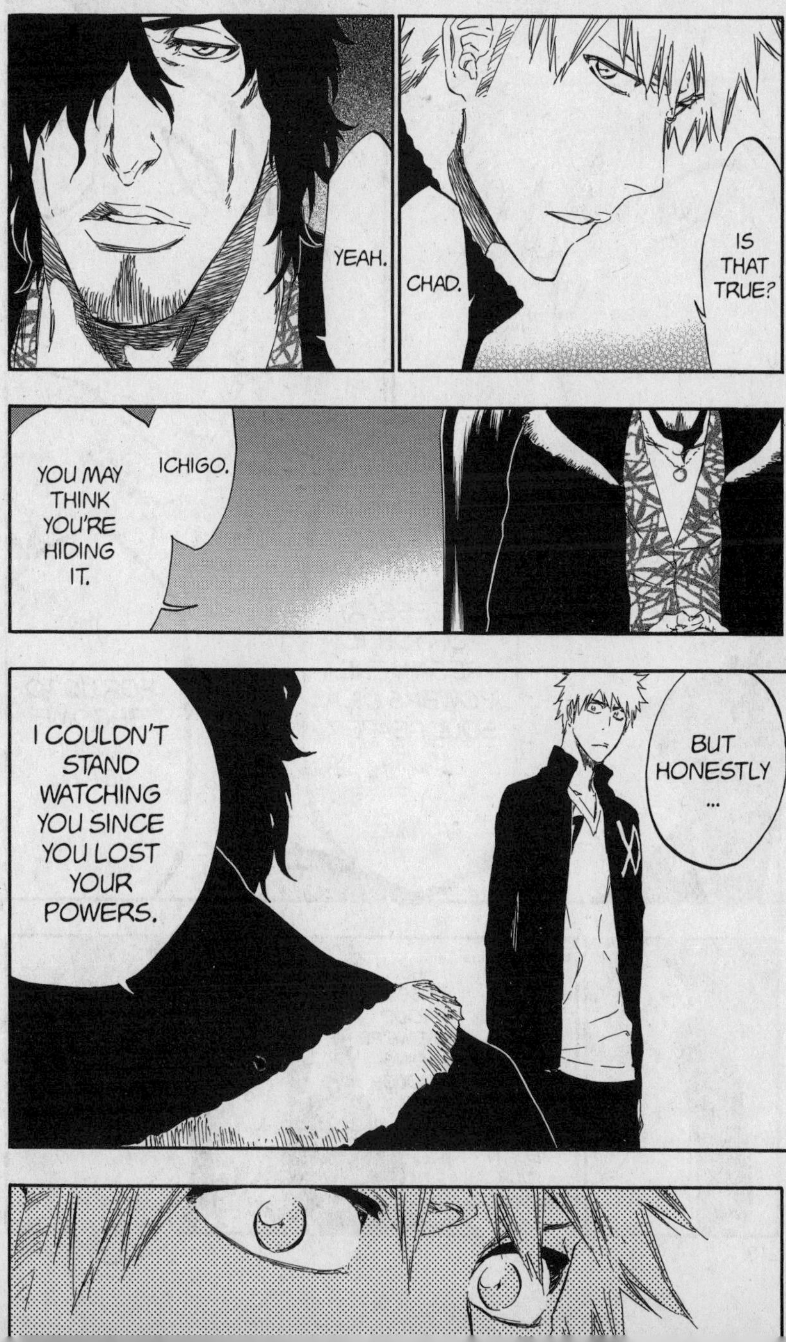

IS THAT TRUE?
CHAD.
YEAH.
ICHIGO.
YOU MAY THINK YOU'RE HIDING IT.
BUT HONESTLY ...
I COULDN'T STAND WATCHING YOU SINCE YOU LOST YOUR POWERS.

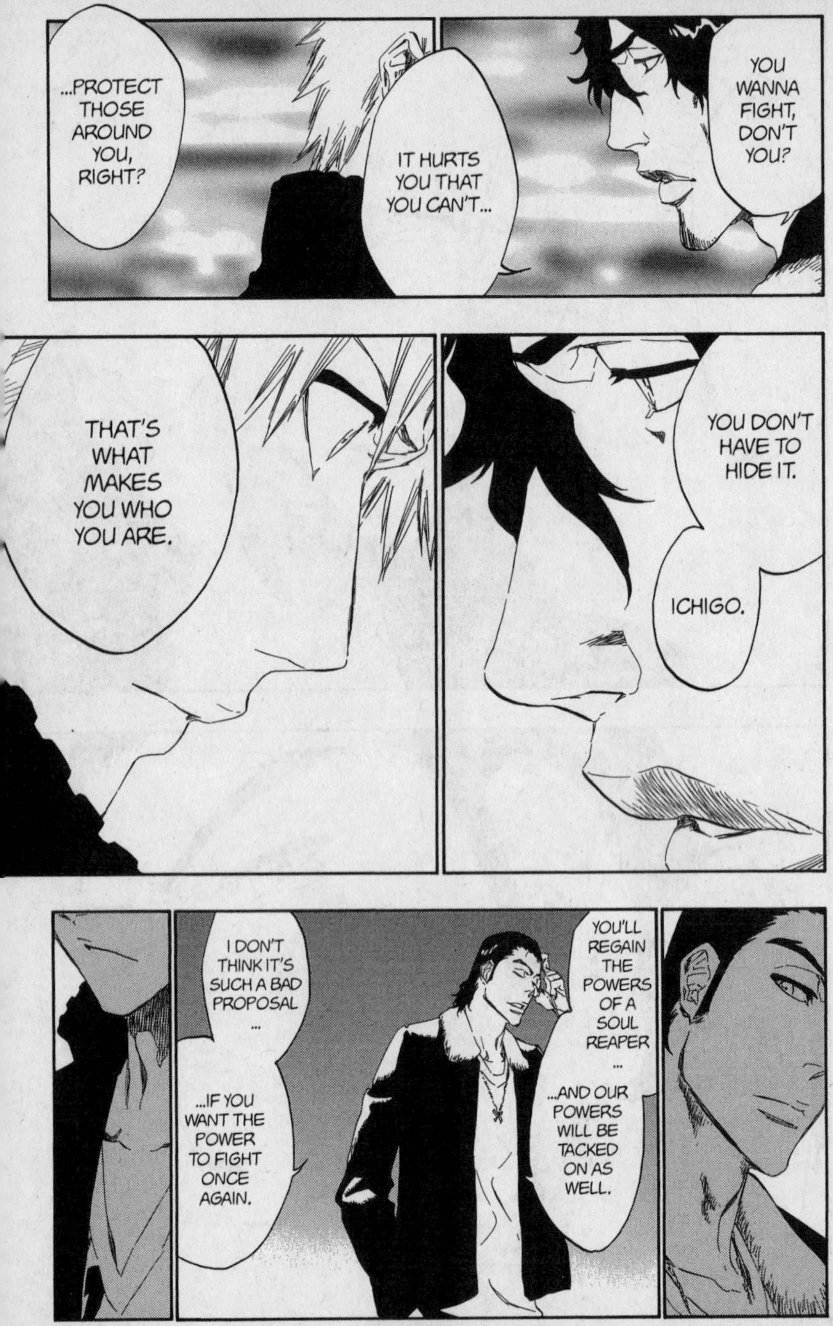
YOU WANNA FIGHT, DON'T YOU?
IT HURTS YOU THAT YOU CAN'T...
...PROTECT THOSE AROUND YOU, RIGHT?
YOU DON'T HAVE TO HIDE IT.
ICHIGO.
THAT'S WHAT MAKES YOU WHO YOU ARE.
YOU'LL REGAIN THE POWERS OF A SOUL REAPER...
...AND OUR POWERS WILL BE TACKED ON AS WELL.
I DON'T THINK IT'S SUCH A BAD PROPOSAL...
...IF YOU WANT THE POWER TO FIGHT ONCE AGAIN.

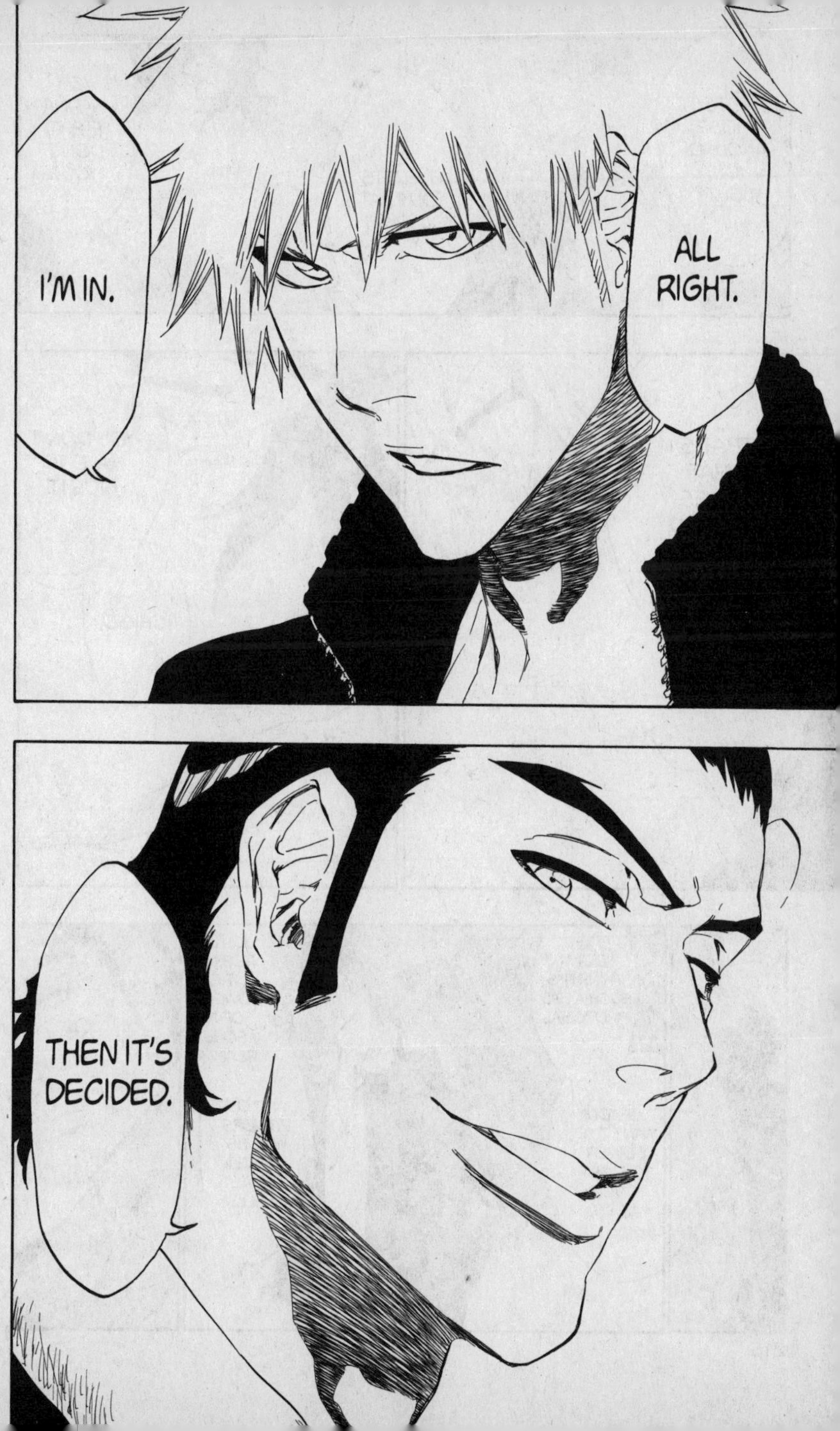
ALL RIGHT.
I'M IN.
THEN IT'S DECIDED.

READ THIS WAY

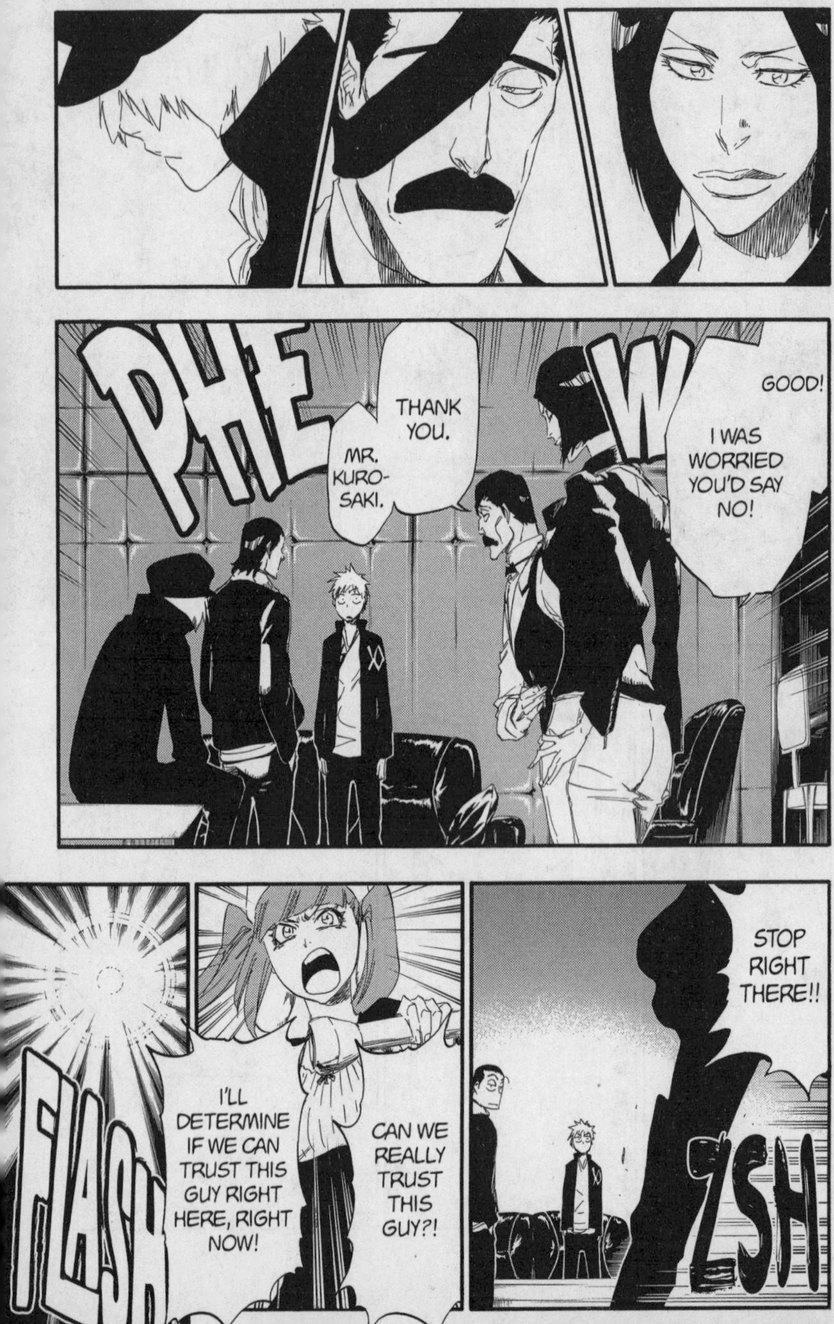
GOOD!
I WAS WORRIED YOU'D SAY NO!
PHEW
THANK YOU.
MR. KURO-SAKI.
STOP RIGHT THERE!!
ZSH
CAN WE REALLY TRUST THIS GUY?!
I'LL DETERMINE IF WE CAN TRUST THIS GUY RIGHT HERE, RIGHT NOW!
FLASH

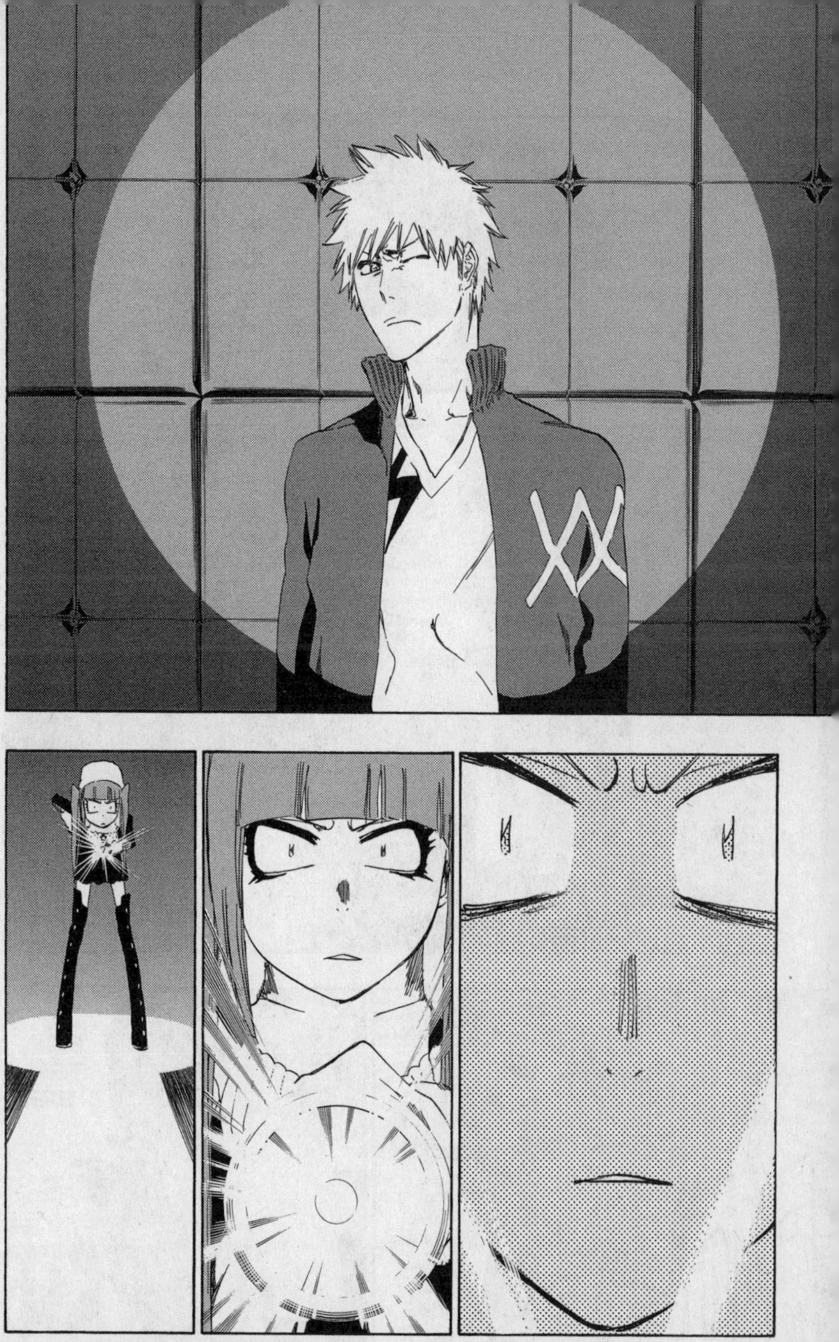

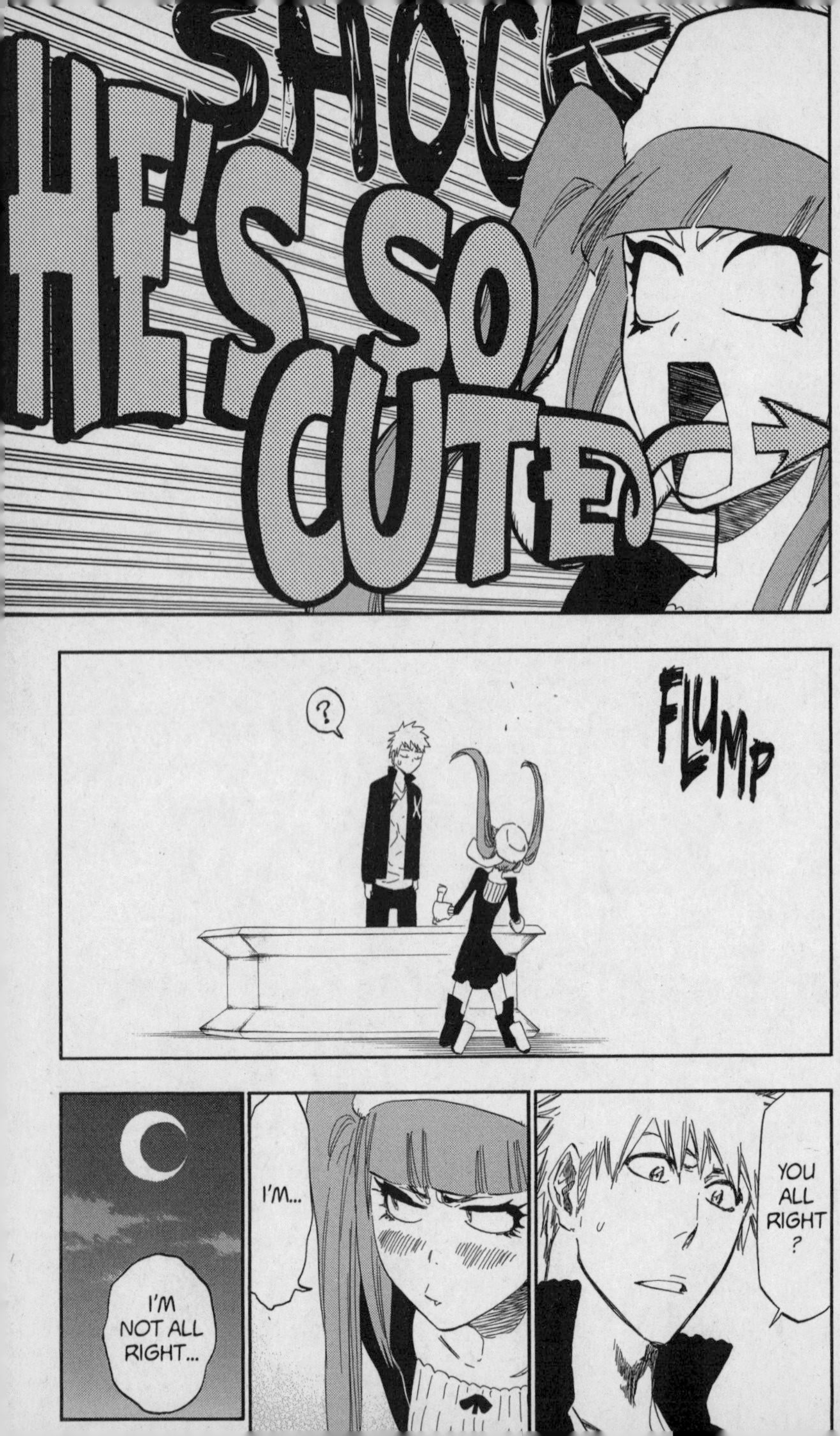
SHOCK
HE'S SO CUTE
FLUMP
?
YOU ALL RIGHT?
I'M...
I'M NOT ALL RIGHT...

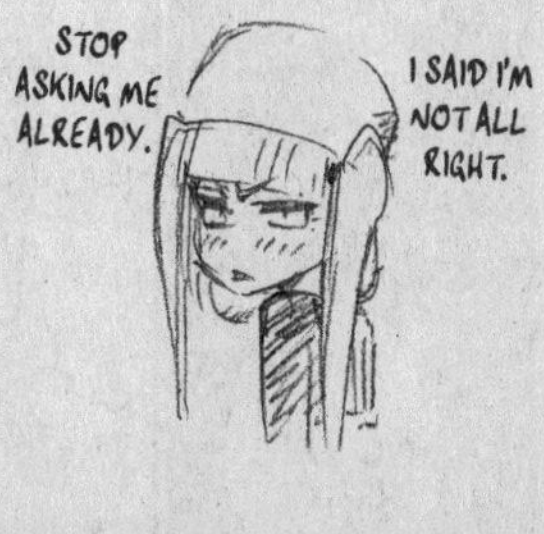
I SAID I'M NOT ALL RIGHT.
STOP ASKING ME ALREADY.

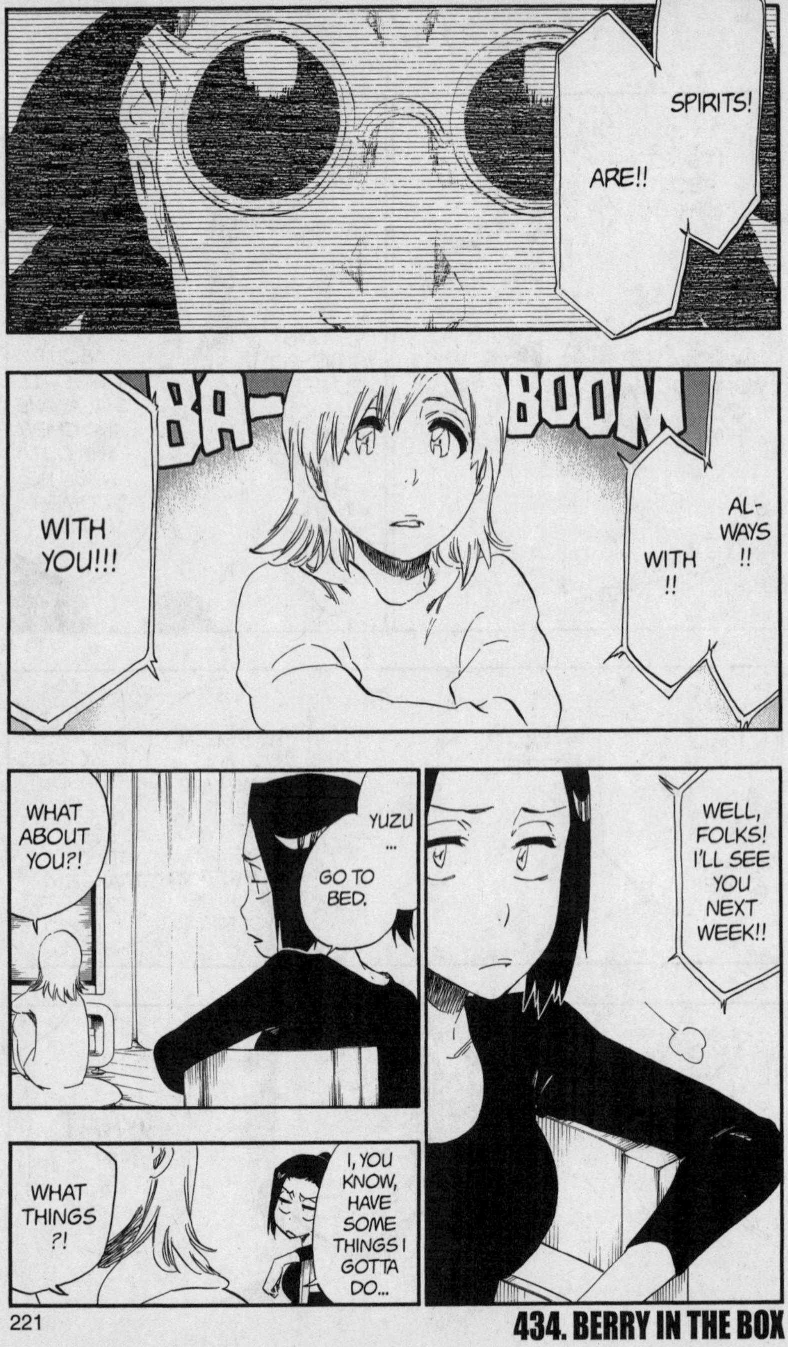
SPIRITS!
ARE!!
BA-BOOM
AL-WAYS!!
WITH!!
WITH YOU!!!
WELL, FOLKS! I'LL SEE YOU NEXT WEEK!!
YUZU... GO TO BED.
WHAT ABOUT YOU?!
I, YOU KNOW, HAVE SOME THINGS I GOTTA DO...
WHAT THINGS?!

434. BERRY IN THE BOX

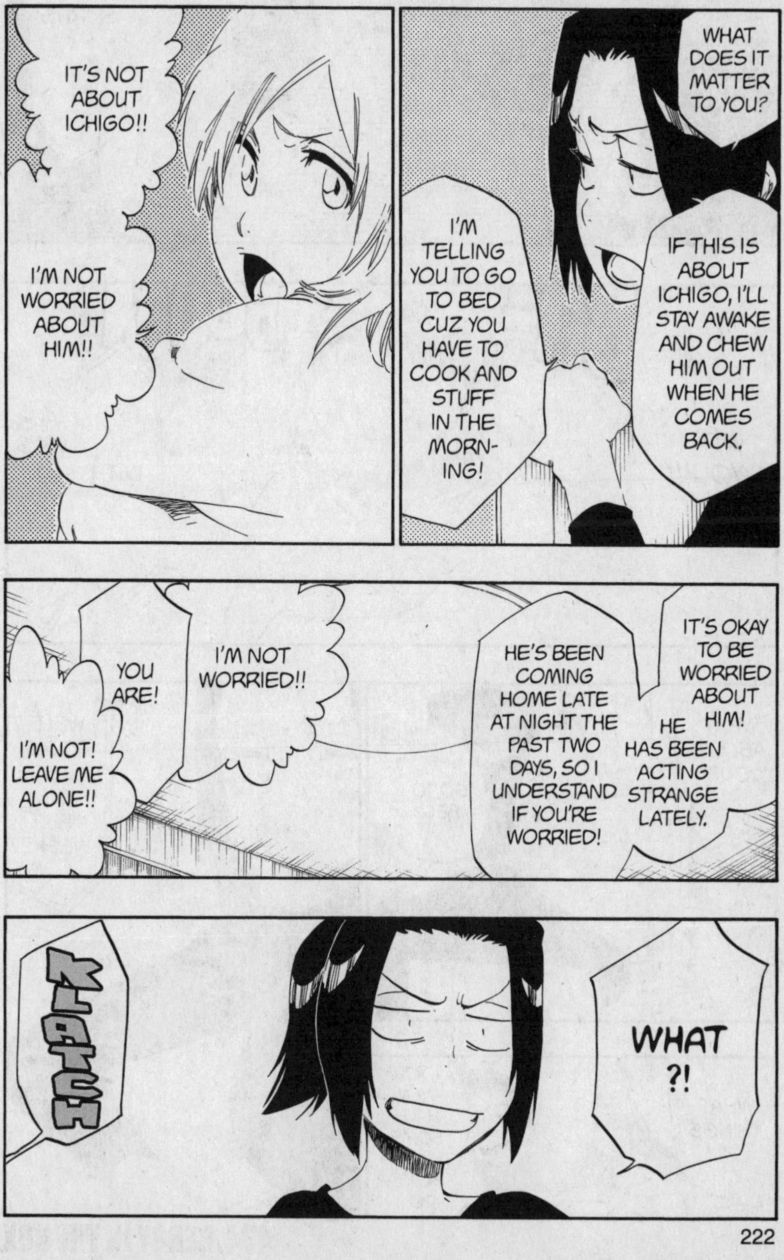
WHAT DOES IT MATTER TO YOU?
IF THIS IS ABOUT ICHIGO, I'LL STAY AWAKE AND CHEW HIM OUT WHEN HE COMES BACK.
I'M TELLING YOU TO GO TO BED CUZ YOU HAVE TO COOK AND STUFF IN THE MORN-ING!
IT'S NOT ABOUT ICHIGO!!
I'M NOT WORRIED ABOUT HIM!!
IT'S OKAY TO BE WORRIED ABOUT HIM!
HE HAS BEEN ACTING STRANGE LATELY.
HE'S BEEN COMING HOME LATE AT NIGHT THE PAST TWO DAYS, SO I UNDERSTAND IF YOU'RE WORRIED!
I'M NOT WORRIED!!
YOU ARE!
I'M NOT! LEAVE ME ALONE!!
WHAT ?!
KLATCH

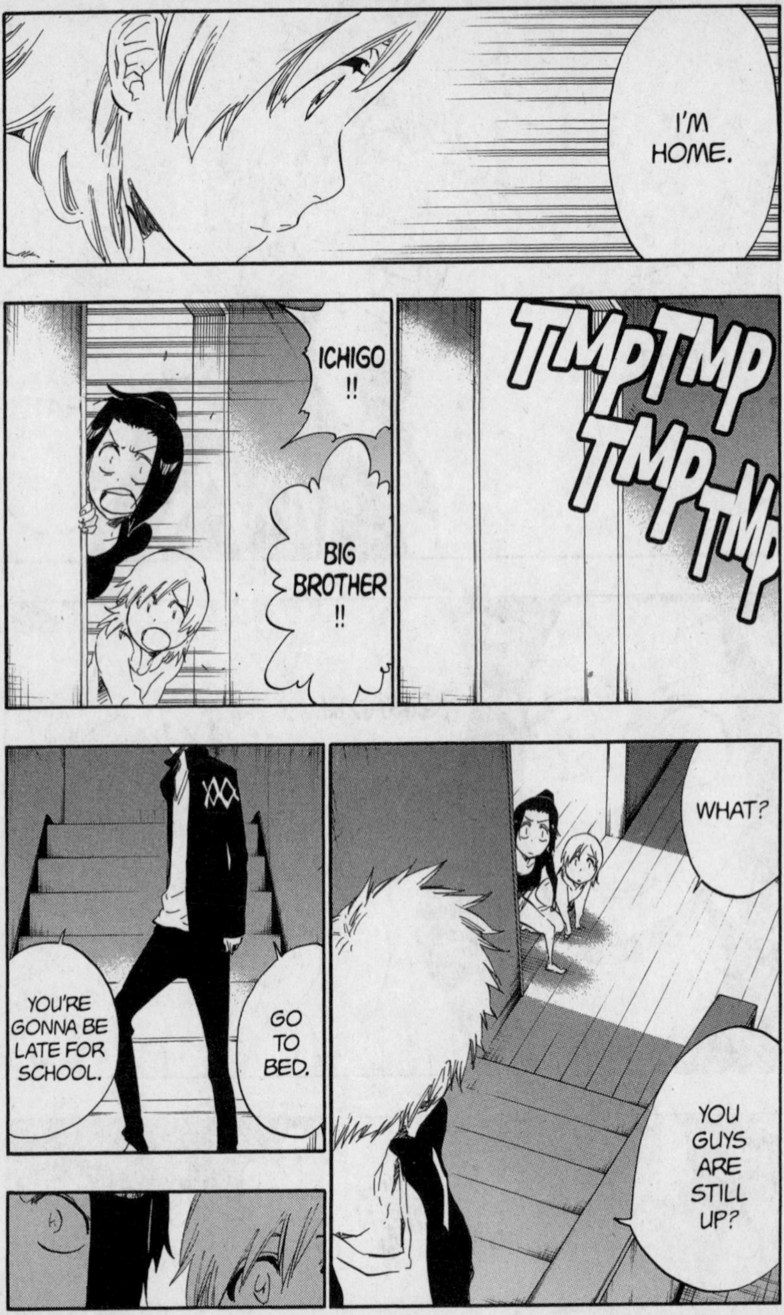
I'M HOME.
TMPTMP TMP TMP TMP
ICHIGO!!
BIG BROTHER!!
WHAT?
YOU GUYS ARE STILL UP?
GO TO BED.
YOU'RE GONNA BE LATE FOR SCHOOL.

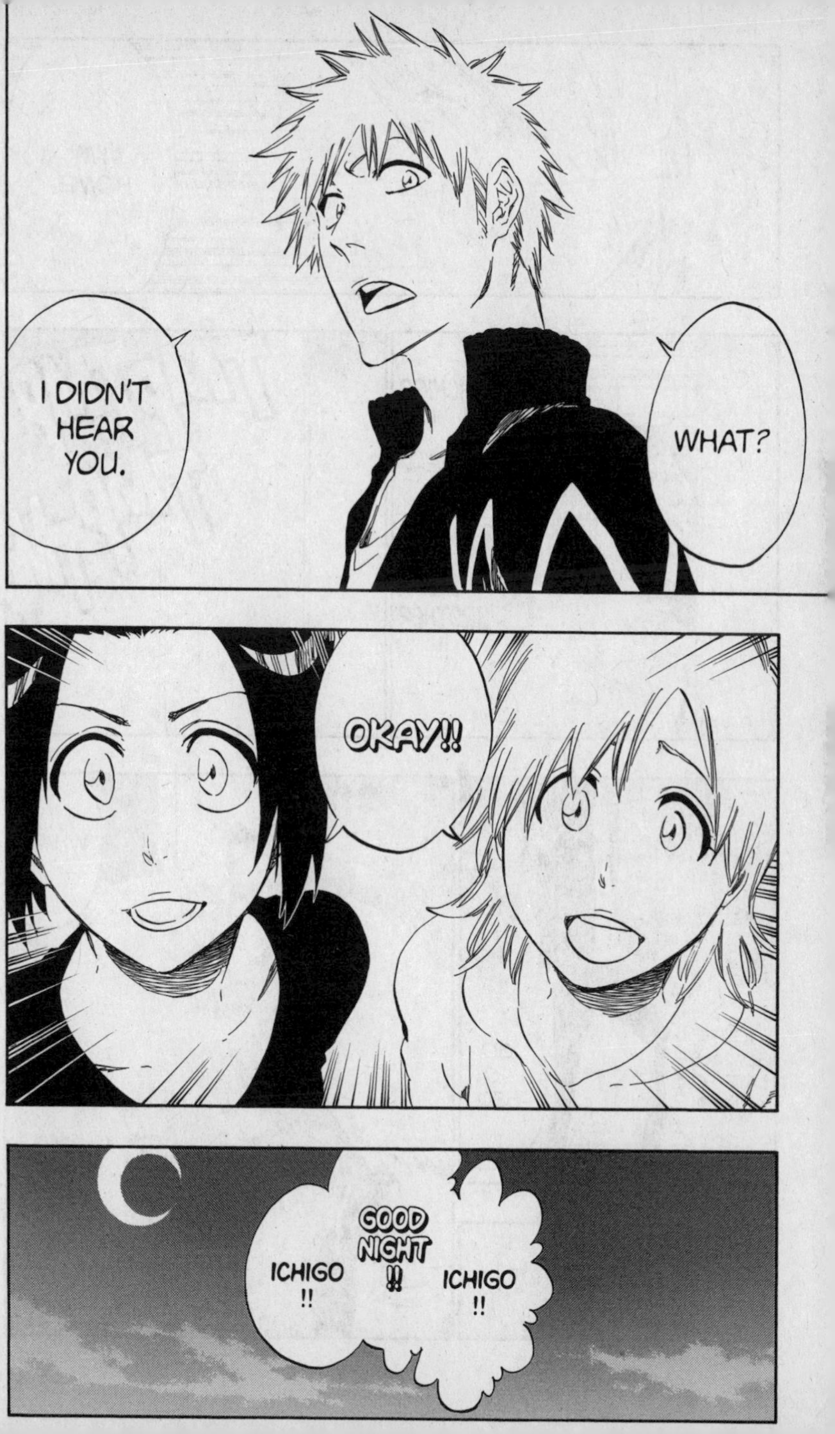
WHAT?
I DIDN'T HEAR YOU.
OKAY!!
GOOD NIGHT!!
ICHIGO!!
ICHIGO!!

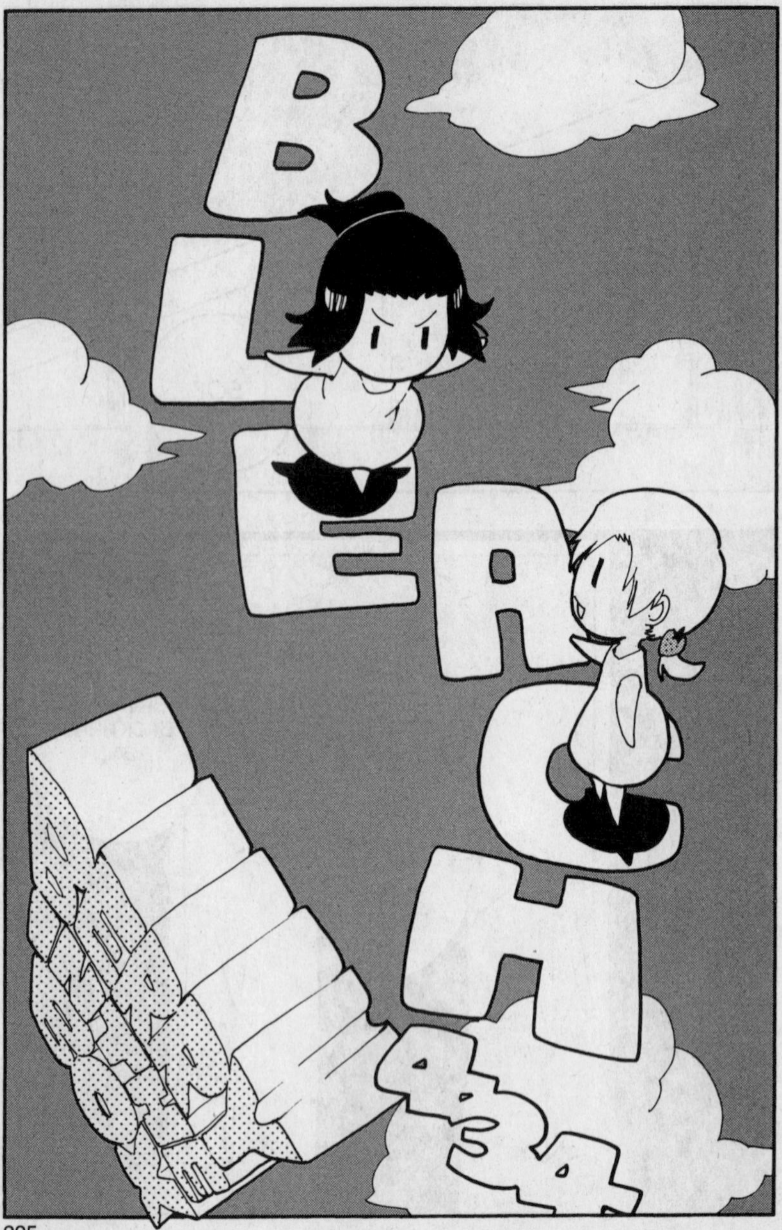
BLEACH

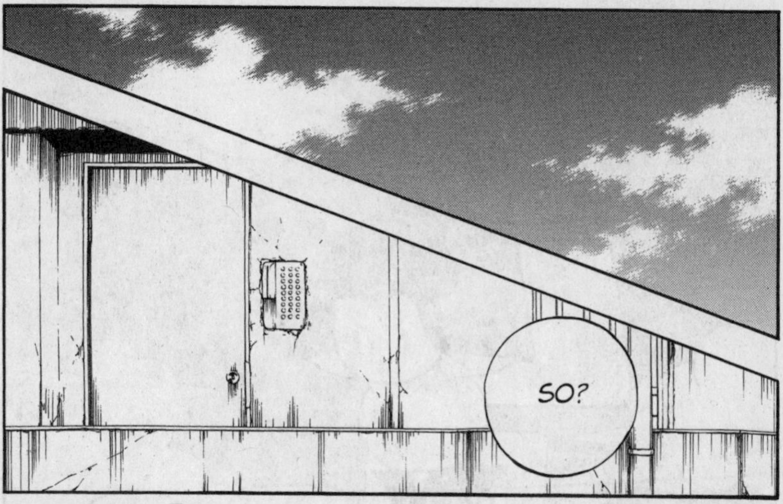
SO?
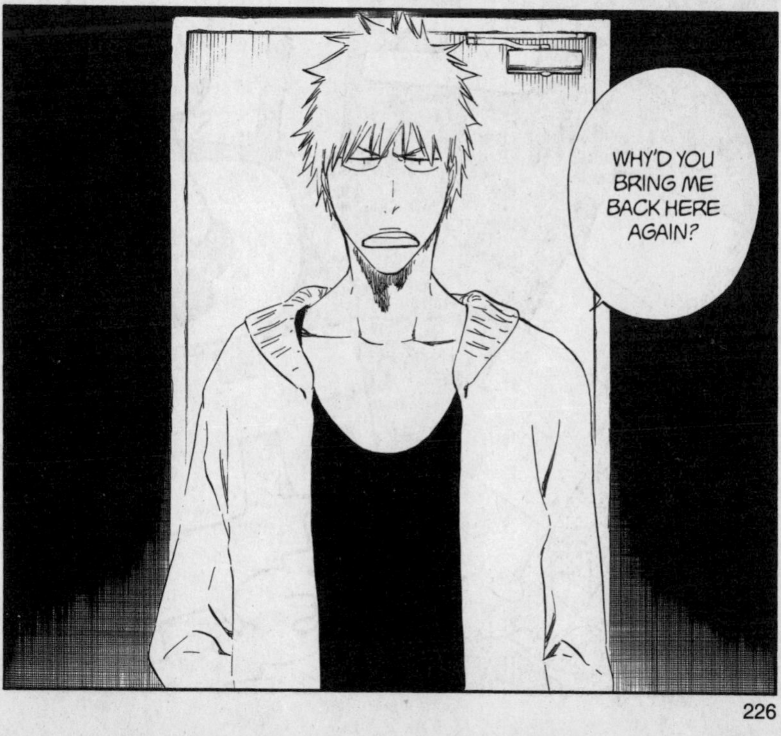
WHY'D YOU BRING ME BACK HERE AGAIN?

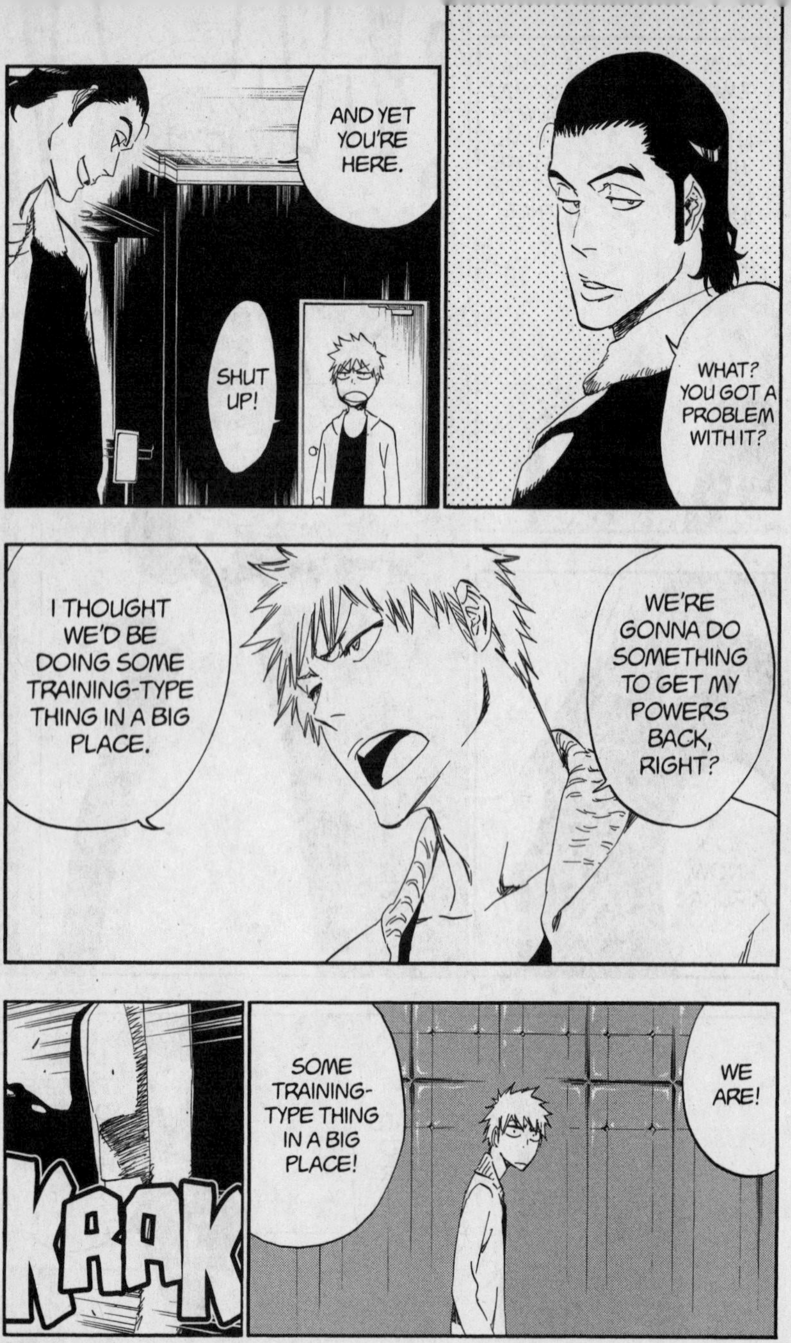
WHAT? YOU GOT A PROBLEM WITH IT?
AND YET YOU'RE HERE.
SHUT UP!
WE'RE GONNA DO SOMETHING TO GET MY POWERS BACK, RIGHT?
I THOUGHT WE'D BE DOING SOME TRAINING-TYPE THING IN A BIG PLACE.
WE ARE!
SOME TRAINING-TYPE THING IN A BIG PLACE!

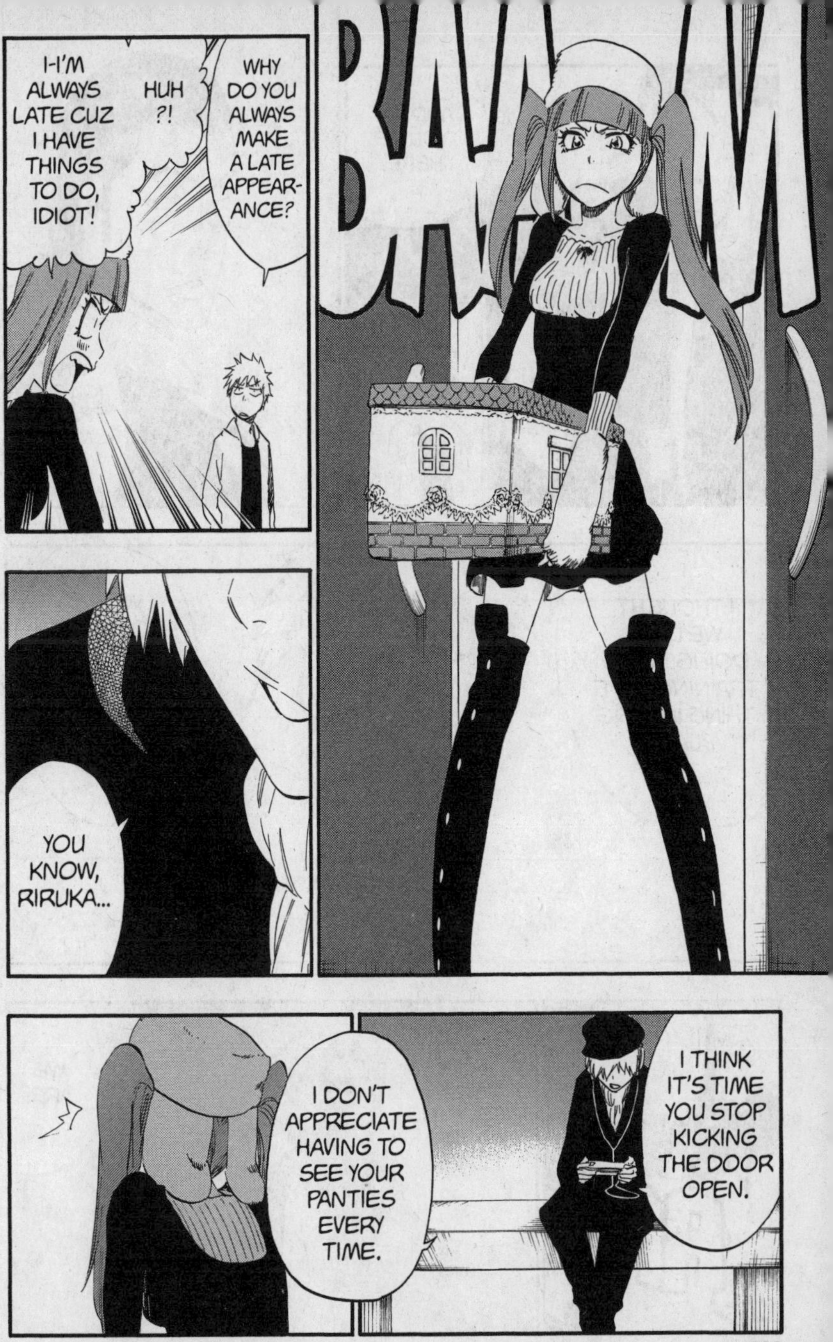
WHY DO YOU ALWAYS MAKE A LATE APPEARANCE?
HUH ?!
I-I'M ALWAYS LATE CUZ I HAVE THINGS TO DO, IDIOT!
YOU KNOW, RIRUKA...
I THINK IT'S TIME YOU STOP KICKING THE DOOR OPEN.
I DON'T APPRECIATE HAVING TO SEE YOUR PANTIES EVERY TIME.

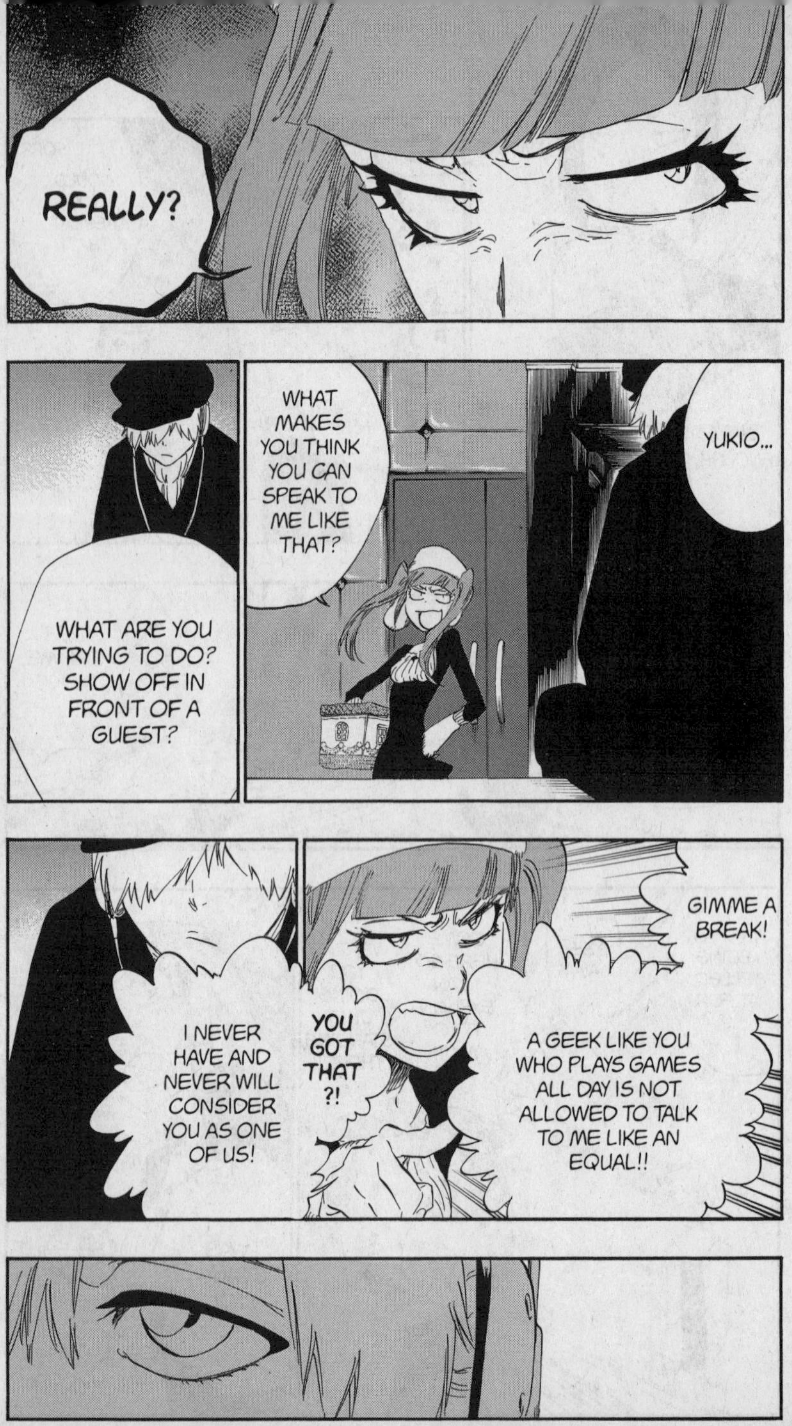
REALLY?
YUKIO...
WHAT MAKES YOU THINK YOU CAN SPEAK TO ME LIKE THAT?
WHAT ARE YOU TRYING TO DO? SHOW OFF IN FRONT OF A GUEST?
GIMME A BREAK!
A GEEK LIKE YOU WHO PLAYS GAMES ALL DAY IS NOT ALLOWED TO TALK TO ME LIKE AN EQUAL!!
YOU GOT THAT?!
I NEVER HAVE AND NEVER WILL CONSIDER YOU AS ONE OF US!

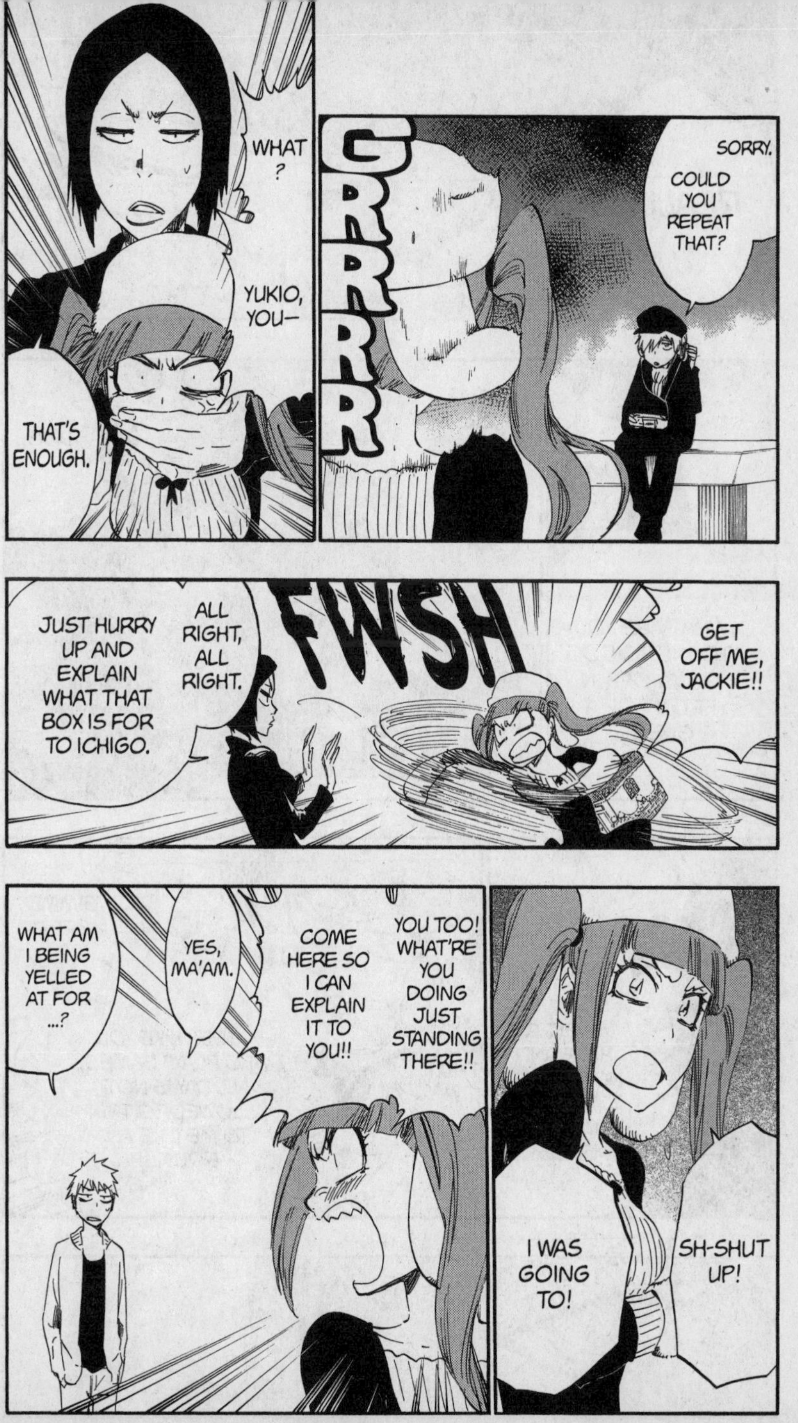
SORRY.
COULD YOU REPEAT THAT?
GRRRR
WHAT?
YUKIO, YOU—
THAT'S ENOUGH.
GET OFF ME, JACKIE!!
FWSH
ALL RIGHT, ALL RIGHT.
JUST HURRY UP AND EXPLAIN WHAT THAT BOX IS FOR TO ICHIGO.
SH-SHUT UP!
I WAS GOING TO!
YOU TOO! WHAT'RE YOU DOING JUST STANDING THERE!!
COME HERE SO I CAN EXPLAIN IT TO YOU!!
YES, MA'AM.
WHAT AM I BEING YELLED AT FOR ...?

READ THIS WAY

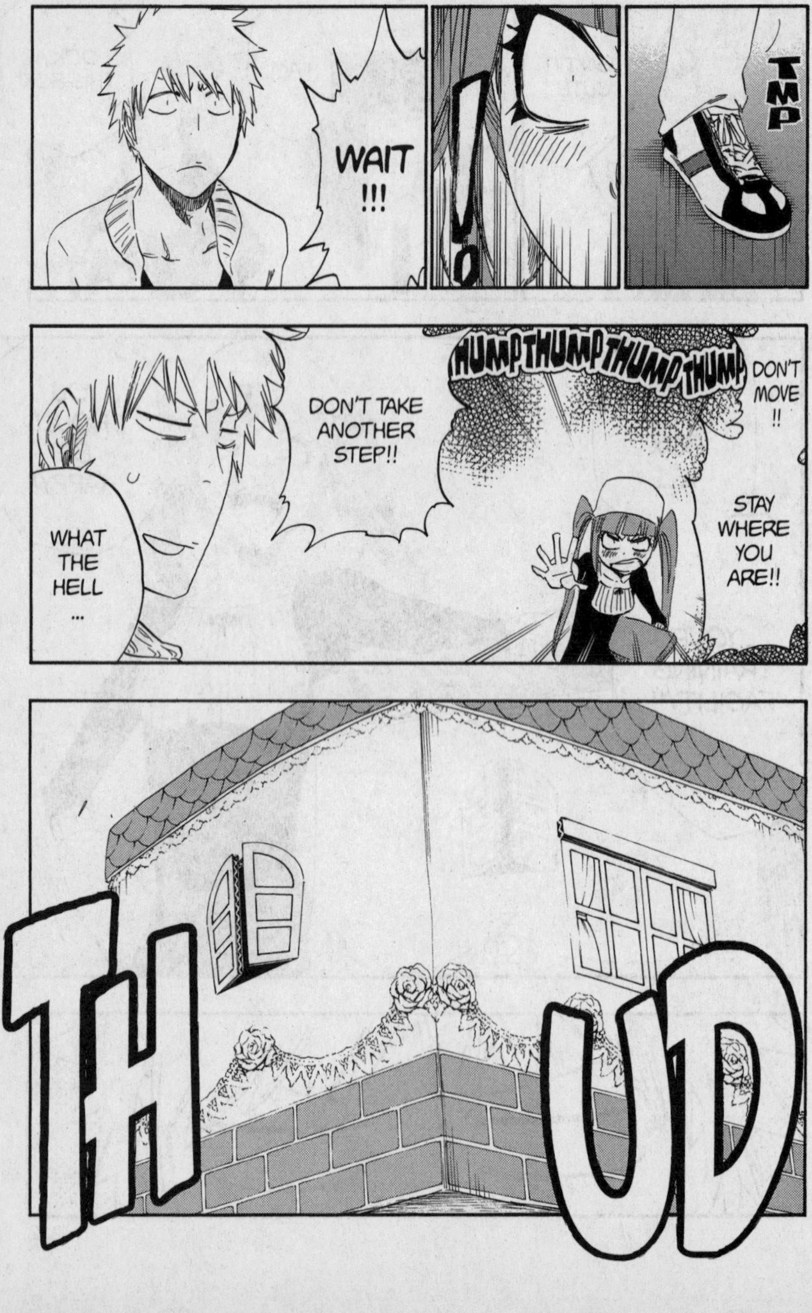
TMP
WAIT !!!
DON'T MOVE !!
THUMP THUMP THUMP THUMP
STAY WHERE YOU ARE!!
DON'T TAKE ANOTHER STEP!!
WHAT THE HELL ...
THUD

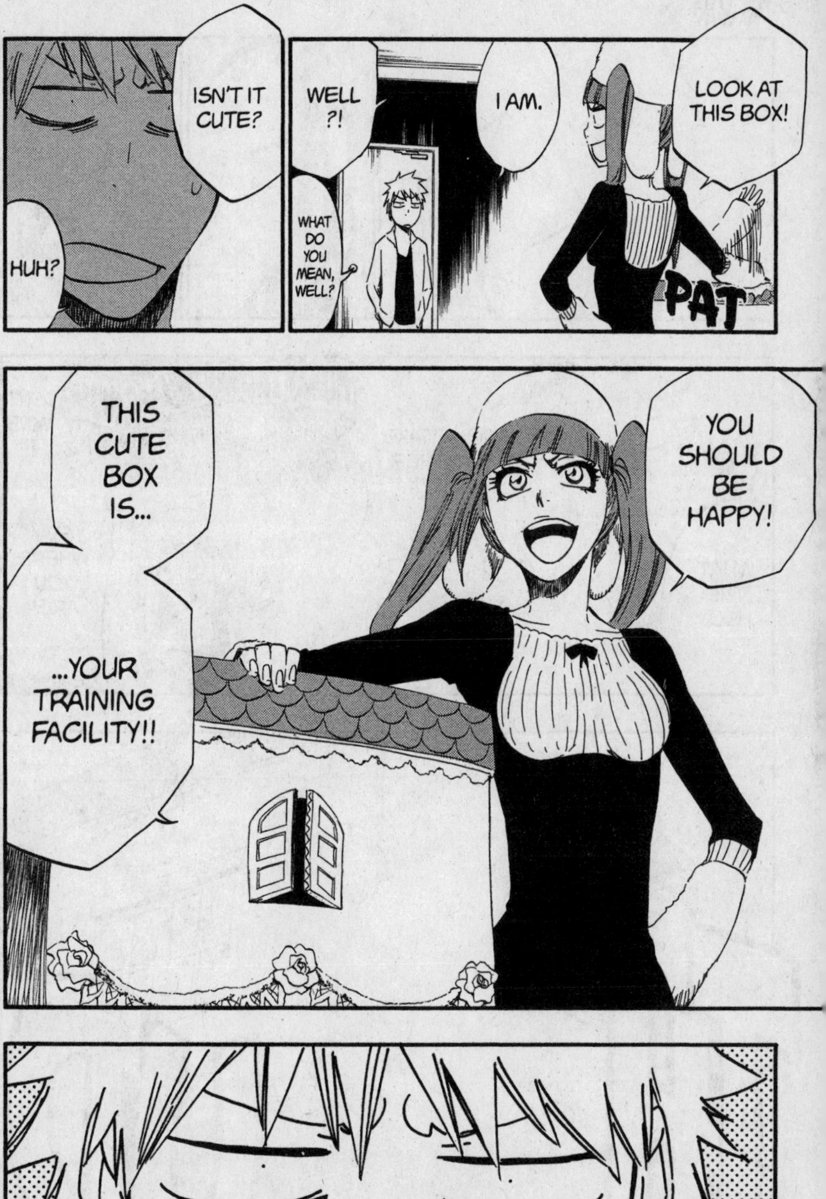
LOOK AT THIS BOX!
PAT
I AM.
WELL ?!
WHAT DO YOU MEAN, WELL?
ISN'T IT CUTE?
HUH?
YOU SHOULD BE HAPPY!
THIS CUTE BOX IS...
...YOUR TRAINING FACILITY!!

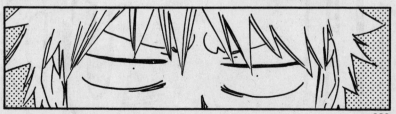

READ THIS WAY

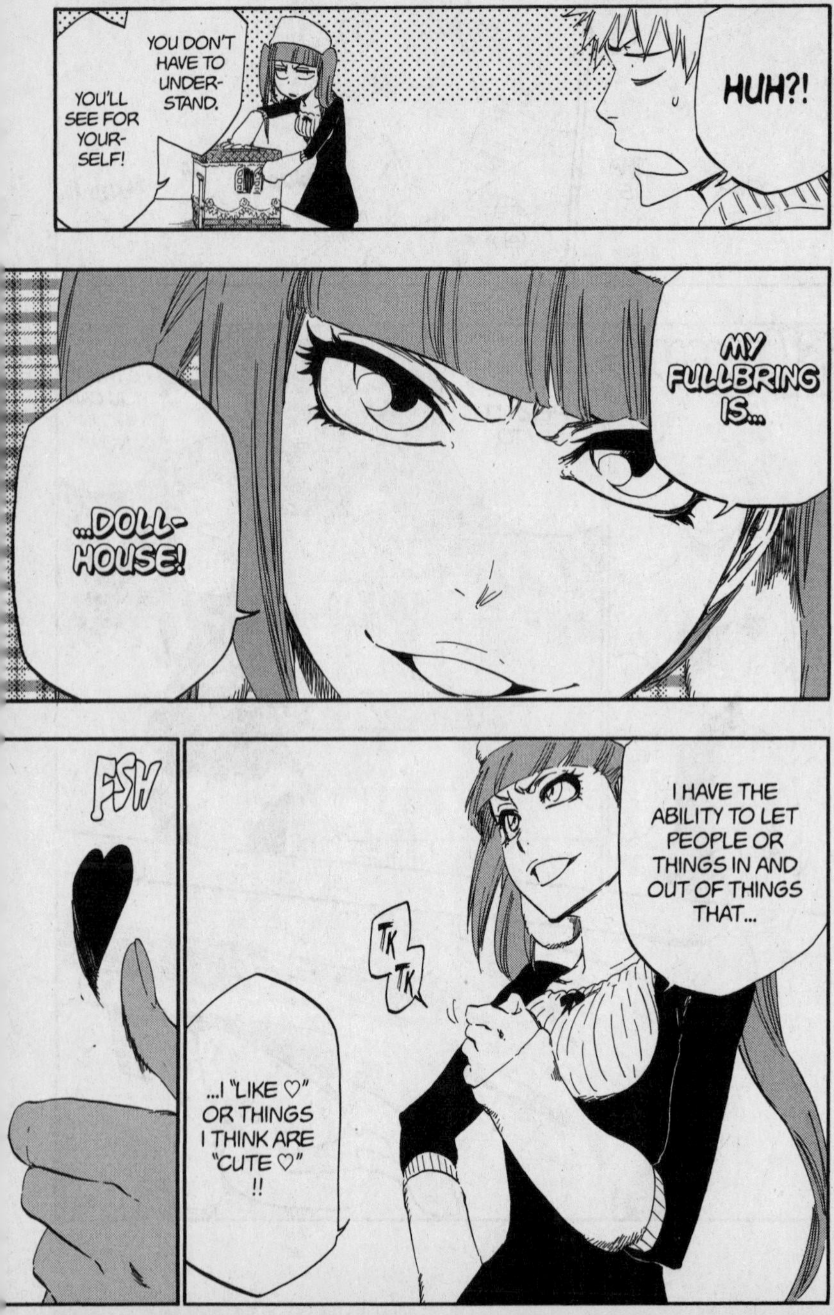
HUH?!
YOU DON'T HAVE TO UNDER-STAND.
YOU'LL SEE FOR YOUR-SELF!
MY FULLBRING IS...
...DOLL-HOUSE!
I HAVE THE ABILITY TO LET PEOPLE OR THINGS IN AND OUT OF THINGS THAT...
TK TK
...I "LIKE ♡" OR THINGS I THINK ARE "CUTE ♡" !!
FSH

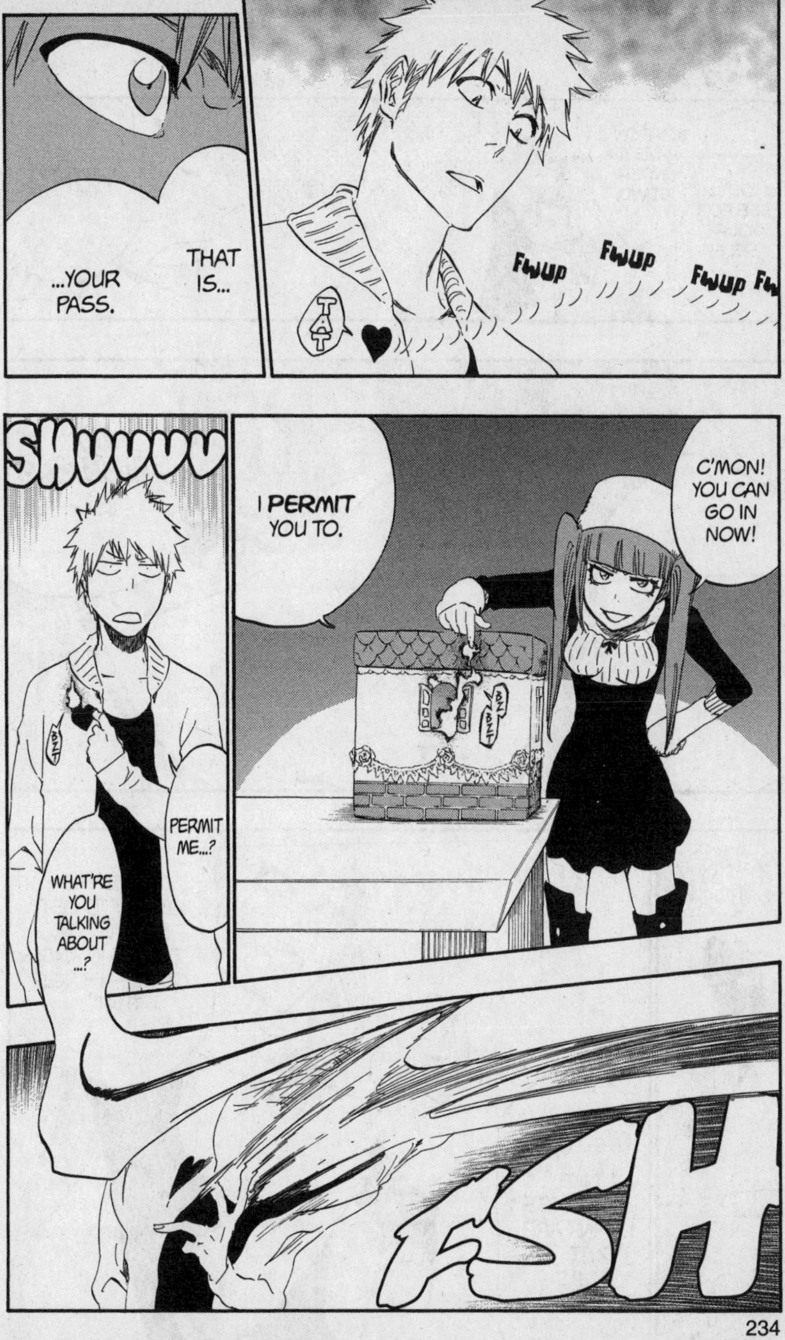
FWUP
FWUP
FWUP
TAT
THAT IS...
...YOUR PASS.
C'MON! YOU CAN GO IN NOW!
I PERMIT YOU TO.
SHUUUU
PERMIT ME...?
WHAT'RE YOU TALKING ABOUT ...?
FSH

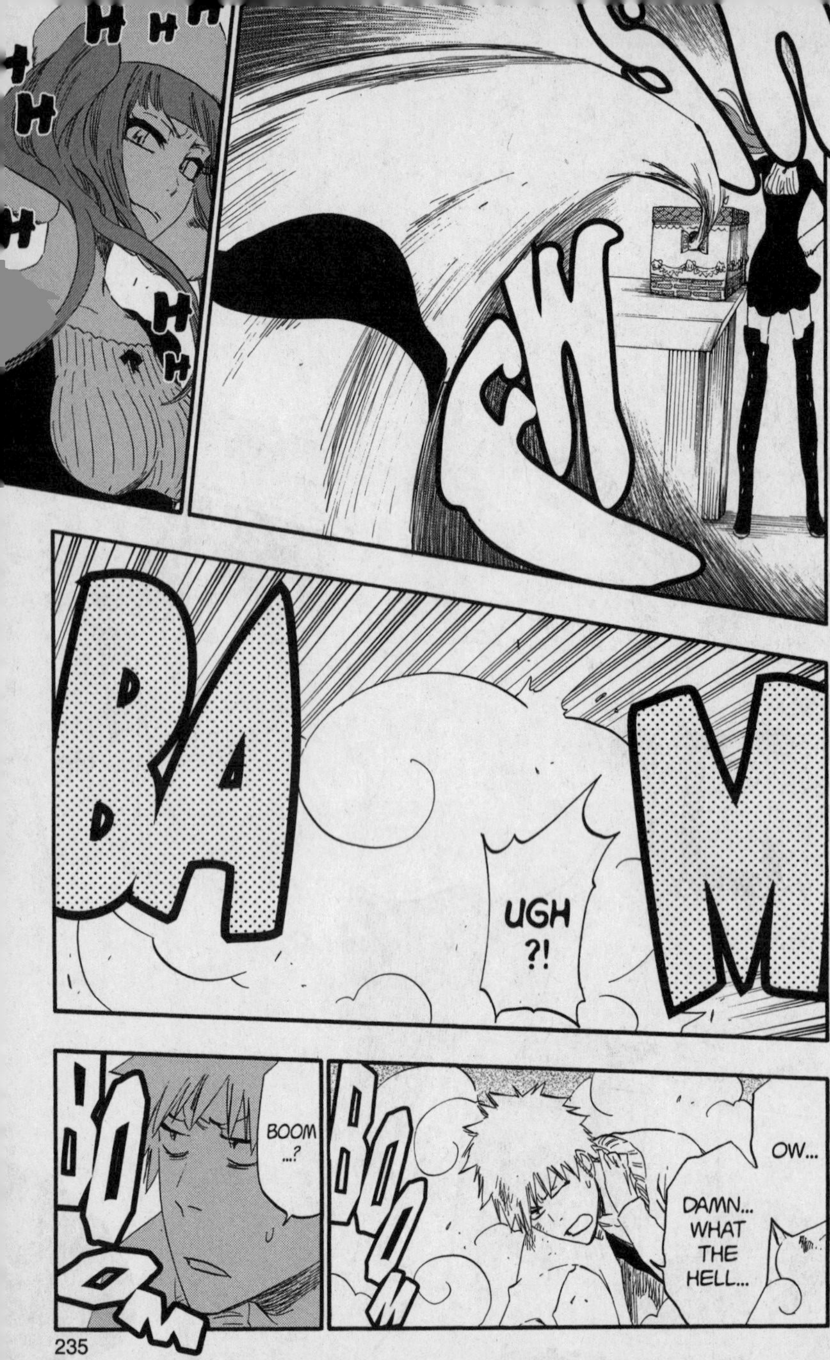
UGH ?!
OW...
DAMN... WHAT THE HELL...
BOOM ...?

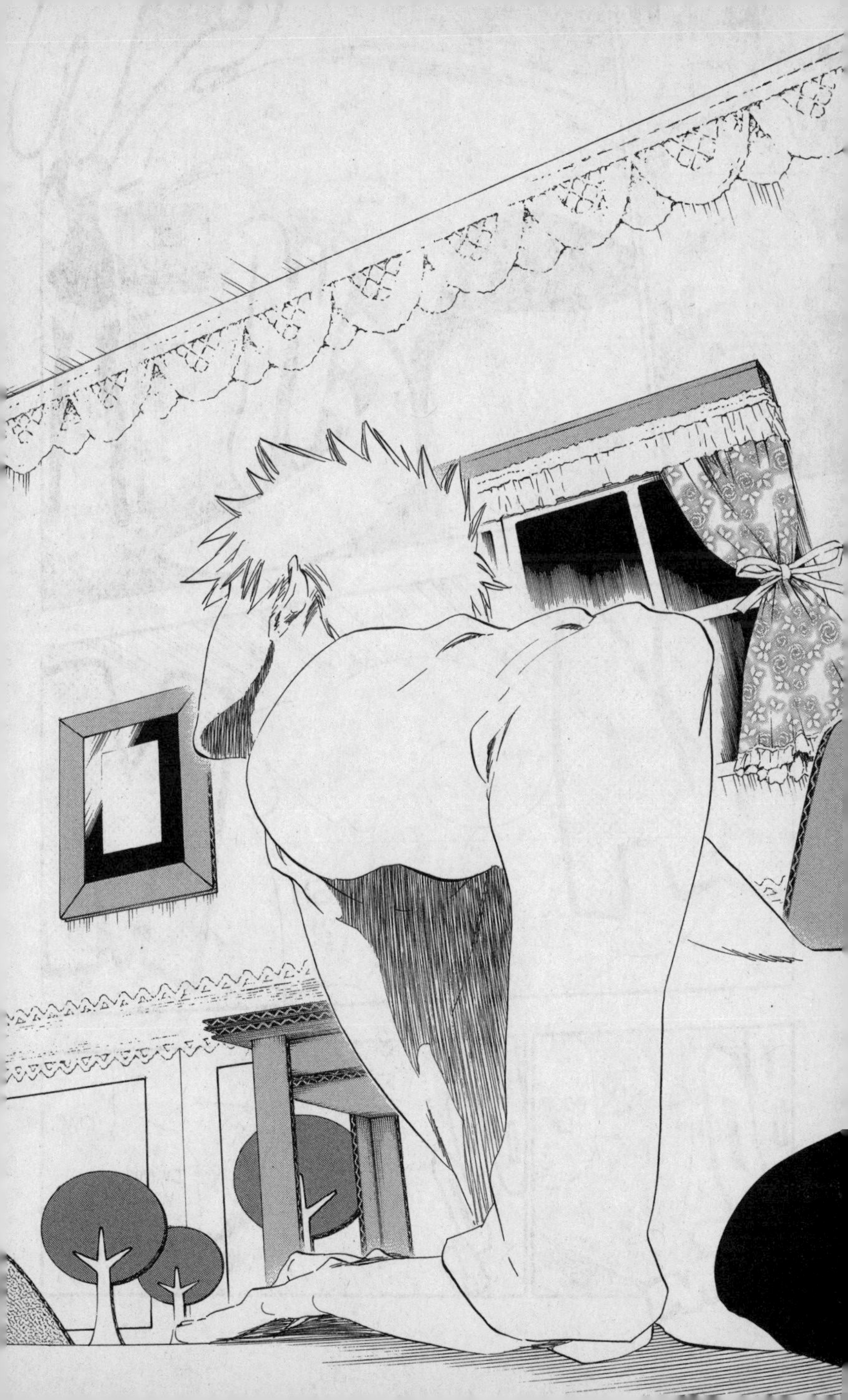

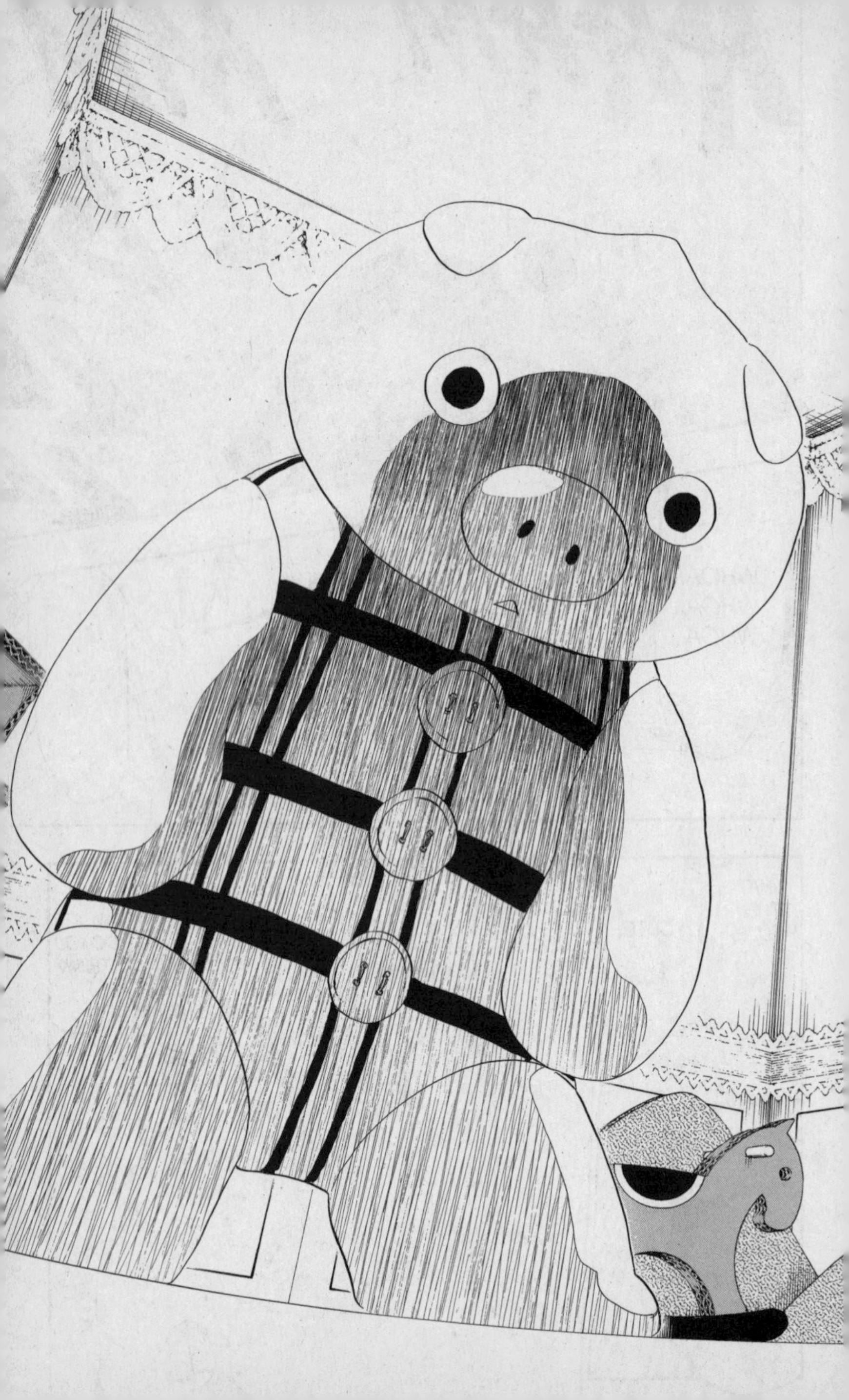

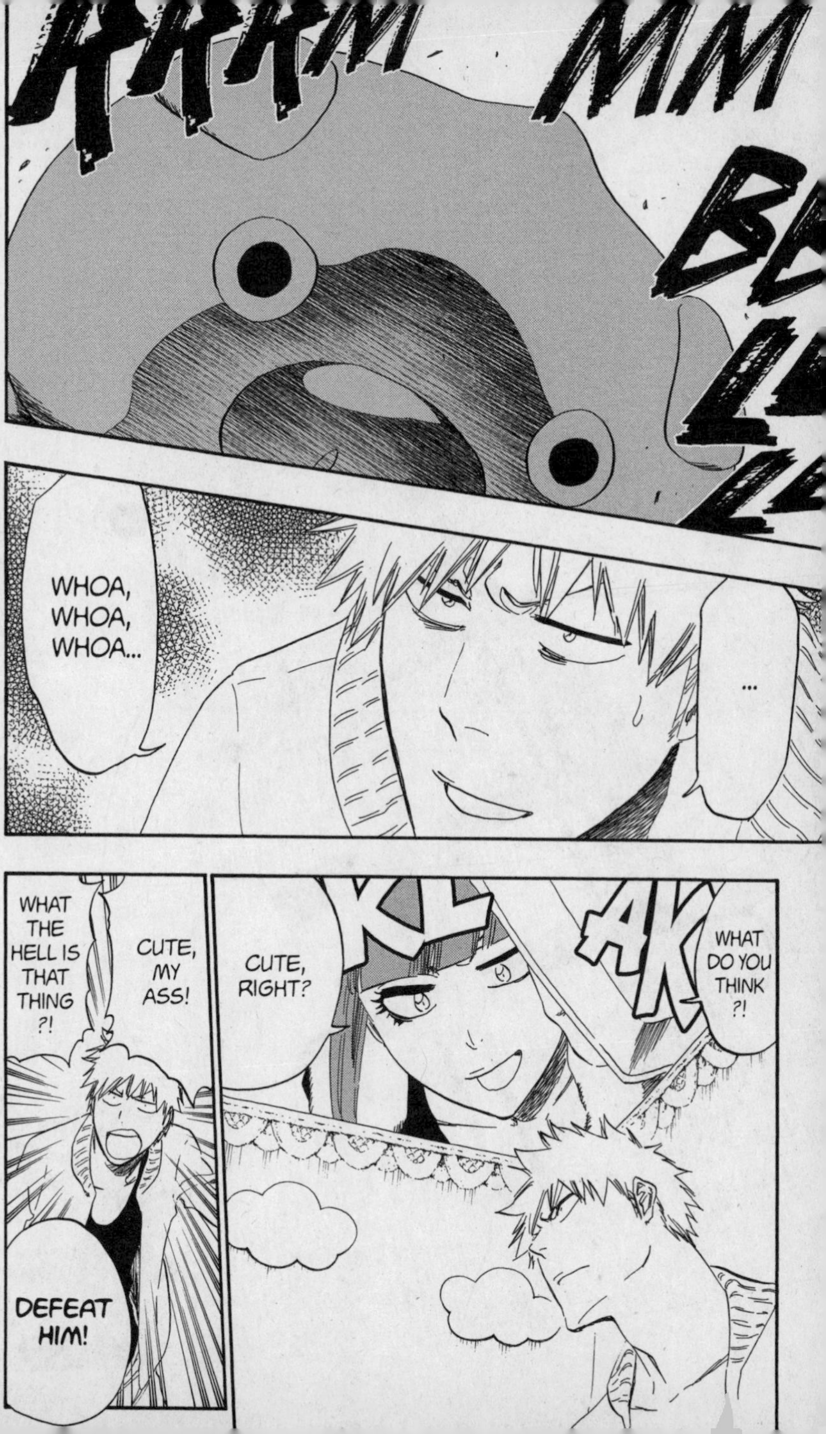
AHHM
MM
BE
LL
LL
...
WHOA, WHOA, WHOA...
KL
AK
WHAT DO YOU THINK?!
CUTE, RIGHT?
CUTE, MY ASS!
WHAT THE HELL IS THAT THING?!
DEFEAT HIM!

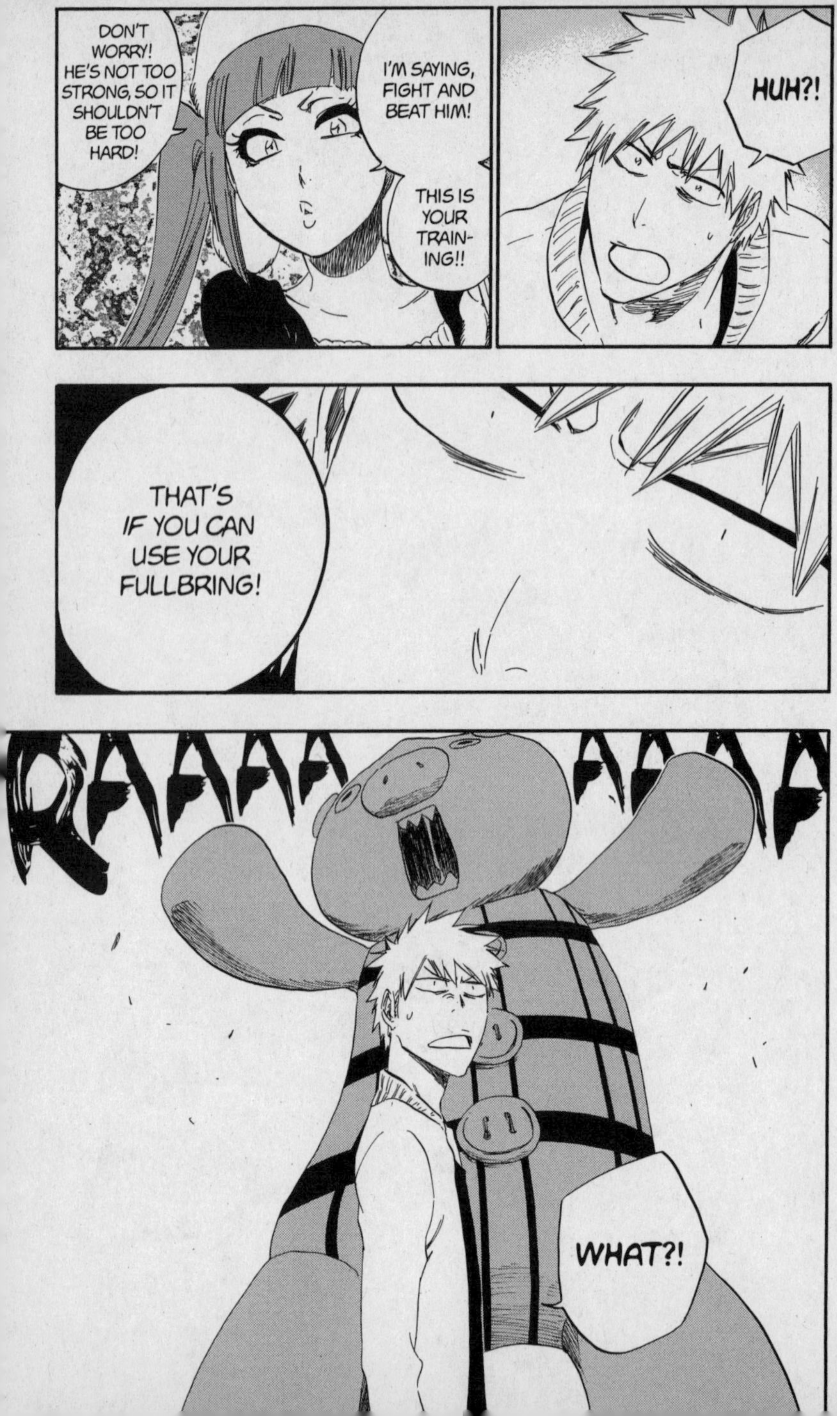
HUH?!
I'M SAYING, FIGHT AND BEAT HIM!
THIS IS YOUR TRAIN-ING!!
DON'T WORRY! HE'S NOT TOO STRONG, SO IT SHOULDN'T BE TOO HARD!
THAT'S IF YOU CAN USE YOUR FULLBRING!
RAAAAAAAA
WHAT?!

I HAVE A LATE-NIGHT SHOW NOW!
PROOF THAT I'M GAINING POPULARITY!

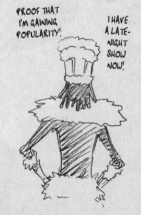

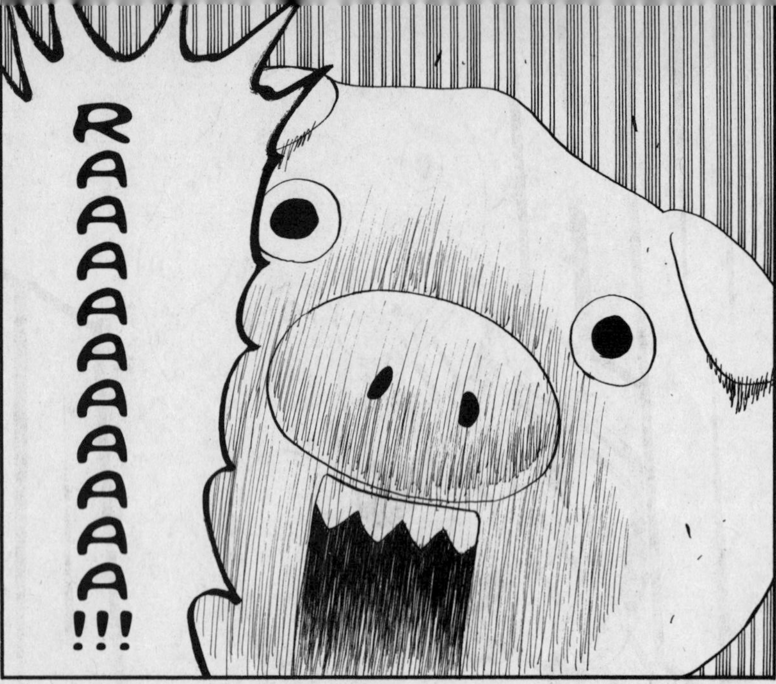
RAAAAAAAAAAA!!!
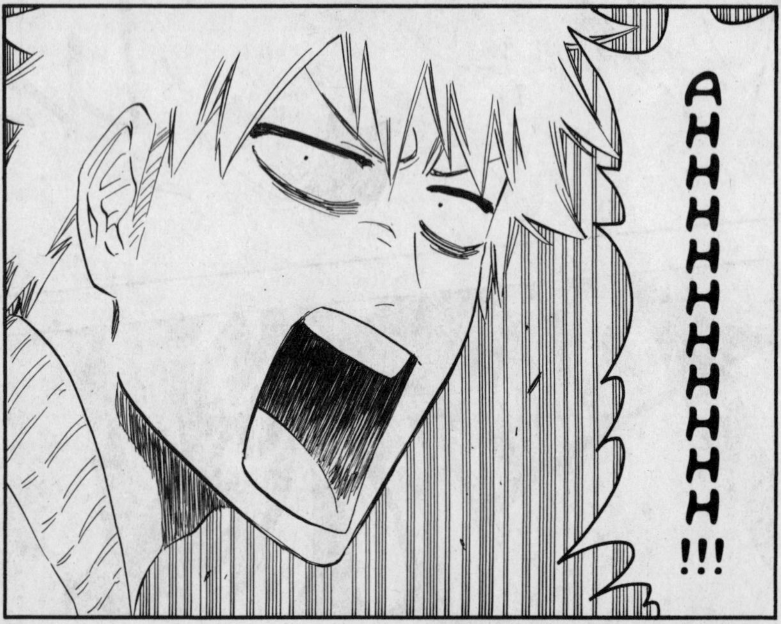
AHHHHHHHHHHH!!!

435. Panic at the Dollhouse

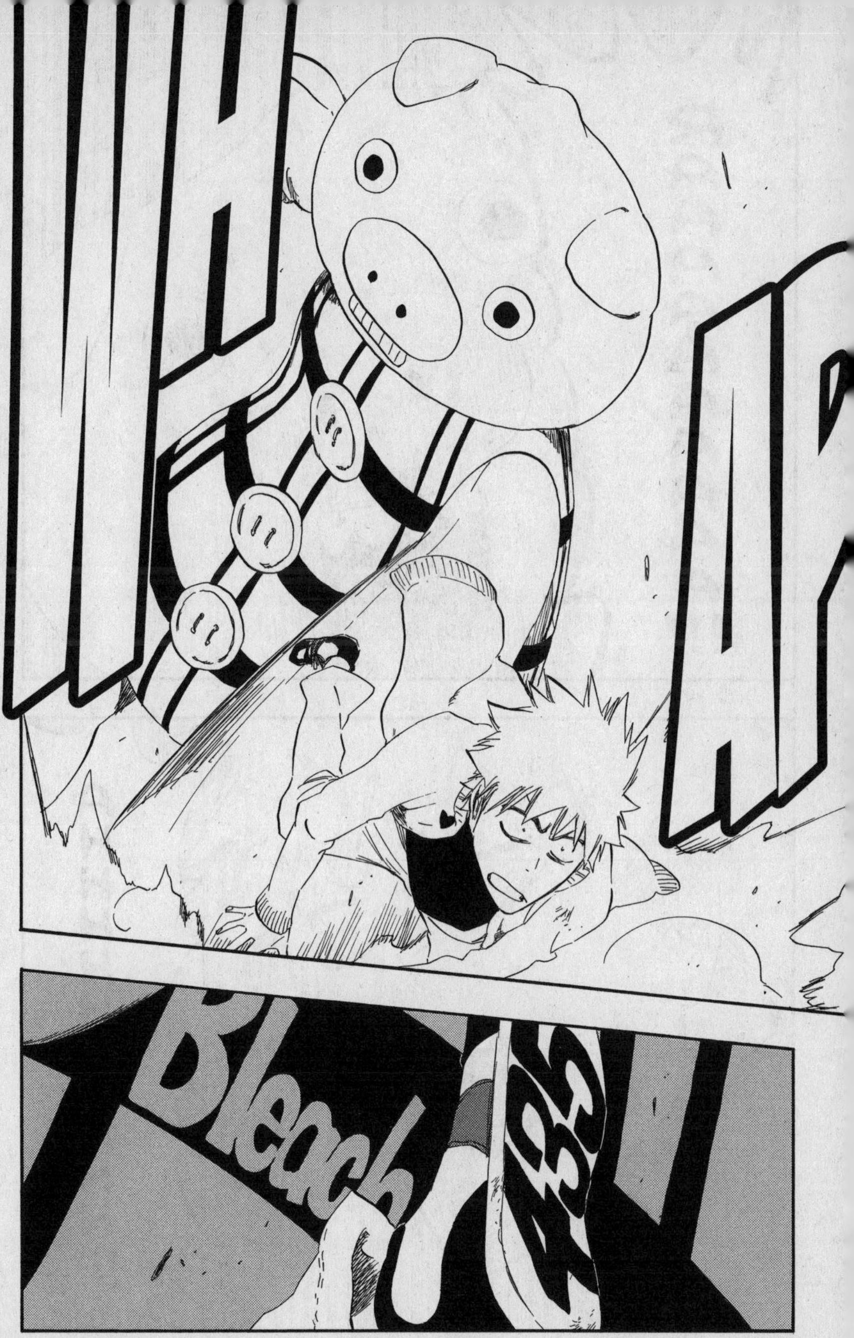
WHA
AH
Bleach
433

READ THIS WAY

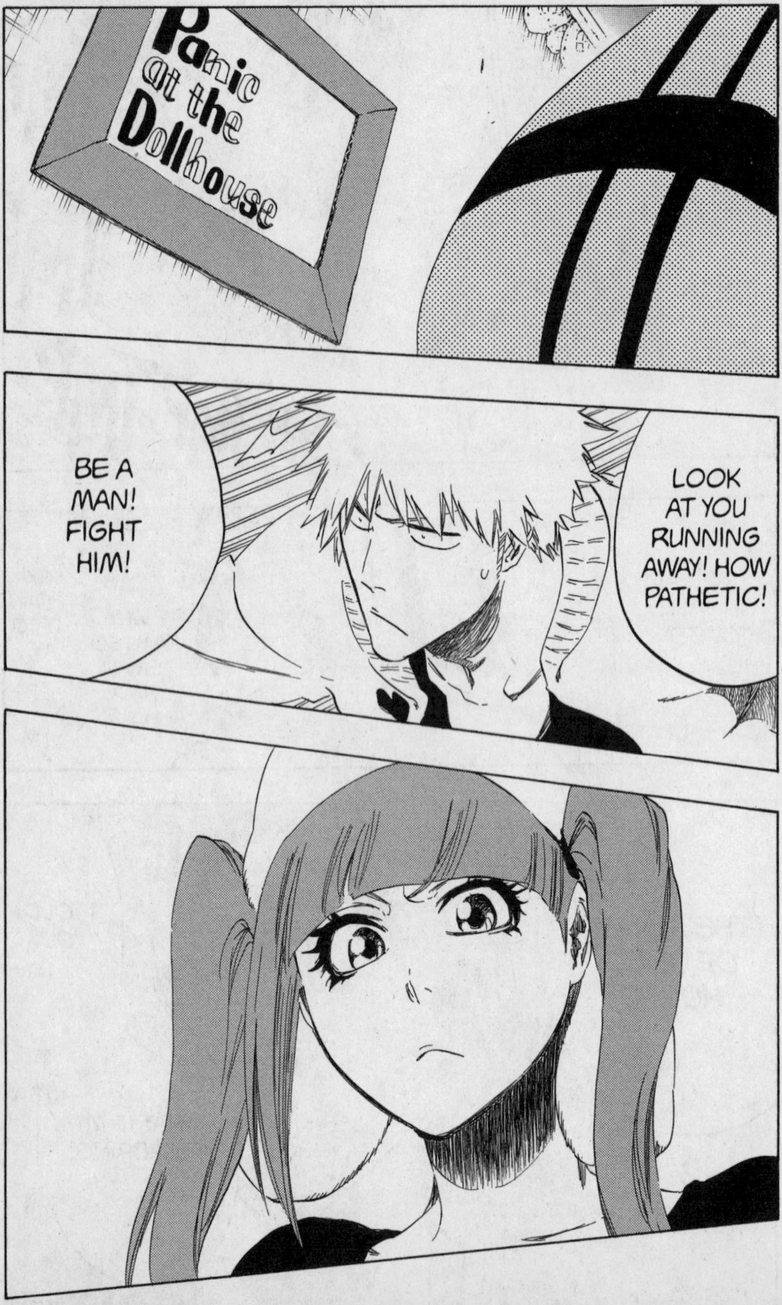
Panic at the Dollhouse
LOOK AT YOU RUNNING AWAY! HOW PATHETIC!
BE A MAN! FIGHT HIM!

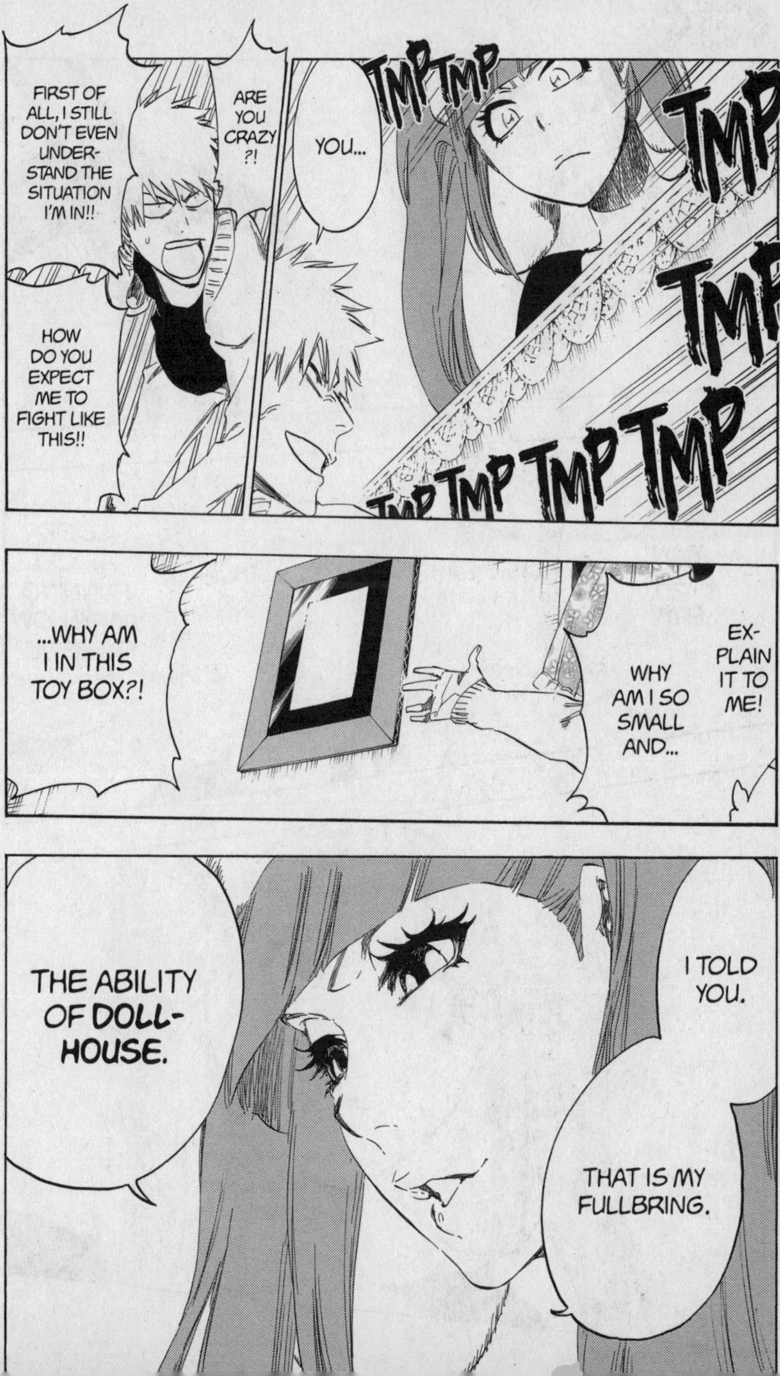
TMPTMP
TMP
TMP
TMPTMPTMPTMP
YOU...
ARE YOU CRAZY?!
FIRST OF ALL, I STILL DON'T EVEN UNDER-STAND THE SITUATION I'M IN!!
HOW DO YOU EXPECT ME TO FIGHT LIKE THIS!!
EX-PLAIN IT TO ME!
WHY AM I SO SMALL AND...
...WHY AM I IN THIS TOY BOX?!
I TOLD YOU.
THAT IS MY FULLBRING.
THE ABILITY OF DOLL-HOUSE.

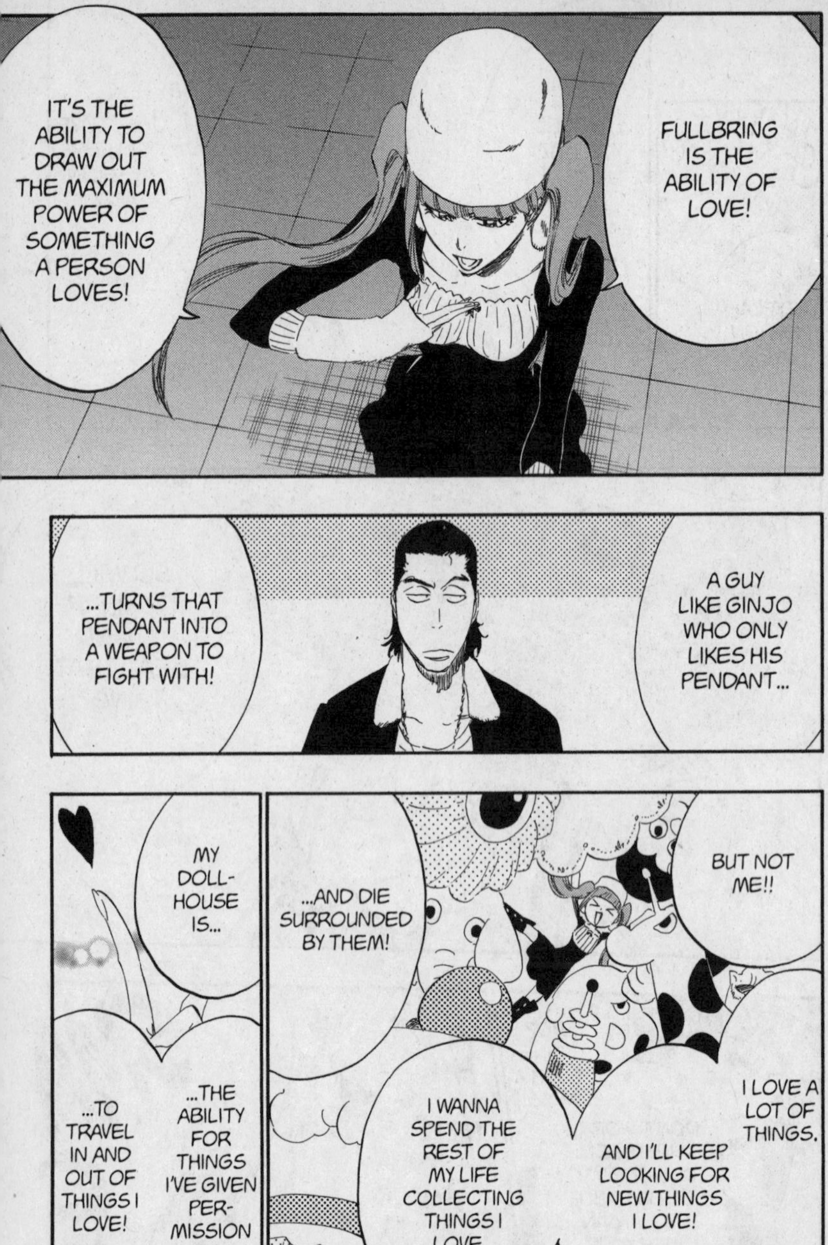
FULLBRING IS THE ABILITY OF LOVE!
IT'S THE ABILITY TO DRAW OUT THE MAXIMUM POWER OF SOMETHING A PERSON LOVES!
A GUY LIKE GINJO WHO ONLY LIKES HIS PENDANT...
...TURNS THAT PENDANT INTO A WEAPON TO FIGHT WITH!
BUT NOT ME!!
I LOVE A LOT OF THINGS.
AND I'LL KEEP LOOKING FOR NEW THINGS I LOVE!
I WANNA SPEND THE REST OF MY LIFE COLLECTING THINGS I LOVE...
...AND DIE SURROUNDED BY THEM!
MY DOLL-HOUSE IS...
...THE ABILITY FOR THINGS I'VE GIVEN PER-MISSION TO...
...TO TRAVEL IN AND OUT OF THINGS I LOVE!

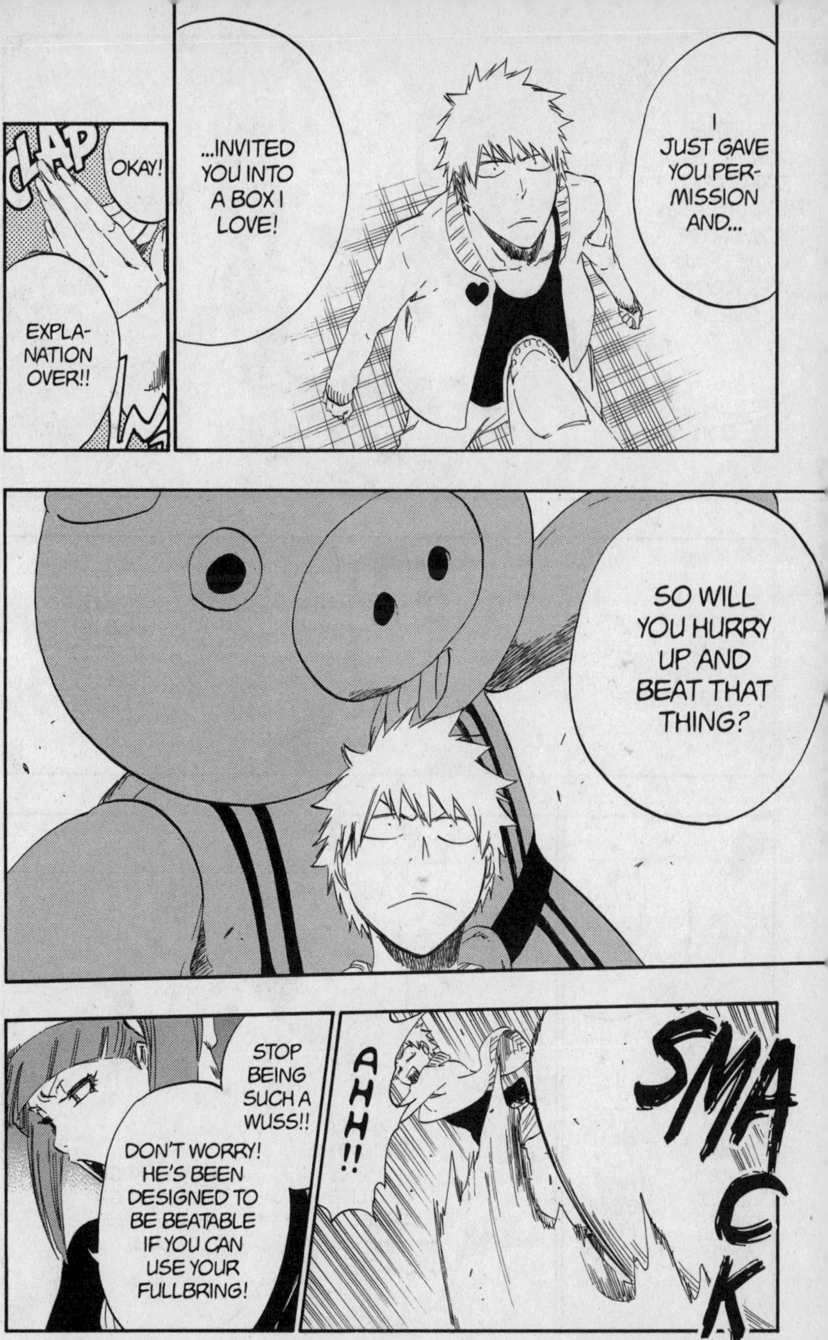
I JUST GAVE YOU PERMISSION AND...
...INVITED YOU INTO A BOX I LOVE!
CLAP
OKAY!
EXPLANATION OVER!!
SO WILL YOU HURRY UP AND BEAT THAT THING?
SMACK
AHHH!!
STOP BEING SUCH A WUSS!!
DON'T WORRY! HE'S BEEN DESIGNED TO BE BEATABLE IF YOU CAN USE YOUR FULLBRING!

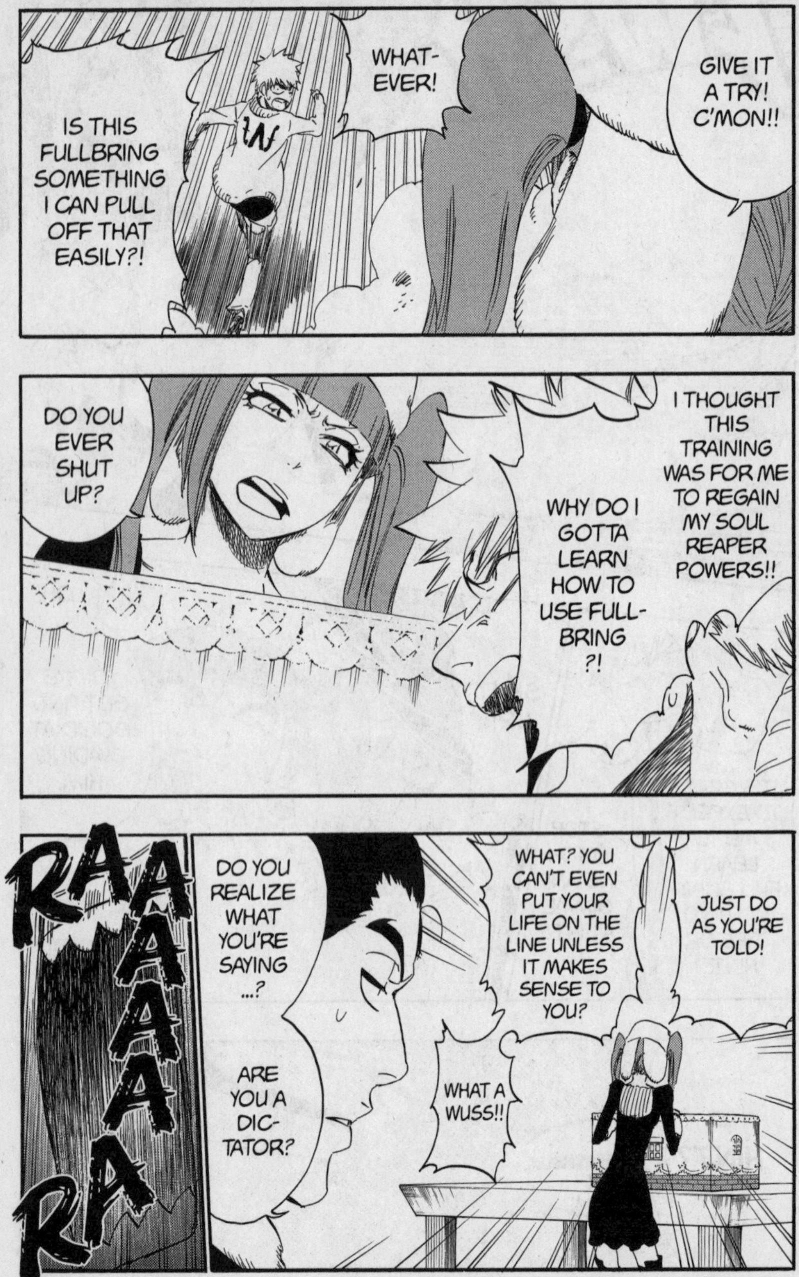
GIVE IT A TRY! C'MON!!
WHAT-EVER!
IS THIS FULLBRING SOMETHING I CAN PULL OFF THAT EASILY?!
I THOUGHT THIS TRAINING WAS FOR ME TO REGAIN MY SOUL REAPER POWERS!!
WHY DO I GOTTA LEARN HOW TO USE FULL-BRING ?!
DO YOU EVER SHUT UP?
JUST DO AS YOU'RE TOLD!
WHAT? YOU CAN'T EVEN PUT YOUR LIFE ON THE LINE UNLESS IT MAKES SENSE TO YOU?
WHAT A WUSS!!
DO YOU REALIZE WHAT YOU'RE SAYING ...?
ARE YOU A DIC-TATOR?
RAAAAAAA
RA

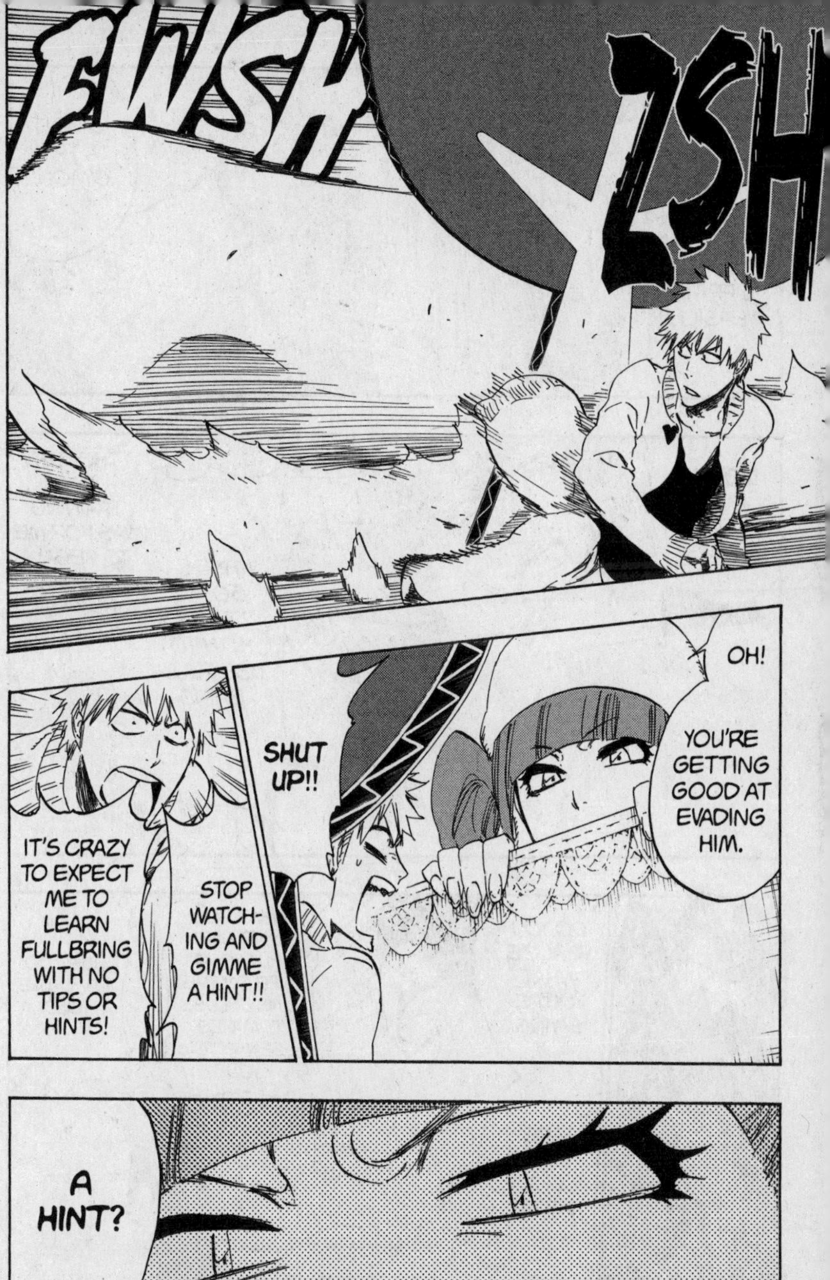
ZSH
FWSH
OH!
YOU'RE GETTING GOOD AT EVADING HIM.
SHUT UP!!
STOP WATCH-ING AND GIMME A HINT!!
IT'S CRAZY TO EXPECT ME TO LEARN FULLBRING WITH NO TIPS OR HINTS!
A HINT?

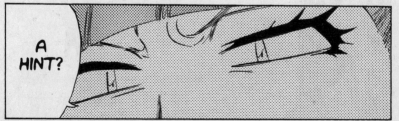

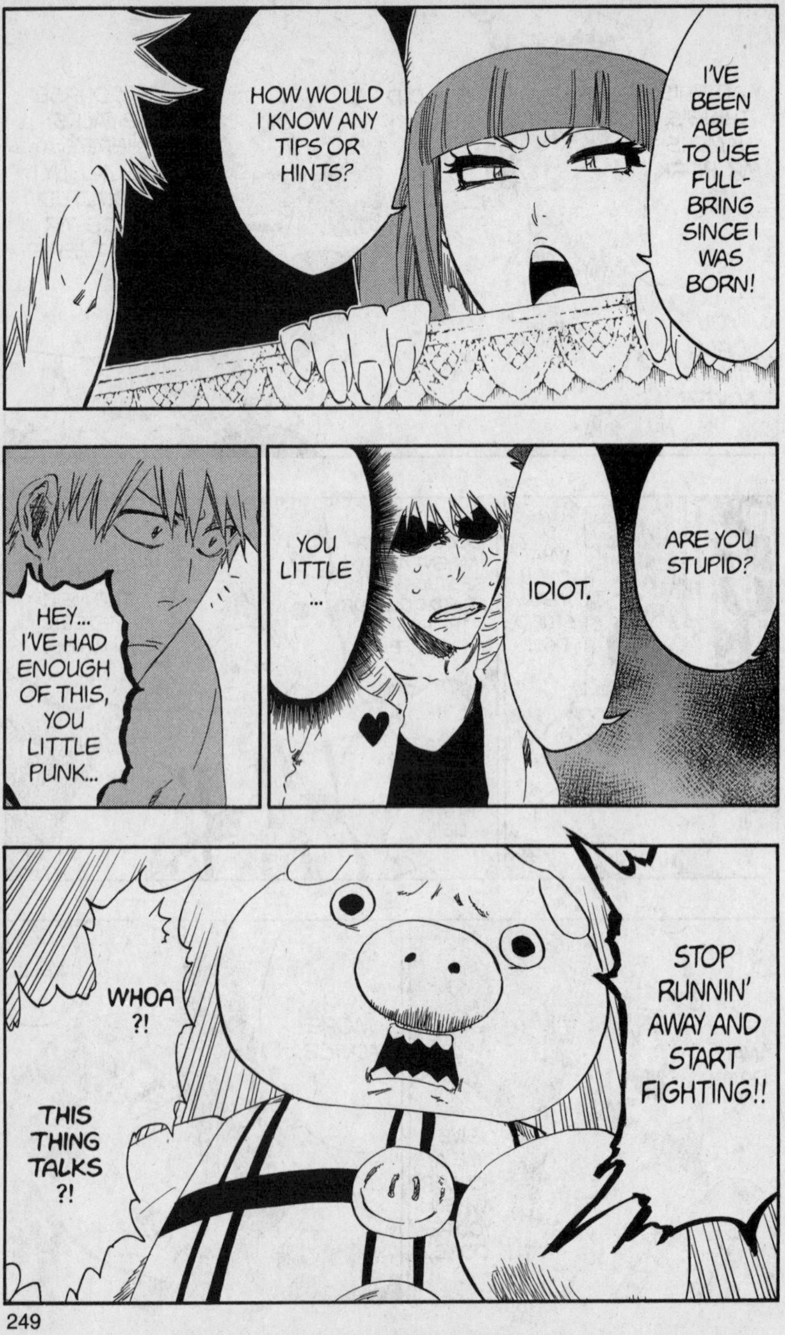
HOW WOULD I KNOW ANY TIPS OR HINTS?
I'VE BEEN ABLE TO USE FULL-BRING SINCE I WAS BORN!
ARE YOU STUPID?
IDIOT.
YOU LITTLE ...
HEY... I'VE HAD ENOUGH OF THIS, YOU LITTLE PUNK...
STOP RUNNIN' AWAY AND START FIGHTING!!
WHOA ?!
THIS THING TALKS ?!

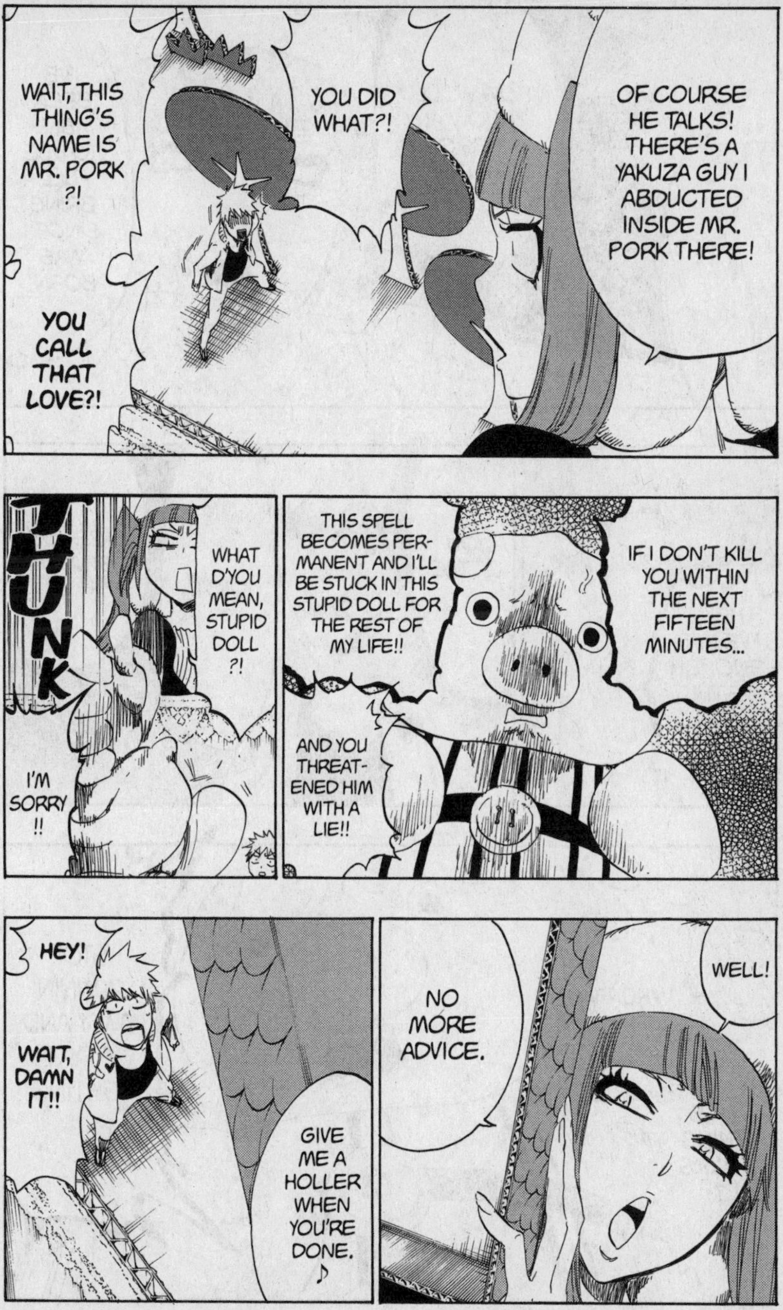
OF COURSE HE TALKS! THERE'S A YAKUZA GUY I ABDUCTED INSIDE MR. PORK THERE!
YOU DID WHAT?!
WAIT, THIS THING'S NAME IS MR. PORK ?!
YOU CALL THAT LOVE?!
IF I DON'T KILL YOU WITHIN THE NEXT FIFTEEN MINUTES...
THIS SPELL BECOMES PERMANENT AND I'LL BE STUCK IN THIS STUPID DOLL FOR THE REST OF MY LIFE!!
AND YOU THREATENED HIM WITH A LIE!!
WHAT D'YOU MEAN, STUPID DOLL ?!
THUNK
I'M SORRY !!
WELL!
NO MORE ADVICE.
GIVE ME A HOLLER WHEN YOU'RE DONE. ♪
HEY!
WAIT, DAMN IT!!

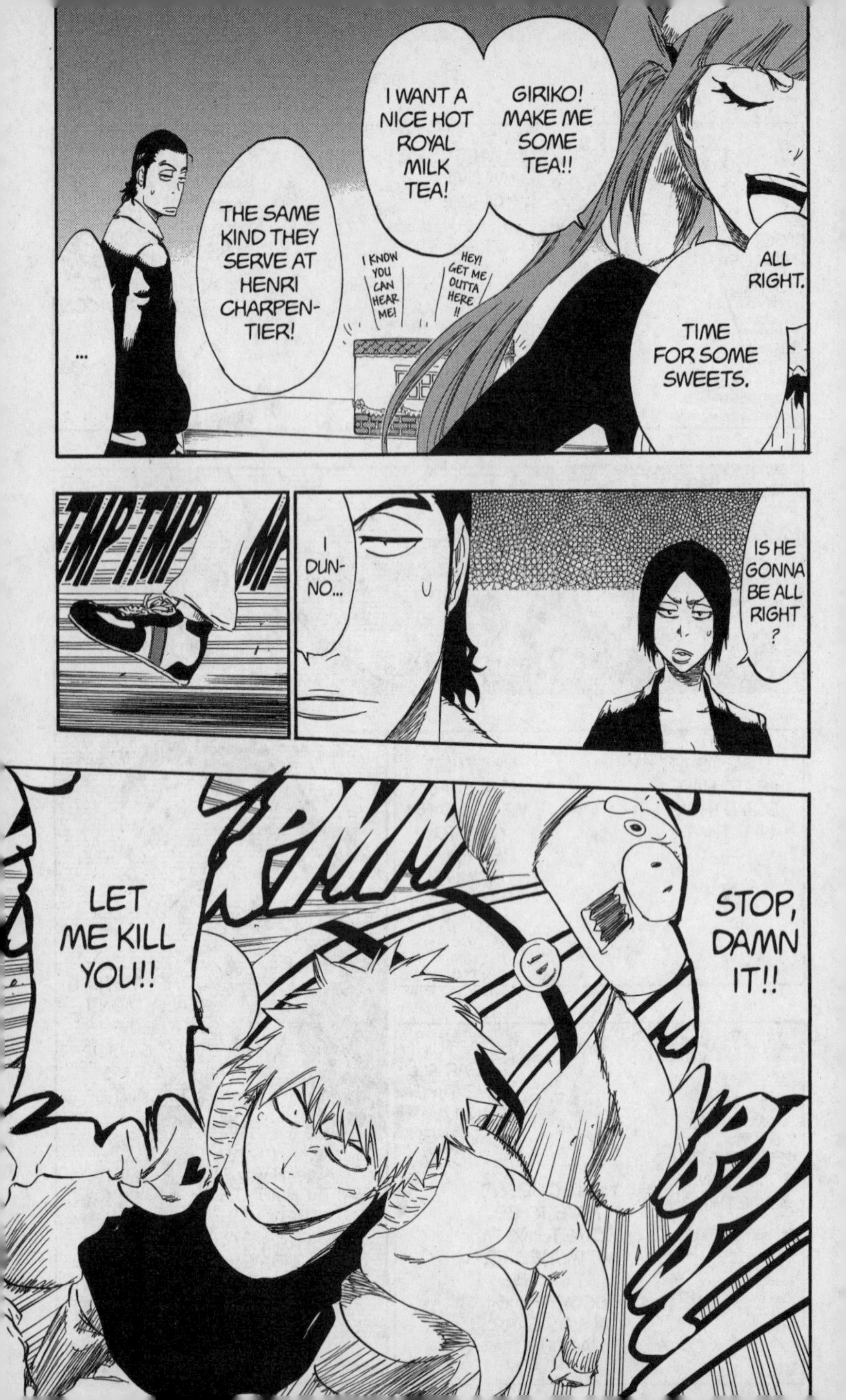
ALL RIGHT. TIME FOR SOME SWEETS.
GIRIKO! MAKE ME SOME TEA!!
I WANT A NICE HOT ROYAL MILK TEA!
HEY! GET ME OUTTA HERE!!
I KNOW YOU CAN HEAR ME!
THE SAME KIND THEY SERVE AT HENRI CHARPENTIER!
...
IS HE GONNA BE ALL RIGHT?
I DUNNO...
TMP TMP
STOP, DAMN IT!!
LET ME KILL YOU!!

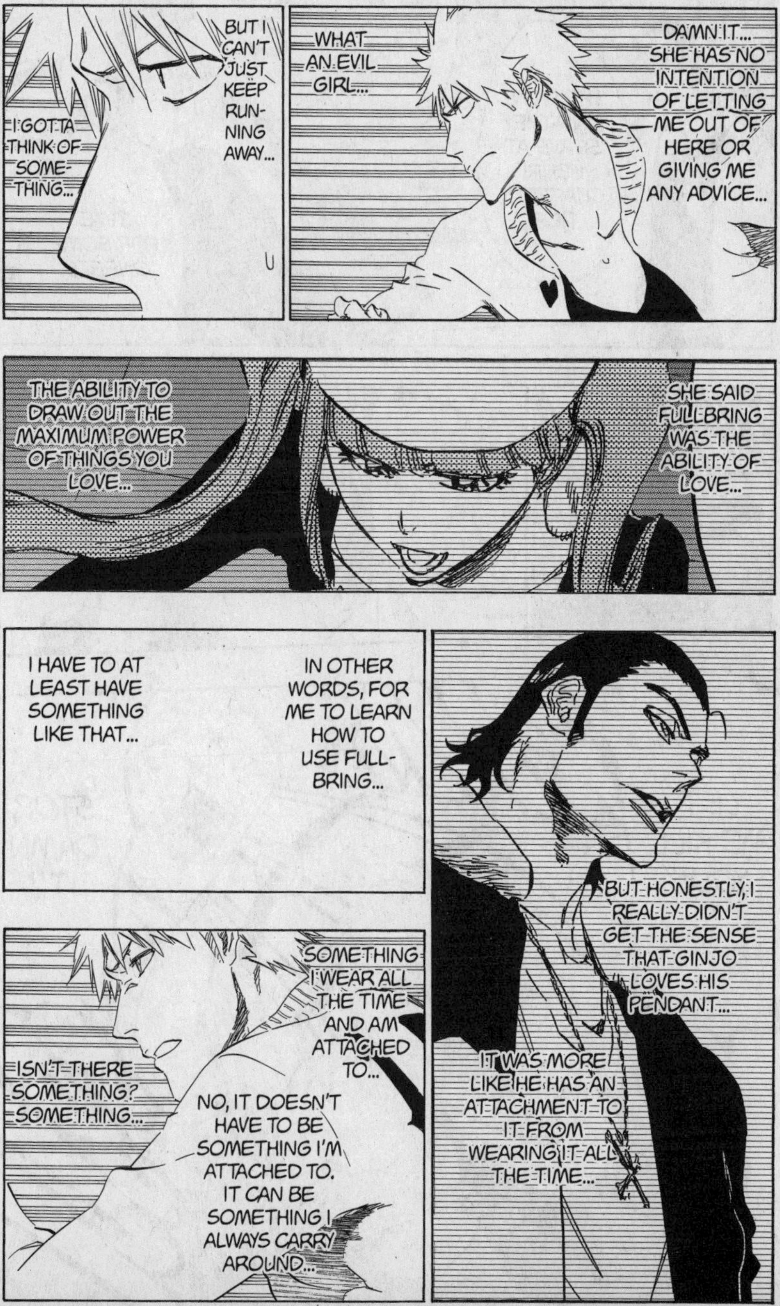
DAMN IT... SHE HAS NO INTENTION OF LETTING ME OUT OF HERE OR GIVING ME ANY ADVICE...
WHAT AN EVIL GIRL...
BUT I CAN'T JUST KEEP RUNNING AWAY...
I GOTTA THINK OF SOMETHING...
SHE SAID FULLBRING WAS THE ABILITY OF LOVE...
THE ABILITY TO DRAW OUT THE MAXIMUM POWER OF THINGS YOU LOVE...
BUT HONESTLY, I REALLY DIDN'T GET THE SENSE THAT GINJO LOVES HIS PENDANT...
IT WAS MORE LIKE HE HAS AN ATTACHMENT TO IT FROM WEARING IT ALL THE TIME...
IN OTHER WORDS, FOR ME TO LEARN HOW TO USE FULL-BRING...
I HAVE TO AT LEAST HAVE SOMETHING LIKE THAT...
SOMETHING I WEAR ALL THE TIME AND AM ATTACHED TO...
ISN'T THERE SOMETHING? SOMETHING...
NO, IT DOESN'T HAVE TO BE SOMETHING I'M ATTACHED TO. IT CAN BE SOMETHING I ALWAYS CARRY AROUND...

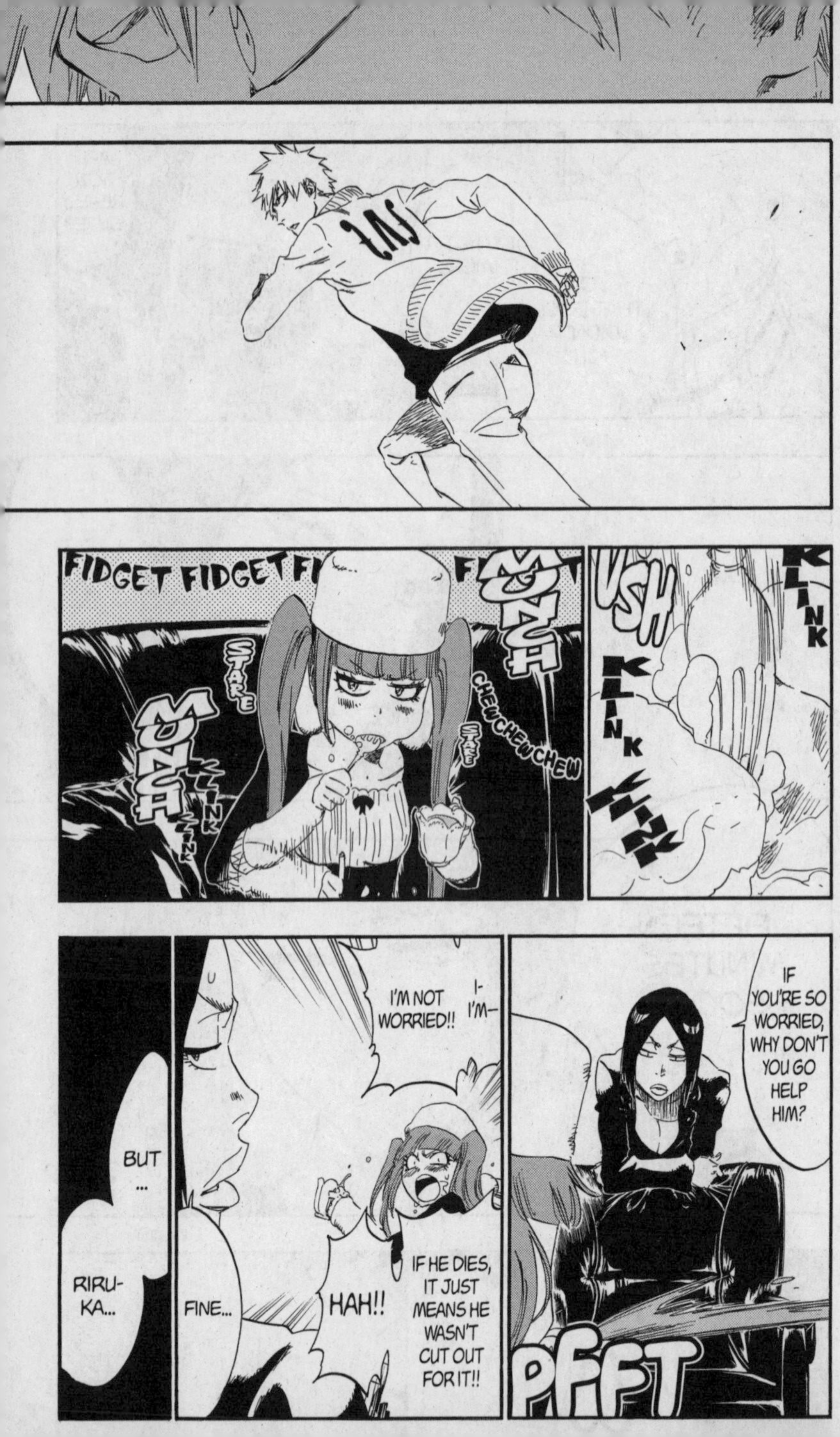
KLINK
USH
KLINK
KLINK
FIDGET FIDGET
MUNCH
CHEW CHEW CHEW
STARE
STARE
MUNCH
KLINK
KLINK
IF YOU'RE SO WORRIED, WHY DON'T YOU GO HELP HIM?
PFFT
I- I'M-
I'M NOT WORRIED!!
IF HE DIES, IT JUST MEANS HE WASN'T CUT OUT FOR IT!!
HAH!!
FINE...
BUT ...
RIRU-KA...

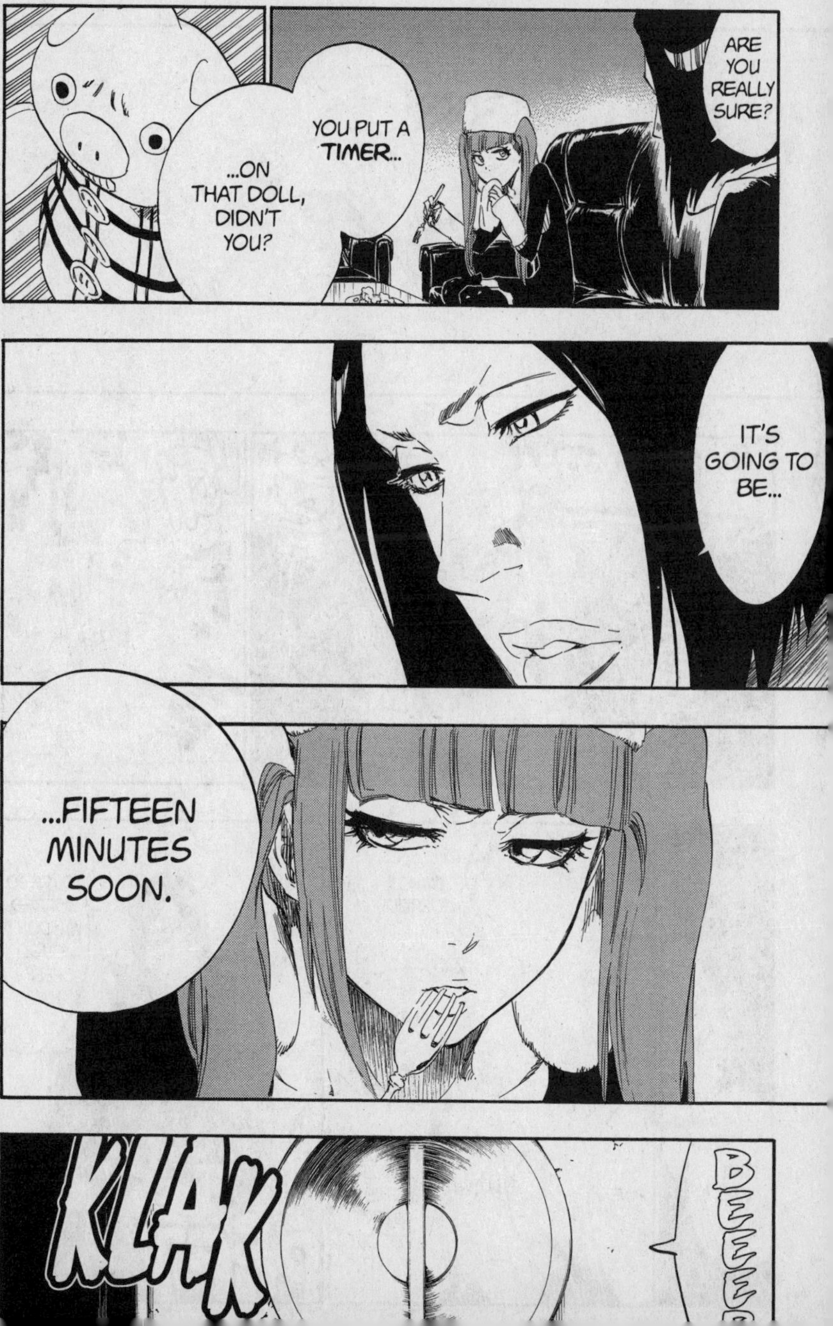
ARE YOU REALLY SURE?
YOU PUT A TIMER...
...ON THAT DOLL, DIDN'T YOU?
IT'S GOING TO BE...
...FIFTEEN MINUTES SOON.
BEEE
KLAK

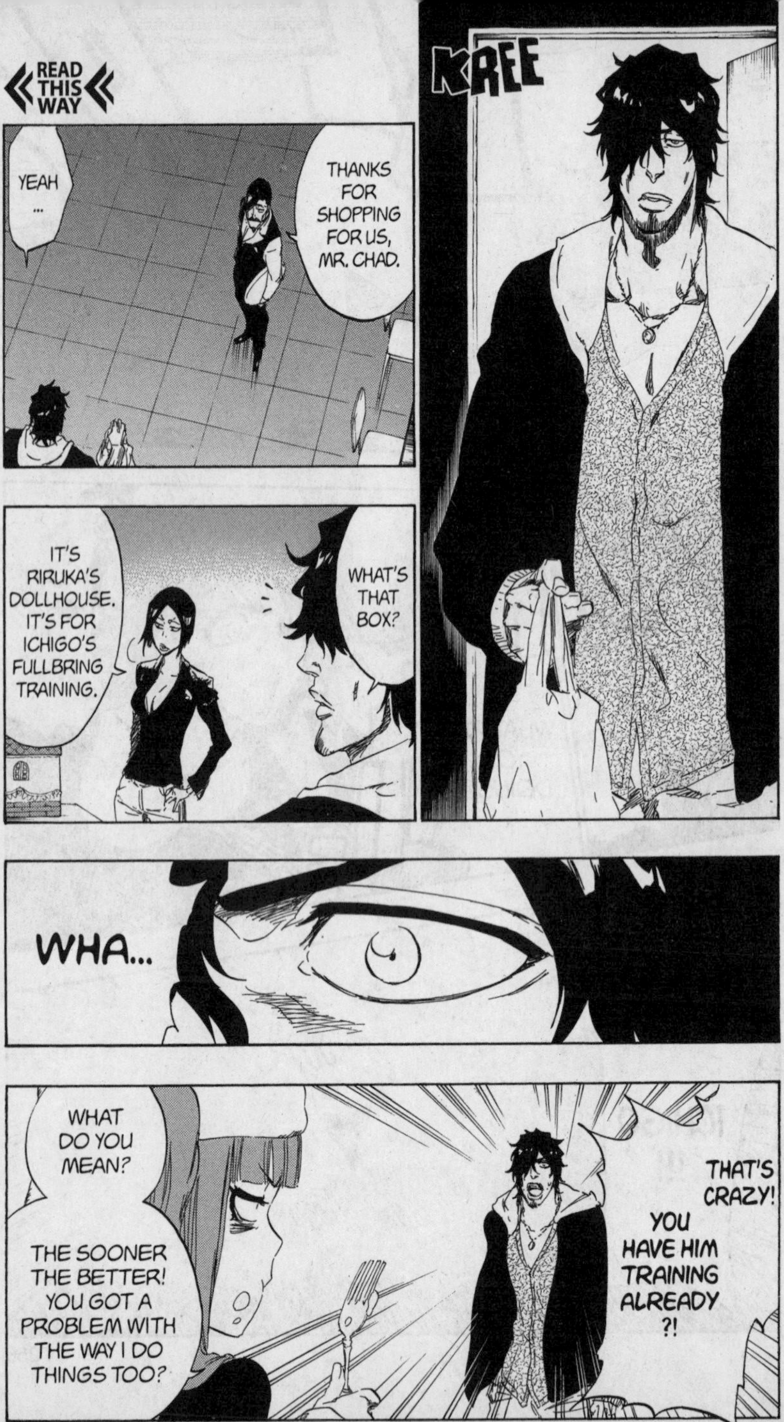
READ THIS WAY
KREE
THANKS FOR SHOPPING FOR US, MR. CHAD.
YEAH ...
WHAT'S THAT BOX?
IT'S RIRUKA'S DOLLHOUSE. IT'S FOR ICHIGO'S FULLBRING TRAINING.
WHA...
THAT'S CRAZY!
YOU HAVE HIM TRAINING ALREADY?!
WHAT DO YOU MEAN?
THE SOONER THE BETTER! YOU GOT A PROBLEM WITH THE WAY I DO THINGS TOO?

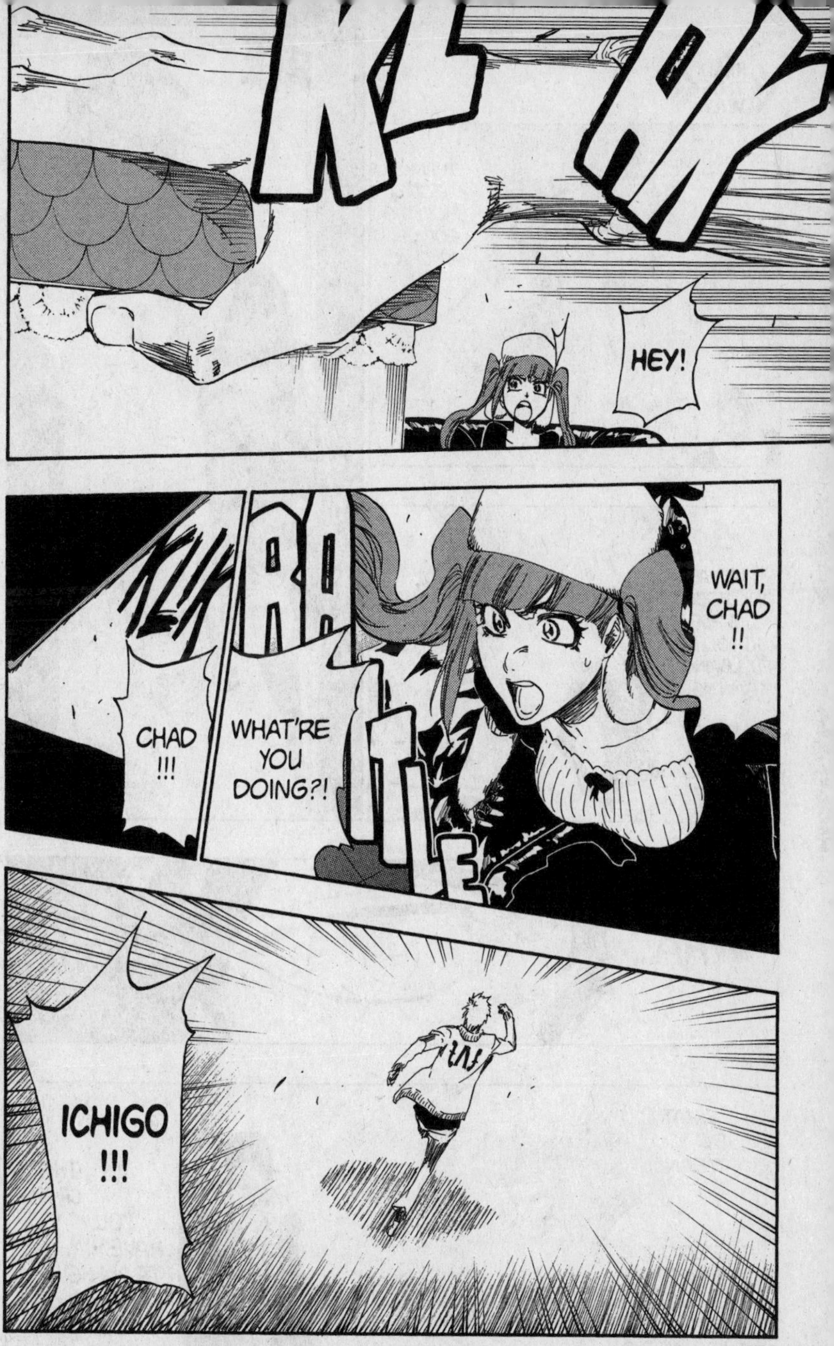
HEY!
WAIT, CHAD !!
WHAT'RE YOU DOING?!
CHAD !!!
ICHIGO !!!

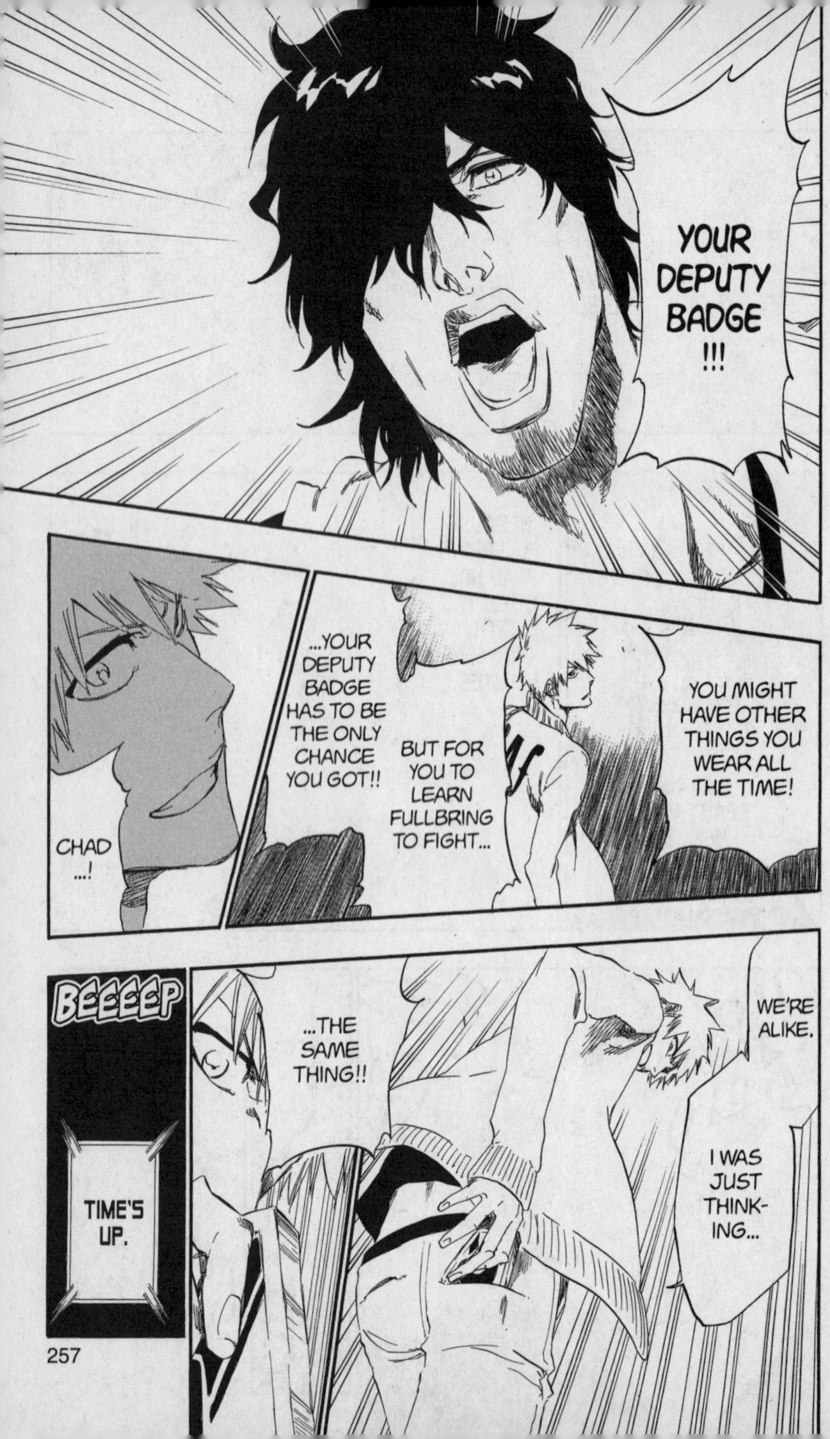
YOUR DEPUTY BADGE !!!
YOU MIGHT HAVE OTHER THINGS YOU WEAR ALL THE TIME!
BUT FOR YOU TO LEARN FULLBRING TO FIGHT...
...YOUR DEPUTY BADGE HAS TO BE THE ONLY CHANCE YOU GOT!!
CHAD ...!
WE'RE ALIKE.
I WAS JUST THINKING...
...THE SAME THING!!
BEEEEEP
TIME'S UP.

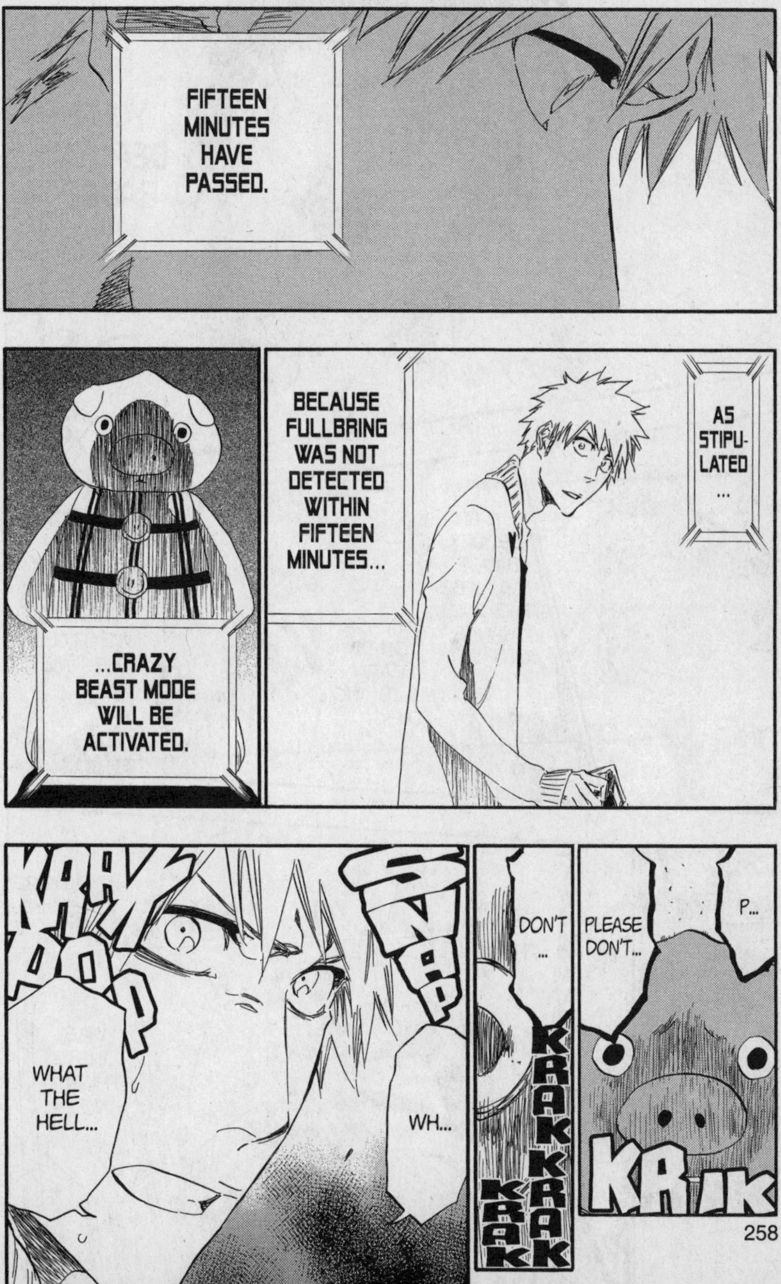
FIFTEEN MINUTES HAVE PASSED.
AS STIPU-LATED ...
BECAUSE FULLBRING WAS NOT DETECTED WITHIN FIFTEEN MINUTES...
...CRAZY BEAST MODE WILL BE ACTIVATED.
P...
PLEASE DON'T...
KRIK
DON'T ...
KRAK KRAK KRAK KRAK KRAK
SNAP
WH...
KRAK
POP
WHAT THE HELL...

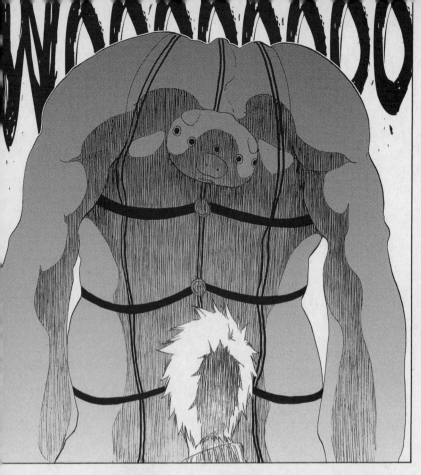

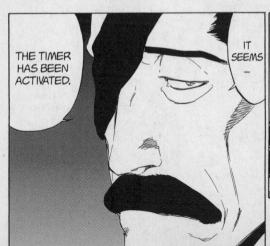

THE TIMER
HAS BEEN
ACTIVATED.

IT
SEEMS
...

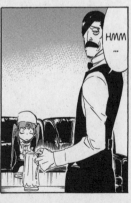

HMM
...

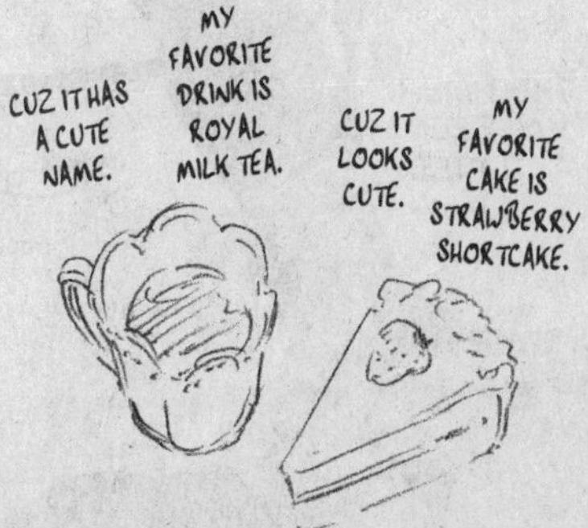
MY FAVORITE CAKE IS STRAWBERRY SHORTCAKE.
CUZ IT LOOKS CUTE.
MY FAVORITE DRINK IS ROYAL MILK TEA.
CUZ IT HAS A CUTE NAME.

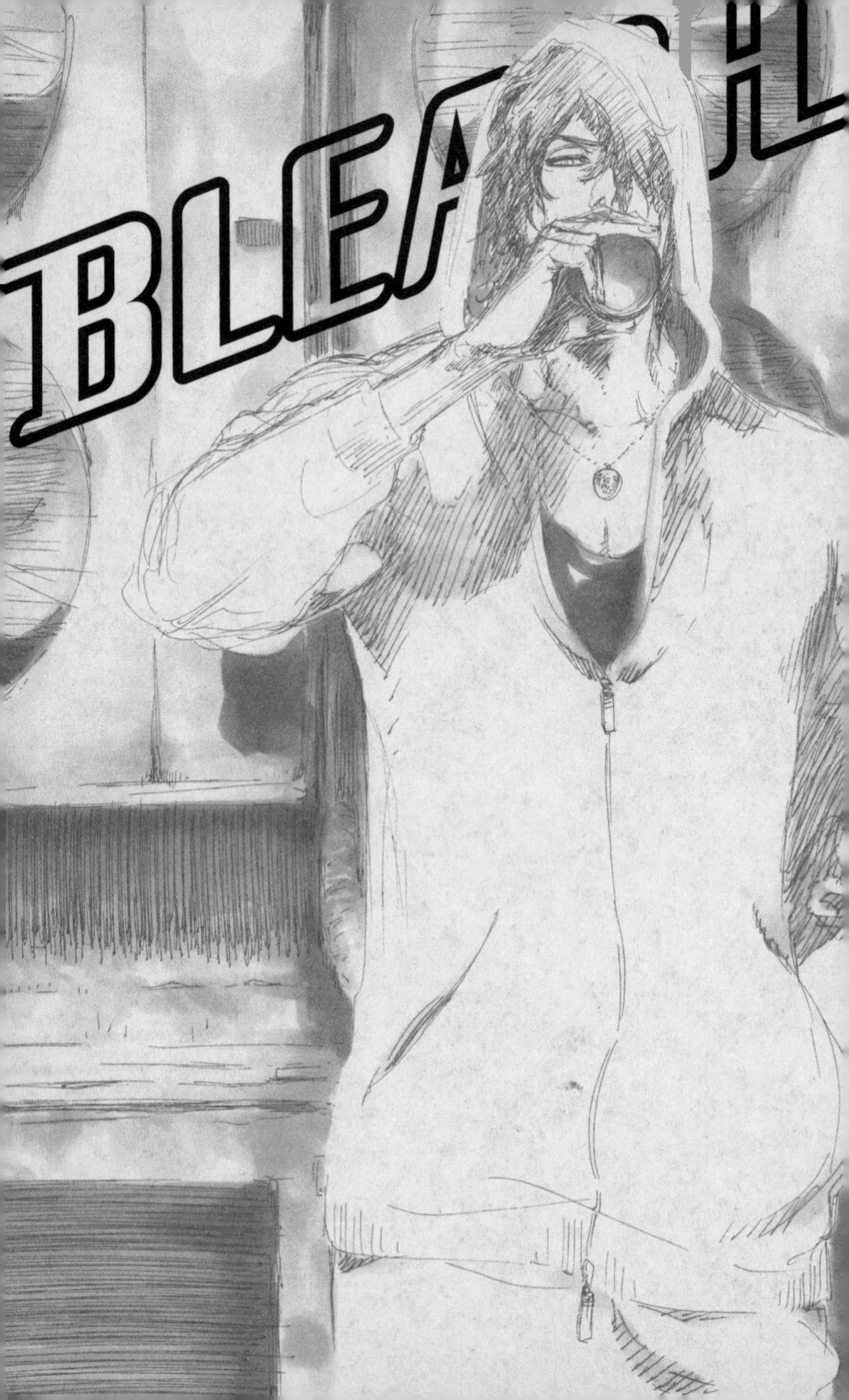
BLEA H

BLEACH
ブリーチ

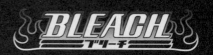

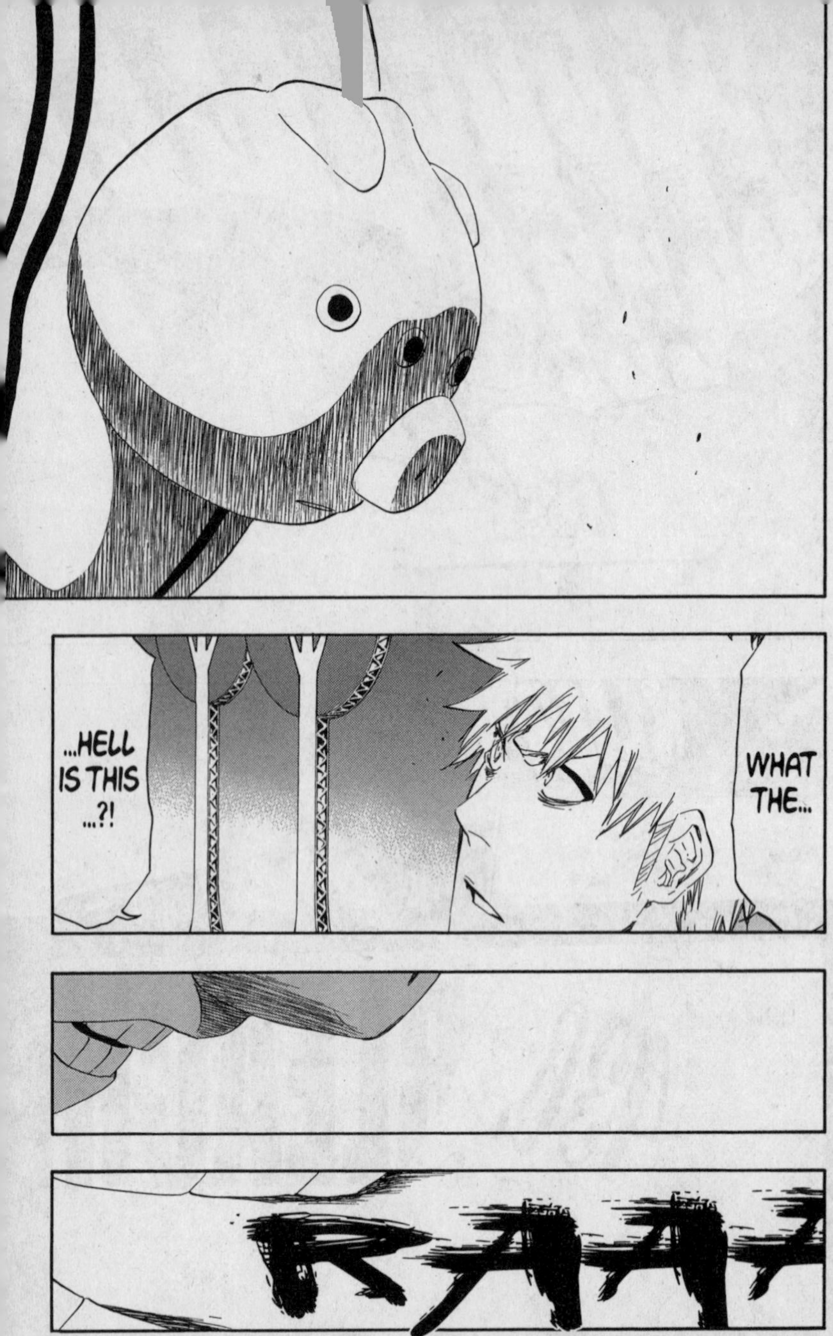
WHAT THE...
...HELL IS THIS ...?!

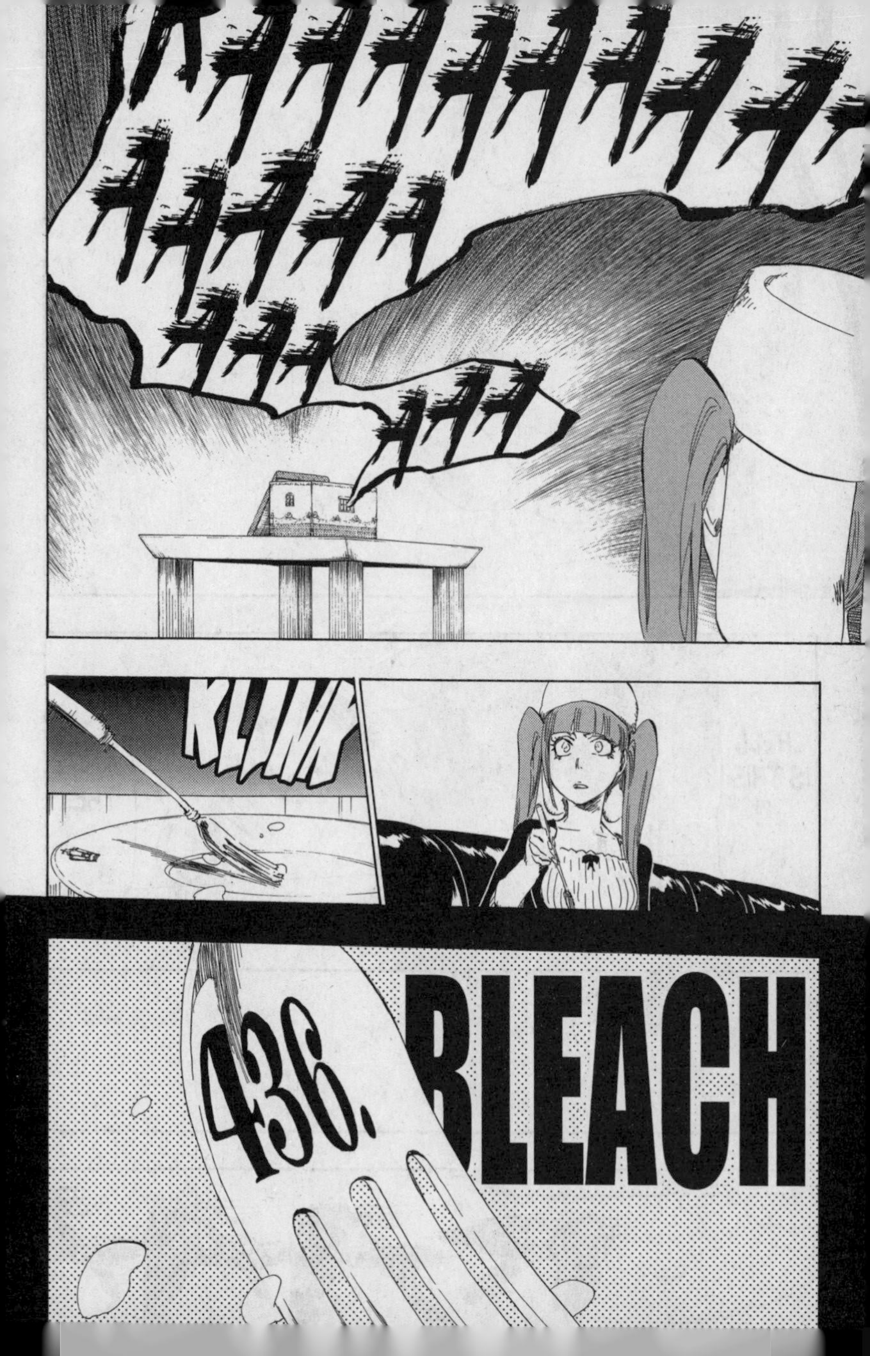
KYAAAAAAAAAAAAAAAAAAAAAAA
KLINK
436. BLEACH

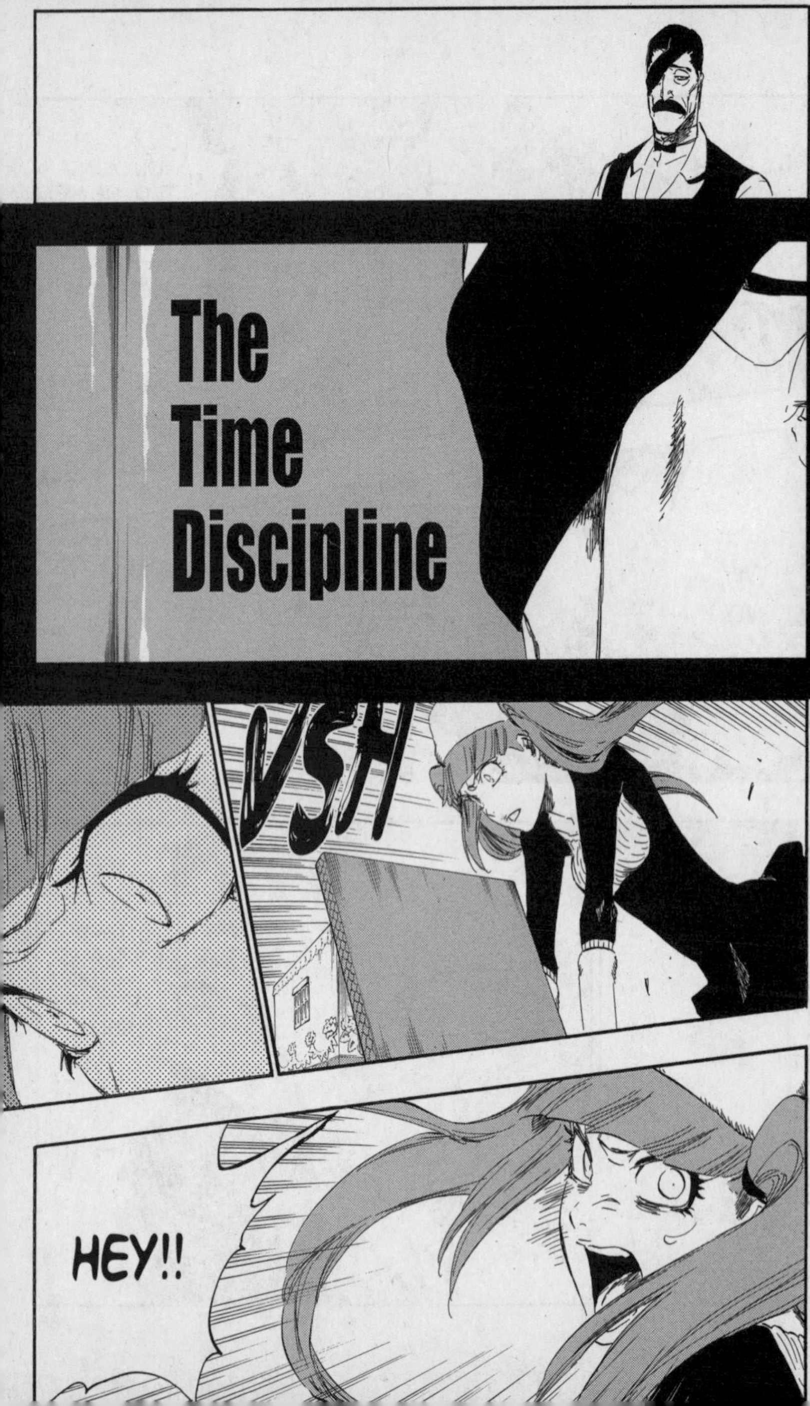
The Time Discipline
SH
HEY!!

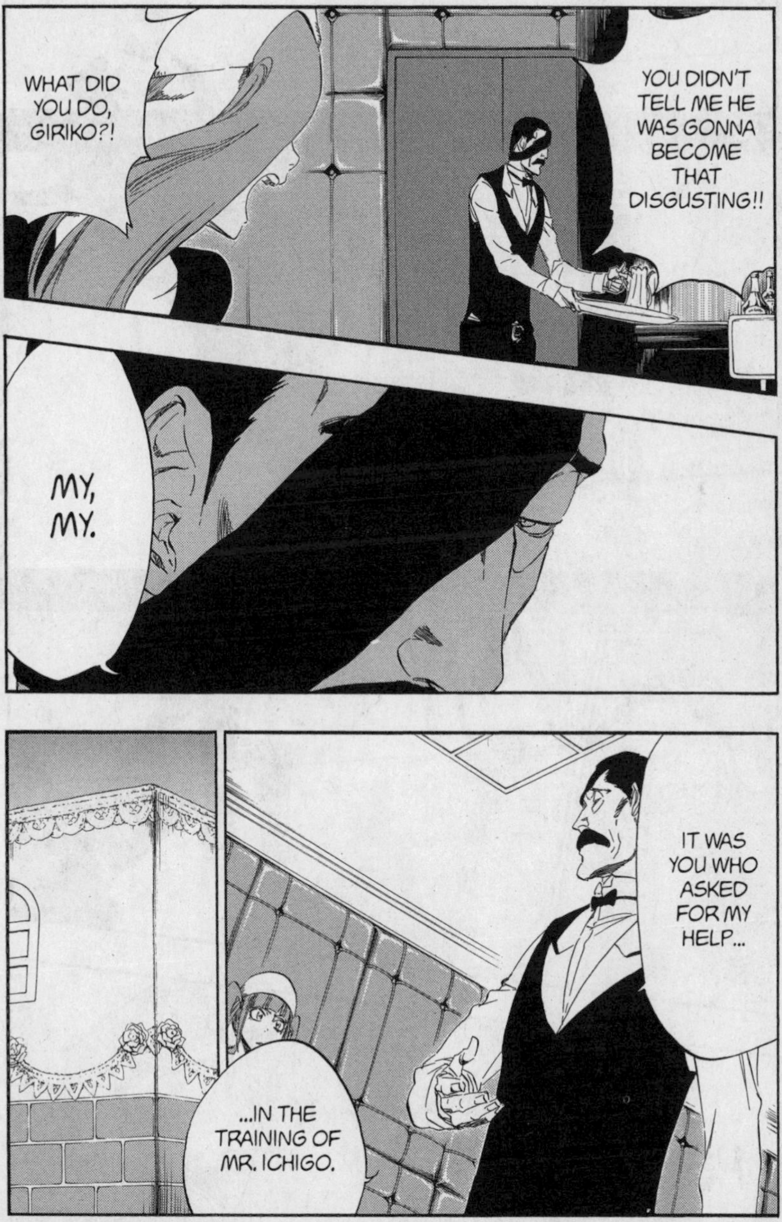
YOU DIDN'T TELL ME HE WAS GONNA BECOME THAT DISGUSTING!!
WHAT DID YOU DO, GIRIKO?!
MY, MY.
IT WAS YOU WHO ASKED FOR MY HELP...
...IN THE TRAINING OF MR. ICHIGO.

READ THIS WAY

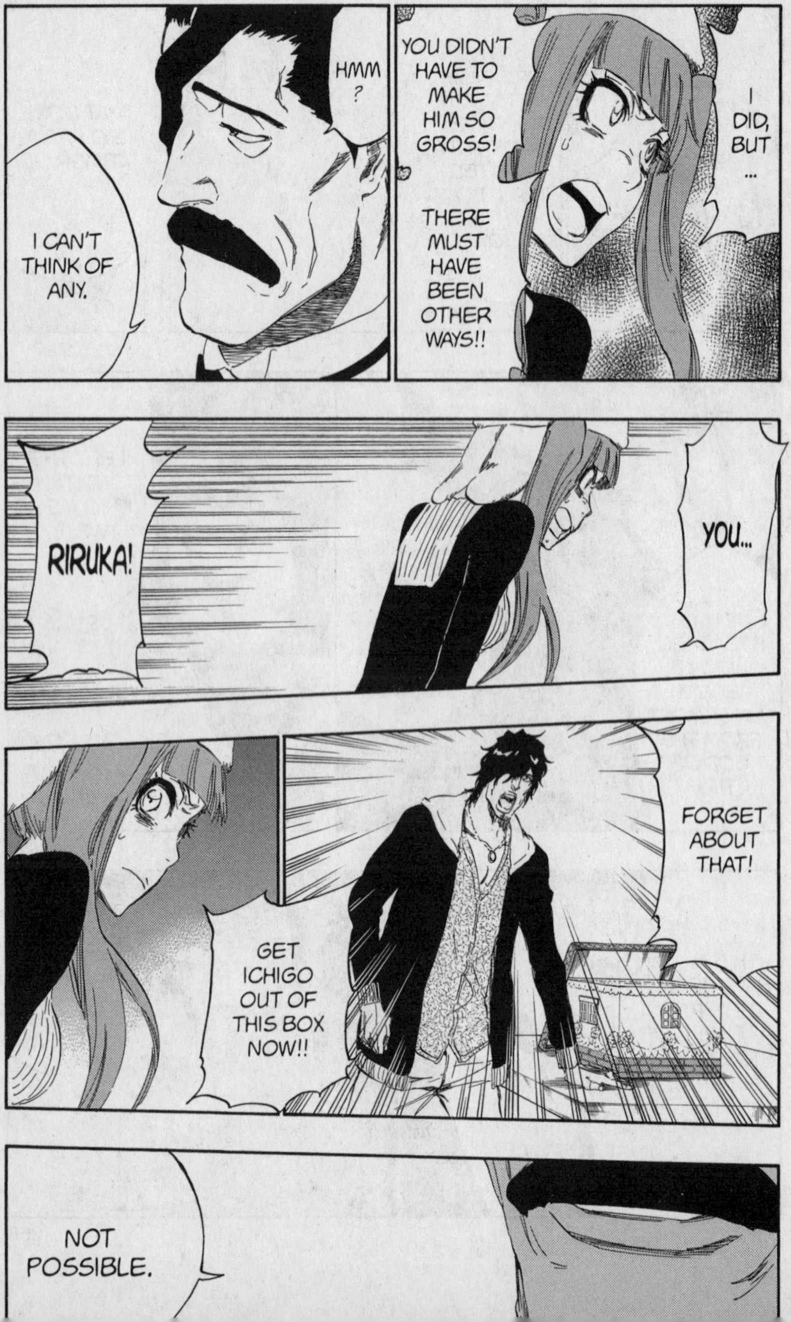
I DID, BUT ...
YOU DIDN'T HAVE TO MAKE HIM SO GROSS!
THERE MUST HAVE BEEN OTHER WAYS!!
HMM ?
I CAN'T THINK OF ANY.
YOU...
RIRUKA!
FORGET ABOUT THAT!
GET ICHIGO OUT OF THIS BOX NOW!!
NOT POSSIBLE.

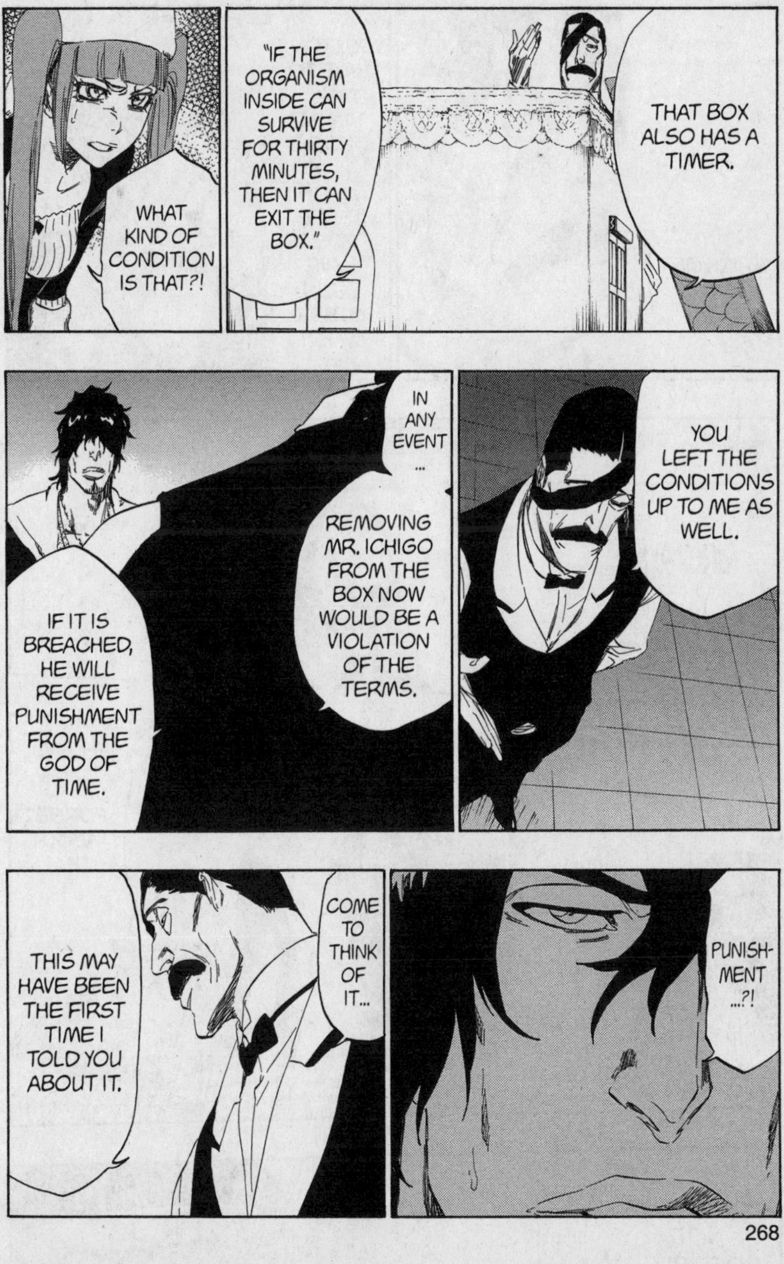
THAT BOX ALSO HAS A TIMER.
"IF THE ORGANISM INSIDE CAN SURVIVE FOR THIRTY MINUTES, THEN IT CAN EXIT THE BOX."
WHAT KIND OF CONDITION IS THAT?!
YOU LEFT THE CONDITIONS UP TO ME AS WELL.
IN ANY EVENT...
REMOVING MR. ICHIGO FROM THE BOX NOW WOULD BE A VIOLATION OF THE TERMS.
IF IT IS BREACHED, HE WILL RECEIVE PUNISHMENT FROM THE GOD OF TIME.
PUNISH-MENT...?!
COME TO THINK OF IT...
THIS MAY HAVE BEEN THE FIRST TIME I TOLD YOU ABOUT IT.

READ THIS WAY

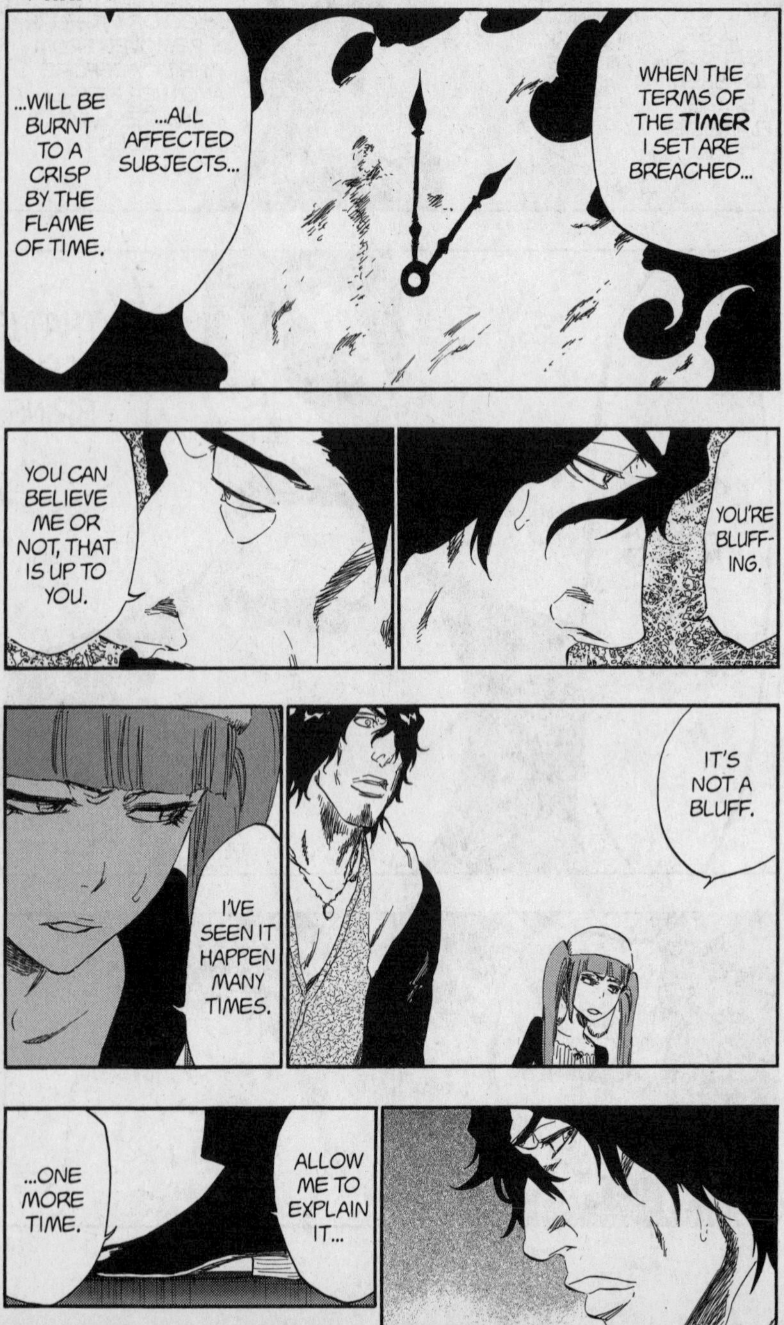
WHEN THE TERMS OF THE **TIMER** I SET ARE BREACHED...
...ALL AFFECTED SUBJECTS...
...WILL BE BURNT TO A CRISP BY THE FLAME OF TIME.
YOU'RE BLUFF-ING.
YOU CAN BELIEVE ME OR NOT, THAT IS UP TO YOU.
IT'S NOT A BLUFF.
I'VE SEEN IT HAPPEN MANY TIMES.
ALLOW ME TO EXPLAIN IT...
...ONE MORE TIME.

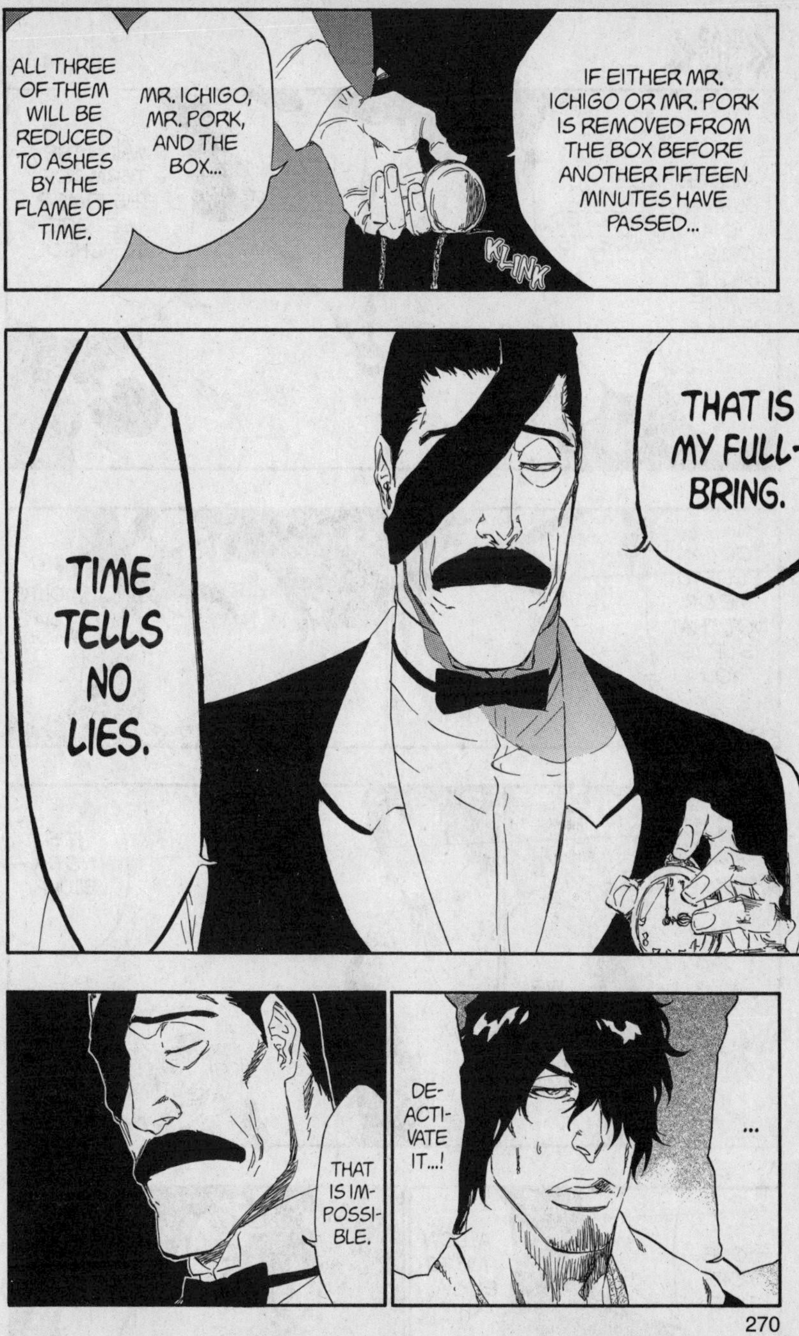
IF EITHER MR. ICHIGO OR MR. PORK IS REMOVED FROM THE BOX BEFORE ANOTHER FIFTEEN MINUTES HAVE PASSED...
MR. ICHIGO, MR. PORK, AND THE BOX...
ALL THREE OF THEM WILL BE REDUCED TO ASHES BY THE FLAME OF TIME.
KLINK
THAT IS MY FULL-BRING.
TIME TELLS NO LIES.
...
DE-ACTI-VATE IT...!
THAT IS IM-POSSI-BLE.

READ THIS WAY

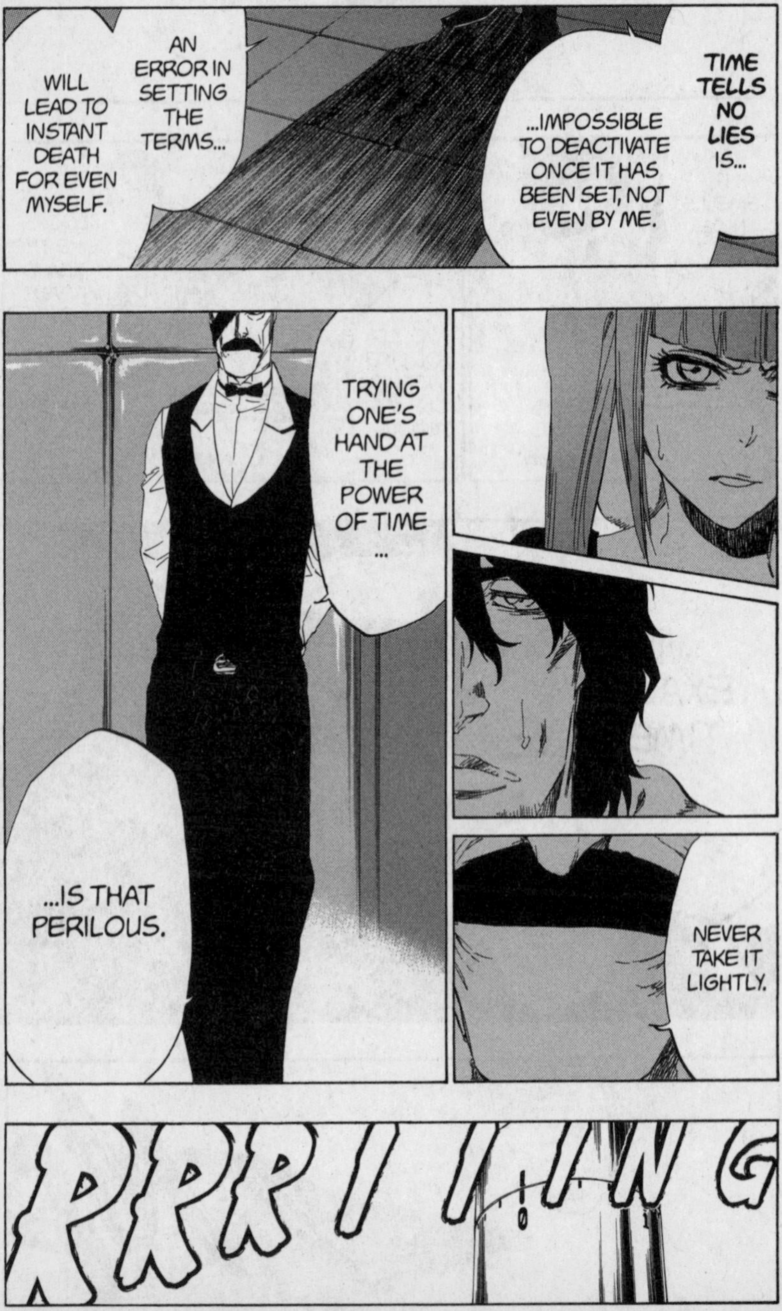
TIME TELLS NO LIES IS...
...IMPOSSIBLE TO DEACTIVATE ONCE IT HAS BEEN SET, NOT EVEN BY ME.
AN ERROR IN SETTING THE TERMS...
WILL LEAD TO INSTANT DEATH FOR EVEN MYSELF.
NEVER TAKE IT LIGHTLY.
TRYING ONE'S HAND AT THE POWER OF TIME...
...IS THAT PERILOUS.
RPRIIING

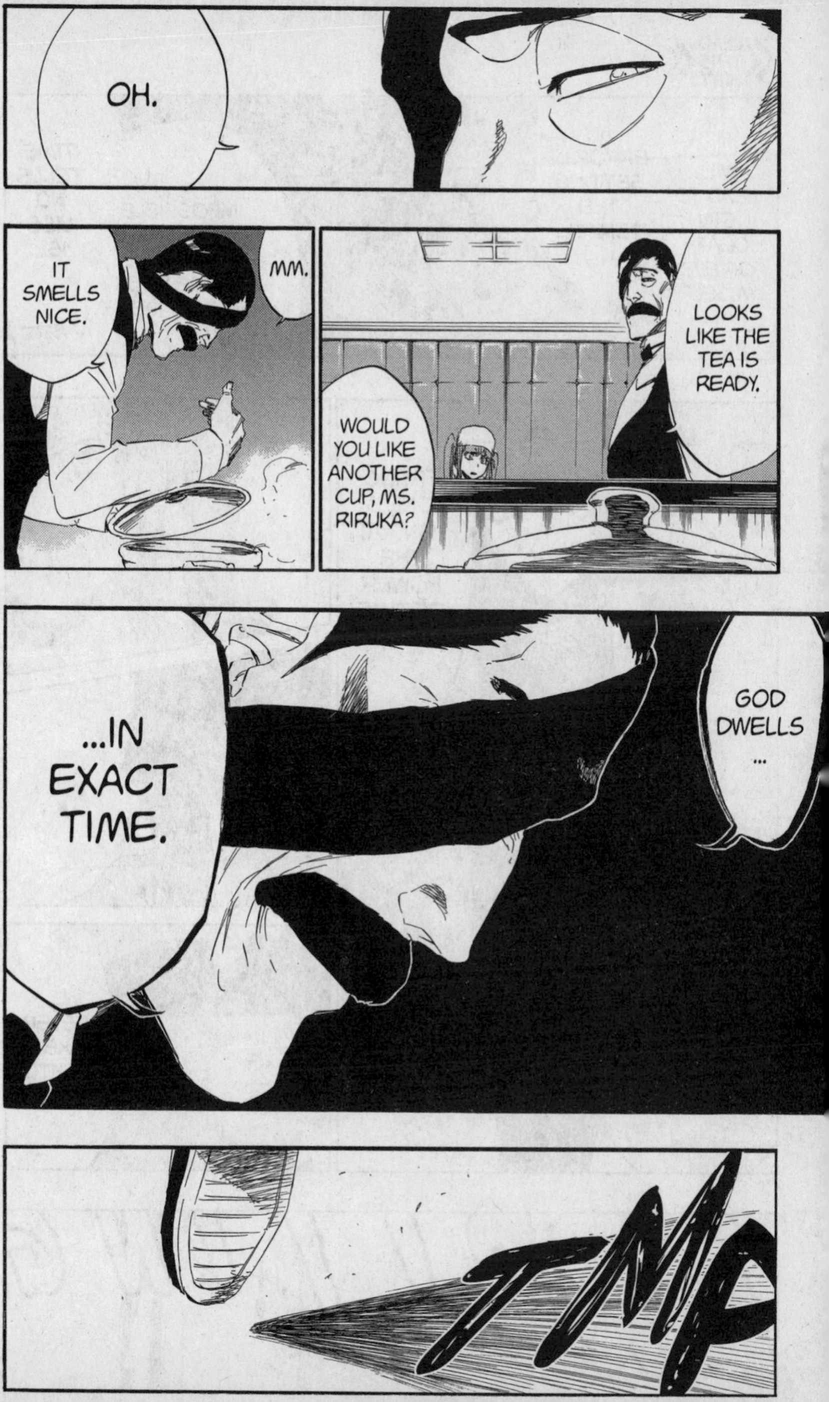
OH.
LOOKS LIKE THE TEA IS READY.
WOULD YOU LIKE ANOTHER CUP, MS. RIRUKA?
MM.
IT SMELLS NICE.
GOD DWELLS ...
...IN EXACT TIME.
TMP

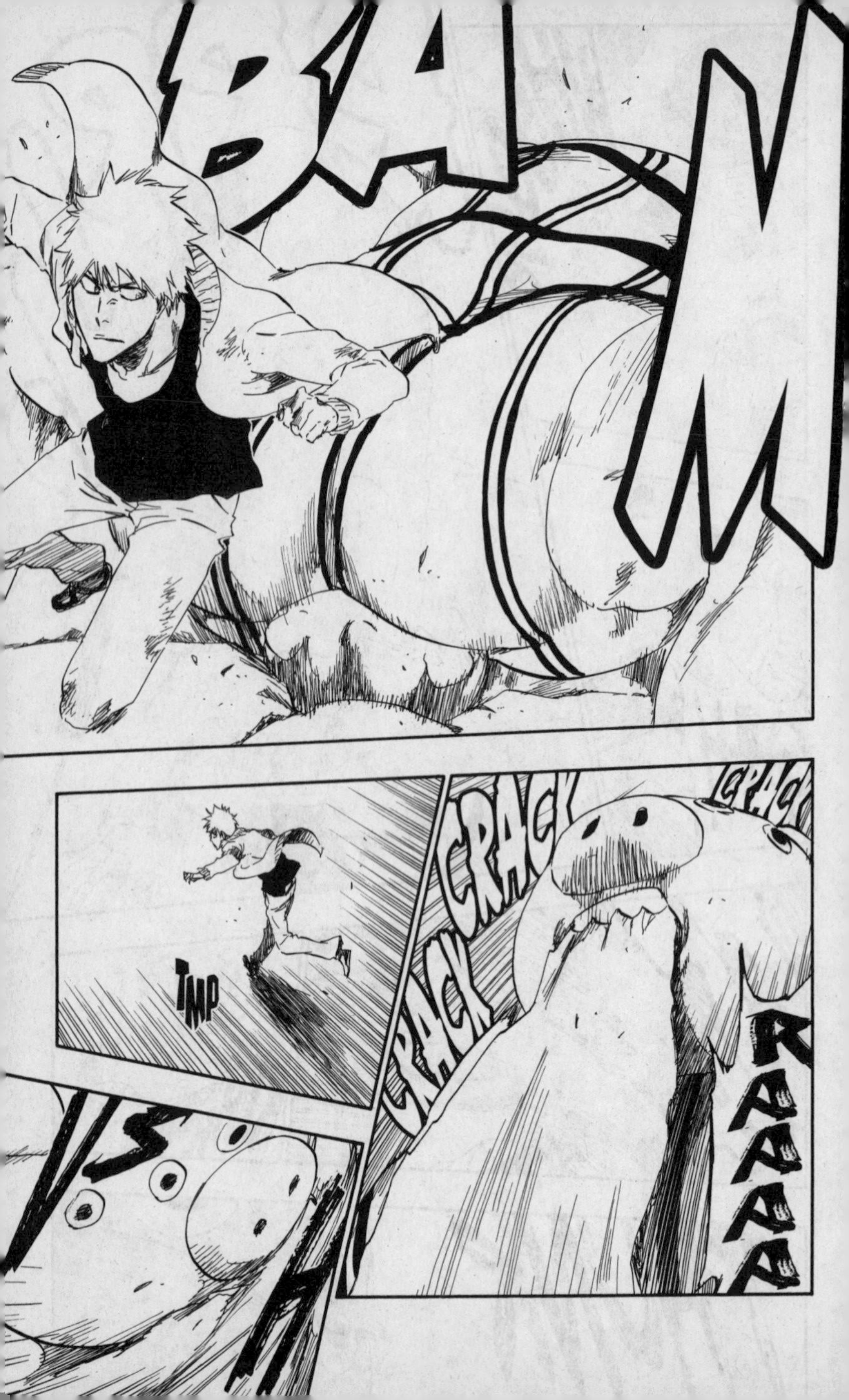
BAM
CRACK
CRACK
CRACK
CRACK
RAAAAA
TMP

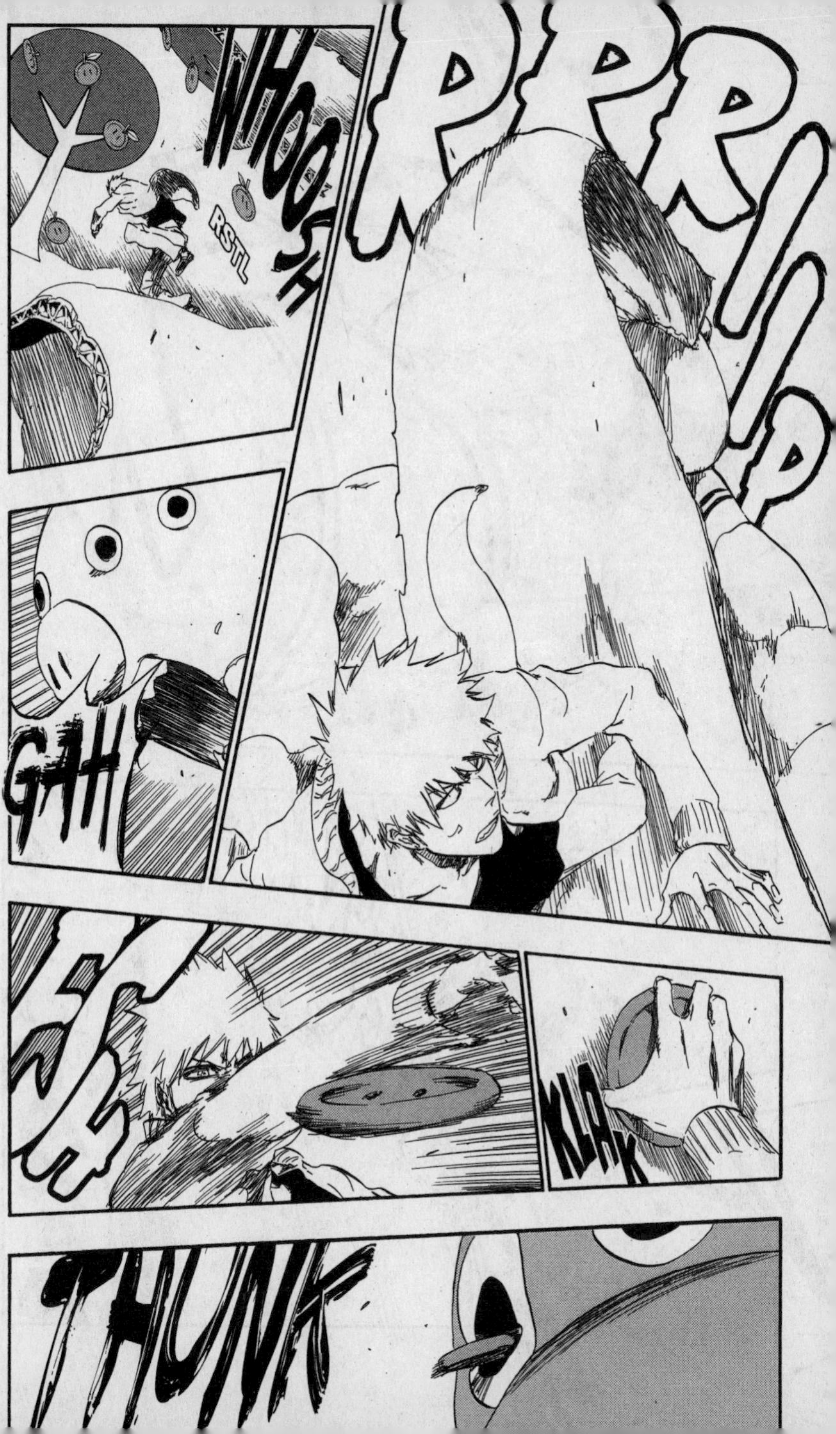
RRRIIP
WHOOSH
RSTL
GAH
KLAK
THUNK

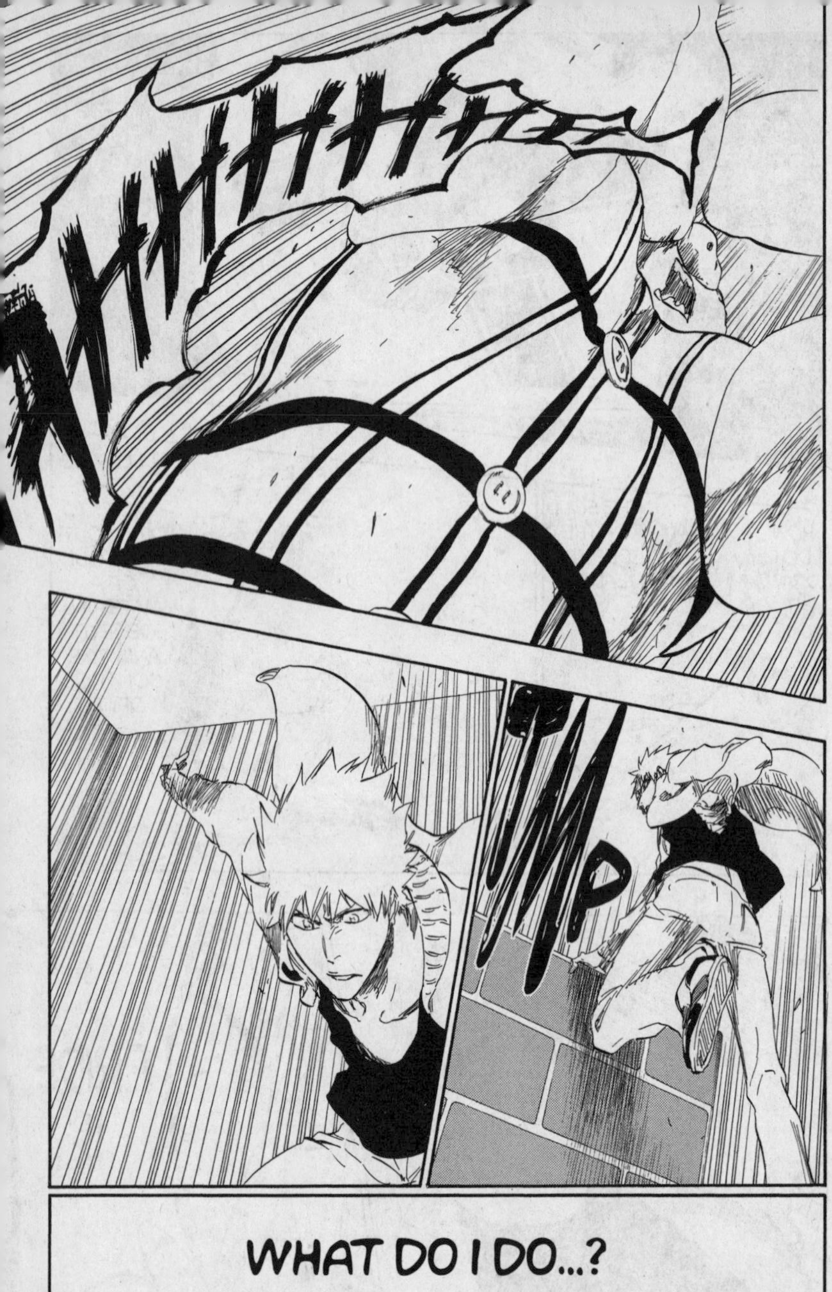
WHAT DO I DO...?

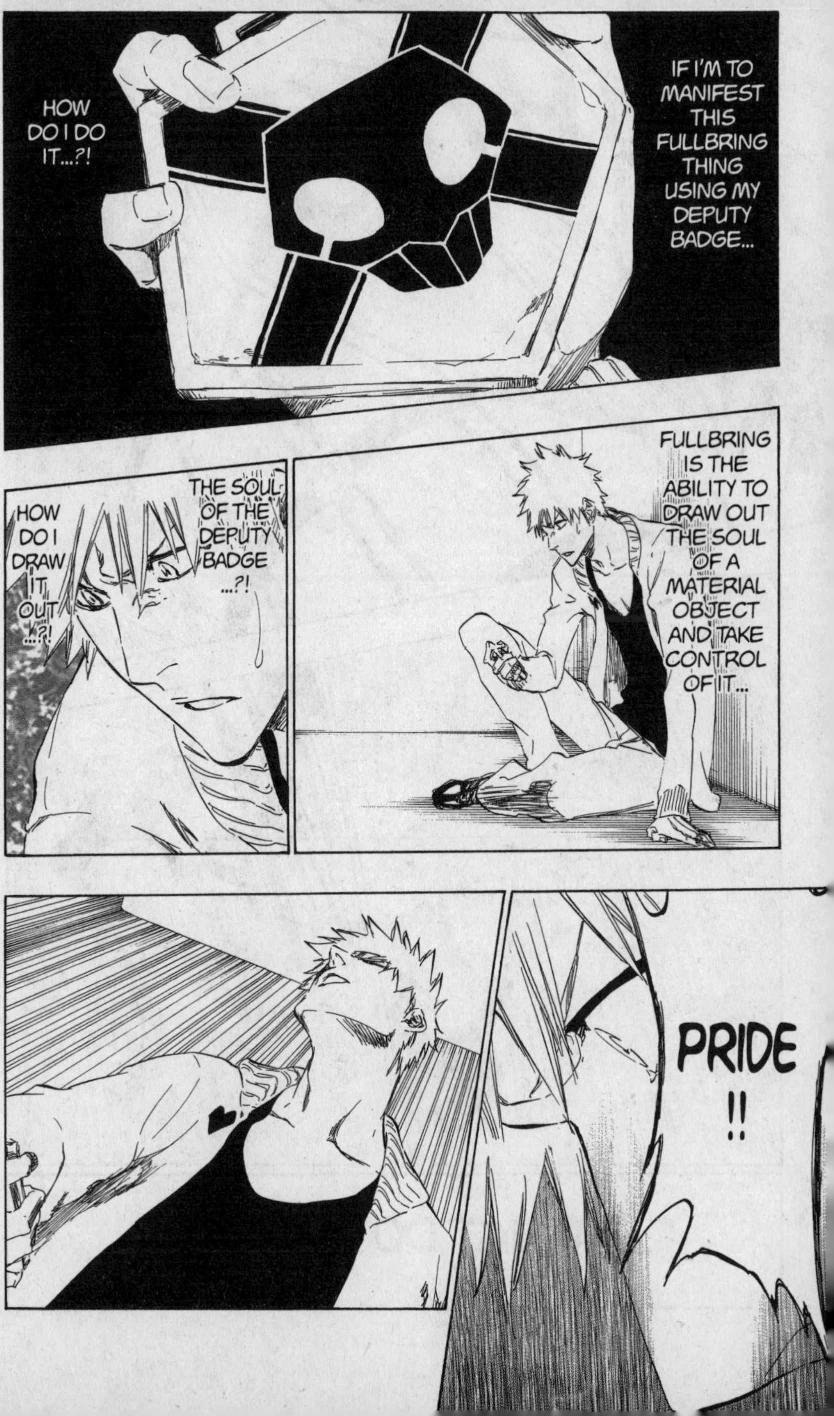
IF I'M TO MANIFEST THIS FULLBRING THING USING MY DEPUTY BADGE...
HOW DO I DO IT...?!
FULLBRING IS THE ABILITY TO DRAW OUT THE SOUL OF A MATERIAL OBJECT AND TAKE CONTROL OF IT...
THE SOUL OF THE DEPUTY BADGE ...?!
HOW DO I DRAW IT OUT ...?!
PRIDE !!

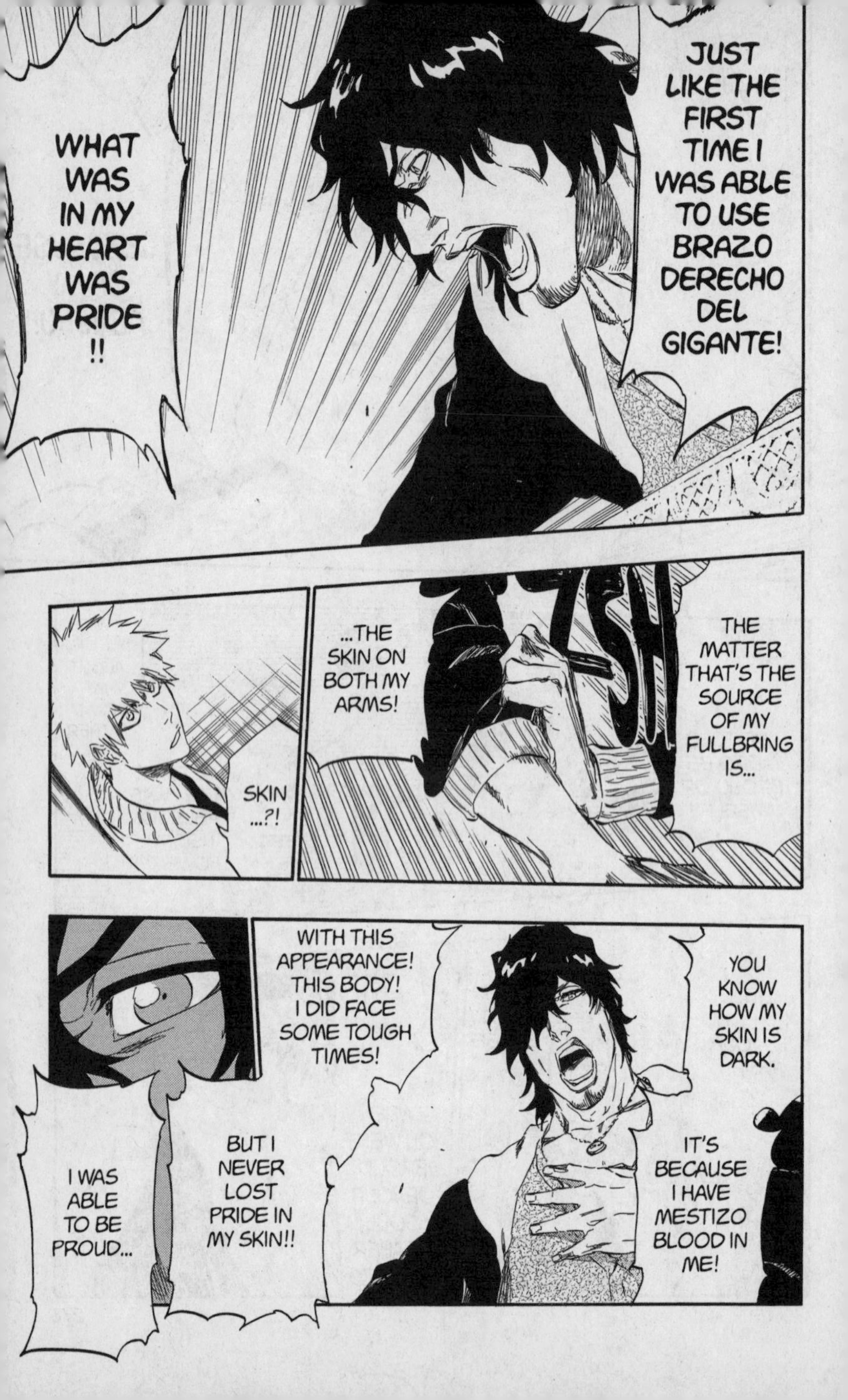

JUST LIKE THE FIRST TIME I WAS ABLE TO USE BRAZO DERECHO DEL GIGANTE!
WHAT WAS IN MY HEART WAS PRIDE !!
THE MATTER THAT'S THE SOURCE OF MY FULLBRING IS...
...THE SKIN ON BOTH MY ARMS!
SKIN ...?!
YOU KNOW HOW MY SKIN IS DARK.
IT'S BECAUSE I HAVE MESTIZO BLOOD IN ME!
WITH THIS APPEARANCE! THIS BODY! I DID FACE SOME TOUGH TIMES!
BUT I NEVER LOST PRIDE IN MY SKIN!!
I WAS ABLE TO BE PROUD...

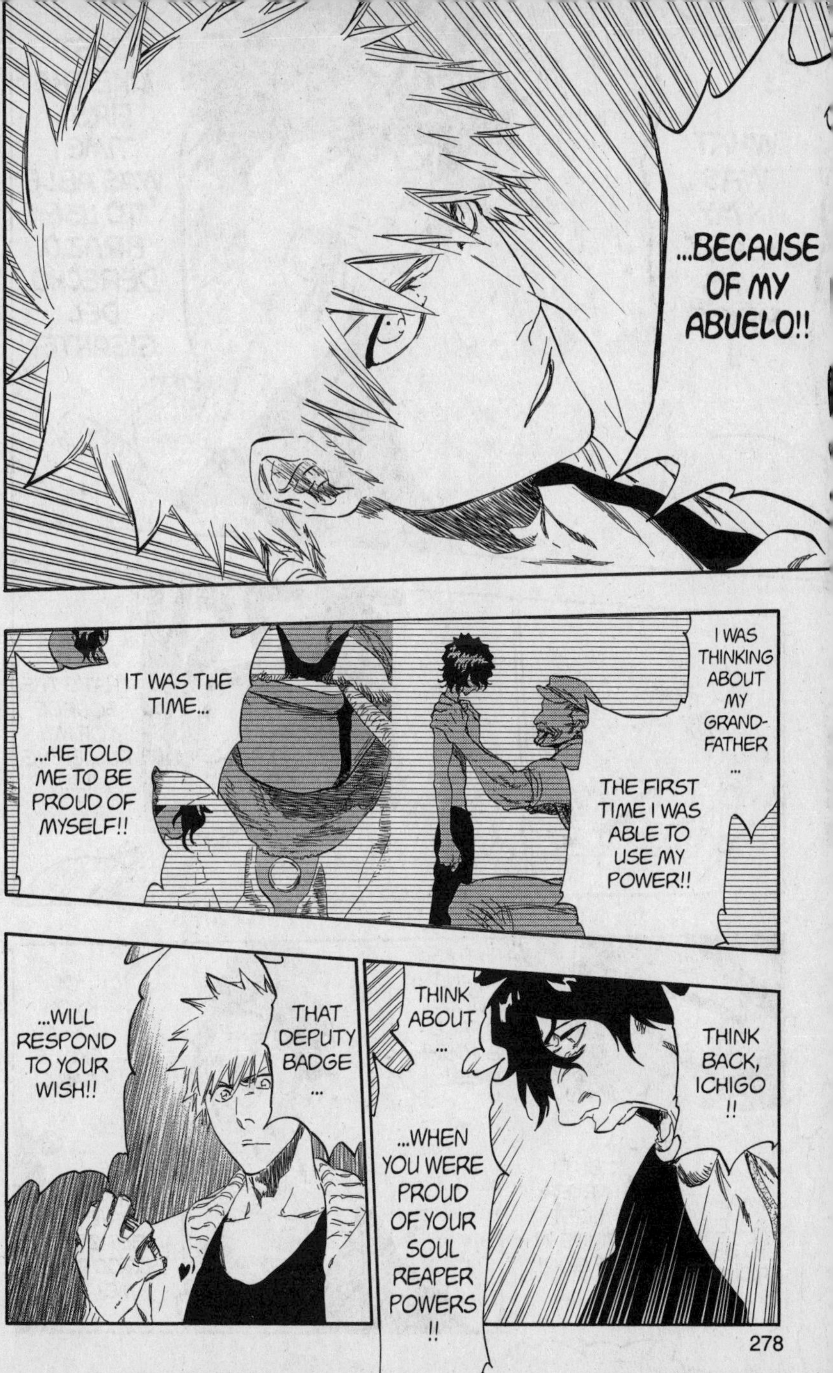
...BECAUSE OF MY ABUELO!!
I WAS THINKING ABOUT MY GRANDFATHER ...
THE FIRST TIME I WAS ABLE TO USE MY POWER!!
IT WAS THE TIME...
...HE TOLD ME TO BE PROUD OF MYSELF!!
THINK BACK, ICHIGO !!
THINK ABOUT ...
...WHEN YOU WERE PROUD OF YOUR SOUL REAPER POWERS !!
THAT DEPUTY BADGE ...
...WILL RESPOND TO YOUR WISH!!

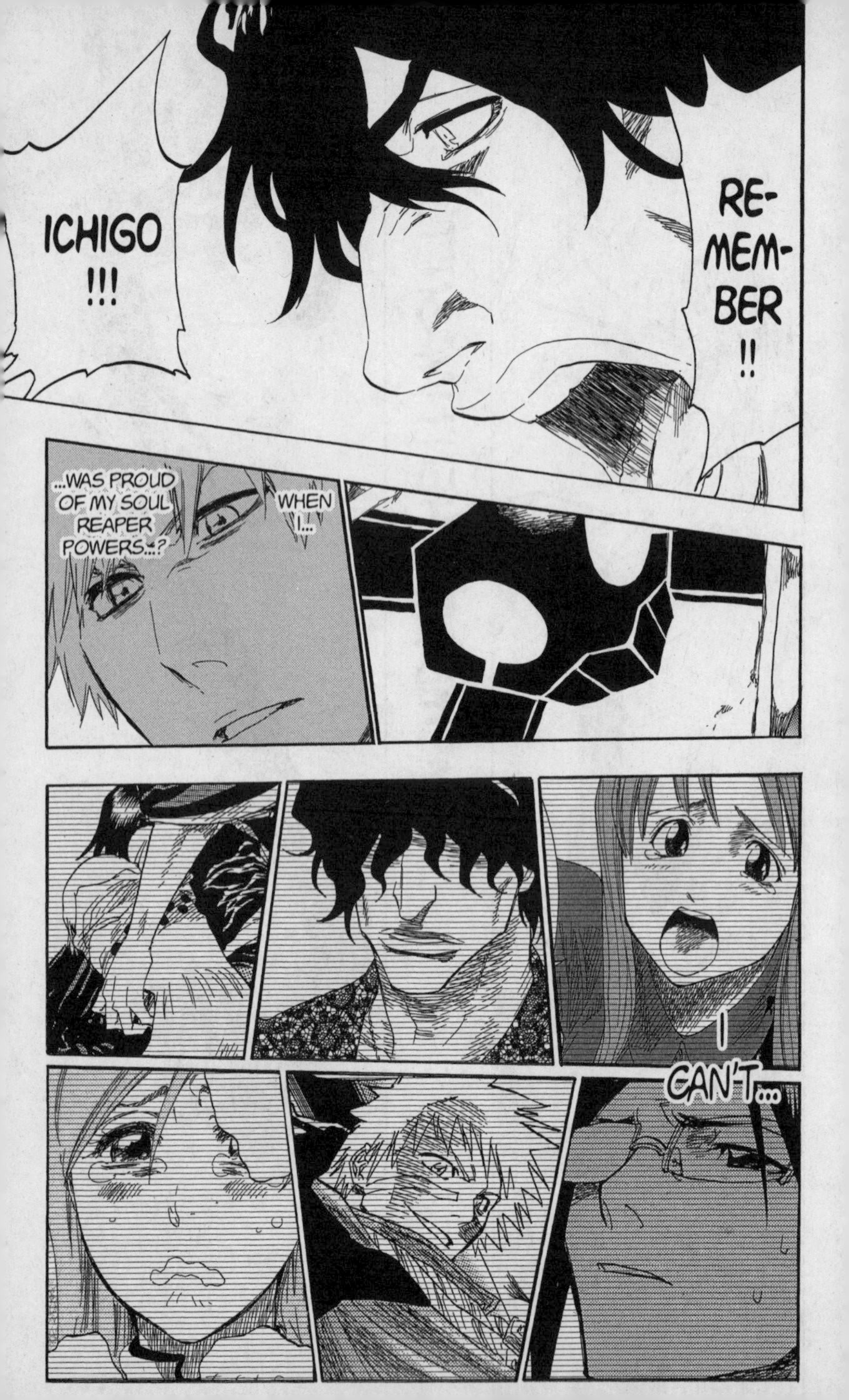
RE-MEM-BER!!
ICHIGO!!!
WHEN I...
...WAS PROUD OF MY SOUL REAPER POWERS...?
I CAN'T...

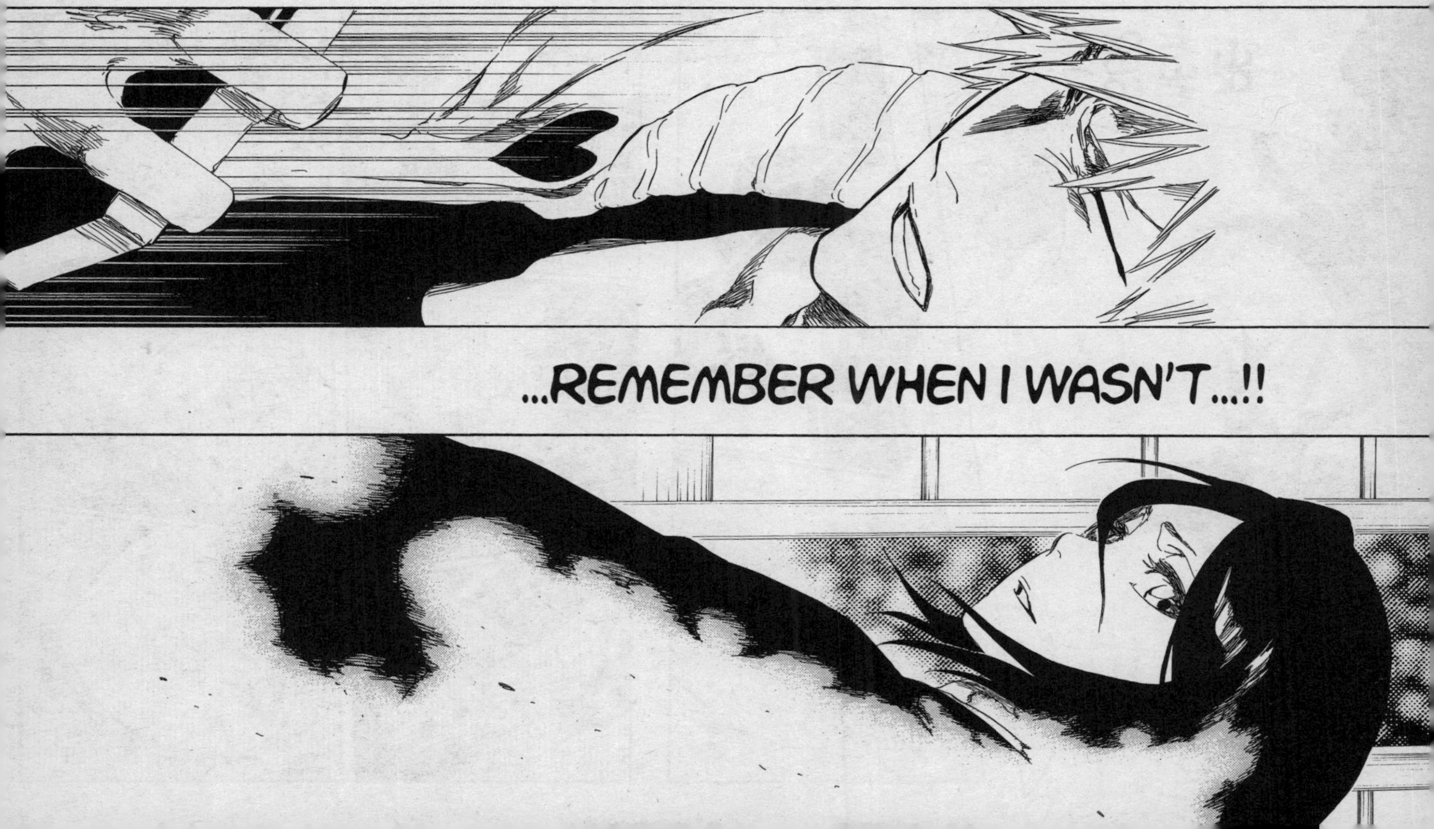
...REMEMBER WHEN I WASN'T...!!

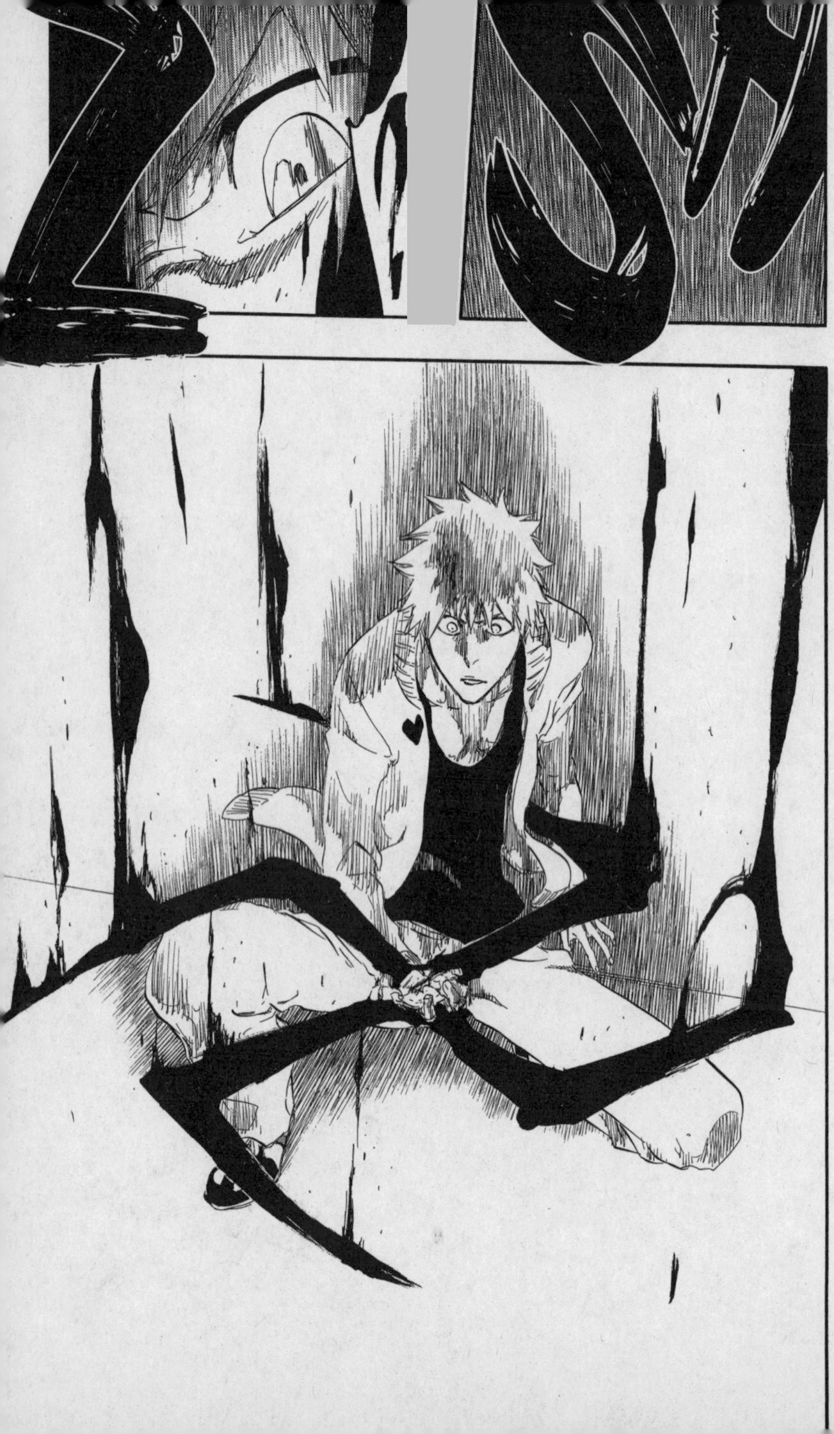

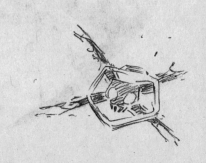

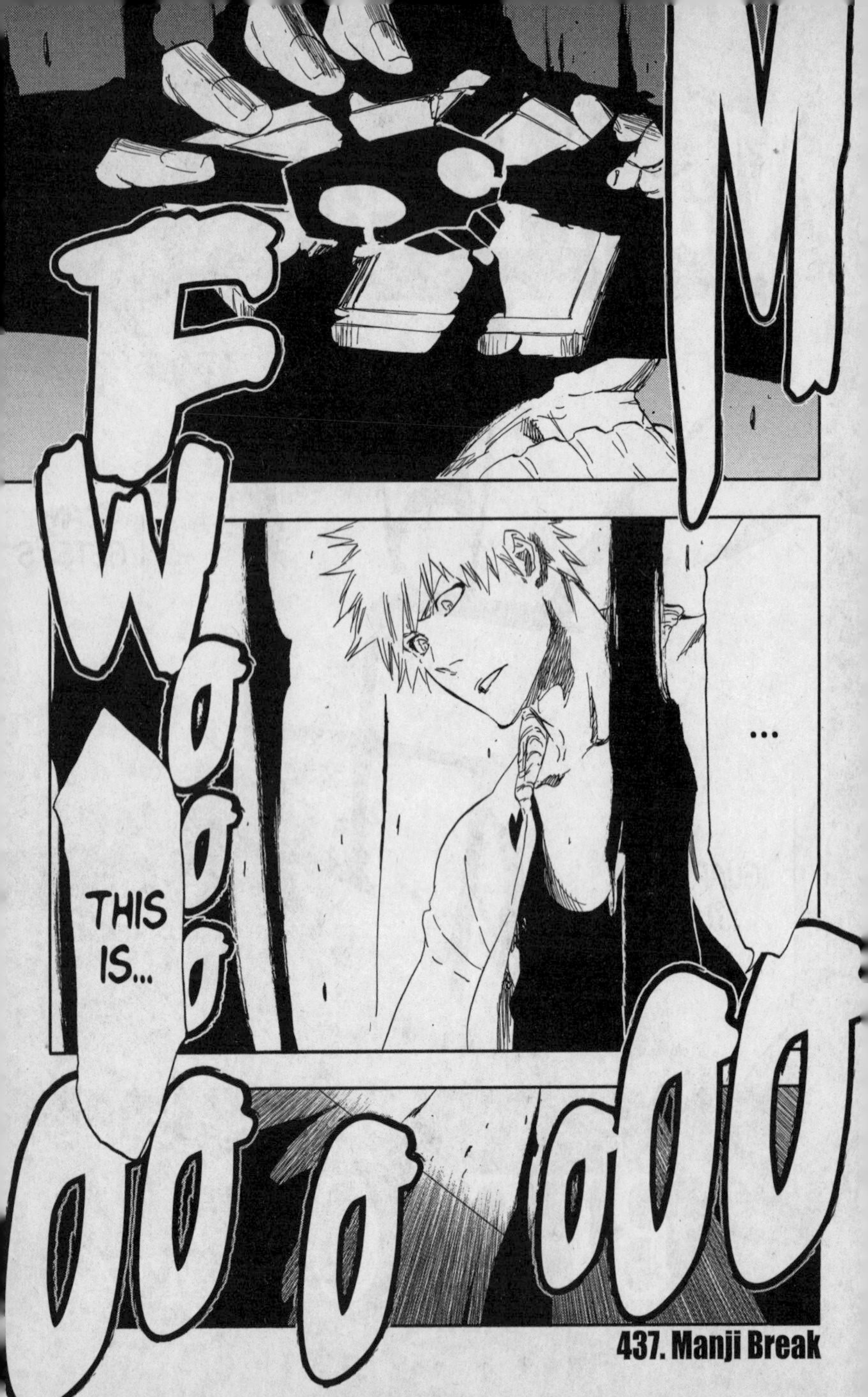
...
THIS IS...

437. Manji Break

Manji Break

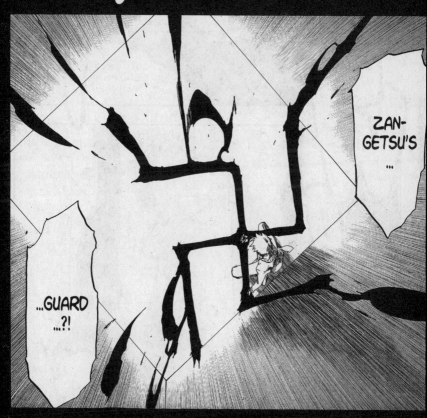

ZAN-GETSU'S...

...GUARD...?!

BLEACH 437.

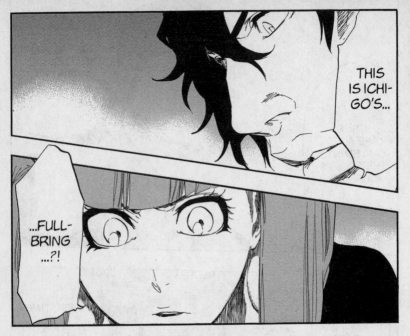

THIS IS ICHI-GO'S...

...FULL-BRING...?!

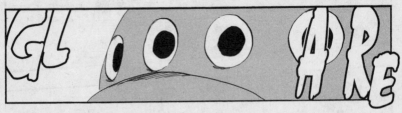

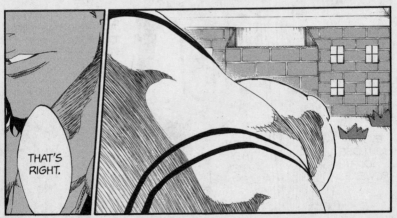

THAT'S RIGHT.

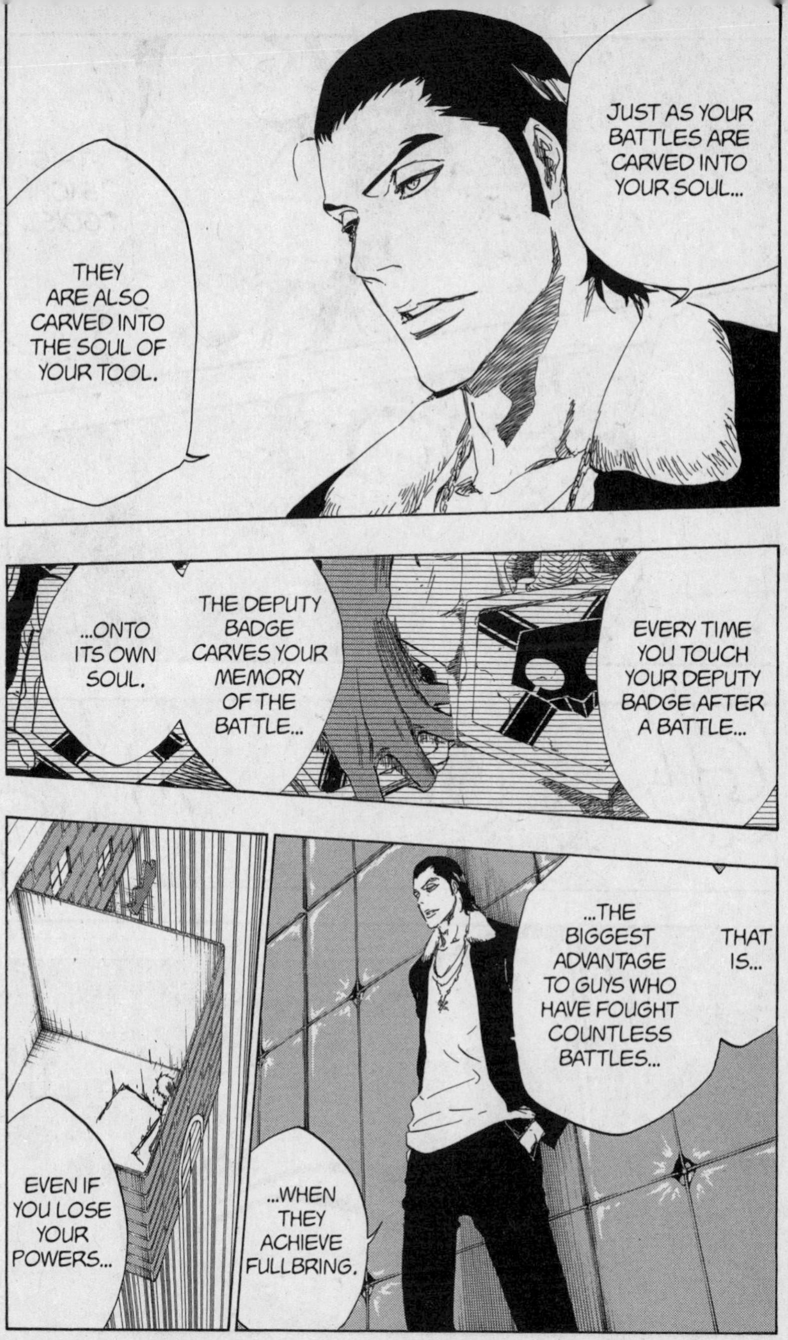
JUST AS YOUR BATTLES ARE CARVED INTO YOUR SOUL...
THEY ARE ALSO CARVED INTO THE SOUL OF YOUR TOOL.
EVERY TIME YOU TOUCH YOUR DEPUTY BADGE AFTER A BATTLE...
THE DEPUTY BADGE CARVES YOUR MEMORY OF THE BATTLE...
...ONTO ITS OWN SOUL.
THAT IS...
...THE BIGGEST ADVANTAGE TO GUYS WHO HAVE FOUGHT COUNTLESS BATTLES...
...WHEN THEY ACHIEVE FULLBRING.
EVEN IF YOU LOSE YOUR POWERS...

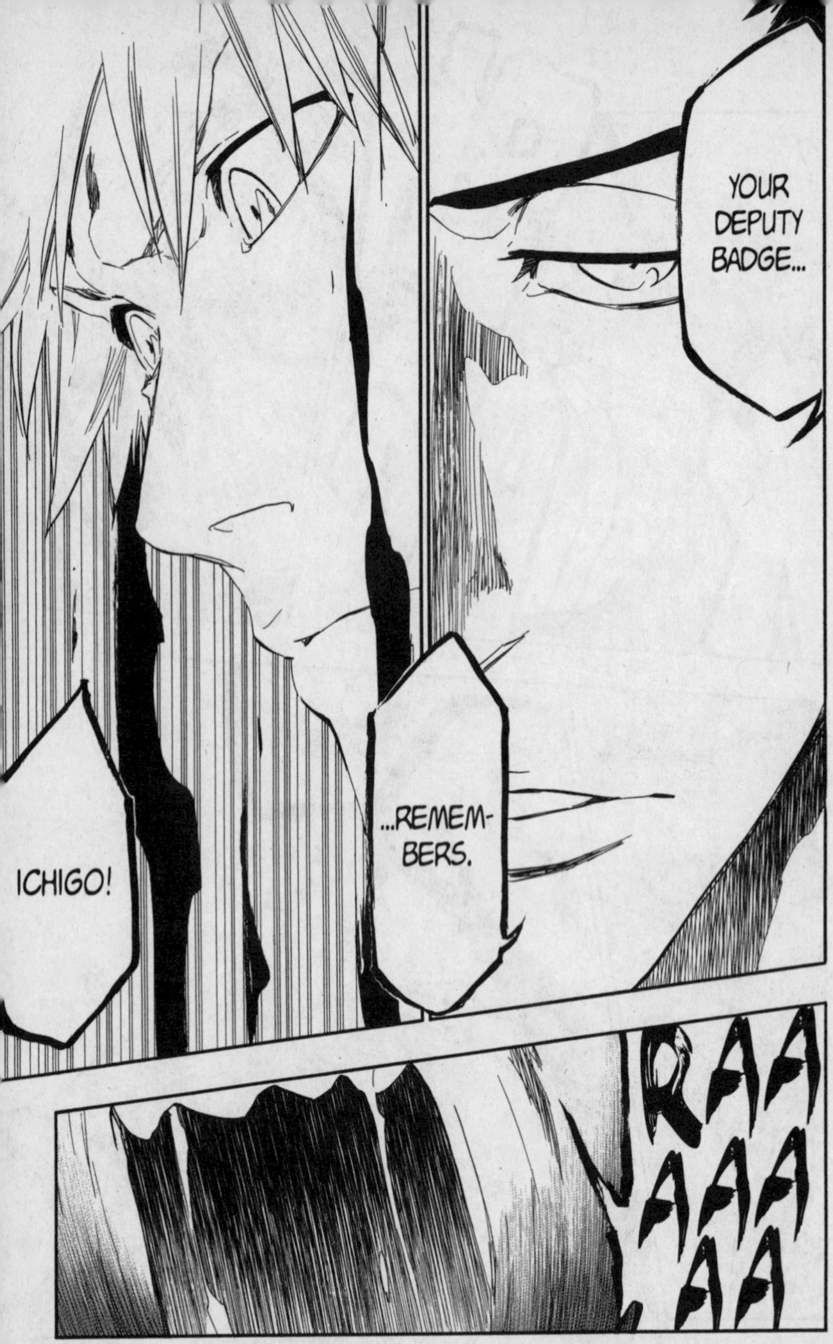
YOUR DEPUTY BADGE...
...REMEMBERS.
ICHIGO!
RAAAAAAAA

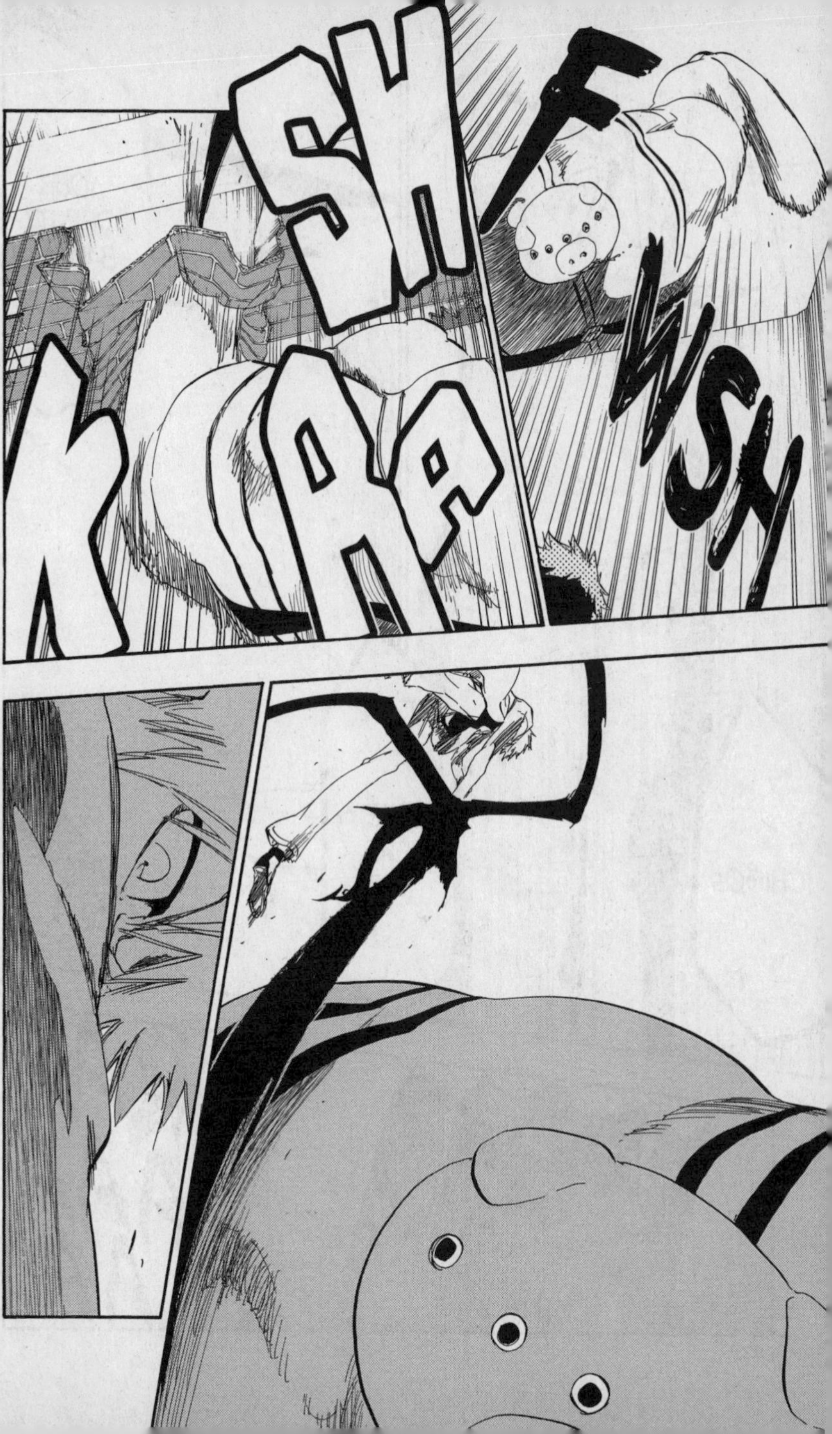
KRASH
WSH

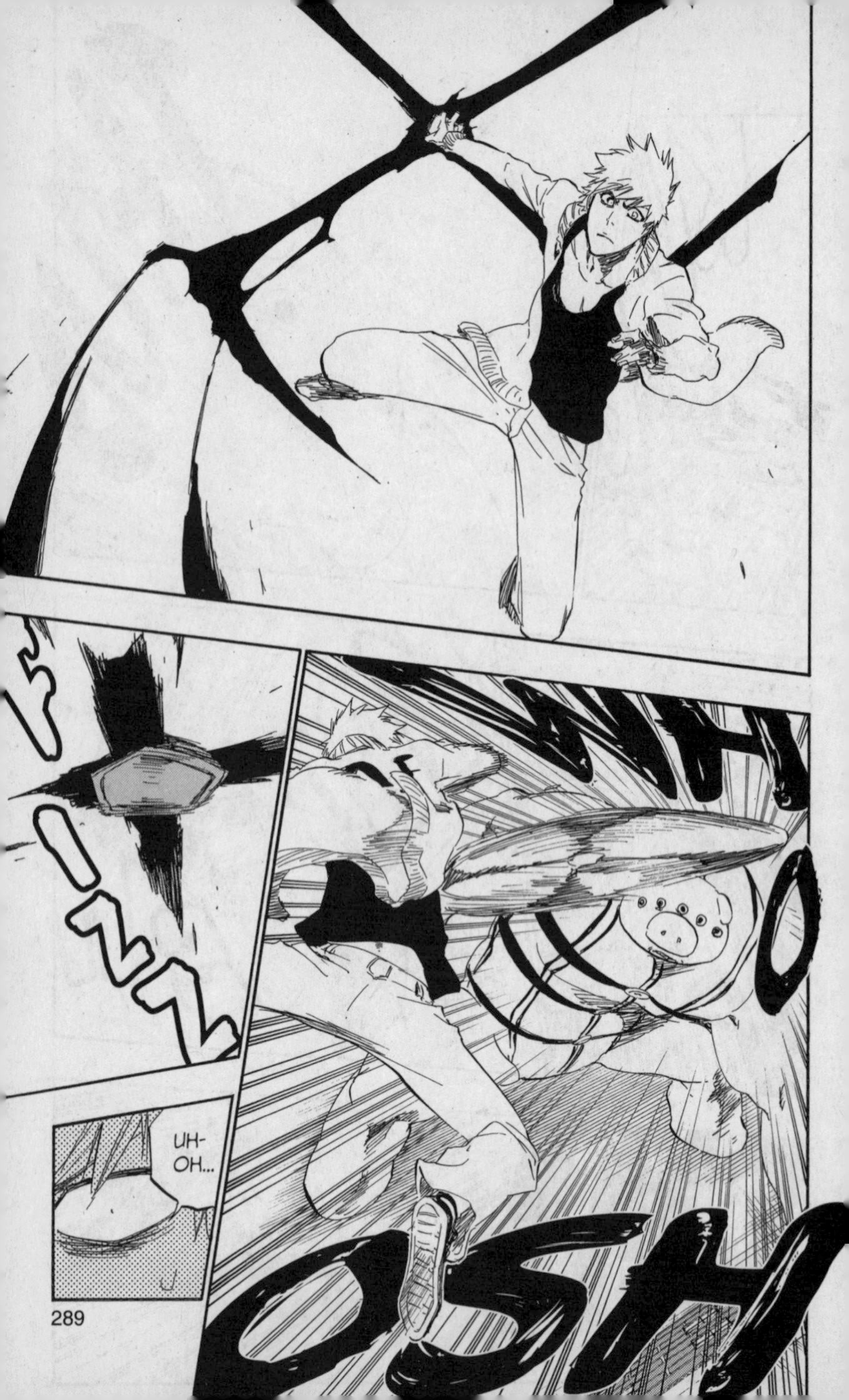
UH-
OH...

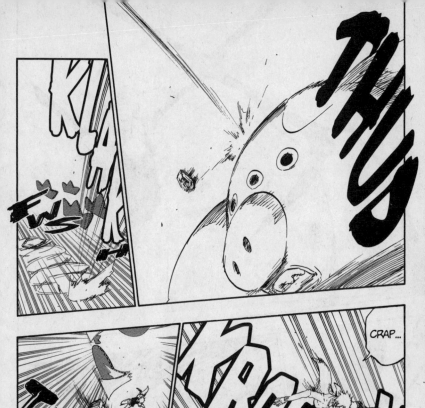

CRAP...

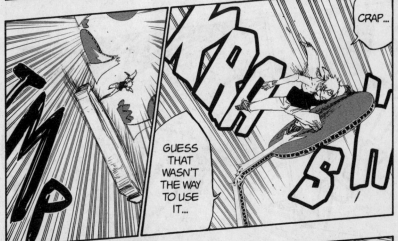

GUESS THAT WASN'T THE WAY TO USE IT...

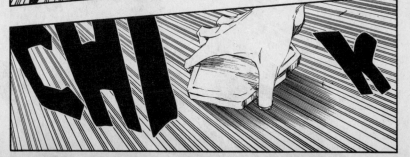

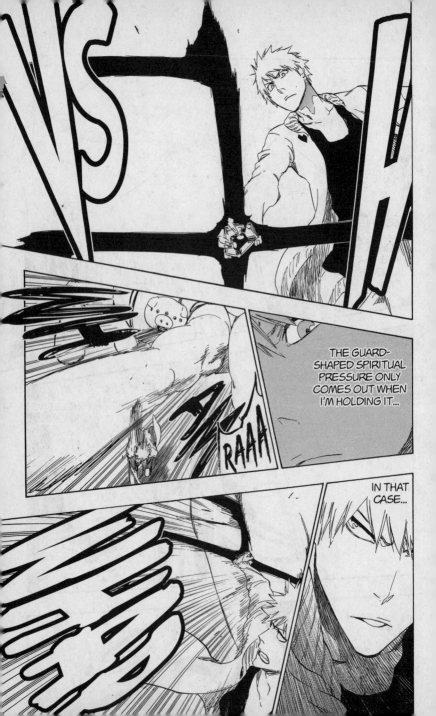

THE GUARD-SHAPED SPIRITUAL PRESSURE ONLY COMES OUT WHEN I'M HOLDING IT...

IN THAT CASE...

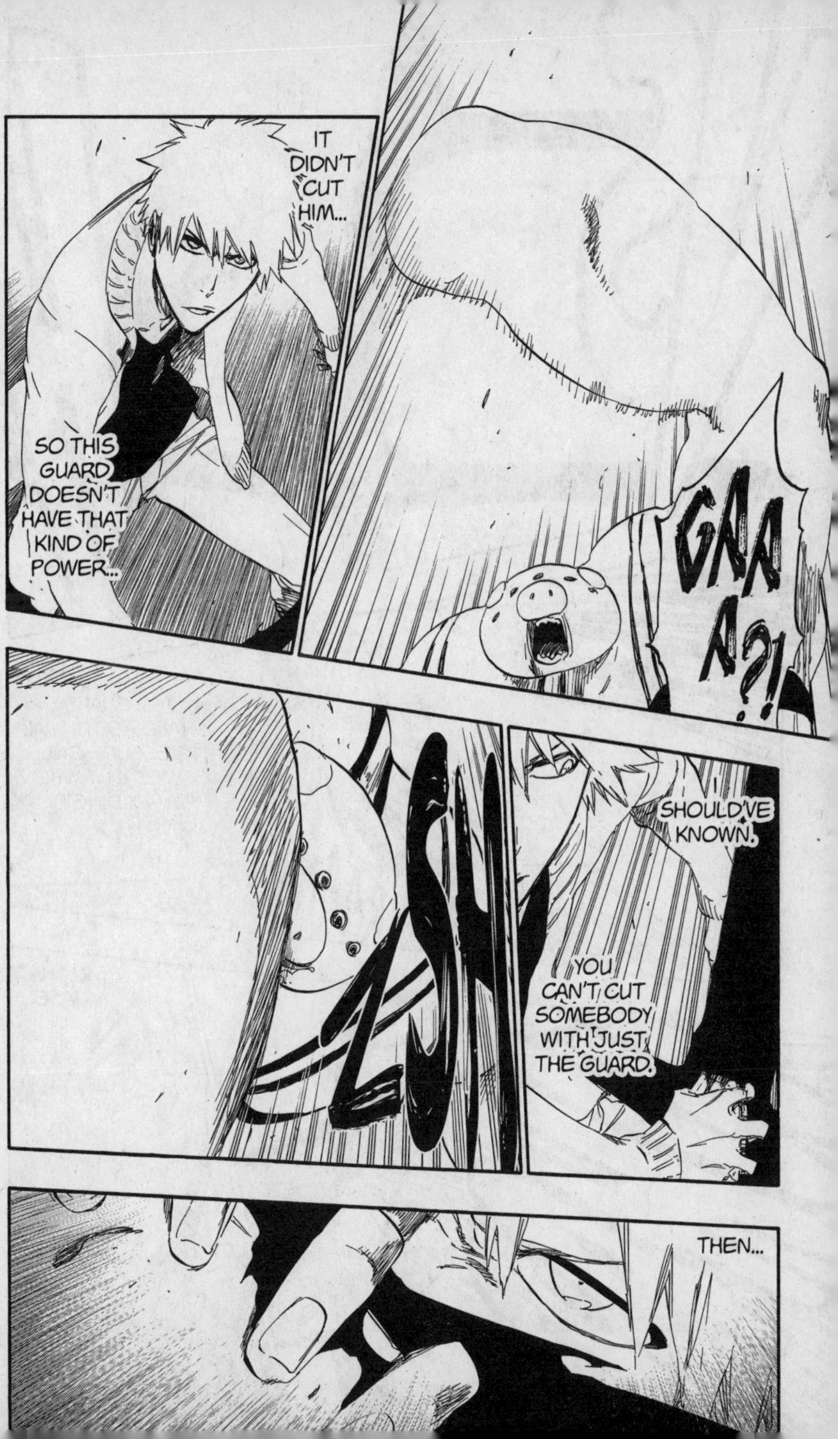
GRAAA?!
IT DIDN'T CUT HIM...
SO THIS GUARD DOESN'T HAVE THAT KIND OF POWER...
SHOULD'VE KNOWN.
YOU CAN'T CUT SOMEBODY WITH JUST THE GUARD.
ZSH
THEN...

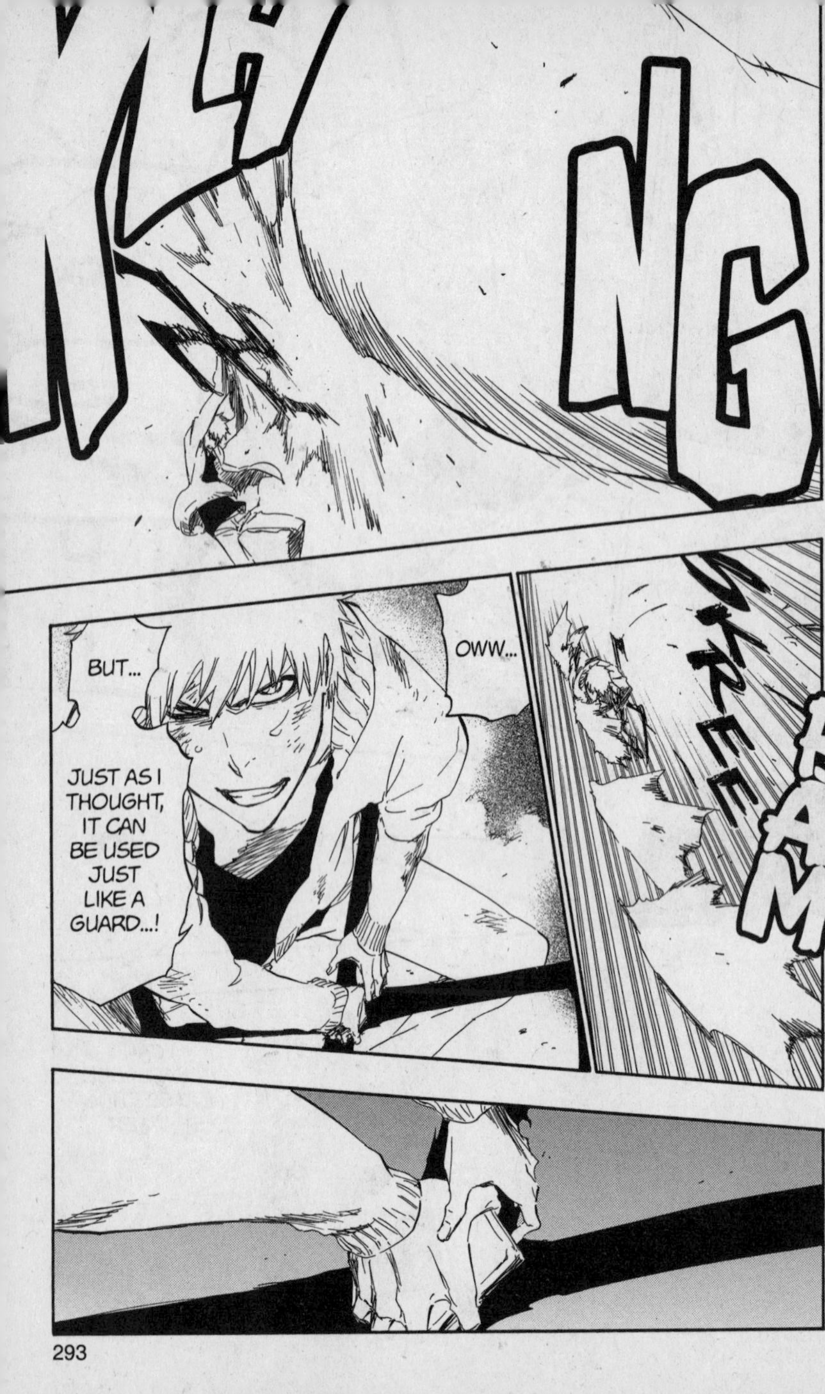
BAM
SKREE
OWW...
BUT...
JUST AS I THOUGHT, IT CAN BE USED JUST LIKE A GUARD...!

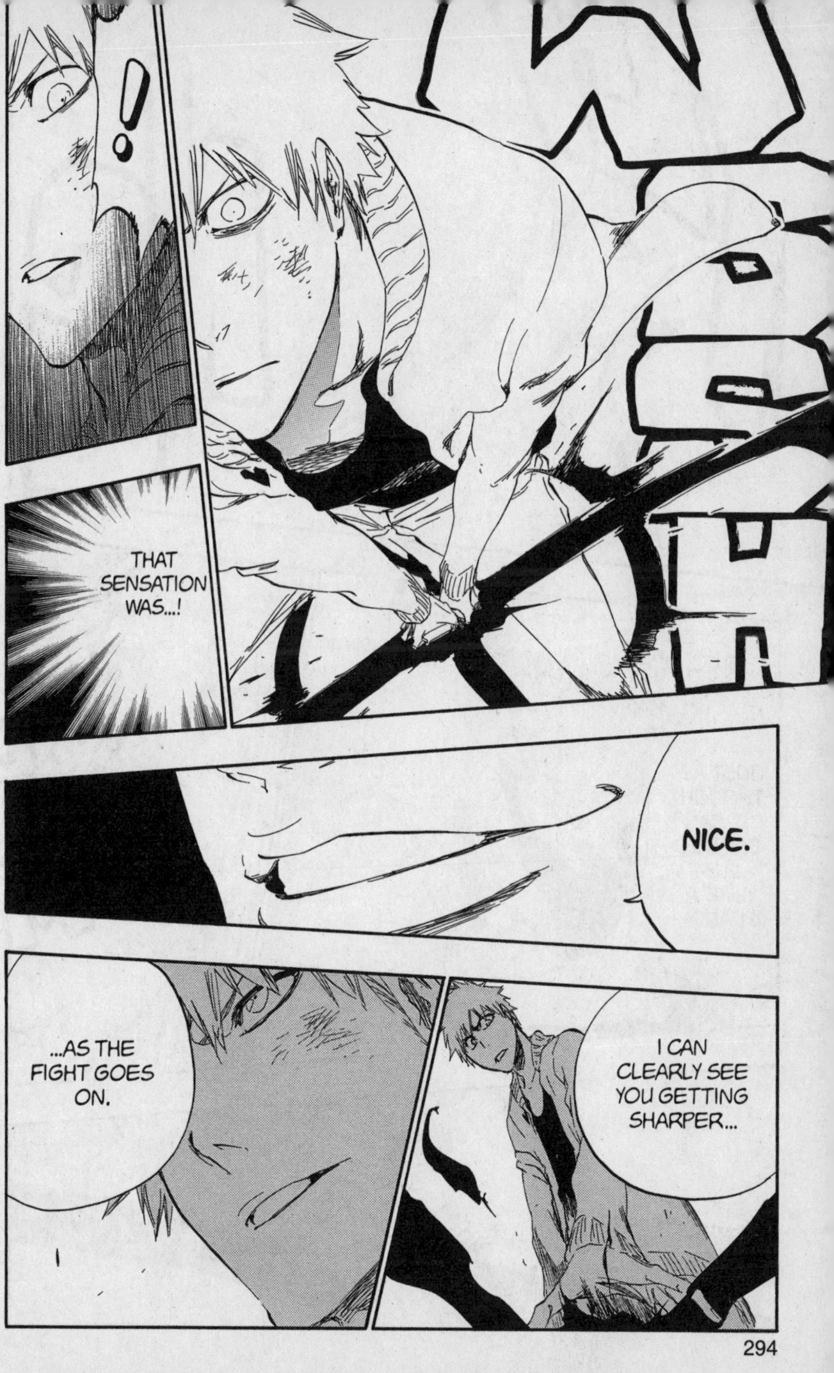
!
THAT SENSATION WAS...!
NICE.
I CAN CLEARLY SEE YOU GETTING SHARPER...
...AS THE FIGHT GOES ON.

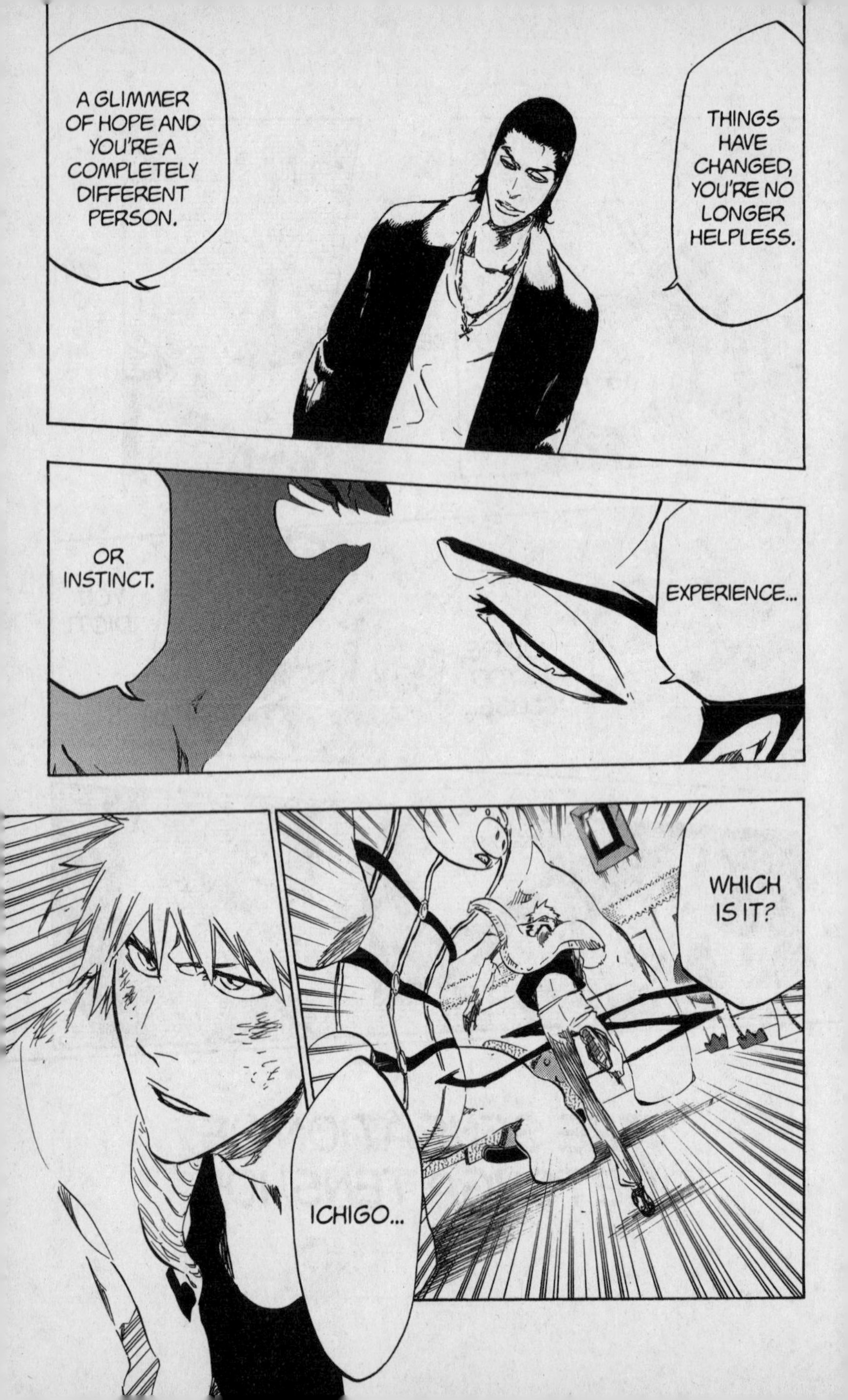
THINGS HAVE CHANGED, YOU'RE NO LONGER HELPLESS.
A GLIMMER OF HOPE AND YOU'RE A COMPLETELY DIFFERENT PERSON.
EXPERIENCE...
OR INSTINCT.
WHICH IS IT?
ICHIGO...

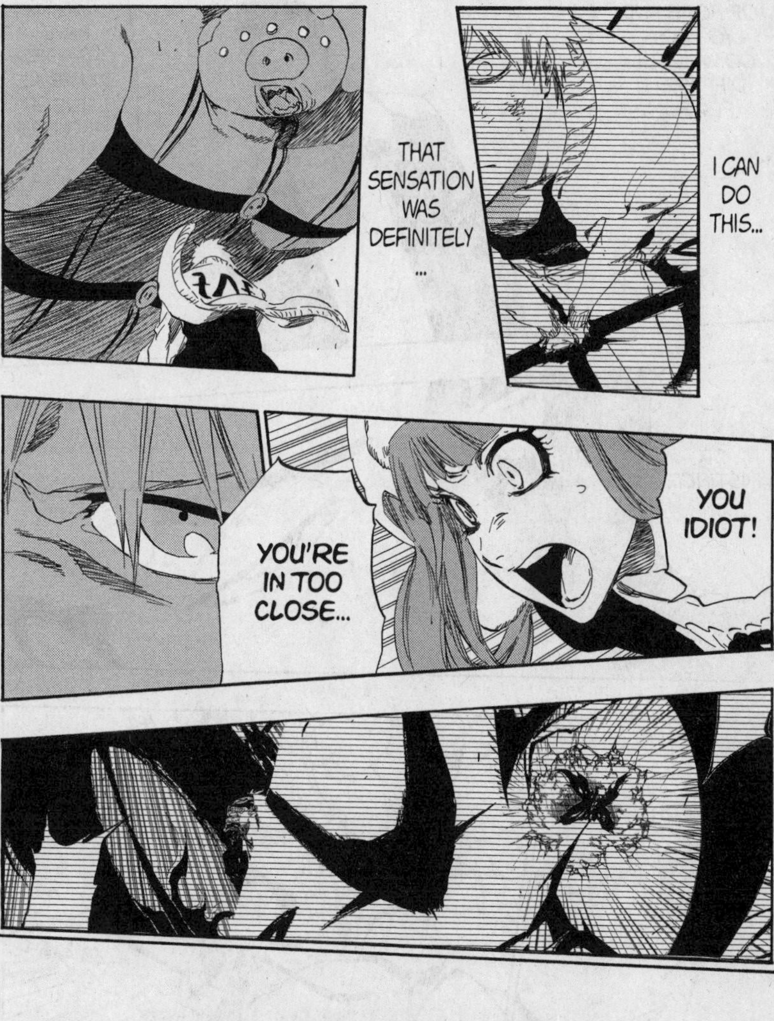
I CAN DO THIS...
THAT SENSATION WAS DEFINITELY ...
YOU IDIOT!
YOU'RE IN TOO CLOSE...

THE SENSATION OF GETSUGA TENSHO!!

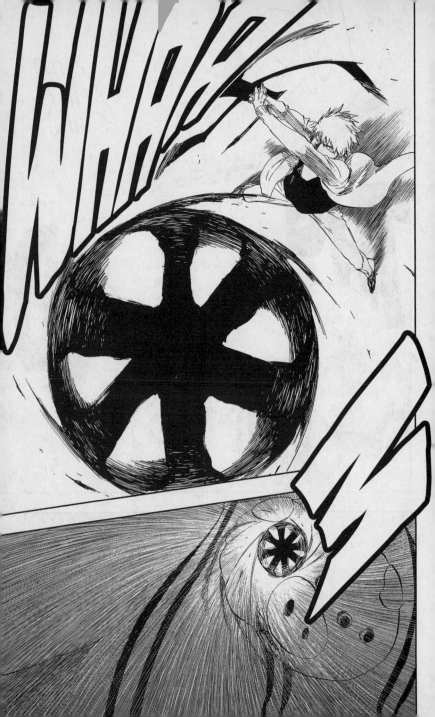

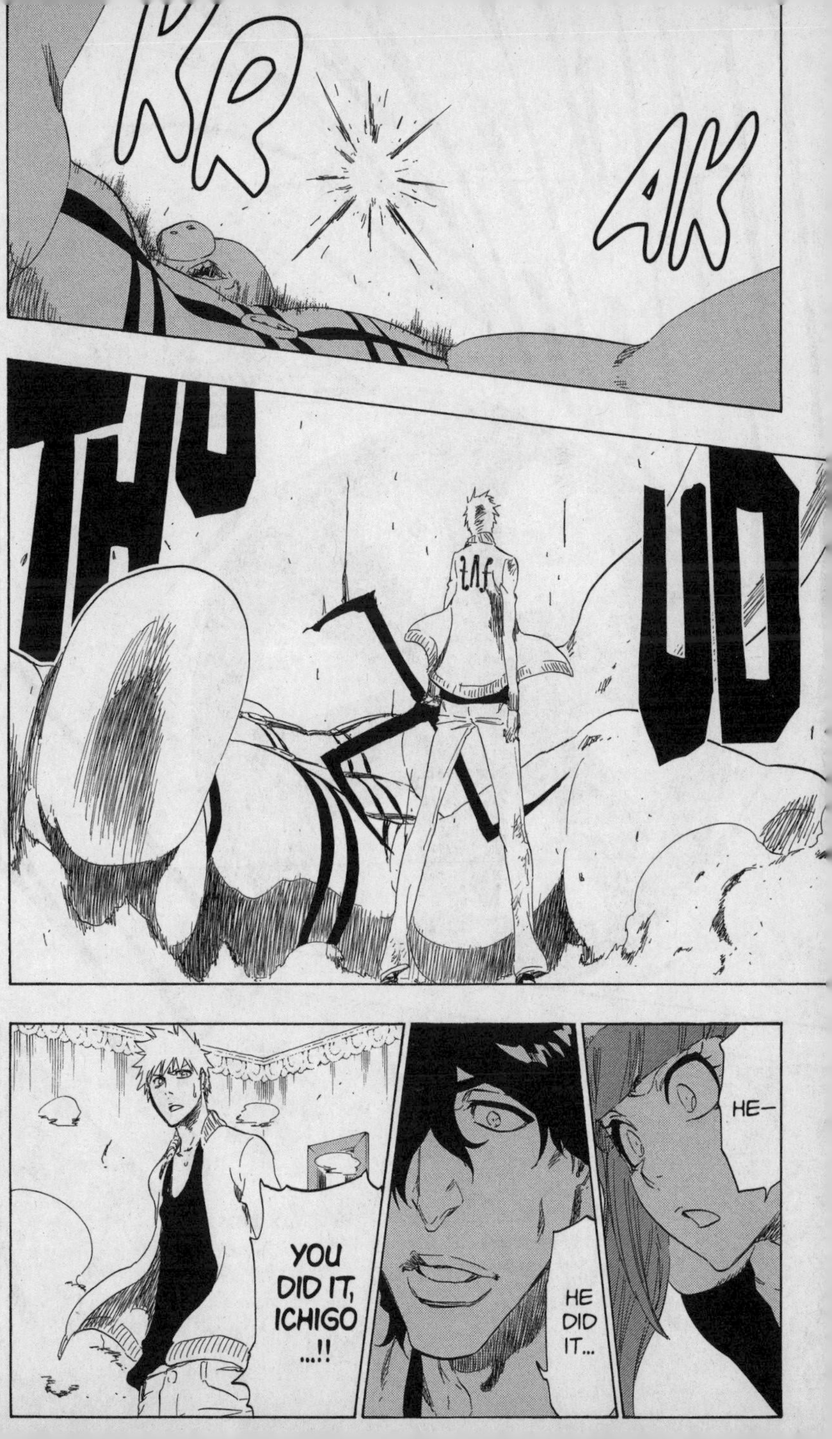
KRAK
THUD
HE—
HE DID IT...
YOU DID IT, ICHIGO ...!!

READ THIS WAY

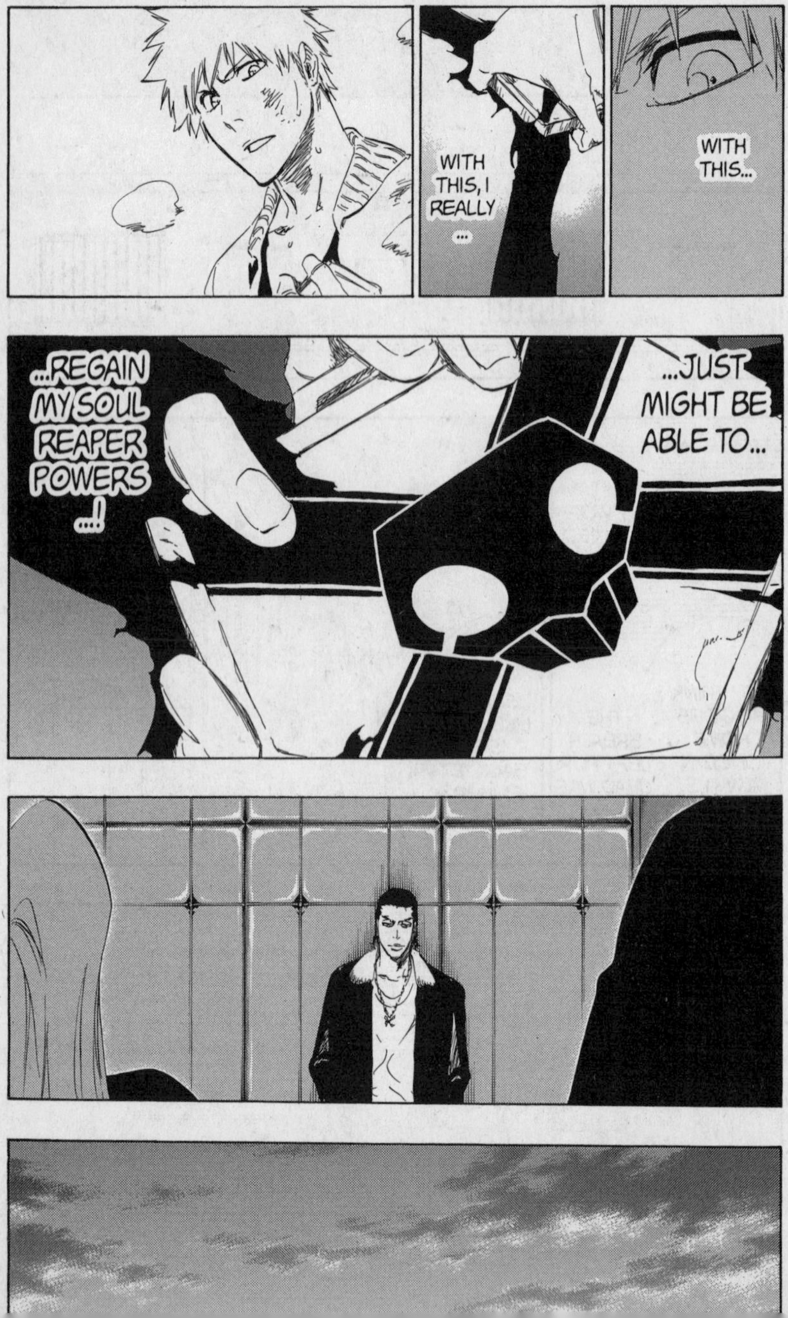
WITH THIS...
WITH THIS, I REALLY ...
...JUST MIGHT BE ABLE TO...
...REGAIN MY SOUL REAPER POWERS ...!

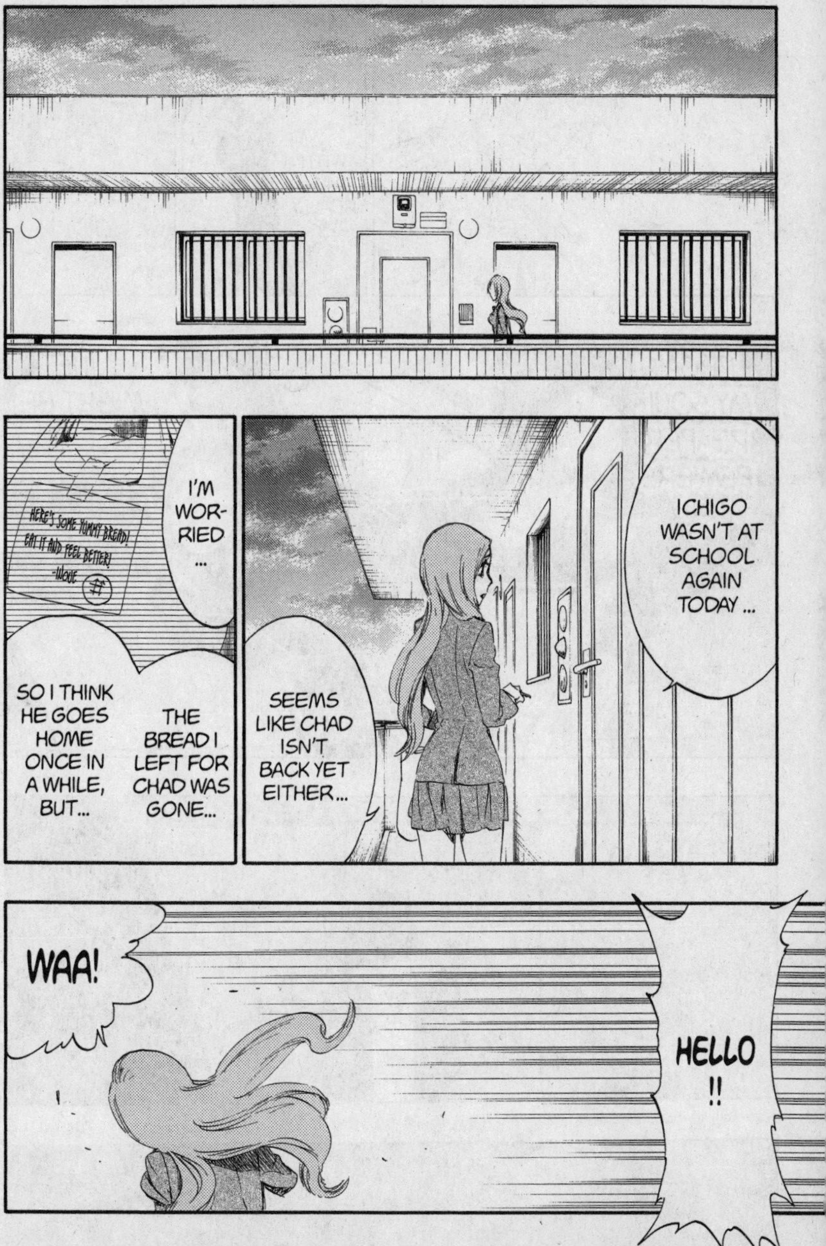
ICHIGO WASN'T AT SCHOOL AGAIN TODAY ...
SEEMS LIKE CHAD ISN'T BACK YET EITHER...
I'M WOR-RIED ...
HERE'S SOME YUMMY BREAD! EAT IT AND FEEL BETTER! -INOUE
THE BREAD I LEFT FOR CHAD WAS GONE...
SO I THINK HE GOES HOME ONCE IN A WHILE, BUT...
HELLO !!
WAA!

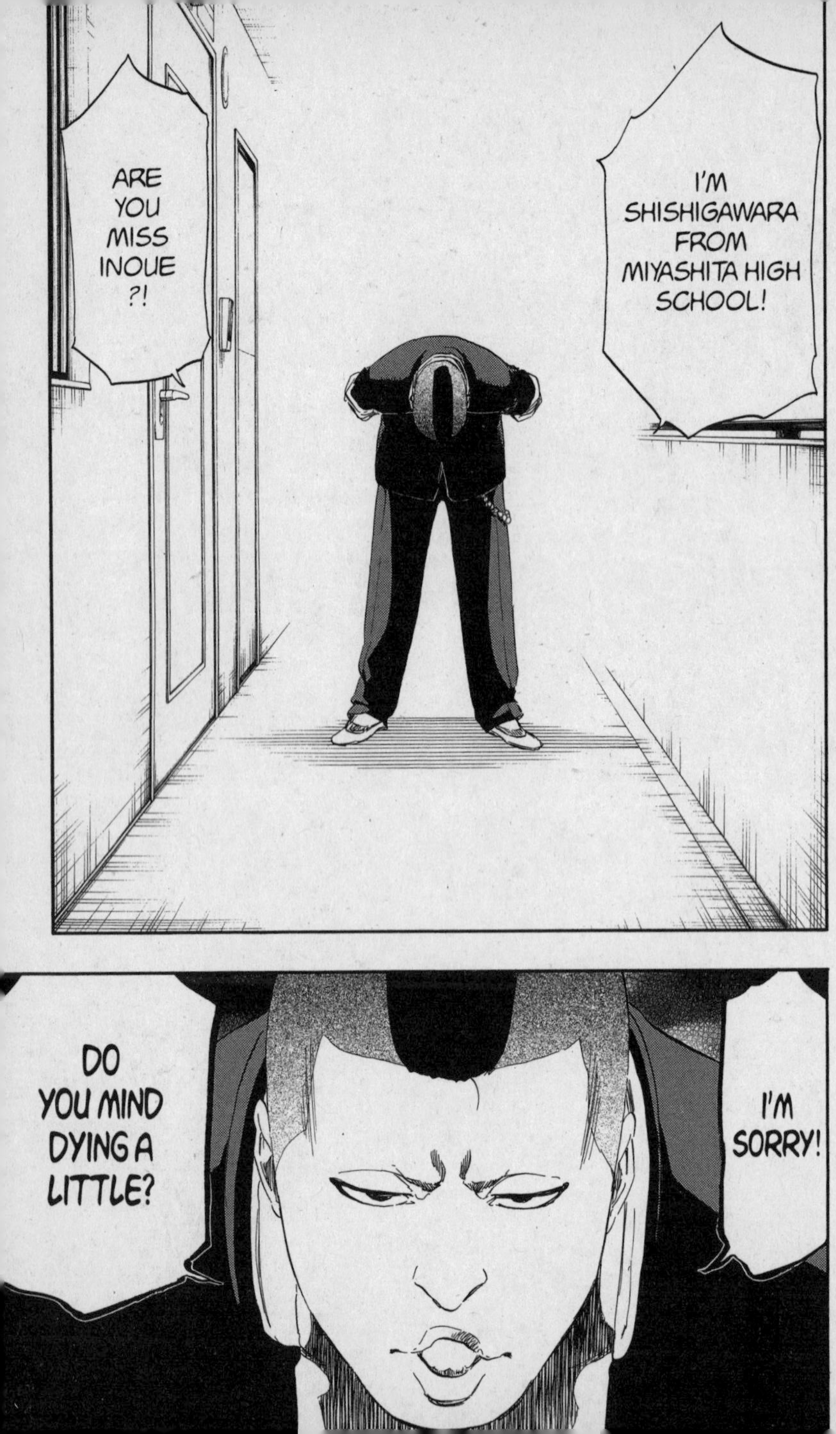
I'M SHISHIGAWARA FROM MIYASHITA HIGH SCHOOL!
ARE YOU MISS INOUE ?!
I'M SORRY!
DO YOU MIND DYING A LITTLE?

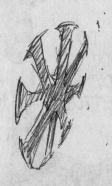

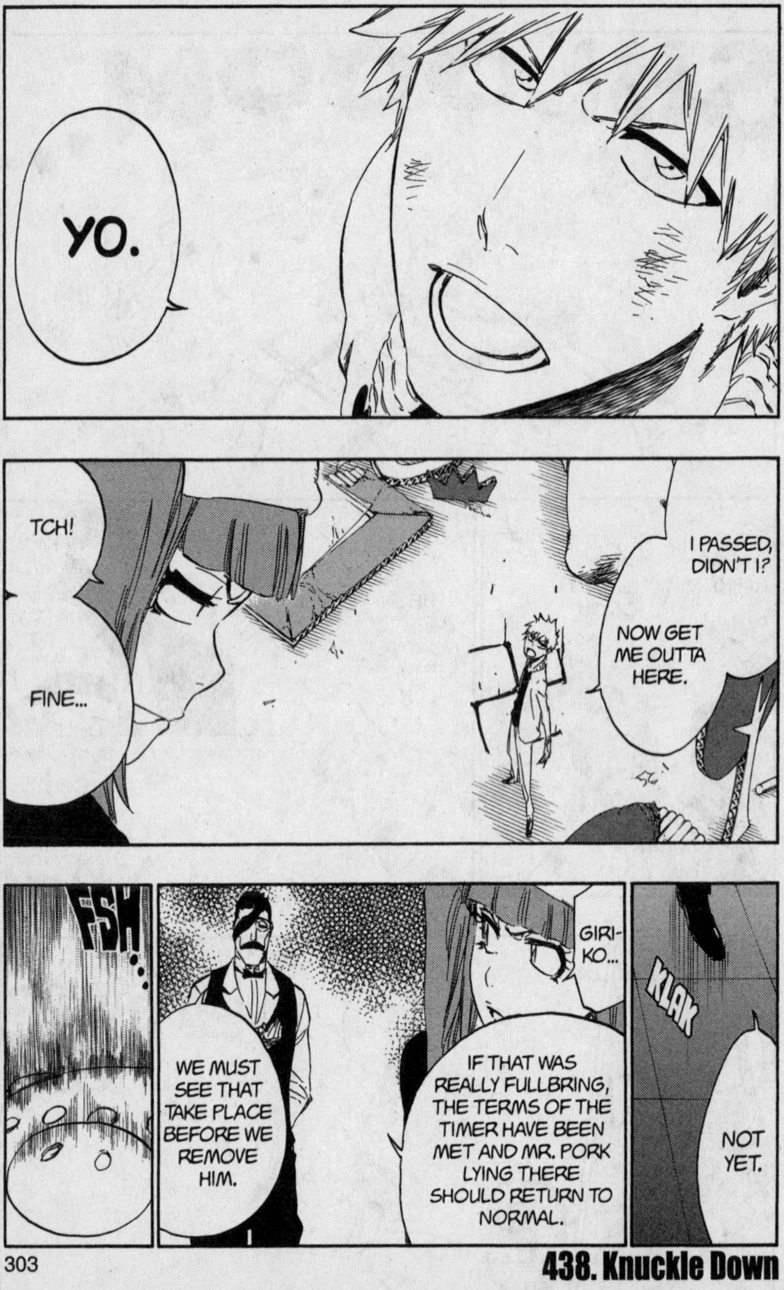
YO.
I PASSED, DIDN'T I?
NOW GET ME OUTTA HERE.
TCH!
FINE...
KLAK
NOT YET.
GIRI-KO...
IF THAT WAS REALLY FULLBRING, THE TERMS OF THE TIMER HAVE BEEN MET AND MR. PORK LYING THERE SHOULD RETURN TO NORMAL.
WE MUST SEE THAT TAKE PLACE BEFORE WE REMOVE HIM.
FSH

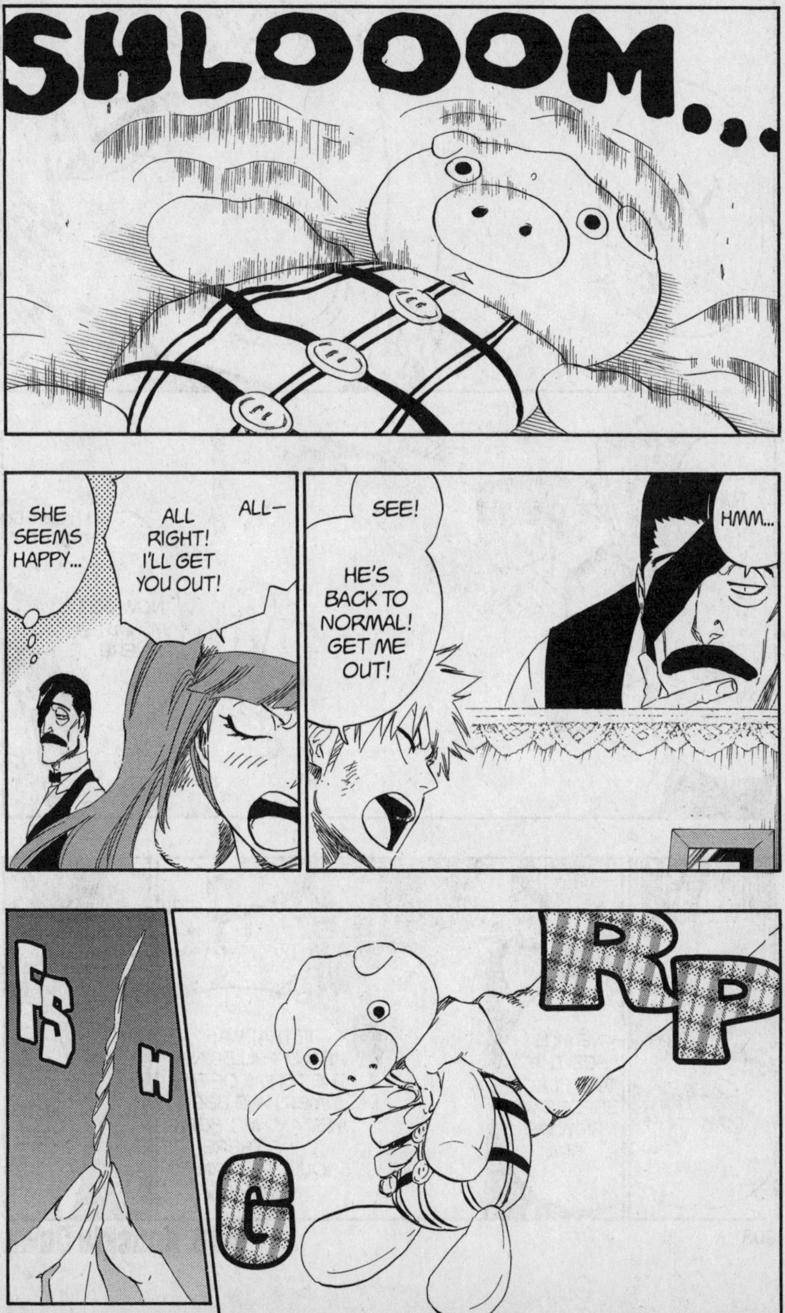
SHLOOOM...
HMM...
SEE!
HE'S BACK TO NORMAL! GET ME OUT!
ALL-
ALL RIGHT! I'LL GET YOU OUT!
SHE SEEMS HAPPY...
RP
G
FS
H

READ THIS WAY

WIGGLE WIGGLE WIGGLE
?
WHAT'RE YOU DOING?
AAAA...
ACHOO!!
SPLSSH
WHOA?!
AWW...
ACHOO!!
SPLSSH
FLASH

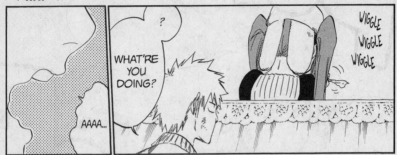

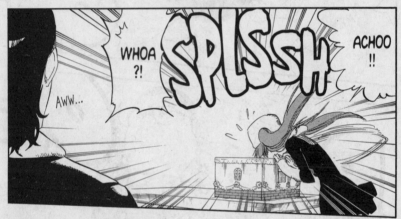

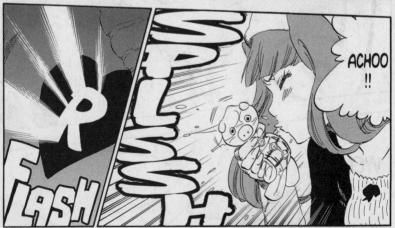

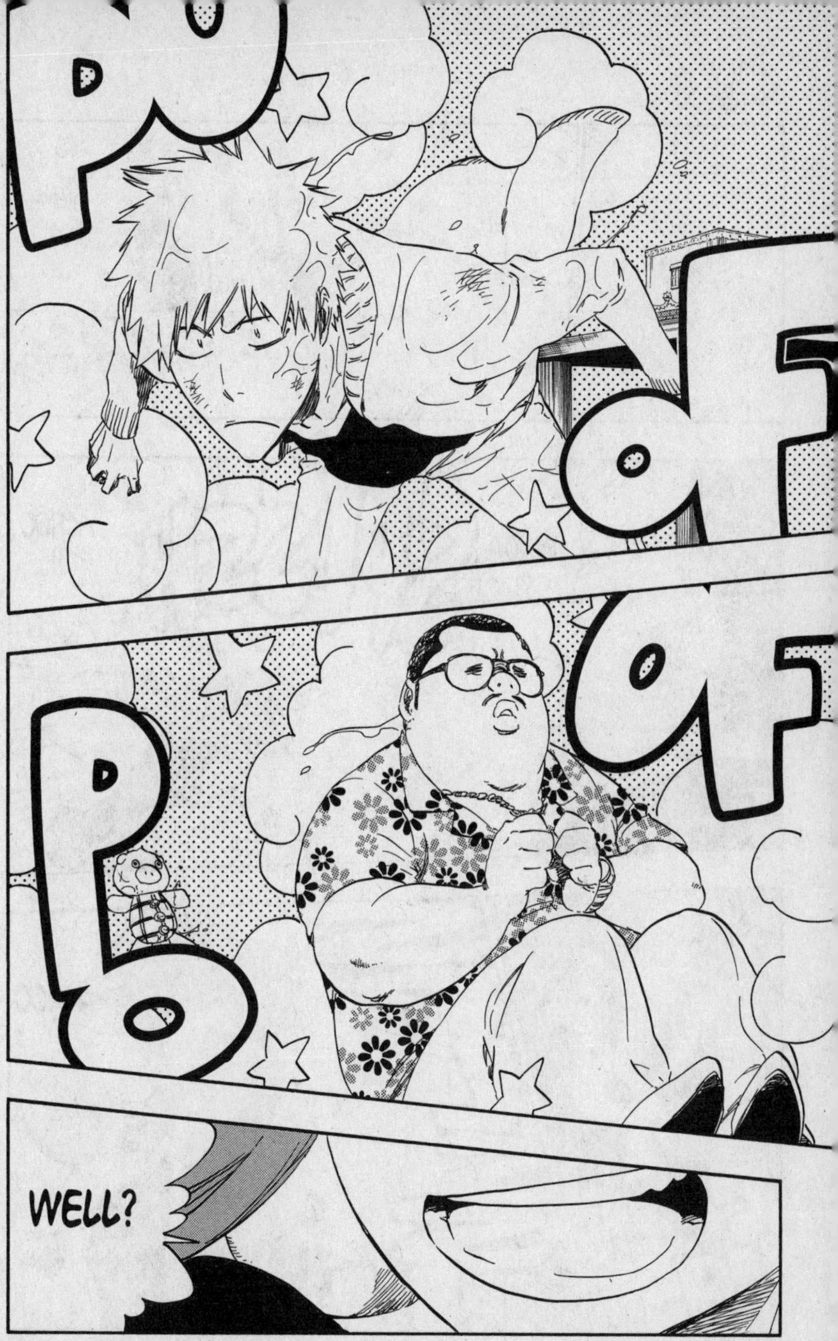
POOF
POOF
WELL?

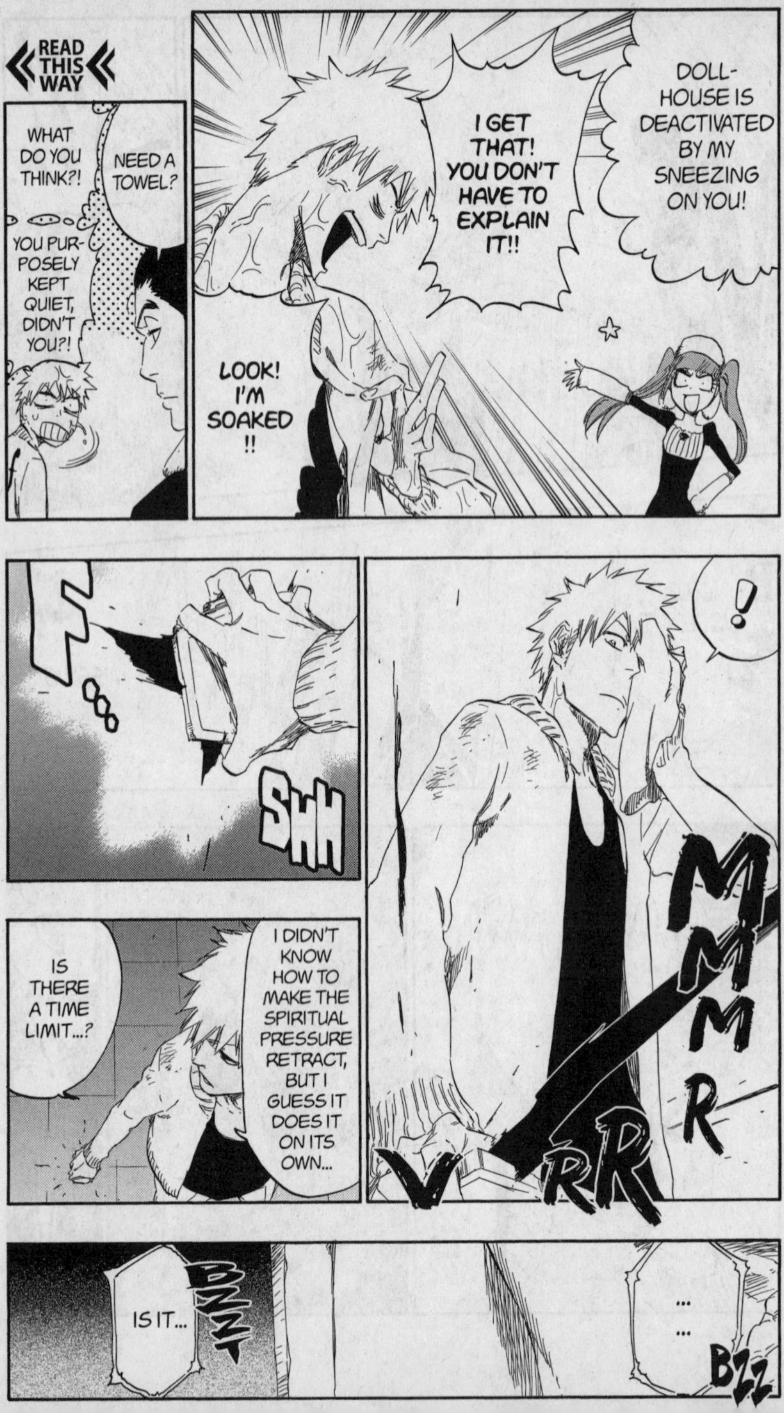
READ THIS WAY
DOLL-HOUSE IS DEACTIVATED BY MY SNEEZING ON YOU!
I GET THAT! YOU DON'T HAVE TO EXPLAIN IT!!
LOOK! I'M SOAKED!!
NEED A TOWEL?
WHAT DO YOU THINK?!
YOU PURPOSELY KEPT QUIET, DIDN'T YOU?!
!
MMMR
VRRR
SHH
I DIDN'T KNOW HOW TO MAKE THE SPIRITUAL PRESSURE RETRACT, BUT I GUESS IT DOES IT ON ITS OWN...
IS THERE A TIME LIMIT...?
... ...
BZZ
BZZT
IS IT...

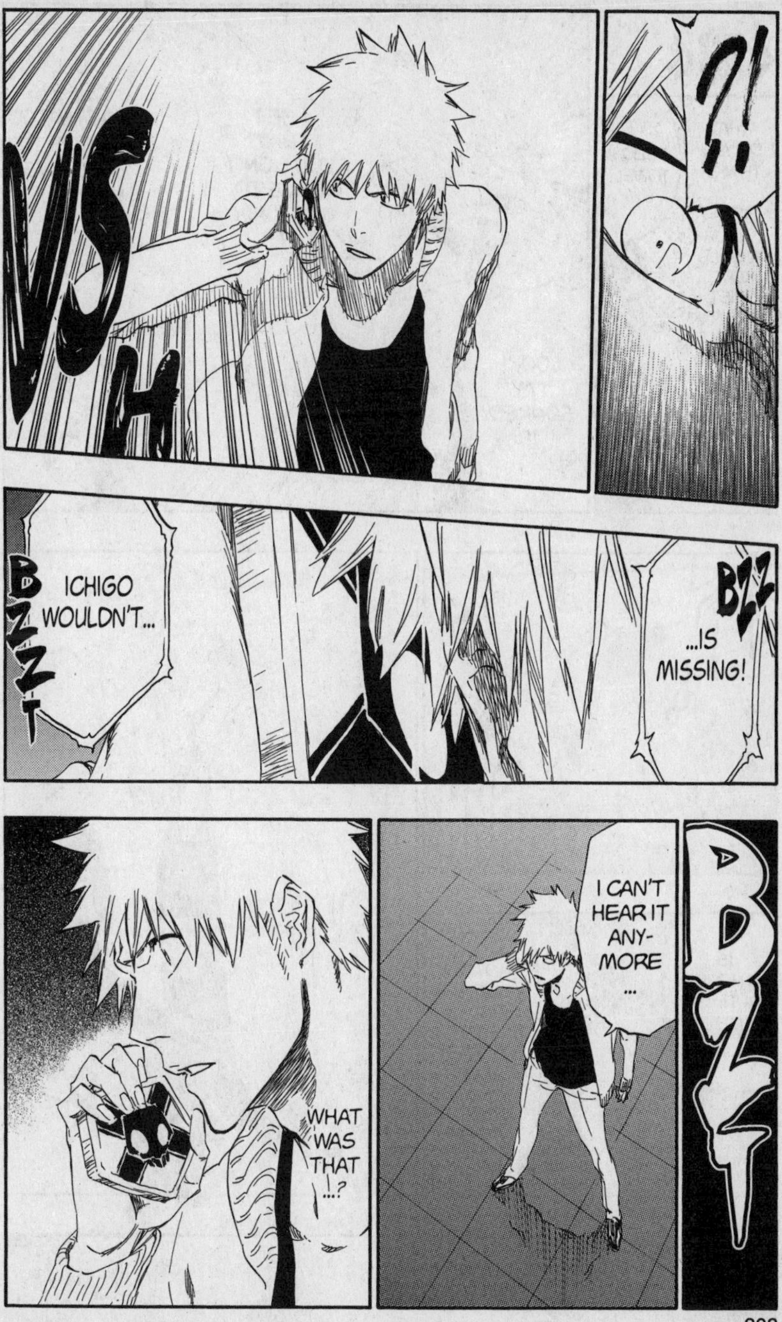
?!
VSH
BZZ
...IS MISSING!
BZZZT
ICHIGO WOULDN'T...
BZZ
I CAN'T HEAR IT ANYMORE ...
WHAT WAS THAT !...?

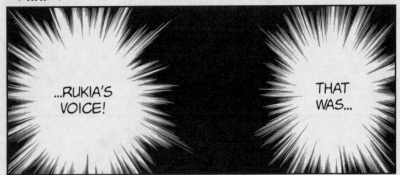

...RUKIA'S VOICE!

THAT WAS...

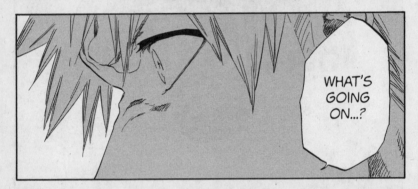

WHAT'S GOING ON...?

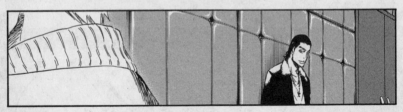

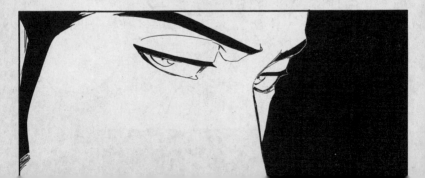

BLEACH 438.

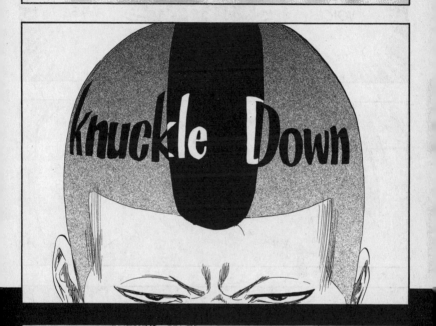

BUT SHE'S A GIRL.

HER?

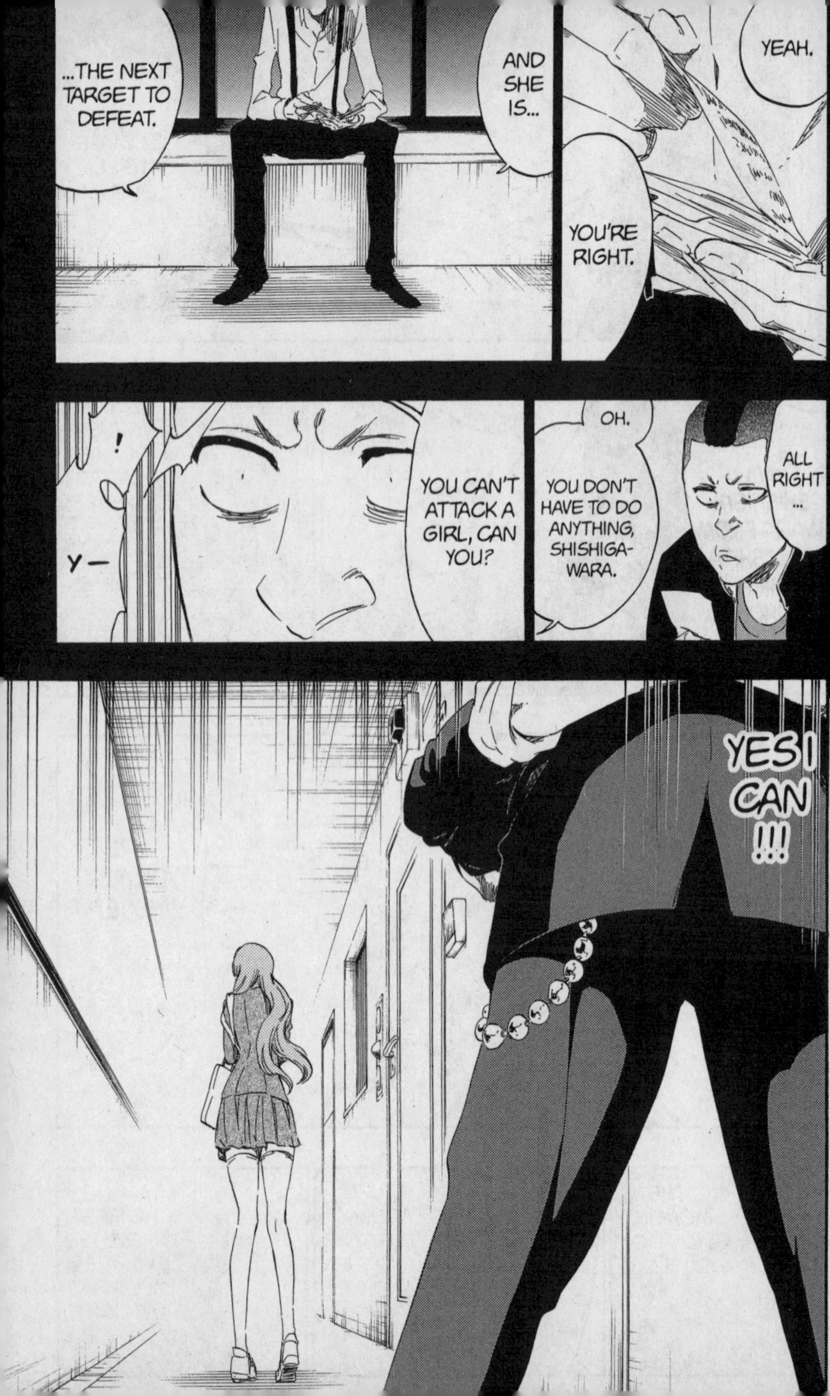
YEAH.
YOU'RE RIGHT.
AND SHE IS...
...THE NEXT TARGET TO DEFEAT.
ALL RIGHT...
OH.
YOU DON'T HAVE TO DO ANYTHING, SHISHIGAWARA.
YOU CAN'T ATTACK A GIRL, CAN YOU?
!
Y—
YES I CAN!!!

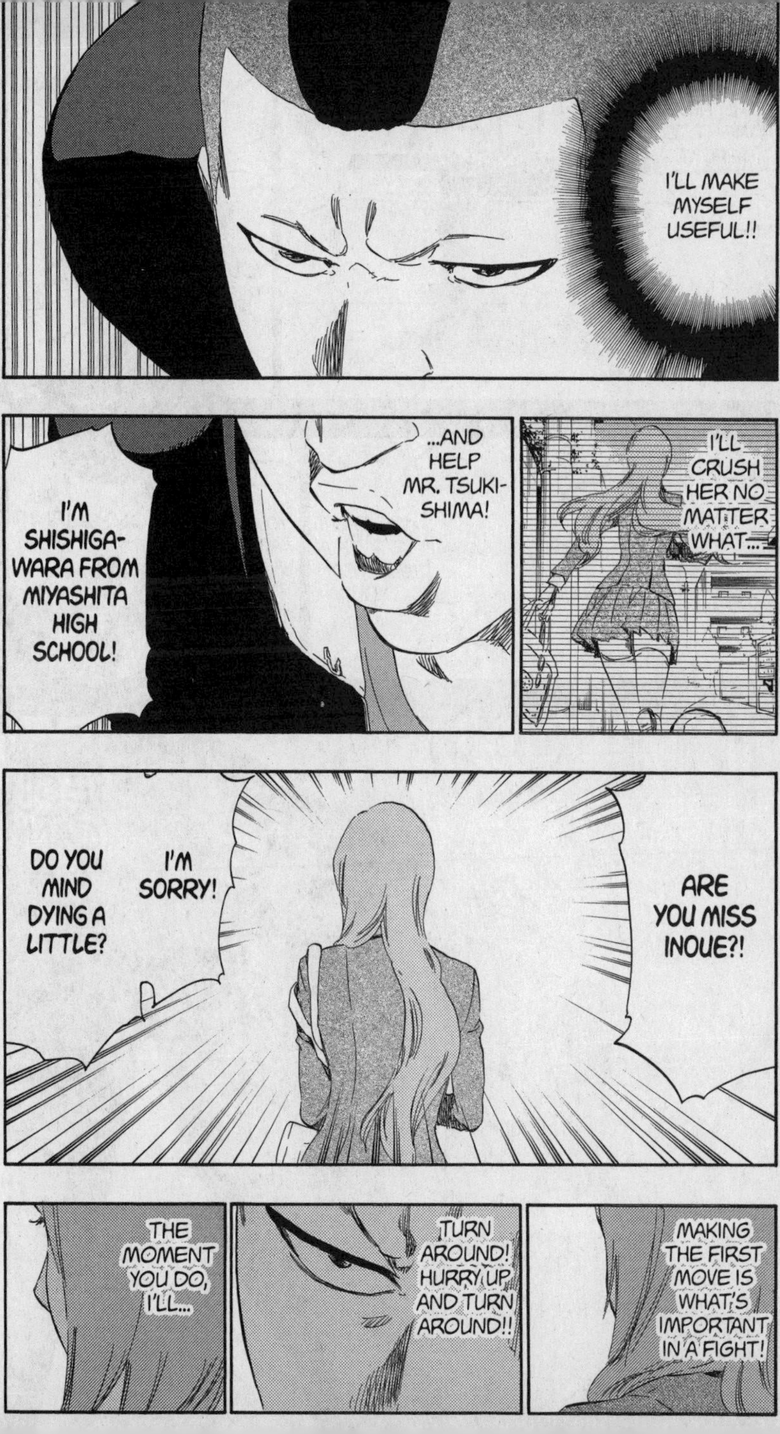
I'LL MAKE MYSELF USEFUL!!
I'LL CRUSH HER NO MATTER WHAT...
...AND HELP MR. TSUKISHIMA!
I'M SHISHIGA-WARA FROM MIYASHITA HIGH SCHOOL!
ARE YOU MISS INOUE?!
I'M SORRY!
DO YOU MIND DYING A LITTLE?
MAKING THE FIRST MOVE IS WHAT'S IMPORTANT IN A FIGHT!
TURN AROUND! HURRY UP AND TURN AROUND!!
THE MOMENT YOU DO, I'LL...

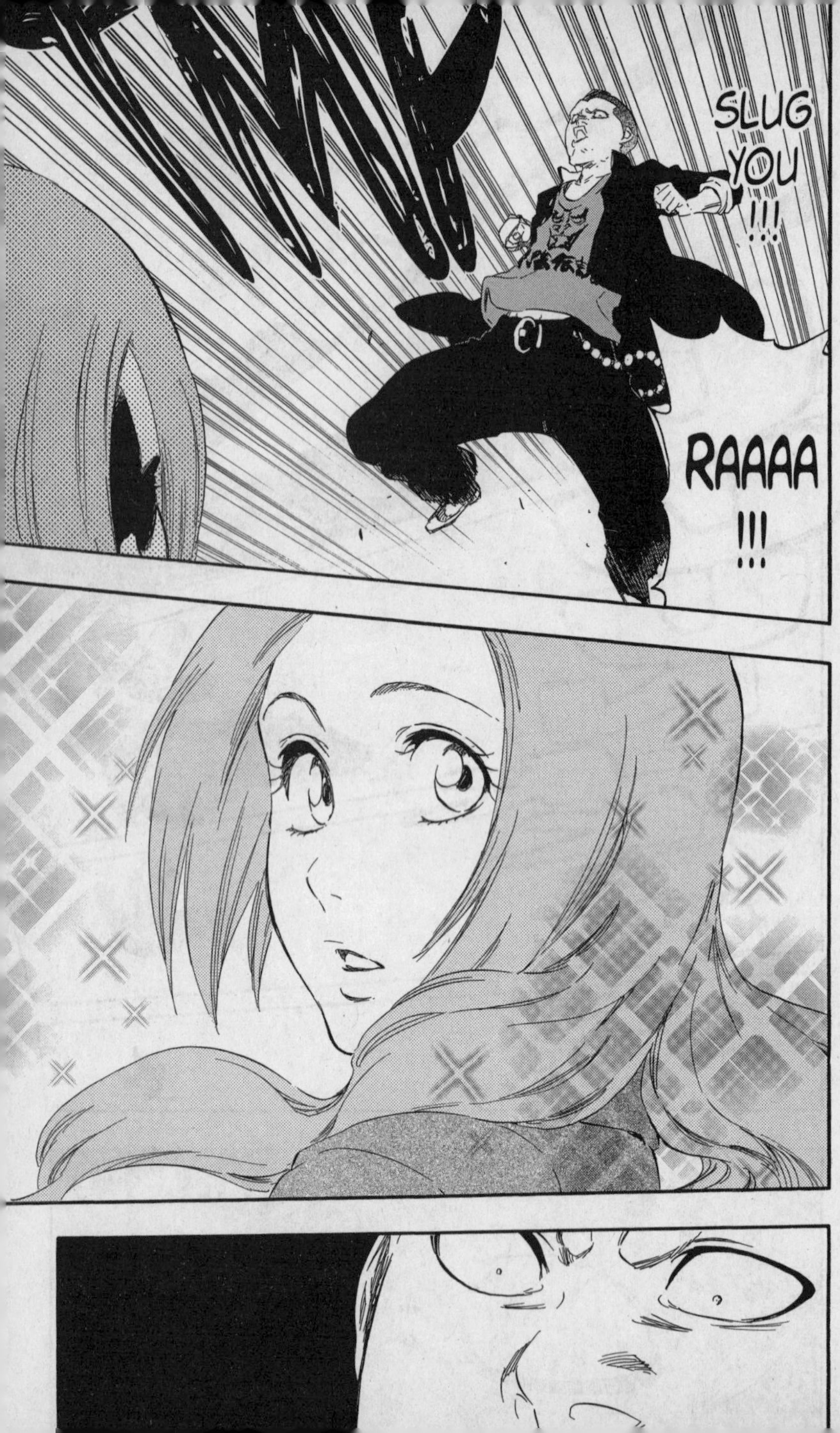
SLUG YOU !!!
RAAAA !!!

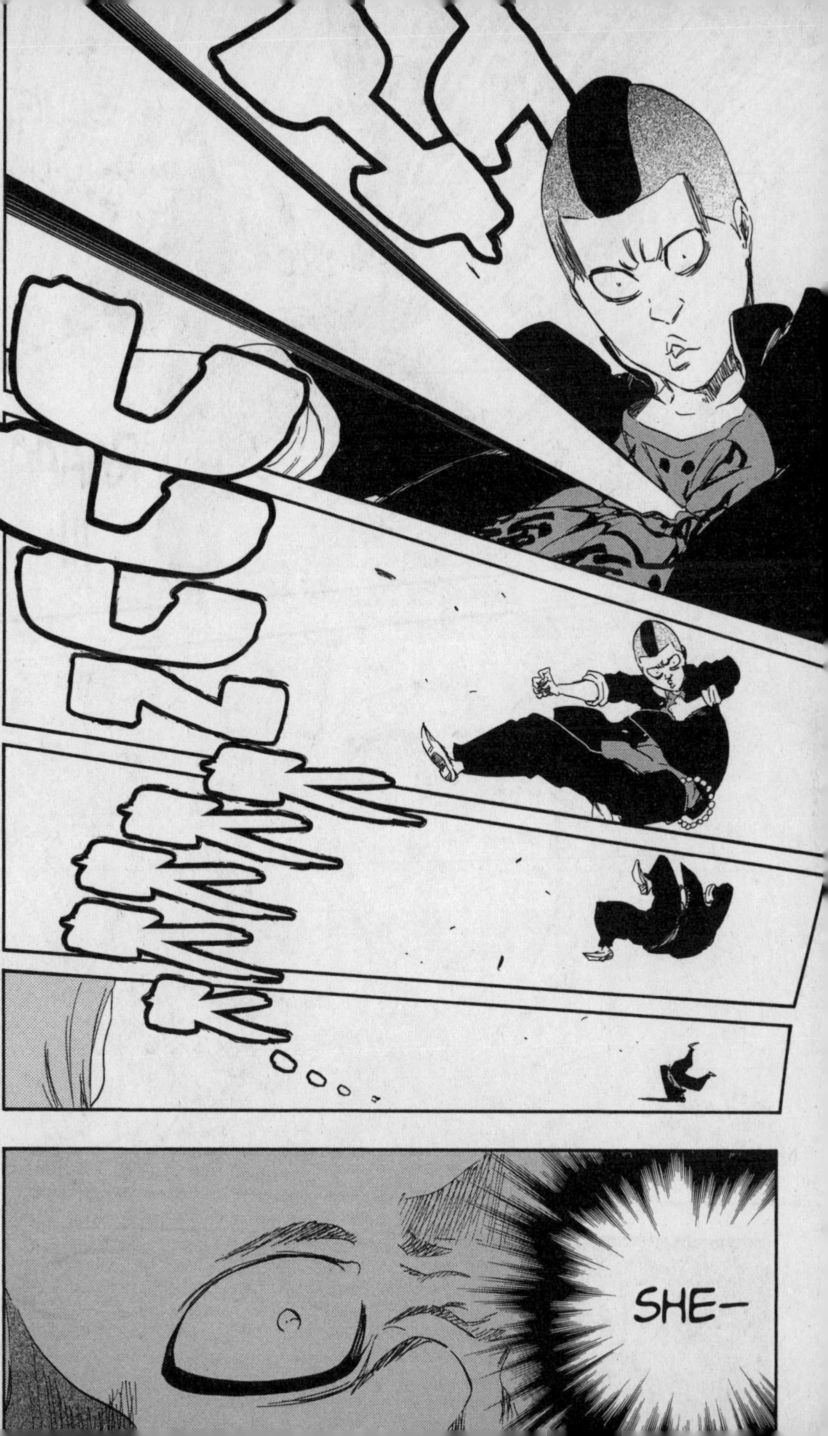
SHE–

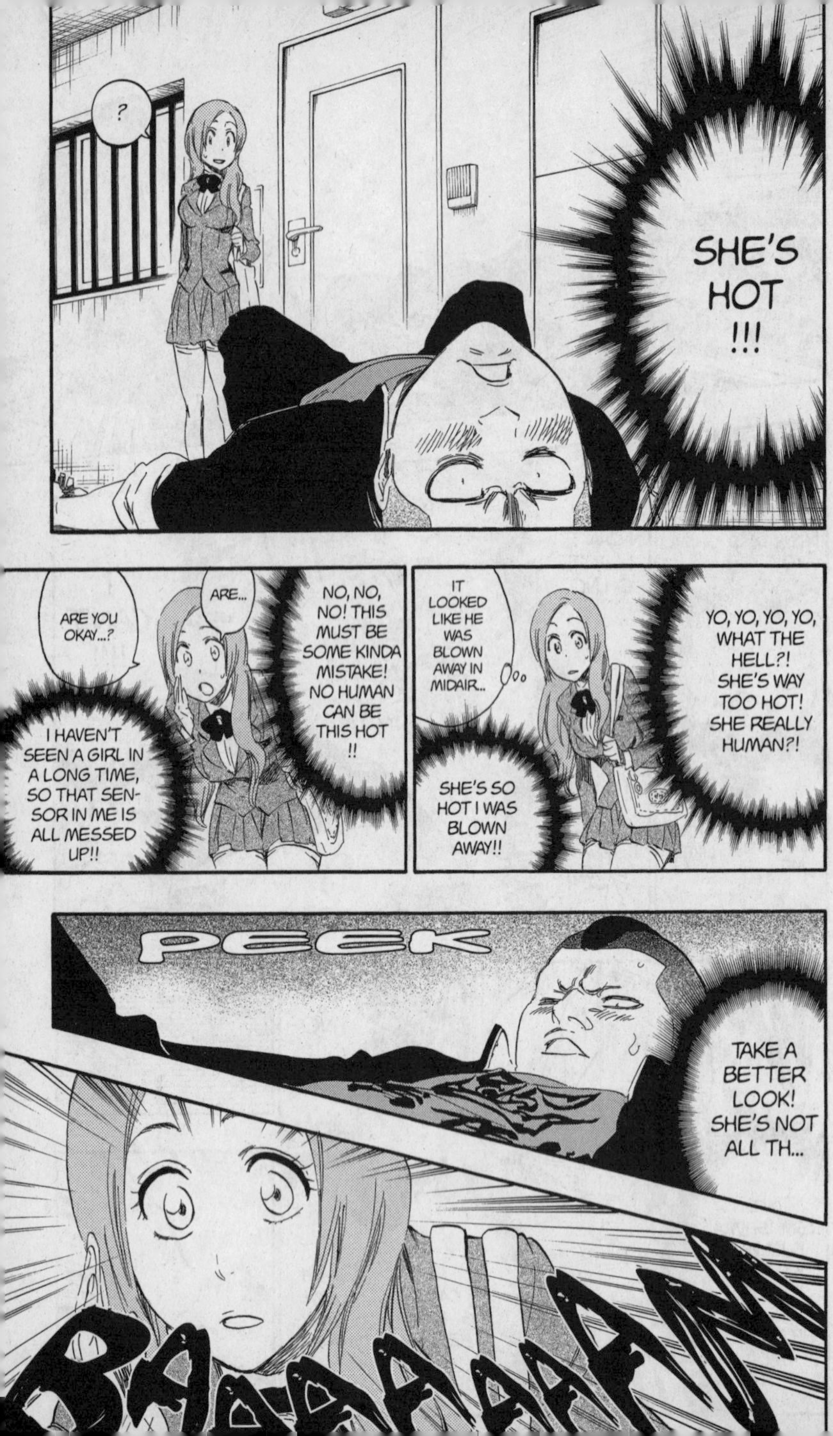
SHE'S HOT !!!
?
YO, YO, YO, YO, WHAT THE HELL?! SHE'S WAY TOO HOT! SHE REALLY HUMAN?!
IT LOOKED LIKE HE WAS BLOWN AWAY IN MIDAIR..
SHE'S SO HOT I WAS BLOWN AWAY!!
NO, NO, NO! THIS MUST BE SOME KINDA MISTAKE! NO HUMAN CAN BE THIS HOT !!
ARE...
ARE YOU OKAY...?
I HAVEN'T SEEN A GIRL IN A LONG TIME, SO THAT SEN-SOR IN ME IS ALL MESSED UP!!
PEEK
TAKE A BETTER LOOK! SHE'S NOT ALL TH...
BAAAAAAAM

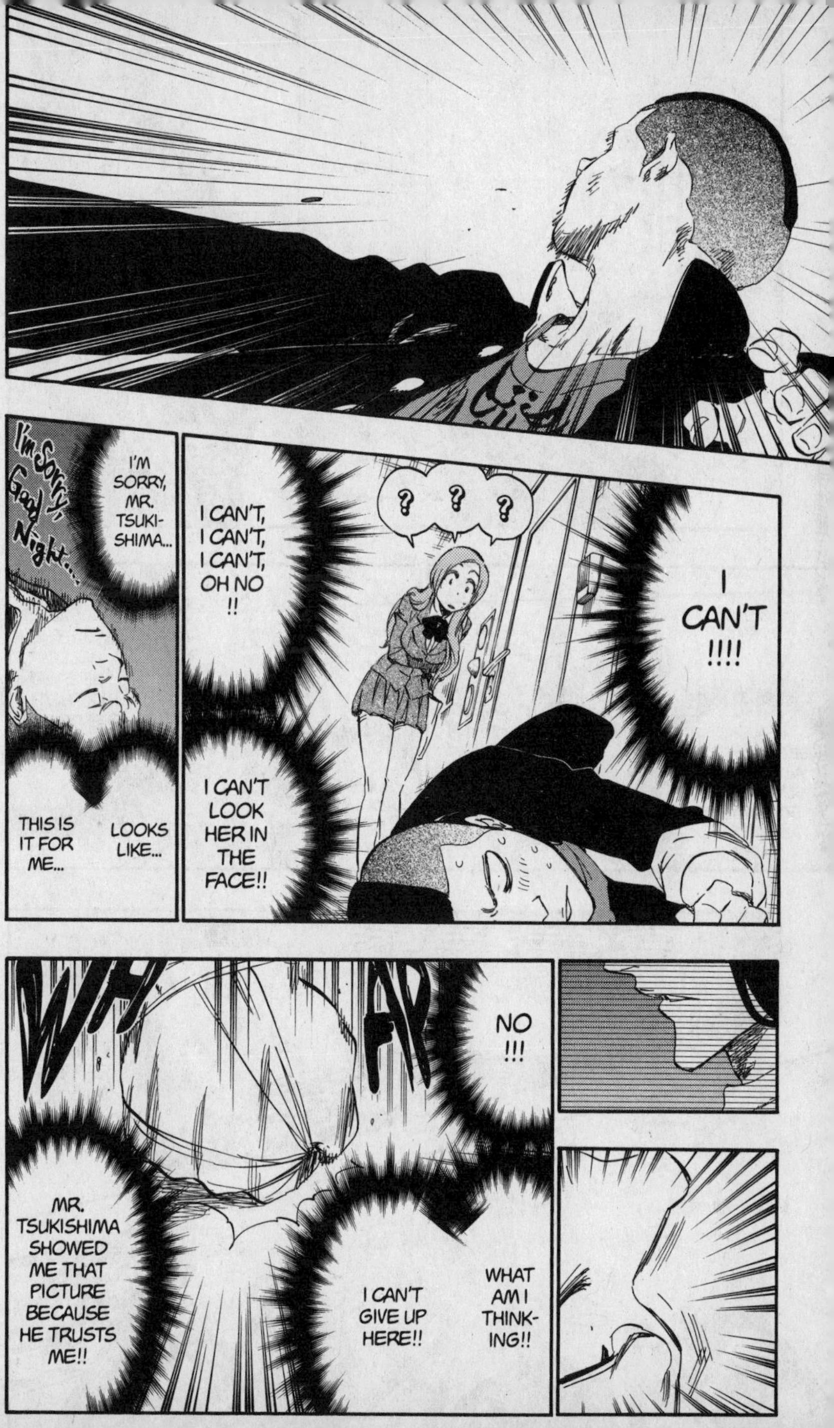
I CAN'T !!!!
? ? ?
I CAN'T, I CAN'T, I CAN'T, OH NO !!
I CAN'T LOOK HER IN THE FACE!!
I'M SORRY, MR. TSUKISHIMA...
I'm Sorry, Good Night...
LOOKS LIKE...
THIS IS IT FOR ME...
NO !!!
WHAT AM I THINKING!!
I CAN'T GIVE UP HERE!!
MR. TSUKISHIMA SHOWED ME THAT PICTURE BECAUSE HE TRUSTS ME!!

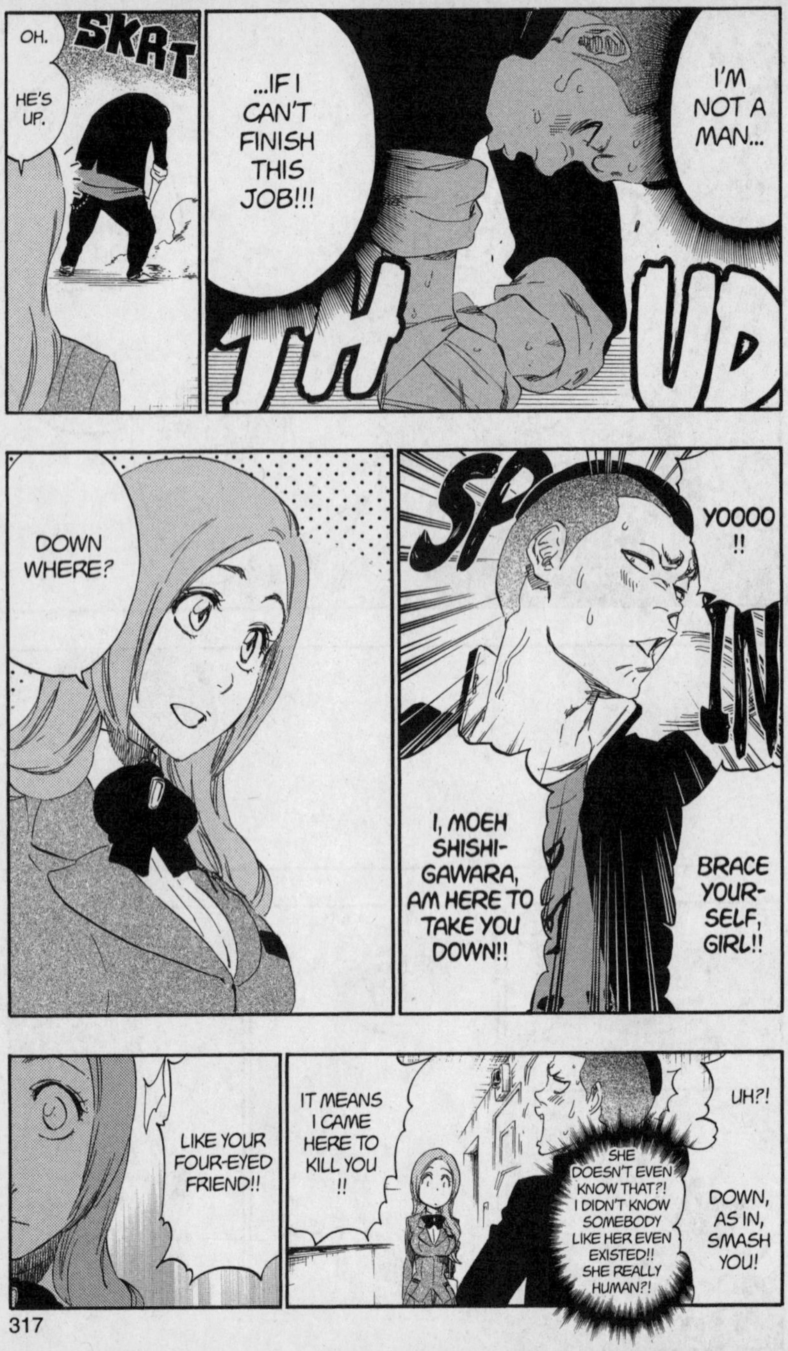
I'M NOT A MAN...
...IF I CAN'T FINISH THIS JOB!!!
THUD
SKRT
OH.
HE'S UP.
SPIN
YOOOO !!
BRACE YOURSELF, GIRL!!
I, MOEH SHISHIGAWARA, AM HERE TO TAKE YOU DOWN!!
DOWN WHERE?
UH?!
SHE DOESN'T EVEN KNOW THAT?! I DIDN'T KNOW SOMEBODY LIKE HER EVEN EXISTED!! SHE REALLY HUMAN?!
DOWN, AS IN, SMASH YOU!
IT MEANS I CAME HERE TO KILL YOU !!
LIKE YOUR FOUR-EYED FRIEND!!

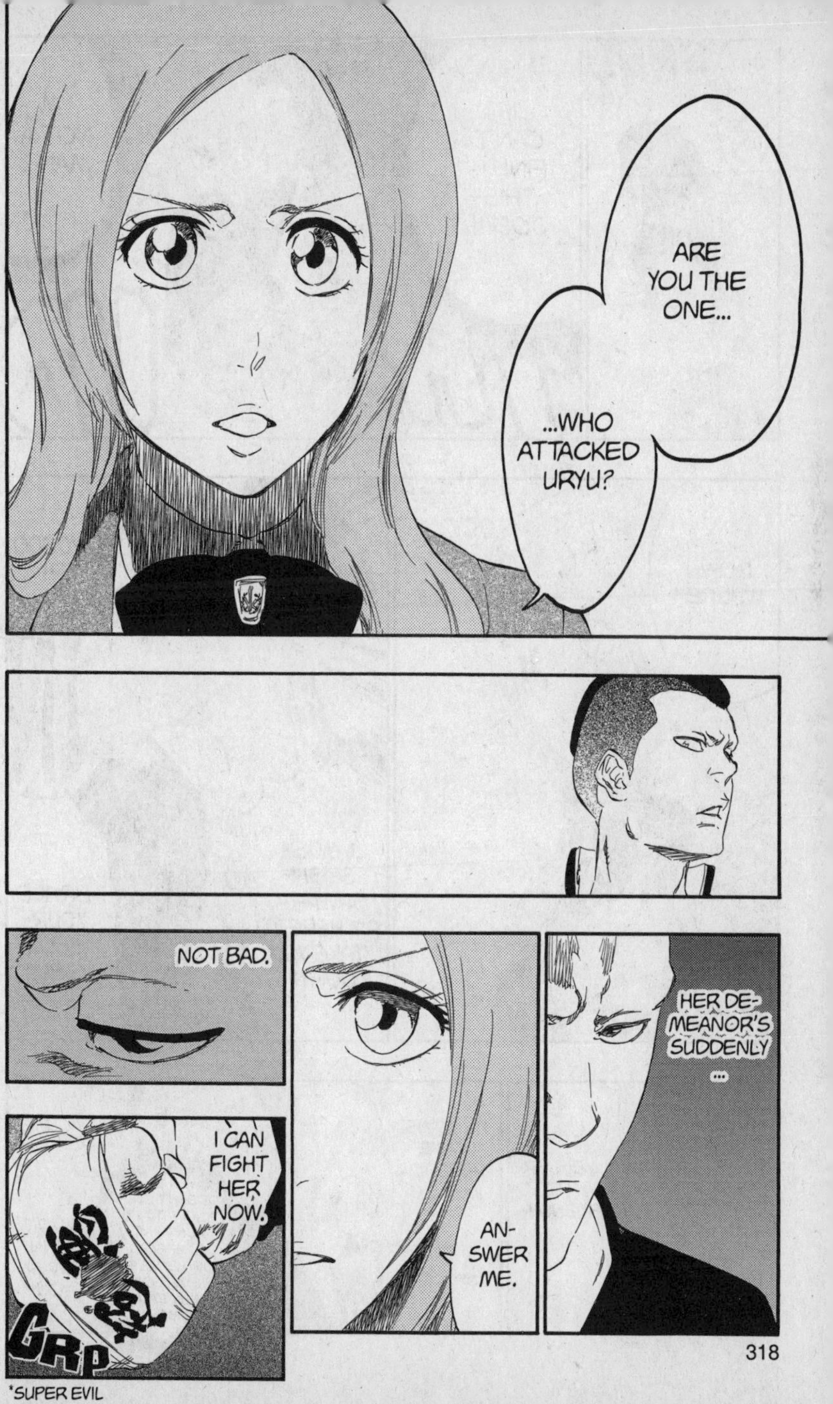
ARE YOU THE ONE...
...WHO ATTACKED URYU?
HER DE-MEANOR'S SUDDENLY ...
AN-SWER ME.
NOT BAD.
I CAN FIGHT HER NOW.
GRP

*SUPER EVIL

READ THIS WAY

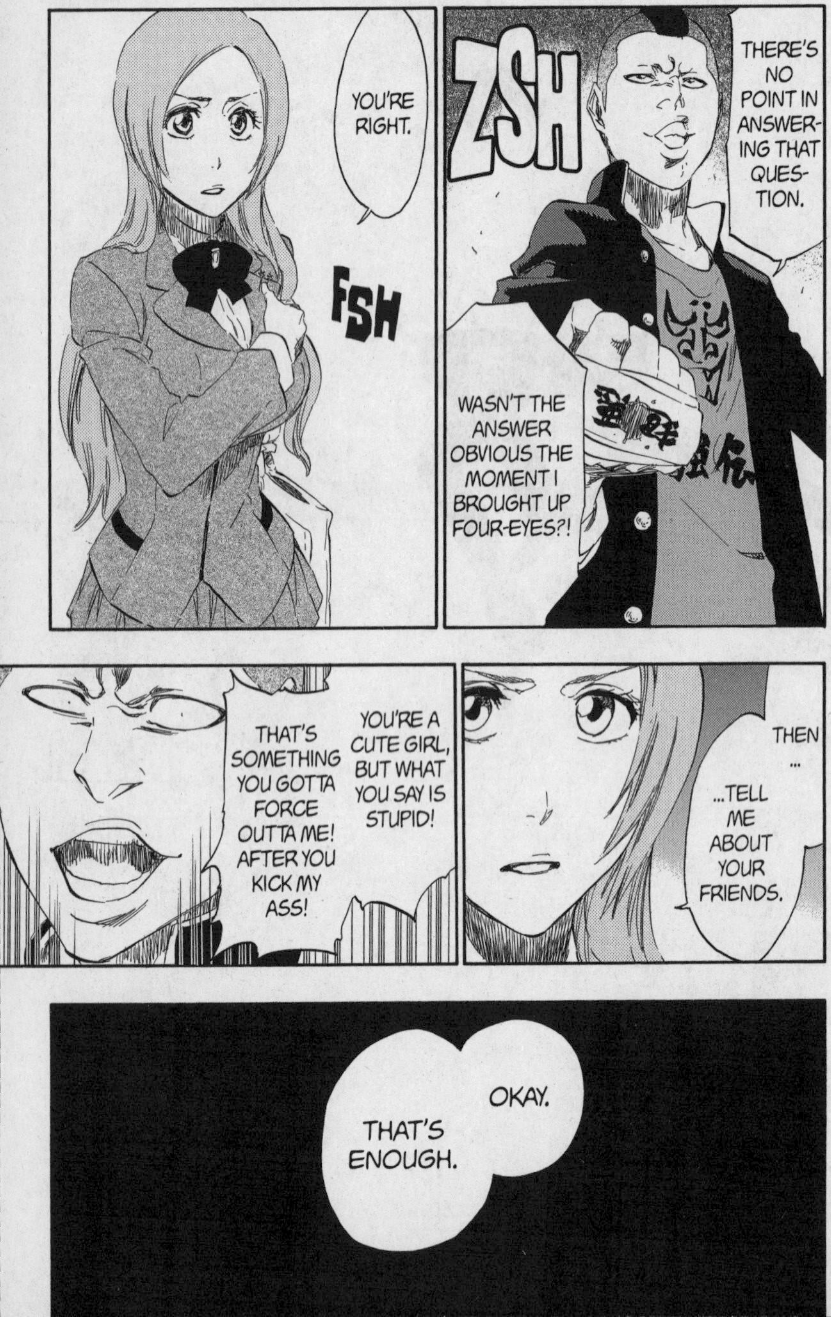
ZSH
THERE'S NO POINT IN ANSWERING THAT QUESTION.
WASN'T THE ANSWER OBVIOUS THE MOMENT I BROUGHT UP FOUR-EYES?!
YOU'RE RIGHT.
FSH
THEN ...
...TELL ME ABOUT YOUR FRIENDS.
YOU'RE A CUTE GIRL, BUT WHAT YOU SAY IS STUPID!
THAT'S SOMETHING YOU GOTTA FORCE OUTTA ME! AFTER YOU KICK MY ASS!
OKAY.
THAT'S ENOUGH.

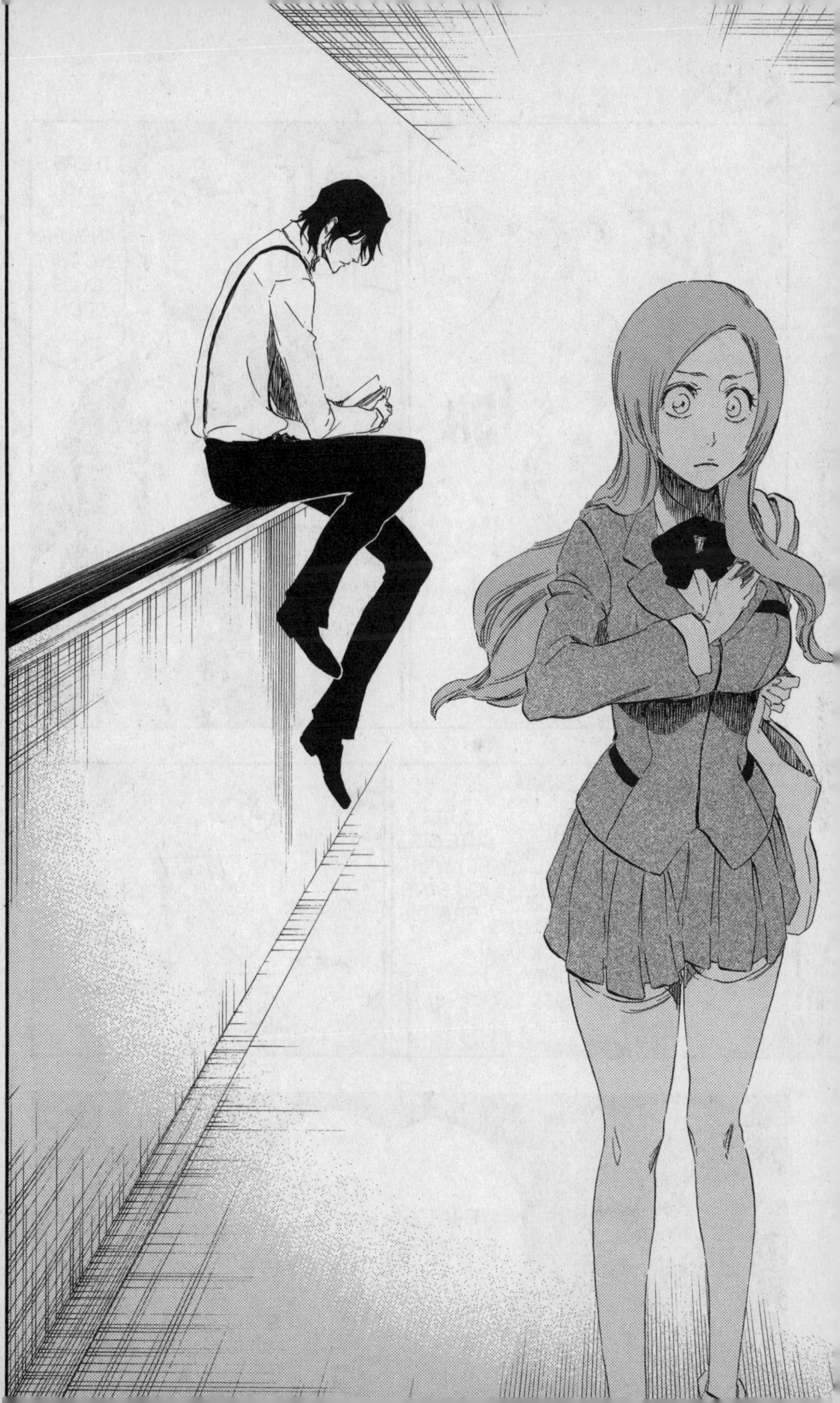

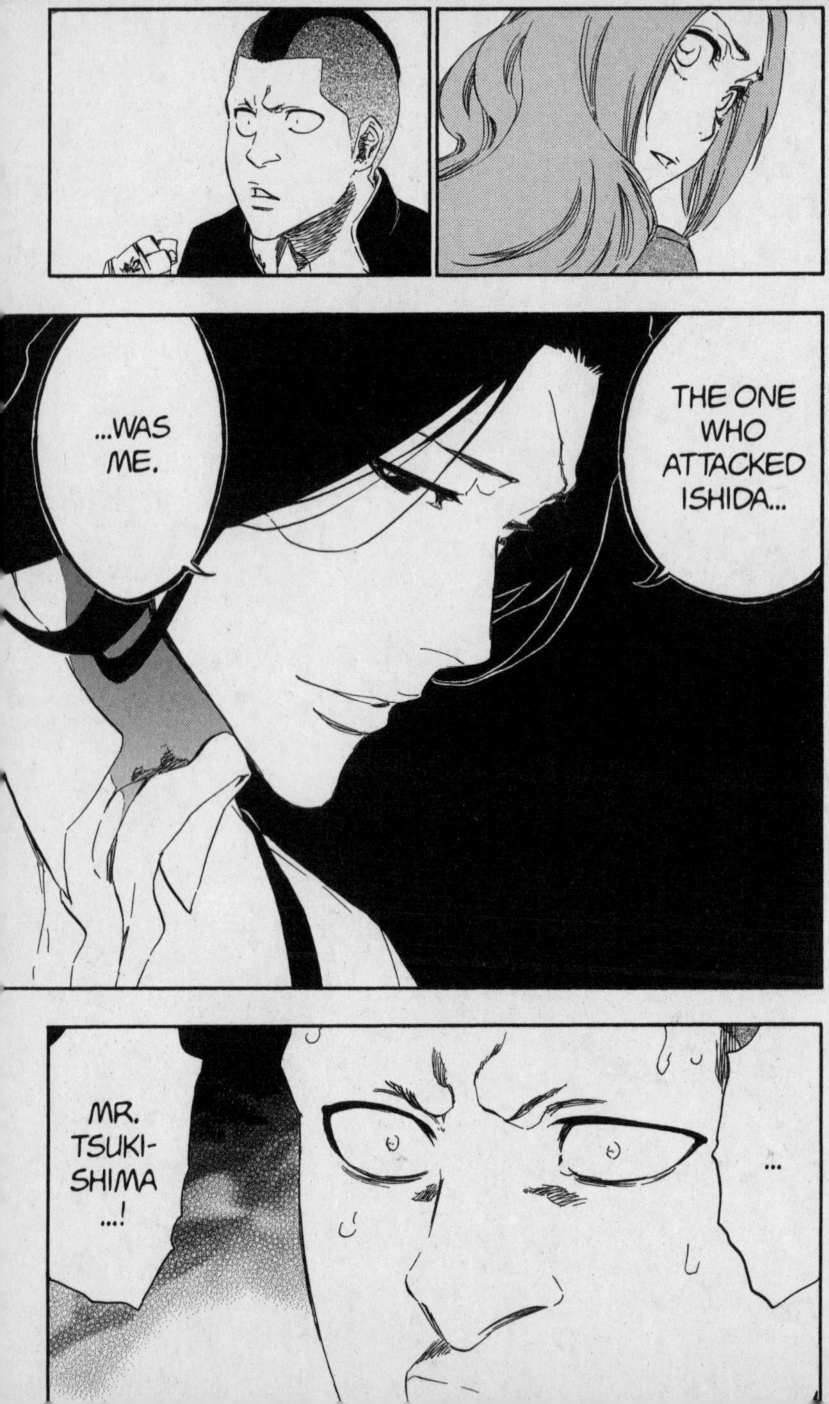
THE ONE WHO ATTACKED ISHIDA...
...WAS ME.
...
MR. TSUKI-SHIMA ...!

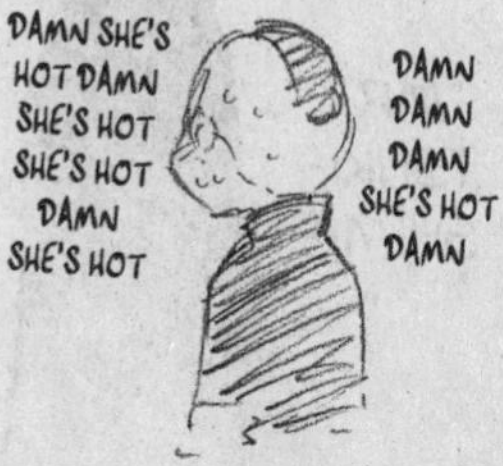
DAMN DAMN DAMN SHE'S HOT DAMN
DAMN SHE'S HOT DAMN SHE'S HOT SHE'S HOT DAMN SHE'S HOT

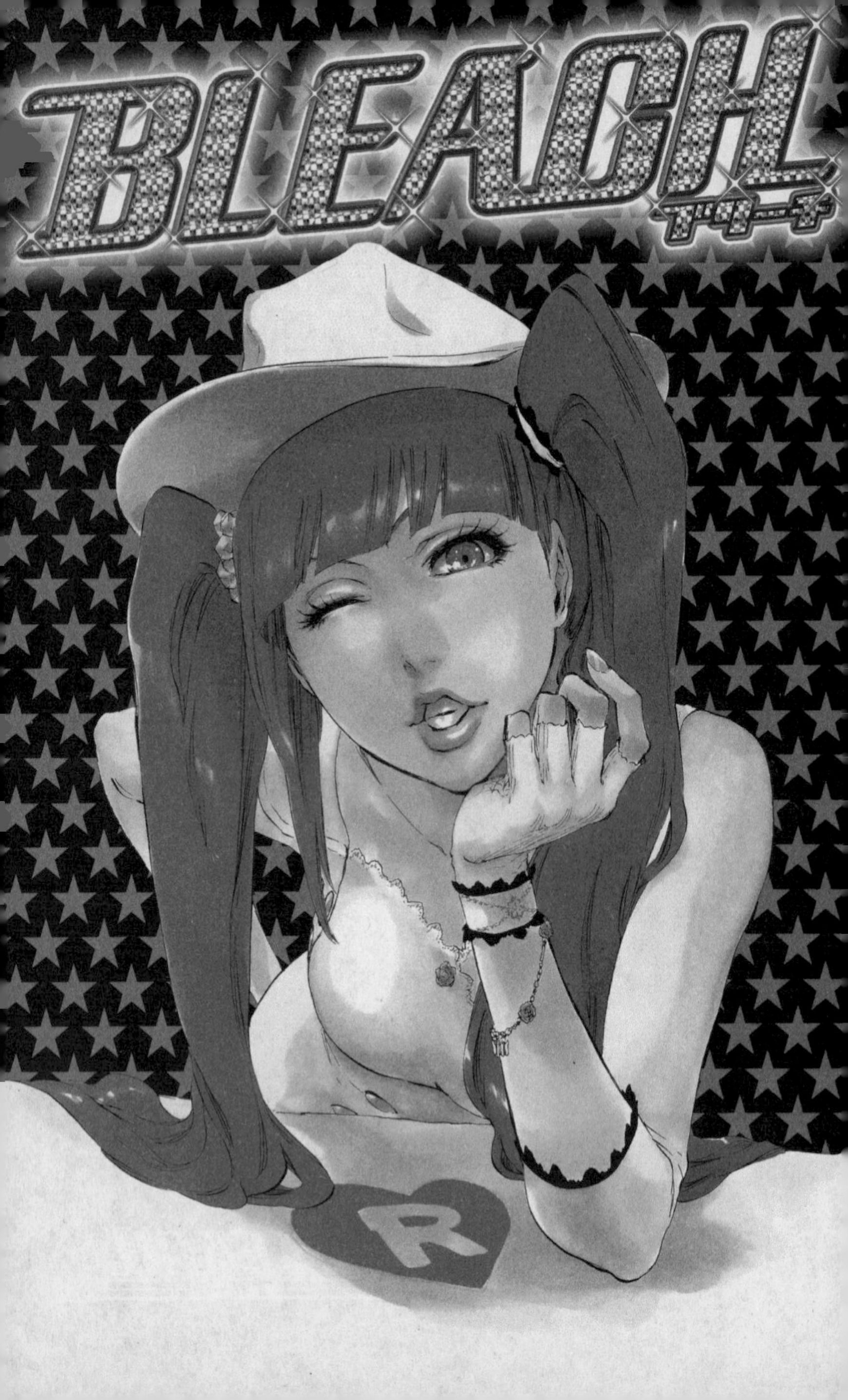
BLEACH
ブリーチ

BLEACH
ブリーチ

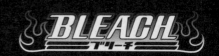

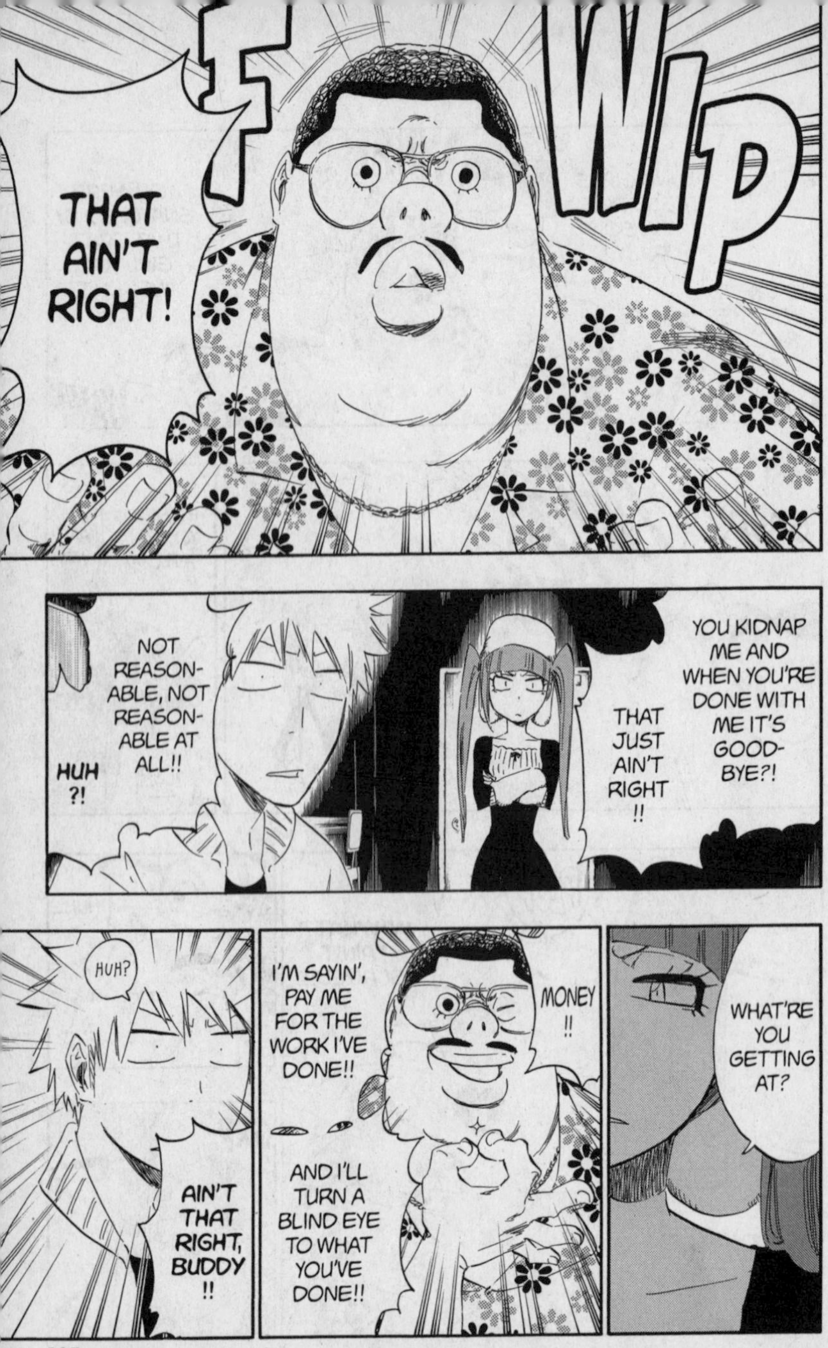
FWIP
THAT AIN'T RIGHT!
YOU KIDNAP ME AND WHEN YOU'RE DONE WITH ME IT'S GOOD-BYE?!
THAT JUST AIN'T RIGHT!!
NOT REASON-ABLE, NOT REASON-ABLE AT ALL!!
HUH?!
WHAT'RE YOU GETTING AT?
MONEY!!
I'M SAYIN', PAY ME FOR THE WORK I'VE DONE!!
AND I'LL TURN A BLIND EYE TO WHAT YOU'VE DONE!!
HUH?
AIN'T THAT RIGHT, BUDDY!!

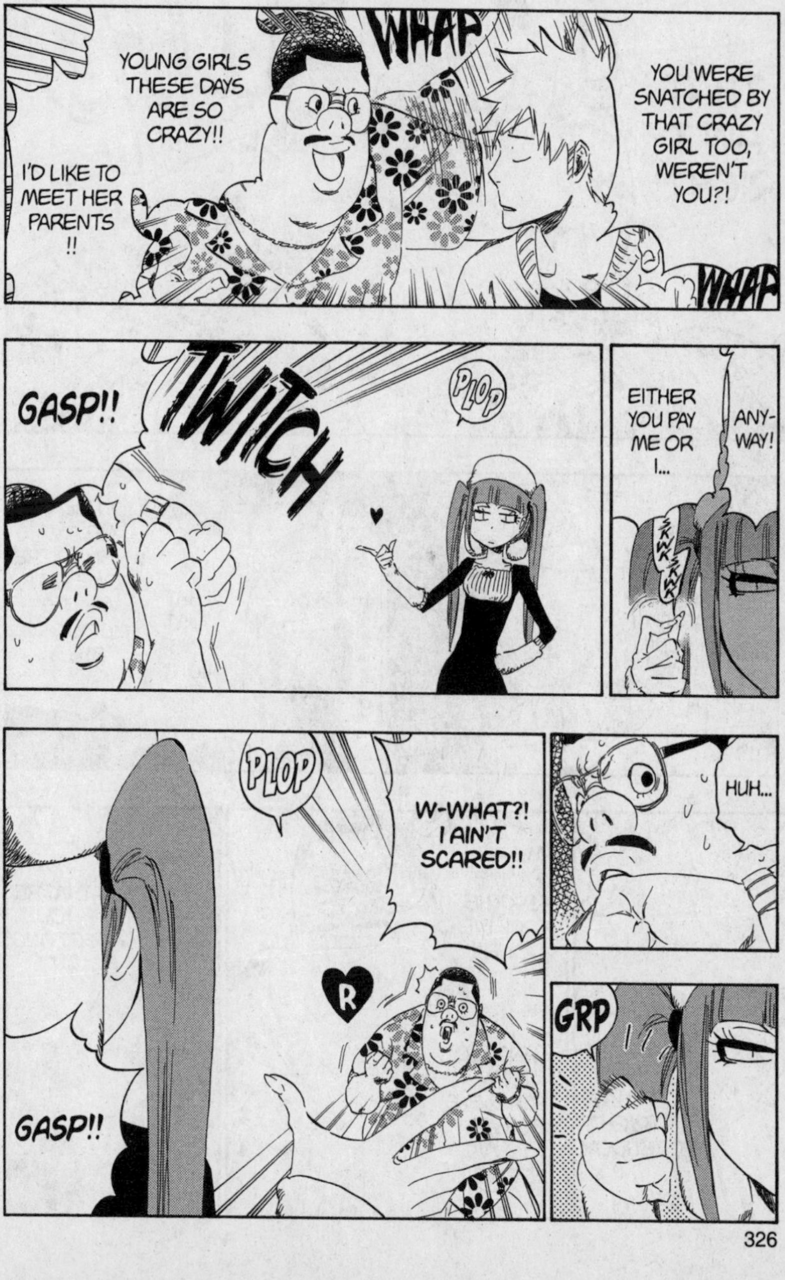
YOU WERE SNATCHED BY THAT CRAZY GIRL TOO, WEREN'T YOU?!
WHAP
YOUNG GIRLS THESE DAYS ARE SO CRAZY!!
I'D LIKE TO MEET HER PARENTS !!
WHAP
ANY-WAY!
EITHER YOU PAY ME OR I...
SKWK SKWK
PLOP
TWITCH
GASP!!
HUH...
GRP
W-WHAT?! I AIN'T SCARED!!
PLOP
R
GASP!!

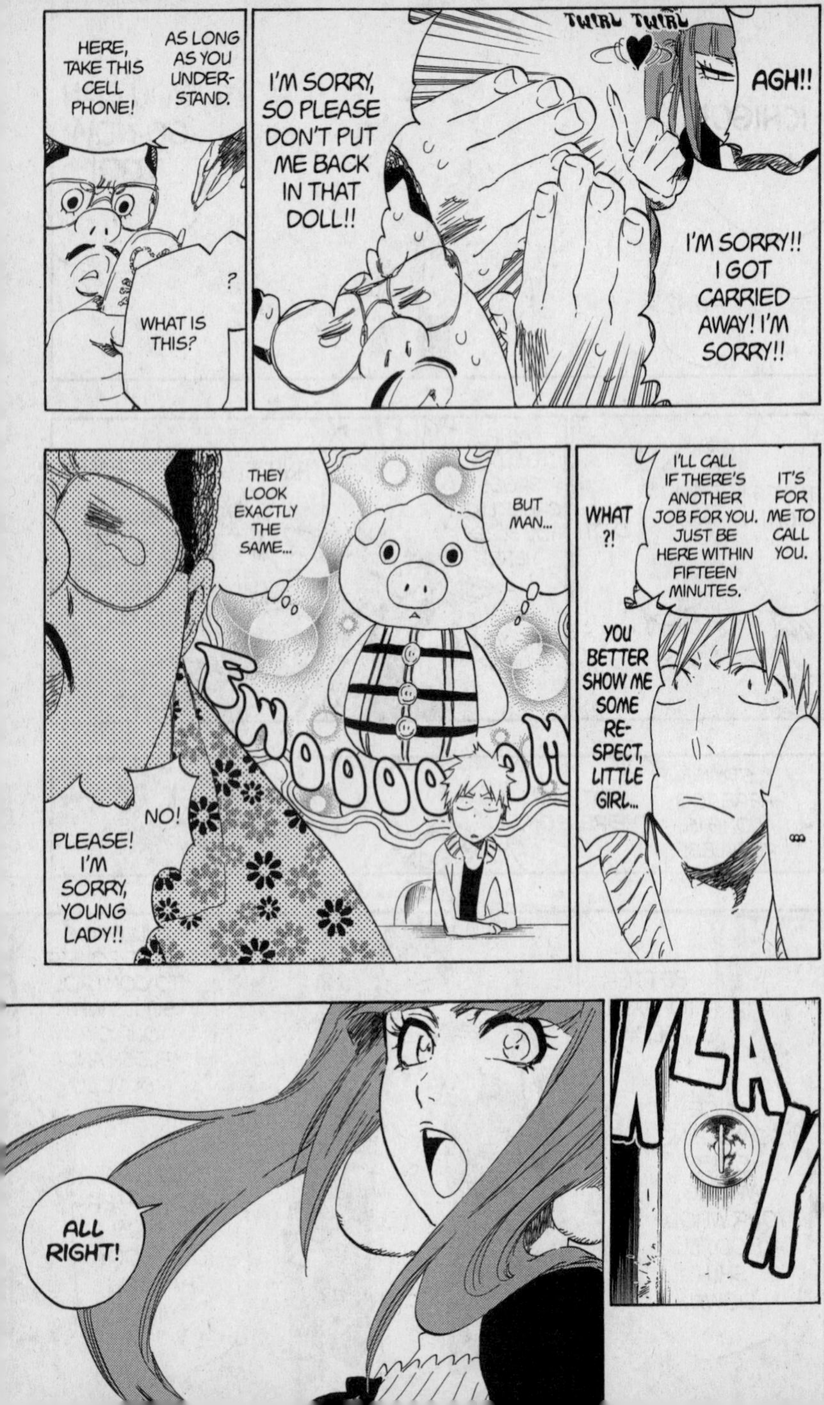
TWIRL TWIRL
AGH!!
I'M SORRY!! I GOT CARRIED AWAY! I'M SORRY!!
I'M SORRY, SO PLEASE DON'T PUT ME BACK IN THAT DOLL!!
AS LONG AS YOU UNDER-STAND.
HERE, TAKE THIS CELL PHONE!
?
WHAT IS THIS?
IT'S FOR ME TO CALL YOU.
I'LL CALL IF THERE'S ANOTHER JOB FOR YOU. JUST BE HERE WITHIN FIFTEEN MINUTES.
WHAT ?!
YOU BETTER SHOW ME SOME RE-SPECT, LITTLE GIRL...
...
BUT MAN...
THEY LOOK EXACTLY THE SAME...
FWOOOOOH
NO!
PLEASE! I'M SORRY, YOUNG LADY!!
KLAK
ALL RIGHT!

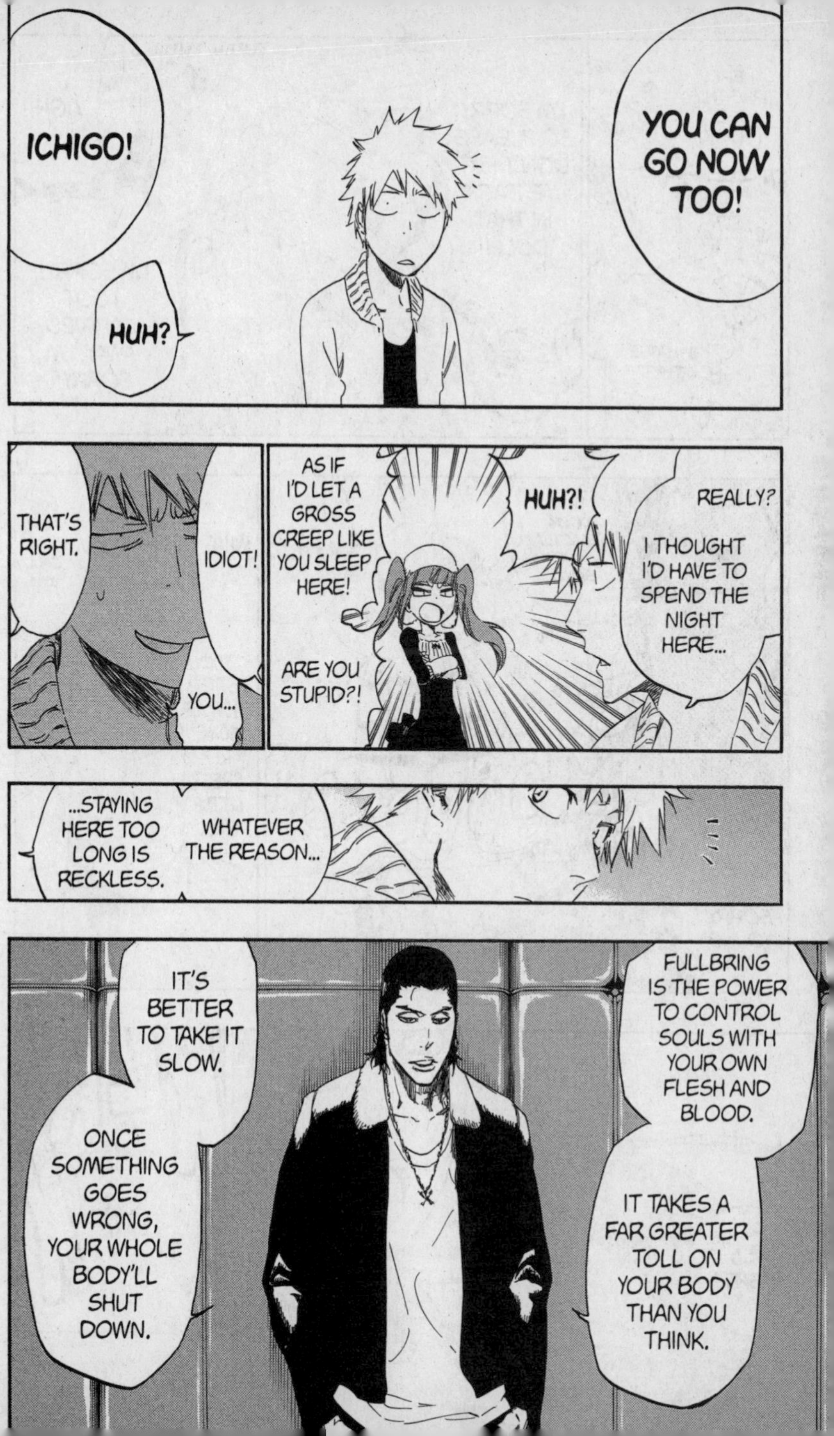
YOU CAN GO NOW TOO!
ICHIGO!
HUH?
REALLY?
I THOUGHT I'D HAVE TO SPEND THE NIGHT HERE...
HUH?!
AS IF I'D LET A GROSS CREEP LIKE YOU SLEEP HERE!
ARE YOU STUPID?!
IDIOT!
YOU...
THAT'S RIGHT.
WHATEVER THE REASON...
...STAYING HERE TOO LONG IS RECKLESS.
FULLBRING IS THE POWER TO CONTROL SOULS WITH YOUR OWN FLESH AND BLOOD.
IT TAKES A FAR GREATER TOLL ON YOUR BODY THAN YOU THINK.
IT'S BETTER TO TAKE IT SLOW.
ONCE SOMETHING GOES WRONG, YOUR WHOLE BODY'LL SHUT DOWN.

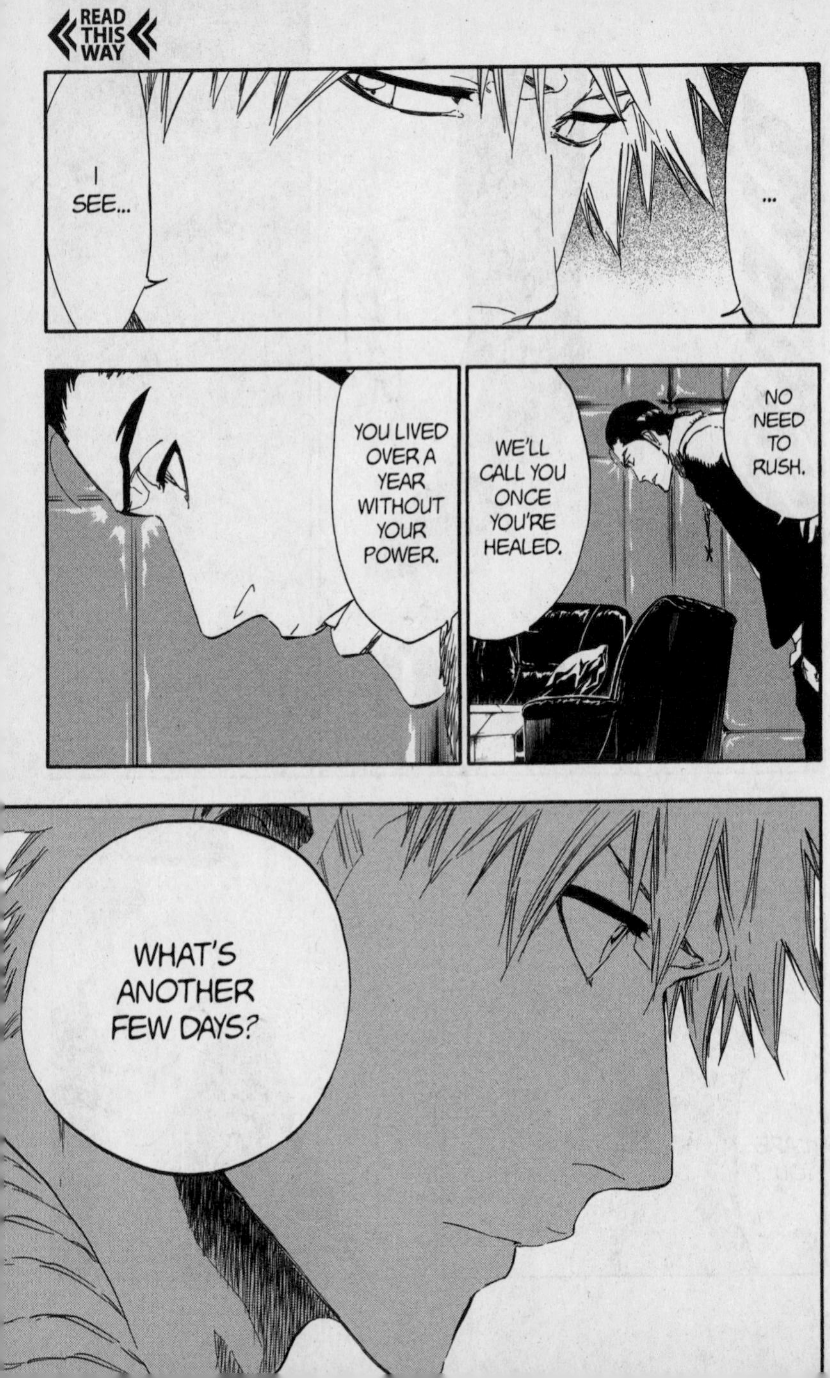
READ THIS WAY
...
I SEE...
NO NEED TO RUSH.
WE'LL CALL YOU ONCE YOU'RE HEALED.
YOU LIVED OVER A YEAR WITHOUT YOUR POWER.
WHAT'S ANOTHER FEW DAYS?

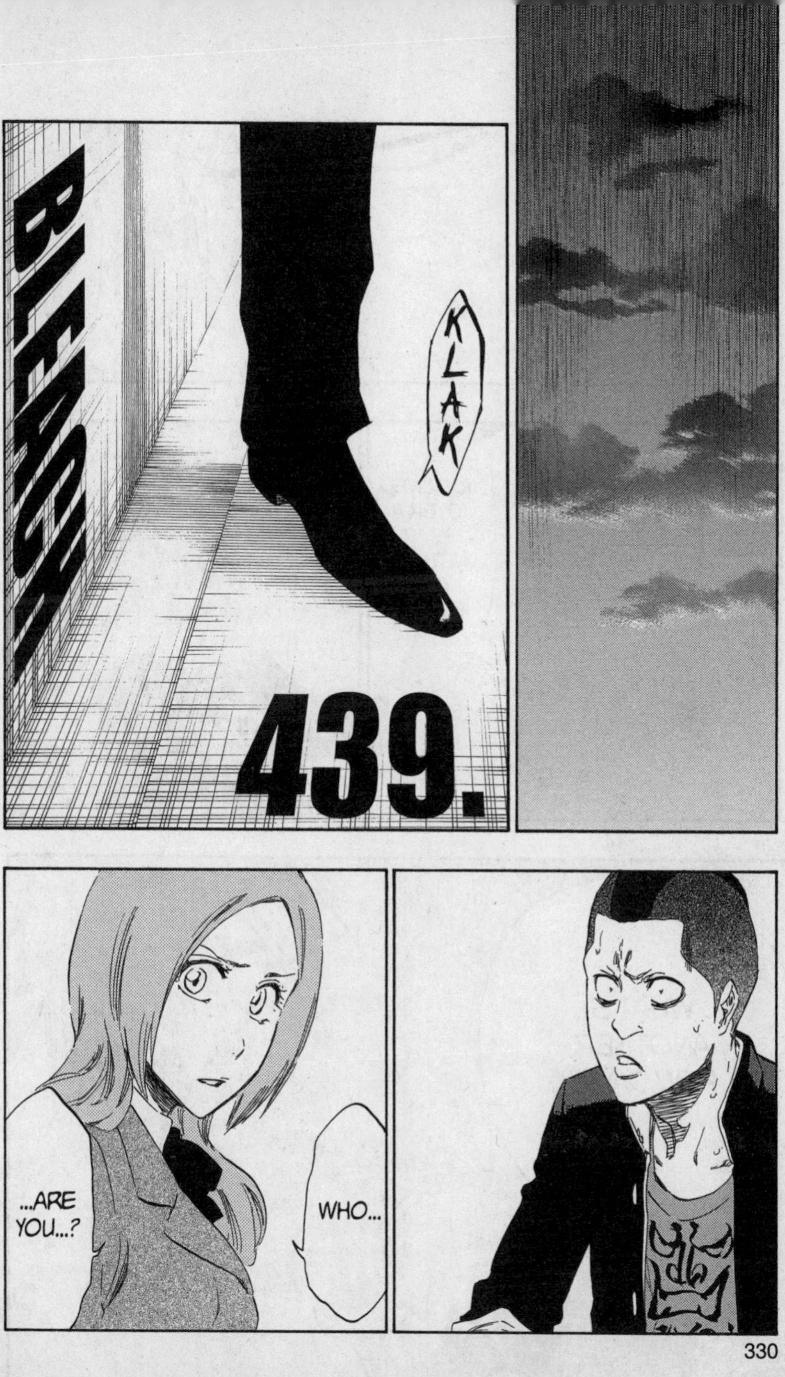
BLEACH
KLAK
439.
WHO...
...ARE YOU...?

READ THIS WAY

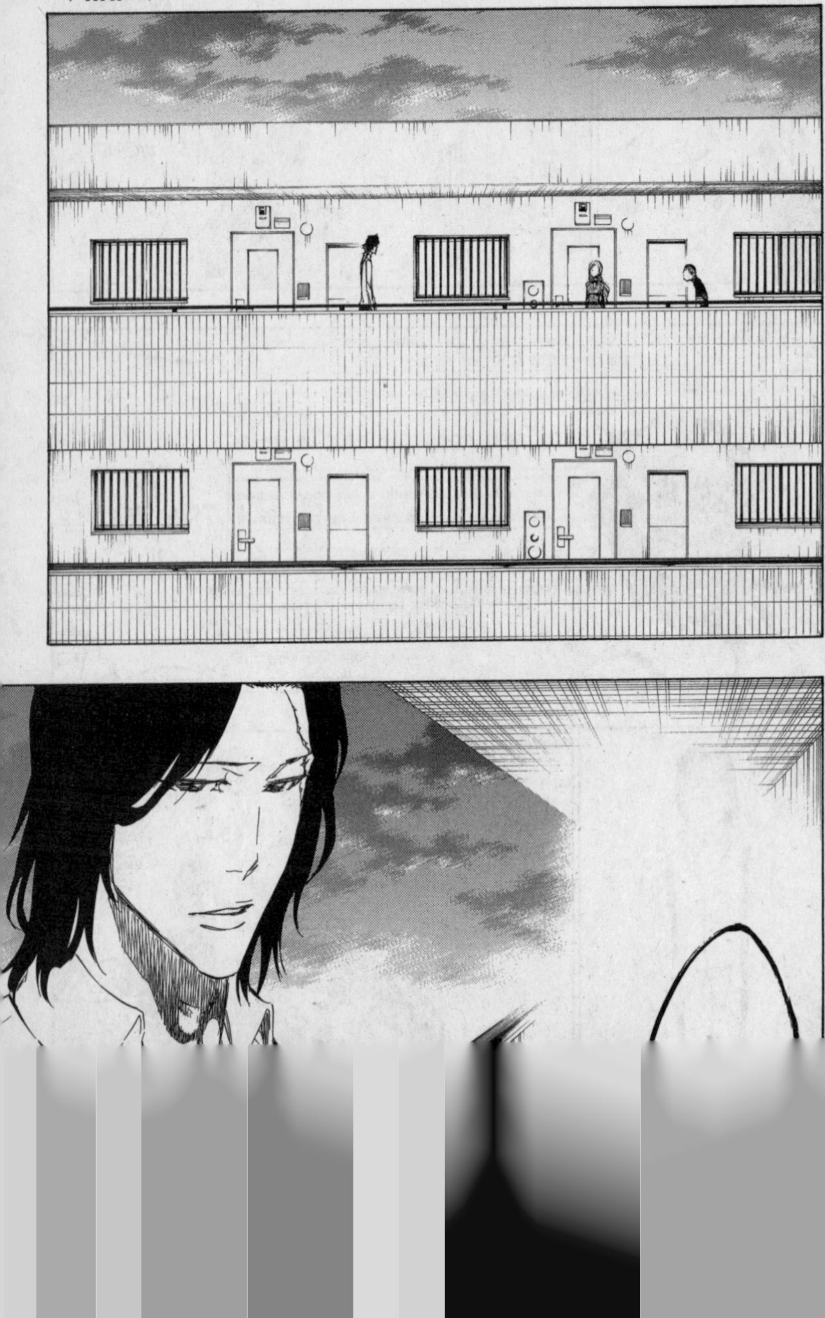

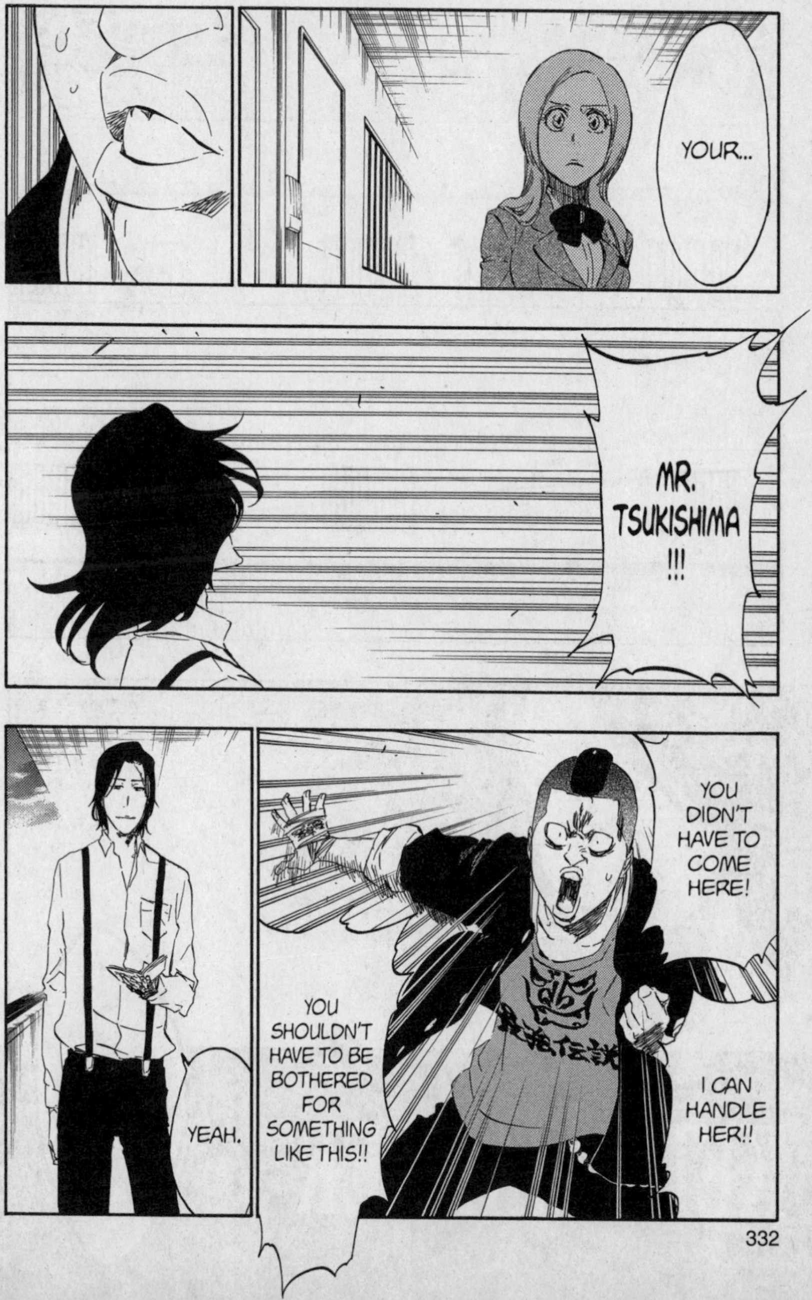
YOUR...
MR. TSUKISHIMA!!!
YOU DIDN'T HAVE TO COME HERE!
I CAN HANDLE HER!!
YOU SHOULDN'T HAVE TO BE BOTHERED FOR SOMETHING LIKE THIS!!
YEAH.

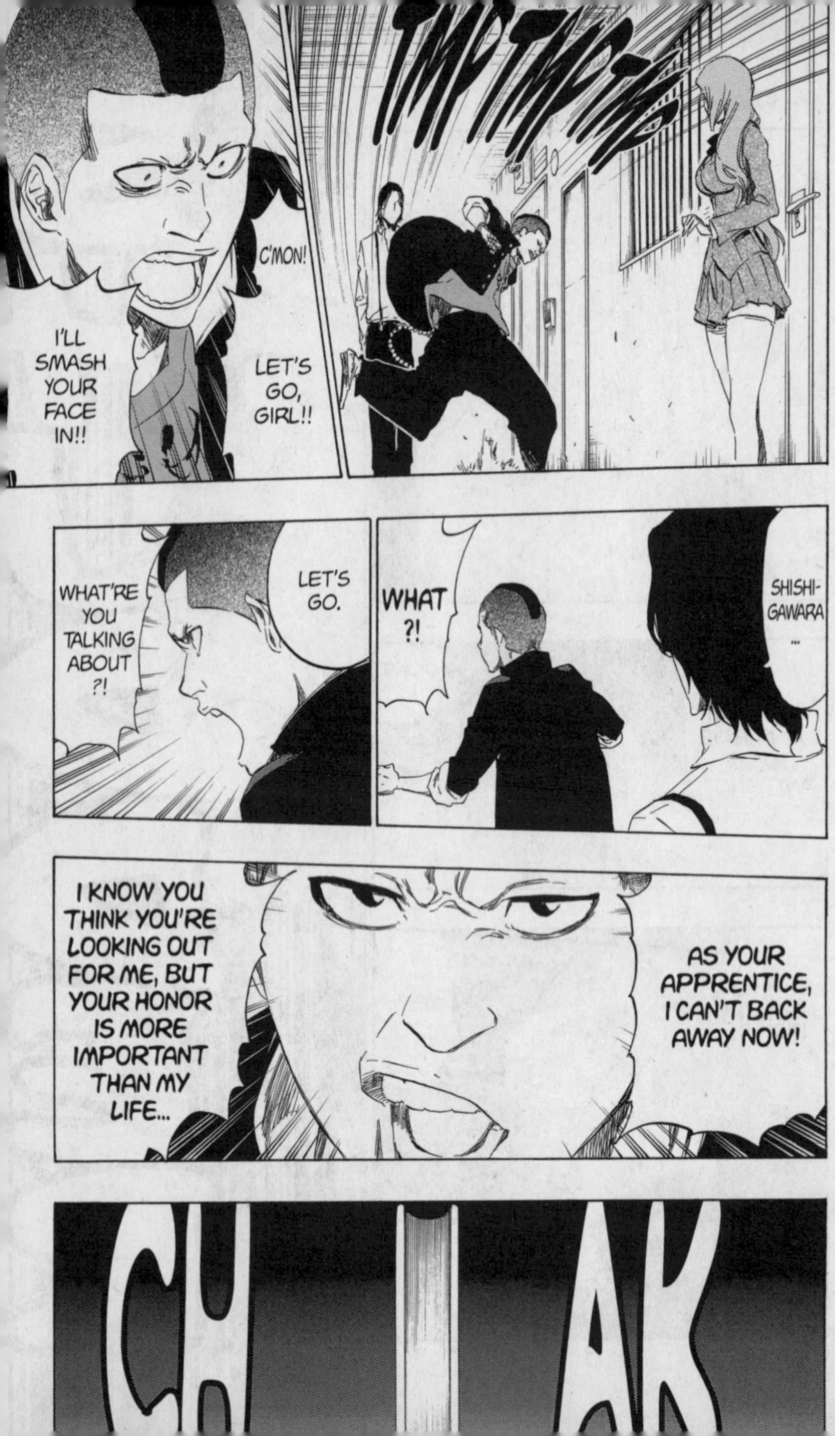
C'MON!
LET'S GO, GIRL!!
I'LL SMASH YOUR FACE IN!!
SHISHIGAWARA...
WHAT ?!
LET'S GO.
WHAT'RE YOU TALKING ABOUT ?!
AS YOUR APPRENTICE, I CAN'T BACK AWAY NOW!
I KNOW YOU THINK YOU'RE LOOKING OUT FOR ME, BUT YOUR HONOR IS MORE IMPORTANT THAN MY LIFE...
CH AK

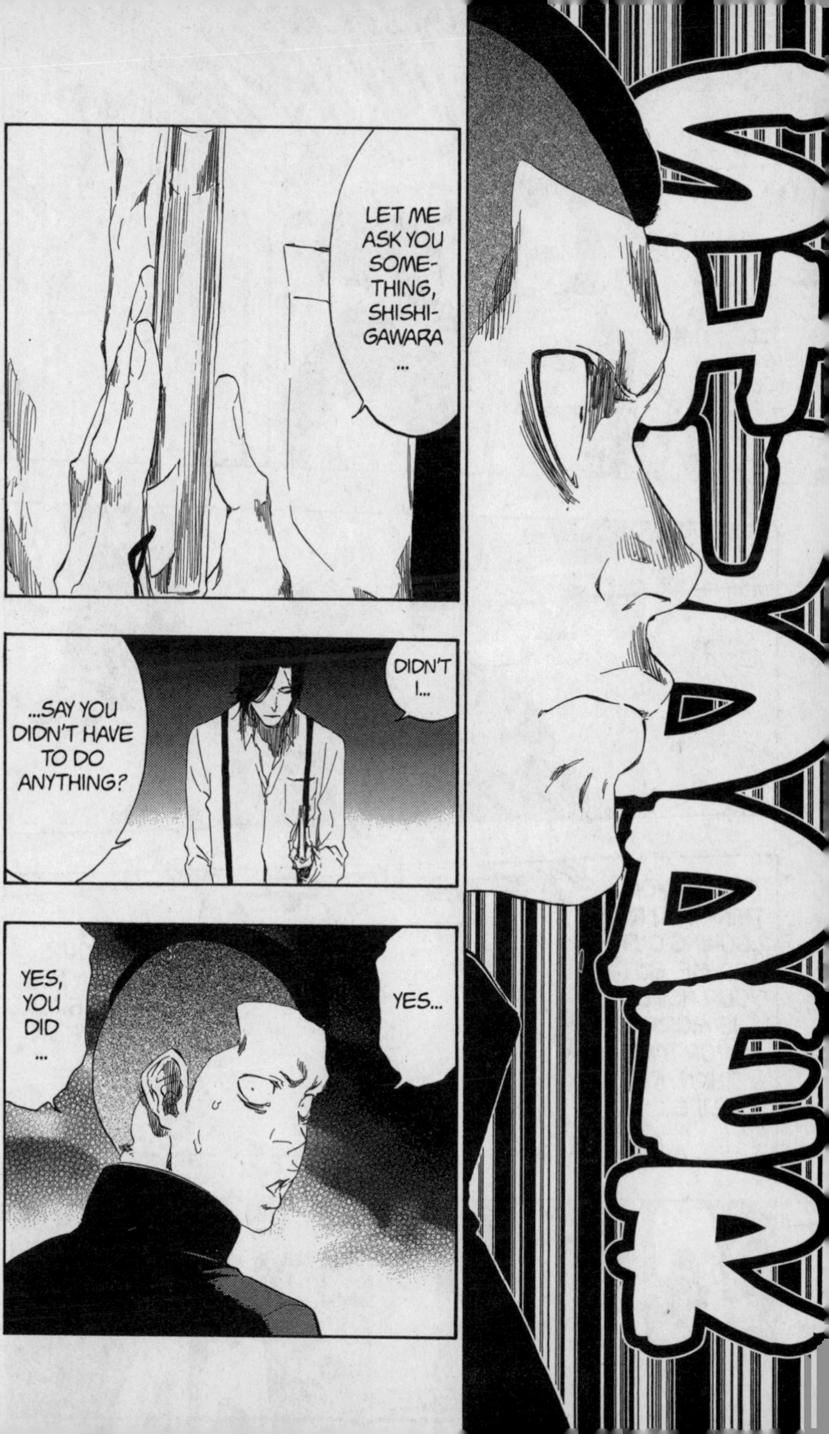
SHUDDER
LET ME ASK YOU SOMETHING, SHISHIGAWARA...
DIDN'T I...
...SAY YOU DIDN'T HAVE TO DO ANYTHING?
YES...
YES, YOU DID...

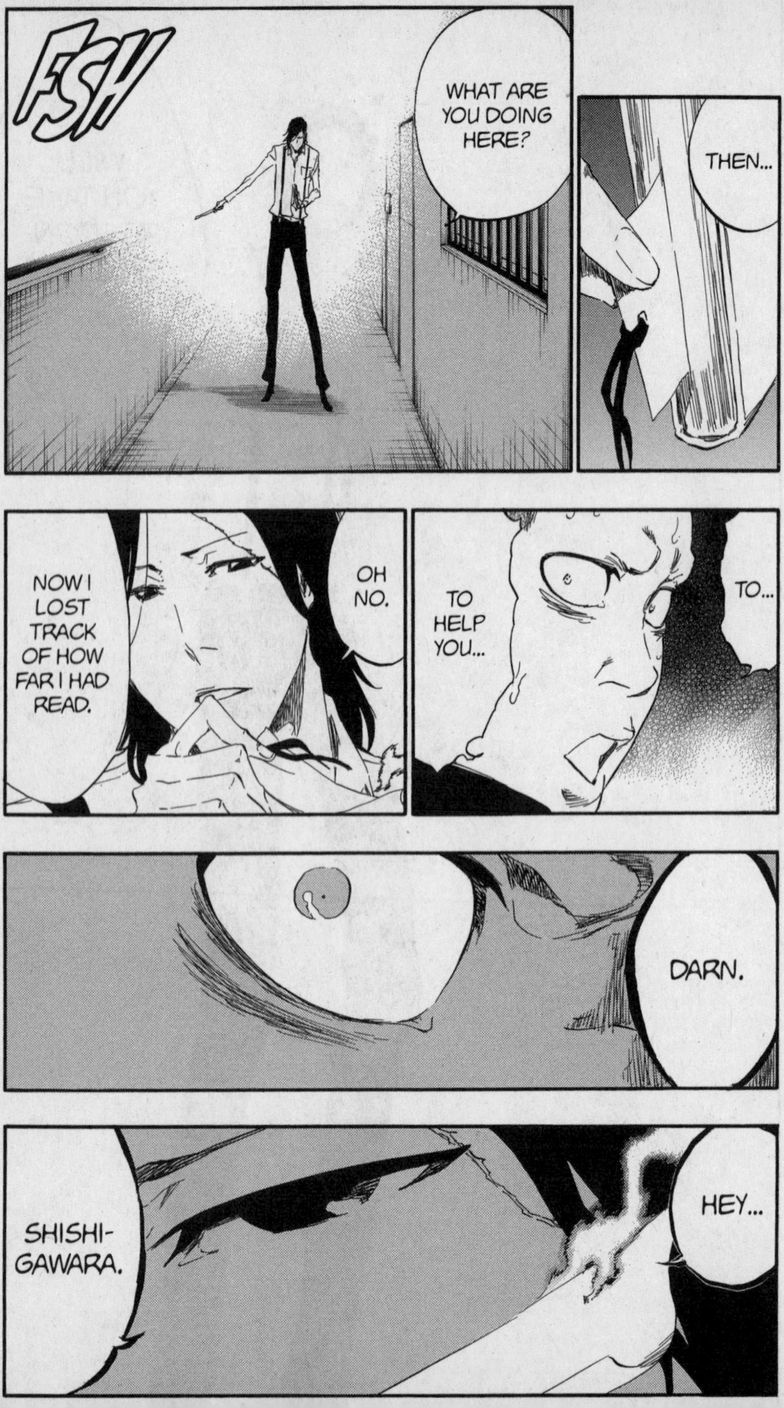
THEN...
WHAT ARE YOU DOING HERE?
FSH
TO...
TO HELP YOU...
OH NO.
NOW I LOST TRACK OF HOW FAR I HAD READ.
DARN.
HEY...
SHISHI-GAWARA.

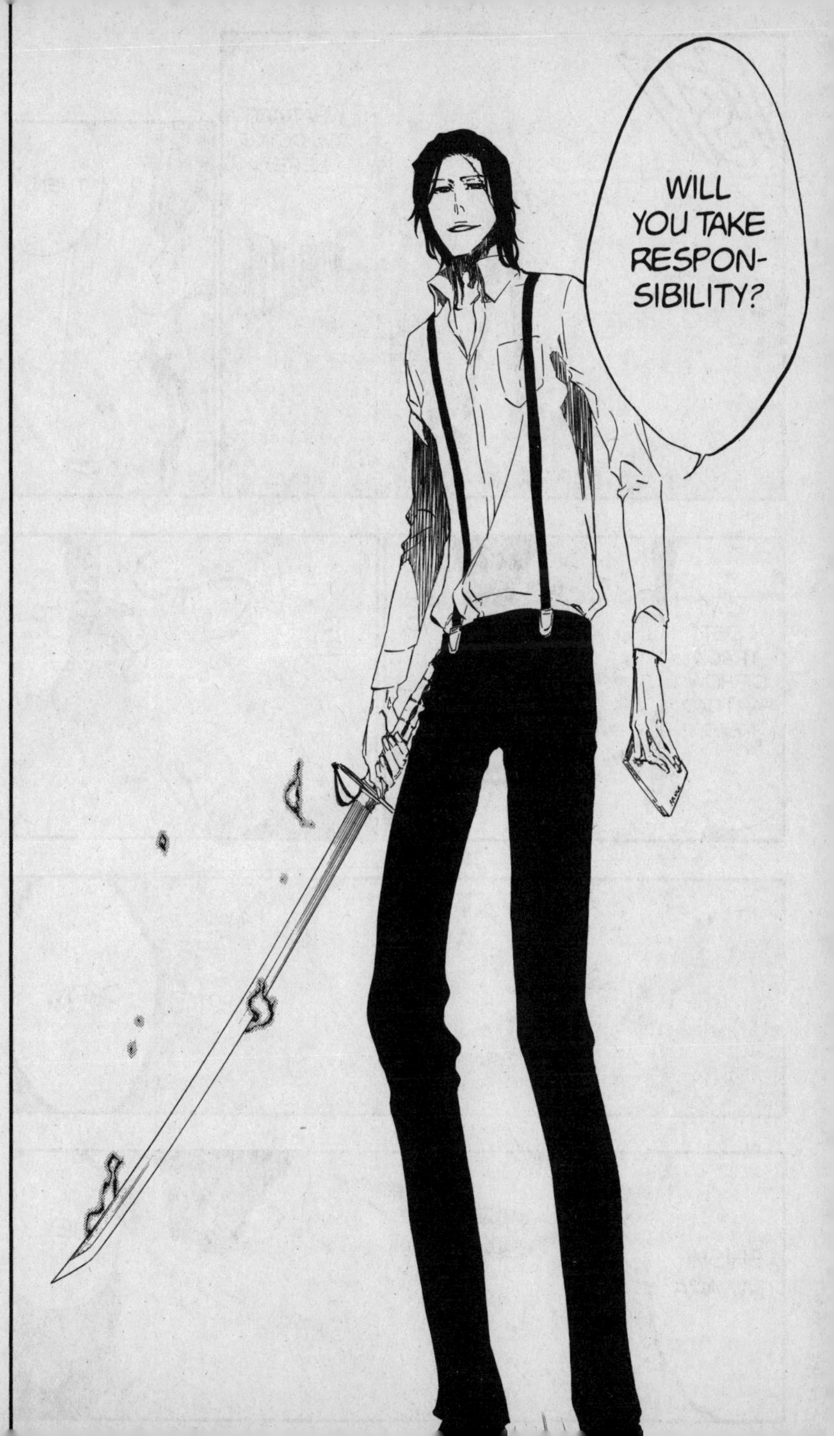
WILL YOU TAKE RESPON- SIBILITY?

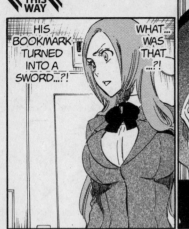

HIS BOOKMARK TURNED INTO A SWORD...?!

WHAT... WAS THAT ...?!

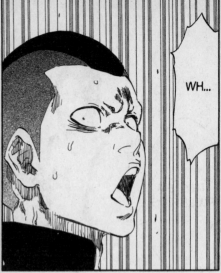

WH...

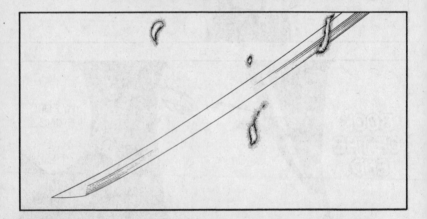

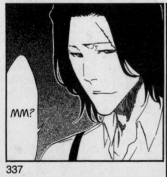

MM?

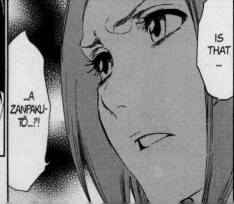

...A ZANPAKU-TÔ...?!

IS THAT ...

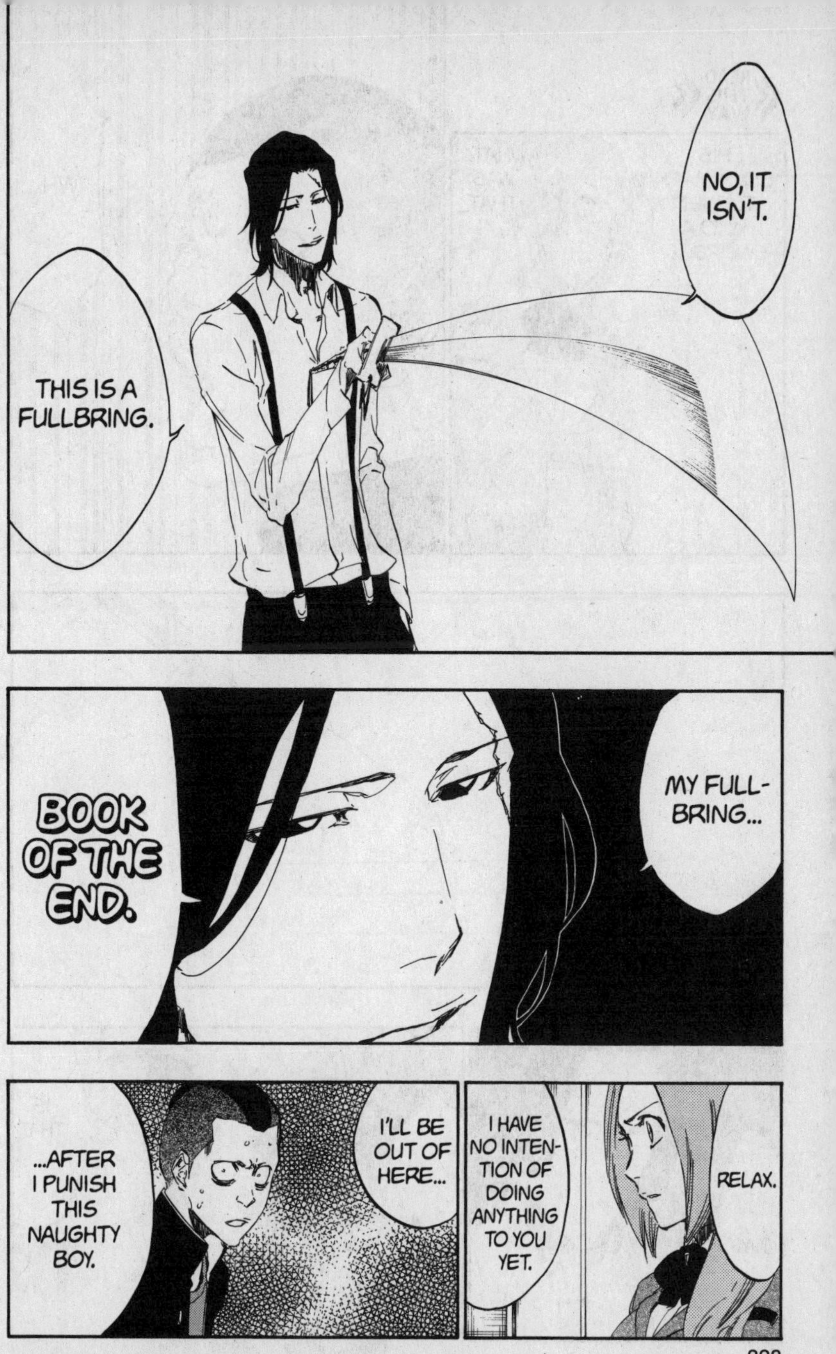
NO, IT ISN'T.
THIS IS A FULLBRING.
MY FULL-BRING...
BOOK OF THE END.
RELAX.
I HAVE NO INTEN-TION OF DOING ANYTHING TO YOU YET.
I'LL BE OUT OF HERE...
...AFTER I PUNISH THIS NAUGHTY BOY.

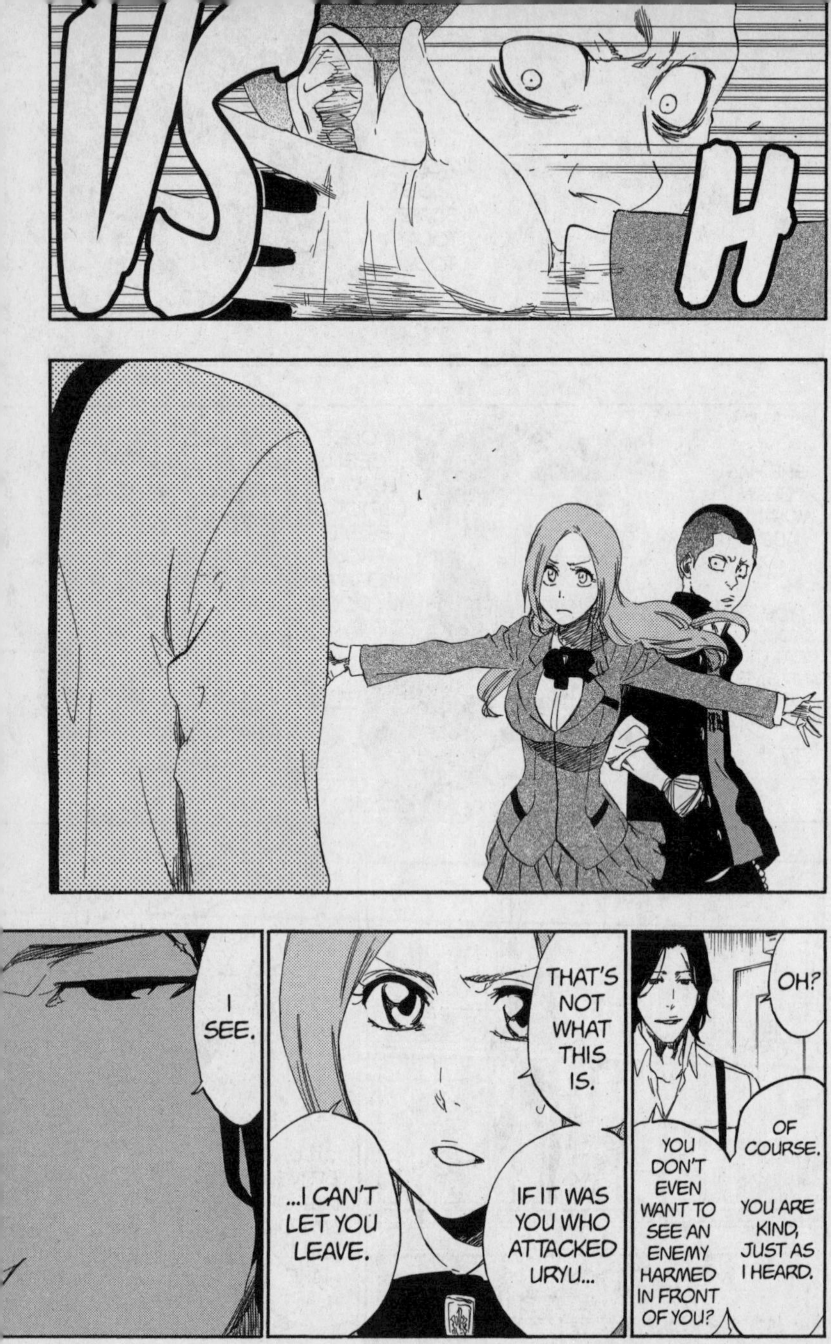
VSH
OH?
OF COURSE.
YOU ARE KIND, JUST AS I HEARD.
YOU DON'T EVEN WANT TO SEE AN ENEMY HARMED IN FRONT OF YOU?
THAT'S NOT WHAT THIS IS.
IF IT WAS YOU WHO ATTACKED URYU...
...I CAN'T LET YOU LEAVE.
I SEE.

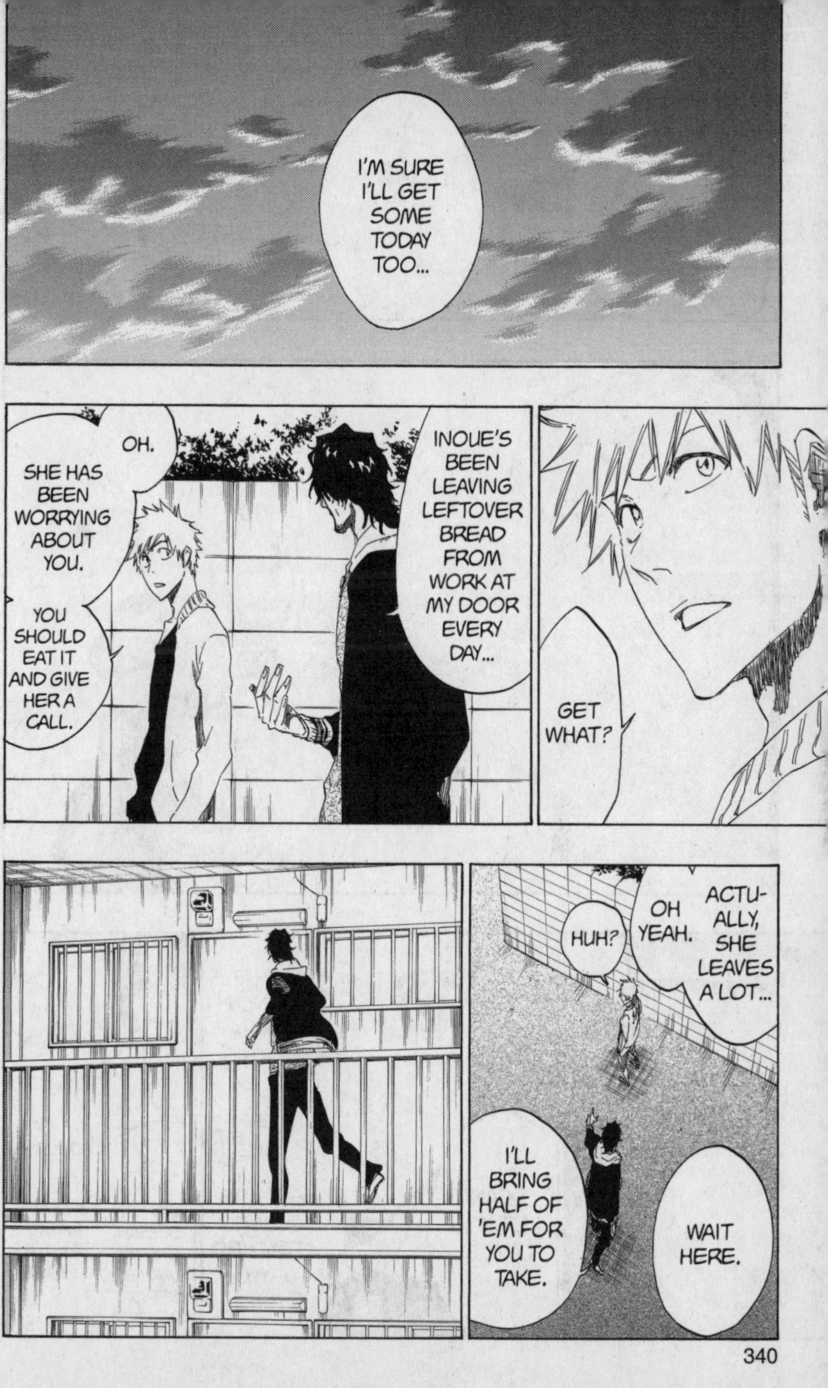

I'M SURE I'LL GET SOME TODAY TOO...
GET WHAT?
INOUE'S BEEN LEAVING LEFTOVER BREAD FROM WORK AT MY DOOR EVERY DAY...
OH.
SHE HAS BEEN WORRYING ABOUT YOU.
YOU SHOULD EAT IT AND GIVE HER A CALL.
ACTU-ALLY, SHE LEAVES A LOT...
OH YEAH.
HUH?
WAIT HERE.
I'LL BRING HALF OF 'EM FOR YOU TO TAKE.

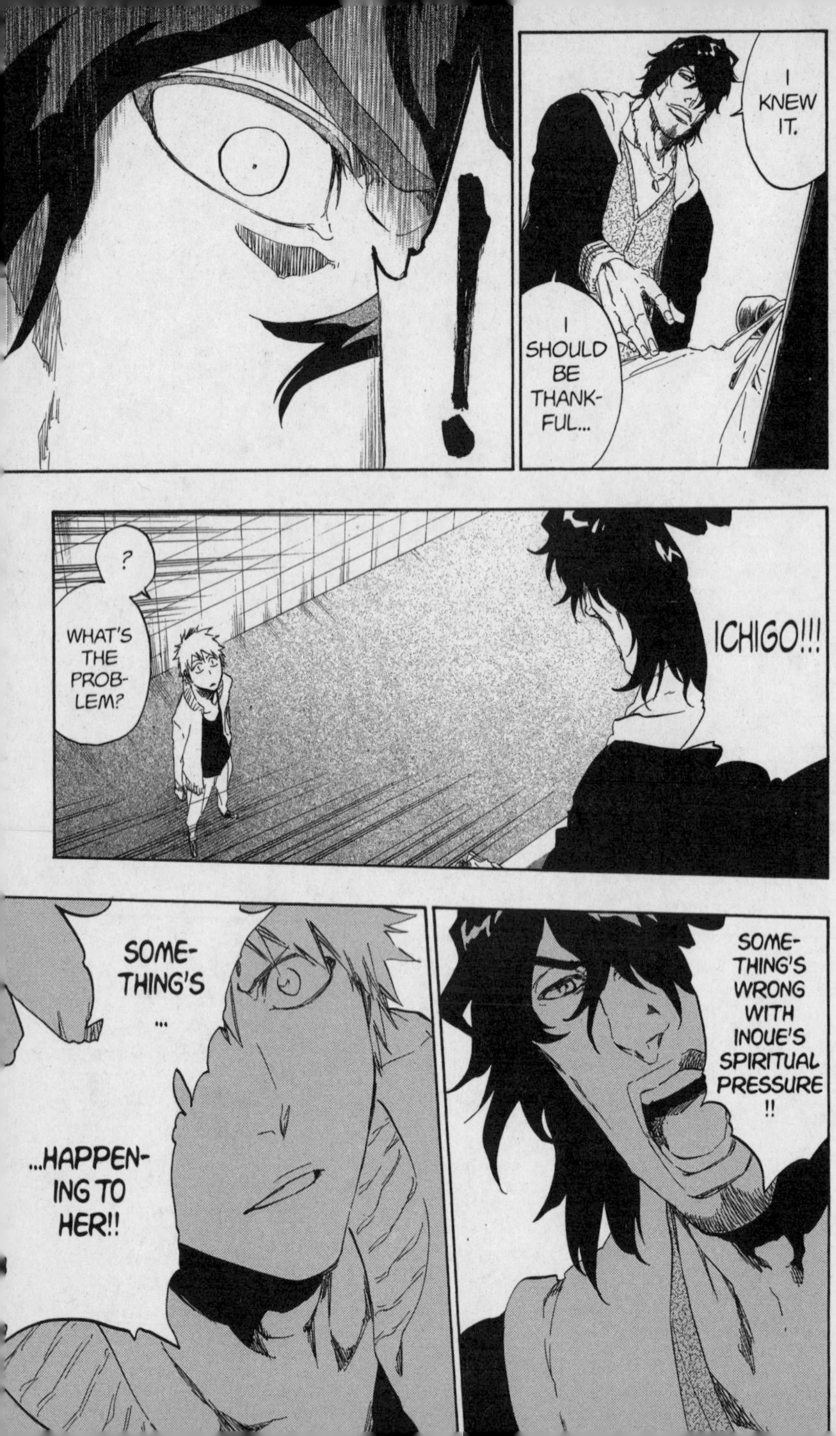
I KNEW IT.
I SHOULD BE THANKFUL...
!
ICHIGO!!!
?
WHAT'S THE PROBLEM?
SOMETHING'S WRONG WITH INOUE'S SPIRITUAL PRESSURE!!
SOMETHING'S...
...HAPPENING TO HER!!

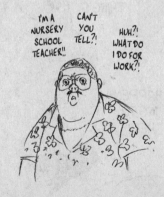

HUH?! WHAT DO I DO FOR WORK?!
CAN'T YOU TELL?!
I'M A NURSERY SCHOOL TEACHER!!

CHAK
WHO YOU CALLING?
INOUE! WHO ELSE?
I WOULDN'T.
THAT SPLIT SECOND THAT SHE'S DISTRACTED BY THE RINGTONE COULD MAKE HER VULNER-ABLE.
IT'S THAT BAD ...?
I DUN-NO...
BUT HER SPIRITUAL PRESSURE IS UNDER TREMEN-DOUS STRAIN ...

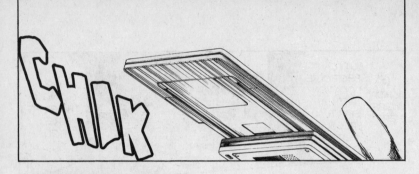

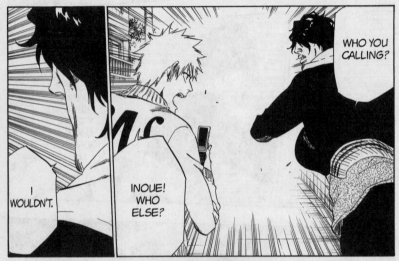

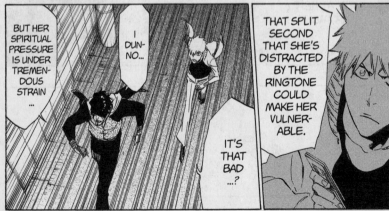

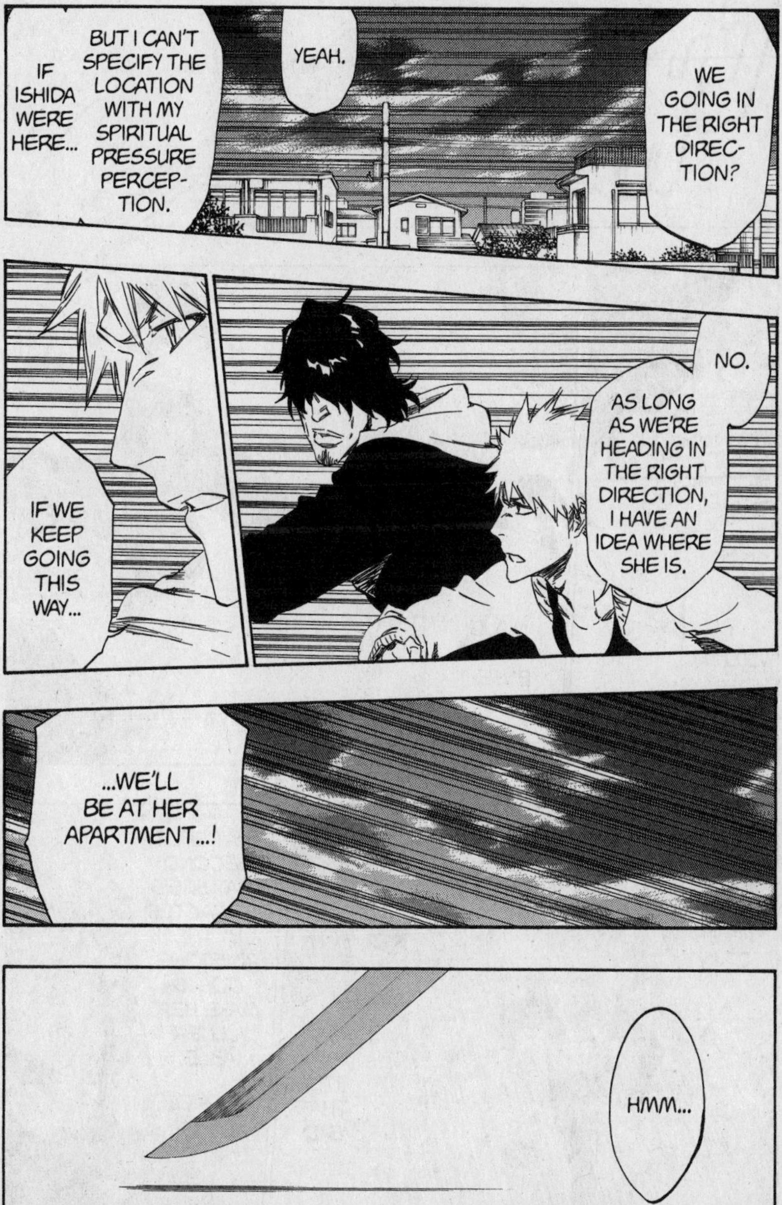
WE GOING IN THE RIGHT DIREC-TION?
YEAH.
BUT I CAN'T SPECIFY THE LOCATION WITH MY SPIRITUAL PRESSURE PERCEP-TION.
IF ISHIDA WERE HERE...
NO.
AS LONG AS WE'RE HEADING IN THE RIGHT DIRECTION, I HAVE AN IDEA WHERE SHE IS.
IF WE KEEP GOING THIS WAY...
...WE'LL BE AT HER APARTMENT...!
HMM...

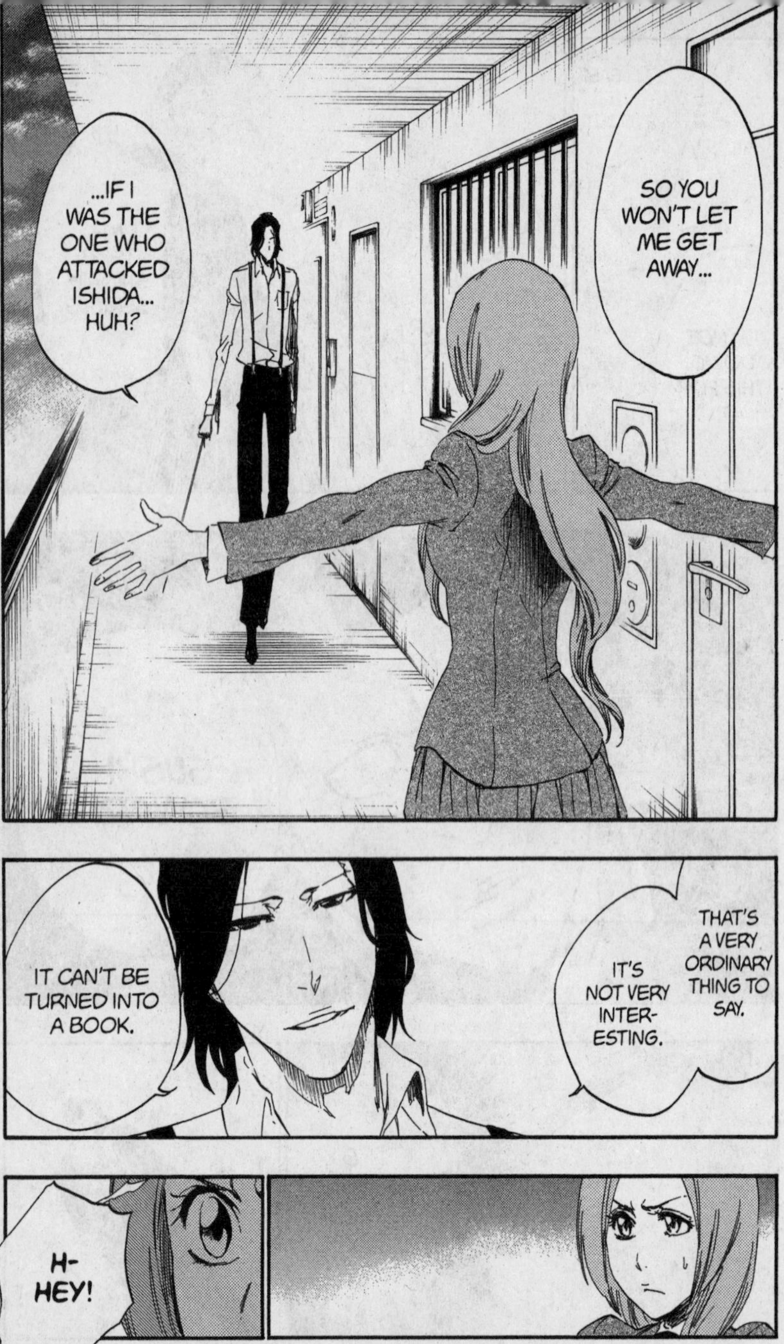
SO YOU WON'T LET ME GET AWAY...
...IF I WAS THE ONE WHO ATTACKED ISHIDA... HUH?
THAT'S A VERY ORDINARY THING TO SAY.
IT'S NOT VERY INTER-ESTING.
IT CAN'T BE TURNED INTO A BOOK.
H-HEY!

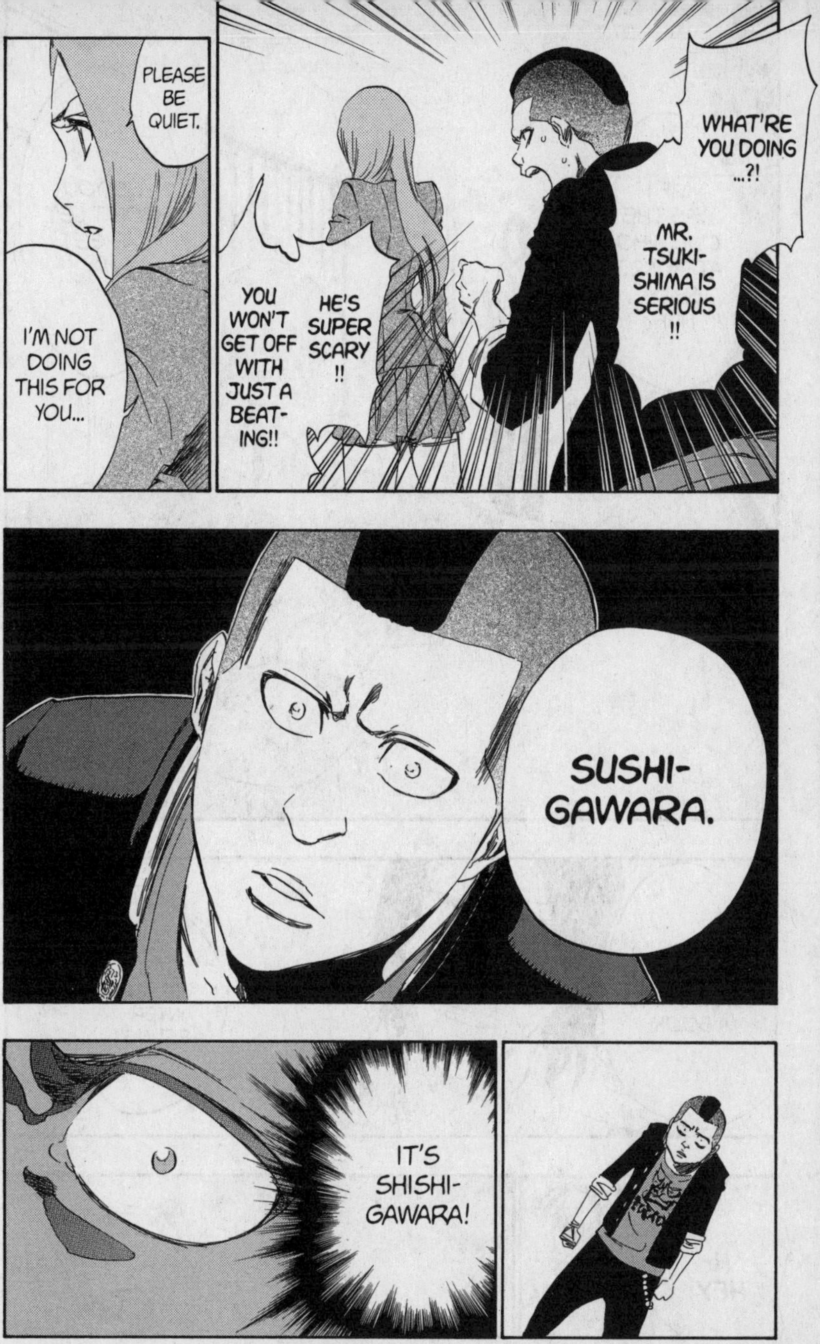
WHAT'RE YOU DOING ...?!
MR. TSUKI-SHIMA IS SERIOUS !!
HE'S SUPER SCARY !!
YOU WON'T GET OFF WITH JUST A BEAT-ING!!
PLEASE BE QUIET.
I'M NOT DOING THIS FOR YOU...
SUSHI-GAWARA.
IT'S SHISHI-GAWARA!

READ THIS WAY

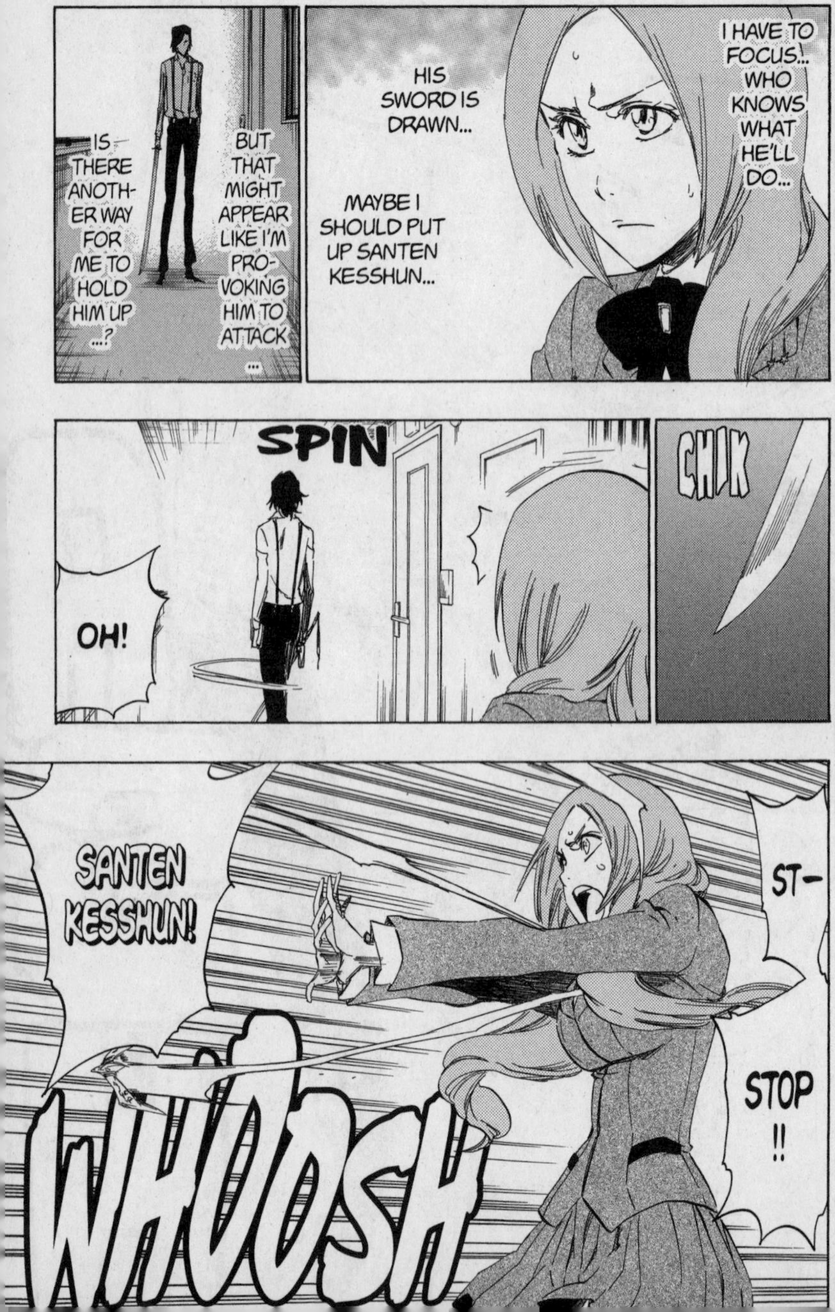
I HAVE TO FOCUS... WHO KNOWS WHAT HE'LL DO...
HIS SWORD IS DRAWN...
MAYBE I SHOULD PUT UP SANTEN KESSHUN...
BUT THAT MIGHT APPEAR LIKE I'M PRO-VOKING HIM TO ATTACK ...
IS THERE ANOTH-ER WAY FOR ME TO HOLD HIM UP ...?
CHIK
SPIN
OH!
ST—
STOP !!
SANTEN KESSHUN!
WHOOSH

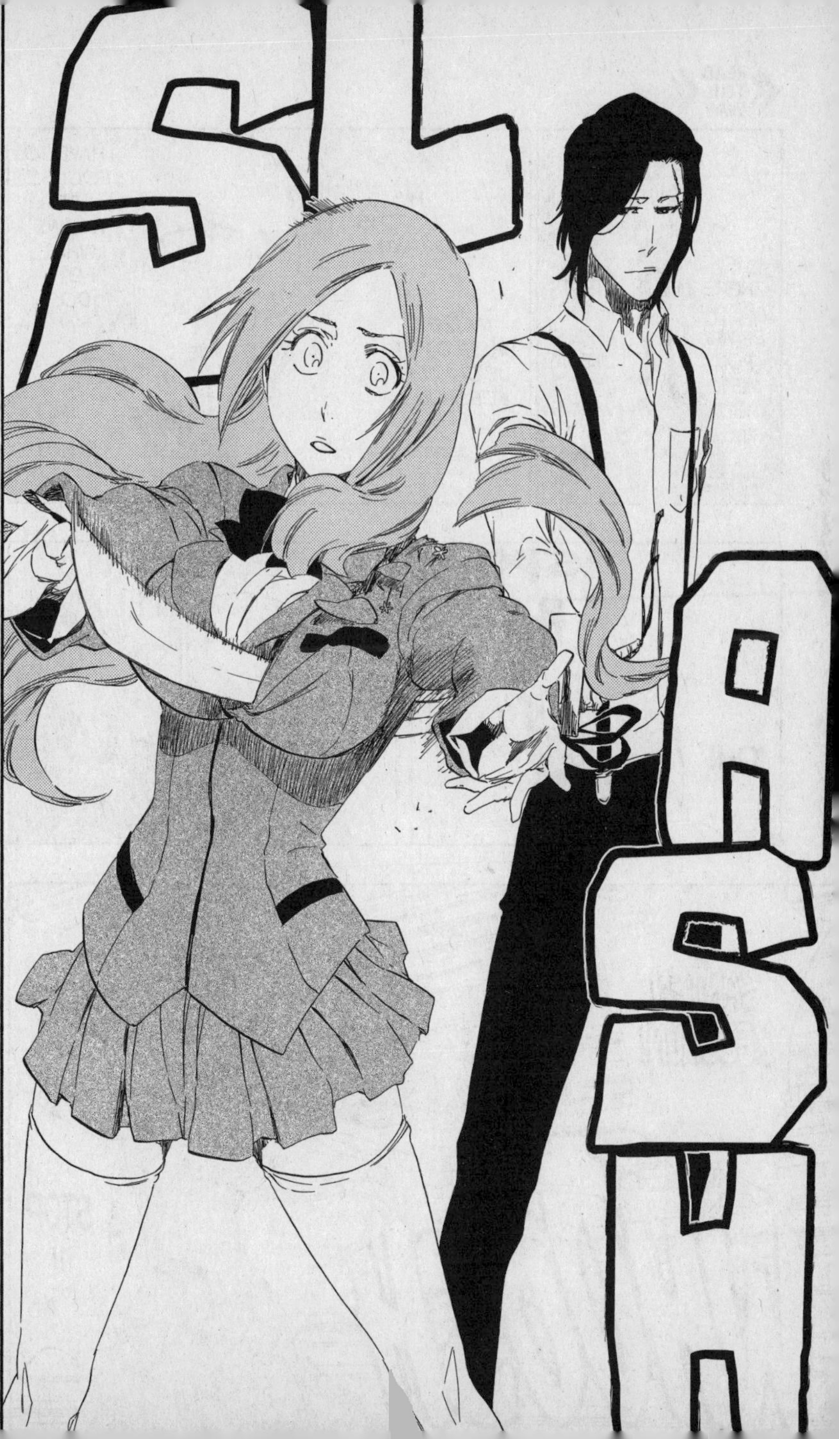
SL
ASH

READ THIS WAY

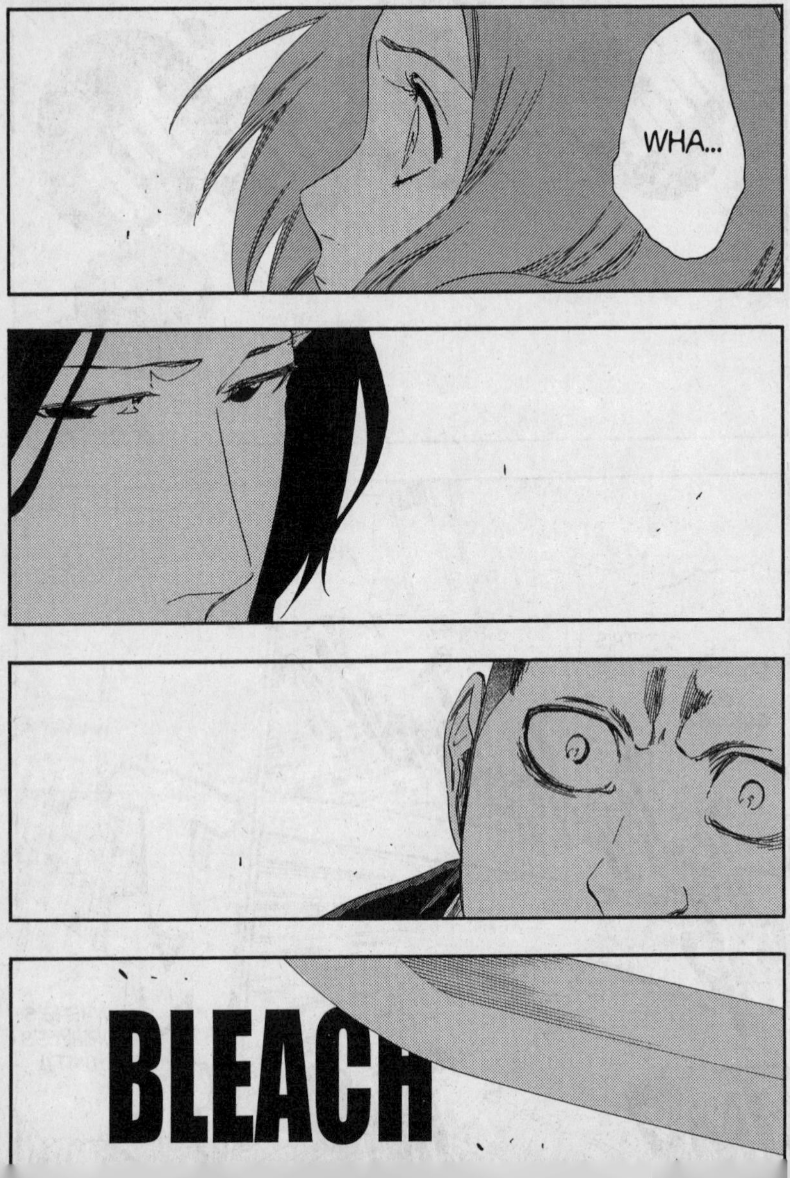
WHA...
BLEACH

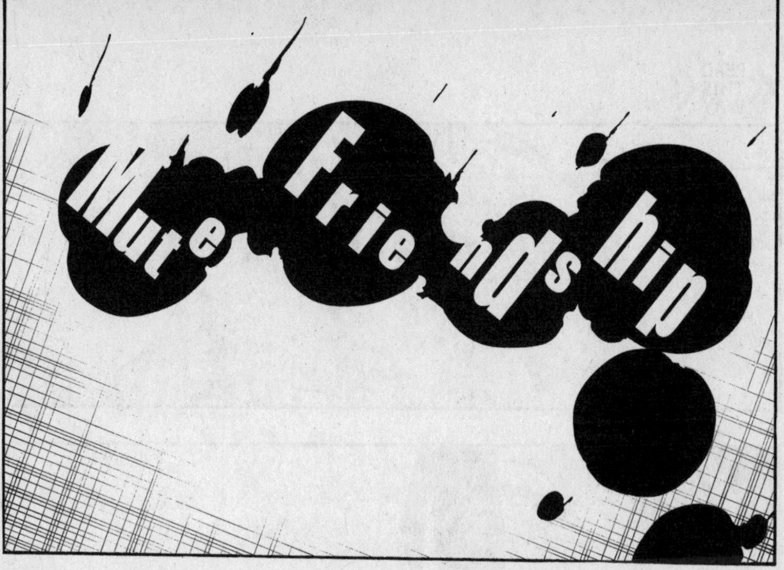
Mute Friendship

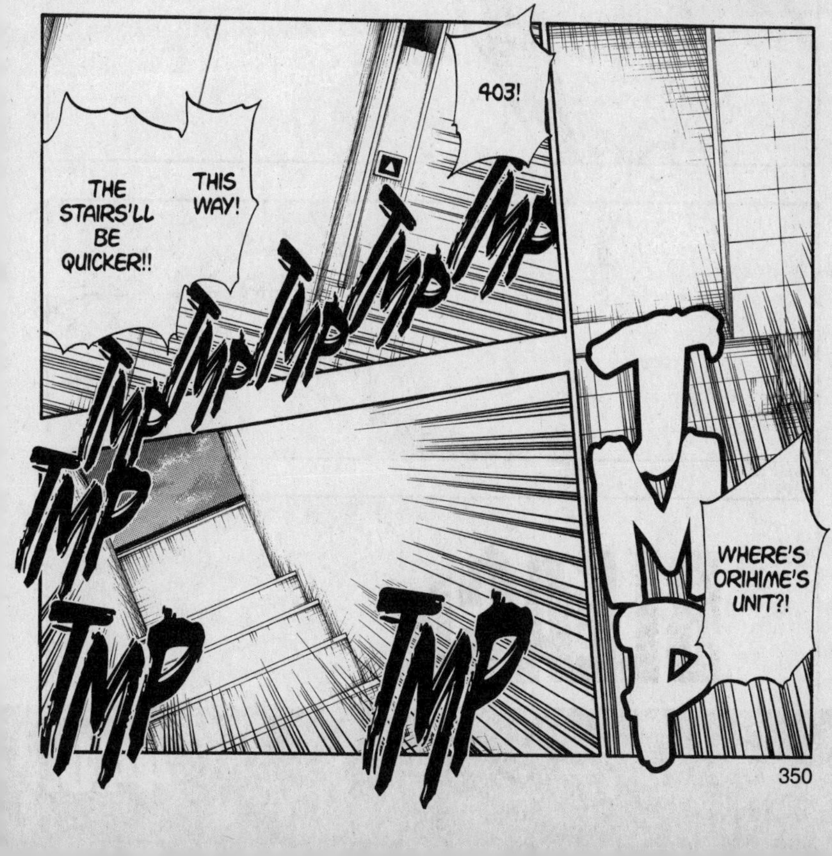
WHERE'S ORIHIME'S UNIT?!
TMP
403!
THIS WAY!
THE STAIRS'LL BE QUICKER!!
TMP TMP TMP TMP TMP
TMP
TMP
TMP

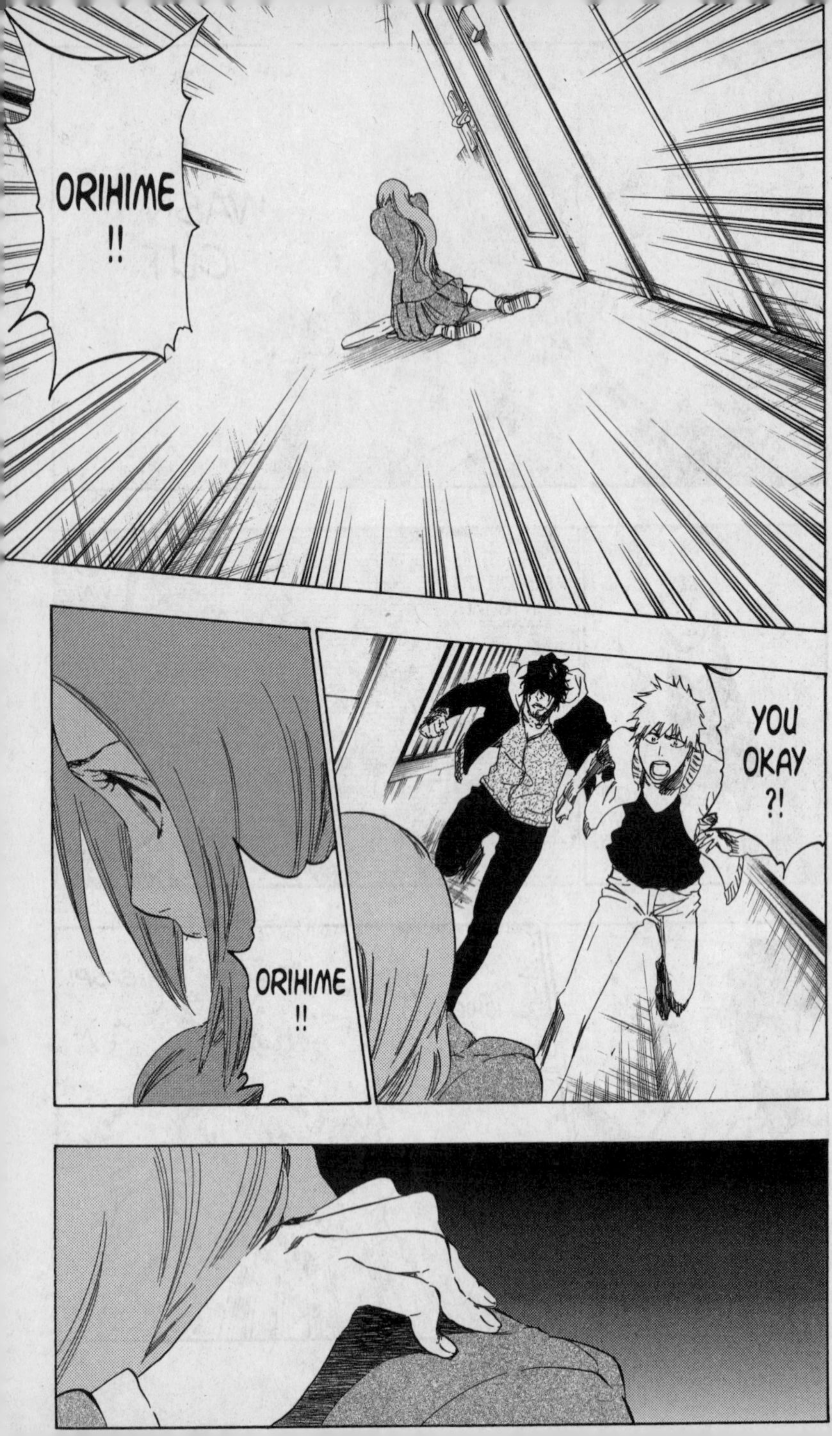
ORIHIME !!
YOU OKAY ?!
ORIHIME !!

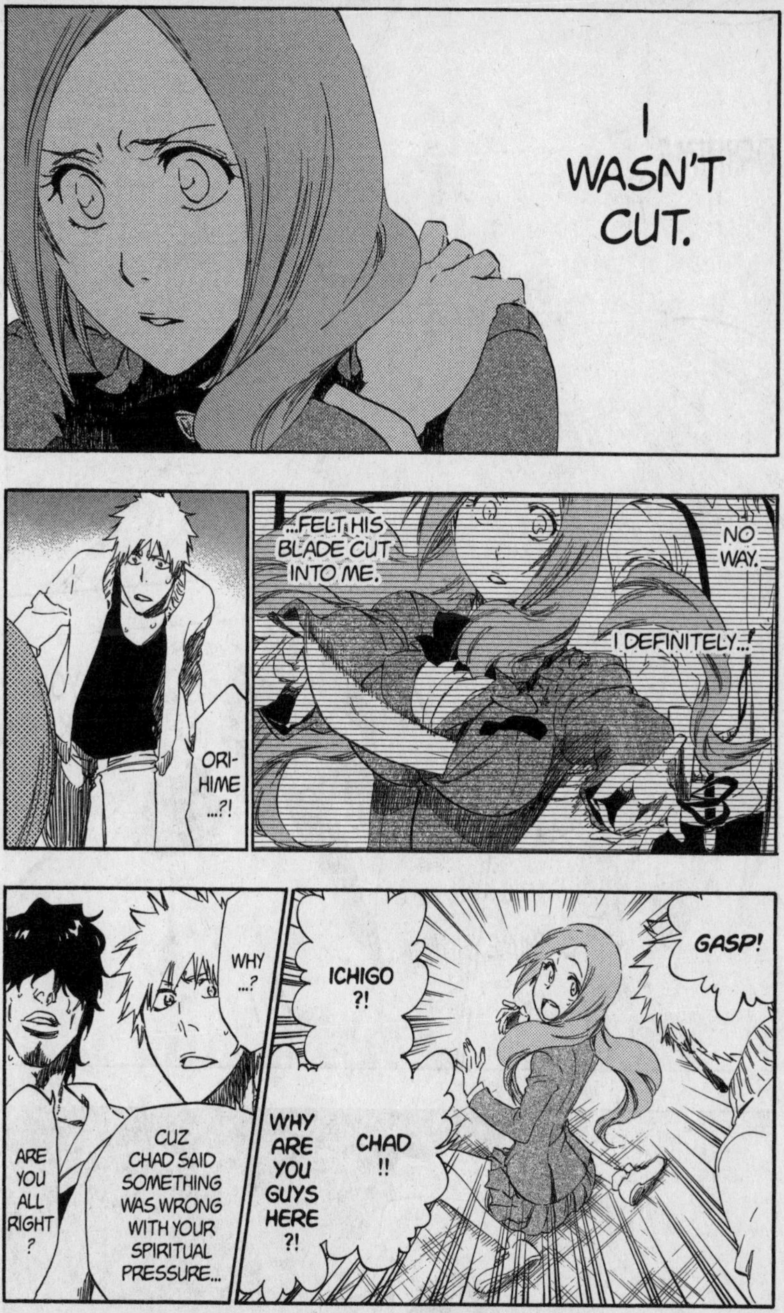
I WASN'T CUT.
NO WAY.
I DEFINITELY...!
...FELT HIS BLADE CUT INTO ME.
ORI-HIME...?!
GASP!
ICHIGO?!
CHAD!!
WHY ARE YOU GUYS HERE?!
WHY...?
CUZ CHAD SAID SOMETHING WAS WRONG WITH YOUR SPIRITUAL PRESSURE...
ARE YOU ALL RIGHT?

READ THIS WAY

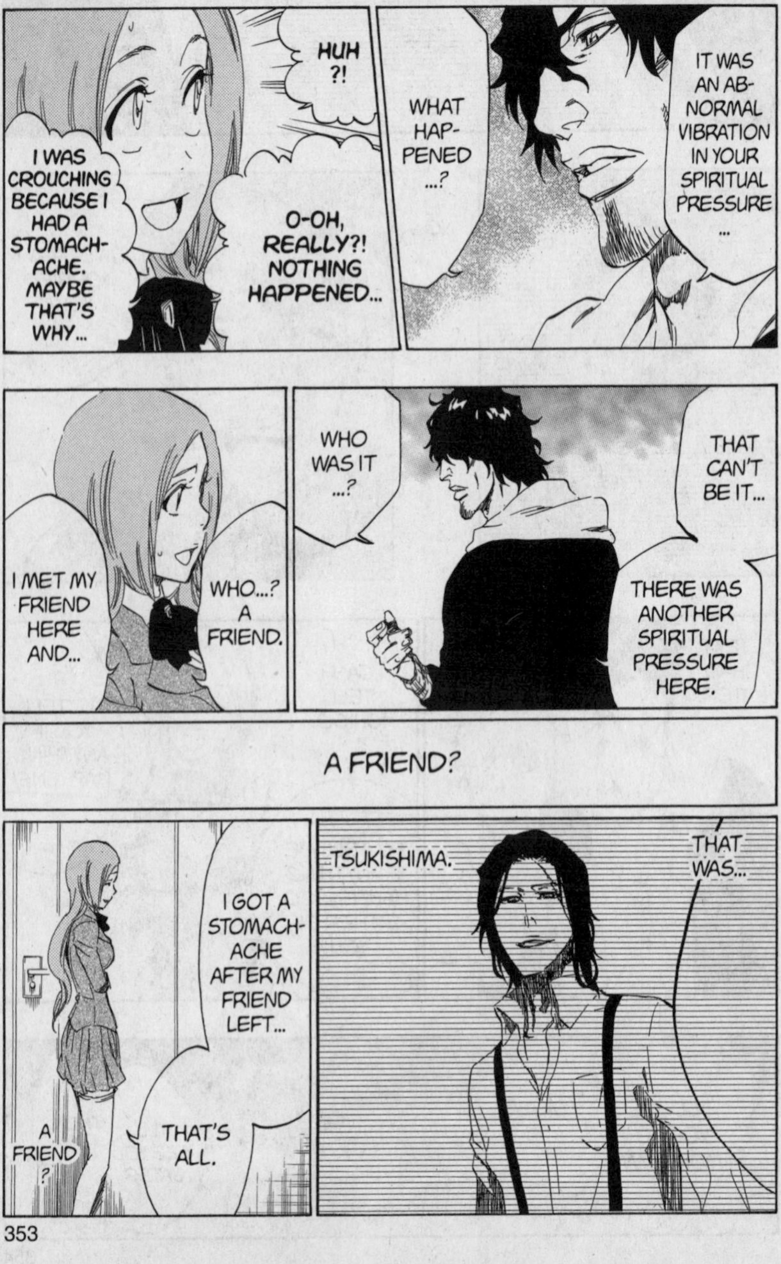
IT WAS AN AB-NORMAL VIBRATION IN YOUR SPIRITUAL PRESSURE...
WHAT HAPPENED...?
HUH?!
O-OH, REALLY?! NOTHING HAPPENED...
I WAS CROUCHING BECAUSE I HAD A STOMACHACHE. MAYBE THAT'S WHY...
THAT CAN'T BE IT...
THERE WAS ANOTHER SPIRITUAL PRESSURE HERE.
WHO WAS IT...?
WHO...? A FRIEND.
I MET MY FRIEND HERE AND...
A FRIEND?
THAT WAS...
TSUKISHIMA.
I GOT A STOMACHACHE AFTER MY FRIEND LEFT...
THAT'S ALL.
A FRIEND?

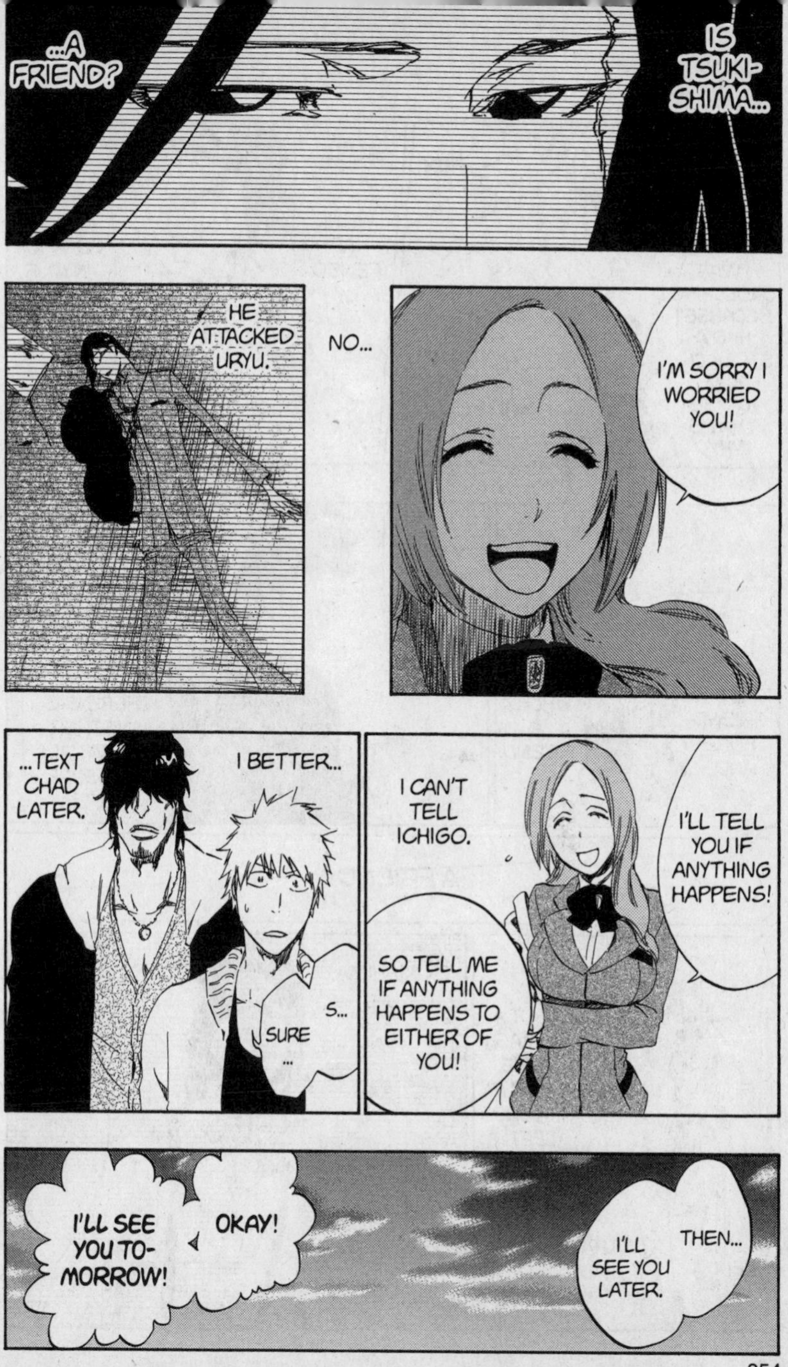
IS TSUKI-SHIMA...
...A FRIEND?
I'M SORRY I WORRIED YOU!
NO...
HE ATTACKED URYU.
I'LL TELL YOU IF ANYTHING HAPPENS!
I CAN'T TELL ICHIGO.
SO TELL ME IF ANYTHING HAPPENS TO EITHER OF YOU!
I BETTER...
...TEXT CHAD LATER.
S... SURE ...
THEN...
I'LL SEE YOU LATER.
OKAY!
I'LL SEE YOU TO-MORROW!

READ THIS WAY

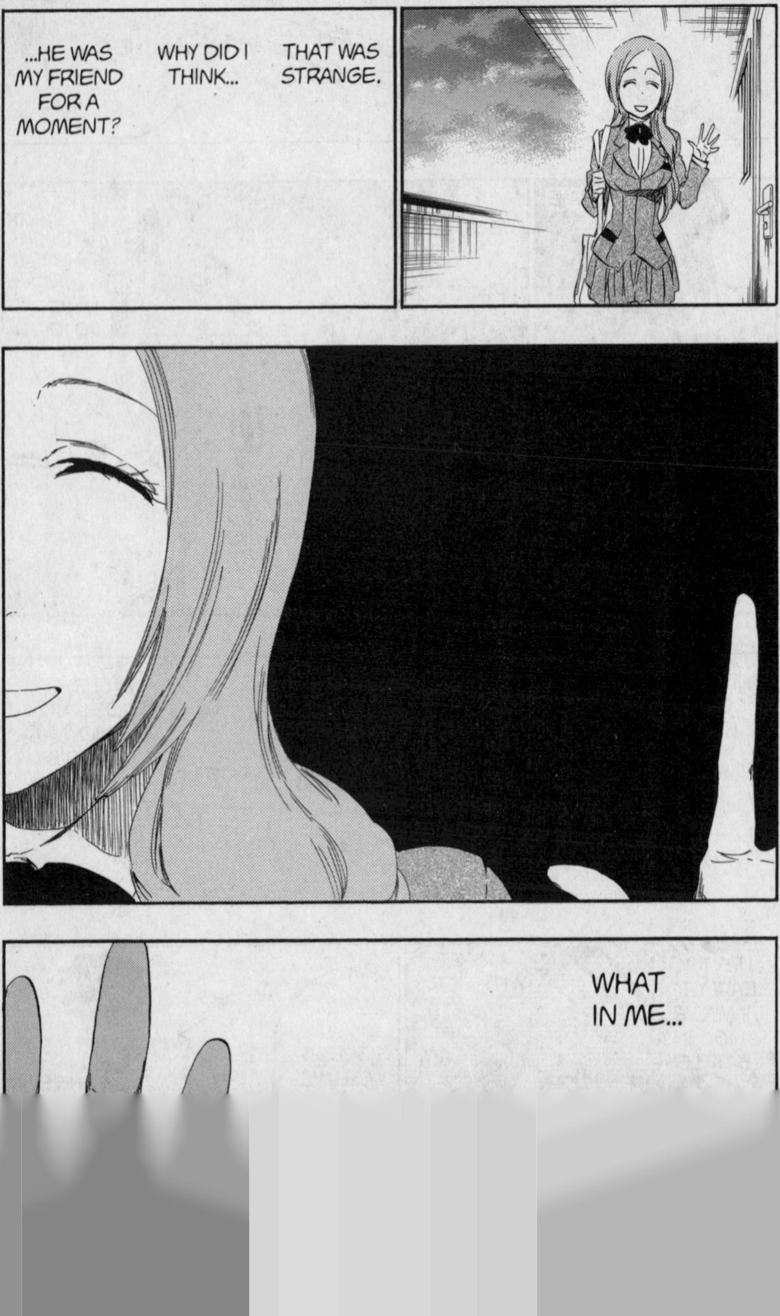
THAT WAS STRANGE.
WHY DID I THINK...
...HE WAS MY FRIEND FOR A MOMENT?
WHAT IN ME...

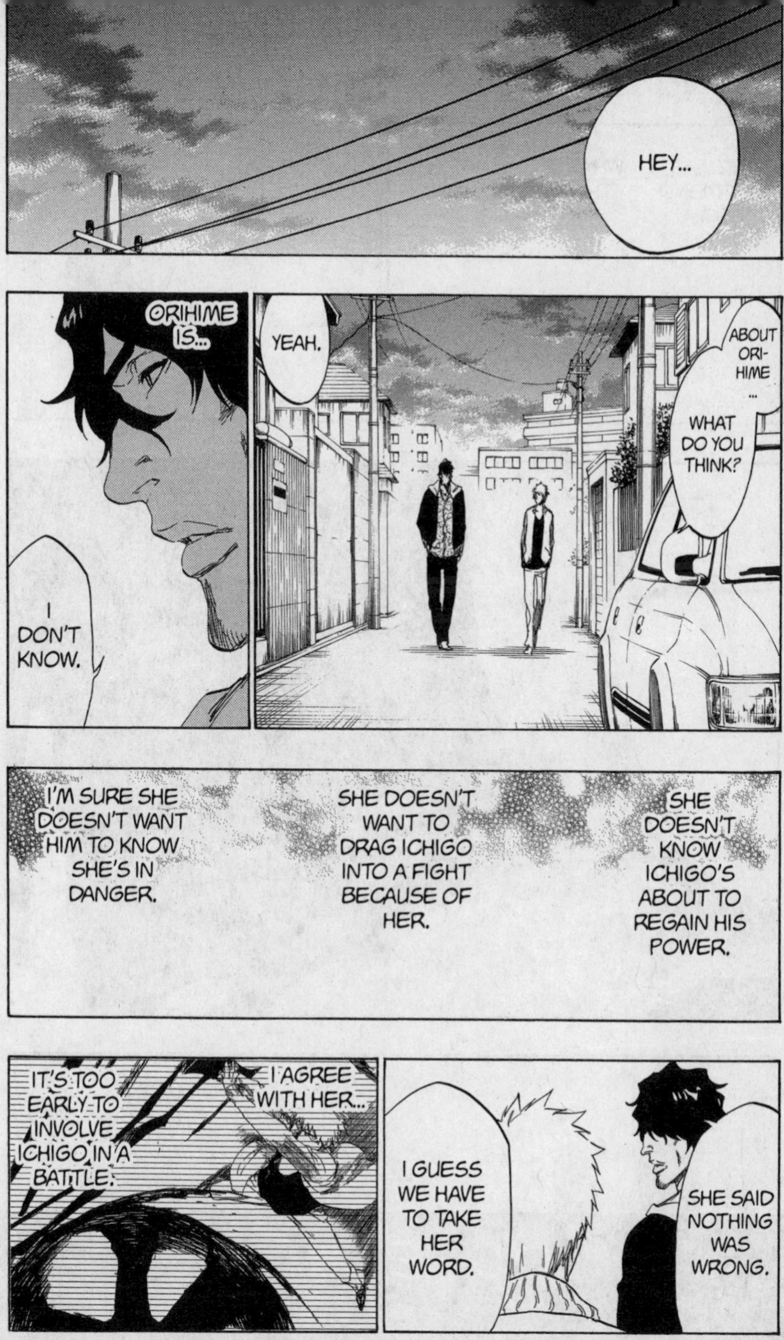
HEY...
ABOUT ORIHIME... WHAT DO YOU THINK?
YEAH.
ORIHIME IS...
I DON'T KNOW.
SHE DOESN'T KNOW ICHIGO'S ABOUT TO REGAIN HIS POWER.
SHE DOESN'T WANT TO DRAG ICHIGO INTO A FIGHT BECAUSE OF HER.
I'M SURE SHE DOESN'T WANT HIM TO KNOW SHE'S IN DANGER.
SHE SAID NOTHING WAS WRONG.
I GUESS WE HAVE TO TAKE HER WORD.
I AGREE WITH HER...
IT'S TOO EARLY TO INVOLVE ICHIGO IN A BATTLE.

READ THIS WAY

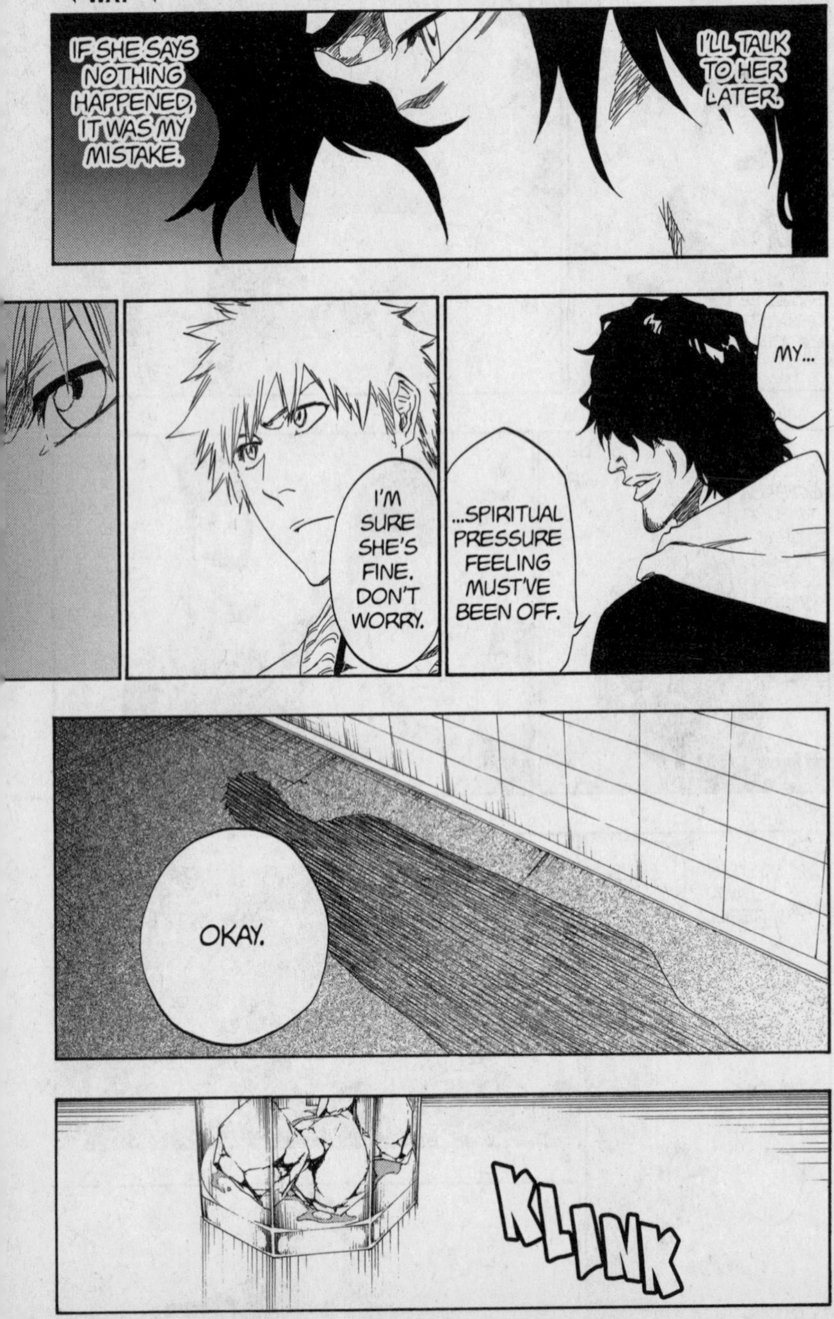
I'LL TALK TO HER LATER.
IF SHE SAYS NOTHING HAPPENED, IT WAS MY MISTAKE.
MY...
...SPIRITUAL PRESSURE FEELING MUST'VE BEEN OFF.
I'M SURE SHE'S FINE. DON'T WORRY.
OKAY.
KLINK

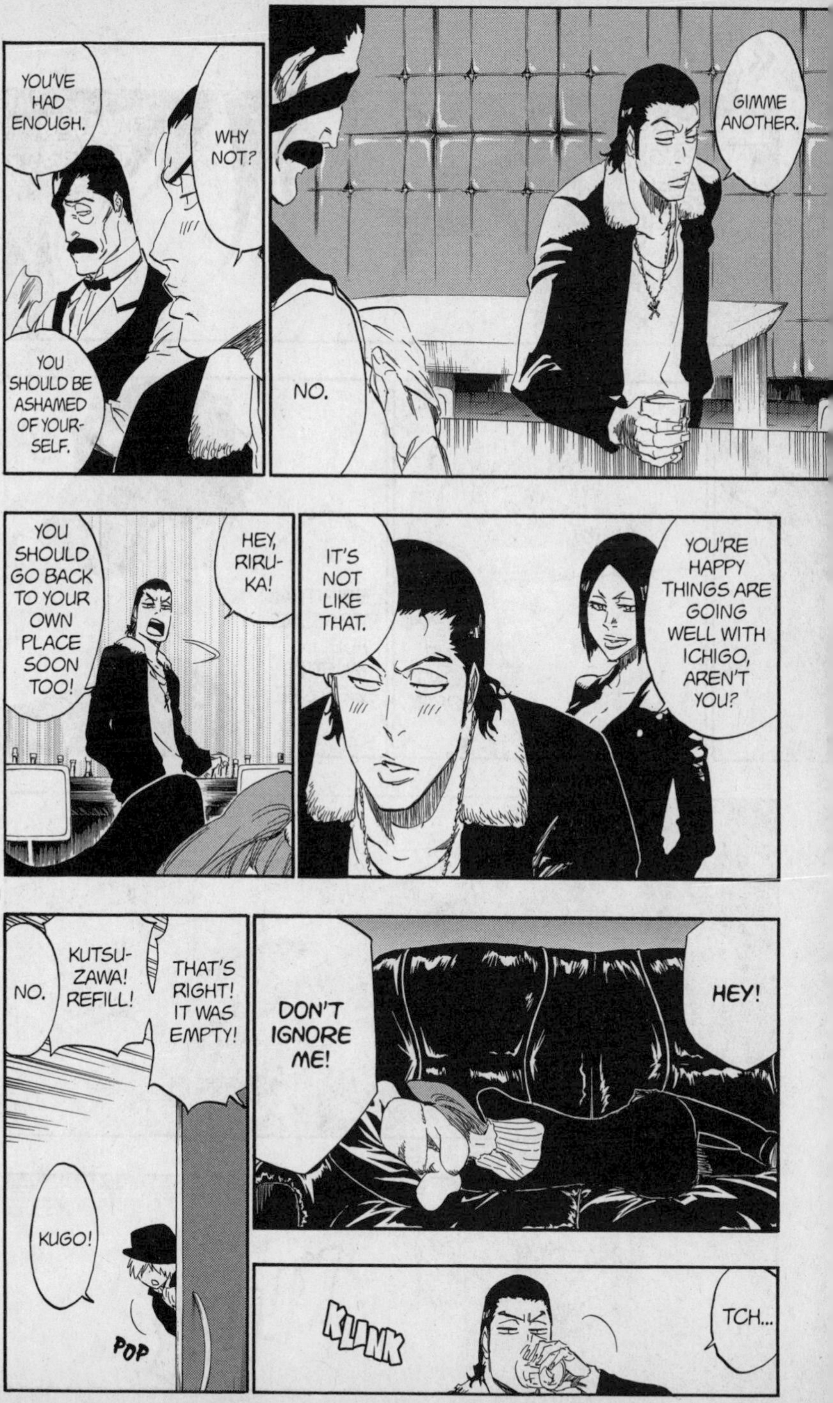
GIMME ANOTHER.
NO.
WHY NOT?
YOU'VE HAD ENOUGH.
YOU SHOULD BE ASHAMED OF YOUR-SELF.
YOU'RE HAPPY THINGS ARE GOING WELL WITH ICHIGO, AREN'T YOU?
IT'S NOT LIKE THAT.
HEY, RIRU-KA!
YOU SHOULD GO BACK TO YOUR OWN PLACE SOON TOO!
HEY!
DON'T IGNORE ME!
TCH...
KLINK
THAT'S RIGHT! IT WAS EMPTY!
KUTSU-ZAWA! REFILL!
NO.
KUGO!
POP

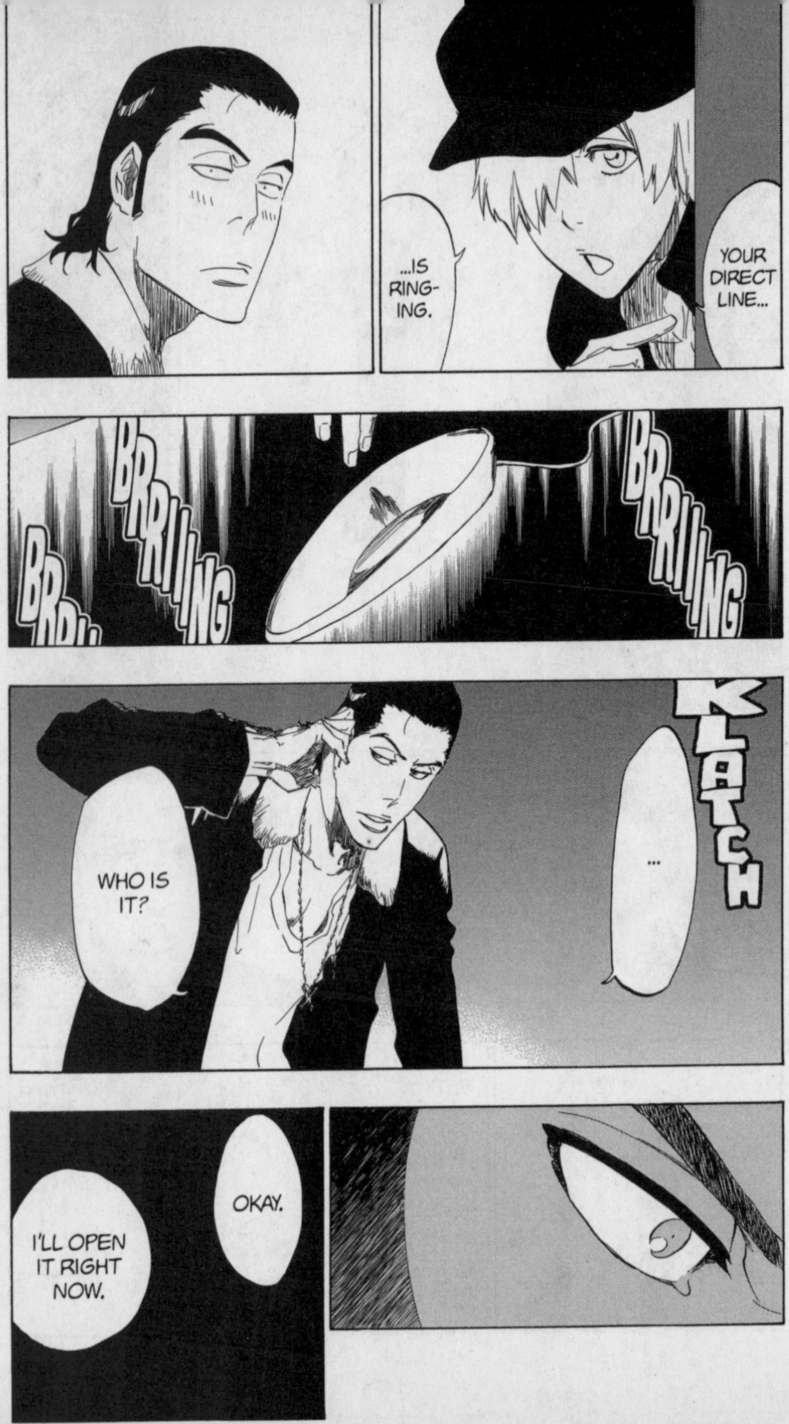
YOUR DIRECT LINE...
...IS RING-ING.
BRRIIING
BRRIIING
KLATCH
...
WHO IS IT?
OKAY.
I'LL OPEN IT RIGHT NOW.

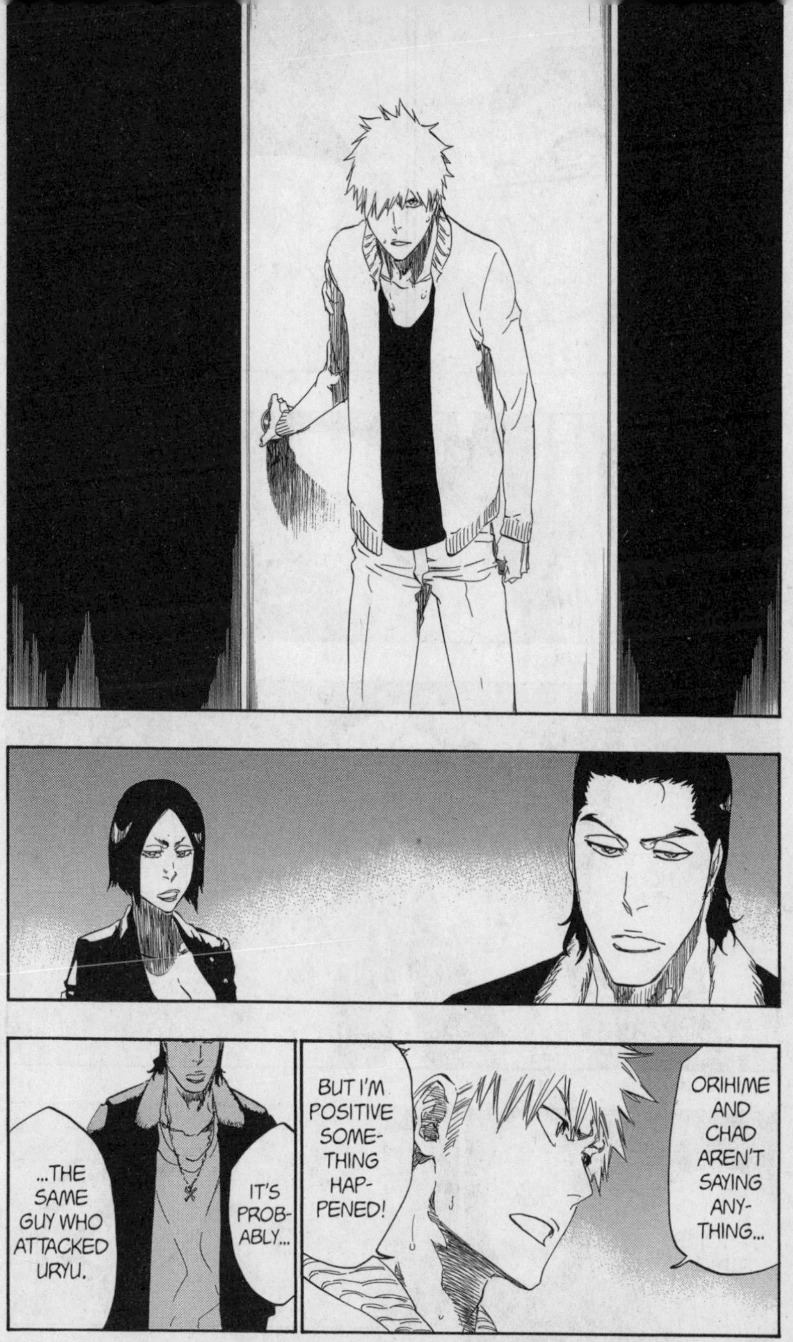
ORIHIME AND CHAD AREN'T SAYING ANY-THING...
BUT I'M POSITIVE SOME-THING HAP-PENED!
IT'S PROB-ABLY...
...THE SAME GUY WHO ATTACKED URYU.

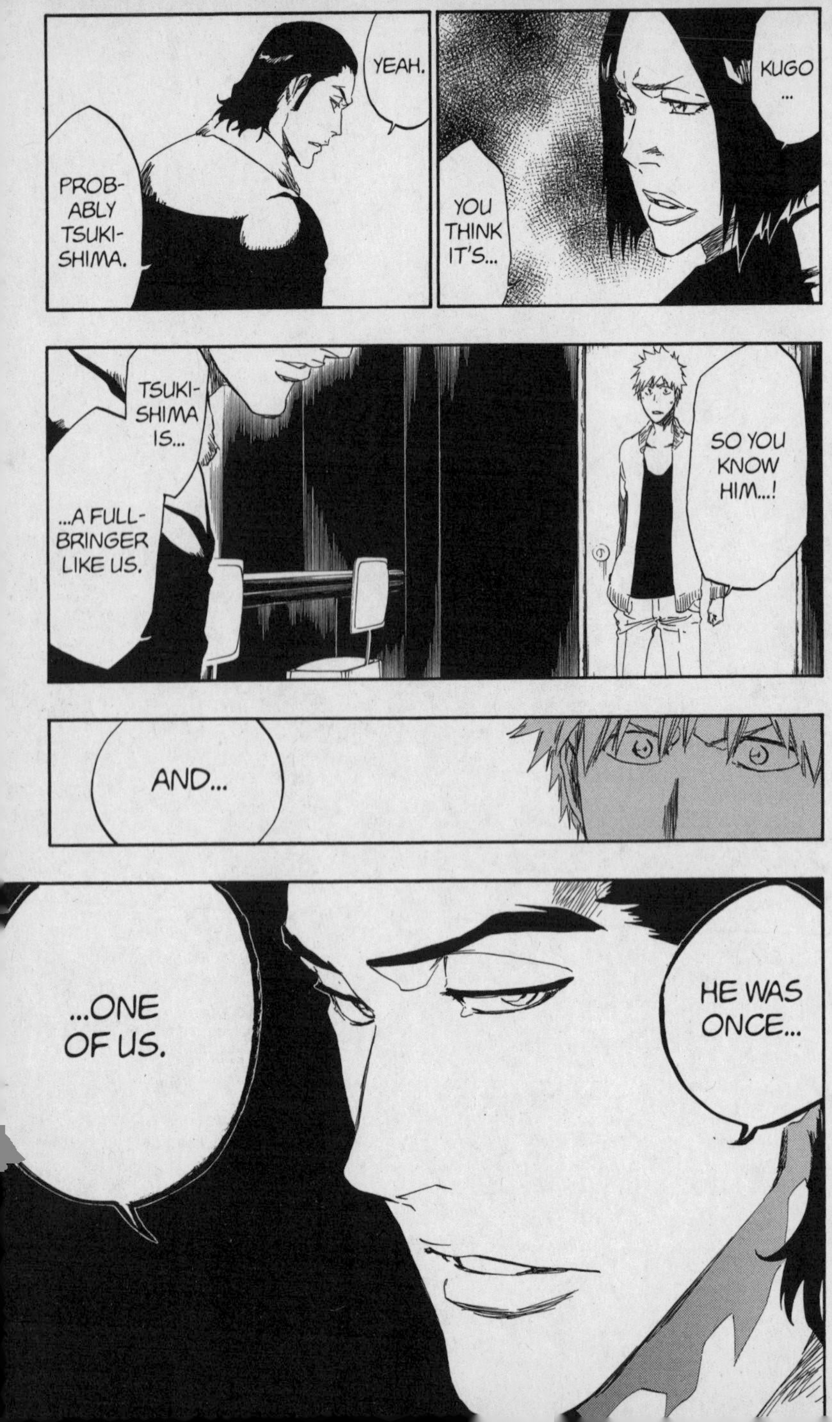
KUGO ...
YOU THINK IT'S...
YEAH.
PROB-ABLY TSUKI-SHIMA.
SO YOU KNOW HIM...!
TSUKI-SHIMA IS...
...A FULL-BRINGER LIKE US.
AND...
HE WAS ONCE...
...ONE OF US.

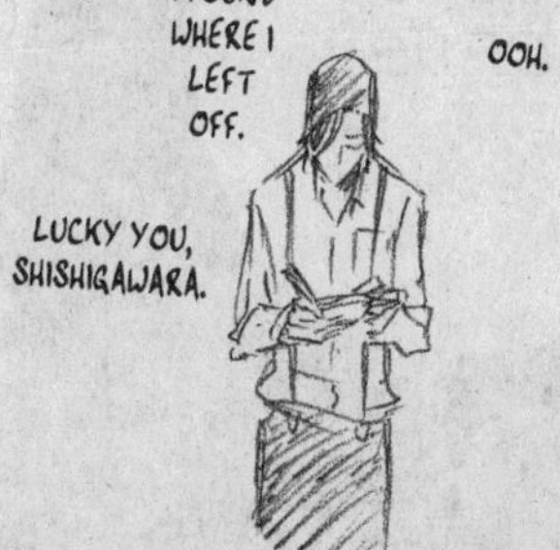
OOH.
I FOUND WHERE I LEFT OFF.
LUCKY YOU, SHISHIGAWARA.

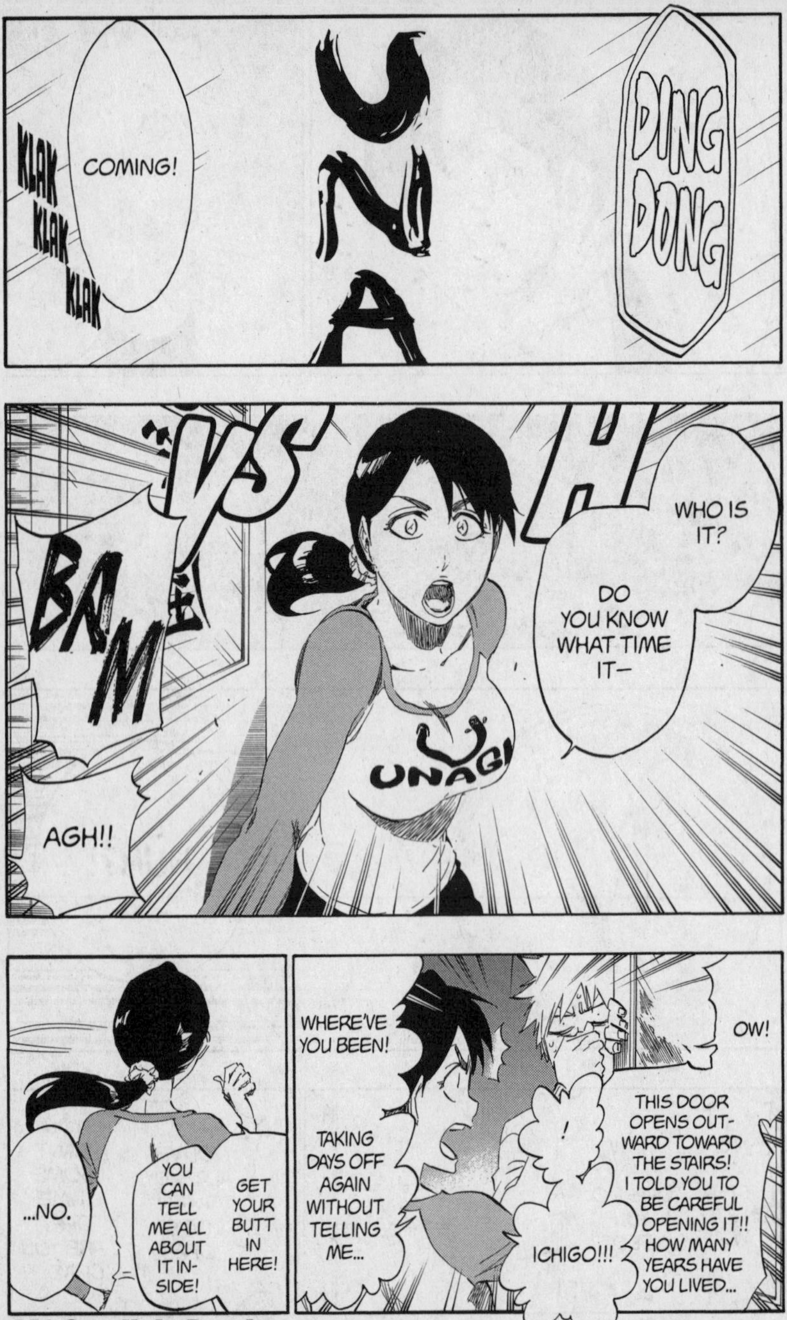
DING DONG
UNA
COMING!
KLAK KLAK KLAK
WHO IS IT?
DO YOU KNOW WHAT TIME IT—
BAM
AGH!!
OW!
WHERE'VE YOU BEEN!
THIS DOOR OPENS OUTWARD TOWARD THE STAIRS! I TOLD YOU TO BE CAREFUL OPENING IT!! HOW MANY YEARS HAVE YOU LIVED...
!
TAKING DAYS OFF AGAIN WITHOUT TELLING ME...
ICHIGO!!!
GET YOUR BUTT IN HERE!
YOU CAN TELL ME ALL ABOUT IT INSIDE!
...NO.

441. Spotlight Brocken

I'M FINE RIGHT HERE.
WHY...?
HUH?!
YOU WANT SOME TIME OFF?! ARE YOU CRAZY?!
YOU'VE ALREADY TAKEN DAYS OFF!!
HOW MANY DAYS DO YOU NEED?!
ARE YOU LISTEN-ING TO ME?!

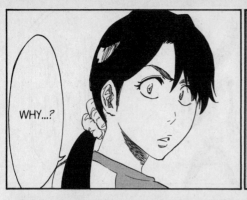

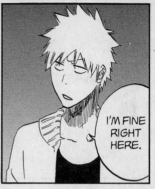

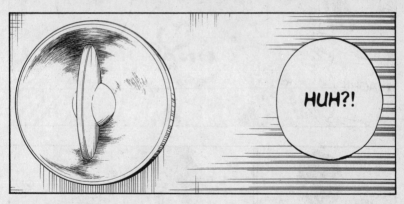

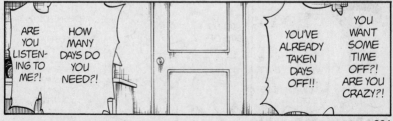

READ THIS WAY

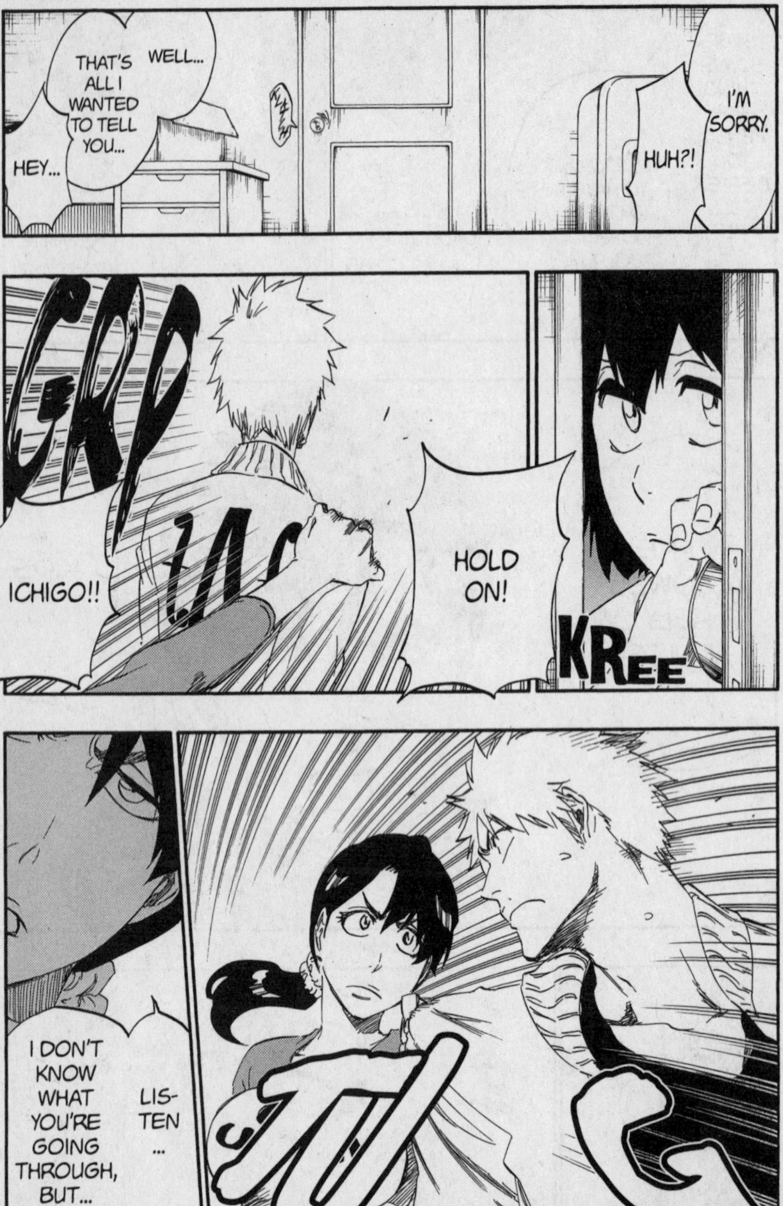
I'M SORRY.
HUH?!
WELL...
THAT'S ALL I WANTED TO TELL YOU...
HEY...
KREE
HOLD ON!
ICHIGO!!
LIS-TEN...
I DON'T KNOW WHAT YOU'RE GOING THROUGH, BUT...

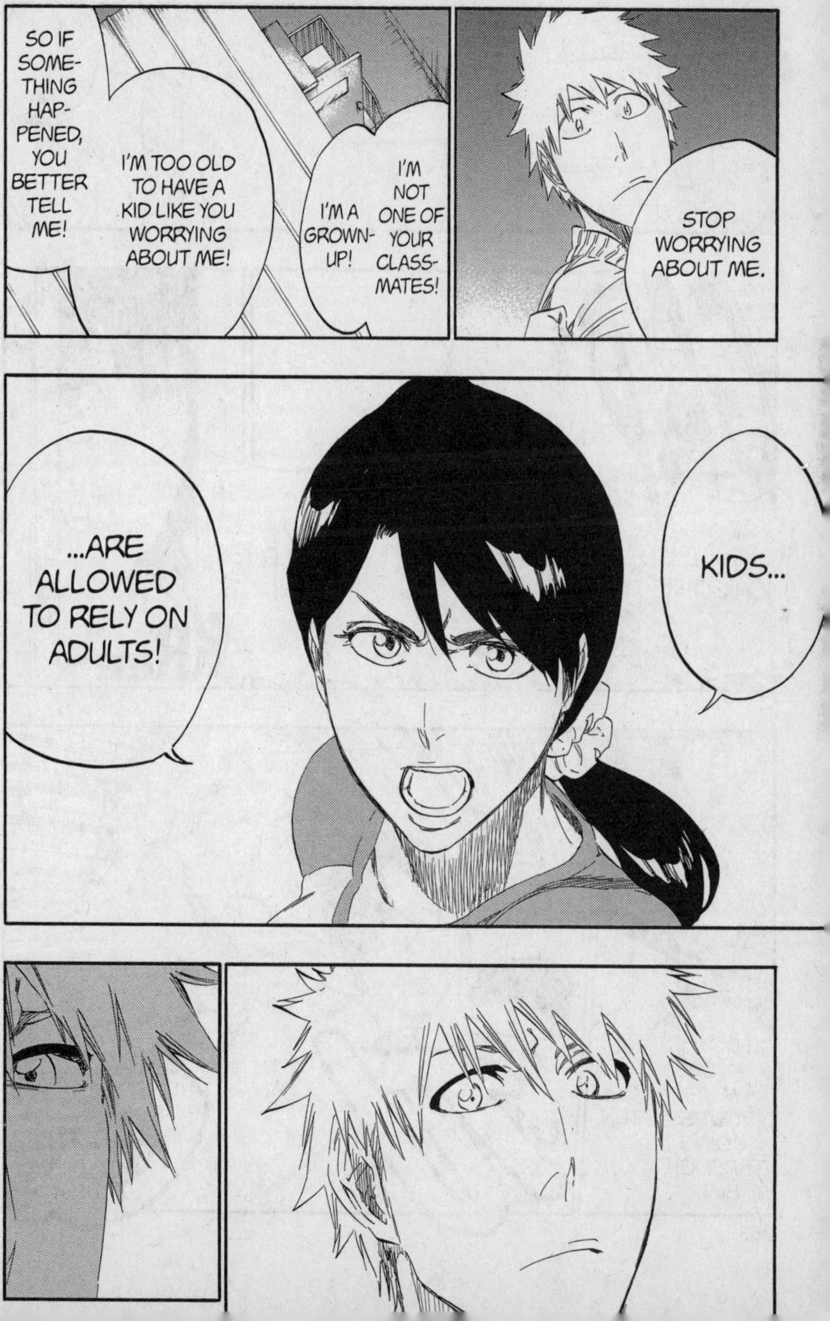
STOP WORRYING ABOUT ME.
I'M NOT ONE OF YOUR CLASSMATES!
I'M A GROWN-UP!
I'M TOO OLD TO HAVE A KID LIKE YOU WORRYING ABOUT ME!
SO IF SOMETHING HAPPENED, YOU BETTER TELL ME!
KIDS...
...ARE ALLOWED TO RELY ON ADULTS!

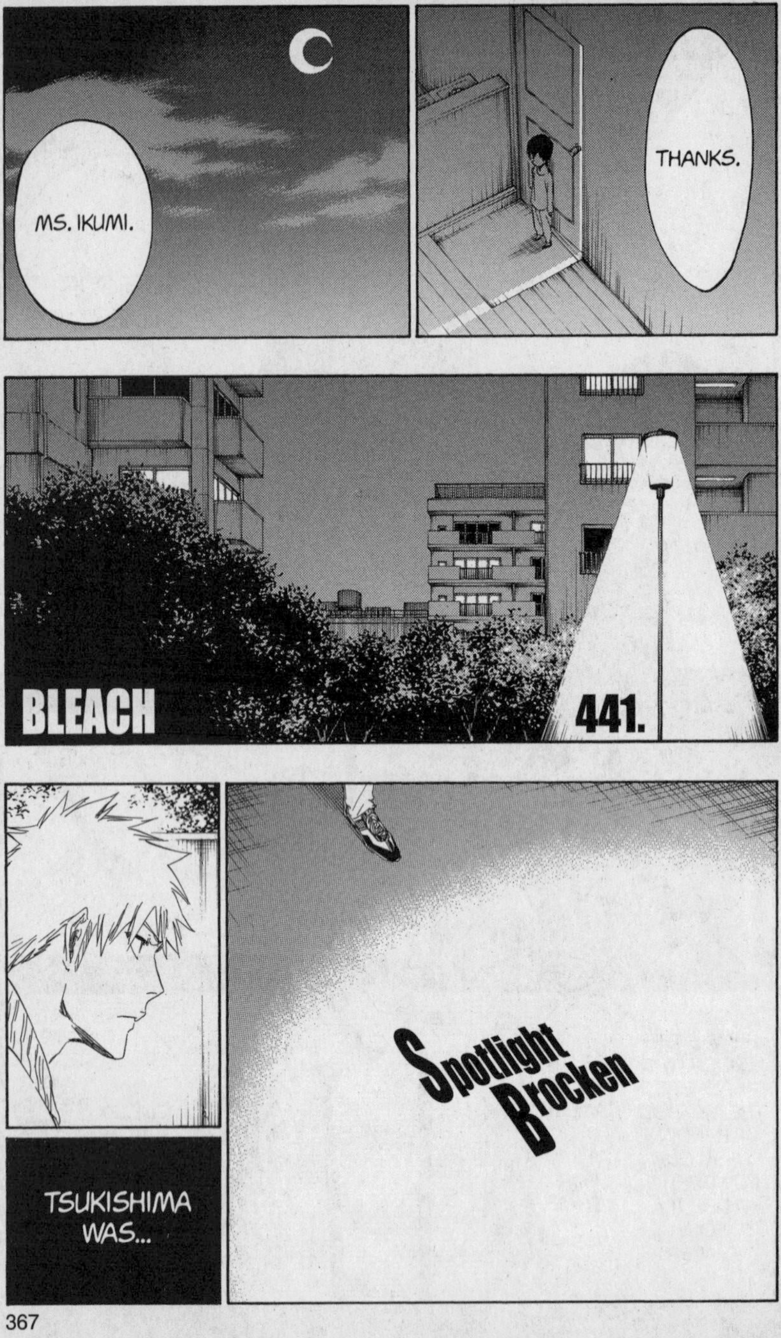
THANKS.
MS. IKUMI.
BLEACH
441.
Spotlight Brocken
TSUKISHIMA WAS...

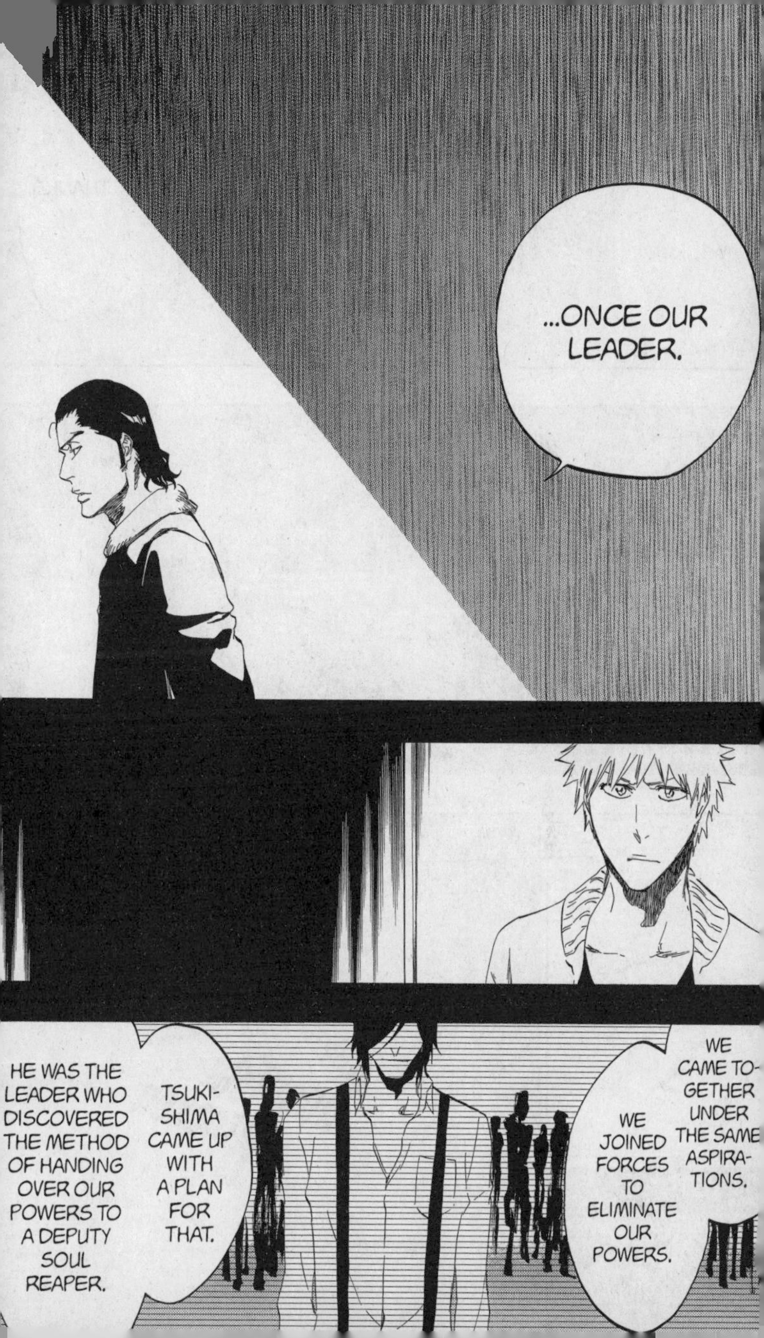
...ONCE OUR LEADER.
WE CAME TO-GETHER UNDER THE SAME ASPIRA-TIONS.
WE JOINED FORCES TO ELIMINATE OUR POWERS.
TSUKI-SHIMA CAME UP WITH A PLAN FOR THAT.
HE WAS THE LEADER WHO DISCOVERED THE METHOD OF HANDING OVER OUR POWERS TO A DEPUTY SOUL REAPER.

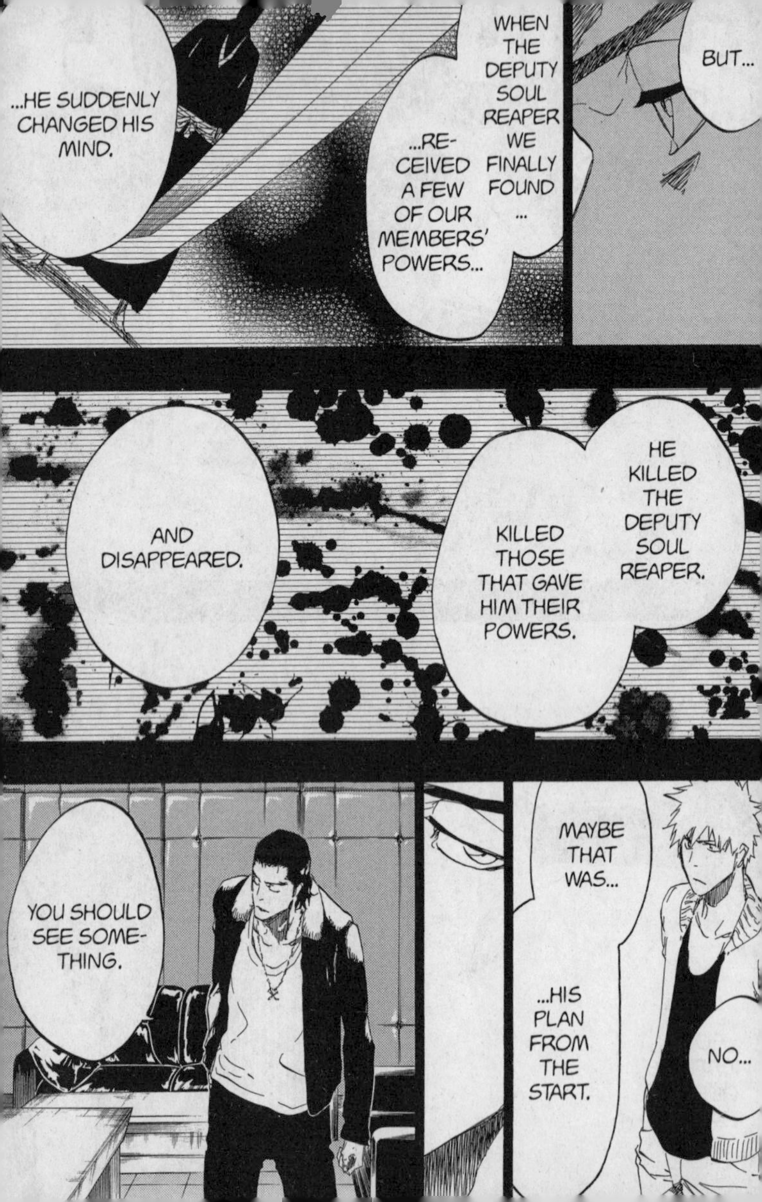
BUT...
WHEN THE DEPUTY SOUL REAPER WE FINALLY FOUND...
...RE-CEIVED A FEW OF OUR MEMBERS' POWERS...
...HE SUDDENLY CHANGED HIS MIND.
HE KILLED THE DEPUTY SOUL REAPER.
KILLED THOSE THAT GAVE HIM THEIR POWERS.
AND DISAPPEARED.
MAYBE THAT WAS...
...HIS PLAN FROM THE START.
NO...
YOU SHOULD SEE SOME-THING.

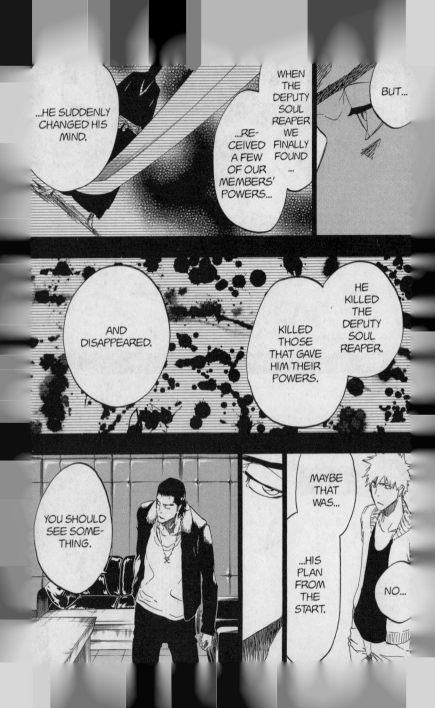

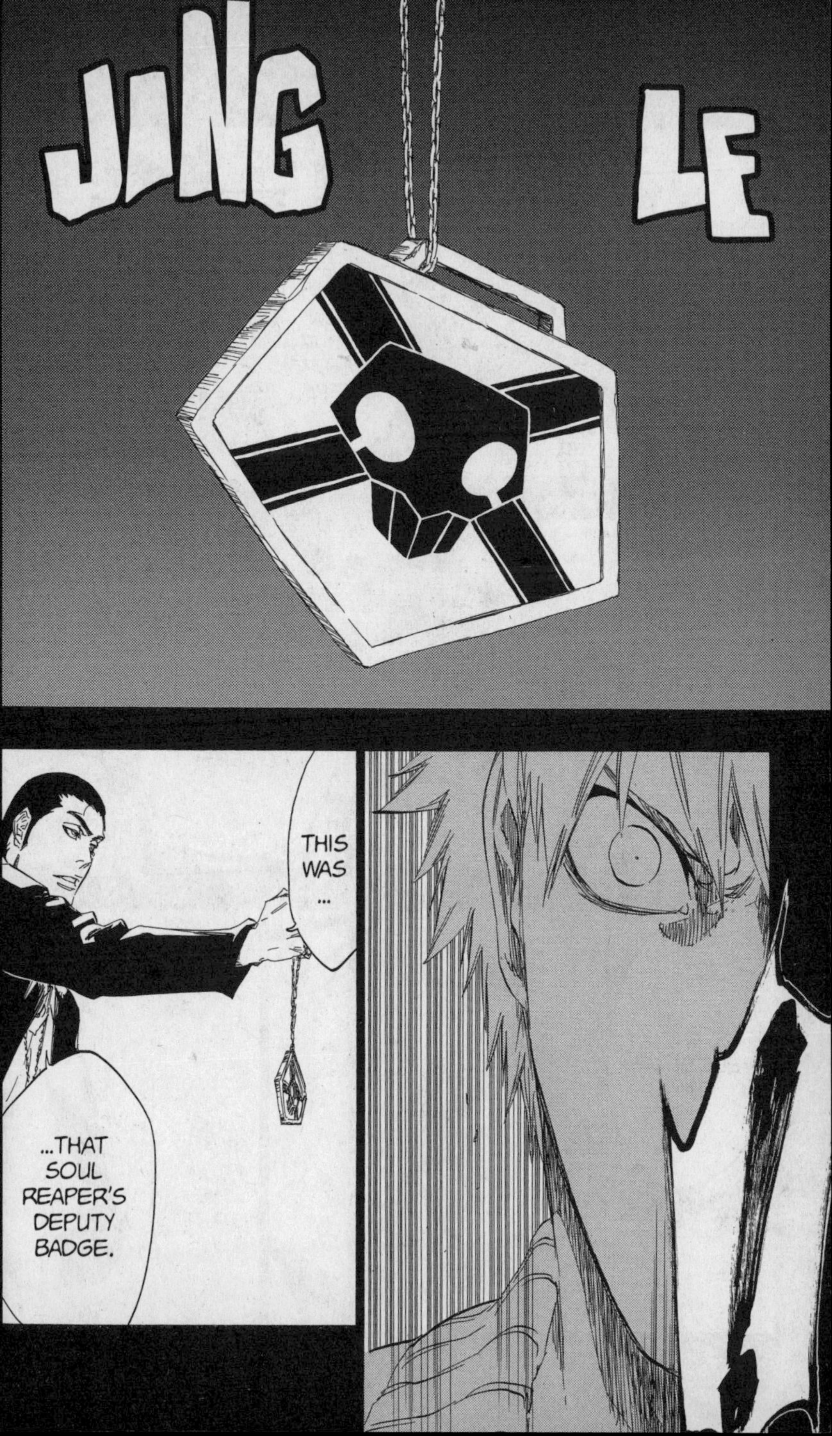
JINGLE
THIS WAS...
...THAT SOUL REAPER'S DEPUTY BADGE.

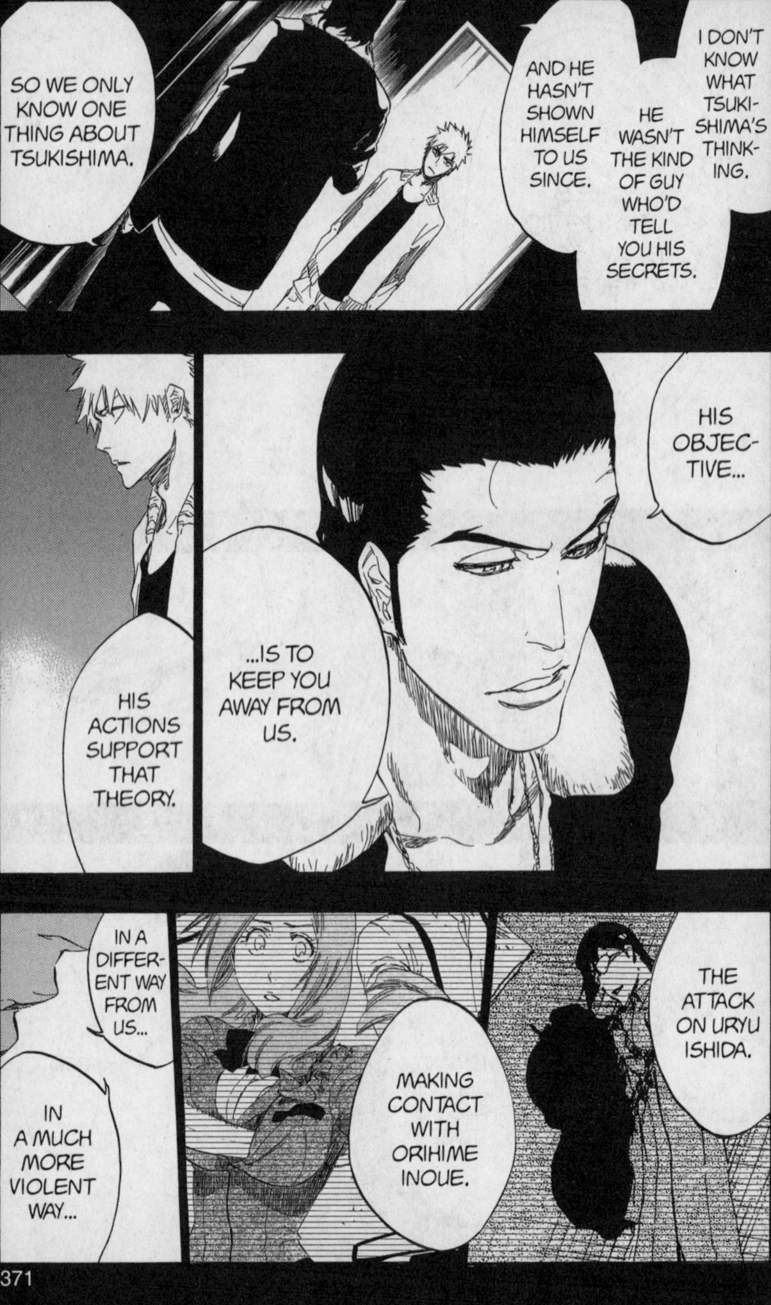
I DON'T KNOW WHAT TSUKISHIMA'S THINKING.
HE WASN'T THE KIND OF GUY WHO'D TELL YOU HIS SECRETS.
AND HE HASN'T SHOWN HIMSELF TO US SINCE.
SO WE ONLY KNOW ONE THING ABOUT TSUKISHIMA.
HIS OBJECTIVE...
...IS TO KEEP YOU AWAY FROM US.
HIS ACTIONS SUPPORT THAT THEORY.
THE ATTACK ON URYU ISHIDA.
MAKING CONTACT WITH ORIHIME INOUE.
IN A DIFFERENT WAY FROM US...
IN A MUCH MORE VIOLENT WAY...

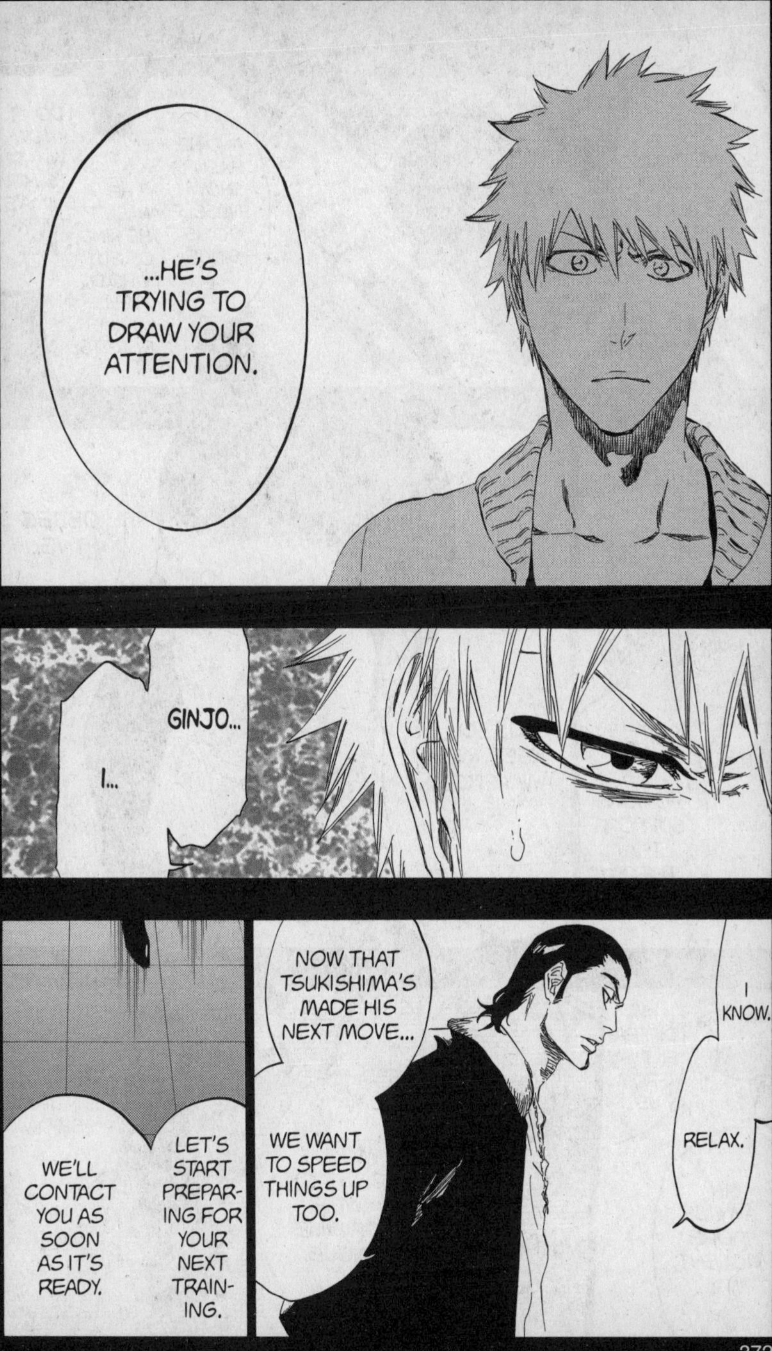
...HE'S TRYING TO DRAW YOUR ATTENTION.
GINJO...
I...
I KNOW.
NOW THAT TSUKISHIMA'S MADE HIS NEXT MOVE...
RELAX.
WE WANT TO SPEED THINGS UP TOO.
LET'S START PREPAR-ING FOR YOUR NEXT TRAIN-ING.
WE'LL CONTACT YOU AS SOON AS IT'S READY.

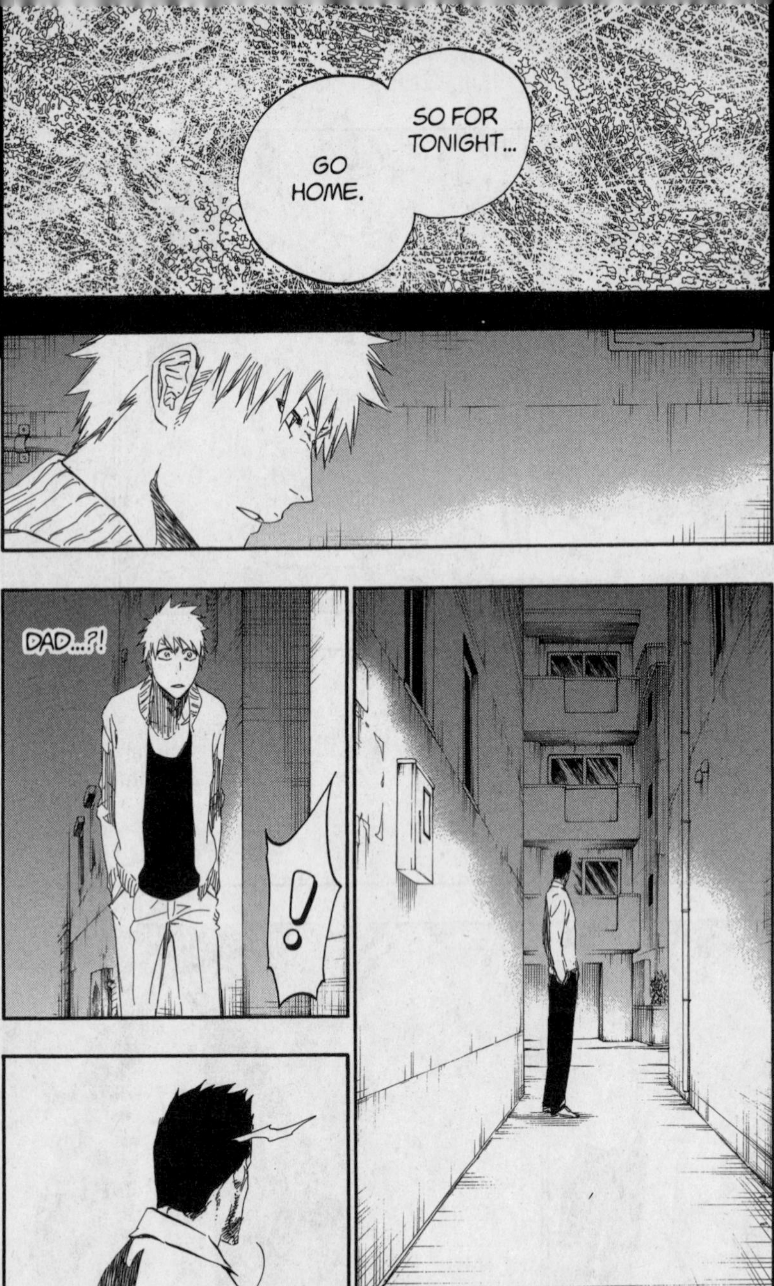
SO FOR TONIGHT...
GO HOME.
DAD...?!
!

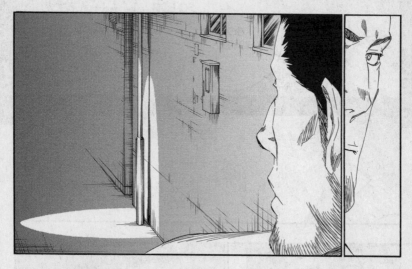

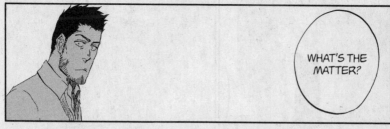

WHAT'S THE MATTER?

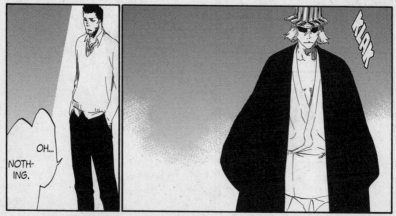

OH... NOTH- ING.

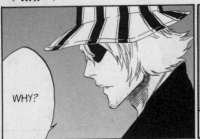

WHY?

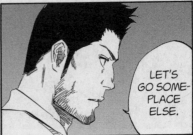

LET'S GO SOME-PLACE ELSE.

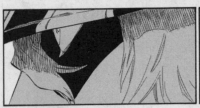

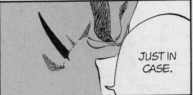

JUST IN CASE.

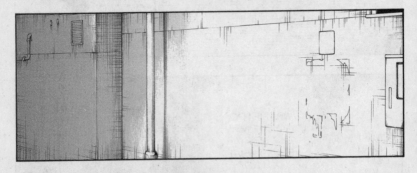

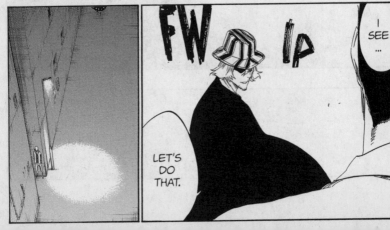

FW IP

I SEE...

LET'S DO THAT.

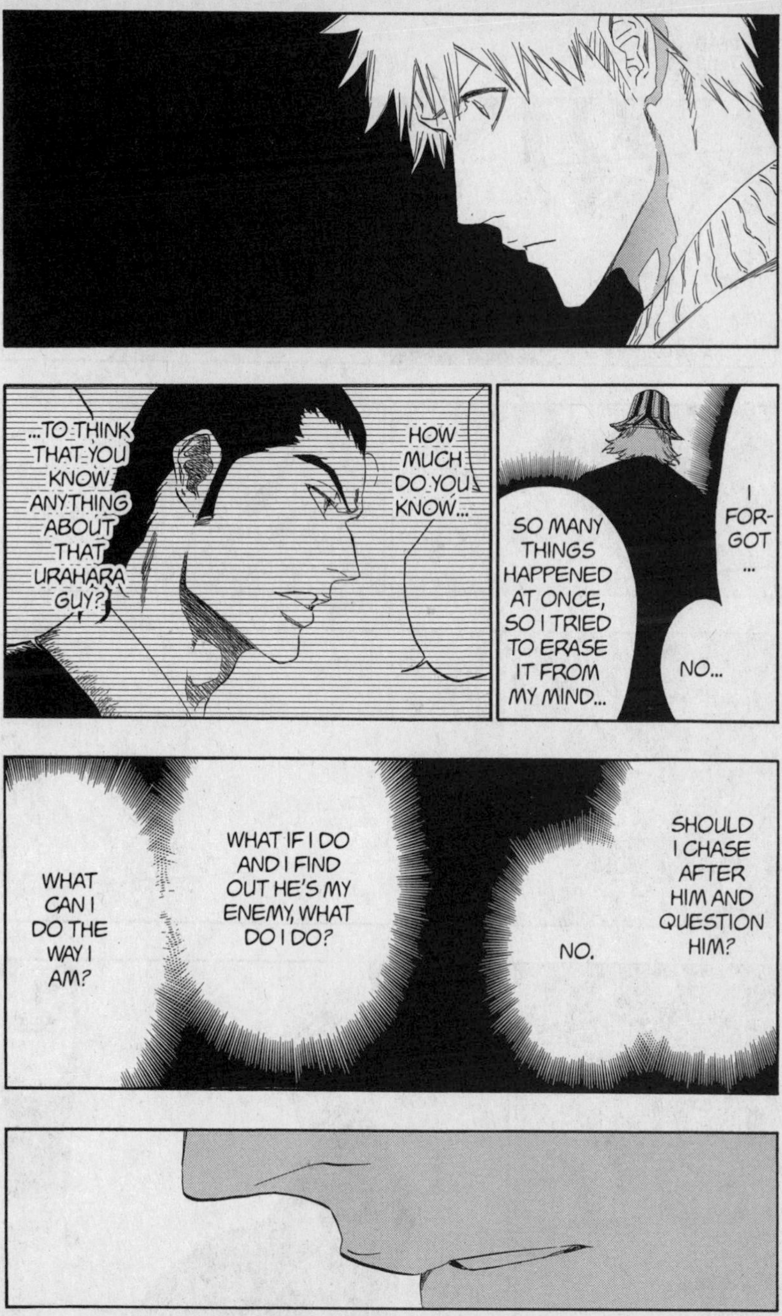
I FORGOT...
NO...
SO MANY THINGS HAPPENED AT ONCE, SO I TRIED TO ERASE IT FROM MY MIND...
HOW MUCH DO YOU KNOW...
...TO THINK THAT YOU KNOW ANYTHING ABOUT THAT URAHARA GUY?
SHOULD I CHASE AFTER HIM AND QUESTION HIM?
NO.
WHAT IF I DO AND I FIND OUT HE'S MY ENEMY, WHAT DO I DO?
WHAT CAN I DO THE WAY I AM?

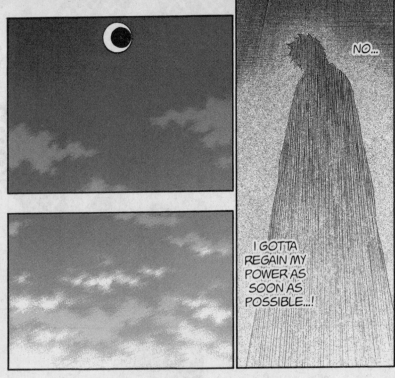

NO...

I GOTTA
REGAIN MY
POWER AS
SOON AS
POSSIBLE...!

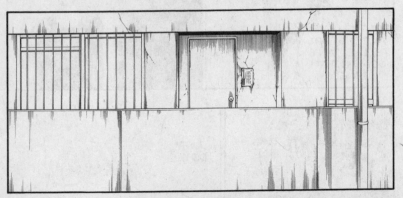

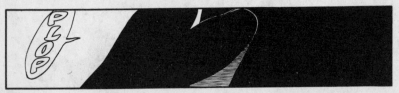

PLOP

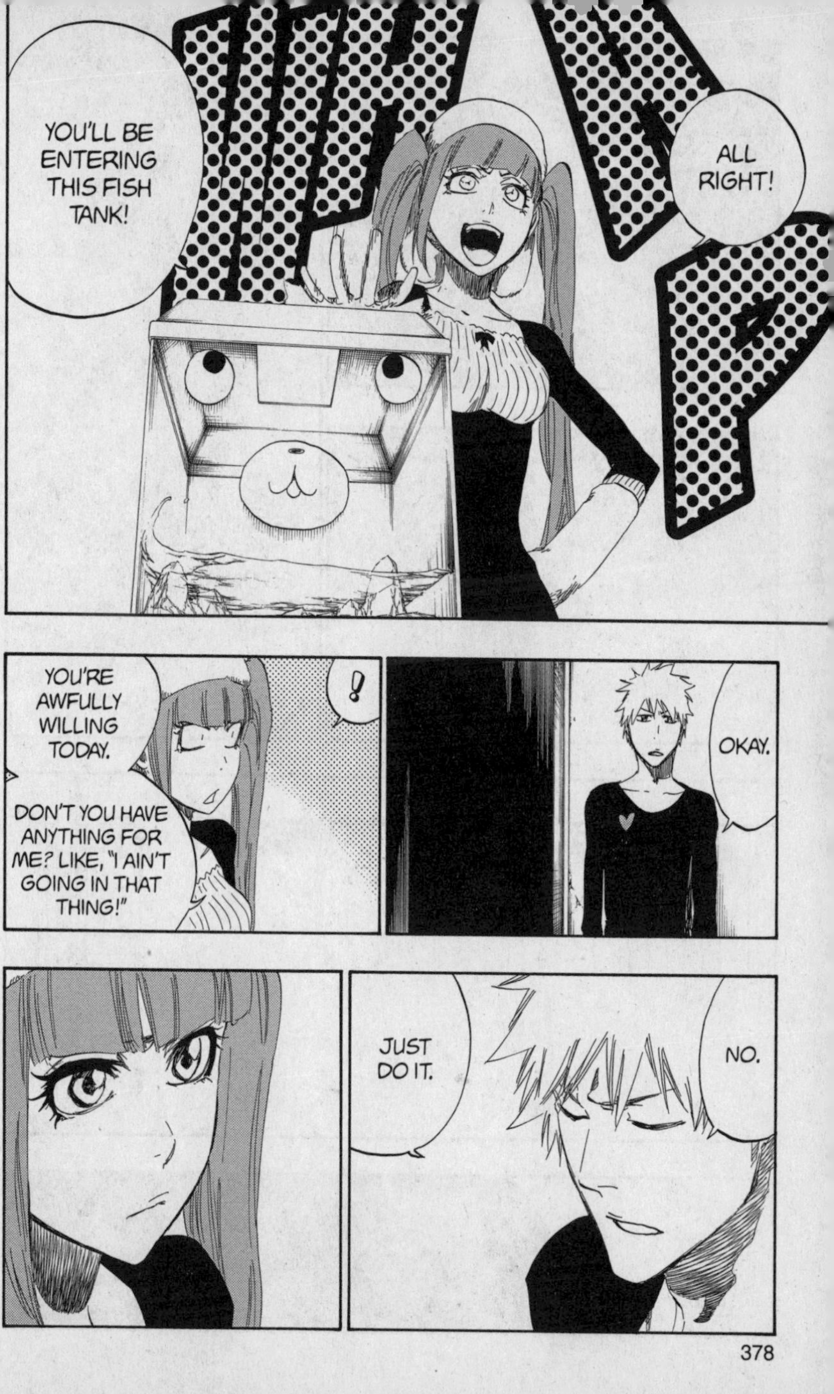
ALL RIGHT!
YOU'LL BE ENTERING THIS FISH TANK!
OKAY.
!
YOU'RE AWFULLY WILLING TODAY.
DON'T YOU HAVE ANYTHING FOR ME? LIKE, "I AIN'T GOING IN THAT THING!"
NO.
JUST DO IT.

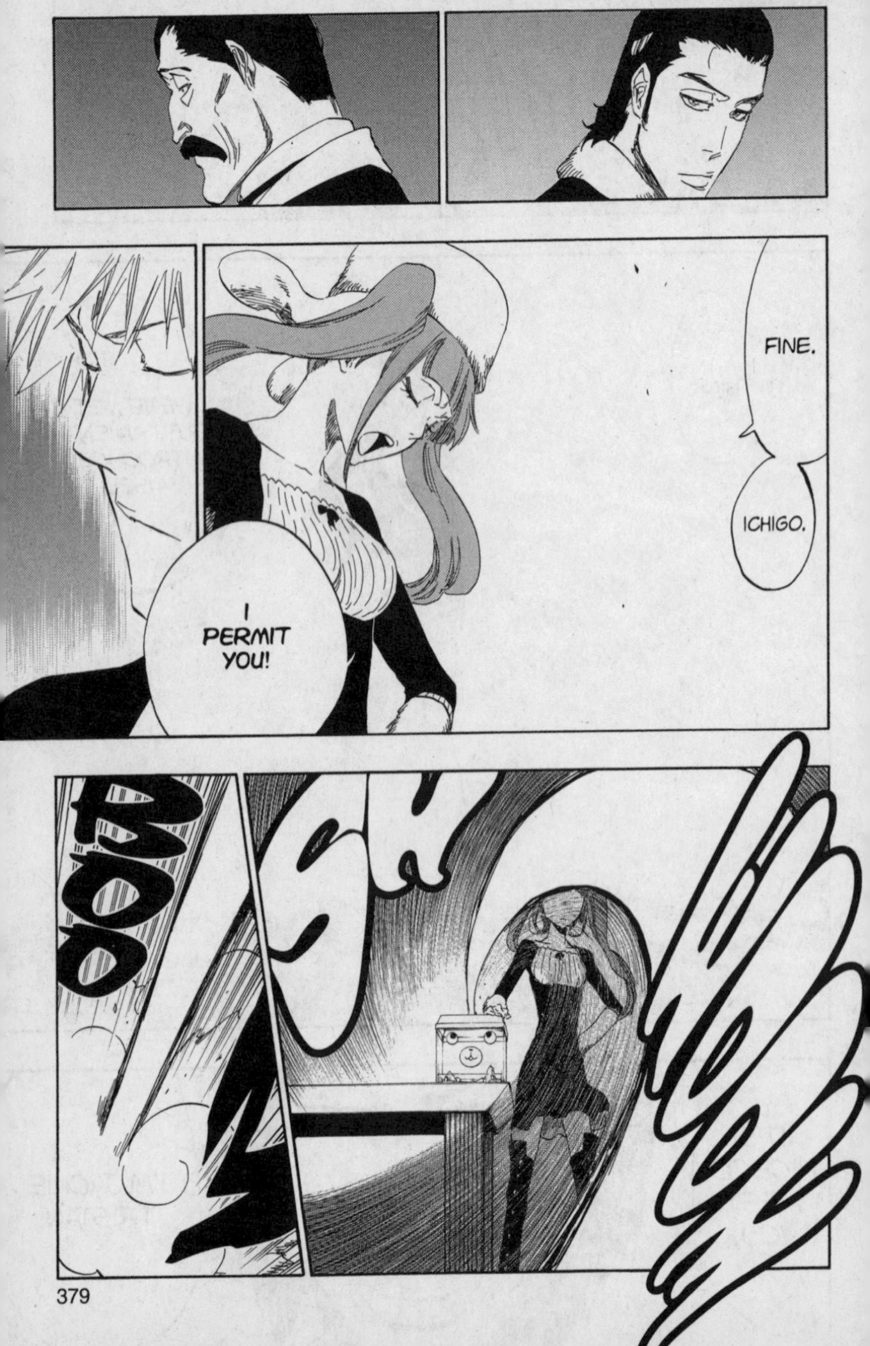
FINE.
ICHIGO.
I PERMIT YOU!

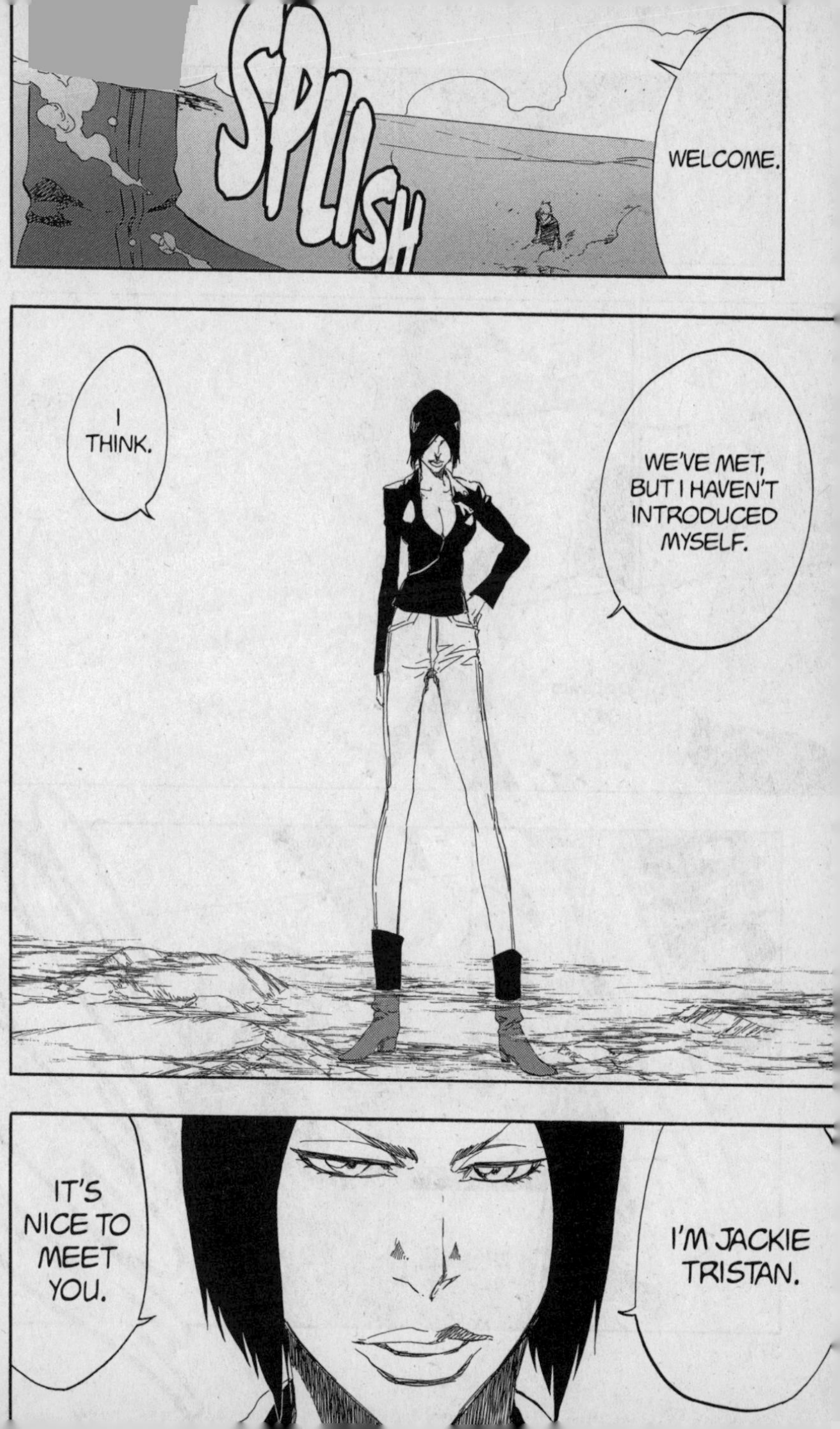
SPLISH
WELCOME.
WE'VE MET, BUT I HAVEN'T INTRODUCED MYSELF.
I THINK.
I'M JACKIE TRISTAN.
IT'S NICE TO MEET YOU.

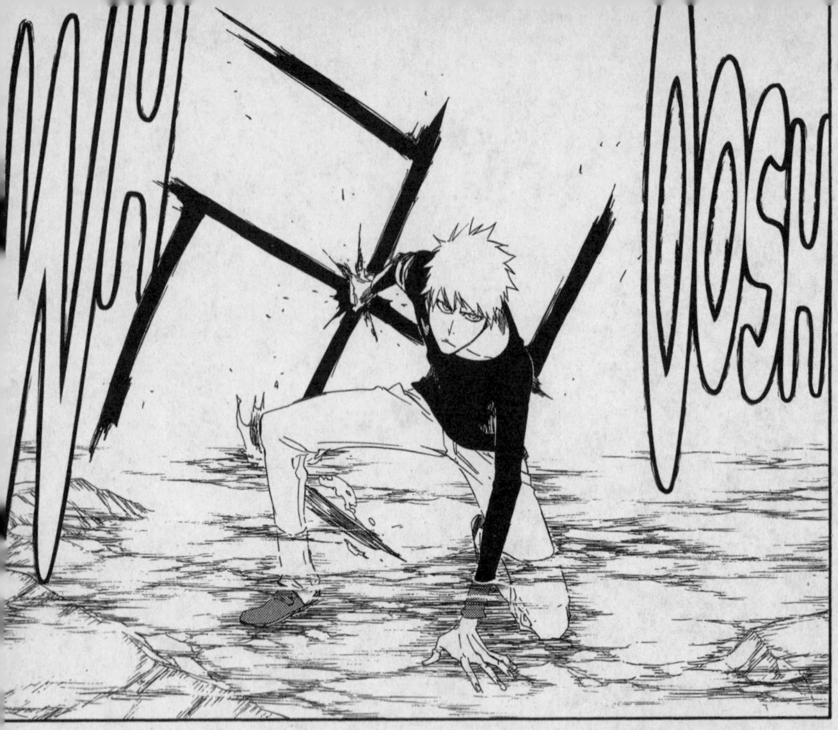
WH
OOSH

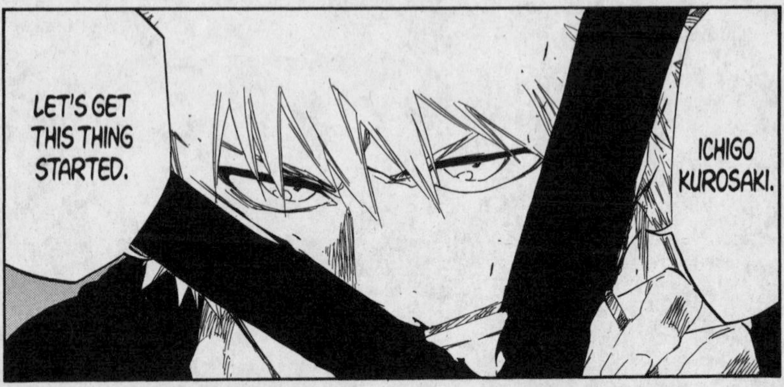
ICHIGO KUROSAKI.
LET'S GET THIS THING STARTED.

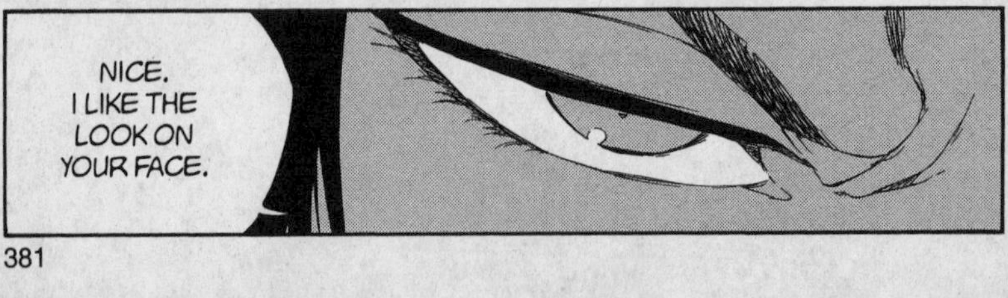
NICE. I LIKE THE LOOK ON YOUR FACE.

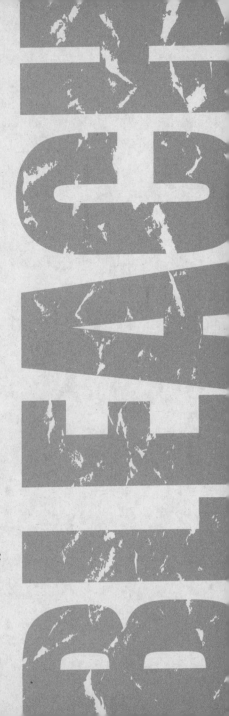

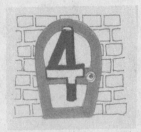

I've been so busy lately for the first time in a while. I haven't been able to go out and play for days. When I can't go out and play, I have nothing to write here. So when I'm busy, I wish this segment didn't exist. I've already spent four hours thinking of what to write. Good, it's filled now!

-Tite Kubo, 2011

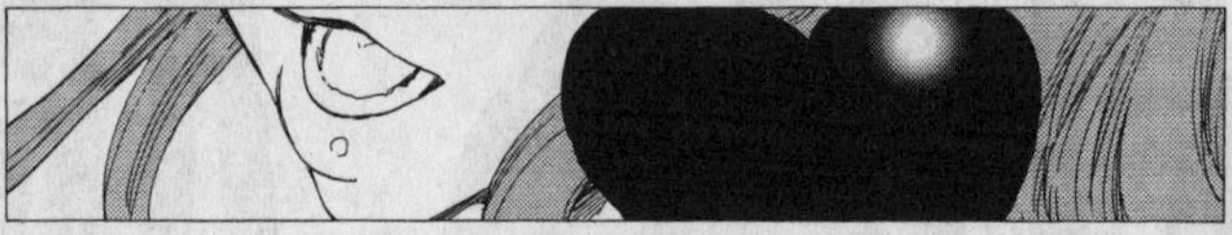

Don't put your finger

In my heart

BLEACH51

Love me Bitterly Loth me Sweetly

Shonen Jump Manga

STARS AND

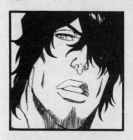

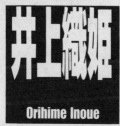

Orihime Inoue

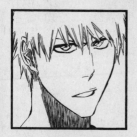

Chad Yasutora

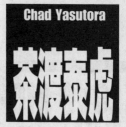

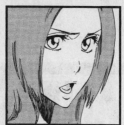

Ichigo Kurosaki

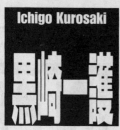

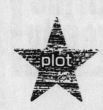

plot

Ichigo Kurosaki meets Soul Reaper Rukia Kuchiki and ends up helping her eradicate Hollows. After developing his powers as a Soul Reaper, Ichigo enters battle against Aizen and his dark ambitions! Ichigo finally defeats Aizen in exchange for his powers as a Soul Reaper.

With the battle over, Ichigo regains his normal daily life. But his tranquil life ends when Ishida is attacked by an unknown assailant. Ichigo then meets Ginjo, whose objective is to help Ichigo regain his Soul Reaper powers. Ichigo then begins his training to gain a new power known as Fullbring. At the same time, Orihime comes in contact with a mysterious figure named Tsukishima. Ichigo grows impatient when he learns he is the target!!

BLEACH ALL

月島秀九郎

Shukuro Tsukishima

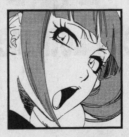

銀城空吾

Kugo Ginjo

Riruka Dokugamine

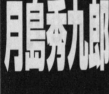

毒ヶ峰リルカ

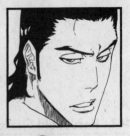

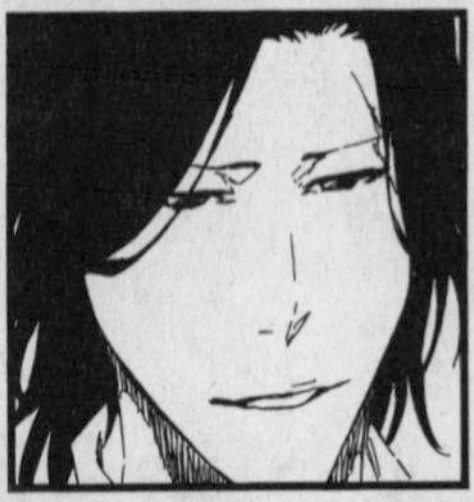

STORIES

BLEACH51

Love me Bitterly Loth me Sweetly

Contents

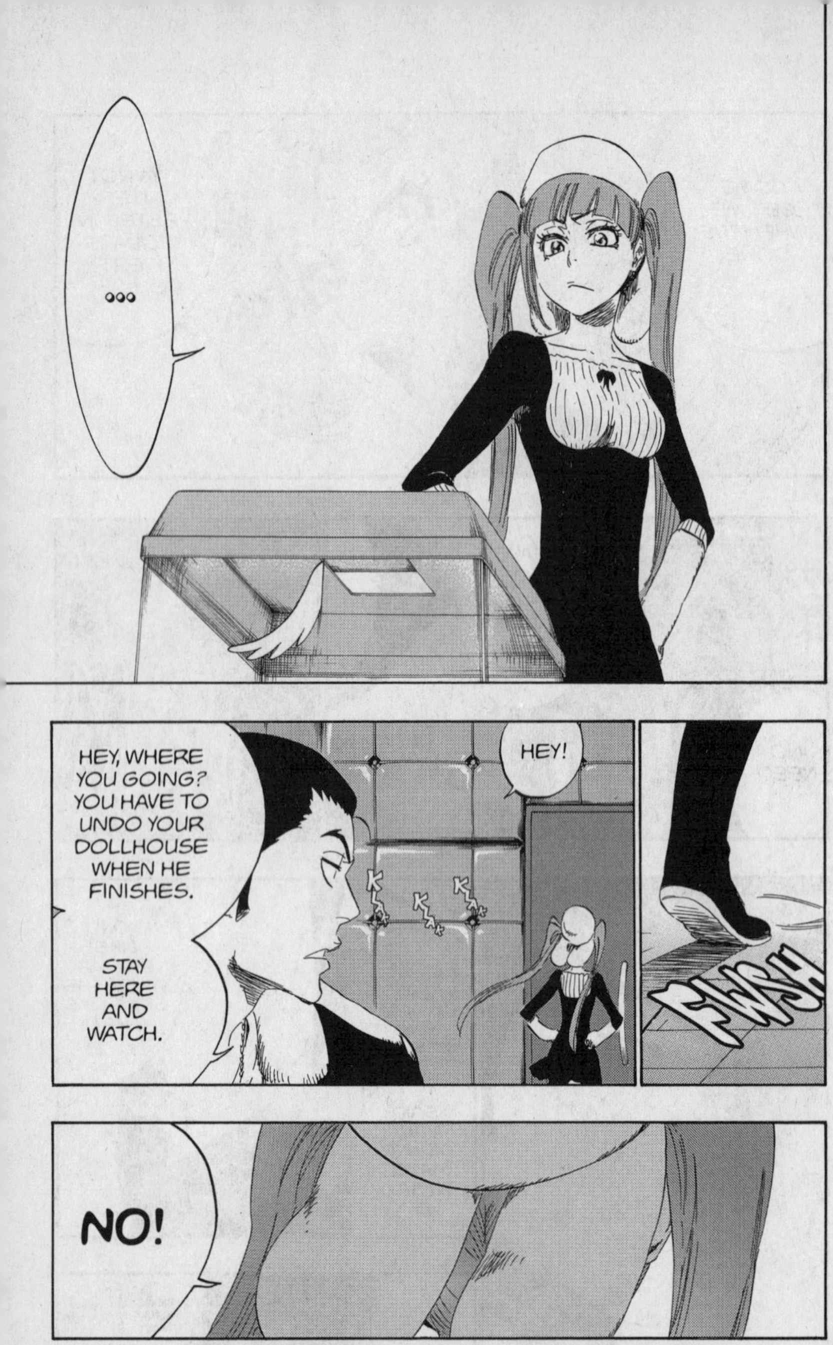
...
FWSH
HEY!
KLAK KLAK KLAK
HEY, WHERE YOU GOING? YOU HAVE TO UNDO YOUR DOLLHOUSE WHEN HE FINISHES.
STAY HERE AND WATCH.
NO!

442. Battlefield Shallows, Otherfield Abyss

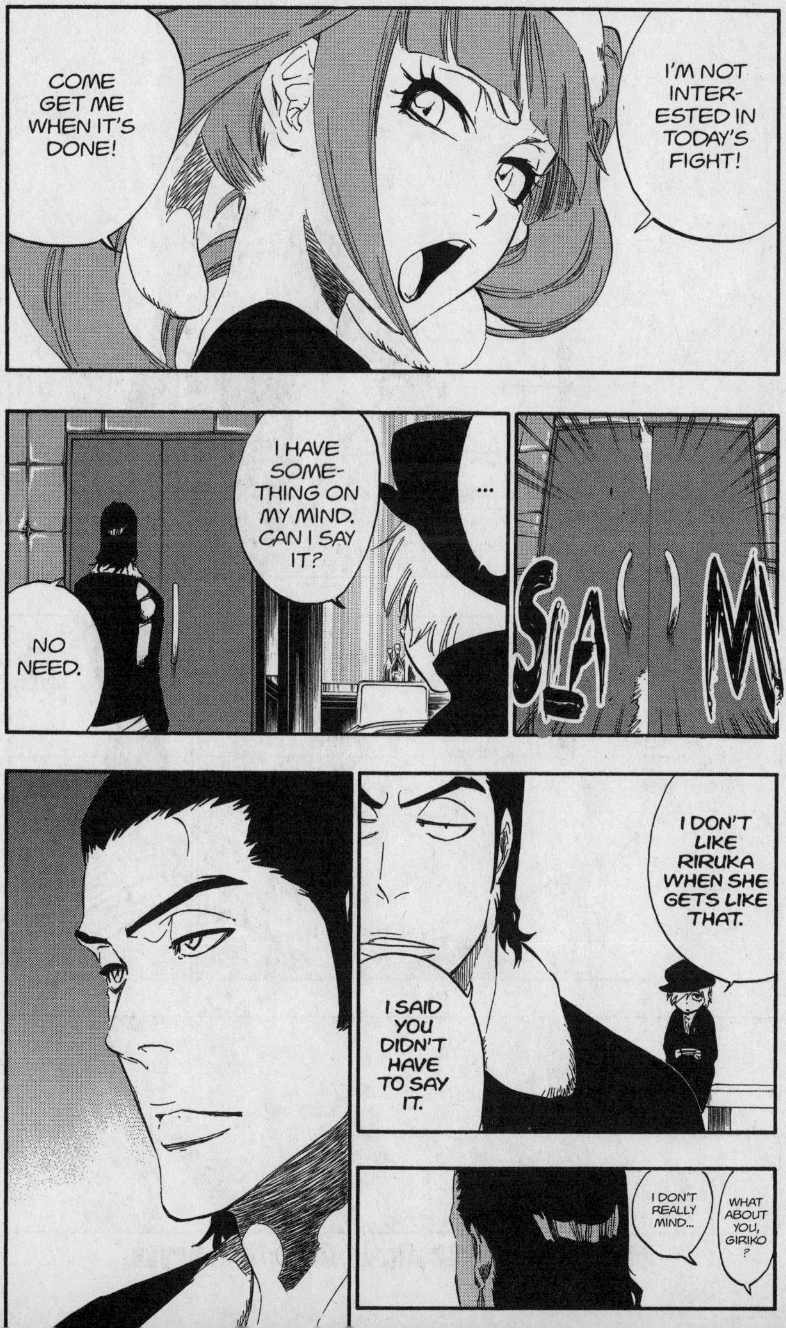
I'M NOT INTER-ESTED IN TODAY'S FIGHT!
COME GET ME WHEN IT'S DONE!
SLAM
...
I HAVE SOME-THING ON MY MIND. CAN I SAY IT?
NO NEED.
I DON'T LIKE RIRUKA WHEN SHE GETS LIKE THAT.
I SAID YOU DIDN'T HAVE TO SAY IT.
WHAT ABOUT YOU, GIRIKO?
I DON'T REALLY MIND...

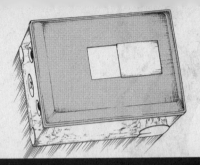

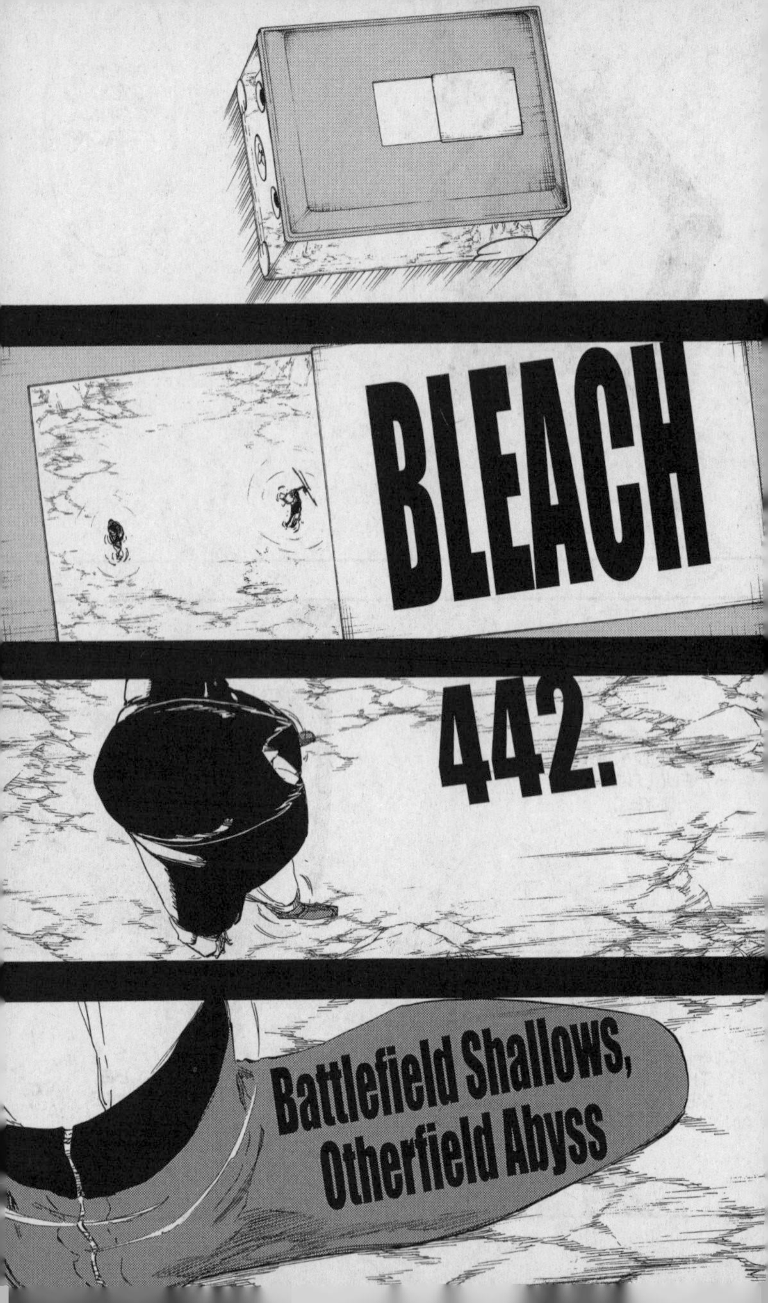

BLEACH

442.

Battlefield Shallows, Otherfield Abyss

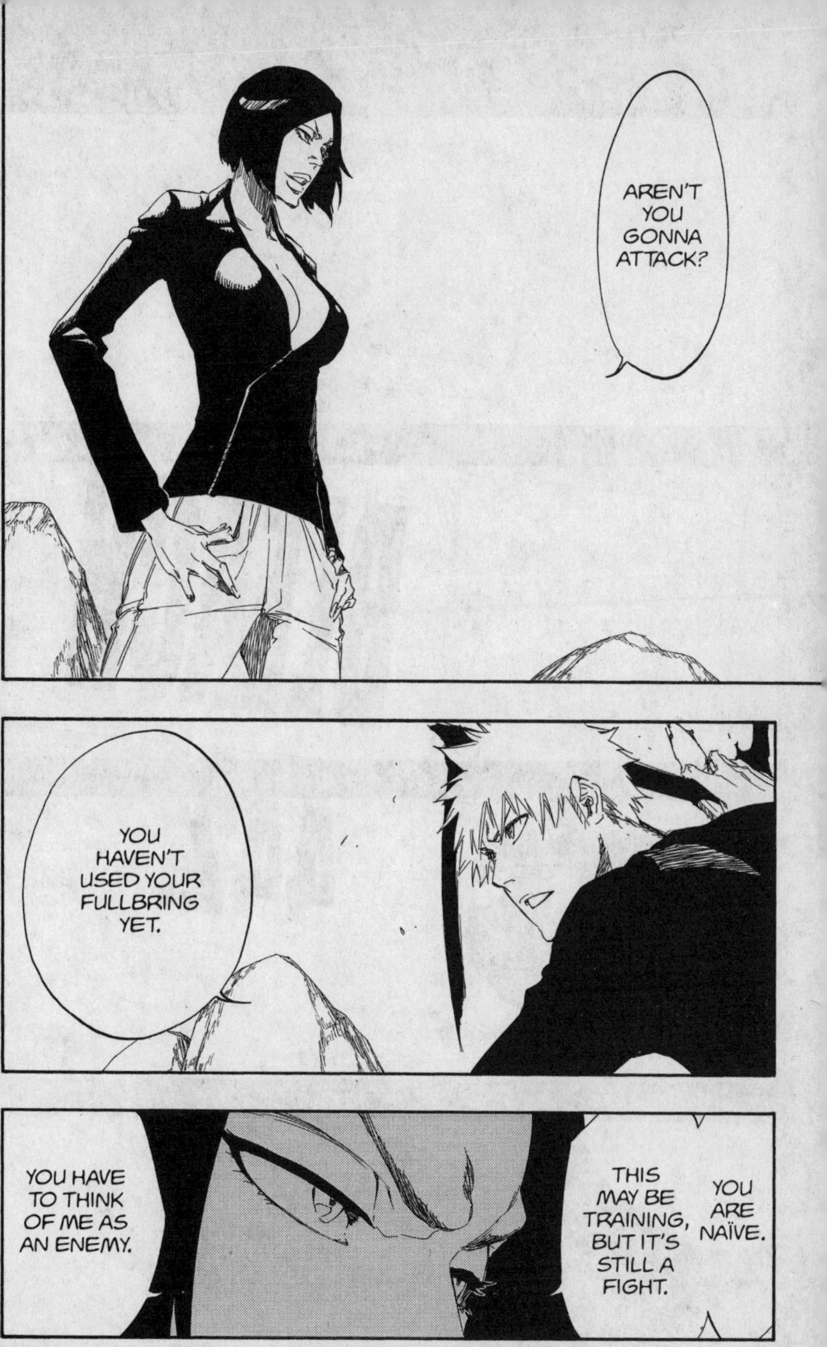
AREN'T YOU GONNA ATTACK?
YOU HAVEN'T USED YOUR FULLBRING YET.
YOU ARE NAÏVE.
THIS MAY BE TRAINING, BUT IT'S STILL A FIGHT.
YOU HAVE TO THINK OF ME AS AN ENEMY.

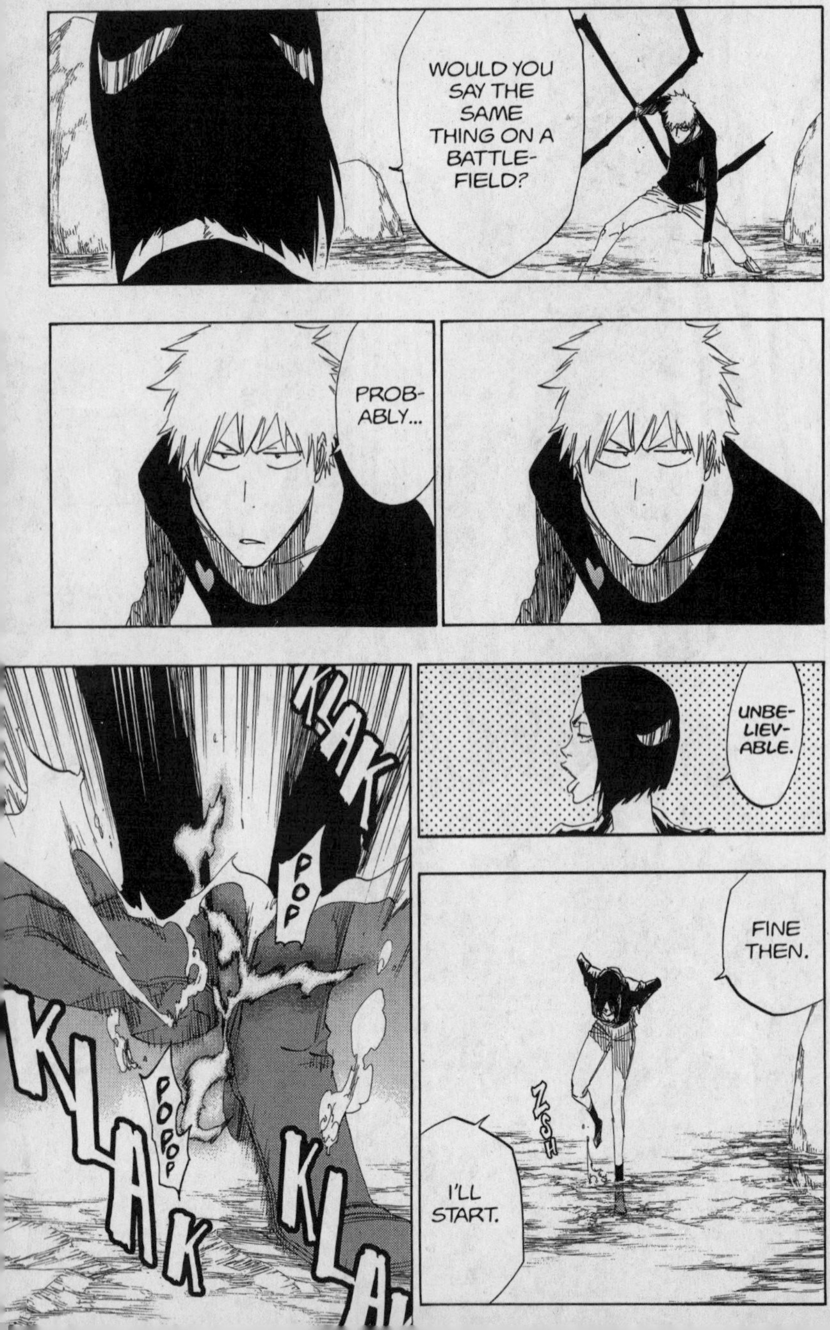
WOULD YOU SAY THE SAME THING ON A BATTLE-FIELD?
PROB-ABLY...
UNBE-LIEV-ABLE.
FINE THEN.
I'LL START.
ZSH
KLAK
POP
POPOPOP
KLAK
KLAK

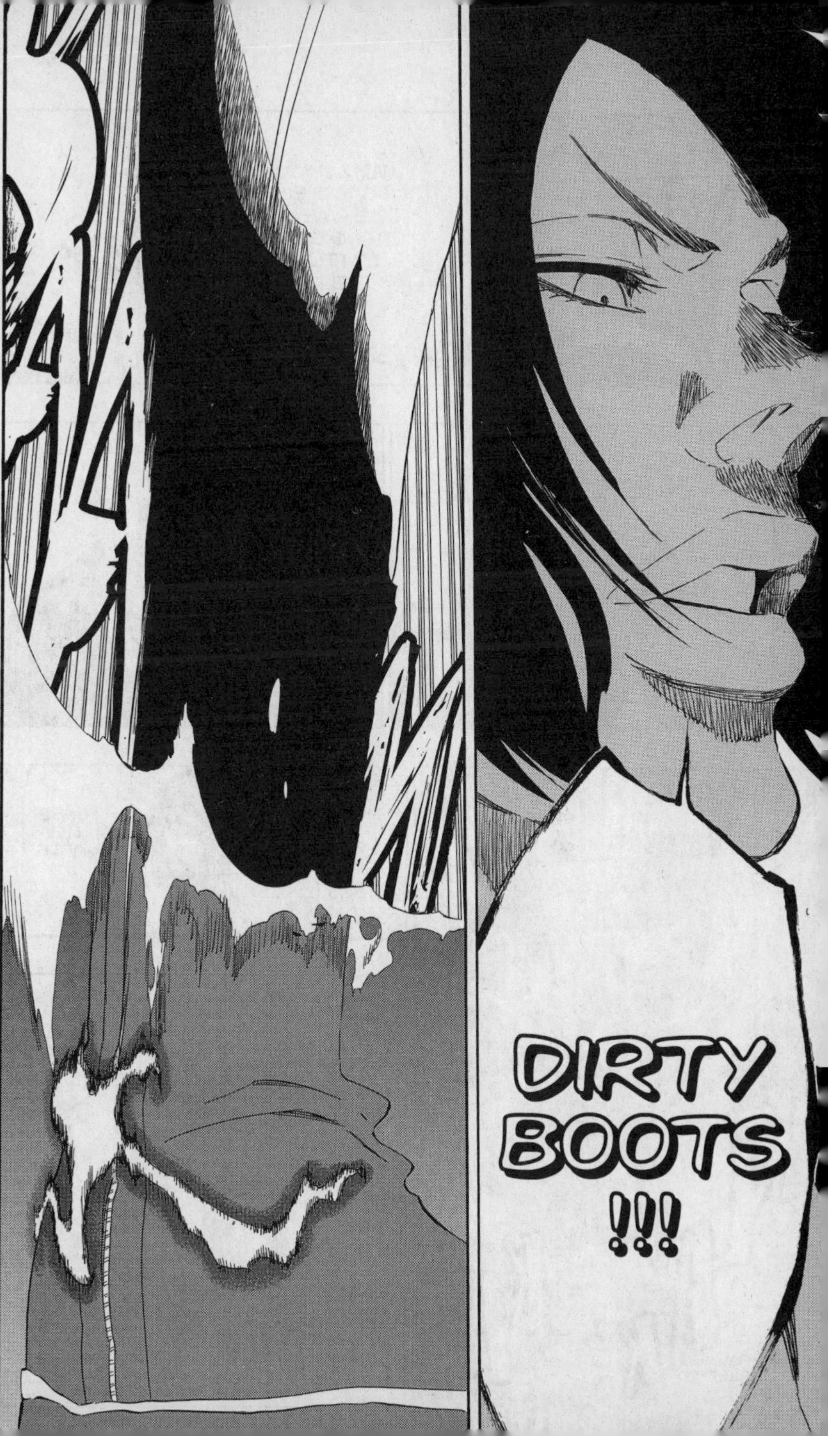
DIRTY BOOTS !!!

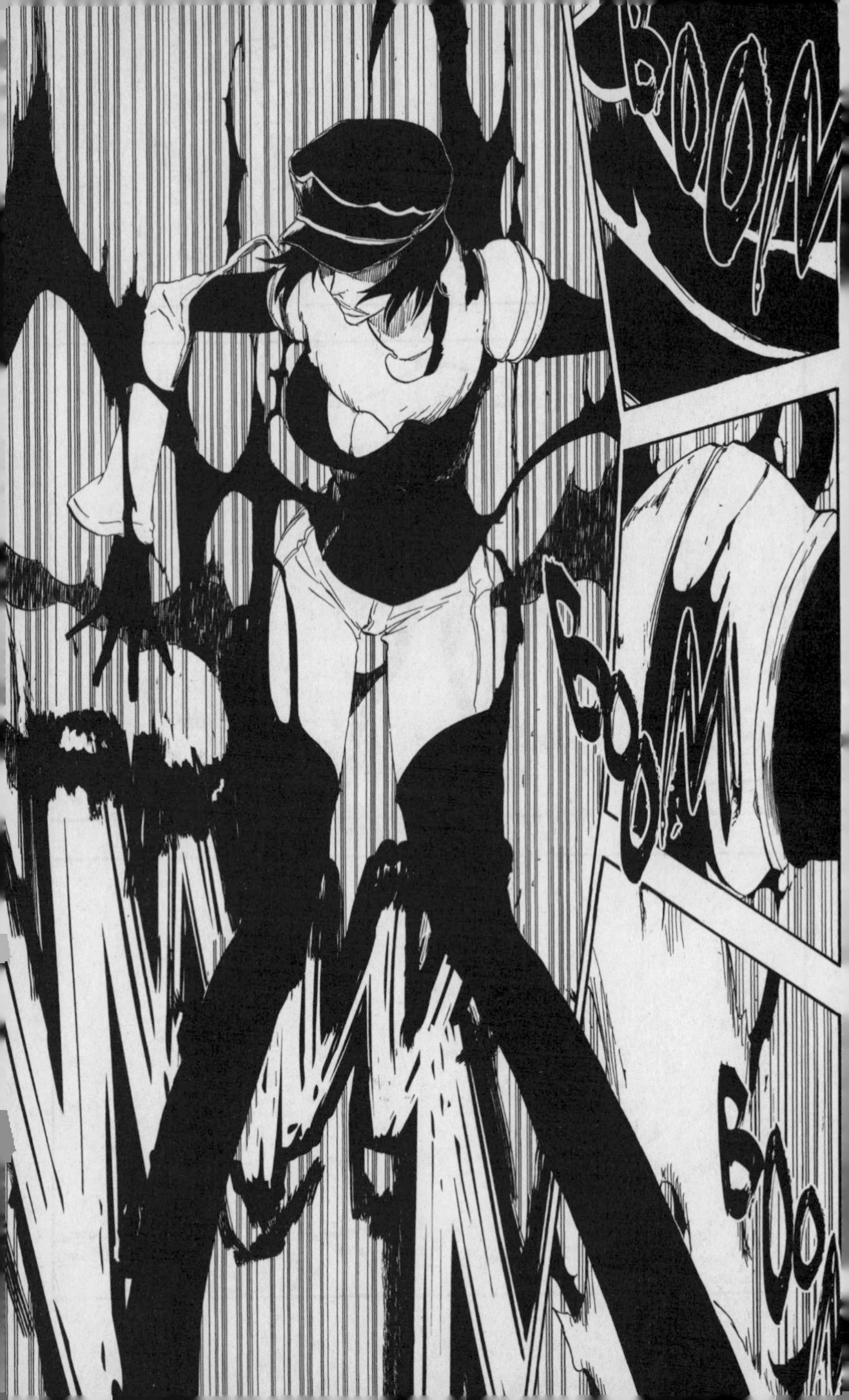
BOOOM
BOOOM
BOOO

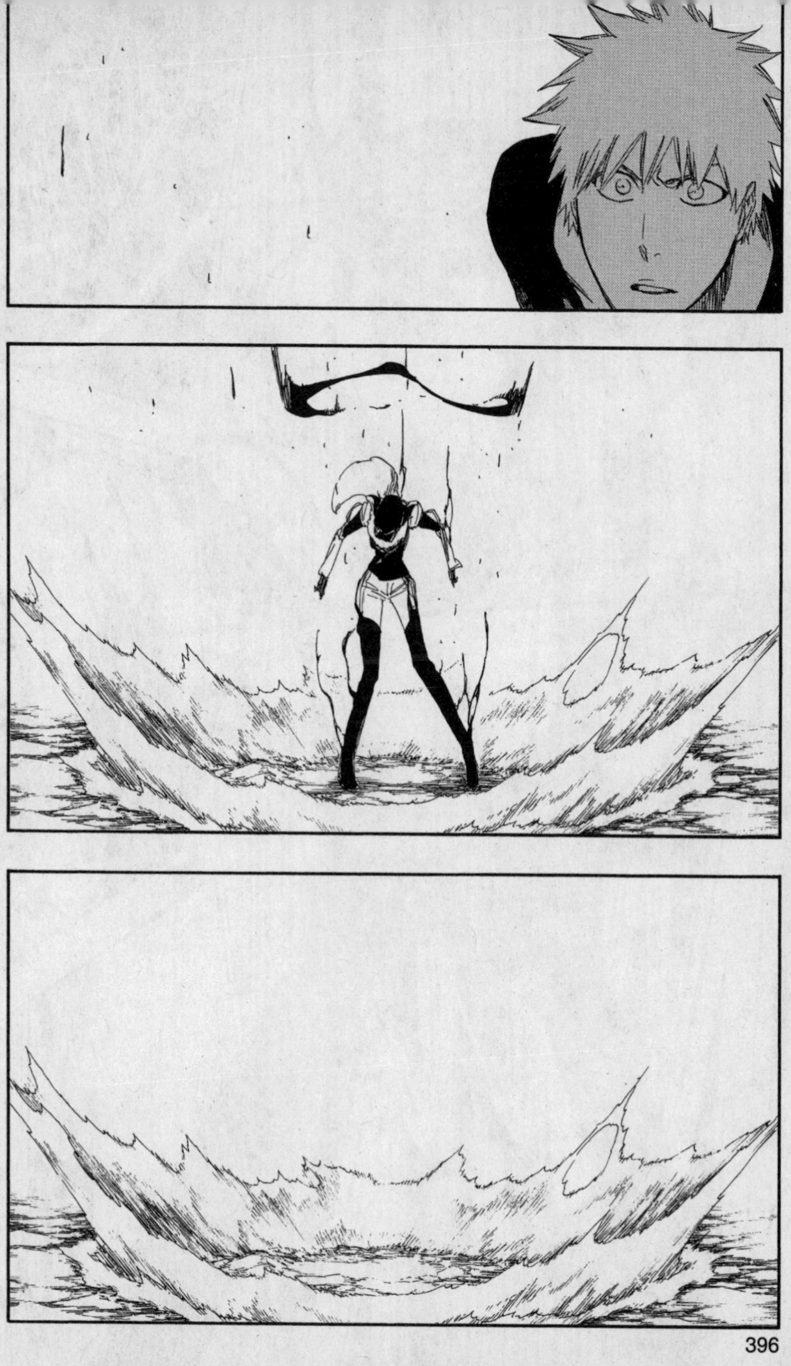

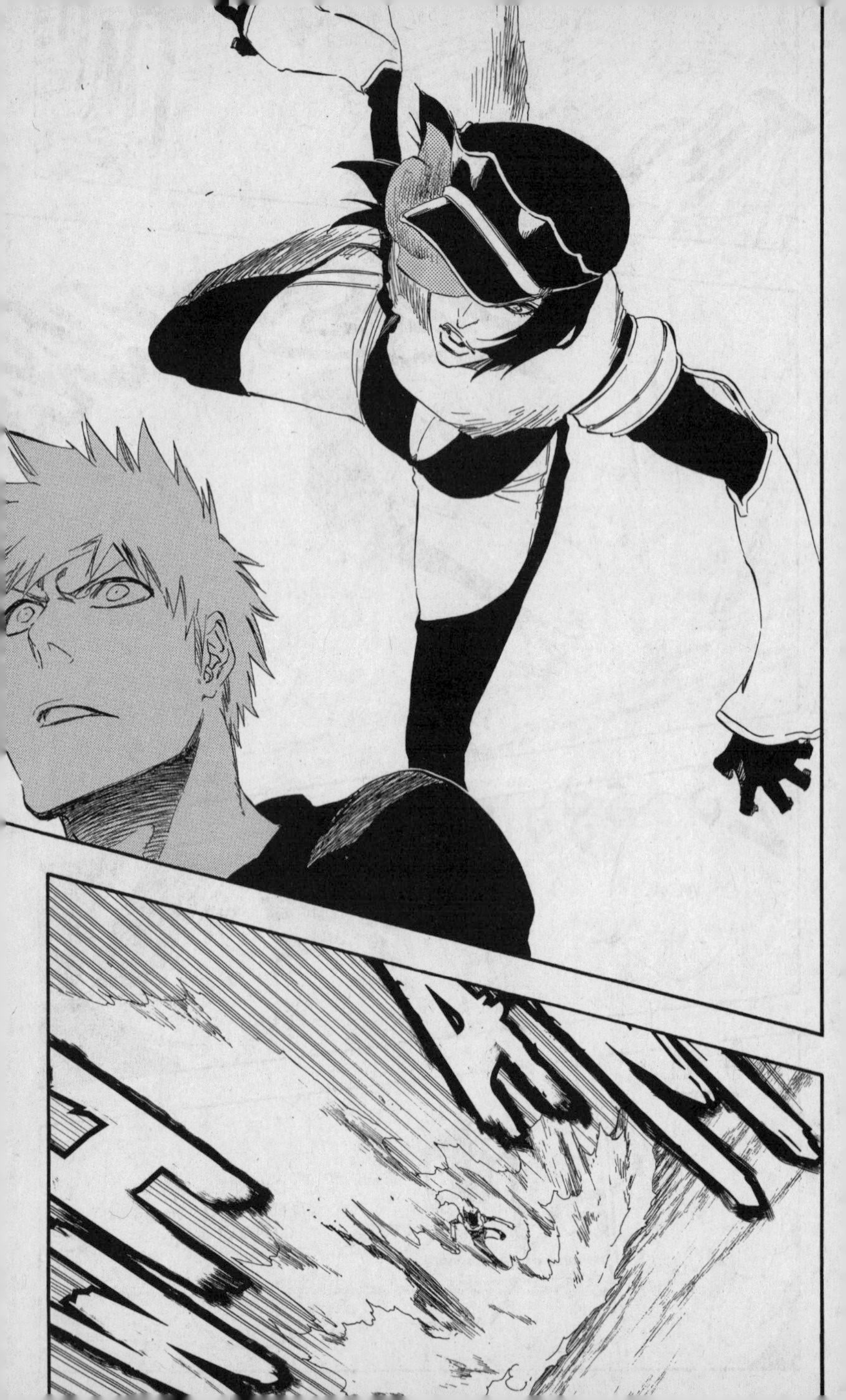

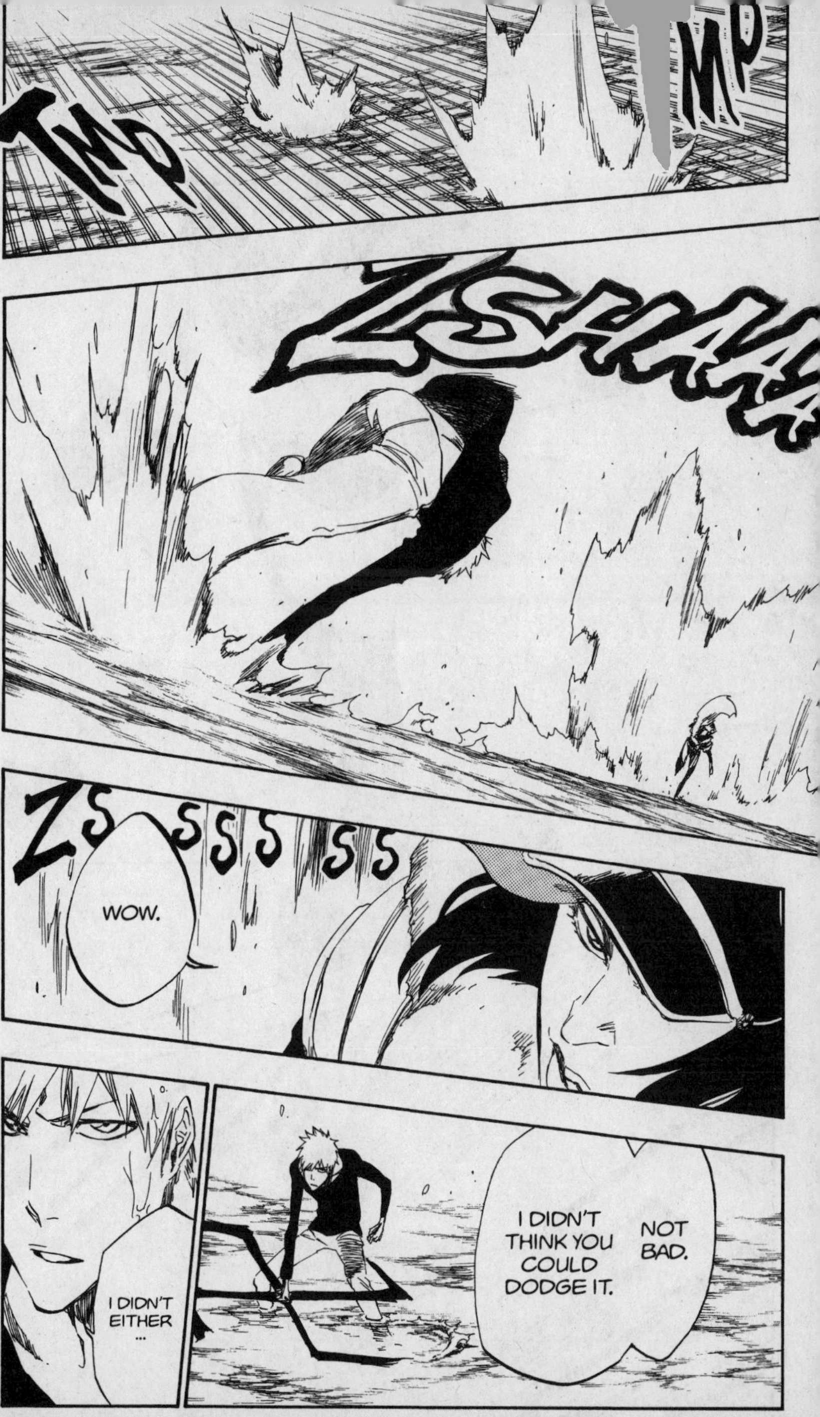

MP
TMP
ZSHAA
ZSSSSSS
WOW.
NOT BAD.
I DIDN'T THINK YOU COULD DODGE IT.
I DIDN'T EITHER...

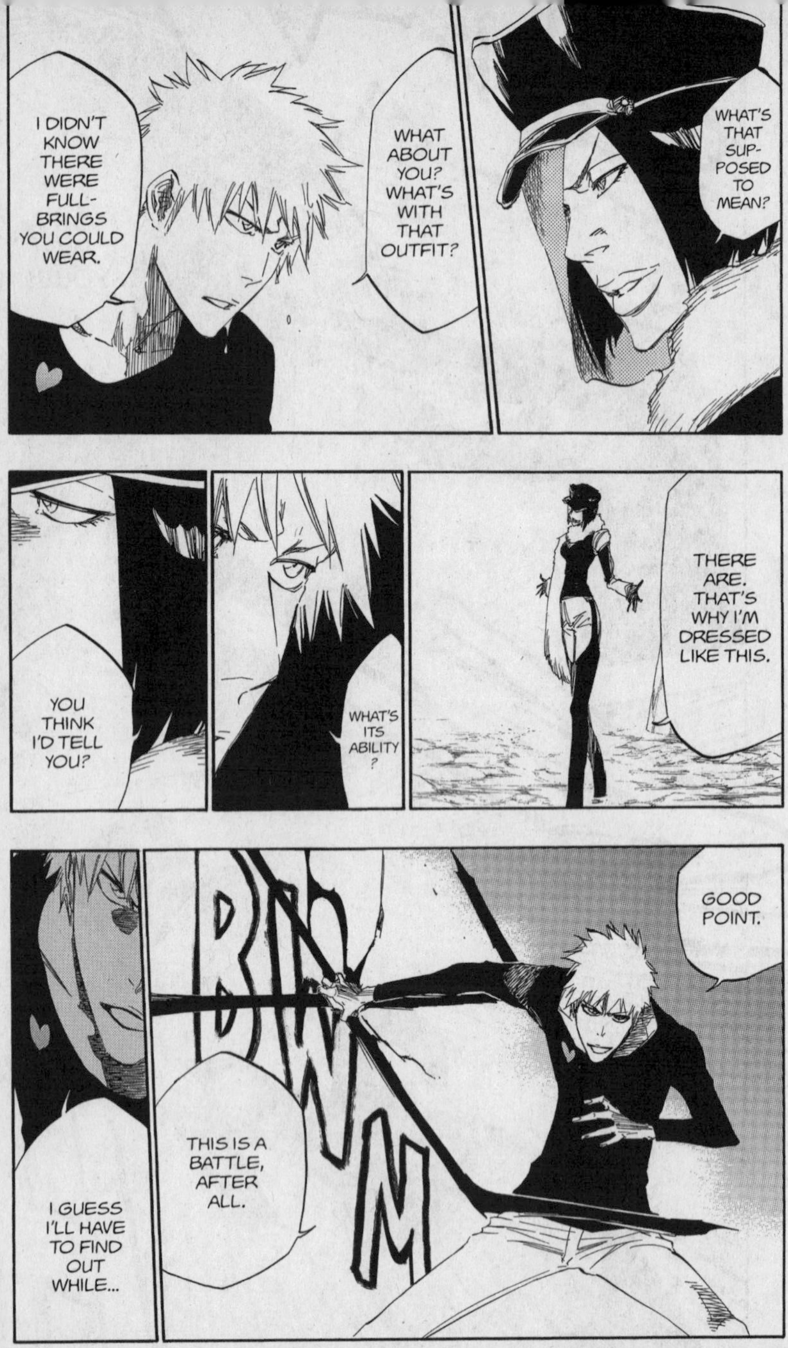
WHAT'S THAT SUP-POSED TO MEAN?
WHAT ABOUT YOU? WHAT'S WITH THAT OUTFIT?
I DIDN'T KNOW THERE WERE FULL-BRINGS YOU COULD WEAR.
THERE ARE. THAT'S WHY I'M DRESSED LIKE THIS.
WHAT'S ITS ABILITY?
YOU THINK I'D TELL YOU?
GOOD POINT.
THIS IS A BATTLE, AFTER ALL.
I GUESS I'LL HAVE TO FIND OUT WHILE...

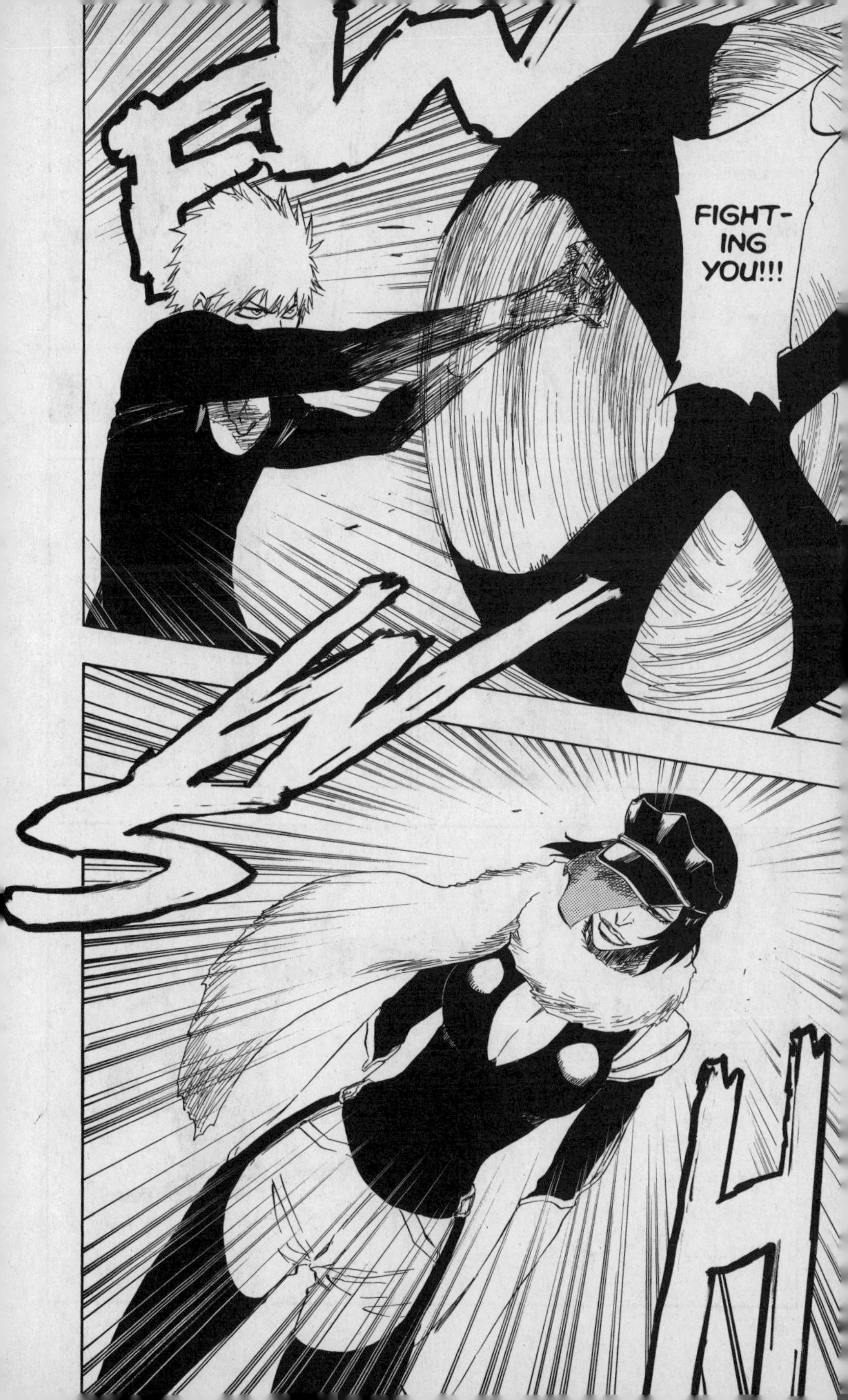
FIGHT-
ING
YOU!!!

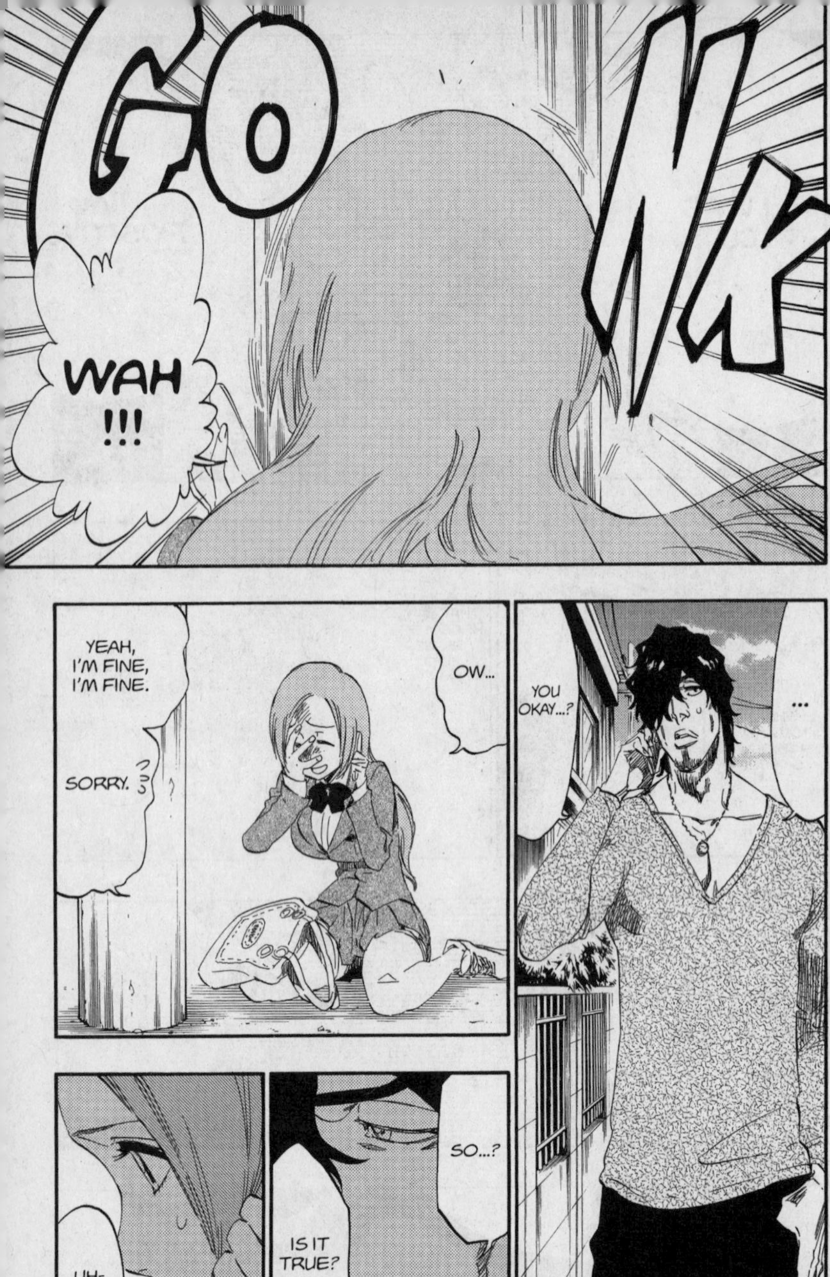
GONK
WAH !!!
...
YOU OKAY...?
OW...
YEAH, I'M FINE, I'M FINE.
SORRY.
SO...?
IS IT TRUE?
UH-HUH...

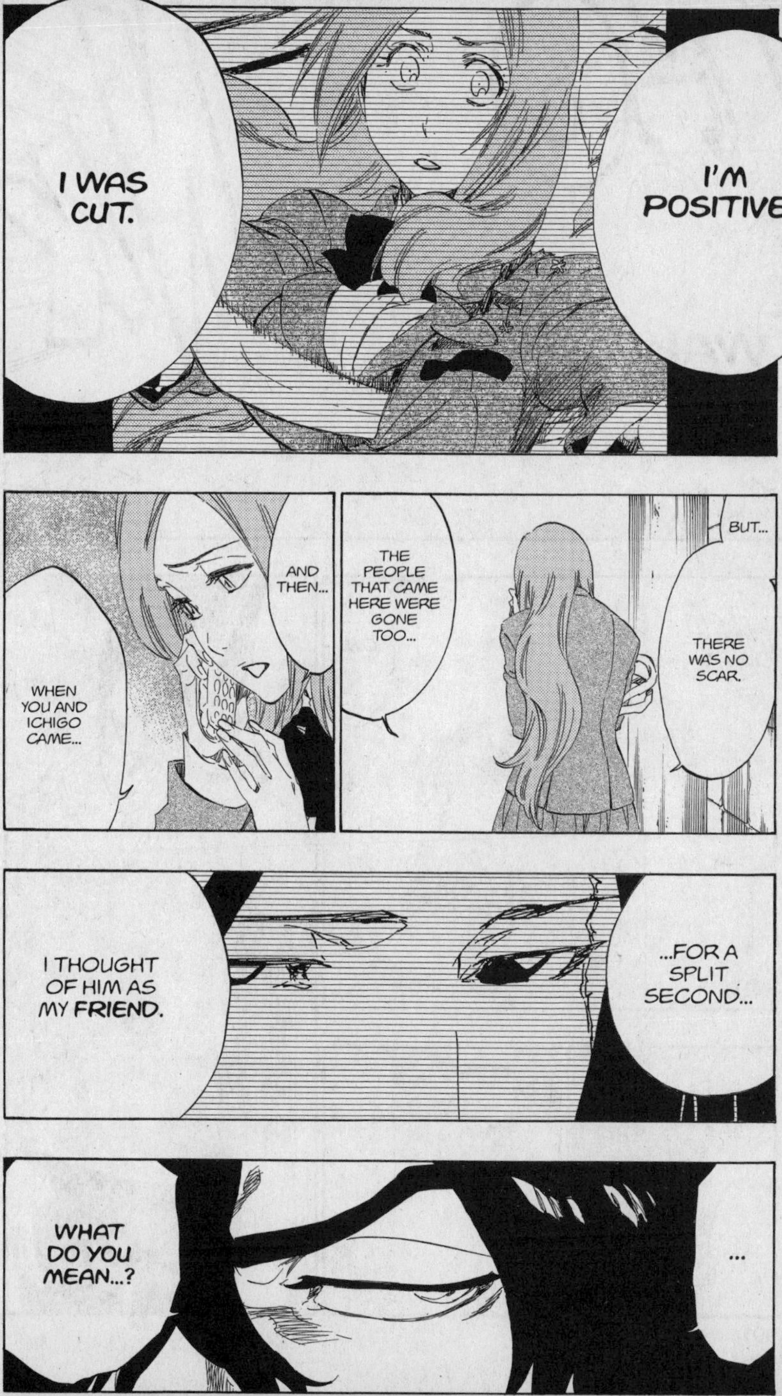
I'M POSITIVE...
I WAS CUT.
BUT...
THERE WAS NO SCAR.
THE PEOPLE THAT CAME HERE WERE GONE TOO...
AND THEN...
WHEN YOU AND ICHIGO CAME...
...FOR A SPLIT SECOND...
I THOUGHT OF HIM AS MY FRIEND.
...
WHAT DO YOU MEAN...?

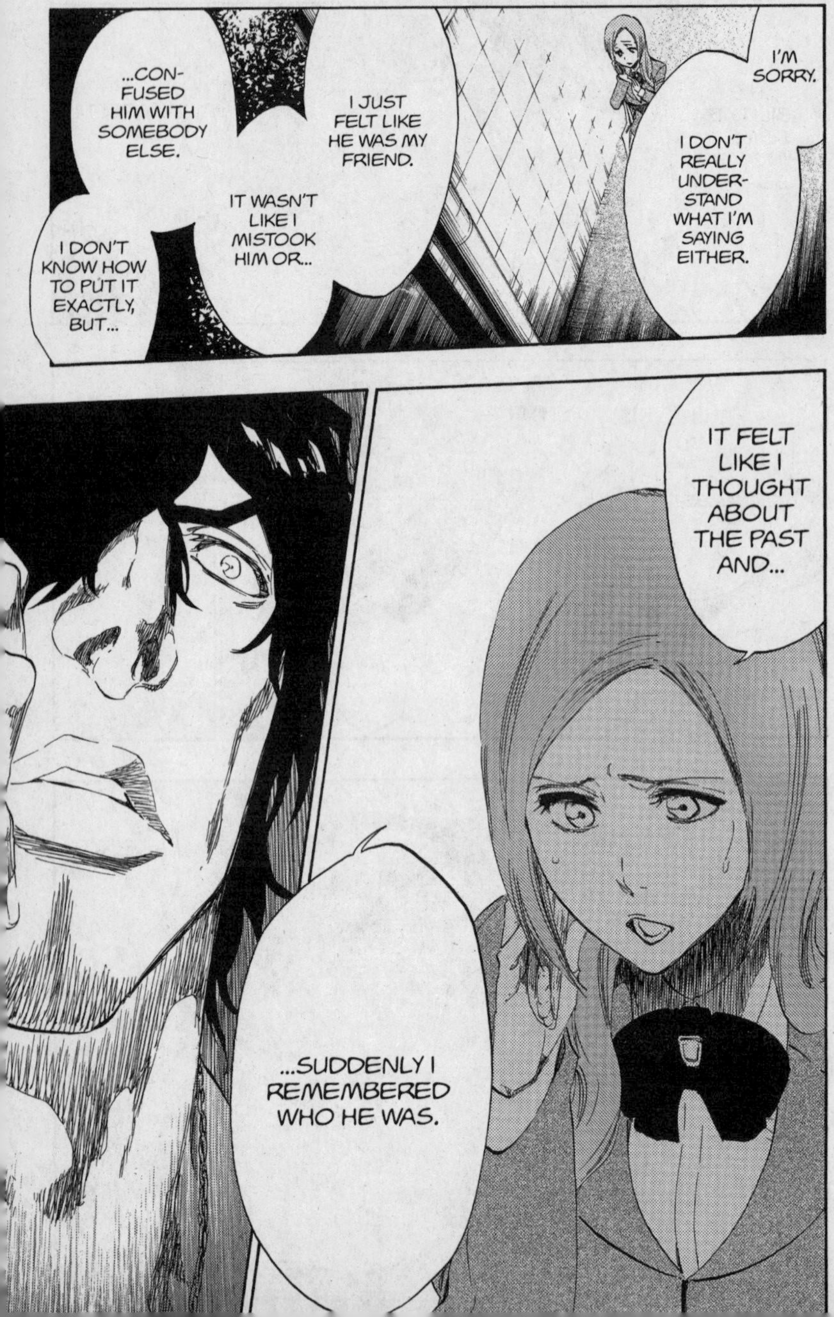
I'M SORRY.
I DON'T REALLY UNDER-STAND WHAT I'M SAYING EITHER.
I DON'T KNOW HOW TO PUT IT EXACTLY, BUT...
IT WASN'T LIKE I MISTOOK HIM OR...
...CON-FUSED HIM WITH SOMEBODY ELSE.
I JUST FELT LIKE HE WAS MY FRIEND.
IT FELT LIKE I THOUGHT ABOUT THE PAST AND...
...SUDDENLY I REMEMBERED WHO HE WAS.

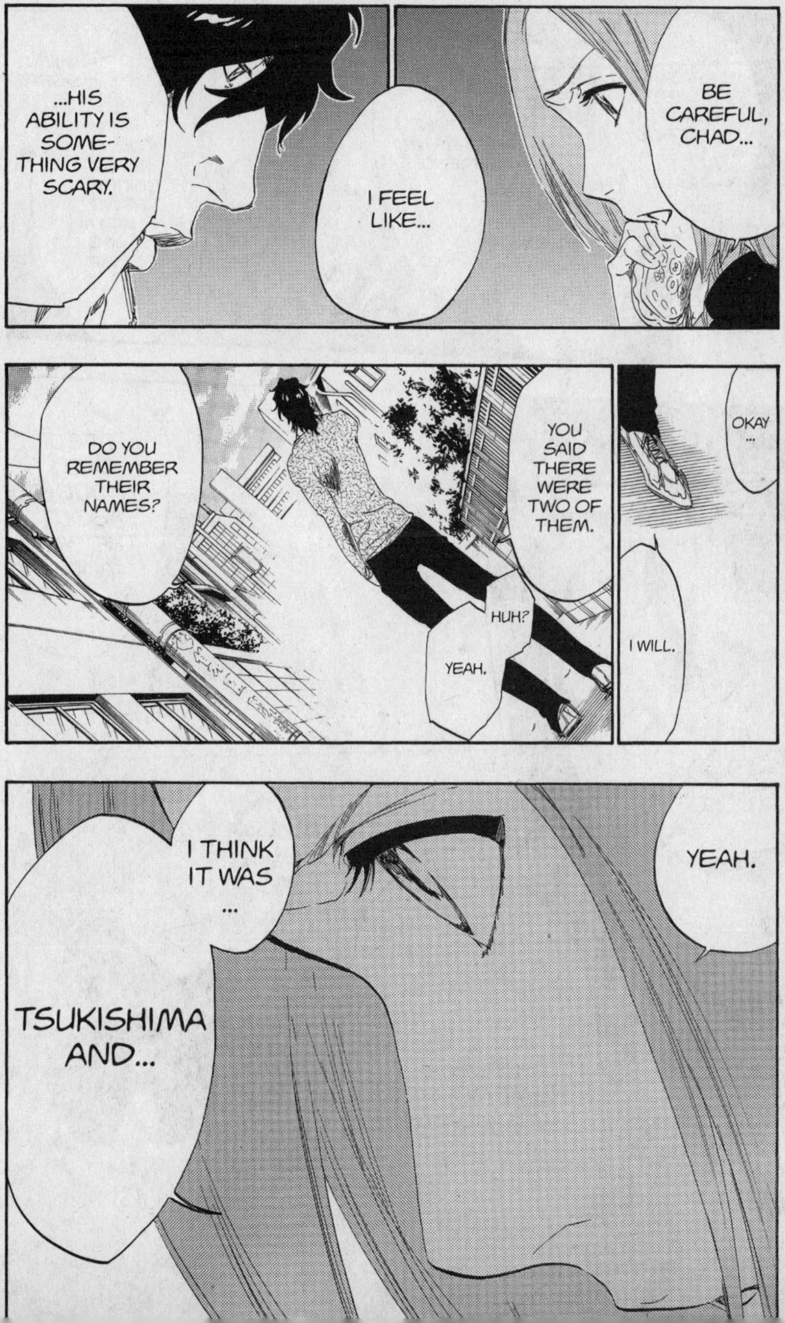
BE CAREFUL, CHAD...
I FEEL LIKE...
...HIS ABILITY IS SOME-THING VERY SCARY.
OKAY...
I WILL.
YOU SAID THERE WERE TWO OF THEM.
DO YOU REMEMBER THEIR NAMES?
HUH? YEAH.
YEAH.
I THINK IT WAS ...
TSUKISHIMA AND...

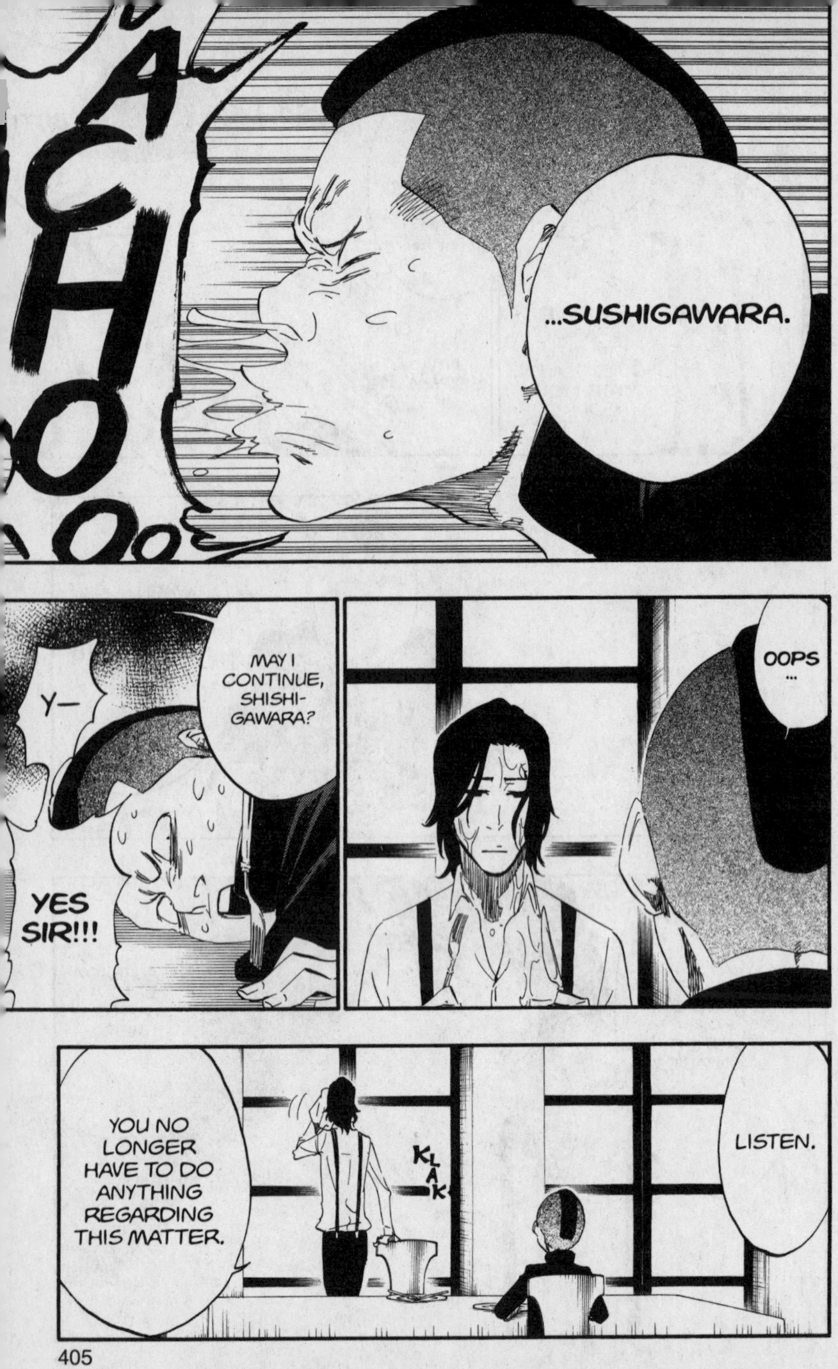
...SUSHIGAWARA.
ACHOO
OOPS ...
MAY I CONTINUE, SHISHI-GAWARA?
Y—
YES SIR!!!
LISTEN.
KLAK
YOU NO LONGER HAVE TO DO ANYTHING REGARDING THIS MATTER.

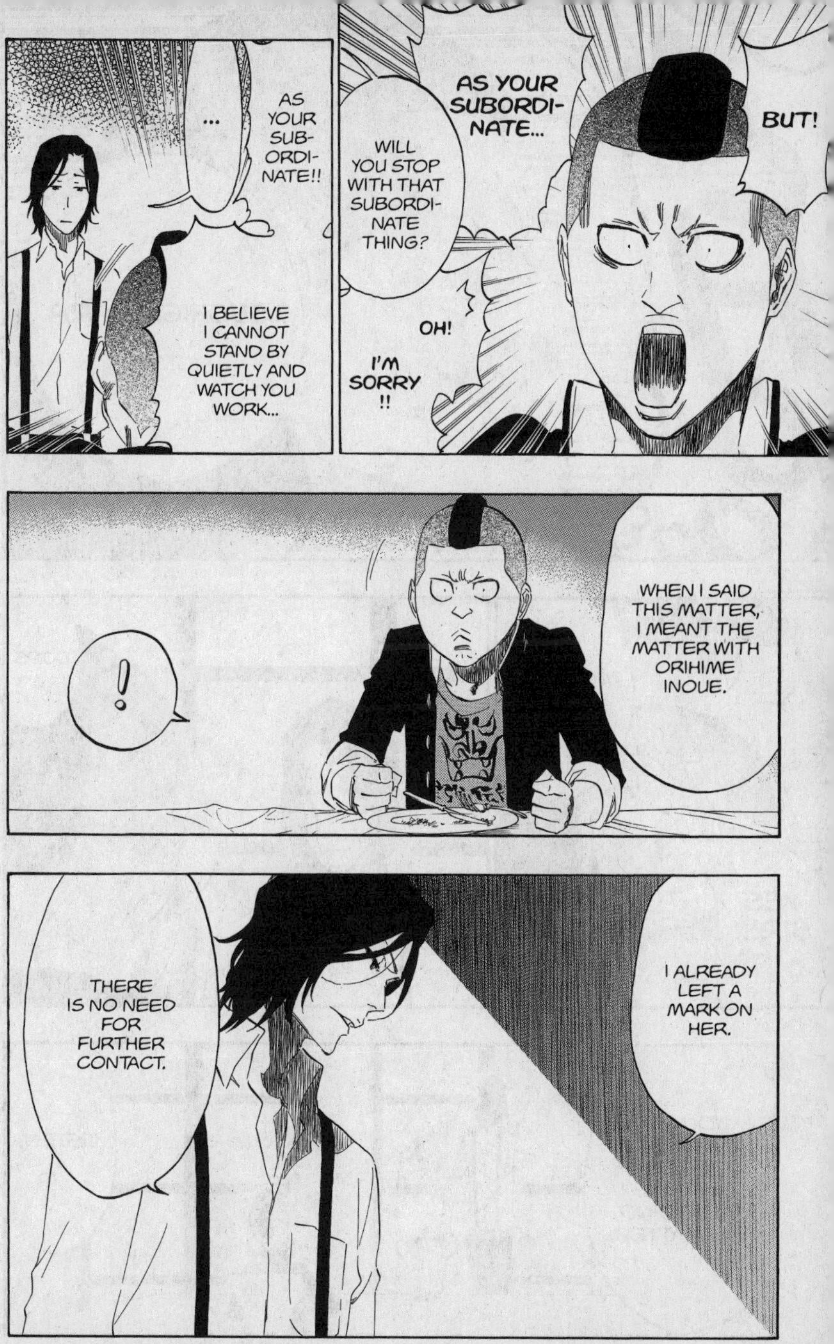
BUT!
AS YOUR SUBORDI-NATE...
WILL YOU STOP WITH THAT SUBORDI-NATE THING?
OH!
I'M SORRY !!
AS YOUR SUB-ORDI-NATE!!
...
I BELIEVE I CANNOT STAND BY QUIETLY AND WATCH YOU WORK...
WHEN I SAID THIS MATTER, I MEANT THE MATTER WITH ORIHIME INOUE.
!
I ALREADY LEFT A MARK ON HER.
THERE IS NO NEED FOR FURTHER CONTACT.

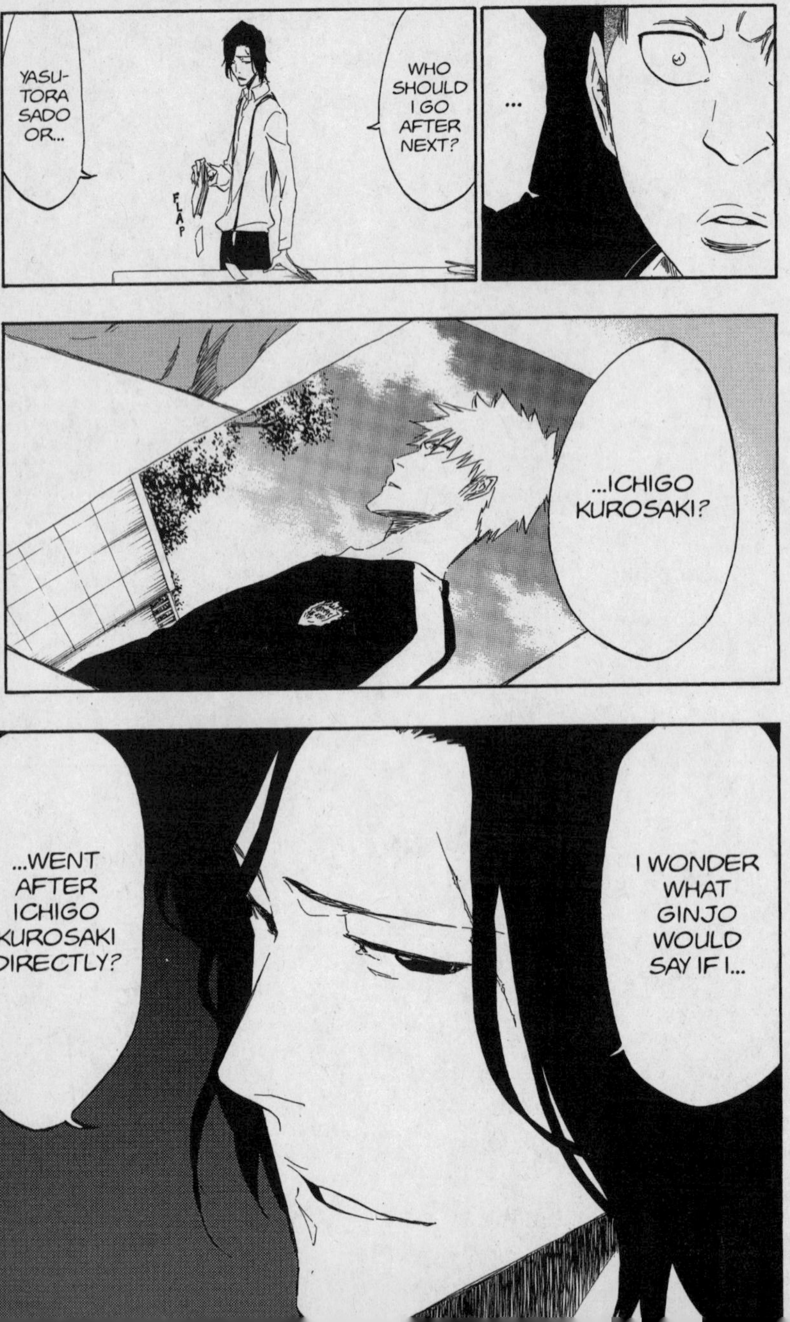
...
WHO SHOULD I GO AFTER NEXT?
FLAP
YASUTORA SADO OR...
...ICHIGO KUROSAKI?
I WONDER WHAT GINJO WOULD SAY IF I...
...WENT AFTER ICHIGO KUROSAKI DIRECTLY?

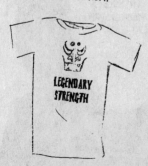

SHISHIGAWARA'S
T-SHIRT

LEGENDARY
STRENGTH

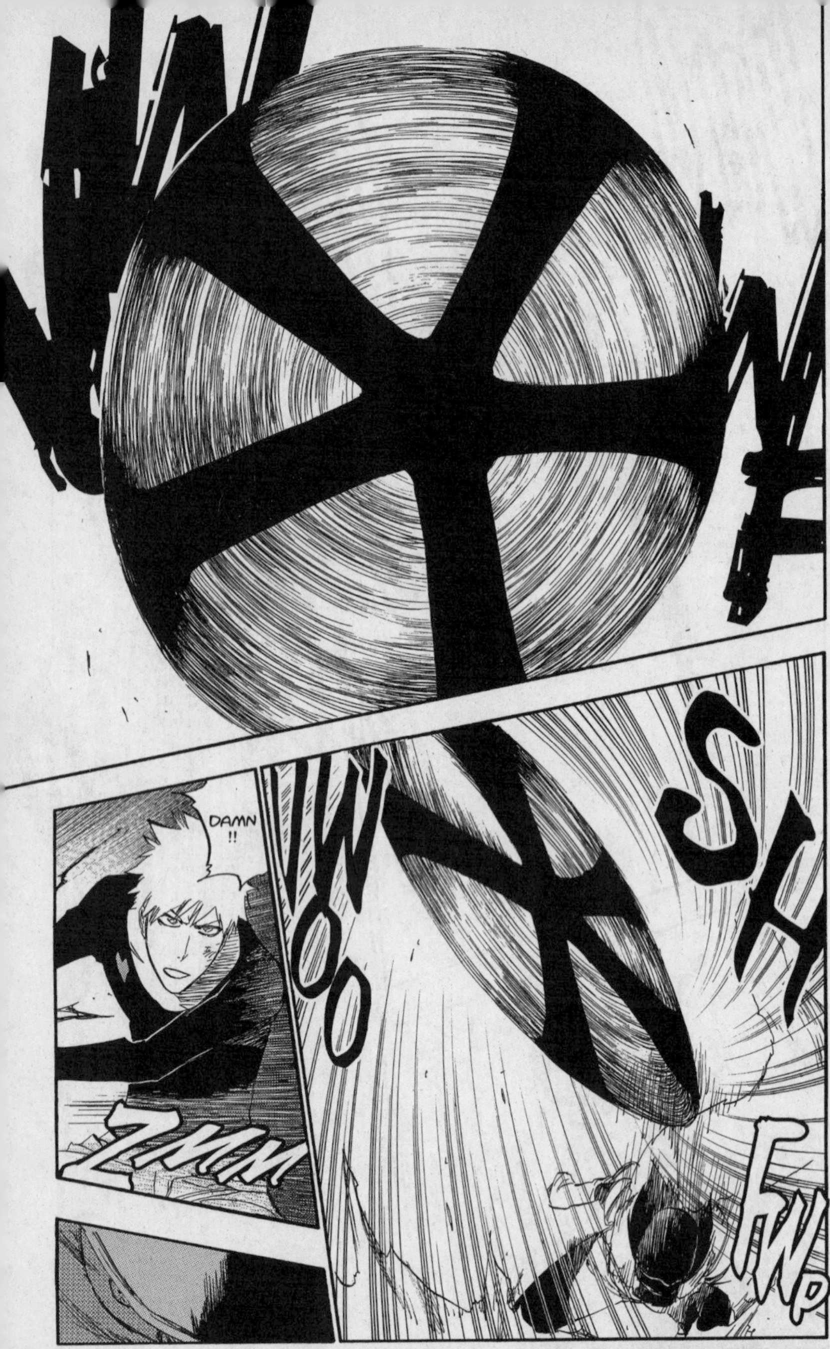
FWP
DAMN !!
ZMMM

443. Dirty Boots Dangers

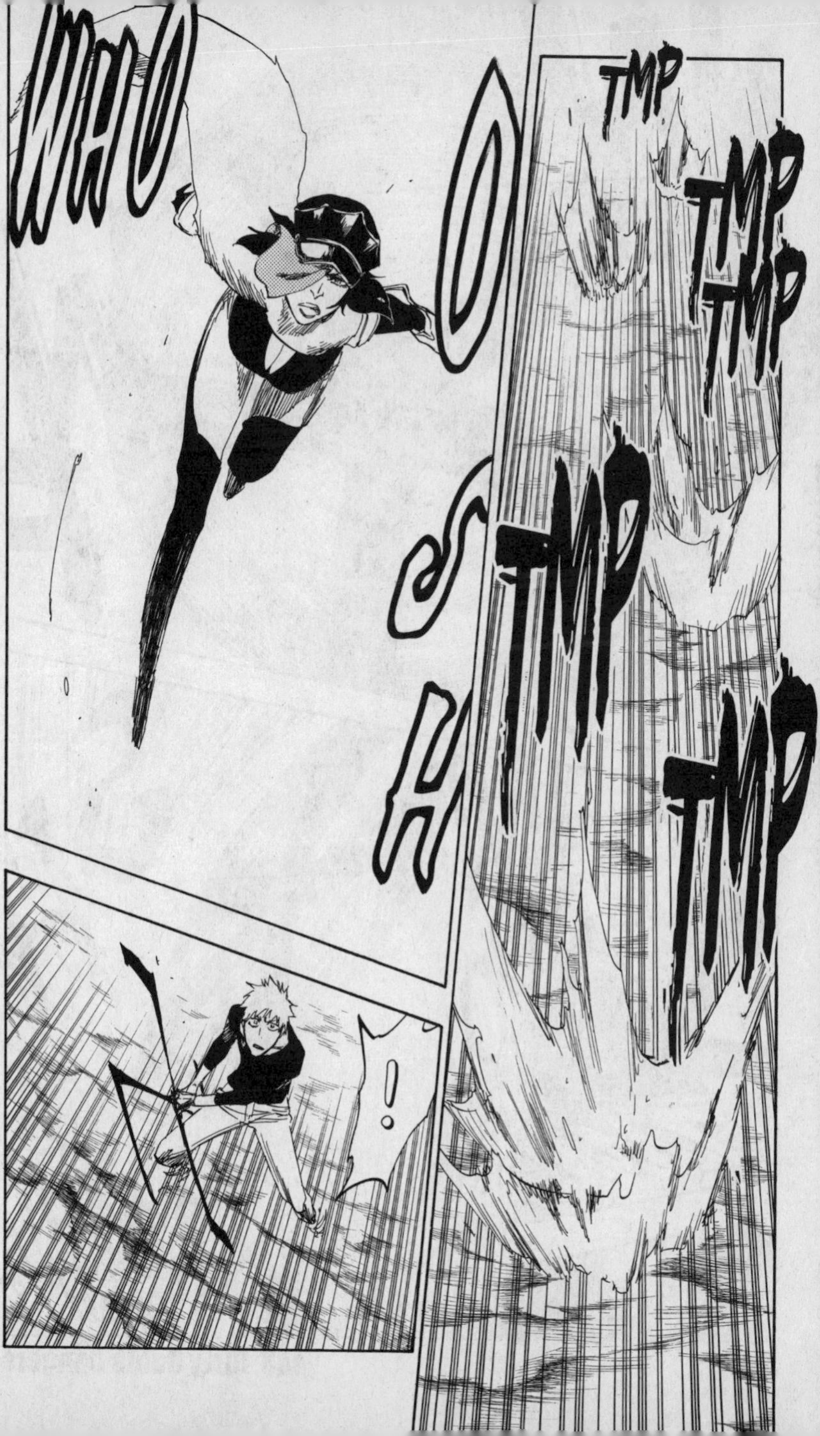
TMP
TMP
TMP
TMP
TMP
!

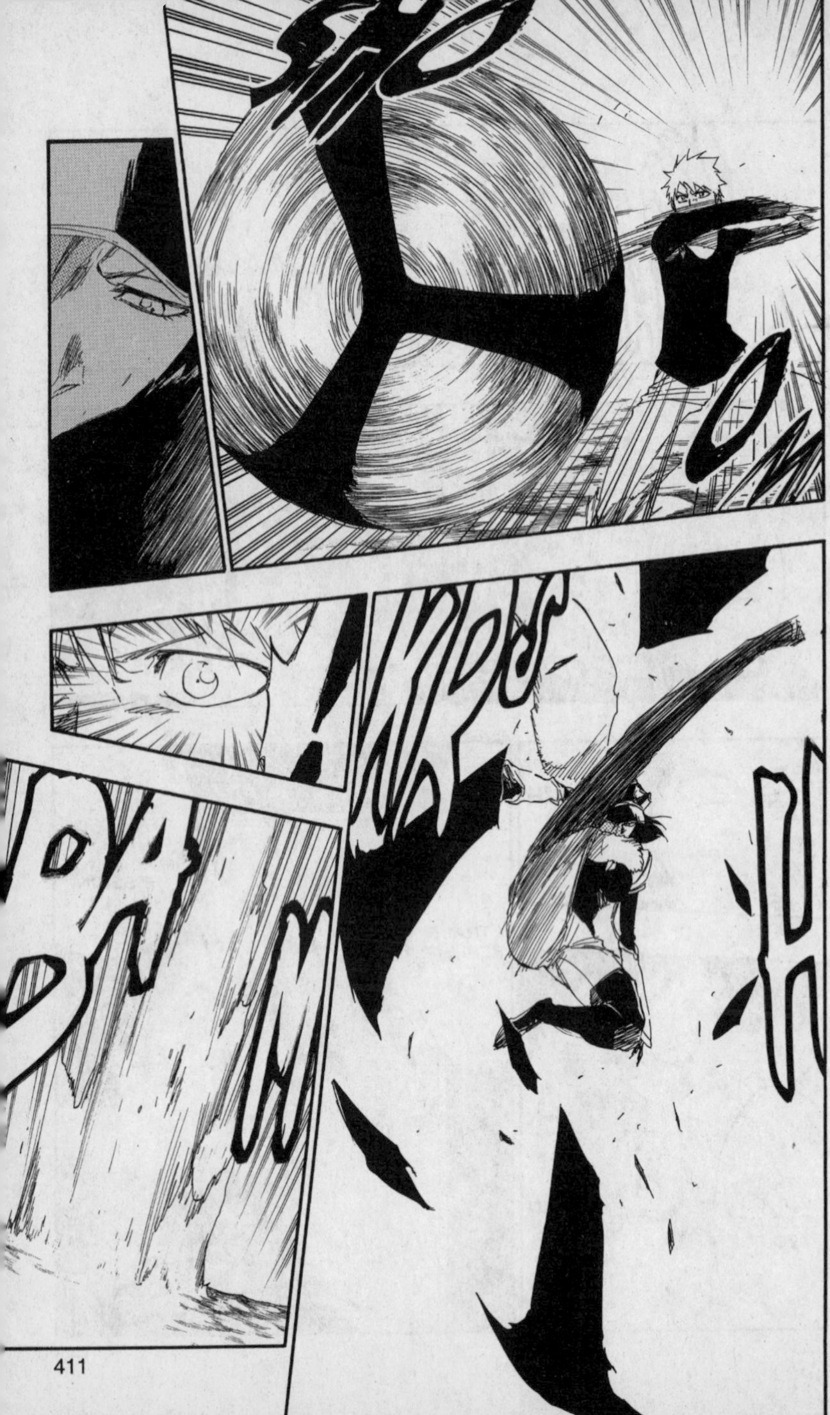

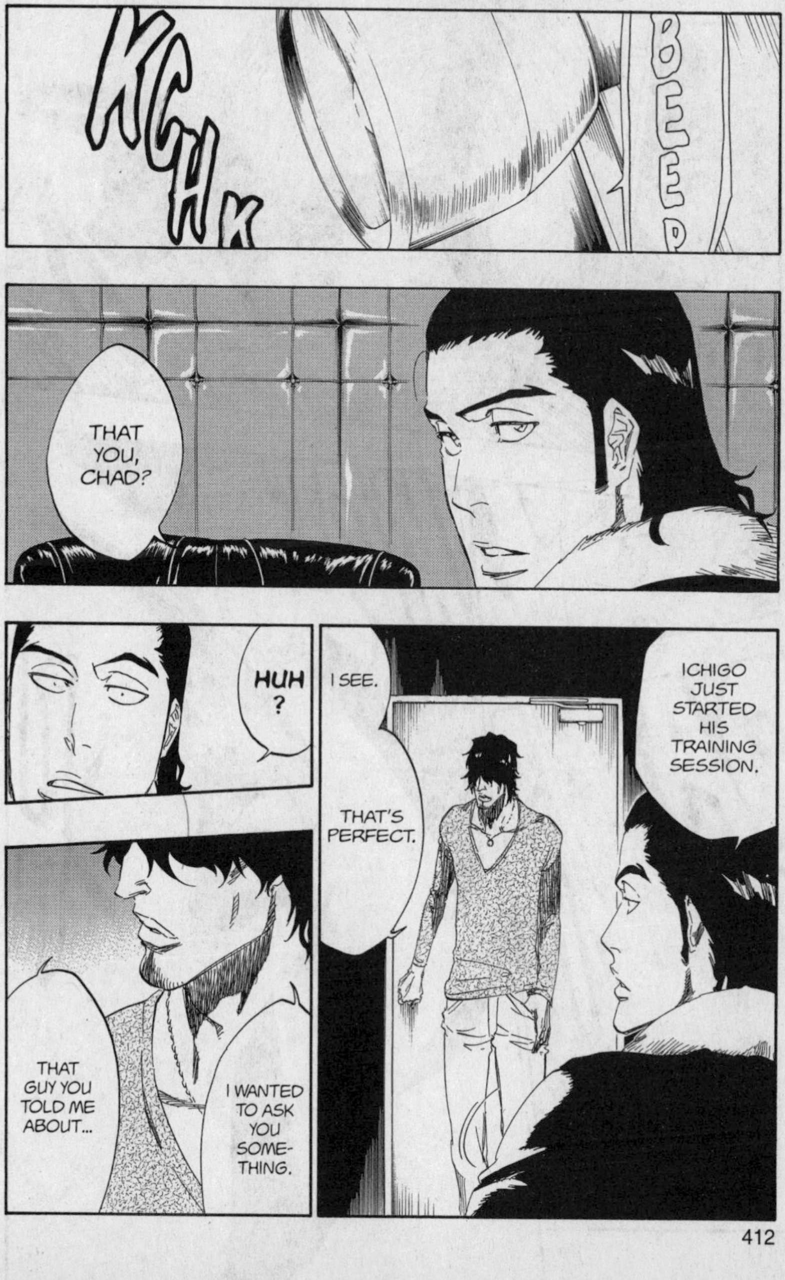
BEEP
KCHK
THAT YOU, CHAD?
ICHIGO JUST STARTED HIS TRAINING SESSION.
I SEE.
THAT'S PERFECT.
HUH?
I WANTED TO ASK YOU SOMETHING.
THAT GUY YOU TOLD ME ABOUT...

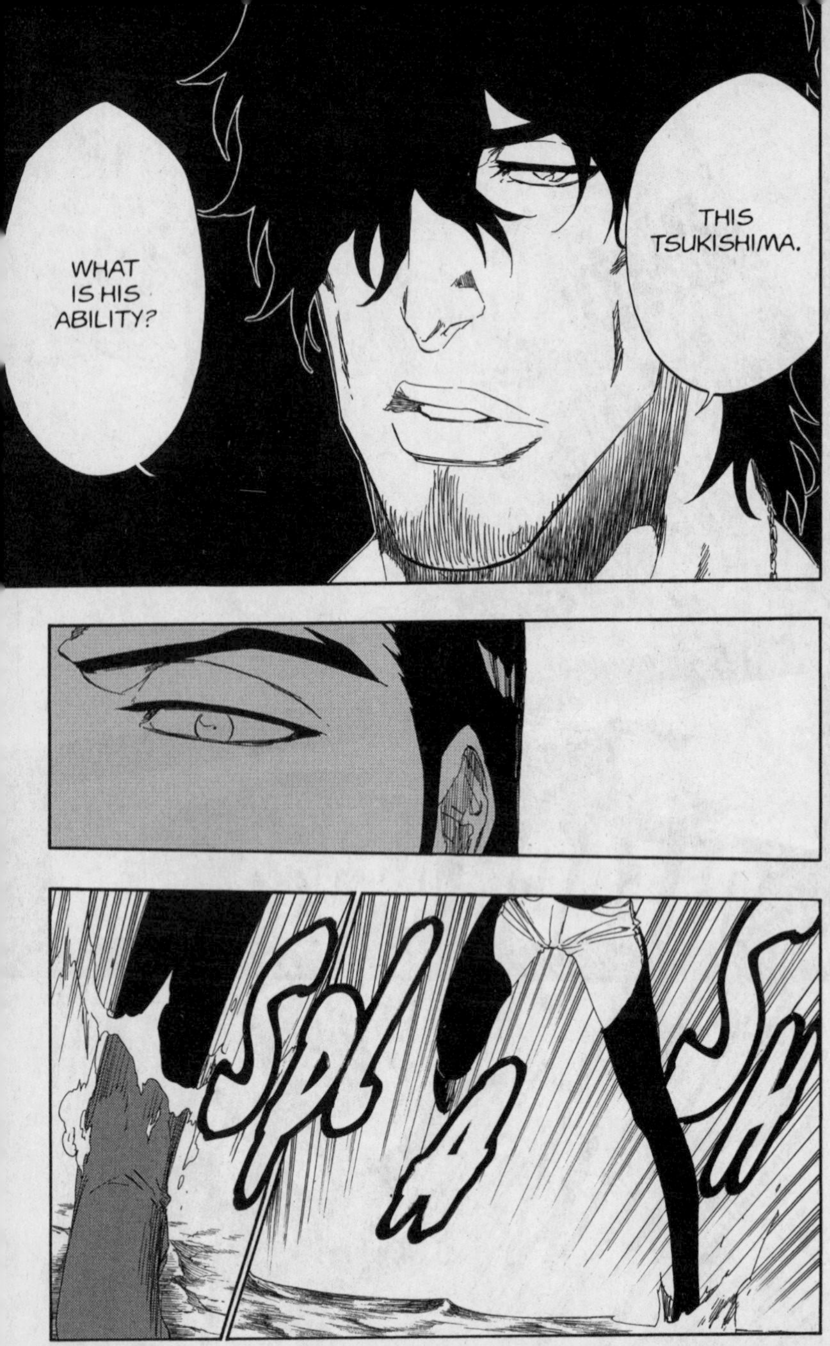
THIS TSUKISHIMA.
WHAT IS HIS ABILITY?

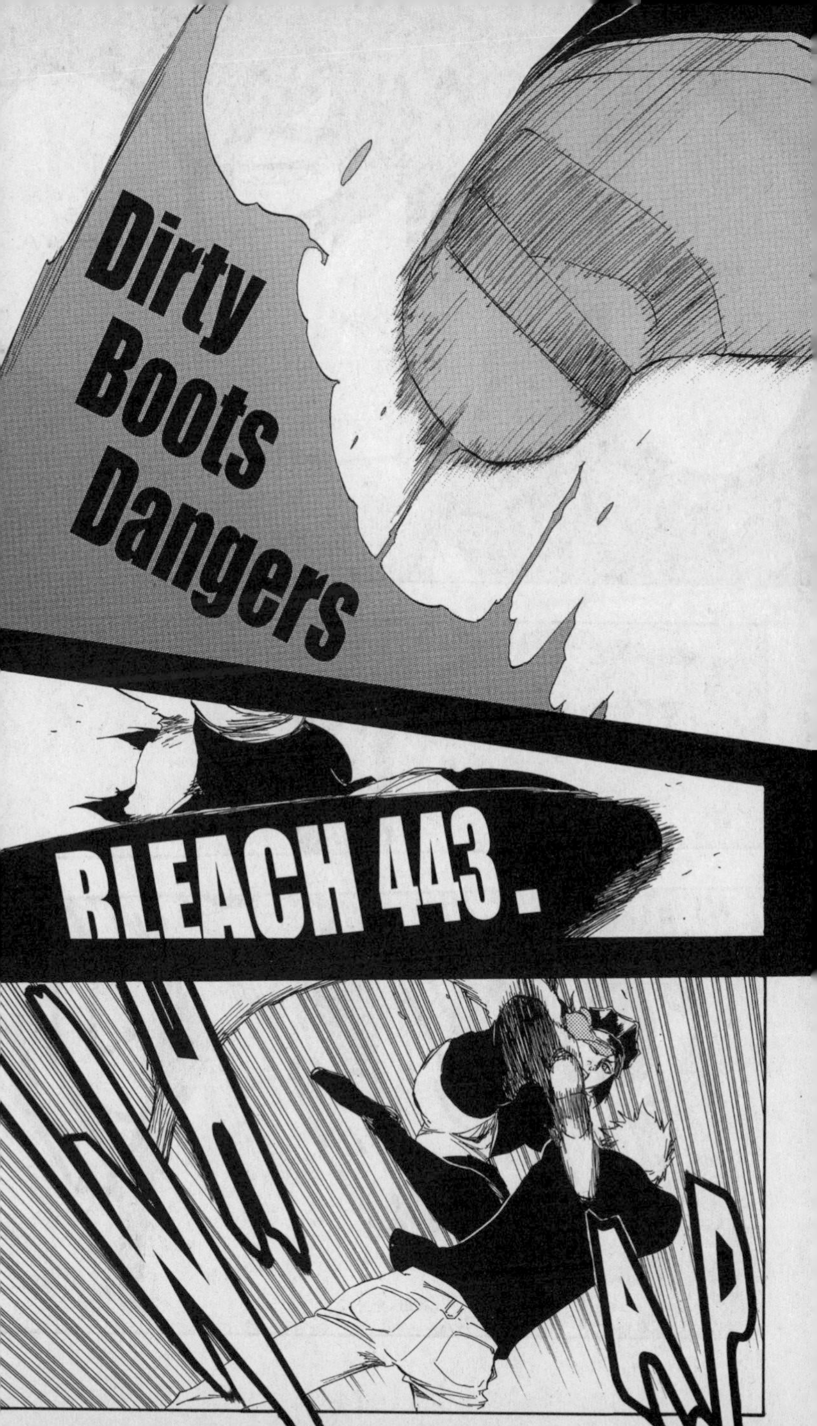
Dirty Boots Dangers
BLEACH 443.

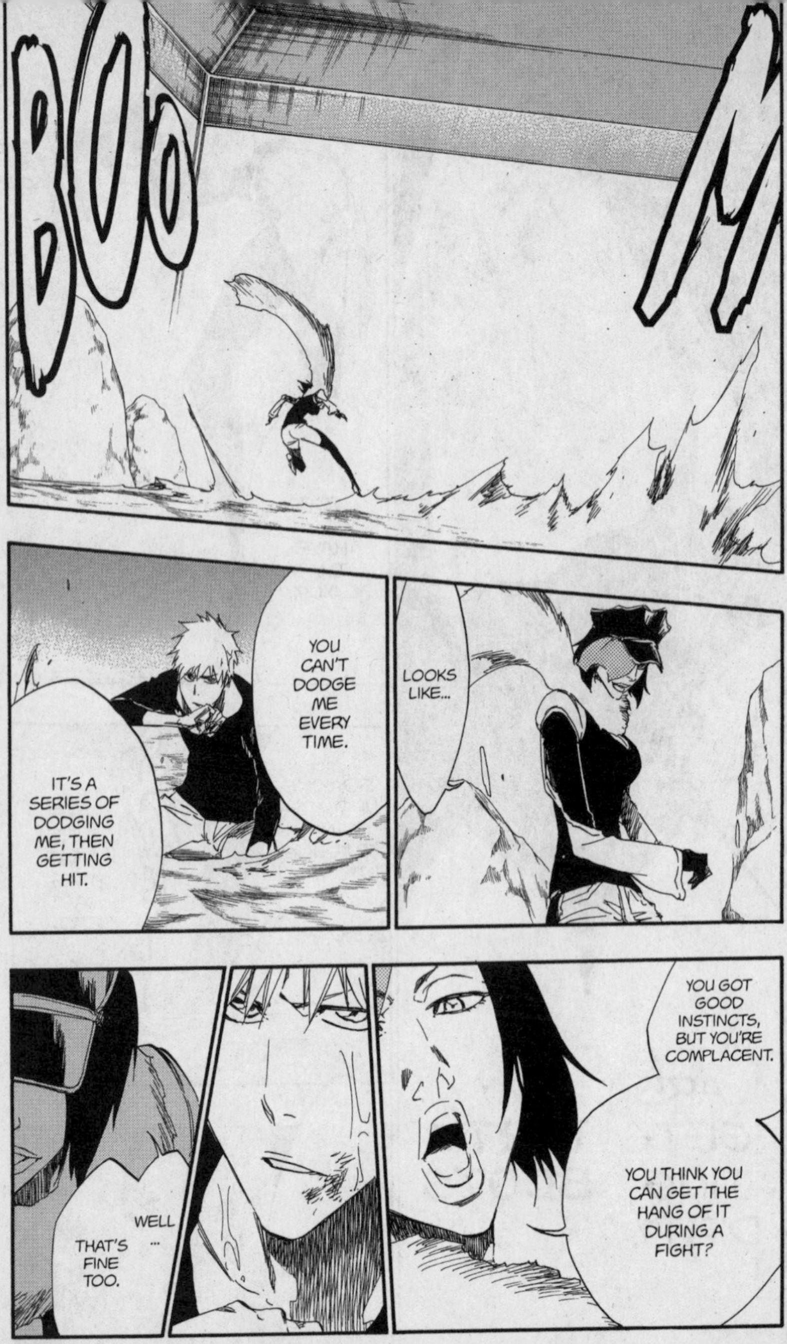
BOOM
LOOKS LIKE...
YOU CAN'T DODGE ME EVERY TIME.
IT'S A SERIES OF DODGING ME, THEN GETTING HIT.
YOU GOT GOOD INSTINCTS, BUT YOU'RE COMPLACENT.
YOU THINK YOU CAN GET THE HANG OF IT DURING A FIGHT?
WELL...
THAT'S FINE TOO.

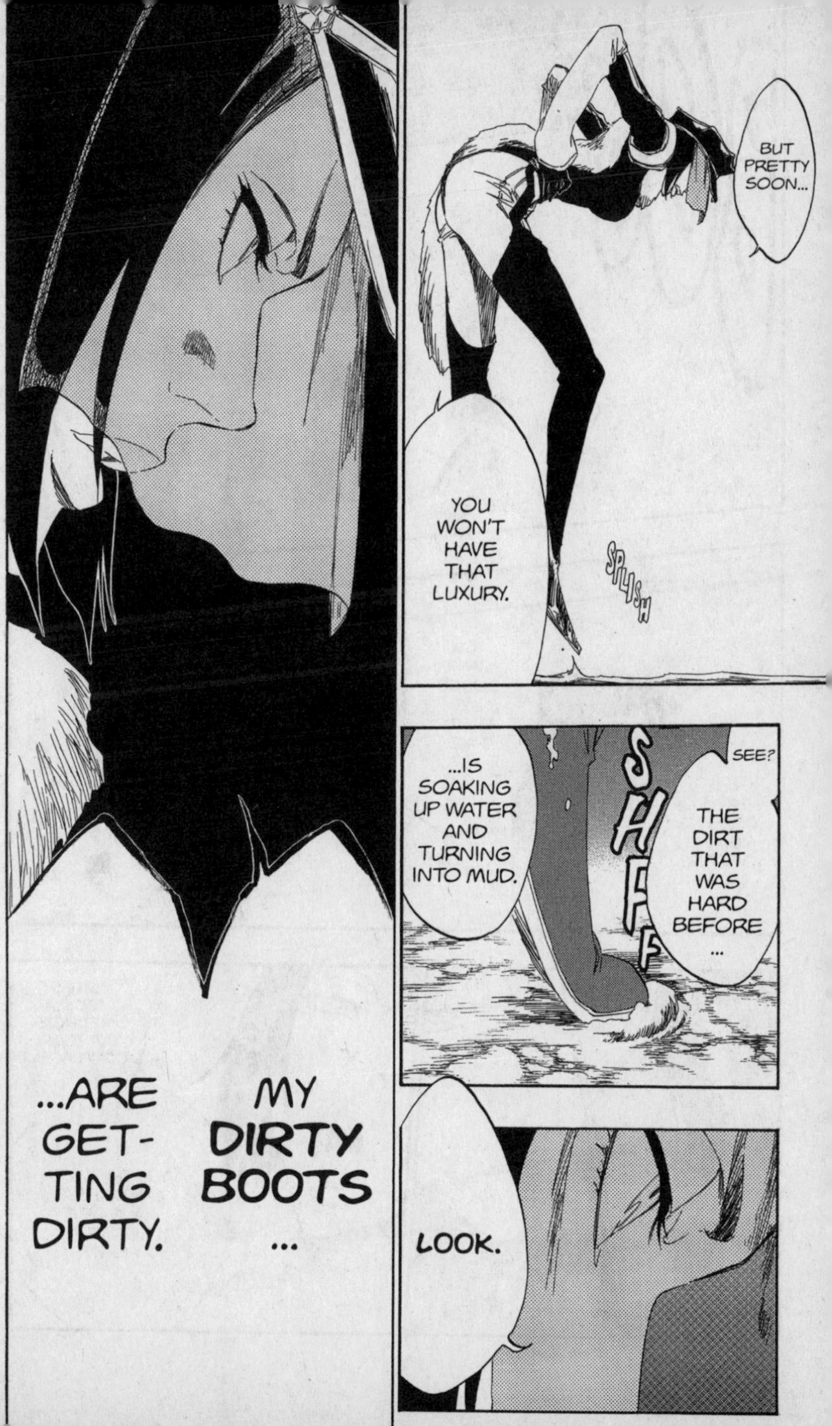
BUT PRETTY SOON...
YOU WON'T HAVE THAT LUXURY.
SPLISH
SEE?
THE DIRT THAT WAS HARD BEFORE ...
...IS SOAKING UP WATER AND TURNING INTO MUD.
SHFF
LOOK.
MY DIRTY BOOTS ...
...ARE GET-TING DIRTY.

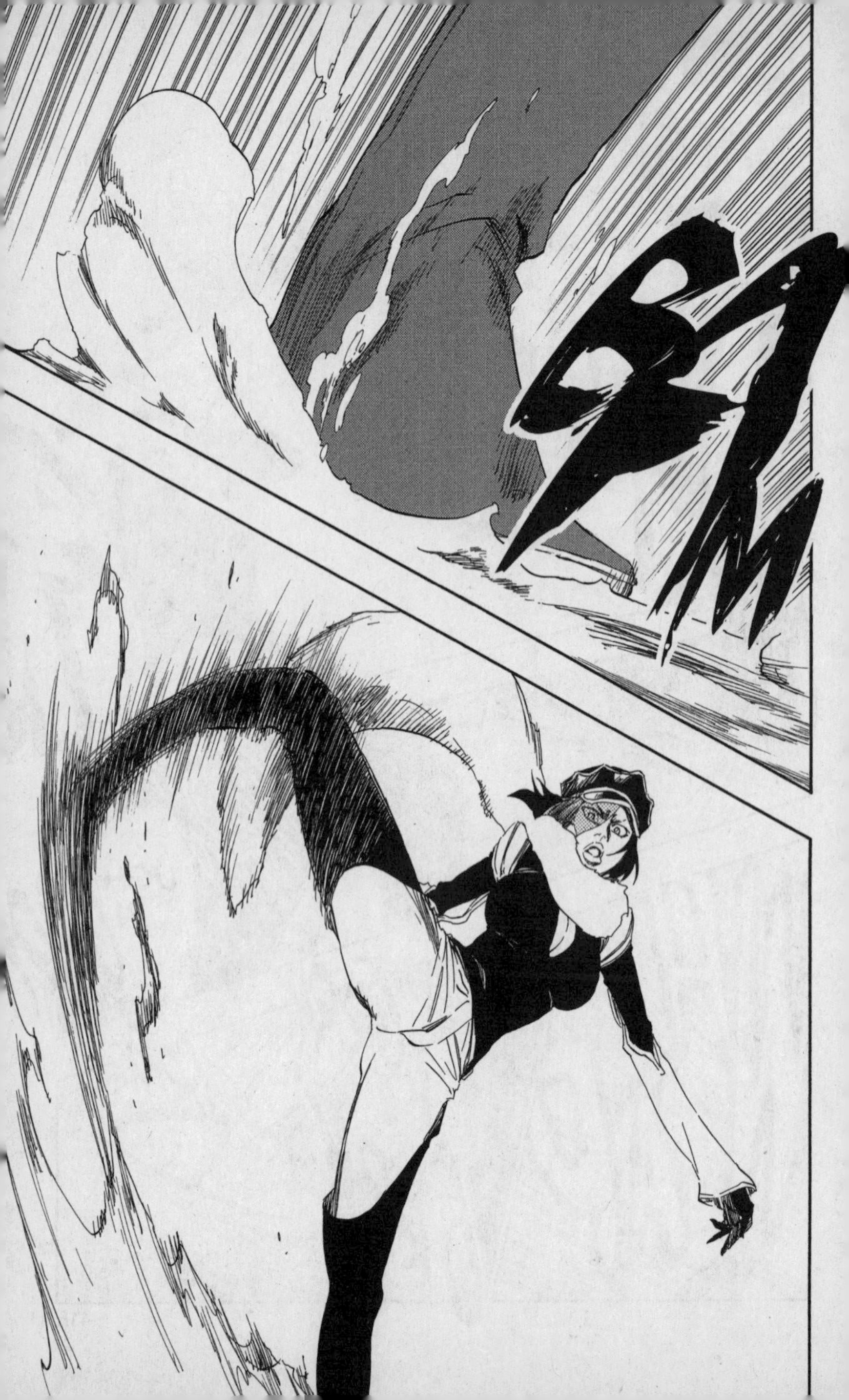
BAM

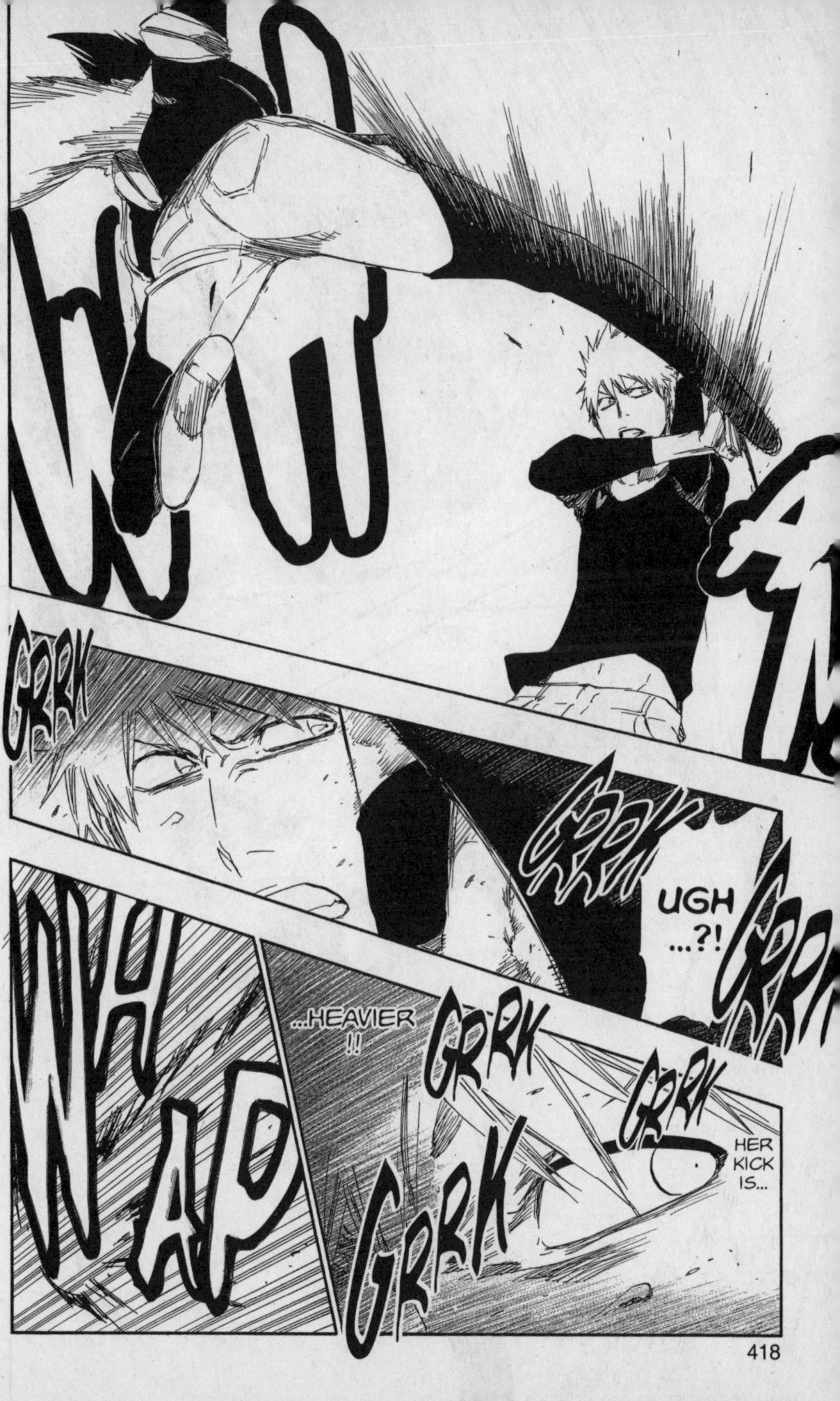
GRRK
UGH
...?!
GRRK
HER
KICK
IS...
GRRK
GRRK
...HEAVIER
!!
WHAP

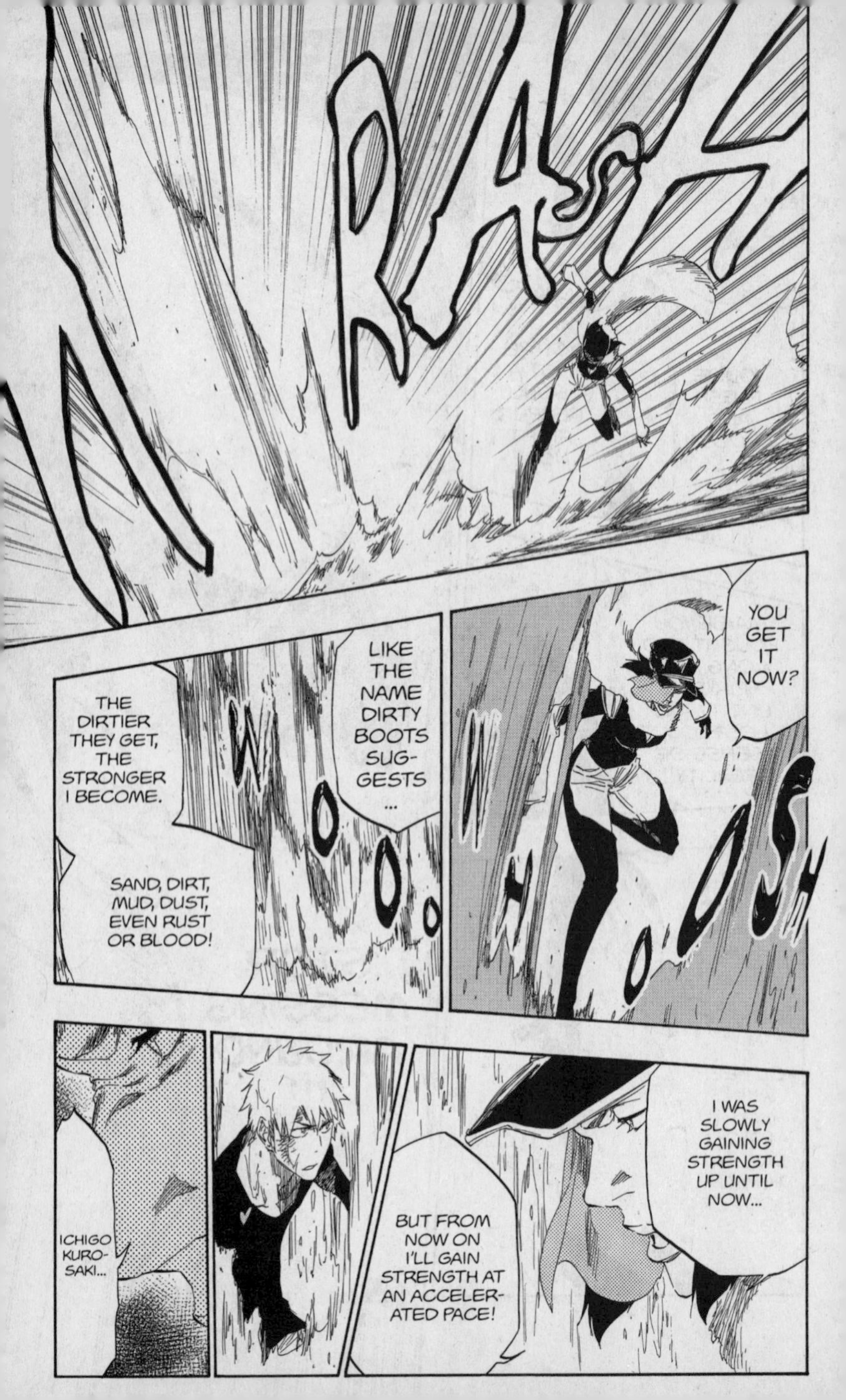
YOU GET IT NOW?
LIKE THE NAME DIRTY BOOTS SUGGESTS...
THE DIRTIER THEY GET, THE STRONGER I BECOME.
SAND, DIRT, MUD, DUST, EVEN RUST OR BLOOD!
I WAS SLOWLY GAINING STRENGTH UP UNTIL NOW...
BUT FROM NOW ON I'LL GAIN STRENGTH AT AN ACCELERATED PACE!
ICHIGO KUROSAKI...

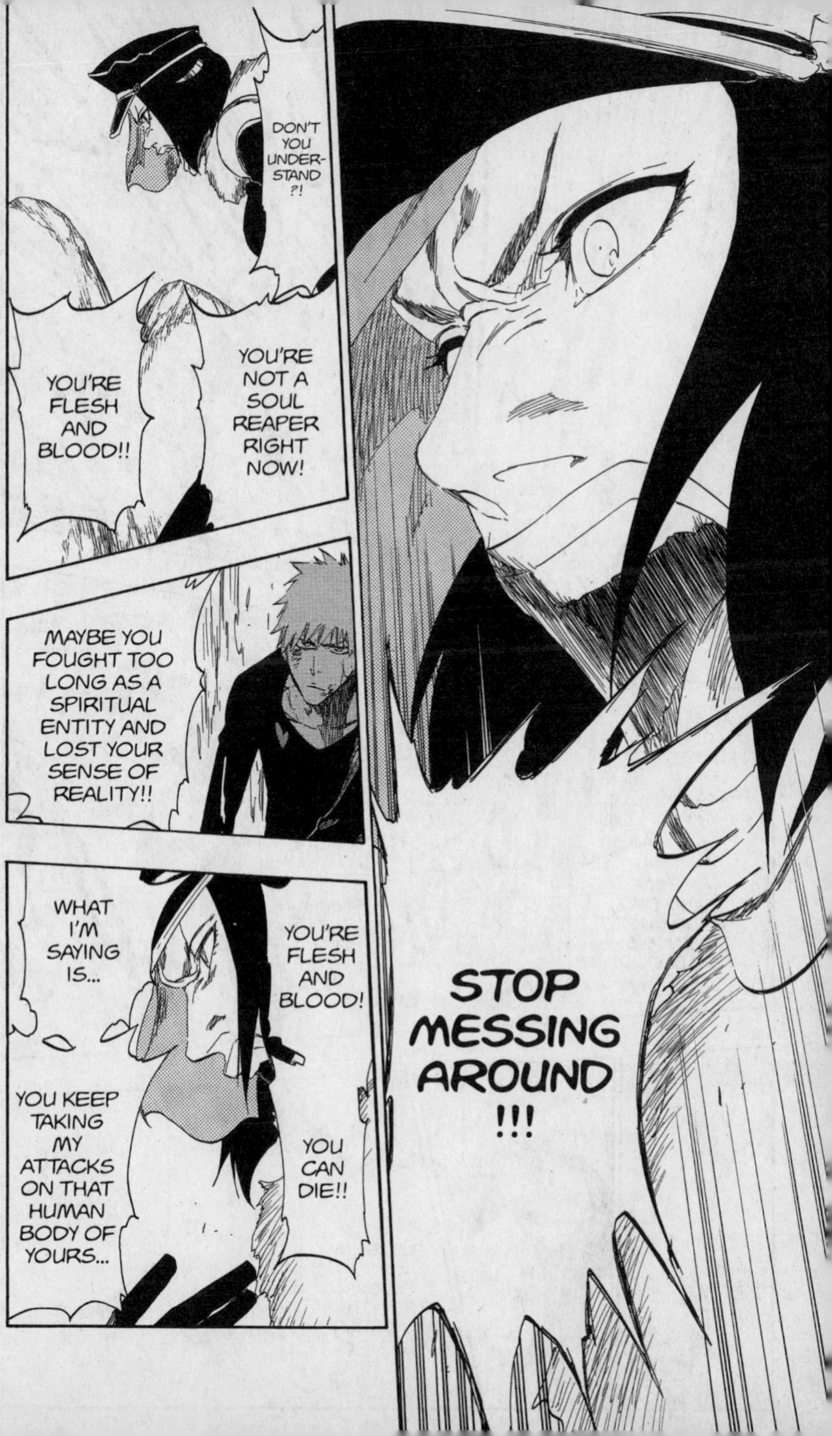
STOP MESSING AROUND!!!
DON'T YOU UNDERSTAND?!
YOU'RE NOT A SOUL REAPER RIGHT NOW!
YOU'RE FLESH AND BLOOD!!
MAYBE YOU FOUGHT TOO LONG AS A SPIRITUAL ENTITY AND LOST YOUR SENSE OF REALITY!!
YOU'RE FLESH AND BLOOD!
WHAT I'M SAYING IS...
YOU CAN DIE!!
YOU KEEP TAKING MY ATTACKS ON THAT HUMAN BODY OF YOURS...

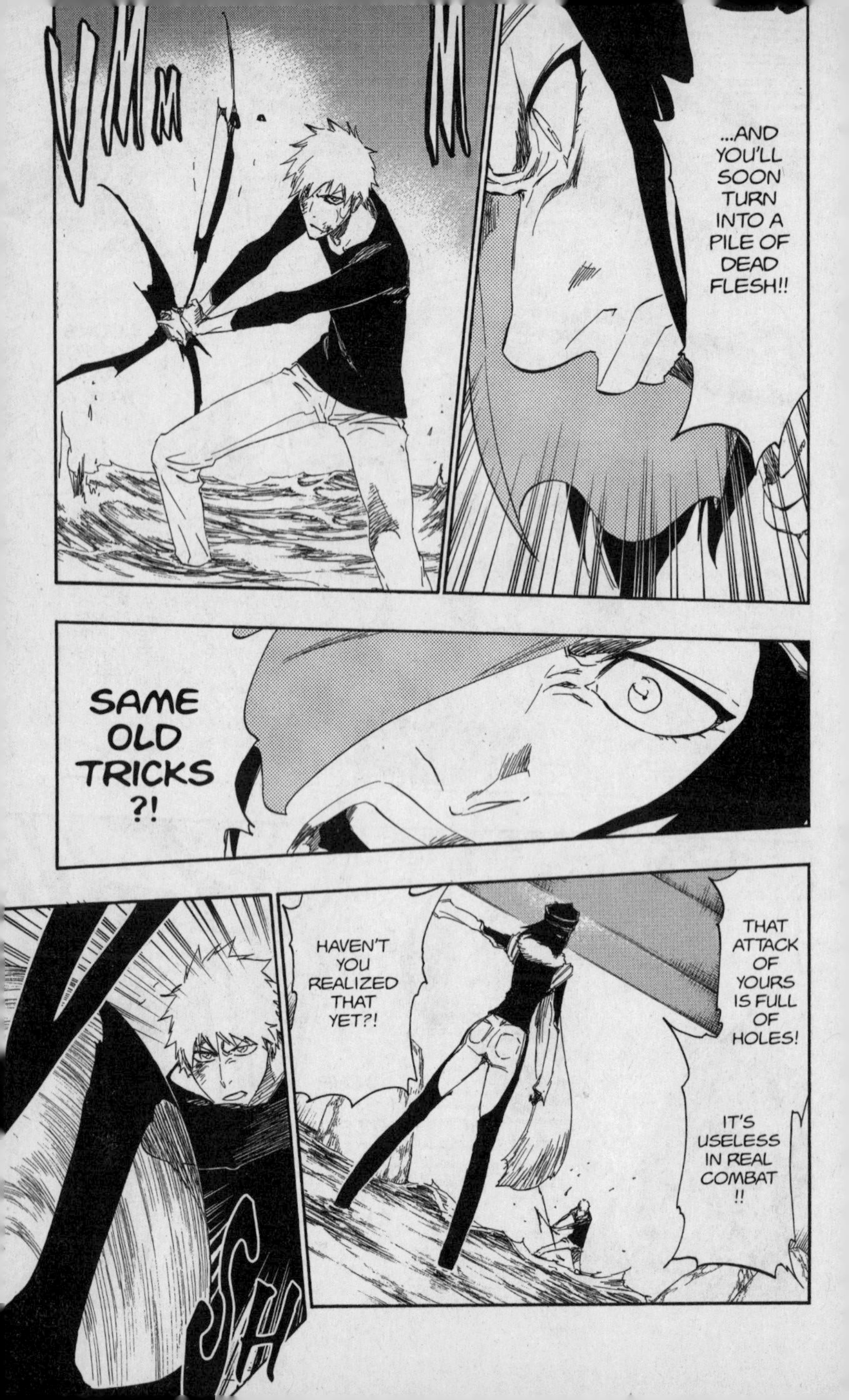
...AND YOU'LL SOON TURN INTO A PILE OF DEAD FLESH!!
VMM
SAME OLD TRICKS?!
THAT ATTACK OF YOURS IS FULL OF HOLES!
HAVEN'T YOU REALIZED THAT YET?!
IT'S USELESS IN REAL COMBAT!!

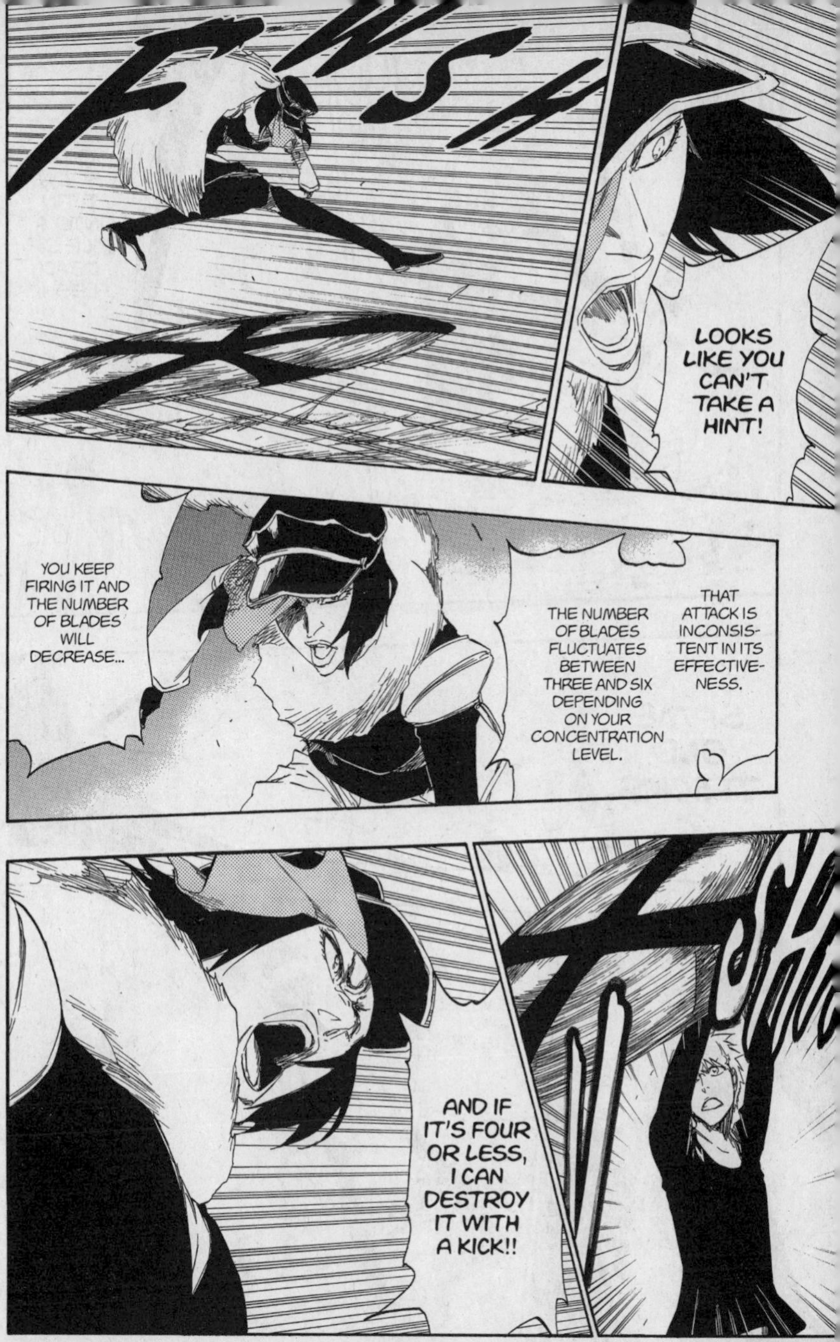
LOOKS LIKE YOU CAN'T TAKE A HINT!
FWSH
THAT ATTACK IS INCONSIS-TENT IN ITS EFFECTIVE-NESS.
THE NUMBER OF BLADES FLUCTUATES BETWEEN THREE AND SIX DEPENDING ON YOUR CONCENTRATION LEVEL.
YOU KEEP FIRING IT AND THE NUMBER OF BLADES WILL DECREASE...
AND IF IT'S FOUR OR LESS, I CAN DESTROY IT WITH A KICK!!

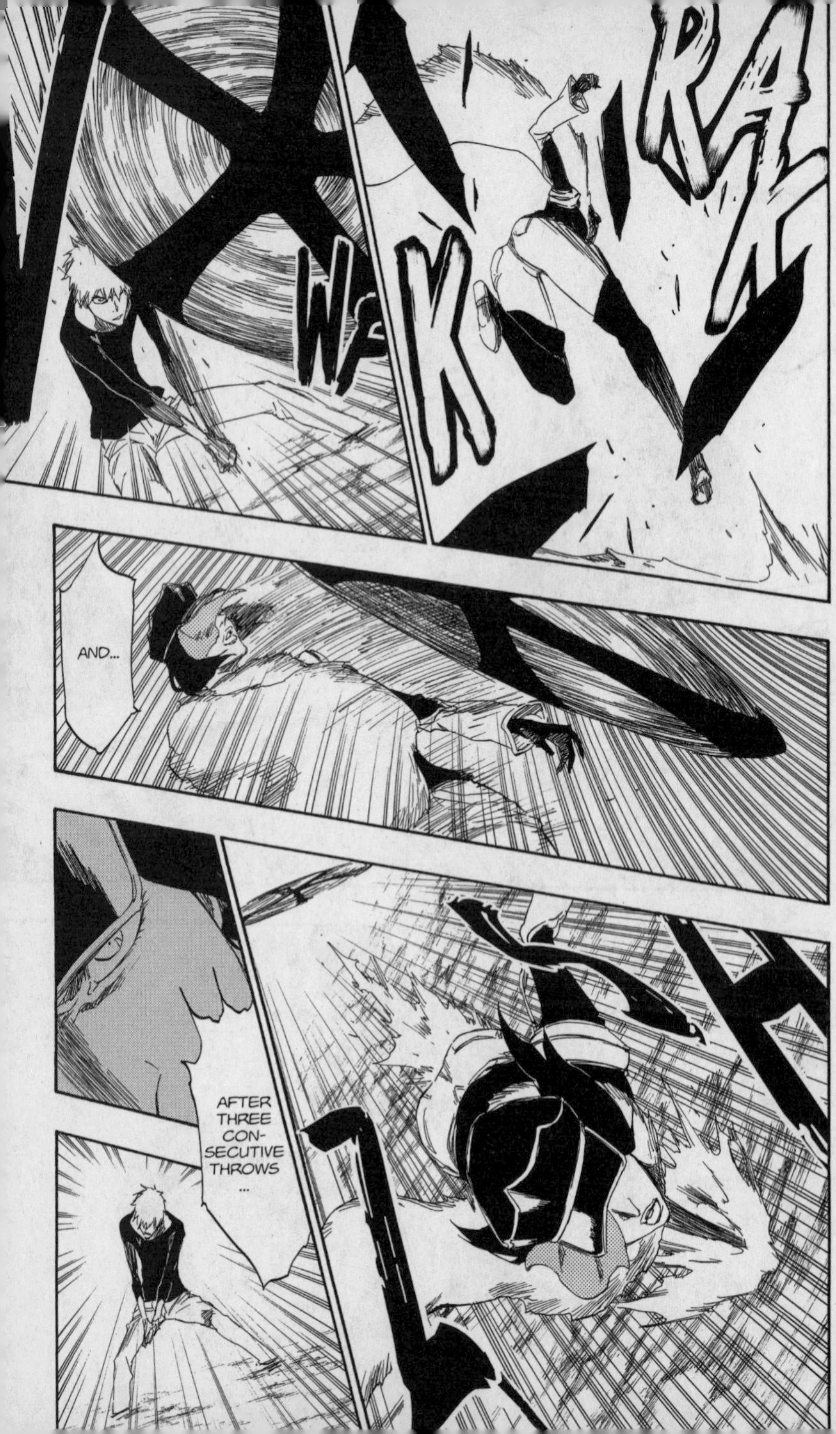
AND...
AFTER THREE CON-SECUTIVE THROWS ...

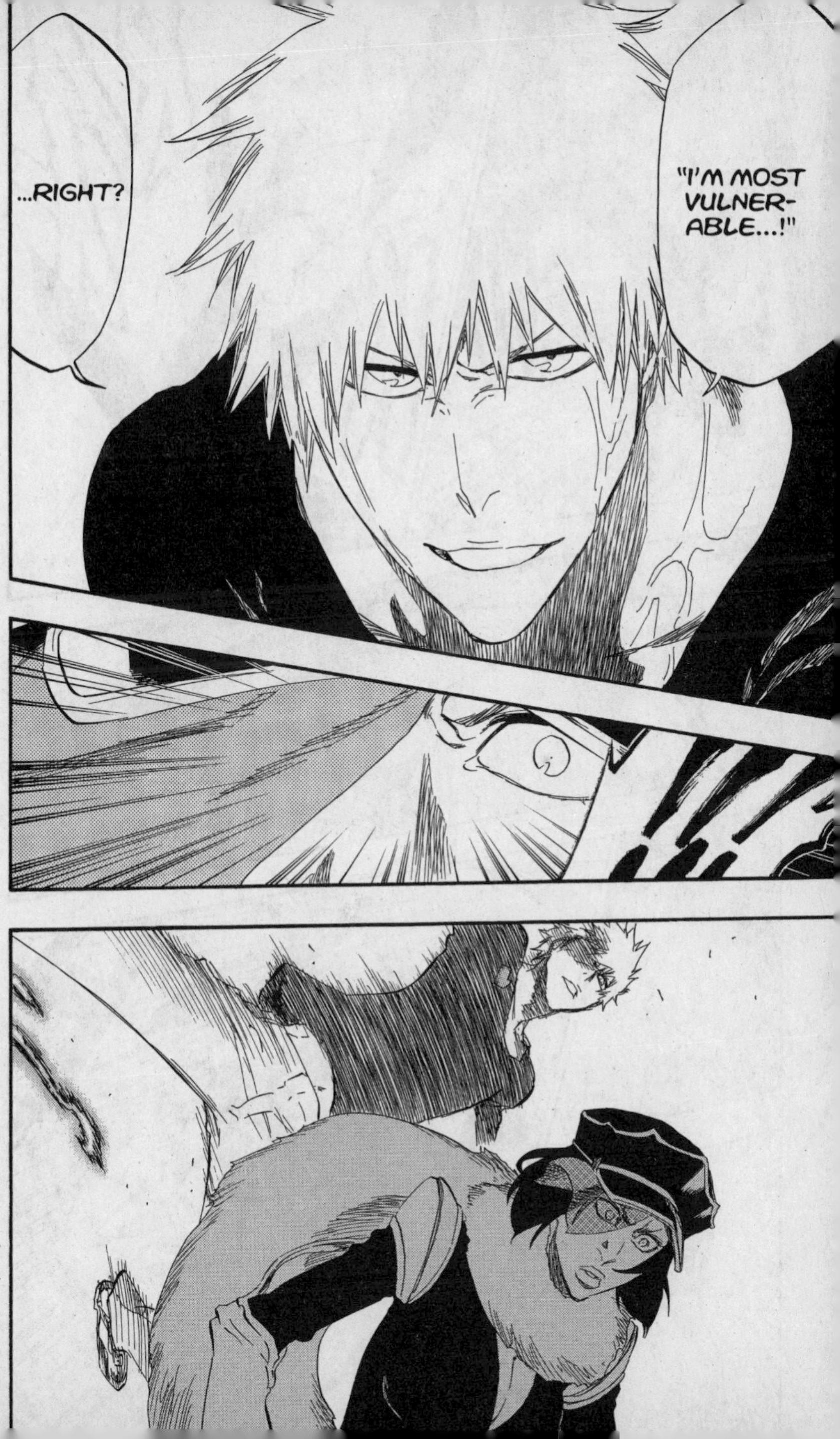
"I'M MOST VULNER-ABLE...!"
...RIGHT?

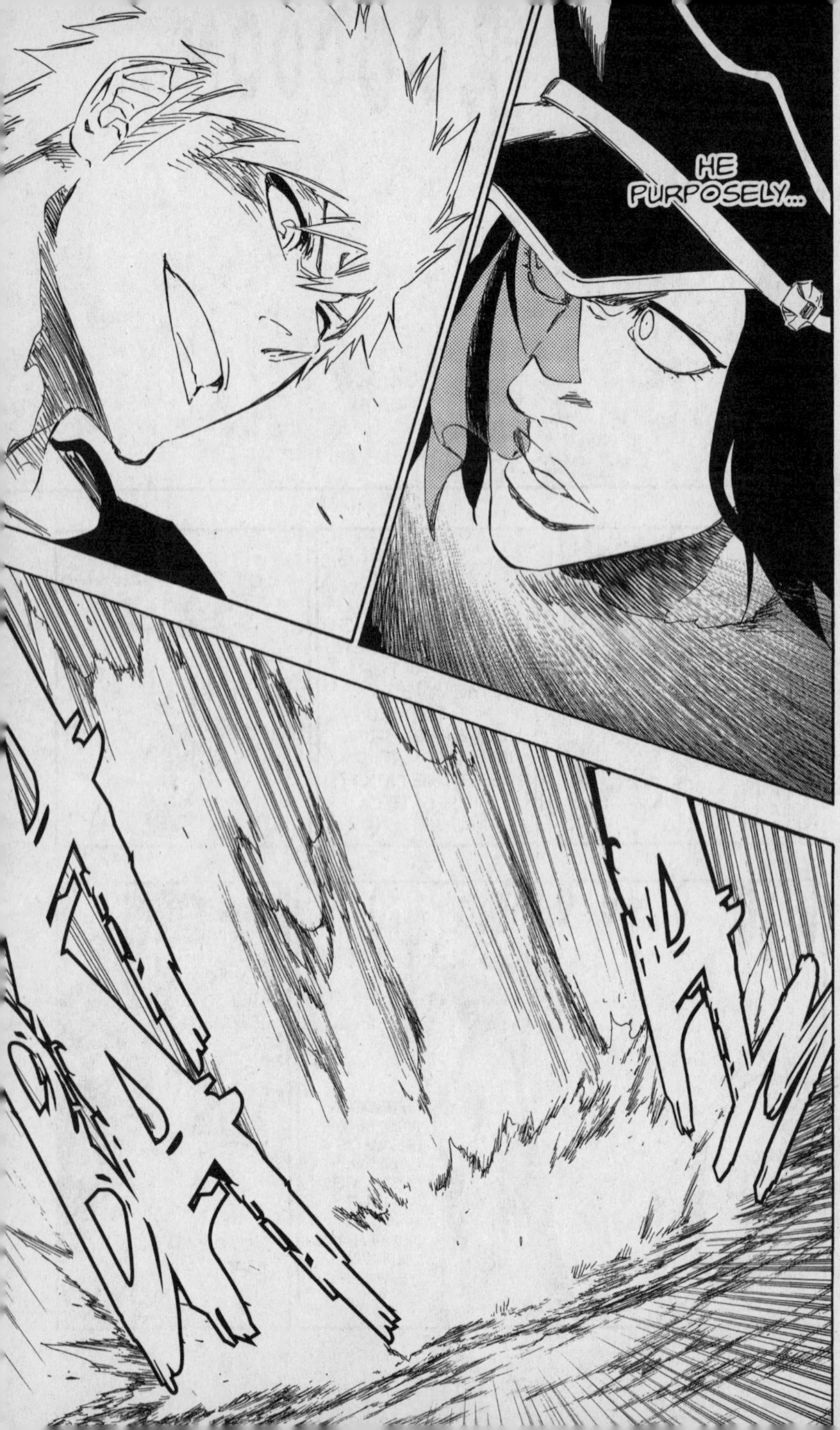
HE PURPOSELY...

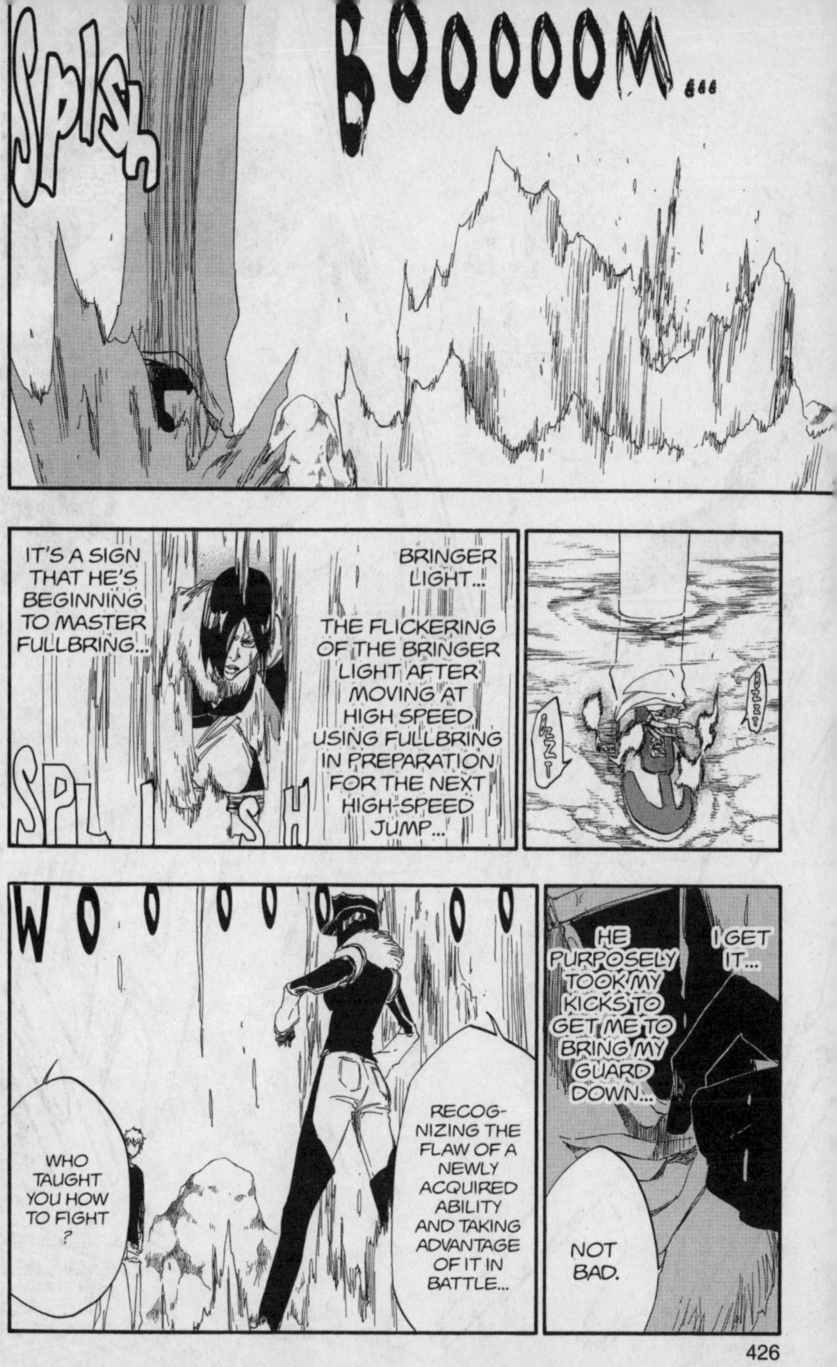
BOOOOOM...
Splsh
DZZT
DZZT
BRINGER LIGHT...
THE FLICKERING OF THE BRINGER LIGHT AFTER MOVING AT HIGH SPEED USING FULLBRING IN PREPARATION FOR THE NEXT HIGH-SPEED JUMP...
IT'S A SIGN THAT HE'S BEGINNING TO MASTER FULLBRING...
SPLISH
I GET IT...
HE PURPOSELY TOOK MY KICKS TO GET ME TO BRING MY GUARD DOWN...
NOT BAD.
WOOOOOO
RECOGNIZING THE FLAW OF A NEWLY ACQUIRED ABILITY AND TAKING ADVANTAGE OF IT IN BATTLE...
WHO TAUGHT YOU HOW TO FIGHT?

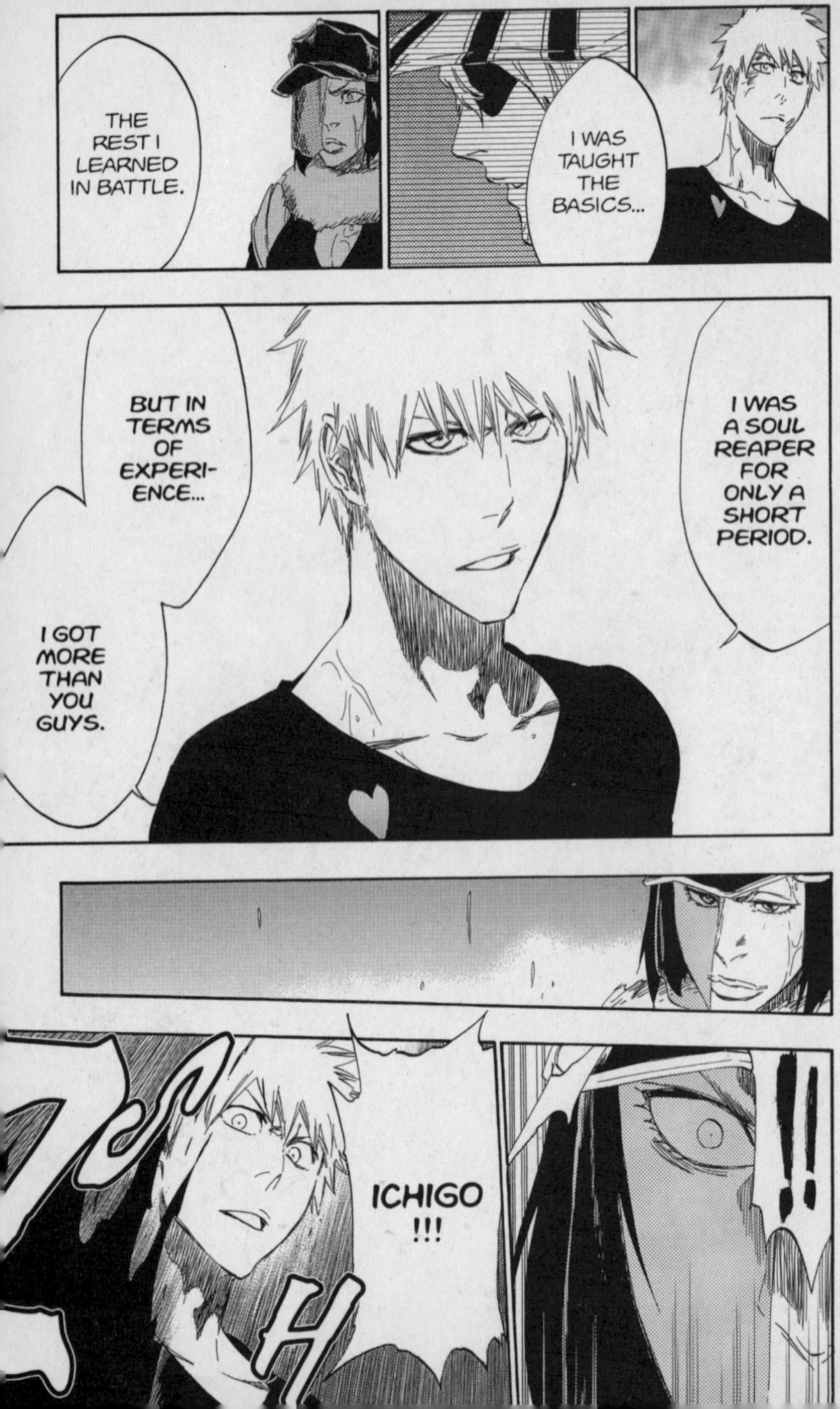
I WAS TAUGHT THE BASICS...
THE REST I LEARNED IN BATTLE.
I WAS A SOUL REAPER FOR ONLY A SHORT PERIOD.
BUT IN TERMS OF EXPERIENCE...
I GOT MORE THAN YOU GUYS.
!!
ICHIGO !!!

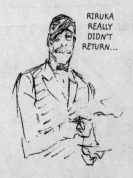

RIRUKA
REALLY
DIDN'T
RETURN...

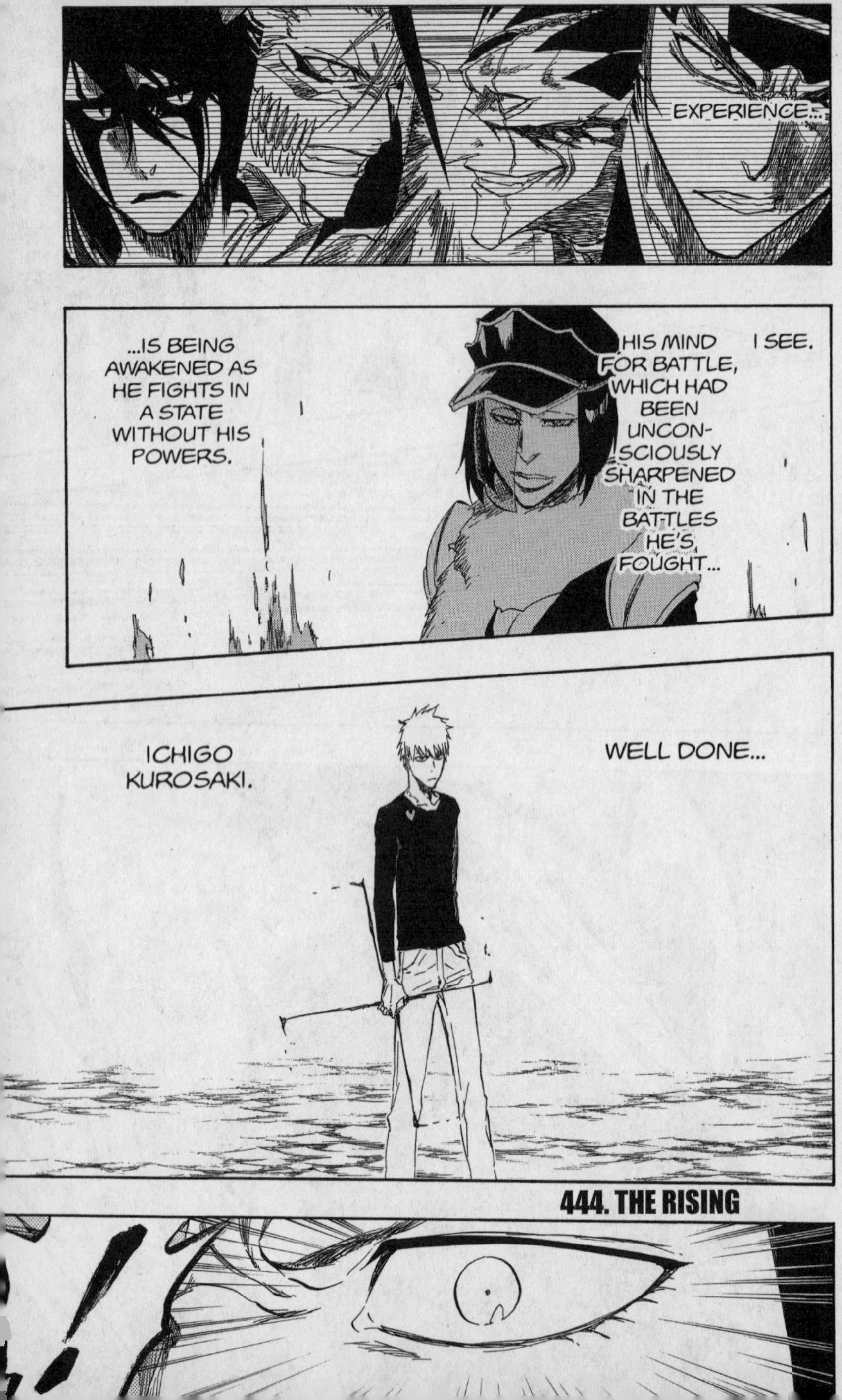
EXPERIENCE...
I SEE.
HIS MIND FOR BATTLE, WHICH HAD BEEN UNCONSCIOUSLY SHARPENED IN THE BATTLES HE'S FOUGHT...
...IS BEING AWAKENED AS HE FIGHTS IN A STATE WITHOUT HIS POWERS.
WELL DONE...
ICHIGO KUROSAKI.
444. THE RISING

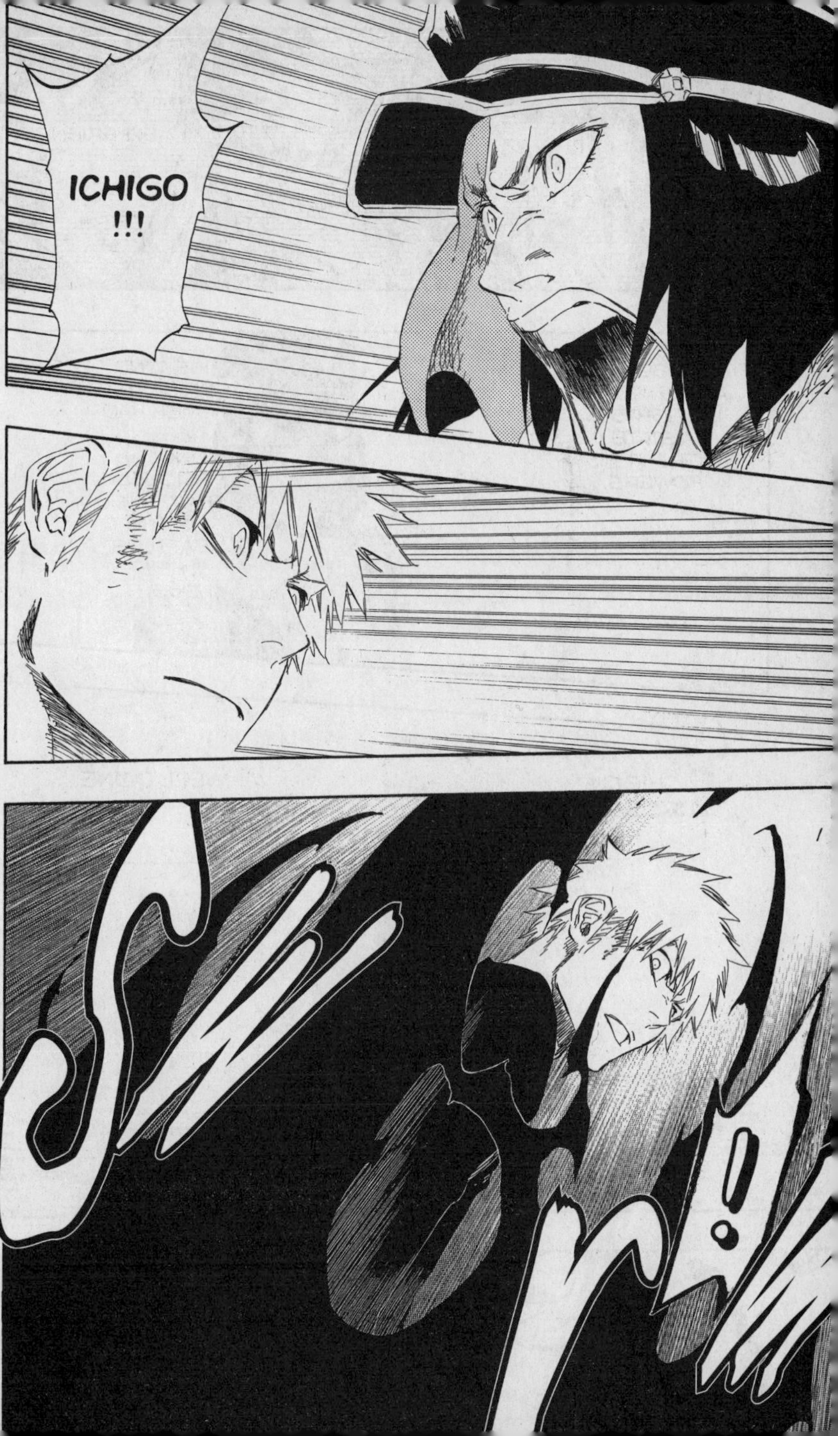
ICHIGO
!!!

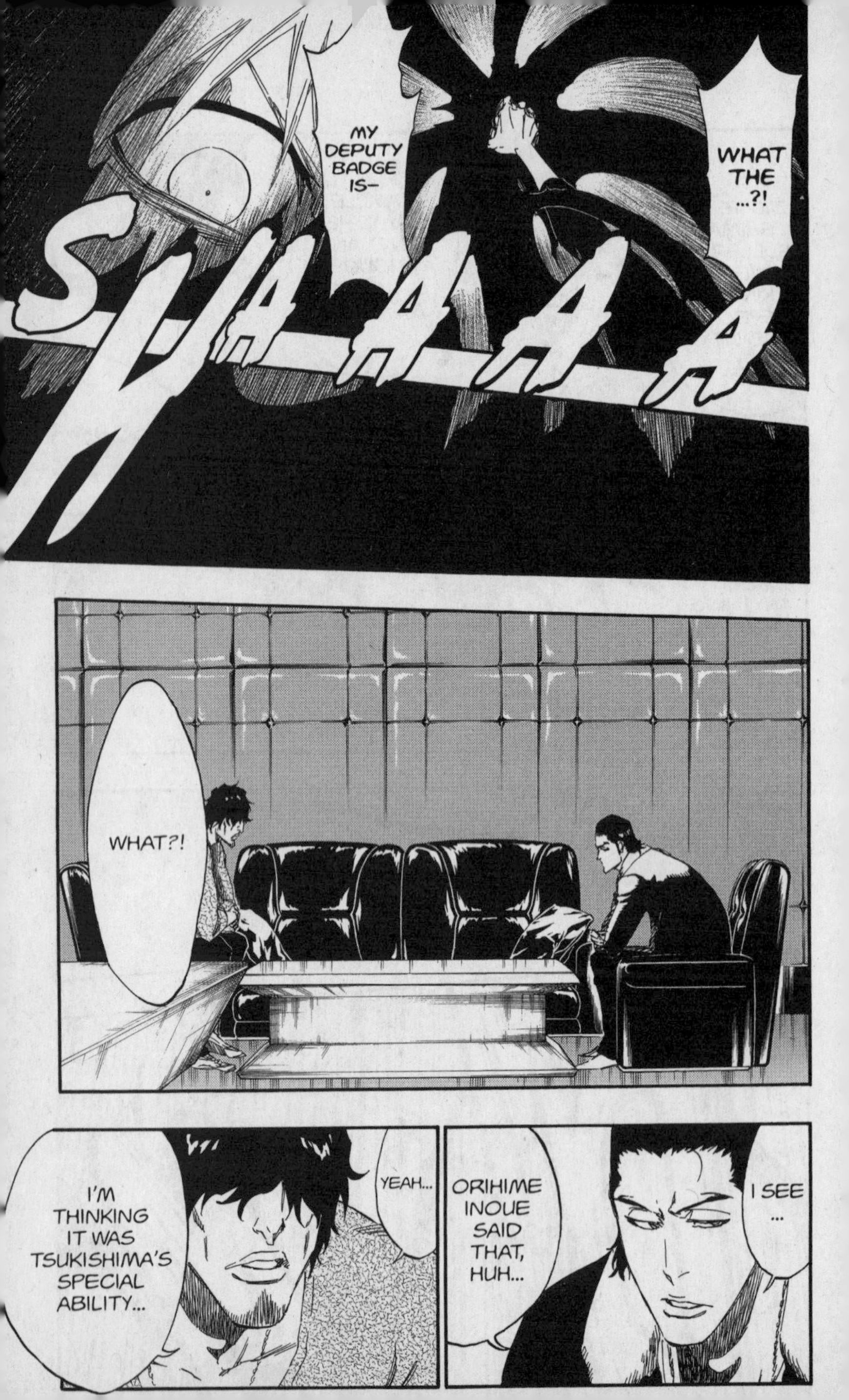
WHAT THE ...?!
MY DEPUTY BADGE IS—
SHAAAA
WHAT?!
I SEE ...
ORIHIME INOUE SAID THAT, HUH...
YEAH...
I'M THINKING IT WAS TSUKISHIMA'S SPECIAL ABILITY...

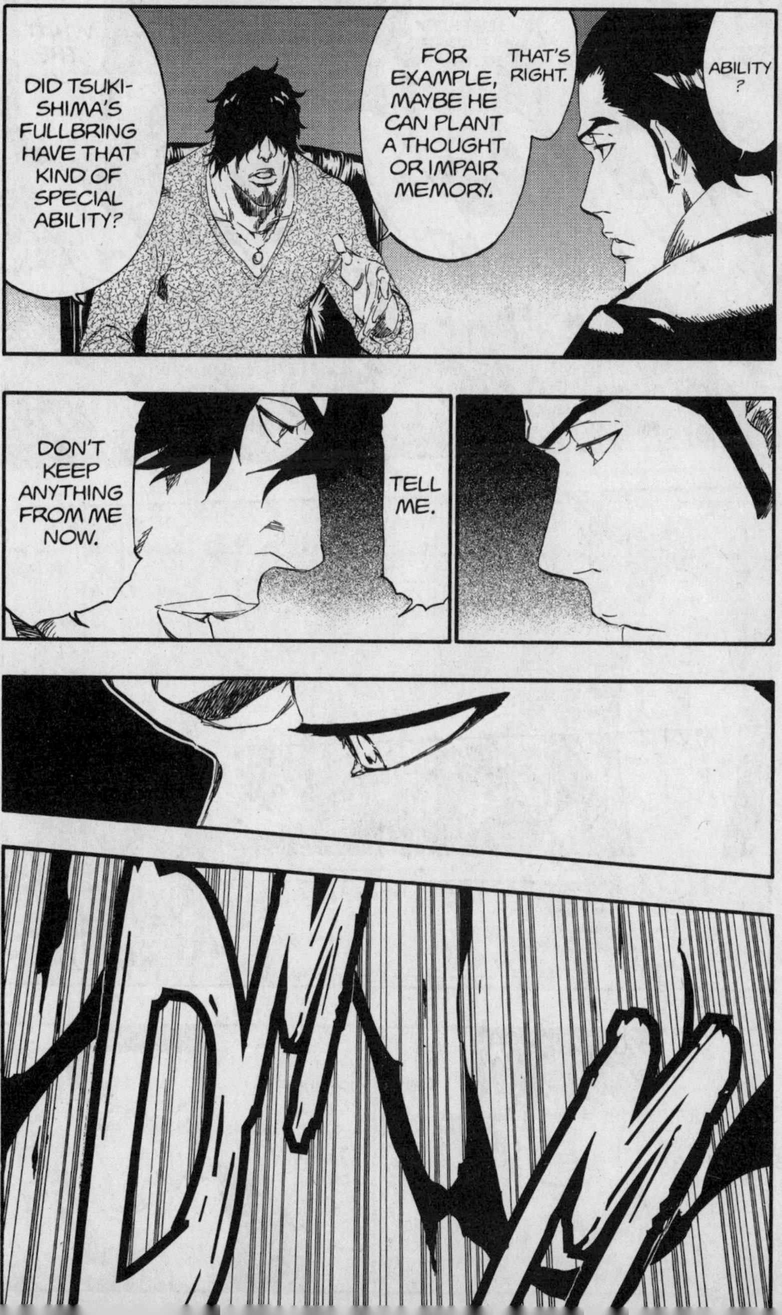
ABILITY?
THAT'S RIGHT.
FOR EXAMPLE, MAYBE HE CAN PLANT A THOUGHT OR IMPAIR MEMORY.
DID TSUKISHIMA'S FULLBRING HAVE THAT KIND OF SPECIAL ABILITY?
TELL ME.
DON'T KEEP ANYTHING FROM ME NOW.

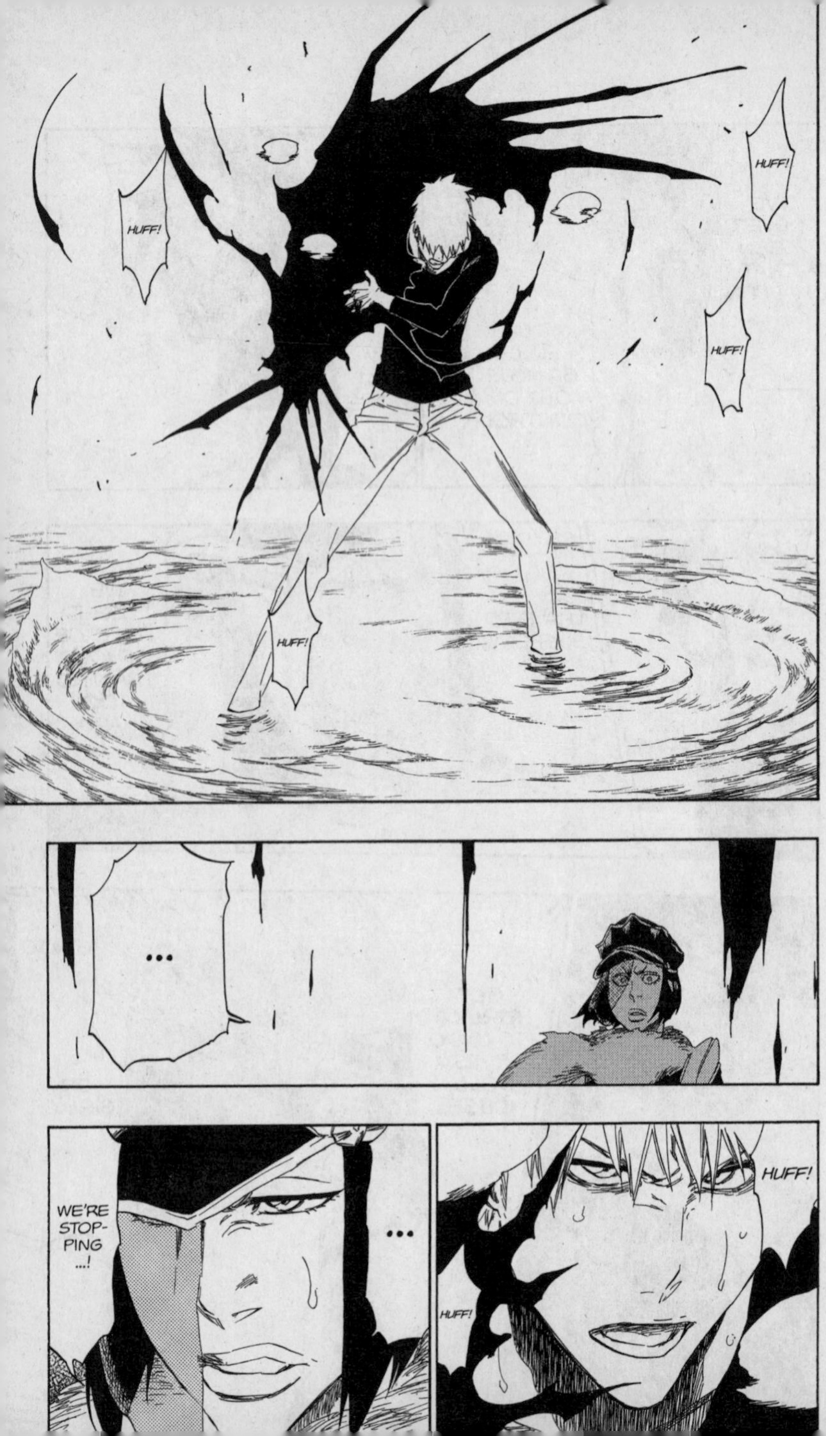
HUFF!
HUFF!
HUFF!
HUFF!
...
HUFF!
HUFF!
...
WE'RE STOP-PING ...!

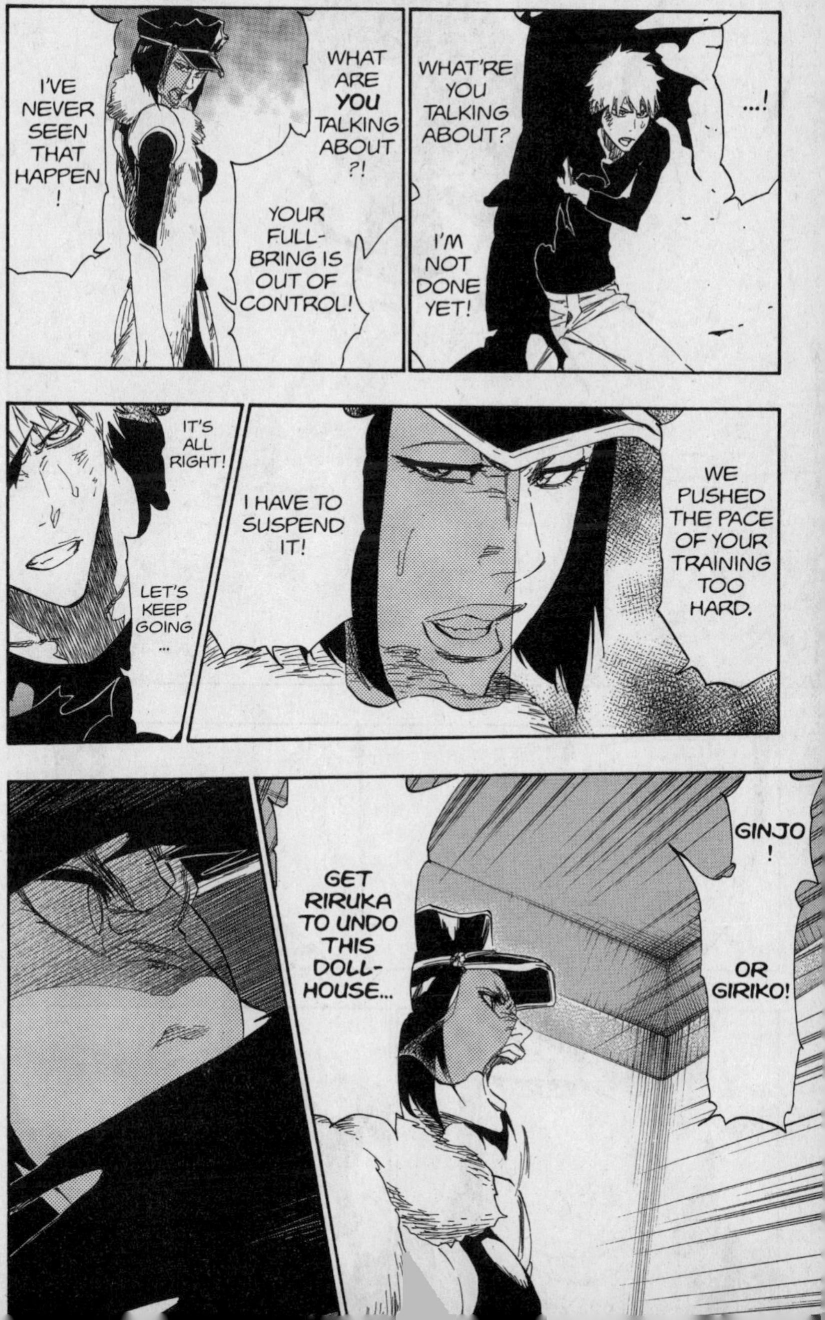
...!
WHAT'RE YOU TALKING ABOUT?
I'M NOT DONE YET!
WHAT ARE **YOU** TALKING ABOUT?!
YOUR FULL-BRING IS OUT OF CONTROL!
I'VE NEVER SEEN THAT HAPPEN!
WE PUSHED THE PACE OF YOUR TRAINING TOO HARD.
I HAVE TO SUSPEND IT!
IT'S ALL RIGHT!
LET'S KEEP GOING...
GINJO!
OR GIRIKO!
GET RIRUKA TO UNDO THIS DOLL-HOUSE...

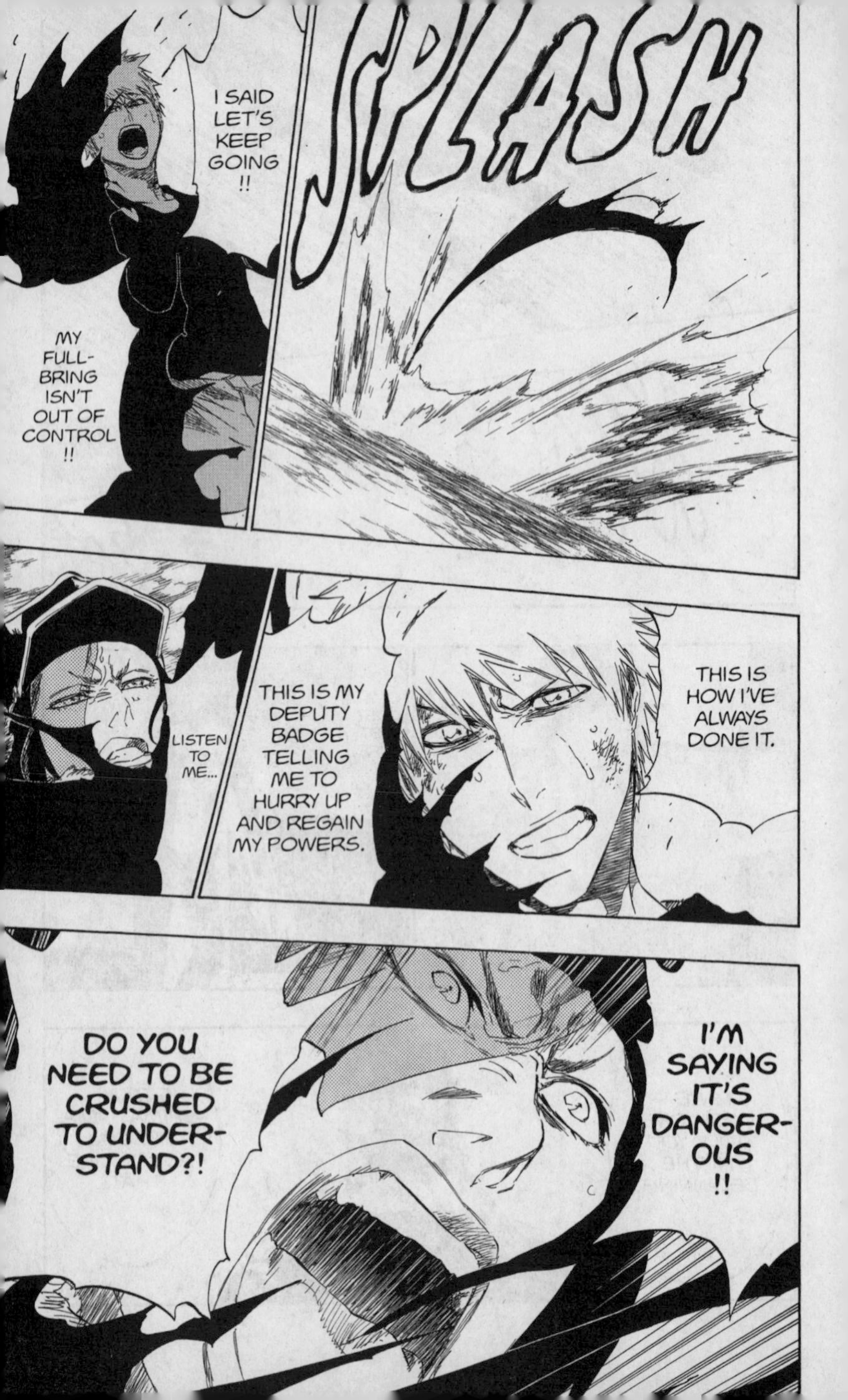
SPLASH
I SAID LET'S KEEP GOING!!
MY FULL-BRING ISN'T OUT OF CONTROL!!
THIS IS HOW I'VE ALWAYS DONE IT.
THIS IS MY DEPUTY BADGE TELLING ME TO HURRY UP AND REGAIN MY POWERS.
LISTEN TO ME...
I'M SAYING IT'S DANGER-OUS!!
DO YOU NEED TO BE CRUSHED TO UNDER-STAND?!

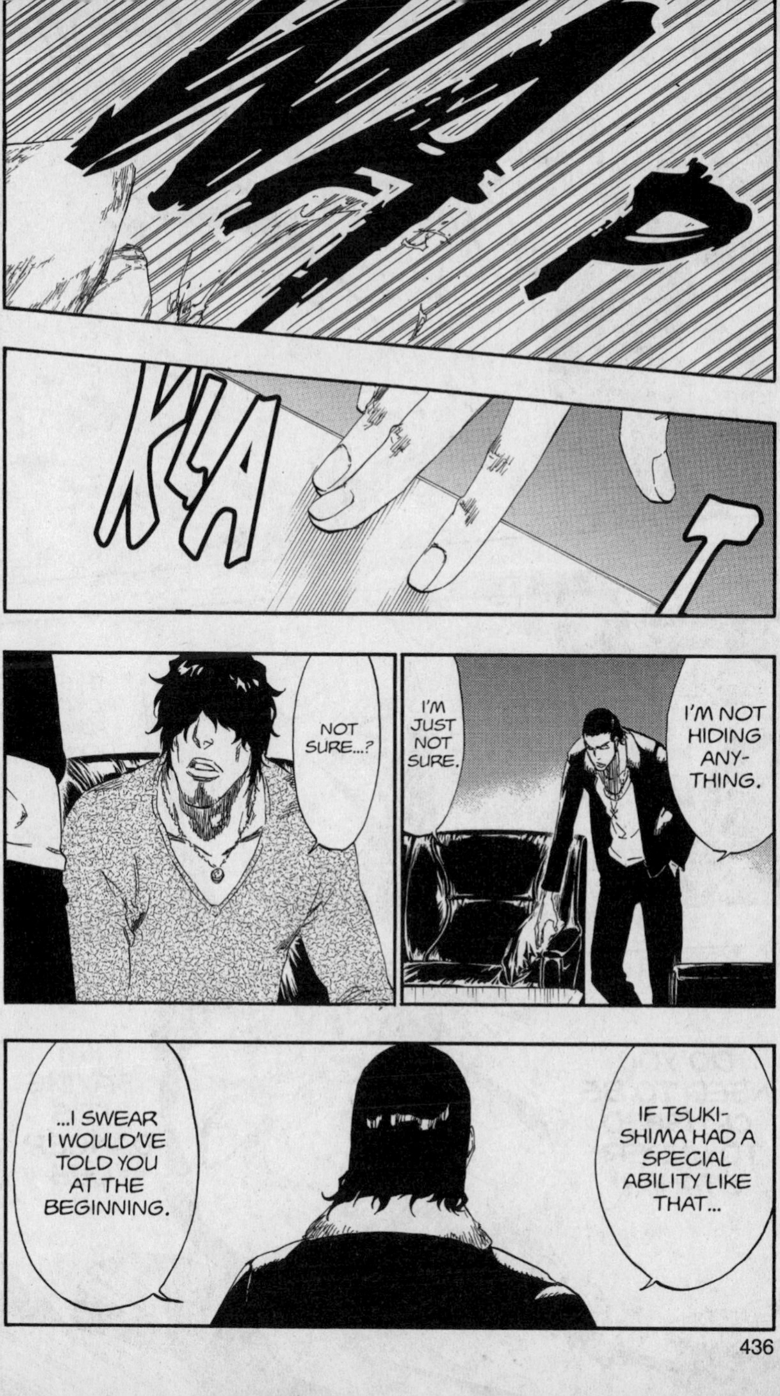
WHAP
KLA
I'M NOT HIDING ANY-THING.
I'M JUST NOT SURE.
NOT SURE...?
IF TSUKI-SHIMA HAD A SPECIAL ABILITY LIKE THAT...
...I SWEAR I WOULD'VE TOLD YOU AT THE BEGINNING.

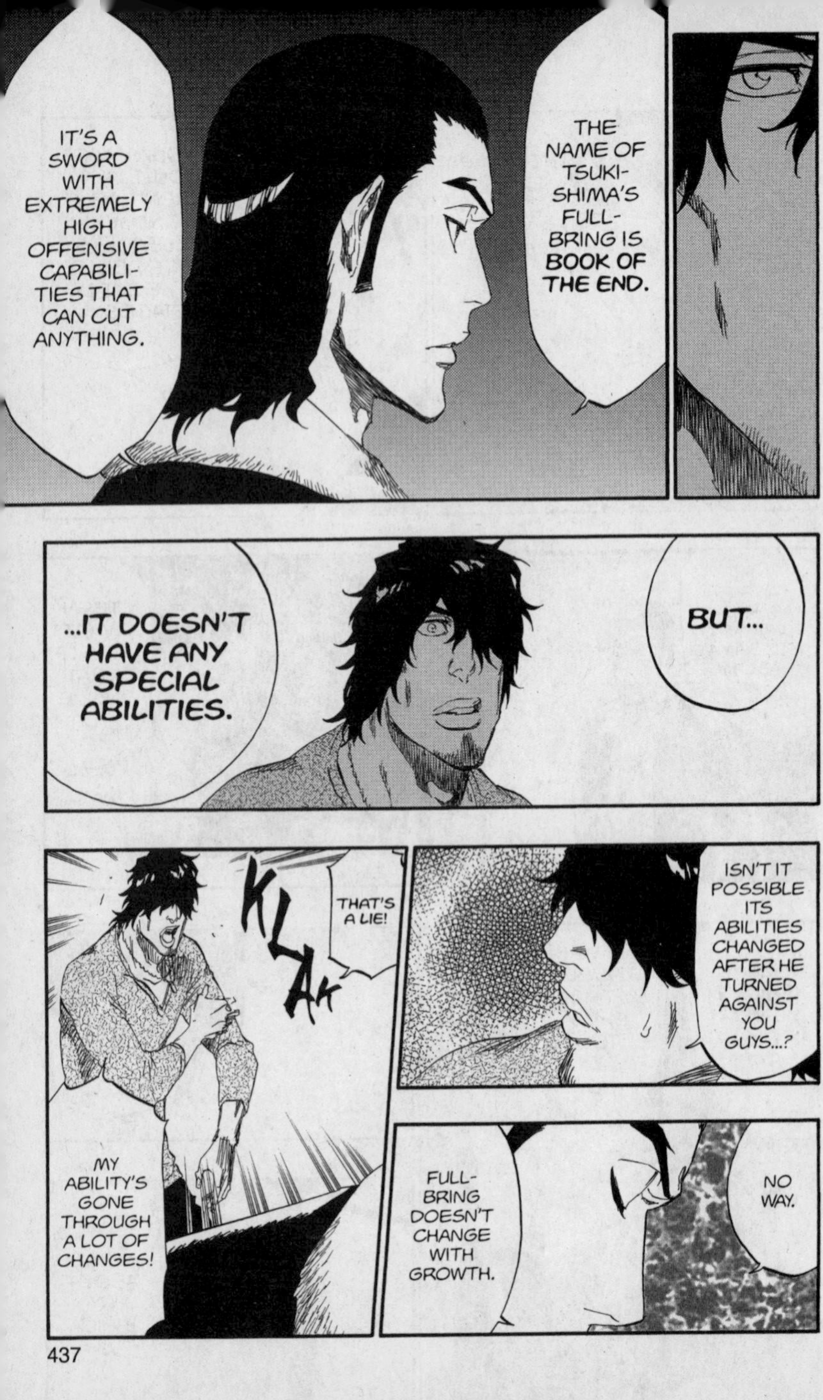
THE NAME OF TSUKISHIMA'S FULLBRING IS BOOK OF THE END.
IT'S A SWORD WITH EXTREMELY HIGH OFFENSIVE CAPABILITIES THAT CAN CUT ANYTHING.
BUT...
...IT DOESN'T HAVE ANY SPECIAL ABILITIES.
ISN'T IT POSSIBLE ITS ABILITIES CHANGED AFTER HE TURNED AGAINST YOU GUYS...?
NO WAY.
FULLBRING DOESN'T CHANGE WITH GROWTH.
KLAK
THAT'S A LIE!
MY ABILITY'S GONE THROUGH A LOT OF CHANGES!

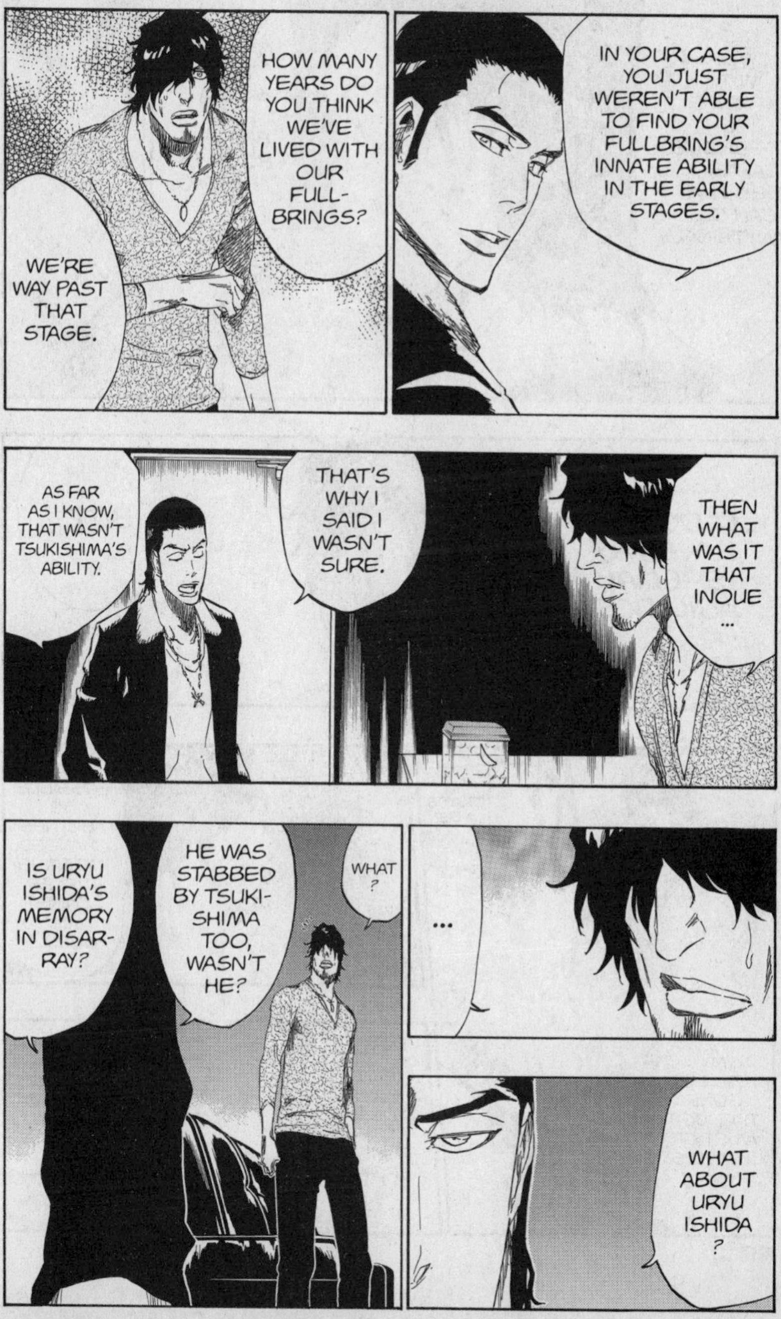
IN YOUR CASE, YOU JUST WEREN'T ABLE TO FIND YOUR FULLBRING'S INNATE ABILITY IN THE EARLY STAGES.
HOW MANY YEARS DO YOU THINK WE'VE LIVED WITH OUR FULL-BRINGS?
WE'RE WAY PAST THAT STAGE.
THEN WHAT WAS IT THAT INOUE ...
THAT'S WHY I SAID I WASN'T SURE.
AS FAR AS I KNOW, THAT WASN'T TSUKISHIMA'S ABILITY.
...
WHAT ABOUT URYU ISHIDA ?
WHAT ?
HE WAS STABBED BY TSUKI-SHIMA TOO, WASN'T HE?
IS URYU ISHIDA'S MEMORY IN DISAR-RAY?

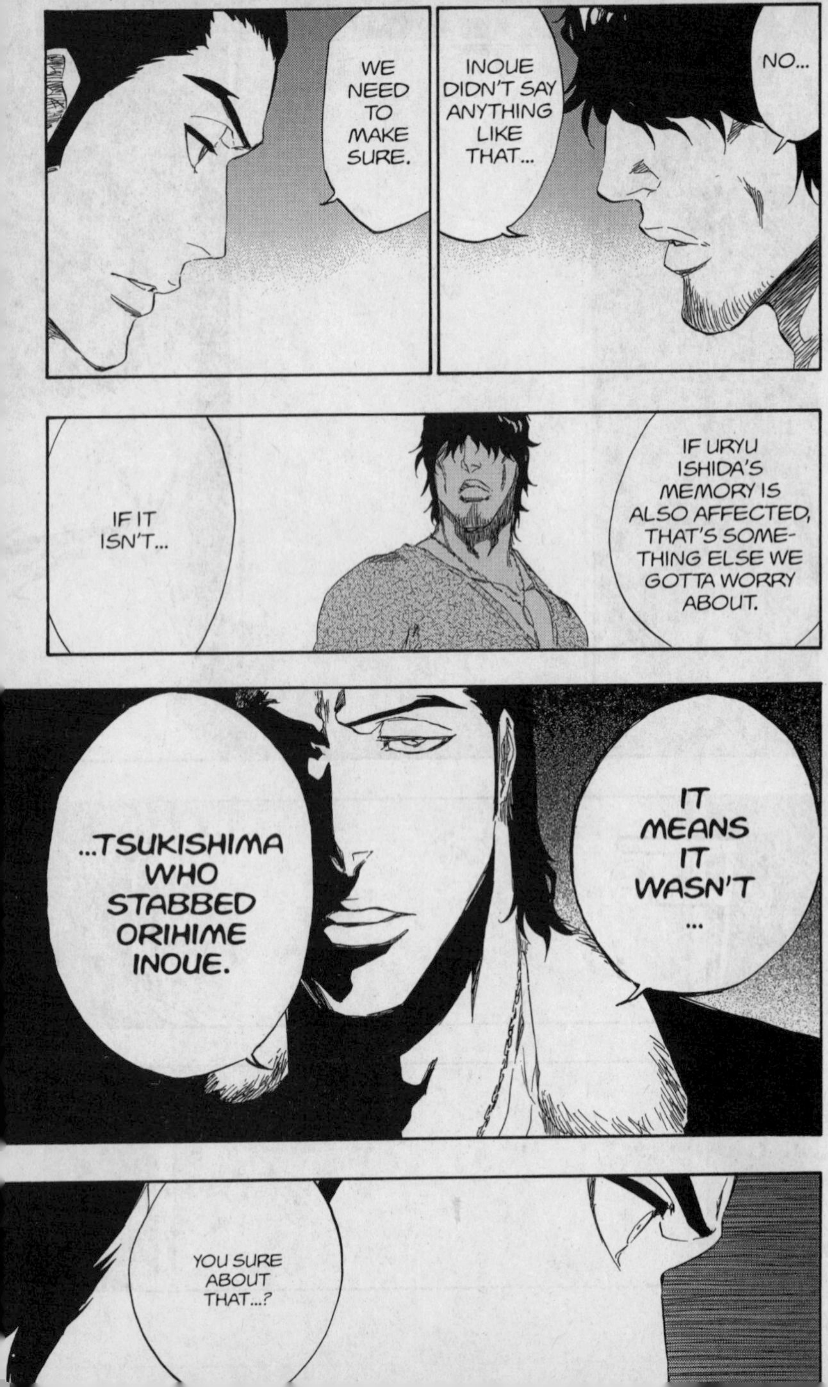
NO...
INOUE DIDN'T SAY ANYTHING LIKE THAT...
WE NEED TO MAKE SURE.
IF URYU ISHIDA'S MEMORY IS ALSO AFFECTED, THAT'S SOME-THING ELSE WE GOTTA WORRY ABOUT.
IF IT ISN'T...
IT MEANS IT WASN'T ...
...TSUKISHIMA WHO STABBED ORIHIME INOUE.
YOU SURE ABOUT THAT...?

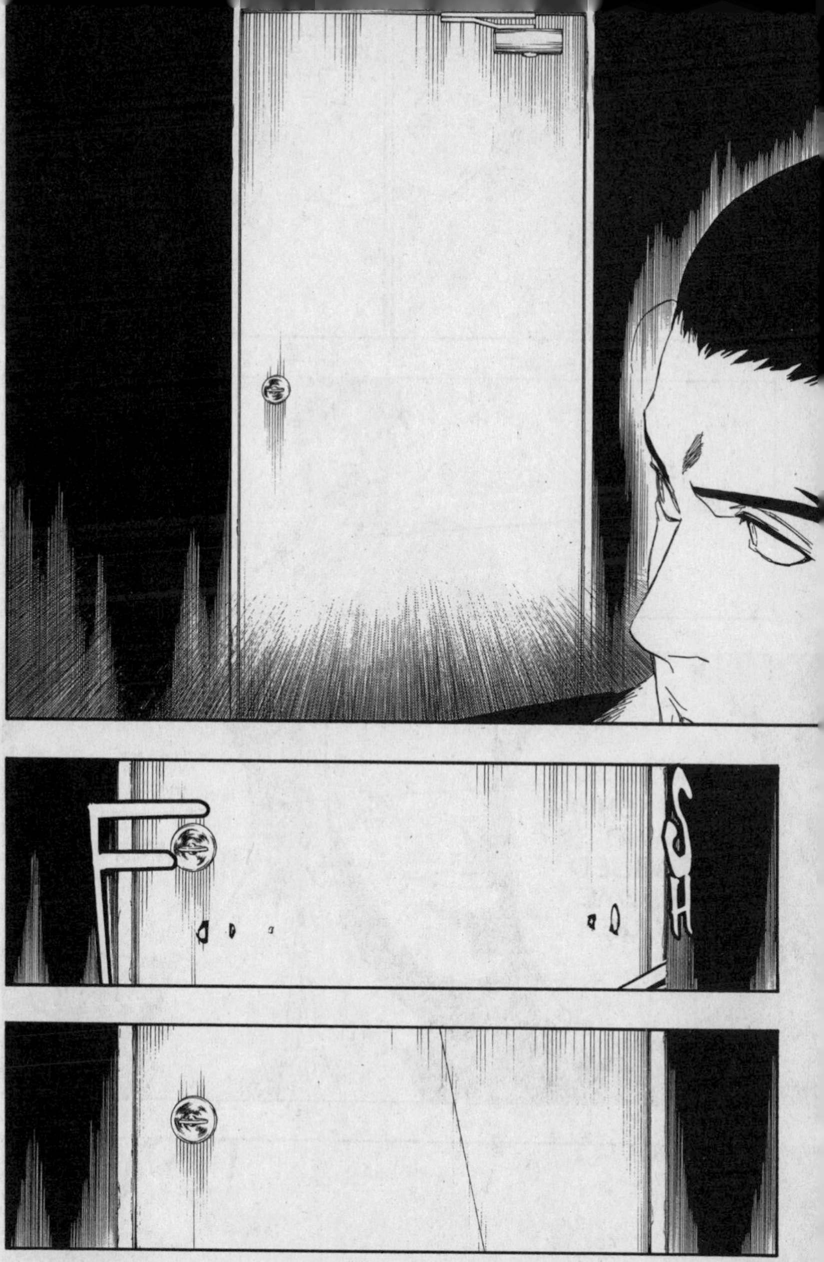
SH

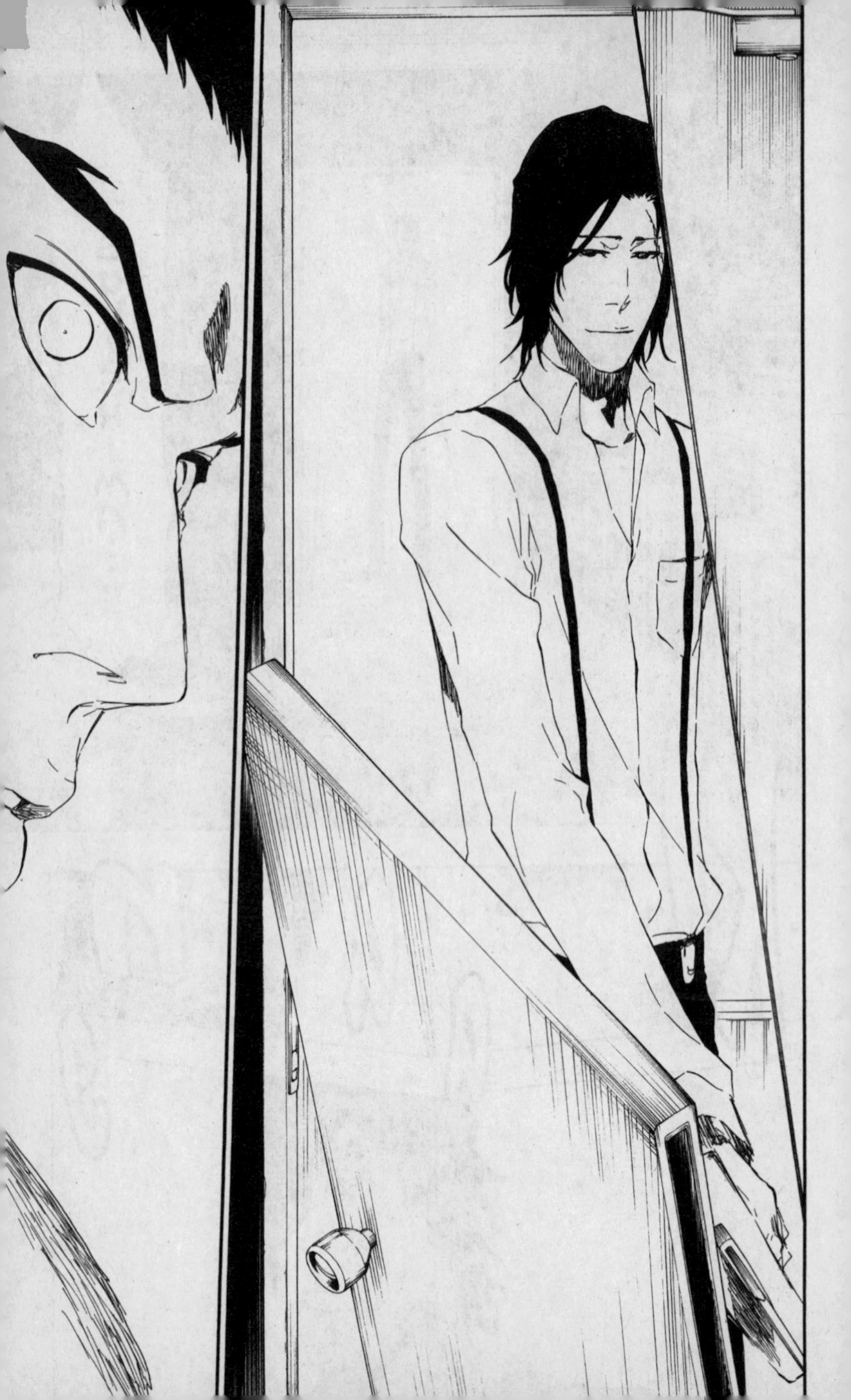

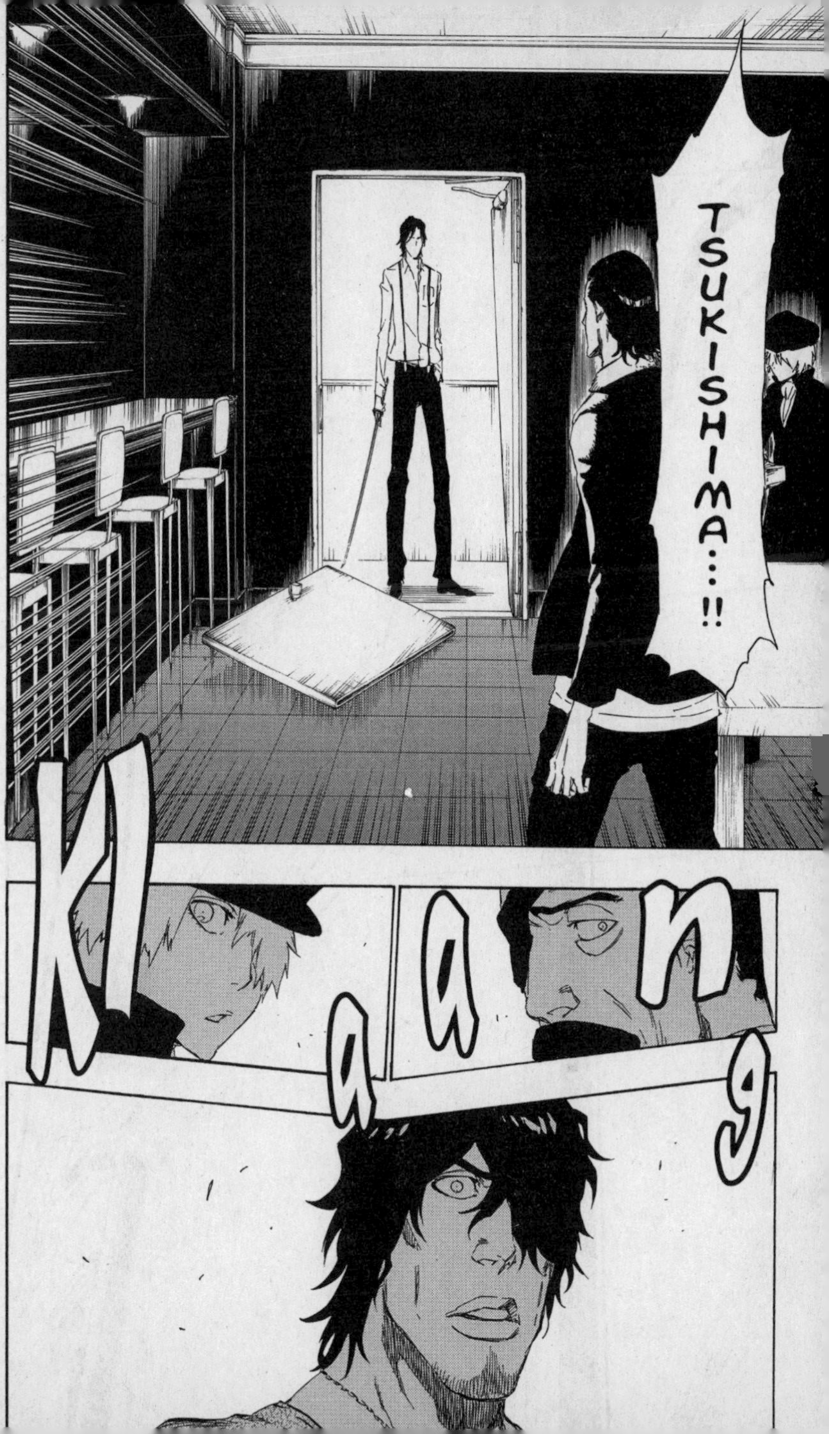
TSUKISHIMA...!!
Klaang

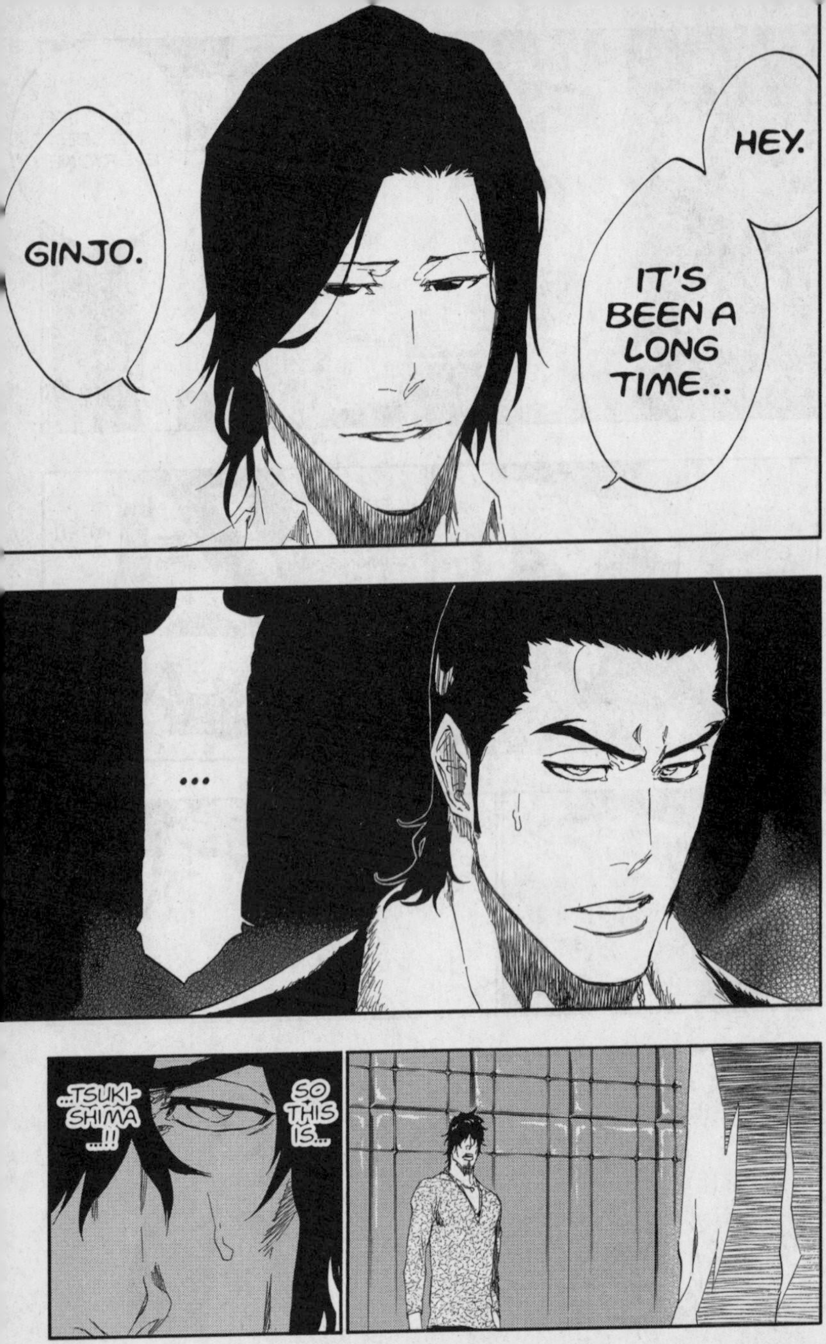
HEY.
IT'S BEEN A LONG TIME...
GINJO.
...
SO THIS IS...
...TSUKI-SHIMA...!!

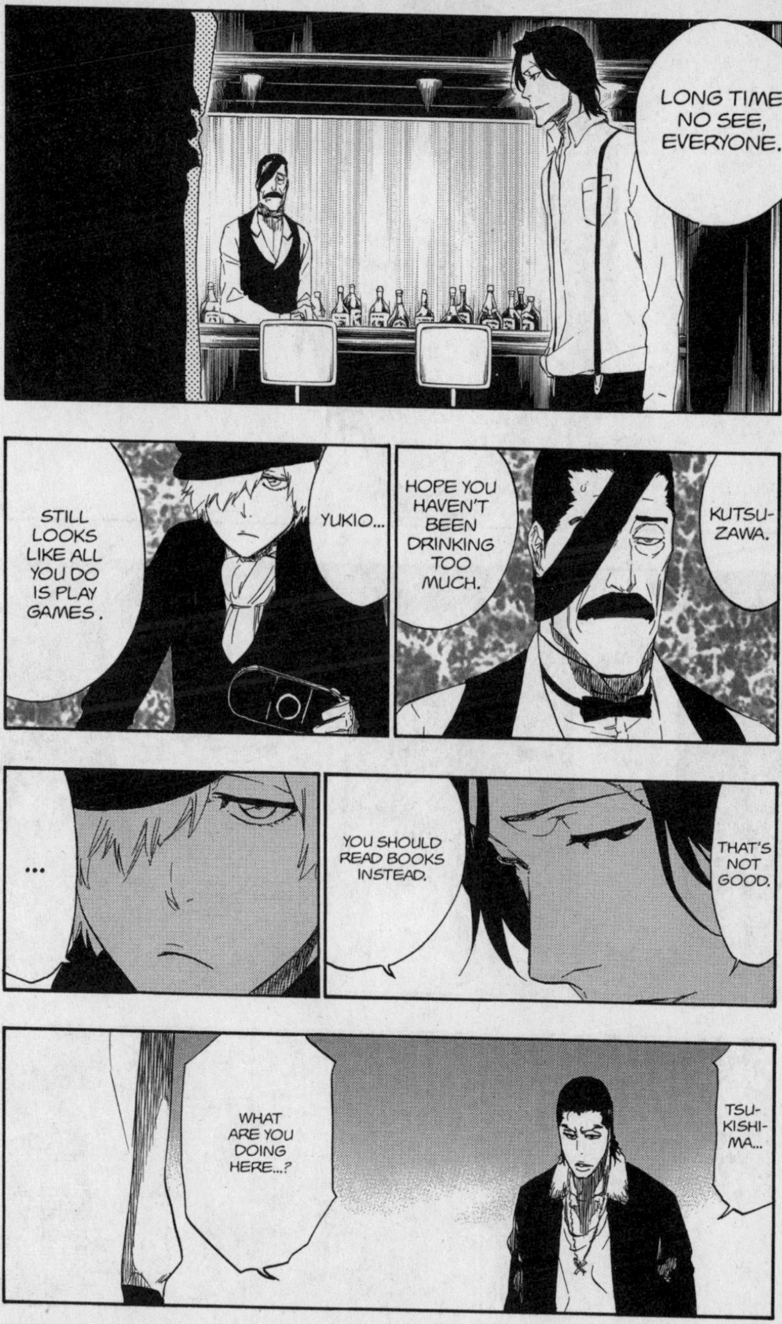
LONG TIME NO SEE, EVERYONE.
KUTSU-ZAWA.
HOPE YOU HAVEN'T BEEN DRINKING TOO MUCH.
YUKIO...
STILL LOOKS LIKE ALL YOU DO IS PLAY GAMES.
THAT'S NOT GOOD.
YOU SHOULD READ BOOKS INSTEAD.
...
TSU-KISHI-MA...
WHAT ARE YOU DOING HERE...?

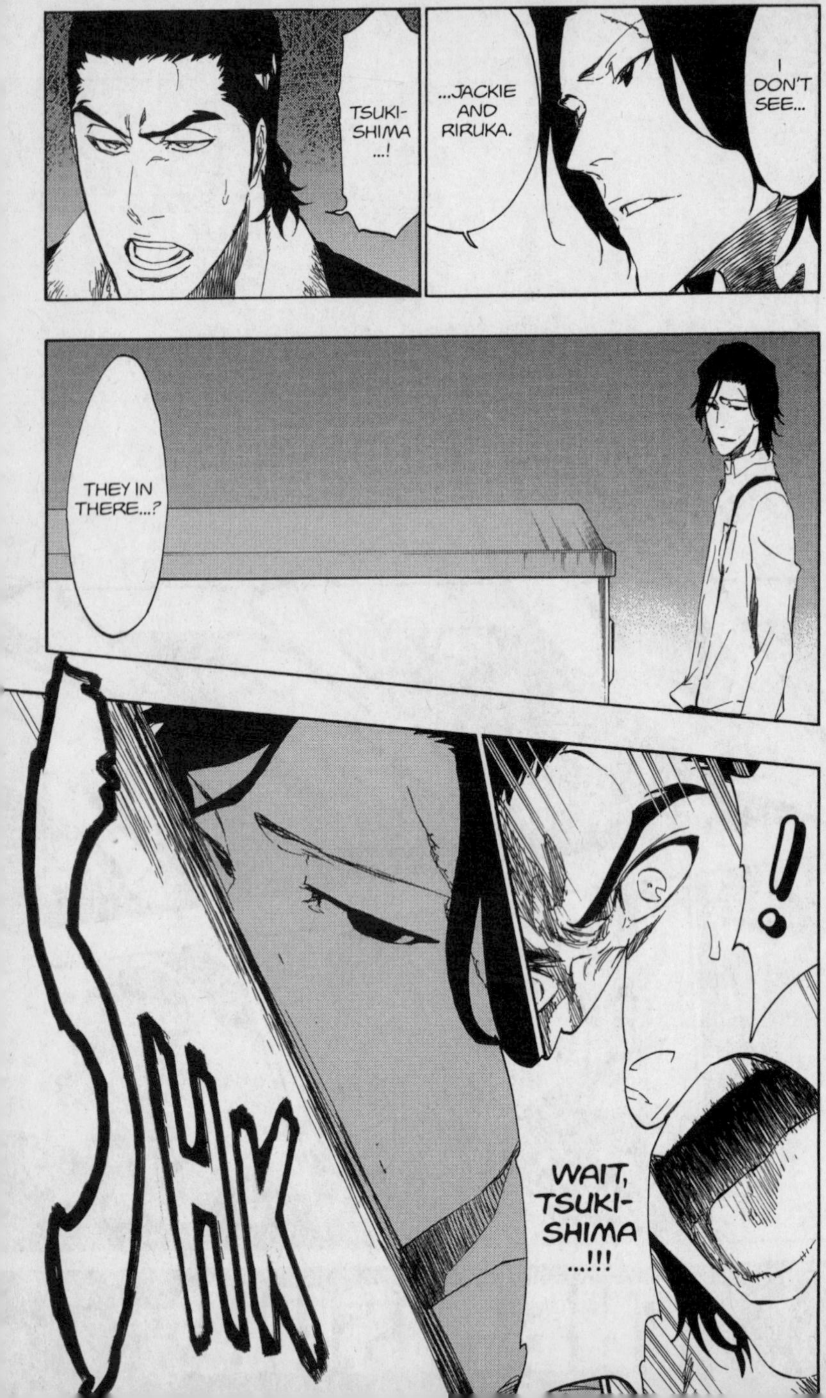
I DON'T SEE...
...JACKIE AND RIRUKA.
TSUKI-SHIMA ...!
THEY IN THERE...?
!
WAIT, TSUKI-SHIMA ...!!!

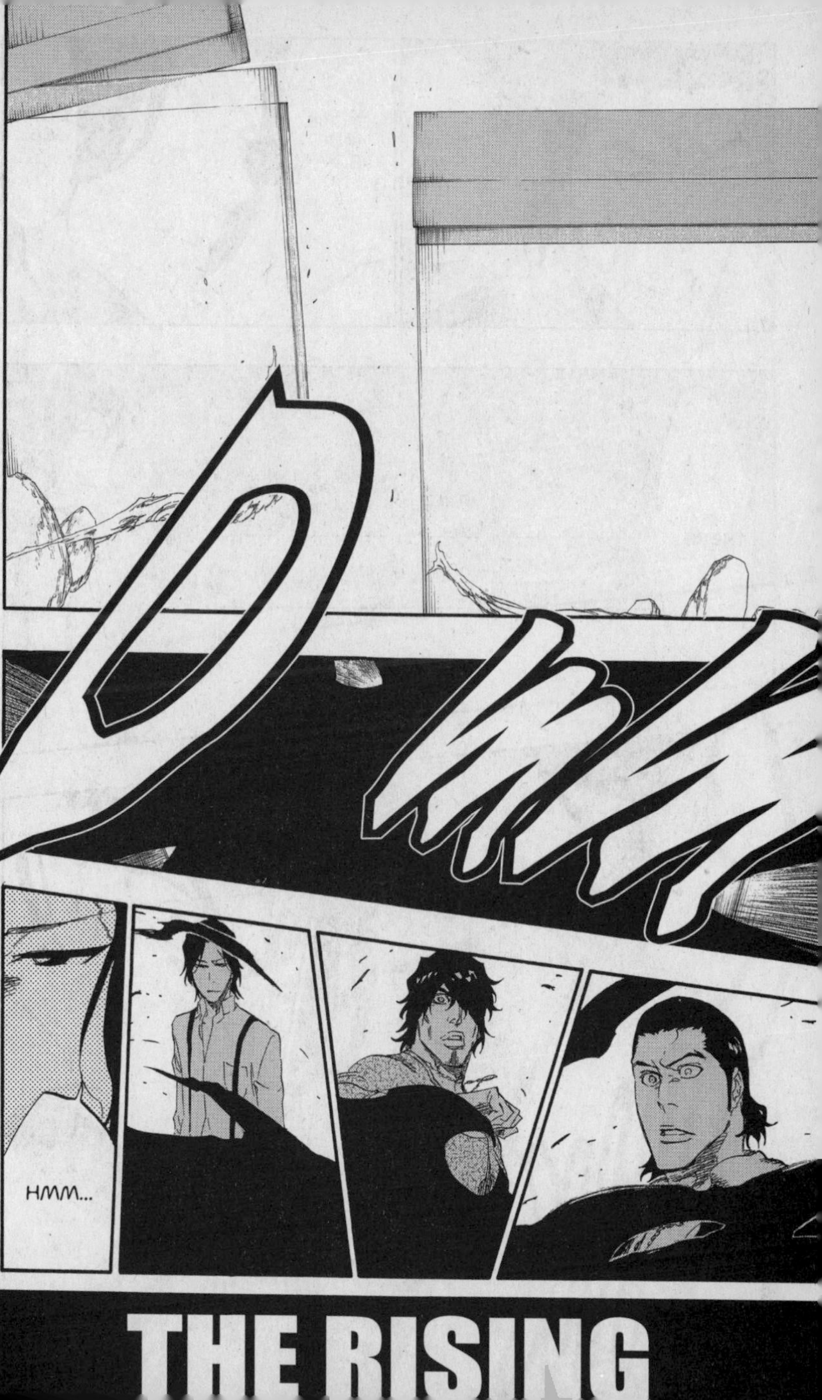
HMM...

THE RISING

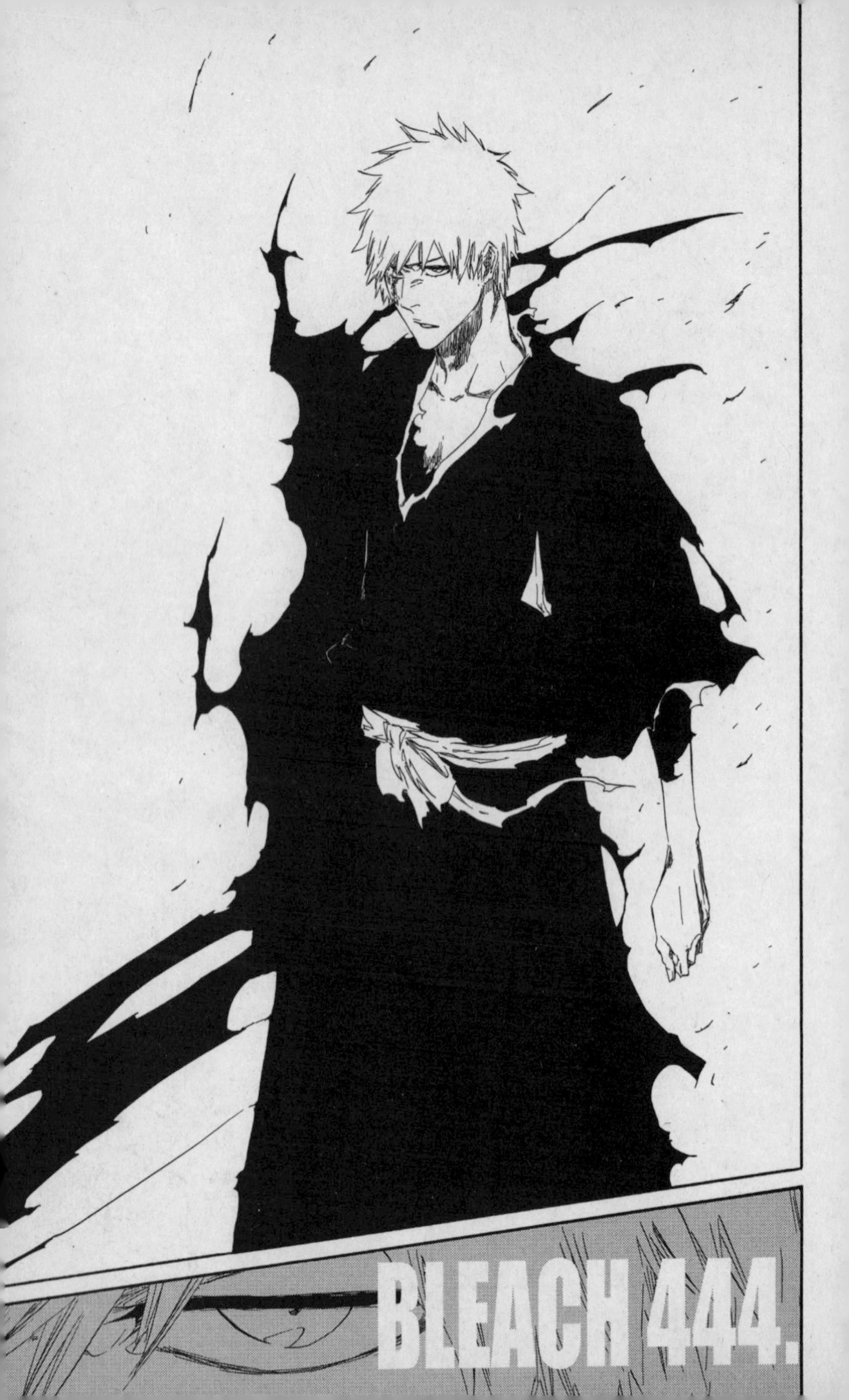
BLEACH 444.

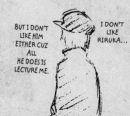

I DON'T LIKE RIRUKA...

BUT I DON'T LIKE HIM EITHER CUZ ALL HE DOES IS LECTURE ME.

445. THE DARK BEAT

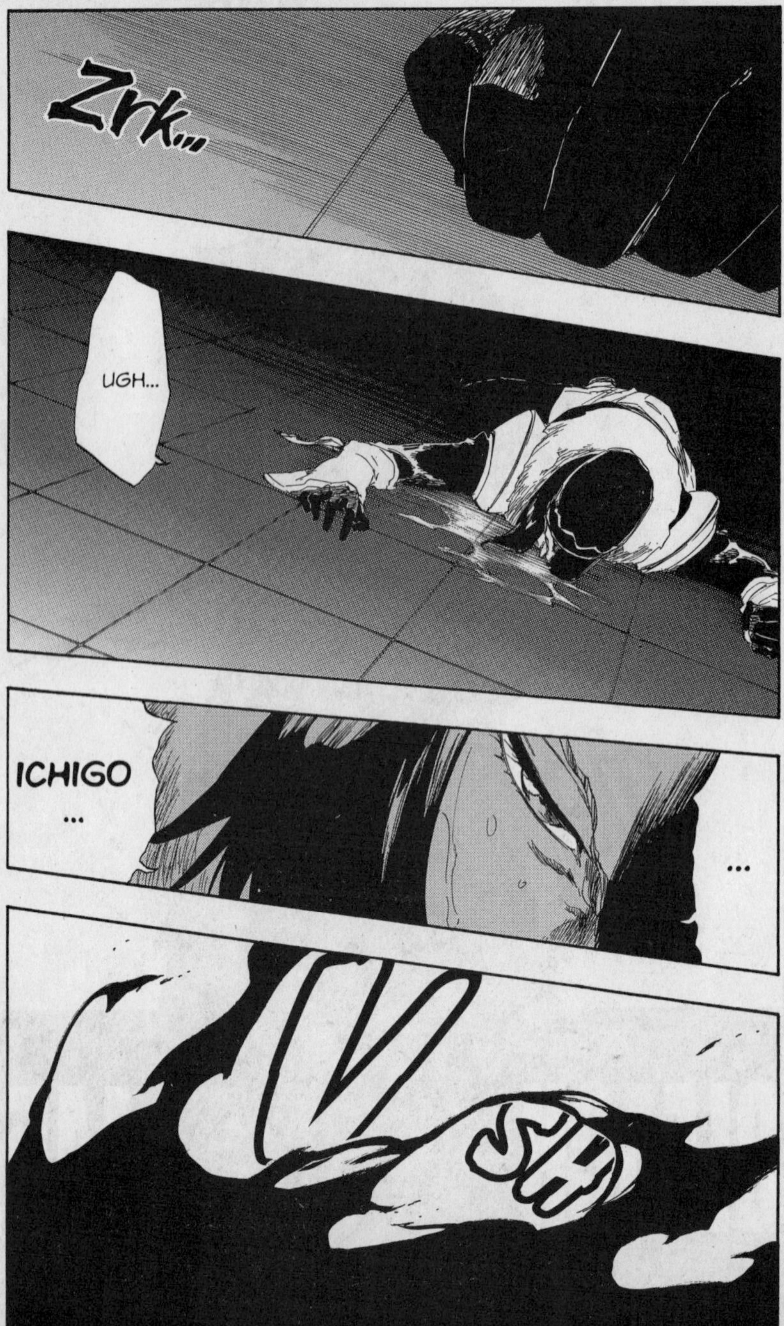
Zrk...
UGH...
...
ICHIGO
...
SH

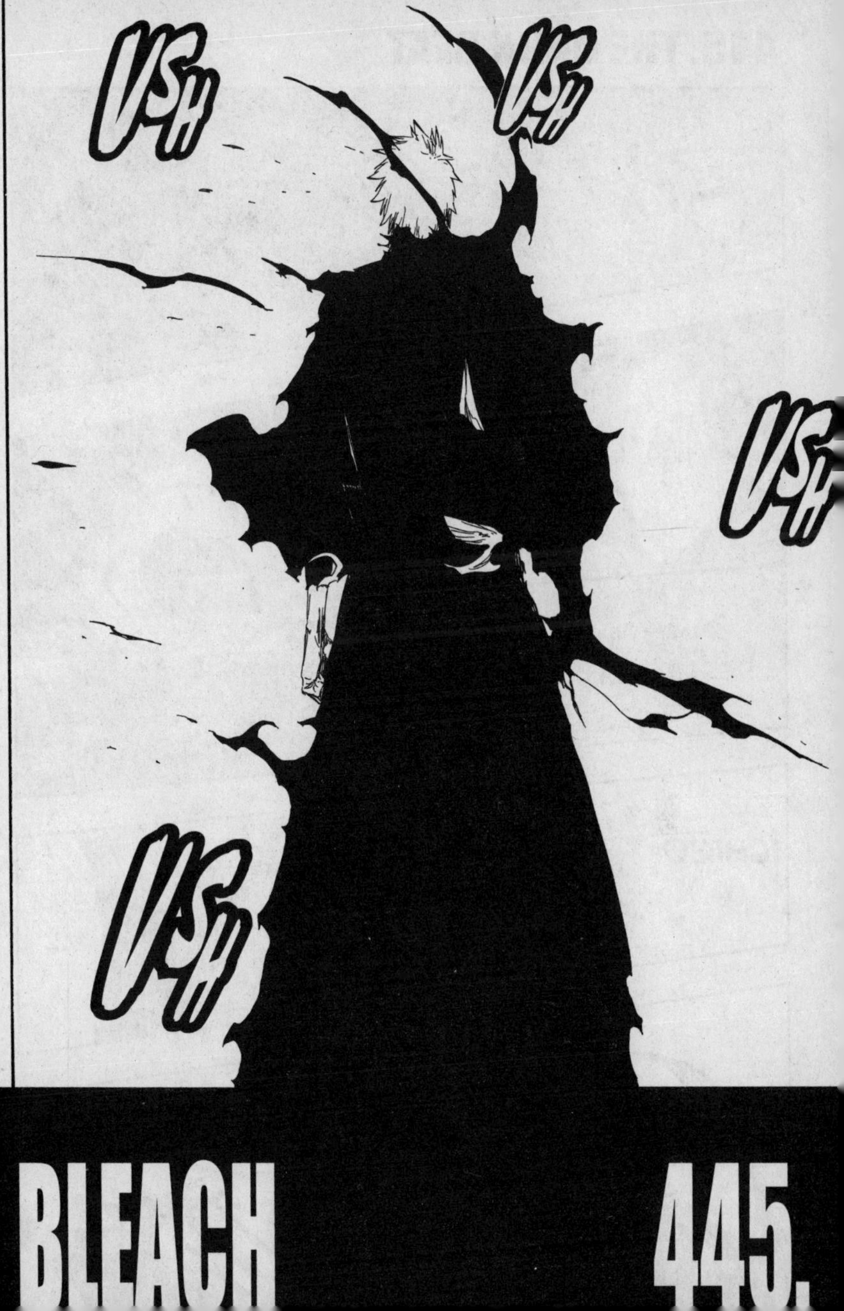
VSH
VSH
VSH
VSH
BLEACH
445.

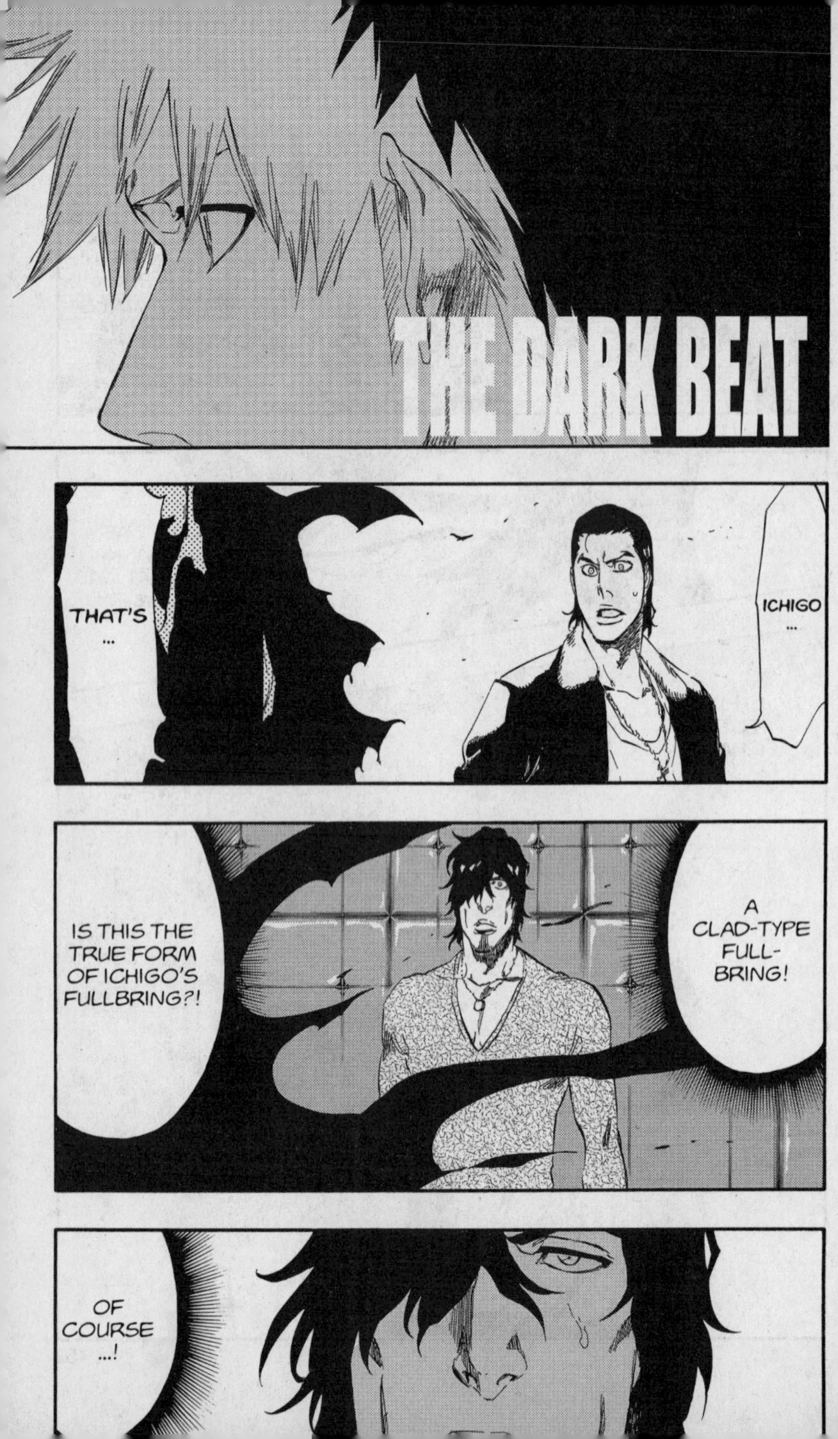
THE DARK BEAT
ICHIGO ...
THAT'S ...
A CLAD-TYPE FULL-BRING!
IS THIS THE TRUE FORM OF ICHIGO'S FULLBRING?!
OF COURSE ...!

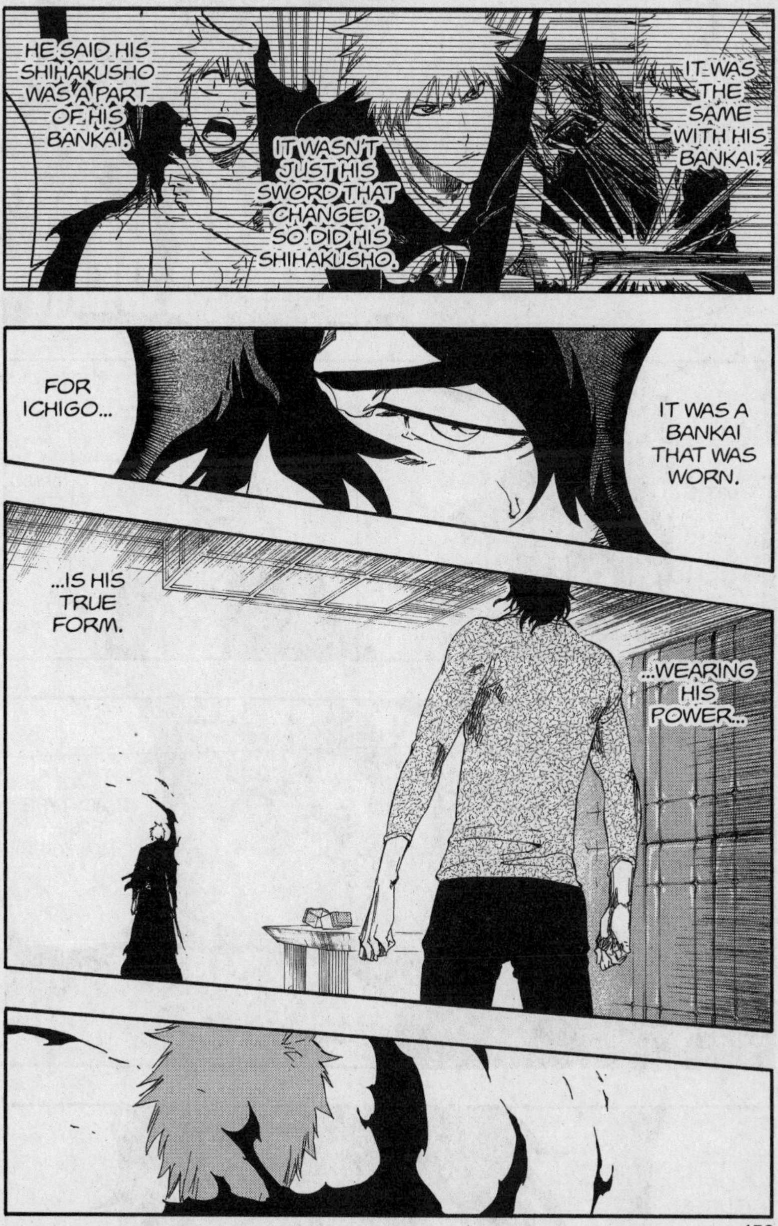

IT WAS THE SAME WITH HIS BANKAI.
IT WASN'T JUST HIS SWORD THAT CHANGED, SO DID HIS SHIHAKUSHO.
HE SAID HIS SHIHAKUSHO WAS A PART OF HIS BANKAI.
IT WAS A BANKAI THAT WAS WORN.
FOR ICHIGO...
...WEARING HIS POWER...
...IS HIS TRUE FORM.

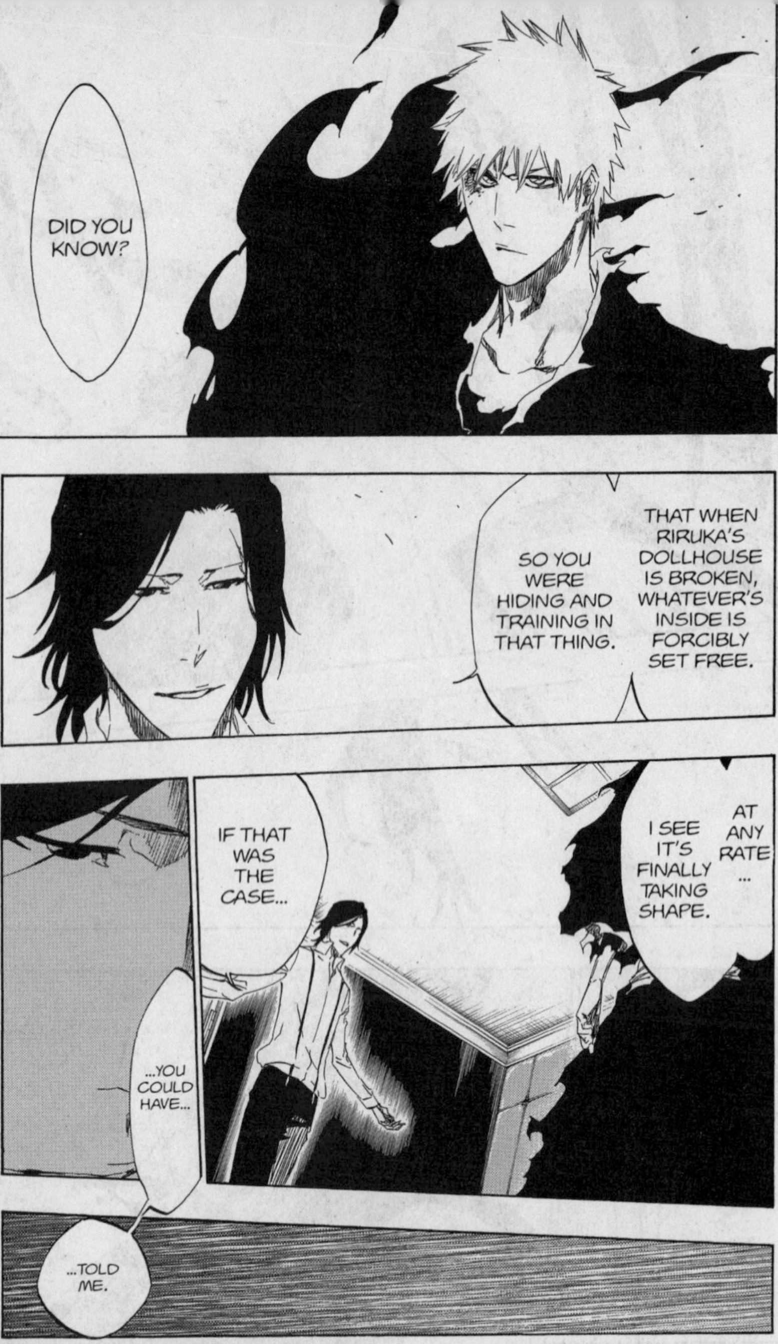
DID YOU KNOW?
THAT WHEN RIRUKA'S DOLLHOUSE IS BROKEN, WHATEVER'S INSIDE IS FORCIBLY SET FREE.
SO YOU WERE HIDING AND TRAINING IN THAT THING.
AT ANY RATE...
I SEE IT'S FINALLY TAKING SHAPE.
IF THAT WAS THE CASE...
...YOU COULD HAVE...
...TOLD ME.

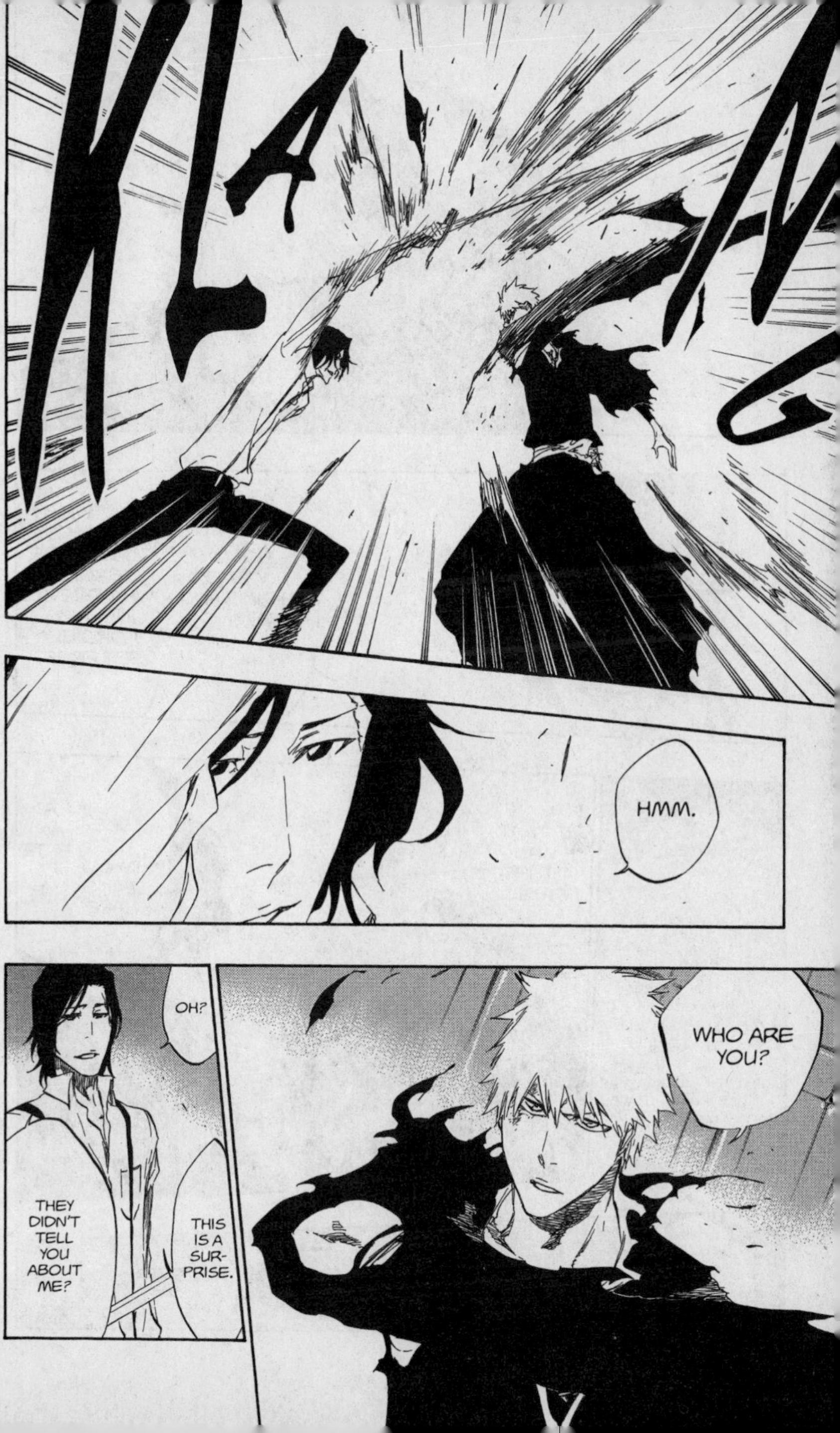
KLANG
HMM.
WHO ARE YOU?
OH?
THIS IS A SUR-PRISE.
THEY DIDN'T TELL YOU ABOUT ME?

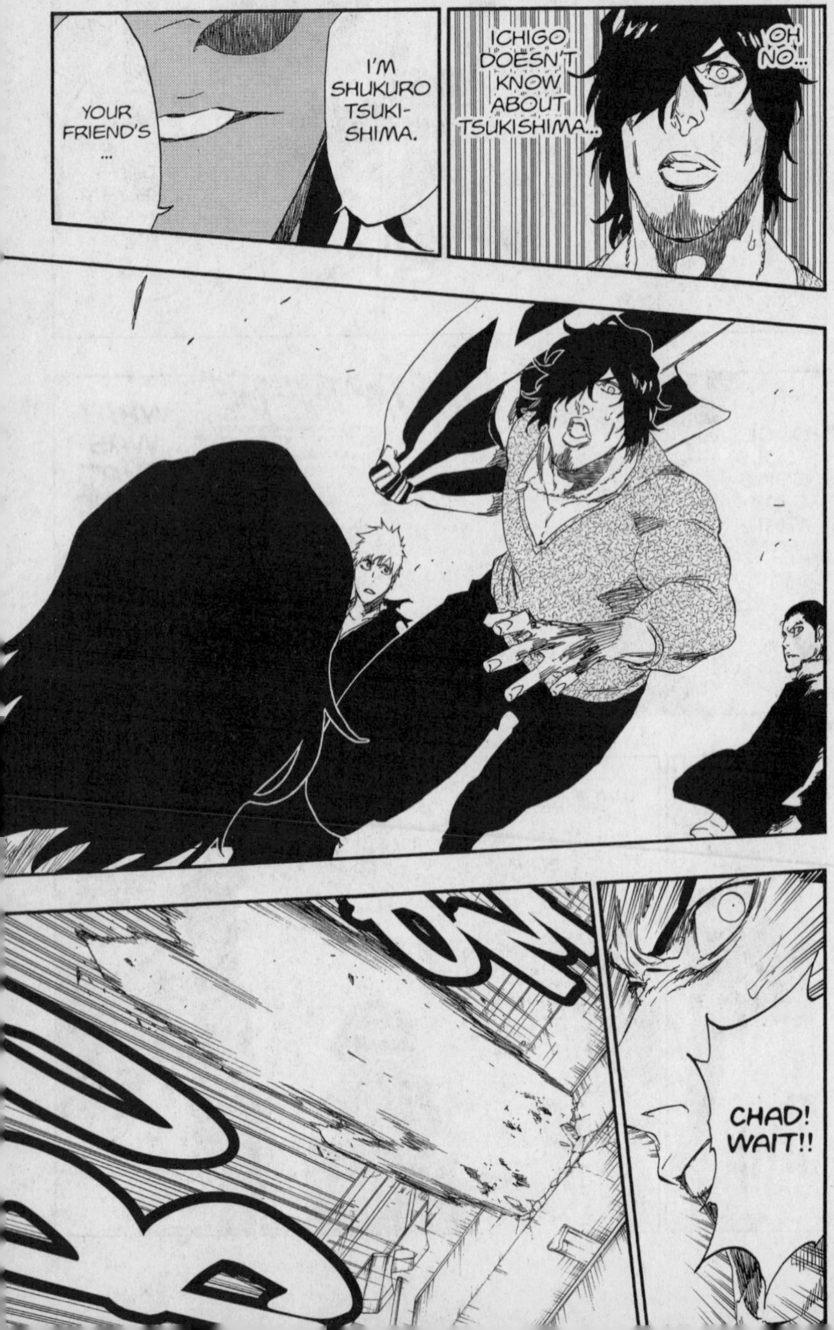
OH NO...
ICHIGO DOESN'T KNOW ABOUT TSUKISHIMA...
I'M SHUKURO TSUKI-SHIMA.
YOUR FRIEND'S ...
CHAD! WAIT!!

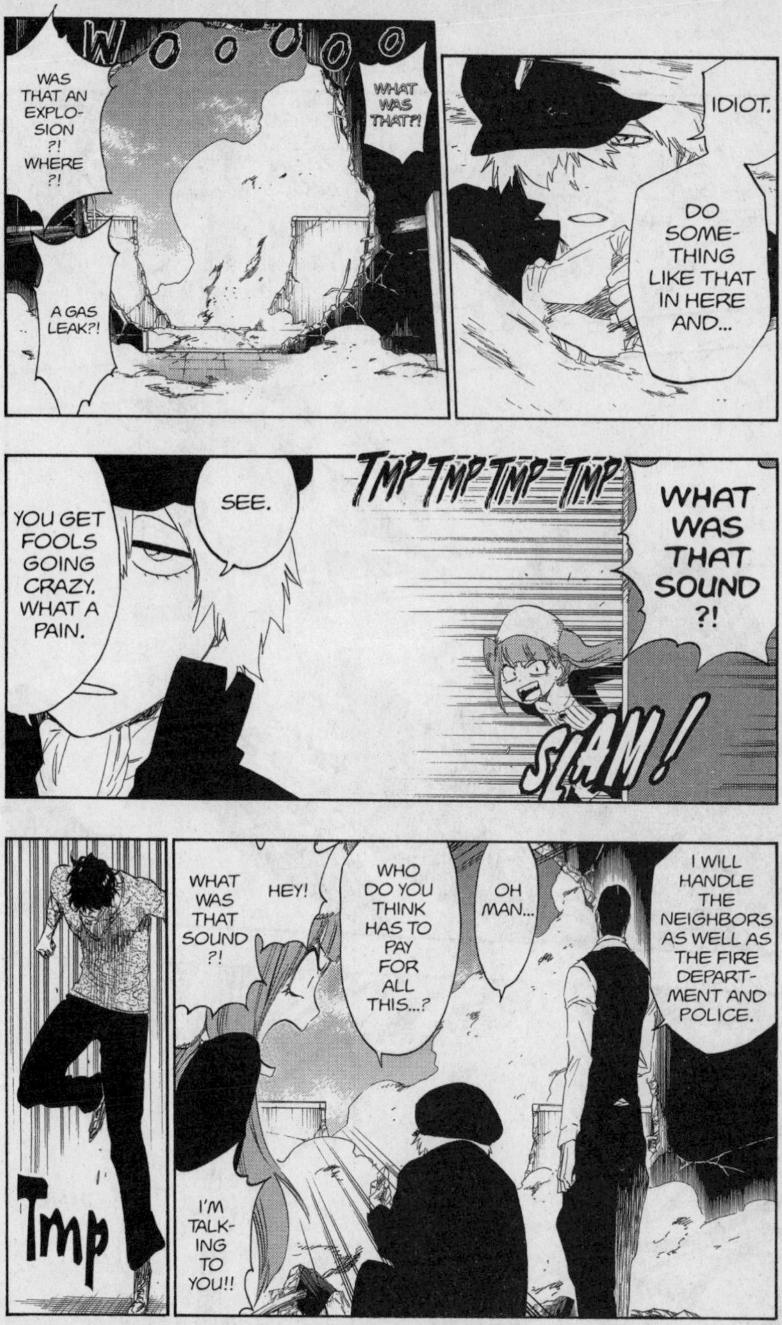
IDIOT.
DO SOMETHING LIKE THAT IN HERE AND...
WOOOOOO
WHAT WAS THAT?!
WAS THAT AN EXPLOSION?! WHERE?!
A GAS LEAK?!
WHAT WAS THAT SOUND?!
TMP TMP TMP TMP
SLAM!
SEE.
YOU GET FOOLS GOING CRAZY. WHAT A PAIN.
I WILL HANDLE THE NEIGHBORS AS WELL AS THE FIRE DEPARTMENT AND POLICE.
OH MAN...
WHO DO YOU THINK HAS TO PAY FOR ALL THIS...?
HEY!
WHAT WAS THAT SOUND?!
I'M TALKING TO YOU!!
Tmp

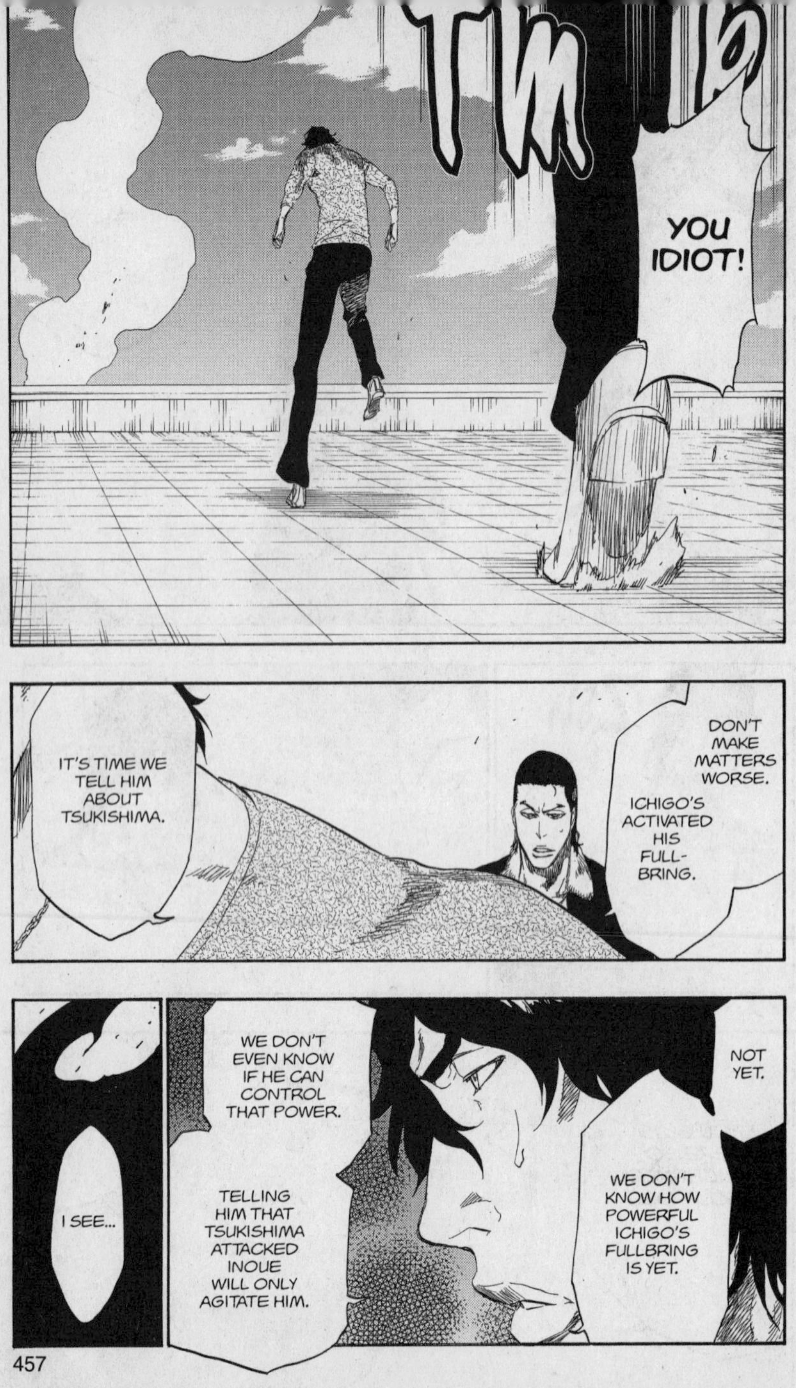
YOU IDIOT!
DON'T MAKE MATTERS WORSE.
ICHIGO'S ACTIVATED HIS FULL-BRING.
IT'S TIME WE TELL HIM ABOUT TSUKISHIMA.
NOT YET.
WE DON'T KNOW HOW POWERFUL ICHIGO'S FULLBRING IS YET.
WE DON'T EVEN KNOW IF HE CAN CONTROL THAT POWER.
TELLING HIM THAT TSUKISHIMA ATTACKED INOUE WILL ONLY AGITATE HIM.
I SEE...

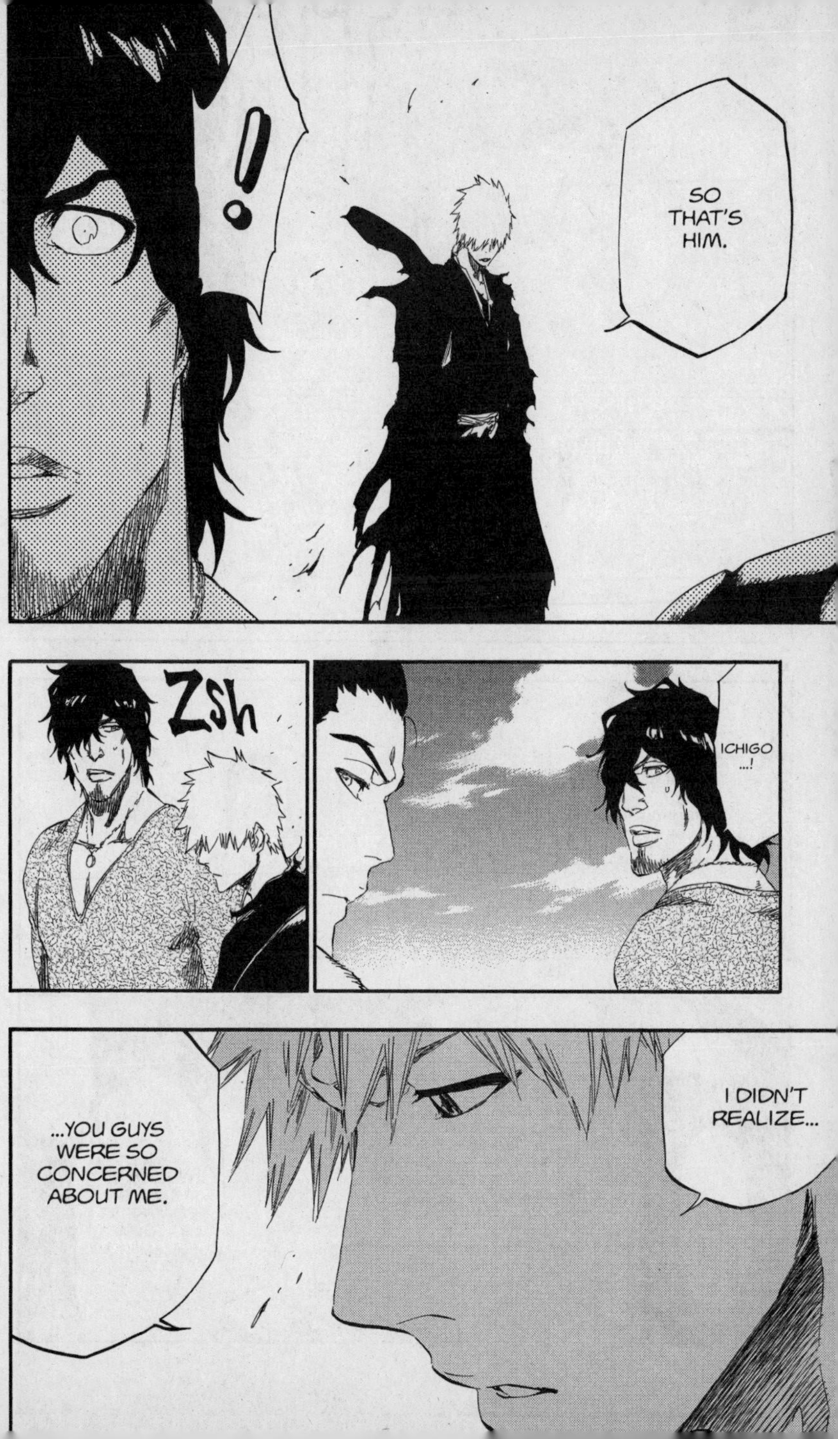
SO THAT'S HIM.
!
ICHIGO ...!
Zsh
I DIDN'T REALIZE...
...YOU GUYS WERE SO CONCERNED ABOUT ME.

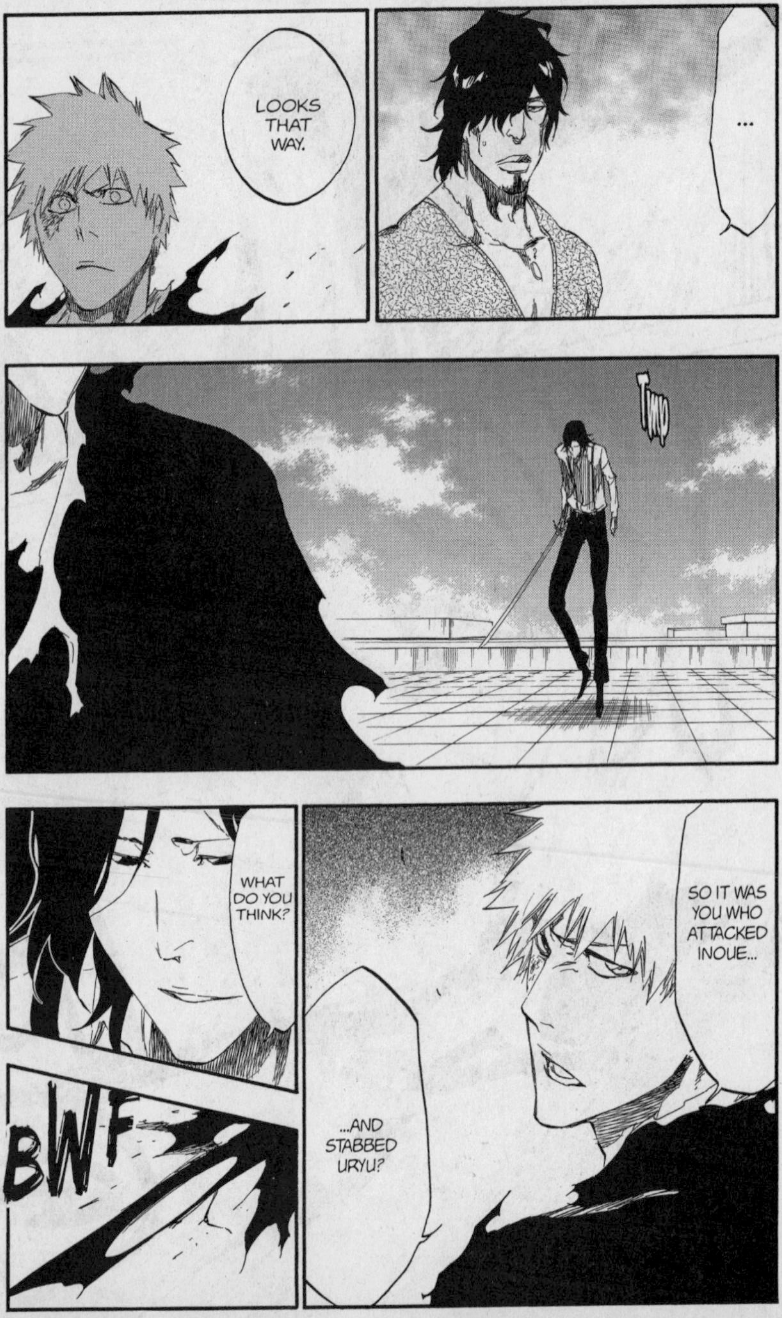
...
LOOKS THAT WAY.
TMP
SO IT WAS YOU WHO ATTACKED INOUE...
...AND STABBED URYU?
WHAT DO YOU THINK?
BWF

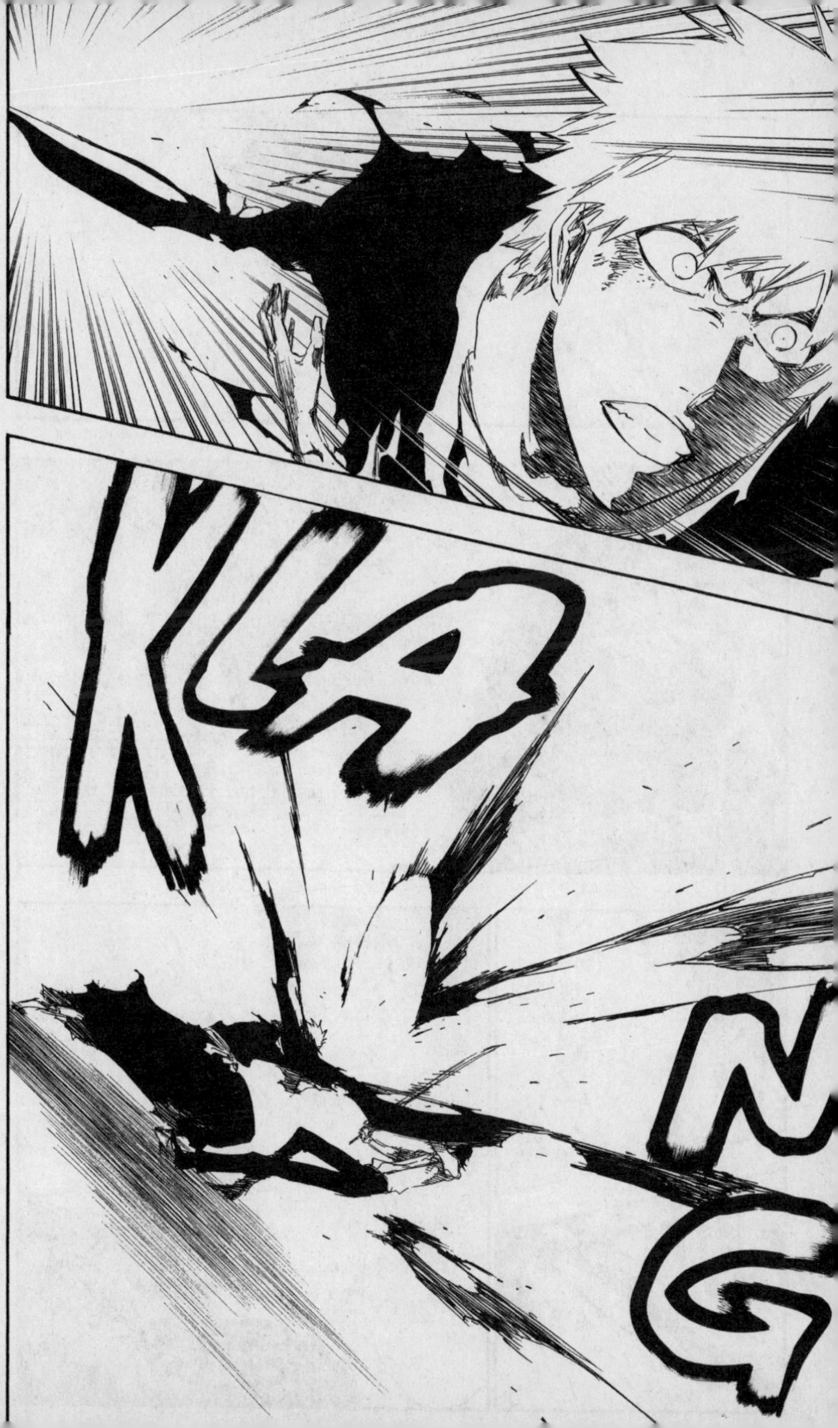
KLANG

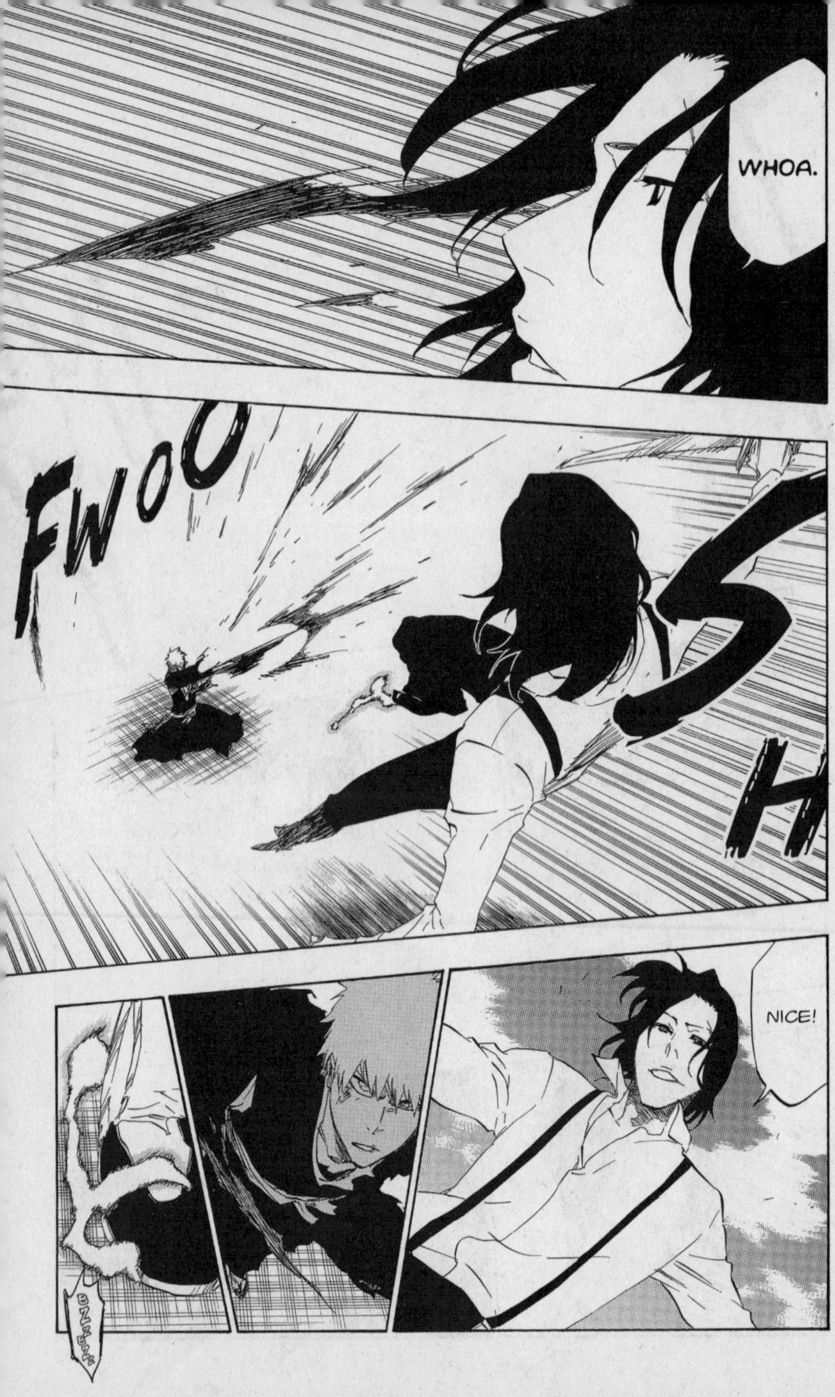
WHOA.
FWOOSH
NICE!
BZZBZZ

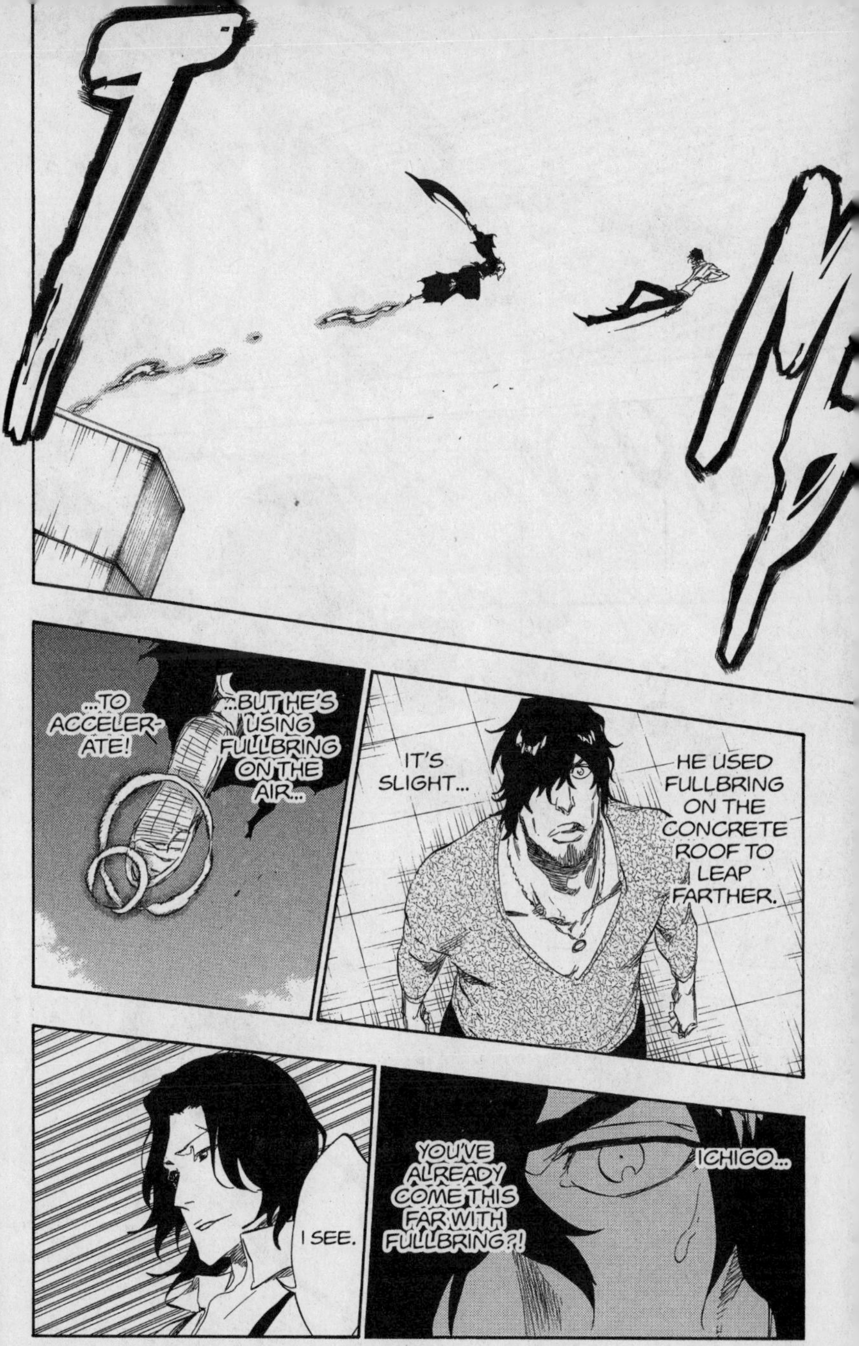
HE USED FULLBRING ON THE CONCRETE ROOF TO LEAP FARTHER.
IT'S SLIGHT...
...BUT HE'S USING FULLBRING ON THE AIR...
...TO ACCELER-ATE!
ICHIGO...
YOU'VE ALREADY COME THIS FAR WITH FULLBRING?!
I SEE.

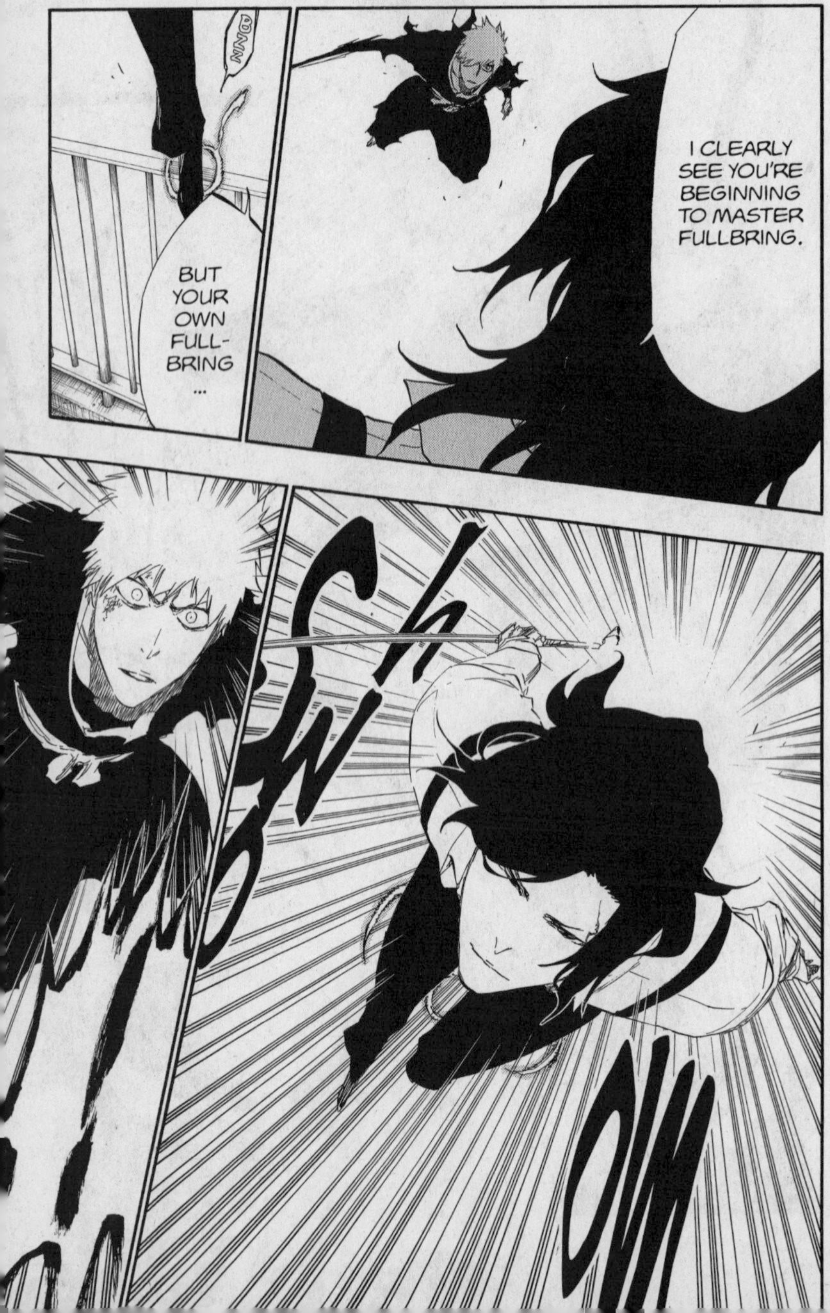
I CLEARLY SEE YOU'RE BEGINNING TO MASTER FULLBRING.
DAMN
BUT YOUR OWN FULL-BRING ...
SHWOOM

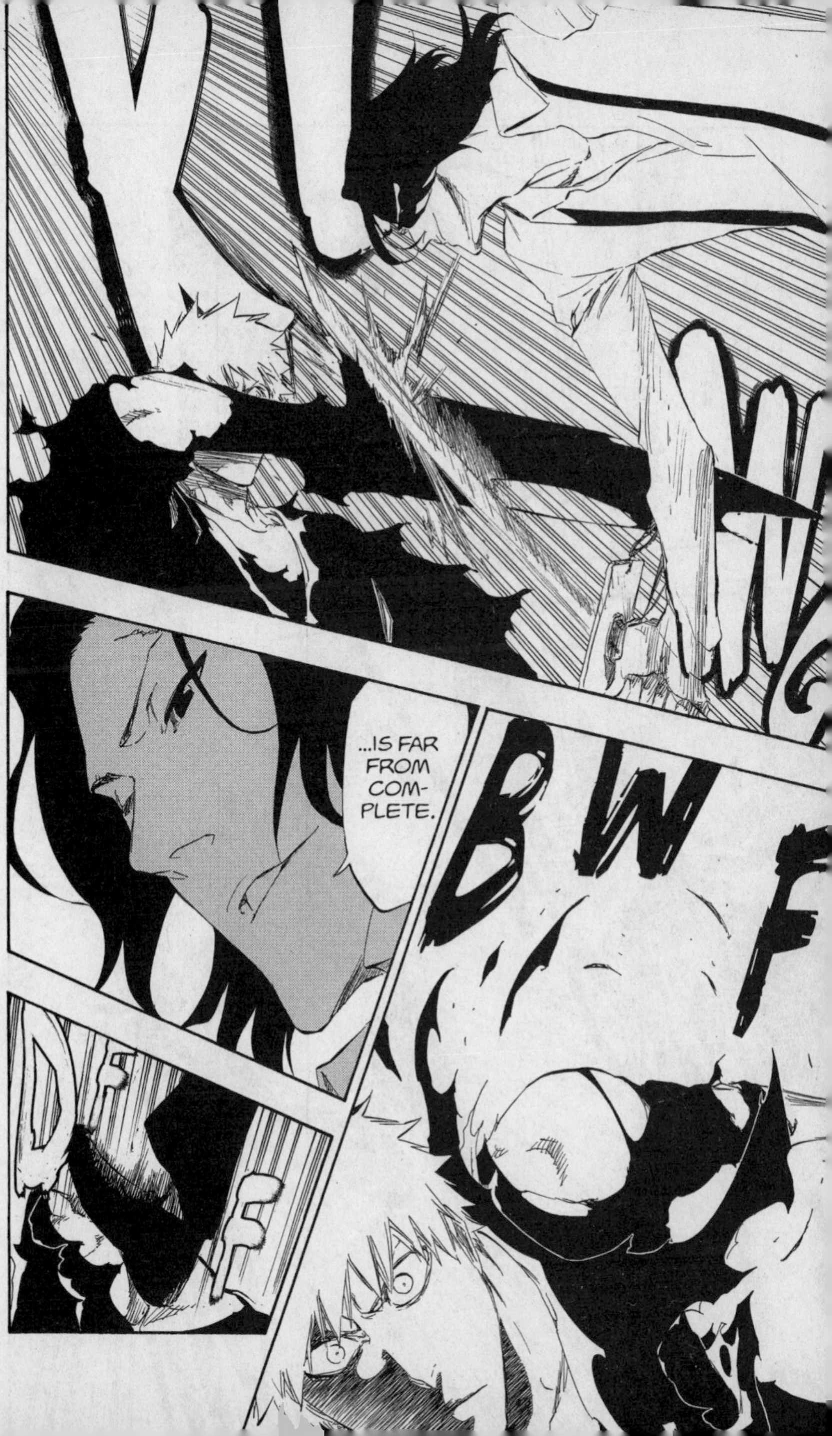
...IS FAR FROM COM- PLETE.
BWF

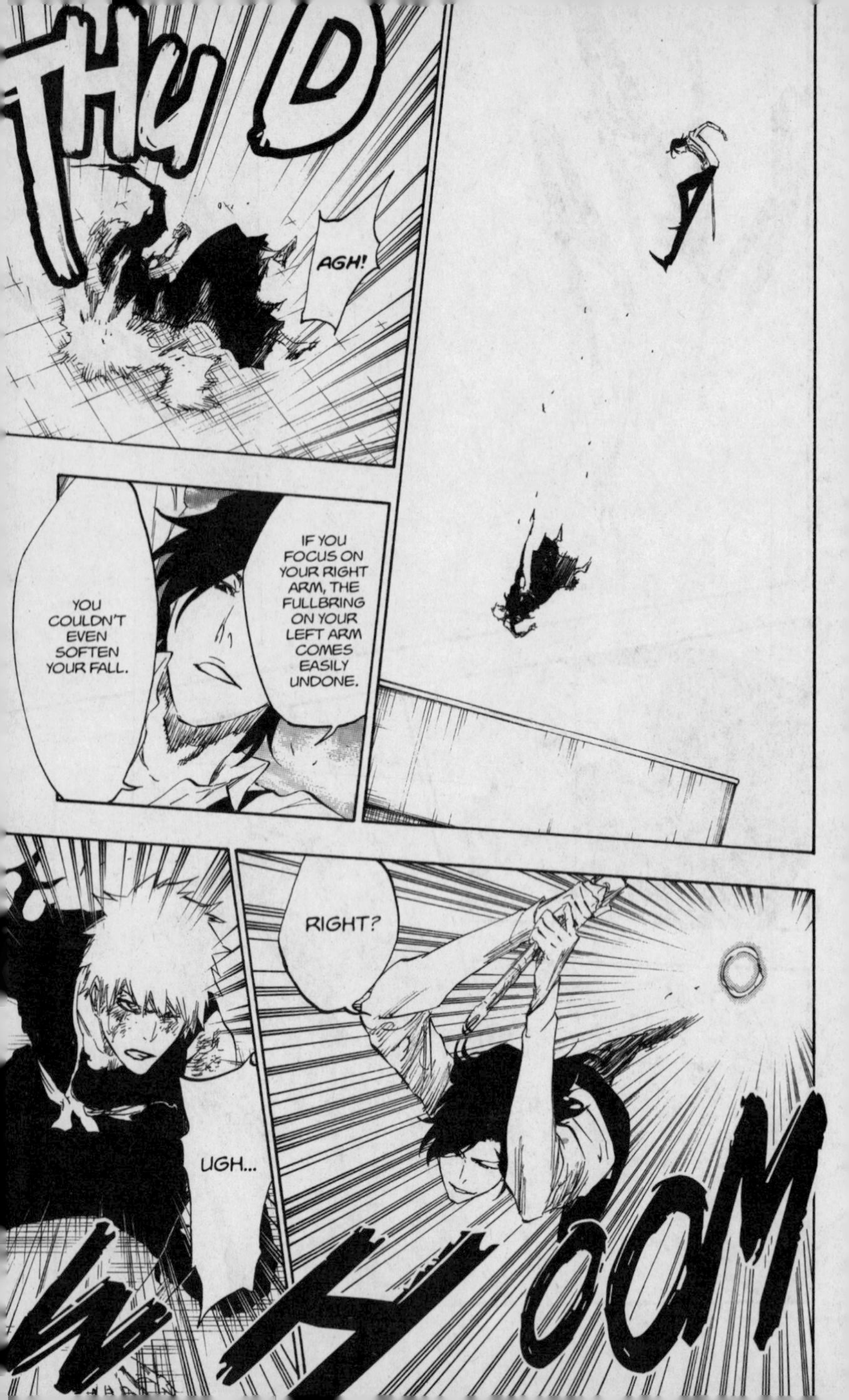
THUD
AGH!
IF YOU FOCUS ON YOUR RIGHT ARM, THE FULLBRING ON YOUR LEFT ARM COMES EASILY UNDONE.
YOU COULDN'T EVEN SOFTEN YOUR FALL.
RIGHT?
WHOOM
UGH...

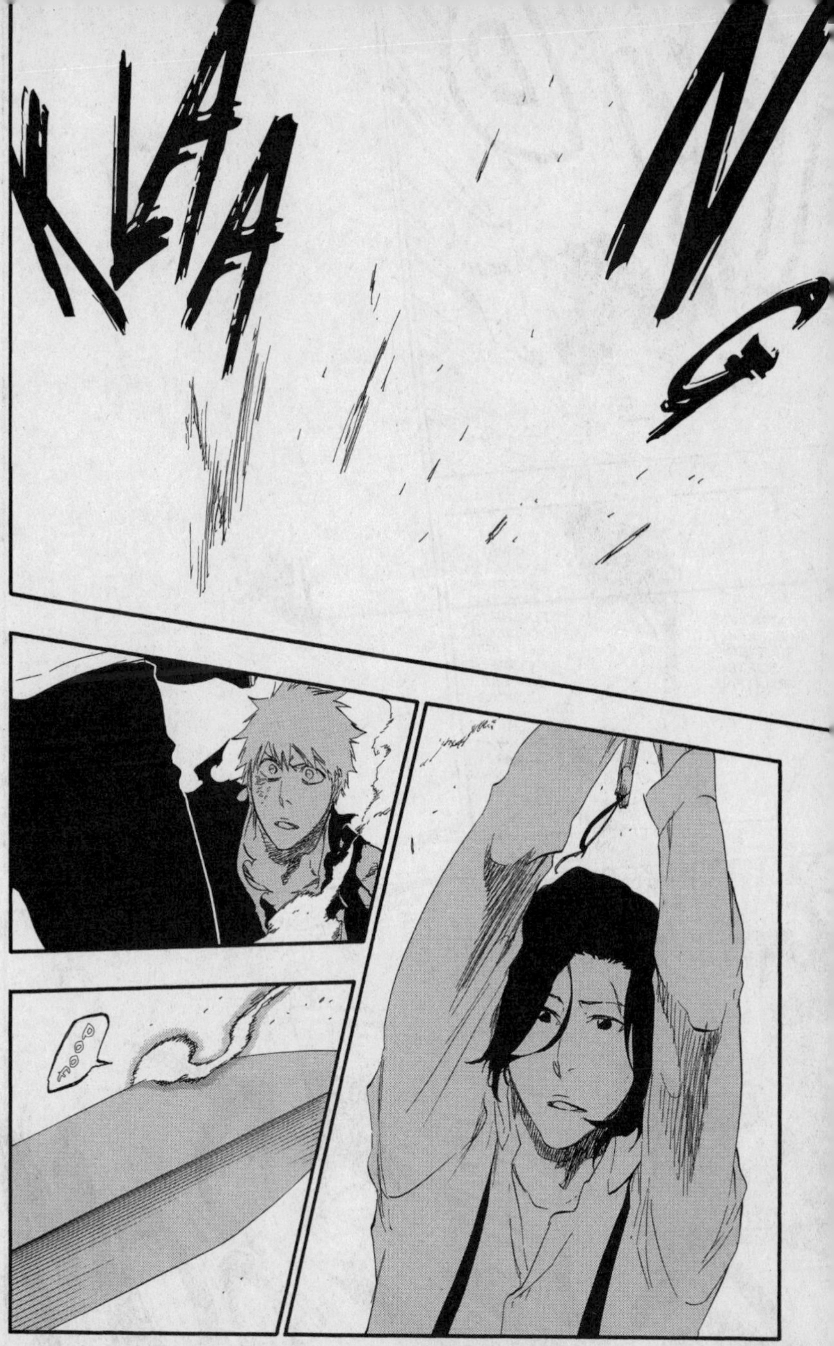
KLANG
POOF

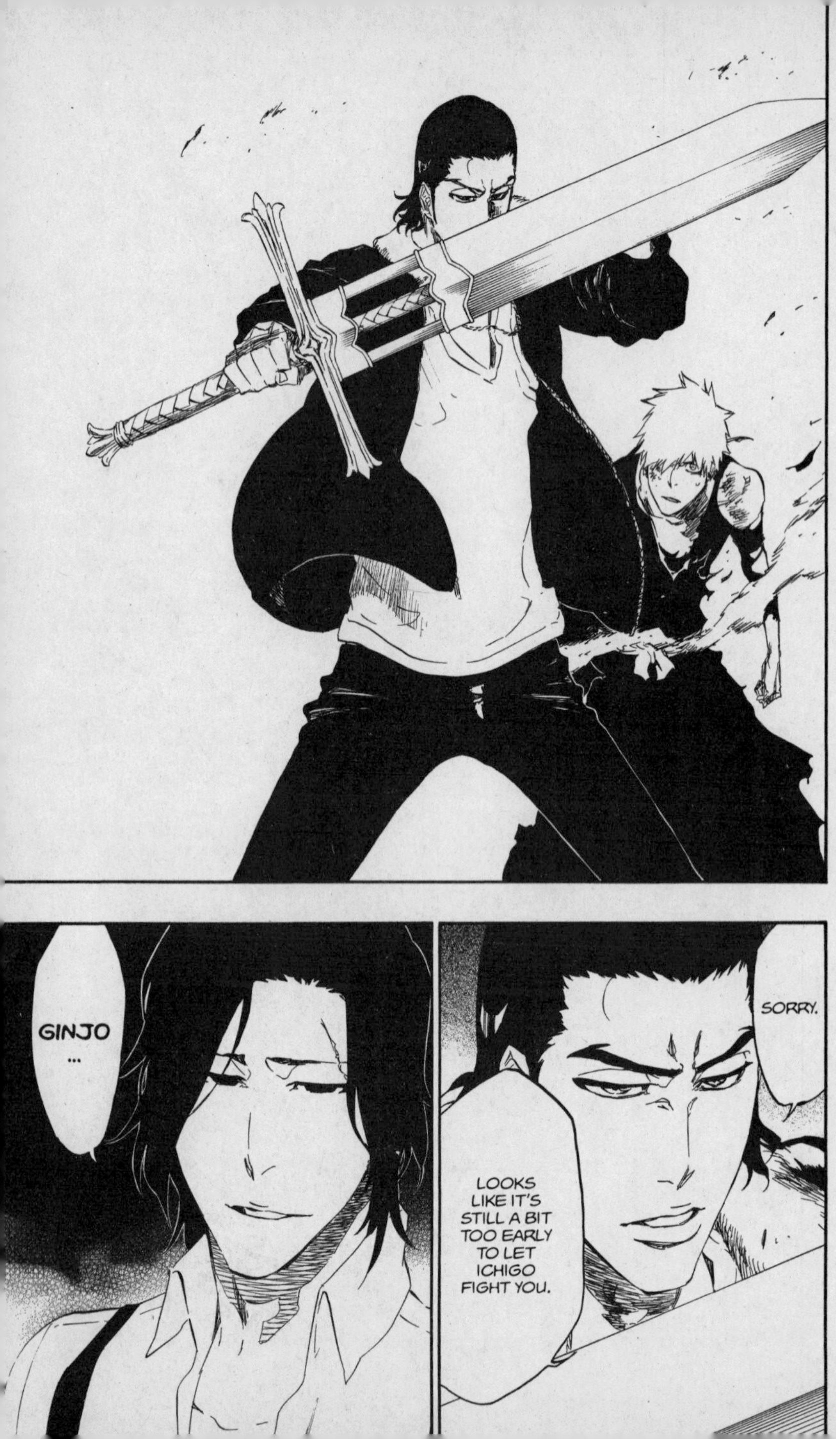
SORRY.
LOOKS LIKE IT'S STILL A BIT TOO EARLY TO LET ICHIGO FIGHT YOU.
GINJO ...

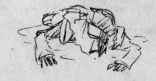

THE STORY
KEEPS
GOING ON
WHILE I'M
LYING
HERE...

446. THE DARK BEAT 2

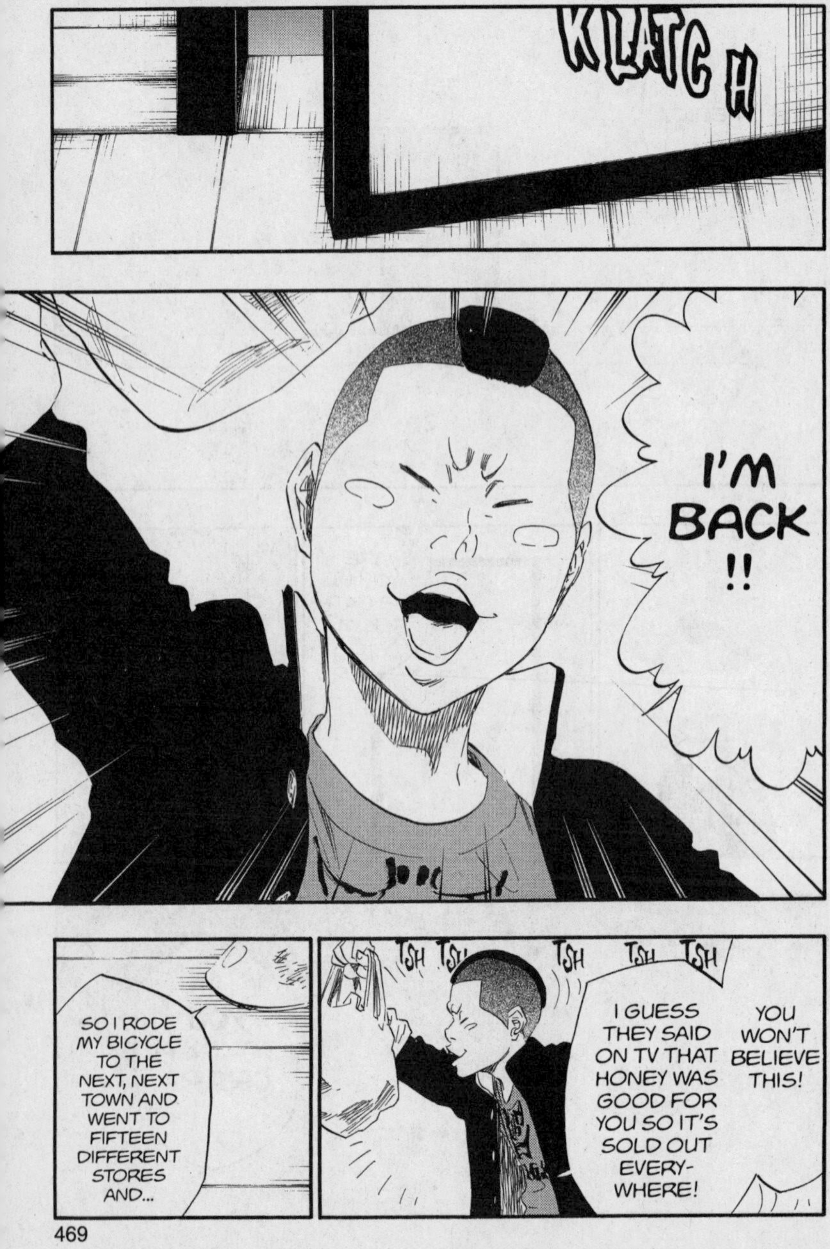
KLATCH
I'M BACK!!
TSH TSH TSH TSH TSH
YOU WON'T BELIEVE THIS!
I GUESS THEY SAID ON TV THAT HONEY WAS GOOD FOR YOU SO IT'S SOLD OUT EVERY-WHERE!
SO I RODE MY BICYCLE TO THE NEXT, NEXT TOWN AND WENT TO FIFTEEN DIFFERENT STORES AND...

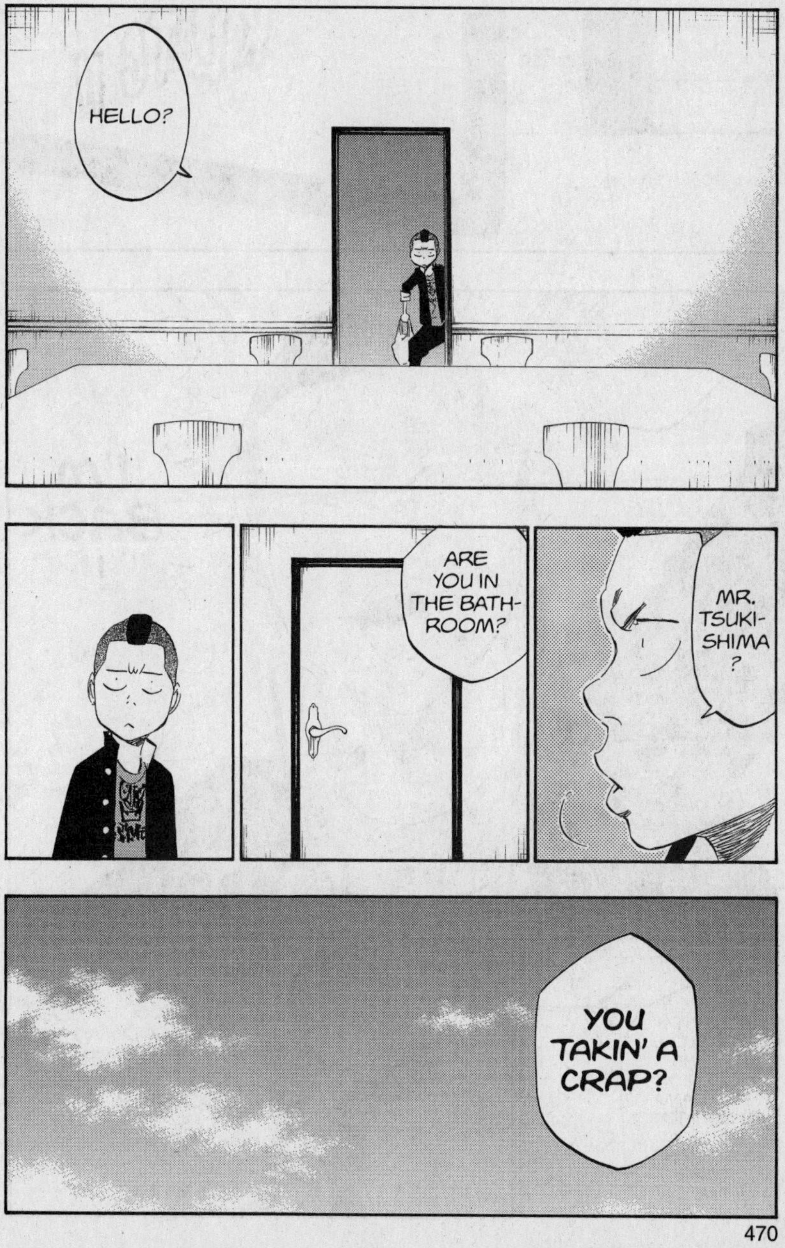
HELLO?
MR. TSUKISHIMA?
ARE YOU IN THE BATHROOM?
YOU TAKIN' A CRAP?

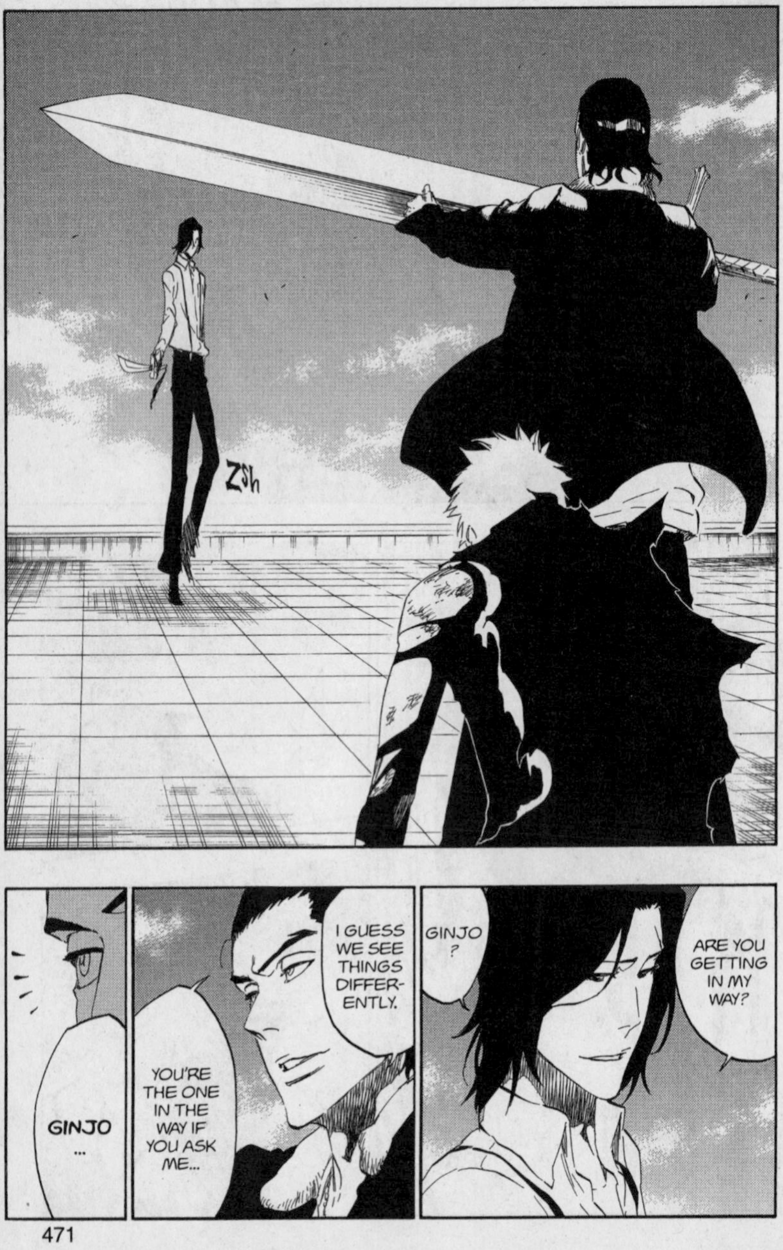
Zsh
ARE YOU GETTING IN MY WAY?
GINJO ?
I GUESS WE SEE THINGS DIFFER-ENTLY.
YOU'RE THE ONE IN THE WAY IF YOU ASK ME...
GINJO ...

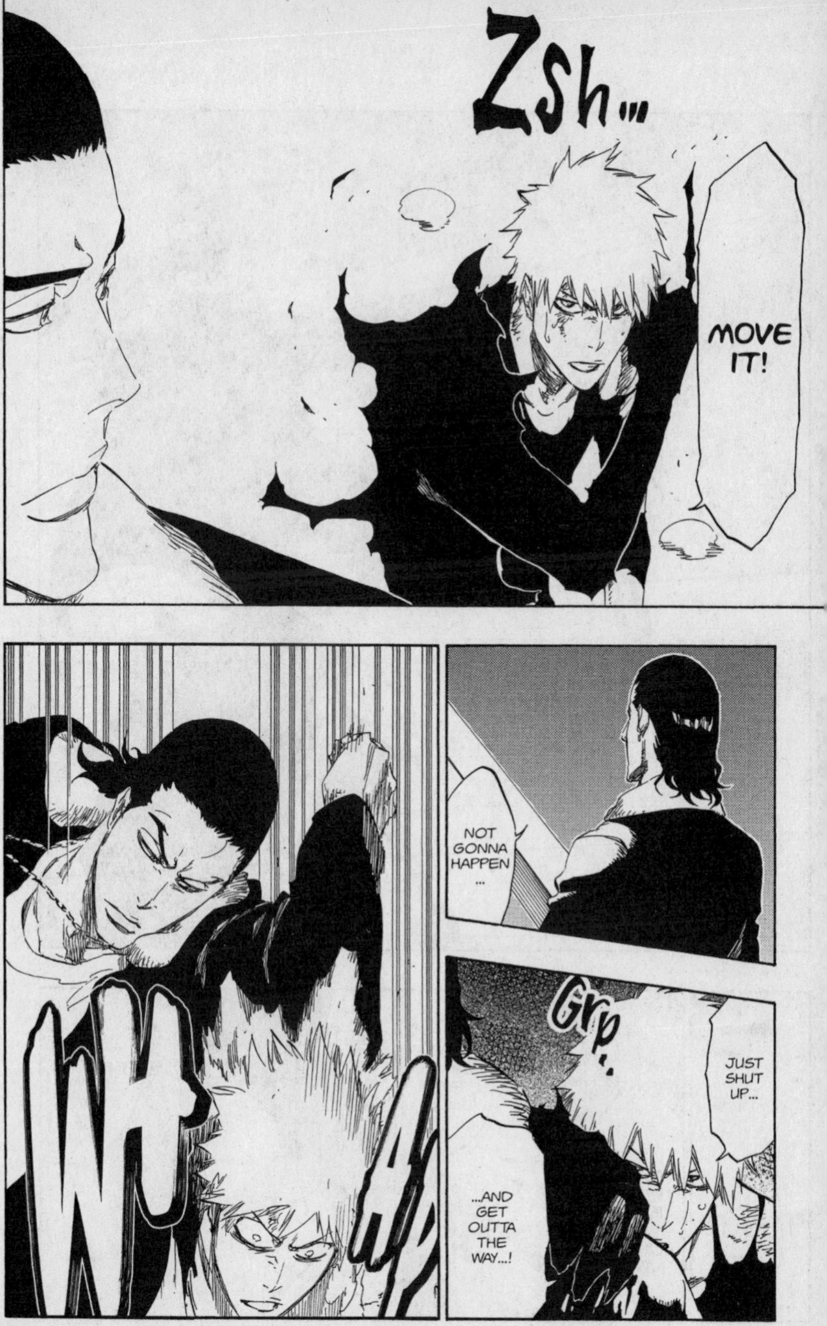
Zsh...
MOVE IT!
NOT GONNA HAPPEN ...
Grp..
JUST SHUT UP...
...AND GET OUTTA THE WAY...!

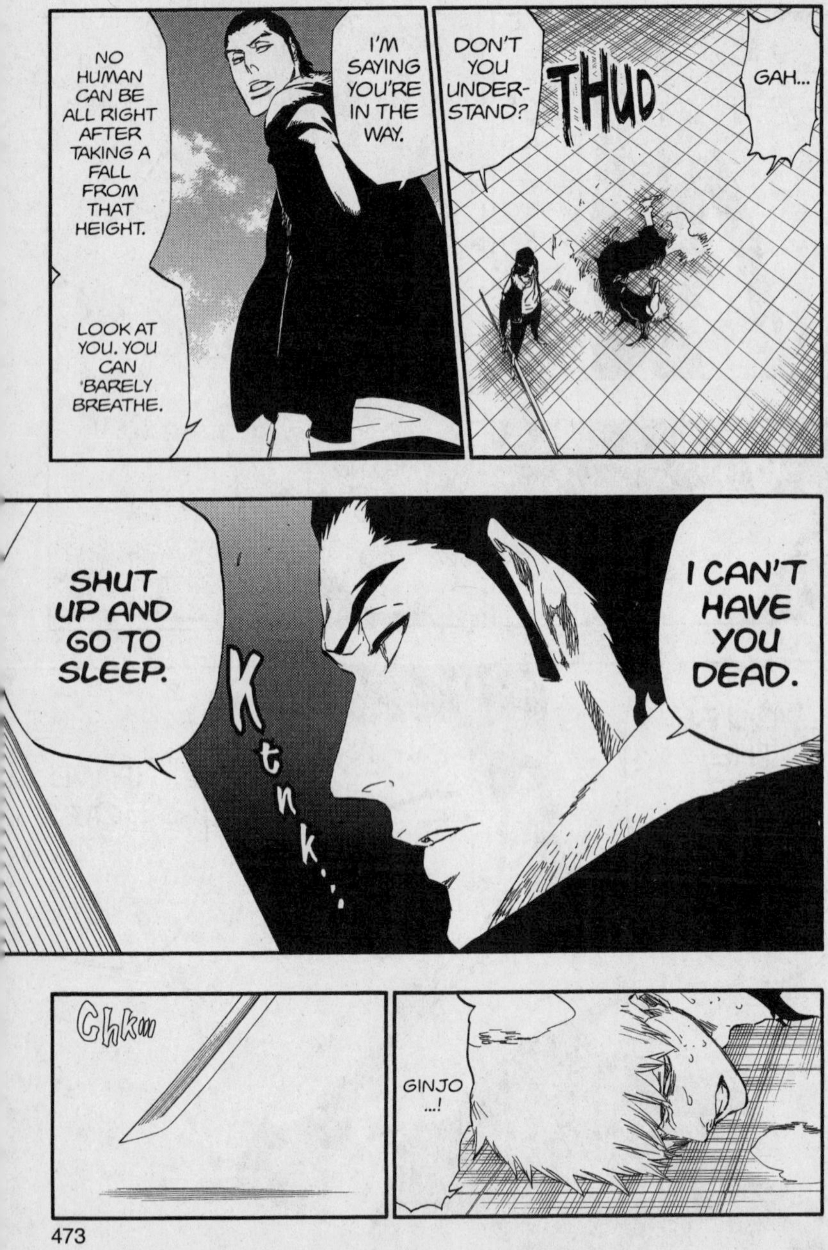
GAH...
DON'T YOU UNDERSTAND?
THUD
I'M SAYING YOU'RE IN THE WAY.
NO HUMAN CAN BE ALL RIGHT AFTER TAKING A FALL FROM THAT HEIGHT.
LOOK AT YOU. YOU CAN BARELY BREATHE.
I CAN'T HAVE YOU DEAD.
Ktnk...
SHUT UP AND GO TO SLEEP.
GINJO ...!
Chk

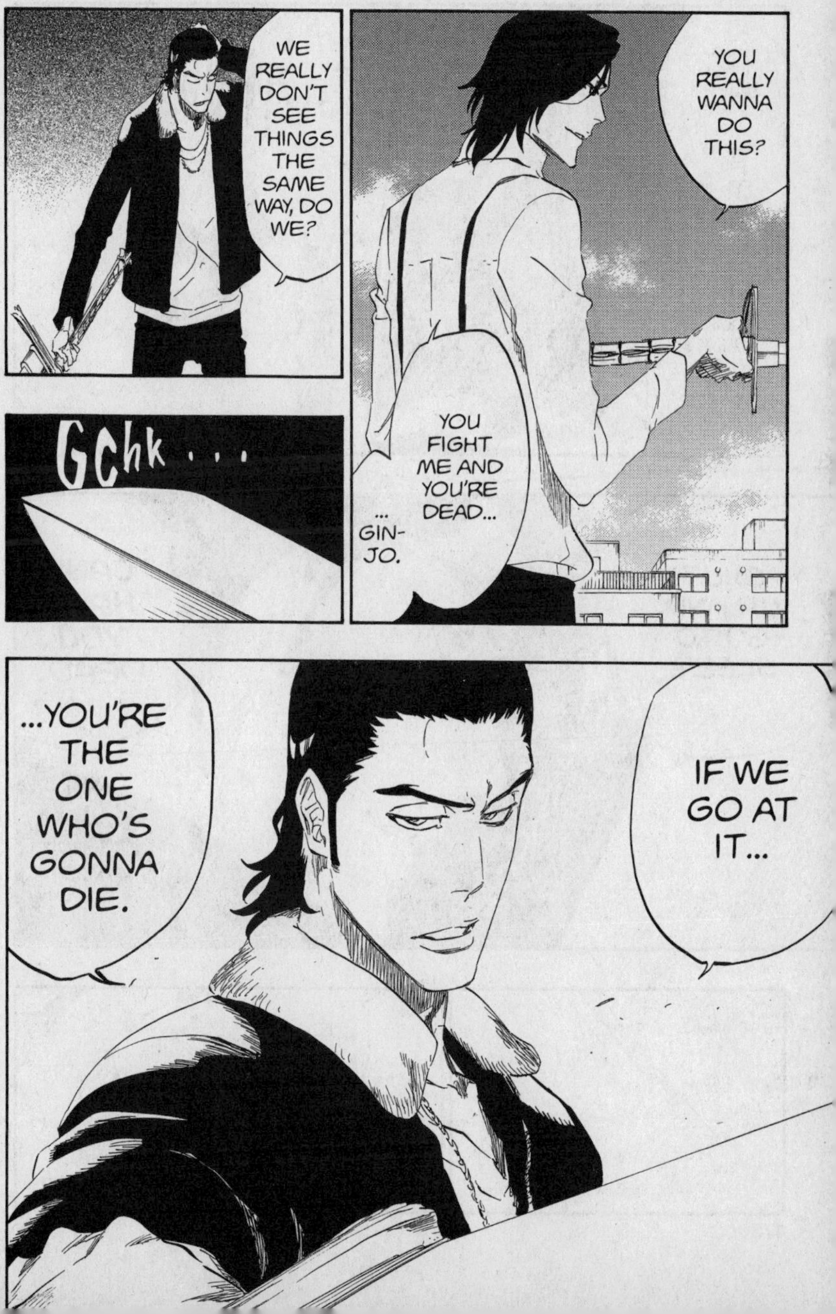
YOU REALLY WANNA DO THIS?
YOU FIGHT ME AND YOU'RE DEAD...
... GIN-JO.
WE REALLY DON'T SEE THINGS THE SAME WAY, DO WE?
Gchk...
IF WE GO AT IT...
...YOU'RE THE ONE WHO'S GONNA DIE.

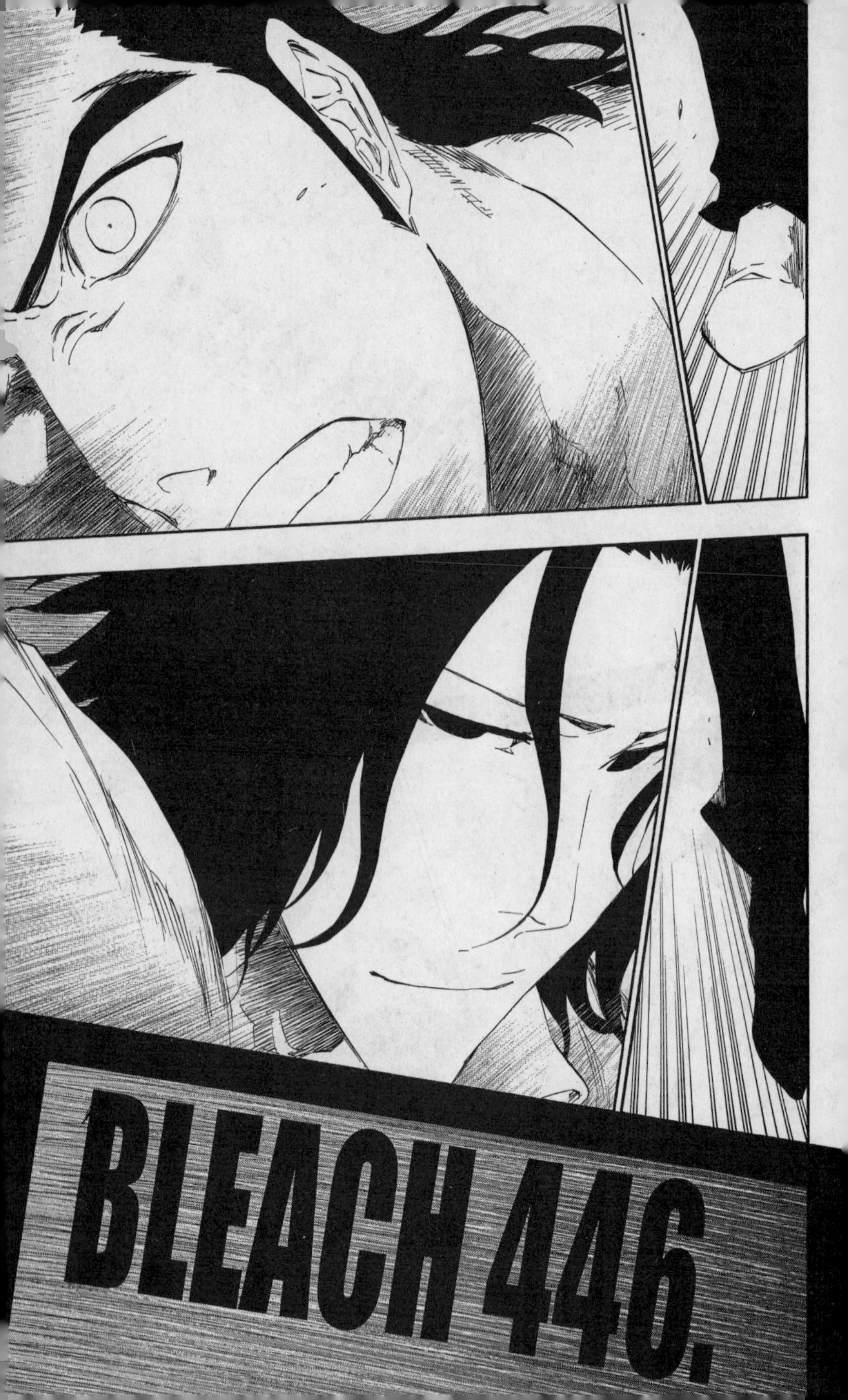
BLEACH 446.

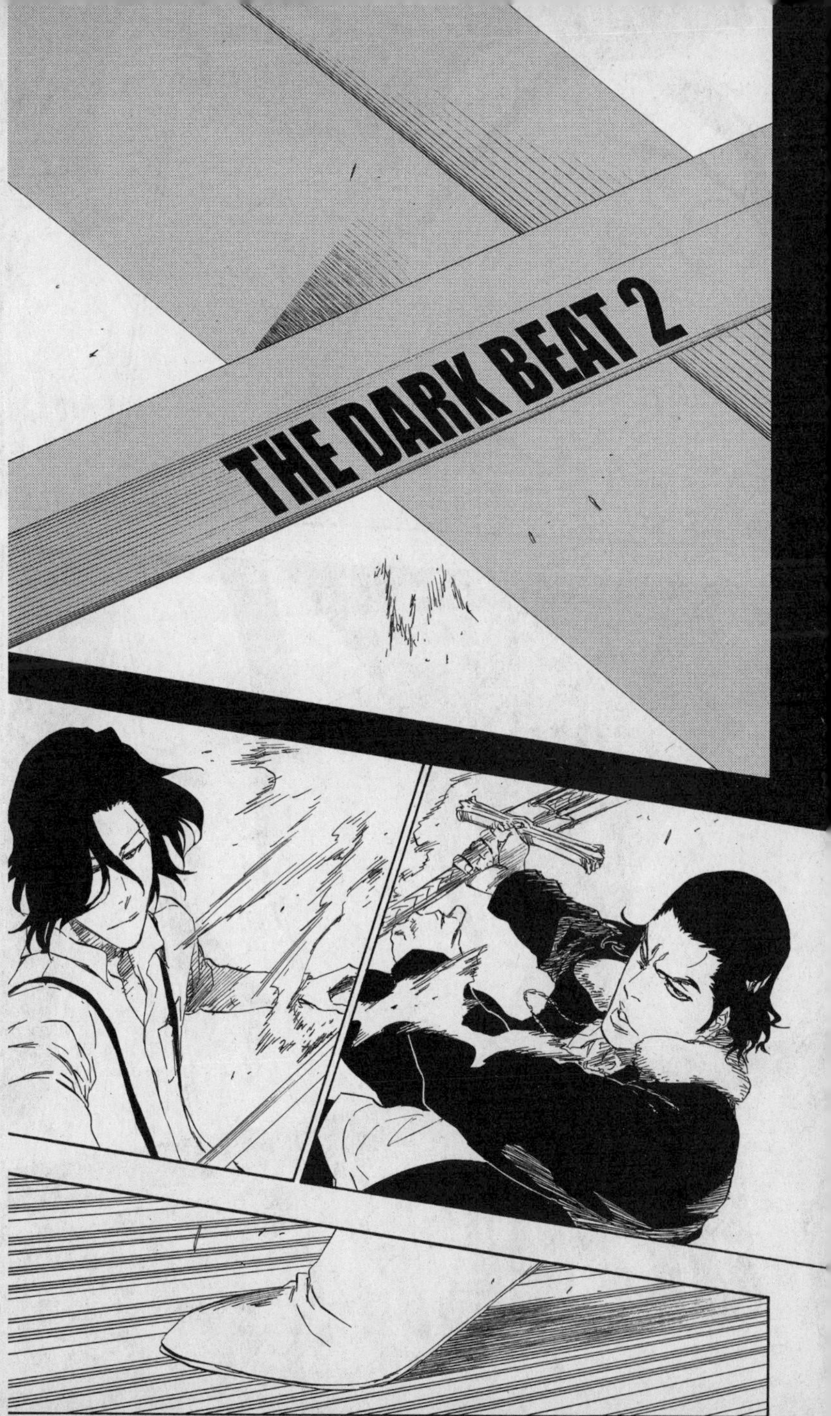
THE DARK BEAT 2

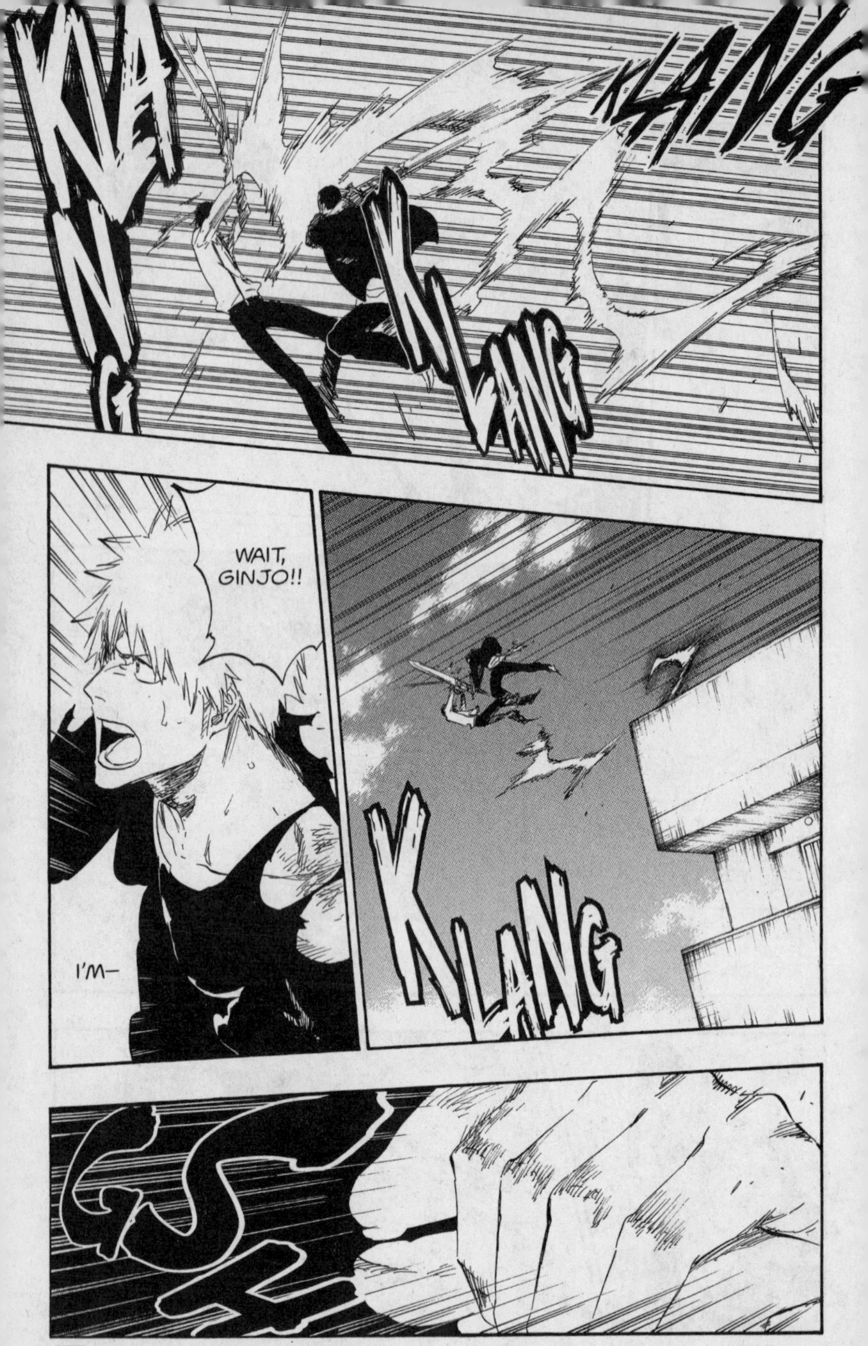
KLANG
KLANG
KLANG
KLANG
WAIT, GINJO!!
I'M—

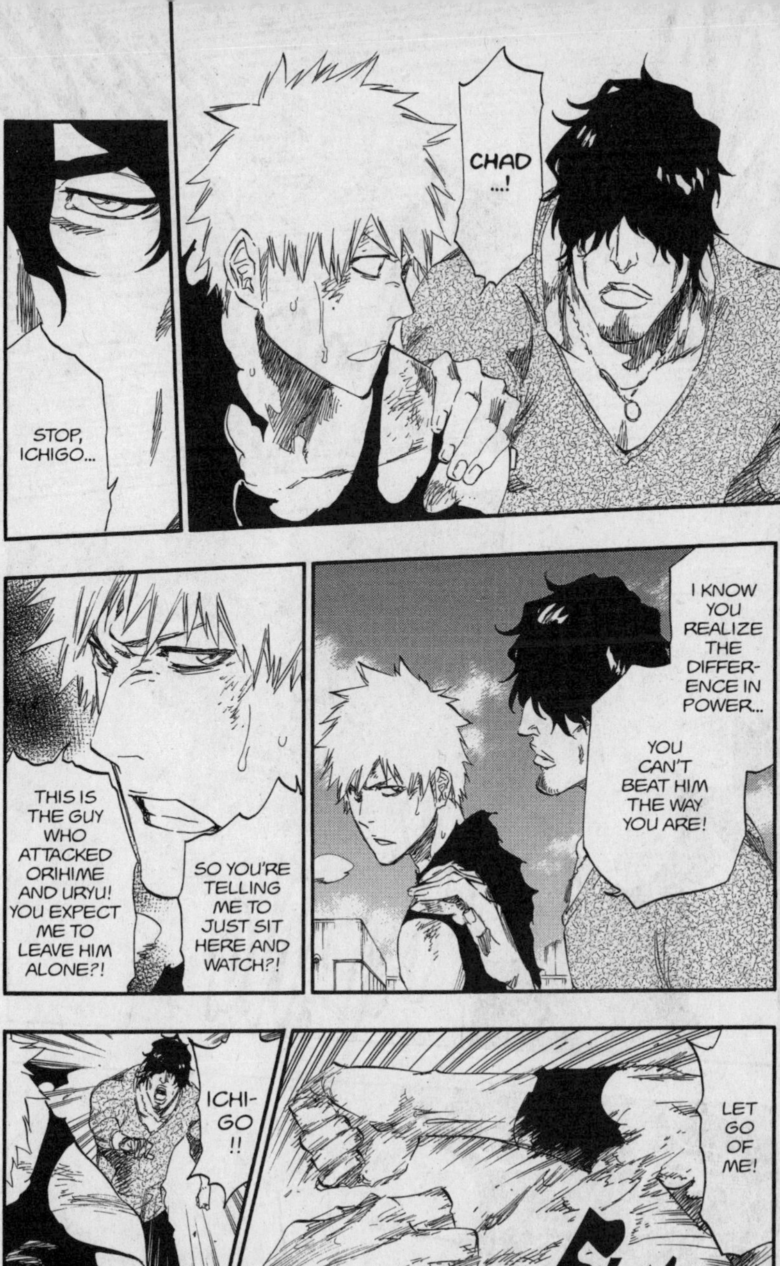
CHAD ...!
STOP, ICHIGO...
I KNOW YOU REALIZE THE DIFFERENCE IN POWER...
YOU CAN'T BEAT HIM THE WAY YOU ARE!
SO YOU'RE TELLING ME TO JUST SIT HERE AND WATCH?!
THIS IS THE GUY WHO ATTACKED ORIHIME AND URYU! YOU EXPECT ME TO LEAVE HIM ALONE?!
LET GO OF ME!
FWP
ICHIGO !!

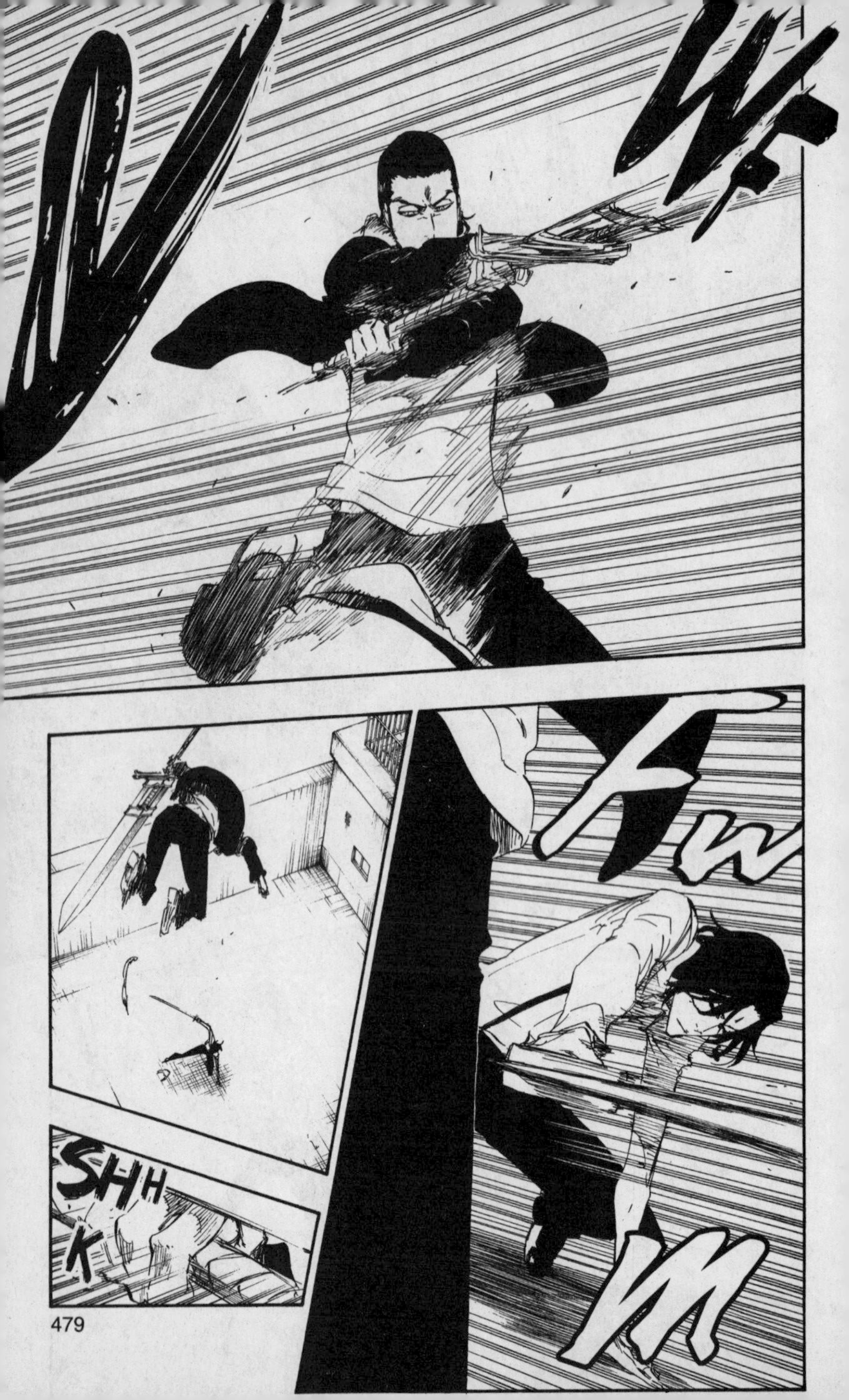
SHHK

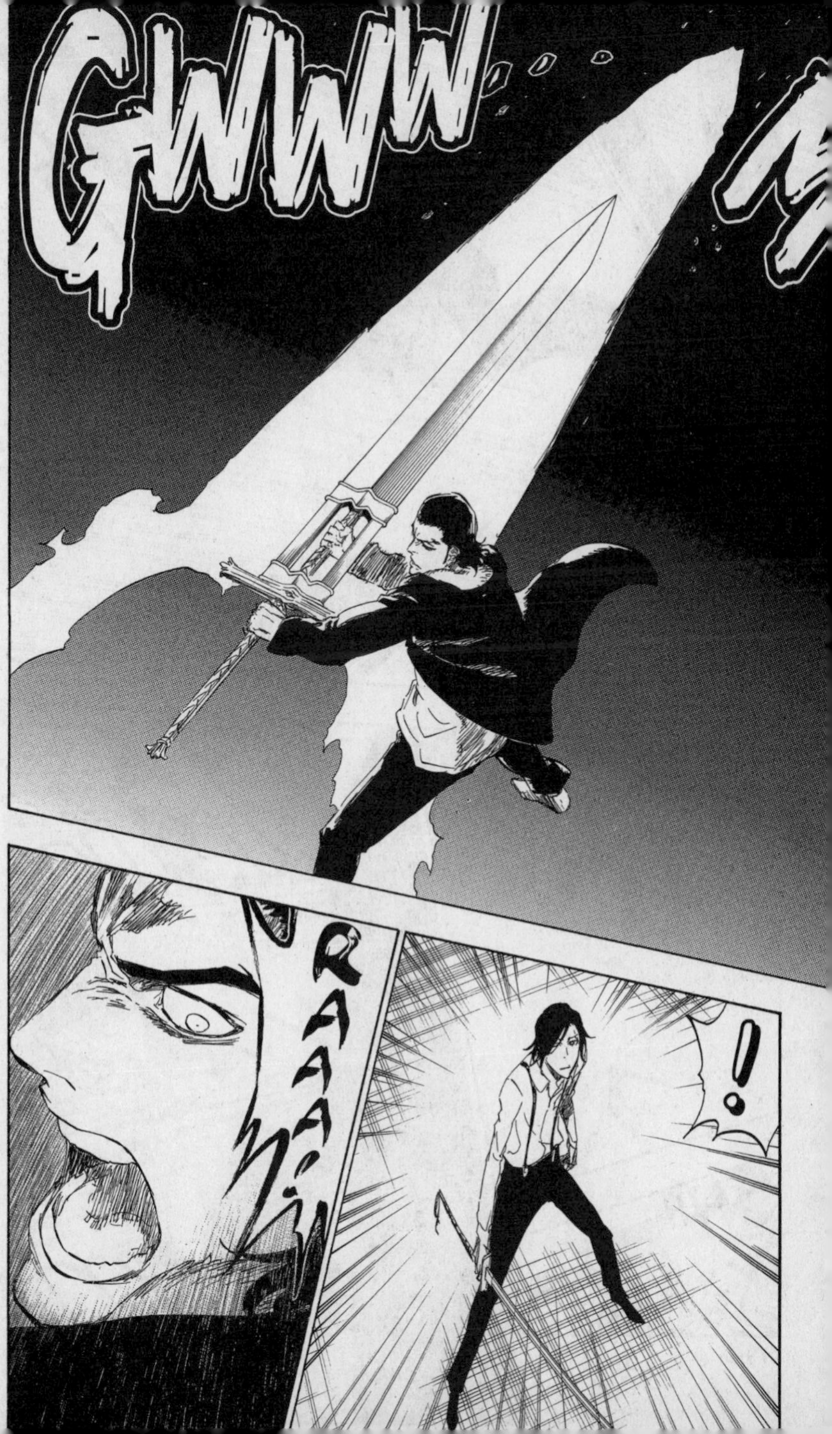
GWWW
!
RAAAA

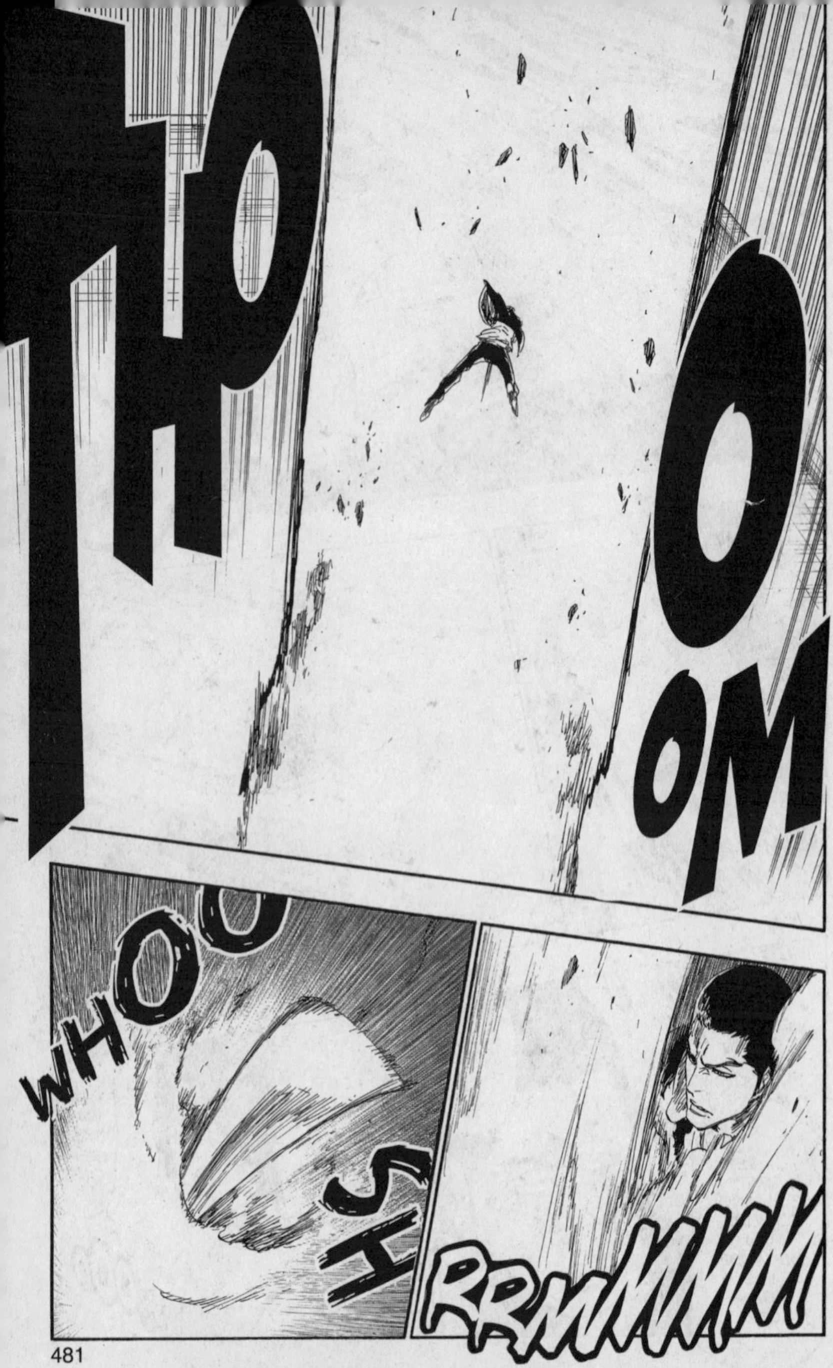
THOOOM
RRMMMMM
WHOOOSH

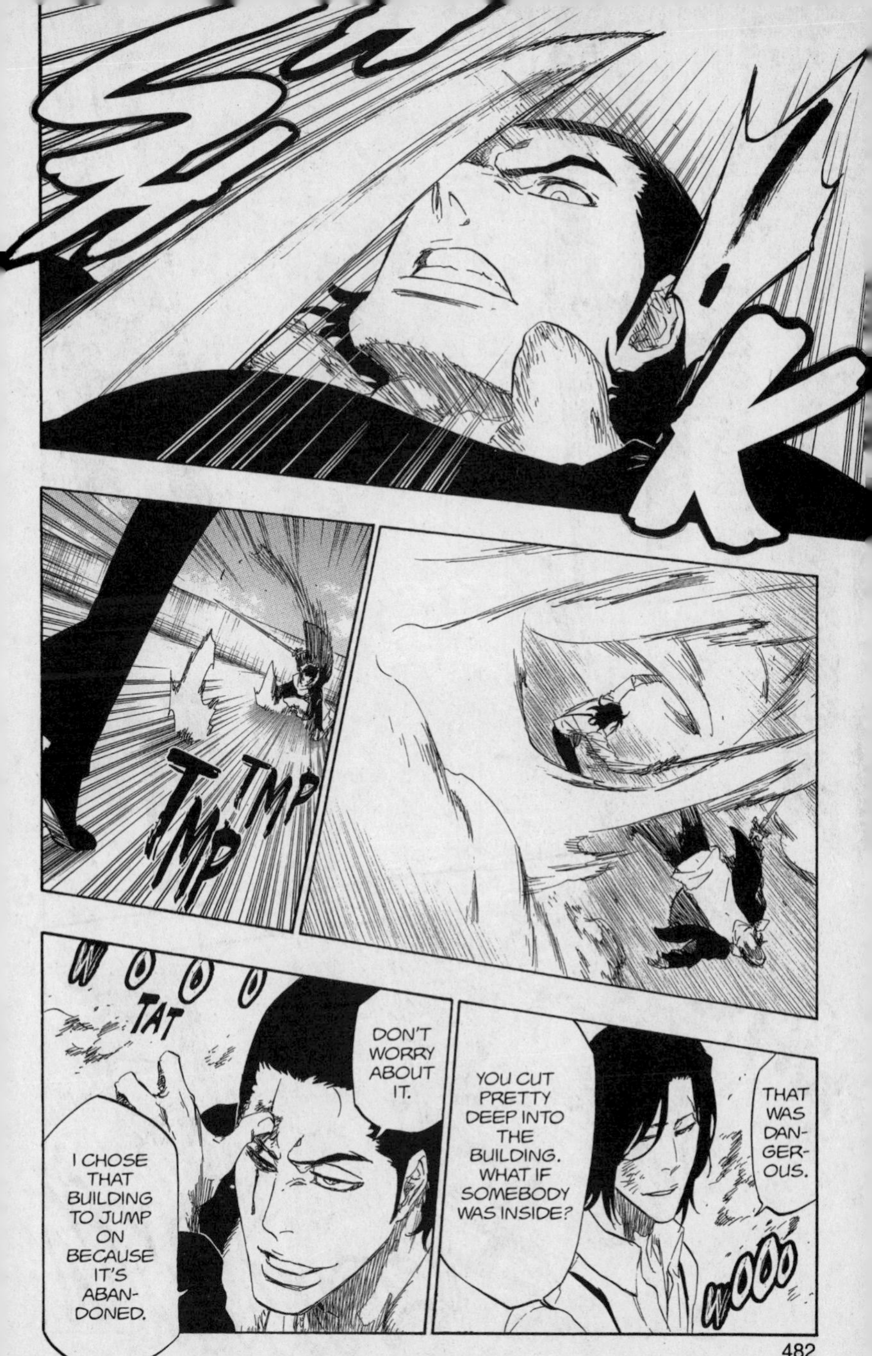
TMP TMP
THAT WAS DANGEROUS.
YOU CUT PRETTY DEEP INTO THE BUILDING. WHAT IF SOMEBODY WAS INSIDE?
WOOO
WOOO
TAT
DON'T WORRY ABOUT IT.
I CHOSE THAT BUILDING TO JUMP ON BECAUSE IT'S ABANDONED.

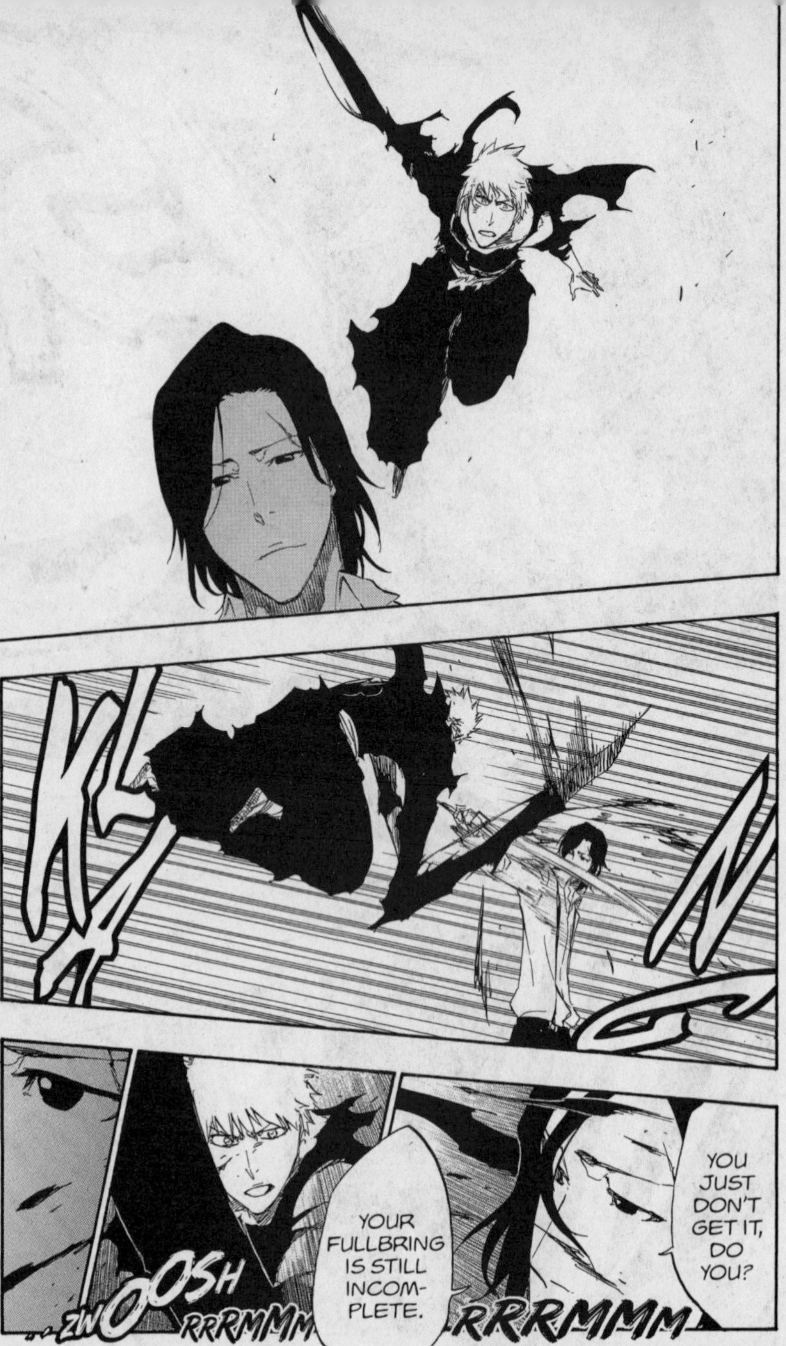
KLANG
YOU JUST DON'T GET IT, DO YOU?
RRRMMMM
YOUR FULLBRING IS STILL INCOMPLETE.
RRRMMMM
ZWOOSH

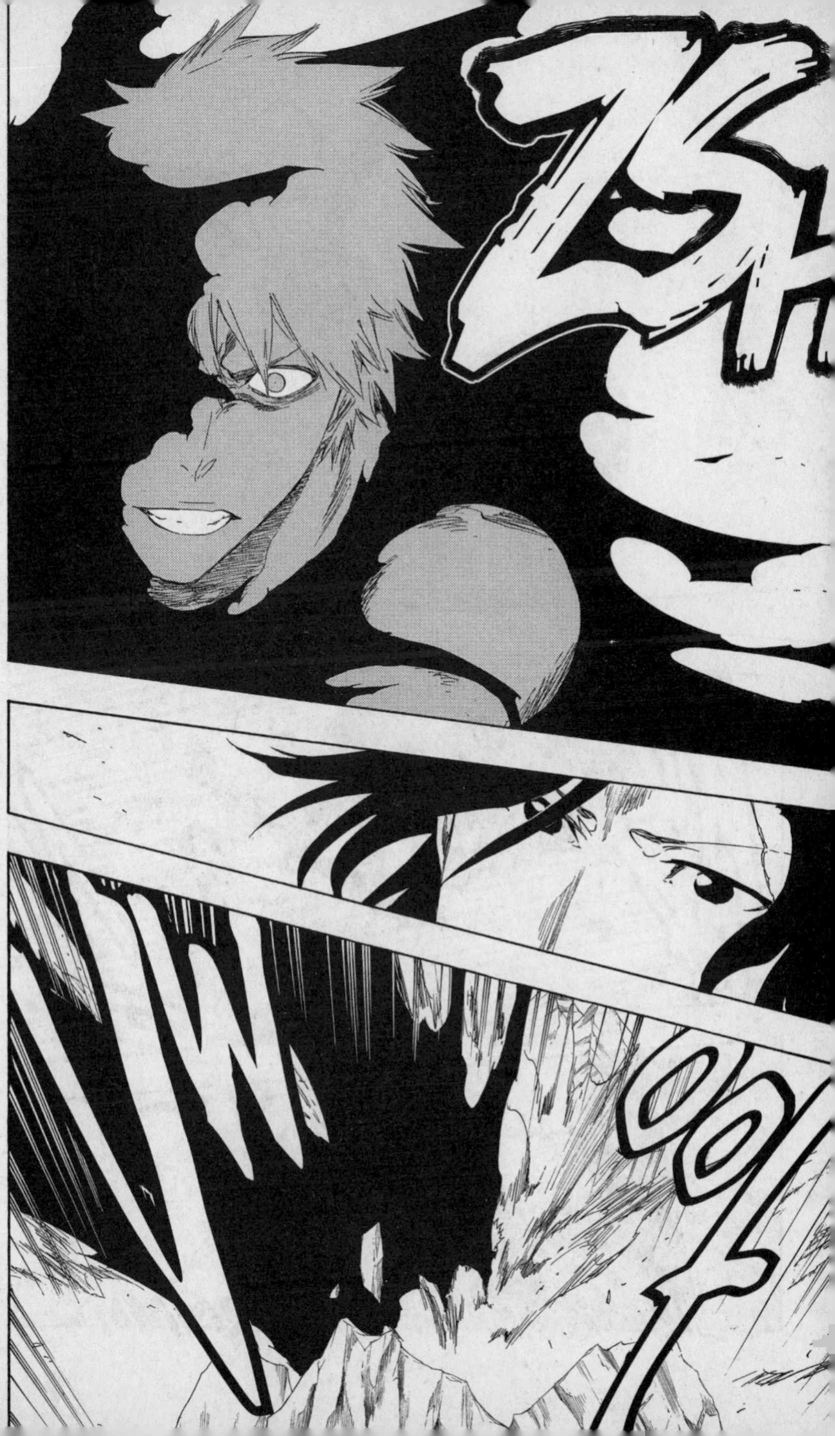

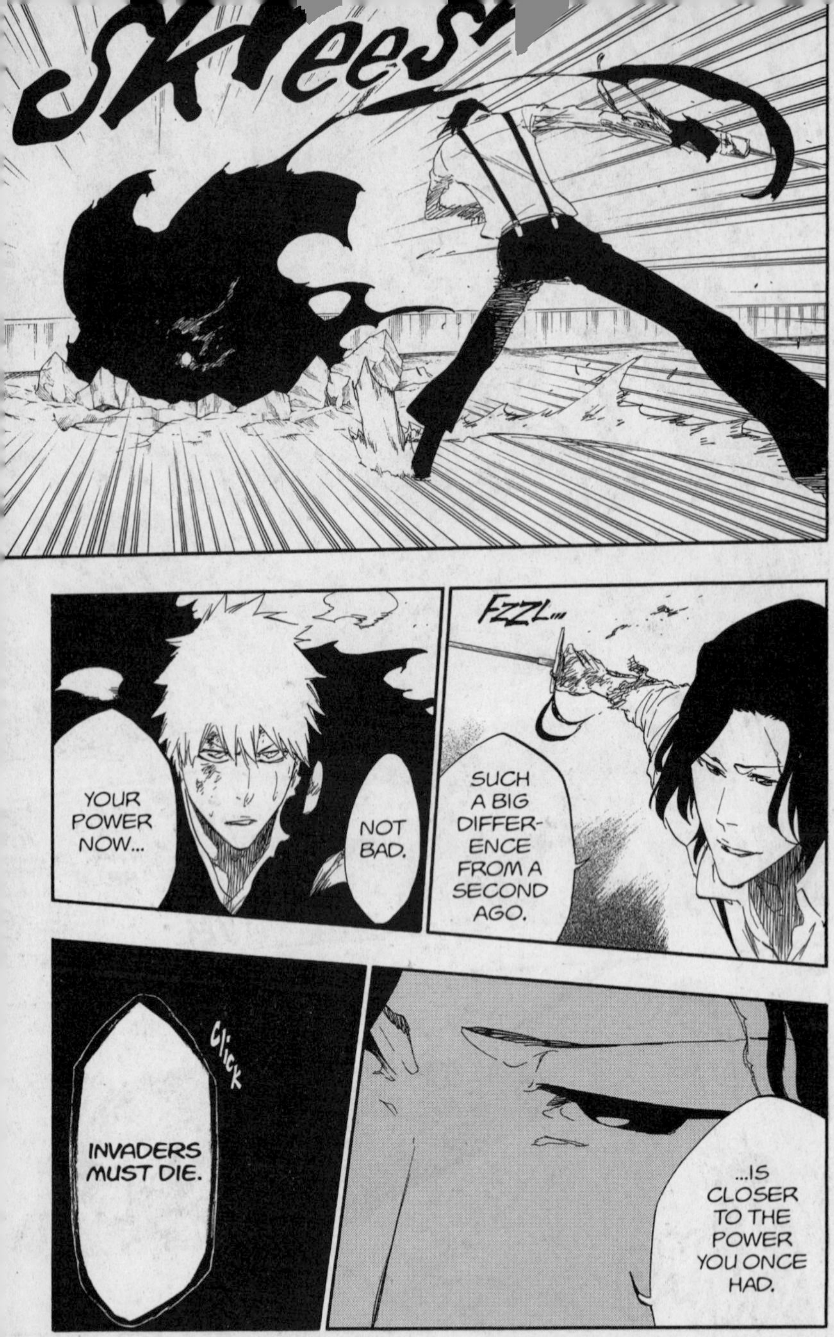
SKEES
FZZL...
SUCH A BIG DIFFER-ENCE FROM A SECOND AGO.
NOT BAD.
YOUR POWER NOW...
...IS CLOSER TO THE POWER YOU ONCE HAD.
Click
INVADERS MUST DIE.

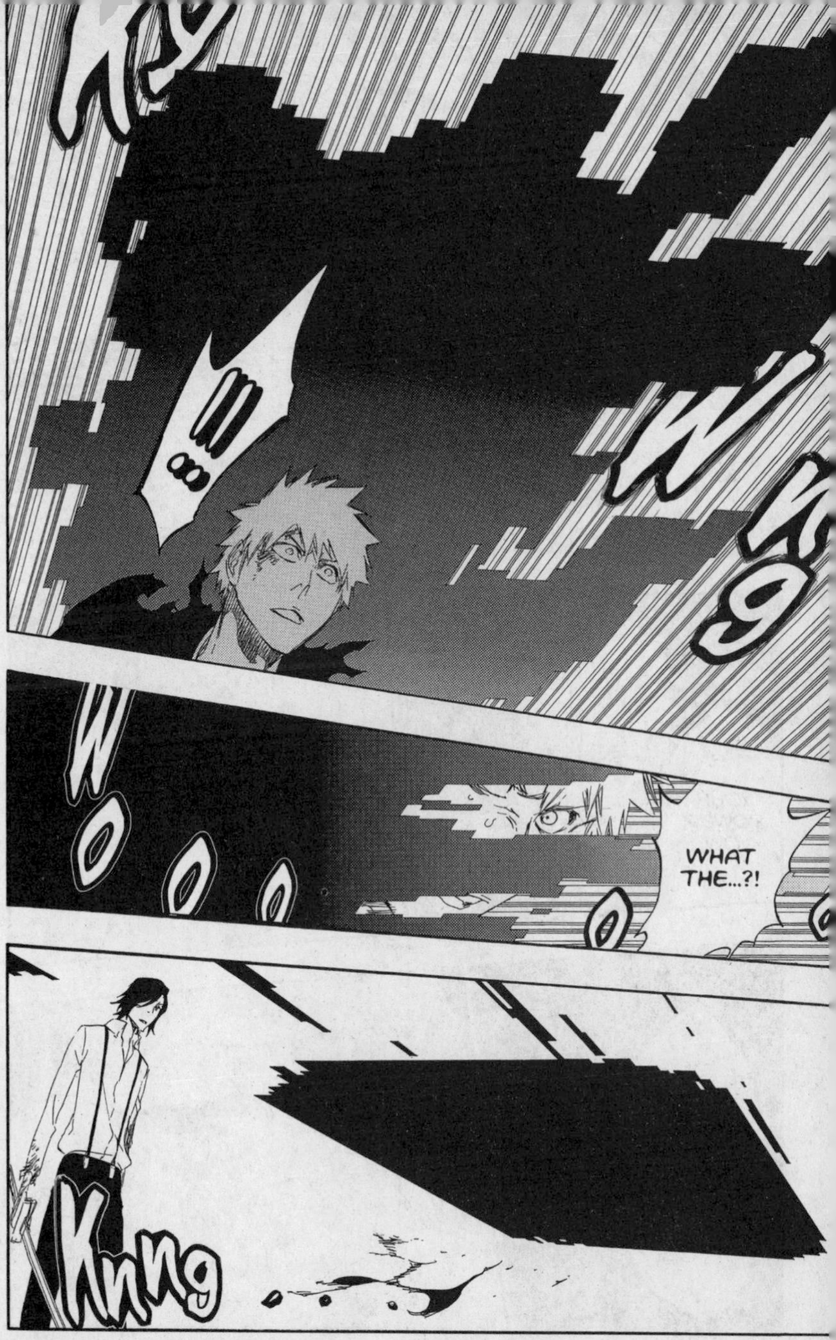
WHAT THE...?!
Knng

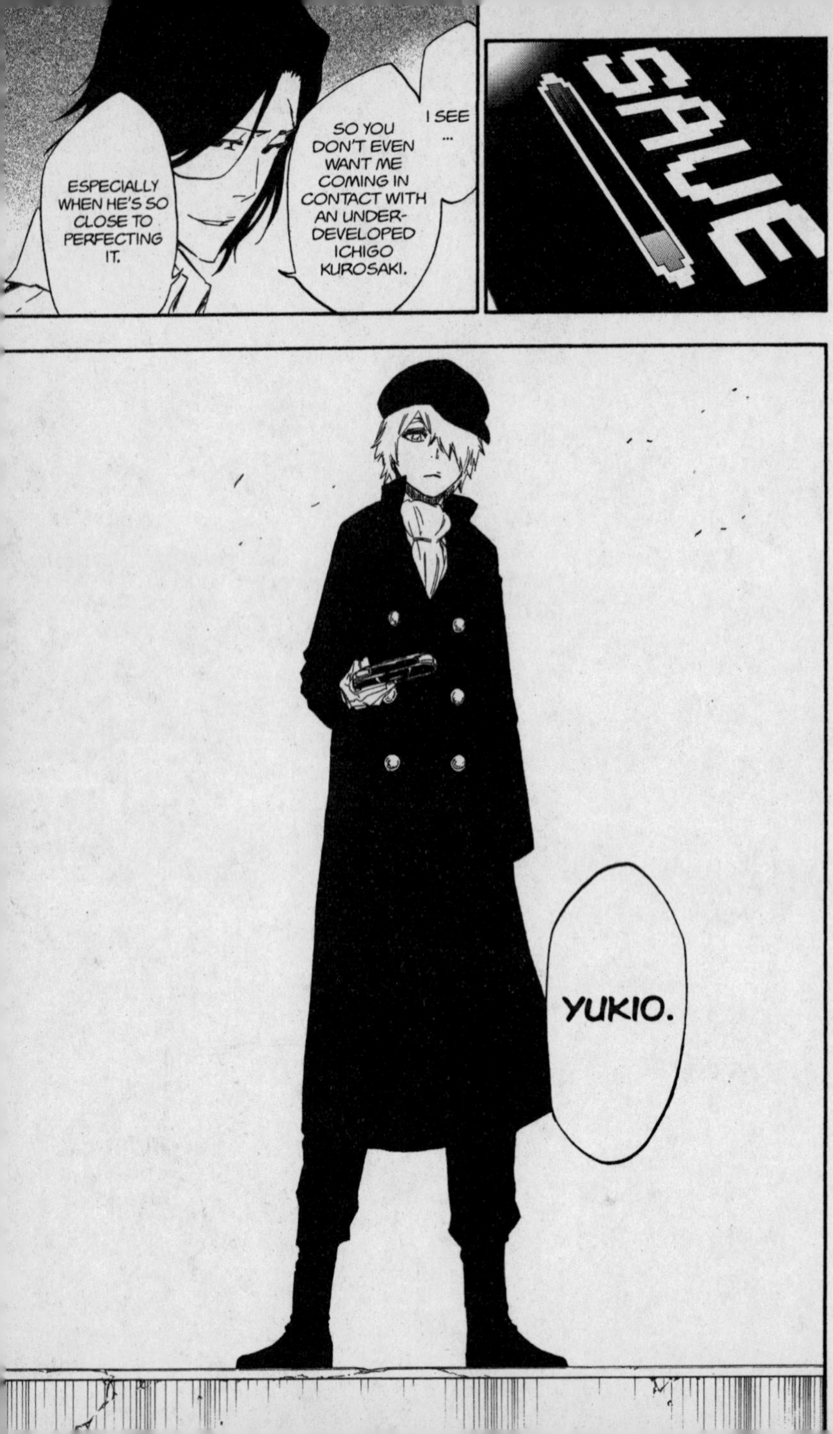
SAVE
I SEE ...
SO YOU DON'T EVEN WANT ME COMING IN CONTACT WITH AN UNDER-DEVELOPED ICHIGO KUROSAKI.
ESPECIALLY WHEN HE'S SO CLOSE TO PERFECTING IT.
YUKIO.

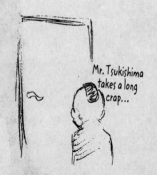

Mr. Tsukishima takes a long crap...

447. Load

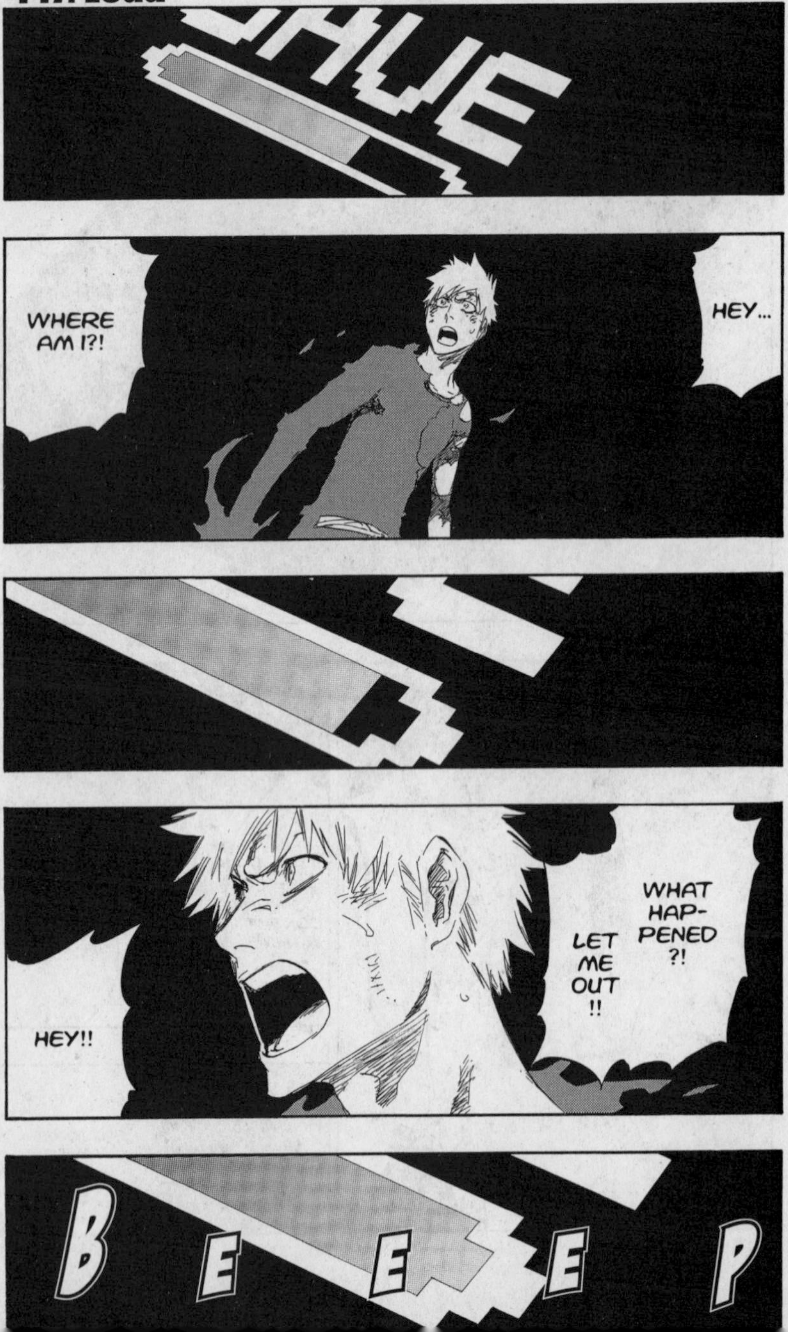
HEY...
WHERE AM I?!
WHAT HAPPENED?!
LET ME OUT!!
HEY!!
BEEEP

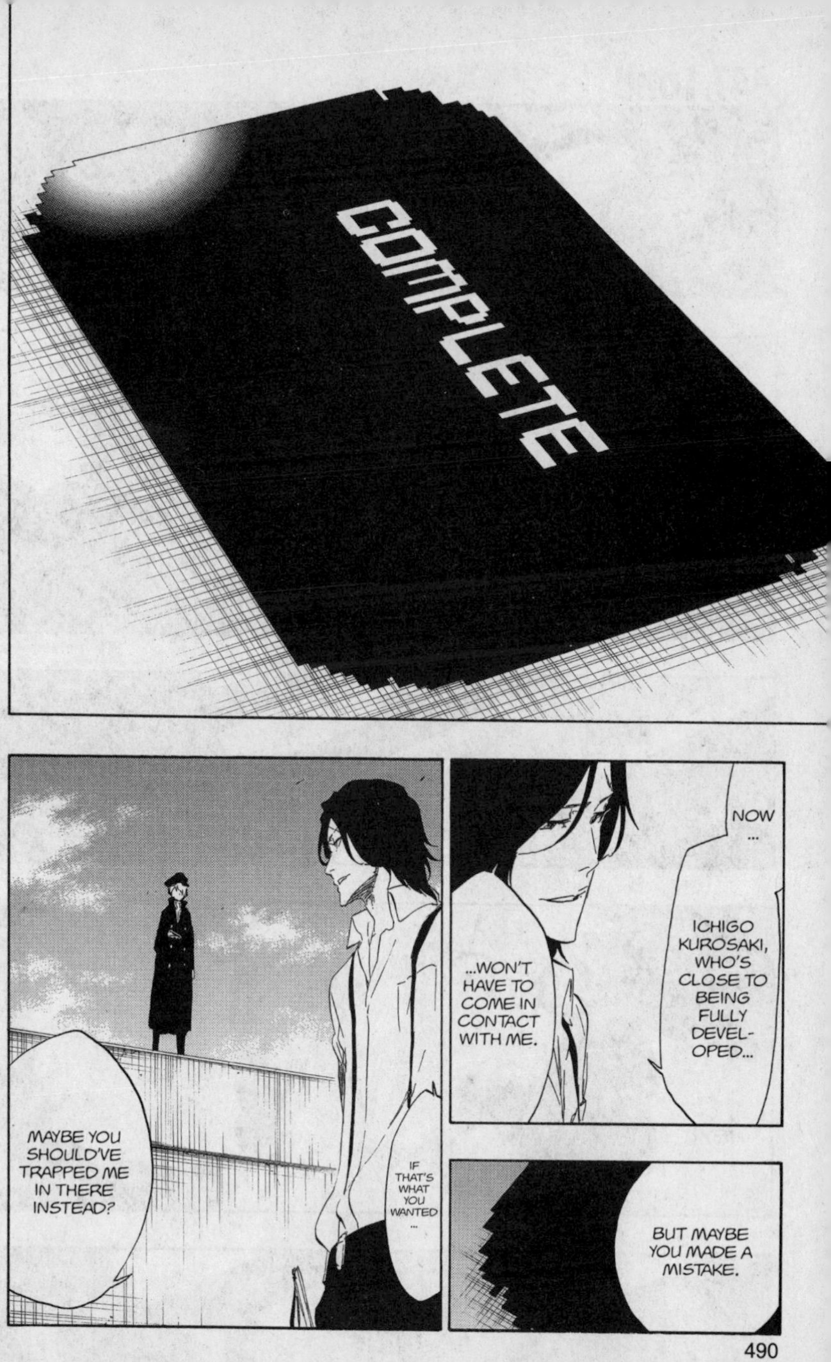
COMPLETE
NOW ...
ICHIGO KUROSAKI, WHO'S CLOSE TO BEING FULLY DEVEL-OPED...
...WON'T HAVE TO COME IN CONTACT WITH ME.
BUT MAYBE YOU MADE A MISTAKE.
IF THAT'S WHAT YOU WANTED ...
MAYBE YOU SHOULD'VE TRAPPED ME IN THERE INSTEAD?

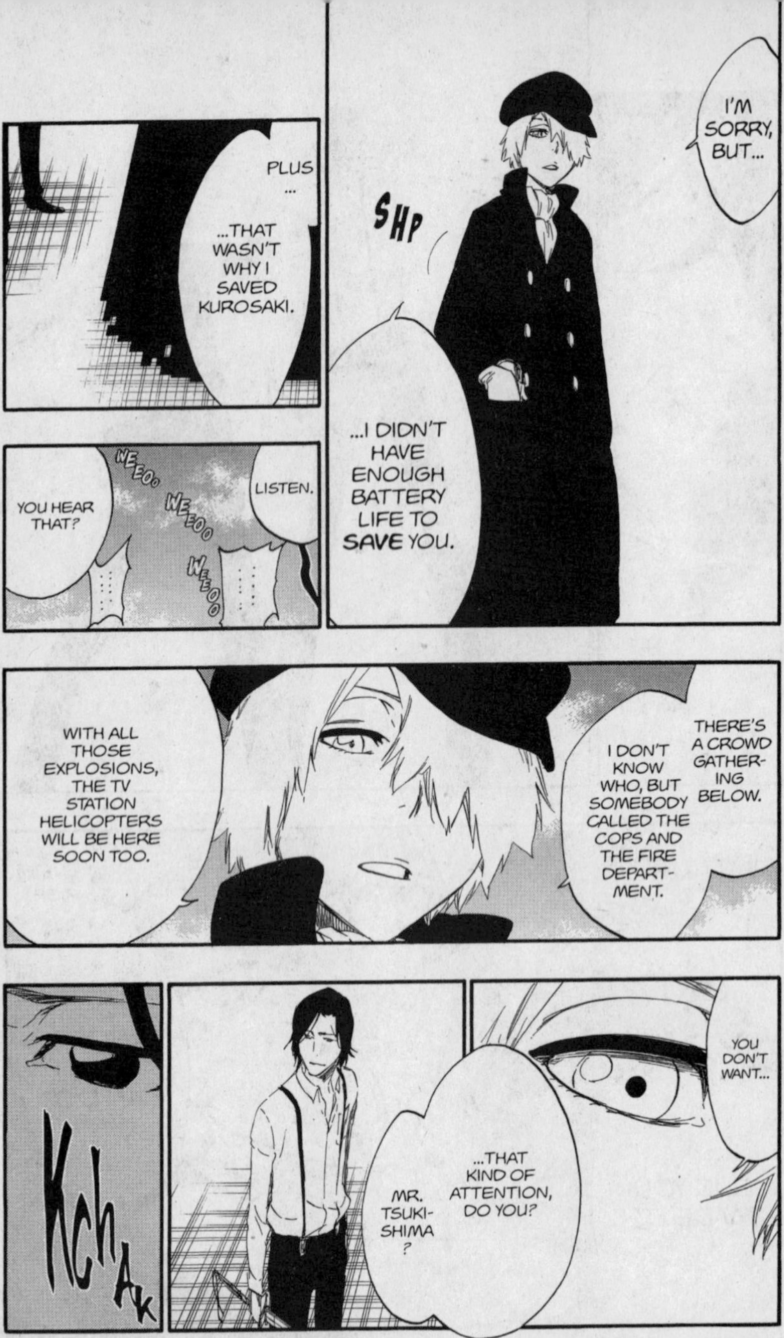
I'M SORRY, BUT...
SHP
...I DIDN'T HAVE ENOUGH BATTERY LIFE TO SAVE YOU.
PLUS ...
...THAT WASN'T WHY I SAVED KUROSAKI.
LISTEN.
WEEOO WEEOO WEEOO
YOU HEAR THAT?
THERE'S A CROWD GATHERING BELOW.
I DON'T KNOW WHO, BUT SOMEBODY CALLED THE COPS AND THE FIRE DEPARTMENT.
WITH ALL THOSE EXPLOSIONS, THE TV STATION HELICOPTERS WILL BE HERE SOON TOO.
YOU DON'T WANT...
...THAT KIND OF ATTENTION, DO YOU?
MR. TSUKISHIMA?
KCHAK

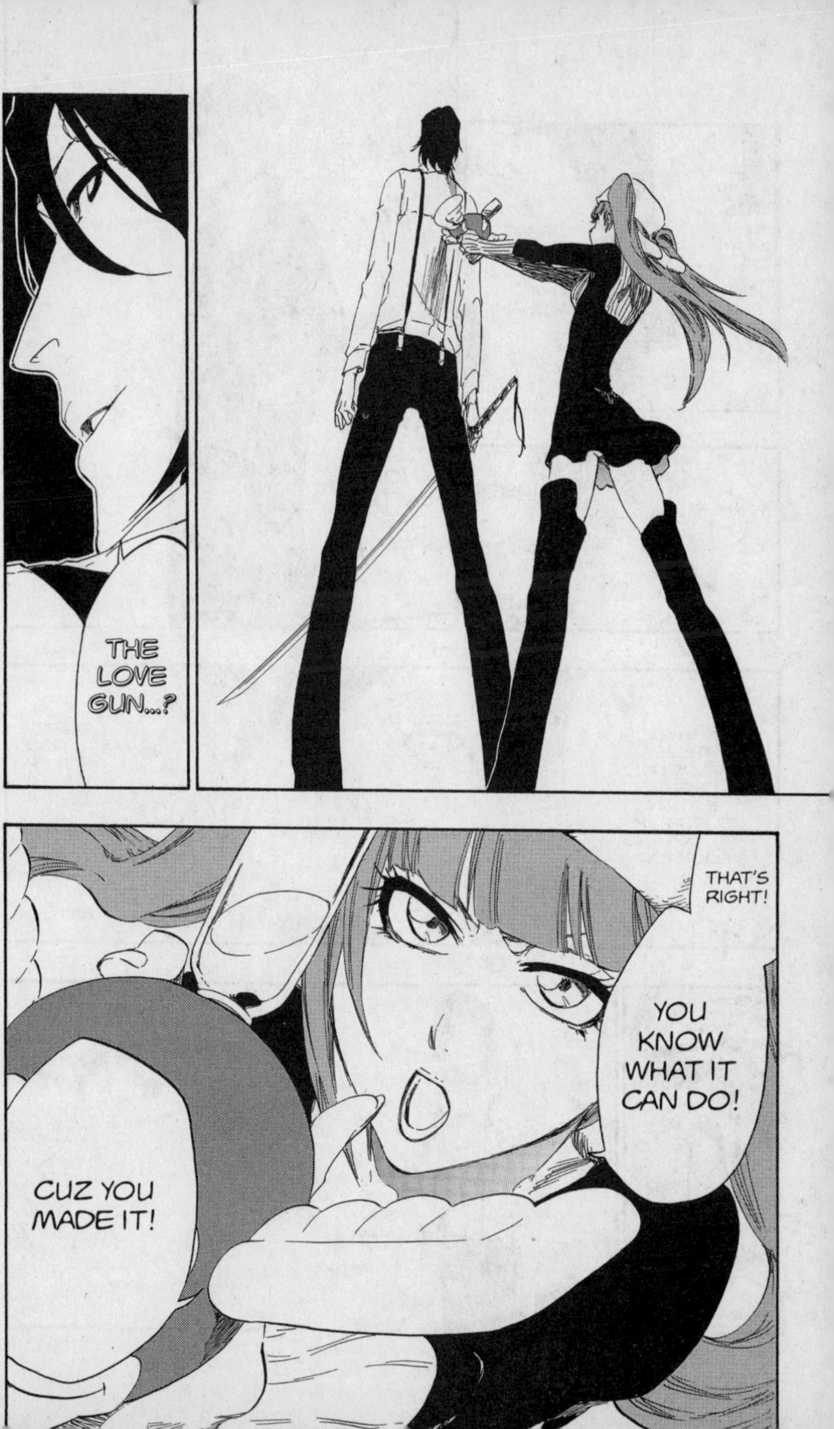
THE LOVE GUN...?
THAT'S RIGHT!
YOU KNOW WHAT IT CAN DO!
CUZ YOU MADE IT!

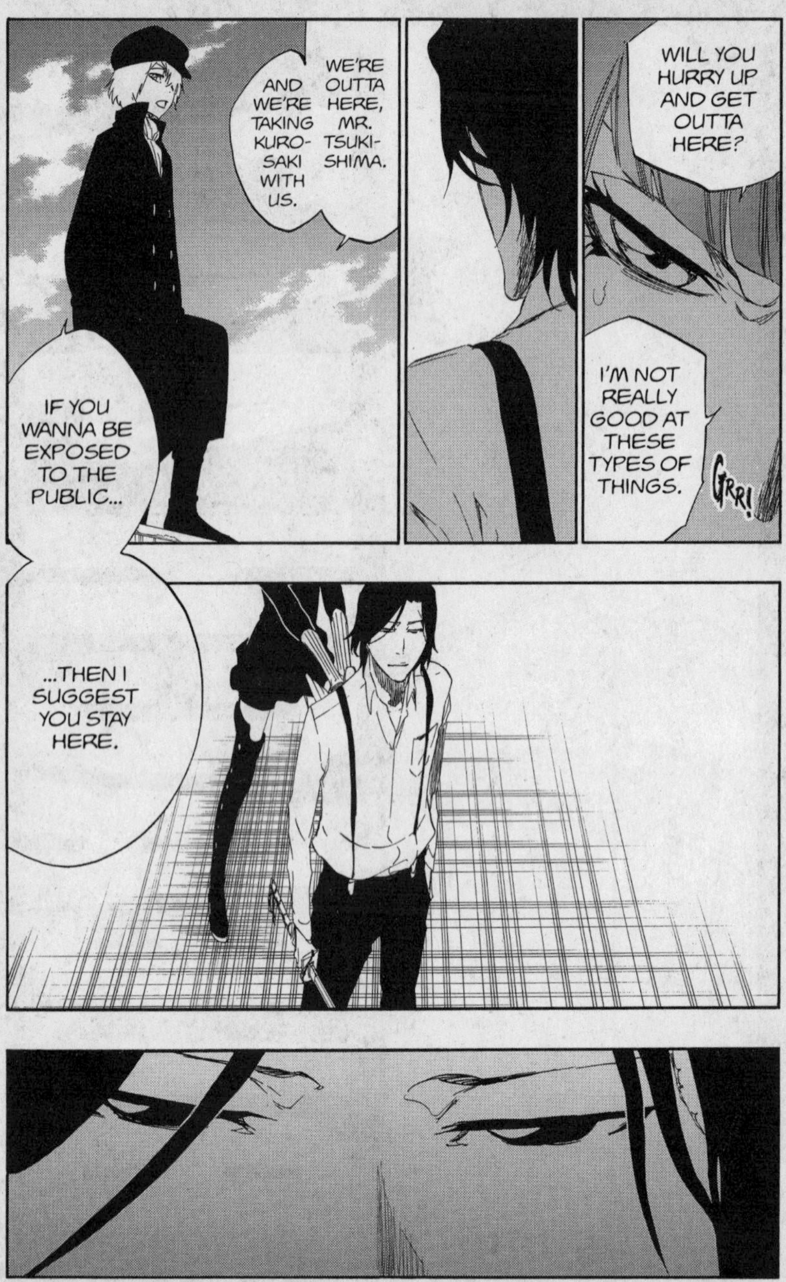
WILL YOU HURRY UP AND GET OUTTA HERE?
I'M NOT REALLY GOOD AT THESE TYPES OF THINGS.
GRR!
WE'RE OUTTA HERE, MR. TSUKISHIMA.
AND WE'RE TAKING KUROSAKI WITH US.
IF YOU WANNA BE EXPOSED TO THE PUBLIC...
...THEN I SUGGEST YOU STAY HERE.

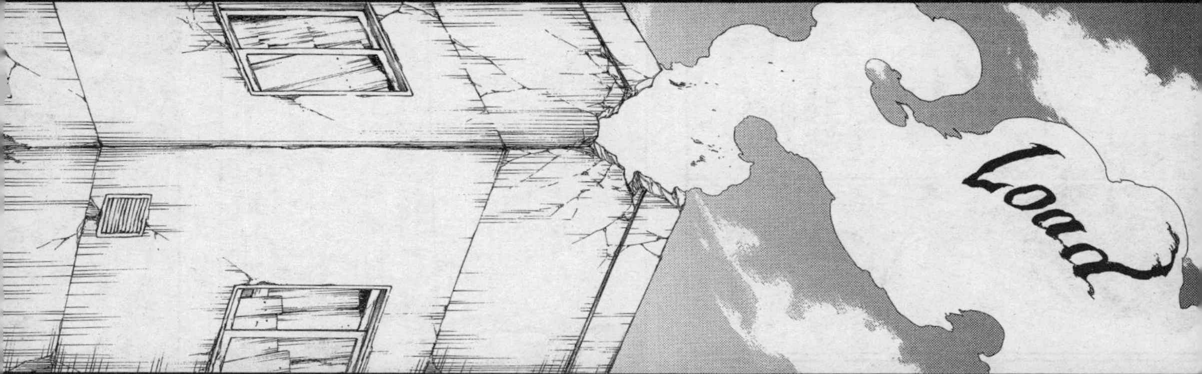
Load

BLEACH 447.

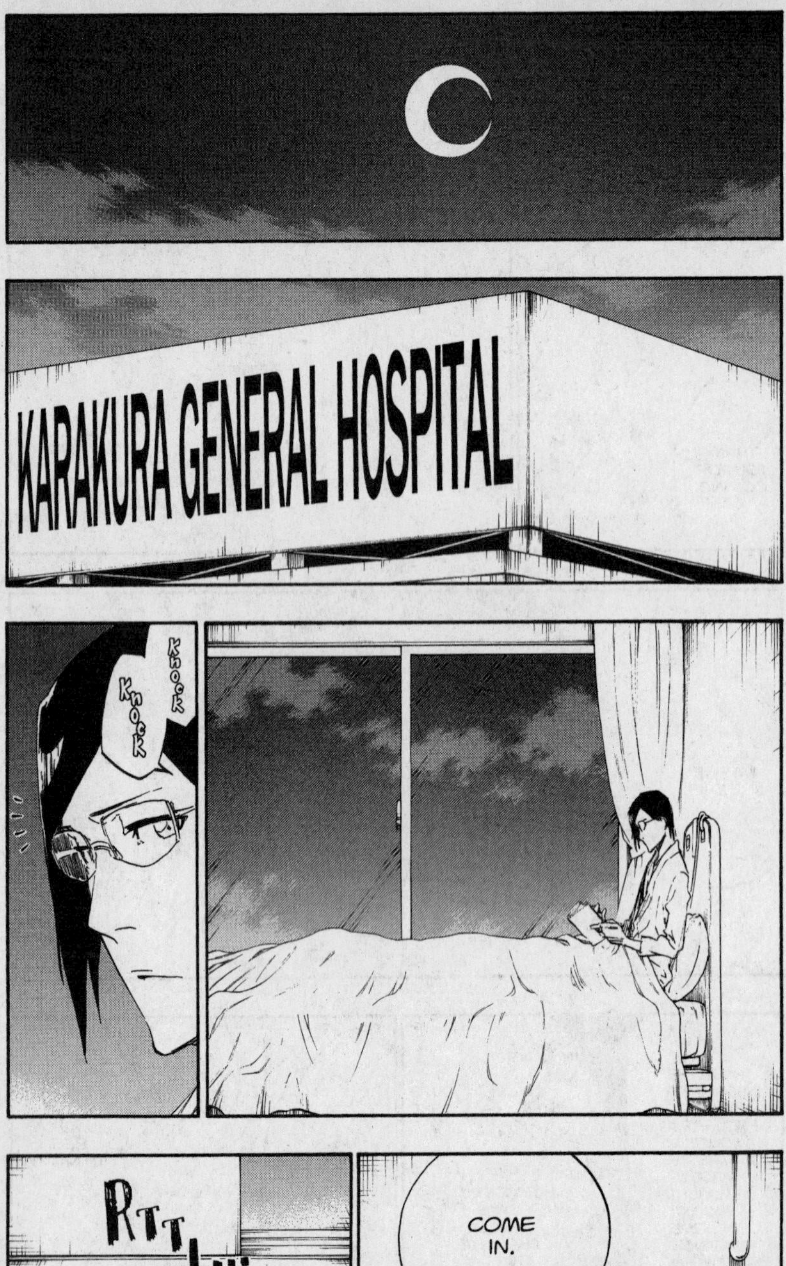
KARAKURA GENERAL HOSPITAL
KNOCK KNOCK
COME IN.
RTTL...

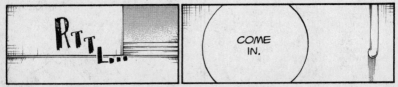

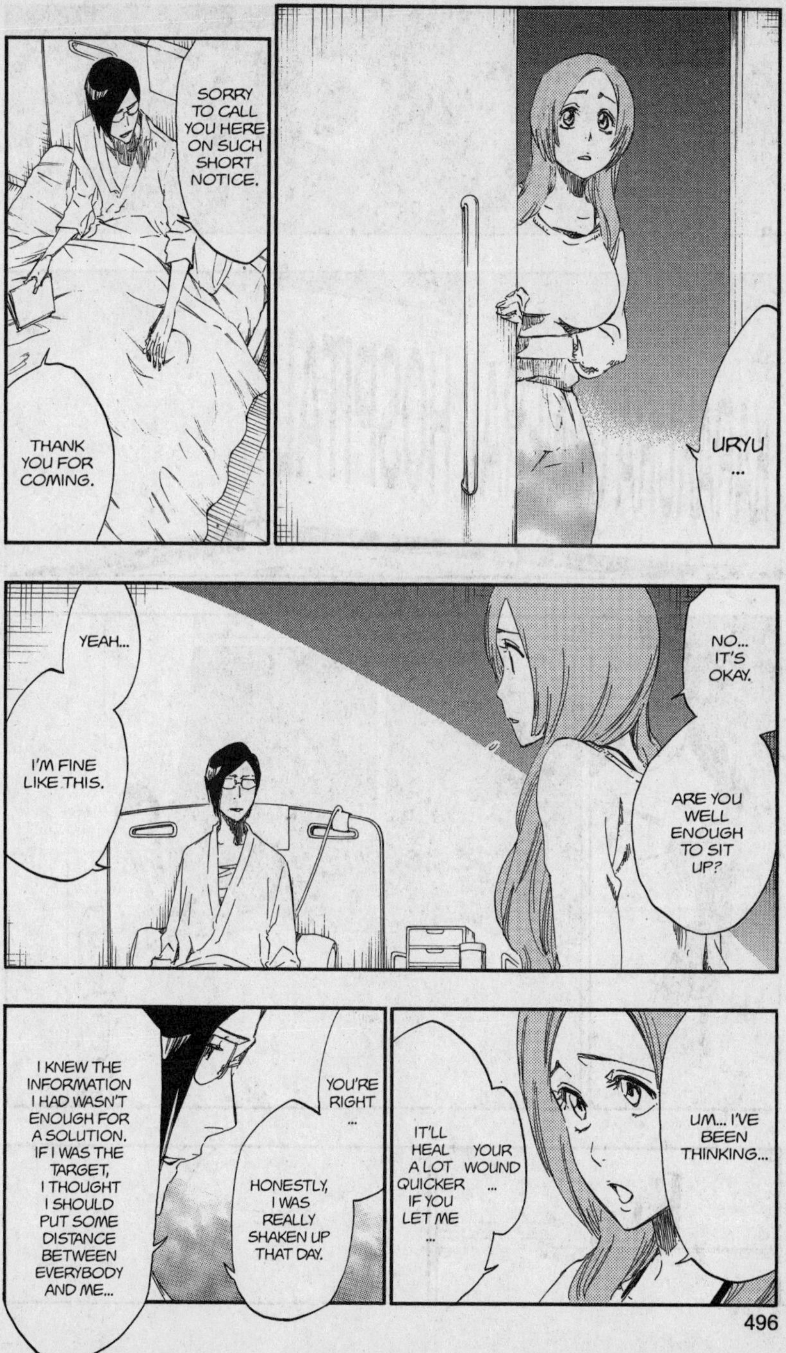
URYU ...
SORRY TO CALL YOU HERE ON SUCH SHORT NOTICE.
THANK YOU FOR COMING.
NO... IT'S OKAY.
ARE YOU WELL ENOUGH TO SIT UP?
YEAH...
I'M FINE LIKE THIS.
UM... I'VE BEEN THINKING...
YOUR WOUND ...
IT'LL HEAL A LOT QUICKER IF YOU LET ME ...
YOU'RE RIGHT ...
HONESTLY, I WAS REALLY SHAKEN UP THAT DAY.
I KNEW THE INFORMATION I HAD WASN'T ENOUGH FOR A SOLUTION. IF I WAS THE TARGET, I THOUGHT I SHOULD PUT SOME DISTANCE BETWEEN EVERYBODY AND ME...

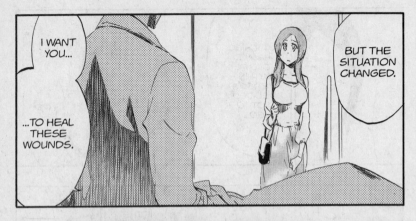

I WANT YOU...

...TO HEAL THESE WOUNDS.

BUT THE SITUATION CHANGED.

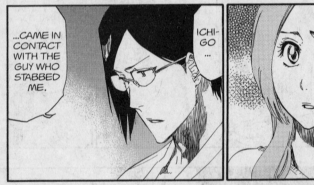

...CAME IN CONTACT WITH THE GUY WHO STABBED ME.

ICHI-GO...

THE SITUATION...?

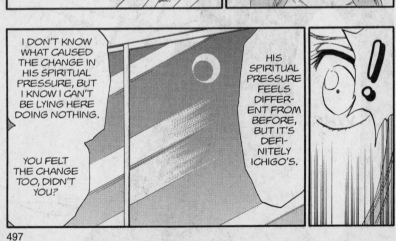

I DON'T KNOW WHAT CAUSED THE CHANGE IN HIS SPIRITUAL PRESSURE, BUT I KNOW I CAN'T BE LYING HERE DOING NOTHING.

YOU FELT THE CHANGE TOO, DIDN'T YOU?

HIS SPIRITUAL PRESSURE FEELS DIFFER-ENT FROM BEFORE, BUT IT'S DEFI-NITELY ICHIGO'S.

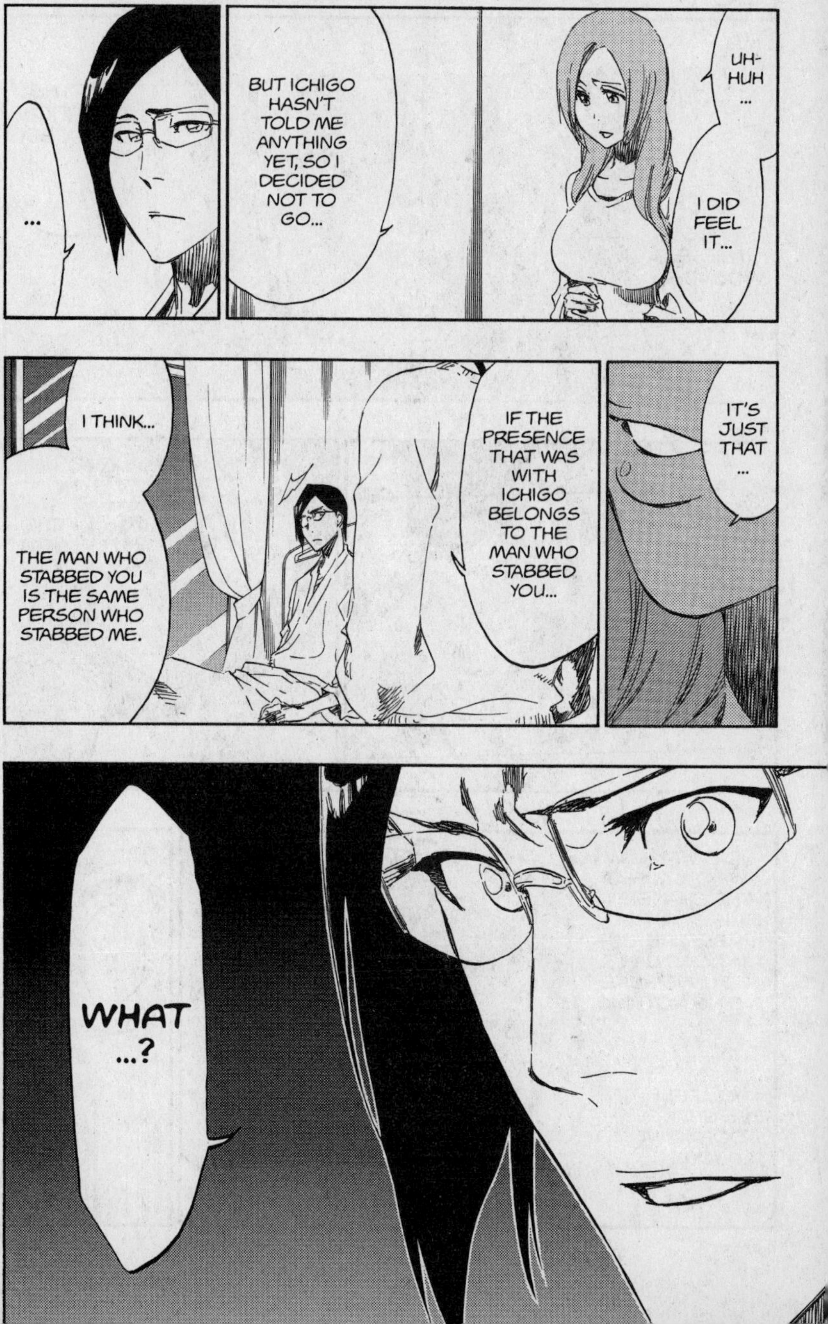
UH-HUH...
I DID FEEL IT...
BUT ICHIGO HASN'T TOLD ME ANYTHING YET, SO I DECIDED NOT TO GO...
...
IT'S JUST THAT...
IF THE PRESENCE THAT WAS WITH ICHIGO BELONGS TO THE MAN WHO STABBED YOU...
I THINK...
THE MAN WHO STABBED YOU IS THE SAME PERSON WHO STABBED ME.
WHAT...?

NOW LOADING...

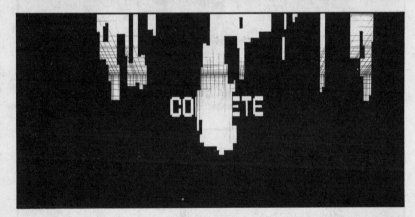

CO█PLETE

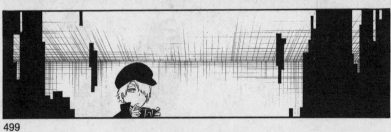

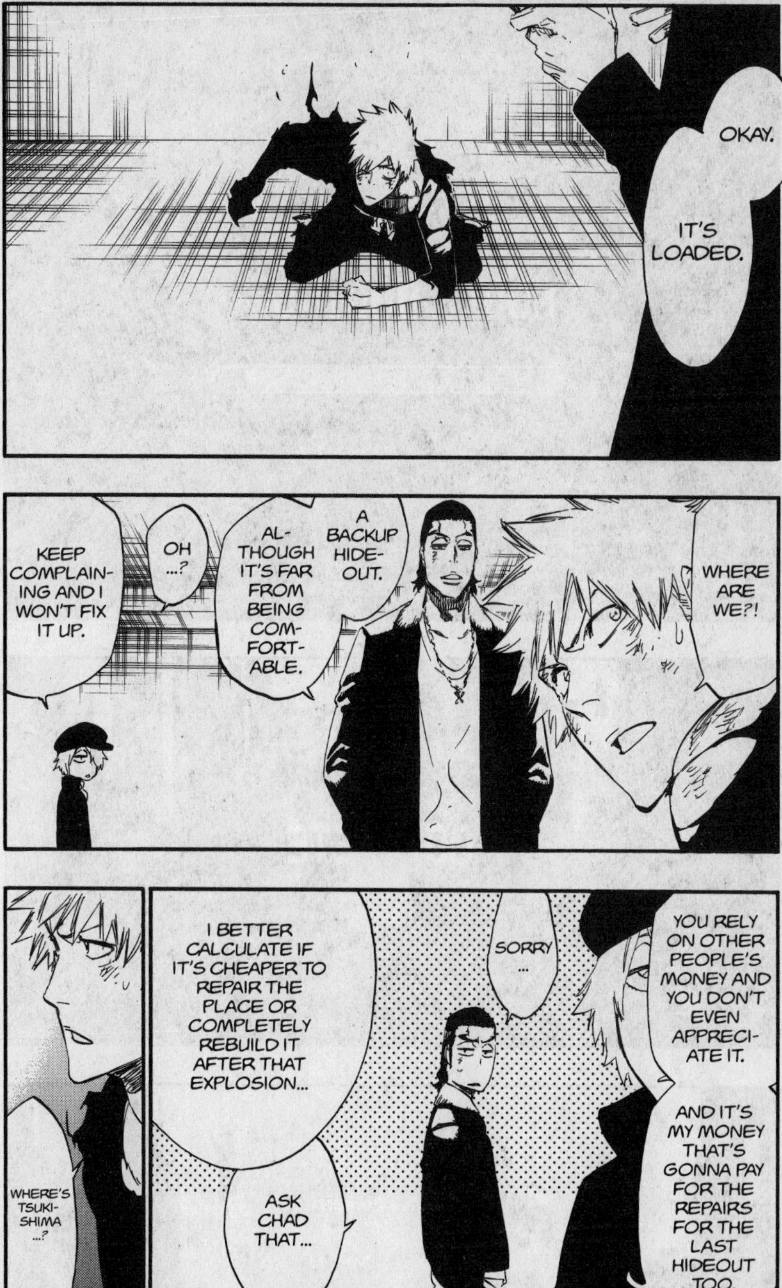
OKAY.
IT'S LOADED.
WHERE ARE WE?!
A BACKUP HIDEOUT.
ALTHOUGH IT'S FAR FROM BEING COMFORTABLE.
OH ...?
KEEP COMPLAINING AND I WON'T FIX IT UP.
YOU RELY ON OTHER PEOPLE'S MONEY AND YOU DON'T EVEN APPRECIATE IT.
SORRY ...
AND IT'S MY MONEY THAT'S GONNA PAY FOR THE REPAIRS FOR THE LAST HIDEOUT TOO.
I BETTER CALCULATE IF IT'S CHEAPER TO REPAIR THE PLACE OR COMPLETELY REBUILD IT AFTER THAT EXPLOSION...
ASK CHAD THAT...
WHERE'S TSUKISHIMA ...?

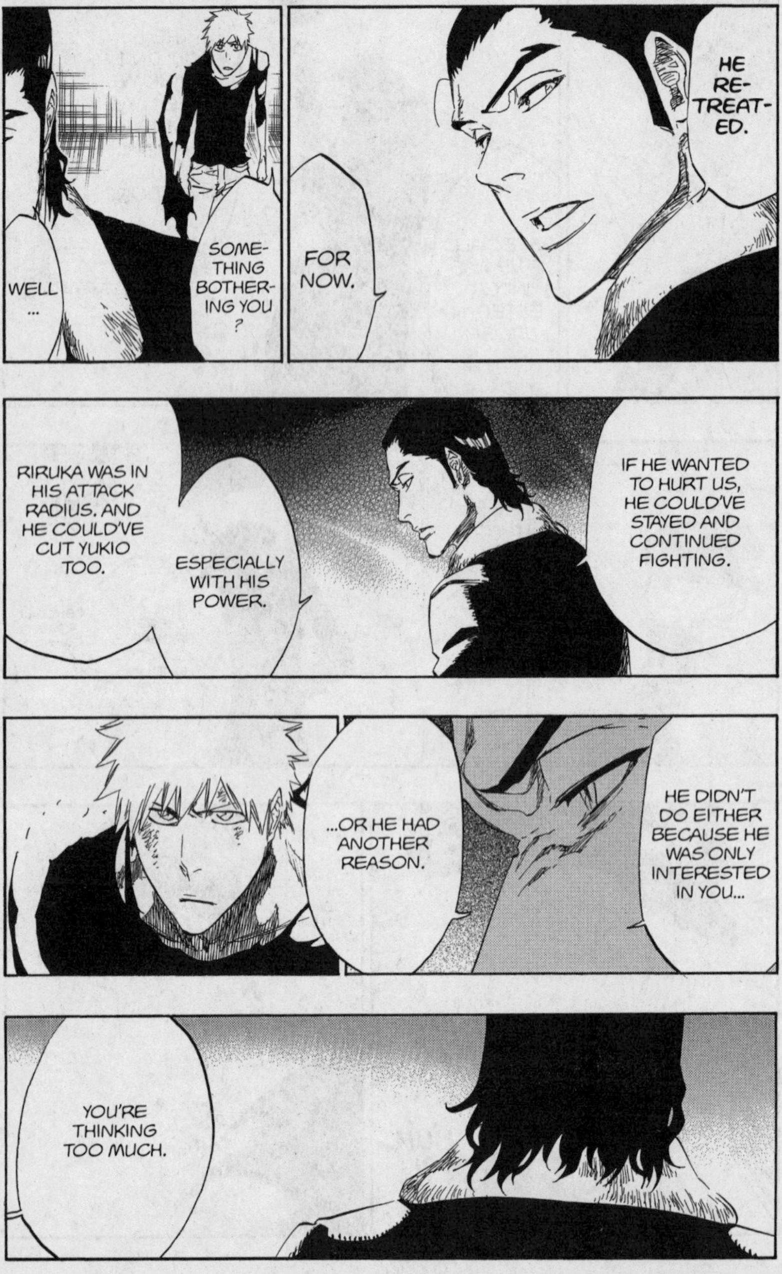
HE RE-TREAT-ED.
FOR NOW.
SOME-THING BOTHER-ING YOU?
WELL...
IF HE WANTED TO HURT US, HE COULD'VE STAYED AND CONTINUED FIGHTING.
ESPECIALLY WITH HIS POWER.
RIRUKA WAS IN HIS ATTACK RADIUS. AND HE COULD'VE CUT YUKIO TOO.
HE DIDN'T DO EITHER BECAUSE HE WAS ONLY INTERESTED IN YOU...
...OR HE HAD ANOTHER REASON.
YOU'RE THINKING TOO MUCH.

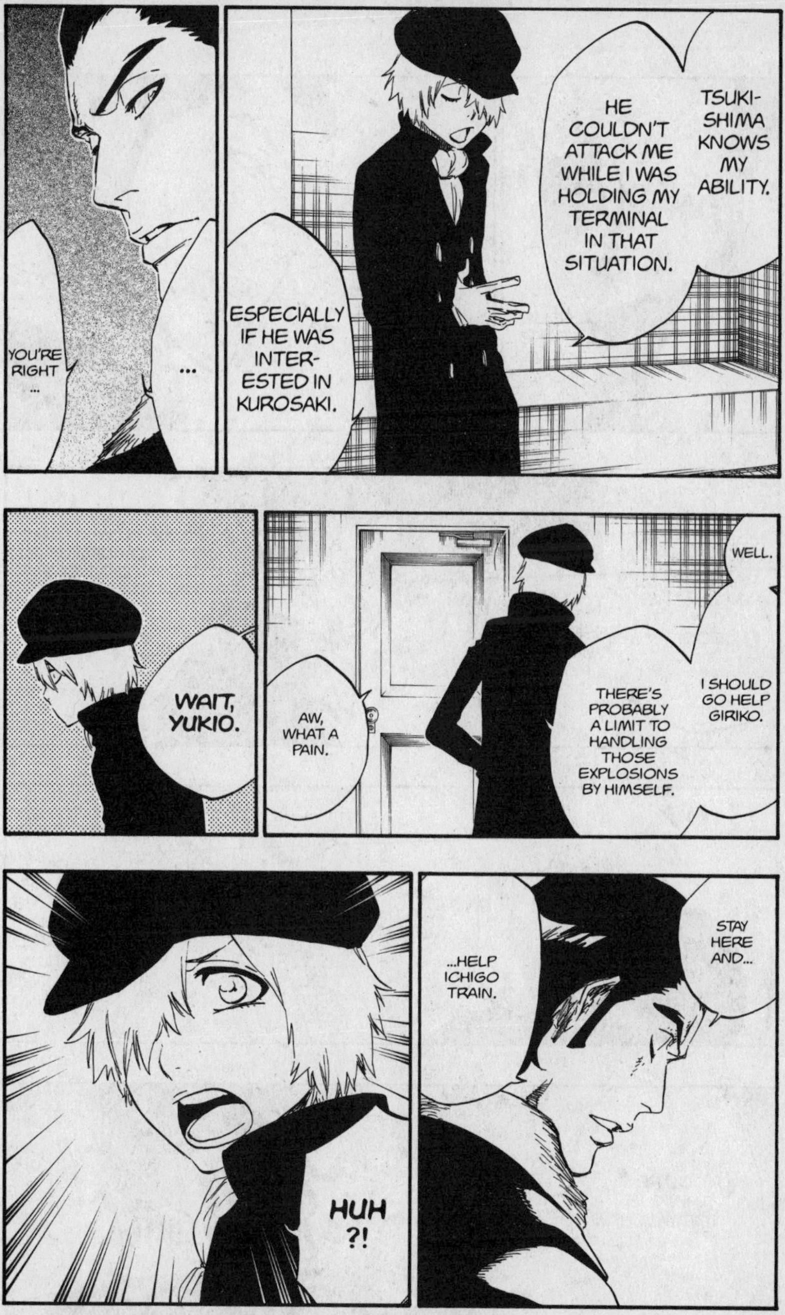
TSUKI-SHIMA KNOWS MY ABILITY.
HE COULDN'T ATTACK ME WHILE I WAS HOLDING MY TERMINAL IN THAT SITUATION.
ESPECIALLY IF HE WAS INTER-ESTED IN KUROSAKI.
...
YOU'RE RIGHT ...
WELL.
I SHOULD GO HELP GIRIKO.
THERE'S PROBABLY A LIMIT TO HANDLING THOSE EXPLOSIONS BY HIMSELF.
AW, WHAT A PAIN.
WAIT, YUKIO.
STAY HERE AND...
...HELP ICHIGO TRAIN.
HUH ?!

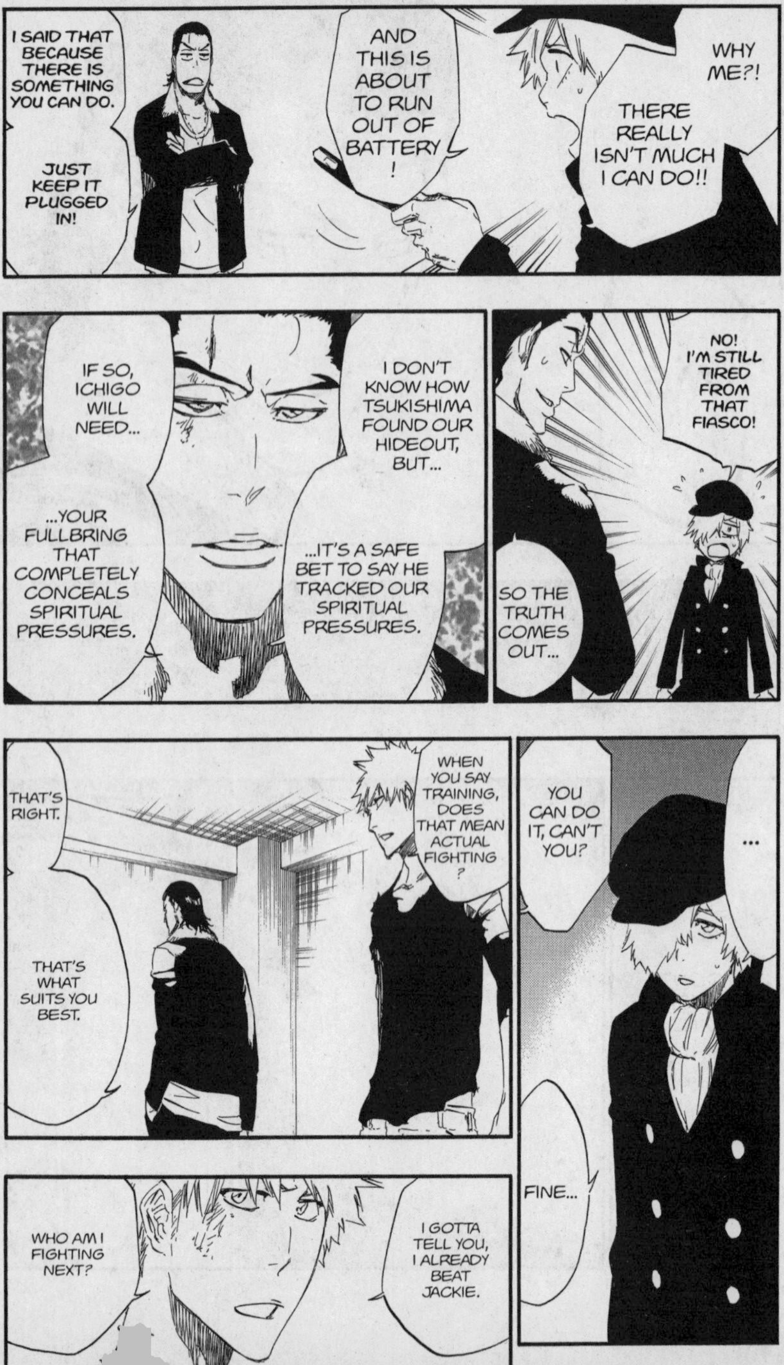
WHY ME?!
THERE REALLY ISN'T MUCH I CAN DO!!
AND THIS IS ABOUT TO RUN OUT OF BATTERY!
I SAID THAT BECAUSE THERE IS SOMETHING YOU CAN DO.
JUST KEEP IT PLUGGED IN!
NO! I'M STILL TIRED FROM THAT FIASCO!
SO THE TRUTH COMES OUT...
I DON'T KNOW HOW TSUKISHIMA FOUND OUR HIDEOUT, BUT...
...IT'S A SAFE BET TO SAY HE TRACKED OUR SPIRITUAL PRESSURES.
IF SO, ICHIGO WILL NEED...
...YOUR FULLBRING THAT COMPLETELY CONCEALS SPIRITUAL PRESSURES.
...
YOU CAN DO IT, CAN'T YOU?
FINE...
WHEN YOU SAY TRAINING, DOES THAT MEAN ACTUAL FIGHTING?
THAT'S RIGHT.
THAT'S WHAT SUITS YOU BEST.
I GOTTA TELL YOU, I ALREADY BEAT JACKIE.
WHO AM I FIGHTING NEXT?

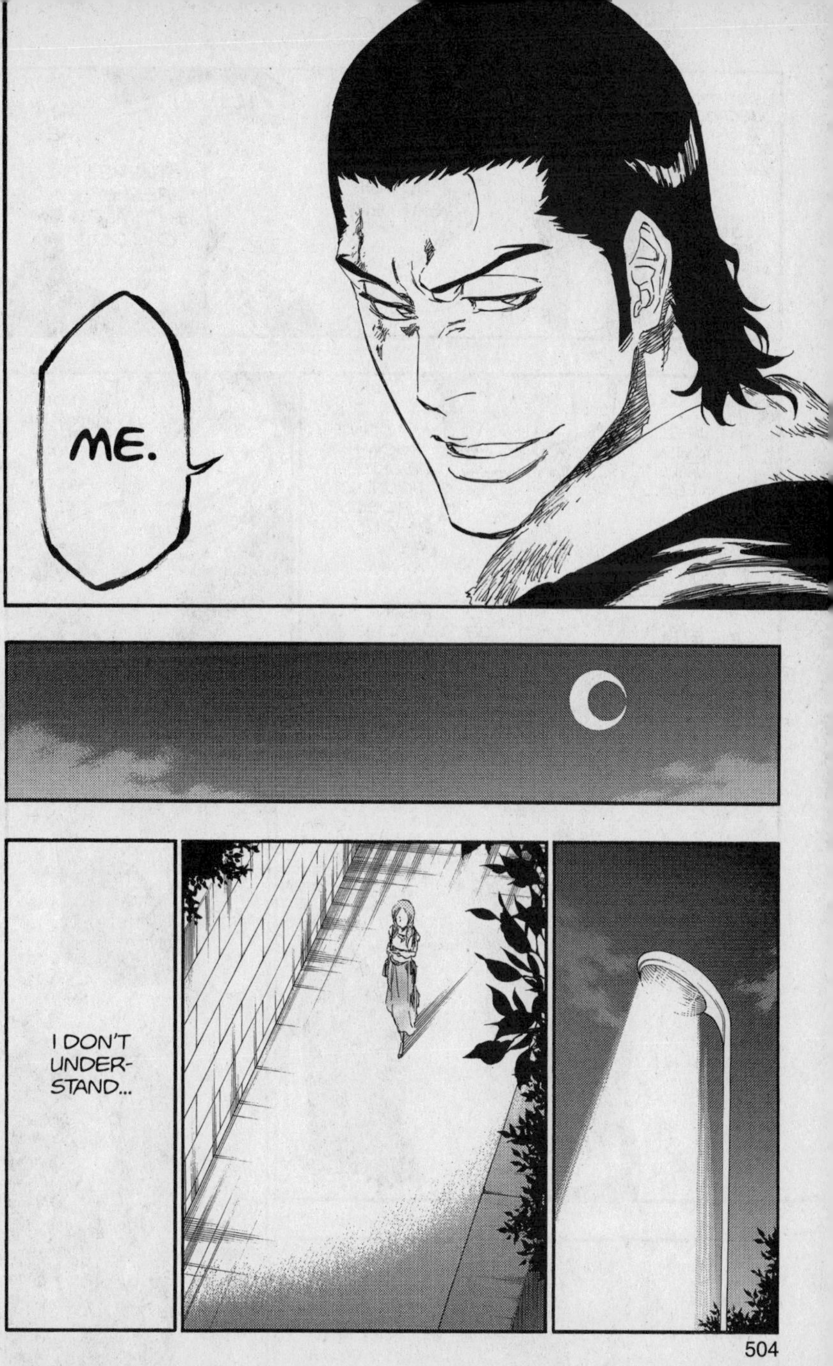
ME.
I DON'T UNDER-STAND...

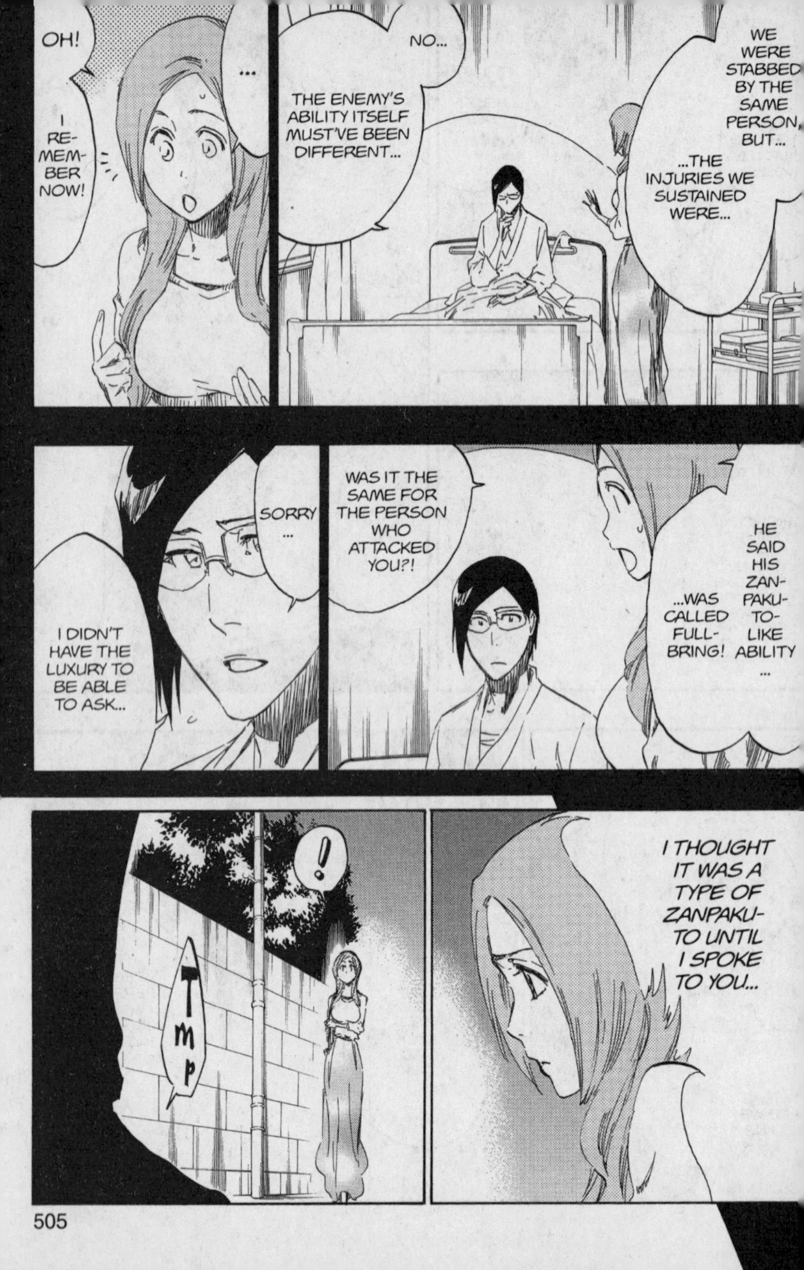
WE WERE STABBED BY THE SAME PERSON, BUT...
...THE INJURIES WE SUSTAINED WERE...
NO...
THE ENEMY'S ABILITY ITSELF MUST'VE BEEN DIFFERENT...
...
OH!
I REMEMBER NOW!
HE SAID HIS ZANPAKU-TO-LIKE ABILITY...
...WAS CALLED FULLBRING!
WAS IT THE SAME FOR THE PERSON WHO ATTACKED YOU?!
SORRY...
I DIDN'T HAVE THE LUXURY TO BE ABLE TO ASK...
I THOUGHT IT WAS A TYPE OF ZANPAKU-TO UNTIL I SPOKE TO YOU...
!
Tmp

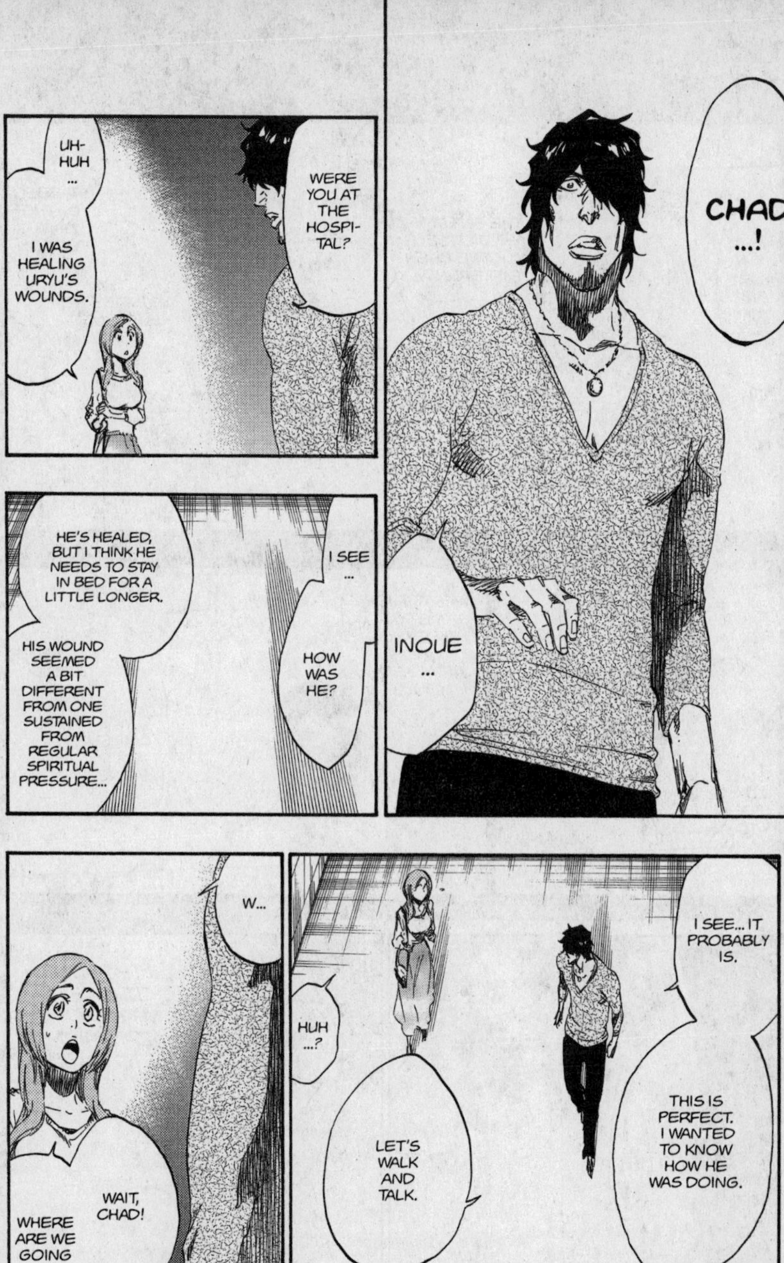
CHAD ...!
INOUE ...
WERE YOU AT THE HOSPITAL?
UH-HUH ...
I WAS HEALING URYU'S WOUNDS.
I SEE ...
HOW WAS HE?
HE'S HEALED, BUT I THINK HE NEEDS TO STAY IN BED FOR A LITTLE LONGER.
HIS WOUND SEEMED A BIT DIFFERENT FROM ONE SUSTAINED FROM REGULAR SPIRITUAL PRESSURE...
I SEE... IT PROBABLY IS.
THIS IS PERFECT. I WANTED TO KNOW HOW HE WAS DOING.
LET'S WALK AND TALK.
HUH ...?
W...
WAIT, CHAD!
WHERE ARE WE GOING ?

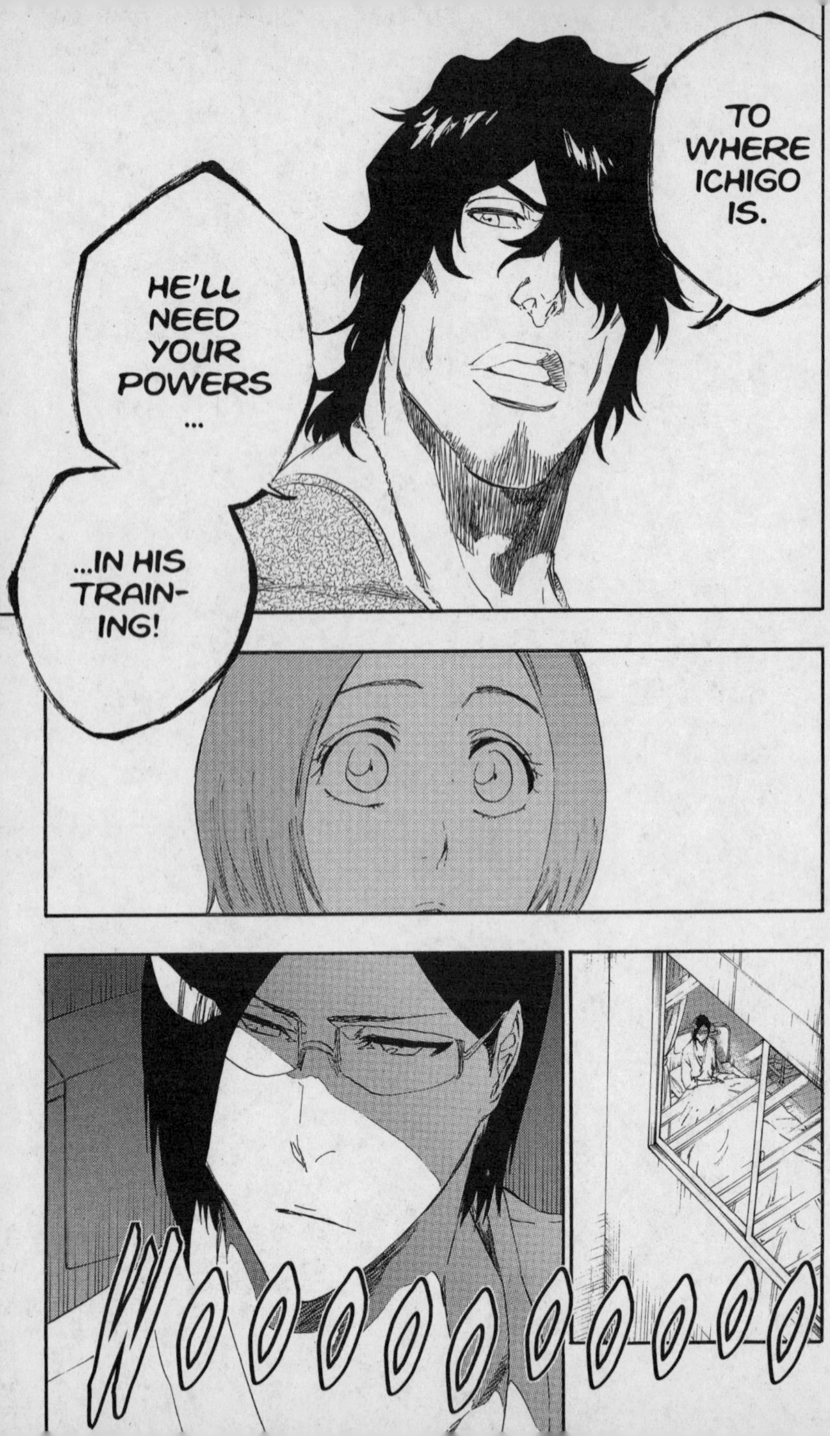
TO WHERE ICHIGO IS.
HE'LL NEED YOUR POWERS ...
...IN HIS TRAIN-ING!
WOOOOOOOOOOO

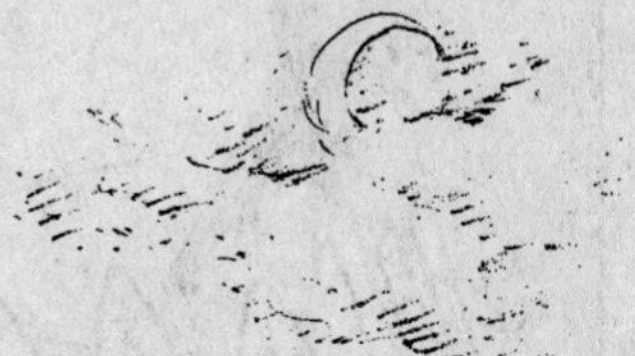

448. LOADING TO LIE

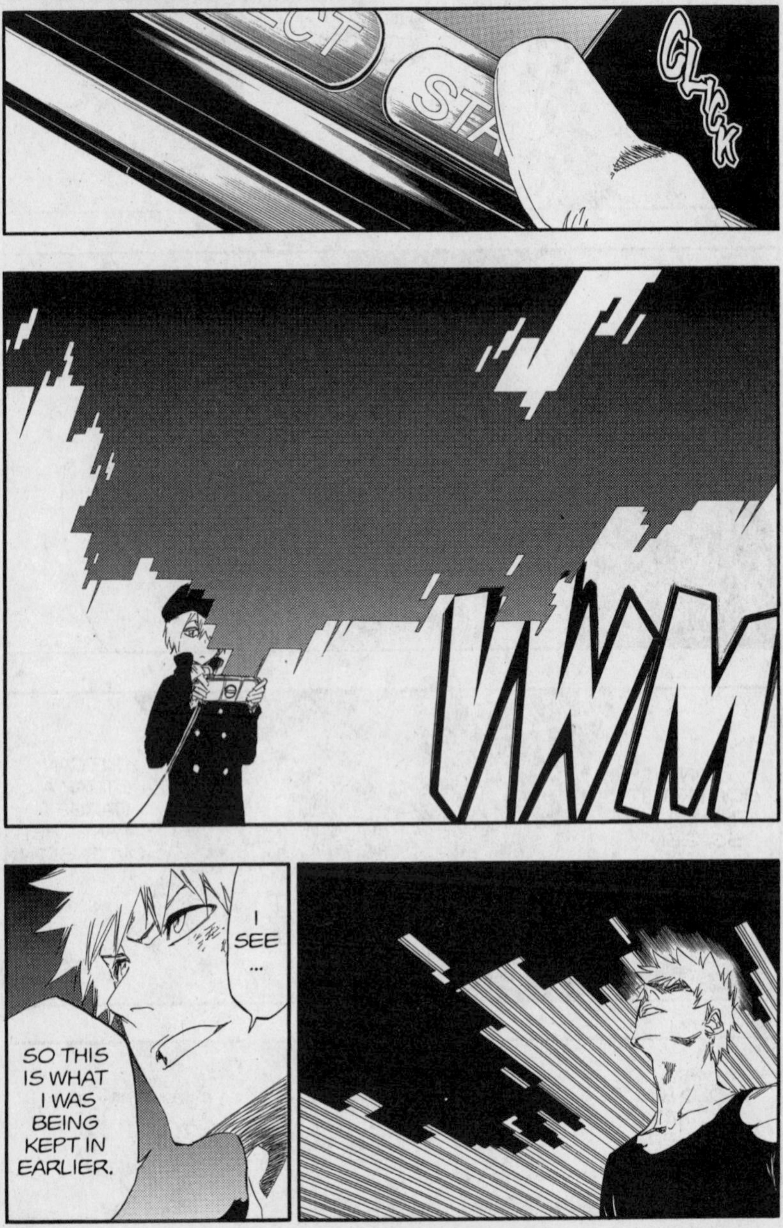
CLICK
VWM
I SEE ...
SO THIS IS WHAT I WAS BEING KEPT IN EARLIER.

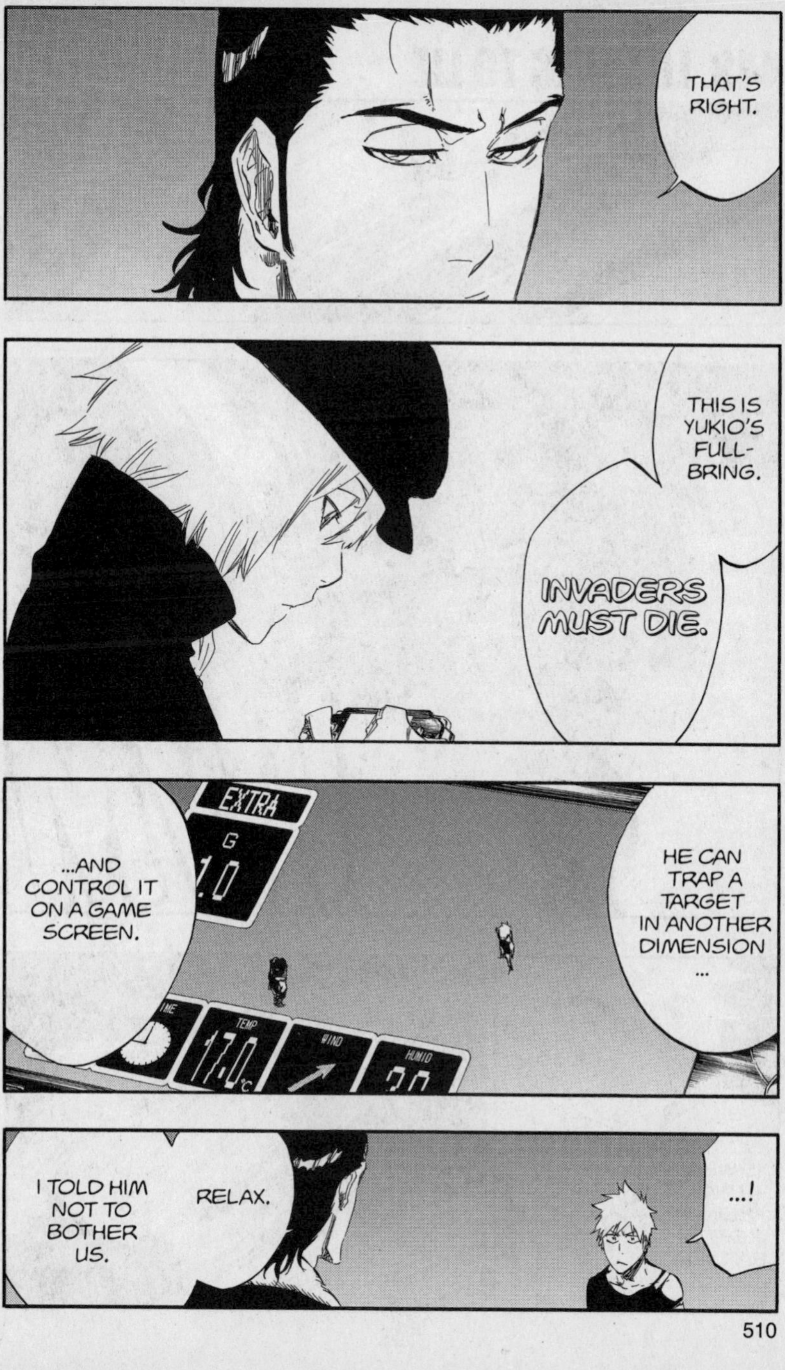
THAT'S RIGHT.
THIS IS YUKIO'S FULL-BRING.
INVADERS MUST DIE.
HE CAN TRAP A TARGET IN ANOTHER DIMENSION ...
...AND CONTROL IT ON A GAME SCREEN.
EXTRA
...!
RELAX.
I TOLD HIM NOT TO BOTHER US.

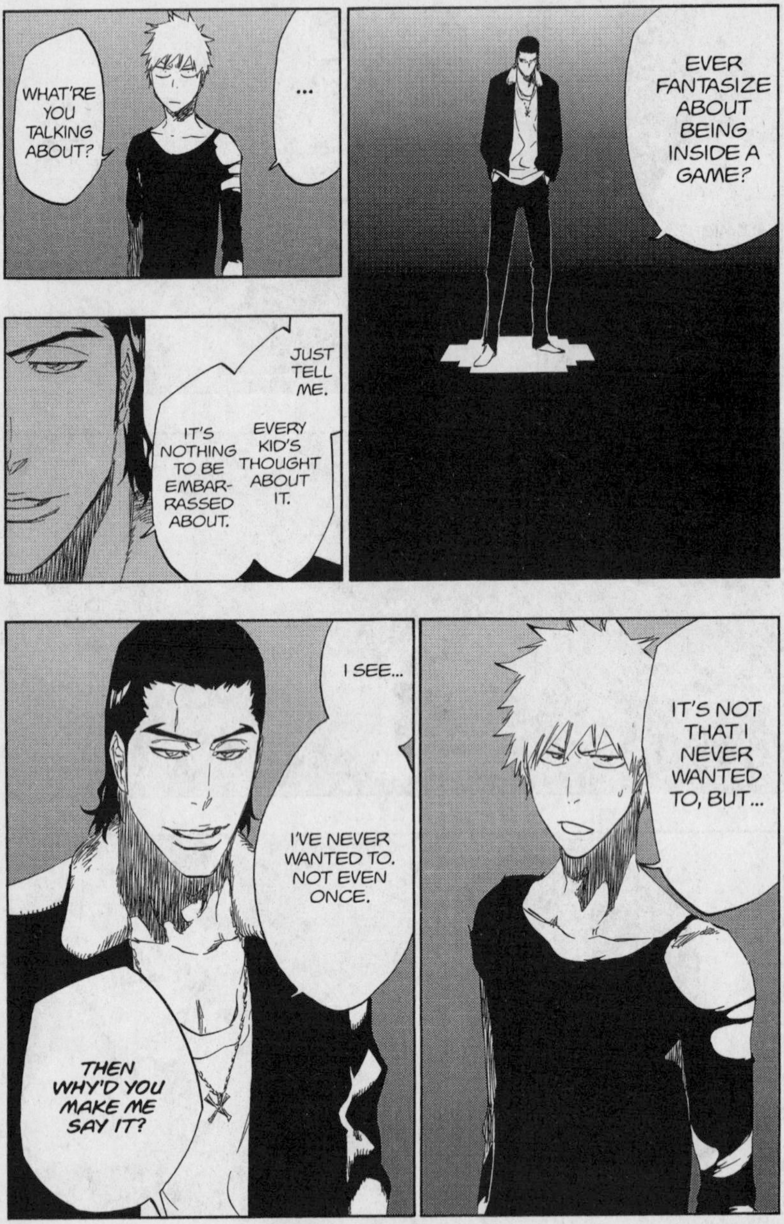
EVER FANTASIZE ABOUT BEING INSIDE A GAME?
...
WHAT'RE YOU TALKING ABOUT?
JUST TELL ME.
EVERY KID'S THOUGHT ABOUT IT.
IT'S NOTHING TO BE EMBARRASSED ABOUT.
IT'S NOT THAT I NEVER WANTED TO, BUT...
I SEE...
I'VE NEVER WANTED TO. NOT EVEN ONCE.
THEN WHY'D YOU MAKE ME SAY IT?

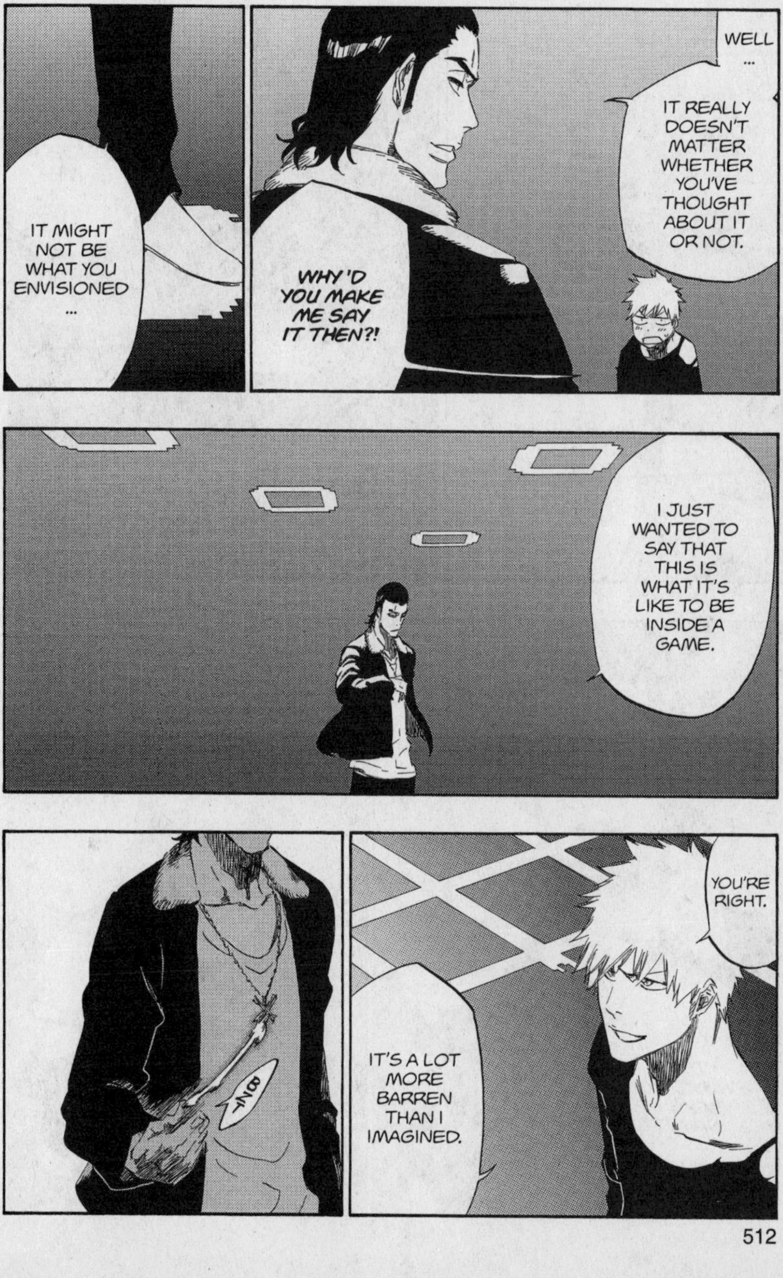
WELL...
IT REALLY DOESN'T MATTER WHETHER YOU'VE THOUGHT ABOUT IT OR NOT.
WHY'D YOU MAKE ME SAY IT THEN?!
IT MIGHT NOT BE WHAT YOU ENVISIONED...
I JUST WANTED TO SAY THAT THIS IS WHAT IT'S LIKE TO BE INSIDE A GAME.
YOU'RE RIGHT.
IT'S A LOT MORE BARREN THAN I IMAGINED.

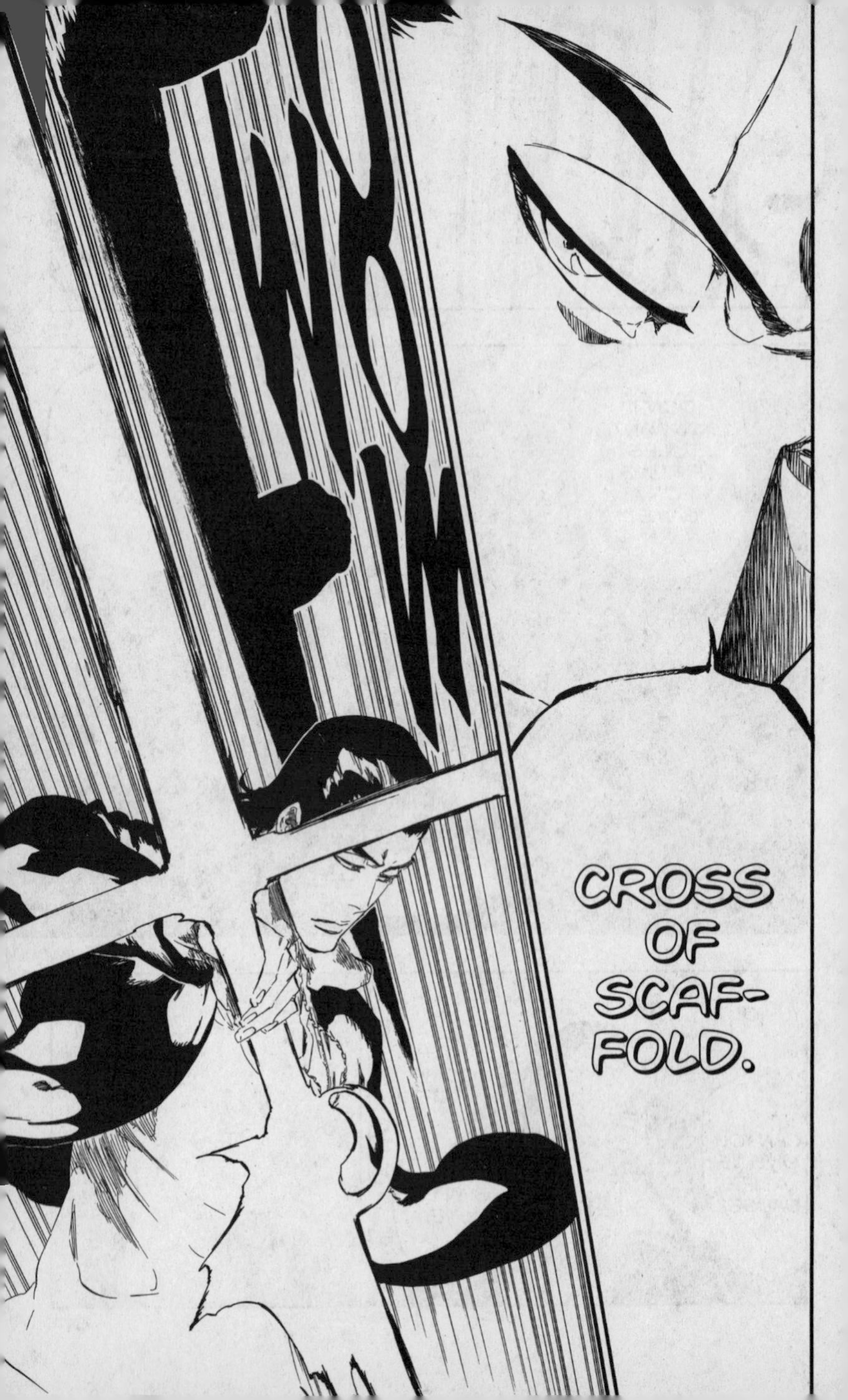
CROSS OF SCAF-FOLD.

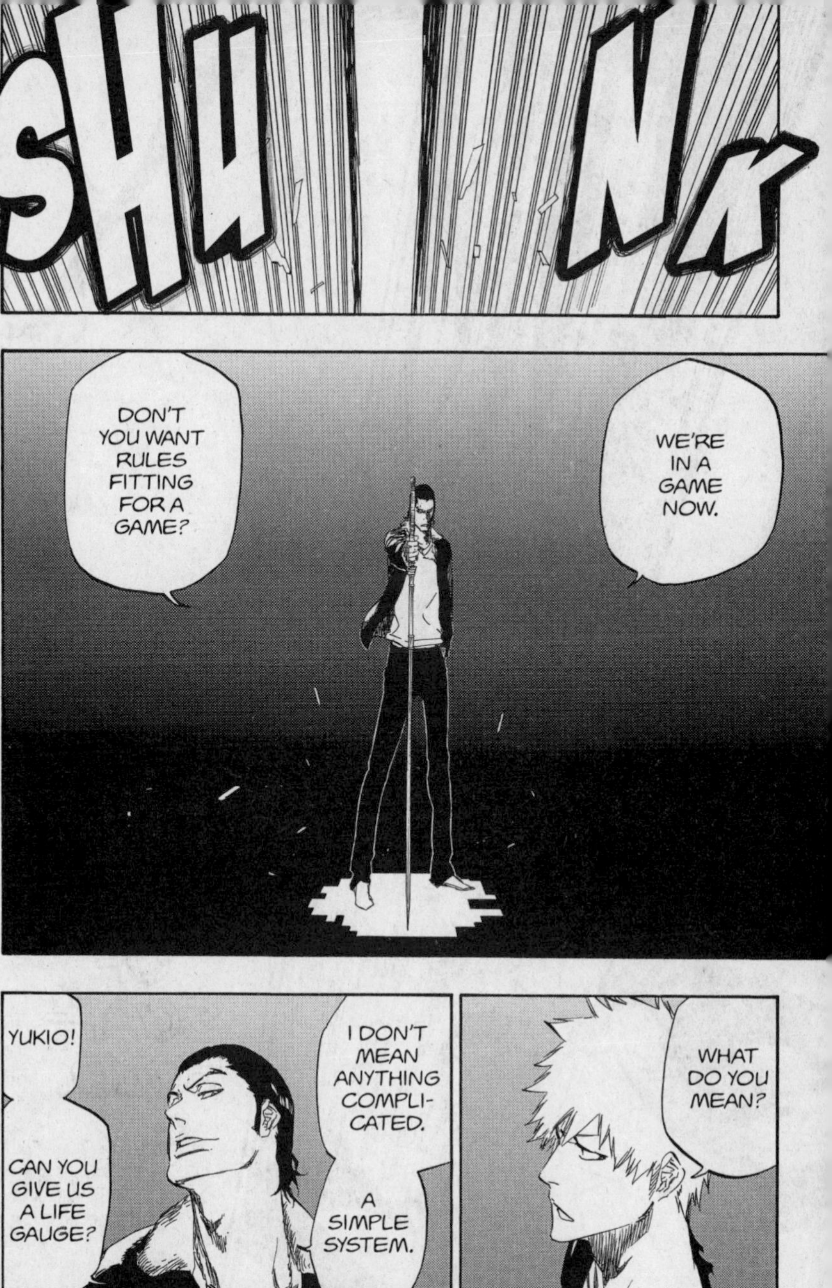
SHUNK
WE'RE IN A GAME NOW.
DON'T YOU WANT RULES FITTING FOR A GAME?
WHAT DO YOU MEAN?
I DON'T MEAN ANYTHING COMPLI-CATED.
A SIMPLE SYSTEM.
YUKIO!
CAN YOU GIVE US A LIFE GAUGE?

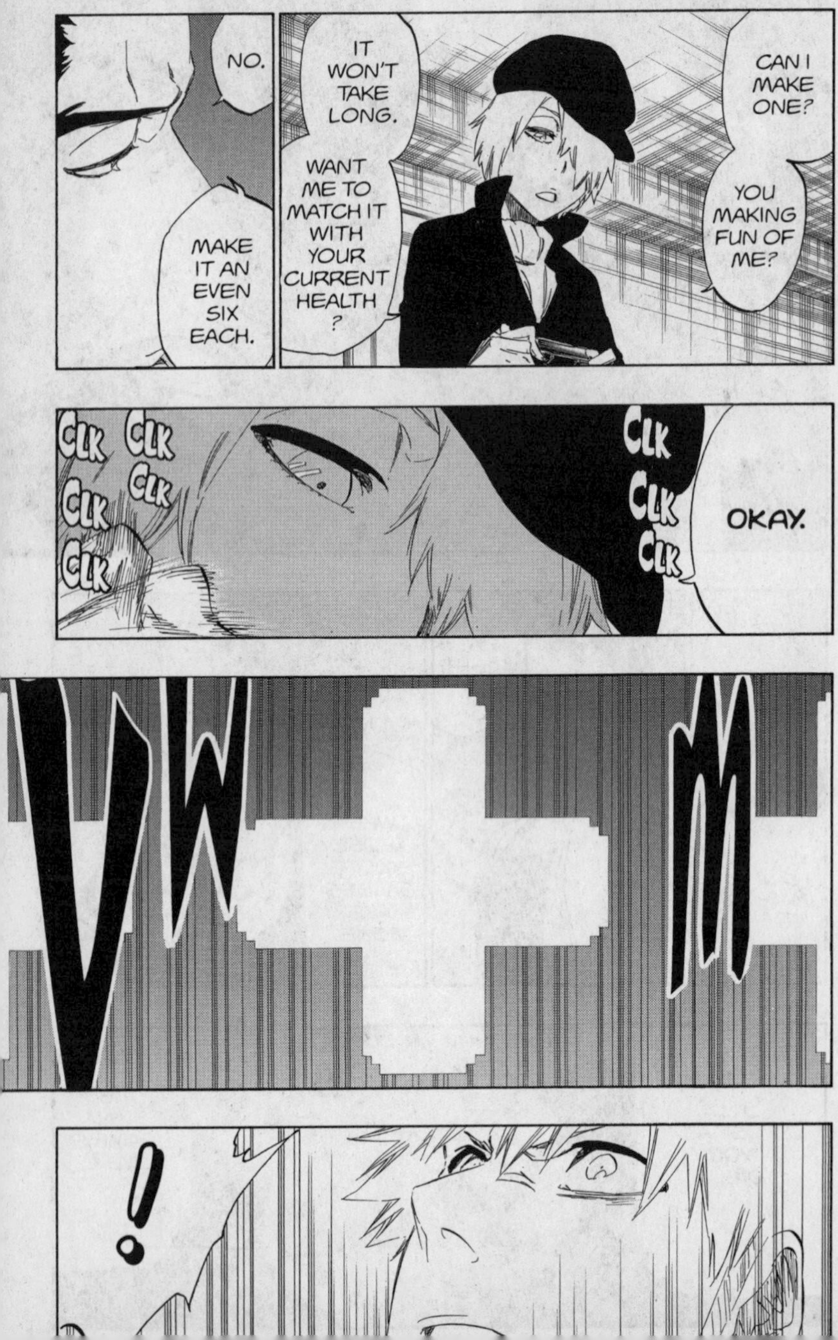
CAN I MAKE ONE?
YOU MAKING FUN OF ME?
IT WON'T TAKE LONG.
WANT ME TO MATCH IT WITH YOUR CURRENT HEALTH?
NO.
MAKE IT AN EVEN SIX EACH.
OKAY.
CLK CLK CLK
CLK CLK CLK CLK CLK
VWM
!

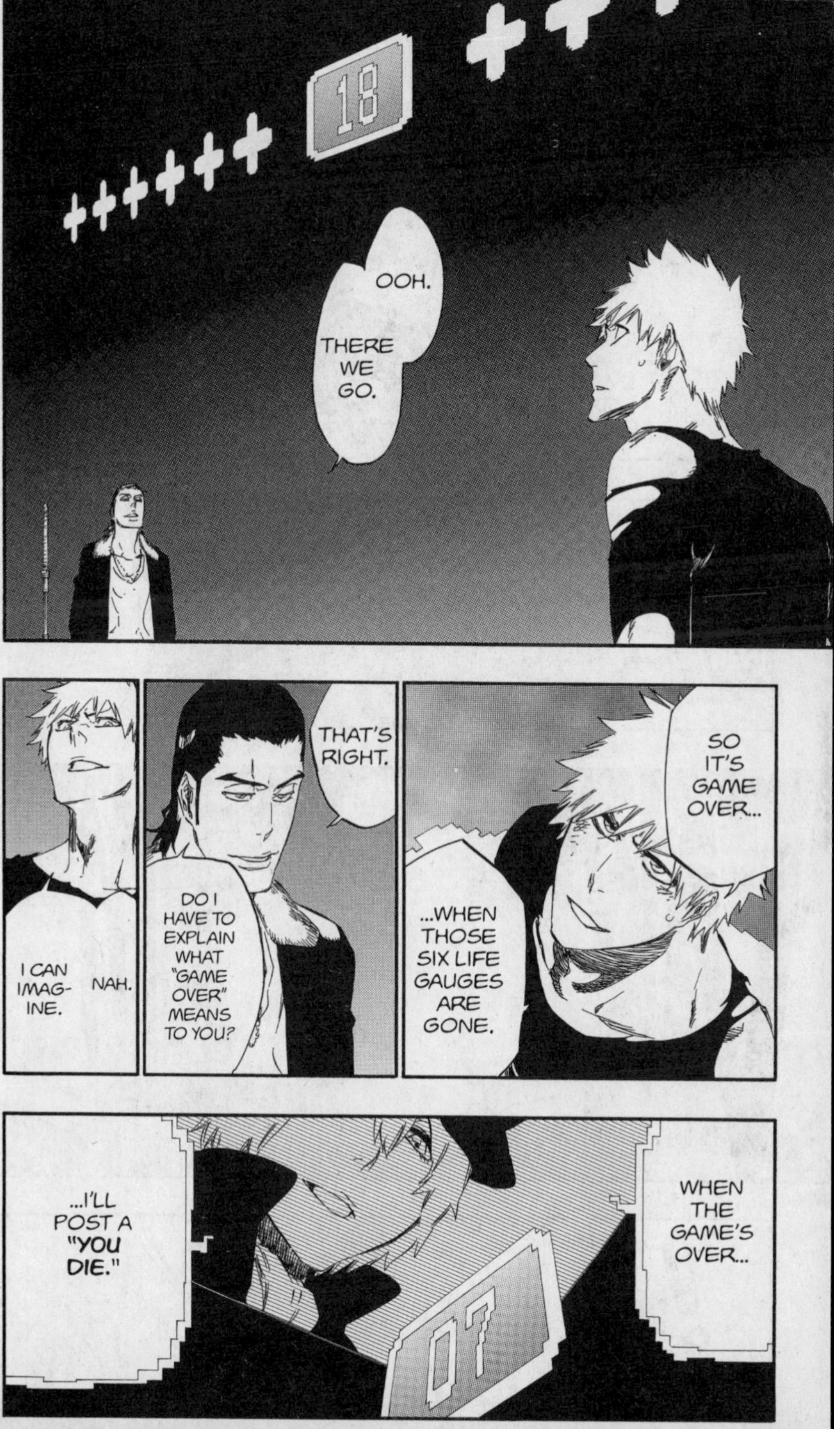
18
OOH.
THERE WE GO.
SO IT'S GAME OVER...
...WHEN THOSE SIX LIFE GAUGES ARE GONE.
THAT'S RIGHT.
DO I HAVE TO EXPLAIN WHAT "GAME OVER" MEANS TO YOU?
NAH.
I CAN IMAGINE.
WHEN THE GAME'S OVER...
...I'LL POST A **"YOU DIE."**
07

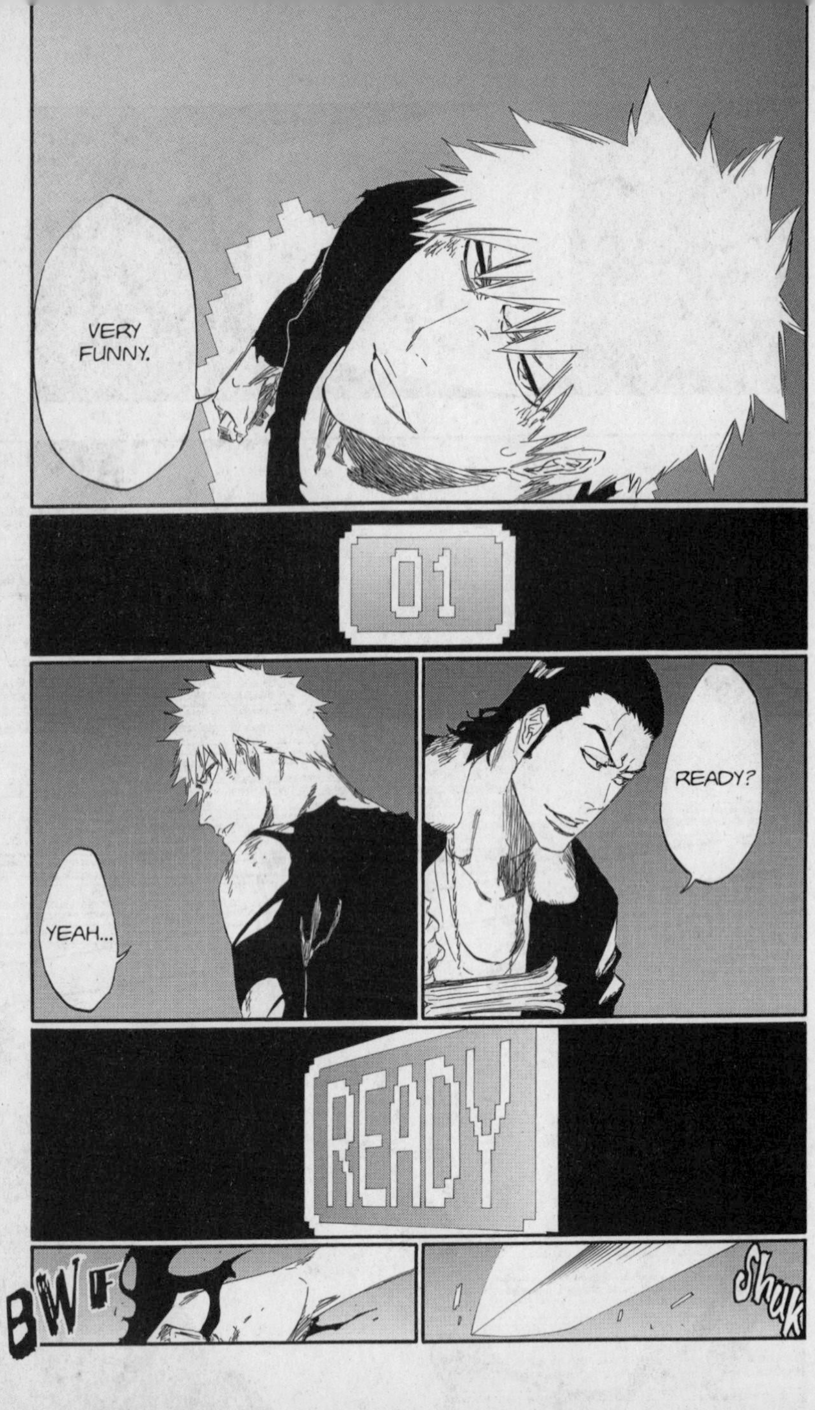
VERY FUNNY.
01
READY?
YEAH...
READY
Shuk
BWUF

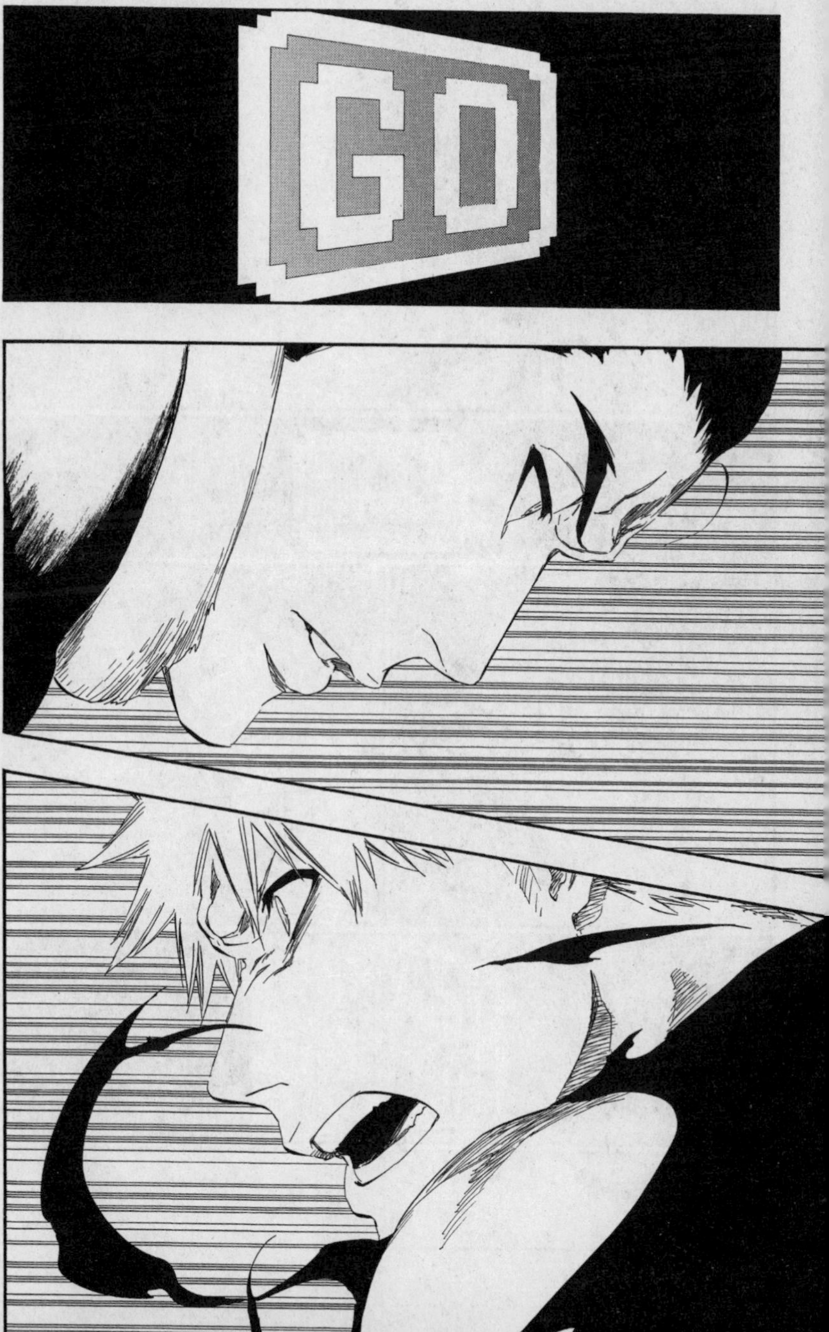
GO

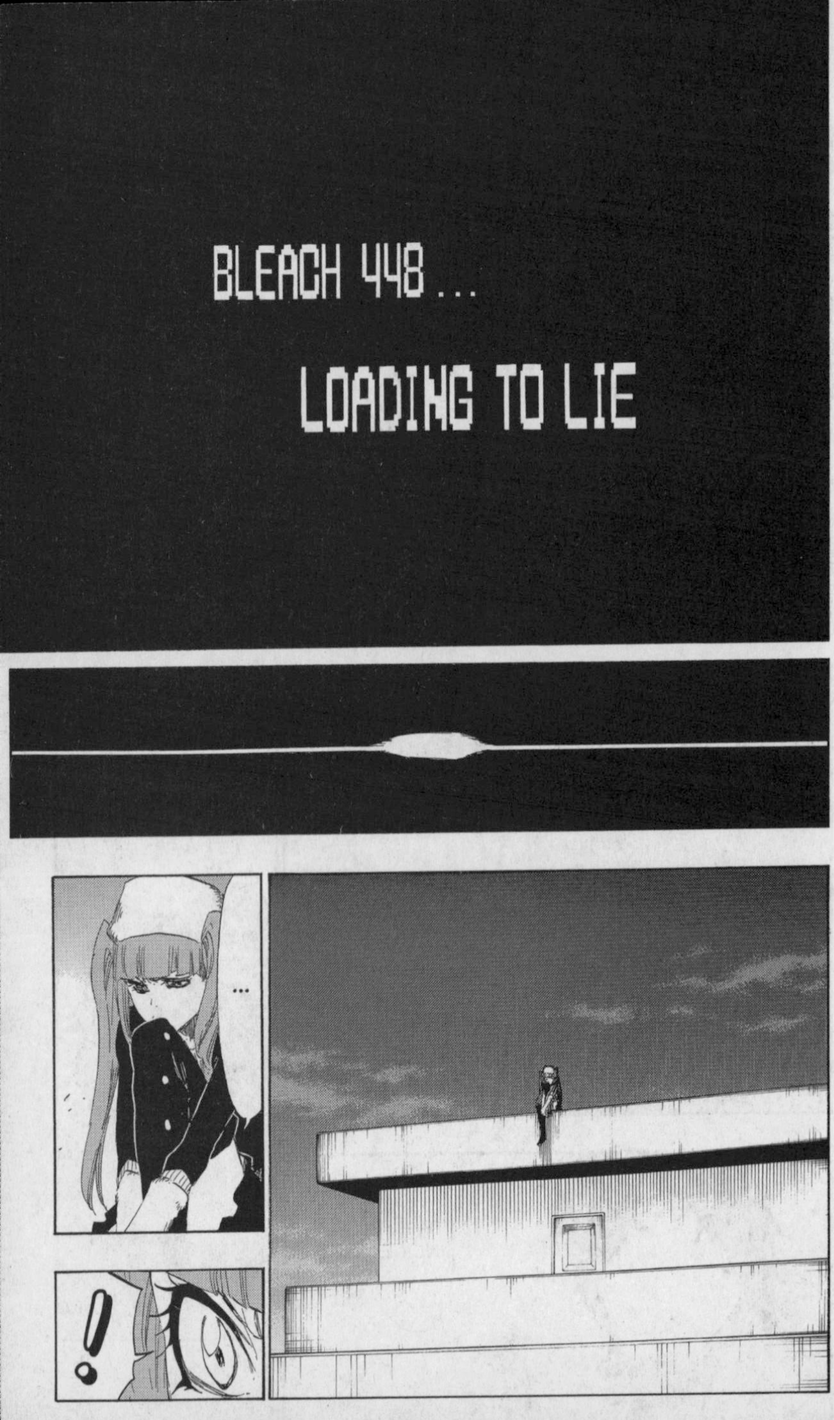
BLEACH 448...
LOADING TO LIE
...
!

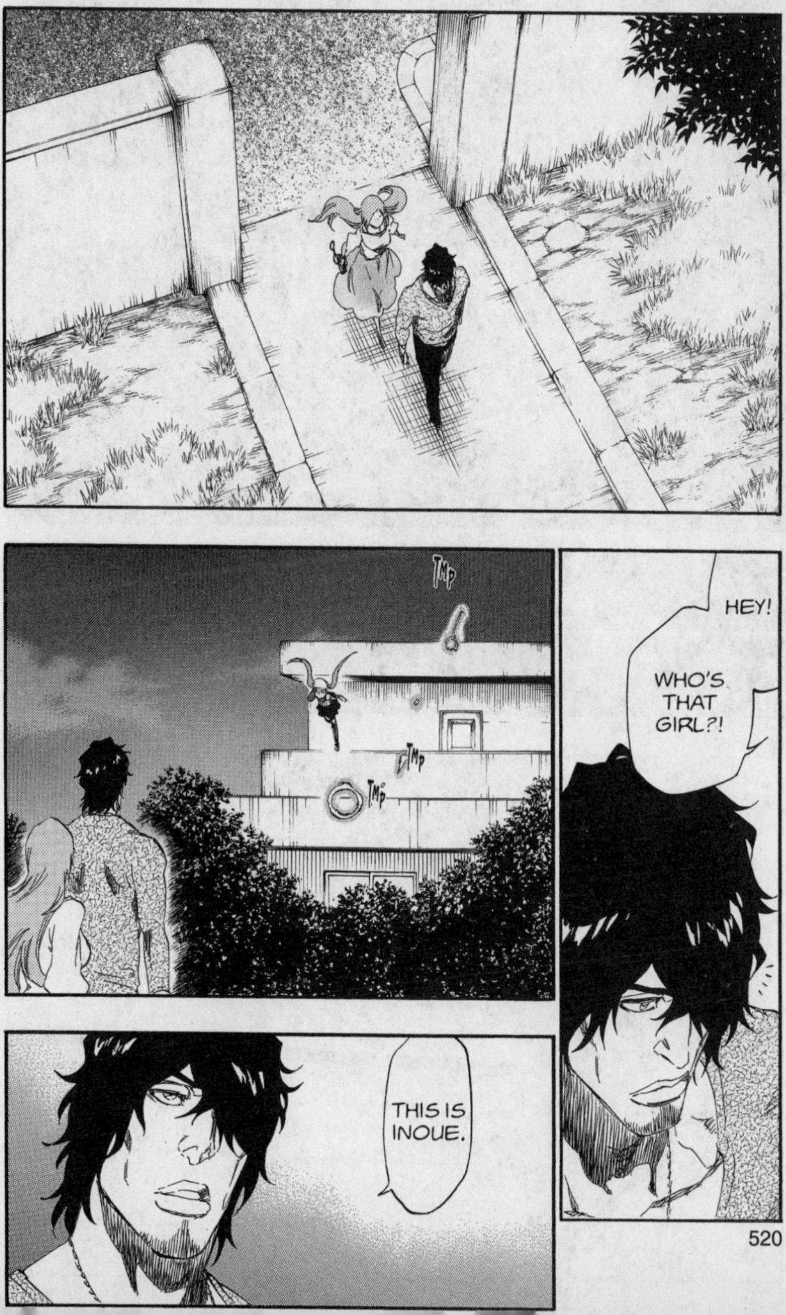
HEY!
WHO'S THAT GIRL?!
TMP
TMP
TMP
THIS IS INOUE.

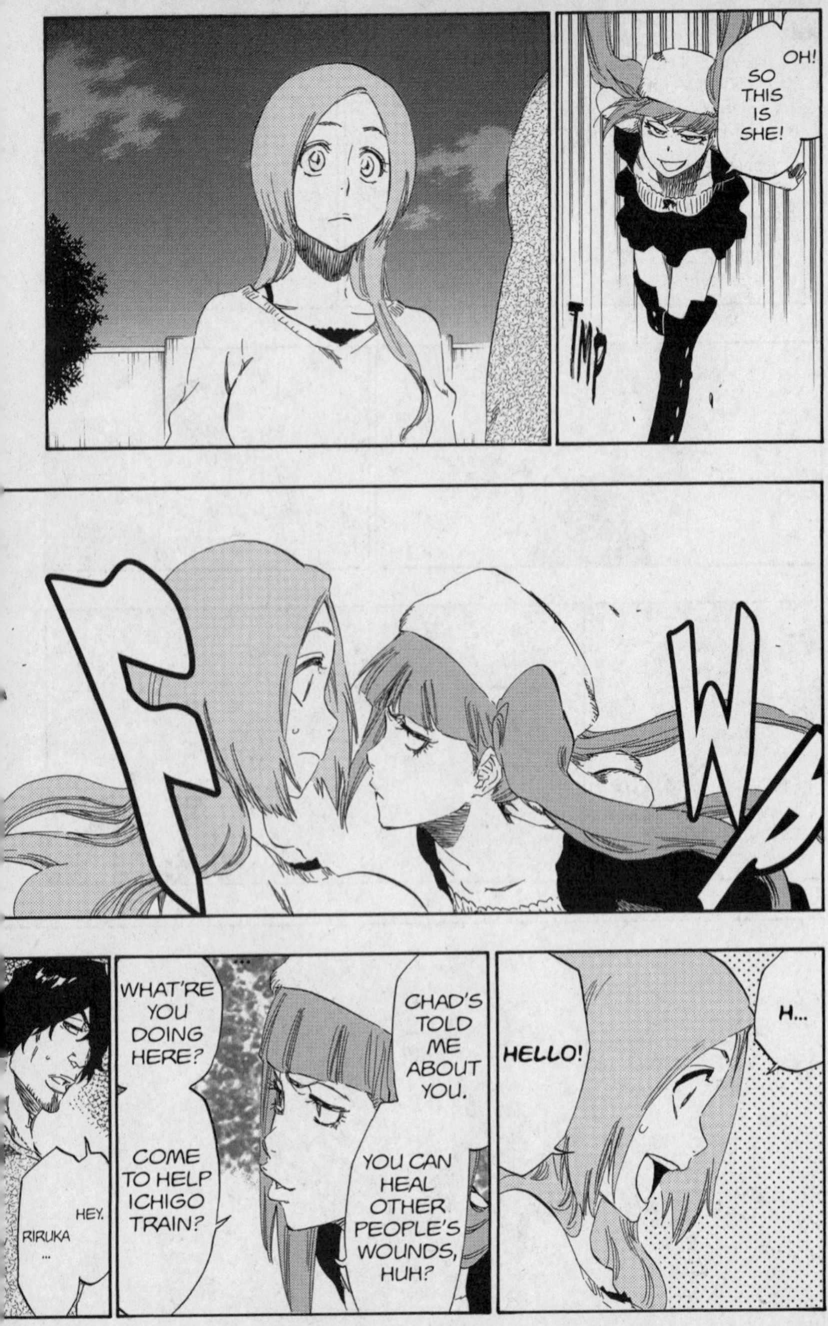

OH! SO THIS IS SHE!
TMP
H...
HELLO!
CHAD'S TOLD ME ABOUT YOU.
WHAT'RE YOU DOING HERE?
YOU CAN HEAL OTHER PEOPLE'S WOUNDS, HUH?
COME TO HELP ICHIGO TRAIN?
...
HEY.
RIRUKA ...

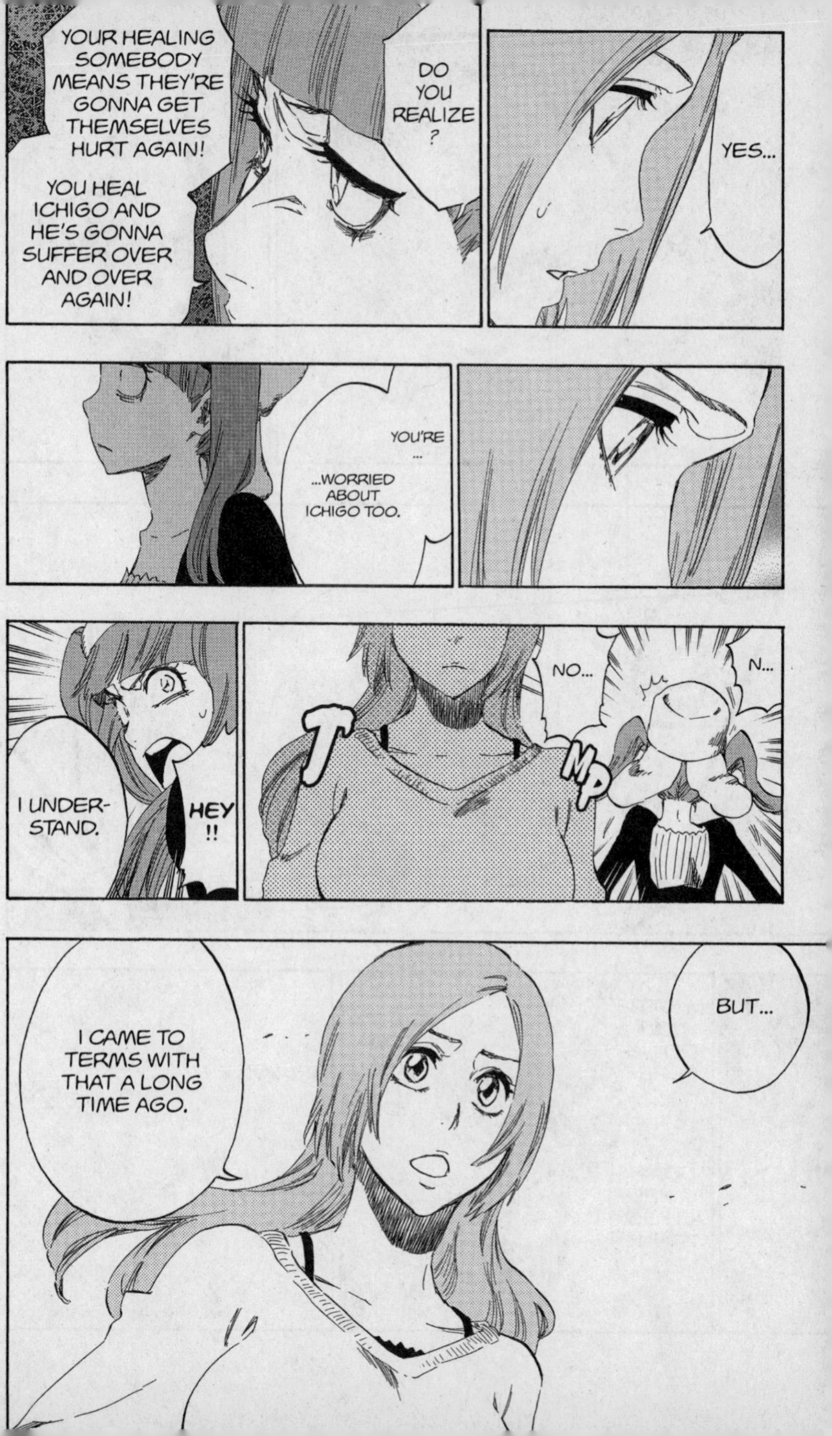
YES...
DO YOU REALIZE?
YOUR HEALING SOMEBODY MEANS THEY'RE GONNA GET THEMSELVES HURT AGAIN!
YOU HEAL ICHIGO AND HE'S GONNA SUFFER OVER AND OVER AGAIN!
YOU'RE ...
...WORRIED ABOUT ICHIGO TOO.
N...
NO...
T
MP
HEY!!
I UNDERSTAND.
BUT...
I CAME TO TERMS WITH THAT A LONG TIME AGO.

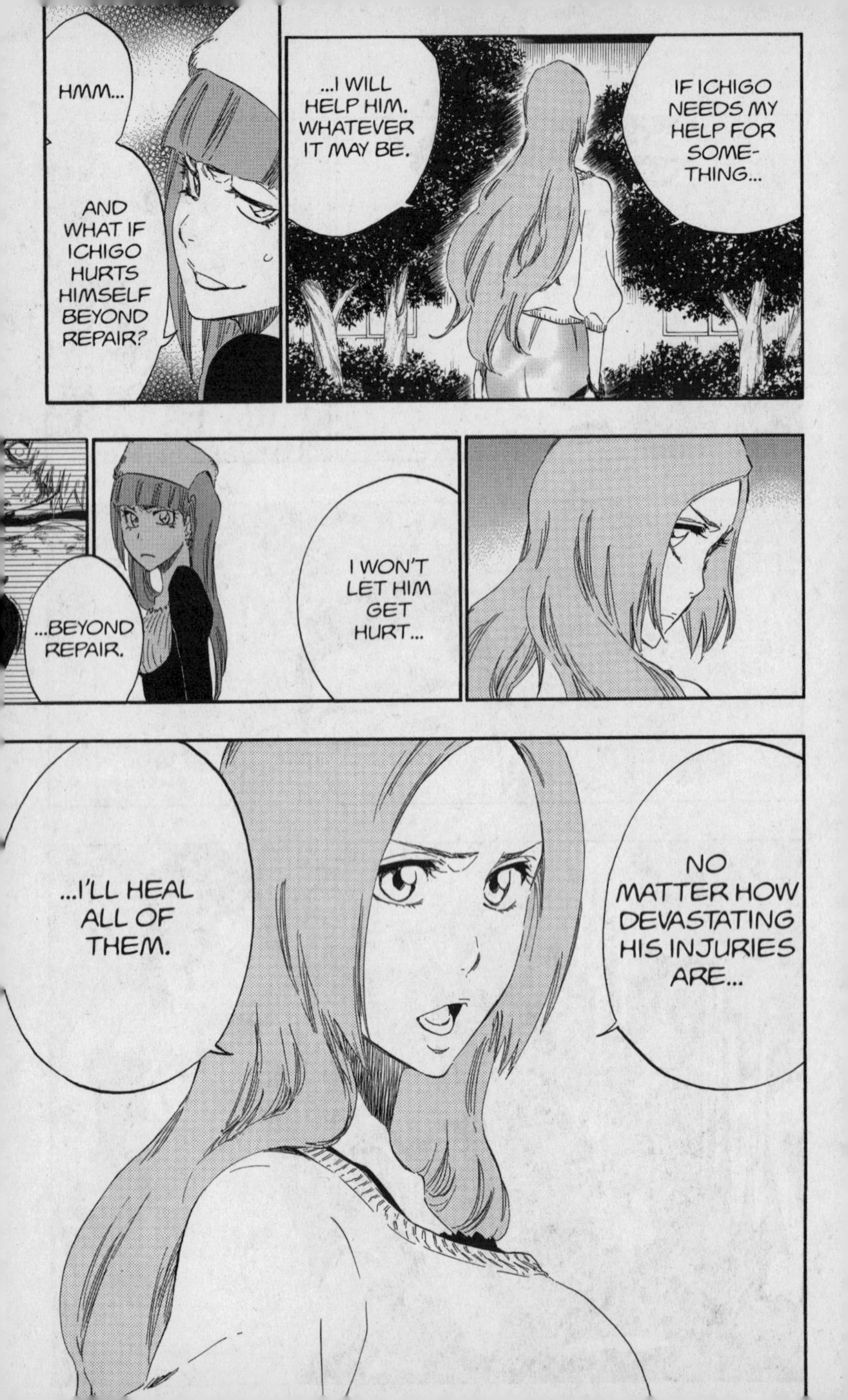
IF ICHIGO NEEDS MY HELP FOR SOME-THING...
...I WILL HELP HIM. WHATEVER IT MAY BE.
HMM...
AND WHAT IF ICHIGO HURTS HIMSELF BEYOND REPAIR?
I WON'T LET HIM GET HURT...
...BEYOND REPAIR.
NO MATTER HOW DEVASTATING HIS INJURIES ARE...
...I'LL HEAL ALL OF THEM.

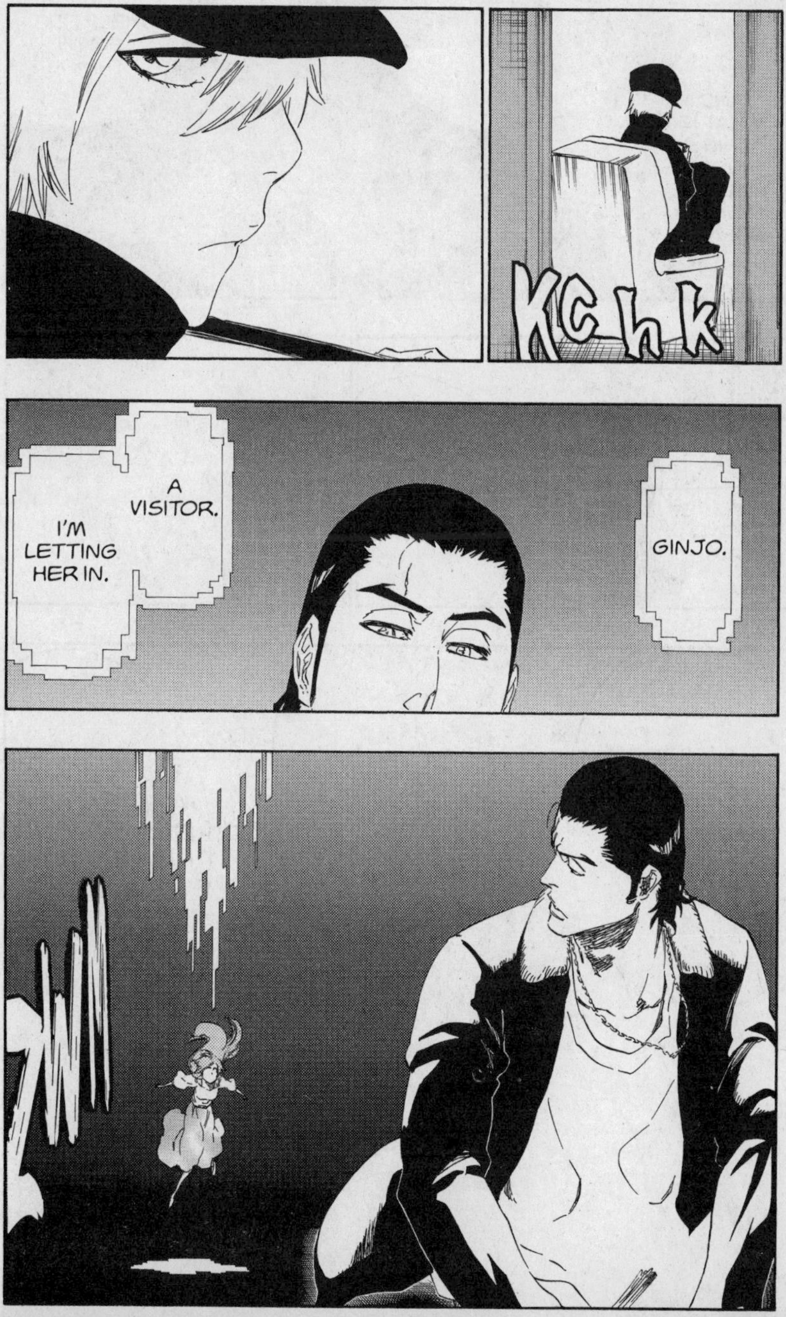
KChk
GINJO.
A VISITOR.
I'M LETTING HER IN.

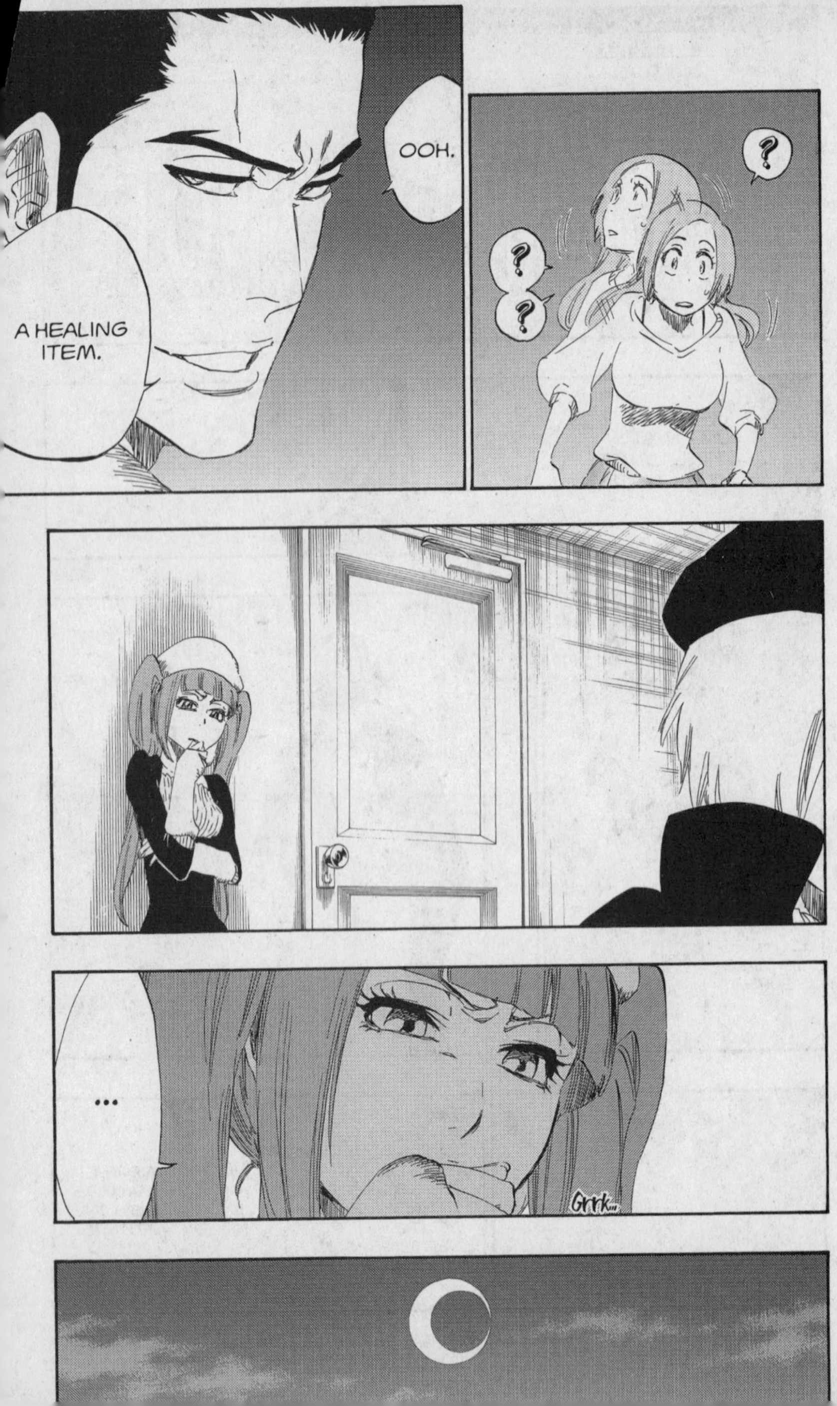
?
?
?
OOH.
A HEALING ITEM.
...
Grrk...

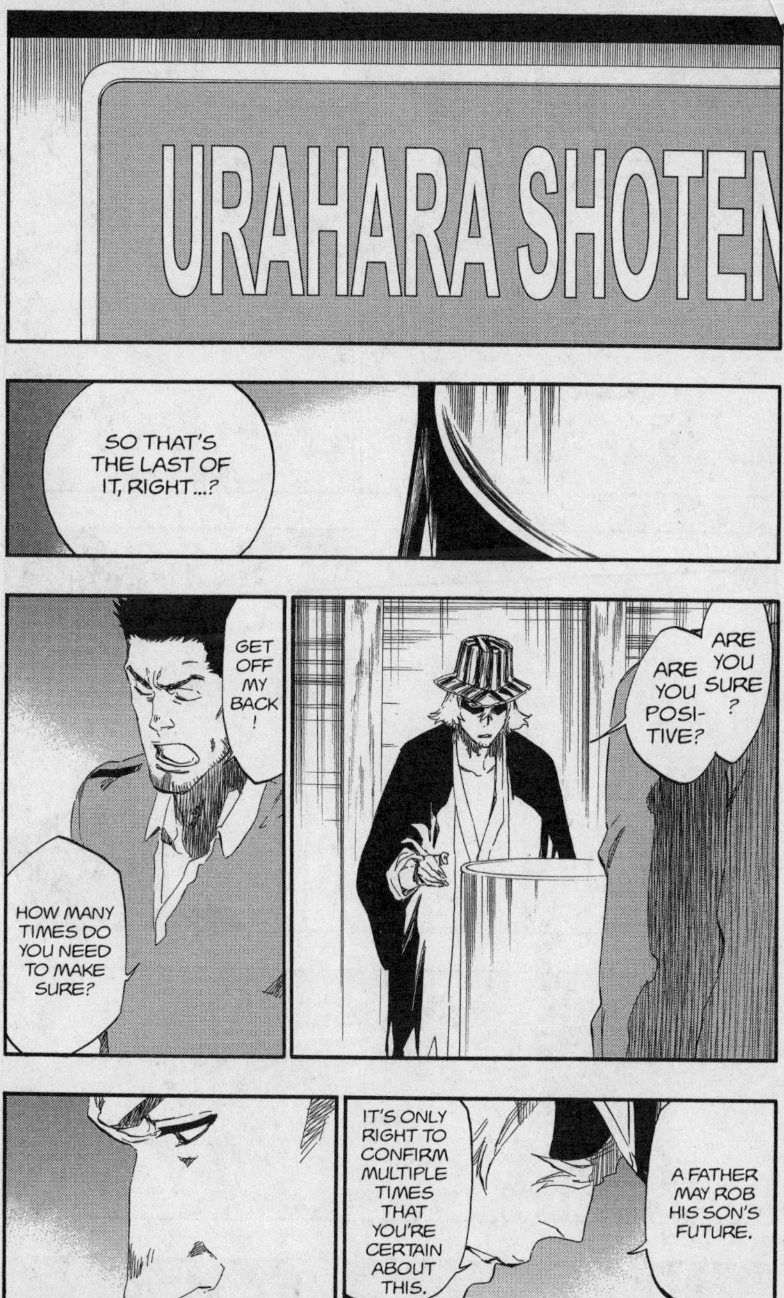
URAHARA SHOTEN
SO THAT'S THE LAST OF IT, RIGHT...?
ARE YOU SURE?
ARE YOU POSITIVE?
GET OFF MY BACK!
HOW MANY TIMES DO YOU NEED TO MAKE SURE?
A FATHER MAY ROB HIS SON'S FUTURE.
IT'S ONLY RIGHT TO CONFIRM MULTIPLE TIMES THAT YOU'RE CERTAIN ABOUT THIS.

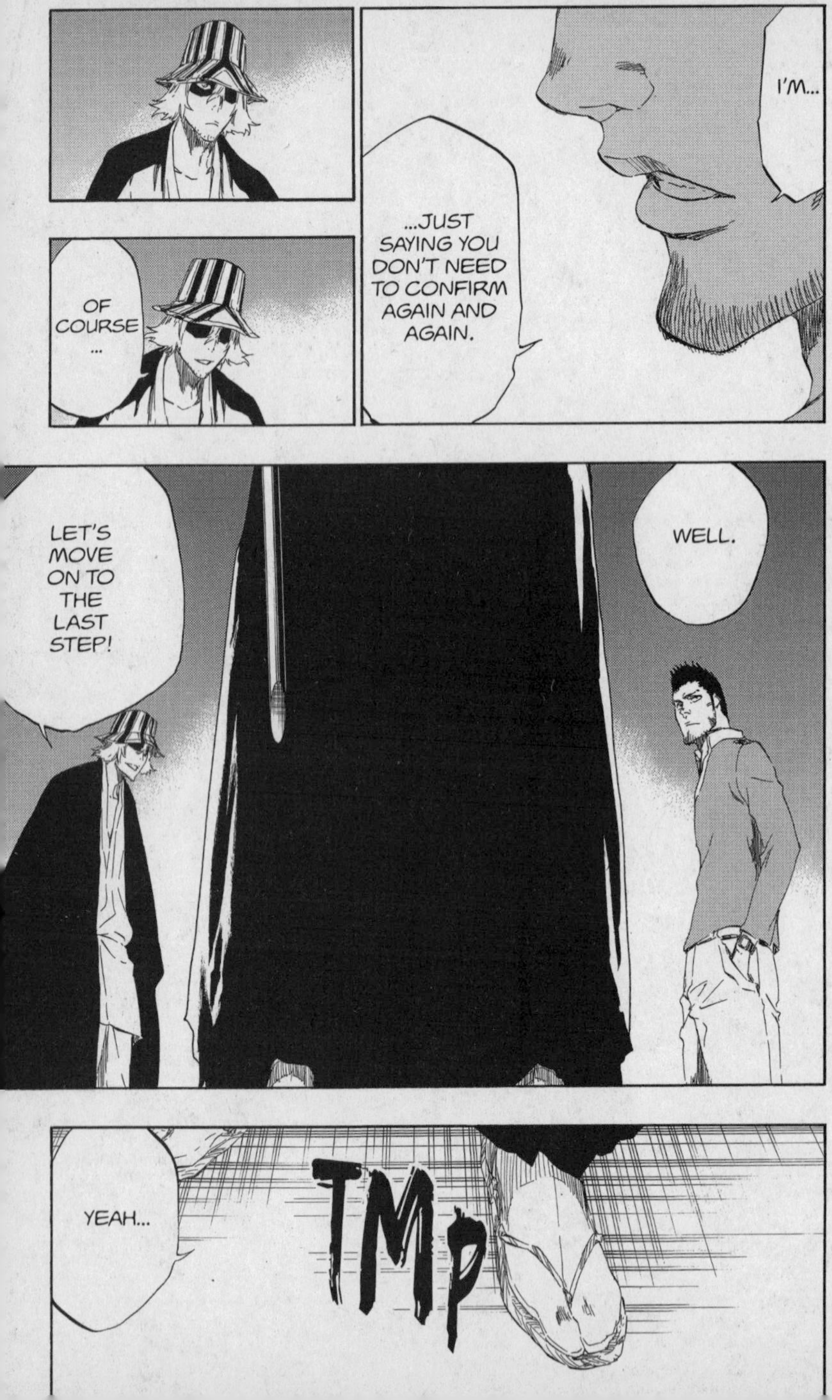
I'M...
...JUST SAYING YOU DON'T NEED TO CONFIRM AGAIN AND AGAIN.
OF COURSE...
WELL.
LET'S MOVE ON TO THE LAST STEP!
TMP
YEAH...

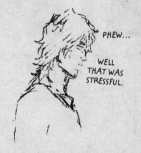

PHEW...

WELL
THAT WAS
STRESSFUL.

449. Not be a Drug

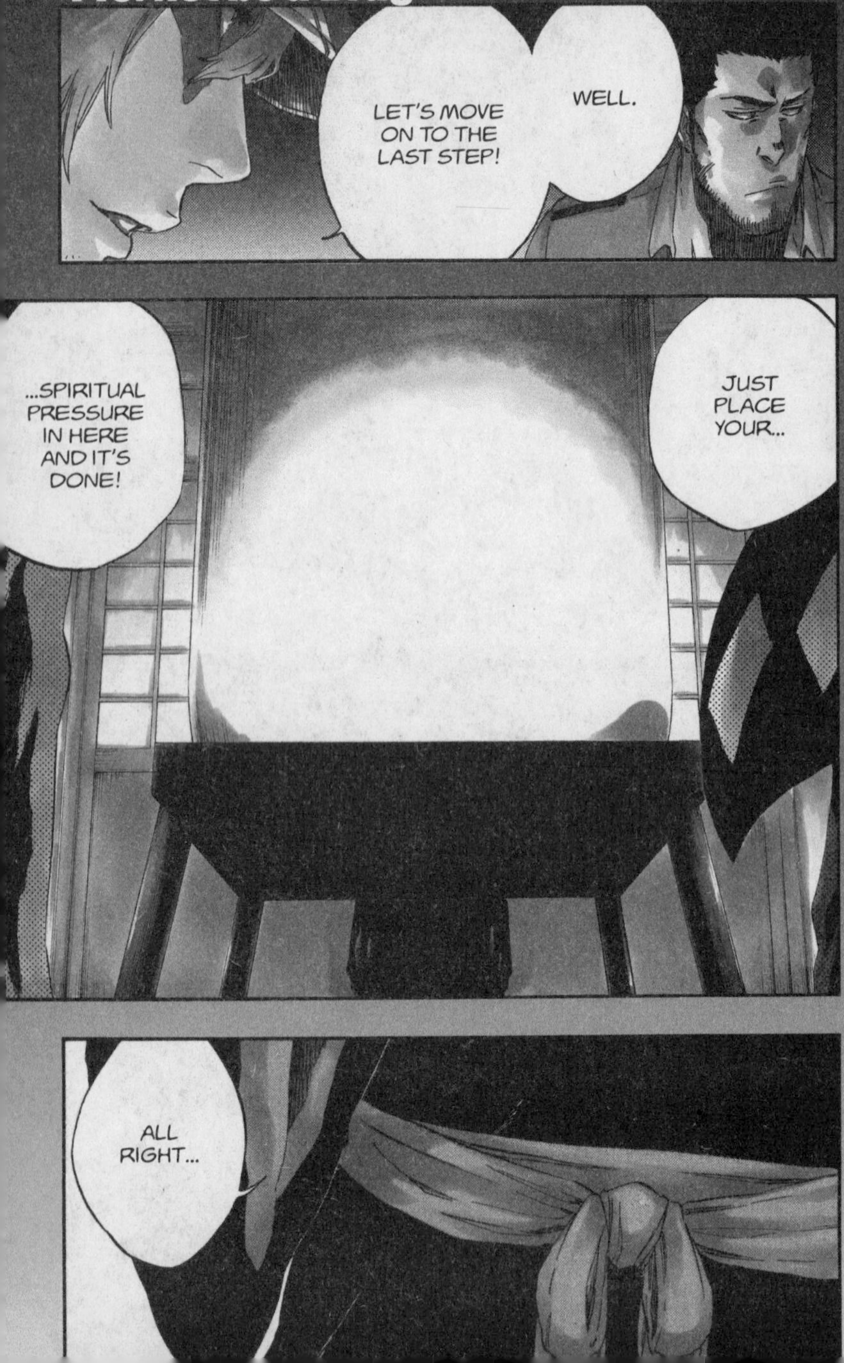
WELL.
LET'S MOVE ON TO THE LAST STEP!
JUST PLACE YOUR...
...SPIRITUAL PRESSURE IN HERE AND IT'S DONE!
ALL RIGHT...

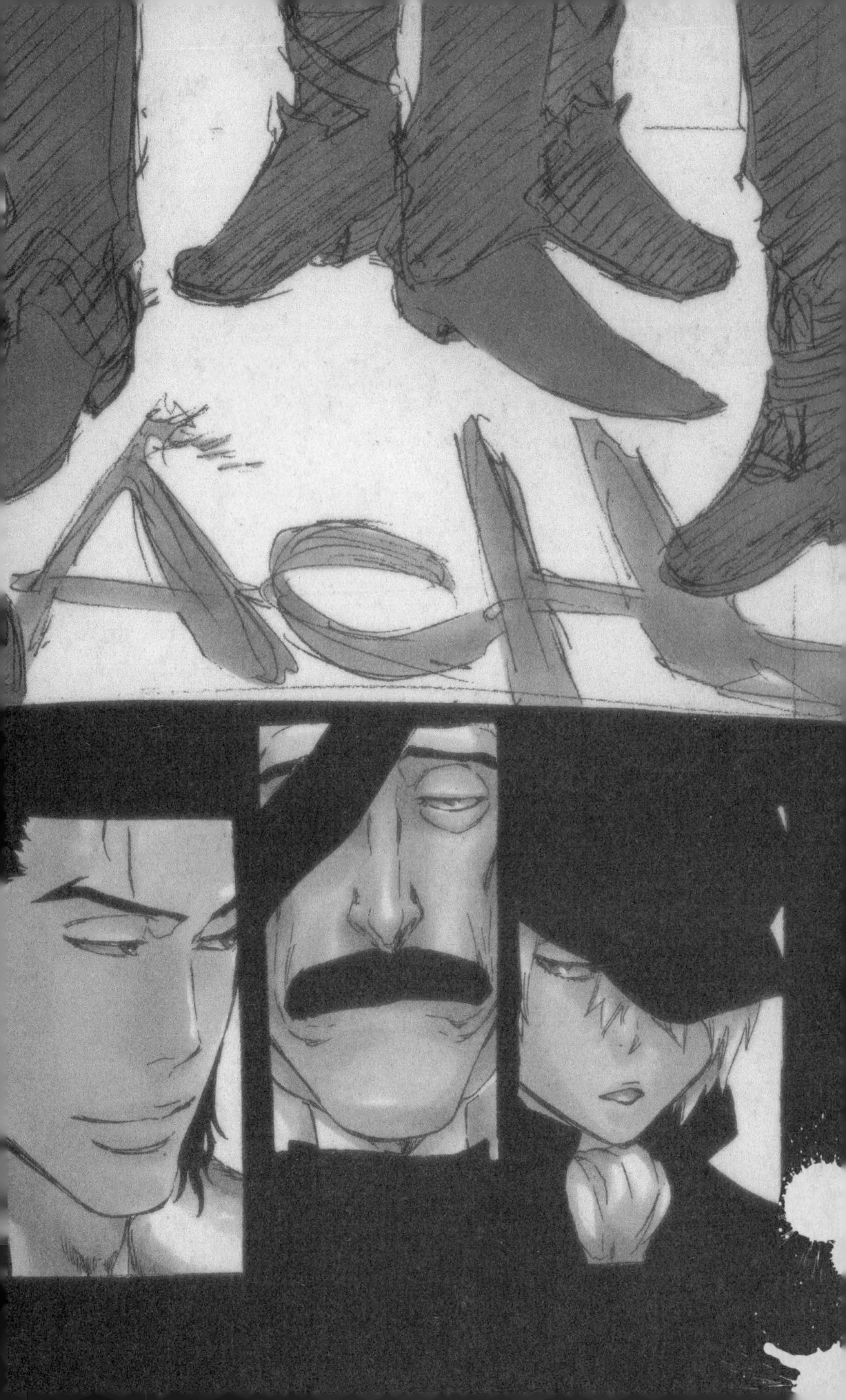

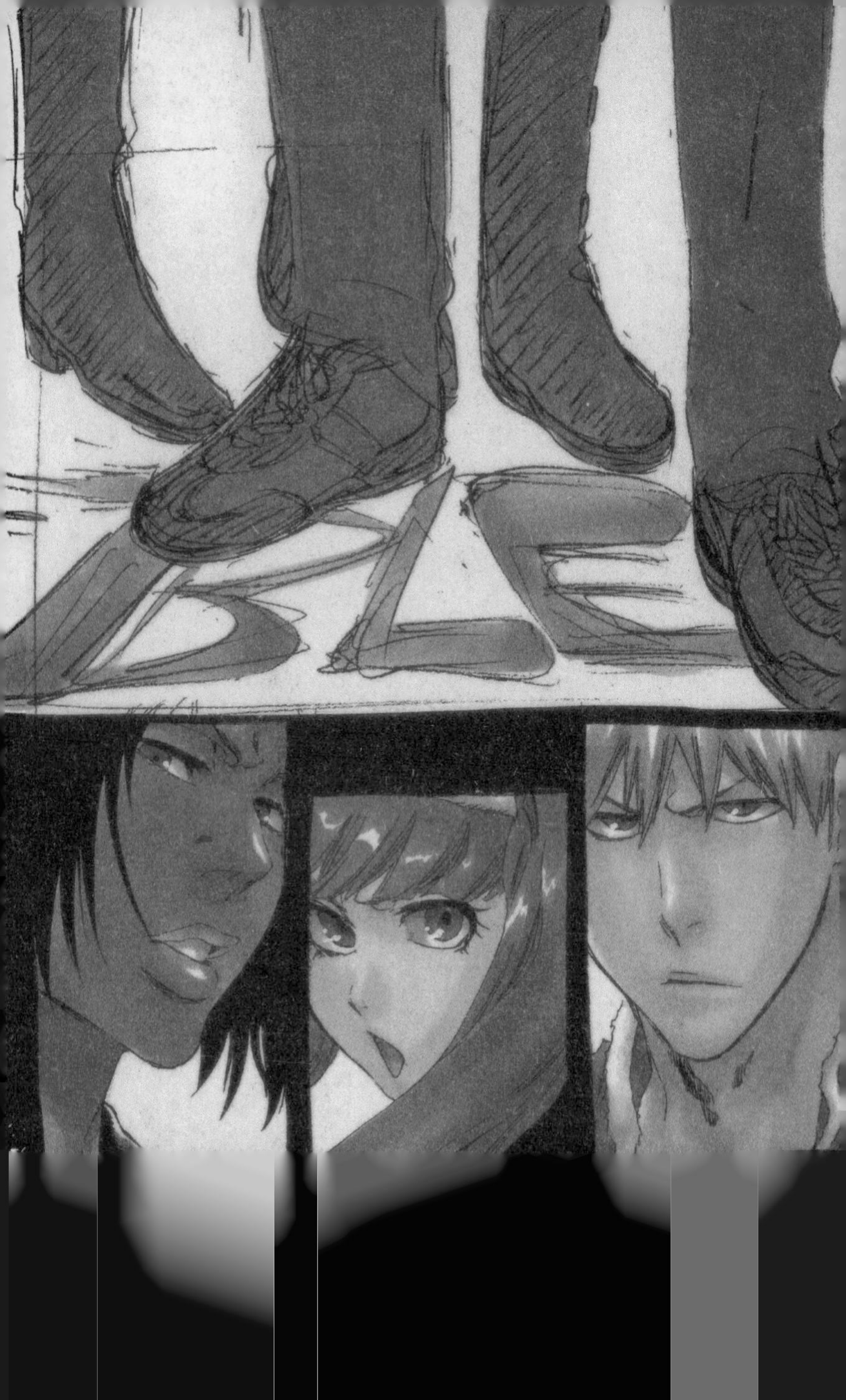
BLE

BLEACH
ブリーチ

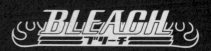

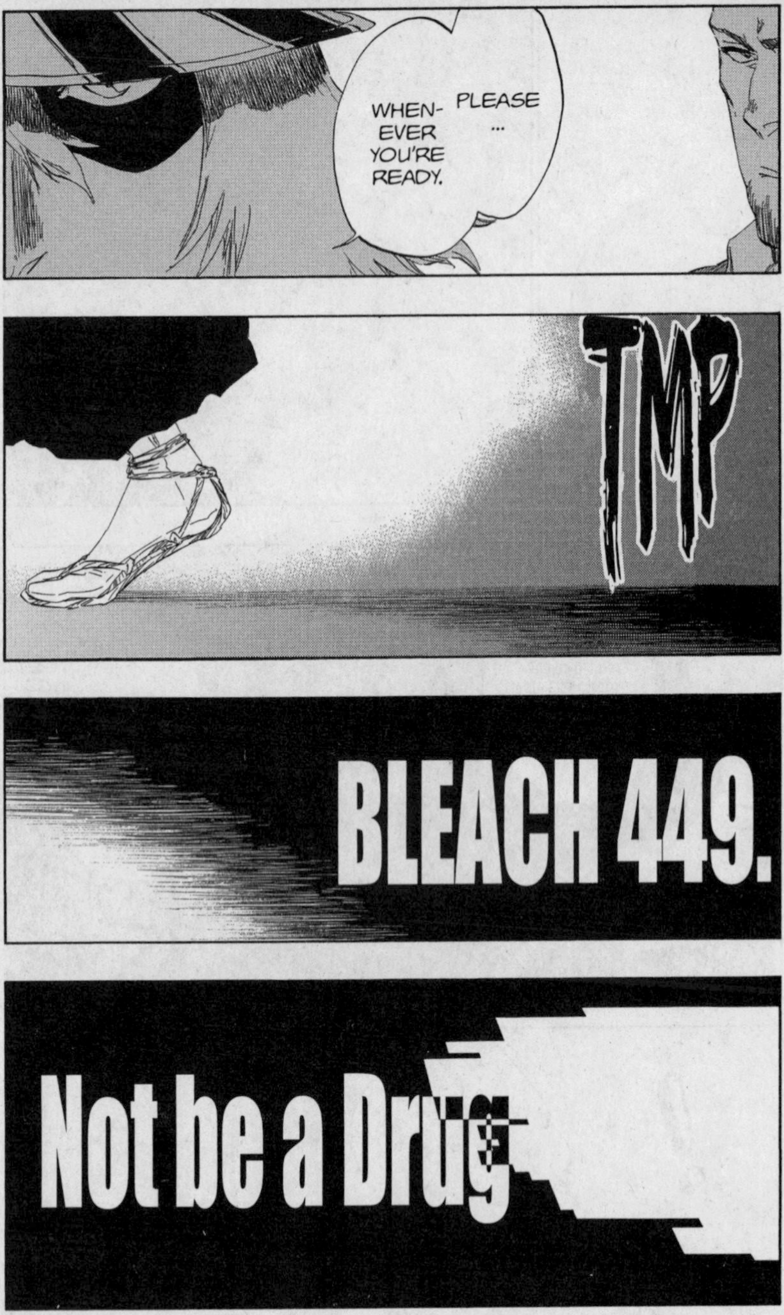
PLEASE ...
WHEN-EVER YOU'RE READY.
TMP
BLEACH 449.
Not be a Drug

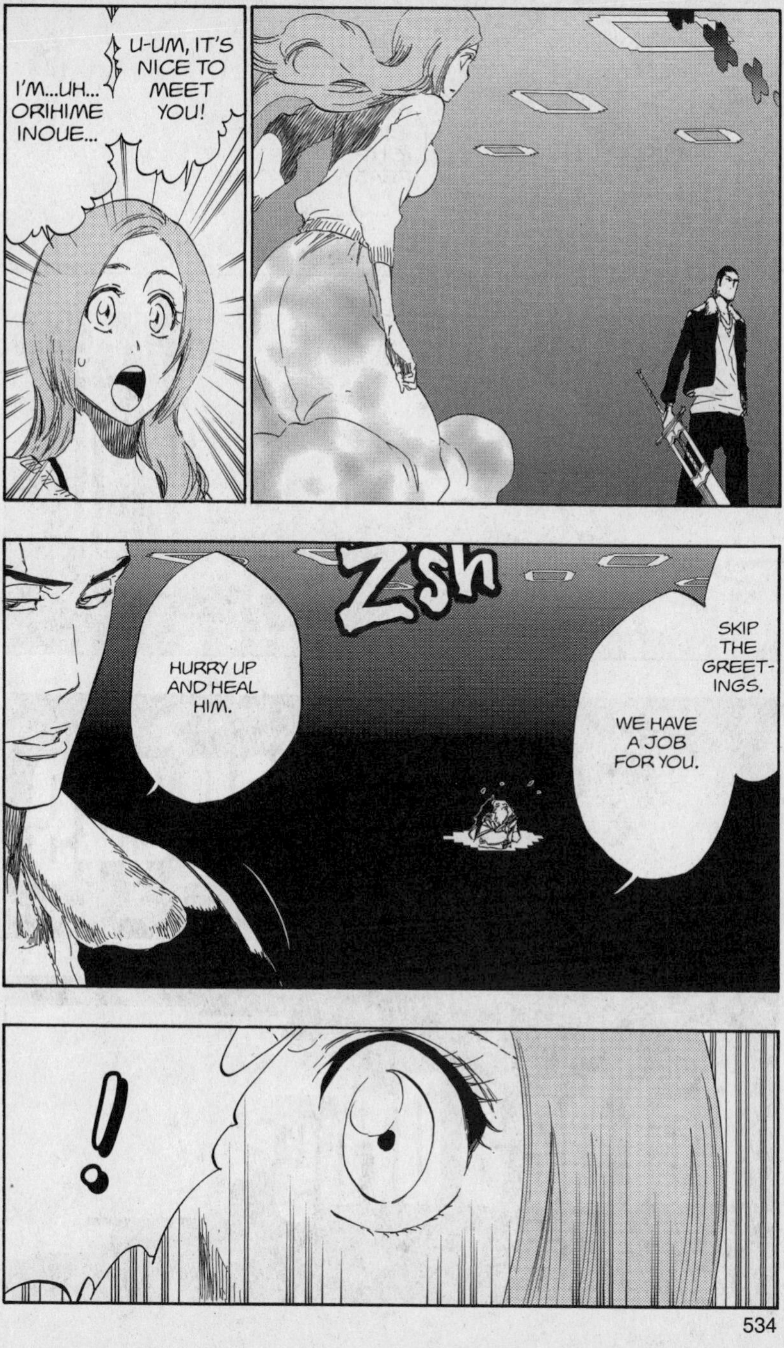
U-UM, IT'S NICE TO MEET YOU!
I'M...UH... ORIHIME INOUE...
SKIP THE GREET-INGS.
WE HAVE A JOB FOR YOU.
Zsh
HURRY UP AND HEAL HIM.
!!

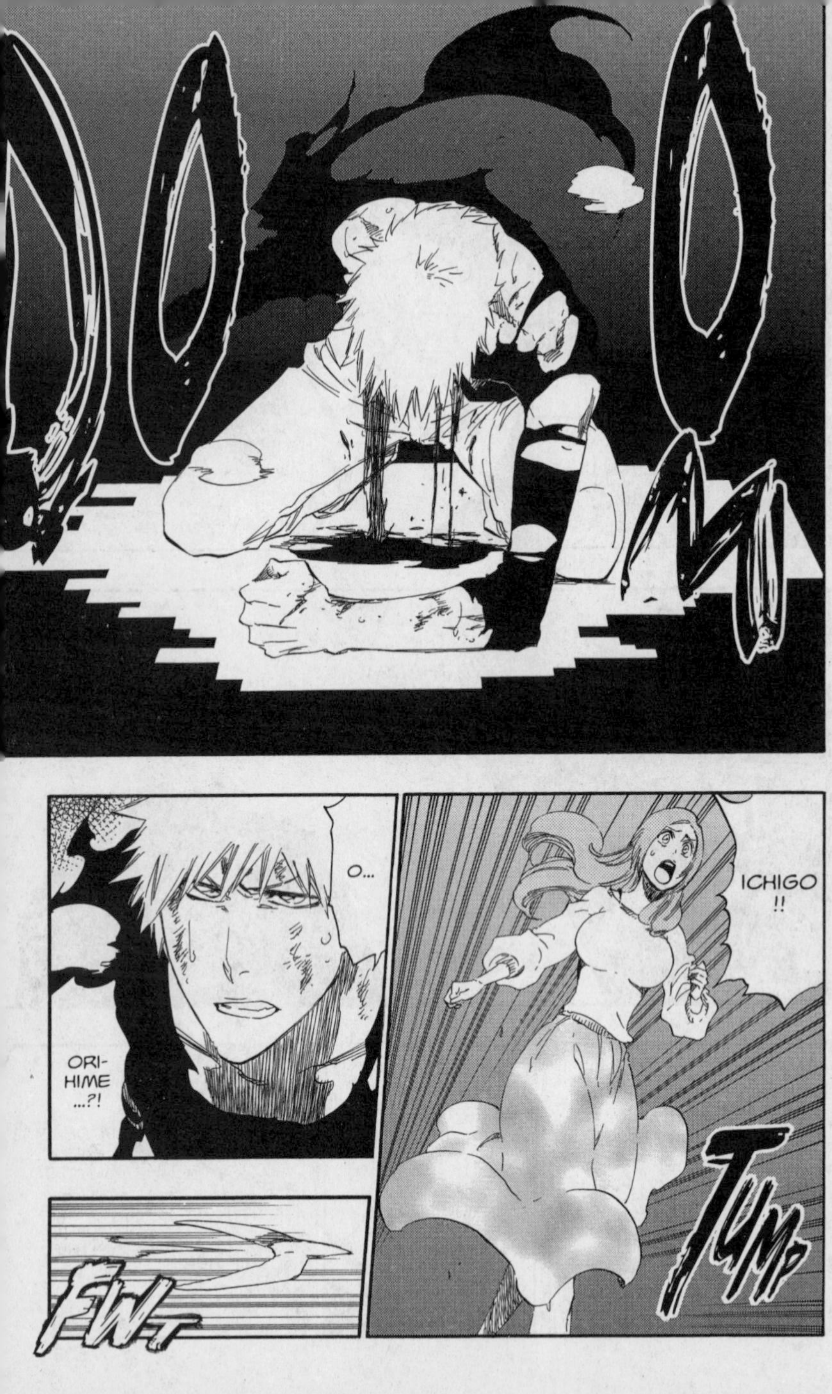
DOOM
ICHIGO !!
TUMP
O...
ORI-
HIME
...?!
FWT

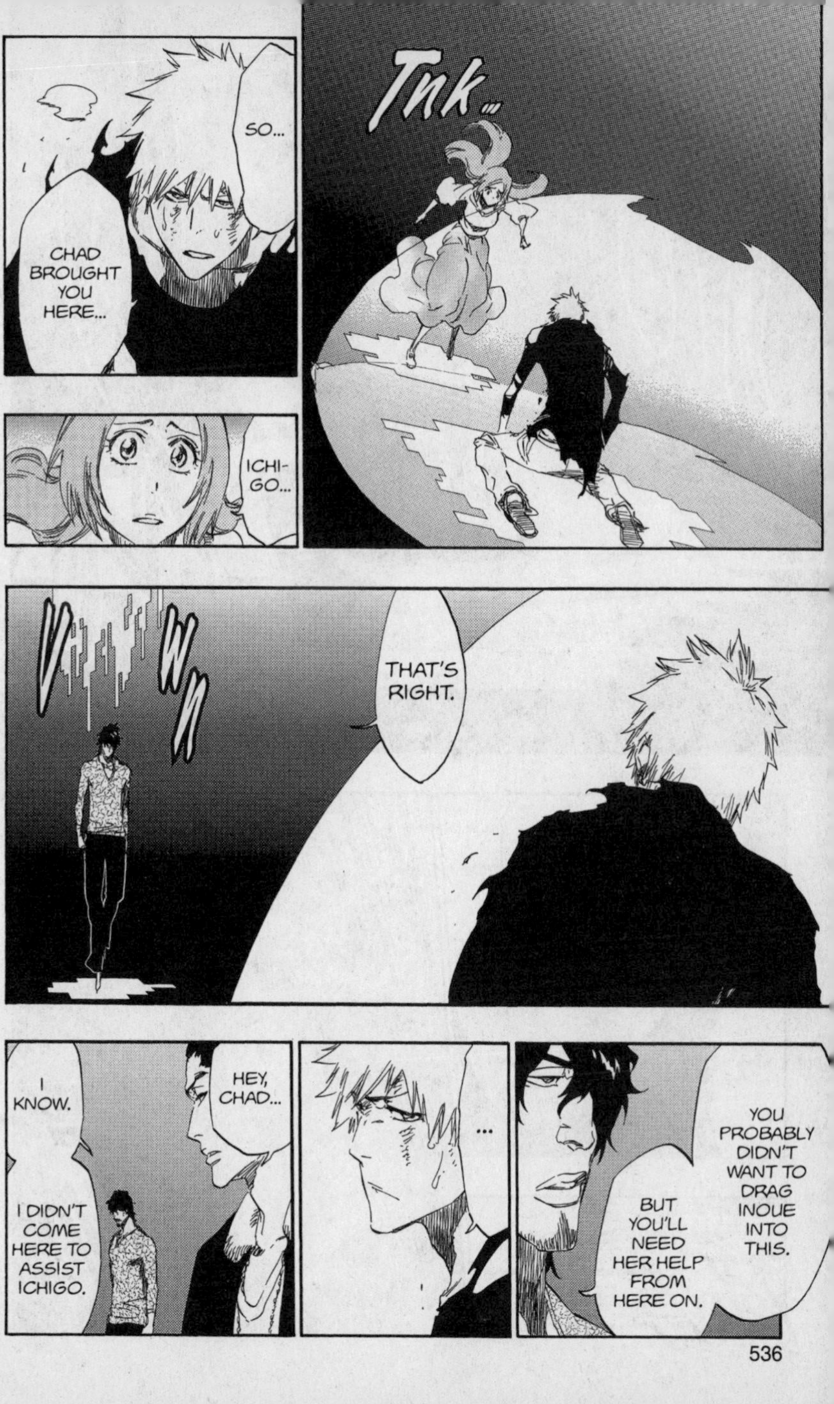
Tnk...
SO...
CHAD BROUGHT YOU HERE...
ICHI-GO...
THAT'S RIGHT.
YOU PROBABLY DIDN'T WANT TO DRAG INOUE INTO THIS.
BUT YOU'LL NEED HER HELP FROM HERE ON.
...
HEY, CHAD...
I KNOW.
I DIDN'T COME HERE TO ASSIST ICHIGO.

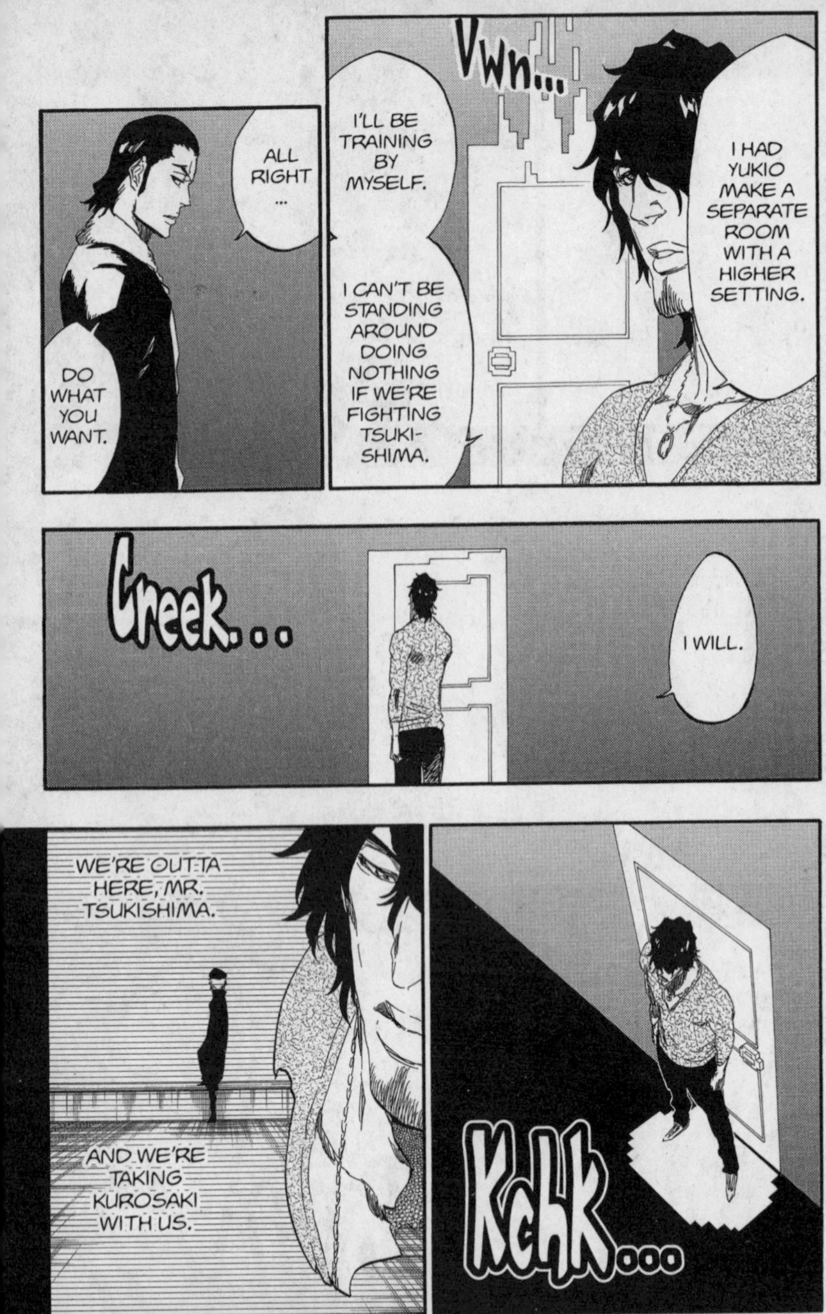
Vwn...
I HAD YUKIO MAKE A SEPARATE ROOM WITH A HIGHER SETTING.
I'LL BE TRAINING BY MYSELF.
I CAN'T BE STANDING AROUND DOING NOTHING IF WE'RE FIGHTING TSUKI-SHIMA.
ALL RIGHT ...
DO WHAT YOU WANT.
I WILL.
Creek...
Kchk...
WE'RE OUTTA HERE, MR. TSUKISHIMA.
AND WE'RE TAKING KUROSAKI WITH US.

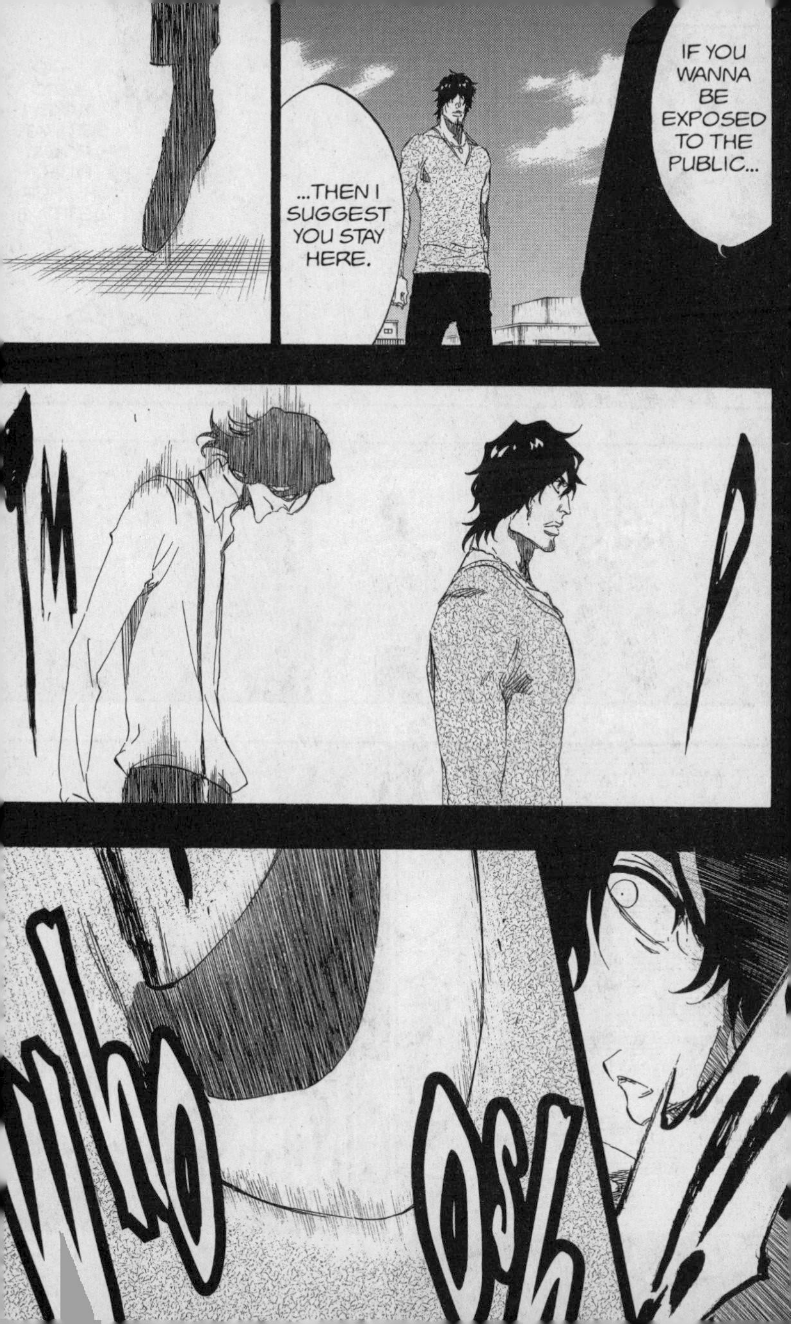
IF YOU WANNA BE EXPOSED TO THE PUBLIC...
...THEN I SUGGEST YOU STAY HERE.

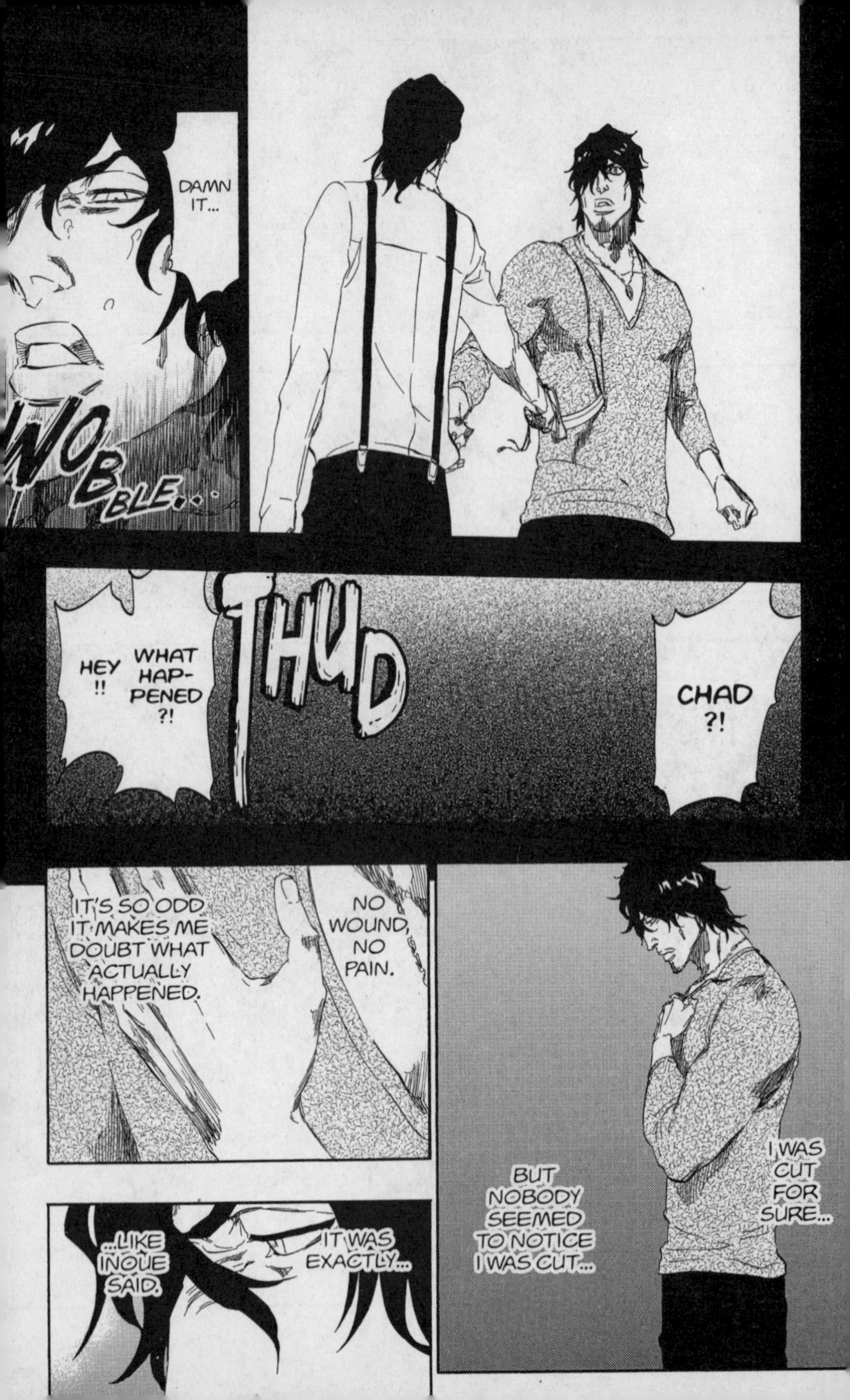
DAMN IT...
WOBBLE...
CHAD ?!
THUD
HEY !!
WHAT HAPPENED ?!
I WAS CUT FOR SURE...
BUT NOBODY SEEMED TO NOTICE I WAS CUT...
NO WOUND, NO PAIN.
IT'S SO ODD IT MAKES ME DOUBT WHAT ACTUALLY HAPPENED.
IT WAS EXACTLY...
...LIKE INOUE SAID.

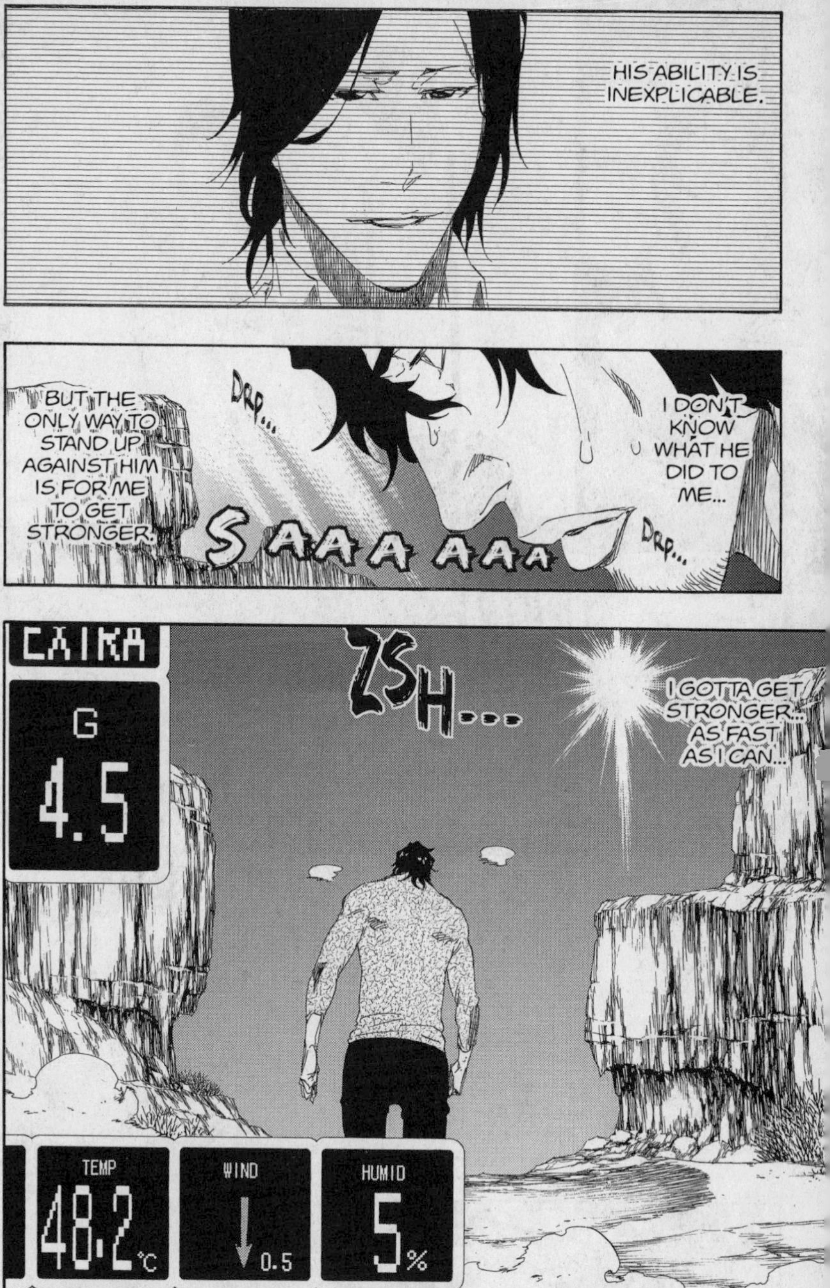
HIS ABILITY IS INEXPLICABLE.
I DON'T KNOW WHAT HE DID TO ME...
DRP...
DRP...
BUT THE ONLY WAY TO STAND UP AGAINST HIM IS FOR ME TO GET STRONGER.
SAAAAAAA
I GOTTA GET STRONGER... AS FAST AS I CAN...
ZSH...
G
4.5
HUMID
5%
WIND
0.5
TEMP
48.2°C

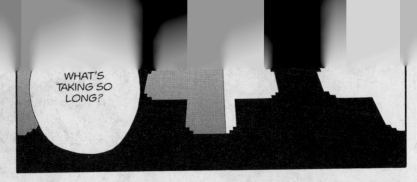

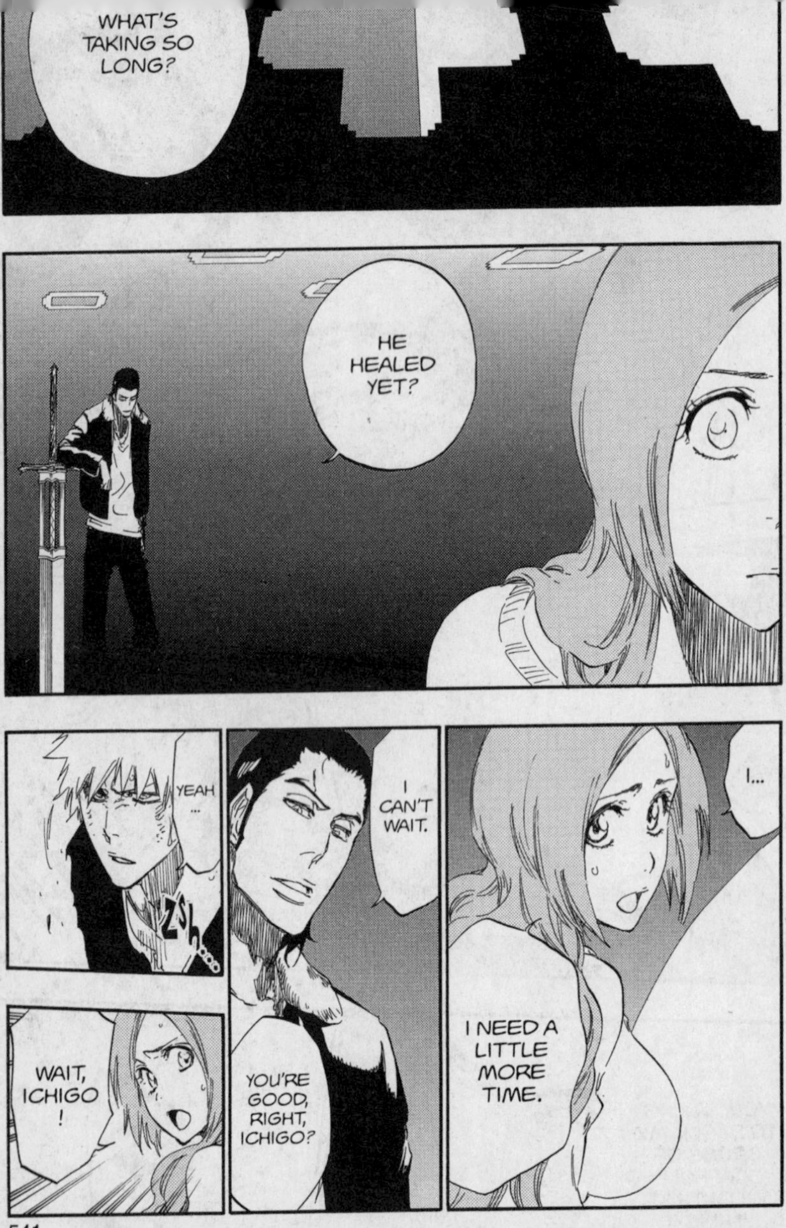
WHAT'S TAKING SO LONG?
HE HEALED YET?
I...
I NEED A LITTLE MORE TIME.
I CAN'T WAIT.
YOU'RE GOOD, RIGHT, ICHIGO?
YEAH ...
ZSH
WAIT, ICHIGO!

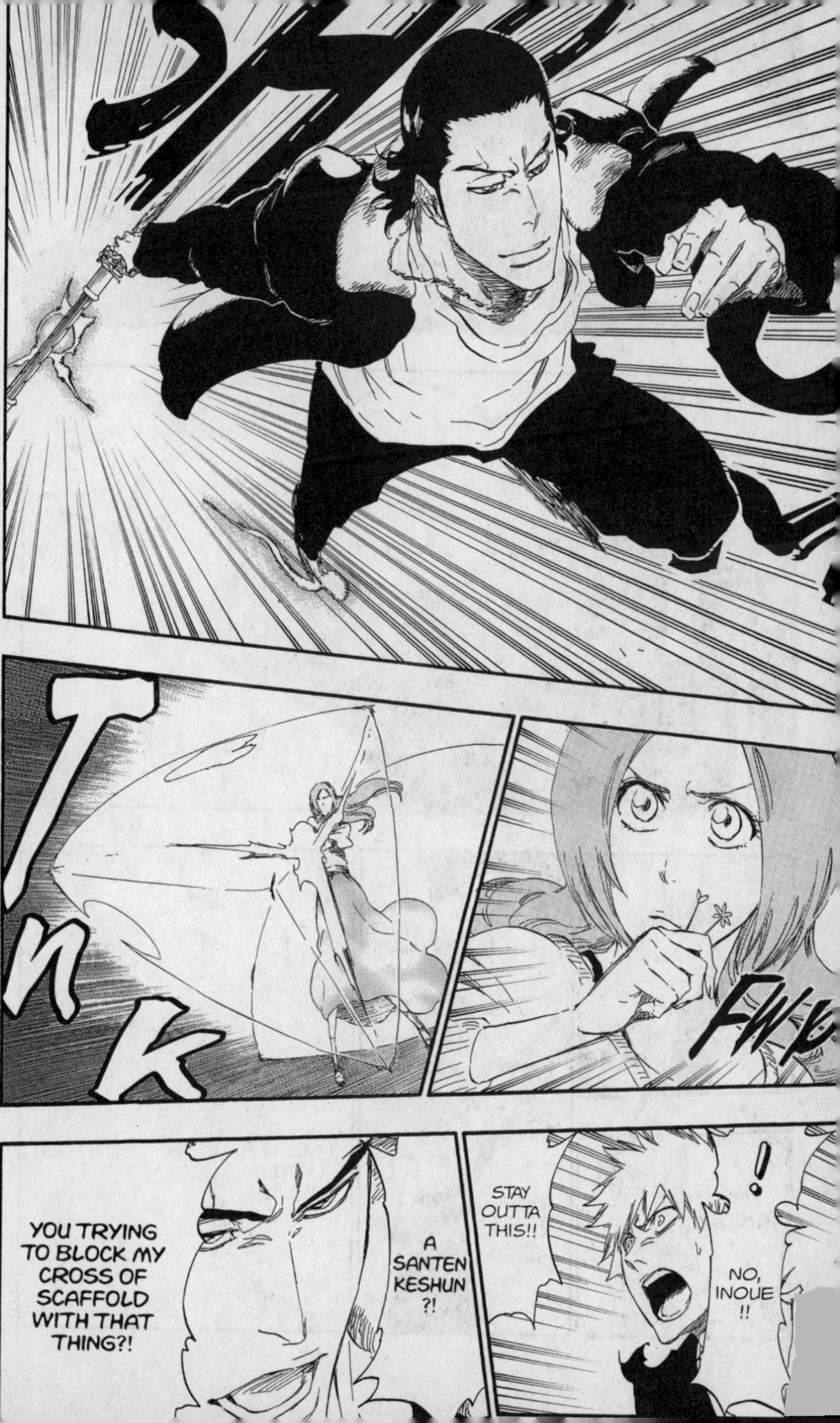
Tink
!
NO, INOUE!!
STAY OUTTA THIS!!
A SANTEN KESHUN?!
YOU TRYING TO BLOCK MY CROSS OF SCAFFOLD WITH THAT THING?!

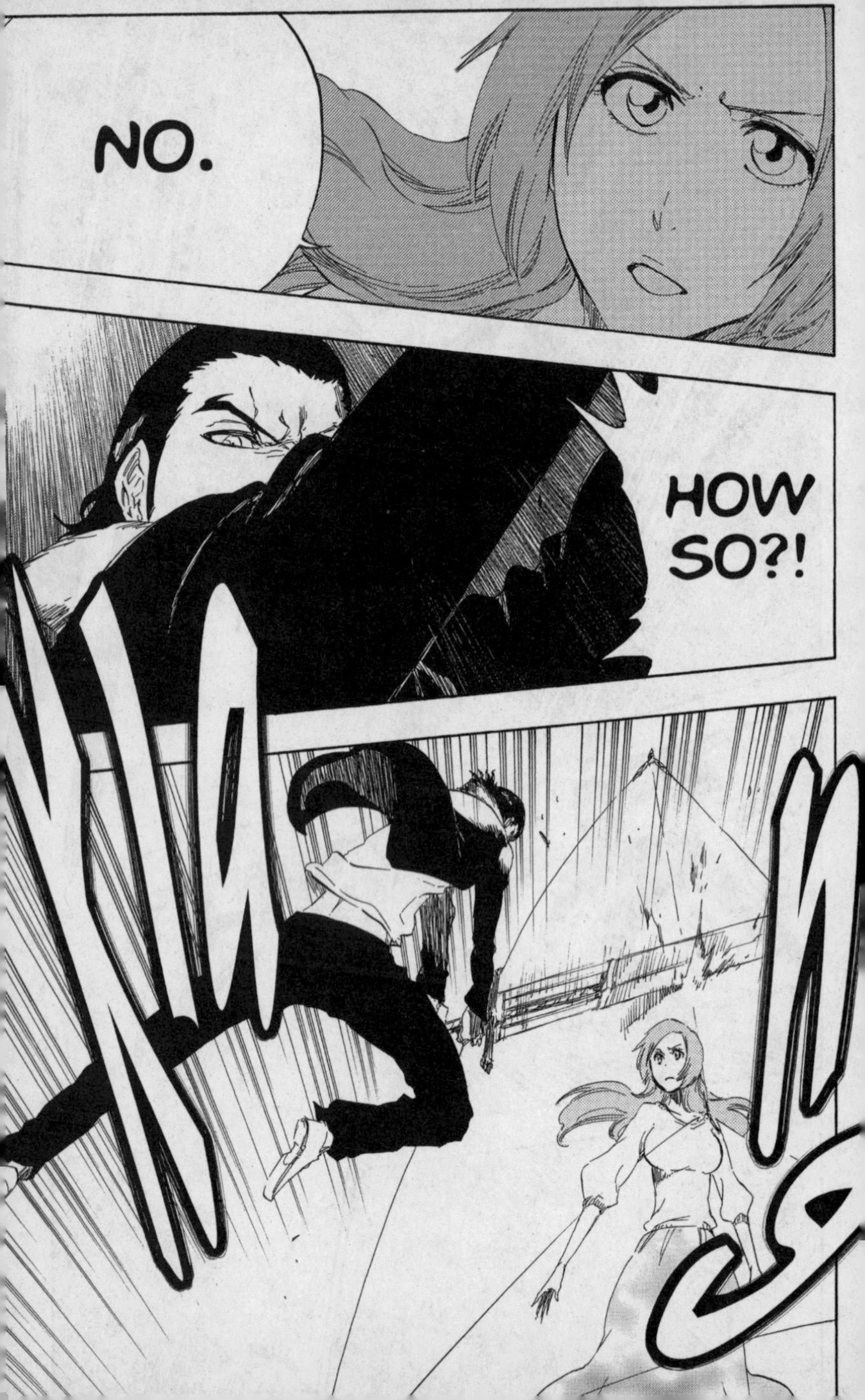
NO.
HOW SO?!

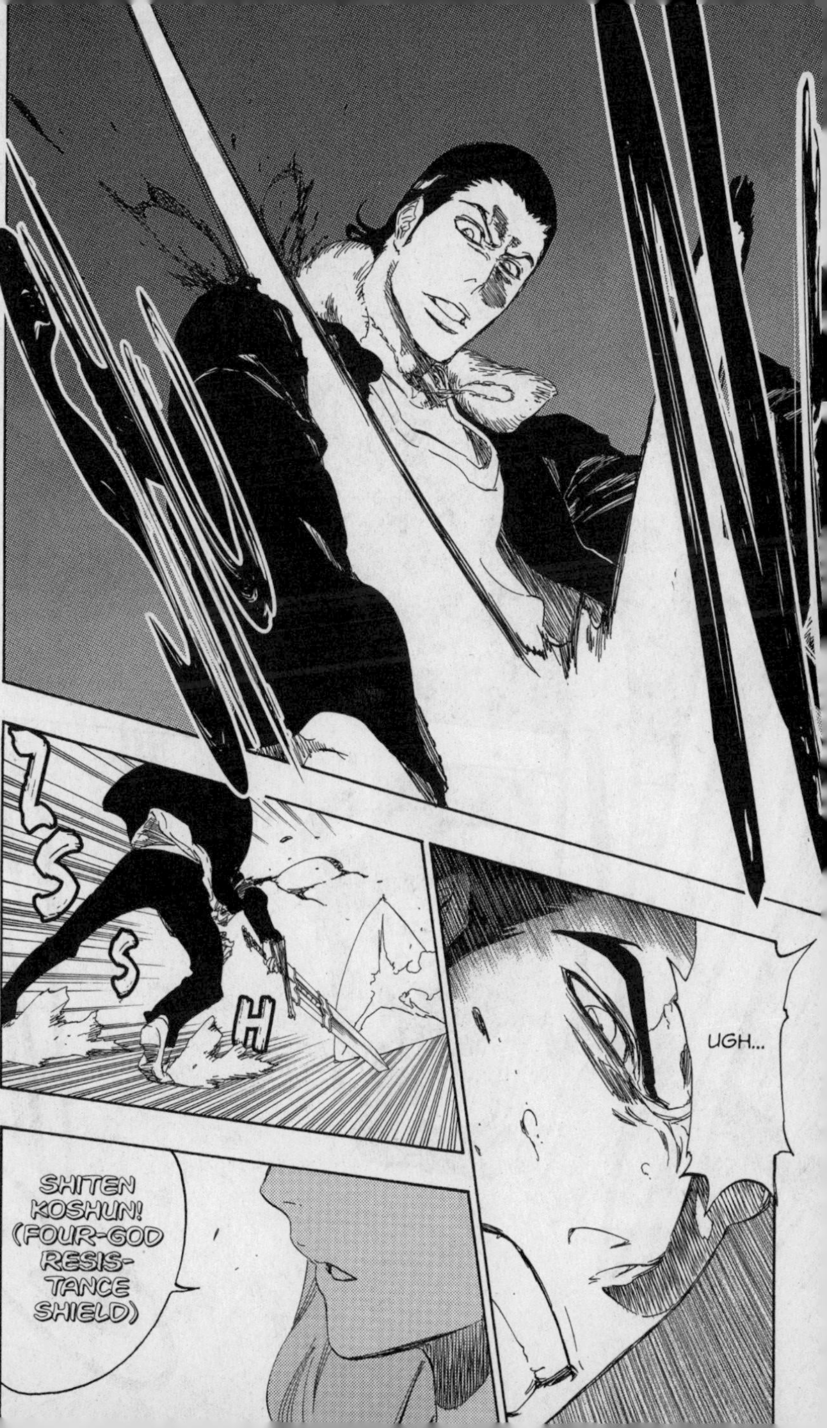

SWISH
UGH...
SHITEN KOSHUN! (FOUR-GOD RESIS-TANCE SHIELD)

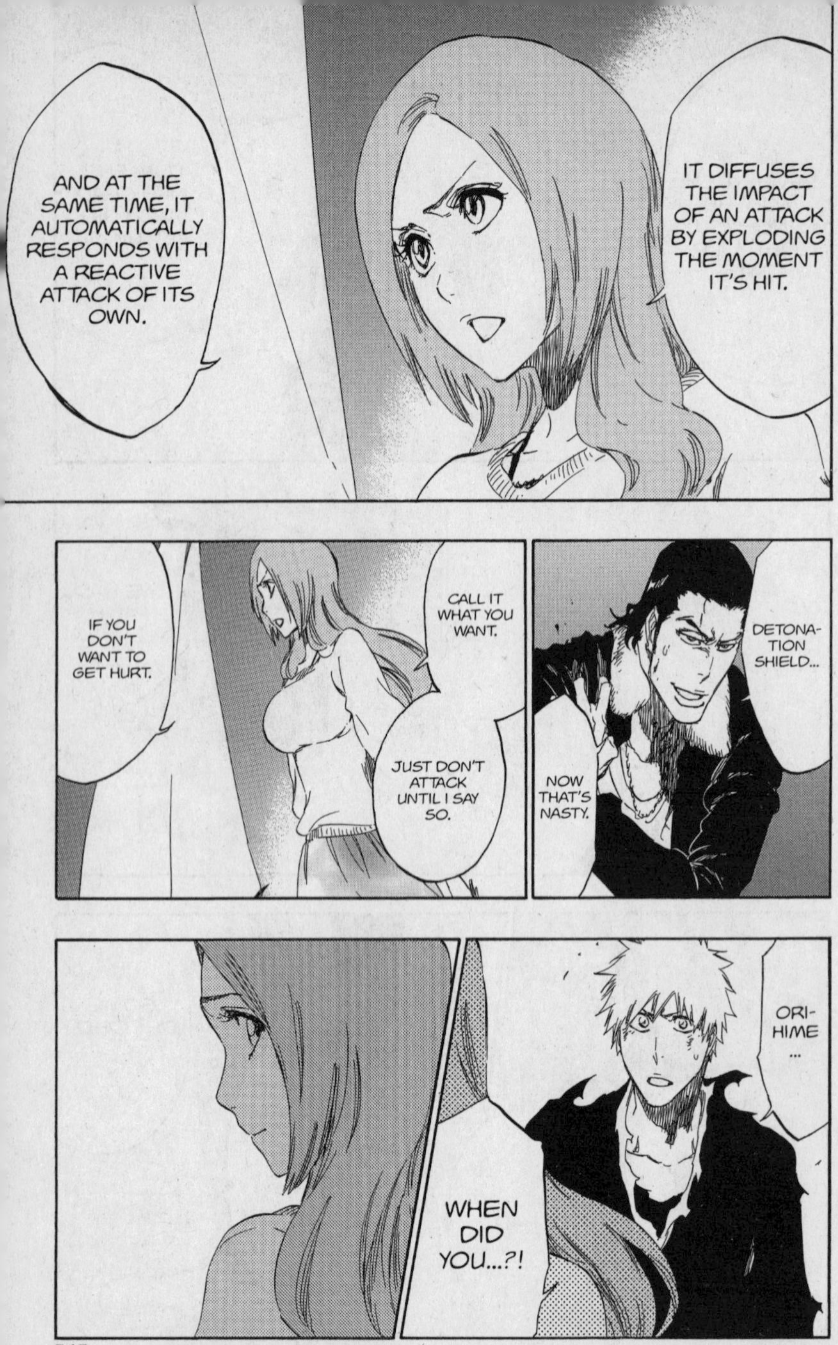
IT DIFFUSES THE IMPACT OF AN ATTACK BY EXPLODING THE MOMENT IT'S HIT.
AND AT THE SAME TIME, IT AUTOMATICALLY RESPONDS WITH A REACTIVE ATTACK OF ITS OWN.
DETONATION SHIELD...
NOW THAT'S NASTY.
CALL IT WHAT YOU WANT.
JUST DON'T ATTACK UNTIL I SAY SO.
IF YOU DON'T WANT TO GET HURT.
ORI-HIME...
WHEN DID YOU...?!

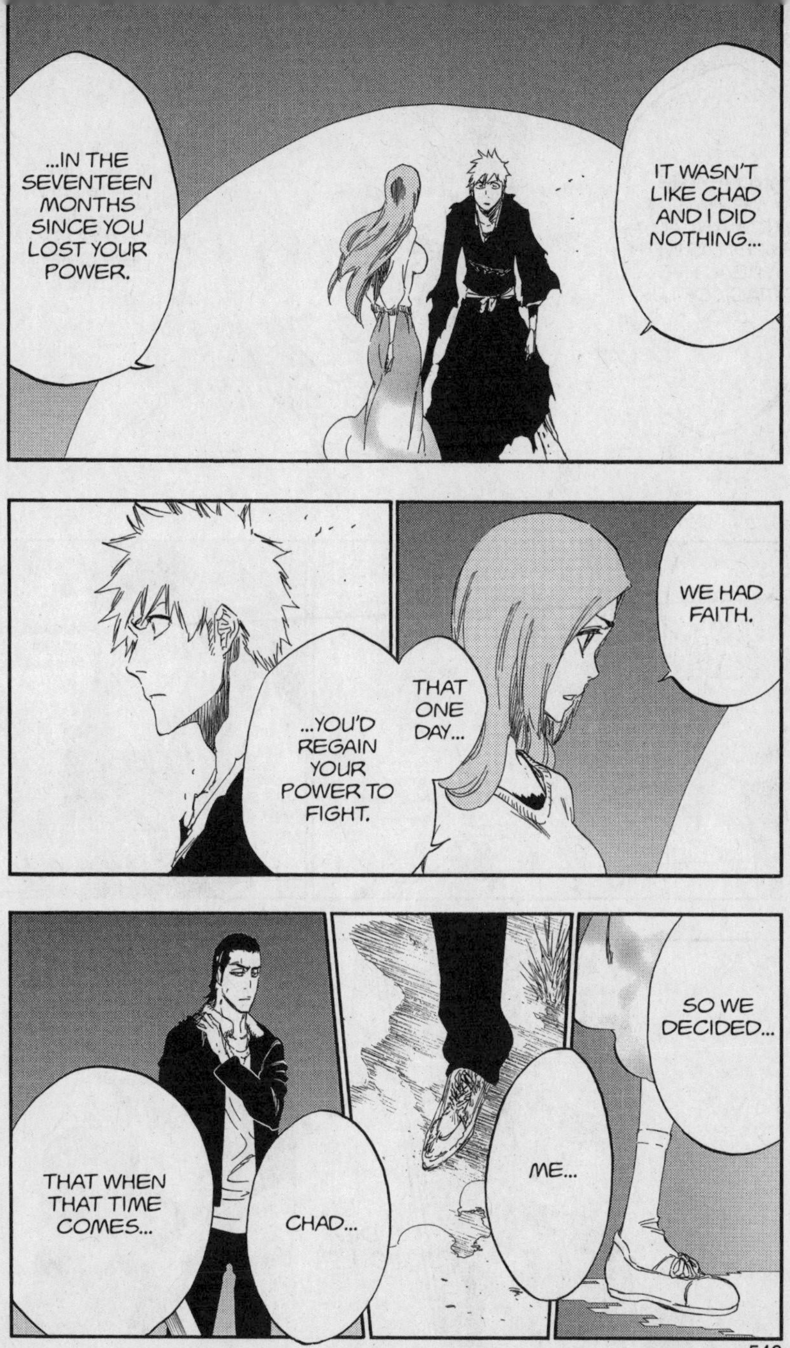
IT WASN'T LIKE CHAD AND I DID NOTHING...
...IN THE SEVENTEEN MONTHS SINCE YOU LOST YOUR POWER.
WE HAD FAITH.
THAT ONE DAY...
...YOU'D REGAIN YOUR POWER TO FIGHT.
SO WE DECIDED...
ME...
CHAD...
THAT WHEN THAT TIME COMES...

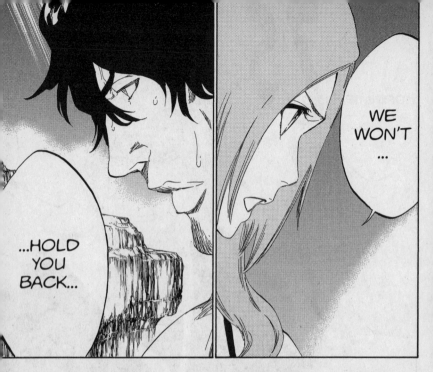

WE WON'T...

...HOLD YOU BACK...

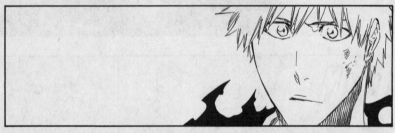

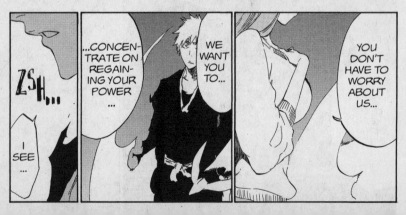

ZSH...

I SEE...

...CONCENTRATE ON REGAINING YOUR POWER...

WE WANT YOU TO...

YOU DON'T HAVE TO WORRY ABOUT US...

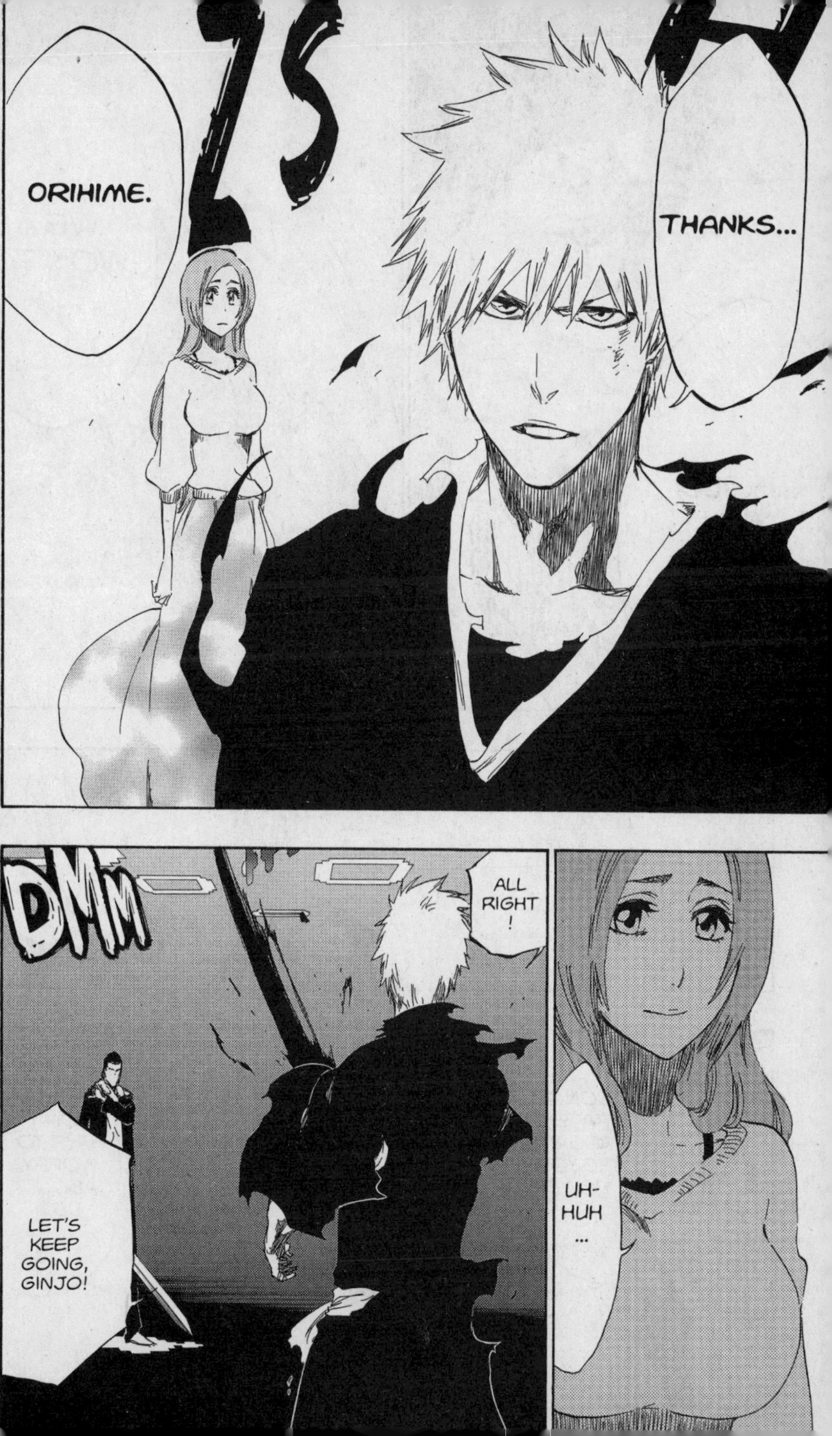
THANKS...
ORIHIME.
UH-HUH...
DMM
ALL RIGHT!
LET'S KEEP GOING, GINJO!

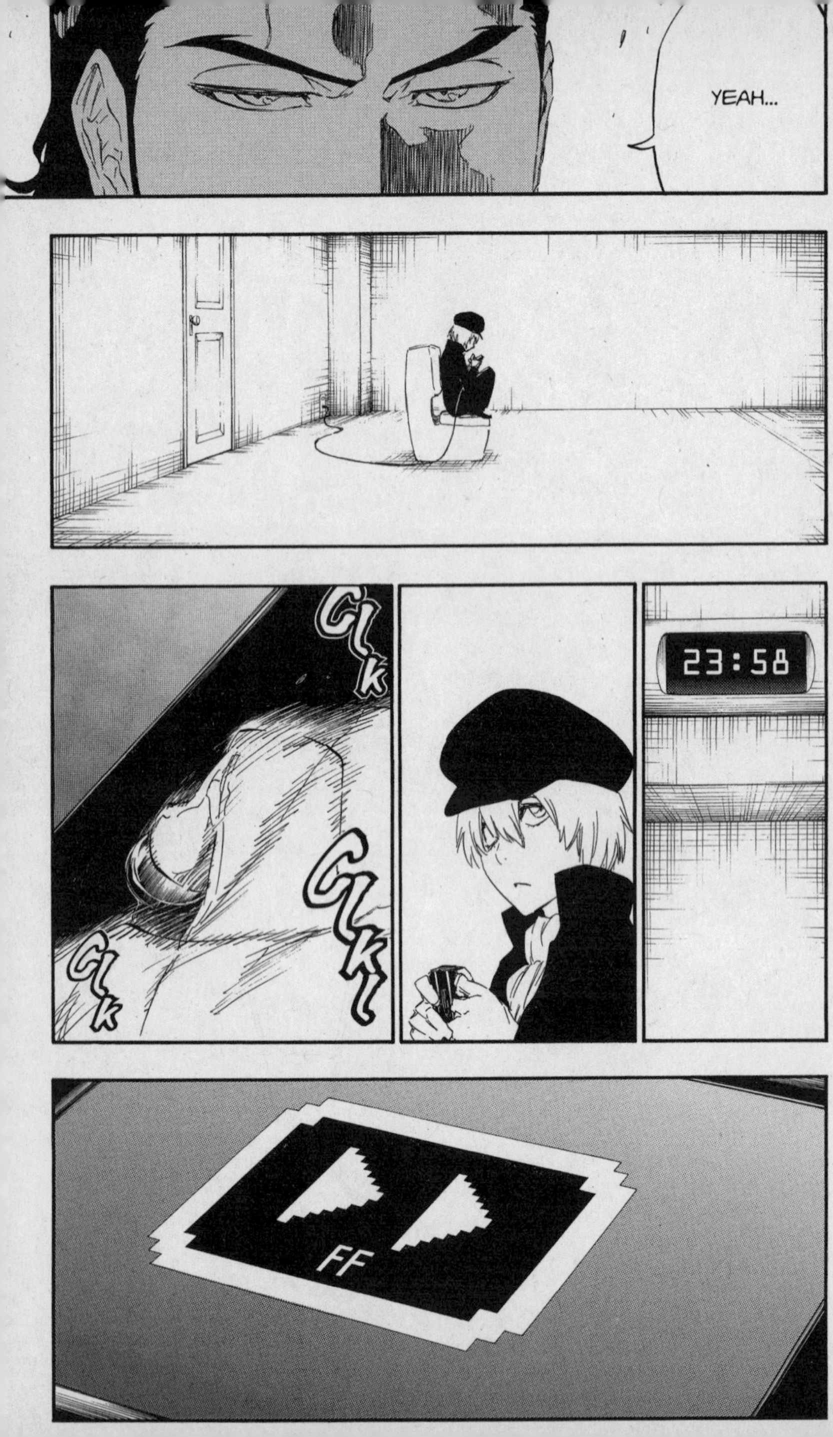
YEAH...
23:58
Clk
Clk
Clk
FF

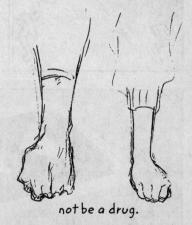

not be a drug.

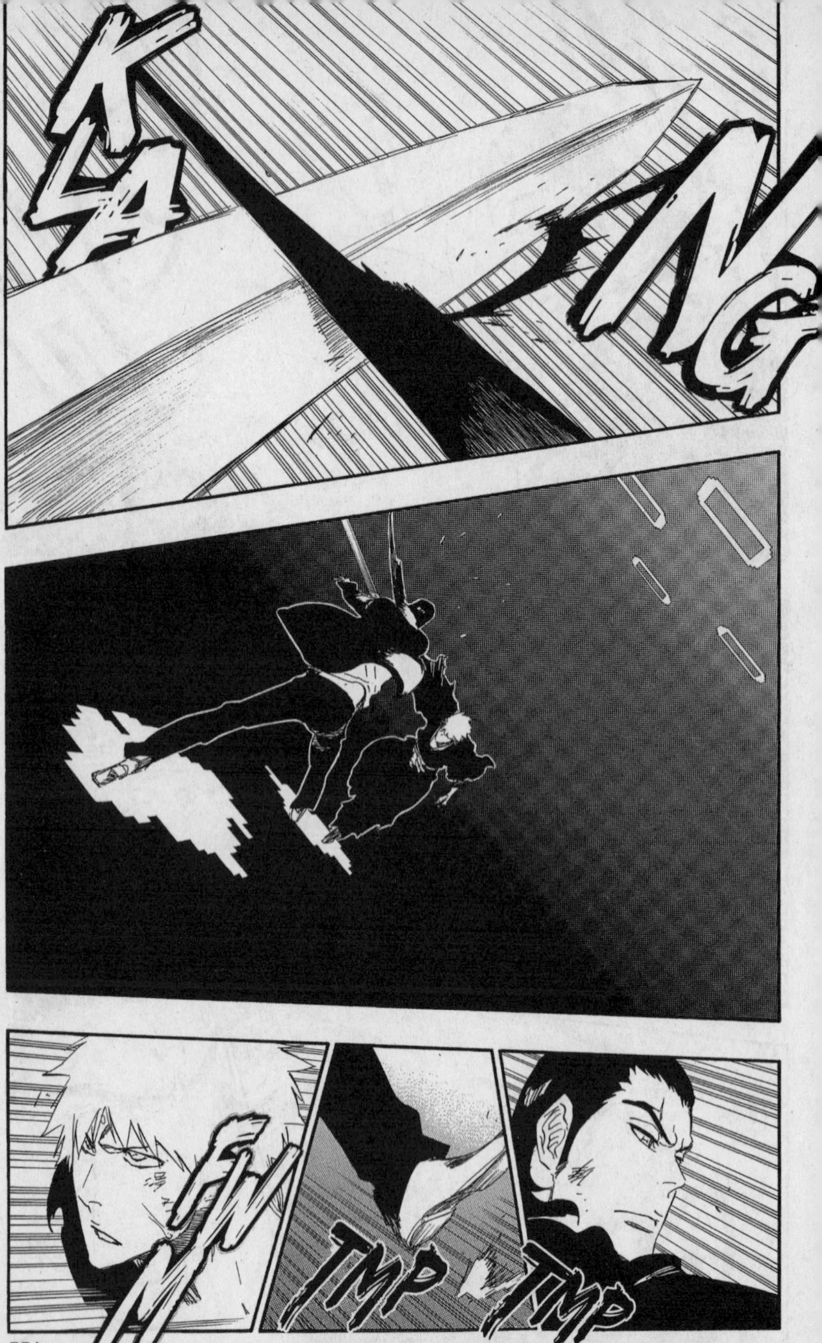
KLANG
TMP TMP
FWM

450. Blind Solitude

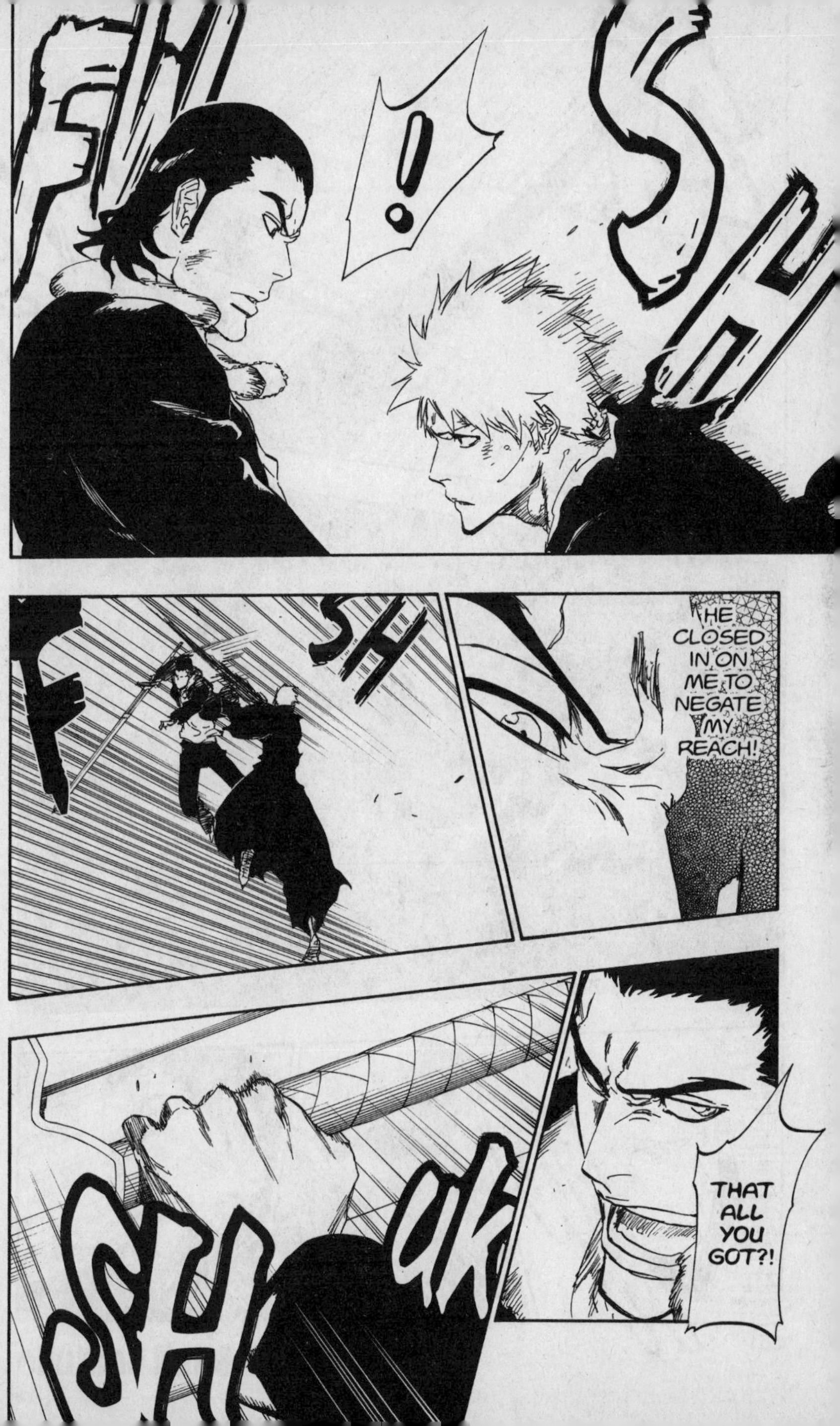
!
HE CLOSED IN ON ME TO NEGATE MY REACH!
SH
THAT ALL YOU GOT?!

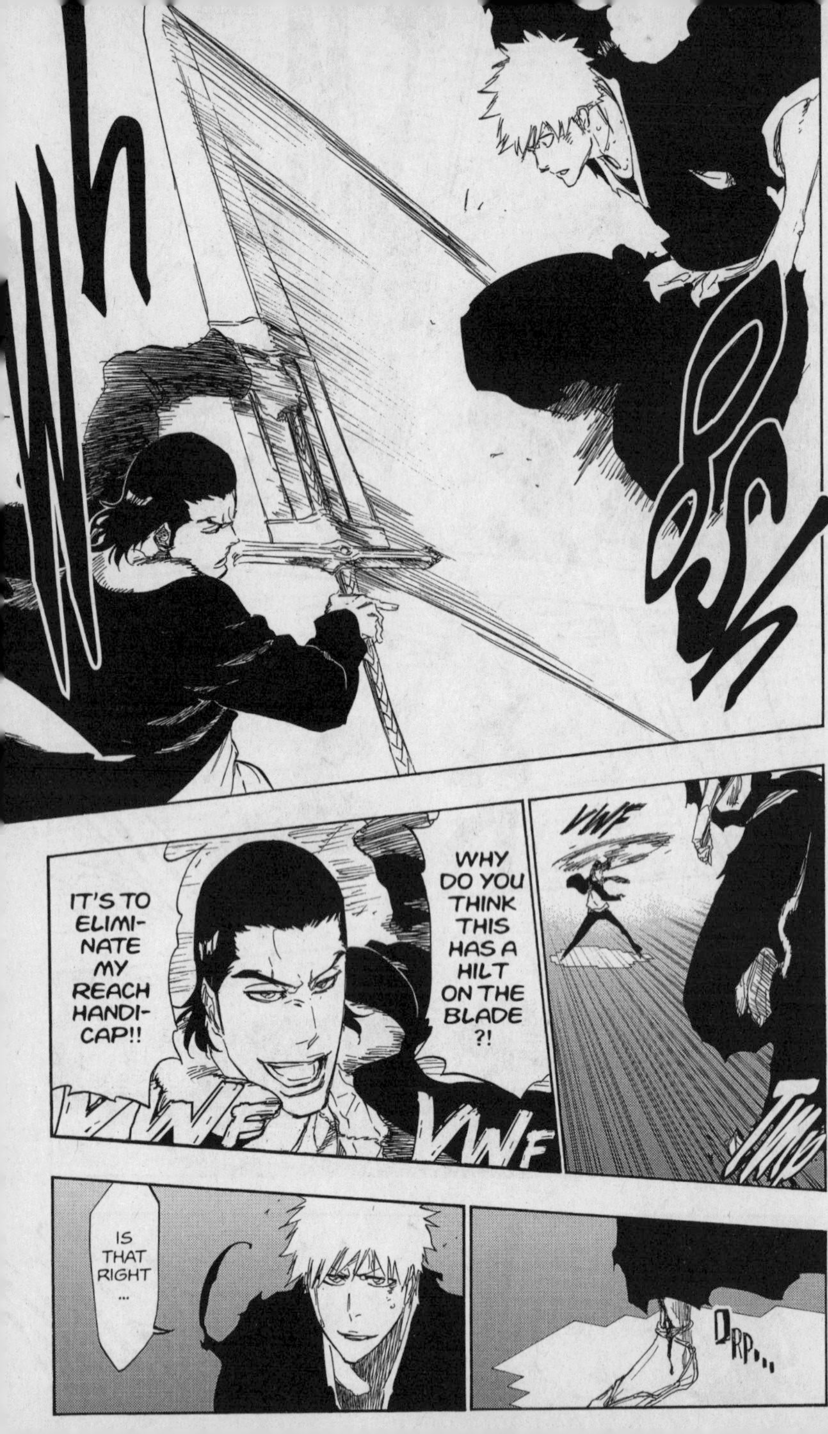
VWF
WHY DO YOU THINK THIS HAS A HILT ON THE BLADE ?!
IT'S TO ELIMI-NATE MY REACH HANDI-CAP!!
VWF
VWF
DRP...
IS THAT RIGHT ...

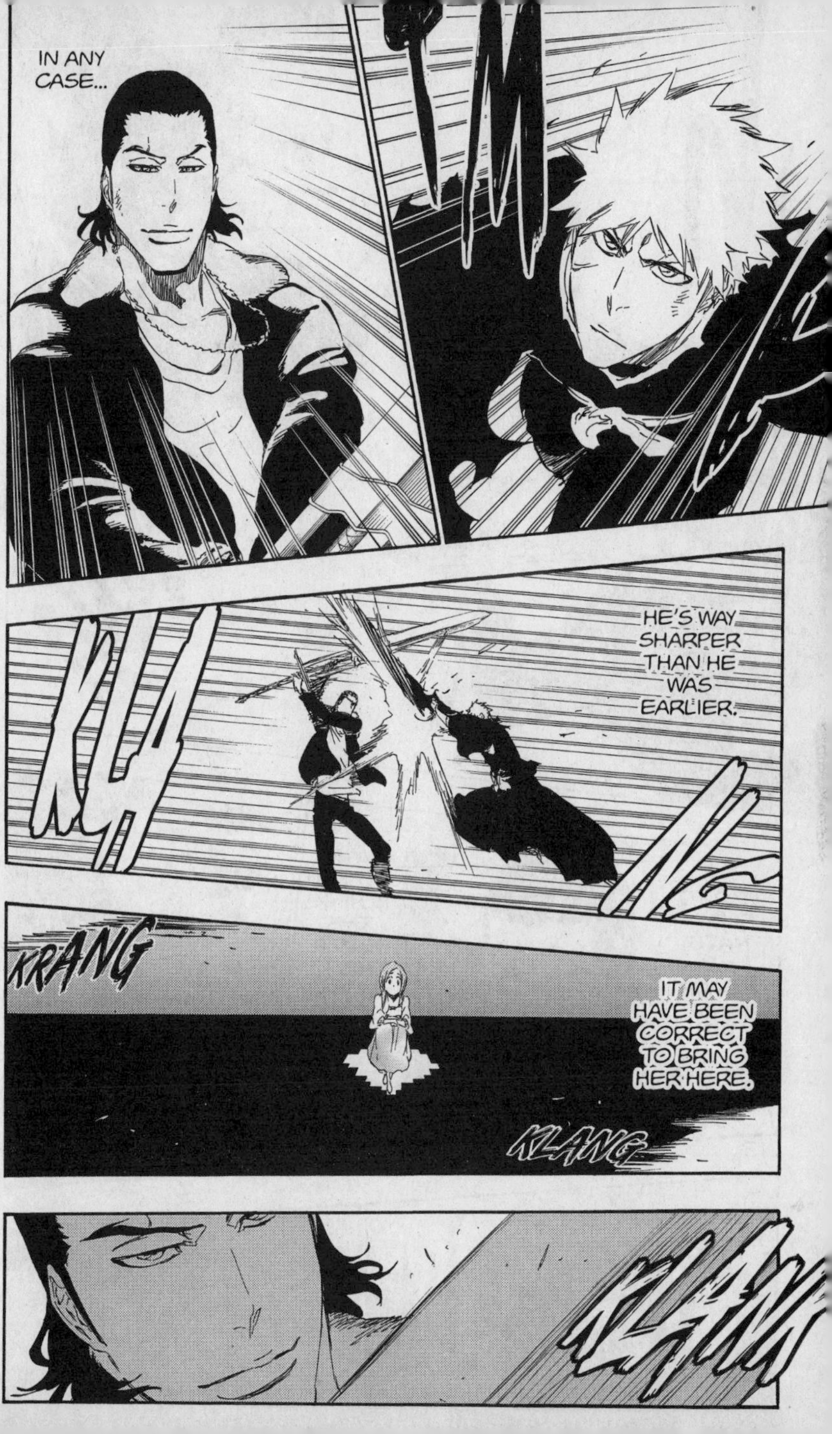
IN ANY CASE...
HE'S WAY SHARPER THAN HE WAS EARLIER.
IT MAY HAVE BEEN CORRECT TO BRING HER HERE.
KRANG
KLANG

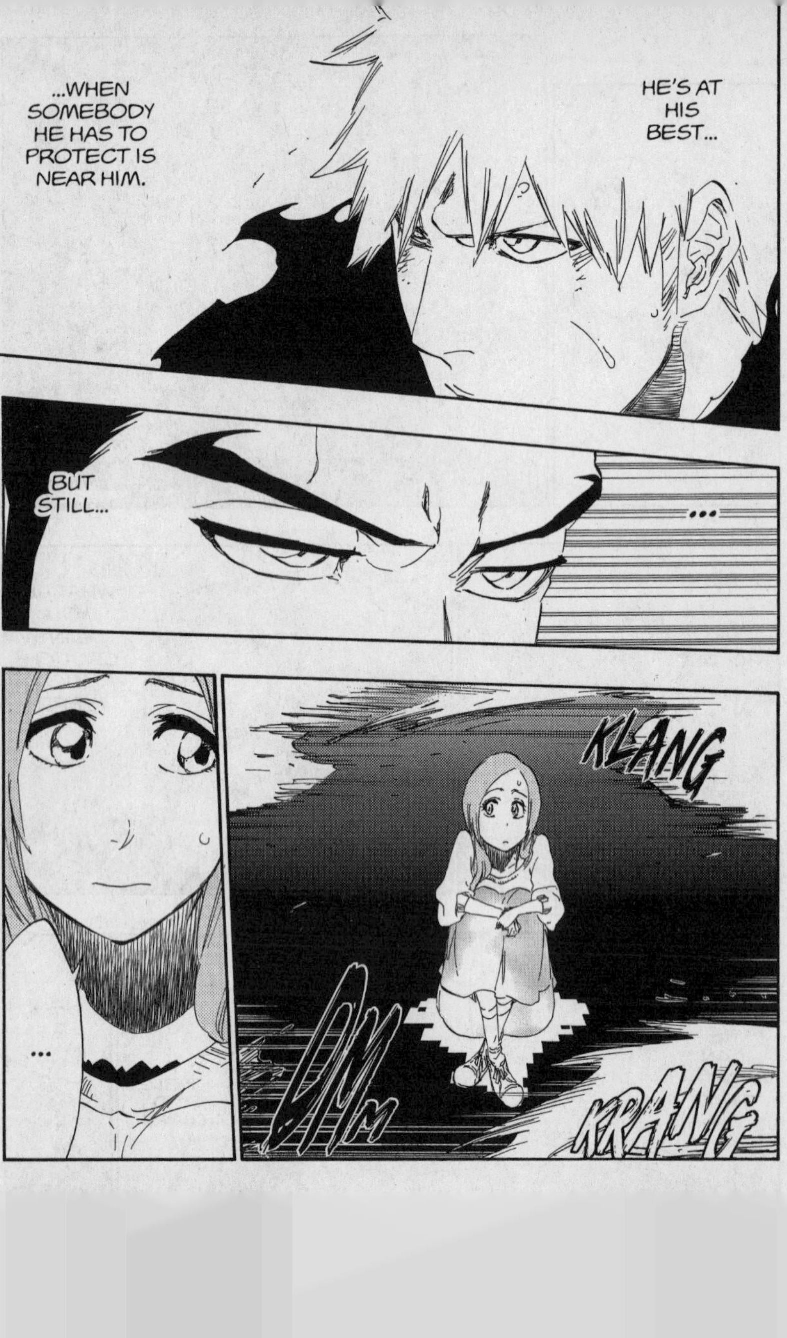
HE'S AT HIS BEST...
...WHEN SOMEBODY HE HAS TO PROTECT IS NEAR HIM.
...
BUT STILL...
KLANG
KRANG
...

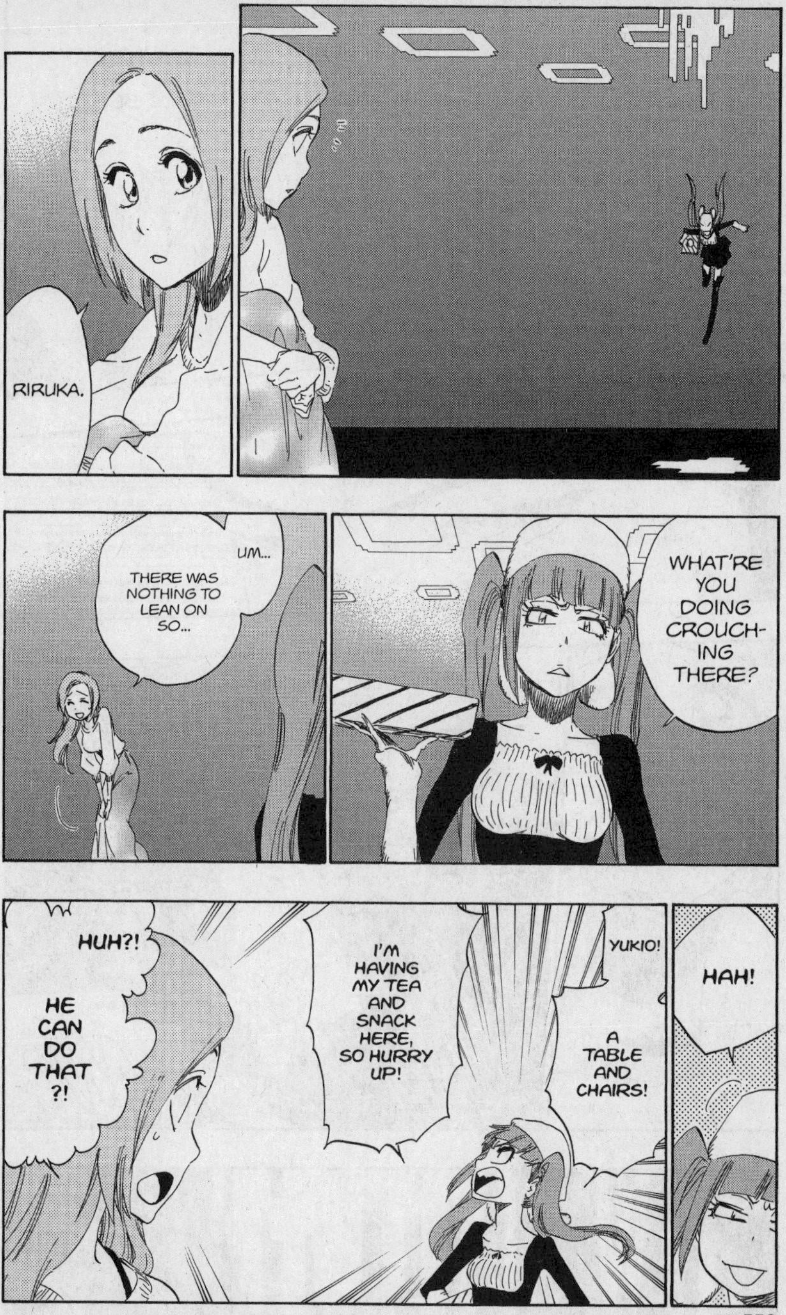
RIRUKA.
WHAT'RE YOU DOING CROUCHING THERE?
UM...
THERE WAS NOTHING TO LEAN ON SO...
HAH!
YUKIO!
A TABLE AND CHAIRS!
I'M HAVING MY TEA AND SNACK HERE, SO HURRY UP!
HUH?!
HE CAN DO THAT?!

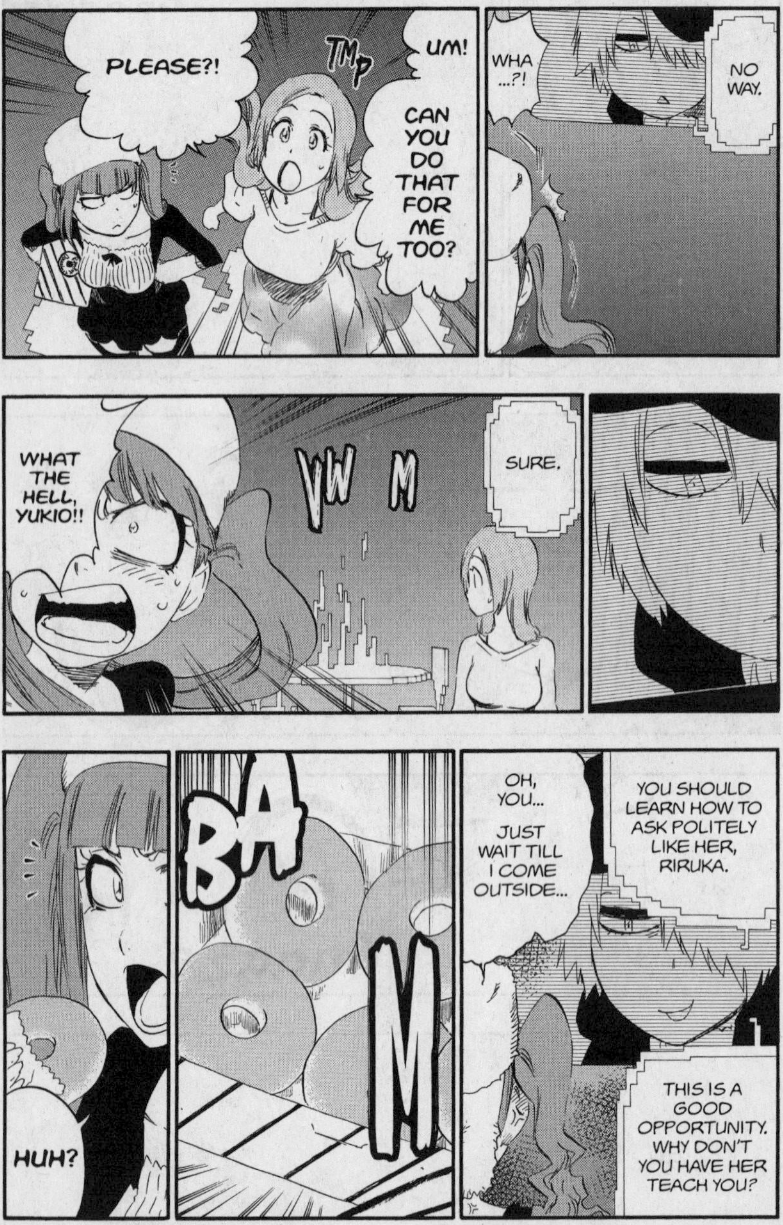
NO WAY.
WHA ...?!
UM!
CAN YOU DO THAT FOR ME TOO?
TMP
PLEASE?!
SURE.
VWM
WHAT THE HELL, YUKIO!!
YOU SHOULD LEARN HOW TO ASK POLITELY LIKE HER, RIRUKA.
OH, YOU...
JUST WAIT TILL I COME OUTSIDE...
THIS IS A GOOD OPPORTUNITY. WHY DON'T YOU HAVE HER TEACH YOU?
BAM
HUH?

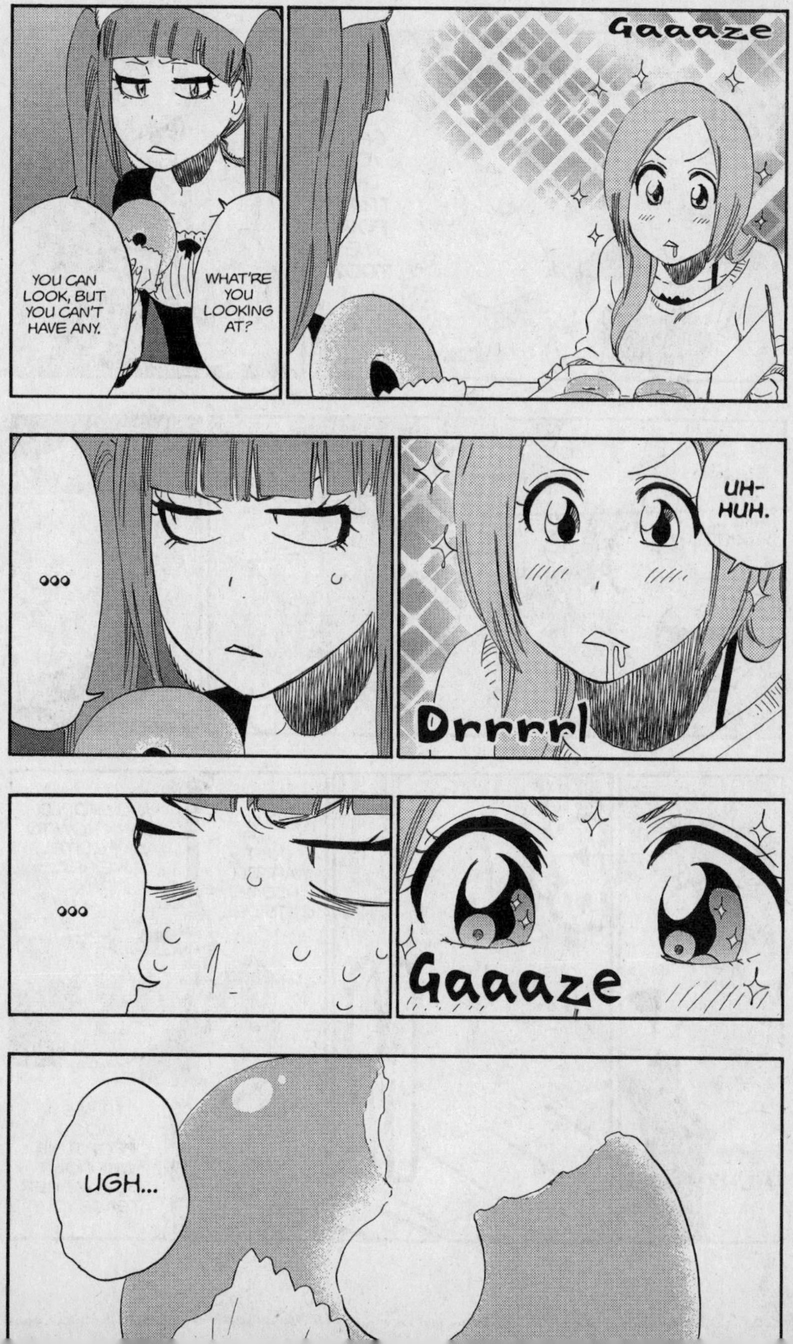
Gaaaze
WHAT'RE YOU LOOKING AT?
YOU CAN LOOK, BUT YOU CAN'T HAVE ANY.
UH-HUH.
Drrrrl
...
Gaaaze
...
UGH...

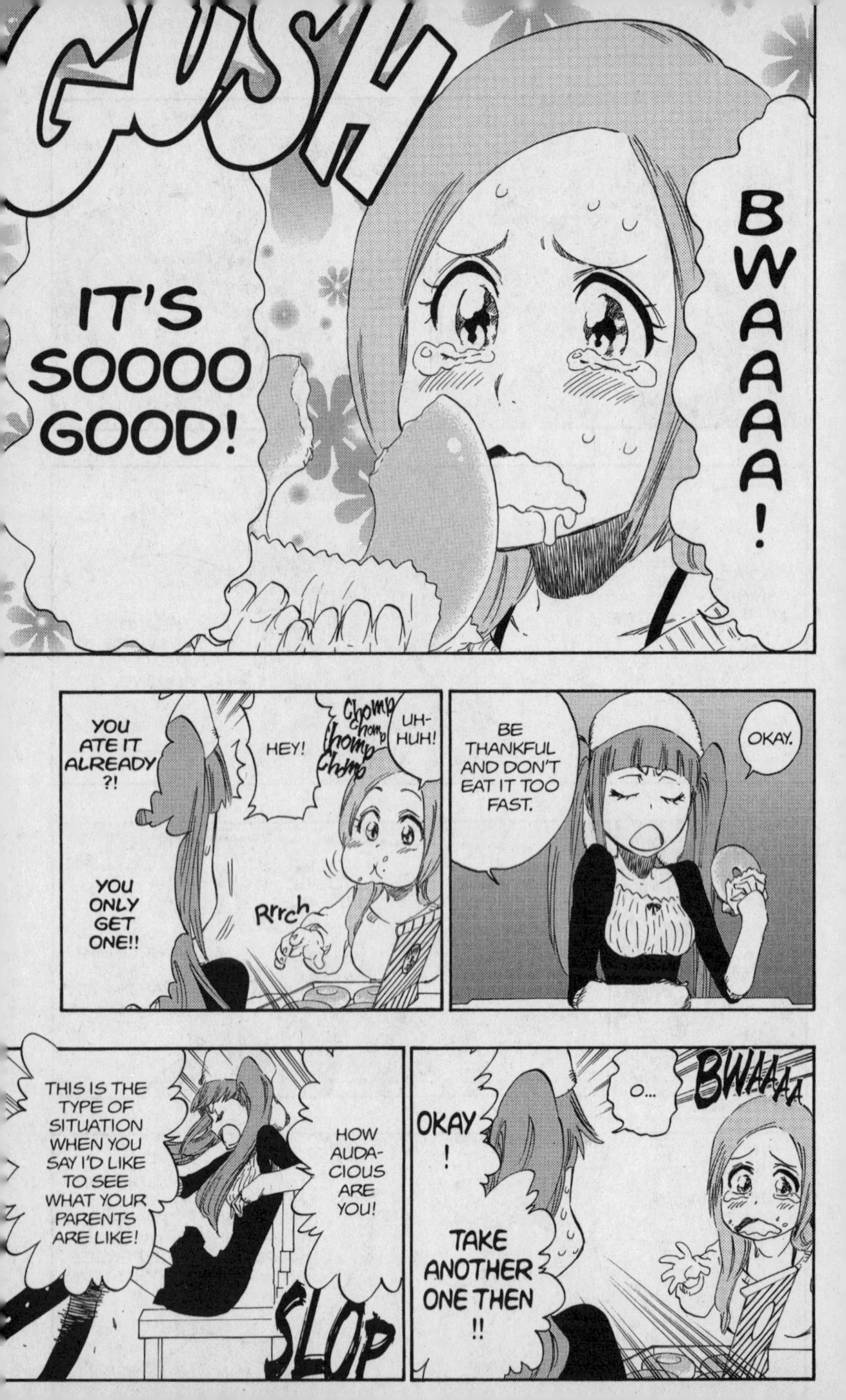

GUSH
BWAAAAA!
IT'S SOOOO GOOD!
BE THANKFUL AND DON'T EAT IT TOO FAST.
OKAY.
UH-HUH!
Chomp chomp chomp chomp
HEY!
YOU ATE IT ALREADY?!
Rrrch
YOU ONLY GET ONE!!
BWAAAA
O... OKAY!
TAKE ANOTHER ONE THEN!!
HOW AUDA-CIOUS ARE YOU!
THIS IS THE TYPE OF SITUATION WHEN YOU SAY I'D LIKE TO SEE WHAT YOUR PARENTS ARE LIKE!
SLOP

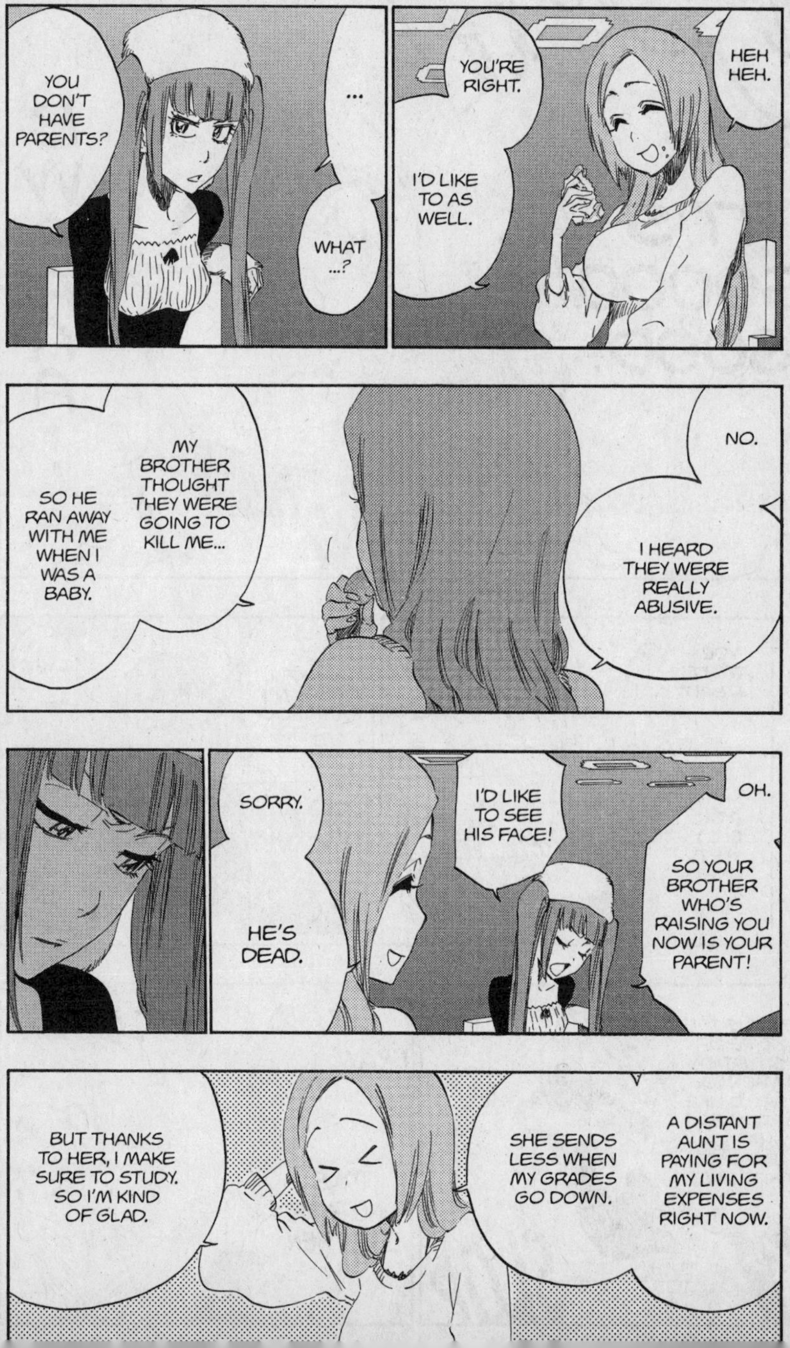
HEH HEH.
YOU'RE RIGHT.
I'D LIKE TO AS WELL.
...
WHAT ...?
YOU DON'T HAVE PARENTS?
NO.
I HEARD THEY WERE REALLY ABUSIVE.
MY BROTHER THOUGHT THEY WERE GOING TO KILL ME...
SO HE RAN AWAY WITH ME WHEN I WAS A BABY.
OH.
SO YOUR BROTHER WHO'S RAISING YOU NOW IS YOUR PARENT!
I'D LIKE TO SEE HIS FACE!
SORRY.
HE'S DEAD.
A DISTANT AUNT IS PAYING FOR MY LIVING EXPENSES RIGHT NOW.
SHE SENDS LESS WHEN MY GRADES GO DOWN.
BUT THANKS TO HER, I MAKE SURE TO STUDY. SO I'M KIND OF GLAD.

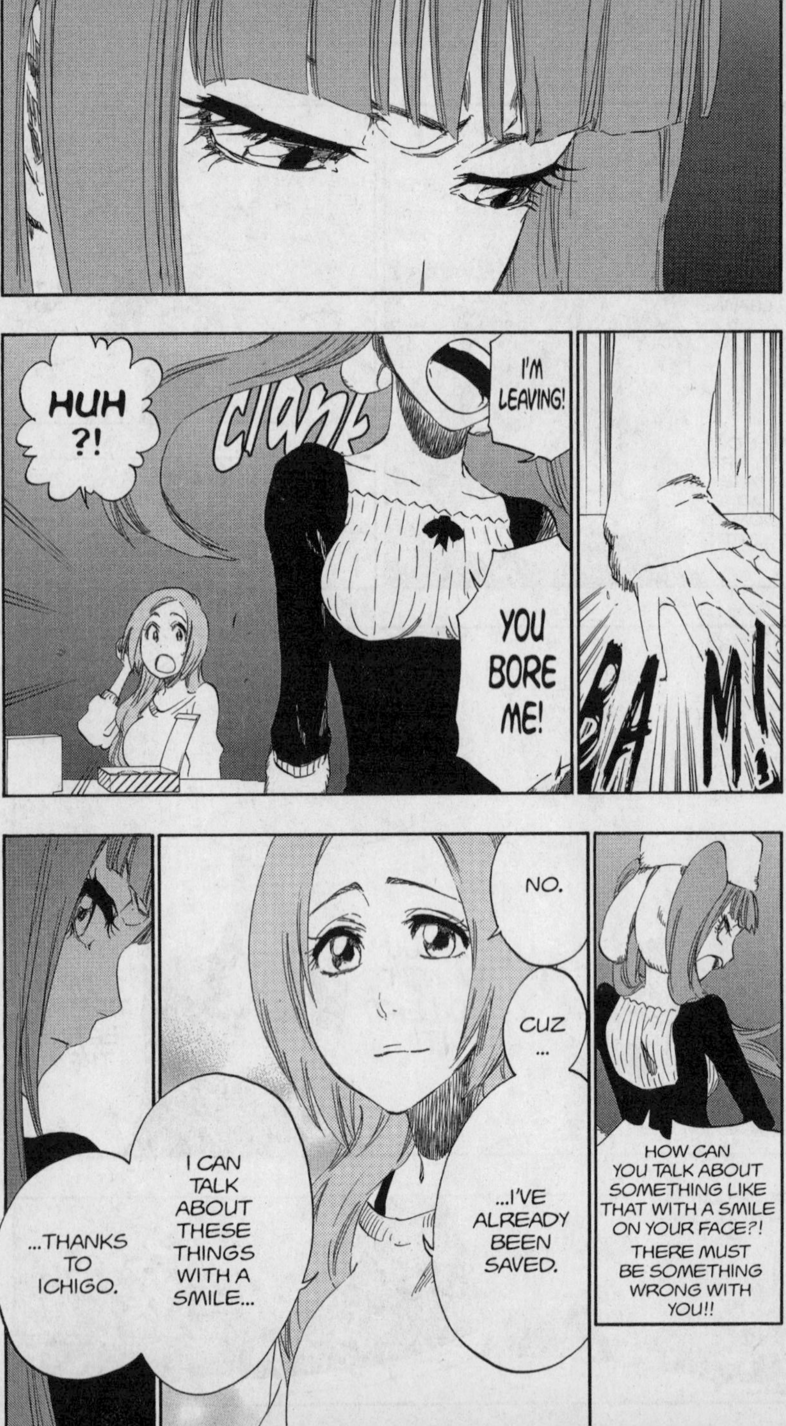

BAM!
I'M LEAVING!
CLANK
HUH ?!
YOU BORE ME!
HOW CAN YOU TALK ABOUT SOMETHING LIKE THAT WITH A SMILE ON YOUR FACE?! THERE MUST BE SOMETHING WRONG WITH YOU!!
NO.
CUZ ...
...I'VE ALREADY BEEN SAVED.
I CAN TALK ABOUT THESE THINGS WITH A SMILE...
...THANKS TO ICHIGO.

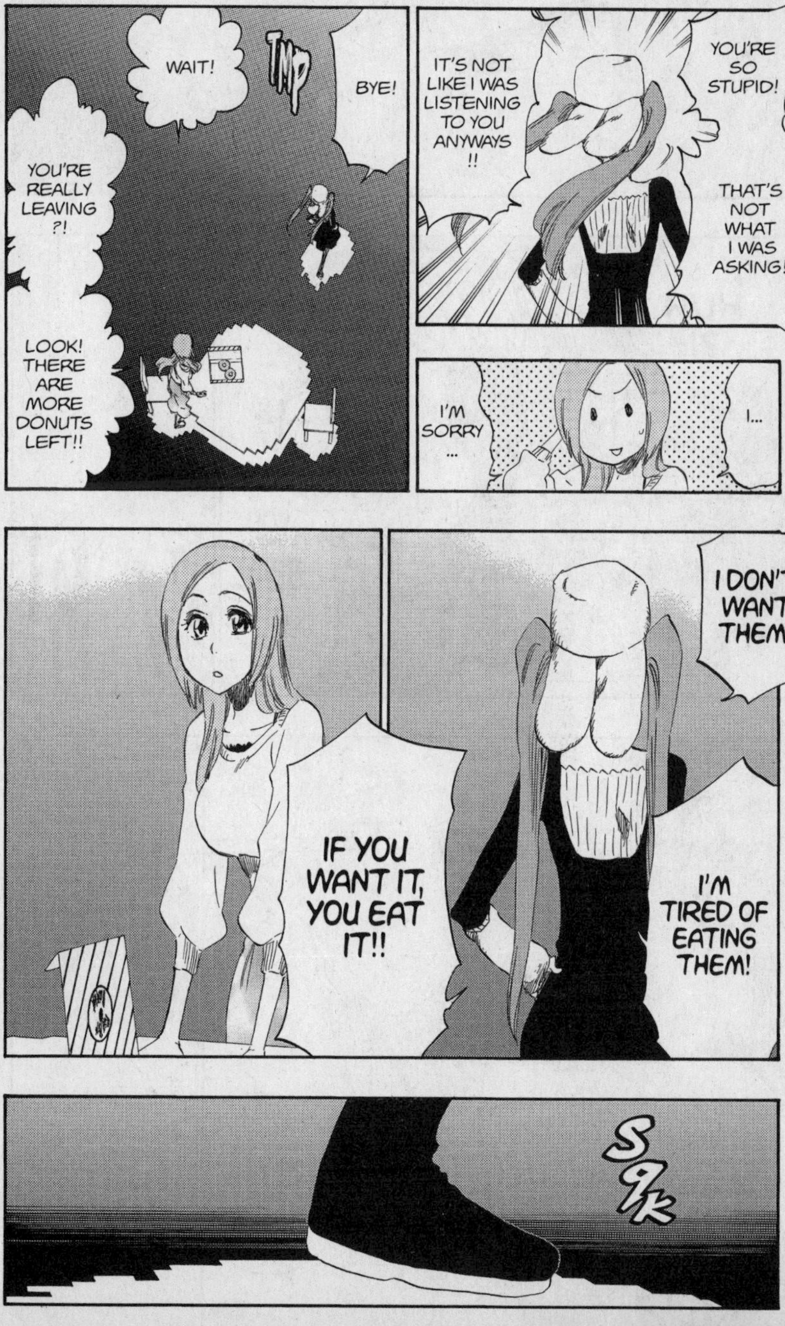
YOU'RE SO STUPID!
IT'S NOT LIKE I WAS LISTENING TO YOU ANYWAYS!!
THAT'S NOT WHAT I WAS ASKING!
I...
I'M SORRY...
BYE!
TMP
WAIT!
YOU'RE REALLY LEAVING?!
LOOK! THERE ARE MORE DONUTS LEFT!!
I DON'T WANT THEM!
I'M TIRED OF EATING THEM!
IF YOU WANT IT, YOU EAT IT!!
SQK

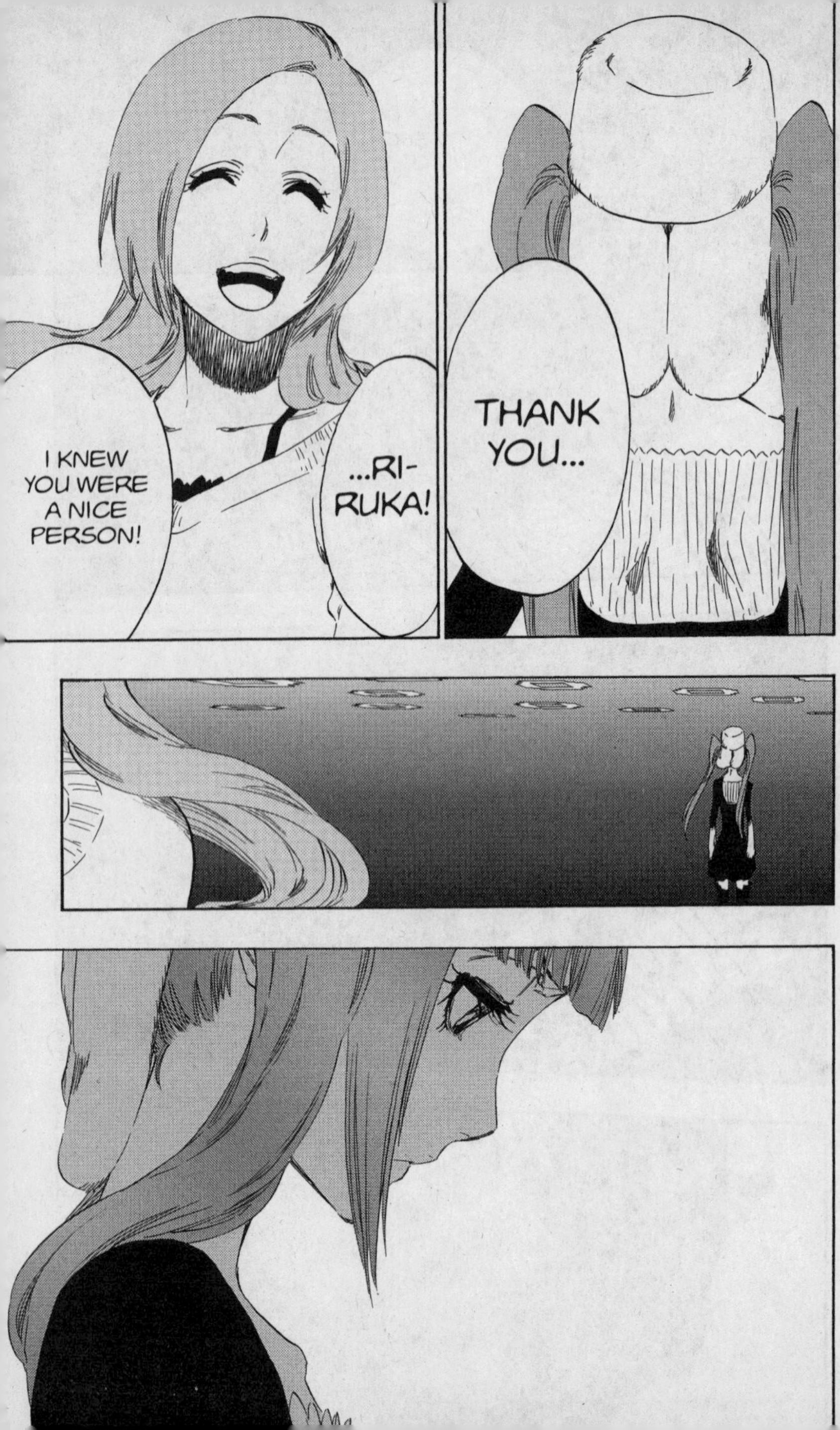
THANK YOU...
...RI-RUKA!
I KNEW YOU WERE A NICE PERSON!

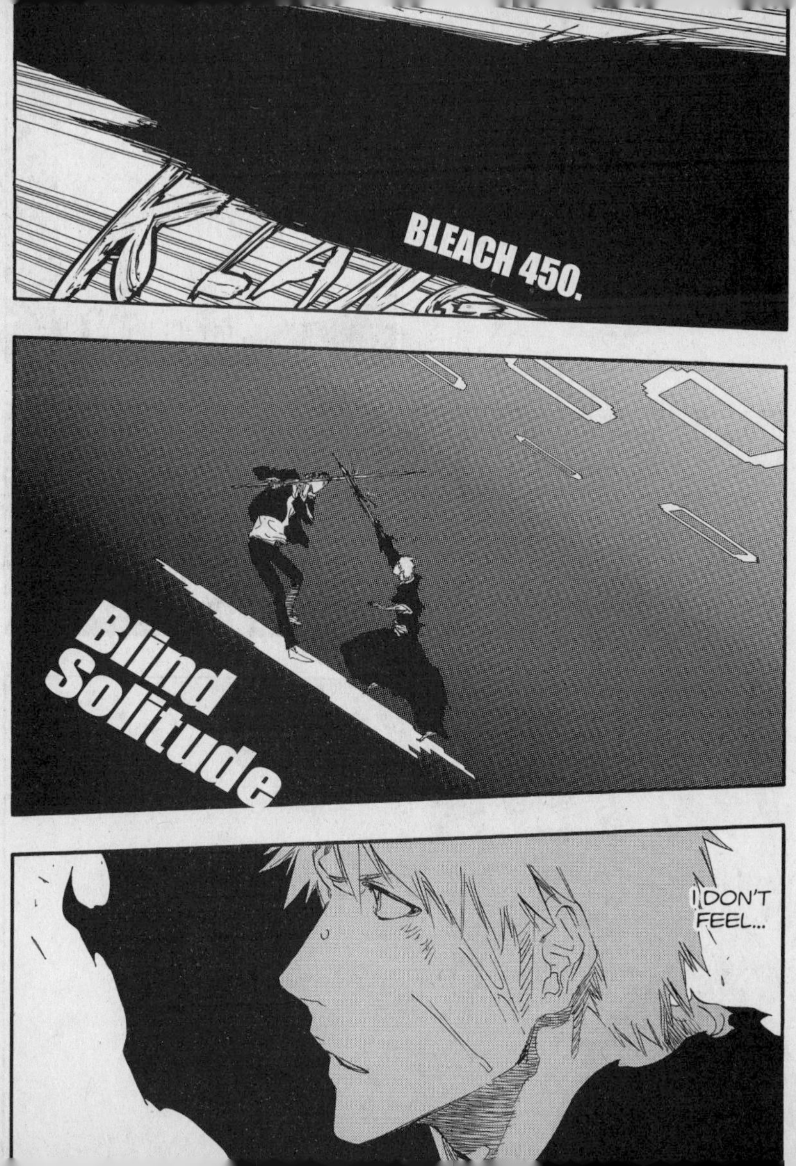
KLANG
BLEACH 450.
Blind Solitude
I DON'T FEEL...

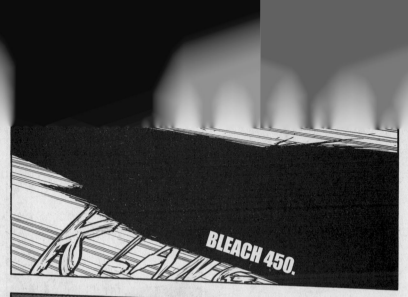

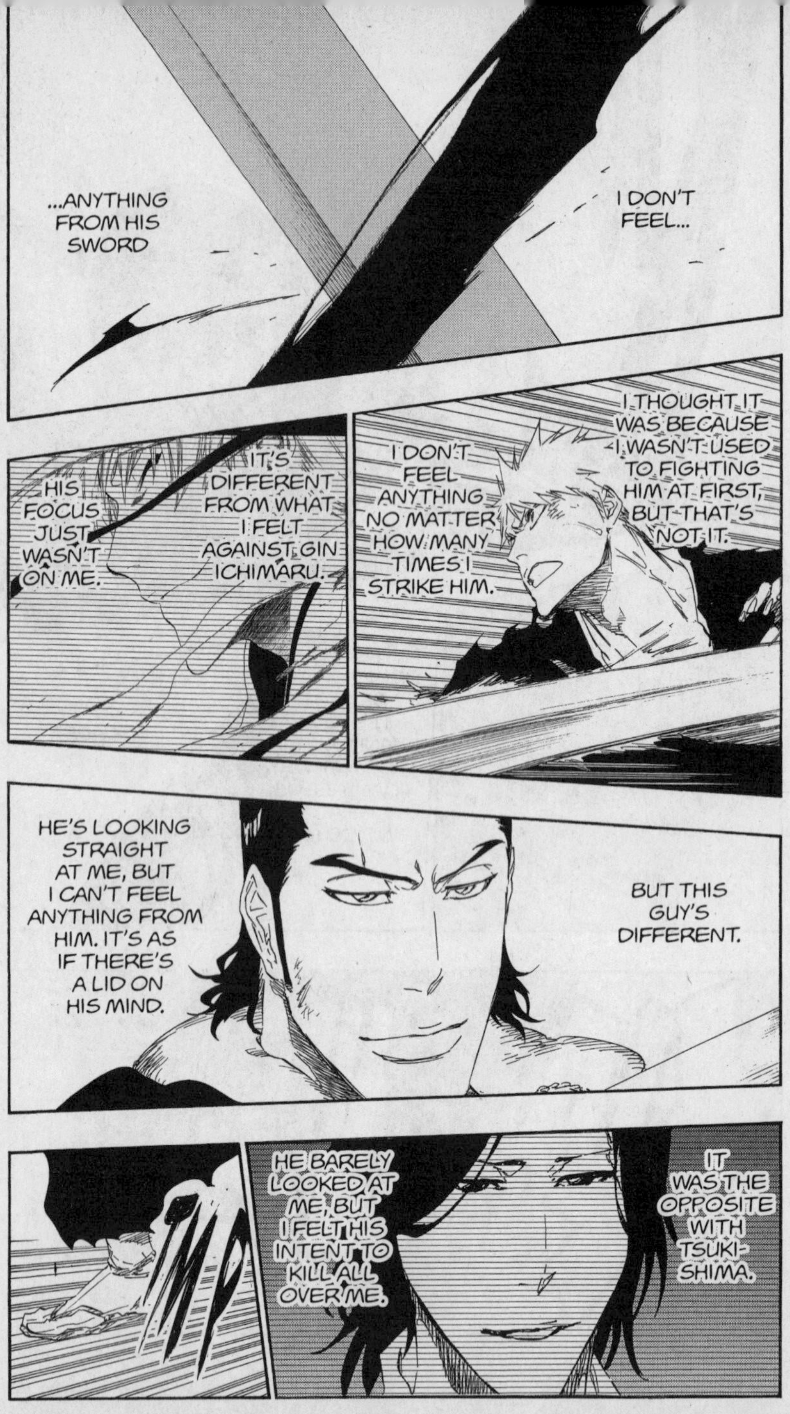
I DON'T FEEL...
...ANYTHING FROM HIS SWORD
I THOUGHT IT WAS BECAUSE I WASN'T USED TO FIGHTING HIM AT FIRST, BUT THAT'S NOT IT.
I DON'T FEEL ANYTHING NO MATTER HOW MANY TIMES I STRIKE HIM.
IT'S DIFFERENT FROM WHAT I FELT AGAINST GIN ICHIMARU.
HIS FOCUS JUST WASN'T ON ME.
BUT THIS GUY'S DIFFERENT.
HE'S LOOKING STRAIGHT AT ME, BUT I CAN'T FEEL ANYTHING FROM HIM. IT'S AS IF THERE'S A LID ON HIS MIND.
IT WAS THE OPPOSITE WITH TSUKI-SHIMA.
HE BARELY LOOKED AT ME, BUT I FELT HIS INTENT TO KILL ALL OVER ME.

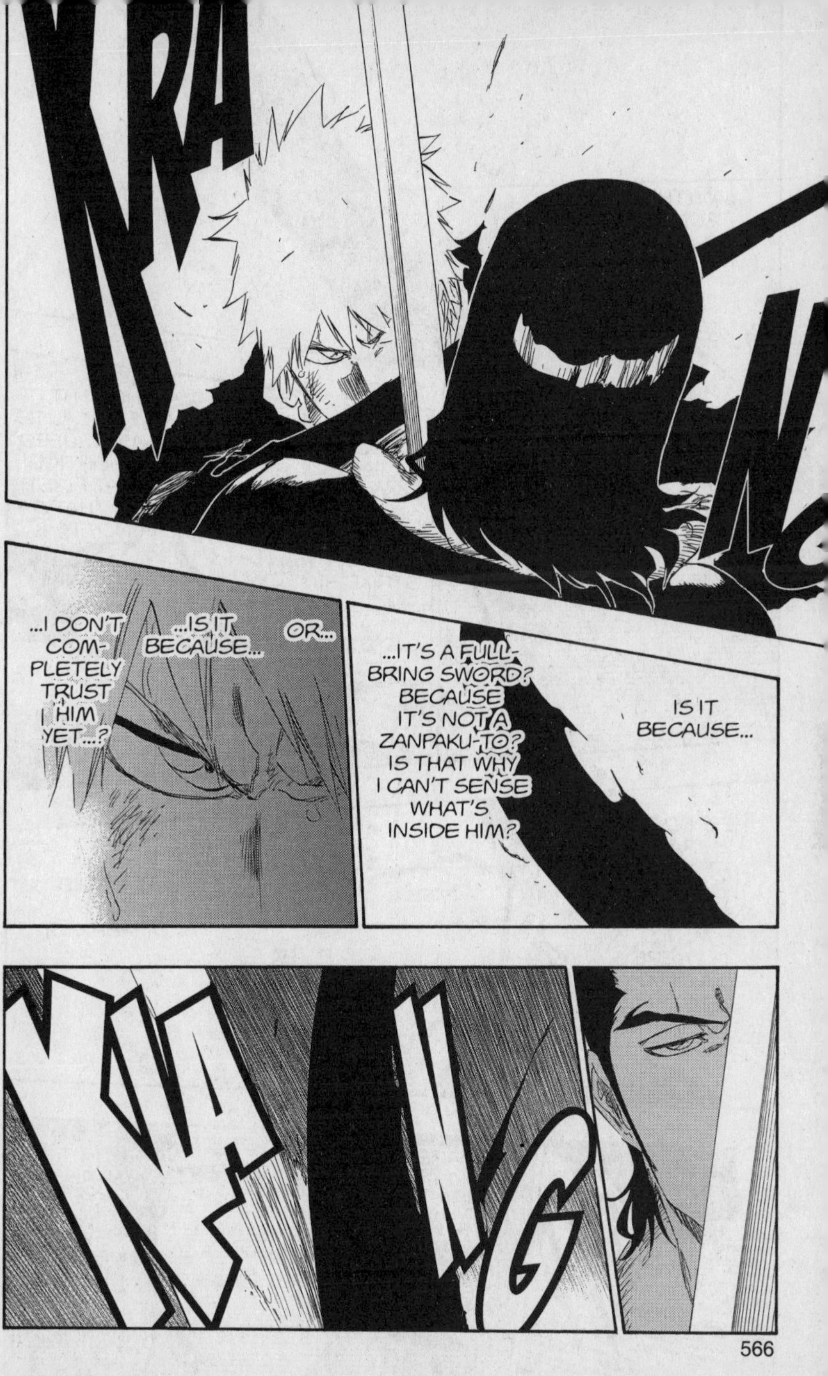
KRANNG
IS IT BECAUSE...
...IT'S A FULLBRING SWORD? BECAUSE IT'S NOT A ZANPAKU-TO? IS THAT WHY I CAN'T SENSE WHAT'S INSIDE HIM?
OR...
...IS IT BECAUSE...
...I DON'T COMPLETELY TRUST HIM YET...?
KRANG

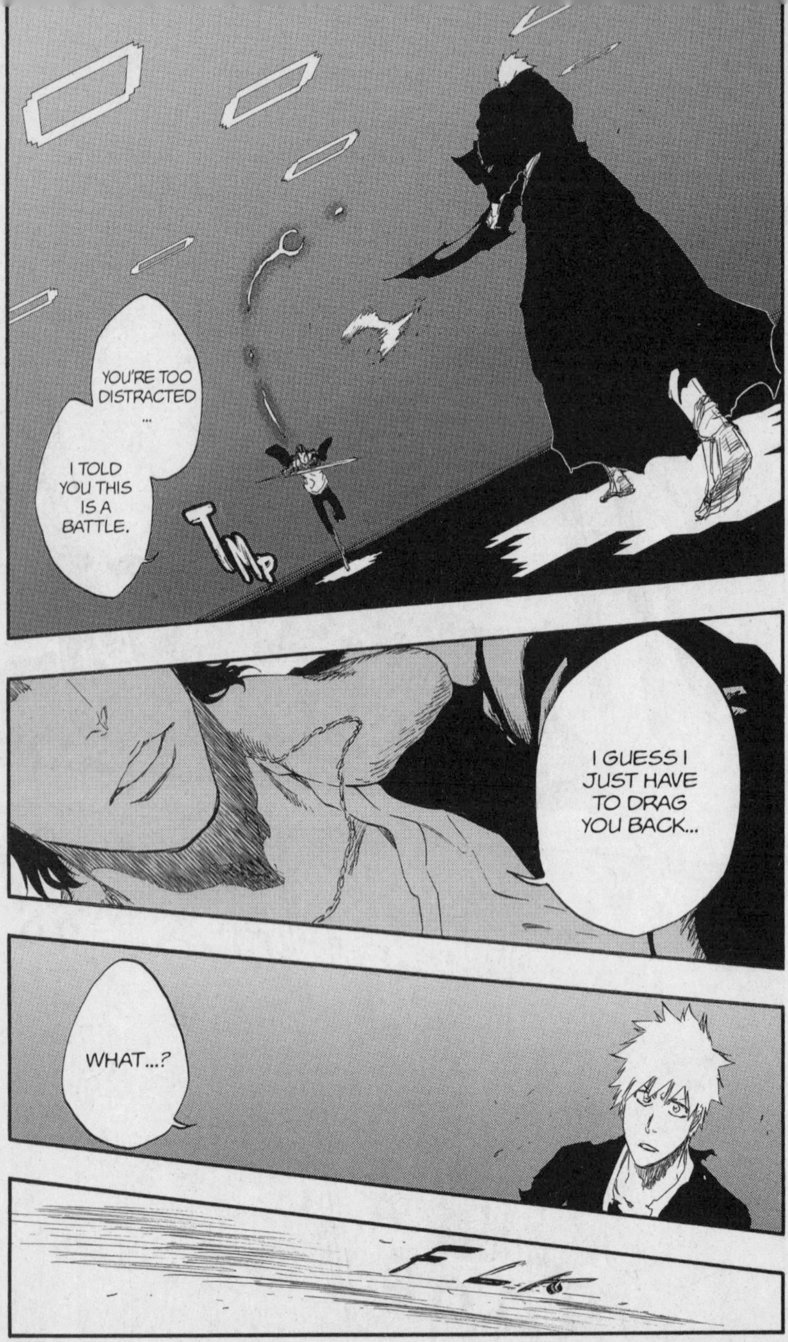
YOU'RE TOO DISTRACTED ...
I TOLD YOU THIS IS A BATTLE.
TMP
I GUESS I JUST HAVE TO DRAG YOU BACK...
WHAT...?

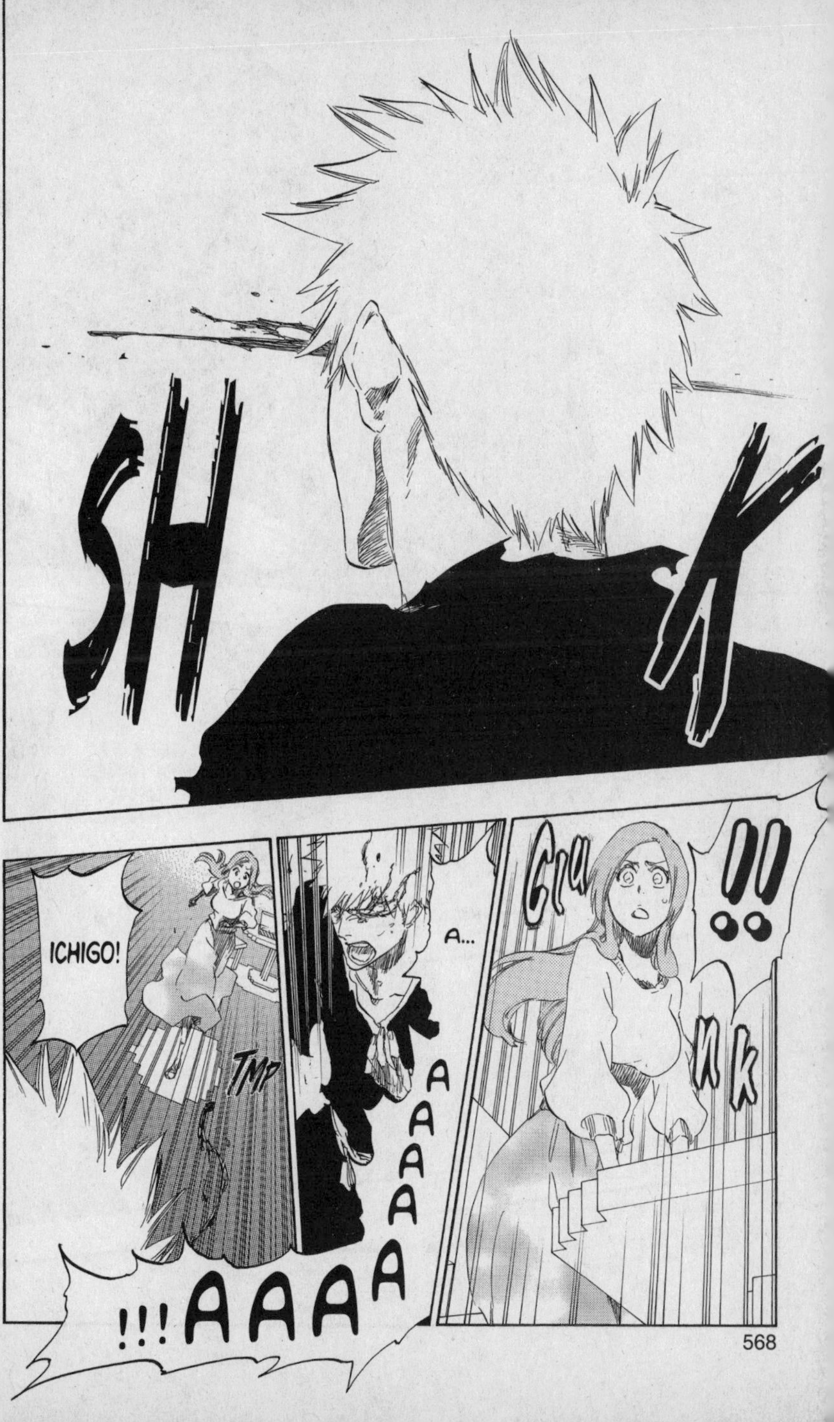
SHK
Clu
!!
nk
A...
AAAAAA
AAAA!!!
ICHIGO!
TMP

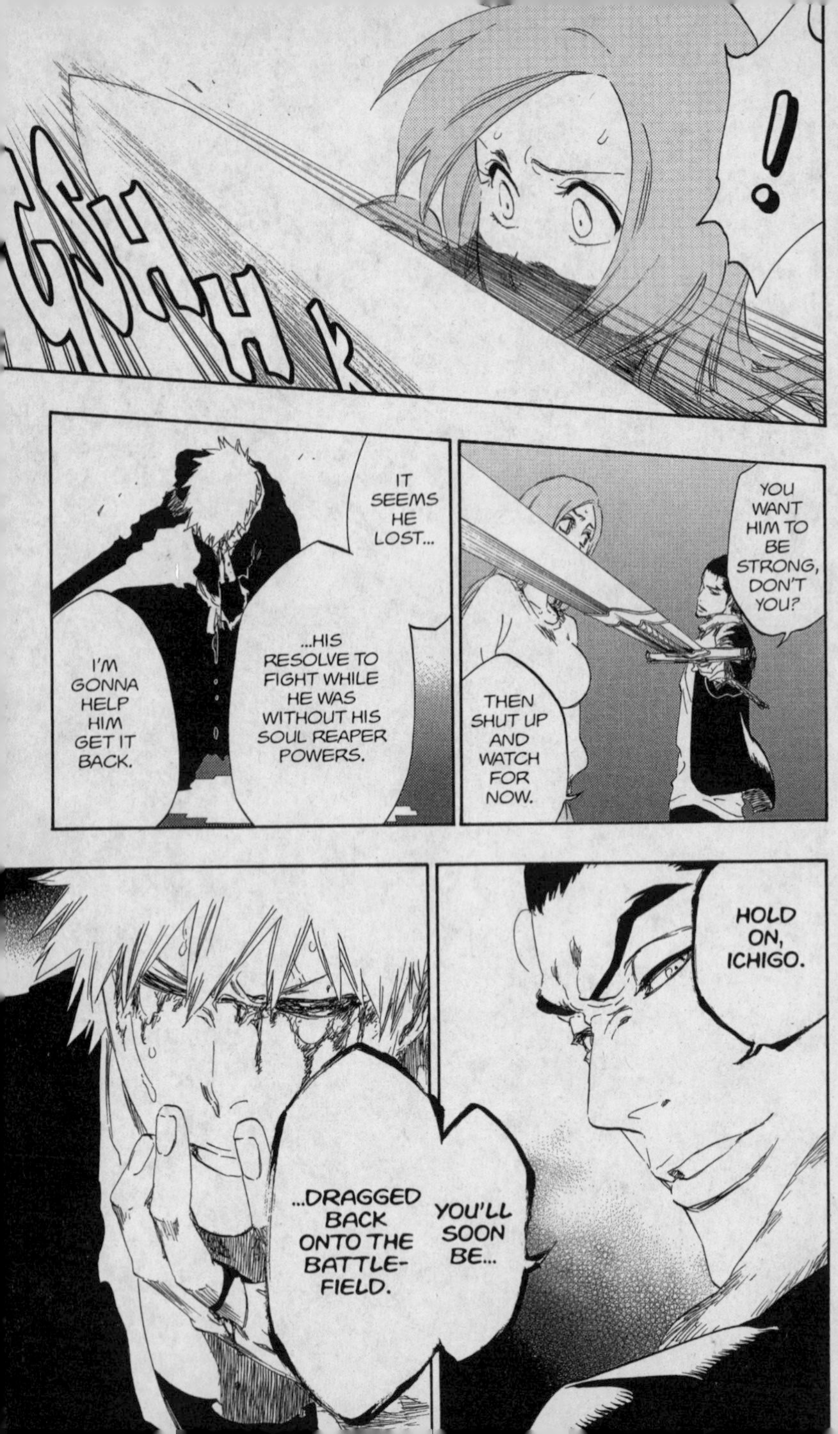
!!
YOU WANT HIM TO BE STRONG, DON'T YOU?
THEN SHUT UP AND WATCH FOR NOW.
IT SEEMS HE LOST...
...HIS RESOLVE TO FIGHT WHILE HE WAS WITHOUT HIS SOUL REAPER POWERS.
I'M GONNA HELP HIM GET IT BACK.
HOLD ON, ICHIGO.
YOU'LL SOON BE...
...DRAGGED BACK ONTO THE BATTLE-FIELD.

Bleach

[The Lost Agent]

Volume

Personal files

1

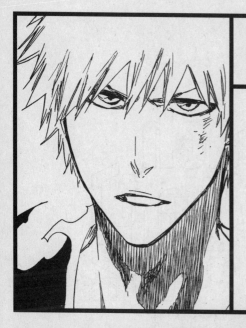

ICHIGO KUROSAKI

Height/181cm
Weight/66kg

Unagiya Employee

Karakura 1st High and

Part-Time Worker

New Member of Xcution

Membership No. 007

KUGO GINJO

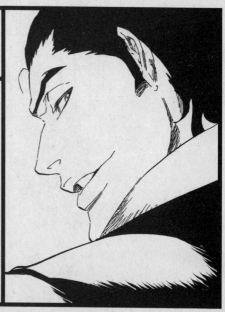

Height/187cm
Weight/90kg

D.O.B. 11/15

Blood Type/AB

Xcution Leader

Membership No. 001

URYU ISHIDA

Height/177cm
Weight/57kg

Karakura 1st High School

25th Student Council

President

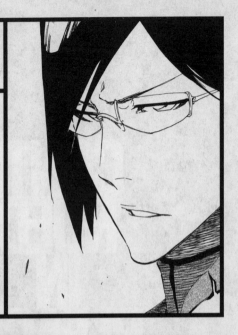

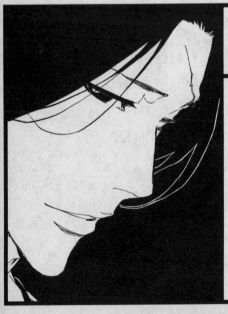

ASHUKURO TSUKISHIMA

Height/198cm
Weight/73kg

D.O.B. 2/4

Blood Type/BB

Xcution Ex-Leader

CONTINUED IN BLEACH 52-54

AVAILABLE FEBRUARY 2017

NARUTO

Story and Art by
Masashi Kishimoto

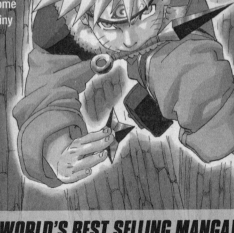

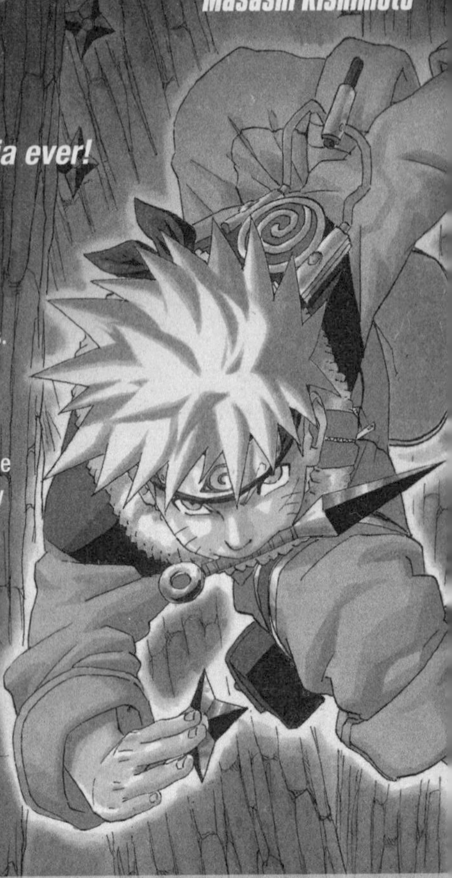

Naruto is determined to become the greatest ninja ever!

Twelve years ago the Village Hidden in the Leaves was attacked by a fearsome threat. A nine-tailed fox spirit claimed the life of the village leader, the Hokage, and many others. Today, the village is at peace and a troublemaking kid named Naruto is struggling to graduate from Ninja Academy. His goal may be to become the next Hokage, but his true destiny will be much more complicated. The adventure begins now!

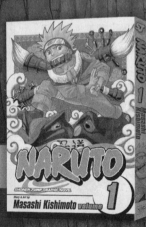

NARUTO
SHONEN JUMP GRAPHIC NOVEL
Story & Art by
Masashi Kishimoto volume 1

WORLD'S BEST SELLING MANGA!

You're Reading in the Wrong Direction!!

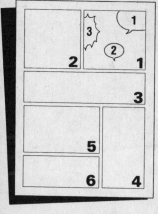

Whoops! Guess what? You're starting at the wrong end of the comic!

…It's true! In keeping with the original Japanese format, **Bleach** is meant to be read from right to left, starting in the upper-right corner.

Unlike English, which is read from left to right, Japanese is read from right to left, meaning that action, sound effects and word-balloon order are completely reversed… something which can make readers unfamiliar with Japanese feel pretty backwards themselves. For this reason, manga or Japanese comics published in the U.S. in English have sometimes been published "flopped"—that is, printed in exact reverse order, as though seen from the other side of a mirror.

By flopping pages, U.S. publishers can avoid confusing readers, but the compromise is not without its downside. For one thing, a character in a flopped manga series who once wore in the original Japanese version a T-shirt emblazoned with "M A Y" (as in "the merry month of") now wears one which reads "Y A M"! Additionally, many manga creators in Japan are themselves unhappy with the process, as some feel the mirror-imaging of their art skews their original intentions.

We are proud to bring you Tite Kubo's **Bleach** in the original unflopped format. For now, though, turn to the other side of the book and let the adventure begin…!

—Editor

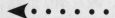

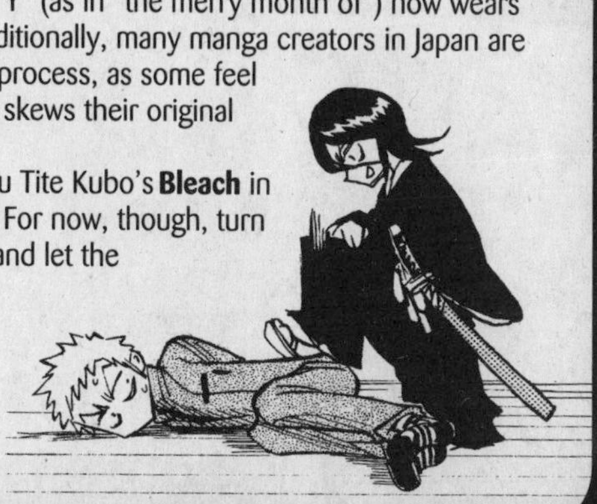